Steve:
(C) 571-216-4669
(H) 703-319-3249

SPORTS AND THE LAW

TEXT, CASES, PROBLEMS

Second Edition

By

Paul C. Weiler
Henry J. Friendly Professor of Law
Harvard Law School

Gary R. Roberts
Professor of Law
Tulane Law School

AMERICAN CASEBOOK SERIES®

ST. PAUL, MINN., 1998

American Casebook Series, the key symbol appearing on the front cover and the West Group symbol are registered trademarks used herein under license.

COPYRIGHT © 1993 WEST PUBLISHING CO.
COPYRIGHT © 1998 By WEST GROUP
                    610 Opperman Drive
                    P.O. Box 64526
                    St. Paul, MN 55164–0526
                    1–800–328–9352

All rights reserved
Printed in the United States of America

Library of Congress Cataloging-in-Publication Data

Weiler, Paul C.
    Cases, materials, and problems on sports and the law / by Paul C. Weiler, Gary R. Roberts. — 2nd ed.
      p.   cm. — (American casebook series)
    Includes bibliographical references and index.
    ISBN 0–314–23128–5 (hard)
    1. Sports—Law and legislation—United States—Cases.
I. Roberts, Gary R., 1948–   . II. Title. III. Series.
KF3989.A7W42 1998
344.73'099—dc21   98–3339
                                                CIP

ISBN 0–314–23128–5

TEXT IS PRINTED ON 10% POST
CONSUMER RECYCLED PAPER

Dedications

* * *

By Paul Weiler
to
Bob and Joe Weiler
for the decades spent debating both sports and law
with their brother.

* * *

By Gary Roberts
to
my coauthor Paul Weiler,
for his patience, understanding, and friendship
that made my contribution to this work possible.

*

Preface

Since *Sports and the Law* first appeared in print in 1993, the sports world has experienced a host of dramatic personal, financial, and legal events. Fans debated throughout the winter of 1997–98 whether Casey Martin should be able to play on the PGA golf tour while riding a cart, or Latrell Sprewell should be able to play NBA basketball after choking his coach. Television networks, aware of the intense fan interest, paid large increases in their broadcast fees, especially for football and basketball. Taxpayers put up billions of dollars in public subsidies in order to attract or keep teams in their communities. Owners and players conducted huge labor battles about how to divide up this surge in sports revenue streams. However, the business as well as popular appeal of the sports market has attracted investment in two new professional sports—men's soccer and women's basketball. Major League Soccer had been in operation for just one season when it suddenly faced a lawsuit by its players challenging the owners' salary cap. But the fact we now have two women's basketball leagues (American Basketball Association and Women's National Basketball Association) testifies to the impact that the law (here Title IX) can have in shaping the sports environment in America.

Most of the specific cases and controversies taking place over the last five years have already appeared in the annual Supplements we have produced for the professors and students who use our book. When it came time to draw all of this material together for this full-blown revision of the original work, that proved to be a somewhat daunting as well as exhilarating task.

One thing we had to do was add two new chapters. Chapter 6, *Sports Broadcasting, Merchandising, and Intellectual Property*, was sparked by the comment made in a book review by Jeffrey Pash (now Executive Vice President and General Counsel of the NFL) about the significance of this legal underpinning to the lucrative licensing deals that teams and leagues have been able to make for the broadcasting and merchandising of their "property." This chapter was also able to draw upon the broader analysis of these issues in the recent book, *Entertainment, Media, and the Law* (Eagan, Minn.: West Publishing, 1997), that one of us has authored. At the same time, the antitrust implications of league rules and restraints in this area, something that was a part of the first edition, have become even more important with the litigation between Jerry Reinsdorf's Bulls and the NBA, Jerry Jones' Cowboys and the NFL, and George Steinbrenner's Yankees and MLB, all of which are now described in a lengthy section in Chapter 7.

There is also a new Chapter 11 entitled *Intercollegiate Sports: Gender Equity*. When we sent our first edition off to the publisher at the end of 1992, Title IX of the Education Amendments Act had been on the books for two decades, but with little indication of its sports law content and implications. However, by the time this book was first being used in classrooms in the 1993–94 academic year, a large number of Title IX decisions were being rendered regarding university treatment of women's sports programs. Shortly afterwards, another burst of litigation took place, directed at the NCAA's treatment of learning disabled student-athletes under the Americans With Disabilities Act. As we began producing this second edition, a major class action suit had been filed under Title VI of the Civil Rights Act on behalf of African American athletes taking on the NCAA's Proposition 48. There now are three chapters (9 through 11) on college sports which address not just these civil rights issues, but their interplay with the educational and economic features of Division I college sports (including the fate of the NCAA's version of a salary cap for "restricted earnings coaches.")

The most turbulent feature of sports off the field continues to be the labor conflicts within professional leagues. Just as we were putting the finishing touches on the first edition in early 1993, the NFL and its Players Association had finally settled their six years of strikes and lawsuits with a combination of free agency and a "hard" salary cap. In the summer of 1994, the NBA began a two-year combination of antitrust litigation, labor decertification, and complex negotiation that largely preserved that sport's "soft" salary cap—something that the owners are likely to revisit in the summer of 1998, just as this edition is appearing in the book stores. The NHL experienced a three-month lockout at the beginning of the 1994–95 season, with an eventual settlement that both sides later agreed to extend past the year 2000 to facilitate the league's expansion. Baseball, as always, had the fiercest labor dispute and the longest-ever work stoppage in sports history. This cost the fans the first World Series in 90 years, and it took three years before a new collective agreement could be signed in the spring of 1997, with a relatively soft salary tax. Meanwhile, the one significant labor dispute that was not settled, the NFL owner's Development Squad salary "cut," produced the Supreme Court's only sports verdict of the 1990s, *Brown v. Pro Football, Inc.*: this decision is already making important changes in the role of law and labor unions in professional team sports. All of these developments are discussed in the significantly-revised Chapters 2 through 5.

The consequences of franchise free agency have become even more visible in the 1990s, as more and more club owners use the leverage of actual or potential relocation of their teams to extract large taxpayer subsidies for new stadiums and arenas. The principal focus of our original Chapter 6 (now Chapter 7), *Franchise, League, and Community*, had been on Al Davis' use of the law in the 1980s to move the NFL Raiders from Oakland to Los Angeles. As we near the end of the 1990s, there is renewed litigation between Davis and the NFL regarding the move of the Raiders back from Los Angeles to Oakland. There have also been important judicial rulings regarding the use of antitrust doctrine to challenge league policies towards television and merchandising deals, corporate ownership of franchises, and the like. Conscious of these legal issues, new league structures were devised by the organizers of Major League Soccer and the ABA and WNBA women's basketball leagues to try to gain "single entity" status that would insulate the leagues from § 1 (if not § 2) of the Sherman Act. These sports developments and legal debates are all reflected in Chapters 7 and 8 of this edition.

Public concerns and debates about the contemporary sports world are not, of course, limited to these financial dimensions. From the point of view of fans, equally if not more important questions are raised about the integrity of the game and its participants. That is why we continue to open this book with a chapter on the *Best Interests of the Sport*, and the role of league governing authorities—in particular, the Commissioner—in establishing and enforcing rules for player behavior off as well as on the field or court. Among the key examples added to Chapter 1 are Latrell Sprewell choking his coach, Roberto Alomar spitting in the face of an umpire, Steve Howe caught with cocaine for the eighth time, and Lawrence Phillips beating up his ex-girlfriend at the University of Nebraska. These kinds of incidents and concerns arise not just in team sports and leagues, but also in individual sports like golf, track and field, and the like. Thus Chapter 12, *Individual Sports*, presents its own important debates about such issues as the use of performance-enhancing drugs (e.g., the Butch Reynolds case), and the most notorious sports episode of all—the 1994 assault of figure skater Nancy Kerrigan allegedly instigated by her rival Tonya Harding (an incident that generated not just litigation, but also the highest-ever Nielsen's rating for an Olympics event). Chapters 1 and 12 not only provide all of the relevant details about these and other cases, but pose for class discussion the broader questions of what should be the appropriate social stance towards private athlete behavior (e.g., drug use or domestic abuse), and to what extent public policies should be enforced through rules that define who can play in private sports.

This combination of new sports developments and new subject matter has made this edition considerably larger in size than the first edition—up from approximately 750 pages to 1,000 pages of text. In order to be able to satisfy our "page cap," we undertook some further editing of the previous cases as well as the new decisions incorporated in the book. While ensuring that all of the key elements of the disputes and legal proceedings are described for the reader, we have focused the judicial opinions on the court's analysis of the legal and policy issues. We have used some of the saved space to expand on our textual description of important but complex features of sports, such as the design of salary caps and taxes, the new organizational structure of Major League Soccer and the women's ABA and WNBA, the evolution of the NCAA's Proposition 48 eligibility standards, and the like. We have also drawn upon (and cited) the recent surge of scholarship in this field to present a broader array of sports law and policy issues for discussion and debate within the classroom. Since more than half the book's pages now consist of our text rather than judicial opinions, we thought it more accurate to change the subtitle to *Text, Cases, Problems*.

* * *

Just as happened with the first edition of our book, we have had the benefit of valuable contributions by a number of our assistants and students to this second version of *Sports and the Law*. Gary Roberts' assistant Patty Cooper played an important role in assembling the new statutory and documentary material that is now incorporated in a fully-updated Statutory Supplement. Paul Weiler's research assistants in the 1994–95 academic year, Jonathan Levey and Ed Rippey, were the ones who gathered and helped organize the material on Intellectual Property and Gender Equity for our 1995 Case Supplement, which became Chapters 6 and 11, respectively. Weiler's former administrative assistant Tasha Hansen was the person who blended together all of the text and cases from the first edition and the four annual Supplements into a first working draft. Not only did this enable the two of us to do all of the necessary additions and refinements, but it also facilitated memos and editorial comments from Weiler's *Sports and the Law* classes in the spring and fall of 1997. And his team of 1997–98 research assistants provided systematic editing of the final manuscript.

Our biggest debt, though, is owed to Weiler's administrative assistant, Michelle Eichelberger. Drawing upon her background in legal publishing, Michelle coordinated the movement of this work between Harvard and Tulane Law Schools and then between West Publishing and the two of us. She also carefully read and edited the entire manuscript, checked all the citations, and then compiled the new index. Michelle's eye for both technical and literary detail generated a host of changes that would otherwise not have been incorporated in the text that you are about to read.

To everyone who helped us bring this project to fruition, and especially to Michelle, our heartfelt thanks.

P.C.W.
G.R.R.

March, 1998

Summary of Contents

	Page
Preface	v
Table of Cases	xxi

Chapter One. Best Interests of the Sport: The Role of the Commissioner and Other Governing Authorities **1**
A. Pete Rose v. Bart Giamatti 3
B. The Legal Scope of the Commissioner's Authority 6
C. Challenges to the Best Interests of the Sport 31

Chapter Two. Constructing a Players Market: From Contract to Antitrust Law **87**
A. Toronto Blue Jays v. Boston Celtics and Danny Ainge 89
B. Evolving Standards for Contract Enforcement 91
C. Reserve System and Restraint of Trade 119

Chapter Three. From Antitrust to Labor Law **150**
A. Antitrust Background 150
B. Antitrust and the Players Market 160
C. Labor Exemption From Antitrust 188
D. Collusion in Baseball 228

Chapter Four. Labor Law and Collective Bargaining in Professional Sports **238**
A. Free Agency Via Labor Arbitration 240
B. Application of the NLRA to Sports 250
C. Union Support and Employer Retaliation 255
D. Certification of the Players' Bargaining Agent 262
E. Union's Exclusive Bargaining Authority 267
F. Duty to Bargain in Good Faith 272
G. Economic Conflict in Sports Labor Relations 289
H. Administration of the Labor Agreement 297
I. Union and Individual Player 304
J. Union Security in Sports 310
K. Salary Caps and Taxes 314

Chapter Five. Agent Representation of the Athlete **322**
A. Union and Agent Representation of Athletes 324
B. Breakdowns in the Agent–Player Relationship 343
C. Emergence of Agent Regulation 360
D. Agents, College Athletes, and NCAA Rules 380

SUMMARY OF CONTENTS

Page

Chapter Six. Sports Broadcasting, Merchandising, and Intellectual Property Law — **389**
A. Right to Broadcast Games — 391
B. Copyright in the Game Broadcasts — 401
C. Player Publicity Rights — 422
D. Owner Trademark Rights — 436
E. Group Marketing of Intellectual Property Rights — 458

Chapter Seven. Franchise, League, and Community — **467**
A. Nature of the League: A Preliminary Look — 468
B. Franchise Ownership Rules — 472
C. Admission and Relocation of Sports Franchises — 500
D. League–Wide Television Contracts — 549

Chapter Eight. Monopoly in Professional Sports — **593**
A. Monopoly Power and the Relevant Market — 596
B. Monopoly Resources and Monopolizing Conduct — 608
C. Break up the Big Leagues? — 643

Chapter Nine. Intercollegiate Sports: Due Process and Academic Integrity — **646**
A. The Tarkanian Saga — 649
B. Procedural Due Process — 661
C. Eligibility Requirements — 675
D. Judicial Scrutiny of Institutional Decisions — 711

Chapter Ten. Intercollegiate Sports: Commercialism and Amateurism — **723**
A. NCAA Eligibility Rules — 725
B. Judicial Reading of the Scholarship Contract — 741
C. Antitrust Scrutiny of NCAA Rules — 749

Chapter Eleven. Intercollegiate Sports: Gender Equity — **799**
A. Pre–Title IX in Action — 801
B. Administrative Development of Title IX — 805
C. Resources — 808
D. Administration — 843
E. Access — 851
F. Afterthoughts — 862

Chapter Twelve. Individual Sports — **864**
A. Umpiring the Game — 866
B. Eligibility to Play — 870
C. Disciplinary Authority of the Tour — 880
D. Organizing a Sports Tour — 885
E. Regulating Playing Equipment — 897
F. Olympic Sports — 906

SUMMARY OF CONTENTS

	Page
Chapter Thirteen. Personal Injury From Sports	**934**
A. Torts and Sports	935
B. Criminal Law and Sports Violence	951
C. Workers' Compensation for Athletes	955
D. Back to Torts	979
E. Disability and the Right to Play	989
INDEX	1007

Table of Contents

	Page
Preface	v
Table of Cases	xxi

Chapter One. Best Interests of the Sport: The Role of the Commissioner and Other Governing Authorities — 1

A. Pete Rose v. Bart Giamatti — 3
B. The Legal Scope of the Commissioner's Authority — 6
    Milwaukee Am. Ass'n. v. Landis — 10
    Charles O. Finley v. Bowie Kuhn — 13
    Questions for Discussion — 20
    Questions for Discussion — 27
C. Challenges to the Best Interests of the Sport — 31
    1. Gambling — 31
        Molinas v. National Basketball Ass'n. — 32
        Questions for Discussion — 34
        Questions for Discussion — 35
        Questions for Discussion — 37
    2. Drug Use — 38
        Major League Baseball Players Association and the Commissioner of Major League Baseball (Steven Howe) — 42
        Questions for Discussion — 47
        Questions for Discussion — 48
    3. Drug Testing — 53
        Hill v. National Collegiate Athletic Association — 57
        Questions For Discussion — 68
    4. Sports and Social Ethics — 71
        a. Treatment of Minorities by Sports — 72
        b. Treatment of Women by Sports — 79
            Ludtke and Time, Inc. v. Kuhn — 80

Chapter Two. Constructing a Players Market: From Contract to Antitrust Law — 87

A. Toronto Blue Jays v. Boston Celtics and Danny Ainge — 89
B. Evolving Standards for Contract Enforcement — 91
    Philadelphia Ball Club v. Lajoie — 91
    Questions for Discussion — 94
    Central New York Basketball, Inc. (Syracuse Nationals) v. Barnett — 95
    Boston Celtics v. Brian Shaw — 101
    Questions for Discussion — 105
    Houston Oilers, Inc. v. Neely — 107
    Questions for Discussion — 111
    Cincinnati Bengals v. Bergey — 113
    Questions for Discussion — 116

TABLE OF CONTENTS

	Page
C. Reserve System and Restraint of Trade	119
American League Baseball Club of Chicago v. Chase	120
Flood v. Kuhn	127
Piazza and Tirendi v. Major	142
League Baseball	142
Questions For Discussion	146

Chapter Three. From Antitrust to Labor Law — 150

A. Antitrust Background	150
Brown v. Pro Football, Inc. (Washington Redskins)	154
B. Antitrust and the Players Market	160
1. Rookie Draft	160
Smith v. Pro Football, Inc.	161
Questions for Discussion	172
Note on Draft Eligibility	175
Questions for Discussion	176
2. Salary Restraints	176
Brown v. Pro Football, Inc. (Washington Redskins)	177
3. Veteran Free Agency	178
Mackey v. National Football League (Part 1)	179
Questions for Discussion	183
C. Labor Exemption From Antitrust	188
Mackey v. National Football League (Part 2)	194
Brown v. Pro Football, Inc.	211
Questions For Discussion	222
Questions For Discussion	226
D. Collusion in Baseball	228
Questions for Discussion	236

Chapter Four. Labor Law and Collective Bargaining in Professional Sports — 238

A. Free Agency Via Labor Arbitration	240
National & American League Professional Baseball Clubs v. Major League Baseball Players Association	241
B. Application of the NLRA to Sports	250
The American League of Professional Baseball Clubs & Ass'n of National Baseball League Umpires	250
Questions for Discussion	254
C. Union Support and Employer Retaliation	255
Seattle Seahawks v. NFLPA & Sam McCullum	256
Questions for Discussion	262
D. Certification of the Players' Bargaining Agent	262
North American Soccer League v. NLRB	263
E. Union's Exclusive Bargaining Authority	267
Morio v. North American Soccer League	268
F. Duty to Bargain in Good Faith	272
Silverman v. Major League Baseball Player Relations Comm.	274
Questions for Discussion	279
Silverman v. Major League Baseball Player Relations Committee	281
Questions for Discussion	287
G. Economic Conflict in Sports Labor Relations	289
NFL Management Council and NFLPA	290
Questions for Discussion	294
Questions For Discussion	296

TABLE OF CONTENTS

	Page
H. Administration of the Labor Agreement	297
Kansas City Royals v. Major League Baseball Players Ass'n	298
Questions for Discussion	303
I. Union and Individual Player	304
Questions for Discussion	305
Peterson v. Kennedy and NFLPA	306
J. Union Security in Sports	310
K. Salary Caps and Taxes	314
Questions For Discussion	317

Chapter Five. Agent Representation of the Athlete ... 322

A. Union and Agent Representation of Athletes ... 324
   1. Standardized and Individualized Contract Terms ... 325
      Alvin Moore & Atlanta Braves ... 325
      Questions for Discussion ... 328
   2. Dealing With the Salary Cap ... 329
   3. Salary Arbitration ... 335
      Raymond Bourque and Boston Bruins ... 336

B. Breakdowns in the Agent–Player Relationship ... 343
   1. Standards for Agent Competence ... 343
      Zinn v. Parrish ... 343
   2. Agent Fee Formulas ... 347
      Brown v. Woolf ... 347
   3. Agent Conflicts of Interest ... 350
      Detroit Lions and Billy Sims v. Jerry Argovitz ... 350
      Questions for Discussion ... 354
   4. Agent Recruiting of College Athletes ... 355
      Norby Walters and Lloyd Bloom v. Brent Fullwood ... 356

C. Emergence of Agent Regulation ... 360
   Collins v. NBPA & Grantham ... 363
   Questions for Discussion ... 369
   Barry Rona and Major League Baseball Players Association ... 375
   Questions For Discussion ... 379

D. Agents, College Athletes, and NCAA Rules ... 380
   United States v. Norby Walters ... 381

Chapter Six. Sports Broadcasting, Merchandising, and Intellectual Property Law ... 389

A. Right to Broadcast Games ... 391
   Pittsburgh Athletic Co. v. KQV Broadcasting Co. ... 392
   Questions For Discussion ... 395
   National Basketball Association v. Sports Team Analysis and Tracking Systems (STATS) and Motorola (SportsTrax) ... 398
   Questions For Discussion ... 401

B. Copyright in the Game Broadcasts ... 401
   New Boston Television v. Entertainment Sports Programming Network [ESPN] ... 404
   Questions For Discussion ... 406
   NFL v. McBee & Bruno's, Inc. ... 408
   Questions For Discussion ... 412
   Questions For Discussion ... 419

C. Player Publicity Rights ... 422
   Questions For Discussion ... 426
   Baltimore Orioles v. Major League Baseball Players Ass'n. ... 428

TABLE OF CONTENTS

Page

C. Player Publicity Rights—Continued
    Questions For Discussion 434
D. Owner Trademark Rights 436
    Indianapolis Colts v. Metropolitan Baltimore Football Club 437
    Questions For Discussion 443
    Questions For Discussion 444
    Boston Professional Hockey Association v. Dallas Cap and Emblem Mfg., Inc. 446
    WCVB–TV v. Boston Athletic Ass'n 452
    Questions For Discussion 455
    Questions For Discussion 457
E. Group Marketing of Intellectual Property Rights 458
    Topps Chewing Gum v. Major League Baseball Players Ass'n. ... 461
    Questions For Discussion 465

Chapter Seven. Franchise, League, and Community 467
A. Nature of the League: A Preliminary Look 468
B. Franchise Ownership Rules 472
    NASL v. NFL 472
    Questions for Discussion 476
    Sullivan v. National Football League 478
    Questions for Discussion 487
    Questions for Discussion 494
C. Admission and Relocation of Sports Franchises 500
    Los Angeles Memorial Coliseum Comm'n. v. NFL (Raiders I) ... 503
    Questions for Discussion 517
    Questions for Discussion 520
    NBA v. San Diego Clippers Basketball Club 522
    Mid–South Grizzlies v. NFL 525
    Questions for Discussion 528
    City of Oakland v. Oakland Raiders (I) 532
    Questions for Discussion 536
    City of Oakland v. Oakland Raiders (II) 538
D. League–Wide Television Contracts 549
    United States v. NFL 550
    Questions for Discussion 555
    Chicago Professional Sports Ltd. & WGN v. NBA 559
    Questions for Discussion 566
    Chicago Professional Sports Limited Partnership & WGN v. National Basketball Association 571
    Questions for Discussion 582
    Note on Merchandising Rights 586
    Note on Revenue Sharing 588

Chapter Eight. Monopoly in Professional Sports 593
A. Monopoly Power and the Relevant Market 596
    AFL v. NFL 597
    Questions for Discussion 606
B. Monopoly Resources and Monopolizing Conduct 608
    1. Players 608
        Philadelphia World Hockey Club v. Philadelphia Hockey Club ... 609
        Questions for Discussion 619
    2. Stadiums 620
        Hecht v. Pro–Football, Inc. 621
        Questions for Discussion 625

TABLE OF CONTENTS

	Page
B. Monopoly Resources and Monopolizing Conduct—Continued	
Weinberg v. Chicago Blackhawk Hockey Team	626
Questions For Discussion	629
3. Television Contracts	629
USFL v. NFL	629
Questions for Discussion	642
C. Break up the Big Leagues?	643

Chapter Nine. Intercollegiate Sports: Due Process and Academic Integrity — 646

A. The Tarkanian Saga	649
National Collegiate Athletic Ass'n. v. Tarkanian	650
Questions for Discussion	658
B. Procedural Due Process	661
The National Collegiate Athletic Ass'n v. Robert F. Miller, Governor, State of Nevada, et al.	663
Questions For Discussion	668
C. Eligibility Requirements	675
1. Admission Standards: Proposition 48	676
Parish v. NCAA	677
Ganden v. NCAA	689
Questions For Discussion	696
2. Academic Progress	698
Hall v. University of Minnesota	698
3. Age and Experience	702
Pottgen v. The Missouri State High School Activities Association	705
D. Judicial Scrutiny of Institutional Decisions	711
Ross v. Creighton Univ.	713
Ross v. Creighton Univ.	717
Questions for Discussion	719

Chapter Ten. Intercollegiate Sports: Commercialism and Amateurism — 723

A. NCAA Eligibility Rules	725
1. Pay Before College	725
Colorado Seminary (Univ. of Denver) v. NCAA	725
2. Pay at College	729
Wiley v. NCAA	729
3. Professional Contracts	736
Shelton v. NCAA	736
B. Judicial Reading of the Scholarship Contract	741
Taylor v. Wake Forest	742
Questions for Discussion	743
English v. NCAA	745
C. Antitrust Scrutiny of NCAA Rules	749
1. Product Market	750
NCAA v. Board of Regents of the Univ. of Oklahoma & Univ. of Georgia Athletic Ass'n.	750
Questions for Discussion	764
Questions for Discussion	768
2. Coaching Market	770
Law v. National Collegiate Athletic Association	771
Questions For Discussion	779

TABLE OF CONTENTS

Page

C. Antitrust Scrutiny of NCAA Rules—Continued
    3. Athletes Market 780
        Banks v. NCAA 782
        Questions for Discussion 791

Chapter Eleven. Intercollegiate Sports: Gender Equity 799
A. Pre–Title IX in Action 801
    Blair v. Washington State Univ. 801
    Questions for Discussion 805
B. Administrative Development of Title IX 805
C. Resources 808
    Cohen v. Brown University 809
    Kelley v. University of Illinois 815
    Cohen v. Brown University 820
D. Administration 843
    Stanley v. University of Southern California 845
E. Access 851
    Hoover v. Meiklejohn 855
    Questions for Discussion 859
F. Afterthoughts 862

Chapter Twelve. Individual Sports 864
A. Umpiring the Game 866
    Crouch v. NASCAR 866
    Questions for Discussion 870
B. Eligibility to Play 870
    Weser v. PGA 872
    Questions for Discussion 876
    Questions for Discussion 878
C. Disciplinary Authority of the Tour 880
    Blalock v. LPGA 880
    Questions for Discussion 882
    Questions for Discussion 884
D. Organizing a Sports Tour 885
    Volvo North Am. Corp. v. Men's Int'l Professional Tennis Council (MIPTC) 888
E. Regulating Playing Equipment 897
    Gunter Harz Sports v. USTA 898
    Questions for Discussion 905
F. Olympic Sports 906
    DeFrantz v. United States Olympic Committee (USOC) 908
    Questions for Discussion 915
    Reynolds v. International Amateur Athletic Federation 916
    Reynolds v. International Amateur Athletic Federation 921
    Questions For Discussion 925

Chapter Thirteen. Personal Injury From Sports 934
A. Torts and Sports 935
    Hackbart v. Cincinnati Bengals & Charles Clark 935
    Hackbart v. Cincinnati Bengals, Inc. 940
    Questions for Discussion 942
    Ordway v. Casella 942
B. Criminal Law and Sports Violence 951
    Questions for Discussion 954

	Page
C. Workers' Compensation for Athletes	955
1. College Athletes	955
Rensing v. Indiana State Univ.	956
Rensing v. Indiana State Univ.	959
Note on NCAA Insurance	962
2. Professional Athletes	964
Palmer v. Kansas City Chiefs	965
Questions for Discussion	969
Gambrell v. Kansas City Chiefs	970
Brumm v. Bert Bell NFL Retirement Plan	974
D. Back to Torts	979
1. Medical Malpractice	979
Bryant v. Fox & Chicago Bears	980
2. Defective Products and Hazardous Facilities	982
Byrns v. Riddell, Inc.	982
Questions for Discussion	985
Maddox v. City of New York	986
E. Disability and the Right to Play	989
Knapp v. Northwestern University	990
Questions for Discussion	1000
Wagenblast v. Odessa School District	1001
Questions for Discussion	1005
INDEX	1007

Table of Cases

The principal cases are in bold type. Cases cited or discussed in the text are roman type. References are to pages. Cases cited in principal cases and within other quoted materials are not included.

Abdul–Jabbar v. General Motors Corp., 427
Abernethy v. State, 386
Acton v. Vernonia School Dist. 47J, 66, 68
Adarand Constructors, Inc. v. Pena, 819, 820, 827
Addyston Pipe & Steel Co., United States v., 159
Air Line Pilots Ass'n, Intern. v. O'Neill, 305
Albrecht v. Industrial Com'n, 972, 973
Ali v. Playgirl, Inc., 426
Allen Bradley Co. v. International Broth. of Elec. Workers, 191
Allied Chemical and Alkali Workers v. Pittsburgh Plate Glass Co., Chemical Division, 305
Amateur Softball Ass'n of America v. United States, 139
American Basketball Ass'n v. AMF Voit, Inc., 455
American Federation of Musicians of United States and Canada v. Carroll, 370
American Football League v. National Football League, 597, 602, 608, 619, 620
American League Baseball Club of Chicago v. Chase, 91, 119, **120,** 125, 179
American League Baseball Club of New York v. Johnson, 7, 9, 10
American League of Professional Baseball Clubs, 250
American Ship Bldg. Co. v. N. L. R. B., 289
American Tel. and Tel. Co., United States v., 643
Andrews, Estate of v. United States, 424
Apex Hosiery Co. v. Leader, 192
Arlosoroff v. National Collegiate Athletic Ass'n, 656
Arnold, Schwinn & Co., United States v., 156
Aspen Highlands Skiing Corp. v. Aspen Skiing Co., 644
Association for Intercollegiate Athletics for Women v. National Collegiate Athletic Ass'n, 844

Association of Independent Television Stations, Inc. v. College Football Ass'n, 765
Atlanta Nat. League Baseball Club, Inc. v. Kuhn, 21, 24, 870
Augusta Nat., Inc. v. Northwestern Mut. Life Ins. Co., 443, 444
Averill v. Luttrell, 950

Babych v. McRae, 952
Baltimore Orioles, Inc. v. Major League Baseball Players Ass'n, 428, 434, 435, 436
Banks v. National Collegiate Athletic Ass'n, 739, 781, **782,** 791, 792, 793, 794, 797
Barry Rona and Major League Baseball Players Ass'n, 375
Bathgate v. NHL Pensions' Society, 305
Bayless v. Philadelphia Nat. League Club, 969
Begley v. Mercer University, 743
Behagen v. Amateur Basketball Ass'n of United States, 915
Bell v. Industrial Vangas, Inc., 979
Berkey Photo, Inc. v. Eastman Kodak Co., 640
Berst v. Chipman, 672
Bias v. Advantage Intern., Inc., 346
Bidwill v. Garvey, 294, 974
Blaich v. National Football League, 557
Blair v. Washington State University, 801, 805, 841
Blalock v. Ladies Professional Golf Ass'n, 880, 882, 883
Blum v. Yaretsky, 656
Board of Regents of State Colleges v. Roth, 657, 658
Board of Regents of University of Oklahoma v. National Collegiate Athletic Ass'n, 776
Boris v. United States Football League, 175
Boston Athletic Ass'n v. Sullivan, 451, 452, 455
Boston Celtics Ltd. Partnership v. Shaw, 91, **101,** 105, 106, 204, 328

TABLE OF CASES

Boston Professional Hockey Ass'n, Inc. v. Cheevers, 609
Boston Professional Hockey Ass'n, Inc. v. Dallas Cap & Emblem Mfg., Inc., 446, 450, 455, 456
Bourque v. Duplechin, 950
Bowen v. United States Postal Service, 310
Bridgeman v. National Basketball Ass'n, 838 F.Supp. 172, pp. 208, 210, 332, 333, 335
Bridgeman v. National Basketball Ass'n, 675 F.Supp. 960, p. 332
Broadcast Music, Inc. v. Claire's Boutiques, Inc., 407
Broadcast Music, Inc. v. Columbia Broadcasting System, Inc., 156, 159, 876
Brown v. Board of Ed. of Topeka, Shawnee County, Kan., 853
Brown v. Pro Football, Inc., 518 U.S. 231, pp. 210, **211,** 222, 223, 224, 225, 227, 228, 234, 240, 266, 794
Brown v. Pro Football, Inc., 50 F.3d 1041, p. 211
Brown v. Pro Football, Inc., 1992 WL 88039, pp. **154, 177,** 178, 186, 188, 293, 294
Brown v. Pro Football, Inc., 782 F.Supp. 125, pp. 210, 619, 770
Brown v. Woolf, 347
Brown University, United States v., 792
Brumm v. Bert Bell NFL Retirement Plan, 974, 978
Bryant v. Fox, 980, 981
Buckton v. National Collegiate Athletic Ass'n, 725, 726, 728
Buffalo Broadcasting Co., Inc. v. American Soc. of Composers, Authors and Publishers, 157
Butler v. NCAA, 696
Butterworth v. National League of Professional Baseball Clubs, 145, 146, 501
Butts v. National Collegiate Athletic Ass'n, 703, 704, 711
Byrns v. Riddell, Inc., 982, 985

Cablevision of Michigan, Inc. v. Sports Palace, Inc., 406, 412
California State University, Hayward v. National Collegiate Athletic Ass'n, 712, 713
Campanelli v. Bockrath, 658
Campbell v. Acuff-Rose Music, Inc., 426
Cardtoons v. Major League Baseball Players Ass'n, 95 F.3d 959, p. 427
Cardtoons v. Major League Baseball Players Ass'n, 868 F.Supp. 1266, p. 427
Carlock v. NFL, 906
Carson v. Here's Johnny Portable Toilets, Inc., 425
Cedars–Sinai Medical Center, 795
Central New York Basketball, Inc. v. Barnett, 91, **95,** 98, 99, 100, 101, 105, 106, 112, 179, 244, 595, 619
Chandler v. Miller, 71
Charles D. Bonanno Linen Service, Inc. v. N.L.R.B., 266

Charles O. Finley & Co., Inc. v. Kuhn, 13, 20, 21, 27, 143, 144, 304, 869, 870
Chevron, U.S.A., Inc. v. Natural Resources Defense Council, Inc., 808
Chicago National League Ball Club v. Francis Vincent, Jr., 24, 25, 26, 27, 870
Chicago Professional Sports Ltd. Partnership v. National Basketball Ass'n, 95 F.3d 593, pp. 570, **571**
Chicago Professional Sports Ltd. Partnership v. National Basketball Ass'n, 874 F.Supp. 844, p. 568
Chicago Professional Sports Ltd. Partnership v. National Basketball Ass'n, 961 F.2d 667, pp. **559,** 566, 568, 582, 583, 588, 606, 766, 894
Chicago Professional Sports Ltd. Partnership v. National Basketball Ass'n, 808 F.Supp. 646, p. 567
Chuy v. National Football League Players' Ass'n, 304, 310
Chuy v. Philadelphia Eagles Football Club, 331
Cincinnati Bengals, Inc. v. Bergey, 91, 101, **113,** 114, 117, 525, 619
Cincinnati Bengals, Inc. v. Thompson, 304
City of (see name of city)
Clark v. Arizona Interscholastic Ass'n, 860
Classen v. Izquierdo, 982
Cohen v. Brown University, 101 F.3d 155, p. **820**
Cohen v. Brown University, 991 F.2d 888, pp. **809,** 814, 815, 819, 823, 827, 838, 839, 841, 842, 843, 860
Cohen v. Brown University, 809 F.Supp. 978, pp. 827, 838
Coleman v. Western Michigan University, 961
Collins v. National Basketball Players Ass'n, 363, 373, 379
Colorado Seminary (University of Denver) v. National Collegiate Athletic Ass'n, 657, **725**
Combined Communications Corp. of Oklahoma, Inc. v. Boger, 673
Communications Workers of America v. Beck, 311
Coniglio v. Highwood Services, Inc., 603
Connecticut v. Teal, 688
Connecticut Professional Sports Corp. v. Heyman, 100
Connell Const. Co., Inc. v. Plumbers and Steamfitters, 191, 222
Connick v. Myers, 76
Consumers Union of United States, Inc. v. General Signal Corp., 446
Container Corp. of America, United States v., 235
Continental T. V., Inc. v. GTE Sylvania Inc., 157, 159, 517, 518, 876
Copperweld Corp. v. Independence Tube Corp., 471, 491, 492, 493, 494, 495, 497, 503, 568, 590
Crawn v. Campo, 949

TABLE OF CASES

Crouch v. National Ass'n of Stock Car Auto Racing, Inc., **866,** 870, 876
CTS Corp. v. Dynamics Corp. of America, 361, 540, 668, 669

Dallas Cowboys Cheerleaders, Inc. v. Pussycat Cinema, Ltd., 456
Dallas Cowboys Football Club, Inc. v. Harris, 100
Dambrot v. Central Michigan University, 75, 77
Dante Pastorini & Oakland Raiders, 329
Davis v. Pro Basketball, Inc., 298, 304
Deesen v. Professional Golfers' Ass'n of America, 871
DeFrantz v. United States Olympic Committee, 908
DelCostello v. International Broth. of Teamsters, 307
Denver Rockets v. All-Pro Management, Inc., 175, 524
Detroit Football Co. v. Robinson, 111
Detroit Lions, Inc. v. Argovitz, 350, 354, 895
Dothard v. Rawlinson, 687
Driskill v. Dallas Cowboys Football Club, Inc., 603
Dr. Miles Medical Co. v. John D. Park & Sons Co., 156
Dryer v. Los Angeles Rams, 304, 310
Duplex Printing Press Co. v. Deering, 190
Duprey v. Shane, 979

Eastern Microwave, Inc. v. Doubleday Sports, Inc., 415
E. I. du Pont de Nemours & Co., United States v., 603, 604, 606, 607
English v. National Collegiate Athletic Ass'n, 745, 749
Erving v. Virginia Squires Basketball Club, 298, 304
Estate of (see name of party)
Eureka Urethane, Inc. v. PBA, Inc., 905
Everett v. Bucky Warren, Inc., 985

Federal Baseball Club of Baltimore v. National League, 126, 131, 137, 138, 140, 144, 145, 146, 148, 250, 251, 477
Feist Publications, Inc. v. Rural Telephone Service Co., Inc., 398, 403
Fibreboard Paper Products Corp. v. N. L. R. B., 274
Firestone Tire and Rubber Co. v. Bruch, 974
First Nat. Maintenance Corp. v. N.L.R.B., 274, 281
Fishman v. Estate of Wirtz, 625
Five Smiths, Inc. v. National Football League Players Ass'n, 234
Fleer Corp. v. Topps Chewing Gum, Inc., 141, 461
Flood v. Kuhn, 407 U.S. 258, pp. 91, 126, **127,** 137, 139, 140, 143, 144, 145, 146, 150, 179, 183, 198, 201, 228, 230, 241, 300, 370, 465, 466, 604, 609, 617, 926
Flood v. Kuhn, 443 F.2d 264, pp. 138, 300
Forbes, State v., 954
Fortnightly Corp. v. United Artists Television, Inc., 407, 413
Franklin v. Gwinnett County Public Schools, 800

Gaines v. National Collegiate Athletic Ass'n, 739, 791
Gambrell v. Kansas City Chiefs Football Club, Inc., 970
Ganden v. National Collegiate Athletic Ass'n, 689, 695, 696, 704, 711, 876, 877
Gardella v. Chandler, 139
Gauvin v. Clark, 948
Gilder v. PGA Tour, Inc., 595, 905
Golden State Transit Corp. v. City of Los Angeles, 297
Green, Regina v., 952, 954
Greenleaf v. Brunswick-Balke-Collender Co., 879
Griffin v. Wisconsin, 66
Griggs v. Duke Power Co., 687
Grinnell Corp., United States v., 608
Grove City College v. Bell, 686, 800, 853
Groves v. Alabama State Bd. of Educ., 687
Grubb v. KMS Patriots, L.P., 404
Gulf South Conference v. Boyd, 711, 713
Gunter Harz Sports, Inc. v. United States Tennis Ass'n, Inc., 898, 903, 905

H. A. Artists & Associates, Inc. v. Actors' Equity Ass'n, 369
Hackbart v. Cincinnati Bengals, Inc., 601 F.2d 516, p. **940**
Hackbart v. Cincinnati Bengals, Inc., 435 F.Supp. 352, pp. **935,** 969
Haelan Laboratories, Inc. v. Topps Chewing Gum, Inc., 423, 424, 425, 460
Haffer v. Temple University, 853, 854
Hall v. University of Minnesota, 657, **698**
Hanna Mfg. Co. v. Hillerich & Bradsby Co., 423
Harlem Wizards Entertainment Basketball, Inc. v. NBA Properties, Inc., 443
Hawaii Housing Authority v. Midkiff, 536
Hawkins v. National Collegiate Athletic Ass'n, 674
Haywood v. National Basketball Ass'n, 175, 176
Hebert v. Los Angeles Raiders, 140, 926
Hecht v. Pro-Football, Inc., 570 F.2d 982, pp. **621,** 625
Hecht v. Pro-Football, Inc., 444 F.2d 931, p. 625
Heldman v. United States Lawn Tennis Ass'n, 887, 988
Henderson Broadcasting Corp. v. Houston Sports Ass'n, Inc., 141, 557
Hendy v. Losse, 979

TABLE OF CASES

Hennessey v. National Collegiate Athletic Ass'n, 771, 779
Hernandez v. Childers, 353
Hill v. National Collegiate Athletic Ass'n, 57, 65, 66, 68, 70, 669
Hirsch v. S.C. Johnson & Son, Inc., 426
HMC Management v. New Orleans Basketball Club, 530
Holmes v. National Football League, 51
Hoover v. Meiklejohn, 855
Hormel Foods Corp. v. Jim Henson Productions, Inc., 457
Horner v. Kentucky High School Athletic Ass'n, 860
Houston Oilers, Inc. v. Neely, 91, 101, 106, **107,** 111, 619, 736
Howard University v. National Collegiate Athletic Ass'n, 656, 658
Hubbard Broadcasting, Inc. v. Southern Satellite Systems, Inc., 417, 419
Hutcheson, United States v., 190, 191

Indianapolis Colts, Inc. v. Metropolitan Baltimore Football Club Ltd. Partnership., 437, 444, 445
International Boxing Club of N.Y., United States v., 139, 604
International Boxing Club of N. Y., Inc. v. United States, 604, 606, 607
International News Service v. Associated Press, 394, 395, 397, 398
International Olympic Committee v. San Francisco Arts & Athletics, 915
International Order of Job's Daughters v. Lindeburg and Co., 450, 456
International Shoe Co. v. State of Wash., Office of Unemployment Compensation and Placement, 917

Jackson v. Drake University, 718
Jackson v. National Football League Players Ass'n, 371
J.I. Case Co. v. N.L.R.B., 267, 271, 304, 363
Jimmy Connors v. Arthur Ashe, 887
Johnson–Kennedy Radio Corporation v. Chicago Bears Football Club, 395
Jones v. Childers, 353
Justice v. National Collegiate Athletic Ass'n, 658

Kansas City Royals Baseball Corp. v. Major League Baseball Players Ass'n, 242, **298,** 304, 379
Kartell v. Blue Shield of Massachusetts, Inc., 152, 153, 155
Kelley v. University of Illinois, 815
Kelley, Walter A., 250
Kelly Communications v. Westinghouse Broadcasting, 395
Kemp v. Ervin, 675, 676
Kennedy v. Long Island R. Co., 190
Kleczek v. Rhode Island Interscholastic League, Inc., 860

Klor's, Inc. v. Broadway–Hale Stores, Inc., 156
Knapp v. Northwestern University, 876, 877, **990,** 1001
Kneeland v. National Collegiate Athletic Ass'n, 673
Koszela v. National Ass'n of Stock Car Auto Racing, Inc., 870
Krueger v. San Francisco Forty Niners, 979, 981

Laborers Health and Welfare Trust v. Advanced Lightweight Concrete Co., Inc., 274
Lafler v. Athletic Bd. of Control, 859
Laing v. Minnesota Vikings Football Club, Inc., 603
Laird v. United States, 547, 548
Law v. National Collegiate Athletic Ass'n, 134 F.3d 1025, p. 779
Law v. National Collegiate Athletic Ass'n, 134 F.3d 1010, p. 779
Law v. National Collegiate Athletic Ass'n, 902 F.Supp. 1394, pp. **771,** 779, 780, 781, 809
Lemat Corp. v. Barry, 114, 244
Lestina v. West Bend Mut. Ins. Co., 949
Levin v. National Basketball Ass'n, 524
Liberty Broadcasting System v. National League Clubs, 394
Linseman v. World Hockey Ass'n, 175
Local 825, Intern. Union of Operating Engineers v. N.L.R.B., 289
Local Union No. 189, Amalgamated Meat Cutters v. Jewel Tea Co., 193, 222, 369
Loeb v. Turner, 395
Loewe v. Lawlor, 189
Los Angeles Memorial Coliseum Com'n v. National Football League, 489, 519, 520, 521, 522, 489, **503,** 517, 518, 519, 520, 521, 522, 523, 524, 529, 537, 566, 583
Los Angeles Raiders v. National Football League, 520
Los Angeles Rams Football Club v. Cannon, 111
Lowe v. California League of Professional Baseball, 951
Ludtke v. Kuhn, 80, 659
Lugar v. Edmondson Oil Co., Inc., 656

Mackey v. National Football League, 99, 175, 178, **179,** 183, 189, 192, 193, **194,** 197, 198, 199, 200, 201, 204, 205, 209, 248, 275, 519, 526, 609
Maddox v. City of New York, 986, 988
Major Indoor Soccer League & Professional Soccer Players Ass'n, 354
Major League Baseball Players Ass'n and the Commissioner of Major League Baseball, 42, 47, 49
Major League Baseball Properties, Inc. v. Sed Non Olet Denarius, Ltd., 444
Maki, Regina v., 953

TABLE OF CASES

Maloney, Regina v., 954
Manning v. Grimsley, 951
Martin Luther King, Jr., Center for Social Change, Inc. v. American Heritage Products, Inc., 424
Mathews v. Eldridge, 658, 662
Matuszak v. Houston Oilers, Inc., 140, 926
Mayor and City Council of Baltimore v. Baltimore Football Club Inc., 537
McCormack v. National Collegiate Athletic Ass'n, 780, 781, 797
McCourt v. California Sports, Inc., 199, 200, 201, 204, 609, 620
McCoy v. Major League Baseball, 145
McHale v. Cornell University, 748
McNeil v. National Football League, 184, 207, 208, 234, 255, 290, 314, 566, 978
Metro Broadcasting, Inc. v. F.C.C., 819, 829
Midler v. Ford Motor Co., 424
Mid-South Grizzlies v. National Football League, 525, 528, 529, 592, 602
Mike Marshall & Minnesota Twins, 328
Milenbach v. Commissioner, 539
Miller v. Universal City Studios, Inc., 403
Milwaukee American Ass'n v. Landis, 10, 12
MLB Players Association v. MLB Player Relations Committee, 29
Molinas v. National Basketball Ass'n, 32, 34, 35, 51
Montana v. San Jose Mercury News, Inc., 427
Morio v. North American Soccer League, 268
Morris v. New York Football Giants, Inc., 304
Morsani v. Major League Baseball, 145
Motschenbacher v. R. J. Reynolds Tobacco Co., 426
Mt. Pleasant, Iowa, City of v. Associated Elec. Co-op., Inc., 568
Muhammad Ali v. State Athletic Commission of N. Y., 883
Munchak Corp. v. Cunningham, 106, 114
Murray v. Nat. Football League, 491
Mutual Broadcasting System v. Muzak Corp., 394

Nassau Sports v. Hampson, 609
Nassau Sports v. Peters, 609
National & American League Professional Baseball Clubs v. Major League Baseball Players Association, 13, 99, 230, **241,** 248, 249, 250, 270, 275, 298, 299, 303, 304, 325, 336, 379, 617
National Basketball Ass'n v. Motorola, Inc., 398, 401, 403, 419, 431, 435
National Basketball Ass'n v. SDC Basketball Club, Inc., 522, 524
National Basketball Ass'n v. Williams, 209, 210, 211, 223, 227, 280
National Broadcasting Co., Inc. v. Copyright Royalty Tribunal, 421

National Collegiate Athletic Ass'n v. Board of Regents of University of Oklahoma, 566, 576, 583, **750,** 763, 765, 766, 768, 769, 771, 772, 773, 779, 781, 793, 894
National Collegiate Athletic Ass'n v. Hornung, 660, 661
National Collegiate Athletic Ass'n v. Miller, 663, 668, 669, 926
National Collegiate Athletic Ass'n v. Tarkanian, 668, **650,** 657, 658, 659, 660, 662, 669, 673, 674, 676, 686, 713, 726, 732, 733, 738, 741, 749, 768, 794, 915
National Exhibition Co. v. Fass, 395
National Exhibition Co. v. Teleflash, 392, 394
National Football League v. Governor of State of Del., 445, 456
National Football League v. McBee & Bruno's, Inc., 408, 412, 430
National Football League v. North American Soccer League, 475
National Football League v. Rondor, Inc., 412
National Football League Management Council v. National Football League Players Ass'n, 50
National Football League Management Council and NFLPA, 290, 294
National Football League Players Ass'n v. National Football League Management Council (Dutton), 249, 250
National Football League Players Ass'n v. Pro-Football, Inc., 312
National Football League Players Ass'n and National Football League Management Council, 54
National Football League Properties, Inc. v. New Jersey Giants, Inc., 455
National Football League Properties, Inc. v. Wichita Falls Sportswear, Inc., 450
National Football League, United States v., 196 F.Supp. 445, p. 555
National Football League, United States v., 116 F.Supp. 319, pp. **550,** 555, 556, 631
National Soc. of Professional Engineers v. United States, 158, 160, 174, 184, 764, 876
National Treasury Employees Union v. Von Raab, 66
Neeld v. National Hockey League, 990, 1000
New Boston Television, Inc. v. Entertainment Sports Programming Network, Inc., 404, 406, 421
New Jersey v. T.L.O., 65
New Jersey Sports and Exposition Authority v. McCrane, 534
New York, City of v. New York Jets Football Club, Inc., 530
New York Football Giants, Inc. v. Los Angeles Chargers Football Club, Inc., 101, 106, 107, 111
Niemczyk v. Burleson, 948

N. L. R. B. v. Acme Industrial Co., 273
N. L. R. B. v. General Motors Corp., 311
N.L.R.B. v. Health Care & Retirement Corp. of America, 255
N. L. R. B. v. Insurance Agents' Intern. Union, AFL–CIO, 273
N.L.R.B. v. Jones & Laughlin Steel Corp., 250
N. L. R. B. v. Katz, 273
N.L.R.B. v. Mackay Radio & Telegraph Co., 289
N.L.R.B. v. Transportation Management Corp., 257
N. L. R. B. v. Wooster Div. of Borg–Warner Corp., 274, 281
Nordstrom v. N.L.R.B., 262
North American Soccer League v. National Football League, 470, 471, **472,** 476, 489, 491, 494, 517, 561, 583, 608
North American Soccer League v. N.L.R.B., 263, 266, 267
Northwest Wholesale Stationers, Inc. v. Pacific Stationery and Printing Co., 157, 160, 876

Oakland, City of v. Oakland Raiders, 220 Cal.Rptr. 153, pp. **538,** 540
Oakland, City of v. Oakland Raiders, 183 Cal.Rptr. 673, pp. **532,** 537, 543
Oates v. District of Columbia, 851
O'Brien v. Pabst Sales Co., 422
O'Grady v. PGA Tour, Inc., 882, 883
Oil, Chemical and Atomic Workers Intern. Union, AFL–CIO v. Mobil Oil Corp., 312
Ordway v. Casella, 942, 950, 951
Orr v. National Football League Players' Ass'n, 312, 313

Pagliero v. Wallace China Co., 450
Palmer v. Kansas City Chiefs Football Club, 965
Parish v. National Collegiate Athletic Ass'n, 506 F.2d 1028, pp. 681, 726
Parish v. National Collegiate Athletic Ass'n, 361 F.Supp. 1220, pp. **677,** 682, 686, 712
Partee v. San Diego Chargers Football Co., 139, 926
Patrick v. Burget, 870
Pattern Makers' League of North America, AFL–CIO v. N.L.R.B., 311
Paul v. Davis, 657
Pavesich v. New England Life Ins. Co., 422
Pederson v. Louisiana State University, 838
People v. _____ (see opposing party)
Pestalozzi v. Philadelphia Flyers Ltd., 951
Peterson v. Kennedy, 306, 311
Pfeiffer v. New England Patriots Football Club, Inc., 603
Philadelphia Ball Club v. Lajoie, 91, 94, 95, 105, 119, 120

Philadelphia World Hockey Club, Inc. v. Philadelphia Hockey Club, Inc., 351 F.Supp. 462, pp. 189, 191, **609,** 620
Philadelphia World Hockey Club, Inc. v. Philadelphia Hockey Club, Inc., 351 F.Supp. 457, p. 198
Piazza v. Major League Baseball, 142, 145, 146, 147, 501, 587
Pirone v. MacMillan, Inc., 423
Pittsburgh Athletic Co. v. KQV Broadcasting Co., 392, 394, 395, 396, 397, 398, 401, 419, 425, 428, 445, 452
Portland Baseball Club, Inc. v. Kuhn, 140
Postema v. National League of Professional Baseball Clubs, 140
Post Newsweek Stations–Connecticut, Inc. v. Travelers Ins. Co., 395
Pottgen v. Missouri State High School Activities Ass'n, 705, 709, 710, 711, 876, 877
Powell v. National Football League, 930 F.2d 1293, p. 205
Powell v. National Football League, 678 F.Supp. 777, pp. 204, 205, 206, 208, 209, 210, 227, 234, 255, 290, 314
Professional Hockey Corp. v. World Hockey Ass'n, 499
Pro–Football, Inc. v. District of Columbia Dept. of Employment Services (Workers' Compensation), 313

Quincy Cablesystems, Inc. v. Sully's Bar, Inc., 412

Radovich v. National Football League, 139
R.A.V. v. St. Paul, Minn., 76
Raymond Bourque and Bostons Bruins, 336, 341
Regents of University of California v. American Broadcasting Companies, Inc., 765
Regents of University of Minnesota v. National Collegiate Athletic Ass'n, 560 F.2d 352, pp. 658, 660
Regents of University of Minnesota v. National Collegiate Athletic Ass'n, 422 F.Supp. 1158, pp. 660, 661
Regina v. _____ (see opposing party)
Rendell–Baker v. Kohn, 656
Rensing v. Indiana State University Bd. of Trustees, 444 N.E.2d 1170, p. **959**
Rensing v. Indiana State University Bd. of Trustees, 437 N.E.2d 78, pp. 794, **956**
Retail Clerks Intern. Ass'n, Local 1625, AFL–CIO v. Schermerhorn, 311
Reynolds v. International Amateur Athletic Federation, 23 F.3d 1110, pp. **921,** 925, 926, 928, 931
Reynolds v. International Amateur Athletic Federation, 505 U.S. 1301, p. 920
Reynolds v. International Amateur Athletic Federation, 841 F.Supp. 1444, pp. **916,** 920, 928

TABLE OF CASES xxvii

Reynolds v. National Football League, 198
Richards v. United States Tennis Ass'n, 879, 932
Riko Enterprises, Inc. v. Seattle Supersonics Corp., 27
Roberson v. Rochester Folding Box Co., 422
Roberts v. Colorado State Bd. of Agriculture, 814, 815, 838
Robertson v. National Basketball Ass'n, 198, 315, 595
Robitaille v. Vancouver Hockey Club, 982
Rose v. Giamatti, 3, 4, 6, 10, 34, 48, 645
Ross v. Creighton University, 957 F.2d 410, p. **717**
Ross v. Creighton University, 740 F.Supp. 1319, pp. **713,** 719, 862
Rothery Storage & Van Co. v. Atlas Van Lines, Inc., 159
Rowe v. Baltimore Colts, 969
Rudy Hackett & Denver Nuggets, 329

Safro v. Lakofsky, 100
Saint v. Nebraska School Activities Ass'n, 859
Salerno v. American League of Professional Baseball Clubs, 140
Sample v. Gotham Football Club, Inc., 331
Sandison v. Michigan High School Athletic Ass'n, Inc., 709, 711
San Francisco Arts & Athletics, Inc. v. United States Olympic Committee, 457
San Francisco Seals, Ltd. v. National Hockey League, 501, 525
Schentzel v. Philadelphia Nat. League Club, 951
Scott v. Kilpatrick, 711
Sealy, Inc., United States v., 156
Seattle Seahawks v. NFLPA, 256
Seattle Totems Hockey Club, Inc. v. National Hockey League, 528
Selig v. United States, 547, 548
Shapero v. Kentucky Bar Ass'n, 388
Sharif by Salahuddin v. New York State Educ. Dept., 687
Sharpe v. National Football League Players Ass'n, 310
Shelton v. National Collegiate Athletic Ass'n, 736, 738
Shubert, United States v., 131
Sielicki v. New York Yankees, 969
Silver v. New York Stock Exchange, 156
Silverman v. Major League Baseball Player Relations Committee, Inc., 67 F.3d 1054, p. 287
Silverman v. Major League Baseball Player Relations Committee, Inc., 880 F.Supp. 246, pp. **281,** 295, 317
Silverman v. Major League Baseball Player Relations Committee, Inc., 516 F.Supp. 588, pp. **274,** 279, 280
Simon & Schuster, Inc. v. New York State Crime Victims Bd., 37
Skinner v. Railway Labor Executives' Ass'n, 66

Smith v. Pro Football, Inc., 161, 166, 172, 173, 175, 177, 183, 188, 198, 248, 519
Socony–Vacuum Oil Co., United States v., 156
Sony Corp. of America v. Universal City Studios, Inc., 406
Sorkin, People v., 343
Southeastern Community College v. Davis, 698
Southern Pac. Co. v. Arizona, 538
Spencer v. Milton, 100
Standard Oil Co. of New Jersey v. United States, 156
Stanley v. University of Southern California, 845
State v. _____ (see opposing party)
State of (see name of state)
Steele v. Louisville & N.R. Co., 304, 305
STP Corp. v. United States Auto Club, Inc., 898, 903, 905
Sullivan v. National Football League, 478, 488, 490, 491, 493, 494, 542, 546, 583
Sullivan v. Tagliabue, 489
Sweeney v. Bert Bell NFL Player Retirement Plan, 975, 978

Tarkanian v. National Collegiate Athletic Ass'n, 657
Taylor v. Wake Forest University, 742, 743, 745, 749
Teleprompter Corp. v. Columbia Broadcasting System, Inc., 407, 414
Titan Sports, Inc. v. Comics World Corp., 427
Toolson v. New York Yankees, Inc., 131, 139, 140, 251
Topco Associates, Inc., United States v., 156
Topps Chewing Gum, Inc. v. Major League Baseball Players Ass'n, 461, 465, 587
Toronto Blue Jays v. Boston Celtics and Danny Ainge, 89, 91, 101, 329, 660
Total Economic Athletic Management of America, Inc. v. Pickens, 371
Trans World Airlines, Inc. v. Hardison, 77
Tunkl v. Regents of University of Cal., 721
Twentieth Century Music Corp. v. Aiken, 407
Twentieth Century Sporting Club v. Transradio Press Service, 401
Twin City Sportservice, Inc. v. Charles O. Finley & Co., Inc., 141

Uhlaender v. Henricksen, 426
United Mine Workers of America v. Pennington, 191, 222
United Paperworkers Intern. Union, AFL–CIO v. Misco, Inc., 298
United States v. _____ **(see opposing party)**
United States Football League v. National Football League, 704 F.Supp. 474, p. 642

TABLE OF CASES

United States Football League v. National Football League, 842 F.2d 1335, pp. **629,** 642

United States Football League v. National Football League, 634 F.Supp. 1155, p. 626

United States Football League Players Ass'n, AFL–CIO v. U.S. Football League, 105, 498

United States Golf Ass'n v. St. Andrews Systems, Data-Max, Inc., 455

United Steelworkers of America v. American Mfg. Co. (Steelworker Trilogy), 298, 303, 304

United Steelworkers of America, AFL–CIO–CLC v. Rawson, 371

University of Colorado v. Derdeyn, 65

University of Pittsburgh v. Champion Products, Inc., 450

Vaca v. Sipes, 305, 310, 320

Ventura v. Titan Sports, Inc., 436

Vernonia School Dist. 47J v. Acton, 66, 71

Virginia, United States v., 819, 820

Volvo North America Corp. v. Men's Intern. Professional Tennis Council, 354, **888,** 893, 894

Wagenblast v. Odessa School Dist. No. 105-157-166J, 1001, 1006

Walters v. Fullwood, 356, 360, 361, 373, 380

Walters v. Harmon, 374, 375, 380, 381, 386

Walters, United States v., 997 F.2d 1219, p. **381**

Walters, United States v., 711 F.Supp. 1435, p. 781

Wards Cove Packing Co., Inc. v. Atonio, 687

Warner Bros., Inc. v. Gay Toys, Inc., 724 F.2d 327, p. 450

Warner Bros., Inc. v. Gay Toys, Inc., 553 F.Supp. 1018, p. 450

Warner Bros., Inc. v. Gay Toys, Inc., 658 F.2d 76, p. 450

Warner Bros., Inc. v. Gay Toys, Inc., 513 F.Supp. 1066, p. 450

Washington v. Davis, 686

Washington Capitols Basketball Club, Inc. v. Barry, 114

Washington State Bowling Proprietors Ass'n v. Pacific Lanes, Inc., 879

WCVB-TV v. Boston Athletic Ass'n, 395, 402, **452,** 455

Weight-Rite Golf Corp. v. United States Golf Ass'n, 766 F.Supp. 1104, p. 905

Weight-Rite Golf Corp. v. United States Golf Ass'n, 1990 WL 145594, p. 905

Weinberg v. Chicago Blackhawk Hockey Team, Inc., 626

Weser v. Professional Golfers' Ass'n. of America, 872, 876

White v. National Football League, 41 F.3d 402, p. 312

White v. National Football League, 836 F.Supp. 1458, pp. 207, 208, 227, 234, 290, 294, 314, 315

White v. Samsung Electronics America, Inc., 424, 425

Wichita State University Intercollegiate Athletic Ass'n v. Swanson Broadcasting, 395

Wiley v. National Collegiate Athletic Ass'n, 729, 733

Williams v. School Dist. of Bethlehem, Pa., 860

Williamson v. Lee Optical of Okl., 361

Winnipeg Rugby Football Club, Limited, v. Freeman, 99, 100, 311

Wisconsin, State of v. Milwaukee Braves, Inc., 140

Wood v. National Basketball Ass'n, 201, 204, 208, 209, 620

Wright v. Columbia University, 1001

Wright Line, a Div. of Wright Line, Inc., 257

WTWV, Inc. v. National Football League, 556

Wynn v. Columbus Mun. Separate School Dist., 851

Zacchini v. Scripps–Howard Broadcasting Co., 395, 424, 425, 428, 434

Zimmerman v. National Football League, 200, 201, 204

Zinn v. Parrish, 343, 346

SPORTS AND THE LAW

TEXT, CASES, PROBLEMS

Second Edition

Chapter One

BEST INTERESTS OF THE SPORT: THE ROLE OF THE COMMISSIONER AND OTHER GOVERNING AUTHORITIES

The most enduring conflicts that bring lawyers and judges into play in the professional sports world involve commercial issues. Thus the bulk of this book will be devoted to the law of labor disputes about player free agency, owner-league-community disputes about franchise free agency, and intellectual property disputes that pit both owners and players against the fans who have to pay to experience more and more features of the sports world. Often, however, the most visible sports controversies involve personal actions that seem to threaten the integrity, not just the image, of the game.

Several of the highly-publicized recent examples involve events that occurred on the field or the court: e.g., Baltimore Orioles' Roberto Alomar spitting on an umpire, Golden State Warriors' Latrell Sprewell choking his coach, and Denver Nuggets' Mahmoud Abdul–Rauf refusing to stand respectfully during the national anthem. More often, though, these player actions take place away from the stadium or arena. Boston College football players were found to have bet on games (including a couple of their own team's games during the 1996 season); the Cowboys' Michael Irvin and Leon Lett used drugs; the Minnesota Vikings' Warren Moon and the Red Sox' Wil Cordero faced charges for physically abusing their spouses. Not just players and coaches, but also owners have generated such *causes célèbres*: e.g., the Cincinnati Reds' Marge Schott used racial and religious slurs about blacks and Jews.

The long-standing popular assumption is that it is the responsibility of the "commissioner" to protect the "best interests of the sport" from such behavior. Any organization needs a chief executive officer—in the case of sports, to establish schedules and league championships, to supervise officials, to negotiate television and merchandising contracts, and the like. What makes sports unique (by comparison with the movie world, for example) is that the office of the commissioner has historically been viewed as the supreme voice about what truly is in the *best* interests (not just the *business* interests) of the game. The Commissioner is empowered to resolve disputes on that score among players, clubs, and other participants.[a] Not just professional team sports, but also individual sports like golf and tennis with their tours, and college sports with the NCAA, have a commissioner (or executive director) to play that role. The one conspicuous exception is boxing, where a large number of "governing" organizations are readily manipulated by promoters like Don King on behalf of fighters like Mike Tyson. This example reinforces the fans' view that any sport that wants to preserve its integrity needs a commissioner.

Ironically, baseball, the sport that gave birth to the role of commissioner in the early 1920s, has functioned throughout much of the 1990s without someone formally occupying this office. Instead, Milwaukee Brewers' owner Allen "Bud" Selig has performed the actual commissioner functions in his role as Chair of Major League Baseball's Executive Committee. Media commentators repeatedly blamed this office vacancy for the long-lasting labor strife that engulfed baseball from 1993 into early 1997. As we shall see later, though, every sport has regularly experienced major labor (and other) disputes even while they were presided over by a commissioner. More fundamentally, serious questions have been raised about whether it really is in the best interests of a sport to have such power reside in a single person selected by one constituency, the team owners, rather than selected by and accountable to players and fans as well.

As we shall see in this chapter, individual disputes that pose that underlying issue have begun to filter into the courts, as aggrieved parties challenge the source and scope of the commissioner's authority, the procedures followed, and the penalties meted out. Even more important than the current legal propriety of such commissioner action is the question of what should be the appropriate division of responsibility among individual freedom, organizational authority, and public scrutiny in addressing gambling, drug use, racial and domestic abuse, and other controversies that bedevil contemporary sports and life.

a. Several popular biographies and histories provide illuminating glimpses of the history and the issues covered in this chapter: e.g., J.G. Taylor Spink, *Judge Landis and 25 Years of Baseball* (St. Louis, Mo.: Sporting News Press, 1974); Harold Seymour, *Baseball: The Golden Age* (New York: Oxford University Press, 1971); Red Barber, *1947: When All Hell Broke Loose in Baseball* (New York: Doubleday, 1982); Bowie Kuhn, *Hardball: The Education of a Baseball Commissioner* (New York: Time Books, 1987); and David Harris, *The League: The Rise and Decline of the NFL* (New York: Bantam Books, 1986). A detailed and readable account of baseball owners' relations with their commissioners (and players and fans) is John Helyar, *Lords of the Realm: The Real History* (New York: Villard Books, 1994). And we now have a more systematic and scholarly treatment of the issues raised in this (and several following) chapters, by Dean Roger I. Abrams, *Legal Bases: Baseball and the Law* (Philadelphia, PA: Temple U. Press, 1998).

A. PETE ROSE v. BART GIAMATTI[b]

A case that dramatically raised these issues about the integrity of the game was the "collision at home plate" between baseball Commissioner Bart Giamatti and baseball superstar Pete Rose.[c] The human dimensions of this tragic affair have been the subject of several books and countless articles. Only the key legal events will be recounted here.

In the early winter of 1989, rumors began to filter into the Commissioner's Office that Rose, then manager of the Cincinnati Reds, had been betting on baseball games, even on games involving his own team. If true, that action would have violated a sixty-year-old Major League Rule that required a one-year suspension for anyone betting on baseball and a lifetime ban for betting on a game involving one's own team. Accordingly, on February 23, newly-elected Commissioner Giamatti hired John Dowd, a Washington lawyer, to investigate this allegation. The Commissioner was acting under the authority granted him by Article I of the "Major League Agreement" among all the clubs making up major league baseball—the "baseball constitution" that now has its equivalents in the National Football League, the National Basketball Association, and the National Hockey League. Under Article I, § 2, "the functions of the Commissioner" include:

> (a) To investigate, either upon complaint or upon his own initiative, any act, transaction or practice charged, alleged or suspected to be not in the best interests of the national game of Baseball, with authority to summon persons and to order the production of documents and, in cases of refusal to appear or produce, to impose such penalties as are hereinafter provided;
>
> (b) To determine, after investigation, what preventive, remedial or punitive action is appropriate in the premises, and to take such action either against Major Leagues, Major League Clubs, or individuals, as the case may be.

In early May, after three months of investigating and interviewing some 40 witnesses, including taking sworn statements from Rose and the two key informants against him, Ron Peters and Paul Janszen, Dowd delivered to Giamatti a 225-page report (with seven volumes of evidence and exhibits) that ended with Dowd's judgment that Rose had regularly bet on Reds' games (although apparently Rose always bet on his Reds to win). Giamatti immediately sent this report to Rose and his lawyers and scheduled Rose's hearing before him for late June.

---

b. The key judicial decision quoted in the text is *Rose v. Giamatti*, 721 F.Supp. 906 (S.D.Ohio 1989). See also Matthew Pachman, *Limits on the Discretionary Powers of Professional Sports Commissioners: A Historical and Legal Analysis of Issues Raised by the Pete Rose Controversy*, 76 Virginia L. Rev. 1409 (1990).

c. See James Reston Jr., *Collision at Home Plate: The Lives of Pete Rose and Bart Giamatti*, (New York: Burlingame Books, 1991). Another useful account of this case is Michael Y. Sokolove, *Hustle: The Myth, Life, and Lies of Pete Rose* (New York: Simon and Schuster, 2d ed. 1992).

On April 18, however, Giamatti had sent a letter to U.S. District Judge Carl Rubin, who was preparing to sentence Peters for federal drug and income tax offenses. Giamatti stated in his letter that Peters had been "candid, forthright and truthful" in providing "critical sworn testimony" about Rose. The Cincinnati-based Judge Rubin, an avowed Reds fan and highly exercised by what he termed the Commissioner's "vendetta against Pete Rose," sent a copy of the letter to Reuven Katz, Rose's principal lawyer. Armed with this letter, Katz filed suit in state court to prohibit Giamatti from going any further with the disciplinary proceeding. The contention was that Giamatti had prejudged the facts of the case, and thus had denied Rose his right to a proceeding conducted with "due regard for all the principles of natural justice and fair play," as the Commissioner's own disciplinary rules required. After Rose won a controversial 10-day restraining order from state court Judge Norbert Nadel, Giamatti sought to remove the case to federal district court on diversity of citizenship grounds.

In arguing for removal, the Commissioner's counsel asserted that this case should be heard only by a "national tribunal":

> In the state court in Cincinnati, I need not describe Mr. Rose's standing. He is a local hero, perhaps the first citizen of Cincinnati. And Commissioner Giamatti is viewed suspiciously as a foreigner from New York, trapped in an ivory tower, and accused of bias by Mr. Rose. Your Honor, this is a textbook example of why diversity jurisdiction was created in the Federal Courts and why it exists to this very day.

But that removal could be obtained only if this case were deemed to be a dispute just between Rose, a citizen of Ohio, and Giamatti, a citizen of New York. If the Cincinnati Reds, also a citizen of Ohio in the eyes of the law, were considered a real party to this conflict, then the complete diversity of citizenship required for federal jurisdiction would be lacking. In applying the arcane rules of federal versus state court jurisdiction, the judicial opinion in *Rose v. Giamatti*, 721 F.Supp. 906, 917, laid bare "the reality ... that Major League Baseball is a unique organization ... [with] extraordinary power invested in the Commissioner."

Rose's argument was quite simple. Rose was the manager of the Reds, under a contract paying him $500,000 a year, a contract whose benefits he was in grave danger of losing because of Giamatti's violation of procedural fairness towards him. Clearly, then, the Reds were an appropriate party in Rose's lawsuit to prevent that from happening.

The commissioner's answer, which the federal court accepted, was that the contract between Rose and the Reds provided that "the Major League and Professional Baseball Agreements and Rules and all amendments thereto hereafter adopted, are hereby made a part of this contract." This feature of Rose's personal employment contract stemmed from the following provision of the Major League Agreement:

> The form of players' contract to be used by the Major Leagues, and all contracts between Major Leagues or Clubs and their officers and

employees, shall contain a clause by which the parties agree to submit themselves to the discipline of the Commissioner, and to accept his decisions rendered in accordance with this Agreement.

The commissioner's disciplinary authority was reinforced by the constituent members' further agreement to "be finally and unappealably bound" by all the disciplinary decisions of the commissioner, and to "waive such right of recourse to the courts as would otherwise have existed in their favor." The judge read this network of contractual relationships as establishing a commissioner's office wielding judicial power totally independently of control by either the Reds individually or the 26 clubs collectively. (As the judge observed, the constitution ordained that "neither the Commissioner's powers nor his compensation may be diminished during his term of office.") That meant that only Rose and Giamatti were real parties to this case, which hence was properly removable to the federal judicial arena.

This procedural ruling came down on July 31. Perhaps because he was then facing even more pressing legal problems with the Internal Revenue Service, Rose agreed on August 23 to settle the case on the terms that Rose would withdraw his suit, accept the Commissioner's jurisdiction and penalty, but neither admit nor deny having bet on baseball. As penalty, Giamatti declared Rose permanently ineligible to associate with any major or minor league baseball club. (After a year, however, Rose would be entitled to apply to the commissioner for termination of this lifetime ban.) A few days later, Giamatti was dead of a heart attack, succeeded in office by his counsel and close friend, Francis "Fay" Vincent. A few months later, Rose went to jail for income tax fraud—in particular, for concealing large cash payments from baseball autograph shows (money that Rose had used to cover his large gambling losses).

As the second edition of this book was being completed in the fall of 1997, Rose was applying for reinstatement in baseball's good graces. Many observers were skeptical that the owners (or a future commissioner) would lift the lifetime ban, and certainly not without Rose admitting and apologizing for having bet on his own team's games. This ongoing Rose saga presents in stark relief, then, baseball's (and other team sports') historic abhorrence of gambling. The case thus poses the *substantive* question whether it is truly in the best interests of the sport to ban the all-time hit leader from the game (and the Hall of Fame) for betting on his own team to win. Later in this chapter we shall consider how this behavior by Rose compares in legal and moral turpitude with other offenses committed by professional athletes—for example, Rose's own income tax evasion (let alone Mike Tyson's rape).

An underlying *institutional* question is why authority over this issue is reserved to the league speaking through its commissioner, rather than left for direct dealings between individual clubs and their managers and players. (In the case of college sports, the alternative would be dealings between colleges and their student-athletes, rather than the NCAA which has a far longer and more detailed rule-book than Major League Baseball.) As we will see in the next several chapters, one of the characteristics that distinguishes sports from other industries is that the clubs make up a league that speaks through a commissioner, and that league pursues objectives that are not necessarily the same as those of individual clubs or their players and fans. A crucial question, then, is whether, when they act collectively as a league, the owners should be treated as a single entity for purposes of contract, antitrust, labor, and other substantive areas of the law.

This brings us to the most fundamental issue posed by *Rose v. Giamatti*—the *constitutional* theme that runs through the entire field of sports and the law. To what extent should public law, speaking through judges, venture to overturn decisions made by private leagues, speaking through their commissioners? The challenge to the law is captured by this passage from George Will's review of *Collision at Home Plate*[d]:

> Reston does not do justice to how close the *Rose* case came to becoming another case of a familiar political pathology. Yet another functioning American institution—the commissioner's office—almost became a victim of judicial overreaching. Today's courts have an unhealthy itch to supervise and fine-tune virtually every equity judgment in American life. Rose's legal strategy was to find a judge willing to insinuate himself into baseball's disciplinary procedures. If Rose had succeeded, the commissioner's office would have been irreparably damaged. Its core function, which is disciplinary, would permanently have been put in question. Another of civil society's intermediary associations—those that stand between the individual and the state—would have been broken to the saddle of government. A nanny-like judiciary would henceforth have made the commissioner's office negligible—another hitherto private institution permeated by state power.

Keep this journalistic version of the "public-private" distinction[e] in mind as you read the entire record presented in this book of the law's involvement in the world of sports.

B. THE LEGAL SCOPE OF THE COMMISSIONER'S AUTHORITY

In fact, Commissioner Giamatti did not assert quite the sweeping insulation from judicial control proclaimed by George Will. In oral argument, Giamatti's counsel stated that the commissioner "has to answer in court as to whether his conduct comported with whatever is required by a court respecting due process." (Should counsel have conceded that the commissioner of a private sports league must observe

---

d. George Will, *Foul Ball*, N.Y. Rev. of Books, June 27, 1991, at 31, 34.

e. This distinction is, of course, one of the principal targets of the entire Critical Legal Studies movement. See Mark Kelman, *A Guide to Critical Legal Studies* 102–09, 253–57, 271–73 (Cambridge, Mass.: Harvard University Press, 1987).

judicial "due process" in his deliberations and decision?) As we have seen, the reason given why the commissioner had to answer to a federal, rather than a state, court is that the commissioner did not have to answer to the Reds. The source and scope of any such judicial scrutiny can be traced in the following cases. As you read each of the decisions reproduced in this chapter, look for and reflect upon the answers to the following questions:

1. What is the source of the commissioner's legal authority to act in the given case? Why is this authority given to the commissioner rather than to an individual club, to an outside arbitrator, or to a public official or judge?

2. What is the scope of the commissioner's power—that is, under the asserted source of authority, in what situations is the commissioner empowered to take action in cases of this type?

3. What procedures should the commissioner follow in deciding on the course of action? What is the source of these procedural requirements?

4. If there are factual doubts or disputes, what standard of proof should the commissioner employ in the given case—reasonable suspicion, preponderance of the evidence, clear and convincing evidence, or proof beyond a reasonable doubt?

5. What remedy or penalty may the commissioner employ in the specific case?

6. Finally, and most importantly, what is (and what should be) the jurisdiction of a court (or an arbitrator) to review the commissioner's action—i.e., the commissioner's answers to questions two through five. What legal theories can legitimately be employed to challenge the action? What standard of review will a court use in these legal challenges?

The legal starting point is *American League Baseball Club of New York (Yankees) v. Johnson*, 109 Misc. 138, 179 N.Y.S. 498 (N.Y.1919). This litigation occurred near the end of the "National Commission" era in major league governance, during which American League President Byron "Ban" Johnson was acknowledged to be the strongest figure in the game. Carl Mays, a pitcher for the Boston Red Sox, walked off the field in the middle of a game, and went fishing the next day. While Johnson waited for the Red Sox to take disciplinary action, Sox owner Harry Frazee instead sold Mays to the Yankees (this was a rehearsal for the next such transaction between the two clubs, which involved Babe Ruth that winter). When he learned of the sale, Johnson himself suspended Mays for "deserting his club and breaking contract." Furious at losing Mays' services in the midst of the pennant race, the Yankees sued Johnson, calling him an "unmolested despot." The case was heard by then Judge, later Senator, Robert Wagner of New York, who eventually authored the National Labor Relations Act of 1935 which was used by

Players Association leader, Marvin Miller, to transform baseball in the 1970s.

Judge Wagner's decision began by stating:

> It is undisputed, and, indeed, a matter of common knowledge, that the commercialization of baseball is a highly profitable undertaking, rendering lucrative returns to the member clubs, to their stockholders, and to their employees. Large capital is invested in the enterprise, and the property representative of this capital consists principally of contracts with individual players, together with the reputation of the club for skill and ability in playing the game. Suspension of a player, therefore, not only interferes with his individual contract, but may also interfere with the reputation and collective ability of the club. Inasmuch as the leading clubs of the league and their players are entitled at the end of the season to certain rights and privileges which are unquestionably to be deemed property rights, this interference with an individual player would confuse and possibly destroy the rights of the respective clubs and their players, for the validity of the games in which Mays participated might be questioned.

Johnson had asserted that the following language of § 20 of the league constitution gave him authority for his action:

> The president, in the performance of his duties, shall have the power to impose fines or penalties, in the way of suspension or otherwise, upon any manager or player who, in his opinion, has been guilty of conduct detrimental to the general welfare of the game.

The Yankees responded, and Judge Wagner agreed, that the wording of § 24 assigned responsibility for these questions to the individual team:

> Each club belonging to this league shall have the right to regulate its own affairs, to establish its own rules, and to discipline, punish, suspend or expel its manager, players or other employees, and these powers shall not be limited to cases of dishonest play or open insubordination, but shall include all questions of carelessness, indifference, or other conduct of the player that may be regarded by the club as prejudicial to its interest, but not in conflict with any provision of the National Agreement or this constitution.

In addition, the President had the authority to exercise disciplinary authority only "in the performance of his duties," which the judge characterized as follows:

> Under these rules it is the right and duty of the president to regulate the actual playing of the game on the field and to enforce the rules instituted for the governing of the game. Doubtless his powers would extend to the discipline of players for any infringement of these rules upon the field, or for an overt act committed by a player on the field in violation of the rules. Beyond that power, however, it does not seem that the president may proceed, for under

the constitution he is given power to discipline only in the performance of his duties, and his duties are only such as are set forth in the constitution and playing rules.

The offense of which Mays was accused was obviously not one of those embraced within the prohibition of these rules. It was not an overt act committed on the field.

Although that literal reading of the constitution did not square with historical practice, the judge stated:

On behalf of the defendant, contention is made that many times in the past the defendant Johnson had exercised power similar to that which he claims the right to exercise under the present circumstances, that his jurisdiction to make orders similar to the one now in dispute has never been questioned, and that the parties to a contract will be bound by the construction which their conduct and acquiescence have placed upon it. Although courts have placed great weight on the construction which parties have put upon contracts existing between them, such considerations must never violate the fundamental concepts of justice. If the original act was unauthorized, repetition does not invest the act with authority. If the construction did not convey power to the president, he cannot prescriptively acquire power by continual usurpation. If the opposite were true he would, in effect, effectuate an amendment of the constitution by usurpation. In his immortal and always useful Farewell Address, Washington said:

"If in the opinion of the people the distribution or modification of the constitutional powers be in any particular wrong, let it be corrected by an amendment in the way which the Constitution designates, but let there be no change by usurpation."

So in this case there can be no change by usurpation. The structure of precedents must fall, unless laid on the foundation of authority.

Accordingly, Judge Wagner granted a permanent injunction against Mays' suspension. The Yankees' celebratory press release stated that "our fight has not been for Mays alone, but to safeguard the vested property rights of the individual club-owners against the continual encroachments on club rights by the president, who has never been clothed with the powers that he has taken unto himself."

Ironically, though, the *Johnson* decision was handed down just after completion of the infamous 1919 World Series, in which gamblers bribed White Sox players to fix the games. When word of the "Black Sox" scandal emerged a year later, both fans and club owners felt that the source of the problem was the lax disciplinary approach of the National Commission (composed of the two league presidents and a chairman selected by the two of them). The owners decided to dismantle the tripartite commission and replace it with a single, powerful commissioner. The man tagged for that position was Kenesaw Mountain Landis, a 38–year–old federal judge in Chicago who had initially caught the owners' eye with his favorable handling of the Federal League antitrust suit a few years earlier (see Chapter 2). Landis agreed to take this new $50,000 per year position only if the Major League Agreement was rewritten to give the commissioner the sweeping powers described in *Rose v. Giamatti*.

There was one reported legal challenge to Landis' authority. Apparently a player named Fred Bennett had been transferred several times between the St. Louis Browns and several minor league teams, but all the clubs were secretly controlled by Browns' owner Phil Ball. When Landis learned of the inter-club relationship, he refused to approve this latest Browns' transaction with the Milwaukee club, and declared Bennett a free agent. The resulting lawsuit revealed a very different judicial attitude to commissioner authority than we saw in the *Johnson* case.

MILWAUKEE AM. ASS'N. v. LANDIS
United States District Court, Northern District of Illinois, 1931.
49 F.2d 298.

LINDLEY, DISTRICT JUDGE.

* * *

Under the Major League Agreement the office of commissioner was created, and his functions were defined.... He was given jurisdiction to hear and determine finally any disputes between leagues and clubs or to which a player might be a party, certified to him, and authorized, in case of "conduct detrimental to baseball," to impose punishment and pursue appropriate legal remedies; to determine finally a disagreement over any proposed amendment to the rules; and "to take such other steps as he might deem necessary and proper in the interest and morale of the players and the honor of the game." Optional agreements with players were defined and assignments thereof required to be filed with, and approved by, the commissioner. The parties agreed to abide by the decisions of the latter and the discipline imposed by him under the agreement and severally waived right of recourse to the courts. Similar covenants appear in the Major–Minor agreement, the National Association agreement and the uniform contracts with players.

The Major–Minor League agreement recognizes the office of commissioner and the jurisdiction aforesaid and provides that, in case of any dispute between any Major club and any Minor club, the disputants may certify the dispute to the commissioner for decision, and that his determination shall be final.

The various agreements and rules constituting a complete code for, or charter and by-laws of, organized baseball in America, disclose a clear intent upon the part of the parties to endow the commissioner with all the attributes of a benevolent but absolute despot and all the disciplinary powers of the proverbial *pater familias*.

* * *

The parties endowed the commissioner with wide powers and discretion to hear controversies that might be submitted to him and of his own initiative to observe, investigate and take such action as necessary to secure observance of the provisions of the agreements and rules, promotion of the expressed ideals of, and prevention of conduct detrimental to, baseball. The code is expressly designed and intended to foster keen, clean competition in the sport of baseball, to preserve discipline and a high standard of morale, to produce an equality of conditions necessary to the promotion of keen competition and to protect players against clubs, clubs against players, and clubs against clubs.

* * *

Certain acts are specified as detrimental to baseball, but it is expressly provided that nothing contained in the code shall be construed as exclusively defining or otherwise limiting acts, practices or conduct detrimental to baseball. It is contended that this phrase should be so construed as to include only such conduct as is similar to that expressly mentioned. However, the provisions are so unlimited in character that we can conclude only that the parties did not intend so to limit the meaning of conduct detrimental to baseball, but intended to vest in the commissioner jurisdiction to prevent any conduct destructive of the aims of the code. Apparently it was the intent of the parties to make the commissioner an arbiter, whose decisions made in good faith, upon evidence, upon all questions relating to the purpose of the organization and all conduct detrimental thereto, should be absolutely binding. So great was the parties' confidence in the man selected for the position and so great the trust placed in him that certain of the agreements were to continue only so long as he should remain commissioner.

Plaintiffs contend that the commissioner has no power to declare a player a free agent. In his answer, the commissioner states that it is his view that, by reason of the alleged breach of the code by plaintiffs and their denial of Bennett's rights, plaintiffs have made it his duty to declare Bennett absolved from any contractual obligations which he may have had with either plaintiff and to declare him a free agent. Obviously declaring Bennett a free agent is a mere declaration of legal effect, that is, the result of finding that the St. Louis Club has forfeited its rights by violating the spirit and intent of the code. Whether there is given to the commissioner the power in so many words to declare Bennett a free agent is immaterial, since the agreements and rules grant to the commissioner jurisdiction to refuse to approve Bennett's assignment by St. Louis to Milwaukee, and to declare him absolved from the burdens of the same and of his contract with St. Louis.

* * *

It is asserted that this wide grant of jurisdiction of the commissioner is an attempt to deprive the court of its jurisdiction and that such a provision as is contained in these agreements, rules, and uniform contract is contrary to public policy. No doubt the decision of any arbiter, umpire, engineer, or similar person endowed with the power to decide may not be exercised in an illegal manner, that is fraudulently, arbitrarily, without legal basis for the same or without any evidence to justify action. The many cases cited upon the power and jurisdiction of such officials are not in serious conflict. An agreement to arbitrate a controverted question and to deprive all courts of jurisdiction, so long as in executory form, is quite commonly held void, but an actual submission to an arbiter or umpire in good faith is proper, and decision under same is binding, unless it is unsupported by evidence, or unless the decision is upon some basis without legal foundation or beyond legal recognition.

Plaintiffs submitted to the defendant as commissioner an optional contract, which under the code could not be effective unless approved by him. After ascertaining the facts, he refused to approve the same. This, if we look at it from the point of arbitration, was an executed agreement for arbitration, and called for more than ministerial action. As we have seen, the commissioner is given almost unlimited discretion in the determination of whether or not a certain state of facts creates a situation detrimental to the national game of baseball. The commissioner rightfully found that the common control of St. Louis and the named Minor Clubs by one person made it possible to create a situation whereby the clear intent of the adopted code that the players under the control of a Major club should not be kept with a Minor club more than two successive seasons without giving other Major clubs the right to claim him was clearly violated, and a result achieved highly detrimental to the national game of baseball. The facts negative any assertion that this decision was made arbitrarily or fraudulently. It was made in pursuance of jurisdiction granted to the commissioner with the expressed desire to achieve certain ends, that is, to keep the game of baseball clean, to promote clean competition, to prevent collusive or fraudulent contracts, to protect players' rights, to furnish them full opportunity to advance in accord with their abilities and to prevent their deprival of such opportunities by subterfuge, covering or other unfair conduct.

Suit dismissed.

Beneath the surface of this technical dispute between Commissioner Landis and the owner of the Browns was a fundamental transformation taking place within organized baseball. Despite his formal constitutional authority, Landis fought a losing struggle against the emergence of the farm system pioneered by Branch Rickey of the St. Louis Cardinals. The *Milwaukee* case had enforced the letter of baseball's rules restricting multiple optioning of players to minor league teams. Just two years after this judicial ruling, though, the "farm bloc" owners used their majority position to push through a revision of the major league rules and baseball's reserve system to facilitate stockpiling of players on a minor league team owned or controlled by the major league club. Who wins and who loses under the farm system arrangement? Keep this question in mind for succeeding chapters when we explore the broader parameters of the owners' reserve system for players.

The last two decades have witnessed a much more active use of commissioner authority in a fast-changing sports environment. In his autobiography, *Hardball*,[f] former baseball commissioner Bowie Kuhn recounts many such cases: two of the most controversial involved maverick club owners Charlie Finley of the Oakland Athletics and Ted Turner of the Atlanta Braves. Both of these cases grew out of a legal ruling reproduced in Chapter 4—the 1976 arbitration decision in the *Andy Messersmith/Dave McNally* grievance. This ruling eviscerated the "reserve clause" that had tied baseball players for life to their original team, and gave players the freedom to move to a new team upon expiration of their current contracts (including one option year). Collective bargaining that summer confirmed the concept of "free agency" in baseball, though it limited such status to players with six years of big league service. The prospect of free agency frightened some team owners, but it was not unwelcome to wealthy owners (like the Yankees' George Steinbrenner) who were yearning to win a pennant.

Charles Finley was the most concerned. Despite an ill-advised move of his Kansas City Athletics to Oakland where they had to compete with the San Francisco Giants for support in the Bay Area, Finley had successfully used the draft system (instituted by baseball in 1965) to build the most powerful team of the early 1970s: five straight divisional titles and three straight World Series championships. Unfortunately, Finley tended to treat his players like "plantation hands" (as Kuhn observed), including even such Oakland stars as Reggie Jackson, Vida Blue, and Jim "Catfish" Hunter. With free agency pending, the A's appeared to be in dire straits. Thus, Finley devised the following strategy: he would sell off his current assets, the veteran stars of his three-time World Series champion A's, and invest the proceeds in development via the farm system of future assets—young stars who could not command high salaries through free agency. There was only one impediment to his plan—Commissioner Kuhn.

CHARLES O. FINLEY v. BOWIE KUHN
United States Court of Appeals, Seventh Circuit, 1978.
569 F.2d 527.

SPRECHER, CIRCUIT JUDGE.

[Just before baseball's trading deadline of June 15, 1976, Finley and the Athletics sold the contract rights to the services of Joe Rudi and Rollie Fingers to the Boston Red Sox for $2 million and of Vida Blue to

---

[f.] See Kuhn, *Hardball: The Education of a Baseball Commissioner*, note a above, at 173–87 and 259–64. A revealing counterpoint to Kuhn's account of these times and these cases can be found in the memoirs of the leader of the Major League Baseball Players Association when it won free agency for its members. See Marvin Miller, *A Whole Different Ball Game: The Sport and Business of Baseball* (New York: Birch Lane Press, 1991).

the New York Yankees for $1.5 million. Rudi and Fingers were to become free agents upon the expiration of their contracts at the end of the 1976 season. Just before the Athletics' transaction with the Yankees, Blue signed a three-year contract extension, the benefit of which was transferred to the Yankees in this sale. The day after a quickly scheduled hearing on June 17, Commissioner Kuhn disapproved the assignments of the contracts of Rudi, Fingers, and Blue to the Red Sox and Yankees "as inconsistent with the best interests of baseball, the integrity of the game and the maintenance of public confidence in it." The Commissioner expressed his concern for (1) the debilitation of the Oakland club, (2) the loss of competitive balance in professional baseball through the buying of success by the wealthier clubs, and (3) "the present unsettled circumstances of baseball's reserve system." A week later, Finley brought this suit challenging Kuhn's authority to take such action.]

II

Basic to the underlying suit brought by Oakland and to this appeal is whether the Commissioner of baseball is vested by contract with the authority to disapprove player assignments which he finds to be "not in the best interests of baseball." In assessing the measure and extent of the Commissioner's power and authority, consideration must be given to the circumstances attending the creation of the office of Commissioner, the language employed by the parties in drafting their contractual understanding, changes and amendments adopted from time to time, and the interpretation given by the parties to their contractual language throughout the period of its existence.

* * *

On September 28, 1920, an indictment issued charging that an effort had been made to "fix" the 1919 World Series by several Chicago White Sox players. Popularly known as the "Black Sox Scandal," this event rocked the game of professional baseball and proved the catalyst that brought about the establishment of a single, neutral Commissioner of baseball.

In November, 1920, the major league club owners unanimously elected federal Judge Kenesaw Mountain Landis as the sole Commissioner of baseball and appointed a committee of owners to draft a charter setting forth the Commissioner's authority. In one of the drafting sessions an attempt was made to place limitations on the Commissioner's authority. Judge Landis responded by refusing to accept the office of Commissioner.

On January 12, 1921, Landis told a meeting of club owners that he had agreed to accept the position upon the clear understanding that the owners had sought "an authority . . . outside of your own business, and that a part of that authority would be a control over whatever and whoever had to do with baseball." Thereupon, the owners voted unanimously to reject the proposed limitation upon the Commissioner's authority, they all signed what they called the Major League Agreement, and Judge Landis assumed the position of Commissioner. Oakland has been a signatory to the Major League Agreement continuously since 1960. The agreement, a contract between the constituent clubs of the National and American Leagues, is the basic charter under which major league baseball operates.

* * *

The Major Leagues and their constituent clubs severally agreed to be bound by the decisions of the Commissioner and by the discipline imposed by him. They further agreed to "waive such right of recourse to the courts as would otherwise have existed in their favor." Major League Agreement, Art. VII, Sec. 2.[14]

Upon Judge Landis' death in 1944, the Major League Agreement was amended in two respects to limit the Commissioner's authority. First, the parties deleted the provision by which they had agreed to waive their right of recourse to the courts to challenge actions of the Commissioner. Second the parties added the following language to Article I, § 3:

> No Major League Rule or other joint action of the two Major Leagues, and no action or procedure taken in compliance with any such Major League Rule or joint action of the two Major Leagues shall be considered or construed to be detrimental to Baseball.

The district court found that this addition had the effect of precluding the Commissioner from finding an act that complied with the Major League Rules to be detrimental to the best interests of baseball.

The two 1944 amendments to the Major League Agreement remained in effect during the terms of the next two Commissioners, A.B. "Happy" Chandler and Ford Frick. Upon Frick's retirement in 1964 and in accordance with his recommendation, the parties adopted three amendments to the Major League Agreement: (1) the language added in 1944 preventing the Commissioner from finding any act or practice "taken in compliance" with a Major League Rule to be "detrimental to baseball" was removed; (2) the provision deleted in 1944 waiving any rights of recourse to the courts to challenge a Commissioner's decision was restored; and (3) in places where the language "detrimental to the best interests of the national game of baseball" or "detrimental to baseball" appeared those words were changed to "not in the best

---

14. ... Also, on the same day, January 12, 1921, that the Major League Agreement was signed on behalf of the two major leagues and sixteen baseball clubs, the league presidents and club presidents individually signed the following "Pledge to Support the Commissioner":

We, the undersigned, earnestly desirous of insuring to the public wholesome and high-class baseball, and believing that we ourselves should set for the players an example of the sportsmanship which accepts the umpire's decision without complaint, hereby pledge ourselves loyally to support the Commissioner in his important and difficult task; And we assure him that each of us will acquiesce in his decisions even when we believe them mistaken, and that we will not discredit the sport by public criticism of him or of one another.

interests of the national game of Baseball" or "not in the best interests of Baseball."

* * *

III

Despite the Commissioner's broad authority to prevent any act, transaction or practice not in the best interests of baseball, Oakland has attacked the Commissioner's disapproval of the Rudi–Fingers–Blue transactions on a variety of theories which seem to express a similar thrust in differing language.

The complaint alleged that the "action of Kuhn was arbitrary, capricious, unreasonable, discriminatory, directly contrary to historical precedent, baseball tradition, and prior rulings and actions of the Commissioner." In pre-trial answers to interrogatories, Oakland acknowledged that the Commissioner could set aside a proposed assignment of a player's contract "in an appropriate case of violation of (Major League) Rules or immoral or unethical conduct."

* * *

The plaintiff has argued that it is a fundamental rule of law that the decisions of the head of a private association must be procedurally fair. Plaintiff then argued that it was "procedurally unfair" for the Commissioner to fail to warn the plaintiff that he would "disapprove large cash assignments of star players even if they complied with the Major League Rules."

In the first place it must be recalled that prior to the assignments involved here drastic changes had commenced to occur in the reserve system and in the creation of free agents. In his opinion disapproving the Rudi, Fingers and Blue assignments, the Commissioner said that "while I am of course aware that there have been cash sales of player contracts in the past, there has been no instance in my judgment which had the potential for harm to our game as do these assignments, particularly in the present unsettled circumstances of baseball's reserve system and in the highly competitive circumstances we find in today's sports and entertainment world."

Absent the radical changes in the reserve system, the Commissioner's action would have postponed Oakland's realization of value for these players.[27] Given those changes, the relative fortunes of all major league clubs became subject to a host of intangible speculations. No one could predict then or now with certainty that Oakland would fare better or worse relative to other clubs through the vagaries of the revised reserve system occurring entirely apart from any action by the Commissioner.

---

27. This realization of value could come in the form of subsequent player transactions involving less cash but some returning-player value, or in box office profits attributable to these players, or possibly in the aggregate value of the club if and when eventually sold as a franchise and team.

In the second place, baseball cannot be analogized to any other business or even to any other sport or entertainment. Baseball's relation to the federal antitrust laws has been characterized by the Supreme Court as an "exception," an "anomaly" and an "aberration." Baseball's management through a commissioner is equally an exception, anomaly and aberration.... In no other sport or business is there quite the same system, created for quite the same reasons and with quite the same underlying policies. Standards such as the best interests of baseball, the interests of the morale of the players and the honor of the game, or "sportsmanship which accepts the umpire's decision without complaint," are not necessarily familiar to courts and obviously require some expertise in their application. While it is true that professional baseball selected as its first Commissioner a federal judge, it intended only him and not the judiciary as a whole to be its umpire and governor.

As we have seen in Part II, the Commissioner was vested with broad authority and that authority was not to be limited in its exercise to situations where Major League Rules or moral turpitude was involved. When professional baseball intended to place limitations upon the Commissioner's powers, it knew how to do so. In fact, it did so during the 20-year period from 1944 to 1964.

The district court found and concluded that the Rudi–Fingers–Blue transactions were not, as Oakland had alleged in its complaint, "directly contrary to historical precedent, baseball tradition, and prior rulings." During his almost 25 years as Commissioner, Judge Landis found many acts, transactions and practices to be detrimental to the best interests of baseball in situations where neither moral turpitude nor a Major League Rule violation was involved, and he disapproved several player assignments.

On numerous occasions since he became Commissioner of baseball in February 1969, Kuhn has exercised broad authority under the best interests clause of the Major League Agreement. Many of the actions taken by him have been in response to acts, transactions or practices that involved neither the violation of a Major League Rule nor any gambling, game-throwing or other conduct associated with moral turpitude. Moreover, on several occasions Commissioner Kuhn has taken broad preventive or remedial action with respect to assignments of player contracts.

On several occasions Charles O. Finley, the principal owner of the plaintiff corporation and the general manager of the Oakland baseball club, has himself espoused that the Commissioner has the authority to exercise broad powers pursuant to the best interests clause, even where there is no violation of the Major League Rules and no moral turpitude is involved.

Twenty-one of the 25 parties to the current Major League Agreement who appeared as witnesses in the district court testified that they intended and they presently understand that the Commissioner of baseball can review and disapprove an assignment of a player contract which he finds to be not in the best interests of baseball, even if the assignment does not violate the Major League Rules and does not involve moral turpitude.

* * *

We conclude that the evidence fully supports, and we agree with, the district court's finding that "[t]he history of the adoption of the Major League Agreement in 1921 and the operation of baseball for more than 50 years under it [strongly indicate] that the Commissioner has the authority to determine whether any act, transaction or practice is 'not in the best interests of baseball,' and upon such determination, to take whatever preventive or remedial action he deems appropriate, whether or not the act, transaction or practice complies with the Major League Rules or involves moral turpitude." Any other conclusion would involve the courts in not only interpreting often complex rules of baseball to determine if they were violated but also, as noted in the Landis case, the "intent of the [baseball] code," an even more complicated and subjective task.

The Rudi–Fingers–Blue transactions had been negotiated on June 14 and 15, 1976. On June 16, the Commissioner sent a teletype to the Oakland, Boston and New York clubs and to the Players' Association expressing his "concern for possible consequences to the integrity of baseball and public confidence in the game" and setting a hearing for June 17. Present at the hearing were 17 persons representing those notified. At the outset of the hearing the Commissioner stated that he was concerned that the assignments would be harmful to the competitive capacity of Oakland; that they reflected an effort by Boston and New York to purchase star players and "bypass the usual methods of player development and acquisition which have been traditionally used in professional baseball"; and that the question to be resolved was whether the transactions "are consistent with the best interests of baseball's integrity and maintenance of public confidence in the game." He warned that it was possible that he might determine that the assignments not be approved....

[In his decision] the Commissioner recognized "that there have been cash sales of player contracts in the past," but concluded that "these transactions were unparalleled in the history of the game" because there was "never anything on this scale or falling at this time of the year, or which threatened so seriously to unbalance the competitive balance of baseball." The district court concluded that the attempted assignments of Rudi, Fingers and Blue "were at a time and under circumstances making them unique in the history of baseball."

We conclude that the evidence fully supports, and we agree with, the district court's finding and conclusion that the Commissioner "acted in good faith, after investigation, consultation and deliberation, in a manner which he determined to be in the best interests of baseball" and that "[w]hether he was right or wrong is beyond the competence and the jurisdiction of this court to decide."[44]

* * *

V

Following the bench trial, the district court reached its decision in favor of the Commissioner without considering the impact of Article VII, § 2 of the Major League Agreement, wherein the major league baseball clubs agreed to be bound by the Commissioner's decisions and discipline and to waive recourse to the courts.

* * *

Oakland has urged us to apply the substantive law dealing with the "policies and rules of a private association" to the Major League Agreement and actions taken thereunder. Illinois has developed a considerable body of law dealing with the activities of private voluntary organizations and we agree that the validity and effect of the waiver of recourse clause should initially be tested under these decisions.

Even in the absence of a waiver of recourse provision in an association charter, "[i]t is generally held that courts ... will not intervene in questions involving the enforcement of bylaws and matters of discipline in voluntary associations."

* * *

Viewed in light of these decisions, the waiver of recourse clause contested here seems to add little if anything to the common law nonreviewability of private association actions. This clause can be upheld as coinciding with the common law standard disallowing court interference. We view its inclusion in the Major League Agreement merely as a manifestation of the intent of the contracting parties to insulate from review decisions made by the Commissioner concerning the subject matter of actions taken in accordance with his grant of powers.

* * *

Even if the waiver of recourse clause is divorced from its setting in the charter of a private, voluntary association and even if its relationship with the arbitration clause in the agreement is ignored, we think that it is valid under the circumstances here involved. Oakland claims that such clauses are invalid as against public policy. This is true, however, only under circumstances where the waiver of rights is not voluntary, knowing or intelligent, or was not freely negotiated by parties occupying equal bargaining positions. The trend of cases in many states and in the

---

44. It is beyond the province of this court to consider the wisdom of the Commissioner's reasons for disapproving the assignments of Rudi, Blue and Fingers. There is insufficient evidence, however, to support plaintiff's allegation that the Commissioner's action was arbitrary or capricious, or motivated by malice, ill will or anything other than the Commissioner's good faith judgment that these attempted assignments were not in the best interests of baseball. The great majority of persons involved in baseball who testified on this point shared Commissioner Kuhn's view.

federal courts supports the conclusion of the district court under the circumstances presented here that "informed parties, freely contracting, may waive their recourse to the court."

Although the waiver of recourse clause is generally valid for the reasons discussed above, we do not believe that it forecloses access to the courts under all circumstances. Thus, the general rule of nonreviewability which governs the actions of private associations is subject to exceptions 1) where the rules, regulations or judgments of the association are in contravention to the laws of the land or in disregard of the charter or bylaws of the association, or 2) where the association has failed to follow the basic rudiments of due process of law. Similar exceptions exist for avoiding the requirements of arbitration under the United States Arbitration Act. We therefore hold that, absent the applicability of one of these narrow exceptions, the waiver of recourse clause contained in the Major League Agreement is valid and binding on the parties and the courts.

* * *

Suit dismissed.

Questions for Discussion

1. Ignoring for the moment the appropriate scope of judicial scrutiny of commissioner decisions, consider the merits of Commissioner Kuhn's ruling. Is there anything wrong with one owner selling a player's services to another? The world of baseball is very different in the late 1990s than it was in the mid–1970s. It is now quite common each summer to see teams that are out of the pennant race transfer star players to top contenders, sometimes for young talent (often to be selected and named later), and occasionally just to move a high salary off a payroll when game attendance is dropping. While baseball still has a version of the *Kuhn* doctrine that bars explicit *sales* of players for excessive (though now much larger) sums, this is not true of all sports. Recall the 1989 blockbuster hockey deal that sent Wayne Gretzky from the Edmonton Oilers to the Los Angeles Kings for $15 million plus players, a deal replicated in 1992 by the Quebec Nordiques who sent Eric Lindros to the Philadelphia Flyers for $15 million and players. Would it have been in the best interests of hockey for then-NHL President John Ziegler to have disallowed either of these transactions, just because of the huge sums of money involved?

2. Would the standard of review articulated in *Finley v. Kuhn* have been any different if the "waiver of legal recourse" clause had not been included in the Major League Agreement? If the court was simply adopting the same "hands off" judicial attitude exhibited towards the actions of private associations or the decisions of private arbitrators, was the validity of the waiver of recourse clause an important issue in the case?

The court in *Finley v. Kuhn* endorsed a broad authority of the commissioner to nullify club transactions. Shortly thereafter came another decision, *Atlanta National League Baseball Club & Ted Turner v. Bowie Kuhn*, 432 F.Supp. 1213 (N.D.Ga.1977), which was issued between the dates of the district and appellate court rulings in *Finley v. Kuhn*. *Turner* dealt with the commissioner's authority to discipline owners and employees of the member teams, and thus raised many issues similar to those posed in Pete Rose's case.

In July, 1976, following the events described in the *Finley* case above, Major League Baseball and its Players Association negotiated a new collective agreement with an elaborate free agency system. Players with six years of service in the major leagues could declare their intention to become free agents before the end of October. In early November, a draft would be conducted for those "declared" free agents, under which up to twelve teams could elect to bid for any one player. Before the draft, though, only his prior club had the right to negotiate with that player.

In August 1976, Commissioner Kuhn issued a series of directives to owners that warned them against any dealings with potential free agents prior to the "reentry draft." In September 1976, the Commissioner found that the Atlanta Braves' General Manager had made improper contact with Gary Matthews of the San Francisco Giants. For this "tampering" offense the Commissioner fined the Braves $5,000 and took away their first pick in the winter amateur draft. Subsequently, at a cocktail party in October 1976, Braves' owner Ted Turner, told Bob Lurie, owner of the Giants, that the Braves would go as high as necessary to get Matthews. Members of the media present at this exchange published the story.

The free agent draft was conducted on November 4, and the Braves succeeded in signing Matthews on November 17. Subsequently, on December 30, Commissioner Kuhn upheld Lurie's complaint against Turner. Kuhn decided, however, not to disapprove Matthews' contract. Instead, the Commissioner suspended Turner from baseball for one year, and deprived Atlanta of its first round pick in the next summer's amateur draft. Turner and the Braves went off to court to try to get Kuhn's ruling overturned.

District Judge Edenfield acknowledged the traditional broad authority of the commissioner to "punish" baseball people "for acts considered not in the best interests" of the game. Complicating this situation, though, was the fact that the Major League Agreement among the owners had to be read in tandem with the new labor agreement between the owners and the Players Association—the document that had created both free agency and a reentry draft for players like Matthews. "The two agreements must now be read together as forming the framework for the government of Major League baseball," which meant that the powers of the Commissioner had to be interpreted "so as to avoid infringing upon the rights secured by the parties to the collective bargaining agreement."

Even with this caveat, the judge concluded ("with some misgivings") that the Commissioner had the authority to issue and enforce directives that barred any owner from "dealing" with another team's players before the draft. With respect to the penalties for the Braves breaching that directive, the judge also found it strange that Kuhn had allowed the Braves to sign and keep Matthews, but forbade Turner, the owner, to operate his Braves team.

> ... [T]he casual observer might call this an Indian massacre in reverse. In their encounter with the Commissioner, the Braves took "nary" a scalp, but lived to see their owner dangling from the lodgepole of the Commissioner, apparently only as a warning to others.

432 F.Supp. at 1222. Ultimately, though, the court did not judge this to be an "abuse of commissioner discretion."

> In Article VII, § 2, of the Major League Agreement the clubs explicitly agreed to be bound by the discipline imposed by the Commissioner and obviously intended to give him a certain amount of leeway to choose the appropriate sanction. Judicial review of every sanction imposed by the Commissioner would produce an unworkable system that the Major League Agreement endeavors to prevent. Here, Turner was warned of the suspension, he asked for the suspension, the contract specifically authorized it, and he got it.

432 F.Supp. at 1223.

The judge however, did feel that he had the authority to rule that Commissioner Kuhn went beyond the scope of his authority by taking away from the Braves their first pick in the next June rookie draft. The court's rationale was that such a draft penalty was not one of the specific commissioner sanctions mentioned in Article II, § 3, of the Major League Agreement. Kuhn's counsel had emphasized the phrasing in § 3 to the effect that "punitive actions by the Commissioner ... *may involve* any one or more of the following ..." (emphasis added). This was the judge's answer:

> [T]he language of the Major League Agreement and Major League Rules seems to imply that the list of sanctions in § 3 is exclusive, and basic rules of contract construction support this conclusion. Prior to the original Major League Agreement, there were no presumed powers vested in a Commissioner. The 1921 agreement created the office of the Commissioner and defined his powers out of whole cloth. In such a situation, the maxim "Expressio unius est exclusio alterius" is particularly applicable. Moreover, in light of the fact that this contract purports to authorize the imposition of a penalty or forfeiture, it must be strictly construed.

432 F.Supp. at 1225. Nor was the court persuaded by the fact that Kuhn's predecessors had regularly imposed disciplinary sanctions that were not listed in § 3, without anyone having gone off to court to seek relief.

> That the Commissioner's authority in those cases went unchallenged does not persuade this court of the Commissioner's unlimited

punitive powers in light of contractual language and established rules of construction to the contrary. If the Commissioner is to have the unlimited punitive authority as he says is needed to deal with new and changing situations, the agreement should be changed to expressly grant the Commissioner that power. The deprivation of a draft choice was first and foremost a punitive sanction, and a sanction that is not specifically enumerated under § 3. Accordingly, the court concludes that the Commissioner was without the authority to impose that sanction, and its imposition is therefore void.

432 F.Supp. at 1226.

The legal scope of the commissioner's powers surfaced once more in the summer of 1992, in a dispute that served as the prelude to major revisions in both the role of the commissioner and the state of free agency in baseball.

The National League was about to expand by adding two teams, each of which had to be assigned to one of the League's two divisions at that time. Everyone naturally assumed that the Colorado Rockies would be in the National League West and the Florida Marlins in the East. However, these league deliberations sparked an effort by several owners to review the overall divisional alignment, with the vast majority of clubs favoring a shift of the Chicago Cubs and St. Louis Cardinals to the West and Cincinnati Reds and Atlanta Braves to the East. This move would ease travel times, enhance geographic rivalries, and keep more away-game telecasts in prime-time viewing in the home markets. The Cubs, however, were strongly opposed. The stated reason for their opposition was the loss of long-standing rivalries with teams such as the New York Mets. The unstated, but widely-assumed, reason was that under the National League's unbalanced divisional schedule, the Cubs would play many more games in western time zones, which would impair the television ratings of the Cub's corporate sibling within the Chicago Tribune empire—the superstation WGN. The Cubs (supported by the New York Mets) exercised their right under the National League constitution to veto their transfer to another division, and thereby blocked the overall proposal.

A number of National League teams decided to pursue the matter further and ask Commissioner Fay Vincent to order realignment through his authority under Article I, § 2 of the Major League Agreement (MLA):

> to investigate ... any act, transaction or practice ... not in the best interests of the national game of Baseball ... [and] to determine ... what preventive, remedial or punitive action is appropriate ... and to take such action....

The Cubs (now supported by several National League teams and National League President Bill White) argued to the Commissioner that his authority in this case was limited to and by Article VII of the MLA, which empowers the Commissioner to decide:

> all disputes and controversies related in any way to professional baseball between clubs ... other than those whose resolution is expressly provided for by another means in this Agreement ... in the constitution of either Major League or the Basic Agreement between the Major Leagues and the Major League Baseball Players Association.

Commissioner Vincent rejected the Cubs' argument, concluded that he did have authority to act under Article I of the MLA, and decided that the best interests of Baseball were not served by the National League's stringent constraints upon realignment decisions. When Vincent ordered that the Cubs (and the Cardinals) be shifted to the National League's Western Division, the Cubs went off to federal district court in Chicago to secure an injunction blocking this move.

In an unreported decision, *Chicago National League Ball Club v. Francis Vincent, Jr.* (N.D.Ill.1992), Judge Conlon concluded that the Commissioner's general authority under Article I was preempted under Article VII by specific language in the National League Constitution which provided that "no member club may be transferred to a different division without its consent." The judge was not prepared to allow the Commissioner to "unilaterally amend the National League Constitution simply because he finds that a constitutional provision or procedure is 'not in the best interests of baseball.'"

> Under Illinois rules for construing contracts, it is clear that the broad authority granted the Commissioner by Article I of the Major League Agreement is not as boundless as he suggests. Giving the language of Article I its common sense and ordinary meaning, the Commissioner's authority to investigate "acts," "transactions" and "practices" and to determine and take "preventive, remedial or punitive action" does not encompass restructuring the divisions of the National League. There has been no conduct for the Commissioner to investigate, punish or remedy under Article I. The veto exercised by the Chicago Cubs as a matter of contractual right merely resulted in the maintenance of long-standing divisional assignments reflected in the National League Constitution.

Echoing the views of the district court in *Turner*, Judge Conlon was not impressed by the long history of untrammelled commissioner authority in baseball.

> The Commissioner also cites two prior actions to support his position: Commissioner Kuhn's 1976 reversal of the National League's rejection of an expansion plan and Commissioner Ueberroth's 1985 approval of a new minority owner of the Texas Rangers. In both of these actions, the Commissioner overrode voting requirements of a league constitution. The Commissioner contends that these actions constitute "strong precedent" for his realignment decision. These incidents did not arise under comparable factual

circumstances and implicated different constitutional provisions. More importantly, the fact that these actions did not result in a court challenge is neither probative nor persuasive evidence that the Commissioner in fact acted within his authority on those occasions.

Thus, an injunction was granted to keep the Cubs in the East.

Chicago Cubs was just one of a series of controversial decisions made in 1992 by Commissioner Vincent that gradually alienated a growing number of owners. Eventually, at a late August meeting, the owners voted (18 to 9 with one abstention) no confidence in Vincent and asked him to resign. Before the meeting, Vincent had asserted that the owners had no power to fire him and that he would not quit his post. However, after reflecting over the Labor Day weekend about the owners' verdict, Vincent decided to leave office—saying that his resignation, not litigation, was in the best interests of baseball. Backed by Jerry Reinsdorf, owner of the Chicago White Sox (and Bulls), Milwaukee Brewers' owner Allen "Bud" Selig was made Chairman of the Major League Baseball Executive Committee, and was placed in charge of the game's day-to-day affairs. The owners stated publicly that no successor to Vincent would be installed as Commissioner until they had secured a new and more favorable labor agreement from the players' union. We shall read about the latter scenario (including the litigation) in Chapter 4.

In the meantime, the owners did address the issues of both commissioner responsibilities and divisional realignment. As regards the latter, the solution they discovered was to break each league down into three divisions, thus permitting the Braves to move East while allowing the Cubs, Cardinals, and Reds to remain together in a new Central Division. Following the lead of the National Football League (and with the consent of the players), a wild card team was added to the baseball playoffs. While that step offended many traditionalists, it did enhance the game's attendance and television ratings, especially in September when more teams now remain in contention for post-season play.

In 1997, though, the baseball realignment problem reared its head once more. Baseball was expanding again into Phoenix and Tampa Bay, which wanted to be assigned to the National League and American League respectively. Existing teams like the Texas Rangers sought to use this occasion to move from the American League West (whose other members are all in the Pacific Time Zone) to the Central Division. For a brief moment, it appeared that baseball was about to embark on a major redistribution of teams among the various divisions within the two leagues. However, disagreement on the part of several owners about where their teams would end up, as well as concern about the reactions of the MLB Players Association which had not yet been consulted on this issue, led to just a modest change in the lineup for the 1998 season. The Tampa Bay Devil Rays were assigned to the American League East, the Detroit Tigers freed up that spot by moving to the American League Central, and filled a vacancy left by Bud Selig's Milwaukee Brewers who had moved to the National League Central in the first-ever switch of a Major League baseball team to a different league. We shall have to wait and see whether this will be the last.

By 1997, baseball had finally attained labor peace, though it still had no commissioner. In 1994, as a sidelight to labor negotiations, the owners created an *ad hoc* Restructuring Committee to study how to alter and improve the office of commissioner. The goals of the Committee were to recommend ways (a) "to preserve the strength and independence of the Commissioner"; (b) "to centralize the administration of Baseball within the Office of the Commissioner"; and (c) "to clarify the scope of the Commissioner's 'best interests' powers." In February 1994, the committee issued a report recommending several changes in the Major League Agreement relating to the office of the commissioner. The owners quickly approved the changes.

The first significant revision to the Major League Agreement added a clause to Article I, § 2(a), which specified that the future commissioner would be the chair of the Player Relations Committee. This would make the commissioner a direct participant and partisan for the owners in the collective bargaining process, a sharp departure from the "neutral" role that previous commissioners had always asserted for themselves in player-club relations. To make sure the commissioner would not intervene unilaterally in labor matters—as Bowie Kuhn did in 1976 by ending the owners' spring training lockout of the players, and as Peter Ueberroth did in the summer of 1985 by ordering the clubs to make their financial records available to the Players Association—a new § 5 was added to Article 1:

> Sec. 5. [T]he powers of the Commissioner to act in the best interests of Baseball shall be inapplicable to any matter relating to a subject of collective bargaining between the Clubs and the Major League Baseball Players Association.

Undoubtedly with an eye on the *Chicago Cubs* case, a new § 4 was also added to Article 1 to clarify another limitation on the commissioner's power to act "in the best interests of Baseball."

> Sec. 4. Notwithstanding the provisions of Section 2, above, the Commissioner shall take no action in the best interests of Baseball that (i) requires the Clubs to take, or to refrain from taking, joint League action (by vote, agreement, or otherwise) on any of the matters requiring a vote of the Clubs at a Joint Major League Meeting that are set forth in Article I, Section 9 or in Article V, Section 2(b) or (c), or (ii) requires the member Clubs of either League to take, or to refrain from taking, League action (by vote, agreement, or otherwise) on any matter to be voted upon by Member Clubs of the League pursuant to their League Constitution; *provided, however*, that nothing in this Section 4 shall limit the Commissioner's authority to act on any matter that involves the integrity of, or public confidence in, the national game of Baseball.

Article VII, § 1, which empowers the commissioner to arbitrate all disputes between clubs or club personnel, had this concluding sentence added to it:

> The procedure set forth in this Section is separate from and shall not alter or affect either the procedure set forth in Article V governing the role of the Commissioner at Joint Meetings of the two Major Leagues *or the Commissioner's powers to act in the best interests of Baseball under Article I*. [Emphasis added.]

Curiously, despite the disagreement between the owners and Vincent over whether the owners had the power to remove him from office during his term, no effort was made to amend the Major League Agreement to clarify this ambiguity. However, a new § 10 was added to Article 1 expressly providing that "[t]he Member Clubs of a League shall be authorized to dismiss their League President only upon the affirmative vote of not less than two-thirds (2/3) of such Clubs."

The basic structure of league governance in the other major team sports is similar, though not identical, to baseball's. Later in this chapter we will encounter the provisions of the National Football League constitution regarding the commissioner's disciplinary authority to protect the "integrity of the sport," provisions that were at issue in the struggle with the NFL Players Association over drug use and drug testing. The National Basketball Association (NBA) (under § 35 of its constitution), like the National Hockey League (NHL) (under § 17 of its by-laws), gives its commissioner the authority to expel, suspend, or fine any club official, employee, or player for conduct "detrimental or prejudicial to the Association" (in the NHL, conduct "dishonorable, prejudicial to, or against the welfare of the League").[g] In both leagues, though, such chief executive decisions can be appealed to the Board of Governors, which consists of all the owners. We note here another legal ruling, *Riko Enterprises (Philadelphia 76ers) v. Seattle Supersonics*, 357 F.Supp. 521 (S.D.N.Y.1973), which held that only the NBA Board of Governors, not Commissioner Walter Kennedy, had the power to award the 76ers the Supersonics' first-round draft pick to the 76ers when Seattle had signed a player, John Brisker, who had remained on the 76ers' reserve player list while playing in the old American Basketball Association.

Questions for Discussion

1. Return now to the *Chicago Cubs* case, and consider how that case might have been resolved on an appeal to the Seventh Circuit, particularly in light of the Eighth Circuit precedent in *Finley v. Kuhn*. Which of the two arguably relevant provisions of the Major League Agreement (MLA) should take precedence—Article I regarding the "best interests" of baseball, or Article VII, regarding "disputes and controversies" in baseball? Suppose the case were to have arisen under the 1995 revisions, with both the new § 4 in

---

g. Of related interest, both basketball and hockey draw a distinction between betting on a game and being involved in the "fix" of a game. While the former is explicitly made a disciplinary offense, only the latter is singled out for immediate expulsion from the sport. The NFL constitution does not explicitly address gambling.

Article 1 and the new sentence at the end of Article VII, § 1: would these make any difference in the legal outcome?

2. Before acquiescing in the 1992 insurgency by Selig, Reinsdorf, and their colleagues against Vincent, the Commissioner and his lawyers said that Article IX of the MLA protected him from being fired:

> Each of the parties hereto subscribes to this Agreement in consideration of the promises of all the others that no diminution of the compensation or powers of the present or any succeeding Commissioner shall be made during his term of office.

(a) Does this clause block the owners from changing the occupant—as opposed to the prerogatives—of the commissioner's office?

(b) Even if a court found that dismissal of the commissioner violated this provision of the MLA (which was incorporated in the commissioner's personal contract), what remedies would be available—specific performance, negative injunction, or monetary damages? (Keep this question in mind for Chapter 2 as well.)

(c) When the owners added the provision to the MLA which expressly authorized the firing of League Presidents, was this step implicitly confirming that the owners had—or did not have—the power to fire the commissioner? Whatever the owners' intent, why would they not have explicitly incorporated it into their own MLA?

3. At the 1994 Senate hearings concerning a bill to remove baseball's antitrust exemption (which we will read about in Chapter 2), Ohio Senator Howard Metzenbaum claimed that the cumulative effect of the pending amendments to the MLA would be to weaken the authority and power of the commissioner to protect the interests of fans and communities in baseball. Bud Selig, testifying as acting Commissioner, responded that these amendments were redefining the office in a manner that not only retained the historic authority of the commissioner's office, but, in key respects, strengthened it. Which of these views is correct—or is the answer somewhere in-between?

4. Taking account of the above legal precedents, what advice would you have given to the Yankees' George Steinbrenner about his chances of overturning the two-year suspension that Commissioner Vincent was prepared to impose on Steinbrenner in July 1990 for paying Howard Spira (a gambler) $40,000 for information about Yankees' star Dave Winfield? Do the above judicial rulings help explain why Steinbrenner "plea bargained" Vincent's proposed two-year suspension into a lifetime ban, which Vincent lifted in July 1992 (effective March 1993)?

5. From a doctrinal perspective, what is the legal foothold upon which judges can scrutinize and overturn any aspect of the decisions made by a private association such as a sports league? From an institutional perspective, should courts be more or less ready to review the decisions of a baseball commissioner than those of a union official, for example?[h] Does your answer

---

h. A classic article on the general common law in this area is Zechariah Chafee, Jr., *The Internal Affairs of Associations Not for Profit*, 43 Harvard L. Rev. 993 (1930). In-depth analysis of the common law treatment of union-member conflicts (prior to

depend upon whether the person challenging the commissioner is an owner, a manager, or a player? On whether the commissioner's decision infringes on specially favored public policies? For example, suppose a team executive is disciplined for speaking out against the commissioner's drug policy or the league's poor record in hiring minorities as managers, coaches, or in front office positions?

The most significant source of external review of baseball's authority has come from arbitrators selected by owners and players to resolve disputes under their collective agreement. In the next section we shall read several such arbitral rulings, relating especially to cases of drug use and drug testing. Here we note the consequences of such arbitral scrutiny in two notorious incidents involving player actions on the field or court.

Just prior to the end of the 1996 regular baseball season, Baltimore Orioles All–Star second baseman Roberto Alomar spit in the face of home plate umpire John Hirschbeck, following a vehement confrontation between the two about a called third strike against Alomar. Alomar was immediately suspended by American League President Gene Budig for five days. A national uproar then erupted when the suspension (which most people thought was too short for this offence) was held in abeyance while Alomar exercised his right to appeal and have a hearing before Budig. That meant that Alomar was able to play in the Orioles-Yankees post-season playoff series, and the suspension did not begin until the start of the 1997 season. Even then, Alomar was paid by Orioles' owner Peter Angelos the $130,000 salary for those five games. By contrast, the Chicago Bulls' owner Jerry Reinsdorf did not pay Dennis Rodman his approximately $1 million in salary during the 11–game suspension meted out by NBA Commissioner David Stern when Rodman kicked a cameraman whom he had tripped over during a 1997 game.

A little-noted fact is that this difference in owner behavior can be attributed to an earlier baseball arbitration decision, *MLB Players Association (Larry Walker) v. MLB Player Relations Committee (Montreal Expos)* (Arbitration, 1994). In 1994, Larry Walker, then a star outfielder with the Montreal Expos, sparked a bench-clearing brawl when he charged the pitcher's mound after being struck by a pitch. National League President Leonard Coleman fined Walker $500 and suspended him for four games. The Expos then told Walker that the team would not pay him the $88,000 otherwise due to him for those games. The Players Association filed a grievance on behalf of Walker, and persuaded the arbitrator that this Expos action was not just a refusal to pay Walker for "failure to render services," but team discipline that could not be

---

enactment of the federal Landrum–Griffin Act of 1959) can be found in Clyde W. Summers, *Legal Limitations on Union Discipline*, 64 Harvard L. Rev. 1049 (1951), and Clyde W. Summers, *The Law of Union Discipline: What the Courts Do in Fact*, 70 Yale L. J. 175 (1960).

added to League action. A key reason for this arbitral reading and application of the language of the labor agreement was the fact that, for as long as witnesses could remember, baseball owners had uniformly paid players their salaries for time lost due to league suspensions for on-the-field (not off-the-field) misconduct. (There had been over 100 such cases and salary payments during the six seasons prior to the Walker episode.) The Expos were bound by such an owner practice and its contractual consequences.

As it turned out, Alomar donated the amount of his salary to charity, and he and Hirschbeck shook hands before the first game in which they appeared together in the 1997 season. However, would it have been in the best interests of players, or owners, or fans for the parties to have altered this practice in the collective bargaining saga that was finally settled during the 1996–97 off-season? Would it have been in the best interests of baseball to keep Alomar out of the 1996 playoffs, rather than just suspend him (even without pay) at the start of the 1997 season?

The next notorious incident took place in basketball just as the second edition of this book was being completed at the end of 1997. Latrell Sprewell was the one All-Star left on the Golden State Warriors roster, playing in the second year of a four-year/$32 million contract. That summer the Warriors had brought in P.J. Carlesimo as their new coach to try to turn the team's performance around. However, in the first month of the 1997–98 season, the Warriors' 1–14 record put them at the bottom of the league standings. Then, in a practice session, Carlesimo made some adverse comments about Sprewell's efforts; the player responded by threatening to kill the coach, and actually choked him for a few seconds before being pulled off by his teammates. After having been banished to the locker room, Sprewell returned 15 minutes later to try to attack Carlesimo once more.

The next day, the Golden State Warriors announced that Sprewell was suspended without pay for ten games. NBPA Executive Director Billy Hunter said the union would not file a grievance to challenge such a penalty for this violent conduct, even though this suspension would cost its member nearly $1 million in salary. The following day, though, the Warriors terminated their contract with Sprewell, citing the provision in the Uniform Player Contract which requires players to "conform to standards of good citizenship and good moral behavior," and prohibits any "acts of moral turpitude." The day after this team action, NBA Commissioner David Stern announced that the league was suspending Sprewell for a full year, which would preclude any other team signing this star player who had just been released by his current team. Stern underlined the fact that Sprewell had returned to "commit a second, and this time clearly premeditated, assault." The NBPA's Hunter responded that the Association would challenge these much more severe actions by the Warriors and the league as far too extreme punishment for "one isolated incident."

The Sprewell case, like Alomar's, created a huge controversy, this time about whether the penalty was too severe. (Unlike Alomar, who lost no pay, Sprewell would lose somewhere between $8 and $25 million.) Among the longest (non-drug) suspensions in NBA history were the 10 games meted out to Houston Rockets' Vernon Maxwell for going into the stands and striking a fan during the 1994–95 season, 11 games to Chicago Bulls' Dennis Rodman for kicking a cameraman at courtside during a 1996–97 game, and 60 days (or 26 games) to the L.A. Lakers' Kermit Washington for slugging the Houston Rockets' Rudy Tomjanovich during a 1977–78 game, fracturing Tomjanovich's skull, and ending his playing career. (We shall read about the personal injury liability issues in the *Washington-Tomjanovich* case in Chapter 13.)

In the NBA, Commissioner disciplinary actions are now reviewable by a neutral arbitrator (though not "for conduct on the playing court"), just to decide whether the action was "arbitrary and capricious," not whether it was for "just cause." By the time this book appears in print, the ruling in the Sprewell case will have been rendered by the parties' arbitrator, Dean John Feerick of Fordham Law School. Whatever the arbitral verdict, the broader question posed by the Sprewell (and Alomar, Rodman, and other such) incidents is what is the appropriate penalty for acts of violence during a game (or practice). How much weight should be given by commissioners to the occurrence of more than one assault, to the player's prior record, to the identity and role of the victim, and to the degree of injury actually inflicted? Given the behavior patterns of present-day players both on and off the field, do we need more or less severe discipline than in the past? Given player salary trends from the days of Kermit Washington to those of Latrell Sprewell, what is the relative impact of suspension in those two eras?

C. CHALLENGES TO THE BEST INTERESTS OF THE SPORT

Let us turn from the question of how much authority and autonomy league owners and judges offer to commissioners, to the more important question of how commissioners (or other sports authorities) should address the host of issues raised in contemporary life about the "best interests" of the sport. Most league discipline responds to conduct on the field that violates the rules of the game. The more difficult challenges arise from actions that take place off the field of play, but nonetheless may threaten the welfare of the game. Besides illustrating the human conflicts in this area, the following cases also display alternative legal ways through which affected participants can challenge the prerogatives and policies of their sport's ruling body.

1. GAMBLING

A perennial sports problem has been gambling. Shortly after his appointment, Judge Landis banned all White Sox players involved in (indeed, one player who merely had knowledge of) the "fixing" of the

1919 World Series, even though a Chicago jury acquitted all the players of criminal charges.[i] In 1942, Landis forced Philadelphia Phillies' owner William Cox to sell his team when it was discovered he had placed about a dozen small bets on the Phillies to win. In 1963, NFL Commissioner Pete Rozelle suspended for a year All–Pros Paul Hornung of the Green Bay Packers and Alex Karras of the Detroit Lions for betting on their own teams to win.

Commissioners have also penalized mere association with gambling, even when no personal betting was involved. For example, Landis' successor, Albert "Happy" Chandler, suspended Dodgers' manager Leo Durocher for the 1947 season just for associating with gamblers. This was the precedent for George Steinbrenner's 1990 removal from the baseball (though not the financial) affairs of the Yankees for paying a gambler, Howard Spira, to produce unsavory information about Dave Winfield. Finally, in 1979 Bowie Kuhn went so far as to ban Willie Mays and Mickey Mantle from any official connections with professional baseball because they took public relations jobs with gambling casinos. (To Kuhn's regret, his successor, Peter Ueberroth, rescinded that ban in 1985.)

The only judicial ruling about the legality of this harsh treatment for gambling came in the following antitrust suit filed by an ex-NBA player, who charged that his lifetime expulsion constituted an illegal antitrust conspiracy of all teams in the league to boycott his services.

MOLINAS v. NATIONAL BASKETBALL ASS'N.
United States District Court, Southern District of New York, 1961.
190 F.Supp. 241.

KAUFMAN, DISTRICT JUDGE.

Plaintiff, Jack Molinas, is a well-known basketball player. In 1953, upon his graduation from Columbia University, Molinas was "drafted" by the Fort Wayne Pistons, then a member of the defendant National Basketball Association (now the Detroit Pistons). Subsequently, in the Fall of 1953, he signed a contract to play with the Pistons. In January of 1954, however, he admitted, in writing, that he placed several bets on his team, the Pistons, to win. The procedure he followed was that he contacted a person in New York by telephone, who informed him of the "point spread" on the particular game in question. The plaintiff [Molinas] would then decide whether or not to place a bet on the game. The plaintiff admitted that he received some $400 as a result of these wagers, including reimbursement of his telephone calls to New York. After the plaintiff admitted this wagering, Mr. Podoloff, the president of the league, acting pursuant to a clause (§ 15) in plaintiff's contract and a

---

i. These events are dramatized in Eliot Asinof, *Eight Men Out* (New York: Henry Holt, 1963), which was later made into a movie of the same name. For a look at more recent sports incidents and legal issues involving gambling, see Thomas J. Ostertag, *From Shoeless Joe to Charley Hustle: Major League Baseball's Continuing Crusade Against Sports Gambling*, 2 Seton Hall J. of Sports L. 19 (1992) (the author is General Counsel for Major League Baseball).

league rule (§ 79 of the League Constitution) prohibiting gambling, indefinitely suspended the plaintiff from the league. This suspension has continued until the present date. Since the suspension, plaintiff has made several applications, both oral and written, for reinstatement. All of these have been refused, and Mr. Podoloff has testified that he will never allow the plaintiff to re-enter the league. He has characterized the plaintiff as a "cancer on the league" which must be excised.

In the meantime, plaintiff attended and graduated from the Brooklyn Law School, and was then admitted to the New York State Bar. He had also been playing basketball for Williamsport and Hazelton of the Eastern Basketball League.

[After synopsizing the procedural history and antitrust background to Molinas' suit, the judge turned to the specific substantive issue of whether the NBA's continued ban against Molinas playing for any team in the league constituted an "unreasonable" restraint of trade in his services.]

* * *

A rule, and a corresponding contract clause, providing for the suspension of those who place wagers on games in which they are participating seems not only reasonable, but necessary for the survival of the league. Every league or association must have some reasonable governing rules, and these rules must necessarily include disciplinary provisions. Surely, every disciplinary rule which a league may invoke, although by its nature it may involve some sort of a restraint, does not run afoul of the anti-trust laws. And, a disciplinary rule invoked against gambling seems about as reasonable a rule as could be imagined. Furthermore, the application of the rule to the plaintiff's conduct is also eminently reasonable. Plaintiff was wagering on games in which he was to play, and some of these bets were made on the basis of a "point spread" system. Plaintiff insists that since he bet only on his own team to win, his conduct, while admittedly improper, was not immoral. But I do not find this distinction to be a meaningful one in the context of the present case. The vice inherent in the plaintiff's conduct is that each time he either placed a bet or refused to place a bet, this operated inevitably to inform bookmakers of an insider's opinion as to the adequacy or inadequacy of the point-spread or his team's ability to win. Thus, for example, when he chose to place a bet, this would indicate to the bookmakers that a member of the Fort Wayne team believed that his team would exceed its expected performance. Similarly, when he chose not to bet, bookmakers thus would be informed of his opinion that the Pistons would not perform according to expectations. It is certainly reasonable for the league and Mr. Podoloff to conclude that this conduct could not be tolerated and must, therefore, be eliminated. The reasonableness of the league's action is apparent in view of the fact that, at that time, the confidence of the public in basketball had been shattered, due to a series of gambling incidents. Thus, it was absolutely necessary for the sport to exhume gambling from its midst for all times in order to survive.

The same factors justifying the suspension also serve to justify the subsequent refusal to reinstate. The league could reasonably conclude that in order to effectuate its important and legitimate policies against gambling, and to restore and maintain the confidence of the public vital to its existence, it was necessary to enforce its rules strictly, and to apply the most stringent sanctions. One can certainly understand the reluctance to permit an admitted gambler to return to the league, and again to participate in championship games, especially in light of the aura and stigma of gambling which has clouded the sports world in the past few years. Viewed in this context, it can be seen that the league was justified in determining that it was absolutely necessary to avoid even the slightest connection with gambling, gamblers, and those who had done business with gamblers, in the future. In addition, conduct reasonable in its inception certainly does not become unreasonable through the mere passage of time, especially when the same factors making the conduct reasonable in the first instance, are still present. At any rate, plaintiff must show much more than he has here in order to compel a conclusion that the defendant's conduct was in fact unreasonable. Thus, it is clear that the refusal to reinstate the plaintiff does not rise to the stature of a violation of the antitrust laws.

Case dismissed.

Questions for Discussion

1. *Molinas* introduces us to the Sherman Antitrust Act's proscription (in § 1) of "contracts, combinations, or conspiracies in restraint of trade," as applied to commissioner discipline. We will explore in several later chapters the application of antitrust doctrine to sports. We simply note here that the antitrust "rule of reason" upon which the court relied in *Molinas* no longer turns on a court's intuitive judgment of whether a particular practice seems sensible and equitable, but rather on economic analysis of whether the challenged practice is, on balance, procompetitive or anticompetitive. This, in turn, requires a judgment about whether the practice enhances or diminishes "consumer welfare" (whatever that term means). If one focuses on that economic question, was the court right in its conclusion that suspending Molinas was "reasonable?"

2. Recall the federal district court's ruling in *Rose v. Giamatti* that the Cincinnati team was not a true party to the suit for jurisdictional purposes, because the individual member clubs had no control over the commissioner in his exercise of disciplinary authority. If that is so, how could a commissioner's suspension or expulsion of a player ever constitute a "contract, combination, or conspiracy?" Is it simply unilateral action beyond the scope of § 1 antitrust review?

The *Molinas* decision had an ironic aftermath. While the litigation was underway, Molinas was actually the ringleader in a nationwide point-shaving scheme in college basketball. When the scandal broke in the spring of 1961 and Molinas was indicted and convicted, Judge Kaufman's ruling seemed even wiser.

Unfortunately, one of the nation's best basketball prospects, Connie Hawkins, was victimized by the fallout from this affair.[j] As the top high school player in New York City, Hawkins met Molinas in the summer of 1960 at playground tournaments. Molinas occasionally bought Hawkins dinner and once loaned him $210 (Hawkins repaid the loan soon thereafter). Then Hawkins went off to the University of Iowa where NCAA rules required him to spend the first year on the freshman team. However, when the point-shaving scandal broke in the spring of 1961, Hawkins was named as a participant. Although he could not have shaved points in a college game—he had not played a game yet—Hawkins was described as both an intermediary between Molinas and other players and a part of Molinas' "farm system" of future point-shavers.

Forced to leave college, Hawkins became the top scorer in the short-lived American Basketball League and then barnstormed with the Harlem Globetrotters. Under NBA rules Hawkins became eligible for its draft in 1964, when his college class graduated. However, the league deemed Hawkins ineligible under the *Molinas* precedent. In 1966, Hawkins launched his own antitrust suit, alleging an illegal boycott of his services.

During the discovery process, which took several years, Hawkins starred in the new American Basketball Association. Eventually, the lawyers uncovered persuasive evidence (partly from Molinas) that Hawkins had been an innocent bystander. As a result, the NBA finally settled the suit in 1969 by paying Hawkins $1.3 million in damages and removing him from its ineligible list. The Phoenix Suns won his draft rights, and in his first season Hawkins led the Suns to the NBA playoffs and made the all-NBA team. In 1992, Hawkins was installed in basketball's Hall of Fame in Springfield, the same year in which Pete Rose was denied eligibility for baseball's Hall in Cooperstown.

Questions for Discussion

1. What are the implications of the Hawkins story? Had the NBA taken the risk of trebled antitrust damages and gone to court, would it (and should it) have won, based on the *Molinas* precedent? What if the facts are murky? Who has the burden of proof and by what standard? What if the facts are clear, but the involvement minor? For example, Doug Moe, a consensus All–American at North Carolina, graduated in 1961, was named as someone who had refused to participate in Molinas' gambling scheme, but was banned from the NBA for failing to report the bribe offer. Should Moe

[j]. See David Wolf, *Foul: The Connie Hawkins Story* (New York: Holt Rinehart, 1972).

have been entitled to sue? (This Moe did not do; instead, after starring in the ABA, Moe went on to become one of the NBA's most successful coaches.)

2. In 1986, Tulane's star center John "Hot Rod" Williams was indicted for allegedly taking money and drugs from gamblers in exchange for "point shaving" in a 1985 game against Memphis State. NBA Commissioner David Stern permitted the Cleveland Cavaliers to draft and pay Williams, but not to play him pending trial, in which Williams was ultimately acquitted by a New Orleans jury. Based on the acquittal, Stern took no action against Williams, who has gone on to a successful and lucrative NBA career with Cleveland and Phoenix. Why no action? Should the Commissioner have felt entitled to take action after indictment, but prior to the criminal trial? Does it depend on the nature of the charge (for example, drug use or domestic abuse, rather than fixing games)? Should the Commissioner's authority be constrained if the criminal proceedings result in a jury acquittal? In dismissal on procedural grounds? Does this imply that in cases where criminal conduct or proceedings are not involved (for example, Pete Rose's gambling as opposed to his tax evasion), the standard of proof for finding the alleged misconduct should be "beyond a reasonable doubt?" In answering these questions, keep in mind that Baseball Commissioner Landis banned for life Shoeless Joe Jackson and the other players involved in the "Black Sox" scandal, even after a jury had acquitted them of all criminal charges related to the alleged "fixing" of the 1919 World Series.

The fall of 1996 witnessed the return of a gambling scandal to college sports, this time involving Boston College. The school suspended thirteen of its football players for having bet on sporting events—some on the World Series or the NFL, some on college football. Two had bet against Boston College itself in a game against Syracuse which their Eagles lost. (One of those players did not play at all, the other just on one kickoff coverage play.) All of these bets were placed (and thence traced) through a B.C. student "runner" for an off-campus professional bookie. The bets typically were in the $25–$50 range, though a few went as high as $1,000 (and the two against B.C. were $200 and $250 respectively). As it turned out, one of the players suspended (for betting, though not against his team) was Brandon King, the grandson of Mike Tyson's boxing promoter Donald King.

The NCAA's anti-gambling rules (in By–Law 10–3) bar any student-athlete from providing gamblers with any game-related information, soliciting a bet on any college team, placing a bet on any of his school's teams, or placing any kind of bet through a bookie. In prior years, players such as Florida quarterback Shane Matthews (in 1989), Maryland quarterback Scott Milanovich (1995), and Northwestern fullback Dennis Lundy (1995) were suspended for violating this rule. In the late 1970s, Boston College experienced an even bigger scandal when it was disclosed that several of its basketball players had shaved points in their games at the request (and payment) of the organized crime figure Henry Hill. (Hill's story eventually triggered both Martin Scorsese's movie

Goodfellas and the Supreme Court's striking down of "Son of Sam" laws under the First Amendment, in *Simon & Schuster v. New York State Crime Victims Board*, 502 U.S. 105 (1991).) In response to this latest gambling incident, Boston College permanently removed from the team (and their scholarships) those players who had bet on B.C. games, and suspended the others for the last three games of the 1996 season and for up to four games in the fall of 1997. The college also suspended from its classes the students whom it discovered had been funneling the bets to bookies.

This Boston College imbroglio occasioned yet another look at the broader phenomenon of gambling in the United States. Apparently in the late 1990s Americans bet over $400 *billion* a year in a variety of legal settings—$300 billion in casinos, and the rest on state and local lotteries, at and off the race track, with church bingos, and the like. An additional $80–100 billion is wagered on sporting events via illegal bookmaking, and no one knows how much more is bet with friends or in office pools on the Super Bowl, the NCAA Final Four, and other notable sporting events. Since the average "take" of betting firms amounts to 10 to 15% of the amount wagered, this means that Americans now cumulatively spend $50 to $60 billion on gambling (compared to $3 billion on going to games and $6 billion on going to movies).

Gambling is especially pronounced among young Americans. A 1991 survey of college students found that 85% had gambled at least once and 25% did so on a weekly basis: 10% of the male students and two percent of female students were judged to have a "pathological" gambling problem. Another 1993–94 survey of Division I football and basketball players found that 25% had bet on college sports, and nearly four percent on games in which they themselves had been playing.

A further irony in the Boston College case is that it received extensive coverage in USA Today and other media around the country. The bulk of such commentary on this episode pressed for firm disciplinary action by Boston College and the NCAA. Yet these same media regularly print or depict the point spreads on professional and college games, with "experts" telling readers and viewers which team to bet on against that spread. After a debate at its January 1997 convention, the NCAA voted to deny press credentials to reporters from any newspapers who print advertisements for "tip or tout sheet" services, though disclosing the point spreads and game picks was judged to be constitutionally protected "speech." USA Today said it would mount a First Amendment attack if any of its reporters were denied access to a press box in a public stadium or arena because it still accepts and prints the tip and tout sheet ads. In March, the NCAA decided not to press forward with this rule, at least for the 1997 Final Four championships.

Questions for Discussion

1. With the above as background, a host of issues are raised. Beginning with the most recent Boston College episode, what are your views about the current NCAA anti-gambling rules? Should a student athlete be barred from

betting only on their own team's games, on any college game, or on any sporting event (e.g., the Super Bowl and the World Series)? Or should the rule focus on whether the bet was made through an illegal bookie, a legal bookie (i.e., in Las Vegas), or with a friend and classmate (and whether the latter is legal under state anti-gambling law)? Should colleges treat betting by any student the same as betting by a student-athlete, and should the focus be on those who *place*, or those who *take* the bets?

2. What about professional sports—the Pete Rose case, for example? Should it have made a difference that the Commissioner found that Rose always bet on his own Reds team to win (by contrast with the two Boston College players who had bet on the Eagles to lose)? What should baseball have done to Albert Belle whose 1997 deposition in a lawsuit admitted that he had lost tens of thousands of dollars betting with bookies on football or basketball (though never baseball) games, something that is a misdemeanor under Ohio state law? Or to the Philadelphia Phillies' Len Dykstra who one year apparently lost $100,000 playing in a privately-organized and illegal poker game during the off-season? Or the NBA to Michael Jordan who created another huge controversy when (with his father) he travelled down from Madison Square Garden after a playoff game with the New York Knicks to gamble at a (legal) casino in Atlantic City? What exactly is it about gambling that makes this behavior (or just associating with it) "detrimental to the best interests of the sport?"

3. Wherever one draws the line against gambling, a further question is how serious is this form of "moral turpitude"—that is, how severe a penalty does it warrant? For example, what actions merited the gravest condemnation from Commissioner Giamatti—Pete Rose's gambling or his income tax fraud? In addition, should betting by a player or manager like Rose be treated the same as betting by an owner such as the Phillies' Cox? Is expulsion of a player or manager such as Rose the same tangible punishment as expulsion of an owner such as Cox or Steinbrenner? Which level of punishment was more appropriate for betting on one's team to win—baseball's lifetime ban of Pete Rose or football's one year suspension of Paul Hornung and Alex Karras?

4. One final episode shows how far the NCAA's formal anti-gambling rules can go. One Miami Hurricanes and two Florida State Seminoles football players were temporarily suspended during the fall 1996 season for violating By-law 10–3 which bars any student-athlete from "accepting a bet on any team representing the institution." The story came to light when the players told a reporter why the Hurricane had given his jersey to the two Seminoles after Florida State had beaten Miami in an October game that year. Apparently this was the payment for a bet the players had made years earlier, while they were playing high school football together, about whose college team would win the most games when they actually played against each other.

2. DRUG USE[k]

As professional league commissioners and NCAA committees continue to define and enforce the standards of behavior they believe to be in

---

k. Useful overviews of this topic in the sports world are Robert Voy, *Drugs, Sports and Politics* (Champaign, Ill.: Leisure Press, 1991); Glenn M. Wong and Richard

the best interests of their sports, the most hotly-debated issue over the last two decade has been drug use, not gambling. The same debate has been taking place in the outside world. Tens of millions of Americans have used marijuana or cocaine at some time in their lives. Unsurprisingly, then, we find a number of drug users among professional and college athletes—especially when the Darryl Strawberrys and Dwight Goodens suddenly reach stardom and high salaries at a young age. Thus, the same sentiment that has impelled American presidents to declare an all-out "War on Drugs" also prompts league commissioners to insist that their players "Just Say No"—or else! But one way that the reaction to drug use differed from gambling, for example, is that the drug problem emerged after players had been organized into unions that engage in collective bargaining under the umbrella of the National Labor Relations Act (which will be canvassed in detail in Chapter 4). Players and their unions naturally took a somewhat different point of view toward this issue than did league owners and commissioners—both about teammates who were found to have abused drugs, and even more so, about league institution of mandatory drug testing of all players. As we will see, the legal and contractual framework for collective bargaining furnished a somewhat more effective base for players challenging the initiatives taken by commissioners to address the drug problem.

In addressing the "drug problem," sports has followed the broader polity in assuming that the major dangers are presented by use of illegal substances such as marijuana and cocaine, rather than by the more widespread but legal consumption of cigarettes and alcohol. (Alcohol advertising—especially of beer—is a major revenue source for sports.) In addition, in the aftermath of the Canadian Ben Johnson's world-record 100–meter victory over Carl Lewis and subsequent disqualification at the 1988 Olympic Games, steroid use became a target of both public criminal law and private commissioner's law. Crucial questions to keep in mind when reading and reflecting on the following materials are whether priority in defending the "best interests of sports" should be placed on "mind-altering" drugs such as cocaine, or on "performance-altering" drugs such as the anabolic steroids, on illegal drugs such as marijuana or on legal drugs such as alcohol.

J. Ensor, *Major League Baseball and Drugs: Fight the Problem or the Players?* 11 Nova L. Rev. 779 (1987); and Edward Rippey, *Contractual Freedom Over Substance-Related Issues in Major League Baseball*, 1 The Sports Lawyers J. 143 (1994). Again, Bowie Kuhn's autobiography, *Hardball* note a above, at 303–322, gives a close-up picture of how this issue looked to one of the major protagonists. Important depictions of the broader issues of drug use and drug enforcement in American life are Mark A.R. Kleiman, *Against Excess: Drug Policy for Results* (New York: Basic Books, 1991); Steven B. Duke and Albert C. Gross, *America's Longest War: Rethinking Our Tragic Crusade Against Drugs* (New York: G.P. Putnam's Sons, 1993); and Erich Goode, *Between Politics and Reason: The Drug Legalization Debate* (New York: St. Martin's Press, 1997).

In baseball, two of the earliest cases of drug abuse involved Alan Wiggins, a second baseman for the San Diego Padres and Baltimore Orioles, and Steve Howe, then a relief pitcher for the Los Angeles Dodgers. After each player went through a lengthy period of drug abuse, attempted treatment, and suspensions from the game, their lives took drastically different turns in 1991—Wiggins died of AIDS, and Howe returned to stardom as a Yankee reliever. But the addictive effect of cocaine was demonstrated once more when Howe was caught in the off-season buying the drug from an undercover Montana police officer—reportedly for "one last party before spring training." After being put on probation by the criminal courts, Howe was banned from baseball for life by Commissioner Fay Vincent.

With the support of the Yankees' owner George Steinbrenner, general manager Gene Michael, and manager Bucky Showalter, Howe sought help from his union, the Major League Baseball Players Association (MLBPA), to try to salvage his career. To assess Howe's legal prospects, MLBPA Executive Director Don Fehr could look back at a long series of drug controversies and rulings in this sport.

The first baseball drug case that really seized both the public and the commissioner's attention involved Kansas City Royals players—Vida Blue, Willie Wilson, Jerry Martin, and Willie Aikens—who were arrested and convicted in 1983 for possession of cocaine, and sentenced to three months in jail. For each of these players, Commissioner Bowie Kuhn imposed a one-year suspension for the entire 1984 baseball season, pursuant to the following rule that had been posted in all clubhouses:

> Anyone involved in the illegal possession or use of drugs or illegal trafficking with drugs of any sort will be subject to discipline. In serious cases, the discipline may include suspension or dismissal and termination of contract guarantees.

This commissioner rule had been issued pursuant to Major League Rule 21(f) which was binding on baseball players under the uniform player contract:

> (1) OTHER MISCONDUCT. Nothing herein contained shall be construed as exclusively defining or otherwise limiting acts, transactions, practices or conduct found not to be in the best interests of Baseball; and any and all other acts, transactions, practices or conduct not to be in the best interests of Baseball are prohibited and shall be subject to such penalties, including permanent ineligibility, as the facts in the particular case may warrant.

However, Wilson and the other players had a legal foothold for challenging the commissioner's exercise of his disciplinary authority. The collective agreement negotiated between baseball owners and the Players' Association (the Basic Agreement) ordained that the Major League Agreement and Major League Rules (the source of the commissioner's powers) bound the players only "to the extent they were not inconsistent with this Basic Agreement." With respect to discipline, Article 11 of the Basic Agreement specified:

A. Just Cause

> The Parties recognize that a Player may be subjected to disciplinary action for just cause by his Club, League or the Commissioner. Therefore, in Grievances regarding discipline, the issue to be resolved shall be whether there has been just cause for the penalty imposed.

Under this provision, which is commonplace in almost every unionized firm in any other industry, a neutral arbitrator selected by the parties decides whether the exercise of the employer's (here the commissioner's) disciplinary authority is, in fact, for "just cause."

In the path-breaking *Wilson* decision of 1984, the arbitrator accepted Commissioner Kuhn's premise that player use of drugs was a matter of legitimate concern regarding "the best interests of baseball":

> At its worst, to the extent that cocaine use becomes habitual or addictive, a player risks both an increased chance of physical deterioration, and a dangerous involvement with the criminals who sell the drug. That involvement may lead to control of the player either because of the addiction or because of the risk of exposure. The consequences of such control over any part of the game are so obviously disastrous as to require no elaboration.
>
> * * *
>
> Nor can there be serious doubt that this type of employee misconduct is of serious impact on the employer. Because baseball players are highly skilled, well compensated and constantly visible, they deserve and receive national attention. Neither the players nor the industry escapes the publicity. And drug involvement, because of its threat to athletes' playing abilities, because it is illegal and because of the related connotation of inroads by organized crime, constitutes a serious and immediate threat to the business that is promoted as our national pastime. Because the perception alone of taint is so potentially damaging, baseball has a substantial interest in the implementation and enforcement of drug prohibitions. This much is clear from the evidence and is not seriously in dispute.

The arbitrator stated that even the Players Association did not seriously challenge the owners' concern about drug use, nor the proposition that discipline might be warranted in appropriate cases. Because Wilson had both served a jail sentence and missed almost all of the 1983 season, the arbitrator concluded that Commissioner Kuhn should have imposed no more than a one-month additional baseball suspension in 1984. However, the suspension of Vida Blue for the whole 1984 season was upheld. While Blue had been treated in the same fashion as Wilson by the criminal justice system, his behavior had involved more extensive use of cocaine in earlier years, as well as serving as a conduit between his drug supplier and his Kansas City teammates (and, occasionally, players from other clubs visiting Kansas City).

With the above as background, let us now read the arbitrator's appraisal of Commissioner Vincent's lifetime expulsion of Steve Howe after his seventh reported incident of illegal drug use during his 12-year baseball career.

MAJOR LEAGUE BASEBALL PLAYERS ASSOCIATION AND THE COMMISSIONER OF MAJOR LEAGUE BASEBALL
(Steven Howe)

(Arbitration, 1992).

NICOLAU, ARBITRATOR.

[Following termination of a short-lived player-management drug program in baseball, Commissioner Peter Ueberroth in 1986 wrote a policy memorandum placing drug testing under the auspices of the Commissioner's Office. That memorandum has been periodically reissued by successor commissioners and is now known as Baseball's Drug Policy and Prevention Program. The MLBPA has neither formally agreed to the policy nor brought an arbitration challenge against it. Instead, the Association has dealt informally with the owners' Player Relations Committee as drug-related issues have arisen.

This arbitration proceeding was a crucial chapter in the lengthy saga of the pitcher, Steve Howe. Between 1982 and 1988, Howe was hospitalized for drug-related treatment on six occasions and suspended from baseball six times. During 1988 and 1989, Howe was under suspension because of violations of his drug aftercare program. In 1990, the MLBPA filed a grievance requesting that Howe be allowed to return to active status. The Commissioner's Office investigated the matter, subjected Howe to medical and psychological examinations, and agreed to permit Howe to return under certain conditions.

Based on medical recommendations, Vincent recognized that Howe needed a stringent aftercare program that would entail testing as frequently as three times per week for the remainder of his career. Vincent also directed that Howe be immediately removed from baseball in the event of a positive drug test. Although the Commissioner never formally approved or implemented such a testing program, Howe was tested over the next two years on a frequent, although irregular, basis. None of the tests yielded a positive result.

Howe succeeded on the playing field, and in November, 1991 signed a contract with the New York Yankees that, with readily attainable performance incentives, promised him a total salary of $2.3 million. Just a month later, however, Howe was arrested in his off-season Montana home town for attempted possession of cocaine. Howe eventually entered an *Alford* plea of guilty to the charge without explicitly conceding the underlying facts. However, in response to this latest drug episode that had followed Howe's history of drug-related suspensions, Vincent imposed a lifetime ban which the MLBPA challenged in arbitration. After an extended review of the medical evidence about Howe's condition (labelled Attention Deficit Hyperactive Disorder (ADHD)) and treatment, the arbitrator formulated the relevant standard of review which he then applied to the facts of this case.]

* * *

The Standard of Review

* * *

As in any disciplinary matter, the burden of establishing just cause is on those imposing discipline. While the Commissioner has a "reasonable range of discretion" in such matters, the penalty he imposes in a particular case must be "reasonably commensurate with the offense" and "appropriate, given all the circumstances," *Nixon* (Panel Decision 84, Nicolau, 1992). Moreover, "offenders must be viewed with a careful eye to the specific nature of the offense, and penalties must be carefully fashioned with an eye toward responsive, consistent and fair discipline," *Wilson/Martin* (Panel Decision 54, Bloch, 1984). There must, in other words, be "careful scrutiny of the individual circumstances and the particular facts relevant to each case."

The need for scrutiny is at its zenith here simply because of the nature of the penalty at issue. Contrary to the analogy counsel seeks to draw, the Commissioner is not an employer who has decided for himself that he will no longer retain an employee who is then free to go elsewhere in the same industry. The Commissioner's imposition of Baseball's "ultimate sanction, lifetime ineligibility," means that no employer in Baseball may hire Howe, no matter what he thinks of his ability, his good faith or his chances of successfully resisting the addiction with which he has been plagued. Thus, the burden on the Commissioner to justify his action transcends that of the ordinary employer inasmuch as he can effectively prevent a player's employment by anyone at any level of his chosen profession.

* * *

Discussion and Analysis

* * *

I fully understand Baseball's institutional interest and its need, in so far as possible, to keep its workplaces free of drugs and to deter drug use among players wherever it might occur. I also appreciate the pressures brought to bear on Baseball by those who only see the "athlete-as-hero." But those considerations, as important as they are, must be examined in the light of the just cause standard. Under that standard, Baseball's conduct, as well as Howe's, is subject to review.

In justifying his decision, the Commissioner told the Panel that Baseball had done all that could have been done and that Howe had simply "squandered" the many chances Baseball had given him. If Baseball had, in fact, done all it could, both before Howe's 1990 return to the game and after, the imposition of a lifetime ban would be more understandable. But it is obvious that reality and what the Commissioner perceived to be the case are quite different.

We now know that Howe has an underlying psychiatric disorder that was never diagnosed or treated; that this disorder has been a contributing factor to his use of drugs; and that, absent treatment for the condition, he remains vulnerable to such use.

We also know that in 1990 the Commissioner's medical adviser cautioned against Howe's return unless he was tested every other day of the year throughout his professional career and that Baseball did not heed this clear warning even though the Commissioner suggested in his March 1990 decision that such testing be imposed.

These two factors cast a very different light on the nature of the chance Howe was given in 1990 and, indeed, on the nature of the chances he had been given in earlier years.

It was clear from Dr. Riordan's report that in his expert view continuous testing, including testing in the off-season, was essential if Howe was to succeed in resisting drugs during his career while also seeking to overcome his addiction through therapeutic means. In his decision allowing Howe to return, the Commissioner quoted Dr. Riordan's report at some length. The Commissioner's order that Howe play in the minors for a year, his directions regarding testing, and his declaration that Howe would be immediately banned if he tested positive were all based on Dr. Riordan's cautionary advice. But the stringent, year-round testing requirement, as we have seen, was not implemented and Howe was unfortunately set on a course without the strategic safeguard Dr. Riordan considered indispensable to his success.

If that safeguard had been firmly in place and if Howe had never been presented with an opportunity to vary its regularity, an opportunity Dr. Riordan had clearly meant to foreclose, it is not at all likely, given the certainty of detection such a regimen would have imposed, that the events of December 19 would have occurred.

While Howe can certainly be faulted for seeking to delay testing at a time of his admittedly increasing sense of vulnerability, the Office of the Commissioner cannot escape its measure of responsibility for what took place in 1991. Based on medical advice the Commissioner had solicited, the need for continuous testing was obvious. To give Howe "yet another chance" of returning to the game without implementing those conditions was not, in my judgment, a fair shot at success.

As to Howe's undiagnosed psychiatric condition and the inadequacy of his prior treatment, the Commissioner considers it unfair to place on his Office the burden of reviewing a player's medical history before imposing discipline. As I pointed out in *Reyes*, a decision rendered three months before the Commissioner's action here, I fail to see the unfairness of such a requirement. Certainly, as the Association attempted to point out prior to the imposition of discipline in this case, it is not unfair to expect an exceptionally scrupulous review of the record when the matter under consideration is a lifetime ban.

What bears repeating here is that the Commissioner does not stand in the isolated position of an individual employer. He can bar the employment of a player at any level of the game regardless of the opinion or wishes of any one of a great number of potential employers. That is an awesome power. With it comes a heavy responsibility, especially when that power is exercised unilaterally and not as the result of a collectively bargained agreement as to the level of sanctions to be imposed for particular actions.

Here, there was little consideration of the medical records and no discernible pre-decision attempt to probe beneath their surface and ascertain if Howe had been properly diagnosed and treated. Even though Dr. Riordan's 1990 report signaled the possibility of a previously undiagnosed and untreated illness affecting Howe's behavior, by 1992, when discipline was to be imposed as a result of Howe's subsequent actions, the Commissioner considered medical matters of little importance when measured against Baseball's interests. But as made manifest by the opinions of Drs. Wender and Kleber, both impartial medical experts, such matters were highly important in that they served to explain events.

It cannot be known what the Commissioner might have done if he had been fully aware of the facts regarding Howe's condition and previous treatment. What we do know is that those facts were not before him and that virtually no effort was made to ascertain them. When considering the permanent expulsion of a player, this failure to examine all the circumstances, irrespective of the cause, is not, in my view, consistent with his responsibility.

The Commissioner seeks to justify his exclusive reliance on institutional considerations by resting Howe's permanent expulsion on an obligation to deter repeated drug use by others. He argues that there was no alternative, that a less severe sanction would have sent the wrong message to players who will view anything short of a lifetime ban as a license to take up and repeatedly use drugs. This hardly seems the case. All available evidence supports the proposition that drug use in Organized Baseball is not what it appeared to be some years ago. As the Association pointed out in *Nixon*, there has not been an "initial offender" in the Major Leagues since 1989, and those who unfortunately repeated an offense are concededly no more than a handful.

To everyone's credit, all this has been accomplished without the imposition of a lifetime ban and, given continued education and awareness at both the minor and Major League levels, this steady progress toward a drug free environment is quite likely to continue. When the industry's goal is the complete elimination of drugs, it can be argued, of course, that a single instance of use is one too many. What cannot legitimately be questioned, however, is the commitment of the industry and the Players Association. No member of the public can seriously contend, given the record, that Baseball's attitude toward drugs is light-hearted or that the manner in which the industry and the Association have previously dealt with the problem has imperiled the integrity of the game.

One further observation on the reasoning the Commissioner advanced in this proceeding is appropriate. Deterrence, however laudable an objective, should not be achieved at the expense of fairness. What was considered vital to Howe's sobriety at this point in his life should have been implemented. Moreover, the Office of the Commissioner should have looked closely at all the circumstances in order to ascertain and evaluate his condition and the adequacy of his treatment before deciding what discipline to impose. These failings lead me to conclude that the Commissioner's action in imposing a lifetime ban was without just cause.

What remains, given this conclusion, is the penalty that should be imposed in lieu of a lifetime ban.... As previously stated, Howe now recognizes, despite his efforts of recent years, that he bears a responsibility for the events of autumn and early winter of 1991 and that what occurred then, however the responsibility of others is assessed, was an "unacceptable failure" on his part. Considering that fact and weighing all other aspects of this unique case, including his conviction on the federal charge, it's my judgment that the interests of deterrence and fairness as well as punishment would be realized if the penalty imposed by the former Commissioner is reduced to time served and Howe is thereafter given a fair opportunity to succeed. A suspension of this length, 119 days, entails a substantial monetary loss to Howe; almost $400,000 in base salary and a lost opportunity to earn upwards of $1,500,000.00 in contract bonuses. A penalty of this magnitude should serve as a clear warning that drug use will continue to be treated with severity. At the same time, a chance to compete coupled with appropriate treatment and rigorous safeguards will give Howe what he was not adequately given in the past.

As is evident from these proceedings, no one can predict whether Howe will succeed even with the treatment and safeguards provided for in the Award. It is not at all certain, as the impartial medical evaluations reflect, that he is quite ready to accept full responsibility for his actions or that he fully understands, even at this juncture, the complex reasons for his behavior. While fundamental fairness requires that his permanent expulsion be set aside, only with his understanding and acceptance of responsibility will his future truly be secure.

Grievance upheld.

Arbitrator Nicolau announced the above reinstatement verdict several months before writing and issuing his more than 50-page opinion, so that Howe could return to the playing field. While Howe, the Yankees, and the Players Association were very pleased with the ruling, Commissioner Vincent was upset, as the following comment indicates:

> "It's like saying you've had seven chances, but eight is the right number. How can there be soundness in that judgment? That makes the whole thing a joke. Nicolau is saying he's giving him one more chance. Well, I did that in '89. What if a medical theory comes up after the next violation? It could excuse the next violation? Then there would be more chances. It's a daisy chain. You never get to the end of it."

As it turned out, not only did Howe not fail any future drug tests, but he performed quite well for the Yankees as their principal left-handed reliever. Howe's skills gradually deteriorated with his age; in June, 1996, the year the Yankees were about to win the World Series, Howe was released. Ironically, as the Howe family was boarding a plane at the Kennedy Airport to return to their home in Montana, Howe was discovered to have a loaded gun in his luggage—something for which he received criminal probation once more.

Questions for Discussion

1. Now that you have read the core parts of the arbitrator's reasoning, with whom do you agree, Vincent or Nicolau? More important, perhaps, than the specifics of the *Howe* case, what is your reaction to the arbitrator's thesis that a commissioner's decision to ban a player from the sport requires more, not less, searching scrutiny than the decision by an ordinary employer to fire a worker?

2. The summer of 1997 witnessed yet another drug controversy, this time involving Tony Phillips, the second baseman with the Anaheim Angels. Midway through the season, Phillips was arrested in an Anaheim motel for having bought cocaine from an undercover police agent, and he faced criminal charges. The Angels then suspended Phillips, who filed a grievance. Supported by the owners' Player Relations Committee (PRC) as well as by the Players Association, Phillips won a unanimous arbitration award reinstating him to play as long as he was undergoing outpatient drug treatment and testing. The Angels are now a part of the Walt Disney entertainment conglomerate, and Disney's head Michael Eisner strongly objected to MLB's labor agreement which required its team to play (or at least to keep on the roster and pay) someone who was publicly known to have used illegal drugs (though had not yet been convicted for possession). One institutional question is why this matter is addressed at the league, rather than at the club level (where presumably it would have to be done through negotiated player contract terms). A second is why a body like Disney feels that it is vital to the integrity of its baseball (and likely its hockey) arm to bar drug-users from playing, but it does not have a similar policy barring anyone who has used drugs from appearing on the screen in movies made by its studio or in television shows broadcast by its ABC network and cable channels.

3. In August 1980, Ferguson Jenkins, then a pitcher for the Texas Rangers, was found to have cocaine in his luggage which was opened at Canadian customs when he flew to Toronto to pitch against the Blue Jays.

(Ironically, Jenkins is the only Canadian baseball player ever elected to the Hall of Fame.) Following his arrest, a preliminary trial date was set for December in Toronto. When Kuhn's staff sought to question Jenkins about the incident to determine what action the Commissioner should take, on advice of his Canadian counsel Jenkins refused to answer. What action should Kuhn be entitled to take as of September 1980 (look back at the scope of the commissioner's investigative authority in the material quoted in *Rose v. Giamatti*)?

4. Pascual Perez, then pitching for the Atlanta Braves, was arrested in the Dominican Republic in January 1984, convicted of possession of cocaine, and fined and released on April 9. Upon his return to the United States, Perez denied having committed the offense. Should the commissioner be able to rely on the court's conviction, or should he have to establish the facts before an American arbitrator? (By the early 1990s, Perez, like Steve Howe, had found his way to the Yankees' pitching staff. Unhappily, as also happened to Howe, in 1992 Commissioner Fay Vincent suspended Perez for having failed a spot drug test during spring training.)

The above cases and questions focused on the role of *commissioner* discipline in addressing illegal drug use by players. The following questions consider possible use of other measures to deal with the drug issue, as well as comparisons of disciplinary reactions to other forms of illegal off-the-field-behavior.

Questions for Discussion

1. David Parker had been a star outfielder with the Pittsburgh Pirates in the late 1970s, and then moved on to the Cincinnati Reds as a free agent in the early 1980s. While with the Reds, it was discovered that Parker had begun using drugs when he was with the Pirates, during a period when his performance on the field had deteriorated. The Pirates filed suit against Parker, claiming that they were entitled to recover at least a part of the salary the team had paid him during these drug-using years. How should a judge (or an arbitrator) interpret the language of the standard player contract as it applies to this issue? Should it matter whether the individual player contract was fully guaranteed? Whether the team sought merely to avoid paying deferred compensation still owed for prior seasons, or to recoup salary payments already made? How feasible is it to determine whether a player's performance during any one season has deteriorated due to drug use, as compared with other factors? If available, is such a contract remedy for the club a sufficient response to the problem of drug use, or was Bowie Kuhn correct in asserting that a commissioner simply cannot trust individual clubs to deal firmly with this problem?

Consider the implications of the Otis Nixon case. Nixon, the star centerfielder of the Atlanta Braves during the 1991 pennant race, failed a drug test (required because of earlier cocaine problems) and was suspended by Commissioner Vincent for the rest of that season and the first month of the 1992 season. Though the Braves narrowly escaped with the National League pennant, they lost the World Series to the Minnesota Twins, in part because of a baserunning blunder in the seventh game by Lonnie Smith, Nixon's replacement in the outfield. Then, in the 1991–1992 off-season, the Braves outbid the California Angels for Nixon's future services, by offering him a multi-million dollar salary increase in a guaranteed three-year contract. What does this case imply about the problem of cocaine use by a baseball player?

2. How does drug use compare with other forms of off-field misbehavior? What about late-night drinking that leads to altercations (as happened to a number of major league players, including the Yankees' Mickey Mantle and Billy Martin)? What about driving a car while impaired and getting into an accident that injures the player and a teammate (as happened to Lenny Dykstra of the Philadelphia Phillies) or even kills another person (as happened to Craig McTavish, then of the Boston Bruins, and Reggie Rogers, then of the Detroit Lions)? A tragic irony of the Rogers case is that just two years earlier, his brother Don Rogers, a star safety for the Cleveland Browns, died from smoking crack cocaine. The deaths not only of Don Rogers, but also of Len Bias (who died the day after the Boston Celtics made him the second pick in the 1986 NBA college draft) put the dangers of cocaine on the front pages of the nation's newspapers. Deaths from drunk driving remain an everyday occurrence. Finally, what about athletes who are arrested for carrying a gun without a license or in an inappropriate public setting (as happened not just to Steve Howe, Jose Canseco, and numerous other athletes, but to then Dallas Cowboys' coach Barry Switzer)? Should sports treat the illegal possession of guns as more or less significant than possession of drugs to the best interests of the game?

3. The above questions have focused on mind-altering drugs, whether illegal drugs such as cocaine or legal drugs such as alcohol. Even more challenging issues are posed by performance-enhancing drugs such as anabolic steroids, which only recently loomed on the sports horizon. Precisely why should we want to prevent athletes such as Ben Johnson in track or Lyle Alzado in football from using steroids to enhance their speed and strength and thus elevate the levels of performance in their sports? Is there something about the nature of athletic competition that makes league efforts to stamp out steroid use a qualitatively different venture in the "best interests" of the sport?[1]

As was graphically displayed in the *Howe* case, baseball players have secured through their labor agreement the right to outside scrutiny of a commissioner decision to discipline players (though not managers like Pete Rose) for behavior the commissioner believes to be contrary to the best interests of the sport. There is a provision (Article XI, § A(1)(b)) in the agreement that gives the commissioner the power to remove a

---

1. An illuminating philosophical discussion of these issues can be found in Robert L. Simon, *Fair Play: Sport, Value, and Society* (Boulder, Colo.: Westview Press, 1991), in particular, Chapter 4, "Enhancing Performance Through Drugs." In Chapter 12 of this book, "Individual Sports" we will look at the issues of steroid use and testing in international track and field and other sports that make up the Olympic Games.

disciplinary case from arbitration, and make his decision in the matter final and binding on the player, by declaring that the matter involves "preservation of the integrity of, or the maintenance of public confidence in, the game of baseball." Baseball owners and players have long disagreed about the scope of this provision. The owners claim that it encompasses a broad range of player conduct, while the Association asserts that the provision covers only behavior that directly affects the integrity of games as played (e.g., players betting on games or taking performance-enhancing drugs). This disagreement has never come to a head, however, because the commissioner has never once invoked the power to declare a case outside the scope of arbitration. The reason, undoubtedly, is the second paragraph of Article XI, § A(1)(b), which gives the union the right to reopen the bargaining agreement if the commissioner ever invokes this power and the union finds his action "unsatisfactory."

The situation in football has followed a different path. The key ruling, *NFL Management Council v. NFL Players Association* (Arbitration, 1979), involved two Miami Dolphins, Randy Crowder and Don Reese. In the spring of 1977, these players were arrested by undercover police detectives for unlawful distribution, not just possession, of cocaine. The two eventually pleaded *nolo contendere* to the criminal charges and were sentenced to one year in jail, which prevented them from playing or being paid for the 1977 season. In August 1978, immediately after their release from the Dade County Stockade, NFL Commissioner Pete Rozelle conducted a disciplinary hearing regarding Crowder and Reese and reached the following verdict.

> As you acknowledged yesterday, you are now fully aware of the fact that NFL players occupy a unique position in the public's perception. The names and images of NFL players are regularly carried into many millions of American homes on television, on radio, and through the print media. NFL players are the focus of wide-spread public attention and are, for good or bad, objects of admiration and emulation for countless American young people.
>
> These unquestioned circumstances impose on every NFL player certain minimal standards of personal conduct—on the field and off. As one court has stated it:
>
>> It is clear that [the NFL has] sought for years to establish a standard of public conduct for professional football participants, including players. This standard (which might be better termed 'image') included the portrayal of players as high-type, admirable young men who are worthy of the respect and emulation of the young.
>
> The resulting obligations of personal conduct are not just owed to the League—they are owed to the public, to the teams with which the players are associated, and to each and every other professional football player. The game itself can be honored—or dishonored—by its own participants.

One such obligation, beyond any doubt, is to avoid criminal involvement with illegal drugs. The use or disposition of illegal drugs, and the seriousness with which it will be viewed by the League, have been repeatedly emphasized within the League in recent years—in team playbooks, locker room notices, and by general discussion.

* * *

[In your] circumstances, I would normally be inclined to impose very severe sanctions. But I recognize that youth and immaturity contributed to the serious mistake you made. I further recognize that the court which heard your case consciously undertook to impose a moderate sentence followed by a strict probation, apparently in a desire to balance deserved punishment against an opportunity for rehabilitation within the line of work you know best. I am also aware that completion of your sentence took you well into the 1978 pre-season training period, and that further suspension action might jeopardize any further opportunity you may have to obtain football employment. Accordingly, I have determined that no suspension from the NFL is warranted at this time. I am proceeding on the premise that you have, as you said yesterday, learned a hard and painful lesson....

I have, however, determined to attach to your return to the NFL [the] condition that you contribute the sum of $5,000 to a drug rehabilitation facility in the state of Florida, subject to approval by this office....

This mandatory "contribution" (in effect, a league assessment or fine of the players) produced a grievance by the NFL Players Association to test the scope and limits of the Commissioner's disciplinary authority. The football arbitrator accepted and applied both the literal wording and negotiating history of Article VIII of the football labor agreement, which allowed the Commissioner to withdraw from general grievance arbitration under Article VII any "action taken against a player by the Commissioner for conduct detrimental to the integrity of, or public confidence in, the game of professional football." Thus, unlike Willie Wilson and Steve Howe in baseball, Randy Crowder and Don Reese (and their successors in football) did not have the right to challenge commissioner reactions to their drug use.

While football players might have the right to go to court, until 1996 none had ever done so, perhaps because their lawyers (after reading the *Molinas* case) believed the players' prospects to be bleak. This view was confirmed by the only such case to raise a challenge, *Holmes v. NFL*, 939 F.Supp. 517 (N.D.Tex.1996). Here the district court upheld Commissioner Tagliabue's authority to reject the appeal of the Dallas Cowboys' Clayton Holmes from his involuntary enrollment in the league's drug treatment program and four game suspension without pay. The league had obtained a first positive drug test that detected marijuana metabolites when Holmes gave a urine specimen to the Detroit Lions while negotiating with them as a restricted free agent. Pursuant to the drug policy established in the collective agreement with the NFLPA, Holmes was involuntarily placed in Stage 2 of the drug program, and subsequently tested positive on two separate occasions. This triggered his suspension without pay by the league. Holmes appealed this sanction to Commissioner Tagliabue, who under the collective agreement serves as the arbitrator for such drug appeals. When Tagliabue upheld the sanctions after a hearing, Holmes sued in federal district court, alleging that because he was not afforded full constitutional due process rights, the commissioner's ruling constituted a breach of the collective agreement. Holmes also claimed that the league's action against him constituted fraudulent inducement, invasion of privacy, intentional infliction of emotional distress, and a breach of the covenant of good faith and fair dealing, all under Texas tort law.

First, the court held that the arbitrator is not required to give full constitutional due process protection, but was only bound by the procedures established in the collective agreement. Then, noting that the parties to the collective agreement voluntarily selected the commissioner as arbitrator in these types of drug cases, the court held that the commissioner's conduct or decision should not be disturbed if it "draws its essence from the collective bargaining agreement and is not based on the arbitrator's 'own brand of industrial justice.'" Thus, the court dismissed the breach of contract claim under the NLRA since "Holmes has not alleged that the Commissioner's ruling was procured by the parties' fraud, or by dishonesty, bad faith, or affirmative misconduct on the part of the Commissioner." It also dismissed the state tort claims as having been preempted by the federal labor laws.

It is evident, then, that judges are not much inclined to overturn decisions made by Commissioners about drug use or other player behavior that the Commissioner believes is a threat to the integrity of the game. The players union can, of course, seek to include in its collective agreement some contractual restraints on such commissioner authority, including review by a neutral arbitrator selected by the two sides. In the most recent round of basketball negotiations (one that was focused primarily on the salary cap), the NBPA did secure a change to their Article XXXI which now allows the Grievance Arbitrator to review Commissioner discipline of players for conduct (though not "on the playing court") that raises concerns about "the preservation of the integrity of, or the maintenance of public confidence in, the game of basketball," and which consists of "a fine and/or suspension that results in a financial impact to the player of more than $25,000." In that situation (which is satisfied by any one game suspension of a player earning approximately $2 million or more), the arbitrator can reverse the Commissioner's ruling only if it is judged to be "arbitrary or capricious." How this new standard will fare in basketball (e.g., in the *Sprewell* case), and whether football or hockey (and perhaps even baseball) will follow suit is something sport law fans will have to wait and see.

While the "moral" authority of commissioners remains generally intact in professional sports, labor negotiations between the players and owners have addressed and resolved specific issues such as drugs. The pioneer in this respect was the NBA. In 1983, when Bob Lanier was President of the NBA Players Association, the union accepted stiff sanctions against its members for drug use. Article 33 of the basketball agreement states that any player detected using, possessing, or distributing a listed "prohibited substance" (at present, heroin or cocaine) shall immediately and permanently be disqualified from the league, and neither the league nor the player's club can dilute this sanction. While the Article does allow the player to petition for reinstatement no earlier than two years from expulsion, approval must be given by both the commissioner and the union. However, the NBA's draconian disciplinary approach to the discovery of drug use is only one component of a policy that emphasizes rehabilitation and education. Under Article 33, any player with a drug problem who comes forward before detection faces no penalty, but instead receives treatment at the club's expense with his salary continued for at least thirty days.

In the 1990s, football and hockey established a graduated system for addressing player drug abuse. The National Hockey League, for example, had previously imposed immediate and indefinite suspension on any player who was found to have used drugs at any time. (In the late 1980s, this happened to then-Edmonton Oilers' All–Star goalie Grant Fuhr, when his wife disclosed Fuhr's earlier drug use during their divorce proceedings.) In 1996, the hockey players and owners agreed to a four-step drug policy that moves from in-patient treatment (with pay) for a first offense, treatment and suspension without pay for a second offense, a minimum six-month suspension for a third offence, and a minimum one-year for a fourth offence, with no assurance of reinstatement. And as this edition was being completed at the end of 1997, NBA owners were saying that marijuana (which, along with guns, had been found in Allen Iverson's car that summer) should also be designated a league-prohibited substance—perhaps in negotiations of a reopened collective agreement in the summer of 1998.

3. DRUG TESTING[m]

Equally important as how to respond to past drug use is what, if anything, should be done to prevent future use. Here the most controversial question, not just in professional (and college) sports, but in workplaces generally, is mandatory drug testing.

m. On drug testing in professional sports see the articles by Wong and Ensor, note k above, and by Ethan Lock, *The Legality Under the National Labor Relations Act of Attempts by National Football League Owners to Unilaterally Implement Drug Testing Programs*, 39 U. of Florida L. Rev. 1 (1987). The best scholarly explorations of this topic in law reviews have been written by Mark A. Rothstein. See his *Drug Testing in the Workplace: The Challenge to Employment Relations and Employment Law*, 63 Chicago–Kent L. Rev. 683 (1987), and *Workplace Drug Testing: A Case Study in the Misapplication of Technology*, 5 Harvard J. of L. and Tech. 65 (1991). A useful presentation of the different viewpoints on this topic is the *Symposium, Drug Testing in the Workplace*, 33 William and Mary L. Rev. 1 (1991).

In 1983, the NBA players and owners pioneered in developing and agreeing to a program for testing players. The parties jointly appointed an independent, experienced expert in drug detection and enforcement to review confidentially any evidence that a particular player had a drug abuse problem. If the expert finds "reasonable cause" for believing this to be true, he issues an "authorization for testing" of this player without notice. Except for a recent provision that allows for one test of all rookies at training camp, NBA clubs have agreed to forego any other drug testing of their players.

Just one year later, baseball followed basketball's lead when the MLB Players Association's Marvin Miller and the owners' Player Relations Committee's Lee MacPhail peacefully negotiated a "reasonable cause-independent review" procedure to try to address the source of the *Wilson-Blue* case. Unfortunately, in 1985 there came a notorious criminal trial of the drug supplier to the Pittsburgh Pirates (the trial that disclosed Dave Parker's drug use and precipitated the Pirates' breach of contract suit against him). The public outcry in this era led the baseball owners to exercise their contractual right to terminate the agreed-to procedure, and to say that baseball needed to test *all* its players. In the winter of 1986, under the guidance of Peter Ueberroth, Bowie Kuhn's successor as Commissioner, the owners insisted that all new player contracts must require the players to submit to random drug testing. However, the Players Association was successful in persuading the arbitrator that such a provision did not fit within the escape valve in the collective agreement, which allowed special covenants in individual player contracts if and only if the covenant was for the "actual or potential benefit of the player."

Football was also experiencing this same sense of crisis. Right after the New England Patriots lost the 1986 Super Bowl to the Chicago Bears in the New Orleans Superdome, the Boston Globe broke the story that six Patriots' players had been using drugs. The ensuing public controversy prompted an immediate effort by NFL Commissioner Rozelle and Jack Donlan, head of the NFL Management Council (NFLMC), to try to persuade Gene Upshaw, Executive Director of the NFL Players Association, to agree to drug testing of all NFL players. While the NFLPA was prepared to accept a variety of anti-drug measures, the union drew the line at mandatory random testing. Thus, on July 7, 1986, Rozelle announced a new drug program, a key ingredient of which were two unscheduled urine tests of all players during the season (conducted exclusively by the league's new drug advisor, Dr. Forrest Tennant).

Upshaw and the Players Association immediately took this issue to arbitration. Rozelle's argument was that he had the right to take this action under the "integrity of the game" provision in the collective agreement. In a lengthy opinion, *NFLPA and NFL Management Council* (Arbitration, 1986), the arbitrator accepted the commissioner's authority to create league-based and standardized drug education and testing procedures. However, with respect to commissioner insistence upon "unscheduled drug testing" of all players, the arbitrator's verdict was different.

"Unscheduled testing" is not addressed, contemplated or permitted by Article XXXI of the collective bargaining agreement. It must be remembered that, as a result of the Commissioner's concern in 1982 regarding abuse and misuse of drugs and his desire to establish urinalysis testing, the League proposed that pre-season and reasonable cause testing be included in the collective bargaining agreement. For a period of time the NFLPA resisted any language being incorporated into the collective bargaining agreement which would permit testing of players for chemical abuse or dependency. When the NFLPA finally conceded to permit certain testing, it qualified the right of the clubs to test by requiring that "there will not be any spot checking for chemical abuse or dependency by the club or club physician." The NFL and the NFLMC have argued that if the NFLPA had wished to prohibit unscheduled testing that their negotiators could have readily drafted language which would have provided that "except as permitted under this agreement, there will be no drug testing of players." The NFL and the NFLMC have further contended that the prohibition on "spot checking" does not prevent the implementation of Commissioner Rozelle's proposed two (2) regular Season unscheduled tests, since those tests cannot be construed as "Spot checks."

The Arbitrator is not persuaded by these arguments. In our opinion the NFL and the NFLMC have improperly attempted to "switch the onus of draftsmanship" to the NFLPA. The "spot checking" prohibition directly follows that sentence in Section 7 of Article XXXI which allows the club physician, upon reasonable cause, to direct a player to Hazelden for chemical abuse or dependency problems. In our opinion, the NFLPA ensured that spot checking was not to be permitted as part of the "reasonable cause" testing right, which the NFLMC obtained for the member clubs as a result of its July 23, 1982 proposal. Accordingly, we find that the "spot checking" prohibition modifies the clubs' rights to conduct reasonable cause testing and is not properly construed as the "only" prohibition on the League's or the clubs' rights to test for chemical use or dependency.

Article XXXI establishes the obligation for players to submit to a pre-season drug test and tests for chemical abuse or dependency problems when a club physician has reasonable cause to direct players to submit to such tests. Article XXXI makes no reference to "two (2) regular season unscheduled tests." The language of Article XXXI is not sufficiently broad to permit unscheduled testing. Further, it is clear that Commissioner Rozelle never contemplated unscheduled testing in 1982, and therefore the negotiators could not have intended that players would be subjected to unscheduled testing.

In none of the professional team sports, then, is there now random drug testing of all players, irrespective of their past history or current indications of drug use. What are the pros and cons of this situation for the fans, the owners, and even the players, with respect to either mind-altering or performance-enhancing drugs?

The situation in college sports is quite different. For reasons we shall read later in Chapter 10, college athletes (even in revenue-generating football and basketball) are considered to be students, and therefore not employees entitled to bargain collectively under labor law. At the same time, many of the colleges for whom student-athletes play are public entities that are governed by the federal and state constitutions, and even private colleges may be subject to laws that apply to all institutions. Thus, college and (most recently) high school athletics have provided the best judicial glimpse of the substantive merits (rather than just the organizational authority) of a policy that requires drug-testing of all—but only—athletes.[n]

Drug-testing of college athletes was also a product of the social and political outcry of the mid–1980s, though with the following important variation. In the 1983 Pan–American Games held in Caracas, Venezuela, a number of American athletes, including college athletes, were found to have been using steroids. This led the United States Olympic Committee to develop a drug-testing program for all athletes competing in international events. The NCAA commissioned a study by scholars at Michigan State University who found that 4% of college athletes reported using steroids, 8% amphetamines, 17% cocaine, and 36% marijuana. A Special Committee proposed a new mandatory testing program modelled on the Olympics.

> The NCAA has a legitimate interest in maintaining the integrity of intercollegiate athletics, including insuring fair competition and protecting the health and safety of all participating student-athletes. The use of "performance enhancing" drugs by individual student-athletes is a violation of the ethic of fair competition, [and] poses a potential health and safety hazard to those utilizing such drugs and a potential safety hazard to those competing with such individuals. The most effective method of ensuring that student-athletes are not utilizing "performance enhancing" drugs is through a consistent, national drug testing program.

[n]. For scholarly explorations of the issues posed by compulsory drug testing of college athletes, see John Allen Scanlan, Jr., *Playing the Drug–Testing Game: College Athletics, Regulatory Institutions and the Rhetoric of Constitutional Argument*, 62 Indiana L. J. 863 (1987); Le Roy Pernell, *Random Drug–Testing of Student Athletes by State Universities in the Wake of* Von Raab *and* Skinner, 1 Marquette Sports L. J. 41 (1990); and Stephen F. Brock, Kevin M. McKenna, and Rhett Traband, *Drug Testing College Athletes: NCAA Does Thy Cup Runneth Over?*, 97 West Virginia L. Rev. 53 (1994).

At the NCAA's January 1986 convention, the membership overwhelmingly endorsed this proposal, but with one key addition: the program would test for mind-altering "street drugs" as well as performance-enhancing steroids and the like.

The new NCAA rules required that every student athlete sign a consent to such testing if he or she wanted to compete. Randomly-selected athletes were required to supply urine in front of an NCAA monitor (of the same sex). The substance was divided into two samples, one of which was tested first, and then the second if the first test was positive.

Two student-athletes from Stanford University challenged their university's effort to institute this program in compliance with NCAA regulations. The students claimed that such testing violated their privacy rights under Article 1 of the California constitution, which applied to private as well as public institutions.

> Section 1. All people are by nature free and independent and have inalienable rights. Among these are enjoying and defending life and liberty, acquiring, possessing, and protecting property, and pursuing and obtaining safety, happiness, and privacy.

(The phrase "and privacy" had been added to the Constitution by a voters initiative in 1972.) Now supported by Stanford, the students won a lower court injunction against NCAA enforcement of this drug-testing policy against any Stanford student-athlete. The Association appealed that verdict to the Supreme Court of California. Following is the Court majority's analysis of the substance of this constitutional claim.

HILL v. NATIONAL COLLEGIATE ATHLETIC ASSOCIATION

Supreme Court of California, en banc, 1994.
7 Cal.4th 1, 26 Cal.Rptr.2d 834, 865 P.2d 633.

LUCAS, CHIEF JUSTICE.

* * *

The trial court found in part that the NCAA drug testing program invades the privacy interests of student-athletes by requiring them: (1) to disclose medications they may be using and other information about their physical and medical conditions; (2) to urinate in the presence of a monitor; and (3) to provide a urine sample that reveals chemical and other substances in their bodies.

The court further found that college athletes do not use drugs any more frequently than college students as a general class. It observed that in 1986–1987, the first year of the NCAA's drug testing program, 34 of the 3,511 athletes tested for drugs were declared ineligible because of proscribed drug use. Of the 34 athletes declared ineligible, 31 were engaged in football, one was in track and field, and two were in basketball. Of the football players, 25 had tested positive for use of steroids. The track and field athlete tested positive for steroids, the two basketball players for cocaine.

From its findings, the court concluded there was no "compelling need" for drug testing to protect the health of college athletes or the integrity of athletic competition. According to the court, the NCAA program was "overbroad" because it banned "useful" over-the-counter medications and prescription drugs "designed to improve the health of the athlete." The court observed the NCAA had not been completely consistent in its professed concern for the health of athletes as shown by its failure to require measles vaccinations of athletes despite previous measles outbreaks at postseason competition or to provide counselling or rehabilitation services for drug-using athletes. The court added that Stanford "believes it is wrong to single out athletes for drug testing" and "favors drug education for its students."

The trial court also found the NCAA had failed to produce evidence that certain banned substances, e.g., amphetamines, diuretics, marijuana, and heroin, actually enhance athletic performance. It did find, however, that marijuana clearly impairs athletic performance and that cocaine may do so. Addressing the alleged perception that use of certain drugs may enhance performance, the court found that drugs are generally not perceived by college athletes and coaches to enhance performance or to be "a major problem." With respect to steroid use, the "perception," according to the court, is that steroids "might only help certain types of positions in football."

* * *

3. APPLICATION OF THE ELEMENTS OF INVASION OF PRIVACY TO THIS CASE

* * *

Plaintiffs correctly assert that the NCAA's drug testing program impacts legally protected privacy interests. First, by monitoring an athlete's urination, the NCAA's program intrudes on a human bodily function that by law and social custom is generally performed in private and without observers.... Second, by collecting and testing an athlete's urine and inquiring about his or her ingestion of medications and other substances, the NCAA obtains information about the internal medical state of an athlete's body that is regarded as personal and confidential....

Observation of urination and disclosure of medical information may cause embarrassment to individual athletes. The first implicates autonomy privacy—an interest in freedom from observation in performing a function recognized by social norms as private. The second implicates informational privacy—an interest in limiting disclosure of confidential information about bodily condition. But, as we have noted, the identification of these privacy interests is the beginning, not the end, of the analysis.

a. Freedom From Observation During Urination

(1) Reasonable expectations of privacy

The observation of urination—a human excretory function-obviously implicates privacy interests.[12] But the reasonable expectations of privacy of plaintiffs (and other student-athletes) in private urination must be viewed within the context of intercollegiate athletic activity and the normal conditions under which it is undertaken.

By its nature, participation in intercollegiate athletics, particularly in highly competitive postseason championship events, involves close regulation and scrutiny of the physical fitness and bodily condition of student-athletes. Required physical examinations (including urinalysis), and special regulation of sleep habits, diet, fitness, and other activities that intrude significantly on privacy interests are routine aspects of a college athlete's life not shared by other students or the population at large. Athletes frequently disrobe in the presence of one another and their athletic mentors and assistants in locker room settings where private bodily parts are readily observable by others of the same sex. They also exchange information about their physical condition and medical treatment with coaches, trainers and others who have a "need to know."

As a result of its unique set of demands, athletic participation carries with it social norms that effectively diminish the athlete's reasonable expectation of personal privacy in his or her bodily condition, both internal and external. In recognition of this practical reality, drug testing programs involving athletic competition have routinely survived Fourth Amendment "privacy" challenges. Drug testing has become a highly visible, pervasive, and well-accepted part of athletic competition, particularly on intercollegiate and professional levels. It is a reasonably expected part of the life of an athlete, especially one engaged in advanced levels of competition, where the stakes and corresponding temptations are high.

The student-athlete's reasonable expectation of privacy is further diminished by two elements of the NCAA's drug testing program—advance notice and the opportunity to consent to testing. A drug test does not come as an unwelcome surprise at the end of a postseason match. Full disclosure of the NCAA's banned substances rules and testing procedures is made at the beginning of the athletic season, long before the postseason competition during which drug testing may take place. Following disclosure, the informed written consent of each student-athlete is obtained. Thus, athletes have complete information re-

---

12. In our culture, urination is generally regarded as private, but perhaps not absolutely private in all conceivable settings. "Men urinate side by side in public restrooms without embarrassment even though there is very little, and often no, attempt to partition the urinals. In hospitals and physicians' offices, urine samples of both men and women are generally taken by female nurses or technicians under conditions of privacy similar to those prescribed by [athletic drug testing rules]." (*Dimeo v. Griffin* 943 F.2d 679, 682 (7th Cir.1991).)

garding the NCAA's drug testing program and are afforded the opportunity to consent or refuse before they may be selected for testing.

To be sure, an athlete who refuses consent to drug testing is disqualified from NCAA competition. But this consequence does not render the athlete's consent to testing involuntary in any meaningful legal sense. Athletic participation is not a government benefit or an economic necessity that society has decreed must be open to all. One aspect of the state constitutional right to privacy is "our freedom to associate with the people we choose." Participation in any organized activity carried on by a private, nongovernment organization necessarily entails a willingness to forgo assertion of individual rights one might otherwise have in order to receive the benefits of communal association.

Plaintiffs and Stanford have no legal right to participate in intercollegiate athletic competition. Their ability to do so necessarily depends upon their willingness to arrive at and adhere to common understandings with their competitors regarding their mutual sporting endeavor. The NCAA is democratically governed by its member institutions, including Stanford. Acting collectively, those institutions, including Stanford, make the rules, including those regarding drug use and testing. If, knowing the rules, plaintiffs and Stanford choose to play the game, they have, by social convention and legal act, fully and voluntarily acquiesced in the application of those rules. To view the matter otherwise would impair the privacy and associational rights of all NCAA institutions and athletes.

(2) Seriousness of invasion

Although diminished by the athletic setting and the exercise of informed consent, plaintiffs' privacy interests are not thereby rendered de minimis. Direct observation of urination by a monitor, an intrusive act, appears to be unique to the NCAA's program. Other decided cases, including those involving athlete drug testing, have involved less invasive testing methods, typically unobserved urination in a restroom stall. (See, e.g., *Dimeo v. Griffin*, supra, 943 F.2d at p. 682 [urine specimen given in "(relative) privacy" of toilet stall with representative standing by but not observing urination].) The NCAA's use of a particularly intrusive monitored urination procedure justifies further inquiry, even under conditions of decreased expectations of privacy.

(3) Competing interests

To justify its intrusion on student-athletes' diminished expectations of privacy, the NCAA asserts two countervailing interests: (1) safeguarding the integrity of intercollegiate athletic competition; and (2) protecting the health and safety of student-athletes. The central purpose of the NCAA is to promote competitive athletic events conducted pursuant to "rules of the game" enacted by its own membership. In this way, the NCAA creates and preserves the "level playing field" necessary to promote vigorous, highlevel, and nationwide competition in intercollegiate sports.

Plaintiffs and Stanford do not contend that the purpose or objectives of the NCAA are contrary to law or public policy. Nor do they attribute bad faith motives to the NCAA or challenge its important role as "the guardian of [the] important American tradition" of intercollegiate athletic competition. (*NCAA v. Board of Regents of Univ. of Okla.*, 468 U.S. 85, 101, fn. 23 (1984).) The NCAA is, without doubt, a highly visible and powerful institution, holding, as it does, a virtual monopoly on high-level intercollegiate athletic competition in the United States. Although the NCAA, like other private businesses and organizations, is subject to numerous regulations, neither Congress nor our Legislature has seen fit to interfere with its general rulemaking functions, whether in the area of drug testing or in other fields. Therefore, we regard the NCAA's stated motives and objectives, not with hostility or intense skepticism, but with a "respectful presumption of validity." (Ibid.) Considered in light of its history, the NCAA's decision to enforce a ban on the use of drugs by means of a drug testing program is reasonably calculated to further its legitimate interest in maintaining the integrity of intercollegiate athletic competition. As one author observed: "[Athletic] competition should be decided on the basis of who has done the best job of perfecting and utilizing his or her natural abilities, not on the basis of who has the best pharmacist." (Zemper, Drug Testing in Athletics, in *Drug Testing: Issues and Options* (Coombs & West eds., 1991) p.120.)

The NCAA began to study drug testing in response to a specific incident of probable drug ingestion by athletes at the Pan American Games. It followed other established and respected amateur sporting organizations—principally the USOC and the International Olympic Committee—in promulgating and enforcing its drug testing program. And, although the NCAA followed the lead of others, it did not do so blindly. Before beginning its testing program, the NCAA commissioned its own study—one that showed significant and widespread use of drugs by student-athletes. Other studies included in the record, as well as testimony from physicians, trainers, and others, confirm substantial, if not extensive, drug use by student-athletes. Despite advance notice and warnings to student-athletes before the testing program began, approximately 1% of the athletes tested in the first two years of operation were declared ineligible because of drug use.[15]

But whatever the provable incidence of drug use, perception may be more potent than reality. If particular substances are perceived to enhance athletic performance, student-athletes may feel pressure (whether internal or external, subtle or overt) to use them. A drug

---

15. Contrary to plaintiffs' argument, we do not regard the results of drug testing after the NCAA announced and began its program as the only persuasive evidence of actual drug use by student athletes. Plaintiffs ignore the self-evident deterrent effect of the program itself, particularly in the context of highly competitive sports activity. Once a program of drug testing is formally announced and in effect, athletes who wish to avoid the disastrous effects of disqualification have a strong incentive to refrain from ingesting prohibited substances. Indeed, one possible yardstick of a drug testing program accompanied by advance consent and publicity is a percentage of positive drug test findings that starts low and continues either at the same level or downward. When so measured, the NCAA's program is successful.

testing program serves to minimize that pressure by providing at least some assurance that drug use will be detected and the user disqualified. As a result, it provides significant and direct benefits to the student-athletes themselves, allowing them to concentrate on the merits of their athletic task without undue concern about loss of a competitive edge. These benefits offset the limited impact on privacy imposed by the prospect of testing.

There was ample evidence in the record that certain kinds of drugs such as anabolic steroids and amphetamines—are perceived by some athletes to enhance athletic performance. Among other findings, the Michigan State University study showed that 69% of the student-athletes who reported taking steroids and 37% of those taking amphetamines admitted doing so "to improve athletic performance." Plaintiffs' own expert, Dr. David Lowenthal, wrote in 1985:

> "In spite of physicians' efforts to provide rational and individual therapy for patients and despite warnings to healthy participants in sports, the consumption of caffeine, salicyclates, nonsteroidal anti-inflammatory drugs ... alcohol, anabolic steroids, and amphetamines to improve athletic performance is rampant."

As to anabolic steroids, Dr. Lowenthal commented:

> "The use of these drugs by athletes has now reached alarming proportions.... In the United States, anabolic steroid use has spread from professional athletes to college and high school athletes.... It would be extremely difficult to determine the number of athletes who use anabolic steroids in different sports. Much of the information in this area comes from former users [and] from informal surveys. It has been suggested that between 80 and 100 per cent of male bodybuilders and weight lifters at the national and international level use these agents during training. Use among shotputters and discus, hammer and javelin throwers is probably comparable. The use of anabolic steroids has spread rapidly to include football players, swimmers and other competitive athletes, as well as non-competitive athletes."

... Finally, the practical realities of NCAA-sponsored athletic competition cannot be ignored. Intercollegiate sports is, at least in part, a business founded upon offering for public entertainment athletic contests conducted under a rule of fair and rigorous competition. Scandals involving drug use, like those involving improper financial incentives or other forms of corruption, impair the NCAA's reputation in the eyes of the sports-viewing public. A well announced and vigorously pursued drug testing program serves to: (1) provide a significant deterrent to would-be violators, thereby reducing the probability of damaging public disclosure of athlete drug use; and (2) assure student-athletes, their schools, and the public that fair competition remains the overriding principle in athletic events. Of course, these outcomes also serve the NCAA's overall interest in safeguarding the integrity of intercollegiate athletic competition.

The NCAA also has an interest in protecting the health and safety of student-athletes who are involved in NCAA-regulated competition. Contrary to plaintiffs' characterization, this interest is more than a mere "naked assertion of paternalism." The NCAA sponsors and regulates intercollegiate athletic events, which by their nature may involve risks of physical injury to athletes, spectators, and others. In this way, the NCAA effectively creates occasions for potential injury resulting from the use of drugs. As a result, it may concern itself with the task of protecting the safety of those involved in intercollegiate athletic competition. This NCAA interest exists for the benefit of all persons involved in sporting events (including not only drug-ingesting athletes but also innocent athletes or others who might be injured by a drug user), as well as the sport itself.

Plaintiffs and Stanford attempt to undermine the strength of the NCAA's interests with a series of factual arguments based on the trial court's findings. However, as we have noted, those findings were premised on the legal assumption that the NCAA bears the burden of establishing a "compelling interest" in its drug testing program that cannot be addressed by any alternative with a lesser impact on privacy interests. No such showing is required. Because the trial court's findings were premised on an erroneous view of the applicable legal standard, they cannot save the judgment....

Without reviewing all of the arguments advanced by plaintiffs and Stanford, it is sufficient to note that most, if not all, are based on matters that are immaterial in light of the elements of invasion of privacy described above. For example, plaintiffs seek to dismiss college athlete drug use as legally insignificant, pointing to a finding that "athletes do not use drugs any more than college students generally" and another that they "actually use drugs less during the athletic season than their peers." The purported comparison between student-athletes and other college students is beside the point. Student-athletes have set themselves apart from their nonathlete peers; as we have noted, they have different and diminished expectations of privacy in the athletic context. If student-athletes' drug use is, or, in the absence of drug testing could be, substantial and detrimental to competition or to the health of student-athletes, the NCAA has a significant interest in conducting a testing program.

Plaintiffs also point to trial court findings that none of the NCAA's banned drugs were "scientifically proven" to enhance athletic performance, noting some controversy among experts respecting certain substances. Plaintiffs cite no authority imposing a "scientific" burden of proof on a defendant in an invasion of privacy case; we have located none. Scientific proof of this nature would require actual drug use under competitive conditions. This kind of human experimentation would pose risks to life and limb of far greater magnitude than plaintiffs' asserted privacy interest in this case. Moreover, the existence of continuing scientific controversy about particular drugs or practices on perceptions in athletic settings can reasonably be viewed as dictating caution and prohibition, rather than total deregulation.

Finally, as we have noted, perception may well overpower reality in this area. Although the trial court found that coaches and athletes in general do not perceive drugs as performance-enhancing or as a "major problem," there is clear evidence of a significant perception to the contrary on the part of some coaches and athletes. Plaintiffs' own expert confirmed the perception and opined that it was growing. Rules are often made and enforced to control the behavior of relatively small numbers of individuals whose conduct, if it became more widespread, would undermine a community goal or objective. If athletic drug use became widespread because of a growing perception that drug users thereby obtained a "competitive edge," the integrity and reputation of NCAA athletic competition could be seriously threatened. The NCAA is not required by state constitutional privacy principles to stay its hand until a "minor" problem becomes a "major" one.

Plaintiffs also challenge the NCAA's list of proscribed drugs, maintaining that it is overbroad because, as the trial court found, it "includes substances which do not enhance performance." Accepting the factual premise of plaintiffs' argument, it is not fatal to the NCAA's drug testing program. Initially, the NCAA's interests are not limited to banning so-called performance-enhancing drugs. It also prohibits street drugs—such as marijuana and cocaine—which are illegal to possess and which probably retard athletic performance. The NCAA's interests in maintaining the integrity of competitive conditions and protecting the health and safety of student-athletes certainly extends to prohibiting the use of illegal and dangerous substances, as well as others that might potentially affect athletic performance, whether positively or negatively.

Moreover, the Privacy Initiative does not empower us to make an item-by-item review of the desirability of retaining each item in the NCAA's prohibited substance list. The privacy interests asserted by plaintiffs are impacted by the manner in which drug testing is carried out; assuming the list contains at least some substances that may potentially injure competitors or competition and thereby justify testing, the impact of monitored urine testing on plaintiffs' privacy interests does not wax or wane depending upon the number of such substances.

* * *

Reversed.

Justice Kennard concurred in the majority's ruling that a private defendant need establish only a reasonable and legitimate, not a compelling, interest in order to justify an invasion of privacy, but would have remanded the case back for a new trial focussed on this new legal standard. Justice George dissented from the holding that a lesser standard was appropriate for private defendants, but concurred in the judgment because he believed the NCAA had established a compelling interest for its drug testing program.

Justice Mosk's dissent in *Hill* relied heavily on *University of Colorado v. Derdeyn*, 863 P.2d 929 (Colo.1993), which involved a challenge against the University of Colorado's random drug testing of its student-athletes throughout their season, on the grounds that this violated the federal Constitution's Fourth Amendment ban on unreasonable searches and seizures, and the Colorado constitution's equivalent provision. (The federal Constitution was implicated because, unlike Stanford and the NCAA, the University of Colorado is a state institution.) There, the Colorado Supreme Court affirmed the lower court injunction against the drug testing program on the grounds that it infringed on reasonable expectations of privacy. The Colorado court took exactly the opposite view to that of the California court about several of the key issues: (a) athletes do not have a diminished expectation of privacy or one that is less than that of other non-athlete students; (b) the university's interest in maintaining the integrity of its athletic program, while valid and commendable, is not that important; and (c) the consent form athletes are required to sign before they can participate in athletics is not voluntary. While avoiding a final decision about whether Colorado had to demonstrate a compelling interest or something less, the court concluded that the university's interest did not outweigh its drug testing program's infringement on the athletes' reasonable expectation of privacy.

At that same time, the issue of mandatory drug-testing of all student athletes was being addressed in the federal courts, this time involving high school athletes. In the mid–1980s, the Vernonia School District in the logging region of Oregon had found that drug use and associated disciplinary problems had begun to increase among its student body. Initially, the District responded to the issue with a drug policy that consisted of special classes, speakers, and presentations about the dangers of drug use. When that policy seemed to be unsuccessful in stamping out the drug problem, the District established a drug-testing program. This new regime however, focused just on students engaged in interscholastic athletics. Each week, ten percent of a school's athletes were randomly selected for urine sample testing. The samples were provided by the student in the bathroom, in front of a monitor, and the drugs tested for were cocaine, marijuana, and amphetamines. If the results of a test were positive, a second test was immediately made. If the second test was also positive, the student was required to participate in an individualized drug abuse program, including weekly testing.

In the fall of 1991, James Acton, a seventh grader who wanted to play football, was told he could be part of the school's team only if he and his parents signed a consent to the drug testing program. Instead, Acton sued, alleging that this program violated his rights under the Fourth and Fourteenth Amendments. Earlier Supreme Court decisions had made it clear that the Fourth Amendment applies to public school officials, *New Jersey v. T.L.O.*, 469 U.S. 325 (1985), and that government-compelled drug testing is a "search" for purposes of the Fourth

Amendment, *Skinner v. Railway Labor Executives Assn.*, 489 U.S. 602 (1989), and *National Treasury Employees Union v. Von Raab*, 489 U.S. 656 (1989). However, it is the general "reasonableness" standard, not the criminal warrant requirement of "probable cause," that governs the constitutionality of such search programs, *Griffin v. Wisconsin*, 483 U.S. 868 (1987). In *Acton v. Vernonia School Dist.*, 23 F.3d 1514 (9th Cir.1994), the Ninth Circuit struck down the Vernonia program, finding that mandatory drug-testing only of those students whose behavior had raised "reasonable suspicion" of a drug problem was a sufficient and less intrusive means of securing the school's objectives here. On appeal, a divided Supreme Court reversed. See *Vernonia School Dist. v. Acton*, 515 U.S. 646 (1995).

Both at the opening and the closing of his majority opinion, Justice Scalia emphasized that "central ... to the present case is the fact that the subjects of the [Vernonia] Policy are (1) children, who (2) have been committed to the temporary custody of the State as Schoolmaster ... [and thus were constitutionally subject to] a degree of supervision and control that could not be exercised over free adults." However, when Justice Scalia addressed the substantive aspects of those attenuated constitutional rights of children, his analysis echoed much of what we read in *Hill*. With respect to privacy claims, not only are all "public school children ... routinely required to submit to various physical examinations, and to be vaccinated against various diseases," but the student athlete has much less in the way of "legitimate privacy expectations."

> School sports are not for the bashful. They require "suiting up" before each practice or event, and showering and changing afterwards. Public school locker rooms, the usual sites for these activities, are not notable for the privacy they afford. The locker rooms in Vernonia are typical: no individual dressing rooms are provided; shower heads are lined up along a wall, unseparated by any sort of partition or curtain; not even all the toilet stalls have doors. As the United States Court of Appeals for the Seventh Circuit has noted, there is "an element of 'communal undress' inherent in athletic participation," *Schaill* by *Kross v. Tippecanoe County School Corp.*, 864 F.2d 1309, 1318 (1988).
>
> There is an additional respect in which school athletes have a reduced expectation of privacy. By choosing to "go out for the team," they voluntarily subject themselves to a degree of regulation even higher than that imposed on students generally. In Vernonia's public schools, they must submit to a preseason physical exam, they must acquire adequate insurance coverage or sign an insurance waiver, maintain a minimum grade point average, and comply with any "rules of conduct, dress, training hours and related matters as may be established for each sport by the head coach and athletic director with the principal's approval." Somewhat like adults who choose to participate in a "closely regulated industry," students who

voluntarily participate in school athletics have reason to expect intrusions upon normal rights and privileges, including privacy.

515 U.S. at 656–57.

Not only were the athlete's privacy expectations considered modest, but the level of intrusion by the testing was deemed to be "negligible" (both in the method through which the urine sample was obtained and the sharing of the testing results only with school personnel). By contrast, the governmental interest in reducing drug use by school children was found to be very important. The reason for focusing testing on student-athletes was partly because the drug problem here was "largely fueled by the 'role model' effect of athletes' drug use," but also because the risk of "immediate physical harm to the [athlete] drug user or those with whom he is playing the sport is particularly high."

Apart from psychological effects, which include impairment of judgment, slow reaction time, and a lessening of the perception of pain, the particular drugs screened by the District's Policy have been demonstrated to pose substantial physical risks to athletes. Amphetamines produce an "artificially induced heart rate increase, peripheral vasoconstriction, blood pressure increase, and masking of the normal fatigue response," making them a "very dangerous drug when used during exercise of any type." Hawkins, *Drugs and Other Ingesta: Effects on Athletic Performance*, in H. Appenzeller, *Managing Sports and Risk Management Strategies* 90, 90–91 (1993). Marijuana causes "irregular blood pressure responses during changes in body position," "reduction in the oxygen-carrying capacity of the blood," and "inhibition of the normal sweating responses resulting in increased body temperature." Cocaine produces "vasoconstriction[,] elevated blood pressure," and "possible coronary artery spasms and myocardial infarction."

515 U.S. at 662. However, having concluded for the above reasons that Vernonia's policy was reasonable and thus constitutional, the Court again emphasized the narrowness of this ruling.

We caution against the assumption that suspicion-less drug testing will readily pass constitutional muster in other contexts. The most significant element in this case is the first we discussed: that the Policy was undertaken in furtherance of the government's responsibilities, under a public school system, as guardian and tutor of children entrusted to its care. Just as when the government conducts a search in its capacity as employer (a warrantless search of an absent employee's desk to obtain an urgently needed file, for example), the relevant question is whether that intrusion upon privacy is one that a reasonable employer might engage in, so also when the government acts as guardian and tutor the relevant question is whether the search is one that a reasonable guardian and tutor might undertake. Given the findings of need made by the District Court, we conclude that in the present case it is.

515 U.S. at 665.

Even more than suspensions for actual drug use, randomized testing of all athletes to deter any future use poses important policy as well as constitutional questions. Indeed, reflecting on these issues is valuable not just for the worlds of professional and college sports, which are the focus of this book, but for the broader workplace and other settings in which drug testing is becoming more and more common.

Questions For Discussion

1. The NCAA did its fourth *Study of Substance Use and Abuse Habits of College Student–Athletes* in 1997. This survey found that, by comparison with 1985 (the year of the first study), steroid use had dropped from four to one percent of college athletes, cocaine use from 17 to two percent, marijuana from 35 to 28%, and alcohol from 88 to 81%. Does this constitute a serious problem of drug use by professional and/or college athletes, either absolutely or by comparison with other performers or students? Is your diagnosis of that problem the same for steroids, for example, as for cocaine? Suppose that there once was a drug problem in the colleges or schools, but no longer; does this imply that drug testing was effective and should be continued or that it is no longer needed?

2. In her brief concurrence in *Acton*, Justice Ginsburg underlined that the Court was upholding the constitutionality of random drug-testing only for students who wanted to play sports, not those who just wanted to attend classes in the school. Justice O'Connor, who authored a dissent joined by Justices Stevens and Souter, observed that this singling out of only student-athletes for testing was a significant part of the problem, not its solution. Should it be a condition at least of the policy (if not constitutional) value of random drug-testing programs that they subject all students to it? Or should Vernonia's program (as well as Stanford's in *Hill*) at least have covered any student who wanted to participate in the school's music, drama, and other extracurricular programs besides athletics?

3. How invasive is drug testing of players' privacy? Does a monitor watching someone urinate significantly intrude on that person's privacy rights (by comparison, for example, with use of public restrooms)? Does your judgment differ between male and female athletes? With respect to either gender, do you agree with Justice Scalia (or with Justice O'Connor) that drug testing is (or is not) qualitatively different than vaccination or physical examinations of students (or employees). Does the more significant feature of a drug-testing program lie not in the initial physical intrusion, but in the eventual suspension of an athlete from the sport if the test detects actual drug use (and is this relevant to the constitutional privacy analysis)?

4. How accurate are drug testing procedures? Are there ways that confidence in drug test results might be enhanced? Is it necessary to watch an athlete urinate in order to be assured of a reliable sample?

5. In *Acton*, the principal basis for the original Ninth Circuit decision and Justice O'Connor's dissent was the fact that the Vernonia School

District had not adopted a less intrusive program of testing only those student athletes whose personal behavior provided a "reasonable basis for suspicion of drug use." The following passage provides Justice Scalia's appraisal of that alternative:

> Respondents' alternative entails substantial difficulties—if it is indeed practicable at all. It may be impracticable, for one thing, simply because the parents who are willing to accept random drug testing for athletes are not willing to accept accusatory drug testing for all students, which transforms the process into a badge of shame. Respondents' proposal brings the risk that teachers will impose testing arbitrarily upon troublesome but not drug-likely students. It generates the expense of defending lawsuits that charge such arbitrary imposition, or that simply demand greater process before accusatory drug testing is imposed. And not least of all, it adds to the ever-expanding diversionary duties of schoolteachers the new function of spotting and bringing to account drug abuse, a task for which they are ill prepared, and which is not readily compatible with their vocation.... In many respects, we think, testing based on "suspicion" of drug use would not be better, but worse.

515 U.S. at 663–64. Justice O'Connor replied that there seemed to be no better setting for using this "individualized suspicion" condition for a drug search than a school in which "the entire pool of potential search targets—students—is under constant supervision by teachers and administrators and coaches, be it in classrooms, hallways, or locker rooms." Focusing not on high schools, but on colleges and professional teams and leagues, what are the pros and cons of this alternative (which, recall, the NBA players and owners pioneered with in their 1983 labor agreement)?

6. Some drugs are not detectable in a person's urine, and can only be discovered in the blood. For example, "blood-doping" drugs greatly increase the red cell blood count, thereby enabling the body to provide itself with much more oxygen for longer than normal periods. Not only do such drugs greatly enhance performance in endurance sports, there is some evidence that they pose a danger to a person's health by thickening the blood and increasing the risks of heart attacks and blood clots. Several years ago, heart attack deaths of over half the Dutch cycling team were later traced to their heavy usage of blood-doping drugs. If the NCAA determined that use of these kinds of drugs was becoming a problem, especially in sports like distance running, swimming, soccer, or basketball where endurance plays a major role, would this justify the Association establishing a program of mandatory random blood tests in all sports? In just those sports most likely affected? If so, once the blood is drawn from an athlete, could it be tested for any illegal substances besides the blood-doping drugs? Is extracting someone's blood a greater intrusion on their privacy than watching them urinate?

7. Some substances banned by various sports authorities are not "drugs" at all. Rather, these are substances that the body naturally produces, but if present at high levels, they significantly enhance athletic performance. The most common example is the male sex hormone testosterone. The difficulty with testing urine for the artificial introduction of testosterone, particularly in women, is that it is hard to determine if high

levels in the body are the result of such artificial action or simply high levels of bodily production. USA Track & Field's controversial four-year suspensions in 1997 of star U.S. runners Mary Decker Slaney and Sandra Farmer–Patrick, on the grounds that their testosterone-to-epitestosterone (t/e) ratios exceeded the 6:1 female guideline, underscored the complexity and difficulty of regulating this type of "drug" use. Should sports authorities even be concerned with such a substance which emerges naturally in everyone's body? Since natural levels of these substances can vary depending on several medical circumstances personal to the individual (such as menstrual patterns or birth control methods), is regulating and testing for testosterone a greater intrusion upon an athlete's privacy than testing for objectively measurable artificial drugs? If so, should the justification for such action have to be more compelling? And what t/e ratio should be required to support a finding of banned artificial introduction—a ratio that cannot possibly be attained by natural production, or one that in a small percentage of cases could be purely natural? In either case, would banning only those female athletes who tested at or above the set ratio solve the problem?

8. In the course of its decision in *Hill*, the California Supreme Court majority made the following observations about why privacy norms may have less compelling weight in the case of a private body (such as the NCAA) as compared to governmental bodies:

> First, the pervasive presence of coercive government power in basic areas of human life typically poses greater dangers to the freedoms of the citizenry than actions by private persons ...
>
> Second, "an individual generally has greater choice and alternatives in dealing with private actors than when dealing with the government." Initially, individuals usually have a range of choice among landlords, employers, vendors and others with whom they deal. To be sure, varying degrees of competition in the marketplace may broaden or narrow the range. But even in cases of limited or no competition, individuals and groups may turn to the Legislature to seek a statutory remedy against a specific business practice regarded as undesirable....
>
> Third, private conduct, particularly the activities of voluntary associations of persons, carries its own mantle of constitutional protection in the form of freedom of association. Private citizens have a right, not secured to government, to communicate and associate with one another on mutually negotiated terms and conditions....

26 Cal.Rptr.2d at 858. Would you put the NCAA (or Major League Baseball, the Professional Golfers Association, and so on) on the private or the public side of the above line that influences the level of judicial intervention on behalf of either athlete or fans?

9. Should the case for drug testing, whether of athletes or of all students and employees, be based not on the needs of the sport, or the school, or the workplace, but of society generally? A key feature of the "demand side" drug policy developed by the Reagan Administration in the mid–1980s was that drug enforcement should try to stamp out the availability of drugs to those who are especially vulnerable to drug use, by punishing any users whose demand for the substance helps create the market that makes this criminal enterprise possible? Would it be even more in the "best

interests of society" to require mandatory drug testing of all performers (not just athletic performers) who appear on the movie or television screens watched by James Acton and his classmates in Vernonia? Still, what is the significance of the most recent Supreme Court decision in this area, *Chandler v. Miller*, 117 S.Ct. 1295 (1997), where the Court (with only Rehnquist, C.J., dissenting) struck down a Georgia statute that required drug testing (by one's personal physician) of all candidates appearing on the ballot in elections for public office. The Court held that, absent tangible evidence of a drug "problem" among political candidates that could not be addressed through normal law-enforcement methods, the only affirmative rationale that Georgia could assert for this mandatory testing was "the image that the state seeks to project," and this constituted an unjustified state action that "diminished personal privacy for a symbol's sake." The Court distinguished its *Vernonia* ruling on the basis, first, that school systems have a special role as the "guardian and tutor of children entrusted to its care," and that student athletes there had been not just drug users but "leaders of the drug culture" that had witnessed a sharp increase in drug use in these schools.

4. SPORTS AND SOCIAL ETHICS

The 1990s have witnessed controversy inside and outside the sports world about testing and reacting to another substance—the HIV virus. This became a major sports issue in the fall of 1991 when Earvin "Magic" Johnson shocked the country by announcing that he was retiring from the L.A. Lakers because he had just been diagnosed as HIV-positive. Several months later, Johnson returned to the basketball court for the 1992 NBA All-Star game, and then to the "Dream Team" in the Summer Olympics in Barcelona. However, Johnson again dropped out of the game in the fall of 1993 when a number of other NBA players (most prominently the Utah Jazz's Karl Malone) raised concerns about the risks of playing against an HIV-infected opponent.

Such concerns were accentuated in the fall of 1995 by the story of Greg Louganis. Louganis won two gold medals in diving at the 1984 Los Angeles Olympic Games and the 1988 Seoul Games. Apparently, though, Louganis had learned some time before the Seoul Games that he was HIV-positive (due to sexual abuse since he was a teenager by a man who had just died of AIDS). At the Seoul Olympics, Louganis hit his head on a diving board during a preliminary event, and he bled profusely into the pool (as well as on the hands of the team physician who was treating him). Needless to say, that incident would have been infinitely more newsworthy in 1988 if Louganis' HIV infection had been disclosed.

By 1995, it was known that a host of other athletes had died of AIDS (most, though not all, contracted after their retirement): e.g., tennis star Arthur Ashe, NFL tight end Jerry Smith, NHL forward Bill Goldsworthy, and NASCAR driver Tim Richmond. Increased consciousness of the scope and limits of the risk had led players like Karl Malone to urge Johnson to return to the Lakers, and the various leagues to make it clear that there was no mandatory testing of players for HIV and no bar to their playing even if they had the condition. There has never been a documented case of HIV transmission during a sporting event, while research indicates the odds of this happening are roughly one of every 400 incidents of unprotected sex with a person of the opposite gender.

The HIV storm broke out again in the winter of 1996, just after Magic Johnson returned for one brief stint with the Lakers. Former WBC heavyweight champion Tommy Morrison was scheduled for a comeback fight in Las Vegas. However, the blood test required by Nevada's state boxing commission disclosed that Morrison was HIV-positive: thus Nevada revoked Morrison's license to fight in that state, a decision that was honored in all other states. Commissioners in New Jersey, New York, and most other states quickly instituted the same mandatory testing and HIV-positive bans. Thus, when Morrison (against the advice of Magic) decided to return to boxing in the fall of 1996, he had to fly to Japan to fight before a modest crowd in the morning so that his 98–second knockout of the opponent could be seen on pay-per-view television that night in the United States. As of the end of 1997, it was doubtful whether any state commission would permit Morrison to fight in his own country.

A host of significant issues are raised by the Johnson–Louganis–Morrison cases. Is there a tangible risk posed to athletes by competing against HIV-positive opponents (or with HIV-positive team-mates)? How does this risk vary from sport to sport: e.g., from Ashe's tennis, to Richmond's stock car racing, Johnson's basketball, Smith's football, Goldsworthy's hockey, and Morrison's boxing? Even if there is a tangible though remote risk, is the proper response of the sports' governing body to ban the athlete or to alter the rules of the sport to avoid the risk? Is some such "reasonable accommodation" feasible for any or all sports, and is it required by the federal Americans With Disabilities Act? Having read the decisions in the prior section, is there a stronger or weaker case for singling out athletes (professional or student) for mandatory testing of HIV than for either steroids or cocaine? Is there a stronger or weaker case for barring from participation in the sport athletes who turn out to be HIV-positive, or steroid users, or cocaine users?

a. *Treatment of Minorities by Sports*[o]

One significant AIDs factor that has not yet been mentioned is the distinct association of this fatal disease with the gay community, and thus the potential disparate impact of HIV regulation on gay athletes. (It should be noted, though, that Johnson and Morrison, unlike Louganis and Smith, contracted this infection from heterosexual, not homosexual, encounters.) There has been little or no evidence of sports discrimination directed against gay athletes. The same, unfortunately, cannot be said of the historic treatment of blacks and women within the sports world.

---

[o] A recent analysis of the broad range of issues noted in this section is Kenneth L. Shropshire, *In Black and White: Race and Sports in America* (New York: NYU Press, 1996). The same author took an in-depth look at one of these topics in *Diversity, Racism, and Professional Sports Franchise Ownership: Change Must Come From Within*, 67 U. Colorado L. Rev. 47 (1996).

The starkest case of discrimination in sports was baseball's total exclusion of black players from the major leagues for more than half a century. True, MLB Commissioner Kenesaw Mountain Landis intoned, rather piously, in 1942:

> There is no rule, formal or informal, or any understanding—unwritten, subterranean, or sub-anything—against the hiring of Negro players by the teams of organized baseball.

But the evidence from the historical record is very much to the contrary. By the 1930s, players in the Negro Leagues such as Satchel Paige and Josh Gibson had amply demonstrated their superstar skills in regular off-season tours against major league stars. Only the cohesive internal structure of the major leagues (under the iron-fisted rule of Judge Landis) can explain why not a single last-place club was tempted to strengthen its team (likely at a low price) by signing such black players whose recognized caliber eventually put them in the Hall of Fame. Not until Landis died in 1944 and his office was filled by Kentucky Senator Albert "Happy" Chandler did the door swing open to allow the Dodgers' Branch Rickey to sign Jackie Robinson in 1945, and bring him up to the major leagues in 1947. The color bar in baseball had finally been broken.

Suppose, however, that Landis had lived to foil Rickey's integration effort (just as he had thwarted Bill Veeck's wartime plan to buy the last place Philadelphia Phillies and restock the team with star black players). What kind of legal attack might have been mounted by Robinson against baseball's segregation, perhaps as part of Charles Houston's and Thurgood Marshall's contemporary strategy at the NAACP? Remember that this was two decades before the nation was prepared to enact the Civil Rights Act prohibiting racial discrimination.

Happily, in 1997, when the country was celebrating the 50th anniversary of Jackie Robinson's breaking the barriers to blacks playing in major league baseball, the MLB owners decided to repair one of the remaining harms from that historic injustice. Larry Doby soon followed Robinson into the American League and starred with the Cleveland Indians. However, a number of still-living African-American players shared the experience of Sam Jethroe, who won the N.L. Rookie of the Year at the age of 30, but was able to play in the major leagues for just four years, which was not long enough to satisfy the five years of service then needed to vest benefits under the pension plan created by team owners in 1947. Since Jethroe had previously starred in the Negro League, he had a legitimate (though perhaps not legally-enforceable) claim that he would have satisfied the five-year vesting condition, but for his discriminatory exclusion from Major League Baseball. However, current team owners have decided that it would be a valuable investment in the integrity of the game to create a special $10 million fund to pay modest pensions (approximately $10,000 a year) to Jethroe and his living colleagues. Indeed, Jethroe's case also moved the owners to extend this pension to other still-living players who had not been able to satisfy the vesting requirement for other non-racial reasons (including Danny Gardella whom we will read about in the next chapter).

By the 1990s, there was no shortage of black players in baseball, nor in football and basketball. Blacks in 1996 made up 17% of baseball players (Hispanics another 20%), 67% of football players, and 80% of basketball players.[p] Not only in number but also in quality of performance and size of salary, black players now occupy the upper echelons of professional team sports in America.[q] However, blacks still comprise only a small fraction of players in certain key positions: for example, blacks make up just 2% of baseball catchers and 9% of football quarterbacks. Even more troubling has been the severe under-representation of blacks in leadership positions with the team or in the front office. Though almost all occupants of head coaching or managerial positions come from the playing ranks, in the early 1990s there had been only two black head football coaches in the entire history of this sport. For decades baseball also lagged behind, with just five black and two Hispanic managers in its history up to 1992. Suddenly, though, four new minority managers (two black and two Hispanic) were added to the two black incumbents—and one of the latter, Cito Gaston, led his Toronto Blue Jays to a World Series triumph that year. By 1996, there were three African–American head coaches in the NFL, three African–American managers in MLB (and one Hispanic American), and five African–American head coaches in the NBA. The minority numbers were somewhat better in senior front office positions (with the exception of baseball).

The issue of racism in sports was catapulted into the national consciousness in 1987, as a result of televised remarks made by Los Angeles Dodgers' Vice President Al Campanis on ABC's Nightline—ironically, on a special program devoted to the fortieth anniversary of Jackie Robinson's first game with the Brooklyn Dodgers. When asked by Nightline host Ted Koppel why there were so few black managers and general managers in the game, Campanis replied:

> I don't think it's prejudice. I truly believe that [blacks] may not have some of the necessities to be, let's say, a field manager or perhaps a general manager.

Immediately after this exchange, Campanis was fired by Dodgers' President Peter O'Malley.[r] More importantly, following the lead of the NBA's David Stern, MLB Commissioner Peter Ueberroth and NFL Commissioner Pete Rozelle instituted affirmative action programs to try to

---

p. See Richard E. Lapchick with Jeffrey P. Brown, *1996 Racial Report Card: Do Professional Sports Provide Equal Opportunities for All Races?* 4 CSSS Digest 1 (Summer, 1996) (a publication of the Center for the Study of Sport and Society at Northeastern University).

q. For a valuable review of the empirical research about minority athlete representation, performance and pay, see Lawrence M. Kahn, *Discrimination in Professional Sports: A Survey of the Literature*, 44 Industrial and Labor Rel. Rev. 395 (1991).

r. For a description of the Campanis episode, see Philip M. Hoosie, *Necessities: Racial Bias in American Sports* at xv-xviii (New York: Random House, 1989).

encourage their leagues' teams to expand the number of minorities in coaching and front office positions, with the modest results noted above.

Unhappily for the sports world, the issue of racism reared its ugly head again at the end of 1992, in a notorious case involving Marge Schott, the managing partner and largest shareholder in the Cincinnati Reds. A wrongful dismissal suit brought by an ex-Reds employee brought into the open the fact that Schott regularly used such epithets as "dumb niggers" and "money-grubbing Jews" to refer to her players, associates, and rivals. It was later reported that in a conference call with other owners, Schott had asserted that she would "rather have a trained monkey working for her than a nigger." The ensuing firestorm of protest across the country caught baseball at a bad time, because it was without a commissioner and engaged in an internal struggle about the future structure and direction of the game. After extensive discussions between her lawyer and baseball's Executive Committee, Schott agreed to accept the penalty of a $25,000 fine and one-year suspension from the day-to-day decisions of the Reds, though she retained her position as managing partner of the club. Then, after apparently having returned to baseball's good graces, Schott created another furor and attracted another suspension in the spring of 1996. She was quoted by ESPN and Sports Illustrated for having praised Adolf Hitler's early efforts in Germany, and said it was only later that the Fuhrer went too far!

The *Schott* case raises several important questions regarding the appropriate governance of sports. Is it appropriate to suspend an owner (or fire an employee, like Campanis) for having made such racial slurs? Should discipline be meted out for similar verbal attacks on other groups—e.g., Muslims, Iranians, or even the Ku Klux Klan? Is different treatment warranted for such epithets when they are uttered in private (like Schott's first ones) or in public (like both Schott and Campanis on television)?

Two other cases in the mid–1990 posed these questions about free speech in sports in an even more troubling form. The first such episode did not get much attention from the national media, but did get it from the courts—producing *Dambrot v. Central Michigan University*, 55 F.3d 1177 (6th Cir.1995). Keith Dambrot was the white coach of Central Michigan University's men's basketball team during the 1992–93 season. Eleven of the 14 players were African–American. The latter regularly used the word "nigger" to refer to each other on campus, in the locker room, in practice, even during games. Concerned about the quality of his team's play in a game, Dambrot asked them at half-time "do you mind if I use the N-word?" After the players had agreed, Dambrot said he wanted them to play like "real niggers," not "half-niggers," a message he believed was "positive and reinforcing" because his players believed their coach was describing someone who was "fearless, mentally strong, and tough." On the other hand, Dambrot told his players not to "act like niggers in the classroom," because he did not want them to be "aggressive, tough, hard-nosed and abrasive" in that setting, behavior that the university had found unacceptable in a dispute between several players and a woman teacher.

Eventually, news filtered out about Dambrot's periodic use of this word, generating campus demonstrations and media criticism. Although the black players defended their coach, the school's affirmative action officer found Dambrot's language to have violated the university's ban on "discriminatory harassment" via expressions "that infer negative connotation about an individual's racial or ethnic affiliation." Thus the University decided not to keep Dambrot on as its coach for the following season. Dambrot sued, alleging that the termination was a violation of his First Amendment rights, and he was joined by several of the players who claimed that the university's harassment policy violated their constitutional rights because of its vagueness and overbreadth.

This case poses two significant questions under the First Amendment (which applied here because Central Michigan is a public university). The first is whether "nigger" is simply a "fighting word" which does not enjoy constitutional protection (in line with the Supreme Court's most recent exploration of this issue in *R.A.V. v. St. Paul*, 505 U.S. 377 (1992)). The second is whether the firing of a public employee like Dambrot is constrained by the First Amendment (under *Connick v. Myers*, 461 U.S. 138 (1983), which requires that the speech "relates to any matter of political, social, or other concern to the community"). Whether the context be public or private sports, the underlying question is whether Dambrot's speech should be treated by the governing authority as the same or different from those of Schott or Campanis.

The NBA had to face that problem during the early winter of 1996. Chris Jackson was born in Mississippi and raised as a Baptist. After reaching the NBA, he converted to Islam and changed his name to Mahmoud Abdul-Rauf. He also became very upset with the foreign policies of the United States, particularly during the 1991 Gulf War against Iraq. Eventually Abdul-Rauf decided that his Islamic beliefs did not permit him to show respect to the American flag, the national anthem, and other symbols of his home country. Like other professional sports dating back to World War II, the NBA rules require every player to stand respectfully during the playing of the national anthem just before each game. Abdul-Rauf, a star guard for the Denver Nuggets, refused to do so during the 1995–96 season, saying that the U.S. flag and the anthem "represent tyranny and oppression," and "I can't be for God and for oppression." For a time the Nuggets had Abdul-Rauf go back into the locker room, or at least into the tunnel, so that the crowd would not notice his stance towards the Star-Spangled Banner. Eventually, though, Abdul-Rauf decided to stay on the bench, or engage in stretching exercises in front of the bench, where his conduct could be easily seen by the NBA fans and commentators. Commissioner David Stern suspended Abdul-Rauf (at a cost of nearly $30,000 a game) until he was prepared to comply with this league rule.

The National Basketball Players Association (NBPA) said that it would file a grievance on Abdul-Rauf's behalf, claiming that Stern's action went beyond the scope of the Commissioner's authority under the NBA Constitution and the terms of the league's labor agreement (which says that the Commissioner can discipline players who are "guilty of conduct prejudicial or detrimental" to the NBA). Many legal commentators said that the league's action constituted discrimination on the basis of religion, in violation of Title VII of the Civil Rights Act (whose key Supreme Court ruling is *Trans World Airlines v. Hardison*, 432 U.S. 63 (1977)). The First Amendment rights of freedom of speech and religion are not directly applicable to the NBA (though there might be some such claim if these rules were being enforced in a public rather than private arena).

Moved perhaps by his NBA colleagues (Hakeem Olajuwon said that "the Muslim teaching is to obey and respect"), Abdul-Rauf announced after one lost game that he would stand for the playing of the anthem, with his eyes closed, his hands cupped close to his face, and praying to Allah. Based on this promise, the NBA lifted the suspension and Abdul-Rauf completed the season without further incident. That summer, though, the Nuggets traded Abdul-Rauf to the Sacramento Kings.

Suppose that this resolution of the issue had not been accepted by both sides. Should a court or arbitrator agree with the Commissioner that a refusal to stand for the anthem was "conduct prejudicial or detrimental to the NBA?" Suppose Abdul-Rauf said that he wanted to stay in the locker room, rather than sit or stretch by the bench, during the anthem. Is his current stance during the anthem a "respectful" one? Whatever the stance Abdul-Rauf took, was this just a political, or is it also a *religious*, statement for purposes of Title VII? Even if it was religious (at least in part), what would the NBA have to do to meet the EEOC Guidelines and case law requirement of "reasonable accommodation to the religious needs of employees ... where such accommodation can be made without serious inconvenience to the conduct of the business?" (It should be noted, by the way, that some players, like the Seattle SuperSonics' Sam Perkins, are Jehovah Witnesses, a religion that has been much more disapproving of national anthems than Islam.) Finally, why do leagues play the national anthem (actually, anthems, including *O Canada* for all games with Canadian teams) before every game? Is attendance at a regular season sports game that different from attendance at a play, a concert, or a movie?

The *Dambrot* and *Abdul-Rauf* cases pose more difficult problems than the *Schott* case about the appropriate social (if not legal) reaction to offensive forms of speech. Even with respect to Schott, a more important question may be what (if anything) baseball authorities should have done when it became clear that Schott's Reds had just one black employee among the 45 members of their front-office staff, far less than the 16% minority representation in front offices across Major League Baseball.

While most people likely accept the premise that racial *action* is more significant than racial *speech*, it may also be more difficult to decide what to do about such actions as hiring practices and patterns. For example, could a minority assistant coach who was not even interviewed, let alone appointed, to a vacant head coach or managerial position challenge the team or league's practice under Title VII of the Civil Rights Act (which forbids discrimination in employment)? Should the commissioner go even further and institute in his sport—pursuant to his "best interests" prerogative—the kind of numerical hiring and promotional guidelines that are prevalent in much of business enterprise? What is the appropriate statistical benchmark for assessing a league's nondiscriminatory practices in filling managerial or front-office positions: is it the minority percentage among players, or in analogous managerial and administrative positions in the broader business world? How significant can a league-wide guideline be in appraising the decision of a particular team (e.g., the Reds) in selecting who is to be its manager or general manager? (Keep this example in mind for later chapters which take up the broader question whether the team or the league is the key entity in the world of sports.) What are the pros and cons of explicit affirmative preferences with respect to the longer-term "best interests" of minority participants in the sports world?

Allegations of racism in sports have recently arisen in yet another context—commissioner discipline for actions taking place on the field. During the 1993 season, Miami Dolphins linebacker Brian Cox made an obscene gesture toward a group of Buffalo Bills fans who he said had yelled racial epithets at him during a game in Buffalo. Commissioner Paul Tagliabue fined Cox $10,000 for the gesture. Cox filed a complaint with and received a "right to sue" letter from the EEOC, and then filed suit against the NFL, alleging that the league had violated Title VII of the Civil Rights Act of 1964 by not maintaining a working environment free from racial harassment, intimidation, or insult. Subsequently, the NFL reduced the fine to $5,000 and Cox withdrew his lawsuit. In 1995, Tagliabue again fined Cox (this time $7,500), for spitting at some Bills fans in Buffalo who, he again claimed, were harassing him. Finally, in 1996, after Cox had moved on to the Chicago Bears, Cox was caught on national television cameras making an obscene gesture toward a game official during a game in Green Bay. For this action, Tagliabue fined Cox $87,500. Since Commissioner discipline is not arbitrable under the football collective agreement, Cox returned to the EEOC, obtained another right to sue letter, and filed another Title VII lawsuit against the league. This letter alleged that the excessive amount of the fine was an unlawful retaliation for his first suit, in violation of § 703, 42

U.S.C.A. § 2000e–2, which prohibits discrimination in employment based on race.

This series of events raises several interesting questions. What steps must the NFL or its teams take during games to protect its players from racially-motivated harassment (e.g., by fans) in order to comply with Title VII's requirement of a safe and healthy working environment? In the same year Cox was fined $87,500, Oakland Raiders tackle Steve Wisnewski was fined $20,000 for making contact with an official while disputing a call, and in 1994 the Indiannapolis Colts' team physician had been fined $500 for making an obscene gesture at an official. Wisnewski and the team doctor are both white, but neither had ever been disciplined by the league before. Do these examples support Cox' legal theory? Are they sufficient by themselves to support his claim? What additional facts, if any, would Cox need to show in order for him to prevail? What would you suspect is the likely outcome of this litigation?

When the Professional Golfers Association (PGA) was created back in 1916, its Charter limited membership to "members of the Caucasian race." As late as the 1950s, the Tour refused to allow stars from the Negro Tour such as Charles Sifford and Ted Rhodes to compete against PGA greats like Ben Hogan and Arnold Palmer. Happily, that racial barrier was removed by the PGA in the early 1960s, and the Tour as well as minorities were reaping the benefits of Tiger Woods' presence in the late 1990s. As this book was going to press in early 1998, the PGA Tour and the country were witnessing another major controversy regarding minority access to professional sports—the much more complicated case of Casey Martin. Martin, who suffered from a severe leg disability, sued and won a trial verdict under the Americans With Disabilities Act (ADA) that required the Tour to allow him to play by riding a cart rather than walking from shot to shot. We shall read about the details of the *Martin* case in Chapter 12 on Individual Sports: e.g., whether the Ninth Circuit on appeal should find that Tour events are places of public rather than private accommodation for players (as opposed to spectators), and whether the cart provides Martin with a "reasonable accommodation" to his disability, or an unfair advantage in golf "as a game of stamina." For purposes of this chapter, reflect on the question whether it is in "the best interests of sport" to include or to exclude a Casey Martin who is playing golf with a cart.

b. *Treatment of Women by Sports*

The treatment of women in and by the sports world raises even more complicated issues than the treatment of blacks and other minorities. For example, there is a full social (as well as legal) consensus that sports must not be segregated into white and black teams and leagues. By contrast, everyone accepts that women athletes should have separate leagues (e.g., for basketball) or tours (e.g., for golf); gender integration of horse racing jockeys or stock car drivers is very much the exception rather than the rule in sports. Indeed, as we shall see in Chapter 11 on *Gender Equality in College Sports*, the tacit assumption that colleges must offer their women students the opportunity to play on their own team, rather than compete for positions on a single integrated team, has now produced a full-blown Title IX debate (in the colleges, the courts, and the Congress) about the relative rosters and resources that the colleges must provide to their women's and men's teams.

In this chapter, we will briefly address a different issue. How must women be treated by players on male teams (whether professional or college)? One aspect of this issue drew widespread public attention in the fall of 1990, when Lisa Olson, a Boston Herald sports writer, covering the New England Patriots, sought to interview Patriots cornerback Maurice Hurst after a practice session. Told that Hurst would be available only in the locker room rather than in the team's media room, Olson went to speak to Hurst at his locker. While there, Olson was confronted by a naked Zeke Mowatt; Mowatt allegedly made an offensive comment to her, which was echoed by several other players in the background. Following a report by his special counsel, new NFL Commissioner Paul Tagliabue fined Mowatt $14,000 and the other players lesser amounts. Later Olson filed a tort suit which was settled by the Patriots, reportedly for $250,000. What is your reaction to the juxtaposition of baseball Commissioner Giamatti's lifetime ban of Pete Rose for betting on his own team to win and Tagliabue's fining Zeke Mowatt the equivalent of one quarter of one game's salary for sexual harassment of a sportswriter?

More interesting legal and policy issues were posed by the activities of Cincinnati Bengals' coach Sam Wyche. Soon after the Olson incident, Wyche, citing his players' need for privacy, refused entry to his locker room after a game to a female USA Today sports writer, Denise Toms. Instead Wyche gave Toms priority in interviewing the player of her choice outside the locker room. For that action, which violated the league's written policy on equal access for female and male reporters, Tagliabue fined Wyche approximately $30,000. Many media accounts of this controversy asserted that female sports writers have an equal legal right to be in the locker room with male reporters, a right that was won in the following case. In reading the opinion, consider whether and to what extent the media's impression is legally correct, especially under the Supreme Court's current "state action" jurisprudence (which we will encounter in Chapter 9 in the litigation between the NCAA and Jerry Tarkanian while he was at UNLV). Are there other sources of legal relief that might have been available if Tagliabue had emulated baseball Commissioner Bowie Kuhn and sided with Wyche? As a policy matter, should female sports writers have automatic locker room access?

LUDTKE AND TIME, INC. v. KUHN

United States District Court, Southern District of New York, 1978.
461 F.Supp. 86.

MOTLEY, DISTRICT JUDGE.

[In April 1975, Commissioner Bowie Kuhn instituted a general ban against admission of women sports writers to baseball clubhouses. By contrast, the National Hockey League and the National Basketball Association had decided earlier to give women reporters access to players in their locker rooms. Despite the contrary wishes of the Yankee players, Kuhn insisted that Melissa Ludtke, a Sports Illustrated sportswriter covering the 1977 World Series between the Yankees and the Dodgers, not be allowed into the Yankees' clubhouse.

This lawsuit involved exclusion of Ludtke from the Yankees clubhouse at Yankee Stadium. Yankee Stadium was owned by the City of New York, having been acquired by eminent domain in the early 1970s, and renovated at a cost of nearly $100 million. The Yankees rented the Stadium from the city for baseball games, under a lease whose rent formula depended on attendance at games.]

* * *

Central to the resolution of this case is the undisputed fact that all accredited female sports reporters are excluded from the Yankee clubhouse at Yankee Stadium solely because they are women, whereas all accredited male sports reporters (to the extent that space limitations permit) are permitted access to the clubhouse after games for the purpose of interviewing ballplayers.

Defendants say women reporters are excluded in order 1) to protect the privacy of those players who are undressed or who are in various stages of undressing and getting ready to shower; 2) to protect the image of baseball as a family sport; and 3) preservation of traditional notions of decency and propriety.

Another pivotal fact which is also not disputed is that fresh-off-the-field interviews are important to the work of sports reporters and will give a competitive advantage to those who have access to the ballplayers at that juncture, particularly during the World Series games.

Another critical consideration is the admission that there are several other less sweeping alternatives to the present policy of blanket exclusion of women reporters. Counsel for defendants admitted that those players who are desirous of undressing can retreat to their cubicles in the clubhouse. There the players can be shielded from the "roving eyes" of any female reporters by having each cubicle furnished with a curtain or swinging door. It is also conceded that the player who is undressed and wishes to move about in that state can use a towel to shield himself from view.

Since the Kuhn policy determination is based solely on sex, and since that policy results in denial of equal opportunity to plaintiff Ludtke to pursue her profession as a sports reporter, and since there are several less restrictive alternatives to the total exclusion of women, and since the material facts regarding New York City's involvement in Yankee Stadium and the lease of those premises to the Yankees are not disputed, the only questions remaining for decision are questions of law.

A. STATE ACTION

The first question is whether New York City's involvement with Yankee Stadium and the lease arrangement with the Yankees is such as to make the Kuhn policy determination state action within the contemplation of the Fourteenth Amendment.

It must by now be regarded as well settled that state action may be found where the direct perpetrator of allegedly discriminatory acts is, though a private entity, "so entwined" with an agency of the state that that agency must be deemed responsible for the private entity's acts. There is, however, no rigid yardstick against which the relationship may be measured to determine the presence of state action. As the Supreme Court has explained:

> Only by sifting facts and weighing circumstances can the nonobvious involvement of the State in private conduct be attributed its true significance.

Burton v. Wilmington Parking Authority, 365 U.S. 715 (1961).

Burton, like the instant case, involved discrimination against the plaintiff on the ground of a class-based characteristic, in that case race. The discrimination there took place on ostensibly private premises (those of the defendant Eagle Coffee Shoppe), operated under lease from a public authority (the Wilmington Parking Authority). Here the discrimination also takes place on ostensibly private premises (the Yankee Clubhouse) located on premises (Yankee Stadium) operated under lease from a public authority (the City of New York). The Court in *Burton* found that the coffee shop, located in an otherwise public building owned by the Wilmington Parking Authority, enjoyed a "symbiotic relationship" with the publicly operated portions of the premises, consisting of parking facilities. The proximity of the coffee shop was found to be essential in establishing the fiscal viability of the parking garage. The Yankee clubhouse in this case has been opened to the press immediately after games, particularly during the World Series, so that players fresh-off-the-field may be interviewed. Moreover, it is undisputed that television cameras were permitted in the clubhouse after the World Series games for the same purpose. Advertising and massive publicity about the Yankees and individual Yankee ballplayers is essential to the profitability of the Yankee Stadium.

* * *

Here, as in *Burton*, the place where the discriminatory acts occurred is owned by the state (the City of New York) and leased pursuant to special legislative provisions to the Yankees. In this case, as in *Burton*, the facility involved is maintained and improved with the use of public funds. The Court noted in *Burton* that the relationship of the public and private entities in that case placed them in a relationship of interdependence. The same observation can be made on these facts, where the annual rentals to be paid to the City for use of the stadium depend directly on the drawing power of Yankee games, and the City has in turn invested substantial sums of public money to enhance that drawing power by modernizing and improving the stadium itself.

In defendants' memorandum, they set forth the objectives underlying baseball's policy of excluding female reporters from the locker room.

Among these conceded objectives were the aim "to protect and preserve the national image of baseball as a family game ... and ... to preserve baseball's audience and to maintain its popularity and standing."

It is an undisputed fact that the City's profit from its lease with the Yankees escalates when attendance at Yankee games increases. Thus the City has a clear interest in the preservation and maintenance of baseball's audience, image, popularity and standing.

* * *

B. SEX DISCRIMINATION

This court finds that the state action complained of here infringes both equal protection and due process rights of plaintiff Ludtke.

1. *Equal Protection*

On the basis of the undisputed facts, plaintiff Ludtke, while in pursuit of her profession as a sports reporter, was treated differently from her male counterparts (other properly accredited sports writers) solely because she is a woman.

* * *

"To withstand constitutional challenge ... classifications by gender must serve important governmental objectives and must be substantially related to achievement of those objectives." *Craig v. Boren*, 429 U.S. 190, 197 (1976). Defendants have asserted, as justification for the complete exclusion of female reporters from the clubhouse at Yankee Stadium, their interest in protecting the privacy of the ballplayers while undressing in the locker room.

The right to privacy is of constitutional dimension, see *Roe v. Wade*, 410 U.S. 113 (1973), and its protection is thus undeniably an important objective. It cannot be said on these facts, however, that there is a sufficiently substantial relationship between that objective on one hand and the total exclusion of women from the Yankee locker room on the other to pass constitutional muster. "Inquiry into the actual purposes of the discrimination ... proves the contrary." *Califano v. Goldfarb*, 430 U.S. 199, 212 (1977).

At least during World Series games, male members of the news media with television cameras have been allowed to enter the Yankee locker room immediately after the games and broadcast live from that location. In this connection, only a backdrop behind the player standing in front of the camera is provided to shield other players from the "roving eye" of the camera. These locker room encounters are viewed by mass audiences, which include many women and children. This practice, coupled with defendants' practice of refusing to allow accredited women sports reporters to enter the locker room, shows that the latter is "substantially related" only to maintaining the locker room as an all-male preserve.

* * *

2. *Due Process*

An analysis of these same facts from the perspective of substantive due process leads us to an identical result. The right to pursue one's profession is a fundamental "liberty" within the meaning of the Fourteenth Amendment's due process guarantee. Further, it is settled law that: Even though the governmental purpose be legitimate and substantial, that purpose cannot be pursued by means that broadly stifle fundamental personal liberties when the end can be more narrowly achieved.

As noted above, the Kuhn policy substantially and directly interferes with the right of plaintiff Ludtke to pursue her profession as a sports reporter. Her male counterparts are able to get to the ballplayers fresh-off-the-field when comments about plays may still be in progress, for example. When a statutory classification significantly interferes with the exercise of a fundamental right, it cannot be upheld unless it is supported by sufficiently important state interests and is closely tailored to effectuate only those interests.

The undisputed facts show that the Yankees' interest in protecting ballplayer privacy may be fully served by [a] much less sweeping means than that implemented here. The court holds that the state action complained of unreasonably interferes with plaintiff Ludtke's fundamental right to pursue her profession in violation of the due process clause of the Fourteenth Amendment.

The other two interests asserted by defendants, maintaining the status of baseball as a family sport and conforming to traditional notions of decency and propriety, are clearly too insubstantial to merit serious consideration. Weighed against plaintiff's right to be free of discrimination based upon her sex, and her fundamental right to pursue her profession, such objectives cannot justify the defendants' policy under the equal protection or due process clauses of the Fourteenth Amendment.

Injunction granted.

The problems encountered by Melissa Ludtke and Lisa Olson are now largely resolved. Women regularly work as sportswriters and broadcasters in the late 1990s, and women fans attend and watch more football (and other men's sports) than ever before. Because the media considers women to be a significantly more valuable audience for commercial advertising than men, leagues have had a real incentive to create a comfortable setting for women reporters to interview and interact with the players whose images are being sold in print or on the screen. Indeed, in the 1997–98 season the NBA took an even more important step when it put two women—Dee Kantner and Violet Palmer—on the court rather than in the locker room, as the first-ever female officials in a professional male team sport.

The sports world is now facing a much more troubling problem regarding the treatment of women. What if anything, should sports (rather than just legal) authorities do about male athletes who physically abuse their wives, girl friends, or even female strangers?[s]

A case that dramatically illustrated the importance of the issue took place in the fall of 1995. Lawrence Phillips was the star running back for the Nebraska Cornhuskers. The night after leading his team to an opening season win over Michigan State, Phillips broke into the apartment of his team-mate Scott Frost, who was then living with Phillips' ex-girlfriend Kate McEwan (herself a Nebraska basketball player). Phillips battered and dragged McEwan down the stairs until he was apprehended by Frost and the neighbors. McEwan was taken to the hospital for treatment and Phillips was brought to the police station for criminal charges.

After pleading no contest, Phillips was convicted that fall of aggravated assault and sentenced to probation with counseling. Initially, he was suspended from his team by Cornhuskers coach Tom Osborne, but late in the season was brought back to lead the team to a Fiesta Bowl victory over Florida and the national championship. Next spring, Phillips was drafted and signed by the St. Louis Rams, and used some of his bonus to settle McEwan's tort suit against him.

The Phillips case was one of dozens of incidents of domestic abuse that have been reported in the sports pages in the 1990s. (The dimensions of the broader social problem were depicted in a 1997 Justice Department report that in 1994, approximately 200,000 women went to hospitals for emergency treatment of injuries stemming from domestic violence.) Among the major athletes who have faced such charges are Warren Moon, Scottie Pippen, Robert Parish, Barry Bonds, John Daly, and in the midst of the 1997 baseball season, Wilfredo Cordero of the Boston Red Sox. There is currently a debate about whether male athletes are especially prone to this type of misbehavior. (One study of 30 Division I schools from 1991–93 found that while male athletes made up three percent of the total male student body, they committed 19% of sexual assaults on campus; however the sample size was too small to meet the test for statistical significance.) The structure of sports does, however, permit a private institutional response to this problem. Thus, several women's and other groups have called on both professional leagues and the NCAA to adopt rules that would automatically bar from competition any athlete like Phillips who was found to have committed domestic abuse (let alone the rape committed by Mike Tyson).

This is an important problem through which to reflect on the range of issues we have encountered in this chapter.

    1. Is such a sexual abuse policy actually in the best interests of the *sport*: is boxing, for example, better or worse off since Mike

---

[s]. One of the first law review analyses of this issue is Note [by Laurence Schoen], *Out of Bounds: Professional Sports Leagues and Domestic Violence*, 109 Harvard L. Rev. 1048 (1996).

Tyson's return to the ring from prison (before or after he bit off Evander Holyfield's ear during their 1997 championship rematch)?

2. Should a sport like baseball treat players like Darryl Strawberry the same or differently for his having regularly used cocaine, or having regularly abused his now ex-wife?

3. If the object is to serve the best interests of *society* rather than just sports, what reason might there be for singling out *athletes* for special sanctions for physical domestic conflicts? For example, does an athlete like Wil Cordero play a more significant role in shaping the attitudes and behavior of his fans than does a sports broadcaster (and sexual abuser) like Marv Albert?

4. What is the appropriate design of any such sanctioning system: should suspension occur, for example, as soon as a player like the Dallas Cowboys' Michael Irvin has rape charges filed against him by a woman during the 1996 NFL playoffs (charges that were later dropped), or only when a player such as the Cleveland Indians' Jose Mesa was indicted by a grand jury (though the trial jury later acquitted him), or only when an athlete such as Mike Tyson has been convicted (though that jury verdict was under appeal)? And should the ban from sports be for life, or only for specified periods of rehabilitation (such as Phillips')?

5. Should commissioners decide that they have the authority to adopt a league-wide policy towards physical abuse of women by players, or should this be done only with the consent and input of the players association (and who will represent student-athletes, male or female, in the deliberations of the NCAA about future Phillips cases)?

You have now seen a much broader sampling of the real-life problems that arise under the rubric of the "best interests of the sport." Consider again George Will's assertion, quoted early in this chapter, that judges should leave these moral dilemmas to commissioners to wrestle with. Alternatively, should leagues and their commissioners leave many, if not all, of these matters to the players and their teams to resolve themselves?[t]

---

[t] Just as this book was going into print, NBA–NBPA arbitrator John Feerick rendered his decision in the *Latrell Sprewell* "coach-choking" case described at pp. 30–31. Feerick concluded that Commissioner Stern's suspension of Sprewell without pay for a full year (or 82 games) should be reduced to the remainder of the 1977–98 season (or 68 games), and he also overturned the Golden State Warriors' termination of the two years remaining on Sprewell's guaranteed contract. Now that you have finished reading this chapter, do you find this verdict to be in the "best interests of the sport"?

Chapter Two

CONSTRUCTING A PLAYERS MARKET: FROM CONTRACT TO ANTITRUST LAW[a]

Chapter 1 focused on a specific set of legal issues implicating a broad spectrum of sports participants—players, managers, owners, even sportswriters. We saw how people who felt aggrieved by commissioner rulings under the time-honored but eminently contestable phrase, "best interests of the sport," sought redress through a number of legal vehicles—contract, antitrust, labor, and constitutional law. Now we undertake an in-depth examination of the situation of one vital segment of the sports world—the players—and consider how the fate of professional athletes has been influenced by the legal structure of their marketplace.

The cases and materials in this and the next chapter focus primarily on one crucial issue: the ability of players to move from one club to another, whether in the same or a different league. (A number of these

---

[a]. An informative law review article on both the law and the sports background to the materials in this chapter (and the next two) is Robert C. Berry and William B. Gould, *A Long Deep Drive to Collective Bargaining: Of Players, Owners, Brawls and Strikes*, 31 Case Western Reserve L. Rev. 685 (1981). The historical background of the development of the "reserve system" in baseball is set out in two books by Harold Seymour—*Baseball: The Early Years* (New York: Oxford University Press, 1960), and *Baseball: The Golden Age* (New York: Oxford University Press, 1971). A Congressional study, Subcommittee on the Study of Monopoly Power of the Committee of the Judiciary, 82d Congress, 2d Session, *Report on Organized Baseball* (Washington, D.C., 1952) (Celler Report), meticulously documents the legal and institutional restraints on player mobility in that sport, which blazed the trail for analogous restraints that emerged in other sports. David Harris, *The League: The Rise and Decline of the NFL* (New York: Bantam, 1986); Terry Pluto, *Loose Balls: The Short, Wild Life of the American Basketball Association* (New York: Simon and Schuster, 1990); and David Cruise and Alison Griffiths, *Net Worth: Exploding the Myths of Pro Hockey* (New York: Viking Penguin, 1991), provide helpful background to the contract disputes in those sports that we will read about in this (and the next two) chapters. Finally, a recent law review article, James R. Devine, *Baseball's Labor Wars in Historical Context: The 1919 Chicago White Sox as a Case-Study in Owner–Player Relations*, 5 Marquette Sports L. J. 1 (1994), provides a valuable perspective on the interplay of the issues we read about in Chapter 1 and those we are going to encounter in this and the following two chapters.

cases and controversies involve managers and coaches—e.g., Bill Parcells and Mike Keenan—whose dealings with their teams and commissioners raised many of the same issues under contract law, though not antitrust and labor law.) In any industry, the worker's ability to play one employer off against another can make a profound difference in benefits received, both in monetary compensation and in satisfactory job conditions.[b] In turn, the legal system has its most powerful impact at precisely this point, as the law chooses whether to enforce, prohibit, or redesign obstacles to employee mobility.

Disputes about player movement from one team to another have been the central preoccupation of sports litigation for over a century, litigation that now takes place within a complex interplay of contract, antitrust, and labor law. From the 1880s to the 1960s, the principal focus was on contract law that defined the relationship between individual player and club. Teams regularly sought to enforce, and players to elude, the network of restrictions epitomized by baseball's "reserve system" (which historically limited players to negotiating contracts with the single team that "owned" their rights). By the end of the 1960s, federal antitrust litigation had been launched against this broad regime of player restraints. A particular target was the reciprocal "anti-tampering" agreement among clubs in the league, a private arrangement that provided the real glue to the reserve system, whatever kind of enforcement the player contract received in the civil courts. That was true, in particular, when there was only one major league in the sport.

As we will see in Chapter 3, the plaintiffs in such antitrust litigation (except for baseball players) enjoyed great success in the 1970s. However, the prime movers in these suits were players associations that at the same time were transforming themselves into labor unions and engaging in collective bargaining under national labor law. By the beginning of the 1980s, the players associations in each of the four major team sports—baseball, football, basketball, and hockey—had negotiated in their collective agreements new rules that specified whether and when a player could become a "free agent," and thence be entitled to move to any other team that made him a better contract offer. Since these relationships also had the legal effect of immunizing the player market from antitrust scrutiny (for reasons explained in Chapter 3), the 1980s were the heyday of labor law in professional sports—a decade that was marked by numerous strikes and lockouts as well as lawsuits. By the end of the decade, though, the National Football League Players Association (NFLPA), which had enjoyed a conspicuous lack of success under labor

b. For a short statement of the case for a freely-competitive labor market, see Milton Friedman and Rose Friedman, *Free to Choose: A Personal Statement* (New York: Harcourt Brace Jovanovich, 1979) at 218–236, which argues that the best source of protection for employees is not their own employer, or their labor union, or their government (legislative or judicial), but *other* employers. For an appraisal of both the force and the limits of this position, see Paul C. Weiler, *Governing the Workplace: The Future of Labor and Employment Law* (Cambridge, Mass.: Harvard University Press, 1990), especially Chapter 4, "The Sources and Instruments of Workplace Governance."

law, declared itself a *non*-union in an effort to bring antitrust back into play for the 1990s. The interplay of antitrust and labor law served as the backdrop for huge confrontations between players and owners—not just in football, but in baseball, basketball, and hockey as well. Happily, by the late 1990s labor peace seemed to have arrived in the sports world, after the two sides in each league had struggled to design different versions of free agency, salary caps, and salary taxes that would reshape the labor market in professional team sports.

A. TORONTO BLUE JAYS v. BOSTON CELTICS AND DANNY AINGE

In line with the historical evolution of this topic, we turn first to contract law's treatment of different versions of the reserve clause in the player contract. To bring into live focus the issues presented by the legal precedents, we first sketch a dispute that produced a jury verdict but no published judicial opinion—the suit brought nearly two decades ago by the Toronto Blue Jays against the Boston Celtics and Danny Ainge.

Danny Ainge's athletic talent made him an early star and eventual professional performer in two sports. First, he was a baseball prospect of some note who was recruited in 1978 by the Toronto Blue Jays, an expansion franchise. After two years in the minor leagues with the Syracuse Nationals, Ainge signed a three-year contract with the Blue Jays for $525,000, including a $300,000 signing bonus. The Blue Jays envisaged Ainge as their third baseman of the future.

Because of NCAA rules that permit professionals in one sport to retain their college eligibility in another sport, Ainge continued playing basketball for Brigham Young University. Although he had been an effective guard in earlier years, Ainge blossomed into a college superstar in the 1980–1981 season. After averaging 25 points per game, he was voted the Eastman Best Player Award by the National Association of Basketball Coaches. However, no NBA team drafted Ainge in the first round of the June 1981 basketball draft because of his apparent commitment to the Blue Jays. But canny Arnold "Red" Auerbach of the Boston Celtics chose Ainge with his second-round pick as a hedge against the possibility that the Celtics' two first-round selections, Charles Bradley and Tracy Jackson, would not satisfy the team's backcourt needs.

Throughout the summer of 1981, Ainge struggled with his baseball career, batting only .180 for the Blue Jays. Eventually, Ainge decided it made most sense to give up baseball and cast his lot with basketball. Although the $300,000 baseball signing bonus had carried an explicit commitment on his part not to play professional basketball, Ainge offered to repay the Blue Jays $350,000 for his release, because he expected to get a much richer contract from the Celtics—in the range of $1.5 to $2 million over three years. The Blue Jays rejected Ainge's offer, though, and told him that they would hold him to his contract. To enforce their position, the Jays sued the Celtics and Ainge in federal district court in New York.

The standard player contract upon which the Blue Jays relied included both an affirmative promise by Ainge to play baseball for the Jays and an undertaking that he would refrain from playing for other professional teams—not only in baseball, but also in basketball, football, hockey, and any other sport "involving a substantial risk of personal injury." For its part, the Blue Jays had agreed to pay Ainge the signing bonus along with a salary that rose over the three years he was to play (from $50,000 to $75,000 to $100,000 per year). The club retained the right to terminate the contract and its obligations if, among other reasons, Ainge "failed, in the opinion of the Club's management, to exhibit sufficient skill or competitive ability to qualify or continue as a member of the Club's team."[c]

Consider the following doctrinal and practical issues posed by the Blue Jays request for injunctive relief against Ainge.[d]

    1. What causes of action, if any, are available on these facts? Have the Blue Jays shown a likelihood of success on the merits of any such legal claim?

    2. If there is some cause of action available to the Blue Jays, why is not the usual monetary damages award the appropriate remedy? Would a failure to grant the Jays an injunction cause the team "irreparable harm?"

    3. If an injunctive remedy is considered, should the judicial order be positive or negative—that is, should the judge order Ainge to play for the Blue Jays or merely not to play for the Celtics? On what legal basis under the contract as well as the standards governing equitable relief?

    4. What are the practical interests of each party to this dispute, and how do you weigh the competing interests against each other? Can you think of any reason why the Celtics might have been prepared to offer Ainge an especially generous monetary package to sign him to an immediate contract? Does the "balance of harms" on this score favor the Blue Jays, or the Celtics and Ainge?

    5. From the broader perspective of the "public interest," what is the ideal legal resolution of cases such as these?

    c. For a useful synopsis of the wording and operation of this termination clause in the contracts in the various professional sports, see Richard J. Ensor, *Comparison of Arbitration Decisions Involving Termination in Major League Baseball, the National Basketball Association, and the National Football League*, 32 Saint Louis U. L. J. 135 (1987).

    d. For a comprehensive review of the evolution of the legal background, see Douglas Laycock, *The Death of the Irreparable Injury Rule* (New York: Oxford University Press, 1991), particularly pp. 168–174 and 184–192 on Personal Service Contracts. A capsule summary of the current doctrines and procedures used in the sports context is Gary Uberstine, "The Enforceability of Sports Industry Employment Agreements," Chapter 9 of Gary Uberstine ed., *Law of Professional and Amateur Sport* (Deerfield, Ill.: Clark, Boardman, and Callaghan, 1991).

6. What do you surmise was the result in and from the litigation, that eventually saw Ainge playing a starring role in two NBA championships won by the Celtics in the mid–1980s?

B. EVOLVING STANDARDS FOR CONTRACT ENFORCEMENT

With the *Ainge* case and these questions in mind, consider the following decisions rendered in cases where clubs sought injunctions against players "jumping" their contracts. The first three decisions portray the unfolding judicial attitude about this contract remedy: at the turn of the last century (*Lajoie*), just before the entry of labor and antitrust law in the 1960s (*Barnett*), and, finally, under the present-day collective bargaining regime (*Shaw*). The next two cases present special issues of allegedly "unclean hands" (*Neely*) and "futures" in player contracts (*Bergey*). Then comes a decision (*Chase*), which brings into focus the background league arrangements within which individual players signed contracts with their respective teams. This last decision serves as a transition to the world of antitrust which we first encounter in the Supreme Court's *Flood* ruling.

PHILADELPHIA BALL CLUB v. LAJOIE
Court of Common Pleas, Philadelphia County, 1902.
202 Pa. 210, 51 A. 973.

POTTER, JUSTICE.

The defendant in this case contracted to serve the plaintiff as a baseball player for a stipulated time. During that period he was not to play for any other club. He violated his agreement, however, during the term of his engagement, and, in disregard of his contract, arranged to play for another and a rival organization. The plaintiff, by means of this bill, sought to restrain him during the period covered by the contract. The court below refused an injunction.

* * *

The learned judge who filed the opinion in the court below, with great industry and painstaking care, collected and reviewed the English and American decisions bearing upon the question involved, and makes apparent the wide divergence of opinion which has prevailed. We think, however, that in refusing relief unless the defendant's services were shown to be of such a character as to render it impossible to replace him he has taken extreme ground. It seems to us that a more just and equitable rule is laid down in *Pom. Spec. Perf.* p. 31, where the principle is thus declared: "Where one person agrees to render personal services to another, which require and presuppose a special knowledge, skill, and ability in the employee, so that in case of a default the same service could not easily be obtained from others, although the affirmative specific performance of the contract is beyond the power of the court, its performance will be negatively enforced by enjoining its breach.... The damages for breach of such contract cannot be estimated with any certainty, and the employer cannot, by means of any damages, purchase the same service in the labor market." ... [W]hen, owing to special features, the contract involves peculiar convenience or advantage, or where the loss would be a matter of uncertainty, then the breach may be deemed to cause irreparable injury.

* * *

The court below finds from the testimony that "the defendant is an expert baseball player in any position; that he has a great reputation as a second baseman; that his place would be hard to fill with as good a player; that his withdrawal from the team would weaken it, as would the withdrawal of any good player, and would probably make a difference in the size of the audiences attending the game." We think that, in thus stating it, he puts it very mildly, and that the evidence would warrant a stronger finding as to the ability of the defendant as an expert ball player. He has been for several years in the service of the plaintiff club, and has been re-engaged from season to season at a constantly increasing salary. He has become thoroughly familiar with the action and methods of the other players in the club, and his own work is peculiarly meritorious as an integral part of the team work which is so essential. In addition to these features which render his services of peculiar and special value to the plaintiff, and not easily replaced, Lajoie is well known, and has great reputation among the patrons of the sport, for his ability in the position which he filled, and was thus a most attractive drawing card for the public. He may not be the sun in the baseball firmament, but he is certainly a bright particular star. We feel, therefore, that the evidence in this case justifies the conclusion that the services of the defendant are of such a unique character, and display such a special knowledge, skill, and ability, as renders them of peculiar value to the plaintiff, and so difficult of substitution that their loss will produce "irreparable injury," in the legal significance of that term, to the plaintiff. The action of the defendant in violating his contract is a breach of good faith, for which there would be no adequate redress at law, and the case, therefore, properly calls for the aid of equity in negatively enforcing the performance of the contract by enjoining against its breach.

[The court then turned to the lower court's argument that the contract lacked "mutuality of remedy," because while Lajoie was bound to "perpetually renewable" obligations, the team could release him (without pay) with just ten days notice. The appeals court first quoted paragraphs in the contract whereby the "consideration" for Lajoie's salary was deemed to be not just performance of services, but also his "concession of the options of release and renewal," and acceptance of equitable relief against performing services for anybody else. The court then continued.]

* * *

We have, then, at the outset, the fact that the paragraphs now criticized and relied upon in defense were deliberately accepted by the defendant, and that such acceptance was made part of the inducement for the plaintiff to enter into the contract. We have the further fact that the contract has been partially executed by services rendered, and payment made therefore, so that the situation is not now the same as when the contract was wholly executory. The relation between the parties has been so far changed as to give to the plaintiff an equity, arising out of the part performance, to insist upon the completion of the agreement according to its terms by the defendant. This equity may be distinguished from the original right under the contract itself, and it might well be questioned whether the court would not be justified in giving effect to it by injunction, without regard to the mutuality or nonmutuality in the original contract. The plaintiff has so far performed its part of the contract in entire good faith, in every detail, and it would therefore be inequitable to permit the defendant to withdraw from the agreement at this late day.

The term "mutuality" or "lack of mutuality" does not always convey a clear and definite meaning. As was said in *Grove v. Hodges*, 55 Pa. 516:

> The legal principle that contracts must be mutual does not mean that in every case each party must have the same remedy for a breach by the other.

In the contract now before us the defendant agreed to furnish his skilled professional services to the plaintiff for a period which might be extended over three years by proper notice given before the close of each current year. Upon the other hand, the plaintiff retained the right to terminate the contract upon 10 days' notice and the payment of salary for that time and the expenses of defendant in getting to his home. But the fact of this concession to the plaintiff is distinctly pointed out as part of the consideration for the large salary paid to the defendant, and is emphasized as such; and owing to the peculiar nature of the services demanded by the business, and the high degree of efficiency which must be maintained, the stipulation is not unreasonable. Particularly is this true when it is remembered that the plaintiff has played for years under substantially the same regulations.

We are not persuaded that the terms of this contract manifest any lack of mutuality in remedy. Each party has the possibility of enforcing all the rights stipulated for in the agreement. It is true that the terms make it possible for the plaintiff to put an end to the contract in a space of time much less than the period during which the defendant has agreed to supply his personal services; but mere difference in the rights stipulated for does not destroy mutuality of remedy. Freedom of contract covers a wide range of obligation and duty as between the parties, and it may not be impaired, so long as the bounds of reasonableness and fairness are not transgressed.... We cannot agree that mutuality of remedy requires that each party should have precisely the same remedy, either in form, effect, or extent. In a fair and reasonable contract, it ought to be sufficient that each party has the possibility of compelling the performance of the promises which were mutually agreed upon.

* * *

The court cannot compel the defendant to play for the plaintiff, but it can restrain him from playing for another club in violation of his agreement. No reason is given why this should not be done, except that presented by the argument, that the right given to the plaintiff to terminate the contract upon 10 days' notice destroys the mutuality of the remedy. But to this it may be answered that, as already stated, the defendant has the possibility of enforcing all the rights for which he stipulated in the agreement, which is all that he can reasonably ask. Furthermore, owing to the peculiar nature and circumstances of the business, the reservation upon the part of the plaintiff to terminate upon short notice does not make the whole contract inequitable.

* * *

Upon a careful consideration of the whole case, we are of the opinion that the provisions of the contract are reasonable, and that the consideration is fully adequate. The evidence shows no indications of any attempt at overreaching or unfairness. Substantial justice between the parties requires that the court should restrain the defendant from playing for any other club during the term of his contract with the plaintiff.

Injunction granted.

There are several interesting facts about this case that are not apparent on the face of the decision.[e] First, Napoleon Lajoie was not just an "ordinary" superstar. Over his 21–year career Lajoie had 3,251 hits and a .339 batting average, and was the first second baseman ever voted into the Hall of Fame. Second, the $2,400 annual salary payable under his Philadelphia Nationals' contract was the amount of the ceiling imposed on players' salaries by the National League. The reason Lajoie moved crosstown to play in the fledgling American League was to avoid this ceiling. Finally, despite their judicial victory, the Nationals failed to retrieve their star second baseman. The Philadelphia Americans simply traded Lajoie to their Cleveland counterparts, and the Ohio courts refused to grant an injunction. Shortly thereafter, the National and American Leagues settled their wars with the major league agreement that established the foundation for organized baseball to this day.

Questions for Discussion

1. Do you agree with the conclusion in *Lajoie* that there was mutuality in the terms of this player contract? Should courts have broad discretion to

[e]. See Seymour, *Baseball: The Early Years*, note a above, at 306–324.

decide whether there is sufficient mutuality to make it equitable to enforce a contract? For all contracts, or only for personal service contracts?

The *Lajoie* case was actually one of the few cases in which a baseball team ever secured an injunction against its own player—and even then, the order had no tangible value. A provocative article[f] observes that this judicial reluctance to issue personal services injunctions was exhibited especially in suits against male workers (including professional athletes). Judges showed quite a different sentiment in suits against women, especially entertainers such as the British opera singer Johanna Wagner and the American actress Lillian Russell. By the 1950s, though, courts had largely overcome such reticence with respect to athletes. As the next case indicates, the courts' attention had shifted from the supposed inequity of the contract toward the player (its lack of mutuality) to the team's need to retain especially talented athletes.

CENTRAL NEW YORK BASKETBALL, INC. (SYRACUSE NATIONALS) v. BARNETT

Court of Common Pleas of Ohio, Cuyahoga County, 1961.
181 N.E.2d 506.

DANACEAU, JUDGE.

[The Syracuse Nationals of the National Basketball Association (NBA) sued both the Cleveland Pipers of the new American Basketball League (ABL) and Dick Barnett. Barnett had been the Nationals' first-round draft choice in 1959. He signed the standard player contract for the 1959–1960 season, and then played the 1960–1961 season pursuant to the option clause in his written contract (at a salary of $8,500). In May 1961, Barnett and Nationals' President Dan Biasone reached a telephone agreement for a 1961–1962 contract of $11,500, with an agreed-to advance payment that was later mailed to Barnett (although the check was not cashed). During the next two months, Barnett was wooed by the Cleveland team (headed by his old college coach), and in July he signed a contract with the Pipers for $14,000. The Nationals then sued for an injunction to prevent Barnett from playing for the Pipers.

The Nationals chose not to rely on the option clause in the earlier written contract. According to the Nationals' construction of the contract—which the judge adopted as "reasonable, rational, [and] practical"—the contract expired at the end of the 1961 season and could *not* be unilaterally renewed by the club, as it had been the previous year. (By contrast, Barnett and the Pipers had construed the contract to be repeatedly renewable by the club in order to argue that it was void as a

---

f. Lea S. Vandervelde, *The Gendered Origins of the* Lumley *Doctrine: Binding Men's Consciences and Women's Fidelity*, 101 Yale L. J. 775 (1992).

perpetual personal services contract.) The case was therefore brought and decided on the basis of the oral agreement between Barnett and Biasone. The Nationals argued that because Barnett's "talents and abilities as a basketball player [were] of a special, unique, unusual and extraordinary character," they were entitled to an injunction preventing him from playing for the Pipers.]

* * *

There is some disagreement in the testimony as to the ability and standing of Barnett as a basketball player. Daniel Biasone, the General Manager of the Syracuse club for the past 16 years, testified that: "As of now I think Richard Barnett is one of the greatest basketball players playing the game." "He is an exceptionally good shooter." "He is above average ... with other foul shooters in the National Basketball Association and that he ranked 19th in the whole league (approximately 100 players) scoring, playing as a guard." He further testified:

Q. What is your opinion as to his ability, this is, as a guard, now, at driving?

A. Terrific.

Q. What is your opinion as to his ability at playmaking as a guard?

A. Good. He has all the abilities a good basketball player should have. He has all the talent of a great basketball player. He is terrific all the way around.

Mr. Biasone also testified on cross-examination that he would place Barnett in the group of some specifically-named nine or ten unusual and extraordinary players in the National Basketball Association.

Mr. Biasone also testified that Barnett was a box office attraction and was asked on cross-examination: "On what basis do you say he was a great box office attraction?" He answered:

A. Because he, in my opinion, he is such a tremendous ball handler and he does things that have crowd appeal, he is noticeable. He appeals to the crowd because he does things extraordinary.

Coach McLendon of the Cleveland Pipers is not so generous in his appraisal. Barnett, in his opinion, is not in the class of the specifically-named outstanding basketball players. McLendon concedes that both Barnett and Neuman, now playing for Syracuse in his first year as a professional, are both "pretty good."

* * *

That the defendant Barnett was 19th among the top 25 scorers in the National Basketball Association in the 1960–61 season is confirmed in the statistics published on page 113 of the official Guide. On page 190 of the Guide is the record of Richard Barnett which indicates that he played in 78 games (out of 79) in the 1960–1961 season for a total of 1,970 minutes; that his F.G.M. percentage was .452; that his F.T.M. percentage was .712 and that he scored 1,320 points for an average of

16.9. The Guide also indicates that Barnett was not among the players in the East–West All Star Game on January 17, 1961, nor was he among the players named in the U.S. Basketball Writers' All–NBA Team for 1961.

The defendant Barnett may not be in the same class with the top ten basketball players. The Syracuse manager is not a disinterested witness, and he may have given an immoderate appraisal of the playing abilities of Barnett. On the other hand, neither are McLendon nor Barnett disinterested witnesses. McLendon's eagerness to secure the services of Barnett at a high salary ($13,000) indicates a higher opinion of Barnett's playing abilities than he was willing to concede at the trial of this case. Barnett was understandably under embarrassment when asked to give opinion of his own abilities and to make comparisons with another named player.

The increase of salary from $8,500 to $11,500 agreed to by plaintiff, the Cleveland Basketball Club's willingness to pay $13,000, and the latter's eagerness to secure his services, all point to a high regard for his playing abilities. Whether Barnett ranks with the top basketball players or not, the evidence shows that he is an outstanding professional basketball player of unusual attainments and exceptional skill and ability, and that he is of peculiar and particular value to plaintiff.

[The court then quoted the provision of Barnett's contract whereby the latter acknowledged his "exceptional and unique skill and ability as a basketball player," whose "peculiar value" to the club could only be remedied by injunctive relief, not just damages for breach of contract—in particular, by Barnett "playing basketball" for any other team.]

* * *

The aforesaid provisions are contained in uniform players' contracts and it would seem that mere engagement as a basketball player in the N.B.A., or A.B.L., carries with it recognition of his excellence and extraordinary abilities.

An important growth in the field of equity has been the use of injunctions against the breach of negative agreements, both express and implied. *Pomeroy's Specific Performance of Contract*, Third Ed. at page 75 reads:

> Another class of contracts stipulating for personal acts are now enforced in England by means of an injunction. Where one person agrees to render personal services to another, which require and presuppose a special knowledge, skill, and ability in the employee, so that, in case of a default, the same services could not easily be obtained from others, although the affirmative specific performance of the contract is beyond the power of the court, its performance will be negatively enforced by enjoining its breach. This doctrine applies especially to contracts made by actors, public singers, artists and others possessing a special skill and ability. It is plain that the principle on which it rests is the same with that which applies to

agreements for the purchase of land or of chattels having a unique character and value. The damages for the breach of such contracts cannot be estimated with any certainty, and the employer cannot, by means of any damages, purchase the same services in the labor market.

* * *

Professional players in the major baseball, football, and basketball leagues have unusual talents and skills or they would not be so employed. Such players, the defendant Barnett included, are not easily replaced.

The right of the plaintiff is plain and the wrong done by the defendants is equally plain, and there is no reason why the Court should be sparing in the application of its remedies.

Damages at law would be speculative and uncertain and are practically impossible of ascertainment in terms of money. There is no plain, adequate and complete remedy at law and the injury to the plaintiff is irreparable.

Professional baseball, football, and basketball require regulations for the protection of the business, the public and the players, and so long as they are fair and reasonable there is no violation of the laws on restraint of trade. The evidence before this Court does not show any unfair or unreasonable act on the part of the plaintiff and the Court concludes that the claim of the defendant that the contract is in restraint of trade is without merit.

* * *

Injunction granted.

An intriguing footnote to *Barnett* is that the principal owner of the Cleveland Pipers was a young George Steinbrenner, demonstrating for the first time his willingness to outbid other teams for the players he wanted. Look closely at the salary figures in this case—both the absolute dollar levels and the relative changes that summer. What do these figures imply about the impact of competition for professional athletes' services? Is this financial impact likely to be the same when competition takes place between two teams in the same league, rather than between two teams in rival leagues?

The heart of Barnett's mutuality claim was that while the contract allowed the team to terminate his services (i.e., cut him from the team) on very short notice, the "option" clause prevented him from ever moving to another club in the same or different league if the club exercised the option and renewed his contract every year. The option clause allowed the team unilaterally to renew the contract during the first ten days of November "for the period of one year on the same terms" (except for the salary, which the team could fix at or above 75% of the prior year's salary).

Barnett argued that when a team renewed the contract under this clause, the new contract thereby included the same option clause, thus permitting the club to renew the contract in each future year—a perpetual right of renewal. The Nationals asserted that the option clause was not included in the renewal option contract; thus the club could exercise this option only once. The court agreed with the Nationals' interpretation, and on that footing held the contract to be valid and enforceable. Had the court agreed with Barnett's interpretation, would that have rendered the contract void (or voidable) for lack of mutuality?

In answering the above question, keep in mind that prior to an arbitration decision and an antitrust decree in the mid-1970s, both Major League Baseball and the National Hockey League had interpreted their respective option clauses as being perpetually renewable, making this clause the cornerstone of their so-called "lifetime reserve system." By contrast, the National Football League had always interpreted its option clause as allowing a club to exercise the option only one time after the principal contract expired. The NFL did use a stringent intraleague "compensation" system to discourage free agent movement to another NFL club (which we will see in the *Mackey v. NFL* case in Chapter 3), but nothing in their contracts prevented NFL players from signing with another league once their option year ended.

For a variety of reasons, the mutuality defense eventually faded from view in sports cases. However, keep the *Barnett* construction of the standard NBA player contract in mind when you read the arbitrator's decision in the *Messersmith* baseball grievance at the beginning of Chapter 4.

By the 1960s the main focus of debate was whether the clubs were likely to suffer "irreparable harm" from losing the services of players with "exceptional and unique skill and ability." The language in Barnett's NBA contract was very similar to the language found in Danny Ainge's Major League Baseball contract, and indeed in the standard contracts in all professional sports. Should this contract wording be decisive in later litigation? In *Barnett*, the court recited pages of testimony relating to Barnett's skills and abilities, but then stated that "mere engagement as a basketball player in the NBA or ABL carries with it recognition of his excellence and extraordinary abilities," and "[p]rofessional players in the major baseball, football, and basketball leagues have unusual talents and skills or they would not be so employed." Are professional clubs irreparably injured just because any athlete breaches his contract (with or without the "unique skill and ability" clause), or is this an issue that should be determined case by case, depending on the special skill and appeal of the particular athlete? If done case by case, under what standards should a court or jury make the determination?

In *Winnipeg Rugby Football Club v. Freeman*, 140 F.Supp. 365 (N.D.Ohio 1955), the court enjoined two players from playing for the

NFL's Cleveland Browns in breach of an ongoing contract with the Winnipeg Blue Bombers of the Canadian Football League (CFL). In finding that the players had unique skill and ability, the court noted that the players were much more valuable to the CFL team because of the lower calibre of play in that league. Does this imply that it would be easier for teams playing at a lower level of professional ball (e.g., the minor leagues, European basketball, or Japanese baseball, as well as the CFL) to get injunctions against players, especially if the team to which they are jumping is in the established major league? In this regard, see *Connecticut Professional Sports Corp. v. Heyman*, 276 F.Supp. 618 (S.D.N.Y.1967); *Spencer v. Milton*, 159 Misc. 793, 287 N.Y.S. 944 (1936) (both refusing to enjoin movement by a minor league baseball and basketball player, respectively); *Safro v. Lakofsky*, 184 Minn. 336, 238 N.W. 641 (1931) (refusing to enjoin a minor league boxer from performing in matches not procured by a party to whom he was under exclusive contract). However, see *Dallas Cowboys Football Club, Inc. v. Harris*, 348 S.W.2d 37 (Tex.Civ.App.1961) (enjoining a player under a one-year option contract with the NFL's Dallas Cowboys from playing for the Dallas Texans in the fledgling American Football League). By the way, should U.S. courts routinely enforce contracts negotiated in foreign countries, such as that of Dino Rajda who was originally enjoined from jumping from his Yugoslavian team to the Boston Celtics, or Pavel Bure who on the eve of his injunction hearing had to pay several hundred thousand dollars to secure release from his Russian contract to play for the Vancouver Canucks of the NHL?

In the *Winnipeg Rugby Football Club* case, an injunction was also issued to bar the Cleveland Browns from doing anything to interfere with the Blue Bombers' players' contracts. A prerequisite to this injunction was that the Browns were, or should have been, aware of the obligation of the players to the old team. Why would the plaintiff team also want to subject the defendant team to an injunction?

Note that the *Barnett* litigation was a product of a new league appearing on the scene. As we will see in Chapter 8, the early 1960s saw the emergence of a number of such competitors to the established leagues in every sport except baseball.[g] Although Barnett's American Basketball League lasted only one year, it was followed five years later by the American Basketball Association (ABA). Hockey saw the World Hockey Association (WHA) challenge the National Hockey League (NHL) in the 1970s. The National Football League (NFL), meanwhile, encountered the American Football League (AFL) in the 1960s, the World Football League (WFL) in the 1970s, and the United States Football League (USFL) in the 1980s. Just as had happened with baseball in the late 19th and early 20th centuries, the presence of two

---

g. In baseball there was a serious threat of a potential competitor, the Continental League, which was organized by Branch Rickey in the late 1950s. Rickey's effort was foiled in the early 1960s when the American and National Leagues, through both expansion and relocation, moved into prime territory in New York, California, Texas, and Minnesota.

leagues competing for the same players produced a burst of contract litigation (exemplified by *Flowers*, *Neely*, and *Bergey*, *infra*). Should the *Barnett* court have focused more squarely on the significance of interleague rivalry? In contrast with the *Ainge* litigation in which the struggle was between two teams in different sports, should the presence of two different leagues in the same sport make a court more or less willing to grant the requested injunction?

The next case presents a player contract dispute in the contemporary context of a collective agreement negotiated by a players' association and interpreted by a labor arbitrator.[h] Brian Shaw was drafted by the Boston Celtics in 1988 and signed to a one-year contract. The next year Shaw signed a two-year contract with the Italian basketball team, Il Messaggero Roma, paying him $800,000 in the first year and $900,000 in the second. That contract also gave Shaw the option to terminate the second year if he wanted to return to the NBA, by sending the team a signed and registered letter to this effect between June 20 and July 20, 1990.

In January of 1990, Celtics executives flew to Rome and persuaded Shaw to sign a five-year deal with them—with a $450,000 bonus and an average salary of slightly over $1 million a year. Shaw specifically undertook to terminate his Il Messaggero contract during the designated window period. At that time, Shaw was without an agent. Later that spring, he retained an agent, who told his client that the Celtics' contract did not reflect Shaw's market value and that he should not leave Il Messaggero that year. The Celtics took the dispute to the arbitrator under the NBA Players Association labor agreement, whose terms were incorporated by reference in Shaw's (and all other players') individual contracts. The arbitrator ruled that Shaw had to deliver the registered termination letter to Il Messaggero, and a federal district judge issued an order of enforcement. Shaw appealed.

BOSTON CELTICS v. BRIAN SHAW

United States Court of Appeals, First Circuit, 1990.
908 F.2d 1041.

BREYER, CIRCUIT JUDGE.

* * *

II. THE LEGAL MERITS

Shaw makes two basic categories of argument in his effort to show that the district court lacked the legal power to enter its order. First, he says that the arbitration award was itself unlawful. Second, he says that

---

[h] For a journalistic account of the battle between Brian Shaw and the Celtics, see Harvey Araton and Flip Bondy, *The Selling of the Green: The Financial Rise and Moral Decline of the Boston Celtics* (New York: Harper Collins, 1992), at 1–19. The title of the book should leave no doubt about the authors' point of view on the *Shaw* case.

regardless of the lawfulness of the award, the district court followed improper procedures. We shall address these arguments in turn and explain why we find each not persuasive.

A. The Arbitrator's Decision

Shaw says that the district court should not have enforced the arbitrator's award because that award was itself unlawful, for any of five separate reasons.

1. *The termination promise.* Shaw argues that the arbitrator could not reasonably find that he broke a contractual promise to the Celtics because, he says, the Celtics had previously agreed with the Players Association that contracts with individual players such as Shaw would not contain promises of the sort here at issue, namely, a promise to cancel a contract to play with a different team. Shaw says that this previous agreement between the Celtics and the Players Association renders his promise to terminate Il Messaggero "null and void." To support this argument, he points to Article I, § 2 of the Collective Bargaining Agreement, which Shaw and the Celtics, through cross-reference, made part of their individual agreement. Section 2 says, "Any amendment to a Uniform Player Contract [of the type Shaw and the Celtics used], other than those permitted by this [Collective Bargaining] Agreement, shall be null and void." The Agreement permits amendments (a) "in ... respect to the compensation ... to be paid the player," (b) "in respect to specialized compensation arrangements," (c) in respect to a "compensation payment schedule," and (d) in respect to "protect[ion]" of compensation in the event of contract termination. Shaw says that his promise to cancel the Il Messaggero agreement was an amendment to the Uniform Players Contract that does not concern compensation, specialized compensation, compensation schedules, or compensation protection; therefore, it is "null and void."

Shaw's argument, while logical, fails to show that the arbitrator's contrary finding is unlawful. The reasons it fails are fairly straightforward. First, the argument concerns the proper interpretation of a contract negotiated pursuant to a collective bargaining agreement. Second, federal labor law gives arbitrators, not judges, the power to interpret such contracts. The Supreme Court, noting the strong federal policy favoring the voluntary settlement of labor disputes, has written that a labor arbitration award is valid so long as it "draws its essence" from the labor contract. See *United Steelworkers v. Enterprise Wheel & Car Corp.*, 363 U.S. 593, 597, (1960). An award "draws its essence" from the contract so long as the "arbitrator is even arguably construing or applying the contract and acting within the scope of his authority." *United Paperworkers Int'l v. Misco*, 484 U.S. 29, 38 (1987).

* * *

Third, one can find "plausible arguments" favoring the arbitrator's construction. Shaw's "rescission" promise defines the beginning of the compensation relationship. It also plausibly determines, at the very least, whether Shaw's compensation will begin at $1.1 million (and continue for three years) or whether it will begin at $1.2 million (and continue for only two years). More importantly, and also quite plausibly, Shaw's overall compensation might have been much different had he declined to promise to play for the Celtics in 1990–91, thereby forcing the Celtics, perhaps, to obtain the services of a replacement for that year. The NBA Commissioner, who reviews all player contracts, found that the term was related to "compensation," as did the arbitrator. We cannot say that their findings lack any "plausible" basis.

* * *

In sum, we find the arbitration award lawful; and, in doing so, it has not been necessary for us to consider the Celtics' additional argument that Shaw bears an especially heavy legal burden in this case because the Players Association does not support him.

B. *The District Court Proceedings*

[The court then turned to the question whether the district court's injunction ordering Shaw to rescind "forthwith" his contract with Il Messaggero and barring him from playing basketball for anyone but the Celtics satisfied the standards for preliminary injunctive relief quoted earlier.]

* * *

To begin with, the Celtics have shown a clear likelihood of success on the merits.... The Celtics also have demonstrated irreparable harm. Without speedy relief, they will likely lose the services of a star athlete next year, see *Wright & Miller* § 2948, at 439 & n. 34 (1972) (collecting cases that have found irreparable harm "in the loss by an athletic team of the services of a star athlete"), and, unless they know fairly soon whether Shaw will, or will not play for them, they will find it difficult to plan intelligently for next season. Indeed, in his contract Shaw expressly:

> represents and agrees that he has extraordinary and unique skill and ability as a basketball player ... and that any breach by the Player of this contract will cause irreparable injury to the Club.

Further, the court could reasonably find that the "balance of harms" favors the Celtics. Of course, a preliminary injunction, if ultimately shown wrong on the merits, could cause Shaw harm. He might lose the chance to play in the country, and for the team, that he prefers. On the other hand, this harm is somewhat offset by the fact that ultimate success on the merits—*i.e.*, a finding that Shaw was not obligated to terminate Il Messaggero after all—would likely result in the following scenario: Shaw might still be able to sign with Il Messaggero and, if not, he would always have the Celtics contract of over $5 million to fall back upon. At the same time, the court's failure to issue the injunction, if the merits ultimately favored the Celtics, could cause them serious harm of the sort just mentioned (*i.e.*, significantly increased difficulty in planning their team for next season). Given the very small likelihood that Shaw would ultimately prevail on the merits, and the "comparative" harms at stake, the district court could properly decide that the overall "balance" favored the Celtics, not Shaw.

Finally, the court could properly find that issuing a preliminary injunction would not harm the public interest. Indeed, as we have pointed out, the public interest favors court action that "effectuate[s]" the parties' intent to resolve their disputes informally through arbitration. Where the dispute involves a professional basketball player's obligation to play for a particular team, one could reasonably consider expeditious, informal and effective dispute-resolution methods to be essential, and, if so, the public interest favoring court action to "effectuate" those methods of dispute-resolution would seem at least as strong as it is in respect to work-related disputes typically arising under collective bargaining agreements. See *New England Patriots Football Club, Inc. v. University of Colorado*, 592 F.2d 1196, 1200 (1st Cir.1979) (collecting cases in which professional sports players were enjoined from playing for rival teams). Shaw, while conceding that the public also has an interest in seeing that contracts between consenting adults are honored, points to a general policy disfavoring enforcement of personal service contracts. That latter policy, however, typically prevents a court from ordering an individual to perform a personal service; it does not prevent a court from ordering an individual to rescind a contract for services and to refrain from performing a service for others.

Shaw makes an additional argument. He notes that courts will not provide equitable relief such as an injunction to a party with "unclean hands," and he argues that the Celtics' hands are not clean. To support this argument, he has submitted an affidavit saying, in effect, that he signed the contract in a weak moment. His trip to Italy had made him "homesick;" he was "depressed" by what he viewed as undeserved and "negative criticism" in the Italian press; he was not represented by an agent; the Celtics had been urging him to sign up; he read the contract only for about 20 minutes while he was driving around Rome with a Celtics official; and no one ever explained to him that if he did not sign and played with Il Messaggero for another year, he would become a "free agent," able to bargain thereafter with any American team, perhaps for an even greater salary than the Celtics were willing to pay him.

Other evidence in the record, however, which Shaw does not deny, shows that he is a college graduate; that he has played under contract with the Celtics before; that the contract is a standard form contract except for a few, fairly simple, rather clear, additions; that he had bargained with the Celtics for an offer that increased from $3.4 million (in December) to $5.4 million (less than one month later); that he looked over the contract before signing it; that he told the American consul in Rome (as he signed it) that he had read and understood it; and that he did not complain about the contract until he told the Celtics in June that he would not honor it.

Given this state of the record, the district court could easily, and properly, conclude that the Celtics' hands were not "unclean." The one case Shaw cites in support of his position, *Minnesota Muskies, Inc. v. Hudson*, 294 F.Supp. 979, 981 (M.D.N.C.1969), is not on point. The player in Muskies had a contract with Team A that permitted Team A, not the player, to renew the contract for additional years. Team B lured the player away from Team A even though it knew that Team A intended to exercise its contractual right to keep the player. The court held that this contractual interference amounted to "unclean hands" and refused Team B's request for an injunction preventing the player from returning to Team A. Here, in contrast, Il Messaggero has no contractual right to retain Shaw; whether or not the contract is renewed or rescinded is entirely up to Shaw, not Il Messaggero. Under those circumstances, we cannot find anything improper, "unclean," or unfair about the Celtics' convincing Shaw (indeed, paying Shaw) to exercise his contractual right in their favor. Cf. Restatement (Second) of Torts § 768 (1979).

* * *

Injunction upheld.

Questions for Discussion

1. Unlike *Lajoie* and *Barnett*, in *Shaw* there was an earlier adjudication of the issues by a labor arbitrator appointed by the NBA and its Players Association under their collective agreement. Should this fact make a court more willing to order equitable relief against a player seeking to move to another league?

2. In the middle of the 1991–1992 season, the Celtics traded Shaw to the Miami Heat for the latter's equally disenchanted point guard, Sherman Douglas. Such trades are made possible by the assignment clause that gives the team, the player's employer, the right to assign the personal services contract to another team in the same league. Though unthinkable in most other employment contexts, this provision is standard in athletes' contracts unless the player can negotiate a "no-trade" clause, or the collective bargaining agreement gives a veteran player some control over his being traded. Should this feature of the contract influence a court's decision about whether to force the player to play for the team with which he originally signed? For the team to which he was traded?

More generally, is this assignment clause itself fair and reasonable, or should it be void as against public policy? Would your answer hinge on whether the players union had agreed to the inclusion of such a clause in the standard contract? For what reasons do club owners want such a clause? What would be the long term effect on player-club relations if such clauses were not enforced by the courts? Does this provision, along with that requiring commissioner approval before the contract can become valid, essentially mean that the player is as much under contract to the league as to the club? Should the league, then, also be liable for any breach of contract (i.e., failure to pay) by the club? See *USFL Players Ass'n. v. USFL*, 650 F.Supp. 12 (D.Or.1986).

3. In *Munchak Corp. v. Cunningham*, 457 F.2d 721 (4th Cir.1972), Billy Cunningham negotiated a "no-trade" clause in his basketball contract with the ABA's Carolina Cougars. Subsequently, the Cougars were sold and all of the team's player contracts were assigned to the new owner. Cunningham sought to avoid being held to his contract by arguing that this assignment made it void. The Fourth Circuit rejected his argument and held that a standard "no assignment" clause merely meant that the player could not be traded to a different club, not that he could not be traded to a different owner of the same club. Is this a fair interpretation of general "no-trade" language? Would your answer be different if the team was sold to a new owner who immediately relocated the franchise to a different city and changed the name of the team?

In assessing the equities of these player contract suits, one factor that influences the reaction of judges, let alone fans, is the salaries paid to players for signing contracts with apparently onerous clauses. Note how dramatically the basketball salary figures in *Shaw* had changed since the days of *Barnett*, and yet how insignificant Shaw's million dollars-a-year deal would seem to a young NBA free agent just a decade later. This salary escalation was due in considerable part to the emergence of union representation and collective bargaining in sports. The impact and the desirability of unionism in sports is the subject of Chapter 4.

An important aspect of the sports world under labor law is that grievance arbitration rather than civil adjudication is the principal method for resolving disputes that affect players (as we saw with drug-testing in Chapter 1). Note the judicial treatment of the arbitration award in *Shaw*, to be recalled in Chapter 4 when we develop the labor law framework for professional sports.

Finally, look carefully at the arbitrator's treatment of whether the collective agreement permitted Shaw to make the special undertaking in his individually negotiated contract. Keep this case in mind when we address the interplay of collective and individual bargaining in sports at the beginning of Chapter 5.

The next cases introduce us to the world of professional football[i] and explore the doctrine of "unclean hands" that was raised at the end of the *Shaw* decision. In *New York Football Giants, Inc. v. Los Angeles Chargers Football Club, Inc.* (*Flowers*), 291 F.2d 471 (5th Cir.1961), Charles Flowers, a star player for the University of Mississippi football team, was signed by the National Football League's New York Giants to a pro

---

[i]. For background on the struggle between the National and American Football Leagues that gave rise to the *Flowers* and *Neely* cases, see Harris, *The League*, note a above, 56–66, 102–06, 132–33.

football contract. If the December, 1959 contract signing had been made public at that time, Flowers would have lost his eligibility to play in the New Year's Day Sugar Bowl against Mississippi's traditional rival, Louisiana State. Accordingly, Giants owner Wellington Mara acceded to Flower's request to keep the contract (and signing bonus) secret until January 2, 1960; thus, the team did not submit the contract to NFL Commissioner Pete Rozelle for his approval.

Later in December, Flowers was offered more money by the Los Angeles Chargers of the new American Football League. Flowers thereupon notified the Giants that he was withdrawing from their contract and returning their uncashed bonus checks. Flowers signed with the Chargers on January 1, immediately after the Sugar Bowl, and the Giants went to court seeking an injunction to enforce its prior agreement. In court, though, the Giants were met with "the age-old but sometimes overlooked doctrine that 'he who comes into equity must come with clean hands.'"

> Here the plaintiff's [Giants'] whole difficulty arises because it admittedly took from Flowers what it claims to be a binding contract, but which it agreed with Flowers it would, in effect, represent was not in existence in order to deceive others who had a very material and important interest in the subject matter. If there had been a straightforward execution of the document, followed by its filing with the Commissioner, none of the legal problems now presented to this court to untangle would exist. We think no party had the right thus to create problems by its devious and deceitful conduct and then approach a court of equity with a plea that the pretended status which it has foisted on the public be ignored and its rights be declared as if it had acted in good faith throughout.
>
> When it became apparent from uncontradicted testimony of Mara that this deceit was practiced in order to bring into being the "contract" sued upon, the trial court should have dismissed the suit without more on the basis of the "clean hands" doctrine.

291 F.2d at 474. While *Flowers* reflects the standard approach to this kind of case, the next decision took a different view.

HOUSTON OILERS, INC. v. NEELY

United States Court of Appeals, Tenth Circuit, 1966.
361 F.2d 36.

PICKETT, CIRCUIT JUDGE.

[Ralph Neely of the University of Oklahoma was one of the top senior college football players in 1964. In those days, the National Football League (NFL) and the new American Football League (AFL) conducted their college player drafts at the end of the college regular season, before bowl games were played. Neely was drafted by both the NFL's Baltimore Colts and the AFL's Houston Oilers. Immediately after the November 28 draft, Baltimore offered Neely a four-year contract with salaries from $16,000 to $25,000 per year and a $25,000 signing bonus.

On November 30, Houston president K.S. "Bud" Adams offered Neely a four-year, "no-cut" contract for $16,000 per year and a $25,000 signing bonus. Adams also promised to get a job for Neely with a local real-estate firm and to have his oil company build a Phillips '66 gas station (at a cost of $30,000 to $60,000) for Neely to own and operate. Neely accepted the Houston offer and the contracts were executed on December 1. Neely, who apparently knew that by signing the contracts he had forfeited his remaining college eligibility, wanted the contracts kept secret so that he could play in the Gator Bowl game on January 2. However, the contracts and bonus check were dated December 1, and the contracts expressly provided that they were binding upon execution and (pursuant to AFL rules) had to be filed with the AFL commissioner within 10 days (and they were).

Neely then learned that Baltimore had traded the right to negotiate with him to the Dallas Cowboys. Neely's father-in-law, who had been involved in the negotiations with Houston, then began secretly negotiating with Dallas. On December 29, Neely returned the $25,000 bonus check and sent letters to Adams and Houston stating that he was withdrawing from his contracts with them. On December 31, Dallas deposited $15,000 in Neely's bank account, and Neely told his Oklahoma coach about the Houston contracts. The next day Neely was declared ineligible for the Gator Bowl game, and that evening he signed a four-year contract with Dallas.

Houston brought suit seeking an injunction to prevent Neely from playing for Dallas (or any other professional football team). The trial court, finding that Neely's contracts with Houston were tainted with fraud, refused to grant the injunction. By the time the appellate court handed down its decision, Neely had already played the 1965 season for Dallas.]

* * *

Disagreement over the validity of these contracts does not arise out of the provisions contained therein, but from an extrinsic oral understanding that their existence was to be kept secret until after the post-season game. The essence of Neely's contentions before the trial court and here is that the contracts are unenforceable because Houston falsely represented that the effective date of the agreement would be January 2, 1965, and that Houston's filing of the contract copies with the Commissioner was a violation of its promise to keep the matter secret. The trial court was of the opinion that these alleged misrepresentations constituted fraud in the inducement of the contract which would subject it to rescission. As has been heretofore stated, each contract specifically provides otherwise. Neely does not say he was so naive that he did not know his eligibility for further intercollegiate football competition would be destroyed when he signed a professional football contract and received the bonus money.

The record is too clear for any misunderstanding that the purpose of secrecy surrounding the execution of the contracts was not to preserve Neely's eligibility, but rather to prevent his ineligibility from becoming known; otherwise there was no need for secrecy.

* * *

The scheme to mislead Neely's school, his coaches, his team, and the Gator Bowl opponents, no doubt would have succeeded but for Neely's own double dealing with Dallas, resulting in his attempt to avoid the Houston contracts. While we do not for a moment condone the ruthless methods employed by professional football teams in their contest for the services of college football players, including the lavish expenditure of money,[7] it must be conceded that there is no legal impediment to contracting for the services of athletes at any time, and the above-mentioned conduct, while regrettable, does not furnish athletes with a legal excuse to avoid their contracts for reasons other than the temptations of a more attractive offer. Although there are many dismal indications to the contrary, athletes, amateur or professional, and those connected with athletics, are bound by their contracts to the same extent as anyone else, and should not be allowed to repudiate them at their pleasure.

* * *

The draft system in professional football limited Neely's negotiations initially to Baltimore and Houston. His collegiate football record was such that he and his father-in-law could anticipate that his services would be in demand and would command a premium contract. The opportunity presented to Neely would come but once in his lifetime, and it is understandable that the situation would be exploited to the maximum. It was with this background that Neely negotiated with Houston and Baltimore. Neely, a bright young man, ably advised by his father-in-law, knew exactly what he wanted.

* * *

There is insufficient evidence to sustain a finding of material misrepresentation on the part of Houston amounting to fraud which would affect the validity of the contracts. It is true that Neely testified that it was his understanding that the contracts were not to become effective until after the game on January 2nd. The contracts, however, provided

---

7. These methods and their adverse effect upon amateur football players were described by Judge Skelly Wright in *Detroit Football Company v. Robinson*, 186 F.Supp. 933, 934 (E.D.La.1960), where he said:

This case is but another round in the sordid fight for football players, a fight which begins before these athletes enter college and follows them through their professional careers. It is a fight characterized by deception, double dealing, campus jumping, secret alumni subsidization, semi-professionalism and professionalism. It is a fight which has produced as part of its harvest this current rash of contract-jumping suits. It is a fight which so conditions the minds and hearts of these athletes that one day they can agree to play football for a stated amount for one group, only to repudiate that agreement the following day or whenever a better offer comes along.

otherwise, and we are not at liberty to rewrite then. Furthermore, the letter of employment, the filling station arrangement, and the $25,000 bonus check which was delivered upon the execution of the contracts, were all dated December 1, 1964.

The trial court, in denying the relief sought, apparently applied the equitable maxim that "he who comes into equity must come with clean hands." This doctrine, fundamental in equity jurisprudence, means that equity will not in any manner aid a party whose conduct in relation to the litigation matter has been unlawful, unconscionable, or inequitable. But the doctrine does not exclude all wrongdoers from a court of equity nor should it be applied in every case where the conduct of a party may be considered unconscionable or inequitable. While it is not contended here that Houston did not have a legal right to sign Neely to a professional player's contract, it is urged that when Houston participated in a scheme to conceal that for the purpose of permitting an ineligible player to participate in a post-season game, it was such deceit upon others that a court of equity should not intervene to assist in the enforcement of the contract. With this argument we cannot agree. It is neither unlawful nor inequitable for college football players to surrender their amateur status and turn professional at any time. Neely was free to bind himself to such a contract on December 1, 1964 as he would have been after January 2, 1965. Nor was Houston under any legal duty to publicize the contract or to keep it secret. Its agreement to keep secret that which it had a legal right to keep secret cannot be considered inequitable or unconscionable as those terms are ordinarily used in contract negotiations. Neely relies on the case of *New York Football Giants v. Los Angeles Chargers*, 291 F.2d 471 (5th Cir.1961), where, in a somewhat similar situation, the court applied the clean hands doctrine. It is quite apparent that the player contract in that case was acquired under circumstances much different from those in this case, but if the rule announced in that case was intended to apply to every instance in which a contract is entered into with a college football player before a post-season game with an understanding that it be kept secret to permit that player to compete in the game, then we must respectfully disagree with the conclusion.

Injunction granted.

The facts in these cases provide a glimpse of the relationship between professional and college football. Do you find anything familiar in Judge Skelly Wright's lament about the "sordid" state of affairs forty years ago—before there were player agents to blame? By the way, do not assume, as did the Fifth Circuit, that there was nothing unlawful in the Houston Oilers signing Neely and keeping that fact secret from his school and the NCAA. We will read a good deal more in Chapters 5 and 10 on the topic of college athletes, player agents, and professional teams.

Questions for Discussion

1. The war between the NFL and the AFL in the early 1960s produced numerous cases of players trying to renege on a secret pre-bowl game contract (and bonus payment) with a team in one league in order to sign with a team in the other league. In addition to the *Neely* and *Flowers* cases, see *Detroit Football Co. v. Robinson*, 186 F.Supp. 933 (E.D.La.1960), and *Los Angeles Rams Football Club v. Cannon*, 185 F.Supp. 717 (S.D.Cal.1960). Only in *Neely* did the court not invoke the "clean hands" doctrine to refuse to enforce the initial contract. Between *Neely* and the other cases, which represents the better legal view? Interestingly, in every one of these cases the court ended up siding with the AFL team and against the NFL team. Is that just a coincidence, or did it reflect a judicial desire to assist the upstart football league against the established league that had far greater market power? Is such a consideration proper in these contract enforcement cases?

2. The *Neely* court made a good deal out of the fact that Neely was intelligent, sophisticated, and knew what he was doing when he helped hide the contract from his college and the NCAA. Is this a factor on which the case should turn? What if the deception were proposed by the club, not by the player? What if the player were relatively naive and uninformed and thus more likely to be led by the professional team?

3. The most obvious form of "unclean hands" argument is the claim that the party seeking injunctive relief has itself violated a key provision in the contract. A possible illustration is a dispute that took place in hockey in the mid–1990s. In the summer of 1993, Mike Keenan signed a five year, $4.5 million contract to coach the New York Rangers. In his first season with the Rangers, Keenan, Mark Messier, and the other Rangers delighted New York fans by winning that team's first Stanley Cup since 1940. Public attention to that long and exciting Stanley Cup playoff helped the NHL to secure a five-year network television commitment from Fox Broadcasting, enabled the Rangers' new ownership to sell the team (along with the Knicks, Madison Square Garden and the MSG sports station) for $1 billion, and earned Keenan a $600,000 contract bonus. However, as in his prior stints with the Philadelphia Flyers and Chicago Blackhawks, Keenan was soon feuding with the Rangers' management. By the end of his first season, Keenan wanted to leave the Rangers for another club where he could be general manager as well as coach. Thus, on Friday, July 15, 1994, after the Rangers had not paid the $600,000 bonus by the July 14th deadline (30 days after Keenan had earned it with the seventh game Stanley Cup victory), Keenan announced that his Rangers contract was terminated because of the team's violation of this essential contract term. After speaking with the Detroit Red Wings on Saturday, Keenan signed a five-year contract on Sunday with the St. Louis Blues to be their coach and general manager.

On Monday, the Rangers filed a complaint with NHL Commissioner, Gary Bettman, and a lawsuit in federal district court. During the next week, Keenan, the Rangers, and the Blues worked out a deal whereby the Blues would get Keenan and two veteran Rangers, Esa Tikkanen and Doug Lidster, and the Rangers would get budding star Petr Nedved and a $400,000 rebate on Keenan's bonus. However, Commissioner Bettman decided that discipline was also necessary: he fined the Rangers $25,000 for suing in court, the Blues and Red Wings $25,000 apiece for tampering with Rangers' personnel, and Keenan $100,000 (plus a 60–day suspension) for terminating his contract without first going to the Commissioner for a decision about the significance of this one-day delay in payment of the bonus. Suppose, though, that Keenan was leaving for a position in another league over which Bettman had no authority, and the bonus payment had been delayed for several weeks because of a dispute about whether Keenan had earned it. Would a court enjoin Keenan from moving to another team? (Ironically, when the Blues dismissed Keenan in the middle of the 1996–97 season, they claimed that this was justified by his having failed to live up to all of his promises under the contract. On the eve of yet another hearing before Bettman, lawyers for the two sides settled the case with the Blues agreeing to pay Keenan approximately two-thirds of the $6 million in salary he was still owed.)

4. The contract Ralph Neely had signed was for four years, and had a "no-cut" clause in it. This type of provision, which requires the team to continue paying the player his salary for the term of the contract even if he is not retained on the playing roster, has been quite rare in professional football, although not in baseball or basketball. (Even in the current era of NFL free agency under a salary cap, players like Deion Sanders receive at the time of signing just a "bonus" in the form of prepayment of part of their future salaries, with the remaining amounts left unguaranteed against release if their value declines.) Can you think of reasons why this might be the case for football players (though not for coaches like Jimmy Johnson or Bill Parcells)? Such a "semi-guarantee" in a contract differentiates it from those the early courts felt might lack mutuality because the team could terminate them at any time. By contrast to Neely's contract, Flower's two-year agreement with the Giants would have allowed the Giants to "cut" him at will. Should the fact that the contract a player was trying to back out of did or did not contain such a "semi-guarantee" affect the equities and perhaps the outcome of the case?

5. Note that in these early 1960's cases (contemporaries of *Barnett*), "unique skill and ability" was not an issue. Courts by this time had apparently adopted the *Barnett* position that the contract clause by which the player represented that he had such skill and ability, plus the very fact of the player being on a professional team roster, satisfied this requirement for an injunction.

The next case brings the story in football up to the 1970s and the challenge launched against the NFL by the World Football League (WFL). (In the course of his opinion, the judge describes comparable litigation involving basketball stars Rick Barry and Billy Cunningham, who were the objects of affection of both the NBA and the American Basketball Association (ABA), a competitor that emerged in the late 1960s.[j]) The interesting legal question is whether it is consistent with a

---

j. On the football background, see Harris, *The League*, note a above, 149–50, 168–70, 185–86, and 215–16. On the basketball rivalry, see Pluto, *Loose Balls*, note a above.

player's contractual obligations to his present team to sign a contract to play for another team in the future.

CINCINNATI BENGALS v. BERGEY
United States District Court, Southern District of Ohio, 1974.
453 F.Supp. 129.

PORTER, DISTRICT JUDGE.

[Bill Bergey, a star linebacker for the Cincinnati Bengals of the NFL, earned slightly less than $40,000 per year under a non-guaranteed contract for 1974 that gave the Bengals an option on his services for 1975. In April 1974 Bergey signed a no-cut, three-year contract with the Virginia Ambassadors of the newly formed WFL, who agreed to pay Bergey $125,000 per year plus a $150,000 signing bonus. This WFL contract was designed to begin with the 1976 football season, but would be accelerated forward if the Bengals released Bergey for any reason. Bergey was one of several Bengal stars pursued by the WFL (including starting linemen such as Bob Trumpy, Bob Johnson, and Rufus Mayes), as part of a WFL effort to stockpile a large number of NFL players for the new league. The threat of competition from the WFL moved NFL teams to elevate sharply their salary levels—the Bengals offered Bergey a new five-year contract for a total of $400,000. Unsuccessful in that bidding war, the Bengals sued Bergey, the Ambassadors, and the WFL, on the grounds that Bergey's future service agreement with the WFL team undermined and interfered with the Bengals' rights under their existing contract with Bergey.

Extensive testimony was offered about the special character of football as a sport and as an enterprise, particularly from Bengals' founder and head coach, Paul Brown, and its assistant coach, Bill Walsh. The judge concluded that, notwithstanding the special emotional demands of football, Bergey's signing of a "futures" contract with another team would not reduce his effectiveness with the Bengals during his existing contract. However, the judge felt there likely would be an adverse impact if several other Bengals' stars were to follow Bergey's lead, because "a football team is a sort of delicate mechanism, the success of whose operation is dependent upon the coordination of various cohesive units."

On the other side of the ledger, though, was the harmful effect on the WFL if its teams were barred from signing NFL contract players for promotion of this new venture. The court noted that "starting a new franchise and a new league is a risky business." It then continued ...]

* * *

Increased television coverage of professional football games has produced a sophisticated audience. The costs of fielding a competitive team are much higher today than in 1960. The cost of acquiring players of exceptional ability has contributed significantly to the substantial increase in ticket prices (though these price increases have not been proportionately as great as the increase in costs). The higher ticket prices mean that sports fans expect major league entertainment for their sports dollar. Faced with the stiff competition for the sports dollar by the NFL, as well as other professional sports organizations, the WFL seeks to ensure its future by signing established NFL players to give the new league "credibility" in the eyes of the public. The signing of professional players is also necessary to overcome the doubts of college players as to the future of the league.... Mr. Putnam stated that the signing of name players to future contracts is "essential" to the WFL's success, since the league's financial future is dependent in great part on the earliest possible public acceptance of the WFL as a marketer of "major league" professional football.

[Turning to the legal issues, the court considered two earlier precedents involving Rick Barry and Billy Cunningham, who had been the subject of a similar tug of war between the National Basketball Association and the American Basketball Association in the late 1960s.

Barry's case was extremely entangled. While under contract with the NBA's San Francisco Warriors for 1967–1968, Barry signed a three-year deal with the ABA's Oakland Oaks. Barry was enjoined from jumping to the Oaks for the 1967–1968 season (see *Lemat Corp. v. Barry*, 80 Cal.Rptr. 240 (Cal.App.1969)), but he did play for Oakland in 1968–69. However, when the Oaks were bought by the Washington Capitols, Barry, who wanted to remain in the Bay area, signed a five-year contract with the Warriors. When the Capitols sought injunctive relief against the NBA team, Barry's argument was that the Oakland contract had been tainted from the outset because of the conflict with his earlier agreement with the Warriors. The Ninth Circuit rejected this argument in *Washington Capitols Basketball Club v. Barry*, 419 F.2d 472 (9th Cir.1969). There was no actionable wrong in an athlete (like any other employee) signing a new contract during the period of his existing contract, as long as "performance and consideration" under the new contract were to begin after expiry of the existing agreement, and there was no "encouragement" to terminate the latter contract early.

A similar ruling was rendered in *Munchak Corp. v. Cunningham*, 457 F.2d 721 (4th Cir.1972), in which the court refused to nullify Cunningham's contract to play for the Carolina Cougars in the 1971–1972 season, even though the three-year agreement had been signed in August 1969 when Cunningham was under contract to the Philadelphia 76ers. The judge in the *Bergey* case then addressed and rejected the Bengals' argument that judicial precedents from basketball should not govern the assertedly different world of professional football.]

* * *

When *Barry* and *Cunningham* are applied to the case at bar, the Court can only conclude that neither the WFL nor Bergey committed a tortious or otherwise unlawful act in entering into negotiations for and reaching agreement upon a contract for Bergey's personal services to commence after the expiration of his contract with the Bengals. In the language of *Cunningham*, there are no more obligations to be protected by either party to the Bengals contract after May 1, 1976.

Plaintiff argues that the acceleration clause of Bergey's WFL contract induces Bergey to seek his release prior to his NFL contract's expiration. We reject this argument, however, because we accept as true Bergey's testimony that he has no intention of seeking an early release. And, notwithstanding plaintiff's interpretation of *Barry*, we do not read the Ninth Circuit's opinion in that case as granting to Barry the right to breach his contract. Bergey will be liable should he breach his contract while its terms are still in effect.

* * *

In short, we conclude that *Barry* and *Cunningham* support the proposition that it is not illegal for either the player or the sports organization, at the time when the player is under a valid contract to one team, to negotiate and enter into a contract with a different, competing, team and league, under the terms of which the player agrees to render his services at the expiration of his current contract.

* * *

Harm To Public Interest

* * *

Next, we flesh out the bare-bones conclusion that plaintiff has failed to show an absence of harm to the public interest if an injunction is granted herein. As we view it, the "public interest" within the meaning of that phrase as it is used here is the policy such as that behind the antitrust laws to encourage to the fullest extent practicable free and open competition in the marketplace. Restraints on competition are not favored.

* * *

The Court would be blind if it did not recognize that there is a public interest of another sort. This is the concern among fans over the actual and prospective loss of key members of a team of which they are devoted followers and the effect this may have on that team's "chances." It is clear that the Court cannot take such "public interest" into consideration. The only public interest that can properly be taken into account is the policy of the law to encourage free competition in the marketplace. Hence, the denial of an injunction is not a case of the Court's turning its back on the fans and the owners of the plaintiff's franchise, as the plaintiff improperly suggested in final argument that it might be.

Harm To WFL And Plaintiff

* * *

The conclusion that plaintiff has not made a clear showing of irreparable injury to itself is a difficult one to make. One reason it is, is that there is nothing to go on because this case is unique. As pointed out by Coach Brown, in all his forty years: "I've never had one like this, where I had a football player playing for me who is also under contract to somebody else." For another, while it may be too late to close the barn door as far as Bergey and Chomyszak are concerned, the threatened damage from the loss of Bob Johnson, et al., may not occur, and will not occur, if the Bengals match any offer they get from a WFL team. The Bengals argue that the fact that in order to match WFL offers they may have to tear up existing contracts and pay more for present services is evidence of irreparable injury.

We recognize that it will cost the Bengals something to bid for the future services of its players to preserve the continuity of the team's performance when present contracts expire. We do not, however, follow the argument that that is evidence of irreparable injury. Prior to the emergence of the World Football League, the teams in the National Football League could rest in relative assurance that the services of their players presently under short-term contracts would remain available beyond the termination dates should the clubs desire to offer players further contracts. The absence of a competitor league justified that self-assurance, for the NFL, until now, has been "the only game in town." With the rise of the WFL, the NFL can no longer rely upon the absence of a competitor for protection of its claims to the future services of players, for which the established teams have neither bargained nor paid consideration.

It is not the players' present services for which the clubs will have to pay more, for those are protected by contracts which can presumably be enforced in the usual manner. It is only when the NFL chooses (and such decision is likely) to join the competition for the later services of its players that it will incur these higher costs. In our best judgment, such higher costs will be attributable to competition and not unfair competition.

* * *

Injunction denied.

Questions for Discussion

1. For reasons that will be explained in Chapter 8, interleague competition for player services had disappeared from all professional sports by the 1990s. The emergence of free agency has, however, generated extensive intraleague competition for player talent. In the case of players, the collective agreements between owners and players associations preclude any discussions, let alone contract signings, between a player and a new team until the prior contract has expired on the specified date when free agency begins. There have, however, been some "futures" contract controversies involving coaches.

The most notable such controversy occurred in January 1997 in football. While Bill Parcells was readying his New England Patriots to play the Green Bay Packers in the Super Bowl, Parcell's lawyer and his agent were telling

Patriots' owner Robert Kraft that their client would be exercising his right to terminate his contract at the end of that season. Parcells would be moving, instead, to New York to try to revive the last-place Jets. The Patriots asked NFL Commissioner Paul Tagliabue to exercise his authority under Article VIII(3)(b) of the NFL constitution, which gives the commissioner "full, complete, and final jurisdiction to arbitrate any dispute between any player, coach and/or other employee of any member of the League ... and any member club ..." While the Patriots lost the Super Bowl, they won the arbitration verdict from Tagliabue, who read Parcell's contract as giving him the right to terminate the contract only for new positions other than coaching or its equivalent.

Parcells then signed a contract with the Jets under which he would coach and manage the Jets beginning in 1998 (when all of Parcell's obligations to the Patriots would have expired), and for 1997 he would serve just as a paid "consultant" to his past (and future) assistant head coach Bill Belichuk. Needless to say, the Patriots immediately went back to the Commissioner, claiming that this "consulting" contract was just a subterfuge, and the Jets were guilty of "tampering" with their coaching property. This time Tagliabue was able to use his position to persuade the two sides to settle the dispute, with Parcells leading the Jets immediately, and the Patriots getting four draft picks over the next three rounds.

Stepping back from this case, as a matter of sports policy should leagues require that all the contracts of its players, coaches, or front office staff have a term precluding any contract discussion, negotiation, or contract signings with any other team until the season is over and the existing contract has expired? Is there more or less justification for such contract limits in the case of players and coaches, or movie stars and directors, or business executives, or law firm partnerships? Is it unfair that league rules do not impose reciprocal contract constraints on players or coaches who may be fired and replaced during midseason (though their remaining salary may have to be paid if it was guaranteed for the full season)? Should the law treat such a rule differently insofar as it is applied to intraleague "futures" contracts (as in the *Parcells* case) than to interleague "futures" (as in the *Bergey* case)?

Litigation about player (or coaching) contracts vividly displays the conflict between two visions of contract and its enforcement. One view pictures contracts as personal promises that create moral obligations and entitlements and are worthy of as much legal teeth as the law can sensibly provide. From this perspective, while judges might reasonably be cautious about issuing a specific order forcing a player to play for the team to which he is under contract, they should not hesitate to enjoin him from playing for another team, even if financial pressures soon yield the first result.

An alternative conception of contract sees it as an economic instrument for whose enforcement the law should be deployed only to the extent such judicial intervention produces an efficient allocation of society's resources. Under this theory, a player should be entitled to break an initial commitment to one team as long as he is willing to pay that team for its financial losses suffered through loss of his services. The assumption is that such contract breaches will be committed only when it is socially efficient to do so—in other words, when someone else finds the player's services more valuable and thus worth enough extra money to leave the player better off after compensation damages are paid to the original team.[k]

The cases we have read leave no doubt that in terms of bottom-line results, if not underlying rationale, the courts have embraced the first view about player contracts. But is this judicial verdict socially desirable? Consider these specific questions about sports cases:

1. Is society (at least the sports community) better off with the athlete playing for the original team or the new team?

2. Is it possible to calculate the actual damages inflicted on a team if a player defects? By analogy, how would you go about calculating the tort damages payable to a team that lost a star player because of physical injuries due to someone else's fault? (As we will see in Chapter 3, precisely that challenge was faced by the court in a suit brought by the NBA Houston Rockets against the Los Angeles Lakers when star Rockets' forward Rudy Tomjanovich was severely injured by a punch thrown by the Lakers' Kermit Washington.)

3. Suppose that the court issues an injunction that forbids a player to move to another team. Is the player likely to stay and perform effectively for his original team? If not, has litigation been fruitless for that team? Or has the club nonetheless gained something of tangible value from the judicial order? Recall the Coase Theorem which you may have encountered in your first year courses, and for which Coase won the 1992 Nobel Prize in Economics: the law's initial allocation of the right to an asset does not dictate its ultimate destination so long as some voluntary transactions are permitted and are feasible regarding disposition of the asset. What does this theorem[l] imply for the way these legal doctrines play themselves out in sports over the longer run?

4. An alternative way of characterizing the issue is the following: whereas limiting the team's remedy to damages treats the contract as simply a *liability* rule, giving the club injunctive relief means that the contract has, in effect, conferred on the team a *property* right in the player's services.[m] In the sports

---

k. For a helpful appraisal of these two competing viewpoints, see Laycock, *The Death of the Irreparable Injury Rule*, note d above, in particular, Chapter 11 "Holmes, Posner, and Efficient Breach."

l. Which, interestingly, was anticipated in one of the key early articles on the economics of sports: Simon Rottenberg, *The Baseball Players' Labor Market*, 64 J. of Political Economy 242 (1956).

m. See Guido Calabresi and A. Douglas Melamed, *Property Rules, Liability Rules,*

world, the latter term is not merely a rhetorical label. As we noted earlier, a standard feature of the player contract in every sport has been a right of the team to sell or trade the player's services to another team. Owners have used that right to sell even the greatest players in the game—Babe Ruth was sold by the Boston Red Sox to the New York Yankees in 1919 and Wayne Gretzky was sold by the Edmonton Oilers to the Los Angeles Kings in 1988. As long ago as *Lajoie*, however, courts have observed that players are paid more than generously for giving the teams that prerogative. Is this judicial sentiment apt?

C. RESERVE SYSTEM AND RESTRAINT OF TRADE

The cases and materials up to this point of the chapter have provided a rather truncated picture of the sports industry setting in which player contracts are initially signed. The next case brings that setting to the fore—in particular, the key ingredients in the reserve system first developed by baseball and then copied in varying ways by the other professional sports.[n] To ease reading of the *Chase* opinion, which dwells on the technical language of the reserve system, we provide this capsule summary of that contractual regime:

1. Each team in a league was entitled to list a certain number of players with whom it had a contract relationship and to which the team claimed exclusive rights.

2. All other teams in the league agreed to respect the reserve lists of their fellow league members and not to "tamper" with another team's players by inducing them to move.

3. All teams in the league agreed to sign players only to a single standard form contract. A key provision in that contract was that when its term expired, the team retained an option to renew the contract for another season with the same provisions as before—including this option clause—except for salary. In case of disagreement over salary, the team had the prerogative to set the salary for the upcoming year.

4. A further feature of the reserve system was the draft, whereby major league teams agreed to select (in reverse order of finish in the previous season) from among minor league players talented enough to play in the major leagues. The modern rookie draft was actually first developed in football in the 1930s, emulated in basketball in the late 1940s, and adopted by baseball and hockey only in the mid–1960s. The players selected were reserved to the

and Inalienability: One View of the Cathedral, 85 Harvard L. Rev. 1089 (1972).

n. On the historical evolution of the reserve clause in baseball, see *Report on Organized Baseball*, note a above, and Seymour, *Baseball: The Early Years*, note a above. For the emergence of the Federal League that gave rise to the *Chase* decision, see Seymour, *Baseball: The Golden Age*, note a above, at 196–213.

drafting club even before they signed the first standard form contract.

With this background, you will now encounter a rather different judicial perspective on the enforceability of player contracts signed in such an environment.

AMERICAN LEAGUE BASEBALL CLUB OF CHICAGO v. CHASE

Supreme Court, Erie County, New York, 1914.
86 Misc. 441, 149 N.Y.S. 6.

BISSELL, JUDGE.

[Hal Chase played first base for the Chicago White Sox in the American League. In March 1914 he signed a one-year contract with the Sox for the upcoming season. However, on June 15, 1914, Chase gave the White Sox notice that he was terminating the contract, and on June 20, he jumped to the Buffalo team in the new Federal Baseball League. The White Sox filed suit for breach of contract and sought an immediate injunction barring Chase from playing for Buffalo.

The court quoted from a number of provisions in Major League Baseball's National Agreement, the Rules of the National Commission, and the terms of the standardized player agreement. This combination of baseball rules gave each team an "absolute right and title" to players it had "selected" (or drafted), required all players to enter into the standard contract prescribed by the National Commission that oversaw baseball, and incorporated in this contract a term that gave the team the option to renew its player's contract (if the team so chose) on the same terms as in the previous year, but also gave the team the right to terminate a player's contract on ten days notice (the provision that had generated the "mutuality" issue in the earlier *Lajoie* case.]

* * *

It appears that originally the defendant was a "selected" player; but whether he was a selected player at the time he entered the service of the plaintiff is immaterial. Had he come from the vacant lots of the cities, or the fields of the country, or from the college campus, and therefore been "a free agent" at the time he made his entry into "organized baseball," the result would have been the same. If a sale or trade is to be made by one major league club to another, § 3 of article VI governs, and "The right and title of a major league club to its players shall be absolute."

If a sale or trade is to be made by a major league club to a minor league club, § 9 of article VI governs, and the sale or trade is not absolute until waivers have been obtained from the other major league clubs. Thus a player in the highest league, without the exercise of any individual choice, may be required to take service with a club of a lower league where smaller salaries are paid, and where both the aggregate of the salary list and the salary of each individual player is subject to strict limitation under the terms of the National Agreement. No opportunity is afforded the player to solicit employment upon his own account. No right is afforded to enable him to resist an unjust limitation upon his power to earn. No consideration is afforded either himself or his family with respect to choosing a home. In short, he is placed where he must, at all times while playing in "organized baseball," consider that his home is only the place in which his services are for the time being controlled.

The baseball player, even though about to be discharged, is still a thing of value to the club owner. The termination of the obligations by the club owner pursuant to the 10-day provision, is not accomplished by him without securing some return. If the player goes to another major league club, it is either in exchange for some other more desired player or players, or for the waiver price; and the same is true if the discharged player is sent to a league of lower grade.

It seems that the promotion of the ball player is also hedged about with such limitations as to make the property in him absolute whether he will accept terms or not, and to make those terms when arrived at only liberal enough to prevent the player from seeking other means of earning his livelihood.

* * *

"Organized baseball" as conducted under the terms of the National Agreement further seeks to enforce and perpetuate its title to and control of its players as follows:

Section 1, Article VI, of the National Agreement provides:

All parties to this agreement pledge themselves to recognize the right of reservation and respect contracts between players and clubs under its protection. No club operating under this agreement shall at any time negotiate for the purchase or lease of the property of another club without first securing the consent of such club.

Section 2 of Article VI is as follows:

Any club or league which harbors a player who refuses to observe his contract with a club member of any party to this agreement, or to abide by its reservation, shall be considered an outlaw organization, and its claim to contractual and territorial rights ignored.

Thus the baseball player is made a chattel; the title of the club to the player ... is made absolute.

Section 2 of Article VI recognizes the property of the club in the player as existing under two conditions: First, under a contract; and, second, under reserve without a contract.

* * *

If the player has ideas of his own, which fail to accord with those of the club, the National Agreement enables the club to enforce its own terms, leaving the player the option to enter some other trade, calling, or profession, if he is not satisfied.

The scheme of the National Agreement to perpetuate control over a player by means of contracts apparently legal is interesting and pertinent. Each term contract, as appears by § 1 of Article VIII, must contain a reserve clause or option to renew, and this article of the National Agreement is further enforced by Section A, Rule 17, of the National Commission, which is as follows:

> A nonreserve clause in the contract of a major league player without the approval of the commission or of a minor league player without the approval of the National Board shall not be valid.

So that each new contract of the player must contain a reserve clause, and so by a series of contracts, "organized baseball" is able to perpetuate its control over the services of the player. But if, upon the other hand, a contract is at any time unobtainable, or even in fact not in good faith sought to be obtained, as the club owner might offer an immoderately low salary, then the provisions for reservation and the respecting thereof, apply and safeguard the "absolute title" of the club.

But why should a player enter into a contract when his liberty of conduct and of contract is thus curtailed? The answer is that he has no recourse. He must either take the contract under the provisions of the National Agreement, whose organization controls practically all of the good ball players of the country, or resort to some other occupation.

[The court then quoted several provisions of the National Agreement and Rules promulgated by the National Commission which prohibited teams from using players who had not signed formal playing contracts that contained the renewable option clause.]

* * *

This somewhat extended analysis shows to what extent the contract between the plaintiff and the defendant presents reciprocal and mutual, enforceable obligations. The plaintiff can terminate the contract at any time on 10 days' notice. The defendant is bound to many obligations under the remarkable provisions of the National Agreement. The Player's Contract executed in accordance with its terms, binds him, not only for the playing season of six months from April 14th to October 14th, but also for another season, if the plaintiff chooses to exercise its option, and if it insists upon the requirement of an option clause in each succeeding contract, the defendant can be held for a term of years. His only alternative is to abandon his vocation. Can it fairly be claimed that there is mutuality in such a contract? The absolute lack of mutuality, both of obligation and of remedy, in this contract, would prevent a court of equity from making it the basis of equitable relief by injunction or otherwise. The negative covenant, under such circumstances, is without a consideration to support it, and is unenforceable by injunction.

[The court then addressed the question of whether this contractual regime in baseball violated federal antitrust law.]

The novel argument is presented with much earnestness by the learned counsel for the defendant that the combination formed by the operation of the National Agreement and the rules and regulations of the National Commission thereunder, with which the defendant is connected through his contract with the plaintiff, is in direct violation of an act to protect trade and commerce against unlawful restraints and monopolies, in force July 2, 1890, and popularly known as the Sherman Antitrust Law. It is apparent from the analysis already set forth of the agreement and rules forming the combination of the baseball business, referred to as "organized baseball," that a monopoly of baseball as a business has been ingeniously devised and created in so far as a monopoly can be created among free men; but I cannot agree to the proposition that the business of baseball for profit is interstate trade or commerce, and therefore subject to the provisions of the Sherman Act. An examination of the cases cited by the defendant confirms rather than changes my conclusion.

* * *

Baseball is an amusement, a sport, a game that comes clearly within the civil and criminal law of the state, and it is not a commodity or an article of merchandise subject to the regulation of Congress on the theory that it is interstate commerce.

[The court then turned to the question of what was the appropriate treatment under the common law of player contracts entered into within this baseball structure.]

Another question to be determined upon this motion is whether so-called "organized baseball," operating under the provisions of the National Agreement and the Rules and Contracts subsidiary thereto, is an illegal combination or monopoly in contravention of the common law. The affidavits read on the hearing of this motion show that a combination of 40 leagues, major and minor, has been formed under the terms of the National Agreement, controlling for profit the services of 10,000 players of professional baseball, practically all of the good or skillful players in the country. The analysis of the National Agreement and the Rules of the Commission, controlling the services of these skilled laborers, and providing for their purchase, sale, exchange, draft, reduction, discharge, and blacklisting, would seem to establish a species of quasi peonage unlawfully controlling and interfering with the personal freedom of the men employed. It appears that there is only one league of any importance operating independently of the National Commission, and that is the newly organized Federal League which comprises eight clubs in eight cities. "Organized baseball" is now as complete a monopoly of the baseball business for profit as any monopoly can be made. It is in contravention of the common law, in that it invades the right to labor as a property right, in that it invades the right to contract as a property right, and in that it is a combination to restrain and control the exercise of a profession or calling.

* * *

If a baseball player like the defendant, who has made baseball playing his profession and means of earning a livelihood, desires to be employed at the work for which he is qualified and is entitled to earn his best compensation, he must submit to dominion over his personal freedom and the control of his services by sale, transfer, or exchange, without his consent, or abandon his vocation and seek employment at some other kind of labor. While the services of these baseball players are ostensibly secured by voluntary contracts, a study of the system as hereinabove set forth, and as practiced under the plan of the National Agreement, reveals the involuntary character of the servitude which is imposed upon players by the strength of the combination controlling the labor of practically all of the players in the country. This is so great as to make it necessary for the player either to take the contract prescribed by the commission or abandon baseball as a profession and seek some other mode of earning a livelihood. There is no difference in principle between the system of servitude built up by the operation of this National Agreement, which as has been shown, provides for the purchase, sale, barter, and exchange of the services of baseball players—skilled laborers—without their consent, and the system of peonage brought into the United States from Mexico and thereafter existing for a time within the territory of New Mexico. The quasi peonage of baseball players under the operations of this plan and agreement is contrary to the spirit of American institutions, and is contrary to the spirit of the Constitution of the United States. It is time to heed the warning of that great jurist, the former Chief Judge of the Court of Appeals, Judge Cullen, who thought it advisable to take for the subject of his annual address at the last meeting of the New York State Bar association "The Decline of Personal Liberty in America," as evidenced by recent legislation and judicial decisions. The sanction by the courts of the system here outlined would indeed be further evidence of "The Decline of Personal Liberty."

The system created by "organized baseball" in recent years presents the question of the establishment of a scheme by which the personal freedom, the right to contract for their labor wherever they will, of 10,000 skilled laborers, is placed under the dominion of a benevolent despotism through the operation of the monopoly established by the National Agreement. This case does not present the simple question of a laborer who has entered into a fair contract for his personal services.

While the question of the dissolution of this combination on the ground of its illegality is not before this court for decision, it has nevertheless been thought necessary for the purpose of ascertaining whether or not this plaintiff comes into a court of equity with clean hands to inquire into the organization and operations of the combination to which the plaintiff is a party. A court of equity, insisting that "he who comes into equity must come with clean hands," will not lend its aid to promote an unconscionable transaction of the character which the plaintiff is endeavoring to maintain and strengthen by its application for this injunction. The court will not assist in enforcing an agreement which is a part of a general plan having for its object the maintenance of a monopoly, interference with the personal liberty of a citizen, and the control of his free right to labor wherever and for whom he pleases, and will not extend its aid to further the purposes and practices of an unlawful combination, by restraining the defendant from working for any one but the plaintiff.

Injunction vacated.

The court refers to Hal Chase as a "special, unique, and extraordinary baseball player." How extraordinary the judge simply did not realize. In his definitive history of baseball, Harold Seymour characterizes Chase as a "malignant genius."[o] While only Lou Gehrig and George Sisler were comparable first basemen on the field, Chase was the "archetype of all crooked ballplayers . . . a full-fledged fixer and gambler." Indeed, at the end of the 1918 baseball season, Chase was charged by his manager, Hall-of-Famer Christy Mathewson, with having tried to persuade his teammates to lose games on which Chase had bets riding. Though three players on his team testified to this effect in a hearing before the National League President, the President absolved Chase by saying that the players had misunderstood the superstar's joking comments. Chase returned to play for the Giants the next season and to serve as the intermediary between the gamblers and the White Sox players who were involved in the fixing of the 1919 World Series. Chase was indicted by a Chicago grand jury for his role in this affair, but the State of California refused to extradite him for trial.[p]

Whether or not Chase himself was a deserving candidate for the judicial sentiment expressed in the prior decision—a victim of "quasi peonage"—his case does cast in a rather different light the contracts signed by Lajoie a decade earlier or even by Barnett fifty years later. One question is whether the league arrangements justify the court's refusal to enforce individual contracts through injunctions. While over the years most courts have answered "no," a more important question is whether even a hands-off approach by courts to player contracts would be a sufficient response to the problems players have with these league arrangements. The next case introduces the potential leverage that antitrust law might give players in their struggle against the reserve system. (As noted earlier, Chapter 9 examines the possible use by rival leagues of antitrust law against that system.)

In *Chase*, the player used antitrust policy as a *shield* against a contract injunction sought by the American League Club that had reserved his services. That tactic was sufficient for Chase's purposes because another club in the rival Federal League had been prepared to

---

o. See Seymour, *Baseball: The Golden Age*, note a above, at 288–93.

p. See Eliot Asinof, *Eight Men Out* (New York: Henry Holt, 1963).

bid handsomely for his services. However, since the demise of the Federal League just a year later, Major League Baseball has faced no such competition in its players market, and other professional leagues have encountered rivals only intermittently. Whether or not a judge enforces the restrictive terms in a contract between a player and his team, if the other teams in the league have agreed not to "tamper" with the services of their respective players except under strictly defined rules and conditions (an agreement enforced by the commissioner), there will be no effective market for the players' services. That is why players have tried to use antitrust law as a *sword* against such an intraleague arrangement.

Federal antitrust law dates back to 1890, the year the Sherman Antitrust Act was enacted. Section 1 of that Act makes illegal any "contract, combination, or conspiracy in restraint of trade," and § 2 prohibits the effort by any person(s) to "monopolize or attempt or conspire to monopolize trade." The Justice Department is authorized to proceed either criminally or civilly against antitrust violators, but it has done so only once in the sports setting (in 1953, against the National Football League's broadcasting restrictions: see Chapter 7). In addition, the Federal Trade Commission (FTC) can issue cease and desist orders against antitrust violators (though not against non-profit violators such as educational institutions), a power that the FTC has considered but never used in the world of sports. In sports, then, enforcement of antitrust law has been left to suits brought by private parties, who can win either treble damages or an injunction (the latter remedy first authorized by the Clayton Antitrust Act of 1914).

Very little use was made of antitrust law in sports until the late 1960s. One reason is that most professional sports did not become thriving business enterprises until that decade. Professional baseball, however, was already becoming a substantial sport and financial presence when the Sherman Act was passed in 1890.[q] The reasons for the lack of antitrust scrutiny of baseball's reserve clause and its other restrictive arrangements must be found within antitrust law itself.

The vast majority of antitrust suits, especially about the players market, have been brought under § 1 of the Sherman Act. There are three key components of this provision: there must be a *contract, combination,* or *conspiracy*; the combination must have produced a *restraint of trade*; and the restraint must affect *trade and commerce among the several states*. The last ingredient became the main obstacle to antitrust litigation against baseball, in a ruling handed down by the Supreme Court in *Federal Base Ball Club v. National League*, 259 U.S. 200 (1922) (in the aftermath of the failure of the Federal League). The subsequent history and the current baseball antitrust status are depicted in the following case.[r]

q. See Seymour, *Baseball: The Early Years*, note a above.

r. The memoirs of two of the key protagonists of the *Flood* litigation contain interesting and naturally conflicting perspec-

Sec. C   RESERVE SYSTEM & RESTRAINT OF TRADE   127

FLOOD v. KUHN

Supreme Court of the United States, 1972.
407 U.S. 258, 92 S.Ct. 2099, 32 L.Ed.2d 728.

JUSTICE BLACKMUN delivered the opinion of the Court.

[Curt Flood was an All–Star center fielder for the St. Louis Cardinals throughout the 1960s, helping lead his team to the World Series in 1964, 1967, and 1968. Flood's salary rose from $4,000 in his initial 1956 contract to $90,000 in 1969. In October 1969, Flood was stunned to learn that, at the age of 31, he had been traded to the Philadelphia Phillies. Although the Phillies offered him a pay raise to $100,000, Flood rejected the trade, declared himself a free agent, and filed suit to establish these rights under federal and state antitrust law (as well as under the Thirteenth Amendment's bar on "involuntary servitude"). After the lower courts had rejected his core antitrust claim based on the judicially-fashioned exemption for baseball, the Supreme Court accepted the case to take yet another look at this issue.]

* * *

For the third time in 50 years the Court is asked specifically to rule that professional baseball's reserve system is within the reach of the federal antitrust laws.[1] Collateral issues of state law and of federal labor policy are also advanced.

I

THE GAME

It is a century and a quarter since the New York Nine defeated the Knickerbockers 23 to 1 on Hoboken's Elysian Fields June 19, 1846, with Alexander Jay Cartwright as the instigator and the umpire. The teams were amateur, but the contest marked a significant date in baseball's

---

tives on the case. One book is by Marvin Miller, the head of the Major League Baseball Players' Association which actually brought and financed the antitrust litigation. See *A Whole Different Ball Game: The Sport and Business of Baseball* (New York: Birch Lane Press, 1991), in particular Chapter 10, "Flood Gate." The other book is by Bowie Kuhn, the Commissioner of Baseball who defended the suit. See *Hardball: The Education of a Baseball Commissioner* (New York: Times Books, 1987), in particular, Chapter 6, "Curt Flood, Meet Marvin Miller." The brief vignette on the *Flood* case in Bob Woodward & Scott Armstrong, *The Brethren: Inside the Supreme Court* 189–92 (New York: Simon and Schuster, 1979), explains why we have reproduced an apparently irrelevant section of the opinion—"The Game." Apparently, the justices spent as much time debating this list of star players as they did the legal issues. Indeed, it was not until Justice Marshall observed the total absence in the draft opinion of any black baseball players that Justice Blackmun added Jackie Robinson, Roy Campanella, and Satchel Paige. Still Justice Blackmun was chagrined to learn later that he had omitted Mel Ott from his list of greats. Finally, the most recent scholarly critiques are by Stephen F. Ross, *Reconsidering* Flood v Kuhn, 12 U. Miami Enter. and Sports L. Rev. 169 (1995), and Andrew Zimbalist, *Baseball Economics and Antitrust Immunity*, 4 Seton Hall J. of Sports L. 287 (1994).

1. The reserve system, publicly introduced into baseball contracts in 1887, centers in the uniformity of player contracts; the confinement of the player to the club that has him under the contract; the assignability of the player's contract; and the ability of the club annually to renew the contract unilaterally, subject to a stated salary minimum....

beginnings. That early game led ultimately to the development of professional baseball and its tightly organized structure.

The Cincinnati Red Stockings came into existence in 1869 upon an outpouring of local pride. With only one Cincinnatian on the payroll, this professional team traveled over 11,000 miles that summer, winning 56 games and tying one. Shortly thereafter, on St. Patrick's Day in 1871, the National Association of Professional Baseball Players was founded and the professional league was born.

The ensuing colorful days are well known. The ardent follower and the student of baseball know of General Abner Doubleday; the formation of the National League in 1876; Chicago's supremacy in the first year's competition under the leadership of Al Spalding and with Cap Anson at third base; the formation of the American Association and then of the Union Association in the 1880s; the introduction of Sunday baseball; interleague warfare with cut-rate admission prices and player raiding; the development of the reserve "clause"; the emergence in 1885 of the Brotherhood of Professional Ball Players, and in 1890 of the Players League; the appearance of the American League, or "junior circuit," in 1901, rising from the minor Western Association; the first World Series in 1903, disruption in 1904, and the Series' resumption in 1905; the short-lived Federal League on the majors' scene during World War I years; the troublesome and discouraging episode of the 1919 Series; the home run ball; the shifting of franchises; the expansion of the leagues; the installation in 1965 of the major league draft of potential new players; and the formation of the Major League Baseball Players Association in 1966.

Then there are the many names, celebrated for one reason or another, that have sparked the diamond and its environs and that have provided tinder for recaptured thrills, for reminiscence and comparisons, and for conversation and anticipation in-season and off-season: Ty Cobb, Babe Ruth, Tris Speaker, Walter Johnson, Henry Chadwick, Eddie Collins, Lou Gehrig, Grover Cleveland Alexander, Rogers Hornsby, Harry Hooper, Goose Goslin, Jackie Robinson, Honus Wagner, Joe McCarthy, John McGraw, Deacon Phillippe, Rube Marquard, Christy Mathewson, Tommy Leach, Big Ed Delahanty, Davy Jones, Germany Schaefer, King Kelly, Big Dan Brouthers, Wahoo Sam Crawford, Wee Willie Keeler, Big Ed Walsh, Jimmy Austin, Fred Snodgrass, Satchel Paige, Hugh Jennings, Fred Merkle, Iron Man McGinnity, Three–Finger Brown, Harry and Stan Coveleski, Connie Mack, Al Bridwell, Red Ruffing, Amos Rusie, Cy Young, Smokey Joe Wood, Chief Meyers, Chief Bender, Bill Klem, Hans Lobert, Johnny Evers, Joe Tinker, Roy Campanella, Miller Huggins, Rube Bressler, Dazzy Vance, Edd Roush, Bill Wambsganss, Clark Griffith, Branch Rickey, Frank Chance, Cap Anson, Nap Lajoie, Sad Sam Jones, Bob O'Farrell, Lefty O'Doul, Bobby Veach, Willie Kamm, Heinie Groh, Lloyd and Paul Waner, Stuffy McInnis, Charles Comiskey, Roger Bresnahan, Bill Dickey, Zack Wheat, George Sisler, Charlie Gehringer, Eppa Rixey, Harry Heilmann, Fred Clarke, Dizzy Dean, Hank Greenberg, Pie Traynor, Rube Waddell, Bill Terry,

Carl Hubbell, Old Hoss Radbourne, Moe Berg, Rabbit Maranville, Jimmie Foxx, Lefty Grove. The list seems endless.

And one recalls the appropriate reference to the "World Serious," attributed to Ring Lardner, Sr.; Ernest L. Thayer's "Casey at the Bat";[4] the ring of "Tinker to Evers to Chance";[5] and all the other happenings, habits, and superstitions about and around baseball that made it the "national pastime" or, depending upon the point of view, "the great American tragedy."

* * *

IV

THE LEGAL BACKGROUND

A. *Federal Baseball Club v. National League*, 259 U.S. 200 (1922), was a suit for treble damages instituted by a member of the Federal League (Baltimore) against the National and American Leagues and others. The plaintiff obtained a verdict in the trial court, but the Court of Appeals reversed. The main brief filed by the plaintiff with this Court discloses that it was strenuously argued, among other things, that the business in which the defendants were engaged was interstate commerce; that the interstate relationship among the several clubs, located as they were in different States, was predominant; that organized baseball represented an investment of colossal wealth; that it was an engagement in moneymaking; that gate receipts were divided by agreement between the home club and the visiting club; and that the business of baseball was to be distinguished from the mere playing of the game as a sport for physical exercise and diversion.

Mr. Justice Holmes, in speaking succinctly for a unanimous Court, said:

---

4. Millions have known and enjoyed baseball. One writer knowledgeable in the field of sports almost assumed that everyone did until, one day, he discovered otherwise:

I knew a cove who'd never heard of Washington and Lee,
Caesar and Napoleon from the ancient jamboree,
But, bli'me, there are queerer things than anything like that,
For here's a cove who never heard of 'Casey at the Bat'!

Ten million never heard of Keats, or Shelley, Burns or Poe;
But they know "the air was shattered by the force of Casey's blow"
They never heard of Shakespeare, nor of Dickens, like as not,
But they know the somber drama from old Mudville's haunted lot.

He never heard of Casey! Am I dreaming? Is it true?
Is fame but windblown ashes when the summer day is through?
Does greatness fade so quickly and is grandeur doomed to die.
That bloomed in early morning, ere the dusk rides down the sky?

"He Never Heard of Casey," Grantland Rice, The Sportlight, New York Herald Tribune, June 1, 1926, p. 23.

5. "These are the saddest of possible words,
'Tinker to Evers to Chance.'
Trio of bear cubs, and fleeter than birds,
'Tinker to Evers to Chance.'

Ruthlessly pricking our gonfalon bubble,
Making a Giant hit into a double—
Words that are weighty with nothing but trouble:
'Tinker to Evers to Chance.''

Franklin Pierce Adams, *Baseball's Sad Lexicon*.

The business is giving exhibitions of baseball, which are purely state affairs.... But the fact that in order to give the exhibitions the Leagues must induce free persons to cross state lines and must arrange and pay for their doing so is not enough to change the character of the business.... [T]he transport is a mere incident, not the essential thing. That to which it is incident, the exhibition, although made for money would not be called trade or commerce in the commonly accepted use of those words. As it is put by the defendant, personal effort, not related to production, is not a subject of commerce. That which in its consummation is not commerce does not become commerce among the States because the transportation that we have mentioned takes place. To repeat the illustrations given by the Court below, a firm of lawyers sending out a member to argue a case, or the Chautauqua lecture bureau sending out lecturers, does not engage in such commerce because the lawyer or lecturer goes to another State.

If we are right the plaintiff's business is to be described in the same way and the restrictions by contract that prevented the plaintiff from getting players to break their bargains and the other conduct charged against the defendants were not an interference with commerce among the States.[10]

* * *

B. In the years that followed, baseball continued to be subject to intermittent antitrust attack. The courts, however, rejected these challenges on the authority of *Federal Baseball*. In some cases stress was laid, although unsuccessfully, on new factors such as the development of radio and television with their substantial additional revenues to baseball. For the most part, however, the Holmes opinion was generally and necessarily accepted as controlling authority. And in the 1952 Report of the Subcommittee on *Study of Monopoly Power*, of the House Committee on the Judiciary, H.R. Rep. No. 2002, 82d Cong., 2d Sess., 229, it was said, in conclusion:

On the other hand the overwhelming preponderance of the evidence established baseball's need for some sort of reserve clause. Baseball's history shows that chaotic conditions prevailed when there was no reserve clause. Experience points to no feasible substitute to protect the integrity of the game or to guarantee a comparatively even competitive struggle. The evidence adduced at the hearings would clearly not justify the enactment of legislation flatly condemning the reserve clause.

---

10. "What really saved baseball, legally at least, for the next half century was the protective canopy spread over it by the United States Supreme Court's decision in the Baltimore Federal League antitrust suit against Organized Baseball in 1922.... It should be noted that, contrary to what many believe, Holmes did call baseball a business; time and again those who have not troubled to read the text of the decision have claimed incorrectly that the court said baseball was a sport and not a business." 2 H. Seymour, *Baseball* 420 (1971).

C. The Court granted certiorari, in the *Toolson, Kowalski*, and *Corbett* cases, and, by a short per curiam (Warren, C.J., and Black, Frankfurter, Douglas, Jackson, Clark, and Minton, JJ.), affirmed the judgments of the respective courts of appeals in those three cases. *Toolson v. New York Yankees, Inc.*, 346 U.S. 356 (1953). *Federal Baseball* was cited as holding "that the business of providing public baseball games for profit between clubs of professional baseball players was not within the scope of the federal antitrust laws," and:

> Congress has had the ruling under consideration but has not seen fit to bring such business under these laws by legislation having prospective effect. The business has thus been left for thirty years to develop, on the understanding that it was not subject to existing antitrust legislation. The present cases ask us to overrule the prior decision and, with retrospective effect, hold the legislation applicable. We think that if there are evils in this field which now warrant application to it of the antitrust laws it should be by legislation. Without re-examination of the underlying issues, the judgments below are affirmed on the authority of *Federal Baseball Club of Baltimore v. National League of Professional Baseball Clubs*, supra, so far as that decision determines that Congress had no intention of including the business of baseball within the scope of the federal antitrust laws.

This quotation reveals four reasons for the Court's affirmance of *Toolson* and its companion cases: (a) Congressional awareness for three decades of the Court's ruling in *Federal Baseball*, coupled with congressional inaction. (b) The fact that baseball was left alone to develop for that period upon the understanding that the reserve system was not subject to existing federal antitrust laws. (c) A reluctance to overrule *Federal Baseball* with consequent retroactive effect. (d) A professed desire that any needed remedy be provided by legislation rather than by court decree. The emphasis in *Toolson* was on the determination, attributed even to *Federal Baseball*, that Congress had no intention to include baseball within the reach of the federal antitrust laws.

[Justice Blackmun then described and quoted from *United States v. Shubert*, 348 U.S. 222 (1955), in which the Court refused to extend professional baseball's antitrust immunity to a nationwide theatre company. Chief Justice Warren's opinion stresses that the result in *Toolson* was based on *Federal Baseball* and stare decisis and concluded that "[i]f the *Toolson* holding is to be expanded—or contracted—the appropriate remedy lies with Congress."]

* * *

E. *United States v. International Boxing Club*, 348 U.S. 236 (1955), was a companion to *Shubert* and was decided the same day. This was a civil antitrust action against defendants engaged in the business of promoting professional championship boxing contests. Here again the District Court had dismissed the complaint in reliance upon *Federal Baseball* and *Toolson*. The Chief Justice observed that "if it were not for

Federal Baseball and *Toolson*, we think that it would be too clear for dispute that the Government's allegations bring the defendants within the scope of the Act." He pointed out that the defendants relied on the two baseball cases but also would have been content with a more restrictive interpretation of them than the *Shubert* defendants, for the boxing defendants argued that the cases immunized only businesses that involve exhibitions of an athletic nature. The Court accepted neither argument. It again noted that "*Toolson* neither overruled *Federal Baseball* nor necessarily reaffirmed all that was said in *Federal Baseball*." It stated:

> The controlling consideration in *Federal Baseball* and *Hart* was, instead, a very practical one—the degree of interstate activity involved in the particular business under review. It follows that stare decisis cannot help the defendants here; for, contrary to their argument, *Federal Baseball* did not hold that all businesses based on professional sports were outside the scope of the antitrust laws. The issue confronting us is, therefore, not whether a previously granted exemption should continue, but whether an exemption should be granted in the first instance. And that issue is for Congress to resolve, not this Court.

The Court noted the presence then in Congress of various bills forbidding the application of the antitrust laws to "organized professional sports enterprises"; the holding of extensive hearings on some of these; subcommittee opposition; a postponement recommendation as to baseball; and the fact that "Congress thus left intact the then-existing coverage of the antitrust laws."

Mr. Justice Frankfurter, joined by Mr. Justice Minton, dissented. "It would baffle the subtlest ingenuity," he said, "to find a single differentiating factor between other sporting exhibitions . . . and baseball insofar as the conduct of the sport is relevant to the criteria or considerations by which the Sherman Law becomes applicable to a trade or commerce." He went on:

> The Court decided as it did in the *Toolson* case as an application of the doctrine of stare decisis. That doctrine is not, to be sure, an imprisonment of reason. But neither is it a whimsy. It can hardly be that this Court gave a preferred position to baseball because it is the great American sport. . . . If stare decisis be one aspect of law, as it is, to disregard it in identical situations is mere caprice.
>
> Congress, on the other hand, may yield to sentiment and be capricious, subject only to due process. . . .
>
> Between them, this case and *Shubert* illustrate that nice but rational distinctions are inevitable in adjudication. I agree with the Court's opinion in *Shubert* for precisely the reason that constrains me to dissent in this case.

Mr. Justice Minton also separately dissented on the ground that boxing is not trade or commerce. He added the comment that "Congress has not attempted" to control baseball and boxing. The two dissenting Justices, thus, did not call for the overruling of *Federal Baseball* and *Toolson*; they merely felt that boxing should be under the same umbrella of freedom as was baseball and, as Mr. Justice Frankfurter said, they could not exempt baseball "to the exclusion of every other sport different not one legal jot or tittle from it."

F. The parade marched on. *Radovich v. National Football League*, 352 U.S. 445 (1957), was a civil Clayton Act case testing the application of the antitrust laws to professional football. The District Court dismissed. The Ninth Circuit affirmed in part on the basis of *Federal Baseball* and *Toolson*. The court did not hesitate to "confess that the strength of the pull" of the baseball cases and of *International Boxing* "is about equal," but then observed that "[f]ootball is a team sport" and boxing an individual one.

This Court reversed with an opinion by Mr. Justice Clark. He said that the Court made its ruling in *Toolson* "because it was concluded that more harm would be done in overruling *Federal Baseball* than in upholding a ruling which at best was of dubious validity." He noted that Congress had not acted. He then said:

> All this, combined with the flood of litigation that would follow its repudiation, the harassment that would ensue, and the retroactive effect of such a decision, led the Court to the practical result that it should sustain the unequivocal line of authority reaching over many years.
>
> [S]ince *Toolson* and *Federal Baseball* are still cited as controlling authority in antitrust actions involving other fields of business, we now specifically limit the rule there established to the facts there involved, i.e., the business of organized professional baseball. As long as the Congress continues to acquiesce we should adhere to—but not extend—the interpretation of the Act made in those cases....
>
> If this ruling is unrealistic, inconsistent, or illogical, it is sufficient to answer, aside from the distinctions between the businesses, that were we considering the question of baseball for the first time upon a clean slate we would have no doubts. But *Federal Baseball* held the business of baseball outside the scope of the Act. No other business claiming the coverage of those cases has such an adjudication. We therefore, conclude that the orderly way to eliminate error or discrimination, if any there be, is by legislation and not by court decision. Congressional processes are more accommodative, affording the whole industry hearings and an opportunity to assist in the formulation of new legislation. The resulting product is therefore more likely to protect the industry and the public alike. The whole scope of congressional action would be known long in advance and effective dates for the legislation could be set in the future without

the injustices of retroactivity and surprise which might follow court action.

* * *

G. Finally, in *Haywood v. National Basketball Assn.*, 401 U.S. 1204 (1971), Mr. Justice Douglas, in his capacity as Circuit Justice, reinstated a District Court's injunction pendente lite in favor of a professional basketball player and said, "Basketball ... does not enjoy exemption from the antitrust laws."

H. This series of decisions understandably spawned extensive commentary, some of it mildly critical and much of it not; nearly all of it looked to Congress for any remedy that might be deemed essential.

I. Legislative proposals have been numerous and persistent. Since *Toolson* more than 50 bills have been introduced in Congress relative to the applicability or nonapplicability of the antitrust laws to baseball. A few of these passed one house or the other. Those that did would have expanded, not restricted, the reserve system's exemption to other professional league sports. And the Act of Sept. 30, 1961, Pub. L. 87–331, 75 Stat. 732, and the merger addition thereto effected by the Act of Nov. 8, 1966, Pub. L. 89–800, § 6(b), 80 Stat. 1515, 15 U.S.C. § 1291–1295, were also expansive rather than restrictive as to antitrust exemption.

V

In view of all this, it seems appropriate now to say that:

1. Professional baseball is a business and it is engaged in interstate commerce.

2. With its reserve system enjoying exemption from the federal antitrust laws, baseball is, in a very distinct sense, an exception and an anomaly. *Federal Baseball* and *Toolson* have become an aberration confined to baseball.

3. Even though others might regard this as "unrealistic, inconsistent, or illogical," the aberration is an established one, and one that has been recognized not only in *Federal Baseball* and *Toolson*, but in *Shubert*, *International Boxing*, and *Radovich*, as well, a total of five consecutive cases in this Court. It is an aberration that has been with us now for half a century, one heretofore deemed fully entitled to the benefit of stare decisis, and one that has survived the Court's expanding concept of interstate commerce. It rests on a recognition and an acceptance of baseball's unique characteristics and needs.

4. Other professional sports operating interstate—football, boxing, basketball, and, presumably, hockey and golf—are not so exempt.

5. The advent of radio and television, with their consequent increased coverage and additional revenues, has not occasioned an overruling of *Federal Baseball* and *Toolson*.

6. The Court has emphasized that since 1922, baseball, with full and continuing congressional awareness, has been allowed to develop

and to expand unhindered by federal legislative action. Remedial legislation has been introduced repeatedly in Congress but none has ever been enacted. The Court, accordingly, has concluded that Congress as yet has had no intention to subject baseball's reserve system to the reach of the antitrust statutes. This, obviously, has been deemed to be something other than mere congressional silence and passivity.

7. The Court has expressed concern about the confusion and the retroactivity problems that inevitably would result with a judicial overturning of *Federal Baseball*. It has voiced a preference that if any change is to be made, it come by legislative action that, by its nature, is only prospective in operation.

8. The Court noted in *Radovich* that the slate with respect to baseball is not clean. Indeed, it has not been clean for half a century.

This emphasis and this concern are still with us. We continue to be loath, 50 years after *Federal Baseball* and almost two decades after *Toolson*, to overturn those cases judicially when Congress, by its positive inaction, has allowed those decisions to stand for so long and, far beyond mere inference and implication, has clearly evinced a desire not to disapprove them legislatively.

Accordingly, we adhere once again to *Federal Baseball* and *Toolson* and to their application to professional baseball. We adhere also to *International Boxing* and *Radovich* and to their respective applications to professional boxing and professional football. If there is any inconsistency or illogic in all this, it is an inconsistency and illogic of long standing that is to be remedied by the Congress and not by this Court. If we were to act otherwise, we would be withdrawing from the conclusion as to congressional intent made in *Toolson* and from the concerns as to retrospectivity therein expressed. Under these circumstances, there is merit in consistency even though some might claim that beneath that consistency is a layer of inconsistency.

The petitioner's argument as to the application of state antitrust laws deserves a word. Judge Cooper rejected the state law claims because state antitrust regulation would conflict with federal policy and because national "uniformity [is required] in any regulation of baseball and its reserved system." The Court of Appeals, in affirming, stated, "[A]s the burden on interstate commerce outweighs the states' interests in regulating baseball's reserve system, the Commerce Clause precludes the application here of state antitrust law." As applied to organized baseball, and in the light of this Court's observations and holding in *Federal Baseball*, in *Toolson*, in *Shubert*, in *International Boxing*, and in *Radovich*, and despite baseball's allegedly inconsistent position taken in the past with respect to the application of state law, these statements adequately dispose of the state law claims.

* * *

[W]hat the Court said in *Federal Baseball* in 1922 and what it said in *Toolson* in 1953, we say again here in 1972: the remedy, if any is indicated, is for congressional, and not judicial, action.

The judgment of the Court of Appeals is affirmed.

JUSTICE MARSHALL, with whom JUSTICE BRENNAN concurs, dissenting.

* * *

To non-athletes it might appear that petitioner was virtually enslaved by the owners of major league baseball clubs who bartered among themselves for his services. But, athletes know that it was not servitude that bound petitioner to the club owners; it was the reserve system. The essence of that system is that a player is bound to the club with which he first signs a contract for the rest of his playing days. He cannot escape from the club except by retiring, and he cannot prevent the club from assigning his contract to any other club.

* * *

We have only recently had occasion to comment that:

Antitrust laws in general, and the Sherman Act in particular, are the Magna Charta of free enterprise. They are as important to the preservation of economic freedom and our free-enterprise system as the Bill of Rights is to the protection of our fundamental personal freedoms.... Implicit in such freedom is the notion that it cannot be foreclosed with respect to one sector of the economy because certain private citizens or groups believe that such foreclosure might promote greater competition in a more important sector of the economy. (*United States v. Topco Associates, Inc.*, 405 U.S. 596, 610 (1972).)

The importance of the antitrust laws to every citizen must not be minimized. They are as important to baseball players as they are to football players, lawyers, doctors, or members of any other class of workers. Baseball players cannot be denied the benefits of competition merely because club owners view other economic interests as being more important, unless Congress says so.

Has Congress acquiesced in our decisions in *Federal Baseball Club* and *Toolson*? I think not. Had the Court been consistent and treated all sports in the same way baseball was treated, Congress might have become concerned enough to take action. But, the Court was inconsistent, and baseball was isolated and distinguished from all other sports. In *Toolson* the Court refused to act because Congress had been silent. But the Court may have read too much into this legislative inaction.

Americans love baseball as they love all sports. Perhaps we become so enamored of athletics that we assume that they are foremost in the minds of legislators as well as fans. We must not forget, however, that there are only some 600 major league baseball players. Whatever muscle they might have been able to muster by combining forces with other athletes has been greatly impaired by the manner in which this Court has isolated them. It is this Court that has made them impotent, and this Court should correct its error.

We do not lightly overrule our prior constructions of federal statutes, but when our errors deny substantial federal rights, like the right to compete freely and effectively to the best of one's ability as guaranteed by the antitrust laws, we must admit our error and correct it. We have done so before and we should do so again here.

* * *

To the extent that there is concern over any reliance interests that club owners may assert, they can be satisfied by making our decision prospective only. Baseball should be covered by the antitrust laws beginning with this case and henceforth, unless Congress decides otherwise.

Accordingly, I would overrule *Federal Baseball Club* and *Toolson* and reverse the decision of the Court of Appeals.

* * *

[Justice Marshall went on to explain that if the Court were to hold baseball subject to antitrust as a general matter, this did not mean that Flood's claim was necessarily actionable. In particular, baseball would still be entitled to offer as a defense the fact that the terms of Flood's player contract were mandatory subjects of collective bargaining between Major League Baseball and its Players Association, and thus arguably protected by the labor exemption from antitrust liability. The unfolding of that argument in other sports is covered in detail in Chapter 3.]

Appeal dismissed.

Justice Oliver Wendell Holmes, Jr., who wrote the Supreme Court's opinion in *Federal Base Ball*, had earlier made the following observations about *stare decisis* in his famous lecture on "The Path of the Law"[s]:

> It is revolting to have no better reason for a rule of law than that it was laid down in the time of Henry IV. It is still more revolting if the grounds upon which it was laid down have vanished long since, and that rule simply persists from blind imitation of the past.

How would (should) Justice Holmes have reacted to Justice Blackmun's adherence in *Flood* to Holmes' decision in *Federal Base Ball*, given that *Flood* rejected every one of the premises upon which *Federal Base Ball* was founded?

[s]. Oliver Wendell Holmes, Jr., *The Path of the Law*, 10 Harvard L. Rev. 457, 469 (1887).

Can the Court's ruling be explained by a judicial feeling that baseball needed a system such as the reserve clause to flourish—remember Justice Blackmun's opening paean to The Game—but that such a restrictive system was difficult to square with the Court's standard antitrust analysis? Imagine what Justice Blackmun thought about this comment in the lower court's opinion:

> [O]rganized baseball existed almost as an enclave or feudal barony throughout the years, managing its own affairs as best calculated to preserve the sport and maintaining its own officialdom for self-regulation purposes—and, except for the brief scandal of the so-called Chicago Black Sox of 1919, apparently has handled its little kingdom and its subjects very well.... As I analyzed the history of organized baseball over the last 50 years, it has shown without Court interference remarkable stability under self-discipline. The Supreme Court in 1922 undoubtedly felt that it should adopt a "hands off" policy as to this one particular sport which had attained such a national standing that only Congress shared the power to tamper with it. And properly so. Baseball's welfare and future should not be for politically insulated interpreters of technical antitrust statutes, but rather should be for the voters through their elected representatives. If baseball is to be damaged by statutory regulation, let the Congressman face his constituents the next November and also face the consequences of his baseball voting record.

Flood v. Kuhn, 443 F.2d 264, 269, 272 (2d Cir.1971). In contrast, consider whether Justice Marshall in his dissent felt some empathy with the following comment by Judge Frank, who was doubtful even in 1949 that *Federal Base Ball* retained much precedential value:

> [W]e have here a monopoly which, in its effect on ball-players like the plaintiff, possesses characteristics shockingly repugnant to moral principles that, at least since the War between the States have been basic in America, as shown by the Thirteenth Amendment to the Constitution, condemning "involuntary servitude," and by subsequent Congressional enactments on that subject. For the "reserve clause," as has been observed, results in something resembling peonage of the baseball player. By accepting the "reserve clause"—and all players in organized baseball must "accept" it—a player binds himself not to sign a contract with, or play for, any club other than the club which originally employs him or its assignee. Although many courts have refused to enforce the "reserve" clause, yet severe and practically efficacious extra-legal penalties are imposed for violation. The most extreme of these penalties is the blacklisting of the players so that no club in organized baseball will hire him. In effect, this clause prevents a player from ever playing with any team other than his original employer, unless that employer consents. Since the right to play with organized baseball is indispensable to the career of a professional baseball player, violations of the clause by such players are infrequent. The violator may perhaps become a judge (a

less exciting and often less remunerative occupation) or a bartender or a street-sweeper, but his chances of ever again playing baseball are exceedingly slim.... I may add that, if the players be regarded as quasi-peons, it is of no moment that they are well paid; only the totalitarian-minded will believe that high pay excuses virtual slavery.

Gardella v. Chandler, 172 F.2d 402, 409–10 (2d Cir.1949)

Finally, how would the *Toolson* Court in 1953 (or the *Flood* Court in 1972) have reacted if, instead of allowing Jackie Robinson to play, baseball had tried to protect its Jim Crow segregation policies from federal antitrust scrutiny? Keep in mind that the Court had greatly expanded the scope of Congress' "trade and commerce" power in the later stages of the New Deal, but Congress did not enact the Civil Rights Act barring employment discrimination until 1964.

Flood did more than maintain baseball's exemption from antitrust law. It also almost offhandedly established an immunity for baseball from state antitrust law.

As Justice Blackmun retraced in his *Flood* opinion, a series of Supreme Court and other rulings had made it clear that no other sport enjoys baseball's special exclusion from the Sherman Act. See *United States v. International Boxing Club*, 348 U.S. 236 (1955) (holding that professional boxing is not exempt); *Radovich v. NFL*, 352 U.S. 445 (1957) (holding that football and other professional team sports are not exempt); and *Amateur Softball Ass'n of America v. United States*, 467 F.2d 312 (10th Cir.1972) (holding that amateur sports such as softball are not exempt). However, baseball's immunity from state antitrust law is based on the "dormant Commerce Clause" principle of federal constitutional law, one that applies just as much to other sports leagues and organizations.

This was the obstacle faced by Dennis Partee, the San Diego Chargers' kicker, when he sought to strike down the NFL's version of the reserve system under California antitrust law. In *Partee v. San Diego Chargers Football Co.*, 34 Cal.3d 378, 194 Cal.Rptr. 367, 668 P.2d 674 (1983), a divided Supreme Court of California highlighted a key feature of dormant Commerce Clause jurisprudence. State business regulation is judged to have imposed an unreasonable burden on interstate commerce where it governs "those phases of the national commerce which, because of the need for national uniformity, demand their regulation, if any, be prescribed by a single authority" (id. at 677). In the majority's view, professional football clearly met that standard:

> Professional football is a nationwide business structured essentially the same as baseball. Professional football's teams are dependent upon the league playing schedule for competitive play, just as in baseball. The necessity of a nationwide league structure for the

benefit of both teams and players for effective competition is evident as is the need for a nationally uniform set of rules governing the league structure. Fragmentation of the league structure on the basis of state lines would adversely affect the success of the competitive business enterprise, and differing state antitrust decisions if applied to the enterprise would likely compel all member teams to comply with the laws of the strictest state.

We are satisfied that national uniformity required in regulation of baseball and its reserve system is likewise required in the player-team-league relationships challenged by Partee and that the burden on interstate commerce outweighs the state interests in applying state antitrust laws to those relationships.

668 P.2d at 678–79.

Another California court concluded that the same Commerce Clause principle precluded quarterback Bobby Hebert from using California's Labor Code (which makes it illegal for any business to deprive a person of the opportunity to earn his livelihood) to move freely from the New Orleans Saints to the Los Angeles Raiders. See *Hebert v. Los Angeles Raiders*, 2 Cal.Rptr.2d 489, 820 P.2d 999 (1991). Earlier decisions to the same effect are *Matuszak v. Houston Oilers*, 515 S.W.2d 725 (14th Tex.Ct.Civ.App.1974) (refusing to apply Texas antitrust law to NFL restraints on player movement), and *State of Wisconsin v. Milwaukee Braves*, 31 Wis.2d 699, 144 N.W.2d 1 (1966), cert. denied, 385 U.S. 990 (1966) (refusing to apply Wisconsin antitrust law to block the move of the Braves from Milwaukee to Atlanta). Does that principle and those precedents block a female umpire, Pam Postema, from filing suit under New York State's Human Rights Act (as well as Title VII of the federal Civil Rights Act), claiming gender discrimination as the reason why she was unable to secure an umpire position in the major leagues? See *Postema v. National League of Professional Baseball Clubs*, 799 F.Supp. 1475 (S.D.N.Y.1992), rev'd in part on other grounds, 998 F.2d 60 (2d Cir.1993).

The *Flood* decision made it clear that the Supreme Court would not be removing the exemption it had created for baseball from federal antitrust law. However, the wording of the *Flood* opinion left important questions unresolved about the scope of an exemption that was no longer attributable to a limited federal authority over interstate commerce. *Flood* and *Toolson* directly, and *Federal Base Ball* indirectly, each involved complaints that baseball's traditional player reserve system amounted to an illegal restraint of trade under the Sherman Act. Two circuit court decisions in the early 1970s applied the exemption to Major League Baseball's dealings with umpires (*Salerno v. American League*, 429 F.2d 1003 (2d Cir.1970)), and with the minor leagues (*Portland Baseball Club v. Kuhn*, 491 F.2d 1101 (9th Cir.1974)). Other cases, however, have refused to extend the exemption to baseball's dealings with outside parties: with concessionaires (see *Twin City Sportservice Inc. v. Charles O. Finley & Co. (Oakland Athletics)*, 365 F.Supp. 235 (N.D.Cal.1972), rev'd on other grounds, 512 F.2d 1264 (9th Cir.1975)); with broadcast outlets (see *Henderson Broadcasting Corp. v. Houston Sports Ass'n (Houston Astros)*, 541 F.Supp. 263 (S.D.Tex.1982)); and with merchandisers (see *Fleer v. Topps Chewing Gum & Major League Baseball Players Ass'n*, 658 F.2d 139 (3d Cir.1981)).

Baseball's antitrust exemption came back to the legal as well as the political scene in the early 1990s—in pursuit of franchise, not player, free agency. (The antitrust and other legal dimensions of franchise movements will be analyzed in depth in Chapter 7.) The immediate focus was a fierce struggle between San Francisco and Tampa Bay for the baseball Giants.[t]

After taxpayer-voters in the San Francisco Bay area had rejected a proposal to finance a new stadium to replace Candlestick Park in the spring of 1992, Giants' owner Robert Lurie accepted an offer from a Tampa Bay Area group that summer to purchase the franchise (for $115 million) with the intention of moving the team to St. Petersburg's Suncoast Dome. Although Lurie had agreed not to negotiate with any other potential buyers of the Giants, the combined efforts of officials from the City of San Francisco and Major League Baseball eventually produced a competing offer (for $100 million) from a San Francisco group led by Peter Magowan. In November 1992, the National League owners rejected the Tampa Bay group's request to relocate the team. Lurie immediately accepted the San Francisco offer and the Giants stayed in Candlestick Park where Barry Bonds helped them win 103 games and attract record-setting crowds during the 1993 season.

These decisions by Major League Baseball precipitated numerous lawsuits, some filed in Florida courts, some in California, and one even in Pennsylvania. The Pennsylvania suit was brought by two residents of the state, Vincent Piazza and Vincent Tirendi. The two were major investors in the Tampa Bay group and, as persons of Italian descent, were aggrieved about reported comments from Baseball's Ownership Committee that the two would not be personally approved as owners because of questions about their "background" that had come up during their "security check." (By the way, Piazza's son Mike was about to become the star catcher for the Los Angeles Dodgers.) Added to Piazza's and Tirendi's charges of defamation and inducing breach of contract was the allegation that rejection by National League owners of the proposed move of the Giants to Tampa Bay constituted a violation of the Sherman Act. Naturally, Baseball's lawyers requested summary dismissal of this claim on the basis of the sport's long-standing antitrust exemption. Following is the response by the federal district judge.

[t]. See Bob Andelman, *Stadium For Rent: Tampa Bay's Quest for Major League Baseball* (Jefferson, N.C.: McFarland & Co., 1993).

PIAZZA AND TIRENDI v. MAJOR LEAGUE BASEBALL

U.S. District Court, Eastern District of Pennsylvania, 1993.
831 F.Supp. 420.

PADOVA, DISTRICT JUDGE.

* * *

(I) SCOPE OF THE EXEMPTION

In each of the three cases in which the Supreme Court directly addressed the [antitrust] exemption, the factual context involved the reserve clause. Plaintiffs argue that the exemption is confined to that circumstance, which is not presented here. Baseball, on the other hand, argues that the exemption applies to the "business of baseball" generally, not to one particular facet of the game.

Between 1922 and 1972, Baseball's expansive view may have been correct. Although *Federal Baseball* involved the reserve clause, that decision was based upon the proposition that the business of exhibiting baseball games, as opposed to the business of moving players and their equipment, was not interstate commerce and thus not subject to the Sherman Act. *Toolson*, also a reserve clause case, spoke in terms of the "business of baseball" enjoying the exemption. Likewise, *Radovich*, a 1957 decision concerning football, recognized the exemption as extending to the "business of organized professional baseball."

In 1972, however, the Court in *Flood v. Kuhn* stripped from *Federal Baseball* and *Toolson* any precedential value those cases may have had beyond the particular facts there involved, i.e., the reserve clause. The *Flood* Court employed a two-prong approach in doing so. First, the Court examined the analytical underpinnings of *Federal Baseball*—that the business of exhibiting baseball games is not interstate commerce. In the clearest possible terms, the Court rejected this reasoning, removing any doubt that "professional baseball is a business ... engaged in interstate commerce."

Having entirely undercut the precedential value of the reasoning of *Federal Baseball*, the Court next set out to justify the continued precedential value of the result of that decision. To do this, the Court first looked back to *Toolson* and uncovered the following four reasons why the Court there had followed *Federal Baseball*:

> (a) Congressional awareness for three decades of the Court's ruling in *Federal Baseball*, coupled with congressional inaction. (b) The fact that baseball was left alone to develop for that period upon the understanding that the reserve system was not subject to existing antitrust laws. (c) A reluctance to overrule *Federal Baseball* with consequent retroactive effect. (d) A professed desire that any needed remedy be provided by legislation rather than court decree.

The emphasized text indicates that the *Flood* Court viewed the disposition in *Federal Baseball* and *Toolson* as being limited to the reserve system, for baseball developed between 1922 and 1953 with the understanding that its reserve system, not the game generally, was exempt from the antitrust laws. This reading of *Flood* is buttressed by (1) the reaffirmation in *Flood* of a prior statement of the Court that "*Toolson* was a narrow application of the doctrine of stare decisis," and (2) the *Flood* Court's own characterization, in the first sentence of its opinion, of the *Federal Baseball*, *Toolson*, and *Flood* decisions: "For the third time in 50 years the Court is asked specifically to rule that professional baseball's reserve system is within the reach of the antitrust laws."

Viewing the dispositions in *Federal Baseball* and *Toolson* as limited to the reserve clause, the *Flood* Court then turned to the reasons why, even though analytically vitiated, the precise results in *Federal Baseball* and *Toolson* were to be accorded the continuing benefit of stare decisis. Like *Toolson*, the *Flood* Court laid its emphasis on continued positive congressional inaction and concerns over retroactivity. In particular, the *Flood* Court "concluded that Congress as yet has had no intention to subject baseball's reserve system to the reach of the antitrust statutes." Finally, the Court acknowledged that "with its reserve system enjoying exemption from the federal antitrust laws, baseball is, in a very distinct sense, an exception and an anomaly. *Federal Baseball* and *Toolson* have become an aberration confined to baseball." Thus in 1972, the Supreme Court made clear that the *Federal Baseball* exemption is limited to the reserve clause.

[The judge then described and disagreed with the Seventh Circuit's contrary ruling in *Finley v. Kuhn*, 569 F.2d 527 (7th Cir.1978), which we read in Chapter 1. That court had quickly dismissed Charles Finley's antitrust claim against Commissioner Kuhn's barring the sale of Athletics players to the Yankees and Red Sox, on the assumption that *Flood* intended to preserve baseball's exemption for its entire business, not just its reserve clause.]

* * *

[T]here is an even more significant flaw in the Seventh Circuit's analysis of *Flood* than in failing to note the extent to which that decision turned upon the reserve clause. Application of the doctrine of stare decisis simply permits no other way to read *Flood* than as confining the precedential value of *Federal Baseball* and *Toolson* to the precise facts there involved. To understand why this is so, one must fully understand the doctrine of stare decisis and its application by lower courts to Supreme Court decisions. The Third Circuit recently offered the following explanation:

> [Supreme Court] ... opinions usually include two major aspects. First, the Court provides the legal standard or test that is applicable to laws implicating a particular ... provision. This is part of the reasoning of the decision, the ratio decidendi. Second, the Court applies that standard or test to the particular facts of the case that the Court is confronting—in other words, it reaches a specific result using the standard or test.

As a lower court, we are bound by both the Supreme Court's choice of legal standard or test and by the result it reaches under the standard or test. As Justice Kennedy has stated, courts are bound to adhere not only to results of cases, but also "to their explications of the governing rules of law." Our system of precedent or stare decisis is thus based on adherence to both the reasoning and result of a case, and not simply to the result alone. This distinguishes the American system of precedent, sometimes called "rule stare decisis," from the English system, which historically has been limited to following the results or disposition based on the facts of a case and thus referred to as "result stare decisis."

Like lower courts, the Supreme Court applies principles of stare decisis and recognizes an obligation to respect both the standard announced and the result reached in its prior cases. Unlike lower courts, the Supreme Court is free to change the standard or result from one of its earlier cases when it finds it to be "unsound in principle [or] unworkable in practice." . . .

Applying these principles of stare decisis here, it becomes clear that, before *Flood*, lower courts were bound by both the rule of *Federal Baseball* and *Toolson* (that the business of baseball is not interstate commerce and thus not within the Sherman Act) and the result of those decisions (that baseball's reserve system is exempt from the antitrust laws). The Court's decision in *Flood*, however, effectively created the circumstance referred to by the Third Circuit as "result stare decisis," from the English system. In *Flood*, the Supreme Court exercised its discretion to invalidate the rule of *Federal Baseball* and *Toolson*. Thus no rule from those cases binds the lower courts as a matter of stare decisis. The only aspect of *Federal Baseball* and *Toolson* that remains to be followed is the result or disposition based upon the facts there involved, which the Court in *Flood* determined to be the exemption of the reserve system from the antitrust laws.

Neither *Finley* nor any other case cited by Baseball in support of its view of the exemption has undertaken such an analysis of the Supreme Court's baseball trilogy. And as none of these decisions is binding upon this Court, I will not follow them. It is well settled that exemptions from the antitrust laws are to be narrowly construed. Application of this principle is particularly appropriate, if not absolutely critical, in this case because the exemption at issue has been characterized by its own creator as an "anomaly" and an "aberration." (*Federal Baseball* is a "derelict in the stream of the law." (Douglas, J. dissenting)). For these reasons, I conclude that the antitrust exemption created by *Federal Baseball* is limited to baseball's reserve system, and because the parties agree that the reserve system is not at issue in this case, I reject Baseball's argument that it is exempt from antitrust liability in this case.

[In the latter part of his decision, the judge addressed the implications of the *Finley* court being correct in reading *Flood* as preserving the *Federal Baseball* "rule" that the "business of baseball," not just the reserve system, is exempt from the Sherman Act. That still left the question of the scope of the "relevant product market" in baseball. The judge noted that the Court in *Federal Baseball* itself had drawn a distinction between "giving exhibitions of baseball" and "moving players and their paraphernalia from place to place:" it was only the latter to which the Sherman Act could apply. The market to which the expansive version of the exemption would apply consisted of the sale by owners of the exhibition of games to buyers who were fans (or perhaps broadcasters). The market to which the *Piazza* suit applied was the sale of baseball teams by the current owners to those who wanted to become owners. The claim of the plaintiffs was that the latter "ownership" market was as distinguishable from the "game exhibition" market as was the "player transportation" market mentioned in *Federal Baseball*. The judge was not prepared at this stage of the proceeding to rule that the sale of teams was sufficiently central to the "exhibitions of baseball" as to be covered by the latter's exemption. He did, however, intimate that if the eventual record were to show that the sale was inseparable from a proposed relocation, something that seemed an integral part of the structure of baseball, then "rule stare decisis" would likely "require application of the exemption."]

* * *

Summary dismissal denied.

The *Piazza* case never came to conclusion because on the eve of trial (not just of the antitrust but also the defamation and inducing contract breach claims), the National League owners settled with an apology and a $6 million payment. However, the federal judge's interpretation of *Flood* was endorsed by the Florida Supreme Court when it upheld the authority of the state Attorney–General to institute proceedings against the National League for having refused to allow the Giants to move to Florida. See *Butterworth v. National League of Professional Baseball Clubs*, 644 So.2d 1021 (Fla.1994). In March 1995, faced with both this litigation and a congressional attack on the exemption sparked by Florida Senators Graham and Mack, Major League Baseball granted new franchises to St. Petersburg and Phoenix to begin play in 1998, in return for an expansion fee of $130 million (plus another $25 million in foregone television revenues for five years).

Even this league action could not, however, forestall a suit by another Florida group who claimed that Major League Baseball had blocked their earlier efforts to buy the Minnesota Twins in 1984 and bring that team to St. Petersburg. In *Morsani v. Major League Baseball*, 663 So.2d 653 (Fla.App.1995), a Florida appellate court followed *Butterworth* and *Piazza* and ruled that baseball could not claim an exemption from this action under either federal or state antitrust law. However, in *McCoy v. Major League Baseball*, 911 F.Supp. 454 (W.D.Wash.1995), a federal district judge in Seattle explicitly disagreed with *Piazza* and

Butterworth, and used the exemption of "the business of baseball" as the principal grounds for rejecting a class action antitrust suit filed against baseball owners on behalf of the Mariners' fans who were left with no games to watch when the players went out on strike in August, 1994.

Questions For Discussion

1. Does the *Piazza* opinion constitute a fair reading of the scope and limits of *Flood* and its depiction of *Federal Baseball*? From the point of view of *stare decisis* in the judicial process, how can one justify the line between baseball's traditional player reserve system and its controls over team ownership and movement? Alternatively, is there a viable distinction between baseball's relations with concession operators, broadcast outlets, and merchandising firms (relations that have been subjected to antitrust scrutiny) and its relations with communities and their stadium authorities (whether San Francisco's Candlestick Park or St. Petersburg's Suncoast Dome)? Finally, if *Piazza's* "result *stare decisis*" approach to *Flood* were to be endorsed, what would this imply for the owner's assertion of antitrust immunity for collective imposition of a salary cap on player contracts and movements?

The fierce labor strife in the mid–1990s over the salary cap greatly intensified popular and political attention to baseball's antitrust exemption. A number of members of Congress, led by Republican Senator (and Judiciary Committee Chairman) Orrin Hatch and Democratic Senator Daniel Moynihan, sponsored legislation in 1995 that would have removed baseball's immunity with respect to Major League Baseball player-owner relations. Their hope was that such legislative action would reduce the players' felt need to strike to block the owners unilaterally imposing a cap on the free agent marketplace. While nothing happened on that score in Congress, the owners and players finally reached a settlement in late 1996, introducing a salary tax rather than a cap. A little-known feature of the new collective agreement was that both sides would "jointly request and cooperate in lobbying the Congress to pass a law clarifying that Major League Baseball players are covered under the antitrust laws (i.e., that major league players will have the same rights under the antitrust laws as do other professional athletes, e.g., football and basketball players), along with a provision that makes it clear that the passage of that bill does not change the application of the antitrust laws in any other context or with respect to any other person or entity ..." Such a joint request was made by the major league owners and players in the spring of 1997, and Senator Hatch introduced the statutory amendment that embodied the above understanding. As of the end of 1997, the political status of this proposal was uncertain.

In the next two chapters, we shall encounter the economic question posed by player free agency and salary caps or taxes, and the interplay of labor and antitrust law that made it easier for owners to accept this specific feature of the 1996 settlement. For purposes of this chapter, what is more significant are the parts of baseball's exemption that will *not* be included in the joint request to Congress. An even more important exclusion than the franchise ownership and relocation matters addressed in *Piazza* is the relationship between major and minor league teams, and the control wielded by major league owners over minor league players. Indeed, perhaps the biggest obstacle to Congress itself addressing this issue on its own initiative in 1995–96, or in response to the major league owner-player request in 1997, is membership concern about the shadow that antitrust law might cast over the quality and appeal of the blossoming minor league game. Minor league ball is now played in 225 communities across the country, and the sale price of Class A franchises, for example, rose from under $10,000 in the late 1970s to more than $5 million by the late 1990s.

The basic structure of organized baseball is defined by the Professional [formerly National] Baseball Agreement (PBA) between Major League Baseball and the National Association of Professional Baseball Leagues (the minor leagues). A key feature of the PBA is the Player Development Contract (PDC) which specifies the terms of all affiliations between major league teams and their minor league farm clubs (the latter in leagues that are grouped in Rookie, A, AA, and AAA classifications). Under the PDC, the major league teams pay all the salaries and benefits of minor league players, coaches, and managers, together with spring training expenses for their farm clubs. The independently-owned minor league clubs pay all other expenditures in operating and promoting their teams, and the minor leagues also pay a percentage share of their gross ticket revenues to the major league clubs. Under the Player Development Contract, minor league players are actually employed by the major league teams. The contracts signed between team and player are, in turn, shaped by the broader institutional arrangements devised by the majors and the minor leagues.

Every June a draft is held of all players who have left high school (and college players after their third season). The draft lasts for as many rounds as the teams may want. (In 1994, while the Oakland Athletics and Texas Rangers stopped drafting players in the 39th round, the Houston Astros continued through the 98th round.) Players who are drafted then sign a standard form contract that gives the major league team the right to renew the contract for three additional seasons. After the first four years have passed, the player is subject to the so-called Rule 5 draft by other teams unless he is put on the 40–player major league off-season roster. And even if he is put on the 40–player off-season roster, the original major league club retains the right to send the player back to the minors for an additional three seasons if the player does not make the regular season 25–man roster. While a number of first-round draft picks have recently negotiated multi-million dollar contracts, the vast majority of players sign at a salary scale that in the mid–1990s reportedly paid the median Class A player approximately $5,000 a season and the Triple A player $15,000 a season.

In the 1990 Professional Baseball Agreement (all of whose key substantive provisions were renewed in 1997), Major League Baseball secured adherence by all of the minor leagues to a new 19–page facility agreement. This pact set minimum standards for conditions on the field, in dugouts and locker rooms, as well as for stadium size, lighting, restrooms, concessions, parking, and the like. Any community whose facility has not been built or upgraded to meet the standards set for clubs in its particular league classification will lose its home team. At the same time, the Agreement permits major league teams to block the location of minor league teams in their home county, plus an additional 15–mile buffer territory.

Absent baseball's antitrust exemption, this broad-ranging Professional Baseball Agreement would certainly face judicial scrutiny in antitrust litigation. For example, in 1993 a dispute arose between Tom Benson, the owner of the NFL's New Orleans Saints, who had an agreement to purchase the class AA Charlotte Knights and move them to New Orleans, and John Diekou, then-owner of the AAA Denver Zephyrs which he wanted to move to New Orleans after being bumped out of Denver by the expansion Colorado Rockies. However, minor league rules giving territorial preference to teams of higher classification allowed Diekou to block the Knights from moving to New Orleans as the Pelicans. Thus, Benson sued the minor leagues (i.e., the National Ass'n of Professional Baseball Clubs) alleging, *inter alia*, that these territorial rights rules violated § 1 of the Sherman Act. That claim in Benson's suit was summarily dismissed by District Judge Martin Feldman, solely on the ground that *Federal Baseball* protected all of the business rules of the minor leagues.

The next several chapters will address a host of questions that have arisen for the player, franchise, and consumer markets in those major league sports that are governed by antitrust. In reading those materials, keep the following questions in mind with respect to minor league baseball (questions that do not apply to football or basketball whose "minor" league player development role is played primarily by college programs).

1. With respect to players, should the draft and the standard player contract be held an unreasonable and illegal restraint of trade in players? How might such a holding affect the current salary structure in minor league baseball? Is there a reason why some such arrangement is crucial to the quality of a sport like baseball, by contrast with the development of talent in entertainment fields such as music or film?

2. With respect to relations between major and minor league clubs, should a uniform Player Development Contract govern all such relationships, or should the terms be individually negotiated between various major and minor league teams? Would such a free marketplace affect the amount being invested by major league teams in player development (now estimated to cost over $6 million for

each of the major league teams that, on average, bring three minor league players a year up to their big league rosters)? Are there ways in which the quality of the minor league baseball product is enhanced and/or is harmed by major league control of all its player (and managerial) talent?

3. Should the Professional Baseball Agreement be permitted to establish uniform standards for stadium facilities that must be met by all minor league communities? What is the purpose and effect of such standards? Should the next such Agreement develop analogous standards for all major league facilities?

4. Should a team like the New York Mets be able to block a proposed 1992 move of a minor league team to Long Island which the Mets claim is their territory, with the result that suburban fans can come into the city to see a major league game for $15 to $25 a seat, but cannot watch minor league games close to home at $5 to $7 a seat?

Chapter Three

FROM ANTITRUST TO LABOR LAW[a]

A. ANTITRUST BACKGROUND

Whatever the Congress chooses to do with *Flood* and baseball's special antitrust exemption, the Major League Baseball Players Association has already demonstrated that it did not need congressional help to dismantle baseball's reserve system. As we shall see in the next chapter, collective bargaining under labor law proved up to that challenge. The Supreme Court, however, confirmed in *Flood* that all other sports were subject to antitrust law—thence launching a burst of antitrust litigation against restrictive practices across the spectrum of professional sports.[b] This chapter recounts the key legal and industry consequences of this litigation over the last quarter century.

One possible source of insulation from § 1 of the Sherman Act of intraleague affairs is the requirement of a "contract, combination, or conspiracy." In contrast with § 2, which speaks of "every person who shall monopolize," § 1 requires that there be at least two distinct legal persons who are parties to a collusive arrangement that restrains trade. The obvious question, then, is whether the league when it adopts

---

a. The best overall account of what happened in both the courts and the various sports in this area is Robert C. Berry, William B. Gould IV, and Paul D. Staudohar, *Labor Relations in Professional Sports* (Dover, Mass: Auburn House, 1986), as updated by Paul Staudohar, *The Sports Industry and Collective Bargaining* (Ithaca, N.Y.: ILR Press, 1989). Three excellent collections of articles, written principally by economists, give us a picture of the sports labor market before and after the arrival of antitrust and labor law: Roger Noll ed., *Government and the Sports Business* (Washington, D.C.: Brookings, 1974); Paul Staudohar and James A. Mangan, eds., *The Business of Professional Sports* (Urbana, Ill.: University of Illinois Press, 1991); and Paul Sommers, ed., *Diamonds Are Forever: The Business of Baseball* (Washington, D.C.: Brookings, 1992). The most recent in-depth analysis of the antitrust issues is Stephen F. Ross, *The Misunderstood Alliance Between Sports Fans, Players, and the Antitrust Law*, 1997 Illinois L. Rev. 519.

b. In addition, as we will see in Chapter 10, the world of intercollegiate sports saw a number of antitrust challenges by students, coaches, and colleges against restrictions imposed by the National Collegiate Athletic Association (NCAA).

intraleague policies is a single entity subject only to § 2 of the Act, or a combination of separate clubs whose internal arrangements are exposed to § 1 scrutiny. This question is clearly relevant to antitrust challenges to league practices that shape the players market; indeed, this will be a key issue in the class action antitrust suit that was filed in 1997 on behalf of Major League Soccer players. To this point, though, the most serious judicial analyses of this question have come in litigation about league restraints that have been initiated by franchise holders (i.e., by people who themselves had been or still were parties to and beneficiaries of the league arrangement). Thus, we will postpone detailed treatment of the "single entity" issue to Chapter 7 on the franchise market.

Still lurking within § 1 (and also § 2) is another potential barrier to antitrust suits by players—the argument that the "trade and commerce" that is protected against collusive restraint (or monopolization) does not include the labor market. The sports arena, including the cases below on the rookie draft and on veteran free agency, constitutes the main category of antitrust litigation about the employment relationship in any industrial setting. Except for a recent district court decision excerpted below (one that was eventually reversed on other grounds), the courts in the sports cases have assumed with little or no discussion that the Sherman Act bars restraint of trade in the labor as well as in the product market. That conclusion, however, raises significant questions within contemporary scholarly and judicial analysis which presumes that the principal, if not exclusive, aim of antitrust law is to enhance consumer welfare through a more efficient allocation of economic resources.[c]

The immediate target of antitrust law is excessive market power, whether in the hands of a single firm or a group of firms that jointly acquire such market power through anticompetitive agreements. Normally when one thinks of market power and its adverse effects, one does so in the context of a firm operating in the product market—selling its goods or services to consumers. Market power exists when consumers have few if any alternatives to the seller's product, thus enabling the seller to dictate terms based on profit maximization rather than competitive pressure. Economists have identified two general consequences of such market power. First, customers who purchase the product have to pay higher prices (or obtain lower quality products), which causes a transfer of wealth from customers to producers. Second, the amount of the good or service produced for and purchased by consumers will drop. This inflicts a "dead-weight loss" upon the economy as a whole, because some factors of production (labor, materials, capital, land, or equipment) that would be most efficient at making the monopolist's product are diverted into producing other goods and services for which they are less well-suited.

---

[c]. Compare Robert Bork, *The Antitrust Paradox: A Policy at War with Itself* (New York: Basic Books, 1978), with Robert H. Lande, *Wealth Transfers as the Original and Primary Concern of Antitrust*, 34 Hastings L. J. 65 (1982). See generally Louis Kaplow, *Antitrust, Law and Economics, and the Courts*, 50 Law & Contemp. Probs. 181 (1987).

There is disagreement about whether the first-mentioned effect of market power—wealth transfer—is the type of harm about which antitrust law is concerned. Conservative "Chicago school" theorists argue that antitrust should not be concerned with who enjoys the fruits of society's output, but only with maximizing the total value of that output. More populist scholars argue that since Congress was concerned about exploitation of consumers when it passed our antitrust laws, wealth transfers from generally less-wealthy consumers to generally more-wealthy producers are properly the concern of antitrust enforcement. There is consensus, however, that the second effect—restriction of output and consequent diversion of resources into less efficient uses—is harmful and should be the target of antitrust law.

Consider, now, the situation in which market power is wielded by the purchaser of a good or service: sellers have few if any other options to which they can turn. The effect of such "monopsony" power is the converse of monopoly power. Sellers are forced to accept lower purchase prices or to invest more effort and resources in production of a higher quality good for the same price; this effects a wealth transfer from sellers to buyers. Faced with that less favorable market environment, sellers will tend to restrict the amount of the good or service sold; again this means that the total value of society's output will be lower because factors of production are diverted into less efficient uses.

Again, there is scholarly agreement that the latter type of deadweight loss from monopsony power is a legitimate concern of antitrust enforcement, but no such consensus exists about the wealth transfer effect. In addition, the political connotations of monopsonistic wealth transfers are more obscure than those stemming from monopoly power. Excess market power wielded by monopoly sellers victimizes the broader population of consumers. But excess power wielded by a firm purchasing goods or services for production may actually lower the cost and enhance the quality of output of that factor of production—in particular, labor—for the benefit of consumers who almost invariably outnumber the producers of any one product.

For example, in *Kartell v. Blue Shield of Massachusetts, Inc.*, 749 F.2d 922 (1st Cir.1984), the First Circuit dismissed an antitrust claim filed by doctors against Blue Shield, the dominant provider of health insurance in Massachusetts, which required all doctors who performed services for Blue Shield insureds to accept its fee schedule as full payment for the service, and not charge the patient any more. As then-Judge Breyer observed,

> ... the prices at issue here are low prices, not high prices. Of course, a buyer, as well as a seller, can possess significant market power; and courts have held that *agreements* to fix prices—whether maximum or minimum—are unlawful. Nonetheless, the Congress that enacted the Sherman Act saw it as a way of protecting consumers against prices that were too *high*, not too low. And the relevant economic conditions may be very different when low prices, rather

than high prices, are at issue. These facts suggest that courts at least should be cautious—reluctant to condemn too speedily—an arrangement that, on its face, appears to bring low price benefits to the consumer.

749 F.2d at 930–31. *Kartell*, then, implies that at least some monopsony power—because it may improve the situation of at least some consumers in the marketplace—may not warrant the same kind of close antitrust scrutiny as does monopoly power, which always threatens the interests of all its consumers.

This analogy is significant for player restraint cases in sports. Players are sellers of a factor of production—their labor—to a league that usually is the only employer in their particular sport. Players associations object to the draft and to restrictions on free agent movement (including salary caps) because by thereby limiting players' options to a single team, the league creates monopsony market power; the buying teams can force players to accept salaries that are less than the players could get in a market where all teams could bid what they want for any one player. Players are not primarily concerned about the impact of such practices on consumer welfare—the prices that fans pay for tickets, or that networks pay for broadcasting rights, or the quality of the product people watch at the park or on the screen. Players are concerned about enhancing their income and avoiding a transfer of wealth from themselves to team owners. The question, though, is whether antitrust law should be concerned about this type of conflict between players and owners. Relevant to that broad question are these specific issues:

1. Would elimination of the rookie draft and limits on veteran free agency substantially raise player salaries? If both restrictions were dispensed with, how would this influence the pattern of salary distribution? With what effect on the supply of players to the league?

2. Assuming that average player salaries would rise to some extent, would higher payroll costs reduce team profits or raise ticket prices and television fees? If both, which effect would predominate?

3. Do league restraints on player mobility, and thence on team competition for players' services, serve to improve competitive athletic balance within the league (by allowing small revenue teams to obtain and retain a larger share of the top players), thus enhancing the attractiveness of the league product to fans? Or might such restraints actually inhibit the ability of weaker clubs to upgrade the quality of their teams, and thence the league product? Again, if both are possible, which would predominate?

The foregoing gives some flavor of the difficult theoretical and empirical questions implicated in the effort to introduce antitrust law into the sports labor market. Following are excerpts from the one sports decision that addresses at even a rudimentary level the question whether antitrust belongs here at all. This case involved a suit lodged against the National Football League for its unilateral imposition of a standard $1,000 per week salary paid to players assigned to a team's development squad, rather than to its regular roster. Further details about the case and its eventual outcome in the Supreme Court will be presented later in this chapter. Here, we reproduce the segment of the district court's opinion dealing with the NFL's motion for summary dismissal of *any* antitrust challenge to employer restraints on the labor market.

BROWN v. PRO FOOTBALL, INC.
(WASHINGTON REDSKINS)

United States District Court, District of Columbia, 1992.
1992–1 Trade Cases (CCH) ¶ 69,747, 1992 WL 88039.

LAMBERTH, DISTRICT JUDGE.

* * *

Contrary to the [NFL teams'] assertion, wage-fixing restraints which affect the labor market are considered price-fixing restraints subject to the antitrust laws. Section 6 of the Clayton Act [which states that "the labor of a human being is not a commodity or article of commerce"] does not exempt such restraints from antitrust liability:

> It is readily apparent that Congress, in enacting § 6, was concerned with the right of labor and similar organizations to continue engaging in [activities that otherwise would be considered antitrust violations], including the right to strike, not with the right of employers to band together for joint action in fixing the wages to be paid by each employer. There is no evidence of the existence of any necessity to protect the latter type of activity at the time when § 6 was enacted. It seems clear that if Congress had wanted to exempt agreements between employers as to the money or compensation that would be paid to their employees, it would not have limited § 6 to exemption of "[t]he labor of a human being" which can be restrained only by the employees or unions controlling the labor itself. Congress would also have provided that compensation offered or paid by employers to employees is not a commodity or article of commerce. This it did not do.

Cordova v. Bache & Co., 321 F.Supp. 600, 606 (S.D.N.Y.1970) (Judge Mansfield). The principle that wage-fixing restraints are price-fixing restraints cognizable under the Sherman Act has been accepted by several courts.... Moreover, the Supreme Court has noted that price fixing by purchasers of goods "is the sort of combination condemned by the [Sherman] Act." *Mandeville Island Farms, Inc. v. American Crystal Sugar Co.*, 334 U.S. 219, 235 (1948). The court finds no discernible reason, given that the Sherman Act applies to services as well as goods, *United States v. National Association of Real Estate Boards*, 339 U.S.

485, 490 (1950) (Sherman Act "aimed at combinations organized and directed to control of the market by suppression of competition 'in the marketing of goods and services'"), why wage-fixing by purchasers of services should be treated differently than price-fixing by sellers of goods.

Other precedent lends further support to the application of the Sherman Act to wage-fixing restraints. The Supreme Court has noted the "broad remedial and deterrent objectives" of the Clayton Act and has recognized that the statute "does not confine its protection to consumers, or to purchasers, or to sellers.... The Act is comprehensive in its terms and coverage, protecting all who are made victims of the forbidden practices by whomever they may be perpetrated." *Blue Shield of Virginia v. McCready*, 457 U.S. 465, 472 (1982). The Supreme Court has clearly stated that the exchange of a "service for money is 'commerce' in the most common usage of that word" and that the Sherman Act applies to restraints involving the sale of services. *Goldfarb v. Virginia State Bar*, 421 U.S. 773, 787–88 (1975).

Furthermore, the Supreme Court has noted that a consumer is injured in his or her business or property when the price of "goods or services is artificially inflated by reason of the anticompetitive conduct complained of." *Reiter v. Sonotone Corp.*, 442 U.S. 330, 339 (1979). By analogy, and applying the broad remedial and deterrent objectives of the Clayton Act, a service provider is injured in his business or property when buyers of those services artificially deflate the price of services through cooperative anticompetitive conduct. See *Chattanooga Foundry & Pipe Works v. Atlanta*, 203 U.S. 390, 396 (1906) (recognizing that a city can be injured in its "business of furnishing water" by an antitrust violation). The law in the District of Columbia Circuit recognizes "that athletes have standing to challenge player restrictions in professional sports since the restraints operate directly on, and to the detriment of, the employee." *Smith v. Pro Football, Inc.*, 593 F.2d 1173, 1175 n. 2 (D.C.Cir.1978). Based on the authority cited above, this court finds that wage-fixing is an antitrust violation to which the Sherman Act applies.

Argument rejected.

How persuasive is the court's analysis of the monopsony issue, especially its conclusion that "wage-fixing" is always an antitrust violation? Is this conclusion compatible with the First Circuit's position in *Kartell*, referred to earlier, in which Blue Shield used its market power to reduce the price paid for doctors' services?

Later in this chapter we will return to the question of the proper role of antitrust in the labor market, with a selection from the voluminous jurisprudence on the labor law exemption of collective bargaining from normal antitrust scrutiny. However, even if antitrust law can be used to challenge league restrictions on players, not all restraints of trade are illegal, only those judged to be *unreasonable* (see *Standard Oil v. United States*, 221 U.S. 1 (1911)). Until well into the 1970s, though, courts tended to find various business arrangements unreasonable *per se*—price fixing (see *United States v. Socony-Vacuum Oil Co.*, 310 U.S. 150 (1940)); market allocation (see *United States v. Topco Assocs.*, 405 U.S. 596 (1972)); group boycotts (see *Klor's, Inc. v. Broadway-Hale Stores*, 359 U.S. 207 (1959)); resale price maintenance (see *Dr. Miles Medical Co. v. John D. Park & Sons Co.*, 220 U.S. 373 (1911)); and vertical territorial restrictions (see *United States v. Arnold, Schwinn & Co.*, 388 U.S. 365 (1967)). Because these categories were vaguely defined, § 1 jurisprudence allowed courts to condemn forms of conduct that the judges disapproved of for social, political, or economic reasons. In this era the Supreme Court delivered several judgments finding various joint venture rules to be illegal *per se*, even though the resulting enterprises appeared to offer consumers lower prices and greater product quality or output. See *United States v. Sealy*, 388 U.S. 350 (1967); *United States v. Topco Assocs.*, 405 U.S. 596 (1972); and *Silver v. New York Stock Exchange*, 373 U.S. 341 (1963). These cases are occasionally cited in the sports cases included in this chapter.

Beginning in the mid-1970s, the Supreme Court sharply altered its antitrust stance by either expressly overruling or drastically limiting application of the various *per se* categories. Here we summarize only a few such decisions—the ones most relevant for analyzing sports cases.

In *Broadcast Music Inc. v. Columbia Broadcasting System, Inc.*, 441 U.S. 1 (1979), the Supreme Court narrowed the *per se* approach to price fixing by holding that an organization that held nonexclusive copyright licenses for the musical compositions of hundreds of composers did not automatically violate antitrust law by selling the right to play all of its licensed music to commercial broadcasters at a set price. The Court reasoned that this "blanket license" achieved major cost savings for purchasers, who otherwise would have had to traverse the globe to obtain individual licenses from the composer of every musical piece they wished to broadcast.

> This substantial lowering of costs, which is of course potentially beneficial to both sellers and buyers, differentiates the blanket license from individual use licenses. The blanket license is composed of the individual compositions plus the aggregating service. Here, the whole is truly greater than the sum of its parts; it is, to some extent, a different product. The blanket license has certain unique characteristics: it allows the licensee immediate use of covered compositions, without the delay of prior individual negotiations, and great flexibility in the choice of musical material.... Thus, to the extent the blanket license is a different product, ASCAP is not really a joint sales agency offering the individual goods of many sellers, but is a separate seller offering its blanket license, of which the individual compositions are raw material. ASCAP, in short, made a market

in which individual composers are inherently unable to compete fully effectively.

441 U.S. at 21–22. Following the remand of the case by the Supreme Court, the lower court concluded that this blanket, but non-exclusive, license satisfied the Rule of Reason standard. See *Buffalo Broadcasting Co. v. ASCAP*, 744 F.2d 917 (2d Cir.1984).

Next, the Court limited "group boycott" illegality in *Northwest Wholesale Stationers, Inc. v. Pacific Stationery & Printing Co.*, 472 U.S. 284 (1985), by holding that a wholesale purchasing cooperative formed by a group of small stationery retailers was not guilty of a *per se* antitrust violation when it expelled one of its members for operating a wholesale stationery supply business in competition with the cooperative. The Court reasoned that the cooperative created purchasing efficiencies for its members, which in turn produced lower prices to consumers, and that enforcement of the rule against members who competed against the cooperative was arguably important for the cooperative to be able to provide these economic advantages. The Court concluded that "[u]nless the cooperative possesses market power or exclusive access to an element essential to effective competition, the conclusion that expulsion [for violating the rule] is virtually always likely to have an anticompetitive effect is unwarranted."

In *Continental T.V., Inc. v. GTE Sylvania Inc.*, 433 U.S. 36 (1977), the Supreme Court expressly overturned the *per se* rule against a manufacturer placing vertical territorial restrictions on its distributors. The Court reasoned that such restrictions on distributors might improve the firm's overall marketing strategy and make the company more efficient and competitive vis-a-vis its rivals, and such competition among producers would ultimately produce lower prices and higher quality for consumers. The Court noted that while vertical restraints may reduce competition among sellers of one manufacturer's brand (intrabrand competition), they might also stimulate greater competition among sellers of different manufacturers' brands (interbrand competition):

> Vertical restrictions reduce intrabrand competition by limiting the number of sellers of a particular product competing for the business of a given group of buyers. Location restrictions have this effect because of practical constraints on the effective marketing area of retail outlets. Although intrabrand competition may be reduced, the ability of retailers to exploit the resulting market may be limited both by the ability of consumers to travel to other franchised locations and, perhaps more importantly, to purchase the competing products of other manufacturers....
>
> Vertical restrictions promote interbrand competition by allowing the manufacturer to achieve certain efficiencies in the distribution of his products.... Economists have identified a number of ways in which manufacturers can use such restrictions to compete more effectively against other manufacturers. For example, [manufacturers] can use the restrictions in order to induce competent and

aggressive retailers to make the kind of investment on capital and labor that is often required in the distribution of products unknown to the consumer, [or] to induce retailers to engage in promotional activities or to provide service and repair facilities necessary to the efficient marketing of their products.... The availability and quality of such services affect a manufacturer's goodwill and the competitiveness of his product. Because of market imperfections such as the so-called "free rider" effect, these services might not be provided by retailers in a purely competitive situation, despite the fact that each retailer's benefit would be greater if all provided the services than if none did.

433 U.S. at 54–55.

These and similar decisions protected antitrust defendants from *per se* rulings of illegality on motions for summary judgment. In each of the cases described above, on remand from the Supreme Court the lower courts found the challenged conduct to be legal after careful Rule of Reason review, thus corroborating the Court's view that productive efficiencies generated by the challenged agreements might render them socially desirable. No longer, then, does the fact that an agreement decreases "competition" in a general sense automatically result in antitrust illegality.

Another noteworthy case was *National Society of Professional Engineers v. United States*, 435 U.S. 679 (1978), which established the relevant factors for Rule of Reason review. The Justice Department had charged the Society governing civil engineers with a *per se* violation of § 1 for adopting a rule that prohibited engineers from quoting a price in their project bids. The Society defended its price ban as necessary to protect the public from unsafe structures that engineers might design if they became too cost conscious in order to win bids and jobs. Again rejecting *per se* analysis (but this time because the defendant was a "learned professional society" that required some self-regulation), the Court established the test for the Rule of Reason: an agreement is unlawful if the anticompetitive injury it causes outweighs the procompetitive benefits it generates. From that premise the Court concluded that a private Society's ban on competitive bidding and lower engineering prices offered to customers, even if justified as a way to prevent unethical behavior and inferior work by this profession, was "nothing less than a frontal assault on the basic policy of the Sherman Act."

> The Sherman Act reflects a legislative judgment that ultimately competition will produce not only lower prices, but also better goods and services.... The assumption that competition is the best method of allocating resources in a free market recognizes that all elements of a bargain—quality, service, safety, and durability—and not just the immediate cost, are favorably affected by the free opportunity to select among alternative offers. Even assuming occasional exceptions to the presumed consequences of competition, the

statutory policy precludes inquiry into the question whether competition is good or bad.

The fact that engineers are often involved in large scale projects significantly affecting the public safety does not alter our analysis. Exceptions to the Sherman Act for potentially dangerous goods and services would be tantamount to repeal of the statute. In our complex economy the number of items that may cause serious harm is almost endless—automobiles, drugs, foods, aircraft components, heavy equipment, and countless others, cause serious harm to individuals or to the public at large if defectively made. The judiciary cannot indirectly protect the public against this harm by conferring monopoly privileges on the manufacturers.

435 U.S. at 695–96.

Clearly, then, the antitrust Rule of Reason requires judges and juries to balance only an agreement's effects on *economic* competition. Courts must weigh the injury to the consumer stemming from any increase in defendants' market power due to the arrangement (allocative inefficiency) against any benefits to the consumer that occur because defendants can make and sell their product(s) at a lower price, or make more and higher quality products at the same price (productive efficiency).

The difficulty is that this approach requires fact-finders to compare apples and oranges, neither of which can be easily identified or precisely quantified. Because economists differ sharply over both the market power and the efficiency effects of any particular business arrangement, this balancing exercise is problematic for judges, let alone lay juries. Judge Robert Bork noted this problem in *Rothery Storage & Van Co. v. Atlas Van Lines, Inc.*, 792 F.2d 210 (D.C.Cir.1986), in an important opinion which resurrected the "ancillary restraints" doctrine that had first been formulated by then-Chief Judge Taft in *United States v. Addyston Pipe & Steel Co.*, 85 Fed. 271 (6th Cir.1898), *aff'd*, 175 U.S. 211 (1899). Though the Supreme Court has not yet explicitly endorsed this concept, we will see it figure in several sports law opinions reproduced in this and the following chapters. In any event, a crucial issue that remains is who has the burden of proving the various facts relevant to each side of the equation and what presumptions apply when the balance of welfare effects appears roughly equal.

When reading the numerous sports cases presented in this chapter (and also in Chapter 7), keep in mind the following issues derived from the four major antitrust precedents we have just seen excerpted. Does a group of separate teams generate large benefits by coming together as a single league, such that the league's distinctive product is more valuable than anything individual teams can offer fans by themselves? (See *Broadcast Music*.) Does a challenged rule produce a superior league product that is more competitive in the (interbrand) entertainment market and thus outweighs whatever antitrust concerns are raised by reduced (intrabrand) competition among league members? (See *GTE*

Sylvania.) Does a challenged league rule confer monopoly power on the league in its market, and if so, how should that finding affect the antitrust analysis under § 1? (See *Northwest Wholesale Stationers*.) And do the harms allegedly suffered by the plaintiffs from a particular rule, or the league's asserted justifications for the rule, reflect only the economic effects that are relevant to Rule of Reason analysis? (See *Professional Engineers*.) These questions are raised by the numerous sports antitrust cases that follow in this chapter and in the rest of this book.

B. ANTITRUST AND THE PLAYERS MARKET

1. ROOKIE DRAFT

With that doctrinal prelude, we now turn to the key substantive issues raised in antitrust litigation by players against restraints imposed on the labor market by leagues, particularly their various reserve systems.[d] The major cases have taken place in football, one involving the rookie draft; the second, development squads; and the third, restraints on veteran free agency.

The draft of college players originated in football in the 1930s and later spread to other professional sports. While there are variations across the sports, the basic structure of the draft is simple. Proceeding in reverse order of finish from the prior season, each team selects a player from the pool of new players available that year. (The NBA and the NHL do conduct a lottery for drafting positions among the teams that miss the playoffs, but this is still heavily weighted towards the clubs with the worst records that season.) The consequence is that a player can either negotiate a contract to play with the team that selected him, or not play in the league at all. When there is no other league in which to play that sport, one would expect an antitrust suit eventually to be lodged by a player unhappy with the contract offer he was able to secure from the team that drafted him. The player in the following case had a somewhat unusual and unfortunate source of his unhappiness.

---

[d]. There has been remarkably little analysis in the legal literature of the specific question whether one or other version of the rookie draft or restraints on veteran free agency are compatible with the principles of antitrust law. Valuable treatments of this subject are found in John C. Weistart and Cym H. Lowell, *The Law of Sports* (Indianapolis: Bobbs-Merrill, 1979), at 500–524, 590–627, and Stephen S. Ross, *Monopoly Sports Leagues*, 77 Minnesota L. Rev. 647, 667–695 (1989). There is, however, no shortage of economic literature on this topic, perhaps because it seems more an economic than a legal inquiry to judge whether such league restraints on competition in the players market are reasonably necessary for a successful league operation and/or risk undue exploitation of players by clubs in the league. Besides the works referred to in note a above, there are two book-length treatments of this issue in connection with baseball. One, Jesse W. Markham and Paul Teplitz, *Baseball Economics and Public Policy* (Lexington Mass.: Lexington Books, 1981), finds such league restraints reasonable. The other, Gerald Scully, *The Business of Major League Baseball* (Chicago, Ill.: University of Chicago Press, 1989), reaches the opposite verdict.

SMITH v. PRO FOOTBALL, INC.
United States Court of Appeals, District of Columbia Circuit, 1978.
593 F.2d 1173.

WILKEY, CIRCUIT JUDGE.

[James "Yazoo" Smith, an All–American defensive back at the University of Oregon, was selected by the Washington Redskins as the twelfth pick in the first round of the 1968 draft. He signed a one-year contract for a total of $50,000—$22,000 in salary and $28,000 in bonuses. Smith suffered a career-ending neck injury in the last game of the 1968 regular season, and the Redskins paid him an additional $19,800 (the amount he would have received had he played out the option year of his contract).

Two years later, Smith filed a lawsuit that, among other things, attacked the legality of the rookie draft under antitrust law. Smith contended that, but for the draft, he would have secured a more lucrative contract that would have better protected him from the financial consequences of his injury. The district court ruled that the NFL's draft violated federal antitrust law and had cost Smith $92,000—the amount the judge calculated as the difference between what Smith would have received in a "free market" without a draft, and what he actually received. These financial losses were automatically trebled to a $276,000 damage award.]

I. BACKGROUND

The NFL draft, which has been in effect since 1935, is a procedure under which negotiating rights to graduating college football players are allocated each year among the NFL clubs in inverse order of the clubs' standing.... In 1968 there were 16 succeeding rounds in the yearly draft, the same order of selection being followed in each round. Teams had one choice per round unless they had traded their choice in that round to another team (a fairly common practice). When Smith was selected by the Redskins there were 26 teams choosing in the draft.

The NFL draft, like similar procedures in other professional sports, is designed to promote "competitive balance." By dispersing newly arriving player talent equally among all NFL teams, with preferences to the weaker clubs, the draft aims to produce teams that are as evenly-matched on the playing field as possible. Evenly-matched teams make for closer games, tighter pennant races, and better player morale, thus maximizing fan interest, broadcast revenues, and overall health of the sport.

The draft is effectuated through the NFL's "no-tampering" rule. Under this rule as it existed in 1968, no team was permitted to negotiate prior to the draft with any player eligible to be drafted, and no team could negotiate with (or sign) any player selected by another team in the draft. The net result of these restrictions was that the right to negotiate with any given player was exclusively held by one team at any given time. If a college player could not reach a satisfactory agreement with the team holding the rights to his services, he could not play in the NFL.

* * *

The NFL player draft differs from the classic group boycott in two significant respects. First, the NFL clubs which have "combined" to implement the draft are not *competitors* in any economic sense. The clubs operate basically as a joint venture in producing an entertainment product—football games and telecasts. No NFL club can produce this product without agreements and joint action with every other team. To this end, the League not only determines franchise locations, playing schedules, and broadcast terms, but also ensures that the clubs receive equal shares of telecast and ticket revenues. These economic joint venturers "compete" on the playing field, to be sure, but here as well cooperation is essential if the entertainment product is to attain a high quality: only if the teams are "competitively balanced" will spectator interest be maintained at a high pitch. No NFL team, in short, is interested in driving another team out of business, whether in the counting-house or on the football field, for if the League fails, no one team can survive.

The draft differs from the classic group boycott, secondly, in that the NFL clubs have not combined *to exclude competitors or potential competitors* from their level of the market. Smith was never seeking to "compete" with the NFL clubs, and their refusal to deal with him has resulted in no decrease in the competition for providing football entertainment to the public. The draft, indeed, is designed not to insulate the NFL from competition, but to improve the entertainment product by enhancing its teams' competitive equality.

In view of these differences, we conclude that the NFL player draft cannot properly be described as a group boycott, at least not the type of group boycott that traditionally has elicited invocation of a *per se* rule. The "group boycott" designation, we believe, is properly restricted to concerted attempts by competitors to exclude horizontal competitors; it should not be applied, and has never been applied by the Supreme Court, to concerted refusals that are not designed to drive out competitors but to achieve some other goal.

* * *

Whether the draft is a group boycott, or not, we think it is clearly not the type of restraint to which a *per se* rule is meant to apply. A *per se* rule is a judicial shortcut: it represents the considered judgment of courts, after considerable experience with a particular type of restraint, that the rule of reason, the normal mode of analysis, can be dispensed with.... A court will not indulge in this conclusive presumption lightly. Invocation of a *per se* rule always risks sweeping reasonable, pro-competitive activity within a general condemnation, and a court will run this risk only when it can say, on the strength of unambiguous experience, that the challenged action is a "naked restraint [ ] of trade with no purpose except stifling of competition...."

The NFL player draft, we think, quite clearly fails to satisfy the "demanding standards" of *Northern Pacific Railway*. Given that the draft's restrictive effect is temporally limited, we would hesitate to describe its impact on the market for players' services as "pernicious." More importantly, we cannot say that the draft has "no purpose except stifling of competition" or that it is without "any redeeming virtue." Some form of player selection system may serve to regulate and thereby promote competition in what would otherwise be a chaotic bidding market for the services of college players. The Redskins, moreover, presented considerable evidence at trial that the draft was designed to preserve, and that it made some contribution to preserving, playing-field equality among the NFL-teams with various attendant benefits. The draft, finally, like the vertical restraints challenged in *Continental T.V.*, is "widely used" in our economy and has both judicial and scholarly support for its economic usefulness.

This is not to say, of course, that the draft in any one of its incarnations may not violate the antitrust laws. It is only to say that the courts have had too little experience with this type of restraint, and know too little of the "economic and business stuff" from which it issues, confidently to declare it illegal without undertaking the analysis enjoined by the rule of reason....

In antitrust law, as elsewhere, we must heed Justice Cardozo's warning to beware "the tyranny of tags and tickets." When anticompetitive effects are shown to result from a particular player selection system "they can be adequately policed under the rule of reason."

* * *

B. Rule of Reason

Under the rule of reason, a restraint must be evaluated to determine whether it is significantly anticompetitive in purpose or effect.... If, on analysis, the restraint is found to have legitimate business purposes whose realization serves to promote competition, the "anticompetitive evils" of the challenged practice must be carefully balanced against its "procompetitive virtues" to ascertain whether the former outweigh the latter. A restraint is unreasonable if it has the "net effect" of substantially impeding competition.

* * *

The draft that has been challenged here is undeniably anticompetitive both in its purpose and in its effect. The defendants have conceded that the draft "restricts competition among the NFL clubs for the services of graduating college players" and, indeed, that the draft "is designed to limit competition" and "to be a 'purposive' restraint" on the player-service market. The fact that the draft assertedly was designed to promote the teams' playing-field equality rather than to inflate their profit margins may prevent the draft's purpose from being described, in subjective terms, as nefarious. But this fact does not prevent its purpose from being described, in objective terms, as anticompetitive, for suppressing competition is the Telos, the very essence of the restraint.

The trial judge was likewise correct in finding that the draft was significantly anticompetitive in its *effect*. The draft inescapably forces each seller of football services to deal with one, and only one buyer, robbing the seller, as in any monopolistic market, of any real bargaining power. The draft, as the District Court found, "leaves no room whatever for competition among the teams for the services of college players, and utterly strips them of any measure of control over the marketing of their talents." The predictable effect of the draft, as the evidence established and as the District Court found, was to lower the salary levels of the best college players. There can be no doubt that the effect of the draft as it existed in 1968 was to "suppress or even destroy competition" in the market for players' services.

The justification asserted for the draft is that it has the legitimate business purpose of promoting "competitive balance" and playing-field equality among the teams, producing better entertainment for the public, higher salaries for the players, and increased financial security for the clubs. The NFL has endeavored to summarize this justification by saying that the draft ultimately has a "procompetitive" effect, yet this shorthand entails no small risk of confusion. The draft is "procompetitive," if at all, in a very different sense from that in which it is anticompetitive. The draft is anticompetitive in its effect on the market for players' services, because it virtually eliminates economic competition among buyers for the services of sellers. The draft is allegedly "procompetitive" in its effect on the playing field; but the NFL teams are not economic competitors on the playing field, and the draft, while it may heighten athletic competition and thus improve the entertainment product offered to the public, does not increase competition in the economic sense of encouraging others to enter the market and to offer the product at lower cost. Because the draft's "anticompetitive" and "procompetitive" effects are not comparable, it is impossible to "net them out" in the usual rule-of-reason balancing. The draft's "anticompetitive evils," in other words, cannot be balanced against its "procompetitive virtues," and the draft be upheld if the latter outweigh the former. In strict economic terms, the draft's demonstrated procompetitive effects are nil.

The defendants' justification for the draft reduces in fine to an assertion that competition in the market for entering players' services would not serve the best interests of the public, the clubs, or the players themselves. This is precisely the type of argument that the Supreme Court only recently has declared to be unavailing. In *National Society of Professional Engineers v. United States*, the Court held that a professional society's ban on competitive bidding violated § 1 of the Sherman Act. In so holding the Court rejected a defense that unbridled competitive bidding would lead to deceptively low bids and inferior work "with consequent risk to public safety and health," terming this justification "nothing less than a frontal assault on the basic policy of the Sherman Act." Ending decades of uncertainty as to the proper scope of inquiry under the rule of reason, the Court stated categorically that the rule, contrary to its name, "does not open the field of antitrust inquiry to any argument in favor of a challenged restraint that may fall within the realm of reason," and that the inquiry instead must be "confined to a consideration of (the restraint's) impact on competitive conditions." The purpose of antitrust analysis, the Court concluded, "is to form a judgment about the competitive significance of the restraint; it is not to decide whether a policy favoring competition is in the public interest, or in the interest of the members of an industry. Subject to exceptions defined by statute, that policy decision has been made by Congress."

Confining our inquiry, as we must, to the draft's impact on competitive conditions, we conclude that the draft as it existed in 1968 was an unreasonable restraint of trade. The draft was concededly anticompetitive in purpose. It was severely anticompetitive in effect. It was not shown to have any significant offsetting procompetitive impact in the economic sense. Balancing the draft's anticompetitive evils against its procompetitive virtues, the outcome is plain. The NFL's defenses, premised on the assertion that competition for players' services would harm both the football industry and society, are unavailing; there is nothing of procompetitive virtue to balance, because "the Rule of Reason does not support a defense based on the assumption that competition itself is unreasonable."

We recognize, on analogy with the Supreme Court's reasoning in *Goldfarb* and *Professional Engineers*, that professional football "may differ significantly from other business services, and, accordingly [that] the nature of the competition" for player talent may vary from an absolute "free market" norm. Given the joint-venture status of the NFL clubs, we do not foreclose the possibility that some type of player selection system might be defended as serving "to regulate and promote ... competition" in the market for players' services. But we are faced here, as the Supreme Court was faced in *Professional Engineers*, with what amounts to a "total ban" on competition, and we agree with the District Court that this level of restraint cannot be justified. The trial judge concluded, with pardonable exaggeration, that the draft system at issue was "absolutely the most restrictive one imaginable." Even though the draft was justified primarily by the need to disperse the best players, it applied to all graduating seniors, including average players who were, in a sense, fungible commodities. It permitted college players to negotiate with only one team. If a player could not contract with that team, *he could not play at all*.

Without intimating any view as to the legality of the following procedures, we note that there exist significantly less anticompetitive alternatives to the draft system which has been challenged here. The trial judge found that the evidence supported the viability of a player selection system that would permit "more than one team to draft each player, while restricting the number of players any one team might sign." A less anticompetitive draft might permit a college player to negotiate with the team of his choice if the team that drafted him failed to make him an acceptable offer. The NFL could also conduct a second draft each year for players who were unable to reach agreement with the team that selected them the first time. Most obviously, perhaps, the District Court found that the evidence supported the feasibility of a draft that would run for fewer rounds, applying only to the most talented players and enabling their "average" brethren to negotiate in a "free market." The least restrictive alternative of all, of course, would be for the NFL to eliminate the draft entirely and employ revenue-sharing to equalize the teams' financial resources, a method of preserving "competitive balance" nicely in harmony with the league's self-proclaimed "joint-venture" status.

We are not required in this case to design a draft that would pass muster under the antitrust laws. We would suggest, however, that under the Supreme Court's decision in *Professional Engineers*, no draft can be justified merely by showing that it is a relatively less anticompetitive means of attaining sundry benefits for the football industry and society. Rather, a player draft can survive scrutiny under the rule of reason only if it is demonstrated to have positive, economically procompetitive benefits that offset its anticompetitive effects, or, at the least, if it is demonstrated to accomplish legitimate business purposes and to have a net anticompetitive effect that is insubstantial. Because the NFL draft as it existed in 1968 had severe anticompetitive effects and no demonstrated procompetitive virtues, we hold that it unreasonably restrained trade in violation of § 1 of The Sherman Act.

[The court, however, remanded the case to the trial judge for recomputation of appropriate antitrust damages, an exercise that admittedly had "a certain Alice-in-Wonderland quality to it...." *Smith* is still the only appellate court decision focusing squarely on the rookie draft's legality under antitrust law. The majority ruling elicited a lengthy and vigorous dissent by Judge MacKinnon, which is the most effective judicial statement of the antitrust point of view consistently presented by all professional sports leagues. It remains to be seen whether the Supreme Court will embrace these arguments when it finally accepts a case raising substantive antitrust issues in professional sports.]

* * *

MACKINNON, CIRCUIT JUDGE, dissenting.

* * *

The Nature of the Business.

* * *

Professional sports teams are in some respects traditional economic units seeking to sell a product to the public. But economic competition between teams is not and cannot be the sole determinant of their behavior. Professional sports leagues are uniquely organized economic entities; the ultimate success of the league depends on the economic cooperation rather than the economic competition of its members. The product being offered to the public is more than an isolated exhibition, it is a series of connected exhibitions that culminate in the annual grand finale contest between the two teams with the best records in the League, which have demonstrated their prowess in organized, rigidly scheduled League competition. The product being offered the public is the "league sport," and the value of this product at the stadium gate and to the television networks depends on the competitive balance of the teams in the league. Spectators and television viewers are not interested in lopsided games or contests between weak teams.

In many respects, the business of professional football as carried on by the NFL resembles a "natural monopoly." The structure of the League as a single entity outside the antitrust laws was also specifically authorized in 1966 by Act of Congress. As defined by two authorities, a natural monopoly is a monopoly resulting from economies of scale, a relationship between the size of the market and the size of the most efficient firm such that one firm of efficient size can produce all or more than the market can take at a remunerative price, and can continually expand its capacity at less cost than that of a new firm entering the business. In this situation, competition may exist for a time but only until bankruptcy or merger leaves the field to one firm; in a meaningful sense, competition here is self-destructive. At the present time, the NFL, as an organized association of various teams (or firms), has a statutorily recognized monopoly over production of the "league sport" of major professional football. Anyone who wishes to watch a major professional football game must watch an NFL game, played under NFL rules with NFL teams and players. History suggests that it is easier for the NFL to expand the number of teams than it is for another league to form and operate successfully. Competition may exist for a time, as the experiences of the American Football League and the World Football League demonstrate, but in the long run such competition is destructive and many teams fail, even as they did within the NFL in its free market formative years.

The History and Effect of the Draft.

[Here Judge MacKinnon detailed a number of features of life in the NFL in the mid–1930s at the time the draft was adopted. There were just nine teams with squads of 22 to 26 players. Though a free market existed for players coming out of college, a career in professional football was not that attractive to many players as they graduated from college. Many opted to go on to graduate or professional school, to go into business, or to begin college or high school football coaching. These alternatives were attractive as compared to the NFL, where salaries were modest, careers were short, and there was always a possibility of a permanently disabling injury. In 1936, the NFL instituted the draft after the last-place Cincinnati team had dropped out of the league. Initially covering 30 rounds, the draft had been cut to 17 rounds by the time that Smith challenged its legality under antitrust law four decades later.]

* * *

In my view, there are compelling reasons why the draft has continued so long without serious challenge. In effect a player draft is *natural* for league sports. Competitive equality among the component teams is an inherent requirement for meaningful sports competition and the survival of a conference or league high school, college, or professional and all of its members. Close rivalries are the backbone of any successful sport. When the NFL established the draft, its objective was to give each team the same fair *opportunity* to be competitive; it sought to achieve a competitive balance among all the League's teams, that is, to "try to equalize the teams." The intended result was to create a situation where each League game would become a closer contest, where spectator interest in the game and the players themselves would be increased, where the interesting individual contests would create an interesting League championship race, and where ultimately the teams and their players would benefit from the greater income resulting from the increased fan interest.

* * *

All major sports, in recognition of the need for competitive balance, have drafts. Hockey and basketball have drafts, and baseball instituted a draft when it became clear from the long domination of the New York Yankees that the farm system was not producing competitive balance.

Since the first college football player draft was held in 1936, the results sought to be accomplished have clearly been achieved. Some argue that this has been caused by other factors, but the preponderance of the factual testimony and record evidence supports a conclusion that the college player draft was the key factor which produced the competitive balance of the teams, which in turn brought about the exciting games and interesting championship races and increased public interest in the sport, which ultimately led to the huge gate receipts and large television contracts that are presently producing enormous benefits for the players themselves. There was no showing to the contrary in the 2,000 page record. The majority argue that it is television that produces the interest and the revenues but the balanced teams produced by the draft came first and caused the close contests which attracted the public and eventually television.

Since 1935, the number of teams has increased from nine to today's League of 28 teams, and the number of players per team has also been increased substantially. Instead of the small squads of around 26 players in the early days of the sport, the modern team's roster once swelled to 47 and was later reduced to 43 players. This has increased the total number of active players in the League as a whole to slightly over 1,200. Gate receipts have increased tremendously due to the increased popular interest in the game. Also important are the television revenues, which constitute a large part of each team's annual income. The NFL television contracts between the League and the television networks have distributed hundreds of millions of dollars to all teams in the League; and current news reports indicate that the payments are to be substantially increased. The lucrative television contract, made possible by an *exemption* from the antitrust laws enacted by Congress, is negotiated for all teams by the League Commissioner. These moneys are distributed *equally* to each team in the League without regard to the size of the team's local television market. In 1968 the revenues from television accounted for approximately 30% of the total revenue of the Redskins and this was approximately the same percentage as the average for all NFL teams in that year. Team revenue from gate receipts, television contracts, and other sources has increased tremendously since 1935, and the NFL teams and their players are the direct recipients of the benefits of the increased national interest in NFL games. College players, 22 years old, coming out of college in 1976 and playing in the NFL were making $20,000 to $150,000 their first year.

* * *

Due to the increased benefits afforded professional football players, the competition for graduating college football players that previously existed from lucrative coaching positions and numerous other business and professional opportunities has been successfully met, if not altogether eliminated as a practical matter. The increasing popularity of pro football and its attractiveness to graduating college players assures those interested in the success of the game, such as television and radio broadcasters and networks, stadium owners, team owners, and players already playing in the NFL, that the best college football players year after year will continue to join the professional ranks and assure the quality and attractiveness of their games. In fact, a great many players now go to college for the sole purpose of establishing a playing record which will result in their being drafted by one of the professional teams; a first-round draft choice in the professional league is viewed by many as the substantial equivalent of *summa cum laude* and first-round draft choices are generally paid much higher starting salaries.

* * *

From my analysis, the testimony of record overwhelmingly supports the conclusion that the growth of football between 1935 and 1968 was largely due to the competitive balance that the League achieved during those years and to the creation of a quality product, the "league sport." This competitive balance, and the consequential tremendous growth in public interest, which has inured greatly to the benefit of the players themselves, is in large part a result of the college player draft.... The draft created the competitive balance, that created the public interest, that led other cities to organize teams, that led to national expansion of the league, that enlarged the total gate receipts, that led to the large revenue-producing television contracts.

[The dissent then addressed the majority's argument that a less restrictive draft system should have been devised by the NFL.]

* * *

A pure draft takes all of the college players that are coming into the market with the teams with the poorest records having preference in the order of their won and lost records. The draft as it existed in 1968 was a pure draft, and it is submitted that the draft should be that extensive if the opportunity for maximum competitive balance is to be assured. If the draft only lasts two rounds, as the trial court here suggested, the rest of the players are left for the free market and the preponderance of those players, or at least the preponderance of the better players in that group, would go to teams with special attractions and the teams owned by super-wealthy millionaires who desire very greatly to own a winning team. Not even a complete sharing of team revenues could overcome the unfair advantage posed by wealthy owners and collateral attractions of a few cities. Large cities such as New York, Chicago, Los Angeles, and Washington offer special advantages for publicity, endorsements, and lucrative off-field jobs in business. Cities with better weather are more attractive to some players, and teams with better prospects of winning in a particular season furnish a certain attraction for some players. Larger cities with larger stadiums realize more income and hence are somewhat able to offer larger salaries than teams with smaller cities and stadiums. So are teams owned by wealthy sportsmen who place a premium on winning and are willing to support their desires with almost unlimited financial resources. The draft has substantially reduced the ability of these owners to dominate the league.

Given these factors that would permit a few teams to corner the "developing players" that in a great many instances eventually surpass developed players, drafted in the earlier rounds, it is necessary to have a draft that reaches the *maximum number of potential players who are absolutely necessary to preserve competitive balance.* When the draft does not reach that many players, the few stronger teams with the natural advantages will be able to corner the best remaining prospects who become free agents. The testimony indicated that a few "super wealthy" owners with a very deep pocketbook could obtain a very substantial advantage if there were a substantial pool of free market players.

* * *

The Rule of Reason and the College Player Draft.

* * *

[T]he important consideration is the *effect* of the draft. The majority concludes that the draft strips the players of "any real bargaining power," lowers their salaries, and suppresses if not destroys competition for their services. I disagree. The majority opinion and the trial court only looked at the draft from the players' side and only at a portion of that. As for bargaining power, the operation of the draft also restrains

Sec. B   ANTITRUST & PLAYERS MARKET   171

the team from dealing with other players (even though there are exceptions, discussed below). This is particularly true when a team drafts for a position, as the Redskins did in drafting Smith as their first-round choice in 1968. The Redskins drafted Smith in the first round to fill a need at the "free safety position." In using their first-round draft choice to select a player for that particular position, they practically put all of their eggs in one basket for that year. In selecting Smith, they passed over or did not reach, all other players of nearly equal ability for that position. After the Redskins had exercised their first draft selection, these other players would be chosen by other teams with later picks, and would thus not be available in later rounds. Even if another player was later available, it would be a waste of a valuable draft choice for the Redskins to use any subsequent choice to draft for that same position, since the position needed only one player and the team had other needs to fill as well. That is the way the 1968 player draft went for the Redskins. After they had drafted Smith first to fill that position, the team practically had to sign him if they wanted to fill what they considered was a vital team vacancy. These circumstances gave Smith very substantial bargaining leverage, as his professional negotiating agent frequently reminded the Redskins. Also, a first-round draft choice commands considerable publicity in the locality, and the team is under very considerable pressure from its fans to sign the player and thereby put the first-round pick in a uniform. Smith was the beneficiary, as a first-round choice, of such public pressure.

While in a free market a player could negotiate with several teams, a team could also negotiate with several players of nearly equal ability and play one off against the others. If Smith had negotiated with the Redskins in a free market, the Redskins could also have simultaneously negotiated with the next-best prospect for free safety as well and the availability of the other player might have served to reduce the salary offers to Smith. Then if Smith and the Redskins could not come to terms, the Redskins could always opt for one of the other prospects they considered to be close to Smith in ability, well realizing, as experience has many times proven, that the ultimate development and performance of the second or third choice might eventually eclipse that of their first favored choice. Drafting college players is not an exact science.

* * *

Simply because the draft is essential to the vitality of the business does not mean that players entering the League, as opposed to veterans already playing in the League, have no interest in the existence of a draft. It would be error to suggest otherwise because without a draft a less stable League with fewer franchises and lower salaries would result. Incoming players receive salaries and bonuses far in excess of what they could command in a free market of teams in a league that did not have the competitive balance which a player draft produces. The vitality of the League, which is admittedly dependent in large measure on the balanced team competition produced by the draft, has attracted so great a public interest that the public in most localities, as referred to above, has subsidized the teams by the erection of huge stadiums without full contribution to their cost by the teams that use them. This fact has enabled salaries paid to draftees to be higher than what they would be in a free market with the attendant destructive competition, unequal competitive balance, and resulting shaky franchises. It cannot be said that rookie players have no interest in the existence of the college player draft.

In short, in my opinion, the evidentiary record here supports the conclusion that the draft also has a favorable effect on the bargaining position of players, which to a considerable extent nets out the adverse effect it has in limiting the players' right to negotiate with other teams. And this bargaining equivalency vitiates the assertion that players' salaries are depressed on account of the draft.

Questions for Discussion

1. Is the *Smith* majority's analysis in the first part of the opinion, which defends the competitive virtues of the draft against a charge of *per se* illegality, fully compatible with its analysis in the second part of the opinion, which condemns the anticompetitive effect of the draft under the Rule of Reason?

2. In several very long footnotes, the *Smith* majority and dissent debated a number of the factual underpinnings to their respective arguments:

   a) Was it the player draft, instituted in 1935, or network television, which emerged in the late 1950s, or some linkage between the two, that was the true source of pro football's economic success?

   b) How much competitive balance can really be contributed by the rookie draft (or restraints on veteran free agency), given the team dynasties associated with head coaches such as Paul Brown, Vince Lombardi, Tom Landry, Don Shula, Chuck Noll, Bill Walsh, and Bill Parcells? Does the NFL need comparable restraints on free agency for coaches (who almost invariably negotiate multi-year no-cut contracts)? Should the league, for example, have had a draft to allocate Jimmy Johnson to a particular team when he decided to move from college football at Miami to professional ball with the Dallas Cowboys?

   c) Is the true secret of evenly balanced athletic competition the sharing of revenues among owners, not just from network and cable television and trademark licensing, but also from gate receipts (though not, as yet, from luxury boxes and other features of lucrative stadium deals)? What effect might such league "socialism" have on teams' ability and incentive to pay their players higher salaries?

3. The *Smith* majority seems to state that it is irrelevant for Rule of Reason analysis that a league practice such as the draft enhances competitive balance within the league. Is that position compatible with the Supreme Court's observations quoted earlier in this chapter, to the effect that improvements in the economic efficiency of an enterprise may actually be procompetitive for the broader economy? Indeed, if a league cannot defend

the legality of restrictive internal practices on the grounds that they improve the quality of the product offered to its fans, how could a less restrictive draft (or any conduct-standardizing rule) pass muster, as the *Smith* majority intimates it could in the latter part of its decision?

4. The principal argument for the draft is that this system is necessary to preserve balanced athletic competition against the threat posed by big market teams. But is there any guarantee that the draft will have that effect, at least as long as teams can sell their top picks to other clubs? Consider, for example, the significance of the Quebec Nordiques dealing Eric Lindros to the Philadelphia Flyers in 1992, for $15 million and five players. (The Nordiques franchise had been purchased in 1989 for $15 million, though it became far more valuable in the late–1990s as the Stanley Cup champion Colorado Avalanche.) In addition, is it possible that the draft also obstructs achievement of such competitive balance? Does not the football draft guarantee the Super Bowl winner the exclusive right to valued players, which may obstruct the ability of weaker teams to make rapid improvements in their relative strength? Can you think of ways to restructure the draft to enhance its contribution to equality on the playing field (as well as its ability to pass the Rule of Reason test)?

5. Opponents of the draft assert that it permits exploitation of new players, who are left with no choice but to accept a "take it or leave it" offer by the drafting team, the only team with which they are permitted to deal. Yet in sports like football or basketball, top rookie draft picks have been signing multiyear contracts worth tens of millions of dollars. For example, in 1992 Shaquille O'Neal received a $40 million, 7–year deal from the Orlando Magic. Even in a less wealthy sport such as hockey, Eric Lindros signed that same year a $21 million, 6–year contract with the Philadelphia Flyers. Presumably teams feel compelled to make such lucrative offers to draft picks they "own," because the player has some negotiating leverage by threatening not to play at all for this team which has not drafted or secured other quality players at this position. The degree of such leverage is shaped by the league's own rules that define how long an unsigned draft pick will remain on the reserve list of the club that drafted him. To address this problem, the leagues in basketball, hockey, and football have each been able to persuade their respective players associations to agree to different versions of a rookie salary cap.

Even in baseball, where top draft picks typically spend some years in the minor leagues, the signing bonus to the number one pick in 1996 (Kris Benson) was $2 million, up from the mere $60,000 paid to the top pick in 1979. At the same time, the economic consequences of a draft system were vividly displayed by that same 1996 baseball draft. Four of the clubs failed that year to comply with the Player Relations Committee's rules that require the drafting team to make a minimum offer to each pick within 15 days of the draft to be able to reserve him. These four accidental free agents (three of whom were high school pitchers) secured a total of $29 million in contract value. Two of them, Travis Lee (the number two pick) and Matt White (number five), were each given more than $10 million in contract guarantees and bonuses by the Arizona Diamondbacks and Tampa Bay Devil Rays, in the hope that these young players would be there when the expansion teams first took the field in 1998. Then, in 1997, the Philadelphia Phillies made

J.D. Drew, a star outfielder at Florida State, the second pick in that year's draft. When the Phillies offered Drew a $2 million rather than a $10 million signing bonus, Drew agreed to play that summer for the St. Paul Saints in the independent Northern Baseball League. Drew's agent Scott Boras was hoping not simply to expose the Phillies to the loss of their pick, but also to exclude Drew from the 1998 draft, which under MLB Rules applies only to "amateur" baseball players. Thus, MLB officials issued a "clarification" of its draft rules which spelled out that amateur players include anyone who has not signed a contract with either a major league or an affiliated minor league club (part of the National Association of Professional Baseball Leagues). The MLBPA responded with a grievance which claimed that such a league position amounted to revision rather than just clarification of the existing rules, a step that requires agreement of the Players Association.

This case, one that is governed by the parties' labor agreement under labor law, was still unresolved at the end of 1997. Certainly if the union's position were to be upheld by the arbitrator, this would offer star prospects a major escape route from the current baseball draft. These recent developments and disputes in that sport pose the broader economic policy issue of whether there are ways in which one can (and should) restructure the draft to ensure that teams do offer drafted players their full economic value, while still preserving sufficient competitive balance among teams on the playing field? Is it good antitrust or other public policy to ensure that star prospects do receive their full economic value?

6. The previous questions suggest the possibility of "more reasonable" or "less restrictive" alternatives to the current "restraint of trade" flowing from the draft. How does the concept of "less restrictive alternative" fit within antitrust law as envisioned by the Supreme Court in *Professional Engineers*? Is such an alternative simply a factor to be considered, or one that dictates the ultimate antitrust result?

For example, if a court believes that professional football with the existing draft is more procompetitive (more attractive to fans) than football without a draft, does the possibility of a less restrictive draft (one that has less anticompetitive impact on the players market) make the existing system illegal? How can one judge which version of the draft is more or less restrictive as far as players are concerned? For example, compare a three-round draft with players tied to the drafting team for two years to a six-round draft with players tied to the team for just one year. How does one then compare the incremental gains to players from relaxing the draft's prohibition against teams bidding for rookies to the incremental losses to fans from a reduction in competitive athletic balance within the league (on the assumption that the draft does contribute at least some measure of competitive equality)? Does the process of antitrust litigation about these issues give the league sufficient guidance in designing its system for allocating new players to the teams? Does the threat of litigation give the league the incentive to explore more optimal solutions along both dimensions of this issue?

7. The NFL's 1993 litigation settlement and subsequent collective bargaining agreement, which authorize a seven-round annual draft, established for the first time in professional sports a maximum limit on the

amount of money that a team could pay each year to its entire group of first year players. In 1996, the NBA and its Players Association went further and agreed to a maximum contract length for rookies (three years), and a salary amount specified for each position in the draft. Unless this system is entitled to a labor exemption from antitrust, it would surely be challenged as a violation of § 1. With what result? If you believe the previous draft system without a rookie salary cap was exploitative, is this system more or less so? Why would the players association be willing to agree to this limitation on the salary amounts that rookies can negotiate? Consider these questions as you read the next section on salary restraints.

Note on Draft Eligibility

First, though, one should note that player draft rules specify not only what happens to the players after the draft, but also which players are eligible to be drafted in the first place.[e] Traditionally, the key eligibility rule in football and basketball was that a player was not included in the draft until four years had elapsed after his high school class had graduated (thus dovetailing with the standard four-year eligibility period in college sports). This historic practice was challenged in 1970 by Spencer Haywood. After graduating from high school in 1967, Haywood starred in junior college basketball for one year, then in the 1968 Olympic Games, and next at the University of Detroit for one year (where he was an All–American). Granted a "hardship" exemption by the new American Basketball Association (*whose* hardship?), Haywood won ABA Rookie of the Year and Most Valuable Player honors in the 1969–1970 season. In 1970, Haywood was interested in playing for the Seattle Supersonics in the NBA, but he was barred by Commissioner Walter Kennedy under the NBA's four-year rule. In response, Haywood launched and won an antitrust suit striking down this eligibility rule in one of the first-ever successful player antitrust cases. See *Denver Rockets v. All–Pro Management, Inc.*, 325 F.Supp. 1049 (C.D.Cal.1971). *Haywood* was followed by *Linseman v. World Hockey Ass'n*, 439 F.Supp. 1315 (D.Conn. 1977), which struck down the WHA's (and implicitly the National Hockey League's) age–20 eligibility rule (which dovetailed with the "graduation" age from Canadian junior hockey), and *Boris v. United States Football League*, 1984–1 Trade Cases (CCH) ¶ 66,012, 1984 WL 894 (C.D.Cal.1984), which invalidated a USFL rule that (like the pre–1990 NFL rule) required football players to exhaust their college eligibility before being drafted. (The USFL had made an exception for Herschel Walker when he left the University of Georgia after his sophomore year to play for Donald Trump's New Jersey Generals.)

In *Haywood*, *Linseman*, and *Boris*, though, the federal district judges applied to these eligibility rules rather strange versions of the *per se* antitrust ban on group boycotts, an approach clearly incompatible with the Rule of Reason analysis now used in all appellate sports cases (including *Smith* above and *Mackey* below). Nonetheless, to some extent because of the specter of antitrust litigation, in 1990 the NFL finally relaxed its own four-year eligibility rule for the football draft, though it still excluded players who

---

e. See Robert A. McCormick & Matthew C. McKinnon, *Professional Football's Draft Eligibility Rule: The Labor Exemption and the Antitrust Laws*, 33 Emory L. J. 375 (1984).

have played less than three years in college. The sports world now has a great deal of experience with drafting young players in basketball, hockey, and football.

Questions for Discussion

1. Should a court reach the same result as in *Haywood* if it embarks on a full-blown Rule of Reason analysis, one that takes into account the interests of the young players (both those drafted and those not) and the leagues (both professional and college or junior leagues)? Suppose, for example, the NFL were to follow the suggestion of Bill Walsh, a great coach in both professional and college football, and set a minimum *age* for draft eligibility. How would one go about determining the appropriate age?

2. Consider also the other side of the coin. Both the NFL and the NCAA continue to require a football player who petitions for inclusion in the NFL draft to renounce his college eligibility. What are the likely market effects of these parallel arrangements? Are they questionable under antitrust law? We shall take this issue up in more detail in Chapter 10.

3. An interesting evolution in the interplay of college and professional eligibility rules took place in the mid–1990s. In 1993, the NCAA amended its by-laws that previously rendered an athlete permanently ineligible for college play if he declared himself eligible for a professional league's draft prior to exhausting his four years of college eligibility; it did so, however, only for basketball, not football. Under the new rule, a basketball player could declare himself eligible for the NBA draft, see whether and how high he got drafted and what kind of contract offer he could receive from the NBA, and then return to play in college if he did not accept the offer or sign with an agent. Recognizing that this option to return to college gave drafted underclassmen real bargaining leverage, the NBA amended its rules to give a team that drafts a player two years of exclusive rights to negotiate with him instead of only one. In the face of this NBA move, as well as substantial pressure from college coaches, the NCAA amended its rule a second time in 1997, to allow only *undrafted* underclassmen to return to college play. What lesson is there in this saga about how the NBA views the effect of the draft on the market for rookies? About how the NCAA views the option of turning professional vis-a-vis the market for star college players? Should players have a viable antitrust suit against the NBA (or the NCAA) for these rules?

2. SALARY RESTRAINTS

As we read earlier, in 1989 the NFL devised a "development squad" system under which each team was permitted to sign as many as six rookies or first-year free agents who could practice but not play with the team. The league collectively fixed the salaries payable to each development squad player at $1,000 per week, rather than continuing to permit individual teams to negotiate amounts that had ranged up to $7,000 per week for some of these players in their previous rookie year. The NFL's stated objective was to "promote competitive equality under fiscally responsible circumstances." However, the federal district judge granted the plaintiffs summary judgment on their antitrust claim, on the grounds that this salary rule was both anticompetitive and not justifiable under the Rule of Reason (as a matter of law, relying on *Smith*).

BROWN v. PRO FOOTBALL, INC. (WASHINGTON REDSKINS)

United States District Court, District of Columbia, 1992.
1992–1 Trade Cases (CCH) ¶ 69,747, 1992 WL 88039.

LAMBERTH, DISTRICT JUDGE.

* * *

Defendants cannot claim that the uniform salary provision was not significantly anticompetitive in its effect. The uniform salary provision prohibited clubs from paying Developmental Squad players anything but $1,000 per week. This prohibition necessarily eliminated all competition and prevented prospective Developmental Squad players from negotiating salary terms among interested NFL clubs. The salary restraint robbed each seller of football services of any bargaining power, left no room "for competition among the teams for the services of [rookie and first year] players, and utterly strip[ped] them of any measure of control over the marketing of their talents." While the impact of the restraint on any given plaintiff, whether positive or negative, is not presently before the court, the effect of the uniform salary provision was to "suppress or even destroy competition."

* * *

Defendants' primary procompetitive claim is that [its] Resolution "promotes competitive balance in the league by eliminating (1) 'stashing' of quality players and (2) consequent disparities in the number of players available for practice purposes." This procompetitive purpose allegedly "enhances the quality of the [NFL's] entertainment product and benefits 'consumers' of NFL football."[14] Defendants claim that "[b]y stashing quality players and consequently accumulating extra players for practice purposes, [some] teams secured an 'unfair' advantage that threatened to undermine the competitive balance crucial to producing the NFL's popular entertainment product." This Circuit has expressly found defendants' proffered "competitive balance" and "better product" purposes to be irrelevant to the rule of reason analysis. *Smith*, 593 F.2d at 1186.

Because the discussion in *Smith* directly addresses and disposes of the issues presently before this court, the discussion will be reproduced

---

14. While the court acknowledges some correlation between the "stashing" point and the salary restraint, the court does not see the correlation of the number of practice players each team has to the salary restraint itself. Because the basis for both the stashing and equalization objectives (promoting competitive balance among the NFL clubs), is irrelevant to the rule of reason inquiry, however, the court need not address the correlation or lack thereof. The court also notes that the rule of reason analysis "does not open the field of antitrust inquiry to any argument in favor of a challenged restraint that may fall within the realm of reason.... [The] inquiry instead must be confined to a consideration of the restraints' impact on competitive conditions." *Smith*, 593 F.2d at 1186.

in its entirety below, replacing the draft restraint in *Smith* with the fixed salary restraint involved in the present case:

> The NFL has endeavored to summarize this justification by saying that the [fixed salary] ultimately has a "procompetitive" effect, yet this shorthand entails no small risk of confusion. The [fixed salary] is "procompetitive," if at all, in a very different sense from that in which it is anticompetitive. The [fixed salary] is anticompetitive in its effect on the market for players' services because it virtually eliminates economic competition among buyers for the services of sellers. The [fixed salary] is allegedly "procompetitive" in its effect on the playing field.... Because the [fixed salary's] "anticompetitive" and "procompetitive" effects are not comparable, it is impossible to "net them out" in the usual rule-of-reason balancing. The [fixed salary's] "anticompetitive evils," in other words, cannot be balanced against its "procompetitive virtues," and the [fixed salary restraint can] be upheld [only] if the latter outweigh the former. In strict economic terms, the [fixed salary's] demonstrated procompetitive effects are nil.

Smith, 593 F.2d at 1186 (citing *National Soc'y of Professional Eng'rs v. United States*, 435 U.S. 679 (1978)).[15] The court finds that the NFL's alleged procompetitive purposes are either insufficient as a matter of law because they fail to justify the necessity of the salary restraint or they are not relevant to the rule of reason analysis.

Judgment granted.

As we will see later in this chapter, the *Brown* case was eventually won by the NFL in the Supreme Court, on the grounds that this salary cap (and cut) was exclusively a matter for collective bargaining, not antitrust challenge by unionized players. Thus, the antitrust merits of the above opinion were never reviewed. In that regard, consider the judge's dismissal of the league's competitive balance argument under antitrust Rule of Reason. Is the above analysis compatible with the Supreme Court's recent pronouncements about the value of economic efficiency in antitrust and the potentially procompetitive impact of certain kinds of internal organizational restraints?

3. VETERAN FREE AGENCY

The following case, *Mackey v. NFL*, posed two different kinds of issues. The first issue was the compatibility with substantive antitrust

---

15. Any claim that the fixed salary provision made the developmental squads themselves more competitive or comparable with each other is likewise rejected. Because the developmental squads did not compete with each other directly, it is obvious that the purpose of any claimed competitive balance among the developmental squads was to promote greater competitive equality among the parent NFL clubs. Such a competitive equality argument, as discussed above, is irrelevant to the antitrust balancing analysis presently before the court.

policy of the "Rozelle Rule," the NFL's practice of requiring the team that signed a veteran free agent to provide what the commissioner judged to be "fair and equitable" compensation (by way of players, draft choices, or both) to the team that had lost the player off its roster. This practice developed in football in the early 1960s (as well as in basketball after the *Barnett* ruling in Chapter 2), in place of the apparently perpetual option contained in baseball's (and hockey's) lifetime reserve system that figured in the *Chase* and *Flood* cases in Chapter 2. The players' objection to the Rozelle Rule was that while football players formally became free agents at the end of their contracts, as a practical matter they had no more ability to sign with other teams than did baseball players bound by the reserve clause—and, unlike baseball, football is subject to antitrust law.

A second key issue introduced in *Mackey* stemmed from the fact that several years after Commissioner Rozelle instituted the compensation rule, this practice was incorporated in the first two collective agreements negotiated between the NFL and its Players Association. The question was whether this free agency restriction had thereby gained a "labor exemption" from antitrust scrutiny.

We first reproduce the portion of *Mackey* that addressed the substantive issue of the compatibility of the Rozelle Rule with antitrust law's bar on "unreasonable restraints of trade."

MACKEY v. NATIONAL FOOTBALL LEAGUE (PART 1)

United States Court of Appeals, Eighth Circuit, 1976.
543 F.2d 606.

LAY, CIRCUIT JUDGE.

* * *

HISTORY.

Throughout most of its history, the NFL's operations have been unilaterally controlled by the club owners. In 1968, however, the NLRB recognized the NFLPA as a labor organization, and as the exclusive bargaining representative of all NFL players. Since that time, the NFLPA and the clubs have engaged in collective bargaining over various terms and conditions of employment. Two formal agreements have resulted. The first, concluded in 1968, was in effect from July 15, 1968 to February 1, 1970. The second, entered into on June 17, 1971, was made retroactive to February 1, 1970, and expired on January 30, 1974. Since 1974, the parties have been negotiating; however, they have not concluded a new agreement.

[The "Rozelle Rule" acknowledged that when a player completed his contractual obligation to a club, usually by playing out the extra "option" year for a 10% pay decrease after his contract term expired, he became a free agent and could negotiate with other NFL teams. However, if the player signed with a new club, that team owed "compensation" (in the form of current players and/or draft picks) to the former team. If the two teams could not agree on what the free agent compensation would be, the commissioner would determine it, and his decision was final and unappealable.]

* * *

This provision, unchanged in form, is currently embodied in § 12.1(H) of the NFL Constitution. The ostensible purposes of the rule are to maintain competitive balance among the NFL teams and protect the clubs' investment in scouting, selecting and developing players.

During the period from 1963 through 1974, 176 players played out their options. Of that number, 34 signed with other teams. In three of those cases, the former club waived compensation. In 27 cases, the clubs involved mutually agreed upon compensation. Commissioner Rozelle awarded compensation in the four remaining cases.

* * *

ANTITRUST ISSUES.

We turn, then, to the question of whether the Rozelle Rule, as implemented, violates § 1 of the Sherman Act, which declares illegal "every contract, combination . . . or conspiracy, in restraint of trade or commerce among the several States." The district court found the Rozelle Rule to be a *per se* violation of the Act. Alternatively, the court held the Rule to be violative of the Rule of Reason standard.

* * *

Per Se Violation.

We review next the district court's holding that the Rozelle Rule is *per se* violative of the Sherman Act [because it significantly deters clubs from negotiating with and signing free agents and thus operates as a group boycott or concerted refusal to deal.]

* * *

There is substantial evidence in the record to support the district court's findings as to the effects of the Rozelle Rule. We think, however, that this case presents unusual circumstances rendering it inappropriate to declare the Rozelle Rule illegal *per se* without undertaking an inquiry into the purported justifications for the Rule.

[T]he line of cases which has given rise to *per se* illegality for the type of agreements involved here generally concerned agreements between business competitors in the traditional sense. Here, however, as the owners and Commissioner urge, the NFL assumes some of the characteristics of a joint venture in that each member club has a stake in the success of the other teams. No one club is interested in driving another team out of business, since if the League fails, no one team can survive. Although businessmen cannot wholly evade the antitrust laws by characterizing their operation as a joint venture, we conclude that the unique nature of the business of professional football renders it inappropriate to mechanically apply *per se* illegality rules here, fashioned in a different context. This is particularly true where, as here, the alleged restraint does not completely eliminate competition for players' services.

* * *

Rule of Reason.

The focus of an inquiry under the Rule of Reason is whether the restraint imposed is justified by legitimate business purposes, and is no more restrictive than necessary.

In defining the restraint on competition for players' services, the district court found that the Rozelle Rule significantly deters clubs from negotiating with and signing free agents; that it acts as a substantial deterrent to players playing out their options and becoming free agents; that it significantly decreases players' bargaining power in contract negotiations; that players are thus denied the right to sell their services in a free and open market; that as a result, the salaries paid by each club are lower than if competitive bidding were allowed to prevail; and that absent the Rozelle Rule, there would be increased movement in interstate commerce of players from one club to another.

We find substantial evidence in the record to support these findings. Witnesses for both sides testified that there would be increased player movement absent the Rozelle Rule. Two economists testified that elimination of the Rozelle Rule would lead to a substantial increase in player salaries. Carroll Rosenbloom, owner of the Los Angeles Rams, indicated that the Rams would have signed quite a few of the star players from other teams who had played out their options, absent the Rozelle Rule. [The court then cited evidence identifying two free agent players who probably would have signed with and moved to new teams but for the Rozelle Rule's deterrent effect on the potential new teams.]

In support of their contention that the restraints effected by the Rozelle Rule are not unreasonable, the defendants asserted a number of justifications. First, they argued that without the Rozelle Rule, star players would flock to cities having natural advantages such as larger economic bases, winning teams, warmer climates, and greater media opportunities; that competitive balance throughout the League would thus be destroyed; and that the destruction of competitive balance would ultimately lead to diminished spectator interest, franchise failures, and perhaps the demise of the NFL, at least as it operates today. Second, the defendants contended that the Rozelle Rule is necessary to protect the clubs' investment in scouting expenses and player developments costs. Third, they asserted that players must work together for a substantial period of time in order to function effectively as a team; that elimination of the Rozelle Rule would lead to increased player movement and a concomitant reduction in player continuity; and that the quality of play in the NFL would thus suffer, leading to reduced spectator interest, and financial detriment both to the clubs and the players. Conflicting evidence was adduced at trial by both sides with respect to the validity of these asserted justifications.

The district court held the defendants' asserted justifications unavailing. As to the clubs' investment in player development costs, Judge Larson found that these expenses are similar to those incurred by other businesses, and that there is no right to compensation for this type of investment. With respect to player continuity, the court found that elimination of the Rozelle Rule would affect all teams equally in that regard; that it would not lead to a reduction in the quality of play; and that even assuming that it would, that fact would not justify the Rozelle Rule's anticompetitive effects. As to competitive balance and the consequences which would flow from abolition of the Rozelle Rule, Judge Larson found that the existence of the Rozelle Rule has had no material effect on competitive balance in the NFL. Even assuming that the Rule did foster competitive balance, the court found that there were other legal means available to achieve that end: e.g., the competition committee, multiple year contracts, and special incentives. The court further concluded that elimination of the Rozelle Rule would have no significant disruptive effects, either immediate or long term, on professional football. In conclusion the court held that the Rozelle Rule was unreasonable in that it was overly broad, unlimited in duration, unaccompanied by procedural safeguards, and employed in conjunction with other anticompetitive practices such as the draft, Standard Player Contract, option clause, and the no-tampering rules.

We agree that the asserted need to recoup player development costs cannot justify the restraints of the Rozelle Rule. That expense is an ordinary cost of doing business and is not peculiar to professional football. Moreover, because of its unlimited duration, the Rozelle Rule is far more restrictive than necessary to fulfill that need.

We agree, in view of the evidence adduced at trial with respect to existing players turnover by way of trades, retirements and new players entering the League, that the club owners' arguments respecting player continuity cannot justify the Rozelle Rule. We concur in the district court's conclusion that the possibility of resulting decline in the quality of play would not justify the Rozelle Rule. We do recognize, as did the district court, that the NFL has a strong and unique interest in maintaining competitive balance among its teams. The key issue is thus whether the Rozelle Rule is essential to the maintenance of competitive balance, and is no more restrictive than necessary. The district court answered both of these questions in the negative.

We need not decide whether a system of inter-team compensation for free agents moving to other teams is essential to the maintenance of competitive balance in the NFL. Even if it is, we agree with the district court's conclusion that the Rozelle Rule is significantly more restrictive than necessary to serve any legitimate purposes it might have in this regard. First, little concern was manifested at trial over the free movement of average or below average players. Only the movement of the better players was urged as being detrimental to football. Yet the Rozelle Rule applies to every NFL player regardless of his status or ability. Second, the Rozelle Rule is unlimited in duration. It operates as a perpetual restriction on a player's ability to sell his services in an open market throughout his career. Third, the enforcement of the Rozelle Rule is unaccompanied by procedural safeguards. A player has no input into the process by which fair compensation is determined. Moreover, the player may be unaware of the precise compensation demanded by his former team, and that other teams might be interested in him but for the degree of compensation sought.

* * *

In sum, we hold that the Rozelle Rule, as enforced, unreasonably restrains trade in violation of § 1 of the Sherman Act.

* * *

Appeal dismissed.

Questions for Discussion

1. Essentially the same questions posed earlier about the rookie draft can also be asked about the system that requires clubs who sign veteran free agents to compensate the players' former teams. Does this arrangement really contribute to stronger competition on the field, or does it inhibit the ability of weaker teams to catch up to their stronger rivals, or does it do some of both? What lessons can be drawn from the experience within baseball before and after 1976 when (as we will see in the next chapter) free agency rights were given to six-year veterans? Or from comparing the level of competitiveness in baseball with that in football over the next fifteen years, with football having reintroduced (through collective bargaining in 1977) a different and even more restrictive system (pursuant to the labor exemption we will explore in the next part of *Mackey*)? Or from football since 1993, when veteran free agency finally arrived, though constrained by a salary cap since 1994?

2. Do limits on competition really produce unacceptable exploitation of players by the teams? Keep in mind that salaries paid by NFL clubs still soared over the same fifteen-year period (to $488,000 in 1992). True, the average football player earned only about half the salary of the average baseball player that year. But what is more important from either an economic or equity standpoint—the *average* or the *median* salary in a sport? The average player *salary* or the average club *payroll*? The proportion of either salary figure to average club *revenues*?

Other than a reduction to 12 rounds, the rookie draft remained virtually the same in the years from *Smith* to the 1993 settlement in football. However, the period since *Mackey* (and *Flood*) has witnessed constant innovation and experimentation with different modes of free agency in all of the leagues. Almost all of those variations were produced through collective bargaining with the players' associations. One new model, however, was introduced unilaterally by NFL owners after a bargaining impasse in 1988—Plan B. Under Plan B, each team was entitled to protect 37 players on its reserve list. Protected players, even if their contract had expired, were permitted to move to other NFL teams only if their current team chose not to match new offers received, and the move was then subject to the new team paying compensation to the player's current team (in the form of draft picks whose number and round varied with the size of the new salary offer). By contrast, all unprotected players (even those still under contract) could try to negotiate a better deal with another club which paid no compensation to the team that lost the player (though just during the months of February and March). If a player did not receive a better offer from another club, he could return to his existing team under whatever contract he enjoyed or was able to negotiate with the latter. In the four years of Plan B, many veteran players moved to other clubs for sizable signing bonuses and salary increases.

In 1989, eight players, backed by the NFLPA, challenged the NFL's Plan B restrictions on each team's 37 protected players, in a case titled *McNeil v. NFL*. As we will see in the next section, the players were able to avoid application of the labor exemption defense after the district judge held that the NFLPA had successfully renounced its status as a union bargaining agent. The merits of the antitrust issues were tried during the summer of 1992, and the jury found that Plan B violated the Rule of Reason. In responding to a series of special interrogatories, the jury indicated that Plan B harmed players by diminishing competition among NFL clubs for their services, that nonetheless the system contributed significantly to competitive balance among NFL teams, but that the system was unreasonable because it was more restrictive than necessary for that purpose. The jury found that only four of the eight plaintiffs actually suffered damages—totalling $1.6 million. Once Judge Doty rendered a final judgment with an injunctive order, the NFL appealed the verdict on several grounds, including that the jury's Rule of Reason analysis reflected in the special interrogatories and dictated by the court's instructions did not properly apply the *Professional Engineers* balancing test discussed earlier in this chapter. (The league also objected to the trial court's allocation of the burdens of proof on specific issues.) Although the case was settled by the players and owners before the Eighth Circuit issued an opinion, how should this case have been resolved on appeal?

The settlement, which was part of an overall resolution of the long-standing legal and labor-relations conflict between the NFL and NFLPA, was spurred by a burst of litigation that ensued after the *McNeil* verdict, involving players other than the eight *McNeil* plaintiffs. A crucial issue presented in all of those cases was whether the NFL would be collaterally estopped by *McNeil* from relitigating the issue of whether the Plan B system violated the rule of reason, or alternatively, whether a different set of restrictions (i.e., a Plan C) was permissible. One such suit filed in

Minneapolis by ten unsigned veteran free agents several weeks into the season sought an injunction declaring them to be unrestricted free agents. After finding that the NFL would likely be estopped by *McNeil* from denying liability, Judge Doty entered a temporary restraining order giving the plaintiffs five days during which they were unrestricted in negotiating with other teams. Three plaintiffs (Keith Jackson, Garin Veris, and Webster Slaughter) then signed contracts with new teams for significantly more money than their original clubs had offered them. The remaining plaintiffs were either released by or signed new contracts with their clubs, resulting in dismissal of their suits as moot. Yet another case was filed in Minneapolis with Philadelphia Eagles' Reggie White as the named plaintiff in a class action seeking to have the Plan B system declared illegal as to all players not otherwise involved in various suits pending around the country. Judge Doty deliberately withheld his judgment about this claim while he prodded both sides to settle the overall conflict.

A comprehensive settlement was finally reached in January 1993. This involved a $195 million payment to satisfy the claims of the players who had been restricted by Plan B (and several other NFL policies that had generated lawsuits). There was also a major change in the legal and public relations positions of both sides, a compromise that became the framework for a new collective agreement (once the union recertified) that will run through at least the 2000 season.

To synopsize the key features of the new regime as it applies to free agency, veteran players are unrestricted free agents when their contracts expire at any time after five full years of service. Each club, however, can protect one free agent by designating him as its "franchise" player, who is then guaranteed a salary of either the average of the highest five players in the league at his position or 120% of his prior year's salary (whichever is higher). In addition, each club can designate two "transition" players among its free agents. For these, the club has a right to match any offer the player receives from another team. If no such offer is received, the club must pay the player the average of the ten highest paid players in the league at his position or 120% of his prior year's salary. Players with two to five years of service are restricted free agents when their contracts expire, subject to the club's right of first refusal and right to receive draft choice compensation from any new club with which the player signs (as under the old agreement).

In exchange for this system of veteran free agency, the Association agreed to continue the rookie draft, though with the number of rounds reduced from twelve to seven. Most important, the Association accepted a team salary cap triggered by the league's overall player costs reaching 67% of total Defined Gross Revenues (DGR) in any one season. The owners agreed that total player costs must be at least 58% of DGR in any season. In the first year of free agency in 1993, average salaries shot up to $650,000 from $488,000 in 1992. Thus, the cap (at 64% of league DGR, divided by the number of teams) immediately was put into effect for 1994, and has remained so since then. As long as the cap is in effect, veteran free agents become unrestricted after four years of service instead of five, and while teams losing players to free agency are compensated with extra draft picks, those picks are not at the expense of the teams signing the free agents.

Why did the parties' negotiating postures evolve in this direction? To what extent did they reflect an accurate perception of the parties respective legal positions? After reading the next section on the labor exemption, and considering that these negotiations took place before the Supreme Court's decision in the *Brown* case, put yourself in the position of counsel advising the NFLPA. Would you have felt there were good *legal* reasons to settle for something considerably short of total free agency? Would you have thought there were good *practical* reasons for constructing a different system? Do your reasons reflect the interests of all Association members, or just some? If the latter, which types of members? Now put yourself in the shoes of the NFL and its counsel, and go through the same legal and pragmatic analysis. Why was there a negotiating zone for creative resolution of this problem, which had bedeviled football for almost a quarter century?

In 1994, a year after the NFL had finally resolved its player-owner conflicts, the United States hosted the World Cup in what is called football in the rest of the world, but soccer in America. The huge audiences for those Championship soccer games led to creation of a new Major League Soccer (MLS) in the United States, which enjoyed a successful opening season in 1996. In early 1997, though, MLS faced a class action antitrust suit filed on behalf of players challenging the League's unilaterally-created system of restraints in the players market.

Under the leadership of its Board Chairman-lawyer Alan Rothenberg, the formal structure of MLS was designed in a fashion that the League hoped would satisfy the "single entity" test that excludes any scrutiny under § 1 of the Sherman Act. Rather than have each team owned by separate persons, the franchises are all owned by the League, which in turn is owned and controlled by the financial investors in this new sports venture. Actual control of decisions by and for seven of the ten original teams (and the first two expansion teams) is wielded by their respective "investor-operators," within the framework of League rules administered by the Commissioner and his Executive Council (which is made up of these investor-operators). For example, that means that Robert Kraft, who clearly owns the New England Patriots of the NFL, is just the "investor-operator" of the New England Revolution in the MLS (both of which play their games in Kraft's stadium). We shall address the details of this MLS league structure and its potential single entity status in Chapter 7, when we read the judicial decisions that have already addressed this key Sherman Act issue for sports.

In practice, the principal impact of this MLS variation from the NFL structure is felt in the players market. All of the players (but only the players) on each team are employed and paid by the league, not the individual club. (By contrast, just as Kraft's Patriots had to do with Bill Parcells and Pete Carroll, his Revolution decides who will be employed and paid by the team as its coach, general manager, front office staff, and the like.) Players are permitted to negotiate contracts and their salaries only with a department in the MLS office, and all the MLS partners have agreed not to bid for and sign contracts with players individually (again by contrast with what Kraft does with his Patriots' quarterback Drew Bledsoe). Once the player contracts have been signed with the MLS, then the players are distributed among the ten clubs. This is done first through a "rookie" draft, after which the team has the freedom to retain, release, or trade the player to another team, depending on how the investor-operator and his staff views the player's performance and the club's needs.

The asserted objective of this MLS structure for its players market was to avoid the fate of the North American Soccer League (NASL), in which "competition among teams ... drove up acquisition costs of the players," thus generating "destructive, economically irrational spending" that eventually led to the dissolution of that league in the early 1980s. Under MLS rules, each player has to sign a Standard Player Agreement which gives the League the unilateral right to renew it for two consecutive years (at five percent salary increases) after the negotiated contract term has expired. Teams are limited to players whose total salary levels do not exceed the league's salary cap—$1.1 million in 1996 and $1.3 million in 1997, or approximately $65,000 in average salary for the 20-man player rosters. MLS also has both a maximum ($175,000 in 1996 and $192,000 in 1997) as well as minimum ($24,000) salary amount that can be paid to any one player. One other potentially significant feature of the Standard Player Agreement is that the player must assign to the League the exclusive right to license on a group basis the player's name and image for merchandising purposes. While players receive two percent of their base salary (i.e., an average of $1,200) for this assignment, the League's control over such group licensing revenues removes the principal instrument that players in other leagues have used to finance the labor organizations that challenged restraints on the players market in football, baseball, and other professional sports.

In late 1997, the MLS salary cap litigation was just getting underway and its ultimate resolution was uncertain.[f] The facts of the case do

---

[f]. Indeed, the first judicial proceeding involved a dispute about whether a particular league restraint on player movement even existed, not whether it could be justified by MLS based on one or more of the standard sports law arguments. MLS is a member of the United States Soccer Federation (USSF), which in turn belongs to the Federation Internationale de Football Association (FIFA). Under FIFA Regulations Governing the Status and Transfer of Football Players, "[i]f a non-amateur player concludes a contract with a new club, his former club shall be entitled to compensation for his training and/or development." Absent agreement among the two teams on the amount of such compensation, FIFA serves as arbitrator of this dispute. Under § 10(d) of the MLS Standard Player Agreement, the FIFA Transfer Rules were said to govern any "loan, transfer, assignment or sale of MLS's right to the Player's services ... [and] this provision shall survive any termination of the Agreement."

raise, though, all of the antitrust questions we have read about, and more (such as the crucial single entity question we will explore in Chapter 7). Does antitrust law apply to the labor as well as to the product market (and is there a difference between the two in a sport like soccer)? What is the appropriate substantive judgment about the rookie draft, salary cap, and restraints on veteran free agency? While MLS is now the only Division I soccer league in the United States, there are a host of similar leagues in other countries. What significance, then, should be attributed to the presence of such player opportunities around the world, and to the agreement between MLS and FIFA (with the U.S. Soccer Federation as intermediary) that imposes transfer fees on player movement?

C. LABOR EXEMPTION FROM ANTITRUST[g]

The Major League Soccer situation also reflects another key feature of antitrust jurisprudence. The players voted not to form themselves into a labor union which would engage in collective bargaining *with* the League. Instead, the players decided to initiate collective litigation *against* the League. The likely explanation can be found in the title of this section.

This version of the labor exemption raises a different question from the one we looked at earlier in connection with *Brown* and *Smith*—

The MLSPA asked the district judge for summary judgment in favor of its claim that at least this soccer version of the traditional Rozelle Rule violated antitrust law (and MLS could not assert that it was part of a single entity that included the 198 other members of FIFA around the world). The principal response of MLS to this claim was that league policy (both in the past and the future) was not to extract transfer fees from non-MLS teams signing MLS "free agents" nor to pay such fees for players coming to the MLS from teams in other leagues. According to MLS, the only role of § 10(a) of its Standard Player Agreement was to ensure that its players had secured an "international transfer certificate" from FIFA before they did leave another league. (It was not clear whether MLS would thus have to refrain from signing any free agents coming from teams that were insisting on such a transfer fee under the FIFA rules to which MLS had subscribed.) As of the end of 1997, the parties were still awaiting a judicial verdict on this first score.

g. Unlike the substantive antitrust questions posed about the rookie draft and veteran free agency, this topic has produced a voluminous legal literature. Among the most notable pieces are, in chronological order, Michael S. Jacobs and Ralph Winter, *Antitrust Principles and Collective Bargaining: Of Superstars in Peonage*, 81 Yale L. J. 1 (1971); John C. Weistart, *Judicial Review of Labor Agreements: Lessons From the Sports Industry*, 44 Law and Contemp. Probs. 109 (Autumn, 1981); Philip J. Closius, *Not at the Behest of Non Labor Groups: A Revised Prognosis for a Maturing Sports Industry*, 24 Boston College L. Rev. 341 (1983); Gary R. Roberts, *Reconciling Federal Labor and Antitrust Policy: The Special Case of Sports League Labor Market Restraints*, 75 Georgetown L. J. 19 (1986); Gary R. Roberts, *Sports League Restraints on the Labor Market: The Failure of Stare Decisis*, 41 U. of Pittsburgh L. Rev. 337 (1986); Lee Goldman, *The Labor Exemption to the Antitrust Laws as Applied to Employers' Labor Market Restraints in Sports and Non–Sports Markets*, 1989 Utah L. Rev. 617; and Ethan Lock, *The Scope of the Labor Exemption in Professional Sports*, 1989 Duke L. J. 339. Valuable treatments of this issue that are not specifically focused on sports include Douglas L. Leslie, *Principles of Labor Antitrust*, 66 Virginia L. Rev. 1183 (1980), and Robert H. Jerry and Donald E. Knebel, *Antitrust and Employer Restraints in Labor Markets*, 6 Indus. Rel. L. J. 173 (1984).

whether antitrust's intrinsic focus on "consumer welfare" implies a lack of antitrust concern about employer power in the labor market. A second key question posed by *Mackey* is whether, even if the Sherman Act was meant to apply to collusive restraints in the overall labor market, antitrust policy must still be subordinate to a separate federal labor policy that has evolved through a number of statutes designed to foster and protect labor organizations and collective bargaining. This question took on real urgency in the sports world in the 1970s, because almost all the important antitrust litigation about free agency restraints (the one exception being the *Philadelphia World Hockey Club* case included in Chapter 8) was either launched or backed by the player unions that had emerged by the late 1960s in all four major professional sports.

As *Mackey* and succeeding decisions exemplify, for over two decades the sports arena was the main battleground in the struggle over the purpose and scope of the labor exemption. Before reading these cases, then, we provide this capsule summary of the broader legal background.

There is a fundamental tension between antitrust law, which bars any "contract, combination, or conspiracy in restraint of trade," and labor unions, whose *raison d'être* is to organize and coordinate the efforts of employees in dealing collectively with their employer. Indeed, for the first two decades of its existence, judges used the Sherman Act more often against trade unions than against business corporations, and in *Loewe v. Lawlor*, 208 U.S. 274 (1908), the Supreme Court made it clear that this Act did apply to unions and their activities (in that case, to a national consumer boycott against a non-union hat manufacturer in Danbury, Connecticut).

Concerned about this threat to their very existence, let alone their effectiveness, unions belonging to the American Federation of Labor persuaded new Democratic President Woodrow Wilson (and his chief advisor on antitrust and labor issues, Louis Brandeis) to include in the 1914 Clayton Act amendments to the Sherman Act a new § 6 which declared:

> That the labor of a human being is not a commodity or article of commerce. Nothing contained in the anti-trust law shall be construed to forbid the existence and operation of labor ... organizations, instituted for the purposes of mutual help ... or to forbid or restrain individual members of such organizations from lawfully carrying out the legitimate objects thereof; nor shall such organizations, or the members thereof, be held or construed to be illegal combinations or conspiracies in restraint of trade, under the antitrust laws.

Samuel Gompers, founder and president of the AFL, celebrated this new section as the "Magna Carta of labor!" To buttress its legal force, § 20 of the Clayton Act went on to state that in disputes between employers and employees about terms and conditions of employment, collective action undertaken by employees through strikes, picketing, and boycotts, should not "be considered or held to be violations of any law of the United States."

Despite the apparent breadth of this legislative directive, the Supreme Court held in *Duplex Printing Press Co. v. Deering*, 254 U.S. 443 (1921), that the Clayton Act protected unions and their members from antitrust liability and federal court injunctions only when the union members were pursuing the "normal and legitimate objects" of a union, not when they "engage in an actual combination or conspiracy in restraint of trade." In *Duplex*, the Court held that a secondary boycott of the only major non-union printing press manufacturer in the country was outside the scope of Clayton Act protection and therefore could be enjoined under § 1 of the Sherman Act.

During the Great Depression and the New Deal of the 1930s, labor was in a political position to secure the protection it thought it had won two decades earlier. Labor's first victory was the Norris–LaGuardia Act of 1932 (authored by Harvard Law Professor Felix Frankfurter). This Act made it clear that regardless of whether a labor dispute went beyond the normal bounds of conflict between an employer and its immediate employees, federal courts could not enjoin strikes, pickets, and other forms of employee self help. Although the language of the Norris–LaGuardia Act expressly barred only federal *injunctive* remedies in "labor disputes," nine years later *Justice* Frankfurter authored the Supreme Court's decision in *United States v. Hutcheson*, 312 U.S. 219, 232 (1941), involving a criminal antitrust prosecution, which read the Act, in conjunction with the 1935 National Labor Relations Act, as having tacitly overruled *Duplex* and restored the Clayton Act's intended protection of labor disputes from substantive antitrust *liability*:

> So long as a union acts in its self-interest and does not combine with non-labor groups, the licit and the illicit under Section 20 [of the Clayton Act] are not to be distinguished by any [judicial] judgment regarding the wisdom or unwisdom, the rightness or wrongness, the selfishness or unselfishness of the end of which the particular union activities are the means.

312 U.S. at 232.

This controversial reading of the Norris–LaGuardia Act was sufficient to give economic pressure by unions a blanket immunity from antitrust liability. Subsequent lower court decisions have held that employer self help through lockouts and strike insurance is similarly protected. (This is why the court in *Kennedy v. Long Island R.R. Co.*, 319 F.2d 366 (2d Cir.1963), dismissed a union antitrust suit against the railroads that had collectively created and financed a plan to insure their members against a strike by the union.) However, this blanket protection for unions and employer groups (commonly referred to under the rubric "statutory" labor exemption) has only applied in cases where one side in a labor-management struggle over union recognition or the terms of a collective agreement has sued the other, alleging that tactics employed in that struggle constituted an illegal restraint of trade. Thus, a major question remained—whether the collective agreement that the union signs with the employer was also insulated from antitrust scrutiny. Although *Hutcheson* extended its antitrust protection to the union only when the latter "does not combine with non-labor groups," it makes little sense to allow a union to strike to get a collective agreement from the employer, but then to subject the agreement itself to antitrust liability. This result seems even more anomalous from the perspective of the second leg of New Deal labor policy, the 1935 Wagner Act, which enacted the National Labor Relations Act (NLRA). The next chapter examines in depth the NLRA as it applies to the world of sports. For now it is sufficient to say that the Wagner Act created an affirmative right of employees to organize themselves into unions, and then imposed on the employer a duty to bargain in good faith with the union to arrive at a collective agreement. In the 1947 Taft–Hartley amendments to the NLRA, the duty to bargain in good faith was also imposed on unions. Both in practice and under the law, such bargaining is often conducted on a wide-ranging multi-employer basis.

The Supreme Court has not, however, been prepared to grant collective agreements the same blanket antitrust exemption that it has extended to strikes and lockouts. Perhaps the most important reason is that unions and employers may find it in their own interest to agree upon restrictive practices whose major impact is felt by outside competitors to the immediate parties. In three key decisions, *Allen Bradley Co. v. IBEW*, 325 U.S. 797 (1945), *UMWA v. Pennington*, 381 U.S. 657 (1965), and *Connell Construction Co. v. Plumbers and Steamfitters*, 421 U.S. 616 (1975), the Supreme Court struggled to formulate a legal test for when the antitrust legality of a collective agreement is challenged. While recognizing the need for a "nonstatutory" (i.e., implicit) labor exemption for collectively bargained agreements in some cases, the Court denied such protection in all three cases where the alleged restraint was on the employers' product market and the plaintiffs were business competitors of the employers who were party to the collective agreement. This same scenario has also arisen in the sports context, when the operation of a collectively-bargained lifetime reserve clause denies a new league access to the available supply of top-flight athletes whom the new league needs to survive as a serious competitor to the established league (see *Philadelphia World Hockey Club v. Philadelphia Hockey Club*, 351 F.Supp. 462 (E.D.Pa.1972)). We will return to this issue and this decision in Chapter 8 when we consider the implications of antitrust for interleague competition.

With respect to situations involving collective employer restraints whose direct impact is felt only inside, not also outside, the employment relationship, the following alternative formulations of the nonstatutory labor exemption have each been advanced by at least one judge or scholar.

1. There should be no nonstatutory exemption from antitrust at all—unions and employers should have no right to do through their agreement what would otherwise be illegal by statute.

2. There should be exemption only for provisions that have been inserted in the agreement at the behest of the union for the benefit of the employees—the historic purpose of the labor exemption is to help workers, not employers.

3. The exemption should protect all, but only, the terms within an existing collective agreement—the essential condition for relief from antitrust must be actual consent to the practice by the employees through their union.

4. The exemption should protect all employment practices that exist in an employee unit represented by a union—since the employees now have the right under labor law to force the employer to negotiate about the practice, they should not also enjoy the right to litigate about the practice under antitrust law.

5. There should be no antitrust liability at all for restraints in employment—as § 6 of the Clayton Act stated, "the labor of a human being is not a commodity or article of commerce" for purposes of antitrust law.

Consider the pros and cons of these options as we trace the history of the labor exemption in sports until its final resolution by the Supreme Court.

The *Mackey* Case

We begin with *Mackey*, whose factual underpinnings and substantive antitrust treatment were presented in an earlier section. In *Mackey*, the pure statutory labor exemption of steps taken by one side in a labor dispute was not discussed by the Court because the NFL apparently failed to raise this as a defense. The League did, however, argue for a partial statutory exemption based not on Norris-LaGuardia, but on § 6 of the Clayton Act which begins by stating that "[t]he labor of a human being is not a commodity or article of commerce." This was the Eighth Circuit's response.

Based on [§ 6], the Supreme Court, in *Apex [Hosiery Co. v. Leader]*, observed:

> [It] would seem that restraints on the sale of the employee's services to the employer, however much they curtail the competition among employees, are not in themselves combinations or conspiracies in restraint of trade or commerce under the Sherman Act.

310 U.S. at 503.

On the surface, the language relied on by defendants lends merit to the defense. However, we cannot overlook the context in which the language arose. Section 6 of the Clayton Act was enacted for the benefit of unions to exempt certain of their activities from the antitrust laws after courts had applied the Sherman Act to legitimate labor activities.... In *Apex*, the Court condoned restrictions on competition for employee services imposed by the employees themselves, not by employers.

In other cases concerning professional sports, courts have not hesitated to apply the Sherman Act to club owner imposed restraints on competition for players' services.... In other contexts, courts have subjected similar employer imposed restraints to the scrutiny of the antitrust laws. We hold that restraints on competition within the market for players' services fall within the ambit of the Sherman Act.

543 F.2d at 617–18.

Since the statutory exemption was largely ignored in *Mackey*, the entire focus of attention was on whether the less comprehensive protection for terms contained in collective agreements (the nonstatutory exemption) applied. This required a somewhat convoluted application of this prong of the exemption; while the Rozelle Rule had been incorporated by reference in the 1970 collective agreement, that contract had expired and the Association was no longer agreeing to its terms. Thus, the NFL was arguing that the nonstatutory exemption not only protects terms in an existing agreement that the union agreed to and was legally bound to accept, but that it also protects terms after they expire and the union no longer consents to them. No previous nonsports case had ever suggested that the implied nonstatutory exemption swept that broadly, because labor disputes had always been analyzed as statutory exemption cases. Thus, *Mackey* posed a difficult conceptual problem for the Eighth Circuit in trying to apply the nonstatutory exemption precedent.

Another problem posed in *Mackey*, and similar litigation in the sports world, is whether there can be antitrust liability when the principal impact of the terms of a collectively-imposed restraint is felt by the parties themselves. For this problem, the single Supreme Court precedent is *Local Union No. 189, Amalgamated Meat Cutters v. Jewel Tea Co.*, 381 U.S. 676 (1965). In that case, the union had insisted on inserting in its collective agreement with the Chicago grocery stores a provision that restricted to daytime hours the sale of fresh meat, in order to protect the unionized butchers from employer pressures to work in the evenings. When one of the stores that was subject to this agreement sued to strike down the provision as an antitrust violation, a divided Supreme Court held that this contract term was protected by the labor exemption. Justice White's decisive opinion (for himself and two other Justices) contains this oft-cited passage on the scope of the exemption:

> Thus the issue in this case is whether the marketing-hours restriction, like wages, and unlike prices, is so intimately related to wages, hours and working conditions [mandatory subjects of collective bargaining under the NLRA] that the union's successful attempt to obtain that provision through bona fide, arms' length bargaining in pursuit of their own labor union policies, and not at the behest of or in combination with non-labor groups, falls within the protection of

the National Labor Policy and is therefore exempt from the Sherman Act.

381 U.S. at 689–90. With this judicial formula in mind as you read *Mackey* and the following cases, consider the ways that courts have treated agreements by players associations to various restrictions on veteran free agency in professional sports.

MACKEY v. NATIONAL FOOTBALL LEAGUE (PART 2)

United States Court of Appeals, Eighth Circuit, 1976.
543 F.2d 606.

LAY, CIRCUIT JUDGE.

THE LABOR EXEMPTION ISSUE.

We review first the claim that the labor exemption immunizes the Commissioner and the clubs from liability under the antitrust laws....

HISTORY.

* * *

The players assert that only employee groups are entitled to the labor exemption and that it cannot be asserted by the defendants, an employer group. We must disagree. Since the basis of the nonstatutory exemption is the national policy favoring collective bargaining, and since the exemption extends to agreements, the benefits of the exemption logically extend to both parties to the agreement. Accordingly, under appropriate circumstances, we find that a non-labor group may avail itself of the labor exemption.

The clubs and the Commissioner claim the benefit of the nonstatutory labor exemption here, arguing that the Rozelle Rule was the subject of an agreement with the players union and that the proper accommodation of federal labor and antitrust policies requires that the agreement be deemed immune from antitrust liability. The plaintiffs assert that the Rozelle Rule was the product of unilateral action by the clubs and that the defendants cannot assert a colorable claim of exemption.

To determine the applicability of the nonstatutory exemption we must first decide whether there has been any agreement between the parties concerning the Rozelle Rule.

[In 1968 negotiations for their first collective agreement, the players requested modification of the Rozelle Rule, but did not put forward any specific proposal as to how to do so. The 1968 labor contract incorporated by reference the NFL Constitution and By-laws, of which the Rozelle Rule was a part. The agreement expressly provided that free agency rules would not be altered during its term. Again, in 1970, the players did not make an issue of the Rozelle Rule which was rarely mentioned in negotiations. While the 1970 agreement made no express reference to the Rozelle Rule, and did not expressly incorporate by reference the terms of the NFL Constitution and By-laws, it did require all players to sign the Standard Player Contract, under which the player agreed to be bound by the Constitution and By-laws. Testimony at trial indicated that it was the understanding of the parties that the Rozelle Rule would remain in effect during the term of the 1970 agreement, through the 1973 season. However, right from the start of the 1974 negotiations, the players consistently sought elimination of the Rozelle Rule and the deadlock between the parties on this issue had so far precluded agreement on a new labor contract.]

* * *

Based on the fact that the 1968 agreement incorporated by reference the Rozelle Rule and provided that free agent rules would not be changed, we conclude that the 1968 agreement required that the Rozelle Rule govern when a player played out his option and signed with another team. Assuming, without deciding, that the 1970 agreement embodied a similar understanding, we proceed to a consideration of whether the agreements fall within the scope of the nonstatutory labor exemption.

Governing Principles.

Under the general principles surrounding the labor exemption, the availability of the nonstatutory exemption for a particular agreement turns upon whether the relevant federal labor policy is deserving of pre-eminence over federal antitrust policy under the circumstances of the particular case.

Although the cases giving rise to the nonstatutory exemption are factually dissimilar from the present case, certain principles can be deduced from those decisions governing the proper accommodation of the competing labor and antitrust interests involved here.

We find the proper accommodation to be: First, the labor policy favoring collective bargaining may potentially be given pre-eminence over the antitrust laws where the restraint on trade primarily affects only the parties to the collective bargaining relationship. Second, federal labor policy is implicated sufficiently to prevail only where the agreement sought to be exempted concerns a mandatory subject of collective bargaining. Finally, the policy favoring collective bargaining is furthered to the degree necessary to override the antitrust laws only where the agreement sought to be exempted is the product of bona fide arm's-length bargaining.

Application.

Applying these principles to the facts presented here, we think it clear that the alleged restraint on trade effected by the Rozelle Rule affects only the parties to the agreements sought to be exempted. Accordingly, we must inquire as to the other two principles: whether the Rozelle Rule is a mandatory subject of collective bargaining, and whether the agreements thereon were the product of bona fide arm's-length negotiation.

Mandatory Subject of Bargaining.

* * *

In this case the district court held that, in view of the illegality of the Rozelle Rule under the Sherman Act, it was "a nonmandatory, illegal subject of bargaining." We disagree. The labor exemption presupposes a violation of the antitrust laws. To hold that a subject relating to wages, hours and working conditions becomes nonmandatory by virtue of its illegality under the antitrust laws obviates the labor exemption. We conclude that whether the agreements here in question relate to a mandatory subject of collective bargaining should be determined solely under federal labor law.

On its face, the Rozelle Rule does not deal with "wages, hours and other terms or conditions of employment" but with inter-team compensation when a player's contractual obligation to one team expires and he is signed by another. Viewed as such, it would not constitute a mandatory subject of collective bargaining. The district court found, however, that the Rule operates to restrict a player's ability to move from one team to another and depresses player salaries. There is substantial evidence in the record to support these findings. Accordingly, we hold that the Rozelle Rule constitutes a mandatory bargaining subject within the meaning of the National Labor Relations Act.

Bona Fide Bargaining.

The district court found that the parties' collective bargaining history reflected nothing which could be legitimately characterized as bargaining over the Rozelle Rule; that, in part due to its recent formation and inadequate finances, the NFLPA, at least prior to 1974, stood in a relatively weak bargaining position vis-a-vis the clubs; and that "the Rozelle Rule was unilaterally imposed by the NFL and member club defendants upon the players in 1963 and has been imposed on the players from 1963 through the present date."

On the basis of our independent review of the record, including the parties' bargaining history as set forth above, we find substantial evidence to support the finding that there was no bona fide arm's-length bargaining over the Rozelle Rule preceding the execution of the 1968 and 1970 agreements. The Rule imposes significant restrictions on players, and its form has remained unchanged since it was unilaterally promulgated by the clubs in 1963. The provisions of the collective bargaining agreements which operated to continue the Rozelle Rule do not in and of themselves inure to the benefit of the players or their union. Defendants contend that the players derive indirect benefit from the Rozelle Rule, claiming that the union's agreement to the Rozelle Rule was a *quid pro quo* for increased pension benefits and the right of players to individually negotiate their salaries. The district court found, however, that there was no such *quid pro quo*, and we cannot say, on the basis of our review of the record, that this finding is clearly erroneous.

In view of the foregoing, we hold that the agreements between the clubs and the players embodying the Rozelle Rule do not qualify for the labor exemption. The union's acceptance of the status quo by the continuance of the Rozelle Rule in the initial collective bargaining agreements under the circumstances of this case cannot serve to immunize the Rozelle Rule from the scrutiny of the Sherman Act.

* * *

Conclusion.

In conclusion, although we find that non-labor parties may potentially avail themselves of the nonstatutory labor exemption where they are parties to collective bargaining agreements pertaining to mandatory subjects of bargaining, the exemption cannot be invoked where, as here, the agreement was not the product of bona fide arm's-length negotiations. Thus, the defendants' enforcement of the Rozelle Rule is not exempt from the coverage of the antitrust laws.

* * *

It may be that some reasonable restrictions relating to player transfers are necessary for the successful operation of the NFL. The protection of mutual interests of both the players and the clubs may indeed require this. We encourage the parties to resolve this question through collective bargaining. The parties are far better situated to agreeably resolve what rules governing player transfers are best suited for their mutual interests than are the courts. However, no mutual resolution of this issue appears within the present record. Therefore, the Rozelle Rule, as it is presently implemented, must be set aside as an unreasonable restraint of trade.

Trial verdict upheld.

John Mackey was the best tight end in professional football for a decade. He was also the President of the National Football League Players Association (NFLPA) and hence the named plaintiff in the above litigation. Not until 1992 was Mackey finally inducted into professional football's Hall of Fame—ironically, the same year as was Raiders' owner, Al Davis, who had been the victor in another major antitrust battle lost by the NFL (regarding Davis' move of the Raiders from Oakland to Los Angeles in the early 1980s), a case we examine in depth in Chapter 7.

The aftermath of *Mackey* was quite different from what happened with respect to the Raiders—who for fourteen seasons were ensconced in Los Angeles before moving back to Oakland in 1995. Shortly after it won *Mackey*, the NFLPA agreed to a new collective agreement with the league. In return for restoration of the Association's "union security" clause (see Chapter 4) and generous improvements in the league's pension and disability plans, the Association agreed to new restrictions on veteran free agency—giving the player's present team either a right of first refusal or compensation in the form of specified future draft picks rather than current players.[h] Over the objections of some dissenting players, the Eighth Circuit approved the new system under the *Mackey* standard. See *Reynolds v. NFL*, 584 F.2d 280 (8th Cir.1978). However, since the compensation for a free agent ranged as high as two first-round draft picks from the signing team, this new system proved even more restrictive than the old Rozelle Rule. Of several thousand players who became free agents from 1977 through 1987, only a tiny handful even received offers from another team and only one player actually changed teams for compensation.

Essentially, the same divergence between antitrust verdict and labor relations outcome occurred in the other sports during the 1970s.[i] In the initial wave of player antitrust litigation in the early 1970s, while baseball players lost in *Flood*, the players won in football (in *Smith*, *Mackey*, and elsewhere), in hockey (in *Philadelphia World Hockey Club v. Philadelphia Hockey Club*, 351 F.Supp. 457 (E.D.Pa.1972)), and in basketball (in *Robertson v. NBA*, 389 F.Supp. 867 (S.D.N.Y.1975)). As we will see in Chapter 4, soon after losing *Flood*, baseball players won from a labor arbitrator full freedom from the game's historic reserve clause. In their next collective agreement, the Players Association gave back six of these years of free agency to the owners (although players had a right to arbitration of their salaries from years three through six), and not until 1996 did the Association agree to some constraints (in the form of a salary tax) upon that lucrative system secured under labor law. In hockey and basketball, as well as in football, the players gave back "equalization" rights to teams that lost free agents: such compensation took the form of players as well as draft picks, but in an amount determined by a neutral arbitrator (*not* the league commissioner). In basketball, such compensation was available for only a five-year period that ended in 1981. Uncompensated free agency in basketball was initially accompanied by a right of first refusal for the player's prior team, and it is now constrained by a salary cap arrangement, which football emulated and expanded on in the 1990s.

The Second Phase

After *Mackey*, sports labor exemption litigation entered a second phase, one that involved challenges by individual players to terms contained in existing collective agreements that had been agreed to and

---

h. See David Harris, *The League: The Rise and Decline of the NFL* 255–57 (New York: Bantam Books, 1986).

i. See Berry, Gould, and Staudohar, *Labor Relations in Professional Sports*, note a above, for detailed accounts of what took place in both litigation and negotiation in each of the major professional team sports.

supported by the unions. As we will see, the formulation of the initial source and purpose of the labor exemption is also crucial for determining the exemption's scope and its duration.

The first of these cases, *McCourt v. California Sports, Inc.*, 600 F.2d 1193 (6th Cir.1979), was from the world of hockey. Here the Sixth Circuit adopted and applied the three-pronged *Mackey* test to find that the exemption protected the system embedded in the 1976 collective agreement, one that required that an "equalization payment" (as determined by a neutral arbitrator, not the Commissioner) be made by the signing team to the team losing a free agent. This restraint on free agency was essentially identical to the league's existing By-law 9A, which the owners had originally proposed in bargaining. The plaintiff, Dale McCourt, an outstanding young forward (who as a rookie had led the Detroit Red Wings in scoring), was awarded by the arbitrator to the Los Angeles Kings as compensation for the Red Wings' signing the Kings' outstanding veteran goaltender, Rogatien Vachon. McCourt refused to report to the Kings, and instead filed suit. The district court rejected the nonstatutory exemption defense after finding that, as in *Mackey*, the "equalization payment" provision in the collective agreement had not been negotiated in *bona fide*, arms-length bargaining. On appeal, the Sixth Circuit reversed.

Contrary to the trial judge's conclusion, the very facts relied upon by him in his opinion illustrate a classic case of collective bargaining in which the reserve system was a central issue. It is apparent from those very findings that the NHLPA used every form of negotiating pressure it could muster. It developed an alternate reserve system and secured tentative agreement from the owner and player representatives, only to have the proposal rejected by the players. It refused to attend a proposed meeting with the owners to discuss the reserve system further. It threatened to strike. It threatened to commence an antitrust suit and to recommend that the players not attend training camp.

For its part, the NHL, while not budging in its insistence upon By-Law Section 9A, at least in the absence of any satisfactory counter proposal by the players, yielded significantly on other issues....

The trial court, while acknowledging that the new collective bargaining agreement contained significant new benefits to the players, held that they were not "directly related to collective bargaining on By-law 9A." This observation and the trial court's conclusion that "the NHLPA never bargained for By-law 9A in the first instance" typifies its approach. It is true that the NHLPA did not "bargain for" By-law Section 9A; it bargained "against" it, vigorously. That the trial judge concluded the benefits in the new contract were wrung from management by threat of an antitrust suit to void the By-Law merely demonstrates that the benefits were bargained for in connection with the reserve system, although he opined that the threat of a suit was a more effective bargaining tool than the threat of a strike....

* * *

From the express findings of the trial court, fully supported by the record, it is apparent that the inclusion of the reserve system in the collective bargaining agreement was the product of good faith, arm's-length bargaining, and that what the trial court saw as a failure to negotiate was in fact simply a failure to succeed, after the most intensive negotiations, in keeping an unwanted provision out of the contract. This failure was a part of and not apart from the collective bargaining process, a process which achieved its ultimate objective of an agreement accepted by the parties.

600 F.2d at 1202–03.

Chief Judge Edwards vigorously dissented. The judge did not dispute that the challenged provision was negotiated in *bona fide*, arm's length bargaining. However, he believed, contrary to the premise of *Mackey*, that an employer group should never be able to claim a labor exemption that was created solely to protect union conduct, one that he characterized as the "labor union exemption."

McCourt was the last antitrust suit filed by hockey players against the NHL restraints on free agency. The 1990s witnessed significant changes in the reserve system accomplished through collective bargaining between the owners, led by new commissioner Gary Bettman, and the players, led by new Players Association head Bob Goodenow. This effort did cost hockey a 10-day strike by the players on the eve of the 1992 Stanley Cup playoffs, and a three-month lockout by the owners at the start of the 1994–95 regular season. The product was a new system that allowed unrestricted free agency to older veterans (initially at 32 years of age, and 31 by 1997–98), and substantial draft pick compensation to teams losing younger free agents (at least if the player had been paid more than the average salary in the prior season). Notwithstanding these major constraints on player mobility, NHL average salaries have risen from $195,000 in 1989–90 to more than $1 million in 1997–98—posing the puzzling question of what is the source of this salary spiral. Part of the answer is to be found in the presence of salary arbitration in hockey and the absence of a salary cap or tax—regimes that we will read about at the end of Chapter 4 and the beginning of Chapter 5.

A second case in this phase, *Zimmerman v. NFL*, 632 F.Supp. 398 (D.D.C.1986), involved a challenge by All–Pro offensive guard Gary Zimmerman to an amended provision in the NFL's 1982 collective agreement. The new term allowed the teams to hold a supplemental draft of players eligible to sign with NFL teams because their contracts with United States Football League teams had terminated with the USFL's demise in 1984. District Judge Barrington Parker also adopted and applied the *Mackey* test, and found that the exemption protected the supplemental draft because it had been agreed to by the union through good faith, arm's-length bargaining.

In the third in this series of cases, the Second Circuit reached a similar result as in *McCourt* and *Zimmerman* but without reference or regard to *Mackey*. This case dealt with an antitrust challenge to a collateral feature of one of the important innovations in sports labor relations—the salary cap, which was developed in professional basketball and was adopted with some significant modifications in professional football in the NFL's 1993 collective agreement.[j] We will describe the NBA and NFL salary caps in detail in Chapter 4. Suffice it to say here that the NBA and its Players Association negotiated a maximum (and a minimum) salary budget that can be spent by any team in signing new players—whether veteran free agents from other teams or rookie draft selections. Any team that was over the salary cap was permitted to offer a new player just the minimum $75,000 salary in a one-year contract. Leon Wood was the 1984 first-round draft pick of the Philadelphia 76ers (who were then over the cap). Thus Wood filed an antitrust suit against this feature of the cap.

After the trial judge dismissed the suit on the basis of the labor exemption, Wood appealed to the Second Circuit. The key person on the appeals panel was Judge Ralph Winter, previously a professor of antitrust and labor law at Yale Law School. While at Yale, not only did Professor Winter write one of the major scholarly examinations of the interplay between these two legal regimes, *Collective Bargaining and Competition: The Application of Antitrust Standards to Union Activities*, 73 Yale L. J. 14 (1963), but he also co-authored the first important analysis of this issue in the sports context, at a time when *Flood v. Kuhn* was still wending its way up to the Supreme Court (see Jacobs & Winter, *Antitrust Principles in Collective Bargaining by Athletes: Of Superstars in Peonage*, 81 Yale L. J. 1 (1971)). That professorial background led Judge Winter to offer a somewhat different judicial perspective in *Wood v. NBA*, 809 F.2d 954 (2d Cir.1987), than the one we saw in both *Mackey* and *McCourt*.

Judge Winter emphasized the fundamental principle of federal labor policy (in § 9(a) of the NLRA) that "employees may eliminate competition among themselves through a governmentally supervised majority vote selecting an exclusive bargaining representative."

> Federal labor policy thus allows employees to seek the best deal for the greatest number by the exercise of collective rather than individual bargaining power. Once an exclusive representative has been selected, the individual employee is forbidden by federal law from negotiating directly with the employer absent the representative's consent, *NLRB v. Allis–Chalmers Mfg. Co.*, 388 U.S. 175, 180, (1967), even though that employee may actually receive less compensation under the collective bargain than he or she would through individual negotiations. *J.I. Case Co. v. NLRB*, 321 U.S. 332, 338–39 (1944).

---

j. See Staudohar, *The Sports Industry and Collective Bargaining*, note a above, at 123–129, for a brief account of the 1983 and 1988 negotiations in basketball, in which the salary cap was first devised and then considerably revised.

The gravamen of Wood's complaint, namely that the NBA–NBPA collective agreement is illegal because it prevents him from achieving his full free market value, is therefore at odds with, and destructive of, federal labor policy. It is true that the diversity of talent and specialization among professional athletes and the widespread exposure and discussions of their "work" in the media make the differences in value among them as "workers" more visible than the differences in efficiency and in value among industrial workers. High public visibility, however, is no reason to ignore federal legislation that explicitly prevents employees, whether in or out of a bargaining unit, from seeking a better deal where that deal is inconsistent with the terms of a collective agreement.

809 F.2d at 959. Wood's counsel objected to the fact that this new basketball system assigned new players coming into the league to work for particular clubs they might not like, for salaries that were set at artificially low levels. Judge Winter pointed out that this collectively-bargained regime, while it might generate lower salaries for some players than their individual talent seemed to justify, had many analogies in the wage systems, hiring halls, seniority clauses, bars on outside contracts, and other standard fare in labor agreements.

If Wood's antitrust claim were to succeed, all of these commonplace arrangements would be subject to similar challenges, and federal labor policy would essentially collapse unless a wholly unprincipled, judge-made exception were created for professional athletes. Employers would have no assurance that they could enter into any collective agreement without exposing themselves to an action for treble damages. Moreover, recognition of a right to individual bargaining without the consent of the exclusive representative would undermine the status and effectiveness of the exclusive representative, and result in individual contracts that reduce the amount of wages or other benefits available for other workers. Wood's assertion that he would be paid more in the absence of the draft and salary cap also implies that others would receive less if he were successful. It can hardly be denied that the NBA teams would be more resistant to benefits guaranteed to all, such as pensions, minimum salaries, and medical and insurance benefits. In fact, the salary cap challenged by Wood is one part of a complex formula including minimum team salaries and guaranteed revenue sharing.

The policy claim that one can do better through individual bargaining is nothing but the flip side of the policy claim that other employees need unions to protect their interests. Congress has accepted the latter position, and we are bound by that legislative choice.

809 F.2d at 961. Finally, Judge Winter emphasized the incompatibility of Wood's antitrust position with that feature of national labor policy that "attaches prime importance to freedom of contract between the parties to a collective agreement."

Freedom of contract is an important cornerstone of national labor policy for two reasons. First, it allows an employer and a union to agree upon those arrangements that best suit their particular interests. Courts cannot hope to fashion contract terms more efficient than those arrived at by the parties who are to be governed by them. Second, freedom of contract furthers the goal of labor peace. To the extent that courts prohibit particular solutions for particular problems, they reduce the number and quality of compromises available to unions and employers for resolving their differences.

Freedom of contract is particularly important in the context of collective bargaining between professional athletes and their leagues. Such bargaining relationships raise numerous problems with little or no precedent in standard industrial relations. As a result, leagues and player unions may reach seemingly unfamiliar or strange agreements. If courts were to intrude and to outlaw such solutions, leagues and their player unions would have to arrange their affairs in a less efficient way. It would also increase the chances of strikes by reducing the number and quality of possible compromises.

The issues of free agency and entry draft are at the center of collective bargaining in much of the professional sports industry. It is to be expected that the parties will arrive at unique solutions to these problems in the different sports both because sports generally differ from the industrial model and because each sport has its own peculiar economic imperatives. The NBA/NBPA agreement is just such a unique bundle of compromises. The draft and the salary cap reflect the interests of the employers in stabilizing salary costs and spreading talent among the various teams. Minimum individual salaries, fringe benefits, minimum aggregate team salaries, and guaranteed revenue sharing reflect the interests of the union in enhancing standard benefits applicable to all players. The free agency/first refusal provisions in turn allow individual players to exercise a degree of individual bargaining power. Were a court to intervene and strike down the draft and salary cap, the entire agreement would unravel. This would force the NBA and NBPA to search for other avenues of compromise that would be less satisfactory to them than the agreement struck down. It would also measurably increase the chances of a strike. We decline to take that step.

809 F.2d at 961–62.

As Judge Winter observed at the end of his opinion, to the extent that this term of the NBA-Players Association contract was believed unjustifiably to discriminate against rookie players, the proper course of legal action was to charge the union with unfair representation of new employees under the NLRA. As we shall see in the next chapter, there are grave doubts about whether such a charge will pass muster under current labor law doctrine. And as we already read in Chapter 2, the limits imposed on rookie salaries by the NBA salary cap were a significant factor in the events leading to the *Brian Shaw* case. Still, most clubs make a serious effort to find room within their salary allotment to sign first-round picks to lucrative contracts. Indeed, after making Wood the initial $75,000 qualifying offer which triggered his lawsuit, the 76ers eventually signed him to a four-year, $1 million contract which was in the range paid to players at his level in the draft that year. Why did the 76ers and other teams go to this trouble?

The Third Phase

The *Wood* decision in 1987 marked the end of the second phase of antitrust litigation about the sports labor market. Whether based on the *Mackey/McCourt* or *Wood* formulation, it seemed clear that leagues enjoyed a labor exemption from player antitrust challenges to terms in collective agreements to which the union had agreed. No such challenges have been brought since *Wood*. However, as both the cases and contracts in *McCourt*, *Wood*, and *Zimmerman* began to expire, the players unions also had become disenchanted with restrictive features of those reserve systems. The Associations, however, confronted strong league resistance to any significant changes in these systems. Thus, once the labor agreements came to an end, the unions themselves filed antitrust challenges to the previously agreed-to restraints on free agency, arguing that the labor exemption had expired along with the agreement, or at least once an impasse had been reached in negotiations for a new agreement. The leagues' position was that the exemption could expire only when the union itself did (and perhaps not even then). Protracted litigation and negotiation that took place in the NFL beginning in 1987 generated the first in-depth judicial exploration of this legal issue.

The first such suit, *Powell v. NFL*, was initiated following collapse of the football players' ill-fated strike during the 1987 season in which games were played for three weeks with replacement players (as we will discuss in more detail in Chapter 4). The sticking point in the negotiations, and the primary target of the antitrust suit, was the set of restrictions on free agent movement that were included in the collective agreement reached at the end of the 1982 strike, and that were substantially similar to the restrictions adopted by the 1977 settlement that followed the Eighth Circuit's decision in *Mackey*.

The free agency system at issue gave teams whose free agents signed with a new club the choice between matching the new offer and retaining the player (a right of first refusal) or letting the player move and receiving compensation in the form of future draft choices, the number and round(s) determined by the player's new salary level. This system proved to be even more restrictive than the prior Rozelle Rule. During the 1977–82 agreement, only a handful of offers were made to free agents (usually when both teams were interested in a trade), and only once did the player move to a new team and compensation become payable. In the 1982 negotiations the NFLPA focused its efforts on a guaranteed revenue share and salary scale. While the union secured a four-year, $1.2 billion package after a lengthy strike, the old free agency system was essentially retained (with adjustments only in the salary levels that triggered various levels of team compensation). This system proved even more restrictive during the 1982–87 agreement: of 1,415 veterans who became free agents, just one received an offer from another team.

When the NFLPA filed the *Powell* suit in Minneapolis, where *Mackey* had been tried, the NFL moved for dismissal on nonstatutory labor exemption grounds, claiming that the exemption survived expiration of the agreement. District Judge David Doty issued an opinion, *Powell v. NFL (#1)*, 678 F.Supp. 777 (D.Minn.1988), with the following language:

> Basic principles of labor law dictate that provisions relating to mandatory subjects of bargaining "survive" formal expiration of the collective bargaining agreement. Typically, the parties to an expired agreement have an obligation [under labor law] to maintain the status quo as to these provisions until a new agreement is concluded or until the parties reach "impasse." The governing principle is that until impasse is reached, an employer is not free unilaterally to change the essential provisions of an expired collective bargaining agreement but must keep those provisions in effect and bargain with the union as to their possible modification.

678 F.Supp. at 784–85. The proper way, then, to accommodate labor and antitrust interests was to rule that the labor exemption for a particular issue survived until and unless the parties had reached an impasse (i.e., "have exhausted the prospects of concluding an agreement" on that issue).

Shortly after this ruling, the National Labor Relations Board found that the NFLPA had not bargained in bad faith during the summer of 1987. Judge Doty thus concluded that an impasse had been reached on the free agency issue and that the NFL's nonstatutory labor exemption had expired. However, recognizing that this was a controlling issue in the case, Judge Doty certified his labor exemption decision for interlocutory appeal, and the Eighth Circuit agreed to hear the issue prior to the antitrust trial.

In late 1989, the Eighth Circuit finally issued its decision reversing Judge Doty's first ruling that the *nonstatutory* exemption had expired at impasse. See *Powell v. NFL (#3)*, 930 F.2d 1293 (8th Cir.1989). The court reaffirmed the basic *Mackey* approach to the exemption. However, the majority then went on to hold that because the parties still had the full range of labor law remedies and resources available to them, the labor exemption from antitrust liability protected terms contained in the collective agreement not only after the agreement had expired, but beyond a bargaining impasse as well. How long past impasse was unclear. Despite a vigorous dissent by Judge Heaney who had sat on the *Mackey* panel 13 years earlier, the court concluded:

> Upon the facts currently presented by this case, we are not compelled to look into the future and pick a termination point for the

labor exemption. The parties are now faced with several choices. They may bargain further, which we would strongly urge that they do. They may resort to economic force. And finally, if appropriate issues arise, they may present claims to the National Labor Relations Board. We are satisfied that as long as there is a possibility that proceedings may be commenced before the Board, or until final resolution of Board proceedings and appeals therefrom, the labor relationship continues and the labor exemption applies.

930 F.2d at 1303–04.

After losing its bid for a rehearing by the Eighth Circuit *en banc,* and its petition for certiorari in the Supreme Court,[k] the NFLPA and its members declared themselves no longer a labor union engaged in collective bargaining. This, the union claimed, ended the bargaining relationship that the Eighth Circuit had made the cornerstone of the labor exemption. The NFLPA then instigated another antitrust suit against the NFL's current player restraints, which in 1988 had been unilaterally modified by the owners (following an impasse in bargaining). This was the Plan B system, under which each club could name 37 players on its roster who would be protected. If the players remained under contract, they were still bound to their team. If they were free agents, they could sign with another team, but subject to the right-of-first-refusal/compensation system contained in the expired labor agreement. All other players, whether under contract or not, were free to negotiate with any other team; if offered a better deal, they could move to the new team without the former team having any rights to their services.

The new suit, filed in New Jersey on behalf of NFLPA President Freeman McNeil and five other players, differed from *Powell* in two respects: not only was the NFLPA no longer purporting to act as a union, but the new system of restraints had been unilaterally implemented by the owners without any earlier agreement of the players. Venue was transferred to Minnesota where, along with the remnants of the *Powell* case, the NFL had also filed a suit asking for a declaratory judgment that its free agency rules were still exempt from antitrust enforcement, and in any event did not violate antitrust laws. All three cases were assigned to Judge Doty. The first issue he had to decide was whether the NFLPA's declaration that it was no longer acting as a union, without the NLRB holding a decertification election, was sufficient to terminate the bargaining relationship and with it the labor

---

k. The issue of the termination of the labor exemption had been the subject of sustained scholarly analysis after the district court and prior to the appeals court rulings in *Powell.* See Lee Goldman, *The Labor Exemption to the Antitrust Laws,* note g above, and Ethan Lock, *The Scope of the Labor Exemption in Professional Sports,* note g above. For commentary on the appeals court ruling, see the exchange between Neil K. Roman, *Illegal Procedure: The National Football Players Union's Improper Use of Antitrust Litigation for Purposes of Collective Bargaining,* 67 Denver U. L. Rev. 111 (1990), and Ethan Lock, *Powell v. National Football League: The Eighth Circuit Sacks the National Football League Players Association,* id. at 135. See also Note (by David Nahmias), *Releasing Superstars from Peonage: Union Consent and the Nonstatutory Labor Exemption,* 104 Harvard L. Rev. 874 (1991).

exemption. Judge Doty ruled, at 764 F.Supp. 1351 (D.Minn.1991), that the labor exemption had ended.

> ... [T]he court holds that the plaintiffs are no longer part of an "ongoing collective bargaining relationship" with the defendants. The NFLPA no longer engages in collective bargaining and has also refused every overture by the NFL defendants to bargain since November of 1989. The NFLPA further has abandoned its role in all grievance arbitrations and has ceased to regulate agents, leaving them free to represent individual players without NFLPA approval. The plaintiffs have also paid a price for the loss of their collective bargaining representative because the NFL defendants have unilaterally changed insurance benefits and lengthened the season without notifying the NFLPA.
>
> Because no "ongoing collective bargaining relationship" exists, the court determines that the nonstatutory labor exemption has ended. In the absence of continued union representation, the Eighth Circuit's rationale for the exemption no longer applies because the parties may not invoke any remedy under the labor laws, whether it be collective bargaining, instituting an NLRB proceeding for failure to bargain in good faith, or resorting to a strike.

764 F.Supp. at 1358–59.

McNeil v. NFL went on to a full-scale Rule of Reason trial. As mentioned earlier in this chapter, a Minneapolis jury found in 1992 that the Plan B restraints did violate Sherman Act § 1, and awarded four of the plaintiffs $1.6 million in damages. Before the Eighth Circuit could issue an opinion in the NFL's appeal of this verdict (including its claim that the NFLPA was really a union in disguise that was refusing to bargain in good faith), the parties settled the litigation in early 1993. The new regime greatly loosened free agency restraints, but created a salary cap that became the heart of the current players-owners relationship in football.

The settlement of the class action that was filed after the *McNeil* verdict on behalf of all NFL players, *White v. NFL*, offered $115 million in compensation to players affected by Plan B, and led the NFLPA to recertify itself. The NFL and the union then signed a new seven-year collective agreement. That agreement instituted unfettered free agency for five-year veteran players in 1993, which brought Reggie White, the lead class action plaintiff and top free agent that year, to the Green Bay Packers whose home city is the smallest in the NFL (and whom White helped lead to the Super Bowl championship in 1997). When total player salaries and related compensation soared to 67% of League revenues in 1993 (up from 56% in 1992), this triggered the contractual salary cap of 64% of league revenues. Because such revenues jumped in 1994 with the NFL's lucrative new television contract with Fox Broadcasting, average player salaries still increased modestly under the cap. The collective agreement also restored the NFLPA's control over the players' group licensing rights for sports merchandise and sharply improved player benefits. For example, the New England Patriots' Darryl Stingley, who had been paralyzed in a game in the late 1970's, saw his annual disability benefits jump from $50,000 a year to $100,000 immediately, with further increases up to $200,000 scheduled during the life of the contract.

More than 95% of the class plaintiffs approved of the settlement, and just as high a percentage of the active players approved the new collective agreement. However, objections were filed before Judge Doty by veteran players who disapproved of the "hard" salary cap, by recent college players who disapproved of the special rookie salary cap, and by Philadelphia Eagles owner Norman Braman who disapproved of the League's granting the NFLPA full control over player licensing (and the $20 million a year in revenues it was generating). After extensive hearings, Judge Doty found the settlement to be "fair, reasonable, and adequate" for the affected class: it gave players a host of tangible benefits in return for giving up a by-no-means-guaranteed legal claim for more extensive damages flowing from an antitrust trial verdict from which the league had filed significant grounds for appeal (see *White v. NFL*, 836 F.Supp. 1458 (D.Minn.1993)). The Eighth Circuit then dismissed the objectors' appeal (see 41 F.3d 402 (8th Cir.1994)). Having lost the case, Eagles' owner Braman sold his team (which he had bought for $65 million in the mid–1980s) for over $190 million. A number of the dissident players, particularly those on the Washington Redskins, continued their legal fight with the Association, under a different legal guise that we shall see in Chapter 4.

While *Powell/McNeil/White* and related ancillary suits were being fought out in Minnesota, the NBPA was fighting its own battle in New York federal courts in its effort to have provisions that it had agreed to in the 1988 collective agreement (the NBA salary cap, the rookie player draft, and the right of first refusal on restricted free agents) removed from the next agreement. The "soft" salary cap, which was the players' primary target, had been negotiated by the NBA with the Players Association in 1983, as a response to the league's economic strains. (The differences between the NBA's "soft" and the NFL's "hard" salary cap are described in sections at the end of Chapter 4 and the beginning of Chapter 5.) After this cap had been successfully defended by both sides against a rookie's antitrust challenge in *Wood*, it was renegotiated in the parties' next agreement in 1988. As the latter contract was coming to an end in 1994, the NBA wanted to tighten up the cap's design to close a loophole displayed in *Bridgeman v. NBA*, 838 F.Supp. 172 (D.N.J.1993) (the Chris Dudley case we will read about in Chapter 5). However, the Players Association (with Charles Grantham having succeeded the deceased Larry Fleisher as Executive Director) wanted to get rid of the salary cap entirely, on the grounds that a sport whose popularity and revenues had soared so much in the prior decade no longer needed this restraint on a free market for players.

With the agreement expiring in June 1994, and players telling owners that maintenance of the cap for that summer's free agent bidding would violate antitrust law, the NBA went to court seeking a declaration that league maintenance of the old cap in place after the agreement expired was protected by the labor exemption. It was clear that the League lawyers wanted to have the case heard in the Second Circuit before Judge Winter. The NBA lawyers' judgment was confirmed when Judge Winter eventually authored a unanimous panel decision affirming a trial court ruling in the league's favor. See *NBA v. Williams*, 45 F.3d 684 (2d Cir.1995).

Just as he had disregarded the Eighth Circuit's *Mackey* analysis in deciding *Wood*, Judge Winter adopted in *Williams* a different analytical approach from the Eighth Circuit's in *Powell* to reach the same result. Noting that multiemployer bargaining was a well-established practice that both Congress and the Supreme Court had recognized as valid, he reasoned that in order to effectuate labor policy properly, the law had to give employers who were bargaining as a group the same flexibility that single employers have. Of course, employees would never be able to file an antitrust case against a single employer because § 1's "contract, combination ... or conspiracy" element could not be met. Thus, Judge Winter reasoned, to allow unionized employees to maintain antitrust suits against the coordinated conduct of multiemployer associations would render multiemployer bargaining *de facto* illegal once an existing collective agreement expired.

As noted, multiemployer bargaining has been a conspicuous feature of collective bargaining since the very formation of unions. To hold at this late date that it—or the essence of practice under it—is illegal under the antitrust laws would cause a massive reshaping of the institution of collective bargaining.

Under the National Labor Relations Act, employers and unions must bargain in good faith over mandatory subjects of bargaining.... It is settled law that employers may formulate proposals to unions and insist upon the proposals so long as they bargain in good faith. It is also settled that employers may implement terms and conditions of employment after good-faith bargaining to an impasse and also resort to economic force, including lock-outs, in support of their demands.... In appellants' view, however, they need not really bargain over mandatory subjects of bargaining because the employers' conduct described above, when engaged in by a multiemployer organization, constitutes illegal price fixing.

... [T]he claim that the NBA Teams may not continue to impose the challenged provisions places the Teams in an impossible position. Those provisions were, of course, part of the 1988 CBA, and, under the Teams' obligation to bargain in good faith, they were obligated to maintain the *status quo* until an impasse was reached. However, appellants claim that imposition of those provisions violated the antitrust laws as soon as the CBA expired, a position that views as illegal, conduct required by the NLRA. Even after impasse, moreover, if employers may impose new terms and conditions of employment, they are surely free to maintain the *status quo*.

* * *

We thus agree with the decision in *Powell* in which the Eighth Circuit held that the nonstatutory labor exemption precluded an antitrust challenge to various terms and conditions of employment implemented after impasse by National Football League teams. The Court noted the soup-to-nuts array of rules and remedies afforded under the labor laws and concluded that application of antitrust principles to a collective bargaining relationship would disrupt collective bargaining as we know it.

45 F.3d at 691–93.

Judge Winter's reasoning in *Williams* not only applied the nonstatutory exemption to the terms contained in the expired agreement for as long as the collective bargaining relationship exists; it also implied that NBA owners were free to implement new terms and conditions after reaching a bargaining impasse under labor law. Thus, the NBA owners would be free under antitrust law unilaterally to close up the Chris Dudley "one year and out" escape valve in their existing salary cap system.

This implication was simultaneously being put to the test in another case then pending against the NFL, one that would finally produce a Supreme Court decision in a sports labor-antitrust case—*Brown v. Pro Football, Inc.*, 518 U.S. 231 (1996). Recall that *Brown* dealt with the NFL's establishment in 1989 of six-player developmental squads for each team at league-mandated salary levels. These squads were to be made up of first or second year players who had not made the regular 47–man roster, but whose teams wanted to keep them for practices and possible replacement of injured or poorly-performing regulars. The system was designed to eliminate the practice of teams "stashing" players who had not made the regular roster on their injured reserve list. This league initiative was not the subject of collective bargaining (let alone agreement) prior to 1989. The NFLPA (which in early 1989 was still acting as the players' bargaining representative) applauded the creation of these squads, but insisted that developmental players' salaries be individually negotiated in the same manner as regular players' salaries. When the NFL went ahead and implemented its fixed salary scale of $1,000 per week, the Association filed an antitrust suit. It is also worth noting that the owners collectively imposed not just a cap, but a huge *cut* in the average salary paid to this category of player (i.e., to new players previously "stashed" on injured reserve), a figure that dropped from about $60,000 per year in 1988 to $16,000 in 1989.

In rejecting the NFL's labor exemption defense to this action, District Judge Royce Lamberth concluded, contrary to all the options embraced in *Bridgeman*, *Powell*, and *Williams*, that the labor exemption expired immediately upon expiration of the agreement. See 782 F.Supp. 125 (D.D.C.1991). As we saw earlier in this chapter, the judge also found (on summary judgment) this salary arrangement to violate antitrust law. After a week-long damages trial in the fall of 1992, a jury determined that $10 million in damages had been inflicted upon the 235 developmental squad players, which was trebled to a $30 million award plus legal costs. Ironically, Tony Brown, the lead plaintiff (who by then was out of football), was awarded $460,000 even though he had been one of the replacement players who enabled the NFL to break the players' strike in 1987.

On appeal, a divided panel of the D.C. Circuit reversed. The majority, adopting the approach of Judge Winter in *Williams*, held that the nonstatutory labor exemption protected a league from all antitrust suits brought by or on behalf of their players' union with respect to conduct engaged in during the collective bargaining process, as long as the bargaining relationship with the union exists. See 50 F.3d 1041 (D.C.Cir. 1995). Both the majority opinion, authored by respected former labor lawyer Harry Edwards, and the dissent by Judge Patricia Wald, were lengthy, cogent, and reflected very different views of the workings and purposes of federal labor law. The players' further appeal from this decision produced the following Supreme Court opinion.[1]

BROWN v. PRO FOOTBALL, INC.

Supreme Court of the United States, 1996.
518 U.S. 231, 116 S.Ct. 2116, 135 L.Ed.2d 521.

JUSTICE BREYER delivered the opinion of the Court.

* * *

[The court began by framing the specific question posed by this case as whether "club owners who had bargained to an impasse with the players union about a wage issue, and had then agreed among themselves (but not with the union) to implement the terms of their own last best bargaining offer" should have their agreement shielded by federal labor laws from antitrust attack. After sketching the history of the "implicit ('nonstatutory')" labor exemption, Justice Breyer stated that its point was to limit] ... an antitrust court's authority to determine, in the area of industrial conflict, what is or is not a "reasonable" practice. It thereby substitutes legislative and administrative labor-related determinations for judicial antitrust-related determinations as to the appropriate legal limits of industrial conflict.

As a matter of logic, it would be difficult, if not impossible, to require groups of employers and employees to bargain together, but at

---

1. *Brown* quickly sparked several major scholarly analyses of the legal and economic issues posed by the labor exemption from antitrust. See Michael Harper, *Multi-Employer Bargaining, Antitrust Law, and Team Sports*, 38 William and Mary L. Rev. 1663 (1997); Jeffrey L. Harrison, Brown v. Pro Football, Inc., *The Labor Exemption, Antitrust Standing, and Distributive Outcomes*, The Antitrust Bulletin 565 (Fall 1997); Gary R. Roberts, Brown v. Football, Inc., *The Supreme Court Gets it Right for the Wrong Reasons*, id., 595; and Stephen F. Ross and Robert B. Lucke, *Why Highly-Paid Athletes Deserve More Antitrust Protection Than Ordinary Unionized Workers*, id., 641.

the same time to forbid them to make among themselves or with each other any of the competition-restricting agreements potentially necessary to make the process work or its results mutually acceptable. Thus, the implicit exemption recognizes that, to give effect to federal labor laws and policies and to allow meaningful collective bargaining to take place, some restraints on competition imposed through the bargaining process must be shielded from antitrust sanctions....

The petitioners and their supporters concede, as they must, the legal existence of the exemption we have described. They also concede that, where its application is necessary to make the statutorily authorized collective-bargaining process work as Congress intended, the exemption must apply both to employers and to employees. Nor does the dissent take issue with these basic principles. Consequently, the question before us is one of determining the exemption's scope: Does it apply to an agreement among several employers bargaining together to implement after impasse the terms of their last best good-faith wage offer? We assume that such conduct, as practiced in this case, is unobjectionable as a matter of labor law and policy. On that assumption, we conclude that the exemption applies.

Labor law itself regulates directly, and considerably, the kind of behavior here at issue—the postimpasse imposition of a proposed employment term concerning a mandatory subject of bargaining. Both the Board and the courts have held that, after impasse, labor law permits employers unilaterally to implement changes in preexisting conditions, but only insofar as the new terms meet carefully circumscribed conditions. For example, the new terms must be "reasonably comprehended" within the employer's preimpasse proposals (typically the last rejected proposals), lest by imposing more or less favorable terms, the employer unfairly undermined the union's status. The collective-bargaining proceeding itself must be free of any unfair labor practice, such as an employer's failure to have bargained in good faith. These regulations reflect the fact that impasse and an accompanying implementation of proposals constitute an integral part of the bargaining process.

Although the caselaw we have cited focuses upon bargaining by a single employer, no one here has argued that labor law does, or should, treat multiemployer bargaining differently in this respect. Indeed, Board and court decisions suggest that the joint implementation of proposed terms after impasse is a familiar practice in the context of multiemployer bargaining. We proceed on that assumption.

Multiemployer bargaining itself is a well-established, important, pervasive method of collective bargaining, offering advantages to both management and labor. See Appendix (multiemployer bargaining accounts for more than 40% of major collective-bargaining agreements, and is used in such industries as construction, transportation, retail trade, clothing manufacture, and real estate, as well as professional sports); *NLRB v. Truck Drivers*, 353 U.S. 87, 95 (1957) (*Buffalo Linen*) (Congress saw multiemployer bargaining as "a vital factor in the effectuation of the national policy of promoting labor peace through strengthened collective bargaining"); *Charles D. Bonanno Linen Service, Inc. v. NLRB*, 454 U.S. 404, 409, n. 3 (1982) (*Bonanno Linen*) (multiemployer bargaining benefits both management and labor, by saving bargaining resources, by encouraging development of industry-wide worker benefits programs that smaller employers could not otherwise afford, and by inhibiting employer competition at the workers' expense). The upshot is that the practice at issue here plays a significant role in a collective-bargaining process that itself comprises an important part of the Nation's industrial relations system.

In these circumstances, to subject the practice to antitrust law is to require antitrust courts to answer a host of important practical questions about how collective bargaining over wages, hours and working conditions is to proceed—the very result that the implicit labor exemption seeks to avoid. And it is to place in jeopardy some of the potentially beneficial labor-related effects that multiemployer bargaining can achieve. That is because unlike labor law, which sometimes welcomes anticompetitive agreements conducive to industrial harmony, antitrust law forbids all agreements among competitors (such as competing employers) that unreasonably lessen competition among or between them in virtually any respect whatsoever. See, e.g., *Paramount Famous Lasky Corp. v. United States*, 282 U.S. 30 (1930) (agreement to insert arbitration provisions in motion picture licensing contracts). Antitrust law also sometimes permits judges or juries to premise antitrust liability upon little more than uniform behavior among competitors, preceded by conversations implying that later uniformity might prove desirable, see, e.g., *United States v. General Motors Corp.*, 384 U.S. 127, 142–143 (1966), or accompanied by other conduct that in context suggests that each competitor failed to make an independent decision, see, e.g., *American Tobacco Co. v. United States*, 328 U.S. 781, 809–810 (1946).

If the antitrust laws apply, what are employers to do once impasse is reached? If all impose terms similar to their last joint offer, they invite an antitrust action premised upon identical behavior (along with prior or accompanying conversations) as tending to show a common understanding or agreement. If any, or all, of them individually impose terms that differ significantly from that offer, they invite an unfair labor practice charge. Indeed, how can employers safely discuss their offers together even before a bargaining impasse occurs? A preimpasse discussion about, say, the practical advantages or disadvantages of a particular proposal, invites a later antitrust claim that they agreed to limit the kinds of action each would later take should an impasse occur. The same is true of postimpasse discussions aimed at renewed negotiations with the union. Nor would adherence to the terms of an expired collective-bargaining agreement eliminate a potentially plausible antitrust claim charging that they had "conspired" or tacitly "agreed" to do so, particularly if maintaining the status quo were not in the immediate economic self-interest of some. All this is to say that to permit antitrust liability here threatens to introduce instability and uncertainty into the collective-bargaining process, for antitrust law often forbids or discourages the kinds of joint discussions and behavior that the collective-bargaining process invites or requires.

We do not see any obvious answer to this problem. We recognize, as the Government suggests, that, in principle, antitrust courts might themselves try to evaluate particular kinds of employer understandings, finding them "reasonable" (hence lawful) where justified by collective-bargaining necessity. But any such evaluation means a web of detailed rules spun by many different nonexpert antitrust judges and juries, not a set of labor rules enforced by a single expert administrative body, namely the Labor Board. The labor laws give the Board, not antitrust courts, primary responsibility for policing the collective-bargaining process. And one of their objectives was to take from antitrust courts the authority to determine, through application of the antitrust laws, what is socially or economically desirable collective-bargaining policy. See *supra*, at 3–4; see also *Jewel Tea*, 381 U.S. at 716–719 (opinion of Goldberg, J.).

III

Both petitioners and their supporters advance several suggestions for drawing the exemption boundary line short of this case. We shall explain why we find them unsatisfactory.

A

Petitioners claim that the implicit exemption applies only to labor-management agreements—a limitation that they deduce from caselaw language, see, e.g., *Connell*, 421 U.S. at 622 (exemption for "some union-employer agreements"), and from a proposed principle—that the exemption must rest upon labor-management consent. The language, however, reflects only the fact that the cases previously before the Court involved collective-bargaining agreements; the language does not reflect the exemption's rationale.

Nor do we see how an exemption limited by petitioners' principle of labor-management consent could work. One cannot mean the principle literally—that the exemption applies only to understandings embodied in a collective-bargaining agreement—for the collective-bargaining process may take place before the making of any agreement or after an agreement has expired. Yet a multiemployer bargaining process itself necessarily involves many procedural and substantive understandings among participating employers as well as with the union. Petitioners cannot rescue their principle by claiming that the exemption applies only insofar as both labor and management consent to those understandings. Often labor will not (and should not) consent to certain common bargaining positions that employers intend to maintain. Similarly, labor need not consent to certain tactics that this Court has approved as part of the multiemployer bargaining process, such as unit-wide lockouts and the use of temporary replacements. See *NLRB v. Brown*, 380 U.S. 278, 284 (1965); *Buffalo Linen*, 353 U.S. at 97.

Petitioners cannot save their consent principle by weakening it, as by requiring union consent only to the multiemployer bargaining process itself. This general consent is automatically present whenever multiemployer bargaining takes place. See *Hi-Way Billboards, Inc.*, 206 N.L.R.B. 22 (1973) (multiemployer unit "based on consent" and "established by an unequivocal agreement by the parties"), enf. denied on other grounds, 500 F.2d 181 (5th Cir.1974); *Weyerhaeuser Co.*, 166 N.L.R.B. 299, 299–300 (1967). As so weakened, the principle cannot help decide which related practices are, or are not, subject to antitrust immunity.

B

The Solicitor General argues that the exemption should terminate at the point of impasse. After impasse, he says, "employers no longer have a duty under the labor laws to maintain the status quo," and "are free as a matter of labor law to negotiate individual arrangements on an interim basis with the union."

Employers, however, are not completely free at impasse to act independently. The multiemployer bargaining unit ordinarily remains intact; individual employers cannot withdraw. The duty to bargain survives; employers must stand ready to resume collective bargaining. And individual employers can negotiate individual interim agreements with the union only insofar as those agreements are consistent with "the duty to abide by the results of group bargaining." Regardless, the absence of a legal "duty" to act jointly is not determinative. This Court has implied antitrust immunities that extend beyond statutorily required joint action to joint action that a statute "expressly or impliedly allows or assumes must also be immune."

More importantly, the simple "impasse" line would not solve the basic problem we have described above. Labor law permits employers, after impasse, to engage in considerable joint behavior, including joint lockouts and replacement hiring. See, e.g., *Brown*, supra, at 289 (hiring of temporary replacement workers after lockout was "reasonably adapted to the achievement of a legitimate end—preserving the integrity of the multiemployer bargaining unit"). Indeed, as a general matter, labor law often limits employers to four options at impasse: (1) maintain the status quo, (2) implement their last offer, (3) lock out their workers (and either shut down or hire temporary replacements), or (4) negotiate separate interim agreements with the union. What is to happen if the parties cannot reach an interim agreement? The other alternatives are limited. Uniform employer conduct is likely. Uniformity—at least when accompanied by discussion of the matter—invites antitrust attack. And such attack would ask antitrust courts to decide the lawfulness of activities intimately related to the bargaining process.

The problem is aggravated by the fact that "impasse" is often temporary; it may differ from bargaining only in degree; it may be manipulated by the parties for bargaining purposes; and it may occur several times during the course of a single labor dispute, since the bargaining process is not over when the first impasse is reached. How are employers to discuss future bargaining positions during a temporary impasse? Consider, too, the adverse consequences that flow from failing to guess how an antitrust court would later draw the impasse line. Employers who erroneously concluded that impasse had not been reached would risk antitrust liability were they collectively to maintain the status quo, while employers who erroneously concluded that impasse had occurred would risk unfair labor practice charges for prematurely suspending multiemployer negotiations.

The Solicitor General responds with suggestions for softening an "impasse" rule by extending the exemption after impasse "for such time as would be reasonable in the circumstances" for employers to consult with counsel, confirm that impasse has occurred, and adjust their business operations; by reestablishing the exemption once there is a "resumption of good-faith bargaining"; and by looking to antitrust law's "rule of reason" to shield—"in some circumstances"—such joint actions as the unit-wide lockout or the concerted maintenance of previously-established joint benefit or retirement plans. But even as so modified, the impasse-related rule creates an exemption that can evaporate in the middle of the bargaining process, leaving later antitrust courts free to second-guess the parties' bargaining decisions and consequently forcing them to choose their collective-bargaining responses in light of what they predict or fear that antitrust courts, not labor law administrators, will eventually decide.

C

Petitioners and their supporters argue in the alternative for a rule that would exempt postimpasse agreement about bargaining "tactics," but not postimpasse agreement about substantive "terms," from the reach of antitrust. They recognize, however, that both the Board and the courts have said that employers can, and often do, employ the imposition of "terms" as a bargaining "tactic." See, e.g., *American Ship Building Co. v. NLRB*, 380 U.S. 300, 316 (1965). This concession as to joint "tactical" implementation would turn the presence of an antitrust exemption upon a determination of the employers' primary purpose or motive. But to ask antitrust courts, insulated from the bargaining process, to investigate an employer group's subjective motive is to ask them to conduct an inquiry often more amorphous than those we have previously discussed. And, in our view, a labor/antitrust line drawn on such a basis would too often raise the same related (previously discussed) problems. See *Jewel Tea*, 381 U.S. at 716 (opinion of Goldberg, J.) (expressing concern about antitrust judges "roaming at large" through the bargaining process).

D

The petitioners make several other arguments. They point, for example, to cases holding applicable, in collective-bargaining contexts, general "backdrop" statutes, such as a state statute requiring a plant-closing employer to make employee severance payments, *Fort Halifax*

Packing Co. v. Coyne, 482 U.S. 1 (1987), and a state statute mandating certain minimum health benefits, *Metropolitan Life Ins. Co. v. Massachusetts*, 471 U.S. 724 (1985). Those statutes, however, " 'neither encouraged nor discouraged the collective-bargaining processes that are the subject of the [federal labor laws].' " *Fort Halifax*, supra, at 21 (quoting *Metropolitan Life*, supra, at 755). Neither did those statutes come accompanied with antitrust's labor-related history.

Petitioners also say that irrespective of how the labor exemption applies elsewhere to multiemployer collective bargaining, professional sports is "special." We can understand how professional sports may be special in terms of, say, interest, excitement, or concern. But we do not understand how they are special in respect to labor law's antitrust exemption. We concede that the clubs that make up a professional sports league are not completely independent economic competitors, as they depend upon a degree of cooperation for economic survival. *National Collegiate Athletic Assn. v. Board of Regents of Univ. of Okla.*, 468 U.S. 85, 101–102 (1984). In the present context, however, that circumstance makes the league more like a single bargaining employer, which analogy seems irrelevant to the legal issue before us.

We also concede that football players often have special individual talents, and, unlike many unionized workers, they often negotiate their pay individually with their employers. But this characteristic seems simply a feature, like so many others, that might give employees (or employers) more (or less) bargaining power, that might lead some (or all) of them to favor a particular kind of bargaining, or that might lead to certain demands at the bargaining table. We do not see how it could make a critical legal difference in determining the underlying framework in which bargaining is to take place. See generally Jacobs & Winter, *Antitrust Principles and Collective Bargaining by Athletes: Of Superstars in Peonage*, 81 Yale L. J. 1 (1971). Indeed, it would be odd to fashion an antitrust exemption that gave additional advantages to professional football players (by virtue of their superior bargaining power) that transport workers, coal miners, or meat packers would not enjoy.

The dissent points to other "unique features" of the parties' collective bargaining relationship, which, in the dissent's view, make the case "atypical." It says, for example, that the employers imposed the restraint simply to enforce compliance with league-wide rules, and that the bargaining consisted of nothing more than the sending of a "notice," and therefore amounted only to "so-called" bargaining. Insofar as these features underlie an argument for looking to the employers' true purpose, we have already discussed them. Insofar as they suggest that there was not a genuine impasse, they fight the basic assumption upon which the District Court, the Court of Appeals, the petitioners, and this Court, rest the case. Ultimately, we cannot find a satisfactory basis for distinguishing football players from other organized workers. We therefore conclude that all must abide by the same legal rules.

* * *

For these reasons, we hold that the implicit ("nonstatutory") antitrust exemption applies to the employer conduct at issue here. That conduct took place during and immediately after a collective-bargaining negotiation. It grew out of, and was directly related to, the lawful operation of the bargaining process. It involved a matter that the parties were required to negotiate collectively. And it concerned only the parties to the collective-bargaining relationship.

Our holding is not intended to insulate from antitrust review every joint imposition of terms by employers, for an agreement among employers could be sufficiently distant in time and in circumstances from the collective-bargaining process that a rule permitting antitrust intervention would not significantly interfere with that process. See, e.g., 50 F.3d at 1057 (suggesting that exemption lasts until collapse of the collective-bargaining relationship, as evidenced by decertification of the union); *El Cerrito Mill & Lumber Co.*, 316 N.L.R.B. at 1006–1007 (suggesting that "extremely long" impasse, accompanied by "instability" or "defunctness" of multiemployer unit, might justify union withdrawal from group bargaining). We need not decide in this case whether, or where, within these extreme outer boundaries to draw that line. Nor would it be appropriate for us to do so without the detailed views of the Board, to whose "specialized judgment" Congress "intended to leave" many of the "inevitable questions concerning multiemployer bargaining bound to arise in the future."

The judgment of the Court of Appeals is affirmed.

JUSTICE STEVENS, dissenting.

In his classic dissent in *Lochner v. New York*, 198 U.S. 45, 75 (1905), Justice Holmes reminded us that our disagreement with the economic theory embodied in legislation should not affect our judgment about its constitutionality. It is equally important, of course, to be faithful to the economic theory underlying broad statutory mandates when we are construing their impact on areas of the economy not specifically addressed by their texts. The unique features of this case lead me to conclude that the Court has reached a decision that conflicts with the basic purpose of both the antitrust laws and the national labor policy expressed in a series of congressional enactments.

I

The basic premise underlying the Sherman Act is the assumption that free competition among business entities will produce the best price levels. *National Soc. of Professional Engineers v. United States*, 435 U.S. 679, 695 (1978). Collusion among competitors, it is believed, may produce prices that harm consumers. *United States v. Socony–Vacuum Oil Co.*, 310 U.S. 150, 226, n. 59 (1940). Similarly, the Court has held, a market-wide agreement among employers setting wages at levels that would not prevail in a free market may violate the Sherman Act. *Anderson v. Shipowners' Assn. of Pacific Coast*, 272 U.S. 359 (1926).

The jury's verdict in this case has determined that the market-wide agreement among these employers fixed the salaries of the replacement players at a dramatically lower level than would obtain in a free market. While the special characteristics of this industry may provide a justification for the agreement under the rule of reason, see *National Collegiate Athletic Assn. v. Board of Regents of Univ. of Okla.*, 468 U.S. 85, 100–104 (1984), at this stage of the proceeding our analysis of the exemption issue must accept the premise that the agreement is unlawful unless it is exempt.

The basic premise underlying our national labor policy is that unregulated competition among employees and applicants for employment produces wage levels that are lower than they should be. Whether or not the premise is true in fact, it is surely the basis for the statutes that encourage and protect the collective-bargaining process, including the express statutory exemptions from the antitrust laws that Congress enacted in order to protect union activities. Those statutes were enacted to enable collective action by union members to achieve wage levels that are higher than would be available in a free market.

The statutory labor exemption protects the right of workers to act collectively to seek better wages, but does not "exempt concerted action or agreements between unions and nonlabor parties." *Connell Constr. Co. v. Plumbers*, 421 U.S. 616, 621–622 (1975). It is the judicially crafted, nonstatutory labor exemption that serves to accommodate the conflicting policies of the antitrust and labor statutes in the context of action between employers and unions.

The limited judicial exemption complements its statutory counterpart by ensuring that unions which engage in collective bargaining to enhance employees' wages may enjoy the benefits of the resulting agreements. The purpose of the labor laws would be frustrated if it were illegal for employers to enter into industry-wide agreements providing supracompetitive wages for employees. For that reason, we have explained that "a proper accommodation between the congressional policy favoring collective bargaining under the NLRA and the congressional policy favoring free competition in business markets requires that some union-employer agreements be accorded a limited nonstatutory exemption from antitrust sanctions."

Consistent with basic labor law policies, I agree with the Court that the judicially crafted labor exemption must also cover some collective action that employers take in response to a collective bargaining agent's demands for higher wages. Immunizing such action from antitrust scrutiny may facilitate collective bargaining over labor demands. So, too, may immunizing concerted employer action designed to maintain the integrity of the multi-employer bargaining unit, such as lockouts that are imposed in response to "a union strike tactic which threatens the destruction of the employers' interest in bargaining on a group basis." *NLRB v. Truck Drivers*, 353 U.S. 87 (1957).

In my view, however, neither the policies underlying the two separate statutory schemes, nor the narrower focus on the purpose of the nonstatutory exemption, provides a justification for exempting from antitrust scrutiny collective action initiated by employers to depress wages below the level that would be produced in a free market. Nor do those policies support a rule that would allow employers to suppress wages by implementing noncompetitive agreements among themselves on matters that have not previously been the subject of either an agreement with labor or even a demand by labor for inclusion in the bargaining process. That, however, is what is at stake in this litigation.

II

In light of the accommodation that has been struck between antitrust and labor law policy, it would be most ironic to extend an exemption crafted to protect collective action by employees to protect employers acting jointly to deny employees the opportunity to negotiate their salaries individually in a competitive market. Perhaps aware of the irony, the Court chooses to analyze this case as though it represented a typical impasse in an unexceptional multiemployer bargaining process. In so doing, it glosses over three unique features of the case that are critical to the inquiry into whether the policies of the labor laws require extension of the nonstatutory labor exemption to this atypical case.

First, in this market, unlike any other area of labor law implicated in the cases cited by the Court, player salaries are individually negotiated. The practice of individually negotiating player salaries prevailed even prior to collective bargaining. The players did not challenge the prevailing practice because, unlike employees in most industries, they want their compensation to be determined by the forces of the free market rather than by the process of collective bargaining. Thus, although the majority professes an inability to understand anything special about professional sports that should affect the framework of labor negotiations, in this business it is the employers, not the employees, who seek to impose a noncompetitive uniform wage on a segment of the market and to put an end to competitive wage negotiations.

Second, respondents concede that the employers imposed the wage restraint to force owners to comply with league-wide rules that limit the number of players that may serve on a team, not to facilitate a stalled bargaining process, or to revisit any issue previously subjected to bargaining. The employers could have confronted the culprits directly by stepping up enforcement of roster limits. They instead chose to address the problem by unilaterally forbidding players from individually competing in the labor market.

Third, although the majority asserts that the "club owners had bargained with the players' union over a wage issue until they reached impasse," that hardly constitutes a complete description of what transpired. When the employers' representative advised the union that they proposed to pay the players a uniform wage determined by the owners, the union promptly and unequivocally responded that their proposal was inconsistent with the "principle" of individual salary negotiation that had been accepted in the past and that predated collective bargaining. The so-called "bargaining" that followed amounted to nothing more than the employers' notice to the union that they had decided to implement a decision to replace individual salary negotiations with a uniform wage level for a specific group of players.

Given these features of the case, I do not see why the employers should be entitled to a judicially crafted exemption from antitrust liability. We have explained that the "the nonstatutory exemption has its source in the strong labor policy favoring the association of employees to eliminate competition over wages and working conditions." *Connell Constr. Co.*, 421 U.S. at 622. I know of no similarly strong labor policy that favors the association of employers to eliminate a competitive method of negotiating wages that predates collective bargaining and that labor would prefer to preserve.

Even if some collective action by employers may justify an exemption because it is necessary to maintain the "integrity of the multiemployer bargaining unit," *NLRB v. Brown*, 380 U.S. 278, 289 (1965), no such justification exists here. The employers imposed a fixed wage even though there was no dispute over the pre-existing principle that player salaries should be individually negotiated. They sought only to prevent certain owners from evading roster limits and thereby gaining an unfair advantage. Because "the employer's interest is a competitive interest rather than an interest in regulating its own labor relations," *Mine Workers v. Pennington*, 381 U.S. 657, 667 (1965), there would seem to be no more reason to exempt this concerted, anticompetitive employer action from the antitrust laws than the action held unlawful in *Radovich v. National Football League*, 352 U.S. 445 (1957).

The point of identifying the unique features of this case is not, as the Court suggests, to make the case that professional football players, alone among workers, should be entitled to enforce the antitrust laws against anti-competitive collective employer action. Other employees, no less than well-paid athletes, are entitled to the protections of the antitrust laws when their employers unite to undertake anticompetitive action that causes them direct harm and alters the state of employer-employee relations that existed prior to unionization. Here that alteration occurred because the wage terms that the employers unilaterally imposed directly conflict with a pre-existing principle of agreement between the bargaining parties. In other contexts, the alteration may take other similarly anticompetitive and unjustifiable forms.

* * *

Accordingly, I respectfully dissent.

Justice Stevens used the latter part of his opinion to document the fact that the principal precedent cited in Justice Breyer's opinion was the earlier opinion written by Justice Goldberg in *Jewel Tea*. As Justice Stevens pointed out, *Jewel Tea* was one of the two major labor exemption decisions rendered by the Court on the same day in 1965, the other being *Pennington*. Both cases involved antitrust suits filed by employers against unions and the wage or hours provisions the latter had secured in collective agreements, with the unions' defense being the labor exemption. The Court's opinions in the two decisions expressed three different positions about the appropriate relationship between antitrust and labor law, each position embraced by three separate groups of Justices.

One view, authored by Justice Goldberg (who had been AFL–CIO General Counsel and then Secretary of Labor before going to the Court), was that labor law should always prevail. A second view, embraced by Justice Douglas, was that antitrust law should always govern. The intermediate view, advocated by Justice White, was that there had to be an accommodation between the two bodies of law, with labor law governing in some cases (such as *Jewel Tea*) and antitrust law taking precedence in others (such as *Pennington*). It was the three-member White group whose votes and opinion were decisive in both cases, not Justice Goldberg's concurring opinion in *Jewel Tea*, any more than his similar dissenting opinion in *Pennington*. Indeed, Justice Stevens went on to document Justice Goldberg's subsequent change of heart in the brief he filed with the Court in the early 1970s, on behalf of his client Curt Flood. (Goldberg had left the Court in 1965 at the request of President Johnson, to replace the deceased Adlai Stevenson as U.S. Ambassador to the United Nations, where he would defend the American role in Vietnam.)

Questions For Discussion

1. In *Pennington*, as well as in a later case, *Connell Construction*, the Supreme Court limited the scope of the labor exemption in situations where it believed the antitrust values of competition in the product market outweighed the labor law values of collective bargaining. In *Jewel Tea*, where industrial relations concerns were judged stronger, the labor exemption precluded use of antitrust law even to strike down a restraint whose immediate impact (though not its purpose) was on the product market. In the *Brown* case, the petitioners argued that there was a strong antitrust interest in precluding employer collusion to eliminate a competitive labor market for development squad players, and a minimal (actually a negative) labor law interest in forcing all the NFL players either to go on strike or to decertify their union in order to allow the development squad players to use antitrust law to remove the large salary cut that the owners had collectively imposed on them. How did the Court's opinion respond to that argument? Even if you were to find that line of argument persuasive, would you still support the *Brown* holding if the Court had rested its decision on the *statutory* exemption (which absolutely bars any antitrust suits by labor, irrespective of competing antitrust interests)?

2. All parties involved in the case recognized that there were significant industrial relations problems in exposing to antitrust scrutiny multi-

employer bargaining associations whose *raison d'etre* was to coordinate and constrain individual employer dealings with their employees. Since unionized employees benefit from the multiemployer bargaining process as much as do employers, everyone agreed that there had to be some measure of labor exemption for such collective employer action. The position of the Solicitor General was that employer associations such as the NFL were fully insulated from antitrust suits *before* bargaining reached an impasse, but that they lost the exemption once it was clear that impasse had been reached. (Even after that point the NFL owners would be entitled to defend their actions under all relevant antitrust doctrines.) The Court's opinion focused on this doctrinal proposal and rejected it. What are your views on this score?

3. The players' formulation was rather different from the Solicitor General's. With respect to bargaining *tactics* used by employer associations, the petitioners proposed that these should be fully insulated from antitrust after as well as before impasse. If the NFL owners had chosen, for example, to lock out the players to secure the union's acceptance of the development squad salary formula, they would enjoy a labor exemption from antitrust suit against use of this tactic. However, when the owners agreed amongst themselves to impose this substantive employment *term* on their players, they should have to defend under antitrust law the propriety of that action, even though it was legal under labor law. This distinction between tactics and terms had already been drawn by the Supreme Court in a series of rulings about when state employment laws could apply to collective bargaining relationships governed by federal labor law. Thus, while a state cannot bar a lockout by an employer to secure lower wage levels from their employees' union, they can set a minimum wage (or other benefit) level which applies to union as well as nonunion workers. The petitioners' argument to the Court was that applicability of the federal antitrust backdrop to labor-management relations should rest on that same basic distinction between tactics and terms. What was Justice Breyer's response to that position?

4. Even with respect to terms of employment, the players also accepted that the labor exemption would protect multiemployer restraints (e.g., a fixed development squad salary) to which the employees union had agreed. Application of that "consent" standard presents no problem during the time that a collective agreement was in force. During the life of a bargaining relationship, though, there are periods when a contract has not yet been negotiated or has expired. A further doctrinal problem facing the players, then, was whether the actions of multiemployer associations were denied any labor exemption at that point. An example offered by the NFL owners came from Judge Winter's opinion in the *NBA-Williams* case: a printers association whose collective agreement with the printers union had expired unilaterally implements its offer of a five percent wage increase rather than the ten percent increase sought by the union. In *Brown*, the players agreed with Judge Winter that such collective action by the employers association was immune from antitrust challenge, because the union in that industry had consented to the standardization of wages in place of competition among employers and employees.

However, the focus of the players' argument was that a key difference in the sports world was that there the players union has always sought to preserve or expand, not to eliminate, a competitive labor market for the setting of salaries. The players noted that sports actually resembled the entertainment, not the printers, labor market. For example, in 1994, following its victory over CBS in the bidding for NFL television rights, Fox Broadcasting won a free agent bidding war for color commentator John Madden, by agreeing to pay him $7.5 million a year. This was more than the $6 million that Dallas Cowboys' quarterback Troy Aikman secured in his new contract that year, but only half the $14 million won by David Letterman in his move from NBC to CBS. John Madden and David Letterman are both members of the American Federation of Television and Radio Artists (AFTRA), a union that bargains collectively with the networks to establish minimum standards of employment. Tom Cruise, John Travolta, and other high-priced movie stars are members of the Screen Actors Guild which bargains with movie studios and producers. Just as in sports, entertainment performers negotiate (through their agents) individual contract terms above the collectively-established minimum floors.

Performers unions supported the players associations, then, in their argument that in industries such as these, unilateral action by employer groups (whether through a sports league like the NFL or an Alliance of Motion Pictures and Television Producers (AMPTP)) to restrain competitive salary bidding against the wishes of their employees should not enjoy a labor exemption from any antitrust scrutiny of the reasonability of such action. Again, what was Justice Breyer's response to that argument? Even if that view of the labor exemption had been accepted for newly-created employment terms, how would it apply to unilateral action by NFL owners to lengthen the playing season, reduce existing pension or disability benefits, expand the commissioner's disciplinary authority, or revise the rookie draft, current restraints on free agency, and the specifics of the existing salary cap?

5. In their brief in *Brown*, the NFL argued that the truly distinctive feature of sports was that the inherently integrated nature of a league's organization and product required that collective bargaining be conducted on a multiemployer basis, to address such league-wide issues as the nature and length of the season, player movement among teams, and so on. During oral argument before the Supreme Court, though, counsel for the NFL owners responded to the petitioners' "consent" theory by claiming that since the players' union had consented to a multiemployer bargaining relationship with the owners, it thereby had consented to the owners acting collectively within that relationship. The other side of that legal coin would be that if employees wanted to assert their rights under antitrust law, they would not have to dispense with unionization under labor law, but instead simply withdraw their consent to multiemployer bargaining. (Because such consent would have to be withdrawn at the beginning of the negotiation round, this would not have benefited the plaintiffs in *Brown*.) Does Justice Breyer's opinion have anything to say on this score? What would be the result if the union refused to consent to bargaining with the league, and insisted instead on negotiating separately with each team? Keep this issue in mind for Chapter 4 where there are some labor law materials on the legality and feasibility of collective bargaining on an individual team rather than league-wide basis in the sports world.

In the D.C. Circuit, Judges Edwards and Wald focused on an aspect of the *Brown* case that was not discussed in the Supreme Court. Read the following excerpts from their respective analyses, first from Judge Edwards' majority opinion.

... While [the Sherman Act § 1] speaks broadly of *every* restraint of trade, the Supreme Court has long since limited its application to only those restraints deemed unreasonable. In an effort to give content to this reasonableness standard, courts have conceived of the Sherman Act as a "consumer welfare prescription." Thus, the Sherman Act's primary focus is the product market, not the labor market. As one prominent commentator has stated, "the antitrust laws are not concerned with competition among laborers or with bargains over the price and supply of labor—its compensation or hours of service or the selection and tenure of employees." Archibald Cox, *Labor and the Antitrust Laws—A Preliminary Analysis*, 104 U. Pa. L. Rev. 252, 255 (1955).

We recognize, of course, that, as a general matter, the antitrust laws may apply to restraints on competition in nonunionized markets. However, we think the inception of a collective bargaining relationship between employees and employers irrevocably alters the governing legal regime. Once employees organize as a union, federal labor law necessarily limits the rights of individual employees to enter into negotiations with their employer.... [O]nce collective bargaining has begun, the Sherman Act paradigm of a perfectly competitive market necessarily is replaced by the NLRA paradigm of organized negotiation—a paradigm that itself contemplates collusive activity on the parts of both employees and employers. Stubborn adherence to antitrust principles in such a market can only result in "a wholesale subversion" of federal labor policy.

50 F.3d at 1054–55. Compare this view with that of Judge Wald:

Admittedly, a few commentators have suggested that antitrust laws should not apply to restraints on labor markets....

It is, however, not possible to square this minority view with the development of our antitrust jurisprudence. The Supreme Court has clearly held that antitrust laws apply not only to restraints on *output* markets, but to *input* markets as well, including both labor and input commodities.

Economists too have long recognized that market inefficiencies created by anticompetitive restraints on input markets can be as destructive of a free market economy (and therefore ultimately damaging to consumers) as restraints on output markets.... [A]ccording to the economists, there is a dead-weight loss associated with imposition of monopsony pricing restraints. Some producers will either produce less or cease production altogether, resulting in less-than-optimal output of the product or service, and over the long run higher consumer prices, reduced product quality, or substitution of less efficient alternative products. So, even proceeding from the premise that the antitrust laws aim only at protecting consumers, monopsonies fall under antitrust purview because monopsonistic practices will eventually adversely affect consumers.

... If team owners join together to suppress the price of athletic services through monopsony practices, most athletes will not be able to switch profitably to other lines of work.... Economic theory tells us, however, that monopsony will diminish output over time. Because *some* talented athletes *will* switch to other sports or other professions, or decide not to enter the field, the overall quality of athletic performance in the sport will then decline, to the detriment of consumers.

50 F.3d at 1060–61.

Questions For Discussion

1. Putting aside all of the direct arguments about whether the labor exemption should apply, which of these two views about the value of antitrust enforcement in the labor market makes more sense to you? After reading Justices Breyer's and Stevens' opinions, do you sense that they have differing views about the efficacy of using antitrust law to police employer conduct in labor markets; if so, is that an important aspect of why they draw the line differently on the exemption issue?

2. Do you agree with Judge Wald's economic analysis that monopsonistic pricing of player salaries will adversely affect the quality of a league's entertainment product, because some players will either not play professional ball at all or will cut their athletic careers shorter than they would have in a competitive labor marketplace? Keep in mind Judge Edwards' observation that once the players unionize, collective bargaining always determines the ultimate shape of the labor market. Will allowing players to bring antitrust suits against their leagues' player practices in order to enhance their bargaining leverage create a labor market that enhances the quality of the product the fans see? How have the current regimes in the NFL or the NBA, both of which were wrung from the owners while under the threat of antitrust liability, affected the attractiveness of NFL and NBA games for the fans?

3. Judges Edwards and Wald had another point of disagreement. Judge Edwards believed that allowing unionized employees to bring antitrust suits against multiemployer bargaining groups would inject antitrust law into collective bargaining and upset the natural balance of power in the bargaining relationship. Judge Wald contended that to deny unionized employees the same protections that nonunion employees enjoy under antitrust law against restraints imposed by an employer group on the labor market upsets the natural balance of power, but in the opposite direction. With whose viewpoint do you agree? Recall that in the unionized context, most such disputes affecting unionized employees will eventually be resolved not by an antitrust verdict but by a collective bargaining settlement, which (like the

NFL's post-*White* hard salary cap) is then immune from antitrust challenge by the employees. Do you think that either the presence or absence of potential antitrust liability will affect the intentions and tactics of either or both sides in their negotiations?

While *Brown* was being briefed, argued, and decided in the Supreme Court, the NBPA's appeal of the *Williams* case was on hold at the Court. During that time, the NBA owners and players had not been able to finalize their collective agreement reflecting the terms of a rough settlement in principle reached in the summer of 1995. (One factor was the Association's dismissal of their new Executive Director, Simon Gourdine, who had replaced Charles Grantham in the previous year, and the efforts by a group of players and their agents to have the union involuntarily decertified and a new antitrust suit filed.) Shortly after the *Brown* ruling came down in mid-June 1996, the two sides executed a formal agreement which preserved and to some extent tightened up the terms of basketball's "soft" salary cap. In early July, bidding for free agent players began under the new contractual regime. Within ten days, Michael Jordan had signed a one year deal with the Chicago Bulls for a reported $30 million, and Shaquille O'Neal had moved from the Orlando Magic to the Los Angeles Lakers for $120 million over seven seasons. What does this experience imply about the role of antitrust or labor law in shaping the employment market in the world of sports?

One final note about the NFL's collective agreement and the labor exemption. The agreement states that (a) the parties do not waive their right to make antitrust claims about provisions in the settlement after it expires; (b) the parties recognize that the labor exemption applies throughout the term of the agreement and that neither party will sue the other for antitrust violations until impasse is reached in bargaining or six months after the agreement's expiry, whichever comes later; and (c) if the NFLPA decides to decertify after impasse, the NFL will not invoke the labor exemption on the ground that the union did not really decertify. In thinking about why the NFL would agree to this provision, consider the difficulties posed for the league by the NFLPA's decision to decertify after *Powell*. The absence of a union certainly made it harder for the two sides to settle all the player litigation and enter into a new collective agreement. Would not both parties have found it in their mutual interest to agree that the NFL would waive any right to invoke the labor exemption in an antitrust suit brought by the union at some point after the new agreement expires? Why might the NFL have opposed such a provision?

D. COLLUSION IN BASEBALL[m]

In *Brown*, the NFL owners had complied with the requirements of labor law in unilaterally instituting the development squad salary. No collective agreement was then in effect, and they first bargained to impasse with the Players Association. Suppose, however, that the owners had acted during the midst of an agreement, or after expiry of the contract but without first discussing the issue with the union (which would be a clear unfair labor practice in violation of labor law). Given *Brown*, would the labor exemption still protect the owners, or would their collective action be subject to antitrust as well as labor law attack? If the latter, since league practices necessarily must be adopted league-wide, would this have the effect of turning every unfair labor practice the league commits into an antitrust issue? The following episode from baseball illustrates that this may not be a purely hypothetical question.

Despite their sport's special immunity from antitrust law, baseball players were the first to achieve broad free agency, and since then they have enjoyed the most favorable market setting for negotiating salaries of any of the professional team sports. The Major League Baseball Players Association (MLBPA) first secured this regime via a 1976 arbitrator ruling we will read at the beginning of the next chapter—one that removed the lifetime reserve system that the Supreme Court had refused to touch in *Flood*. Since 1976, baseball players have been able to rely on their negotiating leverage under labor law to preserve the essentials of their free agency-salary arbitration system. This fact should be kept in mind as you assess the comparative value of antitrust and labor law in the sports labor market—for players, owners, and fans (who have experienced more and longer work stoppages in baseball than in the other three major sports combined).

In the mid-1980's, though, under newly-elected Commissioner Peter Ueberroth, the baseball owners sought to undermine the "free agency" regime that they had been unable to weaken through collective bargaining. Under the auspices of free agency, baseball salaries had soared from an average of $50,000 in 1976 to $370,000 in 1985. Baseball owners were so troubled by this perceived threat to their fiscal viability that at the outset of collective bargaining in 1985, they voluntarily opened their books to the Players Association. After a brief work stoppage in the summer of 1985, the owners succeeded in securing a modest MLBPA concession that postponed players' eligibility for salary arbitration from two to three years of service. In return, the owners agreed to establish a

---

[m]. For an overview of these events, see Stephen L. Willis, *Comment: A Critical Perspective on Baseball's Collusion Decisions*, 1 Seton Hall J. of Sports Law 109 (1991). For contrasting economic analyses see Dan Durland, Jr., and Paul M. Sommers, *Collusion in Major League Baseball: An Empirical Test*, 14 J. of Sports Behavior 19 (1991); Robert A. Baade and Carolyn Tuttle, *Owner Collusion or Sound Fiscal Management: An Analysis of Recent Events in Baseball's Labor Market*, 1 Seton Hall J. of Sports Law 41 (1991); and Andrew Zimbalist, "Salaries and Performance: Beyond the Scully Model," Chapter 7 of *Diamonds are Forever*, note a above.

modified regime for bidding for free agents. When a player declared for free agency before the end of October, his incumbent (or "home") team was given until December 7th to offer the player salary arbitration. If arbitration was not offered, or if the player did not accept the offer within a few weeks, the home team had to re-sign the player by January 8th or lose all rights to negotiate with him until May 1st. The Association's objective was to remove what it felt was a sentiment among the owners to defer to the interests of the home team in deciding whether to bid for a free agent's services.

Subsequently, Commissioner Ueberroth convened the owners for a series of meetings at the end of the 1985 season. His aim was to document why it was bad business for teams to engage in bidding for free agents by offering players not only very high salaries, but also guaranteed long-term contracts. Such behavior by one club forced all the other clubs to adopt similar measures, to the ultimate detriment of the owners collectively.

The owners' response to the Commissioner's message was dramatic. During the previous off-season (in the winter of 1984–1985), 26 of 46 veteran free agents switched teams, and 16 of the 26 clubs signed at least one free agent. The average salary increase of free agents and of other veteran players who signed that year was roughly 14%. In the 1985–1986 off-season, by contrast, only four of 32 free agents signed with other clubs, and all four players had been told by their home team that it was not interested in resigning them. The home team had expressed an ongoing interest in each of the other 28 free agents; none received a single offer from another team. Feeling that strong pressure, all of these players accepted their home club's final offer by the January 8th deadline. One player, Kirk Gibson, did so by phone from New Zealand, five minutes before midnight. The average salary negotiated by veteran players that year was six percent *lower* than it had been in the previous year.

Similar events occurred in the next off-season, 1986–1987, but with some interesting variations. There were more free agents, 79 in total, who as a group tended to be of somewhat higher quality (including All-Stars such as Jack Morris, Tim Raines, Andre Dawson, and Lance Parrish). A few more players changed teams that year, but none of the 79 free agents received a higher outside offer. For example, Jack Morris was arguably the best pitcher to have entered the free agent market up to that time. However, Morris received no offer from any club other than his home team, the Detroit Tigers. Not one outside club (including Morris' preferred choice, his hometown Minnesota Twins) would even accept Morris' offer to sign at a salary to be determined by a neutral arbitrator. Only the Tigers took that offer, and so Morris reluctantly signed with them before the January 8th deadline.

Eight players, though, did not sign before the January 8th deadline. Most experienced the fate of Tim Raines. Even with his home team, the Montreal Expos, apparently shut out of the market for his services,

Raines, the 1986 National League batting champion, received no outside offers, before or after January 8th. Eventually he returned to the Expos on May 1st, after missing the first month of the season.[n] In total, the salaries of that year's cohort of free agents declined 15%, and the vast majority signed only one-year contracts.

The consequence for the owners was that overall players' salaries increased at a far lower rate for the next several years than total league revenues and club profits. Under *Flood*, baseball players could not challenge this pattern of concerted owner behavior under antitrust law. The Players Association was, however, able to lodge a series of grievances under the following provision in the "free agency" article of baseball's collective agreement:

H. INDIVIDUAL NATURE OF RIGHTS

The utilization or non-utilization of rights under this Article XVIII is an individual matter to be determined solely by each player and each club for his or its own benefit. Players shall not act in concert with other Players and Clubs shall not act in concert with other Clubs.

Ironically, this clause had been inserted into the agreement at the owners' insistence in 1976, when the parties were designing their new free agent system after the *Messersmith* arbitration ruling. The owners had been troubled by earlier episodes of the Dodgers' Sandy Koufax and Don Drysdale, and then of the Phillies' Mike Schmidt and Larry Bowa, who had negotiated with their clubs as a tandem: one player would not sign without his friend and teammate also being signed. The owners' concern was that with both free agency and the proliferation of player agents representing multiple players (see Chapter 5), the use of this tactic would spread. The aim of Paragraph H was to ensure that each player negotiated as an individual, not as part of a package. Marvin Miller, Executive Director of the Players Association, eventually agreed to the proposal, but only with the anti-concerted action clause being made equally applicable to the teams.

Both Arbitrator Tom Roberts who heard the players' grievance about the 1985–86 off-season, and Arbitrator George Nicolau who did so regarding the 1986–87 off-season, upheld the Association claims and rejected the League's argument that while the teams may have been acting in a "consciously parallel" fashion, each was doing so as a response to its own financial and competitive needs, not as part of a

---

n. Bob Horner, instead of returning to the Atlanta Braves, finally signed with the Yakuit Swallows in the Japanese Baseball League. Andre Dawson, who desperately wanted to move from the Expos to a team with a natural grass playing surface that would preserve his knees, eventually got an offer from the Chicago Cubs, but only in the following bizarre fashion. His agent offered the Cubs a contract signed by Dawson, but with the salary left blank. The agent then called a press conference to tell the Chicago fans that the Cubs could have Dawson at whatever price the *team* thought was fair. After a written apology to the league's Player Relations Committee, the Cubs signed the contract with Dawson at *their* figure of $500,000, less than half Dawson's salary with the Expos in the previous year. For that price, the Cubs got a player who won the 1987 Most Valuable Player Award.

broader reciprocal arrangement with its colleagues. As Arbitrator George Nicolau wrote:

> Article VIII(H) [of the collective agreement] does not guarantee any particular level of market activity and it may well be, as the Clubs assert, that a growing awareness of the economics of the game and the "learning curve" of free agent performance would lead to fewer offers, perhaps at lower prices. But the period at issue was not one of "declining activity"; the Record demonstrates that there was literally no market; no bid, save one: that of the former club. Those players who only received that one bid "surely had a value [to other clubs] at some price," in Chairman Roberts words, yet there were no bidders "at any price." Only when the former club no longer wanted "its" player, did other clubs "feel free" to bid.
>
> ... What transpired in 1986 occurred because everyone "understood" what was to be done. By common consent, exclusive negotiating rights were, in effect, ceded to former clubs. There was no vestige of a free market as that term is commonly understood. The object was to force players back to their former clubs and the expectation was that all would go back in a replication of 1985, requiring nothing more to be done....

* * *

> In any one year, there may be a great deal of bidding between former clubs and other clubs; in another year, substantially less. But the abrupt cessation of activity in 1985 and the repetition of that pattern [in 1986] ... cannot be attributed to the free play of market forces. Clubs have different personalities, different budgets, and different needs. Rather than reactions on the basis of those realities and those needs, there was a patent pattern of uniform behavior, a uniformity simply unexplainable by the rubric of financial responsibility or by any other factors on which the Clubs have relied in this proceeding. In my opinion, their conduct with respect to the 1986 free agents was in deliberate contravention of Club obligations as embodied in Article VIII(H), for which an appropriate remedy is fully justified.

The remedial phase of these collusion proceedings was as lengthy, complex, and illuminating as was the liability phase. The simple remedy the arbitrators initially adopted was to offer each of the directly affected veteran players a "second look" at free agency. The consequence, though, was that when arbitrator Roberts made this order in January 1988 for the original free agent class of 1985–1986, ongoing collusion by the owners caused these players to fare little better the second time than they had the first. Only Kirk Gibson signed with another team, the Dodgers, and he did so for essentially the same salary that he received under his old contract with the Tigers. (The following 1988 season Gibson was the National League's Most Valuable Player.)

By the winter of 1987–1988, the Roberts ruling had come down, the second arbitration hearing was well under way, and the owners had modified their program to establish an "Information Bank" under the auspices of the Player Relations Committee. Under this arrangement, every team in the league provided detailed information about each and every offer it made (or even contemplated making) to any player. This permitted every team to get an immediate picture of the demand for the services of every player in the free agent market. Any team could know, then, precisely how much it had to bid to gain an edge on its competitors—if not for one player, then for another.

In response to the Association's third grievance, Arbitrator Nicolau found that this arrangement, too, violated Article XVIII's bar against concerted owner action. The 76 free agents in 1987–1988 did receive twelve offers from other teams in competition with their home teams, and three of these players switched clubs. However, the Information Bank was found to have limited considerably the salary offers made by competing teams that year.

When the arbitrators turned to the task of awarding monetary damages to affected players, their calculations required several analytical judgments. Some judgments involved the interlocking features of salary determination. For example, contracts signed by free agents early in the off-season had a demonstrable spillover effect on salary arbitration that winter. Thus, the sizable cohort of players with three to five years of service were also affected even though these players were not yet entitled to free agency. Similarly, artificial restraints imposed on salary levels for any one year's class of free agents had a depressing effect on the subsequent year's salaries; this effect would endure even after collusion had ended because free agents (or arbitration candidates) in those later years would begin their negotiations with considerably lower salary benchmarks than a fully competitive marketplace would have produced. Finally, the removal of effective competition for free agents not only depressed actual salary amounts, but also cut back on valuable contract terms such as long-term salary guarantees, performance bonuses, and no-trade clauses.

With respect to each group of affected players, there remained an even more difficult problem of how to calculate the actual financial losses. Without going into the details of the econometric models used to do the analysis, suffice it to say that damages awarded by the arbitrators amounted to $10 million for lost 1986 salaries, $38 million for lost 1987 salaries (the product of collusion in both 1986 and 1987), and $65 million for lost 1988 salaries. Further damage awards for salary losses in 1989 and 1990 were forthcoming, as well as damages for the lost value of the contract features such as performance bonuses and no-trade clauses. By 1990, baseball had a new commissioner, Fay Vincent, and a somewhat more cooperative cast to its labor-management relationship (the latter sentiment emerging in the aftermath of still another lockout of players from spring training camps in early 1990.) Having received and read several hundred pages of arbitration decisions, the owners and the Players Association finally agreed in the fall of 1990 to a settlement of all claims during the entire collusion period, for a total of $280 million. In addition, several players were given yet another chance at free agency, this time in a much more competitive marketplace. (After collusion ended, average salaries leaped from $430,000 in 1988 to over $1 million in 1992.) Of the "second look" free agents who switched teams in return for considerably more lucrative contracts, the most significant was Jack Morris who signed with the Minnesota Twins and became the Most Valuable Player in the Twins' thrilling 1991 World Series triumph over the Atlanta Braves.

The settlement agreement and payments completed the owners' involvement in the collusion case. The Players Association then had the daunting task of devising a formula for distributing the $280 million among its members. The dimensions of the challenge became clearer in the summer of 1991 when approximately 800 players filed claims totalling over $1 billion. The first awards were made in February 1994, distributing $14 million for lost salary amounts in 1986 and $59 million for 1987. Individual awards of over $1 million were initially made to Jack Clark ($2.1 million), Lance Parrish ($1.8 million), Andre Dawson ($1.3 million), Carlton Fisk ($1.2 million), Tim Raines ($1.1 million), Rich Gedman ($1.1 million), and Tom Seaver ($1 million). Since then, the Association has made awards totalling approximately $75 million for 1988 and $90 million for 1989 (though the latter year's figures still needed approval by Arbitrator Roberts). As of the end of 1997, no awards had been made for any players who might have experienced the impact of this collusion from contracts they signed in the "out years" following 1989.

As a postscript, in their 1990 collective bargaining round the parties amended the "in concert" provision to provide that if the owners (though not the players) violated this clause in the future, affected players would be entitled to receive three times their "lost baseball income," plus full legal fees and interest. However, during the bitter negotiations leading to the strike that wiped out the 1994 World Series, the owners fervently sought to eliminate the "no negotiations in concert" rule in the next agreement. That owner effort failed, however, and the contract finally signed in 1997 contained the same anti-collusion language and treble damages remedy as its predecessor.

The five-year period of baseball owner collusion and union response vividly demonstrates how a system of private negotiation and adjudication undertaken within the umbrella of labor law can replicate the role of public antitrust law in defining and enforcing the conditions for a competitive marketplace. The episode suggests several intriguing questions.

For example, why do we need treble damages, rather than simply full compensation for actual damages, to enforce a ban on collusion? Is payment of $280 million—$11 million per club—not a sufficient deterrent to future incidents of this kind of contract violation?

A second question focuses on how antitrust law would apply to conduct similar to the baseball owners' collusion in a sport other than baseball (or even in baseball if Congress does repeal baseball's special immunity, at least for major league player restraints). If owners act in concert in refusing to bid for other teams' free agents, does this constitute a substantive violation of § 1 of the Sherman Act? Absent specific "no collusion" language in the collective agreement, would such conduct constitute a unilateral change in the terms of employment, such that it would also be an unfair labor practice? If such owner action were to be an unfair labor practice, would the *Brown* formulation of the labor exemption still protect that collusive conduct from antitrust attack?

A third question concerns the owners' use of the "Information Bank" to collect and disseminate salary offers to free agent players. This practice constituted the owners' violation in the third collusion year, after Arbitrator Nicolau had given a rather literal reading to the "in concert" clause in the collective agreement. In the absence of such a clause, though—and in a sport other than baseball—such information sharing could be challenged under antitrust law. Why should this be so? Is not the assumption of "perfect knowledge" a fundamental ingredient of the free market model? What is wrong with each bidder and seller knowing exactly what everyone else thinks a particular player is worth, as long as they do not have an agreement to act collusively with that information (as in traditional bid-rigging conspiracies)?

Information sharing, however, is not a tactic limited to one side of the bargaining table; player agents, as well as owners, can agree to communicate salary offers to one another in order to drive up the "going rate" of certain types of players, such as first-round draft choices. Indeed, in the early 1990s in an offshoot of the *Powell/McNeil/White* litigation, the NFL alleged that the NFLPA and agents representing NFL and college players had done just this. With the help of the Association, agents began to exchange and use information about the current salaries of all players and any new offers being made to them, information that helped the agents extract somewhat better offers for their clients. In *The Five Smiths v. NFL Players Association*, 788 F.Supp. 1042 (D.Minn.1992), Judge Doty rejected the NFL's assertion that this practice violated § 1 of the Sherman Act, noting that the Supreme Court "has determined that, absent some agreement between competitors to restrain price, the exchange of price and other market information is generally benign conduct that facilitates efficient economic activity."

The NFL, however, relied on the Court's ruling in *United States v. Container Corp.*, 393 U.S. 333 (1969). This was Judge Doty's response.

> ... *Container Corp.* ruled that an exchange of price information among competitors, without an agreement to fix prices, was sufficient to raise antitrust concerns, but only in markets where certain structural conditions exist. Those characteristics are: (1) a highly concentrated market dominated by relatively few sellers; (2) a fungible product; (3) competition that is primarily based on price; and (4) inelasticity of demand because buyers tend to order for their immediate short term needs. Examining those characteristics, the court concludes that such market conditions do not exist in the present case. Plaintiffs neither allege nor can allege that there is a highly concentrated relevant market of competing sellers of players' services because there are over 1,500 professional football players, many of whom are represented in salary negotiations by agents, of whom there are hundreds. In addition, most football players do not compete by selling a fungible product as to which purchasing decisions are primarily made on the basis of price, additional structural factors which are necessary for an information exchange to violate the rule of reason. See *Container Corp.*, 393 U.S. at 337. Rather, each player has his own unique attributes and skills, which are of varying desirability to the different teams. Moreover, each player's salary is arrived at during negotiations with his employer club.[1] Finally, the court concludes that there is no inelasticity of demand due to a market of buyers who purchase only for their immediate short term needs. To the contrary, the teams generally sign players to multi-year contracts and the system of player restraints essentially ties each player to his employer club for the duration of his career. Based on the foregoing, the court concludes that the market structure of the National Football League does not have the characteristics required by *Container Corp.* and thus the plaintiffs cannot allege the requisite factors to establish a rule of reason violation based solely on the exchange of salary information.

788 F.Supp. at 1053–54.

The judge also emphasized the fact that absent meaningful free agency, NFL players were then largely confined to negotiating new contracts with a single club, one that already had similar comparative salary data through its league office. Rather than constraining competition, then, the availability of similar information for player agents "can only make the negotiation process fairer because the negotiations can take place without any misunderstanding or misrepresentation about what other players are earning."

---

1. As a result of the plaintiffs' players restraints, specifically the college draft and the first refusal/compensation system, most players are also unable to compete with each other for the same position on the same team because they are bound to their assigned clubs for the duration of their careers.

Questions for Discussion

1. Near the end of the above opinion, the court argues that rather than restrain competition, the agents' information sharing actually enhances it by creating a level playing field between the clubs and the agents. Is this argument sound? If so, does this suggest that the flexible "rule of reason" approach under antitrust law is preferable to the rigid, literal interpretation of a contractual provision such as the "in concert" clause in the baseball collective agreement?

2. In rejecting the NFL's restraint of trade argument, Judge Doty kept emphasizing that the players were not competitors because of the restrictions on free agency in the league. Since the players were able to obtain a substantially greater degree of free agency in the 1993 settlement with the NFL and the subsequent collective agreement, would a league antitrust challenge to players sharing detailed contract information have more validity today under the court's analysis? If not, would the clubs be able to share salary information lawfully?

Consider the broader significance of the club revenue-player salary equation displayed in the collusion cases. From 1985 through 1988, while baseball player salaries rose from an average of $370,000 to $430,000, total baseball revenues soared from $650 million to $1 billion. When owner collusion ended, average salaries spiraled from $430,000 in 1988 to more than $1 million in 1991, but league revenues also shot up throughout this period, to over $1.6 billion by 1992.

By the time the 1994 labor negotiations had begun, baseball owners were concerned not just with the growing share of league revenues devoted to player salaries (approximately 55% in 1994), but even more with the impact of spiraling salaries on particular small market clubs. While all the teams had to compete in the same free agent market (and were subject to the same criteria in salary arbitration), teams in smaller cities like Milwaukee, Kansas City, and Pittsburgh which earned less than a third of the total revenues of teams in the major markets like New York, Los Angeles, and Chicago, were being squeezed out of the star player market altogether. Indeed, in 1997 the Pirates entire 25-player roster earned less than the $10 million salary the White Sox were paying Albert Belle that year.

Would you agree that this poses a problem for either baseball's competitive balance or the financial viability of small market teams? If so, what do think is the optimal solution—holding down player salaries through restraints on free agency, a salary cap, some form of luxury tax on high payrolls, or greater revenue sharing among the clubs themselves?

Alternatively, baseball could require small market teams to relocate to more populous areas where they can generate sufficient revenue; probably more than two teams would end up in the New York, Chicago, and Los Angeles markets, and more than one team in areas like

Philadelphia, Boston, and Toronto. Assuming the owners would ever permit it, would gravitation of teams to fewer but more populous communities be desirable? As yet another alternative, perhaps the small markets would keep their teams, but the mega-markets would be given several new expansion teams to dilute the revenues of the teams currently there. Would that be desirable? What impact would such expansion have on average player salaries? On the quality of team play? Keep all these questions in mind when we explore monopolization in professional sports in Chapter 8.

Interestingly, although the MLB Players Association did successfully fend off efforts by the owners to impose a salary cap in the negotiations in 1994–96, the collective agreement reached in 1996 gave the owners an important concession in the form of a luxury tax of 35% on the amount a team's payroll exceeds $51 million (in 1997). As part of this new regime, the owners agreed amongst themselves (as well as with the players) to a new revenue sharing system. The top 13 revenue-earning teams will contribute different amounts to a fund (beginning at approximately $40 million in 1996 and rising to $70 million in the year 2000) that would be redistributed among the bottom 13 revenue earners. To give some sense of the dimensions of this new program, for the 1996 season the New York Yankees contributed $5.8 million and the Montreal Expos received $5.5 million; by 2,000 the clubs' respective figures would be $14.4 million and $13.5 million (assuming their relative shares of the game's projected revenues that year were not altered in the meantime).

Finally, in his 1991 memoirs, *A Whole Different Ballgame: The Sport and Business of Baseball*, Marvin Miller, founder of the baseball players' union, asserted that the collusive behavior of Commissioner Ueberroth and the owners was a more serious violation of the "best interests of the game" than was Pete Rose's gambling. Miller's point was not so much that the owners violated their contractual undertakings to the players (as would also have been true if the owners had paid less than their proper contribution to the players' pension plan). Miller said that what was special about owner collusion, and worse than Rose trying to make money by betting on his team to win, was that owners such as George Steinbrenner tried to make money by, in effect, choosing to let their teams lose. Is that a valid comparison? What arguments could one make against Miller's assertion?

Chapter Four

LABOR LAW AND COLLECTIVE BARGAINING IN PROFESSIONAL SPORTS[a]

For the last three decades, the world of professional sports has experienced the most tumultuous labor-management relations of any industry in America. The 1990s witnessed perhaps the broadest and deepest of such conflicts in each of the four major leagues.

The 1990s began with the *McNeil* antitrust suit having been filed by the NFL players against their owners, the settlement of which was not achieved and judicially approved until 1993. Just a year later, the NBA owners went to court as their collective agreement was expiring. It took two years of litigation, internal player conflicts (including a failed union decertification effort by players such as Michael Jordan and Patrick Ewing), and negotiations by new union representatives with the owners to settle on a new basketball agreement in 1996. (In 1997, Ewing was elected president of the union.) In hockey, the owners also took the initiative to try to secure a more favorable contract by locking their players out at the beginning of the 1994–95 season. That labor dispute (the only one to be addressed solely through negotiation, rather than litigation) was not resolved until January 1995, after half of the regular

---

a. The first major treatment of both the labor relations history and doctrinal issues in this area is Robert C. Berry, William B. Gould, and Paul D. Staudohar, *Labor Relations in Professional Sports* (Dover, Ma.: Auburn House, 1986). The Symposium, *Strife, Liberty, and the Pursuit of Money: Labor Relations in Professional Sports*, 4 Villanova Sports & Enter. L. J. 1 (1997), offers valuable analyses of the legal and labor relations conflicts in the 1990s. See also Lee Lowenfish, *The Imperfect Diamond: A History of Baseball's Labor Wars* (New York: Da Capo Press, rev. ed. 1991), John Helyar, *Lords of the Realm: The Real History* (New York: Villard Books, 1994), and David Harris, *The League: The Rise and Decline of the NFL* (New York: Bantam, 1986) for interesting depictions of what has taken place in collective bargaining in those two sports. The memoirs of the two principal protagonists in baseball in the critical period, Marvin Miller, the players association's leader, and Bowie Kuhn, baseball's commissioner, offer a provocative counterpoint on the key early decisions made in that sport. See Marvin Miller, *A Whole Different Ballgame: The Sport and Business of Baseball* (New York: Birch Lane Press, 1991), and Bowie Kuhn, *Hardball: The Education of a Baseball Commissioner* (New York: Times Books, 1987).

season (though not the Stanley Cup playoffs) had been lost. Baseball in 1994 seemed to be at its peak; both fan attendance and player salaries were at their highest levels ever. However, the regular season and the World Series were abruptly ended by a player strike in August. It then took three years of litigation at the National Relations Labor Board and in the courts, lobbying at the White House and the Congress, and negotiations between players and a changing owner lineup before a new collective agreement was finally signed in 1997.

By the late 1990s, labor peace seems finally to have appeared in professional sports—though how long it will last remains uncertain. What is clear is that collective bargaining has transformed the rules of the game for dealings between individual teams and players. Veteran free agency has now become the rule rather than the exception, but with different forms of salary constraints imposed on the amount that a team can offer a player (and his agent).

There is an ironic feature to this story. In the late 1960s, when real unionism first came to the sports world, the average salaries in baseball, hockey, basketball, and football ranged from $19,000 to $25,000. By 1995, in the midst of this labor strife, average salaries were $725,000 in football, $735,000 in hockey, $1.1 million in baseball, and $1.8 million in basketball. This huge salary spiral had been accompanied by comparable leaps in fan attendance, television and merchandising deals, league expansion, and team franchise values. Sports is an apt illustration of a basic truth about employment (and other) relationships: intense and visible conflicts about how to divide up the available revenues are more likely when the size of the pie is rising rather than declining. The focus of this chapter is on how labor law and labor negotiations address these employment conflicts.

The first organizations of professional athletes developed more than a century ago, with the formation of the National Brotherhood of Baseball Players. This was the body that, shortly thereafter, tried to establish a Players' League to free its members from the shackles of the dominant National League's reserve clause and $2,000 per year salary cap.[b] However, the seeds of modern collective action by professional athletes were sown in the 1950s, with the formation of player organizations in all four team sports. In each sport these bodies were deliberately named *associations* rather than *unions*, because the latter term was considered appropriate only for the teams' concession vendors or maintenance crews, not for elite athletes. Not until the mid–1960s did players realize that, for all their status in the outside world, if they were to force owners to change the structure of the players' market they would have to engage in full-fledged collective bargaining under professional union leadership—the leadership of Marvin Miller in baseball, Ed Garvey in football, Larry Fleisher in basketball, and Alan Eagleson in hockey.

---

b. For an in-depth look at this and other features of baseball's early history, see Robert F. Burk, *Never Just a Game: Players, Owners & American Baseball to 1920* (Chapel Hill: Univ. of North Carolina Press, 1994).

As we have seen in the previous chapter, from the mid–1970s to the mid–1990s, a major preoccupation of the players associations (less so in baseball) was how to utilize antitrust law to remove the collective constraints that owners have historically placed on the players market. However, both before and after these antitrust efforts took place in the courts (and the Congress), each union established collective allegiance among its player-members and engaged in direct negotiations with the owners—all done under the umbrella of the National Labor Relations Act (NLRA). Now that Justice Breyer has authored the Supreme Court's verdict in the *Brown* case, players realize that if they wish to use the NLRA for purposes of collective bargaining, they must forfeit their rights to use the Sherman Act to challenge collective self-help by the owners. That is why, having read *Brown*, the players in Major League Soccer (MLS) voted to create a Players Association that they say is *not* a labor union, but rather a body designed to bring an antitrust class action against MLS and its owners (a "non-union" characterization that the MLS owners claim is not actually the case).

The NLRA was first enacted in 1935 as the Wagner Act and was sweepingly revised by the Taft–Hartley Act of 1947. The Act confers on employees (via § 7) the rights to organize themselves into a union, to engage in collective bargaining with their employer, and to go on strike or take other concerted action for their mutual aid and protection. The employees' right to engage in (or refrain from) this bargaining process is secured in § 8 by several unfair labor practice provisions that prohibit particular forms of employer (or union) interference and intimidation. The primary responsibility for interpreting and administering the Act, both to protect these employee rights and to preserve a legitimate sphere of action for employers and unions, is conferred on the National Labor Relations Board (NLRB), whose decisions are subject to a measure of judicial review by the federal appellate courts.

Over the last six decades, the NLRB and the courts have developed an elaborate labor law jurisprudence. In the three decades of active union representation in professional sports, this process has produced decisions that illustrate virtually all the important doctrinal spheres in contemporary labor law. Reading the sports labor law cases gives us a bird's-eye view of the tumultuous course taken by labor relations in sports. The cases also provide a revealing perspective on labor law itself, as the NLRB tries both to resolve conflicts between leagues and unions and to reconcile tensions on each side of the bargaining table—on the league side, among the various clubs and their commissioner, and on the union side, between veterans and rookies, superstars and journeymen.

A. FREE AGENCY VIA LABOR ARBITRATION

Before detailing the distinctive jurisprudence that has evolved for sports labor relations, we present a labor law decision that produced the first major change in the sports labor market. This decision was rendered not by a court or by the NLRB, but by a labor arbitrator. Under the statutory framework for labor law, once a union has been able to win a collective agreement from an employer, the standard mechanism for administering this agreement is through private arbitration, not public litigation. Traditionally in the sports world, this role as arbitrator—i.e. a *private* judge—had been performed by the commissioner under both the uniform player contract and the league rules. However, in the early collective agreements negotiated by the player associations, the commissioner was replaced by an independent arbitrator as the person who would finally resolve grievances arising under the labor agreement or the standard player contract.[c]

This little-noticed institutional change, under which Arbitrator Peter Seitz replaced Commissioner Bowie Kuhn as interpreter of both the baseball labor agreement and player contract, had a profound effect on the sport. Just three years after the Supreme Court in the *Curt Flood* case had once again refused to subject baseball's "reserve system" to antitrust scrutiny, Seitz was presented with the following case, which required him to construe the meaning and scope of the key components of that system.

NATIONAL & AMERICAN LEAGUE PROFESSIONAL BASEBALL CLUBS v. MAJOR LEAGUE BASEBALL PLAYERS ASSOCIATION

(Messersmith and McNally Grievances).
66 Labor Arbitration 101 (1976).

SEITZ, ARBITRATOR.

[Andy Messersmith of the Los Angeles Dodgers and Dave McNally of the Montreal Expos had both refused to sign new player contracts at the end of the 1974 season; instead, they played the 1975 season under the terms of § 10(c) of the Uniform Player Contract, which gave their clubs the right to renew the old contract "on the same terms" (except for salary, the amount of which had recently been subjected to binding arbitration in cases of dispute). The question posed to the arbitrator was whether the contract as renewed by the club contained this option clause as well. If it did, the player could be included indefinitely on the club's reserve lists through use of this perpetually renewable option. If, on the other hand, the reserve option clause was spent after its first use, the two players had now become free agents.

In addition to that issue of interpretation, the arbitrator faced a preliminary question whether he even had jurisdiction to entertain this issue, because of the presence of the following provision in the collective agreement:

Except as adjusted or modified hereby, *this agreement does not deal with the reserve system*. The Parties have different views as to the legality and as to the merits of such system as presently constituted.

---

c. As we saw in Chapter 1, though, this displacement was not absolute. Commissioners have retained in varying degrees their responsibility as final arbiter of the "best interests of the sport."

This agreement shall in no way prejudice the position or legal rights of the parties or of any player regarding the reserve system.

During the term of this agreement neither of the parties will resort to any form of concerted action with respect to the issue of the reserve system, and there shall be no obligation to negotiate with respect to the reserve system.

(Emphasis supplied.)

In the first half of his decision, Seitz wrestled with the meaning of this apparent exclusion of the reserve clause from the agreement upon which his authority rested. Eventually, he concluded that he did have jurisdiction to resolve grievances about the meaning of different provisions in the collective agreement and the standard player contract, even though some of these provisions served as more or less important features of the reserve system. The merits of that judgment will be examined later in this chapter, with the decision in *Kansas City Royals v. Major League Baseball Players Ass'n*, 532 F.2d 615 (8th Cir.1976), in which a federal appeals court reviewed the correctness of the arbitrator's jurisdictional ruling. Here we present the arbitrator's analysis of the crucial question of the scope of the reserve clause in baseball.

The arbitrator first reviewed the origins and development of the reserve clause.]

* * *

The Reserve System of the leagues is nowhere defined in a sentence or a paragraph. Reference is commonly and frequently made in the press and by the news media to a "Reserve Clause;" but there is no such single clause encompassing the subject matter. It seems fair to say, on the basis of what has been presented, that the "Reserve System" refers to a complex and a congeries of rules of the leagues (and provisions in the collective Basic Agreement and the Uniform Players Contract) related to the objective of retaining exclusive control over the service of their players in the interest of preserving discipline, preventing the enticement of players, maintaining financial stability and promoting a balance or a relative parity of competitive skills as among clubs. Such "exclusive control," it is said, is exercised by a Club placing the name of a player on its "reserve list" which is distributed to the other clubs in both leagues. A player on such a list, assert the leagues, cannot "play for or negotiate with any other club until his contract has been assigned or he has been released" (Rule 4–A(a)) and may not be the subject of "tampering" as described in Rule 3(g).

This system of reservation of exclusive control is historic in baseball and is traceable to the early days of the organized sport in the 19th century. Over the years, the scheme and structure of provisions designed to establish and maintain that control has been changed in expression. The leagues assert that the system was designed, initially, to combat the institutional chaos that resulted when players under contract with one club defected to another. In an effort to deal with the problem, it is represented, various versions of reserve clauses had been adopted.

The problems facing the National League in the closing years of the 19th century, however, in respect of defecting players, were not limited to the circumstances of a player defecting to another club in the league. Other leagues came into being from time to time and disappeared. The League, in 1899, in an effort to prevent defection of players to other leagues, placed in the individual player's contract a "renewal clause," so-called. This clause, according to the leagues, was the legal basis for clubs applying to the courts of equity to enjoin players from "jumping" to a rival league. As Club Exhibit 16 evidences, contract renewal clauses, over time, differed in their provisions; but all gave an option to a Club to renew its contracts with players for stated periods.

* * *

[The current version of the renewal clause in MLB's Uniform Players Contract was developed in 1947. If the Club had tendered a contract to the player by February 1st and the parties had not agreed to new contract terms by March 1st, the Club had the prerogative under § 10(a) (via written notice to the player within the next ten days) "to renew the contract for the period of one year *on the same terms*." The only exception was salary, which the club could fix at an amount not less than 75% of the prior year's salary. However, arbitrator Seitz rejected the club's argument that this renewal provision incorporated the *option clause* among all the other terms incorporated in the renewed contract. That meant that Messersmith and McNally were no longer under contract to the Dodgers and Expos, respectively, when their 1975 option year had expired.]

* * *

It deserves emphasis that this decision strikes no blow emancipating players from claimed serfdom or involuntary servitude such as was alleged in the *Flood Case*. It does not condemn the Reserve System presently in force on constitutional or moral grounds. It does not counsel or require that the System be changed to suit the predilections or preferences of an arbitrator acting as a Philosopher–King intent upon imposing his own personal brand of industrial justice on the parties. To go beyond this would be an act of quasi-judicial arrogance! ... [T]he scope and effect of a reserve system is for the *Parties* to determine, not the Panel. As stated, the Panel's role is restricted to an interpretation and application of the agreement of the parties.

* * *

No one challenges the right of a Club to renew a Player's contract with or without his consent, under § 10(a), "for the period of one [renewal] year." I read the record, however, as containing a contention by the leagues that when a Club renews a Player's contract for the renewal year, the contract in force during that year contains the "right of renewal" clause as one of its terms, entitling the Club to renew the contract in successive years, to perpetuity, perhaps, so long as the Player is alive and the Club has duly discharged all conditions required of it. This is challenged by the Players Association whose position it is that the contractual relationship between the Club and the Player terminates at the end of the first renewal year. Thus, it claims that there was no longer any contractual bond between Messersmith and the Los Angeles Club on September 29, 1975.

The league's argument is based on the language in § 10(a) of the Player's Contract that the Club "may renew this contract for the period of one year *on the same terms*;" and that among those "terms" is the right to further contract renewal.

In the law of contract construction, as I know it, there is nothing to prevent parties from agreeing to successive renewals of the terms of their bargain (even to what had been described as "perpetuity"), provided the contract expresses that intention with explicit clarity and the right of subsequent renewals does not have to be implied. . . .

There is nothing in § 10(a) which, explicitly, expresses agreement that the Players Contract can be renewed for any period beyond the first renewal year. The point the leagues present must be based upon the implication or assumption, that if the renewed contract is "on the same terms" as the contract for the preceding year (with the exception of the amount of compensation) the right to additional renewals must have been an integral part of the renewed contract. I find great difficulties, in so implying or assuming, in respect of a contract providing for the rendition of personal services in which one would expect a more explicit expression of intention. There are numerous provisions and terms in the Uniform Players Contract that are renewed in the renewal year when a Club exercises its renewal rights under § 10(a). Provision of the right to make subsequent and successive renewals is in an entirely different category, however, than the numerous terms in the Players Contract which deal with working conditions and duties which the Club and the Player owe to each other. That right, critically, concerns and involves the continued existence of *the contract itself* as expressing the mutual undertakings of the parties and the bargain which they struck. All of the other "terms" of the Player–Club relationship stand or fall according to whether the contract, as such, is renewed.

[The arbitrator then discussed two basketball cases—*Lemat Corp. v. Barry*, 275 Cal.App.2d 671, 80 Cal.Rptr. 240 (Cal.Ct.App.1969) and *Central New York Basketball v. Barnett*, 181 N.E.2d 506 (Ohio C.P.Ct. 1961) (both of which we saw in Chapter 2)—involving similar renewal clauses. In *Barnett*, the *club* had argued and the court agreed, that the option clause in basketball's standard player contract was for one renewal year only, not perpetual, and *Barry* followed *Barnett*.]

* * *

In this connection it is also pertinent to observe that the "no tampering rule" (which, in baseball, is contained in Major League Rule 3(g)), has its equivalent, in NBA basketball, in § 35 of the NBA constitution. The prohibition there, however, applies to any player "who is *under contract* to any other member of the Association." (Emphasis supplied.) Thus, in the "reserve system" of the NBA basketball league, the player must have been under contract to be reserved; but in this case, the leagues argue that even if the contract be construed to have expired, the player may be reserved.

In these circumstances I find that § 10(a) falls short of reserving to a Club the right to renew a contract at the end of the renewal year. Accordingly, I find that Messersmith was not under contract when his renewal year came to an end.

[The clubs advanced a second argument for their position. Under Major League Rule 4–A(a), each club was to transmit to the Commissioner, by November 20th, "a list not exceeding forty (40) active and eligible players whom the clubs desire to reserve for the ensuing season ... and thereafter no player on any list shall be eligible to play for and negotiate with any other club until his contract has been assigned or he has been released." The Clubs' Rule 4–A(a) was supplemented and reinforced by Rule 3(g), which provided that "to preserve discipline and competition and to prevent the enticement of players ... there shall be no negotiations or dealings respecting employment, either present or prospective, between any player ... and any club other than the club with which he is under contract ... or by which he is reserved ..."]

* * *

We now turn to the Major League Rules, as to which it has already been stated that, by virtue of § 9(a) of the Uniform Players Contract and Article XIII of the Basic Agreement, they are a part of the agreements of the parties if not inconsistent with the provisions of the Basic Agreement and the Players Contract.

The parties are in sharp conflict on this. The leagues claim that there is exclusive reservation of a player's services under Rule 4–A(a) regardless of the continued existence of any contractual relationship between the Club and the Player. Thus, Counsel for the National League asserted that:

> The club may continue the pattern of career-long control over the player and that this pattern of career-long control is not essentially dependent upon the renewal clause (Section 10–A) at all.

The Players Association, on the other hand, asserts that in the absence of a nexus or linkage of contract between the Player and the Club, there can be no exclusive reservation of the right to his future services.

* * *

These provisions and others in the very Rules which, allegedly, establish the kind of reservation of services for which the leagues contend, all subsume the existence of a *contractual relation*. The leagues would have it that it is only when there is a release or assignment that a contract must have been in existence; but even if there were no contract in existence (the players' contract having expired) a Club, by placing the name of a player on a list, can reserve exclusive rights to his services from year to year for an unstated and indefinite period in the future. I find this unpersuasive. It is like the claims of some nations that persons once its citizens, wherever they live and regardless of the passage of time, the swearing of other allegiances and other circumstances, are still its own nationals and subject to the obligations that citizenship in the nation imposes. This "status" theory is incompatible with the doctrine or policy of freedom of contract in the economic and political society in which we live and of which the professional sport of baseball ("the national game") is a part.

* * *

Finally, on this point, it is evident that traditionally, the leagues have regarded the existence of a contract as a basis for the reservation of players. In Club's Exhibit No. 15 there is set forth the Cincinnati Peace Compact of the National and American Leagues, signed January 10, 1903—probably the most important step in the evolution and development of the present Reserve System. In that document it provided:

> Second—A *reserve rule* shall be recognized, by which each and every club may reserve *players under contract*, and that a uniform contract for the use of each league shall be adopted. (Emphasis supplied.)

This emphasis on the existence of a contract for reservation of a player to be effective was perpetuated in the Major League Rules to some of which I have referred. It is even found in Rule 3(g) in which, however, it is referred to disjunctively along with acceptance of terms "or by which he was reserved." However, *even in Rule 3(g)*, reading it analytically and construing it syntactically, one may reasonably reach the conclusion:— *no contract, no reservation*. The provision says there shall be no dealings between a player and a club other than the one "with which he is under *contract*, or acceptance of terms, *or by which he is reserved*." (Emphasis supplied.) ...

Thus, I reach the conclusion that, absent a contractual connection between Messersmith and the Los Angeles Club after September 28, 1975, the Club's action in reserving his services for the ensuing year by placing him on its reserve list was unavailing and ineffectual in prohibiting him from dealing with other clubs in the league and to prohibit such clubs from dealing with him.

In the case of McNally whom the Montreal Club had placed on its disqualified list, a similar conclusion has been reached.

* * *

[Finally, Arbitrator Seitz addressed the League's concern that the absence of a lifetime reserve system would devastate baseball.]

I am not unmindful of the testimony of the Commissioner of Baseball and the Presidents of the National and American League given at the hearings as to the importance of maintaining the integrity of the Reserve System. It was represented to me that any decision of the Arbitration Panel sustaining the Messersmith and McNally grievances would have dire results, wreak great harm to the Reserve System and do serious damage to the sport of baseball.

Thus, for example, it was stated that a decision favoring these grievants would encourage many other players to elect to become free agents at the end of the renewal years; that this would encourage clubs with the largest monetary resources to engage free agents, thus unsettling the competitive balance between clubs, so essential to the sport; that it would increase enormously the already high costs of training and seasoning young players to achieve the level of skills required in professional baseball and such investments would be sacrificed if they became free agents at the end of a renewal year; that driven by the compulsion to win, owners of franchises would over-extend themselves financially and improvident bidding for players in an economic climate in which, today, some clubs are strained, financially; that investors will be discouraged from putting money in franchises in which several of the star players on the club team will become free agents at the end of a renewal year and no continuing control over the players' services can be exercised; and that even the integrity of the sport may be placed in hazard under certain circumstances.

I do not purport to appraise these apprehensions. They are all based on speculations as to what may ensue. Some of the fears may be imaginary or exaggerated; but some may be reasonable, realistic and sound. After all, they were voiced by distinguished baseball officials with long experience in the sport and a background for judgment in such matters much superior to my own. However, as stated above, at length, it is not for the Panel (and especially the writer) to determine what, if anything, is good or bad about the reserve system. The Panel's sole duty is to interpret and apply the agreements and undertakings of the parties. If any of the expressed apprehensions and fears are soundly based, I am confident that the dislocations and damage to the reserve system can be avoided or minimized through good faith collective bargaining between the parties. There are numerous expedients available and arrangements that can be made that will soften the blow—if this decision, indeed, should be regarded as a blow. This decision is not the end of the line by any means. The parties, jointly, are free to agree to disregard it and compose their differences as to the reserve system in any way they see fit.

* * *

Grievance upheld.

Early in his opinion, Arbitrator Seitz emphatically stated that his role was not to evaluate the merits of baseball's reserve system, but merely to interpret the meaning of its constituent provisions. Look closely at the passages in which the arbitrator considers and selects from the alternative interpretations advanced by the Association and the League about the proper interpretation of the option clause in the player's contract and the reserve clause in the major league rules. Is there such a sharp distinction between evaluation and interpretation of these legal documents?

The legal implication of the *Messersmith* ruling was that any baseball player could become a free agent simply by playing out his option year without signing a new contract. As the *Messersmith* decision was being rendered and judicially reviewed in the winter of 1975–76, the baseball collective agreement was itself expiring and being renegotiated. Naturally enough, free agency became the central issue in these negotiations. After a 17-day owner lockout of the players during spring training—a work stoppage that was unilaterally ended by Commissioner Kuhn in the "best interests of the sport"—the Players Association and the owners' Player Relations Committee reached a new collective agreement in the summer of 1976. The new contract modified free agency considerably. During his first two years in the league, a player had to accept his club's unilateral contract offers or not play, and for years three through six, the player was still contractually bound to his initial club but had the right to final-offer arbitration about the appropriate amount of salary (see later in the chapter). Only after six years' service did full free agency begin. We saw in Chapter 1 how owners such as Charles Finley and Ted Turner reacted to this brand-new regime and how Commissioner Kuhn responded. In Chapter 3, we saw how Commissioner Ueberroth and the owners collaborated in the mid-1980s to stifle competition for free agents, and how the Players Association and Seitz's successor arbitrators responded to that challenge. As we are about to see in this chapter, it took another major labor dispute in baseball in the mid-1990s (two decades after *Messersmith*) to make significant alterations to the basic structure of the baseball player market.

Messersmith and its progeny stand in stark contrast to what happened in football. As we read in Chapter 3, shortly after the arbitral ruling in the *Messersmith* grievance, federal appeals courts held in *Mackey* and *Smith* that football's restraints on competition for players violated federal antitrust laws. Like their counterparts in basketball and hockey, though, the NFL Players Association subsequently agreed in collective bargaining to alternative restraints on free agency.

This regime in football gave the incumbent owner a right of first refusal regarding any offer made by another club to one of the team's free agent players. If the incumbent team chose not to match the offer, it was awarded specified draft picks of the new team intended to compensate for the value of the player being lost. Unlike baseball, then, football did not establish any time at which a veteran player would enjoy untrammelled free agency. Experience soon made it clear that there would be little or no competitive bidding for players under this new system, and as a result the NFLPA sought to emulate their baseball counterpart's success through labor arbitration.

The case of *NFL Players Association v. NFL Management Council (Dutton)* (Arbitration 1980) involved John Dutton, a defensive lineman with the Baltimore Colts. Dutton played out his contract in 1978, received no offers from other teams as a free agent, and thus played the next season with the Colts for 110% of his prior year's salary, as provided for in § 17 of Article XV (Right of First Refusal/Compensation) of the NFL labor agreement. At the expiration of the 1979 season, Dutton again sought but received no free agent offers, even though he was one of the leading defensive ends in the league. The reason was that the NFLMC interpreted the prior club's right to elect first refusal or draft pick compensation as applying to any free agent, even one coming off an option year contract. Thus Dutton and the NFLPA sought a ruling from the football arbitrator similar to *Messersmith*—that these obstacles to free agency applied only after expiry of the contract signed by the player, not after the year of automatic contract renewal via the collective agreement.

Interestingly, Arbitrator Luskin observed that the evidence before him indicated that during the several months of labor negotiations in the winter and spring of 1977, neither side had ever explicitly addressed the *Messersmith* question, though that decision and its impact on baseball had occurred just a year earlier. The football players' argument was that, absent express contract language or clear negotiating history, the general wording of § 17 must not be interpreted as creating a perpetually-renewable option for the teams (though with option year salaries going up, not down, as in baseball). Arbitrator Luskin rejected this argument after he had situated § 17 within the broader array of provisions in Article XV. Section 1 seemed to subject all "veteran free agents" to this regime, not just those who "play out the options in their contracts," and § 18 created an *Extreme Personal Hardship* exception that denied the prior club a right of first refusal to keep the player on that team, but still granted the club a right of compensation. Given these and several other clues in related contract provisions, the arbitrator concluded that he could not "infer from the absence of affirmative or negative language that the parties reached an agreement or understanding that would serve to confer total free agent status to a veteran player who had completed a year of service pursuant to a § 17(b) contract...."

Thus, Andy Messersmith was able to win free agency for his baseball counterparts, but John Dutton failed in his effort in football. While there were some textual variations in the language of the collective agreements in the two sports, differences in the negotiating scenarios that produced the language (and perhaps also in the arbitrators' philosophical inclinations) also account for the opposite verdicts. The stark contrast between baseball's and football's labor markets after *Messersmith* and *Dutton* drove home to both players and owners (in basketball and hockey as well) what a difference a labor agreement could make. Not until the late 1990s (and following fierce legal and industrial relations conflicts) did the governing rules begin to converge across all the games. What we shall now examine are the ways that federal labor law shapes this bargaining process.

B. APPLICATION OF THE NLRA TO SPORTS

Congress enacted the National Labor Relations Act (NLRA) pursuant to its power to regulate interstate commerce. At the time when *Federal Baseball Club of Baltimore v. National League of Professional Baseball Clubs*, 259 U.S. 200 (1922), was decided, "interstate commerce" usually was construed quite narrowly; for that reason, baseball was considered too localized a form of business enterprise to be subject to federal antitrust law. Only a razor-thin 5–4 majority of the Supreme Court in *NLRB v. Jones & Laughlin Steel Corp.*, 301 U.S. 1 (1937), which upheld the validity of the NLRA itself, released Congress from this "dual federalism" constraint on its authority over the national economy.

A side effect of the New Deal constitutional revolution was that the open-ended NLRA gained considerably broader reach over private business and employment than Congress had initially contemplated. As a result, the NLRB has consistently exercised some measure of discretion to decide whether and when certain industries will be subjected to the national labor law. Not until the early 1970s were higher education and health care, for example, brought within the Board's purview. Notwithstanding the changing orientation of player associations in the mid-1960s, then, it was by no means inevitable that sports would come under the umbrella of the NLRA. (In fact, the NLRB refused to apply the Act to horse racing tracks in *Walter A. Kelley*, 139 N.L.R.B. 744 (1962).) Ironically, the decision that gave professional athletes their rights under labor law was rendered in a union certification application by *umpires*.

THE AMERICAN LEAGUE OF PROFESSIONAL BASEBALL CLUBS & ASS'N OF NATIONAL BASEBALL LEAGUE UMPIRES

National Labor Relations Board, 1969.
180 N.L.R.B. 190.

* * *

[The Board first ruled that baseball sufficiently involved interstate commerce so that the NLRA could apply.] ... The Board's jurisdiction under the Act is based upon the commerce clause of the Constitution, and is coextensive with the reach of that clause ... [Notwithstanding *Federal Base Ball* and *Toolson*], since professional football and boxing have been held to be in interstate commerce and thus subject to the antitrust laws, it can no longer be seriously contended that the Court still considers baseball alone to be outside of interstate commerce. Congressional deliberations regarding the relationship of baseball and other professional team sports to the antitrust laws likewise reflect a Congressional assumption that such sports are subject to regulation under the commerce clause. It is, incidentally, noteworthy that these deliberations reveal Congressional concern for the rights of employees such as players to bargain collectively and engage in concerted activities. Additionally, legal scholars have agreed, and neither the parties nor those participating as *amici* dispute, that professional sports are in or affect interstate commerce, and as such are subject to the Board's jurisdiction. Therefore, on the basis of the above, we find that professional baseball is an industry in or affecting commerce, and as such is subject to Board jurisdiction under the Act.

* * *

Section 14(c)(1) of the National Labor Relations Act, as amended, permits the Board to decline jurisdiction over labor disputes involving any "class or category of employers, where, in the opinion of the Board, the effect of such labor dispute on commerce is not sufficiently substantial to warrant the exercise of its jurisdiction...." The Employer and other employers contend that because of baseball's internal self-regulation, a labor dispute involving the American League of Professional Baseball Clubs is not likely to have any substantial effect on interstate commerce; and that application of the National Labor Relations Act to this Employer is contrary to national labor policy because Congress has sanctioned baseball's internal self-regulation. The Employer also contends that effective and uniform regulation of baseball's labor relations problems is not possible through Board processes because of the sport's international aspects.

* * *

We have carefully considered the positions of the parties, and the *amicus* briefs, and we find that it will best effectuate the mandates of the Act, as well as national labor policy, to assert jurisdiction over this Employer. We reach this decision for the following reasons.

Baseball's system for internal self-regulation of disputes involving umpires is made up of the Uniform Umpires Contract, the Major League Agreement, and the Major League Rules, which provide, among other things, for final resolution of disputes through arbitration by the Commissioner. The system appears to have been designed almost entirely by employers and owners, and the final arbiter of internal disputes does not appear to be a neutral third party freely chosen by both sides, but rather an individual appointed solely by the member club owners themselves.

We do not believe that such a system is likely either to prevent labor disputes from arising in the future, or, having once arisen, to resolve them in a manner susceptible or conductive to voluntary compliance by all parties involved. Moreover, it is patently contrary to the letter and spirit of the Act for the Board to defer its undoubted jurisdiction to decide unfair labor practices to a disputes settlement system established unilaterally by an employer or group of employers. Finally, although the instant case involves only umpires employed by the League, professional baseball clubs employ, in addition to players, clubhouse attendants, bat boys, watchmen, scouts, ticket sellers, ushers, gatemen, trainers, janitors, office clericals, batting practice pitchers, stilemen, publicity, and advertising men, grounds keepers and maintenance men. As to these other categories, there is no "self-regulation" at all. This consideration is of all the more consequence for of those employees in professional baseball whose interests are likely to call the Board's processes into play, the great majority are in the latter-named classifications.

We can find, neither in the statute nor in its legislative history, any expression of a Congressional intent that disputes between employers and employees in this industry should be removed from the scheme of the National Labor Relations Act.

* * *

[W]e are not here confronted with the sort of small, primarily intrastate employer over which the Board declines jurisdiction because of failure to meet its prevailing monetary standards. Moreover, it is apparent that the Employer, whose operations are so clearly national in scope, ought not have its labor relations problems subject to diverse state laws.

The Employer's final contention, that Board processes are unsuited to regulate effectively baseball's international aspects, clearly lacks merit, as many if not most of the industries subject to the Act have similar international features.

* * *

We further find that the following employees of the Employer constitute a unit appropriate for the purposes of collective bargaining within the meaning of Section 9(b) of the Act:

All persons employed as umpires in the American League of Professional Baseball Clubs, but excluding all other employees, office clerical employees, guards, professional employees and supervisors as defined in the Act.

Petition granted.

MEMBER JENKINS, dissenting:

My colleagues advance as a reason for asserting jurisdiction herein the absence of a Congressional intent to resolve labor disputes in baseball in a different manner from that established in the NLRA. In my opinion, the question is not whether Congress intended that disputes between employers and employees in the professional baseball industry should be resolved in the same or in a different manner from that established for other industries covered by the Act, but whether Congress, in enacting the NLRA, intended to include such disputes within the reach of the Board's jurisdiction at all. If any inference is to be drawn from Congressional silence on the matter, a very compelling reason exists for nonassertion of jurisdiction.

* * *

Whether fortuitous or otherwise, professional baseball's unique and favored status [in both the Nation's social and business community] had already gained judicial approval long before enactment of the NLRA. It is irrefutable, therefore, that Congress in 1935 harbored no intent to include the labor relations of professional baseball within the reach of the Board's jurisdiction. And while the Supreme Court has since rejected the narrow conception of commerce on which *Federal Baseball* was premised, in large measure prior to any amendments to the Act, my colleagues point to no legislative history in the subsequent amendments to the Act which would support a legislative intent thereafter to include baseball's labor relations within the reach of the Act. Indeed, it would appear that in the present posture, an amendment expressly including the baseball industry within the Act would be required to warrant the Board's assertion of jurisdiction.

* * *

Even assuming in agreement with my colleagues that professional baseball is subject to the Board's jurisdiction, and further, that the Board has the discretion under § 14(c)(1) of the Act to assert or decline jurisdiction, I am of the opinion that no compelling reasons exist for exercising that discretion to assert jurisdiction in the instant case. There is no showing that this industry is wracked with the kinds of labor disputes which are likely to constitute a burden on commerce. Nor am I satisfied that the majority's conclusion, that baseball's "commissioner" system for internal self-regulation of disputes is not likely to prevent such burden or disruption of commerce, constitutes a ground for our taking jurisdiction over the industry. Indeed, I question the propriety of prejudging baseball's arbitral system in this representation proceeding, particularly in view of the fact that the matter has not been litigated and in the absence of an issue which calls for a close scrutiny of the efficacy of that system based on facts spread on the record. In any event, the pendency of a single [unfair labor practice] charge, even assuming it arose as a direct result of the failure of baseball's arbitral system, is hardly ground for discrediting that system any more than it is for rejecting arbitration procedures in any industry. Moreover, my colleagues appear to shoot wide of the mark when they note that other employees, such as clubhouse attendants, bat boys, watchmen, scouts, ticket sellers, ushers, gatemen, trainers, janitors, grounds keepers and maintenance men, are not covered by baseball's arbitral system. Unlike umpires, these employees appear to be directly employed by the individual baseball clubs and it appears that their labor relations would be so handled. While baseball players are likewise hired directly by the individual clubs, the entire league has an interest in the relations between the players and their employers because of the very nature of the game and the need to maintain competition. Thus, there is an urgent need for ultimately settling problems dealing with the players on a league level while no such need is apparent in the case of stadium-oriented employees. Furthermore, it appears from the record that some of the latter employees are already represented by labor organizations in single-employer units and presumably have their own dispute settlement procedures. Finally, there is no showing that any labor disputes of national importance exist among these employees.

For the foregoing reasons I would dismiss the petition herein.

Questions for Discussion

1. What is your reaction to the contrasting observations by the NLRB members about baseball's system of internal self-regulation via the commissioner, in light of what you read in Chapter 1?

2. In the following portion of its decision in the above case, the NLRB dealt with the League's argument that umpires are "supervisors" as defined in § 2(ii) of the NLRA and thus not "employees" entitled to union representation:

> It is not contended that umpires have authority to hire, fire, transfer, discharge, recall, promote, assign, or reward. We think it equally apparent that umpires do not "discipline" or "direct" the work force according to the common meaning of those terms as used in the Act.
>
> The record indicates that an umpire's basic responsibility is to insure that each baseball game is played in conformance with the predetermined rules of the game. Thus, the umpire does not discipline except to the extent he may remove a participant from the game for violation of these rules. Testimony shows that after such a removal the umpire merely reports the incident to his superiors and does not himself fine, suspend, or even recommend such action. As the final arbiter on the field, the umpire necessarily makes decisions which may favor one team over another, and which may determine to some extent the movements of various players, managers, and other personnel on the ball field. The umpire does not, however, direct the work force in the same manner and for the same reasons as a foreman in an industrial setting. As every fan is aware, the umpire does not—through the use of independent judgment—tell a player how to bat, how to field, to work harder or exert more effort, nor can he tell a manager which players to play or where to play them. Thus, the umpire merely sees to it that the game is played in compliance with the rules. It is the manager and not the umpire who directs the employees in their pursuit of victory.
>
> Accordingly, we find that the umpires are not supervisors, and thus the Employer's motion to dismiss on this ground is hereby denied.

180 N.L.R.B. at 192–93.

In early 1997, Scotty Bowman, coach of the Detroit Red Wings, reportedly sought to organize his colleagues into an NHL Coaches Association. Apparently, the average salary of an NHL coach in the 1996–97 season was $385,000, much less than the $890,000 average for players. One important question is whether coaches like Bowman (or the NFL's Bill Parcells and the NBA's Pat Riley, or MLB managers like Tony LaRussa) are legally entitled to union representation and collective bargaining as "employees" under the NLRA. Should the line be drawn between the position of coach and director of player personnel (which Bowman also fills for the Red Wings), or between coach and assistant coach, or between assistant coaches and players? For the most recent Supreme Court decision in this area, see *NLRB v. Health Care & Retirement Corp. of America*, 511 U.S. 571 (1994) (finding that "charge nurses" in nursing homes are potentially excludable from the NLRA as supervisors). As you read the remaining materials in this chapter, though, consider also the question of how much real-life difference NLRA coverage would make to coaches' efforts at self-organization.

C. UNION SUPPORT AND EMPLOYER RETALIATION[d]

One tangible result of NLRA coverage is that employees gain federal legislative protection against employer retaliation for supporting the employees' union and its actions. For most workers, this legal protection is most important in the early days of union organization, in the face of employers determined to stay union-free. In professional sports, however, players had already organized their associations and secured rudimentary collective agreements before they could be sure of NLRA coverage. In addition, sports clubs and leagues are unusual employers because they need and want a union for their players in order to secure and retain the benefit of the labor exemption. (This was the source of the peculiar posture of the parties in the *Powell-McNeil* litigation we read about in Chapter 3, in which the NFL, the employer, was vigorously resisting the efforts of the NFLPA to deunionize football.)

---

d. Unlike the relationship between antitrust law and sports, there has been little systematic scholarly work done on the various aspects of labor law as applied to professional sports. (The principal exception is the book by Berry, Gould, and Staudohar cited in note a above; one of its authors, William Gould, was installed by President Clinton as Chairman of the NLRB in 1994, just as the next wave of labor conflict was about to hit the sports world.) In this chapter, then, we will provide references to some of the recent scholarly work on debates within labor law generally. With respect to the topic in this immediate section, one of us has written extensively: see, Paul C. Weiler, *Promises to Keep: Securing Workers' Rights to Self-Organization Under the NLRA*, 96 Harvard L. Rev. 1769 (1983), and Paul C. Weiler, *Governing the Workplace: The Future of Labor and Employment Law* (Cambridge, MA.: Harvard University Press, 1990), Chapters 3 and 6.

However, the § 7 rights of employees extend beyond initial organization to encompass support of the union in its bargaining efforts—for example, by trying to rally fellow employees in favor of the union and against the employer during a strike. Section 8 of the Act makes it an unfair labor practice for the employer to "interfere with, restrain, or coerce" employees engaged in such "concerted activities," and § 8(a)(3) forbids "discrimination in tenure of employment" (that is, dismissal) on account of such union support.

While these employee rights and employer obligations are firmly embedded in labor jurisprudence, they are inevitably murky in application. Even the most determined antiunion employer, recognizing the presence of the NLRA in the background, is careful to direct such retaliation only against employees whose work history provides some colorable basis for discharge or other punitive action. As a result, unfair labor practice charges based on § 8 involve difficult and time-consuming examinations of both the employer's true motivation for its actions and the employee's record of performance.

This difficulty is greatly exacerbated in professional sports. Unlike workers in almost every other walk of life, athletes have no expectation of keeping their positions just because they are doing a reasonably competent job. Every pre-season (indeed, throughout the season) veteran players face the threat of release and replacement by rookie challengers. Examine the standard NFL player contract, for example:

> *Skill, Performance and Conduct.* Player understands that he is competing with other players for a position on Club's roster within the applicable player limits. If at any time, in the sole judgment of Club, Player's skill or performance has been unsatisfactory as compared with that of other players competing for positions on Club's roster, or if Player has engaged in personal conduct reasonably judged by Club to adversely affect or reflect on Club, then Club may terminate this contract.

A severe test is posed to the NLRB, then, when the Board must decide whether a club's exercise of this judgment about a player's relative skill was contaminated by animus against his union activities. This problem is magnified by the fact that union representatives tend to be respected veterans who may have passed their peak performance years. The following case illustrates the difficulty of this issue.

SEATTLE SEAHAWKS v. NFLPA & SAM McCULLUM

National Labor Relations Board, 1989.
292 N.L.R.B. No. 110.

[From 1976 through 1981, Sam McCullum was a starting wide receiver for the Seattle Seahawks. In 1981, McCullum was selected by his teammates to be their union player representative. McCullum's prominent role in union activities in the following bargaining year (leading up to the lengthy players' strike during the 1982 season) produced severe tensions with Seahawks' coach Jack Patera. In particular, Patera was upset by McCullum's orchestration of the "solidarity handshake" by his teammates with members of the opposing team at the beginning of their first pre-season game. Nevertheless, McCullum started all of the August 1982 pre-season games for the Seahawks. In a trade made at the end of training camp, however, the Seahawks obtained from the Baltimore Colts another wide receiver, Roger Carr, and McCullum was cut from the team's final roster. An unfair labor practice charge was then filed by McCullum and the NFLPA.

The evidence at trial showed that the Seahawks' Director of Football Operations, Mike McCormick, and its General Manager, John Thompson, had been trying for months to trade for Carr on favorable terms. Also, Jerry Rhome, the offensive coordinator, had been closely involved in deciding which of the team's four wide receivers should be let go to make room for Carr. However, the Administrative Law Judge (ALJ) found that both of these team decisions were influenced by the Seahawks'—and especially Patera's—anti-union sentiments directed at McCullum. In this decision, a divided NLRB grapples with the Seahawks' appeal from the ALJ's ruling.

In *Wright Line*, 251 N.L.R.B. 1083 (1980), enf'd, 662 F.2d 899 (1st Cir.1981), cert. denied, 455 U.S. 989 (1982), the NLRB clarified its test for determining when an employer has committed an unfair labor practice by firing an employee. Rather than stopping with the judgment whether antiunion motivation was a cause "in part" of the firing, the Board required the employee first to show that his union activities were a "motivating factor" in the employer's decision to fire him, and then the employer could defend by showing that the employee would have been fired even if he had not engaged in union activities. The Supreme Court accepted this "but for" test in *NLRB v. Transportation Management Corp.*, 462 U.S. 393, 400–03 (1983). The Seahawks first challenged the ALJ's ruling on the ground that it misapplied the *Wright Line* test by finding no more than that McCullum's union activities were "in part" a factor in his release.]

* * *

It is incontestable that the judge, notwithstanding his occasional use of the term "in part" to describe the extent of the Respondent's unlawful motivation, found that antiunion considerations were a motivating factor in the decision that produced McCullum's release, and that he fully considered the Respondent's *Wright Line* defense. We therefore find that his analysis fully comports with the *Wright Line* standard.

The Respondent has also excepted to the judge's implicit finding that certain remarks that Sam McCullum made in his role as the team's player representative at a February 19, 1982 press conference and that produced negative reactions from both the team's general manager, John Thompson, and its head coach, Jack Patera, are in fact protected under § 7 of the Act. In particular, the Respondent argues that McCullum's expression of his view that team doctors, whom he saw as identified with management, released injured players for games too soon, when the players were not fully recovered, constituted "disloyal" disparagement of the employer, which, pursuant to the theory of *NLRB v. Electrical Workers Local 1229 IBEW (Jefferson Standard)*, 346 U.S. 464 (1953), is not protected activity under § 7. The Respondent also argues, as to the "solidarity handshake" episode, that any hostility would naturally be against the Union—as the author of this activity throughout the league—rather than against McCullum. We disagree with both contentions.

In *Jefferson Standard*, the Supreme Court held that a union's public attacks on the quality of the employer's product were not protected under § 7 when they had no connection with the employee's working conditions or any current labor controversy. It seems indisputable, however, that the relative haste with which injured players are returned to the football field is a matter that directly affects the players' working conditions. Although McCullum's views may have been exaggerated or not soundly based, that does not withdraw the protection of the Act from them. Indeed, employees and employers frequently differ greatly in their views whether the employees are properly treated.

We do not mean to suggest, of course, that it was unlawful for either Thompson or Patera to take issue with McCullum's statements. The fact remains, however, that McCullum established himself at this press conference as a fairly aggressive union spokesman. McCullum's role as player representative was highlighted again when he and two other players approached Patera in August to apprise him of the players' intention to support the Union's "solidarity handshake" plan by engaging in such a handshake with the opposing team in the upcoming August 13 game with St. Louis. Although it was another player who mentioned the "union solidarity" symbolism of the handshake, it was McCullum who—after Patera had expressed his opposition—said that the players might go ahead and do it anyway. We agree with the judge that Patera's prediction of the subsequent fines ('I'll fine you as much as I can') and the heavy fines that the Respondent sought to impose reveal animus toward union activity for which, at this point, McCullum was the obvious focus on the team.

* * *

The Respondent attacks the judge's discrediting of Patera—which is essential to his findings of unlawful motive—by insisting that it rests fundamentally not on observations of witness demeanor but rather on a flawed logical analysis of the plausibility of Patera's account of an urgent search, beginning as early as January 1982, for a "deep threat" wide receiver.

* * *

We, of course, recognize that the judge's evaluation of all the testimony was influenced by his view of how it fit together logically or failed to do so, but we are necessarily reluctant to disregard the demeanor component of credibility resolutions by a trier of fact. We therefore decline the Respondent's invitation to reverse the judge's assessment of the credibility of Patera's testimony.

Finally, we address two of the Respondent's arguments concerning alleged inconsistencies between the judge's factual findings and the record evidence. These are both matters raised also by our dissenting colleague.

First, the Respondent argues that a finding that it was seeking to obtain Carr in order to rid itself of McCullum is inconsistent with the evidence that the Respondent had declined to accept Baltimore's offer of Carr in late spring for a first round draft choice, that it had declined another Baltimore offer in August for a "high" draft choice, and that the Respondent had even toughened its position by insisting on September 2 that it would give up only a fourth round draft choice for Carr. We do not see that conduct as inconsistent with the judge's motivation finding for the reasons essentially given by the judge.

An employer may harbor an unlawful intent to rid itself of a troublesome employee but still wish to do so on the most advantageous terms possible. Furthermore, the testimony of the Respondent's own witnesses shows that they reasonably believed that Baltimore wanted to be rid at all costs of the injury-prone Carr.

* * *

It is undeniable that Rhome was responsible for rating the wide receivers throughout training camp and the pre-season games and that Patera would reasonably take seriously his judgment, after the Carr trade, that McCullum should be released rather than Steve Largent, Byron Walker, or Paul Johns. But it is clear from Rhome's testimony that he was not consulted about the desirability of having Carr, as opposed to McCullum, at the point in the season that Carr was finally acquired. Thus, Rhome testified that he could not rate Carr because he had not seen him play very recently. Rhome obviously approached the evaluation process with the realization that Carr was not for cutting. As he testified, "You can't just eliminate Roger Carr because you just got through trading for him." Hence, having Carr as one of the wide receivers going into the new season was essentially imposed on Rhome by the trade. He made no considered judgment that an injury-prone player who had not participated in any training camp that summer and did not know Seattle's system of offensive plays would be more valuable than McCullum.

Although Carr's name was first mentioned by McCormick when he joined the Respondent's organization in March and the initial decision to make inquiries about Carr occurred after a conversation among McCormick, Patera, and Thompson about the matter, Patera made the initial call, while subsequent negotiations with Baltimore were carried out first by McCormick and later by Thompson. But Patera's role was crucial. As Thompson testified, Patera was the one to decide who would make the team. Given the time at which Carr was finally acquired—just before the opening of the season—it was clear that, as Rhome recognized, acquiring him meant bringing him onto the team. Nothing in the record suggests that efforts to acquire players would have been made without continuing consultation with the head coach. Thus, it had to be up to Patera whether negotiations to acquire Carr would continue just before the start of the season, when cuts were to be made....

Given the reports that Rhome says he made to Patera about the progress of players Walker and Johns in the training camp and preseason games, the continued pursuit of Carr is suspect. McCullum was rated a very good wide receiver in many respects—allegedly all except for the ability to go deep and catch "the bomb." But this was an area in which Johns and Walker were now rated highly, so the need to obtain Carr for that particular skill was diminishing rapidly according to the Respondent's own witnesses.

The Respondent simply has not shown that the acquisition of Roger Carr on September 3 would have occurred even in the absence of the animus of the Respondent's management—more notably, but not solely, the animus of Patera—against McCullum as an outspoken representative of union sentiment on the team. The animus against the Union's solidarity had been powerfully expressed, but thwarted in August, when the Respondent imposed fines for the 'solidarity handshake' that greatly exceeded those imposed by any other NFL team and then was forced to rescind the fines. The opportunity for the Respondent to rid itself of the most visible team symbol of that solidarity was finally seized upon in September through the acquisition of Carr.

Charges upheld.

MEMBER JOHANSEN, dissenting.

Despite the undisputed facts regarding the timing and progress of the Carr-trade talks—notably the early initial efforts of McCormick, the hard bargaining techniques of Thompson, and the absence of any role in the process by Patera—the judge and my colleagues nevertheless conclude that the Carr acquisition was central to a carefully designed pretext to justify McCullum's elimination. I cannot agree. The judge's analysis is flawed by his failure to account for Patera's lack of participation in effecting the trade. The judge imputed Patera's apparent hostility toward McCullum to the Respondent generally. By so doing, however, the judge ignored the fact that the Respondent did not stand accused of having committed any unfair labor practices independent of the McCullum discharge, and that there is no union animus on the part of those within the Respondent's organization, i.e., McCormick and Thompson, who actually played a direct personal role in the Carr acquisition.

The judge's analysis also too readily discounts the fact that the attempts to deal for Carr were initiated right after McCormick joined the

Seattle organization after leaving the Colts, and well in advance of McCullum's most "anti-Patera" confrontation, i.e., the "solidarity handshake" incident; and it leaves unexplained the unwillingness of the Respondent's trade negotiators to conclude the Carr-deal quickly so as to assure an excuse for dismissing McCullum. Indeed, it was the Colts who, in the end, were the party most eager to make a trade for Carr.... Yet the Seahawks twice passed by Colt deadlines for trading for Carr.

The judge's analysis also does not refute the Respondent's evidence that it cut McCullum for sound business reasons. In this regard, as with the Carr acquisition itself, the judge again overemphasized Patera's responsibility in the selection process ... failed to account fully for the role of the Respondent's offensive coordinator, Jerry Rhome, in the decision to let McCullum go.

* * *

Rhome proceeded to rate Largent as the [Seahawks'] star. He stated that he could not rate Carr because he had not seen him play in preseason. He declared that Johns, Walker, and McCullum were very close, but that he would take Walker over McCullum. Rhome testified that he had earlier told Patera that Johns should probably be given the starting position over McCullum. Rhome also testified that retaining five players at the wide receiver position would not have been tenable because the extra receiver would cost the team a player at another slot; the team could not afford cutting back on the strength of their offensive line; the possibility of an injury to a quarterback precluded having only two at that position; the tight end position was thought to require three active players; and the Respondent had traditionally carried just four wide receivers. Rhome averred that his fellow assistant coaches agreed with his assessment on the number of receivers that should be carried. Rhome further commented that in any event McCullum was not likely to be happy in a backup role, spending the bulk of the game time on the bench. Rhome stated that the decision boiled down to a choice between McCullum and Walker and that developing the potential of a youthful Walker was an appealing prospect for the team.

After giving his perspective to Patera the decision to terminate McCullum seemed logically to emerge: (1) Largent, as the Respondent's premier wide receiver, would obviously be kept; (2) Carr would be retained in view of the fact that the trade for him had just been effected; (3) Johns was projected as a probable starter over McCullum; (4) Johns was needed as the punt returner—a matter independent of his role as wide receiver; (5) Walker displayed promise as a young talent with his best playing years ahead; and (6) McCullum's starting role was challenged and he was facing the declining years of his playing abilities.

* * *

For all the foregoing reasons, the Respondent's choice of McCullum as the expendable player emerges as one based on a business judgment of the team's personnel needs that would have been made even in the absence of antiunion motivation. Accordingly, I find that the Respondent has met its *Wright Line* burden and I would reverse the judge's conclusion that the Respondent's termination of McCullum violated the Act.

Questions for Discussion

1. The NLRB rendered its decision in 1989, and the D.C. Circuit eventually upheld the Board's unfair labor practice finding and $250,000 back pay award in *Nordstrom v. NLRB*, 984 F.2d 479 (D.C.Cir.1993). That final legal ruling in this case took place eleven years after the Seahawks had let McCullum go for the reasons detailed above. What is the likely effect of such administrative-judicial delays in protecting worker rights of self organization against employer retaliation? Is delay more or less significant in securing the policies of the NLRA in the sports context?[e]

2. What does this issue suggest to the average player who is deciding for whom to vote as the club's union representative? Should he vote for a younger star player who is unlikely to be released but also less likely to be sympathetic to the union's goals on behalf of journeymen players, or for an older journeymen player who is more susceptible to being cut by the team but more committed to union activities?

D. CERTIFICATION OF THE PLAYERS' BARGAINING AGENT

The aim of a union organizing drive is to win the right to represent employees in collective bargaining with their employer. Absent voluntary recognition by the employer (as was extended by the various sports leagues in the late 1960s to what were then comparatively weak player associations), a union enjoying substantial allegiance among the employees must petition the NLRB to conduct a secret ballot election. If the union wins a majority of the votes cast, the Board then certifies the union as the exclusive bargaining agent for all the employees (§ 9(a)). But before any such election can be conducted, the Board must define the scope of the relevant employee constituency—that is, the "unit appropriate for purposes of collective bargaining" (§ 9(b)).

The NLRB and the courts have developed an elaborate jurisprudence for determining which of the many possible employee groupings exhibits the ideal "community of interest" for bargaining together.[f] Although these conclusions were not preordained by precedents from other industrial settings, no one has challenged the assumption that the appropriate unit in professional sports is comprised of *only* the players (thus excluding all other employees of the clubs) and of *all* the players (thus not distinguishing higher-priced positions such as quarterback from lower-priced positions such as defensive back). Just like antitrust law, however, labor law must decide whether the center of gravity in the

---

[e]. See Ethan Lock, *Employer Unfair Labor Practices During the 1982 National Football League Strike: Help on the Way*, 6 U. of Bridgeport L. Rev. 189 (1985).

[f]. See Douglas L. Leslie, *Labor Bargaining Units*, 70 Virginia L. Rev. 353 (1984).

union's bargaining relationship is to be with the individual club or with the entire league. The answer was rendered in a certification petition for players in the North American Soccer League.

NORTH AMERICAN SOCCER LEAGUE v. NLRB

United States Court of Appeals, Fifth Circuit, 1980.
613 F.2d 1379.

RONEY, CIRCUIT JUDGE.

[In 1977, the National Football League Players Association (NFLPA) financed and manned a new North American Soccer League Players Association (NASLPA), which then organized players from the 19 NASL clubs (two of which were Canadian teams) and petitioned the NLRB for certification of a single, league-wide bargaining unit. The division of authority between soccer clubs and their league (under its commissioner) was essentially the same as in other team sports. In the case of player relations, individual teams selected, compensated, traded, and released their players. However, league rules regarding rookie drafts, waivers, free agency, and the like governed such individual team-player dealings, and all players were required to sign a standard NASL contract that accepted the ultimate disciplinary authority of the Commissioner.

Given these facts, the Board accepted the position of the Player Association that a single league-wide unit was *an* (though not the *only*) appropriate bargaining unit in an employment relationship in which the League and individual clubs were "joint employers" of the players, because both exercised a significant degree of control over their respective personnel policies. The Board majority decided, though, not to exercise jurisdiction over the two Canadian-owned and based clubs, the Toronto Metros and the Vancouver Whitecaps, notwithstanding the dissent's observation that these two teams played nearly half their games in the United States and shared in both gate receipts and television revenues from this country. The League and its member clubs appealed the Board's certification of a single unit encompassing all of the players on American teams.]

* * *

JOINT EMPLOYERS.

Whether there is a joint employer relationship is "essentially a factual issue," and the Board's finding must be affirmed if supported by substantial evidence on the record as a whole.

The existence of a joint employer relationship depends on the control which one employer exercises, or potentially exercises, over the labor relations policy of the other. In this case, the record supports the Board's finding that the League exercises a significant degree of control over essential aspects of the clubs' labor relations, including but not limited to the selection, retention, and termination of the players, the terms of individual player contracts, dispute resolution and player discipline. Furthermore, each club granted the NASL authority over not only its own labor relations but also, on its behalf, authority over the labor relations of the other member clubs. The evidence is set forth in detail in the Board's decision and need be only briefly recounted here.

The League's purpose is to promote the game of soccer through its supervision of competition among member clubs. Club activities are governed by the League constitution, and the regulations promulgated thereunder by a majority vote of the clubs. The commissioner, selected and compensated by the clubs, is the League's chief executive officer. A board of directors composed of one representative of each club assists him in managing the League.

The League's control over the clubs' labor relations begins with restrictions on the means by which players are acquired. An annual college draft is conducted by the commissioner pursuant to the regulations, and each club obtains exclusive negotiating rights to the players it selects. On the other hand, as the Board recognized, the League exercises less control over the acquisition of "free agent" players and players "on loan" from soccer clubs abroad.

The regulations govern interclub player trades and empower the commissioner to void trades not deemed to be in the best interest of the League. Termination of player contracts is conducted through a waiver system in accordance with procedures specified in the regulations.

The League also exercises considerable control over the contractual relationships between the clubs and their players. Before being permitted to participate in a North American Soccer League game, each player must sign a standard player contract adopted by the League. The contract governs the player's relationship with his club, requiring his compliance with club rules and the League constitution and regulations. Compensation is negotiated between the player and his club, and special provisions may be added to the contract. Significantly, however, the club must seek the permission of the commissioner before signing a contract which alters any terms of the standard contract.

Every player contract must be submitted to the commissioner, who is empowered to disapprove a contract deemed not in the best interest of the League. The commissioner's disapproval invalidates the contract. Disputes between a club and a player must be submitted to the commissioner for final and binding arbitration.

Control over player discipline is divided between the League and the clubs. The clubs enforce compliance with club rules relating to practices and also determine when a player will participate in a game. The League, through the commissioner, has broad power to discipline players for misconduct either on or off the playing field. Sanctions range from fines to suspension to termination of the player's contract.

Although we recognize that minor differences in the underlying facts might justify different findings on the joint employer issue, the record in this case supports the Board's factual finding of a joint employer relationship among the League and its constituent clubs.

Having argued against inclusion of the Canadian clubs in the NLRB proceeding, petitioners contend on appeal that their exclusion renders the Board's joint employer finding, encompassing 21 clubs, inconsistent with the existence of a 24–club League. The jurisdictional determination is not before us on appeal, however, and the Board's decision not to exercise jurisdiction over the Canadian clubs does not undermine the evidentiary base of its joint employer finding.

Even assuming the League and the clubs are joint employers, they contend that *Greenhoot, Inc.*, 205 N.L.R.B. 250 (1973), requires a finding of a separate joint employer relationship between the League and each of its clubs, and does not permit all the clubs to be lumped together with the League as joint employers. In *Greenhoot*, a building management company was found to be a joint employer separately with each building owner as to maintenance employees in the buildings covered by its contracts. The present case is clearly distinguishable, because here each soccer club exercises through its proportionate role in League management some control over the labor relations of other clubs. In *Greenhoot*, building owners did not exercise any control through the management company over the activities of other owners.

Appropriate Unit.

The joint employer relationship among the League and its member clubs having been established, the next issue is whether the leaguewide unit of players designated by the Board is appropriate. Here the Board's responsibility and the standard of review in this Court are important.

The Board is not required to choose the most appropriate bargaining unit, only to select a unit appropriate under the circumstances. The determination will not be set aside "unless the Board's discretion has been exercised 'in an arbitrary or capricious manner.'"

Notwithstanding the substantial financial autonomy of the clubs, the Board found they form, through the League, an integrated group with common labor problems and a high degree of centralized control over labor relations. In these circumstances the Board's designation of a leaguewide bargaining unit as appropriate is reasonable, not arbitrary or capricious.

In making its decision, the Board expressly incorporated the reasons underlying its finding of a joint employer relationship. The Board emphasized in particular both the individual clubs' decision to form a League for the purpose of jointly controlling many of their activities, and the commissioner's power to disapprove contracts and exercise control over disciplinary matters. Under our "exceedingly narrow" standard of review, no arguments presented by petitioners require denial of enforcement of the bargaining order.

Thus the facts successfully refute any notion that because the teams compete on the field and in hiring, only team units are appropriate for collective bargaining purposes. Once a player is hired, his working conditions are significantly controlled by the League. Collective bargaining at that source of control would be the only way to effectively change by agreement many critical conditions of employment.

Order enforced.

The result of the *NASL* decision was to require all the soccer teams to bargain as a single unit with the players association. In that respect, the labor law treatment of sports leagues is distinctive. The general principle of labor law is that multiemployer bargaining is a purely consensual undertaking, one that must initially be agreed to by the union and each of the employers participating.[g] The principal constraint imposed by the law is that, once all affected parties have voluntarily moved towards such an arrangement, no one party can unilaterally withdraw during a particular round of bargaining just because negotiations have not gone as that party hoped. (Thus, in *Charles D. Bonanno Linen Service v. NLRB*, 454 U.S. 404 (1982), the Supreme Court held that even an impasse reached in negotiations did not warrant an employer leaving the larger multiemployer unit.) Note the way in which the court in *NASL* characterized the relevant employer entity in the sports context in order to distinguish the broader doctrinal principles just mentioned. Recall this labor law treatment of the issue when we take up in Chapter 7 the analogous question of whether the club or the league is the relevant entity under antitrust law—something that is especially relevant to the revival of this sport in a new Major League Soccer (MLS).

Though voluntary in origin, multiemployer bargaining is now a common feature of the industrial relations landscape, particularly in industries such as trucking or construction, in which there are hosts of small firms dealing with a few large unions, such as the Teamsters or the Carpenters. Both employers and unions in these industries find they have a complementary long-term interest in putting their relationship on that broader footing. What might these interests be in the sports context? How is league-wide bargaining helpful or harmful to the clubs or to the players? Does the sports world differ from other industries in that certain types of issues can only be addressed effectively through league-wide, rather than individual club, bargaining?

Recall, also, the *Brown* decision in Chapter 3, in which Justice Breyer placed considerable weight on the voluntary feature of multiemployer bargaining to justify the Supreme Court's ruling that the labor exemption precluded antitrust suits by unionized employees against unilateral imposition of salary or other restraints by a multiemployer association (of NFL owners). How does *Brown* square with *NASL*'s interpretation of multiemployer labor law doctrine in the sports context? In particular, suppose that, prior to the next round of labor negotiations

g. See Douglas L. Leslie, *Multiemployer Bargaining Rules*, 75 Virginia L. Rev. 241 (1989), and Jan Vetter, *Commentary on 'Multiemployer Bargaining Rules': Searching for the Right Questions*, 75 Virginia L. Rev. 285 (1989).

in a particular sport, the players union announced to the owners that it was withdrawing its consent to league-wide bargaining, and was prepared to negotiate just with each club individually. Could the league secure an order from the NLRB that barred this move under labor law? Would such union action suffice to restore to the players their right to antitrust scrutiny of the validity of agreements among the teams to restrain competition amongst themselves for players? Or do the players have to give up their entire labor law rights to union representation and collective bargaining in order to assert any such antitrust protection?

The *NASL* case illustrated another legal complication that now affects the bargaining structure of hockey, basketball, and baseball. Two of the teams in baseball (the Toronto Blue Jays and the Montreal Expos), two in basketball (the Toronto Raptors and Vancouver Grizzlies), and six of the teams in hockey are located in Canadian cities. Though the basic labor law model in Canada resembles that in the United States,[h] there are a number of significant variations in the operation of labor law in the two countries. (Indeed, a fundamental constitutional difference is that Canadian labor law is principally a matter of provincial rather than national jurisdiction, so that the labor law in Quebec governing the Expos is itself somewhat different from that of Ontario law which covers the Blue Jays.) Canadian labor laws, for example (unlike their U.S. counterpart), tend to require mandatory government mediation and secret ballot strike votes before a strike or lockout can be legal, and then the law bars permanent—and in the case of Quebec and British Columbia, even temporary—replacement of the striking or locked-out employees. As we shall see at several points in this chapter, the 1990s witnessed for the first time the use of Canadian labor law in North American sports disputes.

E. UNION'S EXCLUSIVE BARGAINING AUTHORITY[i]

Once the NLRB has certified the union as the majority choice of the employees, the union becomes the "exclusive representative of *all* the employees in the unit for purposes of collective bargaining" (§ 9(a)). Although this was not inevitable from the Act's bare language, the Supreme Court, in its crucial decision in *J.I. Case Co. v. NLRB*, 321 U.S. 332 (1944), read the congressional intent under this provision to make the collective agreement prevail over any individually negotiated employment conditions:

---

h. See Paul C. Weiler, *Reconcilable Differences: New Directions in Canadian Labor Law* (Toronto: Carswell, 1980).

i. See George Schatzki, *Majority Rule, Exclusive Representation, and the Interests of Individual Workers: Should Exclusivity be Abolished?*, 123 U. of Pennsylvania L. Rev. 897 (1975), and Eileen Silberstein, *Union Decisions on Collective Bargaining Goals: A Proposal for Interest Group Participation*, 77 Michigan L. Rev. 1485 (1979).

It is equally clear since the collective trade agreement is to serve the purpose contemplated by the Act, the individual contract cannot be effective as a waiver of any benefit to which the employee otherwise would be entitled under the trade agreement. The very purpose of providing by statute for the collective agreement is to supersede the terms of separate agreements of employees with terms which reflect the strength and bargaining power and serve the welfare of the group. Its benefits and advantages are open to every employee of the represented unit, whatever the type or terms of his pre-existing contract of employment.

321 U.S. at 338. The following decision from the sports context illustrates the doctrine of exclusive union authority in operation.

MORIO v. NORTH AMERICAN SOCCER LEAGUE

United States District Court, Southern District of New York, 1980.
501 F.Supp. 633.

MOTLEY, DISTRICT JUDGE.

[As we saw in the preceding section, following the NLRB's certification of the NASL Players Association as bargaining agent for NASL soccer players, the League sought (unsuccessfully) to challenge the Board's league-wide unit determination in court. During that time frame, the League refused to bargain collectively with the union, and its clubs continued to negotiate new contracts with individual players. League authorities unilaterally instituted a number of changes in the general working conditions that were embodied in these contracts: the summer season was extended by two weeks; a new winter season was created; roster sizes were reduced from 30 to 26 players; and players were required to use the footwear selected by their club (absent consent by the latter). The Association filed charges with the NLRB, alleging that this NASL conduct violated the union's exclusive bargaining authority under the NLRA; the Board then went to court to secure a § 10(j) interim injunction against such post-certification negotiation of new individual contracts (by then covering 97% of league players).]

* * *

The unilateral changes which Respondents admit have occurred since September 1, 1978, in the terms and conditions of employment, may violate the employer's obligations to bargain with the exclusive bargaining representative of the players. The duty to bargain carries with it the obligation on the part of the employer not to undercut the Union by entering into individual contracts with the employees. In *NLRB v. Katz*, 369 U.S. 736 (1962), the Supreme Court noted:

A refusal to negotiate in fact as to any subject which is within § 8(d) and about which the Union seeks to negotiate violates § 8(a)(5).

It is undisputed that Respondents have since September 1, 1978, refused to bargain with the Union. Respondents claim that they had a right to refuse to bargain with the Union since they were pursuing their right to appeal the Board's determination that all of the players referred to above constitute a unit for collective bargaining purposes. ==Respondents' duty to bargain with the Union arose from the time the Union was certified as the exclusive bargaining representative of the players==—September 1, 1978. The fact that Respondents were pursuing their right to appeal did not, absent a stay of the Board's order, obviate their duty to bargain with the Union and does not constitute a defense to an application for relief under § 10(j) of the Act where, as here, Respondents have apparently repeatedly refused to bargain with the Union and have continued to bypass the Union and deal directly with employees. As Petitioner says, Respondents could have bargained subject to later court decision adverse to Petitioner and the Union and can do so now. Negotiations between Respondents and the Union were scheduled to commence August 12, 1980, notwithstanding Respondents' petition for a writ of certiorari.

Respondents' most vigorous opposition comes in response to Petitioner's application for an order requiring Respondents to render voidable, at the option of the Union, all individual player contracts, whether entered into before or after the Union's certification on September 1, 1978. Respondents' claim that such power in the hands of the Union, a non-party to this action, would result in chaos in the industry and subject Respondents to severe economic loss and hardship since these individual contracts are the only real property of Respondents.

It should be noted, at the outset, that the relief requested by Petitioner is not a request to have all individual contracts declared null and void. It should be emphasized that Petitioner is not requesting that the "exclusive rights" provision of the individual contracts, which bind the players to their respective teams for a certain time, be rendered voidable. Moreover, the Board seeks an order requiring Respondents to maintain the present terms and conditions in effect until Respondents negotiate with the Union—except, of course, for the unilateral changes—unless and until an agreement or a good faith impasse is reached through bargaining with the Union. Petitioner does not, however, seek to rescind that unilateral provision which provided for the present summer schedule. The Board has consciously limited its request for relief to prevent any unnecessary disruption of Respondents' business. The Board is seeking to render voidable only those unilateral acts taken by the Respondents, enumerated above, which Respondents admit have in fact occurred.

These unilateral changes appear to modify all existing individual contracts entered into before September 1, 1978, in derogation of the Union's right to act as the exclusive bargaining agent of all employees in the unit.

The court finds that Petitioner is entitled to the temporary injunctive relief which it seeks with respect to all of the individual contracts. The individual contracts entered into since September 1, 1978, are apparently in violation of the duty of the Respondents to bargain with the exclusive bargaining representative of the players. The Act requires Respondents to bargain collectively with the Union. The obligation is exclusive. This duty to bargain with the exclusive representative carries with it the negative duty not to bargain with individual employees. *Medo Photo Supply Corp. v. NLRB*, 321 U.S. 678 (1944).

* * *

In *National Licorice Co. v. NLRB*, 309 U.S. 350 (1940), the Supreme Court held that the Board has the authority, even in the absence of the employees as parties to the proceeding, to order an employer not to enforce individual contracts with its employees which were found to have been in violation of the NLRA. Petitioner is seeking temporary relief to this effect as to those individual contracts entered into before September 1, 1978, as well as relief with respect to those contracts entered into prior to September 1, 1978. The evidence discloses that Petitioner has reasonable cause to believe that Respondents have used, and will continue to use, the individual contracts entered into prior to September 1, 1978, to forestall collective bargaining.

[The court concluded that the Labor Board and the NASL Players Association were entitled to require NASL to "render voidable" the particular contract provisions that the union objected to—relief that "has been carefully tailored to avoid chaos in [the League's] industry and to avoid any economic hardship to [League members]."]

* * *

Injunction granted.

———

By virtue of § 9(a), then, the union is entitled to eliminate all individual bargaining, even bargaining to secure better terms than the collectively-negotiated minimum. But collective bargaining in sports, as in the entertainment industry generally, has followed a different path, under which the union agreement sets out guaranteed benefits and a minimum salary scale and permits a Michael Jordan and a Greg Maddux (like a Tom Cruise and a Jerry Seinfeld) to negotiate whatever extra remuneration the market will bear. Such individual freedom of contract operates at the sufferance of, and within parameters set by, the collective agreement—with the performer's agent serving, in a sense, as delegate for the union.

That free market orientation first became pronounced in baseball, with its free agency system developed after *Messersmith*. Not only were baseball salaries dramatically higher in the mid–1990s than they were two decades earlier, but so also was the salary range; for example, in 1997, salaries ranged from the $150,000 minimum to Albert Belle's $11 million-a-year contract. Nor are these figures just isolated extremes.[j] In

---

j. For close empirical analysis of this phenomenon, see Rodney Fort, "Pay and Performance: Is the Field of Dreams Barren?," Chapter 8 of Paul M. Sommers, ed.,

1967, when Marvin Miller was appointed Executive Director of the MLBPA and set out to turn the organization into a true union, the average baseball salary was $19,000 a year and the median salary was $17,000; in 1976, just before free agency became operative, the average salary was $52,000, the median $40,000; but by the opening of the 1997 season, while the average salary was $1.37 million, the median was only one-third that—just over $400,000. Indeed, in basketball the disparity was even worse. Led by Michael Jordan's $30 million, the salary average was $2.2 in the 1996–97 season. However, 38% of the players were earning the minimum salary (including eight of the 14 players on the Houston Rockets' roster).

In that respect the outcome of sports collective bargaining is sharply different than what one finds in most unionized sectors, where the salary scale tends to tilt towards the average career veteran rather than the exceptional star.[k] How would the salary structure in baseball be different if there were no association and no basic agreement? Does this suggest that the *raison d'être* for a players union is different from that for a traditional trade union?

The one occasion when a players association sought to act like a mainstream labor union was during the 1982 negotiations in football. That year, the NFLPA, under Ed Garvey, tried to establish a salary scale weighted toward seniority and specific accomplishments, and thereby restructure the existing salary pattern that turns more on playing position (for example, quarterback as opposed to defensive back) or original draft position (for example, early in the first round rather than in a later round). The policy rationale for allowing a union to have legal authority to negotiate such constraints on individual salary negotiations was expressed by the Supreme Court in *J.I. Case, supra.*

> But it is urged that some employees may lose by the collective agreement, that an individual workman may sometimes have, or be capable of getting, better terms than those obtainable by the group and that his freedom of contract must be respected on that account. We are not called upon to say that under no circumstances can an individual enforce an agreement more advantageous than a collective agreement, but we find the mere possibility that such agreements might be made no ground for holding generally that individual contracts may survive or surmount collective ones. The practice and philosophy of collective bargaining looks with suspicion on such individual advantages. Of course, where there is great variation in circumstances of employment or capacity of employees, it is possible for the collective bargain to prescribe only minimum rates or maximum hours or expressly to leave certain areas open to individual

Diamonds Are Forever: The Business of Baseball, (Washington, D.C.: Brookings, 1992).

k. See Richard B. Freeman and James L. Medoff, *What Do Unions Do?* (New York: Basic Books, 1984), in particular, Chapter 5, "Labor's Elite: The Effect of Unionism on Wage Inequality."

bargaining. But except as so provided, advantages to individuals may prove as disruptive of industrial peace as disadvantages. They are a fruitful way of interfering with organization and choice of representatives; increased compensation, if individually deserved, is often earned at the cost of breaking down some other standard thought to be for the welfare of the group, and always creates the suspicion of being paid at the long-range expense of the group as a whole. Such discriminations not infrequently amount to unfair labor practices. The workman is free, if he values his own bargaining position more than that of the group, to vote against representation; but the majority rules, and if it collectivizes the employment bargain, individual advantages or favors will generally in practice go in as a contribution to the collective result. We cannot except individual contracts generally from the operation of collective ones because some may be more individually advantageous.

321 U.S. at 338–39.

Having beaten back that salary scale effort by the NFL Players Association in the 1982 negotiations and strike, ten years later the NFL ironically was proposing a salary scale—targeted in particular at rookies. The NFLPA (in return, finally, for somewhat relaxed veteran free agency) would only go so far as to establish a separate salary pool for rookies. This amount would then be divided up by the teams in individual negotiations with their various draft picks. In 1995, though, both the NHLPA and the NBPA used their exclusive bargaining authority rights to define the specific salary range that would be permitted for each pick in each round of the draft. (Given that baseball draft picks almost invariably start play with minor league teams, it is doubtful whether the MLBPA has the authority under the NLRA to define the payments that can be made by major league teams for minor league players who are not within the scope of the MLBPA bargaining unit.) In the late 1990s, though, all players associations continue to reject the idea of any ceiling on the amounts that can be paid to individual veterans. At the end of this chapter, when we look at the new systems of team salary caps and taxes, we shall address the pros and cons of that hands-off union stance.

F. DUTY TO BARGAIN IN GOOD FAITH

Once an employee bargaining agent has been selected, both employer and union come under a statutory duty to bargain collectively with each other. Section 8(d) of the NLRA defines that obligation as follows:

(T)o bargain collectively is ... to meet at reasonable times and confer in good faith with respect to wages, hours, and other terms of employment, ... but such obligation does not compel either party to agree to a proposal or require the making of a concession.

Many volumes of labor law cases and commentary have been written to spell out the meaning and application of the duty to bargain.[1] For our purposes it is sufficient to state that the principal focus of the duty is procedural, rather than substantive. As long as a party does not engage in *surface* bargaining—that is, go through the motions with no real intent to arrive at a settlement—the party is perfectly free to engage in *hard* bargaining—to remain unyielding in its negotiating position, whatever the arguments made by the other side. The statutory policy of free collective bargaining presumes that the ultimate way to break a deadlock at the bargaining table should be through the economic pressure of a strike or a lockout, not through an unfair labor practice charge in which one party tries to persuade the Board that its position is more reasonable than the other side's. As the Supreme Court observed in *NLRB v. Insurance Agents' Int'l Union*, 361 U.S. 477 (1960):

> It must be realized that collective bargaining under a system where the Government does not attempt to control the results of negotiations, cannot be equated with an academic collective search for truth—or even with what might be thought to be the ideal of one. The parties ... still proceed from contrary and to an extent antagonistic viewpoints and concepts of self interest. The system has not reached the ideal of the philosophic notion that perfect understanding among people would lead to perfect agreement among them on values. The presence of economic weapons in reserve, and their actual exercise on occasion by the parties, is part and parcel of the system that the Wagner and Taft–Hartley Acts have recognized.

361 U.S. at 488–89. There is no better illustration of the Court's pessimistic appraisal of peaceful collective bargaining than the sports world's experience with bargaining over free agency and salary caps over the last quarter century.

But while the law has adopted a hands-off attitude to the content of collective bargaining, it has been more interventionist in prescribing standards of behavior in the bargaining process. Perhaps the two most important such doctrines are (i) an obligation of the employer (and, on occasion, the union) to supply all relevant information that is "needed by the bargaining representative for the proper performance of its duties" (see *NLRB v. Acme Industrial Co.*, 385 U.S. 432, 435–36 (1967)),[m] and (ii) the obligation to refrain from unilateral changes in employment conditions under discussion, at least until "impasse" has been reached in bargaining (see *NLRB v. Katz*, 369 U.S. 736, 743, 745 (1962)).[n] The assumption of the Court is that "freezing the status quo ante after a collective agreement has expired promotes industrial peace by fostering a

---

[1]. See Archibald Cox, *The Duty to Bargain in Good Faith*, 71 Harvard L. Rev. 1401 (1958), and Paul C. Weiler, *Striking a New Balance: Freedom of Contract and the Prospects for Union Representation*, 98 Harvard L. Rev. 351 (1984).

[m]. See Leslie K. Shedlin, *Regulation of Disclosure of Economic and Financial Data and the Impact on the American System of Labor–Management Relations*, 41 Ohio State L. J. 441 (1980), and Lee Modjeska, *Guess Who's Coming to the Bargaining Table*, 39 Ohio State L. J. (1978).

[n]. Peter G. Earle, *The Impasse Doctrine*, 66 Chicago–Kent L. Rev. 407 (1988).

noncoercive atmosphere that is conducive to serious negotiations on a new contract" (*Laborers Health & Welfare Trust v. Advanced Lightweight Concrete Co.*, 484 U.S. 539, 544 n. 6 (1988)).

An essential component of each doctrine is whether the issue in dispute comes within the phrase "terms and conditions of employment" under § 8(d), such that the employer must provide information and refrain from unilateral action about it. The inevitable substantive judgments that must be made about the appropriate scope of "mandatory" bargaining *subjects*, if not the legitimate content of bargaining *proposals*, preoccupied the Board and the courts for several decades. The important Supreme Court decision in *First National Maintenance Corp. v. NLRB*, 452 U.S. 666, 673 (1981), held that key management decisions "about the scope and direction of the enterprise" were not mandatory subjects of bargaining, regardless of their direct impact on employee lives.[o] In this respect, the Court majority echoed the sentiment in Justice Stewart's earlier concurring opinion in *Fibreboard Paper Products v. NLRB*, 379 U.S. 203, 223, 226 (1964), that § 8(d) does not detract from the prerogative of private business management under "the traditional principles of free enterprise" to make decisions that "lie at the core of entrepreneurial control." On the other hand, management's prerogative not to bargain about its original *decision*, for example, to close down a facility, does not relieve the employer of its duty to bargain with the union about the *effects* of that action on its employees.

The fact that bargaining about a particular topic is not *mandatory* does not imply that such bargaining is *illegal*. Indeed, purely voluntary negotiation about such *permissive* topics takes place regularly in different bargaining relationships. But the line drawn between mandatory and permissive subjects is significant not only because the employer has no duty to discuss the latter topics (nor to supply information and to remain inactive about them), but also because the union is not entitled to insist—on particular, to the point of a strike—on bargaining about them (see *NLRB v. Wooster Division of Borg-Warner Corp.*, 356 U.S. 342 (1958)).

With this capsule summary of the basic concepts of the duty to bargain in mind, we shall now read applications of the doctrine to two different baseball disputes—with starkly different legal and practical results.

SILVERMAN v. MAJOR LEAGUE BASEBALL PLAYER RELATIONS COMM.

United States District Court, Southern District of New York, 1981.
516 F.Supp. 588.

WERKER, DISTRICT JUDGE.

[Following the arbitrator's ruling in the *Messersmith* grievance, Major League Baseball (MLB) and its Players Association agreed in 1976

---

o. See Michael C. Harper, *Leveling the Road From* Borg-Warner *to* First National Maintenance: *The Scope of Mandatory Bargaining*, 68 Virginia L. Rev. 1447 (1982), and Thomas C. Kohler, *Distinctions without Differences: Effects Bargaining in Light of* First National Maintenance, 5 Ind. Rel. L. J. 402 (1983).

to a four-year labor agreement that gave free agency status to players with six years of big-league service. (Players with between two and six years service had a right to salary arbitration instead.) If a team lost a free agent, it was entitled to receive from the signing club only an amateur draft pick as "compensation." Under this new system, average player salaries rose sharply, from approximately $52,000 in 1976 to $197,000 in 1981.

With the agreement expiring at the end of 1979, the Player Relations Committee (PRC), the clubs' official bargaining arm headed by Ray Grebey, sought to change the compensation system for free agents who met certain specified standards of high performance. The PRC proposed that a team losing such a "premium" or "ranking" free agent would be entitled to select from the roster of the signing team a player who had not been put on the latter team's "protected" list of its top fifteen players (a much more moderate version of the NFL's Rozelle Rule that we read about in the *Mackey* case in Chapter 3).

The Players Association, led by Marvin Miller, objected strongly to the PRC's proposal on the ground that it would deter free agent signings and thus depress overall player salaries. On the eve of the strike in May 1980, the two sides agreed, in effect, to postpone the issue for one year. A joint committee was established to study the issue and report back during the next winter. Absent agreement at that time between the two sides, the owners were left free to implement the new compensation system, and if they did, the players could strike over it during the 1981 season.

There were a number of highly publicized comments made in the winter of 1980–81 by Commissioner Bowie Kuhn and by club owners such as Ted Turner of the Atlanta Braves and Ray Kroc of the San Diego Padres, to the effect that escalating player salaries had caused serious financial problems to the game and even threatened certain clubs with bankruptcy. When Miller formally requested financial data to substantiate this claim, Grebey refused, saying that the owners were seeking expanded compensation for free agents in order to maintain better player balance between the clubs. Rather than have to rely on the vagaries of the amateur draft and minor league prospects, a club losing a free agent would receive a major league player in return. The Players Association then filed a "bargaining in bad faith" charge with the NLRB. The Board found the charge meritorious and sought immediate injunctive relief from a federal district court in New York.]

* * *

The Board alleges in its petition that the public statements by club owners regarding claims of financial difficulties created a reasonable belief on the part of the Players Association that respondents' bargaining position during this second round of negotiations was based, "at least in part, on the present or prospective financial difficulties of certain of Respondents' member clubs." Although Marvin Miller has expressed some doubt as to club owners' inability to pay rising player salaries, he nevertheless takes the position that the Players Association must have the financial information it requests if it is to fulfill its duty of fair representation. If deprived of that information, the Association claims that it must blindly decide whether to press its demands and risk the loss of jobs for its members if the clubs cannot survive under the "compensation" terms proposed by the Association, or to recede from its position and accept the PRC's proposal without verifying owners' claims of financial distress caused by "free agency." Thus, the Association brought an unfair labor practice charge against the PRC for its failure to disclose the requested financial data after the clubs allegedly put into issue their inability to pay.

In *NLRB v. Truitt Manufacturing Co.*, 351 U.S. 149 (1956), the Supreme Court laid to rest the question of whether an employer, bound by the National Labor Relations Act to bargain in good faith, could claim that it was financially unable to pay higher wages and then refuse a union's request to produce financial data to substantiate the claim. Holding that such conduct supported a finding of failure to bargain in good faith, the Court explained:

> Good-faith bargaining necessarily requires that claims made by either bargainer should be honest claims. This is true about an asserted inability to pay an increase in wages. If such an argument is important enough to present in the give and take of bargaining, it is important enough to require some sort of proof of its accuracy.

Id. at 152–53.

However, *Truitt's* progeny have held that an employer is required to disclose its financial condition only when the employer claims an inability to pay, however phrased, during the course of bargaining.

Petitioner admits that at no time during bargaining sessions have respondents made a claim of inability to pay. Nevertheless, petitioner urges the Court to find that public statements made by several club owners as well as the Commissioner of Baseball about the financial condition of the industry are sufficient to support a finding of reasonable cause to believe that respondents have injected the inability to pay into the negotiations.

* * *

Petitioner concedes, as it must, that the Board and courts have never found that an employer has injected financial condition into negotiations, absent statements or conduct by the employer at the bargaining table. Nevertheless, it urges this Court to find, on the basis of statements by Commissioner Kuhn and various owners, that the financial issue has become relevant to the negotiations regarding "compensation" because of the unique nature of collective bargaining in baseball.

Mindful that this Court must be "hospitable" to the views of the Regional Director, however novel, I am nevertheless convinced that the Board's position is wrong, and thus will not "defer to the statutory construction urged by (it)."

It is the PRC Board of Directors which is charged with the exclusive authority to formulate the collective bargaining position of the clubs and to negotiate agreements with the Players Association. Indeed, Grebey, the official spokesman for the PRC in collective bargaining matters, has consistently denied that the clubs' financial status is at issue in the current negotiations.

Commissioner Kuhn's remarks in December 1980 at the convention cannot be imputed to the PRC as a statement of its bargaining position. First, petitioner's attempt to establish an agency relationship between the Commissioner and the PRC is unavailing. As Commissioner of Baseball, Kuhn presides at the regular joint meetings of the Major Leagues, but does not request nor preside at special meetings called by the PRC. Moreover, while Kuhn is responsible for disciplining players who may then file grievances against him in his capacity as Commissioner, he has likewise ordered the clubs to cease certain action when the interests of baseball warranted his intercession, as when he directed the clubs to open their training camps in the spring of 1976.

* * *

In a multi-employer bargaining unit as large and publicly visible as the Major League Baseball Clubs, it is inevitable that extraneous statements will be made by individuals affiliated in some way with the group which are inconsistent with the official position of the unit. This only underscores the necessity, recognized by the PRC, for centralized bargaining responsibility and authority. Clearly, individual expressions of opinion cannot serve to bind the entire bargaining unit in the absence of authority to speak for the group.

Petitioner and the Association strain to emphasize the uniqueness of collective bargaining in the baseball industry to avoid the consequences of the established labor law regarding the inability to pay. However, this Court cannot accept "collective bargaining through the press" as a basis for a 10(j) injunction.

The Act has provided for collective bargaining between the parties through their authorized representatives. If this Court were to find that the several public statements by club officials and the Commissioner were sufficient to support a finding that the PRC and its negotiating team view the respondents' "compensation" proposal as related to the financial condition of the clubs, it would do violence to the intent and purpose of the Act which limits the jurisdiction of this Court.

To accept petitioner's argument would permit disgruntled employers in a multi-employer unit who disagreed with the negotiation policies of their representatives to force negotiation issues into the courts, thereby "conducting labor management relations by way of an injunction," a result clearly contrary to the purpose of the Act. The Players Association and the PRC entered into a valid contract on May 23, 1980. As part of that contract they agreed that if the parties were unable to reach an agreement on the "compensation" issue, the PRC could implement its proposal, thereby triggering one of the Players Association's options, that is, to reopen the agreement on that issue and set a strike deadline of no later than June 1, 1981. This Court will not alter the terms of this contract for which the parties freely bargained by delaying implementation of the proposal and a possible strike on the basis of a tortured reading of the law regarding inability to pay.

Thus, I cannot find that the comments by several club officials and the Commissioner, relied upon by petitioner, are statements of policy on behalf of the PRC which would support a claim of inability to pay.

Moreover, the issue of salary, above a minimum rate, is not a subject of collective bargaining between the Players Association and the PRC. Rather, individual players negotiate independently with the clubs as to their salary. Indeed, it is the high player salaries which have resulted from the negotiation of individual contracts by players and clubs which Commissioner Kuhn addressed in his 1980 speech. Noting that player salaries are increasing at a more rapid rate than revenues, he opined that bargaining of individual contracts has led to this problem. He called upon players and owners to cooperate in this regard to arrest the trend and avoid loss to all, including the fans who will be required to pay higher ticket prices.

* * *

The court is mindful that a strike may result from its denial of petitioner's request for a 10(j) injunction. Indeed, the industry has suffered a strike in the past. Nevertheless, in struggling with a temptation and even compulsion to prevent a strike in the public interest, I am bound by the law. The possibility of a strike, although a fact of life in labor relations, offers no occasion for this Court to distort the principles of law and equity. The resolution of the "compensation" issue is left to the parties through the negotiation process.

PLAY BALL!!!

SO ORDERED.

Contrary to the hopes of the district judge, his decision was quickly followed by a strike that shut baseball down for much of the summer of 1981. The contract dispute was finally settled on the basis that teams losing free agents would receive replacement players drawn from a pool of players left unprotected for this purpose by all teams that had retained the right to sign free agents in that off-season. This compromise arrangement provided some compensation to the team losing a player via free agency, but without directly deterring any team from bidding for that player.

The most notable instance of this compensation system in operation took place in 1984. When the Toronto Blue Jays signed Dennis Lamp, a free agent from the Chicago White Sox, the White Sox selected as compensation Tom Seaver, who had been left unprotected by the New York Mets. The result was that when Seaver, the most illustrious player in Mets' history, won his 300th game in the summer of 1985, he did so while pitching in New York's Yankee Stadium, rather than in Shea Stadium. Even more ironic, Seaver won that game for the White Sox on the eve of yet another baseball strike, in whose settlement the owners scrapped their 1981 innovation and returned to the older model of amateur draft picks payable by the team that won to the team that lost a premium free agent. By this time, baseball owners had become more concerned about the salary arbitration process, for which the association agreed to postpone eligibility for most players until completion of three, rather than just two, years of service.

Silverman was decided favorably for the baseball owners only because the PRC itself had carefully avoided making any claims of financial difficulty during negotiations. It is not uncommon, though, in sports bargaining, for the league to claim financial troubles that may trigger the obligation to provide supporting data. Furthermore, other types of documents that leagues would like to keep confidential may have to be produced for the union. For example, in 1982 the NFLPA won an unfair labor practice claim against the NFL Management Council because the Council refused to produce its television and radio contracts—thereby depriving the union of information it needed to represent the players whose working conditions might be affected by league or club obligations contained in the contracts. Thus, if information is relevant to a bargaining issue, either during collective bargaining or during the administration of an existing agreement, the employer must produce that information if requested by the union.

Questions for Discussion

1. Suppose a players association asks the league for detailed information about team revenues and costs for purposes of bargaining for a fixed percentage share of the gross for the players. Does the league have to supply this data, and if so, in what form? Is it a good idea for sports leagues to disclose their financial situation voluntarily to their players' representatives? (In the summer of 1985, Commissioner Peter Ueberroth overrode the objection of a number of owners and ordered baseball's books opened to the Players Association's auditors and economists.)

The NLRB's Regional Director in New York, Daniel Silverman, returned to the sports pages as well as the labor law reports in the winter of 1995, with yet another novel legal problem of alleged "bad faith bargaining" in baseball. This was a key moment in the protracted labor dispute in baseball, which not only had shut down the great 1994 season, but was seriously endangering the prospects for 1995. (Hockey players and owners had finally ended their three-month lockout with a settlement in January 1995, but basketball was still caught up in the *Williams* antitrust litigation about the NBA's salary cap.) By 1994, average salaries in baseball had reached $1.15 million, up nearly 600% from the $197,000 average in 1981, the year of the first *Silverman* case. From the owners' point of view, this salary spiral was the product of the combination of salary arbitration and veteran free agency that had been created in 1976, preserved in 1981, and only slightly modified in their 1985 and 1990 labor negotiations.

In determining salaries for the 1994 season, baseball players fell into three basic categories. Those in their first three seasons were limited to offers coming from their own team; those with three to six years service could have their final proposal and that of the team assessed by a neutral arbitrator who selected one or the other; those with six or more years of service were entitled to free agency bidding by any major league team. When collective bargaining got underway in June 1994, the owners proposed to eliminate salary arbitration for all players, to permit restricted free agency (with a team right of first refusal) for players with four or five years service, and to maintain unlimited free agency after six years, but constrained by an NFL-style salary cap. While the players were prepared to consider significant changes in the current regime (e.g., substituting full free agency for those now eligible for salary arbitration), they were strongly opposed to the concept of a "hard" salary cap.

The result was that the 1994 season, with the highest game attendance in baseball history, was shut down in mid-August. Once that year's World Series had been lost to the game, the parties returned to the bargaining table with the assistance of a noted mediator, William Usery. By November, the two sides were seriously discussing a salary tax rather than a cap, but with sharply different figures proposed for the tax triggers and percentage rates.

In mid-December, just after the players had made a new proposal that increased their tax numbers, the owners declared that an "impasse" had been reached in bargaining, and implemented their prior position of a salary cap, restricted free agency, and no arbitration for that winter's individual team-player negotiations. The players responded by collectively refusing to sign any new contracts with their teams and filing a failure to bargain charge with the NLRB. (Another aspect of this charge was the fact the owners had decided, after the 1994 All–Star Game had been played, not to follow the long-time practice of paying a portion of the All–Star revenues into the Players Association's pension and disability benefit funds, at least until a new collective agreement was reached.) After investigating the players' charge, the General Counsel of the NLRB made a tentative decision that the owners had violated the NLRA and that a formal complaint should be issued. After their lawyers were informed of that legal prospect, the owners agreed on February 3, 1995, to remove the salary cap and restore the status quo. The General Counsel then held the Board's unfair labor practice proceedings in abeyance.

Just three days later, though, the owners informed the players that there would be no more negotiations between individual teams and players for new contracts. Instead, all player contracts for the upcoming season would have to be worked out between the owners' Player Relations Committee (PRC) and the Players Association. In those negotiations, salary arbitration would not be available to any player, and the prior ban against concerted (i.e., collusive) action by owners or players was revoked. The Association immediately filed new unfair labor practice charges against these three owner moves. President Clinton called both sides to the White House in an unsuccessful effort to secure a settlement, and the parties also spent a great deal of time on Capitol Hill trying to preserve or to roll back baseball's antitrust exemption.

In mid-March, while the teams were conducting spring training with replacement squads (without a single crossover from major league strike rosters), the General Counsel of the NLRB issued a formal complaint against the owners' unilateral elimination of the salary arbitration and anti-collusion employment terms (though not about their transfer of negotiating authority from individual teams to their PRC). Clinton's Chairman, William Gould (on leave from Stanford Law School, where he taught both labor and sports law), and his two Democratic Board colleagues, voted 3–2 to authorize the General Counsel to seek a preliminary injunction in district court barring such ownership action. The owners did not try to defend this unilateral action on the basis that an impasse had been reached on these matters. Instead, the PRC's claim was that these two subjects were *permissive*, not *mandatory*, and thus such employer action was not constrained by the duty to bargain in good faith about them (relying on such Supreme Court precedents as *First National Maintenance, Borg Warner*, and others mentioned earlier in this section). Following is the district court's opinion on this score.

SILVERMAN v. MAJOR LEAGUE BASEBALL PLAYER RELATIONS COMMITTEE

United States District Court, Southern District of New York, 1995.
880 F.Supp. 246.

SOTOMAYOR, DISTRICT JUDGE.

* * *

Collective bargaining in the context of professional sports presents issues different from most other contexts. On the one hand, the talent of an individual athlete can provide him with extraordinary bargaining power, but on the other hand, a player may sell his talent only to a circumscribed group of owners, who have something akin to monopoly power in the sport at issue. These circumstances in professional sports have given rise to the development of the reserve/free agency system, which, perhaps not surprisingly, is quite different from other models of collective bargaining in less specialized and unique industries.

To look for guidance, then, in deciding whether the Board had reasonable cause for making its determination that the provisions changed by the Owners were mandatory, I find most helpful precedent that involves professional sports. Accord, *Wood v. Nat'l Basketball Ass'n*, 809 F.2d 954, 961 (2d Cir.1987) (collective bargaining between athletes and their leagues "raises numerous problems with little or no precedent in standard industrial relations"). And in the sports context, courts have overwhelmingly held that the constituent parts of reserve/free agency systems are mandatory, not permissive, subjects of bargaining.

For example, this Circuit held in *Wood* that the agreement between professional basketball players and team owners "is a unique bundle of compromises," and matters such as salary caps, minimum individual salaries, fringe benefits, minimum aggregate team salaries, guaranteed revenue-sharing, and first refusal provisions are all mandatory subjects of bargaining, as "each of them is intimately related to 'wages, hours, and other terms and conditions of employment.'" Id. at 961–62. Likewise, in *Mackey v. Nat'l Football League*, 543 F.2d 606, 615 (8th Cir.1976), cert. dismissed, 434 U.S. 801 (1977), the Eighth Circuit held that the Rozelle Rule, even though it does not on its face deal with wages, hours, and other terms and conditions of employment, is a mandatory subject of bargaining because it "operates to restrict a player's ability to move from one team to another and depresses player salaries." See also, *Powell v. Nat'l Football League*, 930 F.2d 1293, 1298–99 (8th Cir.1989) (agreements establishing first refusal and compensation system are mandatory subjects).

I recognize that these precedents, which address the question of whether wage topics trump the antitrust laws, do not deal with the issue before me, i.e., the continuation of reserve and free agency systems in which individual owners competitively bid for players after the expiration of a collective bargaining agreement and pending the completion by Player and Owner representatives of negotiations over a successor agreement. The Owners argue that the right to bid competitively or collectively must be a permissive topic of bargaining, because if it were a mandatory topic, the Owners would be forced to give up their statutory right to bargain collectively.

Courts in addressing the antitrust area of law have easily recognized, however, that the essence of collective bargaining in professional sports is the establishment and maintenance of reserve and free agency systems in which owners agree to bid competitively for some players and collectively for others. The Owners' argument has a superficial appeal in its attempt to harken back to the unionizing cry of employees when they banded together to create this nation's labor laws. What the Owners have missed here, and the NLRB has not, is that the statutory right to join collective bargaining units belongs to employees, not to employers.

The NLRA gives only employees the § 7 right to bargain collectively through an elected representative. The only reciprocal statutory right the Act imposes on employers and employees is that they bargain with the other in good faith. In other words, the term "employer union" for collective bargaining purposes is not meaningful.

The extent of statutory protection for an employer is that it may select a representative for the purpose of bargaining free of coercion from a labor union. This right is not a statutory right for a group of employers to bargain collectively through one representative. In fact, while many multi-employer bargaining units, like the PRC, have been formed, the NLRB and the union must consent to the such formation. See, e.g., *NLRB v. Johnson Sheet Metal. Inc.*, 442 F.2d 1056, 1059 (10th Cir.1971) ("the basic test of the appropriateness of a multi-employer bargaining unit is whether it was created with the approval, express or implied, of the parties").

The Owners' attempt to create reciprocal statutory rights to collective bargaining between Unions and Employer groups is simply a wrong presumption from which to start. Hence, any reliance on cases that address prohibitions upon a Union's waiver of its statutory rights to bargain collectively is misguided, as they have no application to an employer's rights or obligations to continue a joint or individual employer bargaining system that has, through arms-length, good faith bargaining, been put into place. As expressed in the Reply Brief of the NLRB, the "valid interest in the selection of [the Owners'] own bargaining representatives ... does not trump employees' § 7 right to have the status quo ante maintained on mandatory bargaining subjects during negotiations." An interest is not a statutory right. It can be waived as the Owners have done here in the Basic Agreement.

Maintaining the reserve/free agency systems in the interim between collective bargaining agreements does not alter the rights of Owners to have the PRC represent them for purposes of negotiating a successor agreement or to continue to oppose the inclusion of the systems in any successor agreement. The Owners can, if they successfully bargain, end the free agency and salary arbitration systems, exclude the anti-collusion provision, and create an entirely new system. What they cannot do is alter particular individual's wages until the system is changed by agreement or until the parties negotiate to impasse. That is the nub of all wage negotiations which are inherently mandatory subjects of bargaining. It must be remembered that many employers are forced to continue sometimes onerous and debilitating wage obligations until the collective bargaining process runs its course, just as many employees may earn less than they would in a system that more closely duplicates the free market. Having freely entered into the free agency and reserve systems in their Basic Agreement, the Owners are bound to that system until they bargain in good faith to an impasse.

In view of the abundant caselaw in the professional sports context that has found that constituent parts of the reserve/free agency system are mandatory subjects of collective bargaining, I find that the Board had substantial reasonable cause to conclude, and a substantial likelihood of success ultimately in establishing, that the unilateral changes made by the Owners to the free agency system before impasse violated the rule against changes to mandatory subjects of bargaining. In summary, the Board has clearly met its injunctive remedy standard in demonstrating that the Owners committed an unfair labor practice by their unilateral abrogation of Article XX(F) and the free agency system.

For substantially similar reasons, I find that salary arbitration for reserve players is also a mandatory part of the collective bargaining process between the Players and the Owners. The Owners argue that their salary arbitration system is indistinguishable from interest arbitration clauses, which are generally classified as permissive subjects of bargaining. Thus, the Owners contend, they have no statutory obligation to preserve salary arbitration until the formation of a new collective bargaining agreement.

The Second Circuit has recognized two basic types of arbitration in the labor context: interest arbitration and rights arbitration. *New York Typographical Union No. 6 v. Printers League Section of the Assoc. of the Graphic Arts*, 919 F.2d 3, 3 n. 2 (2d Cir.1990). Interest arbitration "concerns disputes over terms of new or renewal contracts." Id.; see also *Local 58, Int'l Brotherhood of Electrical Workers v. Southeastern Michigan Chapter, Nat'l Electrical Contractors Ass'n, Inc.*, 43 F.3d 1026, 1030 (6th Cir.1995) (interest arbitrator acts as legislator in fashioning new contractual obligations, rather than as judicial officer who concentrates on construing terms of existing agreement). Rights arbitration, in contrast, is for disputes "over the interpretation or application of a contract." *Printers League*, 919 F.2d at 3 n.2. Because interest arbitration clauses involve "a mechanism for resolving disputes which may arise as to the terms of future contracts," as opposed to existing terms and conditions of employment, they are a non-mandatory topic of bargaining. *Sheet Metal Workers Local Union No. 20 and George Koch Sons, Inc.*, 306 NLRB 834 (1992).

I agree with the Board's conclusion that the salary arbitration clause at issue here is not a traditional interest arbitration clause. The distinction blurred by the Owners' argument is that new future contractual obligations are not being created by the salary arbitrator. By the time a player and owner go to salary arbitration, a UPC, created by the terms of the Basic Agreement, has already been entered into by the parties. The only item missing from the executed contract is a dollar amount. The Owners cannot escape the plain and unambiguous language of Article VI(F)(6), which provides:

> Form of submission: The Player and the Club shall each submit to the arbitrator and exchange with each other in advance of the hearing single salary figures for the coming season (which need not be figures offered during the prior negotiations). At the hearing, the Player and the Club shall deliver to the arbitrator a Uniform

Player's Contract executed in duplicate, complete except for the salary figure to be inserted in paragraph 2. Upon submission of the salary issue to arbitration by either Player or Club, the Player shall be regarded as a signed Player....

Basic Agreement, Article VI(F)(g) (emphasis added); see also id. at Article VI(F)(5) (within 24 hours of hearing arbitrator shall insert salary figure awarded in the duplicate UPC's delivered to him or her). Before the arbitrator rules, there is no question that the player will provide his services to the club for a specified period of time and that the club will pay for those services. The arbitrator's only task is, literally, to fill in the blank where the salary figure goes.

Even if the salary arbitration clause contained in the Basic Agreement is an interest arbitration clause, however, I also agree with the Board's reasoning in *Sea Bay Manor Home for Adults*, 253 NLRB 739 (1980) and *Columbia Univ. in the City of New York*, 298 NLRB 941 (1990) that interest arbitration clauses can survive the expiration of collective bargaining agreements where the clauses

> [are] so intertwined with and inseparable from the mandatory terms and conditions for the contract currently being negotiated as to take on the characteristics of the mandatory subjects themselves.

The essence of the reasoning in *Sea Bay* and *Columbia Univ.* is that in some industries the result of collective bargaining is not to stop talking in the future about a dispute but a recognition that the best continuing process for the parties to establish wages is in arbitration. In these situations, a salary arbitration is a current term of employment. That is the situation in baseball. Salary arbitration is the collectively bargained wage in the parties' Agreement, and the Board's view of it as such is not clearly or otherwise erroneous. For the foregoing reasons, the Board has sustained its burden of proving that the Owners committed unfair labor practices both by eliminating Article XX(F) of the free agency system and the salary arbitration provisions of the Basic Agreement.

* * *

[The court then turned to the question whether an interim injunction was warranted for this NLRB violation. One key value that seemed to require such immediate legal action was the public's interest in more productive and peaceful collective bargaining in baseball.]

... This strike has captivated the public's attention, given the popularity of the sport as well as the protracted nature and well-documented bitterness of the strike. Thus, this strike is about more than just whether the Players and Owners will resolve their differences. It is also about how the principles embodied by federal labor law operate. In a very real and immediate way, this strike has placed the entire concept of collective bargaining on trial. It is critical, therefore, that the Board ensure that the spirit and letter of federal labor law be scrupulously followed. If the Board is unable to enforce the NLRA, public confidence in the collective bargaining process will be permanently and severely undermined.... Issuing the injunction before Opening Day is important to ensure that the symbolic value of that day is not tainted by an unfair labor practice and the NLRB's inability to take effective steps against its perpetuation.

880 F.Supp. at 259.

* * *

[The private interests of players was also a sufficient ground for injunctive relief. In particular, the judge was not persuaded by the owners' argument that monetary damages for lost pay would be sufficient to rectify any losses suffered by affected players. For example, with respect to the obstacles erected to free agent movement,]

... [s]alary is just one factor a free agent considers when seeking and accepting offers. A free agent may wish to join a team because of personal reasons such as family considerations, or because of promises of more playing time. Likewise, a free agent may select a team that pays less money but whose coaching staff and team roster make it a World Series contender.... The protections of the NLRA extend to non-monetary bargaining topics that are "terms and conditions of employment." ... In professional baseball, whether to leave a team, where to go and why are of "deep concern" to the affected players and the loss of those choices in the terms and conditions of employment cannot be adequately recompensed by money.

880 F.Supp. at 259–60.

* * *

[While salary arbitration seemed to be concerned purely with money (as the decision had asserted earlier), the judge believed it would be impossible to reconstruct later what would have been the appropriate arbitration verdicts. One key reason was that the systems of free agency and salary arbitration were "inextricably intertwined," such that illegal alteration of one such feature in the baseball players' market would inevitably change the product of the other.]

Similarly, to the extent the salary arbitration system is intimately intertwined with the choice for both owners and players between free agency or arbitration, it is nearly impossible to reconstruct retrospectively the factors that would have influenced each side's decision at the time of election. Hence, even though it is easier later to reconstruct the actual process of salary arbitration and more precisely determine a lost wage from that process, monetary damages are insufficient to recompense for the harm caused in eliminating the salary arbitration process as a choice in the integrated reserve/free agency systems.

* * *

Thus, a poisoning of the free agency bargaining process will also affect the wage negotiations of reserve and salary arbitration players.

Conversely, the loss of salary arbitration in the reserve system skews the choice of free agency rights. The unusual wage structure in this monopoly industry makes it extraordinarily difficult if not nearly impossible to reconstruct past market conditions for purposes of retroactive damage calculations.

880 F.Supp. at 260–261. [Since monetary damages would be too difficult to ascertain after the fact, injunctive relief was needed before the harm was done.]

Injunction granted.

Judge Sotomayor rendered her decision on Friday, March 31st. Later that fall, the Second Circuit (in an opinion authored by Judge Winter) affirmed the lower court decision on these labor law issues. See *Silverman v. MLBPRC*, 67 F.3d 1054 (2d Cir.1995). In the meantime, the injunction had transformed the situation on the field: this time the two sides did agree to "Play Ball!" The players voted on Saturday to end their strike and return to work, and the owners voted on Sunday to cancel the opening game scheduled for that night with replacements. Instead, the beginning of the regular season was postponed until April 26, and the next three weeks were devoted to signing and training the regular players. There were no further work stoppages during the 1995 and 1996 seasons, and in December 1996, the two sides finally reached a settlement of this three-year labor dispute. We shall learn about the key ingredient of that settlement—a limited salary tax—at the end of this chapter.

Questions for Discussion

1. Do you agree with Judge Sotomayor's judgment that salary arbitration for individual players, as contrasted with interest arbitration for future collective agreements, was a mandatory rather than a permissive subject of bargaining? With her similar judgment about the clubs' and players' earlier undertaking not to act "in concert" in such salary negotiations?

2. The NLRB's General Counsel refused to endorse (i.e., to issue a formal complaint about) the Players Association's charge that the owners had violated the NLRA by unilaterally shifting the authority to conduct such negotiations from individual teams to the Player Relations Committee. Presumably, the General Counsel agreed with the owners that they had a statutory right to bargain collectively with players through a single central body. Is that NLRB position consistent with its judgment (and complaint) that the owners violated the Act by unilaterally removing the bar on concerted salary negotiations by the clubs? Does the fact that the owners have a right to bargain through their PRC to reach a new collective agreement with the MLBPA mean they also have the right to eliminate (before impasse) the existing system of team-player negotiations about individual salaries within the parameters of the prior agreement? And by the way, did the Association have the right to stop all individual player negotia-

tions and signings once the owners imposed the salary cap in December 1994? What if an Association were to take that action even though the clubs had not altered the earlier regime?

3. What are your views about the union's earlier unfair labor practice charge involving the owners instituting their salary cap in December 1994? The Board had reached the informal decision that this action violated the law's requirement that unilateral employer changes in employment conditions can be made only following good faith bargaining to an impasse—i.e., a deadlock—with the union. Was it the lack of good faith or the lack of an impasse that produced that Board judgment (which, recall, the owners and their lawyers did not contest)? Should any significance have been attached to the fact that the owners had held back their contribution to the players' benefit funds for the July 1994 All–Star Game?

4. As a matter of general labor law policy, why is there such a bar on unilateral charges in working conditions until after an impasse has been reached in negotiations (which, as we saw in baseball, can take a long time)? Recall that the NHL owners were entitled to lock out their players (and the MLB owners their umpires) even though these negotiations were still far from an impasse. Should employers be entitled to reduce their employees' pay at work, rather than lock them out without any pay, before a negotiating deadlock has been reached? Or should lockouts (and strikes) also be precluded until impasse?

5. Reflecting on the events from 1994 through 1996, did the baseball owners adopt the most sensible negotiating strategy regarding this contentious salary cap issue? Recall that the owners took eighteen months, from December 1992 to June 1994, to work out their internal differences about this new salary (and revenue-sharing) regime. When negotiations with the players began in mid-June 1994, the owners refused to agree to refrain from the unilateral imposition of a salary cap that winter in return for the players agreeing not to strike during the season. That left the players with the option of striking in mid-August if they wanted meaningful pressure to be felt by the owners (and the players) to compromise in their bargaining positions. Might the owners not have been better advised to take the entire year to explore the salary restraint issues and options with their players, and, if necessary, follow the lead of the NHL owners and lock the players out at the beginning of the 1995 season?

6. Consider finally whether the following range of sports items should be judged to be mandatory subjects for bargaining by owners with players:

    (i) Enlarging the regular schedule or playoffs, adopting interleague or international play, or realigning teams among the leagues and their divisions.

    (ii) Institution (or elimination) of the designated hitter in baseball.

    (iii) Institution (or elimination) of overtime to break ties in hockey or football.

    (iv) Installation of artificial turf in football or baseball parks.

    (v) Hockey's repeal (in 1992) of its rule that players must wear helmets during a game.

(vi) Use of instant replay (here, mandatory bargaining with either the players or the umpires association).

(vii) The league's no-gambling policies.

(viii) Relocation of a team to a new city (for example, the Cleveland Browns to Baltimore), or expansion into new cities (e.g., Phoenix and Tampa Bay in baseball).

(ix) Who the commissioner will be and whether a sitting commissioner can be fired.

G. ECONOMIC CONFLICT IN SPORTS LABOR RELATIONS[p]

We observed earlier that, under our national labor law, the principal means for breaking deadlocks at the bargaining table are supposed to be the economic pressures of a work stoppage, not the legal pressures of an unfair labor practice charge. Section 7 of the original NLRA protected the employees' right "to engage in concerted activities for the purpose of collective bargaining"—that is, to strike. After thirty years of doctrinal evolution, the Supreme Court read the Act as affording employers a reciprocal economic weapon—a lockout of their employees to force the union to compromise at the bargaining table (see *American Ship Building Co. v. NLRB*, 380 U.S. 300 (1965)). From the fans' perspective, both leagues and players associations have been only too ready to exercise these prerogatives in their periodic negotiations.

While each side enjoys the legal right to stop work and thereby try to alter the balance of power in negotiations, the other side does not have to sit back and absorb the economic punishment. In particular, ever since the crucial Supreme Court decision in *NLRB v. Mackay Radio and Telegraph*, 304 U.S. 333 (1938), employers have been told that they are free to continue operating during a strike (if they can), to hire replacements for this purpose, and even to give these replacements priority over the strikers in the jobs available when the strike ends. Interestingly, the issue of "permanent" status for replacements has tended to dominate in popular and political debates about the strike issue over the last decade (in labor disputes ranging from the federal air traffic controllers in the early 1980s to the Detroit Newspapers in the mid–1990s). However, the NFL battle in 1987 shows that the employer's principal weapon is simply the power to recruit and use replacements without any guarantees of job security. And an employer can hire *temporary* replacements even when it is the *employer* that initiates the work stoppage through a lockout. See *Local 825 International Union of Operating Engineers v. NLRB (Harter Equipment)*, 829 F.2d 458 (3d Cir.1987).

Under current federal law, then, both employers and unions have wide leeway to do whatever they can economically to secure a contract settlement on their preferred terms. At some outer point, though, the

---

p. See generally, Weiler, *Striking a New Balance*, note l above, and Weiler, *Governing the Workplace*, note d above, in particular, Chapter 6.

law draws a boundary line between legitimate weapons of self-defense and impermissible forms of retaliation against the exercise of the statutory right. An interesting exploration of where that line should be located is this decision by the NLRB in yet another legal exhibit from the troubled bargaining relationship in football in the 1980s.

NFL MANAGEMENT COUNCIL AND NFLPA

National Labor Relations Board, 1992.
309 N.L.R.B. 78.

[After its experience with the lengthy players' strike in 1982, the NFL Management Council (NFLMC) decided that if the NFLPA went on strike during the 1987 contract negotiations, the league would continue its regular schedule using replacement players. The Council Executive Committee (CEC) and its Executive Director, Jack Donlan, asked CEC official (and former NFL quarterback) Eddie LeBaron, to coordinate this effort, under which the clubs would rely mainly on players who were at their training camps in August that year but who had failed to make the regular roster. The NFL players did go on strike after the third game of the 1987 season. After cancelling the next week's games, the NFL clubs were able to present replacement games in each of the next two weeks. The fact that these games were being played induced a considerable number of striking players to cross their union teammates' line and go back on the football field for pay. The pressures thereby felt by the general union membership forced the Association to call off the strike and send all the players back to work on Thursday, October 15th. (At that time the Association announced that it would use the legal rather than the strike route, via litigation that produced the *Powell-McNeil* verdicts and *White* settlement we read about in Chapter 3.) However, pursuant to the league's labor policy, all the clubs refused to use any of their striking veterans for that weekend's games, because these players had not reported by 1:00 p.m. on Wednesday. At that same time, the clubs were using replacement players who signed as late as 4:00 p.m. on Saturday, October 17th for that Sunday's games (or by 4:00 p.m. Monday for the Monday night game). The NFLPA then filed unfair labor charges with the NLRB on the ground that this NFL policy discriminated against those players who had exercised their statutory right to strike, and thus deprived strikers of one-sixteenth of their annual salaries for the sixteen-game season.]

* * *

The Supreme Court has recognized that "there are some practices which are inherently so prejudicial to union interests and so devoid of significant economic justification . . . that the employer's conduct carries with it an inference of unlawful intent so compelling that it is justifiable to disbelieve the employer's protestations of innocent purpose." *American Ship Building Co. v. NLRB*, 380 U.S. 300 (1965). If an employer's conduct falls within this category, "the Board can find an unfair labor practice even if the employer introduces evidence that the conduct was motivated by business considerations." *NLRB v. Great Dane Trailers*, 388 U.S. 26, 34 (1967).

On the other hand, if the impact on employee rights of the discriminatory conduct is:

> comparatively slight, an antiunion motivation must be proved to sustain the charge if the employer has come forward with evidence of legitimate and substantial business justifications for the conduct. Thus, in either situation, once it has been proved that the employer engaged in discriminatory conduct which could have adversely affected employee rights to some extent, the burden is upon the employer to establish that it was motivated by legitimate objectives since proof of motivation is most accessible to him.

Id. at 34.

Applying these principles to this case, we find as an initial matter that the Wednesday deadline rule clearly constitutes discriminatory conduct which adversely affects employee rights. On its face, the rule discriminates against strikers by applying different, and more stringent, standards for eligibility to participate in NFL games (and to be paid for such participation). Moreover, the rule also adversely affects one of the most significant rights protected by the Act—the right to strike. The Board and the courts, applying the principles of *Great Dane*, have long recognized that the right to strike includes the right to full and complete reinstatement upon unconditional application to return. *NLRB v. Fleetwood Trailer Co.*, 389 U.S. 375, 380–381 (1967); see also *Laidlaw Corp.*, 171 NLRB 1366, 1368–1369 (1968), enf. 414 F.2d 99 (7th Cir.1969), cert. denied 397 U.S. 920 (1970).

As in *Laidlaw*, the Respondents—in reliance on their Wednesday reporting deadline—offered the striking employees who reported for work on October 15 "less than the rights accorded by full reinstatement" (i.e., the right to participate in the games scheduled for October 18–19 and to be paid for those games). Thus, the Wednesday deadline adversely affected the striking employees in the exercise of their right to strike or to cease participating in the strike, by prohibiting the full and complete reinstatement, for the October 18–19 games, of those employees who chose to return to work after the Respondents' deadline had passed.

* * *

The Respondents assert that the Wednesday deadline was justified by the Clubs' need for sufficient time to prepare returning players for game conditions. In this regard, the Respondents presented evidence that the strikers' physical condition would be expected to deteriorate as the strike progressed. In addition, NFL Management Council official Eddie LeBaron testified that players could not maintain their "football condition" without participating in practices involving physical contact. The Respondents also assert that they particularly did not wish to risk injuries to so-called franchise players.

The Respondents also assert that the rule is justified by their goal of ensuring that each Club operates from the same competitive position. Thus, the Wednesday deadline would give each Club the same amount of preparation time with returning players, prevent situations in which a replacement squad was "mismatched" against a squad composed of veterans who had reported late in the week, and ensure that Clubs could prepare for specific players during the Wednesday and Thursday practices when game plans were typically practiced.

Finally, the Respondents assert that the Wednesday deadline was justified in light of substantial administrative difficulties allegedly posed if strikers returned at a late date in the week....

In evaluating the Respondents' justifications, we initially note the unprecedented nature of the Wednesday deadline and the absence of any evidence that the Respondents have imposed a deadline of this type on employees outside of a strike setting. In particular, the record shows that players who withheld their services in pursuit of individual goals (i.e., players holding out for a more lucrative contract) are not subject to comparable restraints on their status on their return. Rather, such players are eligible to play immediately so long as they are included in the Club's active roster. If the Club determines that the player is not in shape to play, he may be placed on an Exempt list, as noted above. However, there is no automatic disqualification from participation in NFL games, or from being paid for a game while on the Exempt list, as was the case with the striking employees in 1987. This is so whether or not the individual is considered a "franchise player." Likewise, after the 1982 strike, players were immediately restored to their prestrike status—including players who did not report or practice until the Thursday prior to the next weekend's games....

It is undisputed that the Wednesday deadline was only applicable to striking players. The Respondents could and did sign nonstrikers to contracts subsequent to the date the strikers were declared ineligible; the nonstrikers were eligible to play in and were paid for the October 18–19 games....

Under these circumstances, we find that the Respondents have not established legitimate and substantial justifications for the deadline rule. While it may be true that some striking employees' physical conditioning declined during the strike, the same considerations were present in the case of holdouts and of replacement players. Likewise, safety concerns did not preclude the immediate reinstatement of the striking players in 1982, even though they had been out for 57 days, while the 1987 strike lasted only 25 days....

We also find that the Respondents' asserted competitiveness concerns are unpersuasive. Although the Respondents were entitled to ensure that all clubs operated under the same rules, adopting a deadline which discriminated against strikers was unnecessary to the achievement of this goal. The Respondents' argument that Clubs needed the practice time provided by the Wednesday deadline to prepare the strikers to play (and, for the purpose of those practices, needed to know who would be playing for its opponent) is contradicted by their willingness to allow nonstrikers with substantially less preparation time to play in those games. Moreover, the Respondents' claim that late-returning strikers would have a disproportionate impact on the game unless Clubs had an opportunity to prepare their players to face them would seem to contradict their prior claim that these same players were so out of shape that it would be unsafe to play them. Again, in the case of returning holdouts, replacement players, and the players returning from the 1982 strike, competitiveness concerns did not dictate the imposition of an eligibility deadline like the Wednesday deadline at issue here. We find that such concerns did not justify that deadline in 1987 either.

In addition, we find that the logistical and administrative burden of reinstating the strikers does not justify the rule either. In this regard, the Respondents' arguments are premised entirely on the burden of reinstating the entire 1100 player complement, even though the rule on its face would apply to a single striker who elected to return to work. The Respondents provide no justification for the application of the rule in these circumstances.[24] We also note that the Respondents maintained a substantial complement of replacement players well after the strikers had been fully reinstated. Accordingly, we find that any administrative burden associated with maintaining two separate squads for the games on October 18–19 is not a legitimate and substantial justification for the Wednesday deadline.

* * *

Complaint upheld.

The NLRB directed NFL teams to compensate each striking player for the salary lost (plus interest) as a result of this unfair labor practice—estimated to total $30 million for 1,100 players. In that same first week in October 1992, a jury in the *Brown* antitrust suit found the NFL liable for $30 million in damages for having imposed the $1,000-a-week cap on salaries payable to 235 development squad players. Just a few months earlier, the NFL had lost its final appeal of another $30 million judgment for disputed contributions (and interest) payable to the

---

24. Indeed, we note that the deadline rule was anomalous in other respects as well. Thus, as the judge noted, it was applied to preclude even specialty players such as kickers from participation in the games, notwithstanding the lack of any evidence that the Respondents' asserted justifications applied in their case. Likewise, the rule was applied to players on injured reserve throughout the strike even though those players would not have been eligible in any event and the only effect of the Wednesday deadline was to prevent them from receiving compensation to which they would otherwise have been entitled as injured players. The Wednesday deadline was also applied to players whose next scheduled game was on Monday, October 19 even though they had as much time to prepare for a Sunday game. The Respondents admit that safety or logistical reasons could not justify the application of the rule to these individuals.

players' pension fund. See *Bidwill v. Garvey*, 943 F.2d 498 (4th Cir. 1991). As part of the *White* class action settlement, in January 1993, of the broader free agency-salary cap issues, the NFL agreed to pay the players the bulk of the sums awarded by the Board and the jury in the *NFLMC* and *Bidwill* cases respectively. Because no such compromise was forthcoming in *Brown*, that case eventually made its way to the Supreme Court, with the consequences we read about in Chapter 3.

Questions for Discussion

1. In the portion of the *NFL Management Council* decision excerpted above, the Board ruled that players who were on the active roster when the strike began were entitled to be paid for the "deadline games" played after the strike ended, despite the League's contention that they would not be ready to play that weekend. Therefore, players who were on "injured reserve" when the strike began and ended—and who were paid their normal salaries before the strike—were even more clearly entitled to payment for the "deadline games," since there was no issue about their readiness to play. But should these players also have been entitled to be paid for games cancelled or played during the strike? Does the answer to this question depend on whether injured reserve players were also on strike? If so, how would you determine whether an injured player was on strike? If you were an association official, would you encourage injured players to "report" for work during a strike or to maintain "solidarity" with the striking players?

2. Consider the broader industrial relations factors that influence the protagonists in deciding how to exercise their statutory rights in a sports labor dispute.

(i) Why did the baseball players choose to strike in August 1994, and the hockey owners choose to lock out in October 1995, while both sides in basketball chose to use legal rather than self-help bargaining weapons during that same time frame?

(ii) Why were replacement players used during the 1987 football strike, not used in the 1994 hockey lockout, but planned for baseball in the spring of 1995?

(iii) Why is it that football stars like Tony Dorsett, Joe Montana, and Laurence Taylor chose to cross the line to play in replacement games in October 1987, but baseball stars like Ken Griffey, Jr., Frank Thomas, and Greg Maddux made it clear they would not do that in April 1995? (Indeed, Cal Ripken announced that he would give up his chance to break Lou Gehrig's historic consecutive games streak, rather than break his commitment to his Association teammates.) And why have basketball players, unlike hockey players, never been prepared to go on strike or face a lockout since their union was first formed?

Are the explanations to be found in the structures or the cultures of the respective sports?

3. Some labor specialists criticized the NFLPA in 1987 for not having utilized the most potent economic weapons at the Association's disposal. Can you think of any strategy a players' union could follow in orchestrating a

work stoppage on the field that might be more effective in pressuring owners to make concessions at the table?

4. Why did the MLB Players Association make it an absolute condition to settling their three-year dispute with baseball owners that the latter had to agree to count as player "service time" the period lost because of the strike late in the 1994 season and early in 1995? Is there a fundamental difference between earning pay during a strike (which the players union did not insist upon) and earning service credit for eligibility for salary arbitration and free agency?

Baseball has experienced yet another difference from football in its life under labor law. This is due to the fact that, unlike the NFL (but like the NHL and now the NBA), Major League Baseball is a North American league with franchises in Toronto and Montreal. The fact that a league does most of its business in the United States does not insulate it from Canadian law governing that part of its operations (just as U.S. law governs Japanese auto manufacturers for their American operations). As was noted earlier, Canadian labor law is largely within the legislative authority of the provinces such as Ontario and Quebec. Unlike the constitutional situation in the United States, the fact that a manufacturer may have plants in different provinces does not put its labor relations within the federal government's authority. So far, no one has argued to the Canadian courts that sports are constitutionally distinctive because of the peculiarly integrated quality of league cooperation and competition.

The major practical significance of this constitutional situation is that the labor laws of several provinces (though not yet the Canada Labor Code) bar use of *temporary*, not just *permanent*, replacements in legal strikes and lockouts. That is why the Toronto Blue Jays (whose home is in Ontario) could not have used replacements for their striking players in games played in the SkyDome. (Apparently, this part of Quebec's labor law applies only to unions that have been formally certified by their provincial labor board, something that the MLB Players Association has never sought: thus the Montreal Expos would have been permitted to use replacements in their home games.) As events transpired following the *Silverman* ruling in the spring of 1995, Ontario's replacement ban never did figure directly in the League's bargaining dispute and eventual settlement with the players association.

The Ontario law did, however, come into play at the end of April, because the owners had begun their season with replacements for the umpires they had locked out that winter. Thus, the Umpires Association filed an unfair labor practice complaint with the Ontario Labor Board. This complaint posed the intriguing legal questions whether the umpires were employed just by the American League (based in New York) and not jointly by the Blue Jays, and even if so, whether Ontario law barred use of replacements for U.S. employees to perform their regular duties in

Ontario. (The flip side of that issue was whether the Blue Jays could legally use replacements for the regular players they employed in Ontario to play games outside Ontario, as the Jays did during spring training in Florida.) A panel of the Ontario Board delivered an expedited ruling in favor of the Umpires Association, and barred future use of replacements in the SkyDome. However, the issue was rendered moot by settlement of the bargaining dispute just a few days later. (Indeed, several months later a new Ontario government removed that province's temporary replacement ban, though this remains the law in Quebec and British Columbia.) This issue of Canadian labor law is important for the future of North American industrial relations in professional baseball, hockey, and basketball. Meanwhile, the sports setting does raise some of the broader policy questions for labor law on both sides of the U.S.-Canadian border.

Questions For Discussion

1. In the United States, whose labor law continues to permit permanent replacements, the principal argument is that employers need the permanent replacement option to be able to recruit workers to keep operating during a strike, and thence maintain a fair balance of bargaining power in their labor disputes. In Canada, the argument in favor of banning even temporary replacements is that blocking the employer from continuing to operate while legally striking (or locked-out) employees are out of work is necessary to maintain a fair balance of bargaining power in the same disputes. How would you appraise those competing positions about the role of law in labor disputes, based on your observations about the effort to use replacements in baseball (and their actual use in football during the 1987 NFL strike)?

2. Employees not only have a legal right to strike, they also have a right *not* to strike, free of retaliation from their union. Does the latter legal rule preclude various expressions of personal displeasure by members of sports (and other labor) unions against their replacements, during and after the strike?

3. A similar issue can confront owners involved in multi-employer bargaining disputes. In baseball, for example, Peter Angelos decided not to allow his Baltimore Orioles to play games with replacements, partly because of his concern for Cal Ripken's historic pursuit of Lou Gehrig's record for consecutive games played. Suggestions were made that Angelos and the Orioles might be penalized—indeed, might have the franchise put into trusteeship—for violating the decision made by the rest of the owners. Under the current NLRA, which grants affirmative rights just to employees, not employers (or unions), it is unlikely that such league reprisals against owner-employers would be deemed illegal under labor law, as are union reprisals against player-employees who cross their teammates' picket lines. Is it players or owners who benefit the most from such disparate protection of dissidents in labor-management conflicts?

4. In the spring of 1995, both the City of Baltimore and the State of Maryland enacted legislation that barred use of replacement players in Camden Yards (in order to head off any overruling of Angelos' policy by his

fellow baseball owners). A number of Supreme Court decisions have made it clear that the employer's rights to use replacements under federal labor law preempts any state laws to the contrary. (See, e.g., *Golden State Transit Corp. v. City of Los Angeles*, 475 U.S. 608 (1986).) The Maryland legislators said, though, that they were acting not in a regulatory, but in a proprietary, capacity to protect the state's and city's investment in its Camden Yards stadium. Do you believe this distinction should make a difference in legal result? Suppose, alternatively, that a city like San Francisco takes the position that the use of replacements by the Giants violates the terms of its lease for the public stadium (originally Candlestick, now 3–Com Park), a lease that requires the club "to field a team of major league baseball players in accordance with major league rules." Is that state action constitutionally permitted?

5. What were the obligations of teams to their season ticket-holders, broadcast stations, and concessionaires with whom teams had contracted to deliver major league baseball? Are the owners permitted to deem any games played in their facilities to be "major league," whatever the quality of replacement players (or umpires)?

H. ADMINISTRATION OF THE LABOR AGREEMENT[r]

However acrimonious the bargaining struggle and work stoppage, eventually labor disputes are settled and contracts signed. The collective agreement almost invariably contains promises by the union not to strike, and by the employer not to lock out, during the contract's term. Because the interest in labor peace is so intense in the sports world, labor agreements here tend to run for four or five years, rather than the two-year or three-year norm in other industries.

During the life of any agreement, especially one that lasts five years, a host of problems inevitably arise—for example, disputes about player discipline or the proper interpretation of contract language (including language in the standard player contract that is incorporated by reference in the collective agreement). While the parties are able to resolve most of these disputes through direct discussions, some differences are not easily reconciled. Having waived their statutory right to strike as a means of breaking the deadlock, employees instead must rely on a system of final and binding arbitration by a neutral person selected by both sides. Baseball's major league umpires discovered that feature of labor law when a federal judge enjoined their threatened strike during the 1996 playoffs between the New York Yankees and the Baltimore Orioles, when the Orioles decided to play Roberto Alomar notwithstanding his having spit in the face of umpire John Hirschbeck just a few days earlier.

---

[r]. See David B. Feller, *A General Theory of the Collective Bargaining Agreement*, 61 California L. Rev. 663 (1973); Theodore St. Antoine, *Judicial Review of Labor Arbitration Awards*, 75 Michigan L. Rev. 1137 (1977); and William B. Gould, *Judicial Review of Labor Arbitration Awards: The Aftermath of* AT&T *and* Misco, 64 Notre Dame L. Rev. 464 (1989).

This development presented a further challenge to labor law: what should be the judicial approach to this institution of grievance arbitration? In its celebrated *Steelworkers Trilogy*, 363 U.S. 564 (1960), the Supreme Court told lower courts in no uncertain terms that they must defer to the parties' choice of this alternative dispute resolution procedure. Therefore, when one side seeks to compel the other to arbitrate a claim (a grievance) under the agreement, the court should—irrespective of its views of the contractual merits of the claim—strongly presume the matter to be arbitrable unless the contract language creating the grievance procedure makes it unmistakable that no such claim of this type was meant to be arbitrated. Likewise, to protect the integrity of the arbitration process, a court may issue injunctions to preserve the status quo pending the outcome of an arbitration. Finally, once the arbitrator has rendered a decision, the court must enforce the decision, whatever its views about the merits of the case, as long as the award appears "to draw its essence from the collective bargaining agreement." The Supreme Court's rationale was that:

> It is the arbitrator's construction which was bargained for, and so far as the arbitrator's decision concerns construction of the contract, the courts have no business overruling him because their interpretation of the contract is different from his.

In the sports context, these principles have been applied on several occasions. See, e.g., *Davis v. Pro Basketball, Inc.*, 381 F.Supp. 1 (S.D.N.Y. 1974), and *Erving v. Virginia Squires Basketball Club*, 349 F.Supp. 716 (E.D.N.Y.1972). However, the most vivid illustration of this judicial hands-off attitude toward arbitration awards—an attitude the Supreme Court emphatically restated in *United Paperworkers Int'l Union v. Misco Inc.*, 484 U.S. 29 (1987)—occurred when Major League Baseball sought judicial reversal of the *Messersmith* decision by Arbitrator Seitz that we read at the start of this chapter, which interpreted the baseball agreement to allow player free agency after a single option year, thus ending baseball's traditional lifetime reserve system. In the following case, the Kansas City Royals, representing Major League Baseball, appealed a federal district court decision upholding Arbitrator Seitz's ruling.

KANSAS CITY ROYALS v. MAJOR LEAGUE BASEBALL PLAYERS ASS'N

United States Court of Appeals, Eighth Circuit, 1976.
532 F.2d 615.

HEANEY, CIRCUIT JUDGE.

[The Players Association and the Owners had entered into two collective bargaining agreements (prior to the 1973 agreement at issue in the *Messersmith* arbitration) that dealt with the arbitrability of the reserve system. The 1968 Basic Agreement established the arbitration procedure for grievances, designated the Commissioner as arbitrator, and specifically excluded two types of disputes (neither relating to the reserve system) from arbitration. With respect to the reserve system, the agreement provided that:

> The parties shall review jointly ... possible alternatives to the reserve clause as now constituted....
>
> The joint review of the reserve clause shall be completed prior to the termination date of this Agreement....
>
> [I]t is mutually agreed that the Clubs shall not be obligated to bargain or seek agreement with the Players Association on [the reserve clause] during the term of this Agreement.

The 1970 Basic Agreement replaced the Commissioner as arbitrator with an independent three-judge panel (such as the one used in *Messer-Smith*), and added two more specific exclusions from arbitration (again neither involved the reserve system). During the negotiations of this agreement, Curt Flood filed a suit (ultimately decided in the Supreme Court opinion discussed in Chapter 2) challenging the reserve system under federal antitrust laws. In the face of this pending litigation, and unable to reach agreement on modifications to the reserve system, the parties inserted the following provision in Article XIV of the Basic Agreement:

> Regardless of any provision herein to the contrary, this Agreement does not deal with the reserve system. The parties have differing views as to the legality and as to the merits of such system as presently constituted. This Agreement shall in no way prejudice the position or legal rights of the Parties or of any Player regarding the reserve system.
>
> It is agreed that until the final and unappealable adjudication (or voluntary discontinuance) of *Flood v. Kuhn* now pending in the federal district court of the Southern District of New York, neither of the Parties will resort to any form of concerted action with respect to the issue of the reserve system, and there shall be no obligation to negotiate with respect to the reserve system. Upon the final and unappealable adjudication (or voluntary discontinuance) of *Flood v. Kuhn* either Party shall have the right to reopen the negotiations on the issue of the reserve system....

A lawyer for the National League claimed that Players Association leader Marvin Miller said during the negotiations that the reserve system "is going to be outside the Agreement. It will not be subject to the Agreement, but we will acquiesce in the continuance of the enforcement of the rules as house rules and we will not grieve over those house rules." Miller denied making the statement.

During the term of the 1970 agreement, players filed grievances involving one or more of the provisions that comprise the reserve system. The owners did not challenge the arbitrator's jurisdiction to rule on these grievances because they felt that the grievances did not concern the "core" or "heart" of the reserve system.

During the negotiations of the 1973 Basic Agreement, the parties agreed to two modifications of the reserve system: the "five-and-ten" rule (a player with ten years of big-league experience, the last five years with the same team, could veto a trade to any other team), and, much more significantly, the arbitration of salary disputes. However, the parties failed to reach agreement on other modifications to the reserve system proposed by the Players Association. Therefore, Article XIV of the 1970 agreement became Article XV of the 1973 agreement, except that the reference to the *Flood* litigation was removed and the phrase "except as adjusted or modified hereby"—which both parties recognized to be ambiguous—was inserted before "this Agreement does not deal with the reserve system." (The owners wanted some recognition of the agreed-upon changes in the reserve system as a safeguard against Miller's efforts to get Congress to repeal baseball's antitrust exemption, which had been upheld by the Supreme Court in the *Flood* case.) In addition, the owners agreed in a letter to Miller that "[n]otwithstanding [Article XV], it is hereby understood and agreed that the Clubs will not during the term of the Agreement make any unilateral changes in the Reserve System which would affect player obligations or benefits."]

* * *

IV

We cannot say, on the basis of the evidence discussed above, that the record evinces the most forceful evidence of a purpose to exclude the grievances here involved from arbitration.

(a) The 1968 agreement clearly permitted the arbitration of grievances relating to the reserve system. It, therefore, cannot be said that the Club Owners never consented to the arbitration of such grievances. The Club Owners might have argued that they agreed to arbitrate such grievances because the Commissioner of Baseball was designated as the arbitrator, and that he, recognizing the importance of the reserve system to baseball, would interpret the disputed provisions to allow perpetual control by a Club Owner over its players. That argument, however, was not advanced before either the arbitration panel, the District Court or this Court. Moreover, the argument would not be particularly flattering to any Commissioner of Baseball.[19]

(b) Article XIV, the predecessor to Article XV, was suggested by the Players Association for rather specific purposes and the Club Owners clearly did what they could to preserve their right to argue that the reserve system remained a part of the collective bargaining agreement. Indeed, if the Club Owners' counterproposals with respect to Article XIV

---

19. Mr. Bowie Kuhn, the present Commissioner of Baseball, testified, in substance, that he felt that Article X of the 1973 agreement gave him the power to withdraw a grievance from arbitration if he felt that the grievance involved the "preservation of the integrity of, or the maintenance of public confidence in, the game of baseball." He testified further that he did not withdraw these grievances from arbitration because he didn't want to do anything to adversely affect the collective bargaining process: he respected the reputation of Mr. Seitz, the impartial arbitrator, and he respected the arbitration process.

had been accepted, the reserve system would clearly have remained subject to arbitration.

Article XV was clearly designed to accomplish the same purposes as Article XIV. If in accomplishing these purposes the players had clearly agreed to exclude disputes arising out of the operation of the reserve system from arbitration, the Messersmith–McNally grievances would not be arbitrable. For the reasons discussed in this opinion, however, no such agreement can be found.

(c) From 1970 to 1973, a number of grievances concerning the reserve system were submitted to arbitration. The Club Owners raised no jurisdictional objections. While this fact alone is not of controlling significance, because the grievances submitted did not go to what the Club Owners regard as the "core" or "heart" of the reserve system, the submission of grievances relating to the reserve system is certainly a fact that detracts from the Club Owners' contention that the parties clearly understood Article XIV to mean that grievances relating to the reserve system would not be subject to arbitration.

(d) The fact that Marvin Miller may have given assurances, during the 1970 negotiations, that the players would not grieve over house rules cannot be viewed as the most forceful evidence of a purpose to exclude the Messersmith–McNally grievances from arbitration. First, there is some dispute in the record as to whether Miller made such a statement. Second, assuming he did, the term "house rules" is ambiguous. Third, and we think most important, the weight of the evidence, when viewed as a whole, does not support the conclusion that Article XV was intended to preclude arbitration of any grievances otherwise arbitrable.

(e) The essence of the Club Owners' arguments on the question of arbitrability was perhaps best articulated in the testimony of Larry McPhail, President of the American League, in which he stated: "Isn't it fair to say that our strong feelings on the importance of the core of the reserve system would indicate that we wouldn't permit the reserve system to be within the jurisdiction of the arbitration procedure?" The weaknesses in this argument have been previously discussed in paragraphs (a), (b) and (c) above. We add only that what a reasonable party might be expected to do cannot take precedence over what the parties actually provided for in their collective bargaining agreement.

V

The Club Owners contend that even if the arbitration panel had jurisdiction, the award must be vacated. They argue that the award exceeded the scope of the panel's authority by "fundamentally altering and destroying the Reserve System as it historically existed and had been acquiesced in by the Association."

As we have previously noted, our review of the merits of an arbitration panel's award is limited. The award must be sustained so long as it "draws its essence from the collective bargaining agreement."

United Steelworkers of America v. Enterprise Wheel & Car Corp., 363 U.S. 593, 597 (1960).

The nub of the Club Owners' argument is that both they and the Players Association understood the reserve system to enable a club to perpetually control a player, that this understanding was reflected in the 1973 agreement, and that the arbitration panel was without authority to alter the agreed-upon operation of the reserve system.

We cannot agree that the 1973 collective bargaining agreement embodied an understanding by the parties that the reserve system enabled a club to perpetually control a player. First, the agreement contained no express provision to that effect. Second, while there is evidence that the reserve system operated in such a manner in recent years,[21] the record discloses that various Players Association representatives viewed the system as allowing a player to become a free agent by playing under a renewed contract for one year.

Moreover, it can be argued that the arbitration panel's award did not "alter" the reserve system. To the extent that the reserve system did enable a club to perpetually control a player, it was not necessarily by virtue of successive invocations of the renewal clause, or application of the reserve list and no-tampering rules in the absence of a contractual obligation. Other provisions operate to deter a player from "playing out his option," as is evidenced by the fact that few players have done so. On this basis, it may be said that the arbitration panel's decision did not change the reserve system, but merely interpreted various elements thereof under circumstances which had not previously arisen.

The 1973 agreement empowered the arbitration panel to "interpret, apply or determine compliance with the provisions of agreements" between the players and the clubs. We find that the arbitration panel did nothing more than to interpret certain provisions of the Uniform Player's Contract and the Major League Rules. We cannot say that those provisions are not susceptible of the construction given them by the panel. Accordingly, the award must be sustained.

Conclusion

We hold that the arbitration panel had jurisdiction to hear and decide the Messersmith–McNally grievances, that the panel's award drew its essence from the collective bargaining agreement, and that the relief fashioned by the District Court was appropriate. Accordingly, the award of the arbitration panel must be sustained, and the District Court's judgment affirmed. In so holding, we intimate no views on the merits of the reserve system. We note, however, that Club Owners and the Players Association's representatives agree that some form of a reserve system is needed if the integrity of the game is to be preserved and if public confidence in baseball is to be maintained. The disagree-

---

21. In *Flood v. Kuhn*, both the majority opinion and Mr. Justice Marshall's dissent viewed the reserve system as involving perpetual player control, although that issue was not squarely before the Court.

ment lies over the degree of control necessary if these goals are to be achieved. Certainly, the parties are in a better position to negotiate their differences than to have them decided in a series of arbitrations and court decisions. We commend them to that process and suggest that the time for obfuscation has passed and that the time for plain talk and clear language has arrived. Baseball fans everywhere expect nothing less.

* * *

Appeal dismissed.

Questions for Discussion

1. Having read the contractual and historical materials in both the arbitral and judicial opinions, what do you think was the proper construction of baseball's collective agreement as it relates to the reserve system? To what extent are your views influenced by your sentiments about the equities of the issue? If you feel that Arbitrator Seitz's reading may have been somewhat dubious, does this affect your evaluation of the *Steelworker Trilogy's* hands-off approach to arbitral construction of labor agreements, an approach that is quite different from judicial sentiment towards an administrative agency's (such as the NLRB's) construction of a statute?

2. Recall that the parties mutually select their arbitrator and that either party can terminate the appointment if displeased with any one ruling. Such dismissal befell Tom Roberts, the baseball arbitrator in 1986, following his decision (mentioned in Chapter 1) striking down the drug-testing covenants in individual player contracts. The same fate overtook Peter Seitz following his *Messersmith* decision. Of even greater interest, though, is the fact that the baseball owners almost dismissed Seitz *before* the *Messersmith* hearing because of Seitz' decision in the Jim "Catfish" Hunter case. Indeed, Commissioner Bowie Kuhn, in his autobiography, *Hardball*, relates that the owners rejected Kuhn's recommendation that Seitz be replaced. The Player Relations Committee felt that Seitz, having ruled for the Players Association in *Hunter*, would likely lean toward the owners in *Messersmith*, with that case's quite different contract footing and more momentous implications.

3. Even though a party may guess wrongly how its current arbitrator will rule, a second key difference between contract arbitration and statutory administration is that the parties can renegotiate the contractual language that an outside arbitrator may have misconstrued, a step the parties certainly cannot take with respect to an administrative interpretation of a statute. In fact, the baseball agreement was expiring around the time the *Messersmith* decision was being rendered, and the agreement was renegotiated long before any more players reached free agent status. According to the Coase theorem so favored within the Law and Economics movement, Seitz's interpretation of the reserve clause, right or wrong, was largely irrelevant to the real-world outcome of those negotiations. Do you agree?

4. In order to re-establish its reserve system after *Messersmith*, did Major League Baseball need to have the consent of the Players Association? Recall that there were two contractual features of the traditional system, the renewable option in the player contract and the anti-tampering clause in the league rules. Could baseball have simply amended its own rules to address

this problem? With what risks under antitrust law? Under labor law? In industrial relations?

5. Coming back to the issue of judicial review, compare the legal standard used by the court in *Kansas City Royals, supra*, with the standard formulated by the court in *Charles O. Finley v. Bowie Kuhn*, 569 F.2d 527 (7th Cir.1978), to govern judicial review of a baseball commissioner's decisions under the owners' major league agreement. (The *Finley* case, as you will recall from Chapter 1, dealt with Bowie Kuhn's rejection of Oakland A's owner Charles Finley's attempt to sell several of his team's star players before they became free agents, post-*Messersmith*.) Should there be more, less, or similar judicial deference to these two types of private rulings?

I. UNION AND INDIVIDUAL PLAYER[s]

The deference given to private arbitration in administration of the labor agreement accentuates the dominance of the association over individual players in the day-to-day life of the bargaining relationship. Thus, a player in a contract dispute with his own club cannot go off to court where he and his attorney might feel more comfortable: he must rely on the private arbitration mechanism endorsed in the *Steelworkers Trilogy* (see *Davis v. Pro Basketball, Inc. (Portland Trail Blazers)*, 381 F.Supp. 1 (S.D.N.Y.1974), and *Cincinnati Bengals v. Jack Thompson*, 553 F.Supp. 1011 (S.D.Ohio 1983)).[t] When the player seeks to use arbitration, he will find in some sports, such as football, that the Association alone controls access to this procedure (see *Chuy v. NFLPA*, 495 F.Supp. 137 (E.D.Pa.1980)). Even in sports such as baseball, where the player has the legal right to take his case to the arbitrator irrespective of the Player Association's views about its merits, as a practical matter the player usually must rely on the experienced Association staff to have any real prospect in front of the arbitrator. Does all of this mean that the player associations are free to wield their legal authority and real-life clout in disregard of the individual player's interests?

The answer is that unions are anything but free in this regard. In a companion decision to *J.I. Case, supra*, described and quoted from earlier, *Steele v. Louisville and Nashville R.R. Co.*, 323 U.S. 192 (1944), the Supreme Court held that the exclusive authority conferred on unions by statute could be upheld as constitutional only if the Act were read as

---

s. See Matthew W. Finkin, *The Limits of Majority Rule in Collective Bargaining*, 64 Minnesota L. Rev. 183 (1980); Michael C. Harper and Ira C. Lupu, *Fair Representation as Equal Protection*, 98 Harvard L. Rev. 1211 (1985); and Clyde W. Summers, *The Individual Employee's Rights Under the Collective Bargaining Agreement: What Constitutes Fair Representation?*, 127 U. Pennsylvania L. Rev. 251 (1977).

t. The statement in the text holds true when the agreed-upon adjudicator is an outside neutral, rather than the League Commissioner—for example, in hockey where the commissioner still decides most player contract disputes. If the adjudicator of a particular dispute is the commissioner or president appointed by the owners, the player is more likely to be able to take the dispute to court. See *Dryer v. Los Angeles Rams*, 40 Cal.3d 406, 220 Cal.Rptr. 807, 709 P.2d 826 (1985); compare *Erving v. Virginia Squires*, 349 F.Supp. 716 (E.D.N.Y. 1972); *Morris v. New York Football Giants, Inc.*, 150 Misc.2d 271, 575 N.Y.S.2d 1013 (1991).

implicitly creating a duty of fair representation (DFR) owed by the union to individual employees. The authoritative judicial statement about the content of this duty is found in *Vaca v. Sipes*, 386 U.S. 171 (1967):

> [A] breach of the statutory duty of fair representation occurs only when a union's conduct toward a member of the collective bargaining unit is *arbitrary, discriminatory, or in bad faith* (emphasis added).

The precedent-setting unfair representation decision, *Steele*, involved a union's negotiation of a collective agreement that put black railroad workers on the bottom rung of the seniority ladder. Absent such clearly illegitimate discrimination, the courts have been loath to overturn the results of collective bargaining between the union and an employer (who, as we saw earlier, owes no corresponding substantive obligations to the employees under its duty to "bargain in good faith"). Thus, in its later decision in *Air Line Pilots Ass'n v. O'Neill*, 499 U.S. 65 (1991), the Supreme Court stated that in applying the *Vaca v. Sipes* "arbitrary, discriminatory, or bad faith" standard to the intense bargaining struggle over the content of the labor contract, courts must offer unions latitude "within a wide range of reasonableness."

Even assuming such a deferential attitude on the part of the courts, though, one can imagine sports cases in which an arguable DFR charge might be filed. One of the most intriguing examples relates to the design of salary caps, which we will see detailed in Section K. For the moment, consider the following examples.

Questions for Discussion

1. Suppose a players association agrees to permit the league to revise the players' pension plan so as to remove an inflation-generated earnings "surplus" that would otherwise have been used to raise the amounts paid to retired players to keep their benefits level with inflation. In return, the owners agree to spend a sizable share of this surplus to pay for a new fringe benefit for active players—severance pay. Ontario Supreme Court Judge Adams found that such a scenario did take place in hockey in the 1980s, and constituted a violation by the league of the terms of its pension plan: the judge awarded approximately $30 million (including interest) in a suit brought by such former NHL greats as Gordie Howe and Bobby Hull. See *Bathgate et al. v. NHL Pensions' Society et al.*, 98 D.L.R.(4th) 327 (1992), aff'd, 110 D.L.R. (4th) 609 (Ont.C.A.1994). Suppose, though, that the wording of the pension agreement would permit such league action if the players association gave its explicit consent, and the retired players then filed a duty of fair representation charge against the association under federal labor law. Does a players association have an obligation to represent fairly the interests of retired players in negotiations with the league? Does the answer turn on whether the association is entitled to negotiate with clubs on behalf of former players? See *Allied Chemical & Alkali Workers v. Pittsburgh Plate Glass Co.*, 404 U.S. 157 (1971).

2. Recall the Sam Jethroe case that was mentioned in Chapter 1. In 1997, on the occasion of the 50th anniversary of Jackie Robinson breaking

the barrier to black players in major league baseball, the owners agreed to repair one of the damages still remaining from that historic injustice. Sam Jethroe had played in the Negro League in the 1940s, and followed Robinson into Major League Baseball in 1950 (when he was named National League Rookie of the year). However, Jethroe was not able to stay in the big leagues long enough to satisfy the five years of service needed for vesting of pension benefits under the plan created by the owners in 1947. The MLB owners have now acknowledged that Jethroe, like a number of his African–American contemporaries in that era, would have been able to meet that pension standard had he not been discriminatorily excluded from the big leagues (something that was legal at that time). The owners have created a special $10 million fund to pay Jethroe and his Negro League counterparts a modest pension benefit. Jethroe has not, however, been able to persuade the MLB Players Association to provide comparable access to its quite generous players pension fund, which is financed by the owners pursuant to the collective agreement. Should present-day players (17% of whom are African American and 20% Hispanic American) feel either a legal or moral obligation to remove these consequences of past discrimination in their sport? Should football, basketball, and hockey, as well as baseball, players feel any such obligation to *all* former players who are still living, but who played at a time when there was no pension fund (or union) in their sport?

In sports, as in labor relations generally, the vast majority of DFR claims involve complaints about the union's handling of an individual contract grievance. One important reason is that the actual terms of the collective agreement negotiated between union and employer provide the court (or the NLRB) some guidance for appraising the union's treatment of the employee in the unit. The following case illustrates the judicial struggle with the content of the duty of fair representation in a concrete sports situation.

PETERSON v. KENNEDY AND NFLPA

United States Court of Appeals, Ninth Circuit, 1985.
771 F.2d 1244.

REINHARDT, CIRCUIT JUDGE.

[James Peterson of the Tampa Bay Buccaneers signed one-year contracts for each of the 1976, 1977, and 1978 football seasons. Besides the standard injury protection clause that provided for payment of that year's salary in case of an injury occurring during any one season, Peterson's contract contained a special clause that entitled him to his salary for the 1977 and 1978 seasons if he were unable to play because of a football-related injury in a previous year. Peterson did injure his knee early in the 1976 season and missed the entire year because of surgery. When Peterson reported to training camp in the summer of 1977, he was cut from the team after one week of drills. This was done pursuant to the standard player contract provision that allows the club to terminate the contract if a player's performance appears "unsatisfactory" compared to other players competing for positions on the squad.

In August 1977, after allegedly talking with Harold Kennedy, a NFLPA staff member (and recent law school graduate), Peterson's agent filed a grievance under the "injury grievance procedure" in the NFL-NFLPA collective agreement in order to recover the salary due for the 1977 and 1978 seasons. The parties disputed whether the NFLPA had been informed at the outset of the special "injury protection" clause in Peterson's contract. However, when Richard Berthelson, the NFLPA General Counsel, learned of that clause in 1978, he sought to channel the grievance into the "non-injury" grievance procedure. Unfortunately, because the switch took place after the sixty days permitted for filing non-injury grievances, the contract arbitrator found the non-injury grievance to be time-barred. Meanwhile, the arbitrator ruled against Peterson's claim under the injury grievance procedure, on the ground that this particular procedure was used only to collect salary payments owed for the year during which the injury occurred.

Having lost both sides of his contract claim against the Buccaneers, Peterson sued the NFLPA for breach of the labor law duty of fair representation—in particular, by erroneously advising him to file an injury grievance and then failing to rectify this error while there still was time to do so. Although the jury found in favor of Peterson's legal claim, the trial judge granted the NFLPA's motion for judgment notwithstanding the verdict (JNOV). The principal ground was that the union's conduct amounted to no more than negligence, and negligence could not constitute unfair representation under the NLRA. Peterson appealed that ruling.]

* * *

The district court concluded that the evidence presented was legally insufficient to sustain the jury's verdict that the union breached its duty of fair representation. We agree. After reviewing all of the evidence in the light most favorable to Peterson, we conclude that the union did not breach its duty of fair representation; the record is devoid of evidence that the union acted in an arbitrary, discriminatory, or bad faith manner.

The duty of fair representation is a judicially established rule imposed on labor organizations because of their status as the exclusive bargaining representative for all of the employees in a given bargaining unit. The Supreme Court [in *DelCostello v. International Bthd. of Teamsters*, 462 U.S. 151 (1983)] recently explained the basis and scope of the duty:

> The duty of fair representation exists because it is the policy of the National Labor Relations Act to allow a single labor organization to represent collectively the interests of all employees within a unit, thereby depriving individuals in the unit of the ability to bargain individually or to select a minority union as their representative. In

such a system, if individual employees are not to be deprived of all effective means of protecting their own interests, it must be the duty of the representative organization to "serve the interests of all members without hostility or discrimination toward any, to exercise its discretion with complete good faith and honesty, and to avoid arbitrary conduct."

462 U.S. at 164, n. 14.

A union breaches its duty of fair representation only when its conduct toward a member of the collective bargaining unit is "arbitrary, discriminatory, or in bad faith." The duty is designed to ensure that unions represent fairly the interests of all of their members without exercising hostility or bad faith toward any. It stands "as a bulwark to prevent arbitrary union conduct against individuals stripped of traditional forms of redress by the provisions of federal labor law."

The Supreme Court has long recognized that unions must retain wide discretion to act in what they perceive to be their members' best interests. To that end, we have "stressed the importance of preserving union discretion by narrowly construing the unfair representation doctrine." We have emphasized that, because a union balances many collective and individual interests in deciding whether and to what extent it will pursue a particular grievance, courts should "accord substantial deference" to a union's decisions regarding such matters.

A union's representation of its members "need not be error free." We have concluded repeatedly that mere negligent conduct on the part of a union does not constitute a breach of the union's duty of fair representation.

* * *

Whether in a particular case a union's conduct is "negligent", and therefore non-actionable, or so egregious as to be "arbitrary", and hence sufficient to give rise to a breach of duty claim, is a question that is not always easily answered. A union acts "arbitrarily" when it simply ignores a meritorious grievance or handles it in a perfunctory manner, for example, by failing to conduct a "minimal investigation" of a grievance that is brought to its attention. We have said that a union's conduct is "arbitrary" if it is "without rational basis," or is "egregious, unfair and unrelated to legitimate union interests." In *Robesky v. Qantas Empire Airways Ltd.*, 573 F.2d 1082, 1089–90 (9th Cir.1978), we held that a union's unintentional mistake is "arbitrary" if it reflects a "reckless disregard" for the rights of the individual employee, but not if it represents only "simply negligence violating the tort standard of due care."

There are some significant general principles that emerge from our previous decisions. In all cases in which we found a breach of the duty of fair representation based on a union's arbitrary conduct, it is clear that the union failed to perform a procedural or ministerial act, that the act in question did not require the exercise of judgment and that there was no rational and proper basis for the union's conduct.

* * *

We have never held that a union has acted in an arbitrary manner where the challenged conduct involved the union's judgment as to how best to handle a grievance. To the contrary, we have held consistently that unions are not liable for good faith, non-discriminatory errors of judgment made in the processing of grievances. We have said that a union's conduct may not be deemed arbitrary simply because of an error in evaluating the merits of a grievance, in interpreting particular provisions of a collective bargaining agreement, or in presenting the grievance at an arbitration hearing. In short, we do not attempt to second-guess a union's judgment when a good faith, non-discriminatory judgment has in fact been made. It is for the union, not the courts, to decide whether and in what manner a particular grievance should be pursued. We reaffirm that principle here.

Sound policy reasons militate against imposing liability on unions for errors of judgment made while representing their members in the collective bargaining process. In *Dutrisac*, we recognized that holding unions liable for such errors would serve ultimately to "defeat the employees' collective bargaining interest in having a strong and effective union." If unions were subject to liability for "judgment calls," it would necessarily undermine their discretion to act on behalf of their members and ultimately weaken their effectiveness. In the long run, the cost of recognizing such liability would be borne not by the unions but by their memberships. Not only would the direct costs of adverse judgments be passed on to the members in the form of increased dues, but, more importantly, unions would become increasingly reluctant to provide guidance to their members in collective bargaining disputes. Such a result would be inconsistent with our oft-repeated commitment to construe narrowly the scope of the duty of fair representation in order to preserve the unions' discretion to decide how best to balance the collective and individual interests that they represent.

* * *

Whether liability for a loss occasioned by ordinary negligence of the union might be spread more equitably among the membership as a whole, rather than be borne by the individual member who is harmed, is no longer an open question.

In applying the foregoing principles to the case at hand, we conclude, as a matter of law, that Peterson failed to establish that the NFLPA breached its duty of fair representation.... The alleged error was one of judgment. Viewing the evidence in the light most favorable to Peterson, the most that can be said is that the union provided him with incorrect advice and did not alter its judgment until it was too late to rectify the error. In this case, deciding whether to file an injury or a non-injury grievance was not a purely mechanical function; the union attorneys were required to construe the scope and meaning of the injury and non-injury grievance provisions of the collective bargaining agreement and to determine which of the two grievance procedures was more appropriate. As we have indicated earlier, the answer was not as simple as a literal reading of the two contract sections might indicate.

* * *

Although the union's representatives may have erred in initially advising Peterson to file an injury grievance and in failing to recognize its mistake in time to file a non-injury grievance in its stead, we are unwilling to subject unions to liability for such errors in judgment. Accordingly, we affirm the district court's conclusion that the evidence presented was insufficient, as a matter of law, to support the jury's verdict against the union.

Appeal Denied.

Suppose that a player files a grievance alleging that his release violated a "no-cut" guarantee in his contract. (This was the contract claim advanced in *Dryer v. Los Angeles Rams*, 40 Cal.3d 406, 220 Cal.Rptr. 807, 709 P.2d 826 (1985).) The Players Association agrees with the club and the league that the contract language will not bear that interpretation and drops the grievance rather than take it to arbitration. Does the player have any legal right to take his claim before an outside adjudicator?

In response to the above question, the Supreme Court devised a carefully qualified remedial structure in *Vaca v. Sipes*, 386 U.S. 171 (1967). The player would have to sue in court both the association and the club, establish first that the union's judgment in dropping the grievance was "arbitrary, discriminatory, or in bad faith" (i.e., that it breached the duty of fair representation owed by the union to the player), and *then* try to sustain the merits of his contract claim against the team (in court, not in arbitration). If the player succeeded on both counts, the club would be responsible for the damage done by the contract violation and the union for the additional costs attributable to use of this more complex procedure, such as legal fees incurred in the lawsuit and additional salary losses incurred because it took longer to get a ruling in litigation than in arbitration (see *Bowen v. United States Postal Service*, 459 U.S. 212 (1983)). For sports cases illustrating this process, see *Chuy v. NFLPA*, 495 F.Supp. 137 (E.D.Pa.1980), and *Sharpe v. NFLPA*, 941 F.Supp. 8 (D.D.C.1996).

J. UNION SECURITY IN SPORTS[u]

A final component of labor law addresses the other side of the tension between the individual interests of particular players and the

---

u. See Kenneth G. Dau–Schmidt, *Union Security Agreements Under the NLRA: The Statute, the Constitution, and the Court's Opinion in Beck*, 27 Harvard J. on Legis. 51 (1990).

group interests of players as a whole. The duty of fair representation described earlier requires the players association to pursue the interests of each member of the bargaining unit, regardless of whether the player has joined and supports the association selected by the majority. Whatever the fate of individual grievances, such as in *Peterson*, supra, all players inevitably enjoy the benefits of the collectively-bargained regime governing their sport—under which average baseball player salaries, for example, have soared from $19,000 in 1967 to $1.31 million in 1997.

On the other side of the coin, what can the players association do to protect the majority of players from the temptation felt by individuals to "free ride"—i.e., to take full advantage of the labor contract, but not to bear any share of the costs of negotiating and administering the agreement? In response to this problem, players associations, like unions in all other industries, have sought to negotiate "union security" arrangements.

Under §§ 8(a)(3) and 8(b)(2) of the National Labor Relations Act, unions and employers are forbidden from requiring actual membership in the union. The practical significance of that statutory ban is that the union can do nothing to employees who choose to go back to work during a strike called by the majority—for example, when the 49ers Joe Montana and the Cowboys Danny White crossed the NFLPA line in the 1987 football strike, notwithstanding the protests of their fellow quarterbacks Dan Marino, John Elway, and Jim Kelly. See *Pattern Makers' League of North America v. NLRB*, 473 U.S. 95 (1985). However, unions can secure from each employee a contribution to the financial cost of the representation effort by requiring even non-members to pay to the union the financial equivalent of the union dues paid by members (see *NLRB v. General Motors Corp.*, 373 U.S. 734 (1963)). A recent Supreme Court decision held, however, that to the extent any union funds are expended on activities not directly related to the fate of the unit (such as political campaigns or organizing drives among non-union workers), a dissenting employee can insist on a *pro rata* rebate of part of this "agency fee" (see *Communications Workers of Am. v. Beck*, 487 U.S. 735 (1988)). Finally, in the twenty or so states (largely in the south or southwest) that have "right-to-work" laws, unions cannot insist on even this limited financial contribution from unit (by contrast with union) members. (See *Retail Clerks Int'l Ass'n, Local 1625 v. Schermerhorn*, 373 U.S. 746 (1963).)

A by-product of the NFL–NFLPA settlement of the *Freeman McNeil* antitrust litigation and the terms of a new collective agreement combining veteran free agency and a salary cap was a legal challenge to the Players Association's union security rights. The NFL labor agreement gives the Association the maximum union security permitted by federal labor law: an "agency shop" requirement that players pay the standard union dues. However, the agency shop is prohibited in the twenty states that have exercised their Taft–Hartley § 14(b) prerogative to bar any such intrusion on the "right to work" within their borders.

At the time, it was assumed that only eight NFL teams were located in such states: the Dallas Cowboys and Houston Oilers (in Texas), the Miami Dolphins and Tampa Bay Buccaneers (in Florida), the Atlanta Falcons (in Georgia), the New Orleans Saints (in Louisiana), the Denver Broncos (in Colorado), and the Phoenix Cardinals (in Arizona). However, a number of Washington Redskins' players also sought to avail themselves of this labor law exemption from payment of the NFLPA's $5,000 annual dues. The Redskins' players were especially aggrieved by the NFL's "hard" cap, because their club's total salary budget (over $45 million in 1993) was considerably higher than the $35 million salary cap that came into force in 1994. That is why Redskin players like Wilbur Marshall, Terry Orr, and others were the key objectors to the *Reggie White* class action settlement and the new NFL–NFLPA collective agreement.

Having lost on that score (see *White v. NFL*, 41 F.3d 402 (8th Cir.1994)), Orr and several other Redskins refused to pay the Players Association the union dues required by the agency shop clause in the labor agreement. Supported by the conservative National Right-to-Work Legal Defense Foundation, these dissidents sought and won favorable verdicts from both a federal district judge (see *NFL Players Association v. Pro–Football, Inc.*, 857 F.Supp. 71 (D.D.C.1994)) and a Virginia state court (see *Orr v. NFLPA*, 147 LRRM 2845 (Va.Cir.Ct.1994)), to the effect that their real place of employment was the anti-union security state of Virginia, where the Redskins practiced, not the District of Columbia, where the team played its home games. For purposes of § 14(b) of Taft–Hartley, the key precedent, *Oil, Chemical, and Atomic Workers International Union v. Mobil Oil Corp.*, 426 U.S. 407 (1976), held that selection of the governing state turns on the "employees' predominant job situs." Rather than focusing just on the place where the employees happen to be hired: "the center of the post-hiring relationship is the job situs, the place where the work that is the very *raison d'être* of the relationship is performed." In the Redskins case, both the federal and state judges applied a quantitative, rather than a qualitative, test: where did the players spend most of their time at work? Since far more hours were spent practicing during the week in Virginia than playing every second Sunday in RFK Stadium in D.C., the Redskins belonged to Virginia, not Washington.

The case poses a host of questions about both the legal rules and larger policies regarding union-employee relationships.

    1. What are the relevant criteria for determining the state in which athletes are employed by teams—where they play their home games, where they practice, where the team offices are located and salary checks written, or any other factors?

    2. Should the locational test be the same for purposes of union security, workers' compensation, income tax, and other legal re-

gimes? (Redskins' owner Jack Kent Cooke was reportedly delighted with the ruling because it diverged from an earlier D.C. decision, *Pro-Football, Inc. v. District of Columbia Dept. of Employment Services*, 588 A.2d 275 (D.C.App.1991), that had applied the District's far more generous workers' compensation law to Redskins' players suffering occupational injuries (such as former quarterback and Super Bowl MVP, Doug Williams).)

3. Who should have primary jurisdiction to decide this union security question: the arbitrator under the collective agreement, the National Labor Relations Board, or the courts (and if the latter, state or federal)?

4. Should a players association have the right to sign an agreement with the league to require players in any state to pay union dues? (And by the way, are these contractual arrangements properly labeled an infringement of the player's "right to work?")

5. Should a players association be given authority under labor law to negotiate with the league a collective agreement that establishes a cap on the salaries that are going to be paid by any team in the league, a contract that binds individual players (and teams) who do not like its terms?

6. Are NFL players—including the Redskins—better or worse off with the new regime secured by their Players Association? What is the standard for making that judgment?

While the above questions are quite important in the broader labor market, the *Orr* decision was of only symbolic significance in football and other professional sports. The reason is that the NFLPA and other players associations have a much more lucrative source of financial support than player dues: group licensing of player names and likenesses.

This avenue was first discovered in the late 1960s by Marvin Miller, head of the baseball players association.[v] Up to that time, baseball players had sold rights to their likenesses on cards on an individual basis—and for a pittance. (As we shall see in Chapter 6, player and other celebrity publicity rights had only begun to be fashioned by the courts in the mid-1950s.) Miller persuaded the players to sign over licensing rights to their associations, which would market the rights collectively. The $70 million or so that the MLBPA now realizes annually from this source provides ample support for the Association's expenses (including the war chest used to cushion the financial effects of the 1994–95 labor dispute with the owners). It also provides a handsome personal dividend to players (and baseball coaches) every year.

v. See Miller, *A Whole Different Ball Game*, note a above, at 91–94, 142–152.

By the early 1990s, the NFLPA was earning over $20 million a year from group licensing of football player images (up from $1 million a year in the mid–1980s). This was the revenue source that financed the expensive *Powell-McNeil* antitrust litigation. It also sparked an effort by NFL Properties to woo name players away from the Association (e.g., into an NFL Quarterback Club) by offering stars a much higher individual return for this asset. However, a key feature of the 1993 *White* class action settlement was that the NFL owners conceded exclusive group licensing rights to the Players Association, which is now earning much more money from that source. In the 1996 basketball labor settlement, the NBA owners agreed to pay a minimum of $25 million a year to the NBPA for distribution to its members from the collective licensing of basketball player images. (Unlike the other sports, these licenses are actually sold by the NBA merchandising office, not by the Players Association.)

In all of these sports, though, a player (such as Terry Orr) can participate in such a group marketing program only if he is a member of the players union and thence able to receive a financial share which is several times larger than the dues that are required from those who want to be union members. Is such association exclusion of nonunion players from this lucrative program a legitimate decision by a private organization engaged in a business venture, or is it illegal discrimination (under the NLRA) against employees for exercising their right to refrain from union membership (a right enjoyed by players in New York, California, and every other state, not just when playing in right-to-work states for the Virginia Redskins)? Alternatively, should a union be able to deny membership (and thence licensing fees) to players who served as replacements in a strike or lockout (such as football's labor dispute in 1987 and baseball's in 1994–95), but who are now playing in the major leagues and want to join and get the benefits of the players association? The NLRB may well answer that last question in connection with an unfair labor practice charge filed in 1997 by ex-replacement baseball players, including Mike Bush of the Dodgers and Rick Reed of the Mets.

K. SALARY CAPS AND TAXES[w]

This chapter began with Andy Messersmith's successful effort to use labor law to eliminate baseball's century-old reserve system—something the Supreme Court had been unwilling to allow Curt Flood to challenge under antitrust law. From the early 1970s to the early 1990s, player litigation and self-help were primarily targeted at securing free agency in all professional team sports. However, by the mid–1990s, the focus of player-owner conflict had shifted. Owners were now prepared to accept

---

w. This is an issue that is beginning to generate a substantial literature. For one of the first systematic treatments in a law journal, see Christopher D. Cameron and J. Michael Echevarria, *The Plays of Summer: Antitrust, Industrial Distrust, and the Case Against a Salary Cap for Major League Baseball*, 22 Florida State U. L. Rev. 827 (1995).

(perhaps even embrace) free movement of players from one team to another. They insisted, though, on creation of league-wide constraints on the amount of money that individual teams could spend to induce such player movement—via salary caps or salary taxes.

This concept of free player movement with salary constraints (and, as we shall see, salary guarantees) was first proposed in the 1982 negotiations by NFLPA Executive Director Ed Garvey. Garvey's idea was that 55% of league revenues should be allocated to player compensation. The bulk of this money would be paid in fixed salary rates determined by position and seniority. The rest would be paid in bonuses for personal and team performance, as measured by statistical factors developed and administered by the NFLPA. The NFL owners, under Commissioner Pete Rozelle, rejected this salary-sharing idea as "socialism in disguise," as an unacceptable inroad upon each team's property rights in a capitalist market. (Interestingly, the same NFL owners had always had by far the largest degree of revenue-sharing among clubs of any sport.)

Just a year later, a revised version of salary capping and sharing came into existence in basketball. By contrast with football, the NBA was in a sorry state in the early 1980s. Two-thirds of its teams were losing money every year, and a few (especially the Cleveland Cavaliers) were both spending and losing so much that the league office was considering whether to take control of them. At the same time, the existing restriction on player free agency (through Commissioner-ordered compensation to the losing team) was about to expire in 1985, pursuant to the 1975 settlement of the *Robertson* antitrust litigation. Thus, NBPA founder and leader Larry Fleisher and Commissioner Larry O'Brien, and O'Brien's chief counsel and soon-to-be successor David Stern, developed a league salary formula designed to accommodate the interests of both sides. Ten years later, a new football leadership (Executive Director Gene Upshaw and Commissioner Paul Tagliabue) agreed to their version of the salary cap as the basis for the *White* class action settlement of two decades of football suits and strikes over free agency.

Salary cap provisions take up dozens of densely-written pages in the NBA and NFL collective agreements. In the next chapter, we shall address some of the technical challenges posed in interpreting, applying, and rewriting the cap language, e.g., to resolve controversies about contracts negotiated by Deion Sanders, Chris Dudley, and Juwan Howard. It is sufficient for our purposes here just to capsulize the core of this sports labor innovation.

Each year the league office and the players association must add up the gross revenue received by all clubs from defined sources—not just gate receipts and television revenues, but merchandising sales, luxury box and club seat rentals, and the like. An agreed-to percentage of that revenue is assigned for player compensation: in basketball in the low 50% range, in football in the low 60%. Part of that compensation fund (approximately four percent in football and two percent in basketball) is reserved for payment of the player retirement, disability, and other benefit funds. The remainder is then divided by the number of clubs in the league to establish a ceiling on the amount of money any one club can pay for its players' salaries—in 1997, $27 million per club in the NBA and $42 million in the NFL.

Here one finds a crucial difference between the NFL and NBA versions of the salary cap. The NBA's is labeled a "soft" cap because it has never restricted the amount that clubs are permitted to spend to sign their current players to new contracts. This feature has always been known as the "Larry Bird" exception, because it was inserted in the 1983 NBA agreement as the instrument though which the Celtics could resign Larry Bird for the salary they knew he was seeking without having to let go of Bird's star teammates (including Robert Parish, Kevin McHale, and Dennis Johnson). The sole aim of the NBA cap, then, was to prevent the Celtics (or the Knicks and Lakers) from using large salary offers to move players from the Cavaliers and other smaller-market teams.

The NFL owners and players agreed, by contrast, to a "hard" cap, one that forced teams to release some of their higher-paid players when their overall salary budget was exceeding the collectively-bargained limit. (The first notable example of this role of the NFL cap came when the New York Giants had to release their long-time star quarterback Phil Simms as the new system went into operation.) But when the NBA owners and Players Association agreed in June 1995 to follow the NFL lead and eliminate the "Larry Bird" exception, this sparked an insurgency (led by Michael Jordan and Patrick Ewing) that forced the two sides to back off and leave the NBA cap in its original "soft" version. Thus, while the NBA's formal cap for the 1996–97 season was set at $24 million, the Bulls paid Michael Jordan $30 million that year, their entire roster $58 million, and only five of the 29 teams in the league were at or below this $24 million mark.

In both leagues, this system imposes not just a ceiling on the amount that teams *may* pay their players, but also a (somewhat lower) floor on the amount that each team *must* pay in salaries. This combination of a cap and a floor means that the NBA and NFL labor agreements actually function to give players a guaranteed *share* in aggregate league revenues. The leagues have also developed a variety of revenue-sharing devices to ensure that each team can and does meet the specified salary floor.

Basketball's and football's respective versions of free agency plus a salary cap set the parameters for individual player negotiations in both sports. (The value of this new regime for football players is evidenced by the fact that average NFL salaries rose from $488,000 in 1992, the year before the settlement, to $650,000 in 1993, the first year of free agency without a cap, to $765,000 in 1996, the third year of the cap.) In 1994, the owners in baseball and hockey set out to secure similar models for their respective sports. Baseball owners wanted the NFL's "hard cap," but with a reduction in the players' share from 55% to 50% of overall league revenues. Since the players were adamantly opposed to the very concept of a cap (not just the specific figures), baseball experienced a shutdown in August 1994 that led to the *Silverman* litigation in the spring of 1995.

Hockey owners, led by the NHL's new commissioner Gary Bettman, proposed a variation—a luxury salary tax rather than cap—to try to address their spiralling salary levels (which had risen from a $195,000 average in the 1985–90 season to $560,000 in 1994–95). However, the owners' proposed tax rate of 200% (later modified to 125%) on team payrolls above the defined ceiling made this "hard tax" the functional equivalent of a hard cap. After a shutdown of the 1994–95 hockey season for three months, the two sides eventually settled without either a cap or a tax, and instead for modest revisions in salary arbitration and free agency. By 1997–98, average NHL salaries had reached approximately $1 million.

In baseball, by contrast, the parties did focus on a real tax alternative to the salary cap. After three years of negotiations, the owners and players finally signed a new collective agreement in early 1997 that contained a "soft tax." The highest-paying five teams in MLB whose payrolls (including their share of player benefits) will pay into league coffers a 35% tax (34% in 1999) on the difference between their payrolls and the mid-point between the fifth and sixth payrolls. (All five taxable payrolls must also exceed $51 million in 1997, $55 million in 1998, and $59 million in 1999.) In 1997, the first tax year, the Yankees paid $4.4 million, the Orioles $4.0 million, the Indians $2.1 million, the Braves $1.3 million, and the Marlins $140,000. All five clubs did play during that post-season when they recouped at least some of this added payroll charge, of which the first $10 million is used to help finance a new MLB revenue-sharing plan for small market teams. Average baseball salaries had actually dropped from $1.15 million in 1994 to approximately $1.1 million in 1995 and 1996 in the aftermath of the devastating 1994 strike, but with the benefit of labor peace, average salaries jumped to $1.31 million in 1997. We shall have to wait and see the longer-term results of this new collective agreement with its salary tax and revenue-sharing regimes.

In the next chapter, we shall address a number of technical issues that have arisen in the administration of salary cap systems, as part of the broader subject of player representation by agents and unions. Here we pose a number of the more fundamental questions about the value of different salary cap (or tax) versions, in their own right as well as compared to the traditional reserve system or unrestricted free agency.

Questions For Discussion

1. What are the pros and cons of the NBA's soft cap versus the NFL's hard cap? Of either cap versus MLB's soft tax or the NHL's proposed hard tax? From the broader perspective of instruments for social control of

private behavior, what are the virtues and limitations of regulatory standards as compared to tax incentives? And by the way, what is the likely interplay of public taxes (state and local as well as federal) with sports caps or taxes?

2. Is it better to have the parties negotiate specific amounts for their salary ceilings (as they did in baseball), or to develop a salary sharing formula based on a numerical percentage of overall league revenues? An obvious virtue of the formula approach is that it automatically adjusts to changes in league revenues over the longer run. That still leaves the question how the parties will define and calculate the revenues for purposes of applying the formula. A regular source of discussion and occasional conflict is how to assess league and team accounting decisions: e.g., when the same entity or person, Time Warner (formerly Ted Turner), owns the Atlanta Hawks and Braves as well as the superstation, WTBS, which is televising their games and is deciding how much the station will "pay" the teams for broadcast rights.

3. An even bigger issue is whether a particular revenue source should be shared with the players. For example, one reason why the NBA salary cap was able to jump from $16 million a team in 1994–95 to $23 million a team in 1995–96, even though the salary percentage was dropping from 53 to 48%, was that NBA owners had agreed to include their spiralling merchandising (and other earnings) sources in the revenue base. The simple answer (and the one the players obviously favor) is to count *all* owner earnings having anything to do with the sport. In football, though, this poses a potentially significant problem because of the lucrative stadium deals enjoyed by certain teams (such as Art Modell's Baltimore Ravens). If these unshared team revenues lift the amount that teams can (indeed, must) pay in salaries, this can create a significant problem for other teams (like Bob Kraft's New England Patriots) that have not been able to extract such deals from their community's taxpayers. (How and why the latter happens we shall examine in Chapter 7.)

4. Even when the two sides do reach an understanding about which and how much revenues are to be counted, this leaves the most difficult question what to select as the relevant percentage figure. The numbers certainly will be very different from sport to sport. For example, football and basketball do not face the substantial expenditures made by baseball and hockey to run farm systems that develop talent for their games. (As we shall see in Chapter 10, it is American colleges that function as the farm system to provide new players for the NFL and NBA.) However, football rosters are four times as large as basketball's, and double the size in baseball and hockey. In initial salary cap negotiations, the parties can select a figure that is reasonably close to the status quo (this is what was done in basketball in 1983). However, over the life of the contract (and its successors), overall league revenues change sharply (usually upward, but in baseball in the mid-1990s, downward). When that happens, the original percentage figure may seem outdated, but the alternative is not obvious. The solution insisted on by the NFLPA in 1993 (and then by the MLBPA in 1996) is to have the final

year (or two) of the labor agreement operate without a cap (or tax). Is that a sensible response to this issue?

A final problem arises not from what is in the salary cap, but from what has been left out. As we have seen, the salary cap systems in both the NBA and the NHL are arrangements between clubs and players about what share of league revenues will be spent on player salaries (and other benefits). The unanswered question is whether there should be an arrangement for sharing those salaries amongst the players themselves (something the NFLPA's Ed Garvey was seeking when this story began in 1982).

Since sports unionism established its base in the late 1960s, the world of sports has witnessed a remarkable increase in the total amounts being paid in player salaries (and a significant rise in the share of overall league revenues that go for player compensation). As we have noted several times in this chapter, there has been an even more stunning increase in the dispersion and inequality of salaries within each league. In the 1997 season, the Bulls' Michael Jordan was paid $30 million, the Chicago White Sox's Albert Belle $10 million, the Pittsburgh Penguins' Mario Lemieux $11 million, and the Green Bay Packers' Brett Favre nearly $7 million. In that same season, approximately one-third of the players in three leagues were paid at or around the minimum salaries (ranging from $150,000 to $260,00). The exception was hockey, partly because its labor agreement grants unrestricted free agency after ten years of professional (not just NHL) play only to veterans whose most recent contract amount was *less* than the League's salary average. In the other sports, the explanation for the stark salary disparity is quite simple. As teams spend more and more money on a few topflight stars and free agents, there is less and less money left to spend on players who are valuable enough to perform (perhaps even start) for a major league team but who do not have quite the talent and name recognition to extract a large premium for their services. Formal salary caps clearly accentuate this trend, but the same phenomenon had taken place in baseball where every team felt the pressure to operate within its own salary budget. The result is that sports has become one of the most vivid illustrations of a broader trend in American life—the Winner Takes the Lion's Share.

Traditionally, organization of labor has always been designed to address both sides of this phenomenon: unions seek to establish a salary floor to make sure that certain workers do not earn too little for their services and a salary ceiling to ensure that other workers do not earn too much for theirs. Player unions in sports have almost always pursued the first and opposed the second. It is only in the recently-created (and non-union) leagues in soccer and women's basketball that dollar limits have been imposed on individual salaries. (In Major League Soccer in 1997, the team salary cap was $1.3 million, the individual player cap was

$192,000, and the floor $24,000.) In the 1990s, though, the players associations were persuaded by owners to accept this dollar limit feature of a salary cap regime, though targeted only at rookies.

When the NFL players agreed in 1993 to an overall cap on team payrolls, they added to it a specific limit on the amount that could be paid by each team for all its rookies (with the actual amount varying in accordance with the number and level of draft picks the team had that year). No direct limit was placed on the amount that the New England Patriots, for instance, were permitted to pay the number one selection that year, Drew Bledsoe; however, the more the team paid to Bledsoe, the less that was available to pay other draft picks. Next, in the NHL labor settlement in early 1995, the only salary cap the NHLPA would agree to was placed on rookie salaries. The ceiling for the 1995 draft was set at $850,000 for any player, to rise gradually to $1.075 million by the year 2000. This limit on salaries for individual rookie players was set at roughly half of what had been paid in prior years to notable draft picks such as Eric Lindros, Alexander Daigle, and Paul Kariya. Agreeing to that cap enabled the NHLPA to fend off the "hard" luxury tax that NHL owners wanted to impose on what teams paid to all their players. Finally, in the basic NBA settlement reached in the fall of 1995, the parties agreed to establish a specified salary level (with just a small range for individual agent negotiations) that was to be paid to every rookie, with the figure tailored to the position of the player in that year's draft. In return for this concession by the Players Association, the owners agreed to preserve the "Larry Bird" exception from their soft salary cap for free agent veterans.

As we have seen in Section E, players' unions do have the legal authority (under § 9(a) of the NLRA) to negotiate such constraints on individual salaries. It is also clear from Chapter 3 that Leon Wood, Anthony Brown, and their rookie successors cannot sue team owners for violating antitrust law by agreeing to and enforcing such a league cap on the amount an individual team will offer its rookies. Suppose, though, that rookies were to file a complaint against the players union under labor law, contending that the union had violated its duty to represent them fairly by agreeing to such a limit on rookie, but not on veteran, salaries. Recall the duty of fair representation standard articulated by the Supreme Court in *Vaca v. Sipes*, 386 U.S. 171 (1967); a union's conduct is prohibited if it is "arbitrary, discriminatory, or in bad faith" in its treatment of certain unit constituents. How should that legal standard be applied to this sports problem? Are there differences in the specific designs of rookie salary constraints in the NFL, NHL, or NBA (as well, perhaps, as in their broader market contexts) that make one of these arrangements more or less defensible than the others?

Even if one believes that there is a problem (whether legal or ethical) with singling out rookies for such special salary constraints, is the ideal solution to remove the rookie cap or to expand it to encompass veterans? Should sports agreements specify a ceiling on the amount that can be spent on the salary of any one player, while at the same time raising the minimum floor on the amount that is paid to players who are at or near the bottom rung of the salary ladder? Perhaps, for example, the parties could adopt a salary ceiling (or tax trigger) as a designated multiple (e.g., 25 times) of the minimum salary, with both figures adjusted annually in accordance with league revenues and the overall salary cap. Is there a tension here between salary equity and performance efficiency (e.g., are Michael Jordan and his successors likely to train and perform better if they know they can or cannot earn $30 million for a single season)? Is there actually a distributional problem in present-day sports from either a fairness or an efficiency standpoint, (e.g., Michael Jordan earning $33 million in 1997–98 and his teammate Scottie Pippen earning $3 million), and is any redistributional effort appropriate for a players association? If you were the leader of a players association, how would you assess the political and organizational factors that would incline you in one direction or the other?

Chapter Five

AGENT REPRESENTATION OF THE ATHLETE[a]

This chapter introduces another important participant in the sports world—the player agent. Ever since William Morris began representing vaudeville performers in the late 1890s, agents have been a key factor in the entertainment industry, helping to secure work and earnings for actors, musicians, and writers. However, because of the tradition in sports that each player was the "property" of the club that originally brought him to the major leagues, there was far less room for effective representation of the player's interests *vis-a-vis* the team. Indeed, one of the first reported instances of athlete representation—by Bob Woolf of Earl Wilson, a pitcher for the Boston Red Sox in the mid–1960s—came about because Wilson happened to consult Woolf about a minor automobile accident. In those early days, team general managers often refused to deal directly with Woolf and his agent colleagues in salary negotiations, which forced the agents to advise their clients from behind the scenes.[b] A portrait of how dramatically the sports world had changed in the next three decades is the 1996 movie *Jerry Maguire*, in which Tom Cruise plays an agent grappling with the personal and ethical challenges in representing an athlete who wants someone to "show [him] the money."

a. This part of the law of sports has produced a considerable body of legal scholarship. Valuable overviews are provided by Kenneth Shropshire, *Agents of Opportunity: Sports Agents and Corruption in Collegiate Sports* (Philadelphia: University of Pennsylvania Press, 1990), and Lionel S. Sobel, "The Regulation of Player Agents and Lawyers," Chapter 1 of Gary Uberstine ed., *Law of Professional and Amateur Sports* (Deerfield, Ill: Clark, Boardman, and Callaghan, 1991) (an earlier version of Sobel's piece appeared at 39 Baylor L. Rev. 701 (1987)). For book-length treatments of the agent's role by two highly-regarded performers in it, see Randal A. Hendricks, *Inside the Strike Zone* (Austin, Tex.: Eakin Press, 1994), and Ron Simon, *The Game Behind the Game: Negotiating in the Big Leagues* (Stillwater, Minn. Voyageur Press, 1993). And a very readable and revealing account of the creation and evolution of talent agencies in the broader entertainment world is Frank Rose, *The Agency: William Morris and the Hidden History of Show Business* (New York: Harper Collins, 1995).

b. Bob Woolf, *Behind Closed Doors* 42–46 (New York: Atheneum, 1976).

As viewers of *Jerry Maguire* will have witnessed, a key reason for the current prominence of agents is the variety of roles they now play for their clients. The principal role is negotiating the player's contract with the team. This task is now far more important because of the huge amounts of money involved in such negotiations—thanks to the interplay of labor and antitrust law described in the previous chapters. Recall from Chapter 4 that collective action by players has helped propel average salaries from the $20–25,000 range in all sports in 1967–68, to $2.2 million in basketball, $1.3 million in baseball, $1 million in hockey, and $800,000 in football (in 1997–98).

The new sports marketplace is different from other industries not only because of these very high average salary levels, but also because of the huge spread between the minimum and maximum amounts earned by different players (in 1997–98, ranging in basketball from the League's $270,000 minimum salary to Michael Jordan's $33 million, and in baseball from the $150,000 minimum to Albert Belle's $10 million.) Because far more money rides on the outcome of individual salary negotiations, it is worthwhile for players (at least those earning more than the league minimum) to pay someone with talent and experience in this work to deal with the seasoned general managers who bargain on behalf of their "clients," the team owners. Added to this financial value is an emotional factor—minimizing the impact on the player's personal feelings and team morale of frank discussion (about the player's shortcomings as well as strengths) that takes place in such negotiations to determine where the player should fit within the game's overall salary scale.

Negotiating contracts with teams is still at the core of the sports agent's role: in one week in July 1996, David Falk negotiated contracts on behalf of six of his basketball clients (Jordan, Mourning, Howard, Mutombo, Anderson, and Mayberry) whose total value was more than $400 million (of which Falk would receive three to four percent). However, agents such as Falk, football's Leigh Steinberg, baseball's Randy Hendricks, and others now do much more on behalf of their clients.[c] Just as is true in the entertainment industry, good agents can secure lucrative endorsements and promotional activities for their clients. In non-team sports such as golf and tennis, athletes' direct earnings from the sport depend on how they fare in the tournaments; thus the principal focus of people like Mark McCormack of International Management Group (who began with Arnold Palmer and now represents Tiger Woods) and Donald Dell of ProServ (who began with Arthur Ashe but recently lost Pete Sampras) has been to generate revenue opportunities for their

---

[c]. See Lloyd Z. Remick and David S. Eisen, *The Personal Manager in the Entertainment and Sports Industries*, 3 Ent. and Sports L. J. 57 (1986), and W. Michael Robertson, "Financial Planning and Professional Money Management for the Athlete," Chapter 3 of Uberstine, ed., *Law of Professional and Amateur Sports*, note a above.

clients outside the sport.[d] Even in team sports, the outside earnings of a star athlete such as Michael Jordan (more than $40 million a year) exceed the huge salaries that Jordan finally received from the Bulls for his accomplishments on the court.

Full-service agents are concerned not only with revenue generation, but also with revenue management for their clients. This task may involve simply planning the athlete's budget for daily living and seeing that his bills are paid. More importantly, it usually involves development and execution of an investment program (including tax planning) that maximizes the long-term value of monies that are saved by the player. This financial management role is crucial now that high draft picks in all sports regularly receive more money from their signing bonuses alone than their families could ever have dreamed of saving from a lifetime of work. Invested wisely, this money can provide long-term financial security for the player, regardless of what fate has in store for him in the usually short and always unpredictable career of a professional athlete.

A. UNION AND AGENT REPRESENTATION OF ATHLETES

Because of the glamour as well as the financial prospects from representing star athletes, the number of agents has spiraled in recent years. No one knows the exact number of practitioners, but it is safe to say that there are as many (perhaps even more) agents as there are professional athletes. One reason that there is no precise count of agents is that no formal training—in particular, no legal training—is required to become one. Indeed, it is sometimes observed that the only qualification for practicing in this profession is that one have a client.

Yet most prominent agents are lawyers, however little they may have learned about negotiating, promoting, and investment planning while they were at law school. There is, however, an important element of legal expertise in athlete representation: knowledge not only of the general law of contract and taxes, but also of the distinctive law of the collective agreement for a sport. The agreement negotiated by the players association and the league in each sport exercises considerably greater influence on the outcome of individual player contracts than does statutory labor and antitrust law upon the terms of the collective agreements themselves.

As a brief reminder of what we saw in Chapter 4, a union selected by a majority of the employees has the exclusive authority to negotiate all terms and conditions of employment for all members in the bargaining unit. Like their counterparts in the entertainment industry, though, players associations have exercised this statutory authority only to the extent of negotiating minimum salaries, benefits, and job protection—a level of basic compensation that is guaranteed to every player, whether a rookie or superstar. The collective agreement thus allows every player to try to negotiate more advantageous terms—in particular, high guaran-

---

d. See Mark McCormack, *What They Don't Teach You at Harvard Business School* (New York: Bantam, 1984), and Donald Dell, *Minding Other People's Business* (New York: Villard, 1989).

teed salaries. A critical step was taken in the 1970 baseball agreement, which opened the door to agents by giving the player a positive right to have a representative negotiate his individual contract.

The collective agreement exerts a powerful influence on the outcome of such individual negotiations.[e] The share of league revenues channeled into team payrolls through collective bargaining—in minimum salaries and fringe benefits—determines how much is left for individual bargaining. Different versions of the salary cap or tax constrain how much any one team can spend on its player roster. Moreover, the way in which the collective agreement structures the individual player market—e.g., who is entitled this year to free agency or salary arbitration, and under what conditions—is crucial in determining the leverage deployed by the player (and his agent) in direct dealings with his team. Finally, the collective agreement and its arbitration jurisprudence define the meaning of crucial terms in the player contract—such as incentive clauses and long-term guarantees. Representatives of both the players and the teams must be fully aware of these legal nuances to know precisely what rides on their negotiation of particular contract language.

We will not attempt to present a detailed picture of the background law of the player contract in every sport; to do so would require another book of nearly the same size as this one.[f] We will, however, provide capsule descriptions of several controversies and decision excerpts that convey some sense of the importance of this branch of the law of sports in the day-to-day work of a player agent.

1. STANDARDIZED AND INDIVIDUALIZED CONTRACT TERMS

The first case depicts the manner and degree to which a league-wide labor agreement leaves room for individualized drafting of contract terms. At issue was the first set of rules drafted for free agency in baseball, following the *Messersmith* decision. That 1976 labor settlement not only specified when a player could become a free agent and what compensation (in the form of draft picks) was owed to the former team, but also created a draft procedure whereby a specified number of teams could secure the right to bid for the free agents the teams wanted to pursue. That last feature of the free agency system was dispensed with in the 1981 baseball agreement, but not before requiring an arbitrator to interpret its meaning and scope.

ALVIN MOORE & ATLANTA BRAVES
(Arbitration, 1977).

PORTER, ARBITRATOR.

[In April 1977, Alvin Moore signed a one-year contract with the Atlanta Braves. That contract contained a clause which said that if

---

[e.] The best theoretical statement of how this happens—albeit written for a different setting—is Robert M. Mnookin and Lewis A. Kornhauser, *Bargaining in the Shadow of the Law: The Case of Divorce*, 88 Yale L. J. 950 (1979).

[f.] That task has actually been undertaken in four separate chapters in Uberstine, ed., *Law of Professional and Amateur Sports*, note a above: Chapter 5, by Jeffrey S. Moorad, on Major League Baseball; Chapter 6, by Leigh Steinberg, on the National Football League; Chapter 7, by Ted Steinberg, on the National Basketball Association; and Chapter 8, by John Chapman, on the National Hockey League.

Moore told the Braves he was "not satisfied with his playing time by June 15, 1977," the Braves had to trade him to another team (approved by Moore). If such a trade had not been consummated before the end of the season, Moore would "become a free agent if he so desires." National League President Feeney disapproved of this "special covenant" as "inconsistent with the Reserve System Article of the new Basic Agreement." The Players Association filed a grievance on Moore's behalf, based on the Article II Recognition clause in the MLB Agreement, which permitted players to negotiate not just individual salaries above the prescribed league minimum, but also "Special Covenants ... which actually or potentially provide additional benefits to the Player." The issue for the arbitrator was whether this provision in the Moore/Braves contract met the test.]

* * *

According to the Association, there are only three valid reasons for a League President to disapprove a special covenant. He may do so: (1) if the covenant does not meet the test of Article II in that it does not "actually or potentially provide additional benefits to the Player;" (2) if the covenant violates an applicable law or is specifically prohibited by a Major League rule which is not inconsistent with the Basic Agreement (e.g., if the covenant provides for the giving of a bonus for playing, pitching or batting skill or a bonus contingent on the Club's standing, types of bonuses specifically prohibited by Major League Rule 3[a]); or (3) if the covenant purports to bind some third party whom the Club and the Player have no authority to bind (e.g., a covenant stating that, regardless of what a Player does on the field, an Umpire cannot eject him from a game or the League President or the Commissioner cannot discipline him)....

The Clubs reply that the Moore covenant strikes at the very heart of the reserve system which the parties negotiated following the Arbitration Panel's Decision No. 29, the so-called *Messersmith–McNally* case. In the wake of the *Messersmith–McNally* case, all players were theoretically free to play out their contracts and become free agents after an additional renewal year. Confronted by the impending collapse of the reserve system, the Clubs observe, the parties, for the first time, jointly negotiated a new reserve system and incorporated the new system in Article XVII of the 1976–1979 Basic Agreement. In the Clubs' view, Article II of the Basic Agreement does not provide authority for an individual Club and Player to negotiate what, in their opinion, is an entirely new reserve system, merely because such a system would provide a benefit to the Player....

The Clubs concede that, in practice, the League Presidents have approved particular covenants which differ from and hence are arguably "inconsistent" with the provisions of the Basic Agreement. In their view, however, the inconsistencies in these approved covenants involved interests of the individual Clubs and Player alone—e.g., covenants guaranteeing a player's salary for one or more years, covenants waiving a Club's rights regarding commercial endorsements, medical examinations, etc. They did not involve covenants, such as the Moore covenant, wherein the Club and the Player sought to waive the interests of others—in this case the 25 other Clubs' interest in maintaining the kind of competitive balance among the various Clubs which the Reserve System of Article XVII was and is designed to provide.

The Moore covenant is said by the Clubs to contravene the scheme of Article XVII in three main respects. First, it grants to Moore, who presently has less than one year of Major League service, a conditional right to demand a trade, should he "not be satisfied with his playing time by June 15, 1977...."

Second, if a trade is not consummated by the end of the 1977 season, the Moore covenant renders Moore eligible to become a free agent, if he so desires, despite the fact that he will then have only a little more than a year's Major League service....

Third, the Moore covenant does not expressly make him subject to the [free agent] re-entry procedure, with its quota and compensation provisions....

The objective of this re-entry procedure, the Clubs contend, is to provide for an even and equitable distribution of players among all the Clubs and prevent a few of the richer Clubs from buying up a disproportionate share of the available free agent talent. To permit the Atlanta Club and Player Moore to by-pass the re-entry procedure would defeat this objective and allow the Atlanta Club to waive the rights which the other 25 Clubs have in maintaining the competitive balance which the re-entry procedure is designed to foster, the Clubs conclude. They ask, accordingly, that league President Feeney's disapproval of the Moore covenant be sustained by the Panel.

* * *

In the Chairman's judgment, both parties have advanced sound positions in support of their respective claims, but each has pushed his position to an unsound extreme. For reasons to be given more fully below, the Chairman is convinced the Moore covenant can be interpreted in a way which does not impinge upon the legitimate interests of the other Clubs and could and should have been approved on that basis. No reason appears why the Atlanta Club may not accord to Moore conditional rights to demand a trade and to become a free agent under Article XVII, B(2), despite the fact that he does not have the requisite years of Major League service to claim these rights unilaterally. The 5–and 6–year service requirements for Players seeking to exercise such rights unilaterally under Article XVII, D and B(2), respectively, are for the individual Club's benefit; and no persuasive evidence or argument has been presented to show why the benefit of long-term title and reservation rights to Moore's contract may not be waived by his club. But if Atlanta may waive the length of service requirements designed for its benefit, it may not waive the reentry procedure designed for the benefit of all 26 Clubs....

Negotiations between individual Clubs and Players are not ... conducted in a vacuum. To the contrary, and at the risk of belaboring the obvious, individual Player–Club negotiations are conducted not only within the framework of applicable law but within the framework of organized professional baseball and the attendant rules, agreements and regulations by which the sport or industry is governed and by which the Association on behalf of the Players and the Clubs comprising the two Major Leagues have agreed to be bound. Within the latter framework are innumerable matters affecting the interests and rights of all the Clubs and Players, such as the number of Player contracts to which each Club may have title and reservation rights, the number of Players each Club may retain on its active roster, the length of the intra or interleague trading periods, etc. Variations in any one of these provisions might give a Player "additional benefits" but are beyond the Club's power to make....

To the extent the Association seeks to push its "additional benefit" argument to the point where the Moore covenant is to be interpreted as exempting Moore from the free agent quota system and other aspects of the reentry procedure designed to protect the interests of all 26 Clubs, the Chairman believes it presses its argument too far.

* * *

Grievance upheld in part.

Questions for Discussion

1. Suppose the individual contract specifies that, at its termination, the player becomes a free agent without compensation—that is, the team waives its right to whatever draft pick it would receive from a new team signing the player. Is this provision valid (see *Mike Marshall & Minnesota Twins* (Arbitration, 1978))?

2. The basketball collective agreement adopts a different approach to the permissible language in individual contracts. Article I of the NBA agreement states "that the player and team can supplement the provisions of the Uniform Player Contract [UPC], but may not agree upon terms that contradict, change, or are inconsistent with a UPC provision, nor provide for a waiver by a player of any benefit or sacrifice of any right to which the player is entitled under the collective agreement." The agreement then goes on to list numerous provisions in the individual contract that can be amended, and presents the carefully-drafted contract terms that can be inserted in their place. Recall the arbitrator's decision in the *Brian Shaw* case (in Chapter 2) about the compatibility with the NBA labor agreement of a specific clause that had been inserted in Shaw's contract with the Boston Celtics.

3. A unique feature of baseball's Major League Rules, incorporated by reference in the collective agreement, prohibits (through Rule 3(A)) "the giving of a bonus for playing, pitching or batting skills; or ... the payment of a bonus contingent on the standing of the club at the end of the championship season." That is why incentive clauses in baseball contracts are always defined in terms of the number of games played, at-bats, pitching starts, or other kinds of appearances. What is the rationale for this contract restriction, one that does not exist in other sports? Is it a sensible sports policy? Consider the case of Dennis "Oil Can" Boyd, to whom the Montreal Expos promised to pay an extra $300,000 if he started 32 games in the 1990 season. However, rather than start Boyd for the 32nd time at his regular turn in the rotation on the final day of the season, the Expos used a rookie pitching prospect? What do you think was—and should have been—the outcome of Boyd's grievance?

4. As we saw in the *Danny Ainge* case and decisions following in Chapter 2, the standard player's contract gives the team the right to terminate the contract if the "player fails, in the opinion of the Club's management, to exhibit sufficient skill or competitive ability to qualify or continue as a member of the Club's team" (this is the language in baseball's standard player contract). A regular problem with that language is that the team may well choose to release a veteran player with a high salary in favor of a less-accomplished younger player with a much lower salary, when the team judges the gap in performance insufficient to warrant the salary differential. To avoid such problems, agents seek to negotiate "guaranteed" contracts if and when their clients have the market leverage to do so. That guarantee provision poses another problem: what happens when the team still decides to release the player, who is then picked up by another team at a lower, but still significant, salary amount? Arbitrators in two cases, *Rudy Hackett & Denver Nuggets* (1977), and *Dante Pastorini & Oakland Raiders* (1984), refused to read either league's existing collective agreement (or general contract principles) as requiring the player to offset against his guaranteed salary claim the amount paid by the new team. The NBA and its Players Association amended their agreement to require such offset by "any amounts earned by the Player (for services as a player) from any NBA member during the period covered by the terminated contract." Is such language likely to address the problem, given the deal the agent for the released player would likely seek to negotiate with the new team?

2. DEALING WITH THE SALARY CAP

More recent controversies have witnessed teams and players trying to figure out ways to finesse the constraints of the salary cap. We read at the end of Chapter 4 about the evolution of salary caps (or taxes) in sports and the key structural features negotiated by players associations and league offices in different sports. Once the basic design is in place, though, both player agents and individual team executives have strong market incentives to find loopholes in the labor agreement that permit the team to show the player enough money to entice him to sign. These individual contracts must go back to the Commissioner for approval, and possibly to the Players Association or an outside adjudicator to decide whether the contract does or does not satisfy the existing rules. Even if the answer is affirmative, the parties may well agree to modify the rules to block off such loopholes for the future.

In football, the biggest such case and controversy involved Deion Sanders. Sanders' 1994 contract with the San Francisco 49ers had a $1 million base salary, with a $750,000 bonus payment after Sanders helped the team win that year's Super Bowl. Cowboys' owner Jerry Jones, having experienced the break in his team's Super Bowl winning streak, was willing to offer Sanders the money the latter wanted to move to the Cowboys in 1995—a seven-year, $35 million contract with a $13 million signing bonus.

Such a contract size posed a serious salary cap problem for the Cowboys who already had high-priced stars such as Troy Aikman, Michael Irvin, and Emmitt Smith. Under the collective agreement, signing bonuses were prorated across the length of player contract for purposes of salary cap calculations. In the case of Sanders, this meant that his $13 million bonus, while paid immediately, was attributed at $1.87 million apiece to each of the seven years of his contract. Jones then agreed to pay Sanders only $178,000 a year in base salary for the first three years, leaping to $5 or $6 million for each of the remaining years (plus the prorated bonus). The reason for the latter move was not simply to postpone the Cowboys' payment, but to allow the team to void the contract in 1998, which it would be likely to do, thereby causing $4/7$ (the still unamortised amount) of the signing bonus to be "counted" in 1999, the year in which the salary cap expired under the labor agreement. Even if the Cowboys did not void the contract, the bulk of the money paid under it would be pushed into the uncapped "out years" (in the hope, however, that the labor agreement and thus the cap would not be extended past 1998).

When NFL Commissioner Tagliabue saw the terms of this deal worked out by Jones and Sanders' agent, he disallowed the contract as violating the spirit, if not the explicit terms, of the League's salary cap system. Following a grievance filed by the Players Association on behalf of Sanders, the parties eventually worked out a settlement that increased by $400,000 the amount attributed from Sanders' bonus to the Cowboys salary cap figures in each of the first three years.

NFL and NFLPA officials also revised their collective agreement for the future, to bar more than a 50% gap between the size of the prorated signing bonus and the lower base salary for that year. In return for that concession to the League, the players union extracted an increase in the minimum salary from $178,000 to $250,000 (and adjusted annually thereafter). Deion Sanders not only helped return the 1995 Super Bowl to Dallas, but his agent's contract device actually produced a pay hike for a large number of minimum salaried players in the League.[g]

---

g. A further feature of the Sanders and other player contracts is worth noting at this point. Signing bonuses paid to football players are not bonuses in the usual sense

An analogous loophole had been discovered in the NBA version of the salary cap. In the summer of 1993, a new provision was inserted in several player contracts negotiated by free agents—by Craig Ehlo with the Atlanta Hawks, Tony Kukoc with the Chicago Bulls, A.C. Green with the Phoenix Suns, and Chris Dudley with the Portland Trail Blazers. Each of these multi-year agreements guaranteed the player the maximum amount the signing team could pay under the League's salary cap. However, the player also had the right unilaterally to terminate the contract after one year when, as a veteran now renegotiating with his current team, he would not be limited by the NBA's "soft" version of the salary cap.

Chris Dudley, for example, a low-scoring but effective rebounder and shot-blocker for the New Jersey Nets, had earned $1.2 million as the Nets' second-string center during the 1992–93 season. With his contract having expired in June 1993, the Nets offered Dudley a new seven-year, $21 million deal, with annual salaries ranging from $1.6 million in 1993–94 to $4.4 million in 1999–2000. However, Dudley and his agent, Dan Fagan, believed that the player's potential market value was considerably higher than the amount the Nets had offered. After negotiating with a number of teams, Dudley eventually signed a seven-year contract for a total of $10.5 million with the Portland Trail Blazers, starting in 1993–94 with the $790,000 slot the Blazers had available under the cap, and then increasing by the maximum 30% per year to $2.2 million for the 1999–2000 season. But while this Trail Blazers' contract guaranteed Dudley only half the amount contained in the Nets' offer, Dudley was

of that term—extra money over and above the guaranteed salary. These bonuses are really a prepayment of the agreed-to salaries that are not otherwise guaranteed by the team. The bonuses serve principally as a deterrent to teams releasing players for whose services they have already paid in part. Except for brief periods of interleague competition, football players have almost never enjoyed the benefit of contracts that are guaranteed against loss of skill and lowered performance, or even against a disability that lasts beyond the season in which the injury occurred. In the past, NFL contracts provided that a player unable to play due to an injury incurred in performance of the contract would be paid only "for the term of the contract." When teams began in the 1960s to sign players to multi-year deals, rather than amend the standard-form contract language, the League practice was to have players sign a series of one-year contracts so that presumably an injured player would still only be paid for the remainder of the year in which he was injured. See *Sample v. Gotham Football Club (Jets)*, 59 F.R.D. 160 (S.D.N.Y.1973). However, after the Third Circuit held that it was a factual question that had to be left to the jury to determine whether a series of one-year contracts evidenced an intent to provide multi-year injury protection (see *Chuy v. Philadelphia Eagles Football Club*, 595 F.2d 1265 (3d Cir.1979)), the League finally amended its standard-form player contract to provide that an injured player would be paid his salary "during the season of injury only and for no subsequent period." Thus, it is now clear that a team can exercise its option to release a player in the off-season if his performance has dropped off for any reason (especially relative to a new draft pick or free agent acquisition), or even if he has become disabled due to an injury. Why is it that supposedly long-term football contracts give owners that one-way opt-out—just for players, not coaches like Jimmy Johnson or Bill Parcells—even in the current world of free agency? To what extent does the signing bonus ameliorate this feature in football deals (a feature that rarely is found in multi-year baseball or basketball contracts)?

entitled to terminate the contract after one year and to negotiate a new deal at whatever amount the Blazers were then willing to pay him.

NBA Commissioner David Stern rejected these contracts as contravening League standards. The NBA Players Association used Dudley's contract as the test case through which to challenge the Commissioner's rulings in front of the New Jersey District Judge who had presided over *Junior Bridgeman v. NBA*, 675 F.Supp. 960 (D.N.J.1987), the antitrust-labor exemption lawsuit whose settlement in 1988 had produced the existing version of the salary cap in the NBA collective agreement. The Special Master under the Bridgeman Settlement Agreement (BSA) found that there had been no specific understanding between Dudley and the Trail Blazers about what would be the salary amount in a new contract. It was, however, clearly understood by everyone that once he had the chance to display his talent as the Blazers' starting center, Dudley would be able to negotiate a far more generous deal than his current one. The NBA argued that it was precisely this understanding that rendered the Dudley contract invalid under § 3 of the BSA, which provided:

> 3. Neither the parties hereto, nor any Team or player shall enter into any agreement, Player Contract, Offer Sheet or other transaction which includes any terms that are designed to serve the purpose of defeating or circumventing the intention of the parties as reflected by (a) the provisions of this Article VII with respect to Defined Gross Revenues, salary cap and Minimum Team Salary and (b) the terms and provisions of this Stipulation and Settlement Agreement.

The judge was not prepared to bar such an opt-out contract provision at this stage of the proceedings, although his opinion hinted that the verdict might well change if broader use of the device seemed to be having a serious adverse impact on the goals of the salary cap system. See *Bridgeman v. NBA* (re: *Chris Dudley*), 838 F.Supp. 172 (D.N.J.1993). While playing for the Blazers under this contract, Dudley broke his leg early in the 1993–94 season, and played very little that year. Notwithstanding that fact, in the summer of 1994 the Trail Blazers signed Dudley to a six-year, $24 million contract. Meanwhile, other star free agents were moving to new teams with similar deals. For example, Horace Grant went from the Chicago Bulls to the Orlando Magic with a one-year-out option in his multi-year contract. Commissioner David Stern rejected the Dudley and Grant contracts, and the matter went back to Judge Debevoise. The judge upheld the new Dudley contract, but cast sufficient doubt on his willingness to do so in the future that Grant, the Magic, and Stern agreed to restructure Grant's contract with a two-year-out option for the player. After opting-out in 1996, Grant was able to secure a contract from the Magic that paid him $15 million for the 1996–97 season (the season during which the Magic lost Shaquille O'Neal to the Lakers).

Even with that modest modification to the *Dudley* ruling, this was a major issue for the NBA in the 1994–95 negotiations for renewal of its labor agreement. The solution proposed by Commissioner Stern, and initially agreed-to by new Association leader Simon Gourdine in June 1995, was to eliminate the "Larry Bird" exception (which placed no limit on what the free agent's prior team could pay him). The NBA would substitute the NFL's "hard" cap for its traditional "soft" cap, in return for which the cap levels were to be raised from $16 to $23 million. A player rebellion, whose most prominent figure was Michael Jordan, forced the NBA to retreat on that score, while still moving the cap to $23 million. (Indeed, it was the continued absence of any cap on what teams paid their own veteran free agents that allowed the Bulls to raise Jordan's salary from $3 million in 1995–96 to $30 million in 1996–97.) However, the League and the union did largely close up this *Dudley* exception. A team that signs a free agent from another team must wait another three years before they can sign him to a new contract at a rate higher than the league's average salary.

Ironically, Chris Dudley generated yet another major legal issue about the interpretation and application of the new labor agreement to individual free agent contracts. As of the summer of 1997, Dudley still had three years remaining on his contract with the Portland Trail Blazers, for a total of $13 million in salary. However, after averaging 3.9 points and 7.3 rebounds per game during the 1996–97 season, Dudley exercised his right to terminate that contract, and as a free agent he turned down a four-year, $17 million offer from the Detroit Pistons. Instead, in late August, Dudley signed a new one-year contract with the Blazers that would pay him the minimum $272,000 salary. The explanation is found in the following understandings negotiated by Dudley's agent with three clubs.

 i. The New York Knicks would trade John Williams to the Toronto Raptors in return for a first-round (non-lottery) draft pick. This trade would free up $1.35 million in the Knicks salary cap allowance to offer a new player during the 1997–98 season.

 ii. Dudley and the Knicks agreed to a $1.35 million, one-year deal for that season, with both sides saying there were no understandings about future contract amounts.

 iii. Dudley then signed the $272,000 1997–98 contract with the Blazers, pursuant to which the Blazers agreed to trade him to the Knicks for a first-round (also non-lottery) draft pick.

The assumption of the immediate parties was that this arrangement would make Dudley a "Qualifying Veteran Free Agent" for purposes of the "Bird" exception, which under Article I(ak) was applicable not just to players who played three seasons with their "Prior Team," but also those who changed teams "by means of assignment" by the Prior Team. However, all of the contracts and trades were made subject to league approval of the validity of Dudley's status under the agreement.

Commissioner Stern quickly ruled against this new "sign-and-trade" arrangement on the grounds that it denied rather than "preserved the essential benefits achieved by both parties to the [Collective] Agreement," and that it was "designed to serve the purpose of defeating or circumventing the interests of the parties as reflected by all of the provisions of this Agreement" (either of which are grounds for striking down a player-team deal under Article XIII:1(a)). Under the new collective agreement, the parties substituted private arbitration for judicial interpretation of these (and other) terms of their contracts. Dudley and the NBPA won the same favorable verdict under this new procedure. From the point of view of broader free agency/salary cap policy, what are the similarities and differences between Dudley's move from the Nets to the Blazers in 1993 and his move back to the New York area with the Knicks in 1997?

A third such salary cap controversy took place in the summer of 1996. While the immediate dispute was resolved, the broader issue remains open.

In the spring of 1996, the Miami Heat and head coach Pat Riley released or traded a number of players with a view to clearing up salary cap room to sign one or more of the highly-rated free agents during the upcoming summer season. A key Heat target was Washington Bullets' forward Juwan Howard, who had become a big star during the past year when he was paid "only" $2 million under a contract he had the right to terminate (which he did). Even more important to the Heat, though, was retention of their center Alonzo Mourning, whose contract was also expiring. Happily for everyone, or so it seemed, Mourning and Howard had the same agent, David Falk, who was negotiating on behalf of both players with the Heat (and other teams).

The Heat could sign Mourning for any amount under the "Bird exception," but they were constrained by that year's $24 million salary cap in what they could offer Howard. If Mourning had not yet reached a new agreement with the Heat, the team had to count only his prior salary (times 1.5) against that cap figure, and thence could afford to offer Howard a seven-year $101 million contract, significantly higher than the Bullets' last offer. (That contract began at $8.8 million for 1996–97, and increased by 20% a year for seven years, the maximum length and increases permitted under the new NBA collective agreement.) However, when the Howard–Heat contract went to League offices for checking and approval, Commissioner Stern learned that Mourning had told an ESPN interviewer that his agent Falk had already worked out a $112 million/seven year contract with Riley and the Heat; in tandem with the Howard contract, this amount would put the Heat over the cap. Thus, Stern rejected the Howard contract on the basis that the Heat had violated the bar on any "undisclosed agreements" in its dealings with Mourning and Falk. Article 13, § 2 of the collective agreement says:

> At no time shall there be any undisclosed agreements of any kind, expressed or implied, oral or written, or promises, undertak-

ings, representations, commitments, inducements, assurance of intent, or understandings of any kind between a player and any team concerning . . . any future renegotiation, extension or amendment of an existing player contract or entry into a new player contract.

The NBPA immediately said it would file a grievance on Howard's behalf, posing the significant question whether an understanding between a player and a team about just the salary and duration of a new deal amounted to a binding agreement for purposes of the salary cap. However, this dispute then took a very different route than the *Sanders* and *Dudley* cases described above. The Bullets were now prepared to offer even more money than the Heat ($105 million, or $15 million-a-year) to Howard, who had preferred to stay in D.C. all along. Such a Howard–Bullets deal faced an obstacle, though, because after Howard had said he was going to the Heat, the Bullets had "renounced" their rights to him to free up salary cap room that they had already used up on other players. To resolve that problem, Stern allowed the Bullets to put Howard back on their pre-free agent roster (in return for giving up their first 1997 draft pick), so that Howard could be signed under the "Bird exception." The players association accepted that resolution which made Howard, their union member, better off, especially given the risk to his negotiating leverage if the arbitrator were to invalidate the Howard–Heat contract. The NBPA made it clear, though (with the agreement of the NBA), that the *Howard* case would not be used as a precedent for future disputes about whether and when an "undisclosed agreement" exists. The only loser that summer was the Heat, though that winter Riley's team with Mourning played far better than did the Bullets (now the Wizards) with Howard.

The *Sanders*, *Dudley*, and *Howard* cases offer interesting real-world views about the design and operation of salary caps. They also reinforce the point made at the start of this chapter—about how complex a job the negotiating of player contracts has become for agents and team executives, and how important it is to have developed the skills ordinarily used in corporate financing and tax avoidance. The leaders and lawyers for the leagues and player unions have to perform much the same role as the SEC, the IRS, and the Congress in minimizing the availability of contract devices that seem to satisfy the letter, but not the spirit, of their system of salary constraints.

3. SALARY ARBITRATION[h]

When most sports fans think of arbitration, what comes to mind is not *grievance*, but *salary*, arbitration. These two collectively-bargained

---

[h]. See James B. Dworkin, *Owners versus Players: Baseball and Collective Bargaining*, 136–172 (Dover, Mass.: Auburn House, 1981), and David M. Frederick, William H. Kaempfer, and Richard L. Wobekind, "Salary Arbitration as a Market Substitute," Chapter 2 of *Diamonds Are Forever: The Business of Baseball* (Washington, D.C.: Brookings, 1992).

procedures resemble each other in their presentation of the positions of player and club at a private, informal proceeding in front of a neutral arbitrator. One difference is that the player's case in salary arbitration is presented by his personal agent, although the players association also has someone present to assist the player's agent. A more fundamental jurisprudential difference, though, is that whereas grievance arbitration interprets and enforces contract rights already created by the collective agreement, salary arbitration itself establishes this key term in the individual player's contract.

Salary arbitration first emerged in the early 1970s in hockey. By contrast with football or basketball, hockey resembled baseball (at least prior to *Messersmith*) in its assumption that the player contract was perpetually renewable. That posed the question of how to fix the salary figure in each year's contract. Traditionally, that prerogative had been reserved for the owners. With the emergence of independent players associations in the late 1960s, the perceived unfairness of this traditional practice led to substitution of a neutral party as salary arbitrator—in hockey in 1970 and in baseball in 1973.

The procedures operate quite differently in the two sports. Hockey utilizes the more conventional arbitration model, in which hearings are conducted by named arbitrators at various times throughout the year; after listening to both sides' arguments, the arbitrator issues a detailed written decision several weeks (even months) later. In baseball, by contrast, each salary arbitration is conducted before one of a large number of arbitrators (or a panel) during a three-week period in February, and each arbitrator simply gives his final verdict on the day after the hearing. In addition to that procedural difference, hockey arbitrators are asked to decide what they think is the appropriate salary amount, typically somewhere between the numbers proposed by each side. The baseball arbitrator, by contrast, can only select one or other of the two figures proposed, rather than compromise between them.

As noted above, hockey is the place where salary arbitrators issue awards with extensively-reasoned opinions. The summer of 1993 produced a heated negotiating dispute between the Boston Bruins and their future Hall-of-Fame defenseman Raymond Bourque. Reading the arbitrator's opinion offers a revealing look at what player agents and team executives have to do by way of salary comparisons and appraisals, not just for purposes of arbitration, but also for negotiation.

RAYMOND BOURQUE AND BOSTON BRUINS
(Arbitration, 1993).

BLOCK, ARBITRATOR.

Raymond Bourque joined the Boston Bruins as a first-round draft pick in the 1979 Entry Draft and has been a centerpiece on that team every year thereafter. The current dispute involves the terms of his

1993–94 contract and the option year, 1994–95. His previous contract, signed at the beginning of the 1990–91 season, established a base salary of $1,100,000 for each season, with an additional $175,000 per season as deferred compensation.

In certain respects, the parties to this dispute are in agreement. They agree, for example, that Bourque should be paid more than any other defenseman in the NHL. The Club offers $1,850,000 on a "one-plus-one" basis with a bonus plan identical to that contained in his current agreement. The player, for his part, proffers a salary, on a "one-plus-one" basis, of $4,250,000 for each of the next two years. The finding here, for the reasons set forth below, is that the Club's figure fails to properly recognize Bourque's capabilities and contributions and that the Player's figure ignores the realities and opportunities of the particular contract structure he has chosen.

While there is no real dispute as to Bourque's achievements, they warrant recounting. They are stunning.... [The arbitrator here detailed Bourque's accomplishments during his fourteen-year NHL career. Suffice it to say that Bourque had been named to the All–Star team every season, and twelve times had been the winner or runner-up for the Norris trophy as the game's best defenseman.]

The Memorandum of Understanding between the NHL and the NHLPA specifies a series of considerations to be reviewed for purposes of salary arbitration. They include, in part, the following:

> (i) the overall performance, including official statistics prepared by the League (both offensive and defensive) of the player in the previous season or seasons;
>
> (ii) the number of games played by the player, his injuries or illness during the preceding seasons;
>
> (iii) the length of service of the player in the League and/or with the Club;
>
> (iv) the overall contribution of the player to the competitive success or failure of his Club in the preceding season;
>
> (v) any special qualities of leadership or public appeal not inconsistent with the fulfillment of his responsibilities as a playing member of his team.

It is not overstating the case to conclude that, measured by these standards, Raymond Bourque is generally unmatched in terms of the quality and consistency of his play. He is, by any definition, a franchise player. Given his pre-eminence in the field and accepting the undisputed premise that he should be paid more than any other defenseman in the League, the question is: how much more?

The parties' Memorandum directs the arbitrator's attention to consideration of comparable players and their salaries, including:

(vi) the overall performance in the previous season or seasons of any player(s) who is alleged to be comparable to the player whose salary is in dispute;

(vii) the compensation of any player(s) who is alleged to be comparable to the Player;

An immediate dilemma exists in terms of attempting to rank, comparatively, someone who is already acknowledged to be at the top. Unquestionably, reasonable comparisons may be drawn between Bourque and Messrs. Coffey (Detroit), Chelios (Chicago), Housley (Winnipeg), Murphy (Pittsburgh), and Macinnis (Calgary), among others, in terms of seniority and general accomplishments among the premier defensemen in the NHL.

In the immediately preceding season ('92–'93), Bourque ranked sixth among twenty-three top defensemen, considering Season Games played, Season Goals, Assists, Total Points, Power Play Goals, Power Play Assists, Power Play Points, Plus/Minus, and Penalty minutes.[1] Over the last *three* seasons, ranked by the same standards, Bourque placed first; third if one considers the last *five* seasons. Ranked over a career, he stands second.

The playoff statistics are less imposing (relatively speaking), at least with respect to 1992–93. His average ranking among the twenty-three defensemen was fifteen. On one hand, the overall success of the team during playoffs is a critical factor in individual statistics, inasmuch as that success directly impacts the number of games played and, consequently, the opportunity to score goals, accumulate assists and other points. Notwithstanding this, Bourque ranks third overall (behind Murphy and Chelios) when measured over the last three and the last five seasons. He ranks third, as well (behind Coffey and Chelios) on a career basis.

In terms of recent performance, therefore, Bourque ranks clearly among the leaders, measured by virtually any standard. Were one to base a decision solely on those types of snapshots, it might be concluded that a salary closely comparable to the others would be appropriate. But viewed in the overall, there are reasons to set this player apart. Both Chelios and Coffey have won the Norris trophy twice—Coffey was runner-up twice. But as indicated above, Bourque has won the Norris trophy four times and has been in the running eight more seasons. In terms of consistent contributions over an extended career which, as indicated above, shows no sign of recent flagging, Bourque has established himself not simply as an outstanding defenseman but as an important fixture in the National Hockey League.

---

1. In this [penalty minutes] category, Bourque ranked twenty-one of twenty-three, having spent forty minutes on the bench as compared to the 282 of Chris Chelios. The team attributes this to a lack of intimidating style. The player testifies, however, that his style of play in this respect has never been criticized. He assumes, he says, that the team wants him on the ice.

Phil Housley, of St. Louis, earned a position on the 1991–92 second team All–Stars, but has never been a factor in the Norris trophy consideration. Housely will earn $1,700,000 in '93–'94 season. Paul Coffey, is comparable, in certain respects, and bests Bourque in terms of offensive capabilities. Bourque, however, is more of a two-way, offensive/defensive player. Coffey has, in his thirteen-year career, been selected to an All–Star team on seven occasions, compared to Bourque's fourteen in fourteen years. Coffey will receive $1,300,000. Chelios, a 10–year defenseman with Chicago, is a two-time Norris Trophy winner and a three-time All Star. He will receive $1,100,000 for the '93–'94 season, as part of a 5–year package. Brian Leetch, of the Rangers, will receive $1,805,000. He is, unquestionably, a brilliant defenseman whose success and statistics need not be restated here. It suffices to say that, while Leetch's accomplishments and potential are unquestioned, they cannot be reasonably compared (yet) with the consistency of Bourque. His accomplishments warrant recognition with a salary that reflects his status as an overall player and a consistent contributor to his team and to the League.

Comparisons to other NHL standouts, including Mark Messier, Brett Hull, Steve Yzerman, Patrick Roy, Wayne Gretzky, and Mario LeMieux, while not inappropriate, are elusive for a number of reasons. Beyond the difficulty of dealing with the purely statistical aspects, the vagaries of the individual contract constructions make specific year-to-year assessments potentially misleading. As noted in the case of *Olyczyk and the New York Rangers* (June, 1993):

> To be sure, the existence of variations on the payment theme, such as signing bonuses and deferred compensation, for example, may make it more difficult, in a given case, to draw precise comparisons between and among salaries for individual players. And, as the Club notes, these compensation devices can potentially distort figures, depending on the assumptions made as to the allocation of various stipends. But this should not require the conclusion that all such compensation should be disregarded. Salary packages are constructed in many varied and wonderful ways. While some careful scrutiny may be required to ensure that apples are being compared to apples, the parties to this process, and its arbitrators are capable of just such adjustments. It is true that a signing bonus is most likely (but not always) associated with long term, multi-year contracts. But it is not the bonus itself that is the problem; rather, it is the fact that the multi-year contract is more likely to reflect higher figures (the price of extended stability) and may thus be seen as not necessarily comparable to the single year agreement. The remedy for this, however, is not to ignore the signing bonus, any more than it is to ignore any other element of true compensation. Similarly, deferred compensation cannot be carved out merely because it represents dollars to be paid in later years. This is compensation for the Player's performance during the season in question. That it is to be deferred, for a host of reasons that may benefit one or the other

party, or both, is virtually irrelevant, other than to note (for whatever it may be worth) that the deferred payment will, in all likelihood, be a relatively less expensive way of settling the debt. The proper approach is simply to account for the disparate nature of the respective agreements, to adjust, to the extent reasonable, to attempt to compare fairly, and, finally, having done this, to draw whatever conclusions are appropriate under the circumstances.

The players set forth above, as well as others offered by the Player for comparison, are universally involved in long-term contracts. It is possible, as the Player contends, that situations may exist where a player will find such an agreement attractive, primarily for security reasons, to the extent of accepting less compensation. But by and large, the stability inherent in a long-term agreement comes at a price to the club, the player having traded away his ability to test the market. Nor may one accept the contention that this particular player is somehow at risk by opting for the shorter format of the "one-plus-one" arrangement. While it is true that the second year is not in all circumstances guaranteed, the Player has access to the market relatively quickly. Indeed, Bourque can return to the bargaining table and, if necessary, to arbitration, after one year. To the extent that certain players somewhere will accept (and that clubs will offer) lower salaries in return for security, one cannot expect those dynamics to apply to the likes of Bourque and his colleagues.

It is fully appropriate, in the course of fashioning the contract award, to place one's self in the parties' position, considering the "market" for a player or given category of player and attempting to discern, to whatever extent possible, the respective positions and the responses. In this context, even accepting a frame of reference that would accommodate non-defensemen players, for comparison purposes, the long-term nature of those arrangements and the impact on salary may simply not be ignored.

Top paid forwards in the NHL for 1993–94 include Messrs. Yzerman, Lindros, Messier, Turgeon, Hull, Sakic, and LaFontaine, all of whom will earn between $2,000,000 and $2,800,000 this year. These are all quality players who figure prominently in their club's fortunes and in that respect may be seen as comparable to Bourque. If, as the Player notes, none has reached his level of consistent accomplishments, it is also true that their salaries all derive from the early years of multi-year contracts. On balance, while one may conclude that Mr. Bourque should be compensated well ahead of other NHL defensemen, given his two-way capabilities and the quality and consistency of his achievements, it may not be said that a ranking that would place him considerably above and beyond virtually all players in the NHL is appropriate, either taken in the abstract or considered in the light of his ability to return to the bargaining table in a very short period of time. Considering these observations, the conclusion is that Raymond Bourque should receive a salary of $2.25 million on a "one plus one" basis, including continuation of all existing bonus provisions.

So awarded.

Bourque and his agent were as disappointed in this arbitral verdict as the Bruins and its management were delighted. (By the way, the Bruins case was argued by the special counsel who handle all salary arbitration cases for the clubs. Why do you think that NHL Commissioner Gary Bettman instituted this League procedure? Can and should NHL Players Association leader, Bob Goodenow, direct the same mode of representation on the player side?) However, the story did have a happy ending. A few weeks after the salary award came down for the 1993–94 season, Bourque and the Bruins agreed on a five-year $12.5 million contract that almost certainly will keep Bourque with the Bruins until the end of his hockey career. What influence did the arbitration decision likely have on the parties' ability to reach such a deal?

Whatever may have been the verdict in *Bourque*, owners in hockey (as in baseball) have always treated arbitration as a major source of rising salary levels in their sport. Thus, as part of the January 1995 settlement of hockey's lockout and bargaining dispute, the players agreed to lighten the force of salary arbitration as felt by the owners (and thereby fend off the latter's salary tax effort). Hockey owners now have the right (which each club can exercise up to three times over two years) to reject an award in excess of average League salaries (approximately $1 million in the 1997–98 season). (The owner can also elect to have the arbitrator resolve the contract for two years, rather than just one.) If the owner "walks away" from a particular award, the affected player then becomes a free agent. If the player does not get a better outside offer, he can "walk back" to his prior club and take the latter's pre-arbitration offer. Now that you have seen hockey arbitration in operation in the *Bourque* case, do you think this revision was necessary or desirable? Are there any cases in which owners are taking advantage of it?

Baseball's version of salary arbitration (by contrast with hockey's more conventional model) is perhaps the most visible and most studied example of "final offer selection," an idea that emerged in 1960s theorizing about dispute resolution. The assumption is that such a constraint on the arbitrator's decision-making authority expands the incentives felt by the parties to agree to a voluntary settlement without outside adjudication. What do you think is the logic of that theory? In actual practice, during the first two years of arbitration in baseball, only half the salary cases were settled; however, by the mid–1990s, of 60 to 80 players entering the process each season, only five to ten needed an arbitral ruling.

Of course, the mere availability of this procedure does make a major contribution to rising baseball salaries. Though owners typically win more verdicts than they lose, the entire class of players eligible for arbitration secures an average salary increase of 75% to 150%. Even the players "losing" their cases secured average annual salary increases of 50% to 75%, amounting to a raise of a half million dollars or more.[i]

That is why salary arbitration has been just as much an object of baseball owners' ire as free agency. In 1985, for example, the owners took a strike to get eligibility for arbitration lifted from two to three years of service; then, in 1990, the owners locked out the players to hold any reduction in eligibility time to just the highest one-sixth of players with between two and three years service; finally, in 1994, owners not only insisted on the imposition of an overall salary cap or hard tax, but they also asked for the total abolition of salary arbitration.

It is easy to understand why leagues would want to avoid arbitral review of the merits of the two sides' salary proposals and instead let the owner's final offer govern. That is why MLB's 1994 proposal was to eliminate arbitration for all players and to give free agency to players with four or five years service (but not those previously eligible for arbitration after two or three years service); even then, the current team would retain a right of refusal of any other club's offer. The MLBPA's position was that it would agree to abolish salary arbitration, but only if every otherwise eligible player thereby got the same unrestricted free agency as six-year veterans. The parties' eventual settlement of this dispute altered arbitration only by gradually moving to three-member panels making the decisions. Again, as in hockey, we shall have to see whether this procedural change makes any difference in substantive salary outcome.

The more interesting and fundamental question concerns the comparative effects and values of salary arbitration and free agency. Would salary arbitration be inflationary if there were no free agency? Would players actually fare better if they gave up neutral salary arbitration entirely in favor of free agency (e.g., as in basketball or football, subject to whatever salary cap exists in the game)? The current system in baseball every year has a handful of free agents with far more players entitled to arbitration if necessary. Does this provide a reasonable balance between the two sides, or does it tilt in one direction or the other? And finally, how should one appraise the current rule in both baseball and hockey that focuses on the *player's* performance and play, but excludes any reference to the *team's* financial position and ability to pay?

---

i. The cash value of salary arbitration is demonstrated even more clearly by recent econometric research which finds that, after taking account of actual performance on the field, the mere fact of becoming eligible for arbitration raises the salaries of players by anywhere from 55% to 90%, depending on the player's position: see Paul C. Burgess and Daniel L. Marburger, "Bargaining Power and Major League Baseball," Chapter 3 of *Diamonds Are Forever*, note h above.

B. BREAKDOWNS IN THE AGENT–PLAYER RELATIONSHIP

The prior section conveys some of the flavor of the sports agent's role and expertise. The principal focus of this chapter, though, is not the law used by agents in their dealings with clubs, but rather the law governing the relationship between agents and players. The cases selected for this section provide a further glimpse of the working life of an agent and illustrate the types of conflict that can arise between an agent and his or her client.

A heavily publicized legal proceeding against an agent in the mid–1970s rated only a brief notation in the law reports: *People v. Sorkin*, 64 A.D.2d 680, 407 N.Y.S.2d 772 (1978). In this case, a New York appeals court upheld a substantial jail term meted out to Richard Sorkin, a prominent New York representative of hockey players. Sorkin misappropriated over $1 million of his clients' funds, which he then lost in gambling at the race track and on the stock market.

While the Sorkin affair cast a blemish on the reputation of sports agents generally, the more important question posed by that case and the ones that follow is whether such misconduct is merely the occasional abuse that occurs in any type of commercial undertaking, or instead is symptomatic of a deeper imbalance in the player-agent relationship. Can we trust the marketplace to drive out most of the bad agents in favor of the good, relying on general criminal or civil law to deal with the few "bad apples" that remain? Or should we devise a systematic regulatory program targeted at sports agents generally? If we should, who should devise and enforce the program, and with what objectives?

1. STANDARDS FOR AGENT COMPETENCE[j]

We turn first to the question of what standard the law establishes for the level of agent competence and quality of representation owed by agents to their player-clients. The one appellate case that has explored this problem involved one of the early agents in professional football.

ZINN v. PARRISH
United States Court of Appeals, Seventh Circuit, 1981.
644 F.2d 360.

BARTELS, SENIOR DISTRICT JUDGE.

[At the recommendation of Lemar Parrish's college football coach, Leo Zinn agreed to serve as agent for Parrish when he was selected by the Cincinnati Bengals in the 1970 NFL draft. Under their Professional Management Contract, Zinn received a 10% commission in return for agreeing to use his "reasonable efforts" on Parrish's behalf in "negotiating job contracts, furnishing advice on business investments, securing

---

[j]. For an outline of the legal framework to the player-agent relationship, see Gregory W. McAleenan, "Agent–Player Representation Agreements," Chapter 2 of Uberstine, ed., *Law of Professional and Amateur Sports*, note a above.

professional tax advice at no additional costs, and obtaining endorsement contracts." Zinn was also supposed to try to secure "gainful off-season employment" for Parrish if he so requested, from which Zinn would receive a commission only if the work was "in the line of endorsements, marketing, and the like." The agency contract was to be automatically renewed every year, unless one side gave 30 days written notice of termination.

For Parrish's first four years with the Bengals, Zinn negotiated base salaries for his client of $16,500, $18,500, $27,000, and $35,000. By the end of the 1973 season, Parrish had become a Pro Bowl cornerback and the rival World Football League (WFL) had appeared on the scene. In the spring of 1974, Zinn had some preliminary conversations with the WFL's Jacksonville Sharks, but decided not to pursue this option (in a league that folded midway through the 1975 season). Instead, Zinn negotiated a new four-year deal with the Bengals, which was to pay Parrish $250,000 over the four seasons, as well as a $30,000 signing bonus. While Parrish signed the four contracts with the Bengals covering the 1974–1977 seasons, he then told Zinn by phone that he "no longer needed his services," something that Parrish reiterated by letter in October 1975. Parrish refused to pay Zinn any commission on those new contracts, and thus Zinn sued.

With respect to the other features of their relationship, Zinn had arranged for Parrish's tax returns to be prepared by H & R Block, and he had forwarded to him stock market recommendations that Zinn had screened. The agent had helped his client purchase and manage a four-unit apartment building, and he had procured one endorsement contract with All–Pro Graphics. However, Zinn had not been able to obtain any off-season work for Parrish. Instead, he had advised his client to return to college in the off-season to secure a degree and thence prepare himself for life when his NFL career had ended.

The appeals court first rejected the district court's conclusion that the contract between Zinn and Parrish was void under federal securities law on the grounds that this was a contract for investment advice and Zinn was not a registered adviser. The court said that isolated transactions with a client as an incident to the main purpose of his management contract to negotiate football contracts did not constitute engaging in the business of advising others on investment securities.]

* * *

We consider next the district court's judgment that Zinn failed to perform the terms and conditions of his contract....

Employment Procurement

Zinn's obligation under the 1971 Management Contract to procure employment for Parrish as a pro football player was limited to the use of "reasonable efforts." At the time the contract was signed, Parrish was already under contract with the Cincinnati Bengals for the 1970–1971 season, with a one-year option clause for the 1971–1972 season exercisable by the Bengals. Parrish could not, without being in breach of his Bengals contract, enter into negotiations with other teams for the 1971–72 season. The NFL's own rules prevented one team from negotiating with another team's player who had not yet attained the status of a "free agent." At no time relevant to this litigation did Parrish become a free agent. Thus, unless he decided to contract for future services for the year following the term of the option clause with the Canadian or World Football League, Parrish's only sensible course of action throughout the time Zinn managed him was to negotiate with the Bengals.

Parrish had no objection to Zinn's performance under the professional management contract for the first three years up to 1973, during which time Zinn negotiated football contracts for Parrish. A drastic change, however, took place in 1974 when a four-season contract was negotiated with the Bengals for a total of $250,000 plus a substantial signing bonus. At that time, the new World Football League came into existence and its teams, as well as the teams of the Canadian Football League, were offering good terms to professional football players as an inducement to jump over to their leagues from the NFL. In order to persuade Parrish to remain with the team, the Bengals club itself first initiated the renegotiation of Parrish's contract with an offer of substantially increased compensation. This was not surprising.

Parrish claims, however, that Zinn should have obtained offers from the World Football League that would have placed him in a stronger negotiating position with the Bengals. This is a rather late claim. It was not mentioned in Parrish's letter of termination, and is entirely speculative. Given what Zinn accurately perceived as the unreliability of any offers he might have obtained from the WFL, his representation of Parrish during this period was more than reasonable.

* * *

OTHER OBLIGATIONS

We focus next on the other obligations, all incidental to the main purpose of the contract. The first of these refers to "[n]egotiating employment contracts with professional athletic organizations and others." . . . [T]he evidence clearly shows that Zinn performed substantial services in negotiating with the Bengals by letter, telephone, and in person when he and Parrish were flown at the Bengals' expense to Cincinnati for the final stage of negotiations on the 1974–1977 series of contracts.

Zinn was further obligated to act in Parrish's professional interest by providing advice on tax and business matters, by "seek[ing] . . . endorsement contracts," and by making "efforts" to obtain for Parrish gainful off-season employment. Each of these obligations was subject to an implied promise to make "good faith" efforts to obtain what he sought. Under Illinois law, such efforts constitute full performance of the obligations. Until Parrish terminated the contract, the evidence was clear that Zinn made consistent, good faith efforts to obtain off-season employment and endorsement contracts. Indeed the district court found that Zinn at all times acted in good faith, with a willingness "to provide assistance within his ability." The district court confused success with good faith efforts in concluding that Zinn's failure to obtain in many cases jobs or contracts for Parrish was a failure to perform. Moreover, Zinn did give business advice to Parrish on his real estate purchases, and he did secure tax advice for him.

Parrish fully accepted Zinn's performance for the years 1970, 1971, 1972, and 1973 by remitting the 10% due Zinn under the contract. Parrish was at all times free to discharge Zinn as his agent before a new season began. Instead, he waited until Zinn had negotiated a series of contracts worth a quarter of a million dollars for him before letting Zinn know over the phone that his services were no longer required. That call, coupled with Parrish's failure to make the 10% commission payments as they came due, was a breach of the 1971 contract.... Therefore Zinn has a right to recover a 10% commission on all amounts earned by Parrish under the 1974, 1975, 1976, and 1977 Bengals contracts.

Appeal granted.

How does the court formulate the standard of performance expected of a sports agent? How does this standard compare with the duty of "fair representation" imposed by labor law on the players association (see Chapter 4)? With the standard of care required of a lawyer who represents a player in any transaction? Is the standard used in *Zinn* appropriate for the sports agent business?

A suit that alleged negligent performance by an agent was *Bias v. Advantage International, Inc.*, 905 F.2d 1558 (D.C.Cir.1990). This case was an outgrowth of the tragic death of Len Bias from cocaine use, only two days after the Boston Celtics had made the Maryland star the second pick in the 1986 NBA draft. The Bias estate sued his agent, Lee Fentress, for allegedly not moving quickly enough to finalize a million-dollar insurance policy and an endorsement contract with Reebok. The suit was summarily dismissed on the grounds that, even though agent and client had discussed these contracts before the rookie draft, the agent could not reasonably have been expected to finalize arrangements before Bias' death made that impossible.

Surprisingly, no suits have ever been brought by a player alleging agent malpractice in the routine aspects of his agent's duties—e.g., for negligently negotiating a below-market salary, or failing to seek various contract guarantees or injury protection, or giving bad advice about what salary to "hold out" for. Indeed, virtually no agents now carry malpractice insurance. (Would a lawyer-agent's attorney malpractice cover such a case?) Why do you think players have never brought this kind of litigation, although suits for medical and legal malpractice have become quite common?

2. AGENT FEE FORMULAS

From the point of view of both agents and players, an equally important subject is how much agents are entitled to be paid for the services they provide their client. As was mentioned at the outset of this chapter, Bob Woolf was perhaps the founding father of agent representation of athletes in professional team sports. Woolf not only authored best-selling books on his profession, but he also generated several disputes and lawsuits, one of which produced the following ruling.

BROWN v. WOOLF

United States District Court, Southern District of Indiana, 1983.
554 F.Supp. 1206.

STECKLER, DISTRICT JUDGE.

* * *

[Andrew Brown played hockey for the Pittsburgh Penguins during the 1973–74 season under a contract negotiated by Bob Woolf, his agent. In July, 1974, the Penguins offered Brown a non-guaranteed two-year contract at $80,000 a year. Woolf advised Brown to reject that offer and to sign instead with the Indianapolis Pacers in the World Hockey League that had begun competing with the NHL three years earlier. The Pacers deal was a five-year guaranteed contract, at $160,000 per season. Unfortunately, the Pacers soon encountered financial difficulties that led Woolf to negotiate two reductions in Brown's pay. These and other cost savings did not save the Pacers from bankruptcy, and Brown ended up collecting just $185,000 on his five-year deal. However, as part of these ongoing discussions, the Pacers agreed to pay Woolf $40,000—his five percent fee applied to the full $800,000 contract promise. When Brown heard of that fact, he sued Woolf, alleging both material misrepresentation and breach of fiduciary duty for failing to investigate the financial situation of the Pacers while receiving full payment of his agency fee.]

* * *

Indiana cases contain several formulations of the tort of constructive fraud. Generally it is characterized as acts or a course of conduct from which an unconscionable advantage is or may be derived, or a breach of confidence coupled with an unjust enrichment which shocks the conscience, or a breach of duty, including mistake, duress or undue influence, which the law declares fraudulent because of a tendency to deceive, injure the public interest or violate the public or private confidence. Another formulation found in the cases involves the making of a false statement, by the dominant party in a confidential or fiduciary relationship or by one who holds himself out as an expert, upon which the plaintiff reasonably relies to his detriment. The defendant need not know the statement is false nor make the false statement with fraudulent intent.

The Court believes that both formulations are rife with questions of fact, inter alia, the existence or nonexistence of a confidential or fiduciary relationship, and the question of reliance on false representations, as well as questions of credibility.

Defendant argues that despite the customary existence of such fact questions in a constructive fraud case, judgment is appropriate in this instance because plaintiff has produced nothing to demonstrate the existence of fact questions. He makes a similar argument in the motion for partial summary judgment on the punitive damages issue.

In this case, defendant has offered affidavits, excerpts of depositions, and photocopies of various documents to support his motions. He contends that such materials demonstrate that reasonable minds could not conclude that defendant did the acts with which the complaint charges him. In response, plaintiff rather belatedly offered portions of plaintiff's depositions as well as arguing that issues such as those raised by a complaint based on constructive fraud are inherently unsuited to resolution on a motion for summary judgment.

Having carefully considered the motions and briefs and having examined the evidentiary materials submitted, the Court concludes that summary judgment would not be appropriate in this action. The Court is not persuaded that there are no fact questions remaining unresolved in this controversy such that defendant is entitled to judgment as a matter of law.

Summary dismissal refused.

Was the true source of Brown's dispute with Woolf the player's fee arrangement with his agent? What precisely was the problem with the fee formula? How would you recast the formula?[k]

An interesting claim has recently been lodged by agent Bucky Woy against former Braves' and Cardinals' first baseman Bob Horner, to recover fees for the money Horner received as damages in the baseball collusion proceedings we read about in Chapter 3.

Woy represented Horner throughout the 1980s, under an oral agreement whereby Horner agreed to pay Woy 10% of his negotiated compensation. In 1986, Horner's contract with the Braves expired and Woy tried to negotiate a new multi-year contract for Horner either with the Braves or another team. As was later determined during the collusion arbitration described at the end of Chapter 3, Woy was unable to negotiate a contract with any other MLB team because of the owners' collusive

---

k. See Saul Levmore, *Commissions and Conflicts in Agency Arrangements*, 36 J. of Law and Econ. 503 (April 1993), for an illuminating analysis of the incentives and conflicts generated by fee structures in a variety of principal-agent relationships—for example, personal injury litigation, real estate, and securities underwriting.

practices. Thus, in 1987 Horner played for the Yakuit Swallows in Japan for $2 million, for which he paid Woy his $200,000 fee. The union later determined that in 1987, Horner would have earned $1,900,000 had collusion not occurred, but he received no damages because his Japanese salary fully mitigated those losses. However, in 1988 Horner returned to the United States and played for the St. Louis Cardinals for $950,000. Again, the union concluded that Horner would have been receiving $2 million in 1988 under a multi-year contract that would have been signed prior to 1987 had there been no collusion. Thus, Horner received $1,050,000 in collusion damages for 1988. Horner retired prior to the 1989 season (even though he had a guaranteed contract to play for the Baltimore Orioles that year), but he still may receive some collusion damages for 1989 and later years.

Woy claims that he is entitled to his 10% fee on that $1,050,000, because the money Horner received in collusion damages for the 1988 season was in lieu of the salary in a guaranteed contract that Woy would have been able to negotiate in 1987 but for owner collusion. Horner responds that the Hendricks firm in Houston had processed his collusion claim and thus only it is entitled to a fee on these damages. The case was heard and decided by Michigan labor law professor Ted St. Antoine, the arbitrator selected by the union to resolve disputes between players and their union-certified agents. Oddly, this is the only time the issue has been raised of whether an agent who represented a player during a collusion year for which the player later received damages is entitled to his fee on those damages. What do you think was the appropriate verdict by Professor St. Antoine?

Another such case and controversy arose in the summer of 1997. James "Patsie" Farrior, a Virginia U. linebacker, was the first pick of the New York Jets and their new coach Bill Parcells in the 1997 draft. Farrior chose Brad Blank as his agent, and Blank negotiated with the Jets in the late spring and early summer. A tentative agreement was reached between Blank and the Jets that would pay Farrior $11.544 million over six years, of which $6.7 million was guaranteed (including $1.8 million in the first year). Upset by the fact that Blank had not secured a signing bonus, Farrior replaced him with Ralph Cindrich as his agent, and Cindrich soon secured a five-year, $8.844 million contract, of which $4 million was a signing bonus. Blank apparently did not dispute that Farrior had the right to replace him with Cindrich and to sign that new financial deal. The issue the parties are pursuing in arbitration is how much (if any) compensation Blank is entitled to secure from Farrior for the time and effort Blank put into getting the Jets offer to the stage it was when he left that role.

3. AGENT CONFLICTS OF INTEREST[1]

We now turn to more fundamental ethical as well as legal issues posed by agent representation of actual, or even potentially, conflicting interests in a comparatively closed sports world.

DETROIT LIONS AND BILLY SIMS
v. JERRY ARGOVITZ

United States District Court, Eastern District of Michigan, 1984.
580 F.Supp. 542.

DeMascio, District Judge.

[This lawsuit arose when Billy Sims, a star running back for the Detroit Lions, signed a contract with the Houston Gamblers of the USFL and then, less than six months later, signed a contract with the Lions. Sims and the Lions sued to have his contract with the Gamblers declared unenforceable.

Sim's agent was Jerry Argovitz (and his associate Burrough). As Argovitz was negotiating a new contract for Sims and the Lions in the spring of 1983, he became part owner and president of the Gamblers. Sims knew that Argovitz had applied for the Gamblers franchise, but he did not know the extent of Argovitz's interest in the Gamblers and, according to the court, he would not have understood the conflicts of interest inherent in Argovitz's dual roles as owner and agent.

On April 5, 1983, Argovitz asked the Lions for $6 million over four years, a $1 million interest-free loan, and guarantees that Sims would be paid in case of injury or decline in skills. By May 30, Argovitz had reduced his demands to $3.5 million over five years, an interest-free loan, an injury (though not a skills) guarantee, and $400,000 to purchase an annuity. The court found that, on June 1, "Argovitz and the Lions were only $500,000 apart," and on June 22, "the Lions and Argovitz were very close to reaching an agreement on the value of Sims' services."]

* * *

Apparently, in the midst of his negotiations with the Lions and with his Gamblers franchise in hand, Argovitz decided that he would seek an offer from the Gamblers. Mr. Bernard Lerner, one of Argovitz's partners in the Gamblers, agreed to negotiate a contract with Sims. Since Lerner admitted that he had no knowledge whatsoever about football, we must infer that Argovitz at the very least told Lerner the amount of money required to sign Sims and further pressed upon Lerner the Gamblers' absolute need to obtain Sims' services. In the Gamblers' organization, only Argovitz knew the value of Sims' services and how critical it was for

---

[1]. See Robert E. Fraley and Fred Russell Harwell, *The Sports Lawyer's Duty to Avoid Differing Interests: A Practical Guide to Responsible Representation*, 11 Hastings Comm. and Ent. L. J. 165 (1989), and Jamie E. Brown, *The Battle the Fans Never See: Conflicts of Interest for Sports Lawyers*, 7 Georgetown J. of Legal Ethics 813 (1994).

the Gamblers to obtain Sims. In Argovitz's words, Sims would make the Gamblers' franchise.

On June 29, 1983, at Lerner's behest, Sims and his wife went to Houston to negotiate with a team that was partially owned by his own agent. When Sims arrived in Houston, he believed that the Lions organization was not negotiating in good faith; that it was not really interested in his services. His ego was bruised and his emotional outlook toward the Lions was visible to Burrough and Argovitz. Clearly, virtually all the information that Sims had up to that date came from Argovitz. Sims and the Gamblers did not discuss a future contract on the night of June 29th. The negotiations began on the morning of June 30, 1983, and ended that afternoon. At the morning meeting, Lerner offered Sims a $3.5 million five-year contract, which included three years of skill and injury guarantees. The offer included a $500,000 loan at an interest rate of one percent over prime. It was from this loan that Argovitz planned to receive the $100,000 balance of his fee for acting as an agent in negotiating a contract with his own team. Burrough testified that Sims would have accepted that offer on the spot because he was finally receiving the guarantee that he had been requesting from the Lions, guarantees that Argovitz dropped without too much quarrel. Argovitz and Burrough took Sims and his wife into another room to discuss the offer. Argovitz did tell Sims that he thought the Lions would match the Gamblers financial package and asked Sims whether he (Argovitz) should telephone the Lions. But, it is clear from the evidence that neither Sims nor Burrough believed that the Lions would match the offer. We find that Sims told Argovitz not to call the Lions for purely emotional reasons. As we have noted, Sims believed that the Lions' organization was not that interested in him and his pride was wounded. Burrough clearly admitted that he was aware of the emotional basis for Sims' decision not to have Argovitz phone the Lions, and we must conclude from the extremely close relationship between Argovitz and Sims that Argovitz knew it as well. When Sims went back to Lerner's office, he agreed to become a Gambler on the terms offered. At that moment, Argovitz irreparably breached his fiduciary duty. As agent for Sims he had the duty to telephone the Lions, receive its final offer, and present the terms of both offers to Sims. Then and only then could it be said that Sims made an intelligent and knowing decision to accept the Gamblers' offer.

During these negotiations at the Gamblers' office, Mr. Nash of the Lions telephoned Argovitz, but even though Argovitz was at his office, he declined to accept the telephone call. Argovitz tried to return Nash's call after Sims had accepted the Gamblers' offer, but it was after 5 p.m. and Nash had left for the July 4th weekend. When he declined to accept Mr. Nash's call, Argovitz's breach of his fiduciary duty became even more pronounced. Following Nash's example, Argovitz left for his weekend trip, leaving his principal to sign the contracts with the Gamblers the next day, July 1, 1983. The defendants, in their supplemental trial brief, assert that neither Argovitz nor Burrough can be held responsible for following Sims' instruction not to contact the Lions on June 30, 1983. Although it is generally true that an agent is not liable for losses occurring as a result of following his principal's instructions, this rule of law is not applicable when the agent has placed himself in a position adverse to that of his principal.

During the evening of June 30, 1983, Burrough struggled with the fact that they had not presented the Gamblers' offer to the Lions. He knew, as does the court, that Argovitz now had the wedge that he needed to bring finality to the Lions' negotiations.

* * *

... The evidence here convinces us that Argovitz's negotiations with the Lions were ongoing and it had not made its final offer. Argovitz did not follow the common practice described by both expert witnesses. He did not do this because he knew that the Lions would not leave Sims without a contract and he further knew that if he made that type of call Sims would be lost to the Gamblers, a team he owned.

On November 12, 1983, when Sims was in Houston for the Lions game with the Houston Oilers, Argovitz asked Sims to come to his home and sign certain papers. He represented to Sims that certain papers of his contract had been mistakenly overlooked and now needed to be signed. Included among those papers he asked Sims to sign was a waiver of any claim that Sims might have against Argovitz for his blatant breach of his fiduciary duty brought on by his glaring conflict of interest. Sims did not receive independent advice with regard to the wisdom of signing such a waiver.

* * *

Argovitz's negotiations with Lustig, Jim Kelly's agent, illustrates the difficulties that develop when an agent negotiates a contract where his personal interests conflict with those of his principal. Lustig, an independent agent, ignored Argovitz's admonishment not to "shop" the Gamblers' offer to Kelly. Lustig called the NFL team that he had been negotiating with because it was the "prudent" thing to do. The Gamblers agreed to pay Kelly, an untested rookie quarterback, $3.2 million for five years. His compensation was $60,000 less than Sims', a former Heisman Trophy winner and a proven star in the NFL. Lustig also obtained a number of favorable clauses from Argovitz; the most impressive one being that Kelly was assured of being one of the three top paid quarterbacks in the USFL if he performed as well as expected. If Argovitz had been free from conflicting interests he would have demanded similar benefits for Sims. Argovitz claimed that the nondisclosure clause in Kelly's contract prevented him from mentioning the Kelly contract to Sims. We view this contention as frivolous. Requesting these benefits for Sims did not require disclosure of Kelly's contract. Moreover, Argovitz's failure to obtain personal guarantees for Sims without adequately warning Sims about the risks and uncertainties of a new league constituted a clear breach of his fiduciary duty.

* * *

We are mindful that Sims was less than forthright when testifying before the court. However, we agree with plaintiff's counsel that the facts as presented through the testimony of other witnesses are so unappealing that we can disregard Sims' testimony entirely. We remain persuaded that on balance, Argovitz's breach of his fiduciary duty was so egregious that a court of equity cannot permit him to benefit by his own wrongful breach. We conclude that Argovitz's conduct in negotiating Sims' contract with the Gamblers rendered it invalid.

* * *

Rescission granted.

Argovitz was one of the protagonists in another highly-publicized tug of war between the NFL and the USFL, this one for Arkansas star Gary Anderson. The 1983 first round draft pick of both the NFL's San Diego Chargers and the USFL's Tampa Bay Bandits, Anderson became an Argovitz client without being told of Argovitz's USFL interests in Houston. Argovitz succeeded in channeling Anderson to the Bandits without giving the Chargers a real chance to outbid its USFL rival.

Shortly thereafter, though, Anderson became friendly with Lloyd Wells, an ex-Kansas City Chiefs' scout and an aspiring agent. When Anderson switched allegiance to Wells, Chargers' owner Gene Klein loaned Wells $30,000 to finance his representation of Anderson. Wells soon negotiated a new four-year, $1.5 million contract with the Chargers, one that topped the Bandits' $1.375 million deal. The Bandits, however, secured an injunction against Anderson playing for the Chargers from a Texas judge who did not find the Bandits' contract to be flawed by Argovitz' wearing these two hats as agent and owner. (Also of interest was the evidence at trial that, despite four years at the University of Arkansas, Anderson had not learned to read; that is one reason he could not understand the various documents he kept signing.)

A more recent illustration of the conflict between the player's and the agent's personal interests is illustrated by litigation against John Childers and his Talent Services, Inc. (TSI): see *Jones v. Childers*, 18 F.3d 899 (11th Cir.1994) (involving the Tampa Bay Buccaneers' Gordon Jones), and *Hernandez v. Childers*, 806 F.Supp. 1368 (N.D.Ill.1992) (involving the St. Louis Cardinals' and the New York Mets' Keith Hernandez). In both cases, the courts found a breach of fiduciary duty on the part of Childers and TSI for advising Jones and Hernandez to invest in high risk, non-IRS approved tax shelters, without Childers telling the clients that his TSI was receiving a sales commission for investments Childers generated in these financial ventures.

Questions for Discussion

1. Is the *Anderson* case different from *Sims* as far as Argovitz was concerned? Of what relevance to the Bandits case is the reported fact that Wells, Anderson's second agent, took loan money from the Chargers' owner? Would an agent ever be able to represent an athlete properly with a team if the team owner is the agent's creditor? With any team in that league?

2. Contrast the *Argovitz* cases with the following situations:

(a) Jerry Kapstein, one of the most prominent baseball agents for two decades, married the daughter of Joan Kroc, then owner of the San Diego Padres, and regularly advised his mother-in-law about her ownership interests. Should that relationship have barred Kapstein from representing players on the Padres? On the Dodgers? On the Yankees? On the Chicago Bears?

(b) Larry Fleisher and Alan Eagleson were the founders and longtime leaders of the NBA and NHL Players Associations, respectively. They also had full rosters of individual clients among their association members. Was this appropriate? See *Major Indoor Soccer League & Professional Soccer Players Ass'n (PROSPA)*, NLRB Ruling, Nov. 15, 1983.

(c) Recall the Juwan Howard case which was described earlier in the section on *Salary Caps and Taxes*. Here, a potentially significant fact is that David Falk's Associate Management Enterprises (FAME) represented not just Howard and Alonzo Mourning, but also Heat guard Rex Chapman who, after all the team budget had been spent on Falk's other clients, ended up moving to the Phoenix Suns at the league's minimum salary. Falk has long believed (and said) that his star clients such as Mourning and Howard (and even more, Jordan and Ewing) should get the lion's share of salary money because, as in movies, it is the star's name and appeal that puts fans in the seats (especially expensive seats). Does that policy pose any problem of agent ethics? What about the further fact that Falk is also agent for Georgetown coach John Thompson, who has advised his stars such as Mourning, Ewing, Allen Iverson, and others to use Falk as their representative when they leave college for the professional ranks?

(d) Multifaceted firms such as International Management Group (IMG) and ProServ not only represent many tennis players but they also promote, manage, and even sponsor tournaments on the tennis tour. Is this dual representation legitimate? Should the body responsible for the tour be able to impose limitations on such inter-relationships? See *Volvo North America Corp. v. Men's International Professional Tennis Council (MIPTC)*, 857 F.2d 55 (2d Cir.1988) (included in Chapter 12).

3. With respect to each of the potential conflicts suggested above (including Argovitz'), if the player is explicitly told of the situation and still enters into or maintains a relationship with his agent, should the player

then be bound to contracts negotiated by the agent? Should the agent be immune from malpractice suits brought by the player alleging poor performance by the agent due to the conflict? Should the agent's conduct be deemed "proper" according to the rules of professional ethics enforced by bar associations? What might lead a player to make such a choice?

4. AGENT RECRUITING OF COLLEGE ATHLETES[m]

The single feature of the player agent trade that contributes the most to what star agent Leigh Steinberg himself has characterized as "the ultimate sleazoid profession" is the way that some agents (presumably not Steinberg) recruit clients from college. Here, rather than the player paying the agent above the table for his necessary services, the agent pays the player below the table, at a time when the player is in college and supposed to be competing as an amateur athlete. (We shall examine in detail the situation of amateur athletes in commercialized college sports in Chapter 10.) Agents often deliver this money through an intermediary (their "runner"), who is often of the same age and with the same interests as the athletes. The runner befriends the athlete, picks up the bills for his entertainment, and then delivers the athlete as a client to the agent when he is about to give up college eligibility and turn professional. Of course, if these payments are ever disclosed (even after the fact), this can cost the school significant penalties for having played someone who was no longer an amateur in NCAA-regulated events. Recent such episodes involved athletes on the Florida State and Southern California football teams, and the U. Mass basketball team (whose star player Marcus Camby received from two agents not just cash, food, drinks, stereos, and jewelry, but even sex with prostitutes while he was leading U. Mass to the 1996 Final Four).

One of the most notorious cases in this vein, and the one that produced the most litigation, involved Norby Walters and his runner-partner Lloyd Bloom. By the mid–1980s, Walters had become a successful representative of many musicians and entertainers, including Marvin Gaye, Dionne Warwick, Lou Rawls, Luther Vandross, and Patti Labelle. At the suggestion of Bloom, a young acquaintance, Walters decided to begin representing athletes as well, especially young football players. The technique Walters and Bloom adopted was for Bloom to approach the player while he was still in college and offer him a cash sum and subsequent monthly payments, in return for which the player signed an agency contract post-dated to January 2nd of the player's senior year. The whole arrangement was to be kept confidential so that the player would not lose his collegiate eligibility, something that would diminish his professional marketability.

[m.] The best treatment of this broad topic is Shropshire, *Agents of Opportunity*, note a above. A very interesting account of the *cause célèbre* described in this section and later on in this chapter is Chris Mortensen, *Playing for Keeps: How One Man Kept the Mob From Sinking its Hooks Into Pro Football* (New York: Simon and Schuster, 1991).

Walters and Bloom quickly enjoyed remarkable success. They signed ten players in 1985, two of whom (Ron Harmon of Iowa and Tim McGee of Tennessee) were 1986 first-round NFL draft picks. In 1986, the two signed up 35 players, of whom eight were 1987 first round draft picks (including Brent Fullwood by the Packers, Reggie Rogers by the Lions, and Rod Woodson by the Steelers), and several others (such as Jerry Ball and Ron Morris) were prominent early round picks. All in all, Walters and Bloom invested roughly $800,000 in recruiting some 60 college players (a few of whom, such as Brad Sellers and Derrick McKey, were star basketball players).

However, this economic venture unraveled and spawned numerous legal proceedings for reasons exhibited in the next case.

NORBY WALTERS AND LLOYD BLOOM v. BRENT FULLWOOD

United States District Court, Southern District of New York, 1987.
675 F.Supp. 155.

BRIEANT, CHIEF JUDGE.

[In the summer of 1986, Norby Walters and Lloyd Bloom induced Brent Fullwood, star running back for Auburn University, to sign a post-dated representation agreement in return for an immediate payment of $4,000 (secured by a promissory note) and another $4,000 during the fall football season. This modest investment by the new agency partnership seemed highly worthwhile when the Packers selected Fullwood as the fourth pick in the 1987 NFL draft. By that time, however, Fullwood had defected to another agent, George Kickliter of Alabama, and had repudiated his deal with Walters and Bloom. Thus Walters and Bloom sued Fullwood, seeking not only to recover the $8,000 they had already paid him, but also to collect the promised 5% commission on Fullwood's multi-million dollar contract. The key issue posed to the federal judge was whether the secret arrangement between the agents and Fullwood, which had put the player in violation of NCAA regulations, was an enforceable contract under New York law.]

* * *

"We are living in a time when college athletics are honeycombed with falsehood, and when the professions of amateurism are usually hypocrisy. No college team ever meets another today with actual faith in the other's eligibility."

—President William Faunce of Brown University, in a speech before the National Education Association, 1904.

The N.C.A.A. was organized in 1906 largely to combat such evils. Its constitution provides in relevant part that:

Any individual who contracts or who has ever contracted orally or in writing to be represented by an agent in the marketing of the individual's athletic ability or reputation in a sport no longer shall be eligible for intercollegiate athletics in that sport.

N.C.A.A. Constitution, sec. 3–1–(c).

Section 3–1–(a) prohibits any player from accepting pay in any form for participation in his college sport, with an exception for a player seeking, directly without the assistance of a third party, a loan from an accredited commercial lending institution against future earnings potential solely in order to purchase insurance against disabling injury.

This Court concludes that the August 1986 loan security agreement and the W.S. & E. agency agreement between Fullwood and the plaintiffs violated §§ 3–1–(a) and 3–1–(c) of the N.C.A.A. Constitution, the observance of which is in the public interest of the citizens of New York State, and that the parties to those agreements knowingly betrayed an important, if perhaps naive, public trust. Viewing the parties as *in pari delicto*, we decline to serve as "paymaster of the wages of crime, or referee between thieves." We consider both defendant Fullwood's arbitration rights under the N.F.L.P.A. Agents' Regulations, and plaintiffs' rights on their contract and promissory note with Fullwood, unenforceable as contrary to the public policy of New York. "The law 'will not extend its aid to either of the parties' or 'listen to their complaints against each other, but will leave them where their own acts have placed them.'"

Absent these overriding policy concerns, the parties would be subject to the arbitration provisions set forth in section seven of the N.F.L.P.A. Agents' Regulations, and plaintiffs' rights under the contract and promissory note with Fullwood also would be arbitrable. However, under the "public policy" exception to the duty to enforce otherwise-valid agreements, we should and do leave the parties where we find them.

It is well settled that a court should not enforce rights that arise under an illegal contract.

* * *

An agreement may be unenforceable in New York as contrary to public policy even in the absence of a direct violation of a criminal statute, if the sovereign has expressed a concern for the values underlying the policy implicated. *In re Estate of Walker*, 476 N.E.2d 298, 301 (1985), the Court of Appeals refused to enforce a bequest of adoption decrees to the testator's adopted daughters, concluding that such a bequest, though not criminal, was contrary to public policy. The court concluded, " '[W]hen we speak of the public policy of the state, we mean the law of the state, whether found in the Constitution, the statutes or judicial records.' Those sources express the public will and give definition to the term. A legacy is contrary to public policy, not only if it directly violates a statutory prohibition ... but also if it is contrary to the social judgment on the subject implemented by the statute."

* * *

The New York State legislature has spoken on the public policies involved in this case, by expressing a concern for the integrity of sporting events in general, and a particular concern for the status of amateur athletics. See, e.g., New York Tax Law sec. 1116(a)(4) (McKinney's supp. 1987) (granting tax exemption to any organization "organized and operating exclusively ... to foster national or international amateur sports competition"); New York Penal Law Secs. 180.35, 180.40 (McKinney's supp. 1987) (establishing criminal sanctions for sports bribery).

Even were we not convinced of the legislative concern for the values underlying sec. 3-1-(c) of the N.C.A.A. Constitution, New York case law prevents judicial enforcement of contracts the performance of which would provoke conduct established as wrongful by independent commitments undertaken by either party. Not all contracts inducing breaches of other agreements fall within this rule, but those requiring fraudulent conduct are unenforceable as contrary to the public policy of New York.

In the case before us, no party retains enforceable rights. To the extent plaintiffs seek to recover on the contract or promissory note signed by Fullwood, their wrongful conduct prevents recovery; to the extent Fullwood seeks to compel arbitration, as provided for in the N.F.L.P.A. Agents' Regulations, his own wrongs preclude resort to this Court.

All parties to this action should recognize that they are the beneficiaries of a system built on the trust of millions of people who, with stubborn innocence, adhere to the Olympic ideal, viewing amateur sports as a commitment to competition for its own sake. Historically, amateur athletes have been perceived as pursuing excellence and perfection of their sport as a form of self-realization, indeed, originally, as a form of religious worship, with the ancient games presented as offerings to the gods. By demanding the most from themselves, athletes were believed to approach the divine essence. Through athletic success, the Greeks believed man could experience a kind of immortality.[3]

There also is a modern, secular purpose served by Secs. 3-1-(a) and 3-1-(c) of the N.C.A.A. Constitution. Since the advent of intercollegiate sports in the late 19th century, American colleges have struggled, with varying degrees of vigor, to protect the integrity of higher education from sports-related evils such as gambling, recruitment violations, and the employment of mercenaries whose presence in college athletic programs will tend to preclude the participation of legitimate scholar-athletes.

Sections 3-1-(a) and 3-1-(c) of the N.C.A.A. Constitution were instituted to prevent college athletes from signing professional contracts

---

3. As expressed by the classical poet Pindar of Thebes (518-438 B.C.): "Creatures of a day/ What is someone?/ What is no one?/ Man is merely a shadow's dream/ But when god-given glory comes upon him in victory/ A bright light shines on us and life is sweet/ When the end comes the loss of flame brings darkness/ But his glory is bright forever." C. Boara, *Classical Greece*, at 23.

while they are still playing for their schools. The provisions are rationally related to the commendable objective of protecting the academic integrity of N.C.A.A. member institutions. A college student already receiving payments from his agent, or with a large professional contract signed and ready to take effect upon his graduation, might well be less inclined to observe his academic obligations than a student, athlete or not, with uncertainties about his future career. Indeed, he might not play at his college sport with the same vigor and devotion.

The agreement reached by the parties here, whether or not unusual, represented not only a betrayal of the high ideals that sustain amateur athletic competition as a part of our national educational commitment; it also constituted a calculated fraud on the entire spectator public. Every honest amateur player who took the field with or against Fullwood during the 1986 college football season was cheated by being thrown in with a player who had lost his amateur standing.

In August 1986, Brent Fullwood was one of that select group of college athletes virtually assured of a lucrative professional sports contract immediately upon graduation, absent serious injury during his senior year. The fruits of the system by which amateur players become highly paid professionals, whatever its flaws, were soon to be his. That is precisely why plaintiffs sought him out. Both sides of the transaction knew exactly what they were doing, and they knew it was fraudulent and wrong. This Court and the public need not suffer such willful conduct to taint a college amateur sports program.

Suit dismissed.

Far more unsavory features of the Walters–Bloom style of sports practice were not adverted to in the above proceeding. In the background as partners and investors in this venture were Sonny and Michael Franzese, key members of the Colombo organized crime family in New York. Apparently Walters and Bloom drew upon these backers for help in enforcing their contracts, with threats of physical violence against players who reneged on their deal, and against agents such as Kickliter, who wooed the players away. Indeed, the whole scheme came to light in March 1987, when a masked man beat Kathy Clements (wife of the former Notre Dame quarterback, Tom Clements) because she was an associate of Steve Zucker, a Chicago-based sports agent. Zucker had been among the first agents to attract a client away from Walters and Bloom (Tim McGee, the Bengals first round pick in 1986), and he had just done the same with two others (Reggie Rogers of Washington and Doug Dubose of Nebraska). When rumors of an organized crime connection with college and professional athletes emerged, the Chicago offices of the U.S. Attorney and FBI took charge of the investigation, with legal ramifications we will see later in this chapter.

While Walters and Bloom might have been unique in their "gangland" approach, they certainly were not unique in paying college players money to sign post-dated agency contracts. The key to the success of such an arrangement was keeping it secret. Neither the agent nor the client would disclose the contract or the payments which, under NCAA rules, made the player ineligible for future collegiate competition; as a result, the player's college risked costly NCAA sanctions for using an ineligible player, even unknowingly. This not uncommon practice invited not only judicial nullification of the agency contract (as in *Fullwood*), but also criminal prosecution of both the players and the agents engaged in such a practice.

Even aside from its deceptive nature, this practice raised significant ethical and legal questions. Why would Walters and Bloom believe it was financially worthwhile to pay clients to sign with them? If a player takes a "signing bonus" from an agent, should the player not be held to that contract later on? Is there any difference from a contract entered into by the player with a team? Suppose that the agent offers no money. Is it proper for an agent to pursue college athletes as potential clients? Should it matter whether the athlete's college eligibility has expired? Consider the following Model Rule of Professional Conduct:

> 7.3. A lawyer may not solicit professional employment from a prospective client with whom the lawyer has no family or prior professional relationship, by mail, in person or otherwise, when a significant motive for the lawyer's doing so is the lawyer's pecuniary gain.

To what extent should a sports agent who happens to be a lawyer feel constrained by this rule?

C. EMERGENCE OF AGENT REGULATION[n]

The substantive issues and cases presented in the prior section raise a broader institutional question. Can and should we rely on market competition shaped by general laws (in particular, contract law or criminal fraud law) to secure a sufficiently high quality of agent representation of athletes? Whatever the merits on that score, the political reality is that expanding control of sports agents has been a conspicuous exception to the broader trend toward deregulation of the marketplace (including owner regulation of player movement via the reserve system). Popular distaste for a profession that includes people like Norby Walters has generated extensive regulation by both state legislatures and players associations. A proposed Collegiate Athletics Integrity Act has been introduced on several occasions in Congress in the late 1990s in an

---

[n] An illuminating perspective on the broader issues posed by these materials is David B. Wilkins, *Who Should Regulate Lawyers?*, 105 Harvard L. Rev. 799 (1992). This article's in-depth analysis of the promise and the limits of different institutional candidates for the regulation of lawyers is of interest not simply by way of analogy. Many agents may not be lawyers, but because the most successful and visible are, most players tend to have a lawyer as their agent.

attempt to federalize one key component of this problem. And in early 1997, the National Conference of Commissioners on Uniform State Laws, at the urging of both the NCAA and the Sports Lawyers Association, formed a drafting committee to develop a proposed state agent regulation law that should be ready for full Conference approval by the summer of 1998. This proposed statute could then go to the states for adoption in place of the existing hodge-podge of different laws currently in place in close to 30 states.

Not until the early 1980s was systematic regulation of the sports agent business undertaken. This effort was pursued along two parallel tracks: one in the state legislatures, the other within the players associations. The pioneers for each were the California legislature, which in 1982 enacted the Athletic Agents Act, and the NFL Players Association, which in 1983 adopted a set of regulations for what it labeled "contract advisors." With some interesting variations, the NFLPA example was followed by the NBPA in 1985, the MLBPA in 1987, and the NHLPA in 1995. While a few state legislatures (such as Alabama and North Carolina) have emulated the broad-based California model (which that state itself abandoned in 1996), the majority of the 28 states that have now passed some form of agent regulation have focused on just the single problem area exemplified by the *Walters & Bloom* case—agent recruiting of college athletes whose eligibility has not yet expired. Such regulation, which addresses the rights and expectations of a third party to the player-agent relationship—the college—will be treated separately in the next section. Here we canvass the issues posed by the efforts of legislatures and unions to protect athletes from possible harm inflicted by their own agents.

Regardless of whether the regulations are adopted within the legislative or the player association forum, they are remarkably similar in the manner in which they tackle the issues posed in the cases and problems depicted earlier in this chapter.[o] There are, however, important differences in the authority and the competence of these respective regulatory sources. The authority of the state legislature in this area is not entirely clear. The representation of athletes is an occupation that can be subjected to the kinds of legal controls that now govern activities ranging from medicine to hairdressing (as to which see *Williamson v. Lee Optical*, 348 U.S. 483 (1955)). While some agents have argued that these regulatory schemes violate the federal Constitution's "dormant" commerce clause by imposing an unreasonable burden on interstate commerce, this argument seems unlikely to prevail under current constitutional standards. See *CTS Corp. v. Dynamics Corporation of America*, 481 U.S. 69 (1987).

o. For a comprehensive overview, see Sobel, *The Regulation of Player Agents and Lawyers*, note a above.

The appropriate scope and practical effects of such state regulation are much murkier than its constitutional validity. For example, given the national cast to professional sports, should the reach of the state regulation turn on the agent's home base, or the player's, or that of the college from which the player is coming, or the professional team to which he is going, or all of the above? State legislatures are naturally prone to spread their regulatory net as far as possible, but such action poses a serious difficulty to agents, especially when the states follow the original California model. California required any aspiring agent to apply for registration (with payment of a fee) with the state Department of Labor. After investigation, the agency granted a license (which had to be periodically renewed) to practice in this field, subject to legal constraints on fees, bonds, and agency contracts. With more and more states insisting on registration (at least 14 by 1997), each requiring its own registration fees, surety bonds, and administrative paperwork, the cumulative cost of such regulation inevitably reduces either the number of agents who are competing to work on behalf of athletes or the number of agents who are complying with the licensing requirements. As it turned out, the latter result is what has largely happened. Initially, only 30 or so agents bothered to register in California, and by the mid–1990s when the total number of agents had soared, the number of California registrants had dropped to less than 20.

As a result, in 1996 California enacted a new *Miller-Ayala Athlete Agents Act* (something that was actively sought by California colleges, not California athletes). Substantive requirements were significantly enlarged, but administrative licensing was eliminated. Instead, if an agent violates the rules governing relations with athletes and/or schools, any "adversely affected" party can file suit in state court for actual and punitive damages (plus attorney fees), with a minimum award of $50,000. In the same year that California enacted this law, Missouri and Kansas were became the 27th and 28th states to regulate agents, and each of these added the registration requirement. (In fact, California also brought this back in late 1997.)

Another possible agent challenge to such state legislation is that it is preempted by federal *labor* law, which makes NLRB certified unions the exclusive bargaining representatives of employees. Since the players association can and does delegate some of this exclusive authority to agents whom it certifies, state regulation which precludes any of these agents from representing union members may infringe upon that congressionally-granted, union-delegated authority.

Whatever the validity of such a labor law-federalism argument, most observers believe that players associations are better equipped to regulate agents than are state governments (at least with respect to the interests of players, if not colleges). Once an agent has learned and complied with the single set of requirements adopted by the unions, he or she can represent any player and deal with any team in that sport (and players associations in several team sports have cooperated in developing similar requirements). In addition, the players' unions have both the incentives and the resources to develop the regulatory competence needed to improve the quality of agent representation.

Regulation by players associations, however, faces its own legal problem—the source of an association's authority to impose binding regulations on agents. The solution comes from labor law. Recall from Chapter 4 that under the NLRA, a union such as a players association has the exclusive authority to represent all employees in its unit (members or not) for purposes of collective bargaining about the terms and conditions of employment (see *J.I. Case Co. v. NLRB*, 321 U.S. 332 (1944)). Under labor law, unions are free to limit the scope of the labor agreement to a set of guaranteed employment terms, and to permit individual bargaining about salaries and benefits above these minimum standards. In sports, as in other entertainment industries, individual negotiation has become the established practice. But while unions can and do delegate their exclusive authority to the individual employee and his agent, a union may choose to waive its statutory prerogatives conditionally, and only in favor of agents of whom the union approves. When players associations adopt the latter posture, both the collective agreement and the labor laws preclude a club from negotiating individual contracts with agents who are not certified for that purpose by the association. In effect, then, the clubs become the enforcer of the association's regulatory program, because they must refuse to deal with any agent who has not secured and retained the association's stamp of approval.

But while its bargaining relationship with the league may give the players association the leverage to impose its certification program on agents, this power secured under labor law does not necessarily insulate the regime from challenge under other laws—in particular, antitrust law.[p] Indeed, player regulation of agents bears an ironic resemblance to the traditional "reserve clause" system under which owners sharply constrained player prerogatives. In effect, the association members agree to a standard set of terms upon which they will purchase the service of player agents—one term being the maximum agency fee—and the players collectively require agents to subscribe to these terms as a condition of doing business in this sport. Should such restraints on the agent market be considered an illegal restraint of trade under the Sherman Act? As one might suspect, players associations answer this question in the negative—asserting the same labor exemption from antitrust that leagues have relied on to protect their limitations on player mobility and salary. In the following case, the NBPA attempted to ward off the first, and as yet only, legal challenge to association regulation of agents.

COLLINS v. NBPA & GRANTHAM

United States District Court, District of Colorado, 1991.
850 F.Supp. 1468 affirmed *per curiam*, 976 F.2d 740 (10th Cir.1992).

MATSCH, DISTRICT JUDGE.

[Starting in the mid–1970s, Thomas Collins had become a successful agent for several NBA stars, including Ralph Sampson, Terry Cum-

---

[p.] See Lori J. Lefferts, *The NFL Players Association's Agent Certification Plan: Is it Exempt from Antitrust Review?* 26 Arizona L. Rev. 599 (1984).

mings, Alex English, Lucius Allen and, most prominently, Kareem Abdul–Jabbar. Collins received certification by the NBPA in 1986, soon after the latter's regulations came into force. Shortly thereafter, though, Collins allowed his certification to lapse because he had become the target of a highly publicized lawsuit by Jabbar. The suit alleged a variety of breaches of fiduciary duty on the part of Collins:

—Failure to prepare and file Jabbar's tax returns for several years, which eventually cost Jabbar $300,000 in interest and penalties.

—Commingling of various clients' funds, including transfer of approximately $200,000 of Jabbar's money to the accounts of other players, from which it could not later be recouped.

—Converting a corporate indebtedness of $290,000 into a personal debt of Jabbar, without Jabbar's authorization.

—Most costly to Jabbar, investing much of his assets in speculative and ill-fated real estate ventures (such as in hotels and restaurants), rather than in the conservative and more secure investments that Jabbar said he had requested.

Eventually, in late 1989, Collins and Jabbar settled their litigation before trial. The terms of that settlement were kept confidential, with the exception of specific acknowledgement by Jabbar that "there has been no finding that [Collins] engaged in misrepresentation, misappropriation, conversion, breach of fiduciary duty or negligence." Although a separate suit by Lucius Allen was still pending, Collins then applied for recertification. At the personal request of Terry Cummings, the NBPA Committee on Agent Representation (which included NBPA Executive Director Charles Grantham) granted Collins interim certification to represent Cummings in his contract negotiations with the San Antonio Spurs.

The Committee, however, undertook an extensive informal investigation of the Jabbar–Collins affair. This involved not only examining the documents and speaking to the lawyers and accountants, but also a lengthy personal meeting with Collins and Jabbar together, without their lawyers. On that basis, the Committee eventually decided, in October 1990, *not* to recertify Collins. The latter was informed of his right to challenge this decision in an evidentiary hearing before a named arbitrator. Instead, Collins brought suit under antitrust law, alleging that the NBPA was guilty of a concerted boycott of his services as an agent, pursuant to an Association effort to monopolize representation of professional basketball players. The following decision considered the NBPA's motion for summary dismissal of Collins' suit.]

* * *

Like other sports and entertainment unions, the NBPA believes that the collective good of the entire represented group is maximized when individualized salary negotiations occur within a framework that permits players to exert leverage based on their unique skills and personal contributions. The NBPA therefore has authorized the players or their individually selected agents to negotiate individual compensation packages. This delegation of representational authority to individual players and their agents has always been limited solely to the authority to negotiate individual compensation packages, and to enforce them through the grievance-arbitration procedure established by the NBPA–NBA Agreement.

Player agents were unregulated by the NBPA before 1986. By the mid–1980s, a substantial number of players had complained to the officers of the NBPA about agent abuses. Specifically, players complained that the agents imposed high and non-uniform fees for negotiation services, insisted on the execution of open-ended powers of attorney giving the agents broad powers over players' professional and financial decisions, failed to keep players apprised of the status of negotiations with NBA teams, failed to submit itemized bills for fees and services, and, in some cases, had conflicts of interest arising out of representing coaches and/or general managers of NBA teams as well as players. Many players believed they were bound by contract not to dismiss their agents regardless of dissatisfaction with their services and fees, because the agents had insisted on the execution of long-term agreements. Some agents offered money and other inducements to players, their families and coaches to obtain player clients.

In response to these abuses, the NBPA established the Regulations, a comprehensive system of agent certification and regulation, to insure that players would receive agent services that meet minimum standards of quality at uniform rates. First, the Regulations provide that a player agent may not conduct individual contract negotiations unless he signs the "Standard Player Agent Contract" promulgated by the Committee. The "Standard Player Agent Contract" limits player agent fees by prohibiting any fee or commission on any contract which entitles the player to the minimum salary and by limiting agent fees on all contracts. Second, the Regulations contain a "code of conduct" which specifically prohibits an agent from providing or offering money or anything of value to a player, a member of a player's family or a player's high school or college coach for the purpose of inducing the player to use that agent's services. The code also prohibits agents from engaging in conduct that constitutes an actual or apparent conflict of interest (such as serving as an agent for a player while also representing an NBA team, general manager or head coach), engaging in any unlawful conduct involving dishonesty, fraud, deceit, misrepresentation, or engaging in any other conduct that reflects adversely on his fitness to serve in a fiduciary capacity as a player agent or jeopardizes the effective representation of NBA players.

Third, the Regulations restrict the representation of players to individuals who are certified player agents, and set up a program for the certification of agents who are then bound by the Regulations' fee restrictions and code of conduct. Prospective player agents must file the "Applications for Certification as an NBPA Player Agent" with the Committee. The Committee is authorized to conduct any informal investigation that it deems appropriate to determine whether to issue certification and may deny certification to any applicant:

(1) Upon ... determining that the applicant has made false or misleading statements of a material nature in the Application;

(2) Upon ... determining that the applicant has ever misappropriated funds, or engaged in other specific fraud, which would render him unfit to serve in a fiduciary capacity on behalf of players;

(3) Upon ... determining that the applicant has engaged in any other conduct that significantly impacts adversely on his credibility, integrity or competence to serve in a fiduciary capacity on behalf of players; or

(4) Upon ... determining that the applicant is unwilling to swear or affirm that he will comply with these Regulations and any amendments thereto and that he will abide by the fee structure contained in the standard form player-agent contract incorporated into these Regulations.

Any prospective agent whose application for certification is denied may appeal that denial by filing a timely demand for arbitration.... The arbitrator is empowered to order certification if he determines, based on the evidence, that the Committee did not meet its burden of establishing a basis for denying certification. The arbitrator's decision is final and binding on all parties and is not subject to judicial review....

After unilaterally promulgating the Regulations, the NBPA obtained, in arms length collective bargaining, the NBA's agreement to prohibit all member teams from negotiating individual player salary contracts with any agent who was not certified by the NBPA.

* * *

Both the Regulations and Article XXXI are within the statutory exemption from antitrust regulation. When promulgating the Regulations and when negotiating Article XXXI, the NBPA acted in its own interest, independently of any employers and without denying access to rival employers. The number and identity of the employers remains unchanged regardless of the Regulations or Article XXXI. A union's actions are in its "self-interest" if they bear a reasonable relationship to a legitimate union interest. *Adams, Ray & Rosenberg v. William Morris Agency, Inc.*, 411 F.Supp. 403 (C.D.Cal.1976). The NBPA regulatory program fulfills legitimate union purposes and was the result of legitimate concerns: it protects the player wage scale by eliminating percentage fees where the agent does not achieve a result better than the collectively bargained minimum; it keeps agent fees generally to a reasonable and uniform level, prevents unlawful kickbacks, bribes, and fiduciary violations and protects the NBPA's interest in assuring that its role in representing professional basketball players is properly carried out. Although Collins claims any benefit is in the *player's* self-interest, not the union's, it is impossible to separate the two—the union is composed of its members and exists solely to serve the players. When the players benefit, the union benefits as well.

The second prong of the [labor exemption] test is also met. Collins incorrectly claims that when enacting the Regulations, the NBPA combined with a non-labor group and thus fails to earn a statutory exemption. The most analogous case is *H.A. Artists and Associates v. Actors' Equity Assn.*, 451 U.S. 704 (1981), in which the Supreme Court upheld similar regulations against an antitrust challenge. In *H.A. Artists*, theatrical agents who represented members of Actors' Equity Association for purposes of procuring employment and negotiating individual salaries above the collectively bargained minimum, challenged that union's licensing system, which regulated the agents and required union members to employ only union-licensed agents. The Equity regulations, like the NBPA regulations at issue here, permitted only those agents who were licensed by the union to represent union members in individual salary negotiations with employers. The Equity regulations protected and sought to maximize wages by requiring agents to renounce any commission on any portion of a contract under which an actor or actress received no more than the collectively bargained minimum wages, and by limiting commissions in other respects. The Equity regulations also allowed actors to terminate their representation contracts with agents, and required agents to honor their fiduciary obligations. The Equity regulations were a response to historical abuses by agents, and were designed to secure better services from agents at lower rates.

The Court held that the Actors' Equity regulations met the *Hutcheson–Allen Bradley Co.* test for the statutory labor exemption. First, the Regulations were designed to promote the union's legitimate self-interest. Second, there was no combination with either a non-labor group or a non-party to a labor dispute. The Court held there was no combination between the union and the employers—the theatrical producers—to create or maintain the regulation system. Rather, the union unilaterally developed the regulatory system in response to agent abuses and to benefit union members. The Court concluded that although some agents agreed to the regulations, there was no combination with a non-labor group or persons who were not party to a labor dispute. The agents themselves were a labor group because they had an "economic interrelationship" with the union and its members "affecting legitimate union interest." That is, "the[y] represented ... union members in the sale of their labor ... [a function] that in most nonentertainment industries is performed exclusively by unions." Thus, any dispute between the agents and the union regarding the representation of union workers was a "labor dispute"—which was outside of the purview of the antitrust laws.

The NBPA Regulations similarly meet the second part of the *Hutcheson–Allen Bradley Co.* test. The NBPA did not combine with a non-labor group or a non-party to a labor dispute when promulgating the Regulations or negotiating Article XXXI. The NBPA unilaterally developed its Regulations in response to agent abuses and to benefit its members. It did not develop them in collusion with the employer group or to assist the employer group effort to restrain competition or control the employer group's product market.

Like the Equity agents, the player agents are a labor group. Although basketball players, unlike actors, can and do obtain employment without an agent, most players employ agents to negotiate their salaries and can fall victim to unscrupulous agent behavior. The player agents have a clear economic interrelationship with the players they represent; their remuneration is directly dependent on the relationship set up with the player and the salary obtained for him. Because they represent persons in the negotiation of terms of employment, the agents are clearly parties to a labor dispute within the meaning of the NLRA. As such, they would meet the second prong of the test regardless of whether there is a combination with a non-labor group.

Article XXI of the NBPA–NBA Agreement also meets the second prong and is entitled to the statutory exemption. Article XXI was obtained in arms-length collective bargaining at the urging of the NBPA after it unilaterally promulgated the Regulations. It was not agreed to at the behest of or in combination with the NBA, the employer group. Regardless of Article XXXI, pursuant to § 9 of the NLRA, the NBA member teams may not negotiate salaries with anyone other than the NBPA without NBPA approval. It therefore follows that Article XXXI of the NBPA–NBA Agreement does little more than memorialize in explicit terms what the NBA member teams' legal duty would be under the NLRA: to deal only with the NBPA or agents specified by the NBPA. The provision adds no new requirements to the NBA and thus creates no problem for the statutory exemption of the Regulations.

Article XXXI of the NBPA–NBA Agreement presents none of the concerns contained in the cases in which employer-union activities have been found to fall outside of the statutory exemption. Unlike *Allen Bradley*, the union activity is not designed to help employers control competition and prices. In fact, Article XXXI which requires teams to negotiate only with NBPA certified agents has no effect on the market for teams' services or on the market relating to any team. There is no combination with employer interests. With respect to the teams, the situation after the agreement is identical to the situation before it. The union serves its legitimate goals of protecting its representational function and the employer group's market is unchanged.

* * *

Even if Article XXXI of the Agreement were not entitled to the statutory exemption, it would be immune from antitrust review under the nonstatutory exemption to the antitrust laws. The Supreme Court has determined that when a union-employer agreement falls within the protection of the national labor policy, a proper accommodation between the policy favoring collective bargaining under the NLRA and the congressional policy favoring free competition in business markets requires that some agreements be accorded a limited nonstatutory labor exemption from antitrust sanctions. *Connell Construction Inc. v. Plumbers and Steamfitters Local 100*, 421 U.S. 616, at 622; *Meat Cutters v. Jewel Tea Co.*, 381 U.S. 676 (1975). Unlike the statutory exemption which immunizes activities that are expressly described in the Clayton and Norris LaGuardia Acts, the nonstatutory exemption immunizes labor arrangements that are the ordinary implication of activities contemplated by the federal labor laws. When the agreement is reached through bona fide, arms-length bargaining between the union and the employers, and the terms of the agreement are not the product of an initiative by the employer group but were sought by the union in an effort to serve the legitimate interests of its members, it is free from antitrust scrutiny.

[After reviewing the *Jewel Tea* decision which we read about in Chapter 3, the court concluded.]

* * *

The nonstatutory exemption similarly immunizes the Regulations from Sherman Act scrutiny. The Regulations were unilaterally developed in response to player complaints and to further NBPA labor policies. The NBPA–NBA Agreement, including Article XXXI, was agreed to in arms-length collective bargaining. The provision was not sought "at the behest of or in combination with" any employer or other non-labor group as forbidden by *Jewel Tea*. There is no economic benefit to the NBPA or the NBA member teams as a result of this provision and there is no effect on the employer's product or service market as a result of the provision.

Summary dismissal granted.

Questions for Discussion

1. Questions have been raised about the applicability of *H.A. Artists and Associates v. Actors' Equity Ass'n.*, 451 U.S. 704 (1981), (and the earlier precedents upon which this decision relied) to the sports context. In *H.A. Artists*, the Supreme Court emphasized the peculiar features of the theatrical world: actors are employed on an intermittent basis for specific productions; agents serve as a vital link in securing scarce work for performers (in place of the union hiring hall that performs this function in other industries in which workers move from job to job and employer to employer); and the primary aim of the Actors' Equity regulations was to ensure that, in return for a chance at getting a job through an agent, actors were not required to pay the agent a fee that left net earnings from the job below the union-negotiated minimum scale. In addition, the Court emphasized that not only did Actors' Equity act unilaterally in devising its program of agent regulation, but it relied on self-compliance by its own members for enforcement, rather than on a collective agreement negotiated with producer-employers.

In each of these respects, the sports industry is quite different from the theatrical industry (and also from the music industry, where an analogous union program passed Supreme Court muster in *American Fed'n of Musicians v. Carroll*, 391 U.S. 99 (1968)). Should these variations make a legal difference? What arguments could sports agents advance that the policy behind the labor exemption for collectively negotiated restraints on players (or owners) does not apply to restraints imposed on agents? If the labor exemption were held not to protect player association regulation of sports agents, would antitrust law apply to the program in baseball (notwithstanding *Flood v. Kuhn*)?

2. One further aspect of the Collins case was adverted to by the Tenth Circuit in its brief *per curiam* decision: no one ever alleged that Collins was incompetent or acted improperly in negotiating player contracts with his clients' professional teams, though this is the function over which unions have exclusive authority and the role that gives players associations the legal hook to regulate agents. The NBPA's refusal to certify Collins only prevented him from negotiating with NBA teams; it did not prevent Collins from handling a player's endorsements, taxes, or investments. Thus, the grounds for not certifying Collins were unrelated to the function that he was being prevented from performing for a player who wanted him to perform it. Is this appropriate? Should unions be allowed to regulate agents for misconduct or incompetence other than as a contract negotiator? If not, should certification be denied to an agent because, for example, he is convicted of drug use? Because he publicly disagrees with the union's bargaining strategy? On the other hand, what is an appropriate standard of incompetence in contract negotiations? Could certification be denied because an agent negotiated a contract the union believed was far below market value?

3. Bruce Pickens had been a star wide receiver for the Nebraska Cornhuskers. In early January 1991, after returning from the Orange Bowl in his senior year, Pickens went to a Lincoln, Nebraska, car dealership owned by Howard Misle. Misle let Pickens select and keep a new Audi in return for just a signed note and no down payment. At that time or shortly thereafter (exactly when was disputed), Pickens signed an agency contract with Misle's Total Economic Athletic Management (TEAM) of America, which had been certified by the NFL Players Association as a player agent and had represented a dozen or so players in the League. Pickens claimed that, in signing this document, he was told by Misle that he was thereby only evidencing his willingness to consider Misle for that role. Misle did not send that document to the NFLPA, and no one's attention was drawn to the fact that Association rules prohibit certified agents giving athletes anything of value to players to induce them to sign agency contracts.

Some time later, at the suggestion of one of his Nebraska coaches, Pickens met and eventually signed an agency agreement with Tom Condon, a former Kansas City Chief and President of the NFLPA and now one of the leading football agents (with a roster of more than 200 clients). Pickens told Misle he was signing with Condon, returned the Audi, and repaid the $3,000 in money and goods he had received from Misle. In that spring's draft, Pickens was selected by the Atlanta Falcons as the third player picked in the first round. In contract negotiations, the Falcon's original offer was $2.7 million over three years, and the contract finally signed by Pickens paid him a $2.5 million signing bonus and promised him $4.4 million in (nonguaranteed) salary and incentives over five years—figures that were midway between those secured by the number two and number four draft picks that year.

Misle sued Pickens in Missouri state court, seeking as damages for breach of the agency contract the specified fee rate of four percent of the Falcons' contract value. A Missouri jury found that there was an actual agency agreement and awarded Misle $20,000 in contract damages. Both sides appealed that verdict to a Missouri appeals court. Does the fact that the Pickens–Misle agreement may have violated the NFLPA rules affect its validity under state contract law? What significance, if any, should be attributed to the fact that at that time, the NFLPA had decertified itself as part of its antitrust litigation against the League (which we read about in Chapter 3)? Suppose that the agency contract were to be held legally enforceable against Pickens: under standard contract damages law, what is the appropriate amount that should be awarded to Misle, the agent? See *Total Economic Athletic Management of America v. Pickens*, 898 S.W.2d 98 (Mo.1995).

4. In the early 1990s, a number of Pittsburgh Steelers (including their All–Pro center Dermontti Dawson) discovered that their agent and investment counsellor, Joe Senkovich, Jr., had misappropriated and lost their savings. While civil, as well as criminal, proceedings were launched against Senkovich, he was by then effectively judgment-proof. Thus the players filed suit against the NFLPA, alleging that the union should have known of Senkovich's dishonesty before or after it certified him as an agent, and should have informed the players of this problem. Again, this case was complicated by the fact that, during part of the period of Senkovich's certification and representation of the players, the Association had renounced its rights under labor law in order to sue the NFL under antitrust law. With respect to the period covered by the NLRA, the Third Circuit affirmed the district court's judgment that there was no basis for suing the union (see *Jackson v. NFLPA*, 26 F.3d 122 (3rd Cir.1994)). Any state law claim of negligent union action on behalf of its unit members was preempted by the union's duty of fair representation under the NLRA, which was not violated by simple negligence. See *United Steelworkers of America v. Rawson*, 495 U.S. 362 (1990). Rather than mere allegations that the NFLPA should have known of Senkovich's dishonesty, the plaintiffs had to provide tangible proof (which they could not) that the NFLPA actually knew of Senkovich's misconduct and had failed to decertify him and inform the plaintiffs. (The court reached the same conclusion with respect to the non-union period.) The court noted that the concerns from which the duty of fair representation arose—the union's exclusive bargaining authority—were remote from this case.

> Here, plaintiffs were free to choose their own contract advisor and to scrutinize his conduct. Plaintiffs were free to confer on their contract advisor whatever degree of control of their financial affairs they wished. Thus, it is clear that the NFLPA's contract certification did not prevent Plaintiffs from protecting their own interests.

Do you agree?

Whatever the ultimate answer to these legal policy questions, players association regulation has evoked remarkably little complaint from established practitioners in this field, many of whom have served as advisers in the development and administration of these programs. One reason for this acceptance among the target group might be the reasonably relaxed character of the programs, which we will see in operation later in this chapter. At this point it is useful to highlight the key issues in the design of any regulatory program by either states or unions.[q]

1. *Coverage.* Who is an "agent" for purposes of such regulation? Should "agents" include only the people who negotiate player contracts with teams, or also people who pursue promotional opportunities for the player or manage his money? What about the "runners" who assist in recruiting clients? Should such regulation (particularly by state legislatures) apply to agents who are also lawyers licensed to practice in the relevant jurisdiction? Should the regulations govern dealings between agents and college players or graduates who are not yet on a professional roster?

2. *Eligibility.* What qualifications should be demanded of someone seeking certification as an approved agent? A law degree? Participation in a training program? A passing score on a test of knowledge of the relevant material in this area of practice? (Should such a test be a one-time entrance exam or one that has to be taken and passed periodically?) A probationary term until successful negotiation of a certain number of player contracts?

3. *Financial Responsibility.* Should the agent have to demonstrate financial responsibility to practice in this field? Through posting a surety bond? For how large an amount? Just for money managers or also for contract negotiators?

4. *Solicitation of Business.* Should any active solicitation of players by agents be permitted? Should the agent be permitted to provide something of value to a player as an inducement to sign the agency contract? Should the agent be able to pay third parties for referrals of players? Most important of all, should agents be restricted from even contacting college players whose eligibility has not yet expired?

5. *Fees.* Within the players associations, the driving force behind regulatory efforts tends to be player concerns about the size of agent fees. An important issue is whether any ceiling at all should be imposed on agent fees, especially a ceiling devised by the players' own association.

---

q. Besides the pieces noted earlier, helpful analyses of these problems can be found in Bart I. Ring, *An Analysis of Athlete Agent Certification and Regulation: New Incentives With Old Problems*, 7 Loyola Ent. L. J. 321 (1987), and Miriam Benitez, *Of Sports, Agents, and Regulations—The Need for a Different Approach*, 3 Ent. and Sports L. J. 199 (1986).

If there is to be such a fee scale, should it be based on an hourly rate or a percentage figure? If a percentage, should it be a single rate or one that rises and falls depending on the size of the underlying contract? What is the appropriate percentage figure (it is now generally four percent)? Should the base exclude the minimum salary amounts mandated by the collective agreement or amounts paid as incentive bonuses? What about non-guaranteed contract amounts, especially those contained in long-term deals?

Is the same fee percentage appropriate for the negotiation of a player's contract with the team as for the negotiation of an endorsement contract with a product manufacturer or a promotional contract with an outside business? (These fees are now not regulated by player associations, and generally run in the 15–20% range.) How will the association's answer to these issues likely influence the agent's incentives in negotiations (e.g., to pursue incentive bonuses and long-term deals)? And by the way, does *Collins* establish a labor exemption from antitrust scrutiny for union regulation of agent fees on endorsement contracts?

There are many other problems addressed by one or other of these regulatory schemes. A broader question of principle, however, runs through all these topics. A players association (and to a lesser extent, a state authority) can gather together all the relevant material about agent qualifications, experience, financial responsibility, fee levels, and potential conflicts of interest, and then make these data available and reasonably comprehensible to players in the sport, ideally on a comparative basis. Is the facilitation of such "comparison shopping" by players—veterans or rookies—a sufficient response to the problems seen in the earlier cases? Is there any danger in having an association or state authority go farther and mandate a set of rules that govern all player-agent relationships?

That question is posed by yet another episode in the Walters and Bloom drama, this time involving Ron Harmon from the University of Iowa and the Buffalo Bills. Harmon was one of the first athletes Walters and Bloom recruited. At a March 1985 meeting (which was secretly taped by Harmon's father), Harmon signed a post-dated representation contract, in return for which he received an immediate $2,500 (evidenced by a promissory note) and an additional $250 per month until he left Iowa. In addition, Walters and Bloom paid travel expenses for Harmon and his family and friends, a "finder's fee" for putting Walters and Bloom in touch with one of his Iowa teammates, and a $32,000 down payment on a new Mercedes as he left school in June 1986. Despite the receipt of more than $50,000 from Walters and Bloom, Harmon switched agents midway through his negotiations with the Bills in the summer of 1986. As in *Fullwood*, Walters and Bloom filed suit against their former client to recover their promised five percent of Harmon's four–year, $1.425 million contract (a $70,000 commission), plus their payments to and expenditures on behalf of Harmon. This time, however, the New York state judge sent the case to arbitration under the NFLPA's agent certification regime (see *Walters v. Harmon*, 135 Misc.2d 905, 516 N.Y.S.2d 874 (1987)).

The arbitrator, John Culver, a former U.S. Senator from Iowa, first indicated that even though the contract between Harmon and World Sports & Entertainment, Inc. ("WSE"—Bloom and Walters' firm) violated NCAA rules, this was neither illegal nor in violation of the NFLPA regulations. Thus, the arbitrator did not take the NCAA rules into consideration in his decision. Likewise, he did not regard Harmon as an innocent victim of fraud or unequal bargaining power. Harmon understood exactly what he was doing and the terms of the agreement, which he signed over the objections of his father. Nonetheless, the arbitrator voided the agreement between Harmon and WSE because Walters and Bloom had induced Harmon to sign it by payments of substantial amounts of cash and travel expenses, all in violation of the NFLPA regulations.

> The fact that Mr. Harmon may have freely accepted or even requested the money does not make their conduct acceptable under the Regulations.... [T]he correct remedy is to render the Agreement null and void. Otherwise, if the Agreement were enforced, the Contract Advisor who provided something of significant value to an NFL player in order for the player to execute a representation agreement would benefit from his or her wrongful conduct.... If such unfettered "bribery" were permitted, the result could be bidding wars between contract advisors for the rights to represent athletes.

The arbitrator did find that Bloom and Walters had provided services of value to Harmon and should be paid *quantum meruit* of $125 per hour for 25.23 hours of work, or $3,153.75. He also required Harmon to reimburse WSE for its out-of-pocket representation expenses, and to repay the $2,500 loan evidenced by a promissory note (although not the other $54,000 unmemorialized payments by WSE on Harmon's behalf).

Interesting questions emerge from these and other arbitration decisions involving soured relationships between players and agents. Should agents who have behaved in reproachable fashion and/or in violation of the union's regulations be awarded fees on a quantum meruit basis and reimbursement of expenses and loans? Or should they get no redress as a punitive deterrent against such behavior? To what extent should your answer depend on the degree of "innocence" of the player involved?

An even more basic question is why it is considered unethical or even reprehensible for an agent to provide cash or other inducements to an athlete to sign with him, as long as the terms of this "gift" or "loan" are made clear to the athlete-client. Is this not just a form of discounting the agent's future fees by the latter, in effect, providing a lending or support service to the athlete? One objection, of course, is that most of these payments are made to college athletes who thereby lose their "amateur" eligibility status under NCAA rules whose legality and legitimacy we shall explore in Chapter 10. But the current rules enacted by both state legislatures and players associations typically bar such advance payments even to athletes who never had or have now exhausted college eligibility, and may already be embarked on a professional career (in the minor leagues, for example). What sports policy is served by legal bars on such agent-player transactions?

Finally, we noted earlier that Walters and Bloom spent roughly $800,000 to induce nearly 60 players to sign agency contracts, and 10 of their clients (including Harmon and Fullwood) were selected in the first round of the 1986 and 1987 NFL drafts. Look closely at the hours and dollar figures in the *Harmon* case to understand why such a large amount seemed a sensible investment in starting up this new enterprise.

The fall of 1993 produced an even more challenging case for association regulation and arbitral scrutiny of agent behavior. Application for certification as a baseball player agent was filed with the MLBPA by Barry Rona. Rona had served from 1974 to 1986 as General Counsel, and from 1986 to 1990 as Executive Director, of MLB's Player Relations Committee, the Association's counterpart on the other side of the bargaining table. During those 16 years Rona had gained an enormous amount of experience and understanding of player relations in baseball. However, as we saw at the end of Chapter 3, one portion of that time (from 1985 to 1988) had been spent by baseball owners colluding to eliminate bidding for free agents, and thence hold down player salaries. Although after leaving the PRC, Rona had already begun representing some football and basketball players, the MLBPA refused to certify him to represent their baseball player-members. Rona challenged that Association decision in front of the program's arbitrator, NYU Law Professor Daniel Collins.

BARRY RONA AND MAJOR LEAGUE BASEBALL PLAYERS ASSOCIATION

(Arbitration, 1993).

COLLINS, ARBITRATOR.

[The basis for the MLBPA's rejection of Rona's application was § 2(C) of its Regulations, which barred certification of anyone whose conduct "may adversely affect his credibility [or] integrity ... to serve in a representative and/or fiduciary capacity on behalf of players." Following are the Association's conclusions on that score about Rona.

In the Association's judgment, your conduct during the conspiracy cannot be explained away or excused as simply a matter of typical adversarial behavior. For the fact is that you were, if not the architect, then at least a master builder of a devastating, profound, and prolonged violation of Players' rights, the extent of which cannot be overestimated. Over an extended period of time, the Clubs undertook a scheme intended to deprive all declared free agents of the market for their services, a market that was established through the Association's good faith, arm's length negotiations with the Clubs—and you.

* * *

In sum, it is the Association's conclusion that because you engaged in the above-described conduct and, indeed, had principal responsibility for it, you are unfit to be certified to represent players. Indeed, in the circumstances, we think it is extreme ill grace that, for your own economic interests, you now seek to align yourself with the interests of the very players you helped victimize.

Arbitrator Collins was limited to determining whether the Association's factual findings were supported by "substantial evidence on the record as a whole," and its legal conclusions were "arbitrary and capricious." The arbitrator quoted extensively from the New York Code of Professional Responsibility which spells out both the client's right to "zealous legal representation" and the lawyer's obligation "not to assist clients to engage in wrongful acts." From these premises, the arbitrator analyzed the Association's reasons for denying Rona certification as a player agent.]

* * *

It is clear to this Arbitrator that any institutional policy which by its terms or application would penalize a lawyer for providing, or would create a disincentive for a lawyer not to provide, zealous representation within the limits of the code, would transgress the public policy on which the Code rests. A corollary to this is that lawyers acting as such can only be judged, in terms of the ethics of their behavior, by the standards set forth in the Code. In addition there would seem to be serious questions whether determinations as to whether or not a lawyer has acted ethically can be made by other than the courts and whether or not such determinations can be based on anything less than a preponderance of the evidence.

The evidence in this proceeding establishes that the PRC is a New York corporation domiciled in New York, that from 1974 or 1975 until late 1985, sometime before January 1, 1986, Rona served the PRC only in a legal capacity, first as Counsel and later General Counsel, and that from late 1985 until his termination in December 1989 he also was the PRC's Executive Director, a post to which he was formally named in August 1986. Thus the collusion that the Roberts Panel found existed in the 1985 free agent market must have been devised and implemented when Rona was acting solely in a legal capacity for the PRC. While he thereafter assumed an additional leading role in the PRC, the evidence establishes only that his subsequent relationship to the collusion in the 1985 and 1986 free agent markets was only in his capacity as a lawyer—evaluating his clients' cases, advising them, questioning them, speaking publicly on their behalf, and serving on the Roberts and the first Nicholau Arbitration Panel. In fact neither Chairman Roberts nor Chairman Nicholau mentioned Rona in their opinions dealing respectively with the 1985 and 1986 free agent markets. As to 1987, there is evidence that Rona was a knowing participant in activities that related directly to the collusion that the Nicholau Panel found existed in that year's free agent market. However, all such activities by Rona, whatever their propriety, were conducted by Rona in his capacity as the principal inside lawyer for the PRC, working in conjunction with PRC outside counsel O'Connor. While the Players Association asserts that Rona bore some other responsibility for the collusion because of his role as PRC Executive Director, that is purely speculative. Since Rona's relationship to the collusion was only that of lawyer representing clients, the significance of Rona's actions for his credibility and integrity, in this Arbitrator's opinion, had to be judged solely in terms of the applicable New York law—the New York Code of Professional Responsibility.

It is mystifying why the Players Association failed to measure Rona's actions against the standards in the Code or even to acknowledge that such standards existed. On this point, Fehr and Orza are very experienced lawyers, and are long-time members of the New York bar. Furthermore Orza testified that although Fehr no longer did the regular work of Association General Counsel, he kept that "title because it would aid him in retaining his lawyer confidentiality privilege...." The lawyer's special privilege to which Orza referred is to be found in Canon 4 of the New York Code, particularly DR4–101.

The Arbitrator is strongly inclined to view the Players Association's evaluation of Rona's credibility and integrity without any reference to the applicable official standards as itself constituting arbitrary and capricious action within the meaning of the Regulations. In any event, even when the evidence is measured by the Code's standards, the Arbitrator finds that the Players Association acted arbitrarily and capriciously in rejecting Rona's application.

The Players Association's conclusion that Rona was part of the collusion in the 1985 and 1986 free agent markets because he was a leading figure in the PRC is fundamentally at odds with the Code's very clear position that lawyers do not act unethically merely because they represent individuals or institutions that are found to have engaged in wrongful activities. And there is no evidence, nor any finding by Chairman Roberts or Chairman Nicholau that it was or should have been obvious to Rona that his clients were acting "merely for the purpose of harassing or maliciously injuring any person" within the meaning of DR2–110 or DR7–102. On the contrary, he expressed his "concerns" to his clients, asked them directly whether they were involved in collusion to destroy the free agent markets in 1985 and 1986 and, when they replied negatively, allowed them to so testify under oath before the Roberts and Nicholau Panels. Rona acted entirely properly within the meaning of EC7–5—his allowing his clients to have their day in court to attempt under oath to refute the circumstantial evidence that they were engaged in collusion can hardly be termed taking a "frivolous legal position" in contravention of EC7–5. This Arbitrator believes that these are not even close questions. For the foregoing reasons the Arbitrator concludes that the Players Association's rejection of Rona's application because of his alleged involvement in the 1985 and 1986 collusion was arbitrary and capricious.

The Players Association argues, though, that independently of what occurred in 1985 and 1986, there is substantial evidence that Rona actively participated in the collusion as to the 1987 free agent market by his creation and administration of the Information Bank. Such conduct might arguably be a violation of the Code. However, the Arbitrator does not believe that the Association's position on this point even recognizes, no less meets the problem created by its arbitrary and capricious conclusion that Rona bore responsibility for the 1985 and 1986 collusion. Only if it viewed Rona's application in the context of his not having been responsible for any collusion prior to 1987 could the Association have responded fairly to his application. Stated another way, Rona was and is arguing that any conclusion that, through the Information Bank, he attempted, deliberately and secretly, to subvert the 1987 free agent market is first of all, based on selective and insubstantial circumstantial evidence; and that in any event such a conclusion is a problematical judgment call; and that when it is weighed against his long, productive and otherwise unblemished professional career there is no justification for finding that he lacks credibility and integrity to be certified as a Player Agent. Under the Regulations the Arbitrator has no jurisdiction to judge the merits of Rona's argument; he only has jurisdiction to review, on a substantial evidence, arbitrary-capricious basis the Association's response to Rona's argument. However, Rona's argument is not [in] the Arbitrator's opinion frivolous—he was entitled to have the Association consider the merits of his argument. That the Association never considered the argument, and could not have considered it, is clear to the Arbitrator. The Association's denial letter makes no effort to treat Rona's activities in 1987 separate and apart from his alleged participation in the 1985 and 1986 collusion. On the contrary, it refers to 1987 as a "graphic illustration of [his] central role ... in the conspiracy." And, even more importantly, the Association never considered the possibility that Rona could be viewed as not bearing any responsibility for the 1985 and 1986 collusion. On the contrary, in its rejection letter, in its statements to this Arbitrator, and in the testimony in this proceeding of its representatives, it has heaped extraordinary opprobrium on Rona, much of which, for example the assertion by former Players Association Executive Director Marvin Miller that Rona was mounting a "Nuremburg defense," is referable only to the events in 1985 and 1986, and not 1987, or is explainable only in terms of Rona's alleged involvement in the collusion in all three years. Having failed to consider, in fact having been incapable of fairly considering the arguments Rona advanced in support of his application, the Association acted, in this Arbitrator's opinion, arbitrarily and capriciously.

Agent certification ordered.

The major legal objection made by the MLBPA to Professor Collins' ruling was that he had exceeded his arbitral authority by focusing on external law, rather than on the standards established in the Association's Player Agent Regulations. Do you agree with that objection? What are the odds that the Association would win a challenge in court, given the standards for judicial review of arbitration awards we saw (in Chapter 4) applied in the Association's favor to sustain the *Messersmith* arbitration ruling that first established free agency in baseball? See *Kansas City Royals v. MLPA*, 532 F.2d 615 (8th Cir.1976).

Several other developments took place in the mid-1990s that posed interesting questions about the legitimate scope of union regulation of the agents who represent their members.

Questions For Discussion

1. Once the NFLPA had reestablished itself in mid-1993 as a union with a collective agreement, the Association also restored its program of mandatory agent certification and regulation. One new addition to the rules was a bar against players' agents also representing general managers and coaches. Is that a sensible idea? Or would you allow (even encourage) the practice in the broader entertainment industry, in which agents for performers have regularly functioned as agents for studio heads?

2. In the winter of 1994-95, Jose Canseco not only moved from the Texas Rangers to the Boston Red Sox, but he also tried to create a new sports management firm targeted especially at Latin American players. Canseco proposed to hire a certified agent to represent players in their direct negotiations with clubs. The plan foundered, though, when the MLBPA deemed it to be an unacceptable conflict of interest for one player's firm to be representing other players. Do you agree with that judgment, at least from the point of view of the Players Association (as distinct from the League)?

3. That same winter, faced with the prospect of baseball replacement games being organized by the owners, the MLBPA was reportedly considering a ban against any of its certified agents representing replacement players. Recall what we saw in Chapter 4, that players (and umpires or other employees) have a legally protected right *not* to strike as well as to do so. If you were an agent wanting to represent a player who proposed to cross the association's picket line, could you distinguish the *Collins* precedent and develop an argument that the labor exemption would not insulate this players association rule from antitrust challenge?

D. AGENTS, COLLEGE ATHLETES, AND NCAA RULES[r]

We return for one final look at the issue of agent integrity, this time focusing on agents' dealings with college athletes. Both the *Harmon* arbitration ruling and the earlier *Fullwood* decision testify to a weakness in the legal sanctions available against agent impairment of college eligibility. The agent who signs a college player—especially the agent who pays money to get the player's signature—risks that the contract will not be legally enforced and that the money paid to the athlete will be lost. However, this risk will materialize only if the player becomes sufficiently dissatisfied with his agent's performance to go elsewhere. Thus, both judge-made contract law and player association regulatory law directly protect the interests only of the athlete, not of the college that is not a party to this agency relationship.

Agents do not appear to have been greatly deterred by the lack of legal enforceability of their players' commitments. In the early 1990s, it was estimated that a large majority of top draft picks in football and basketball had signed with agents before their eligibility had expired, many of these players doing so in return for money or other financial benefits. The elaborate nature of these arrangements is exemplified by the 1987 deal between Kevin Porter, a star cornerback for Auburn University, and an agent named Jim Abernathy. Just before his senior year at Auburn, Porter signed an agreement with Abernethy that promised the latter five percent of Porter's professional salary and ten percent of his endorsement earnings, in return for an immediate $2,000 "signing bonus" paid to Porter, $900 monthly payments, Thanksgiving and Christmas bonuses, and $100 for each interception that season.

These kinds of deals not only constitute symbolic violations of the NCAA principles of "amateur" intercollegiate sports, they also subject the college to a considerable risk of tangible loss. For example, although Walters and Bloom had secretly signed Alabama's star basketball forward, Derrick McKey, to an agency contract, the school used McKey in the next NCAA tournament. When the NCAA discovered this fact, it required Alabama to forfeit two games it had won and repay the $250,000 the university had received from the tournament. And even if the university does learn of an agency contract in time to declare the player ineligible (as happened with Porter prior to Auburn's appearance in the Sugar Bowl), the university loses one of its best players and thus the chance for a successful season, both artistically and financially.

Understandably, then, there is widespread popular sentiment in favor of putting some legal teeth behind the NCAA eligibility rules.

---

r. Besides the books by Shropshire, *Agents of Opportunity*, note a above, and Mortensen, *Playing for Keeps*, note n above, see also Robert J. Ruxin, *Unsportsmanlike Conduct: The Student–Athlete, the NCAA, and Agents*, 8 J. of Coll. and Univ. Law 347 (1981–82), and Charles W. Ehrhardt and J. Mark Rodgers, *Tightening the Defense Against Offensive Sports Agents*, 16 Florida State U. L. Rev. 633 (1988).

However, the NCAA is a private body and its rules are not directly enforceable in court. The attitude of many agents was candidly expressed by Mike Trope, one of the early exponents of this behavior:[s]

> The NCAA rules are not the laws of the United States. They are simply a bunch of hypocritical and unworkable rules set up by the NCAA. I would no sooner abide by the rules and regulations of the NCAA than I would with the Ku Klux Klan.

Norby Walters echoed Trope, saying that he believed that ignoring the NCAA code was "no different than bending the Knights of Columbus rules." However, organized crime's intrusion with physical threats and violence brought the federal authorities into the *Walters* picture.

To establish its jurisdiction in the case, the Chicago U.S. Attorney's office developed the theory that it was a legal fraud for the player and his agent to hide their relationship in order to maintain the player's scholarship and his NCAA eligibility. This became a breach of the federal Mail Fraud Act when the school mailed the player's annual signed eligibility form to the NCAA head office.[t] And as far as agents were concerned, their repeated use of this practice constituted a violation of the Racketeer Influenced and Corrupt Organizations Act (RICO) (to which, of course, were added the allegations of extortion). Under that theory, any time an agent signed a contract with a player who continued to play college ball, both the player and the agent were committing a federal crime, irrespective of whether any money was changing hands (let alone whether there was any of the sleazy quality of the Walters venture). After a long and complex journey through the criminal justice system, the Seventh Circuit was finally required to appraise the legal validity of that theory.

UNITED STATES v. NORBY WALTERS

United States Court of Appeals, Seventh Circuit, 1993.
997 F.2d 1219.

EASTERBROOK, CIRCUIT JUDGE.

* * *

"Whoever, having devised ... any scheme or artifice to defraud, or for obtaining money or property by means of false or fraudulent pretenses, representations, or promises ... places in any post office or authorized depository for mail matter, any matter or thing whatever to be sent or delivered by the Postal Service ... or knowingly causes [such matter or thing] to be delivered by mail" commits the crime of mail fraud. Norby Walters did not mail anything or cause anyone else to do so (the universities were going to collect and mail the forms no matter what Walters did), but the Supreme Court has expanded the statute beyond its

---

[s.] Mike Trope, *Necessary Roughness*, 68 (Chicago: Contemporary Books, 1987).

[t.] See Landis Cox, *Targeting Sports Agents With the Mail Fraud Statute:* United States v. Norby Walters & Lloyd Bloom, 41 Duke L. J. 1157 (1992).

literal terms, holding that a mailing by a third party suffices if it is "incident to an essential part of the scheme," *Pereira v. United States*, 347 U.S. 1, 8 (1954). While stating that such mailings can turn ordinary fraud into mail fraud, the Court has cautioned that the statute "does not purport to reach all frauds, but only those limited instances in which the use of the mails is a part of the execution of the fraud." *Kann v. United States*, 323 U.S. 88, 95, (1944). Everything thus turns on matters of degree. Did the schemers foresee that the mails would be used? Did the mailing advance the success of the scheme? Which parts of a scheme are "essential?" Such questions lack obviously right answers, so it is no surprise that each side to this case can cite several of our decisions in support....

"The relevant question ... is whether the mailing is part of the execution of the scheme as conceived by the perpetrator at the time." *Schmuck v. United States*, 489 U.S. 705, 715 (1989). Did the evidence establish that Walters conceived a scheme in which mailings played a role? We think not—indeed, that no reasonable juror could give an affirmative answer to this question. Walters hatched a scheme to make money by taking a percentage of athletes' pro contracts. To get clients he signed students while college eligibility remained, thus avoiding competition from ethical agents. To obtain big pro contracts for these clients he needed to keep the deals secret so the athletes could finish their collegiate careers. Thus deceit was an ingredient of the plan. We may assume that Walters knew that the universities would ask athletes to verify that they were eligible to compete as amateurs. But what role do the mails play? The plan succeeds so long as the athletes conceal their contracts from their schools (and remain loyal to Walters). Forms verifying eligibility do not help the plan succeed; instead they create a risk that it will be discovered if a student should tell the truth. And it is the forms, not their mailing to the Big Ten, that pose the risk. For all Walters cared, the forms could sit forever in cartons. Movement to someplace else was irrelevant. In *Schmuck*, where the fraud was selling cars with rolled-back odometers, the mailing was essential to obtain a new and apparently "clean" certificate of title; no certificates of title, no marketable cars, no hope for success. Even so, the Court divided five to four on the question whether the mailing was sufficiently integral to the scheme. A college's mailing to its conference has less to do with the plot's success than the mailings that transferred title in *Schmuck*.

To this the United States responds that the mailings were essential because, if a college had neglected to send the athletes' forms to the conference, the NCAA would have barred that college's team from competing. Lack of competition would spoil the athletes' pro prospects. Thus the use of the mails was integral to the profits Walters hoped to reap, even though Walters would have been delighted had the colleges neither asked any questions of the athletes nor put the answers in the mail. Let us take this as sufficient under *Schmuck* (although we have our doubts). The question remains whether Walters caused the universities to use the mails. A person "knowingly causes" the use of the mails when he "acts with the knowledge that the use of the mails will follow in the ordinary course of business, or where such use can reasonably be foreseen." . . .

No evidence demonstrates that Walters actually knew that the colleges would mail the athletes' forms. The record is barely sufficient to establish that Walters knew of the forms' existence; it is silent about Walters' knowledge of the forms' disposition. The only evidence implying that Walters knew that the colleges had students fill out forms is an ambiguous reference to "these forms" in the testimony of Robert Perryman. Nothing in the record suggests that Perryman, a student-athlete, knew what his university did with the forms, let alone that Perryman passed this information to Walters. So the prosecutor is reduced to the argument that mailings could "reasonably be foreseen." Yet why should this be so? Universities frequently collect information that is stashed in file drawers. Perhaps the NCAA just wants answers available for inspection in the event a question arises, or the university wants the information for its own purposes (to show that it did not know about any improprieties that later come to light). What was it about these forms that should have led a reasonable person to foresee their mailing? Recall that Walters was trying to break into the sports business. Counsel specializing in sports law told him that his plan would not violate any statute. These lawyers were unaware of the forms (or, if they knew about the forms, were unaware that they would be mailed). The prosecutor contends that Walters neglected to tell his lawyers about the eligibility forms, spoiling their opinion; yet why would Walters have to brief an expert in sports law if mailings were foreseeable even to a novice?

In the end, the prosecutor insists that the large size and interstate nature of the NCAA demonstrate that something would be dropped into the mails. To put this only slightly differently, the prosecutor submits that all frauds involving big organizations necessarily are mail frauds, because big organizations habitually mail things. No evidence put before the jury supports such a claim, and it is hardly appropriate for judicial notice in a criminal case. Moreover, adopting this perspective would contradict the assurance of *Kann*, 323 U.S. at 95, and many later cases that most frauds are covered by state law rather than § 1341. That statute has been expanded considerably by judicial interpretation, but it does not make a federal crime of every deceit. The prosecutor must prove that the use of the mails was foreseeable, rather than calling on judicial intuition to repair a rickety case.

There is a deeper problem with the theory of this prosecution. The United States tells us that the universities lost their scholarship money. Money is property; this aspect of the prosecution does not encounter a problem under *McNally v. United States*, 483 U.S. 350 (1987). Walters emphasizes that the universities put his 58 athletes on scholarship long before he met them and did not pay a penny more than they planned to do. But a jury could conclude that had Walters' clients told the truth, the colleges would have stopped their scholarships, thus saving money. So we must assume that the universities lost property by reason of Walters' deeds. Still, they were not out of pocket to Walters; he planned to profit by taking a percentage of the players' professional incomes, not of their scholarships. Section 1341 condemns "any scheme or artifice to defraud, or for obtaining money or property" (emphasis added). If the universities were the victims, how did he "obtain" their property?, Walters asks.

According to the United States, neither an actual nor a potential transfer of property from the victim to the defendant is essential. It is enough that the victim lose; what (if anything) the schemer hopes to gain plays no role in the definition of the offense. We asked the prosecutor at oral argument whether on this rationale practical jokes violate § 1341. A mails B an invitation to a surprise party for their mutual friend C. B drives his car to the place named in the invitation. But there is no party; the address is a vacant lot; B is the butt of a joke. The invitation came by post; the cost of gasoline means that B is out of pocket. The prosecutor said that this indeed violates § 1341, but that his office pledges to use prosecutorial discretion wisely. Many people will find this position unnerving (what if the prosecutor's policy changes, or A is politically unpopular and the prosecutor is looking for a way to nail him?). Others, who obey the law out of a sense of civic obligation rather than the fear of sanctions, will alter their conduct no matter what policy the prosecutor follows. Either way, the idea that practical jokes are federal felonies would make a joke of the Supreme Court's assurance that § 1341 does not cover the waterfront of deceit.

Practical jokes rarely come to the attention of federal prosecutors, but large organizations are more successful in gaining the attention of public officials. In this case the mail fraud statute has been invoked to shore up the rules of an influential private association. Consider a parallel: an association of manufacturers of plumbing fixtures adopts a rule providing that its members will not sell "seconds" (that is, blemished articles) to the public. The association proclaims that this rule protects consumers from shoddy goods. To remain in good standing, a member must report its sales monthly. These reports flow in by mail. One member begins to sell "seconds" but reports that it is not doing so. These sales take business away from other members of the association, who lose profits as a result. So we have mail, misrepresentation, and the loss of property, but the liar does not get any of the property the other firms lose. Has anyone committed a federal crime? The answer is yes—but the statute is the Sherman Act, 15 U.S.C. § 1, and the perpetrators are the firms that adopted the "no seconds" rule. *United States v. Trenton Potteries Co.*, 273 U.S. 392 (1927). The trade association we have described is a cartel, which the firm selling "seconds" was undermining. Cheaters depress the price, causing the monopolist to lose money. Typically they go to great lengths to disguise their activities, the better to increase their own sales and avoid retaliation. The prosecutor's position in our case would make criminals of the cheaters, would use § 1341 to shore up cartels.

Fanciful? Not at all. Many scholars understand the NCAA as a cartel, having power in the market for athletes. E.g., Arthur A. Fleisher

III, Brian L. Goff & Robert D. Tollison, *The National Collegiate Athletic Association: A Study in Cartel Behavior* (1992); Joseph P. Bauer, *Antitrust and Sports: Must Competition on the Field Displace Competition in the Marketplace?*, 60 Tenn. L.Rev. 263 (1993); Roger D. Blair & Jeffrey L. Harrison, *Cooperative Buying, Monopsony Power, and Antitrust Policy*, 86 Nw. U. L.Rev. 331 (1992); Lee Goldman, *Sports and Antitrust: Should College Students be Paid to Play?*, 65 Notre Dame L.Rev. 206 (1990); Richard B. McKenzie & E. Thomas Sullivan, *Does the NCAA Exploit College Athletes? An Economic and Legal Reinterpretation*, 32 Antitrust Bull. 373 (1987); Stephen F. Ross, *Monopoly Sports Leagues*, 73 Minn. L.Rev. 643 (1989). See also *NCAA v. University of Oklahoma*, 468 U.S. 85 (1984) (holding that the NCAA's arrangements for the telecasting of college football violated the Sherman Act); *Banks v. NCAA*, 977 F.2d 1081 (7th Cir.1992) (showing disagreement among members of this court whether the NCAA's restrictions on athletes violate the Sherman Act). The NCAA depresses athletes' income—restricting payments to the value of tuition, room, and board, while receiving services of substantially greater worth. The NCAA treats this as desirable preservation of amateur sports; a more jaundiced eye would see it as the use of monopsony power to obtain athletes' services for less than the competitive market price. Walters then is cast in the role of a cheater, increasing the payments to the student athletes. Like other cheaters, Walters found it convenient to hide his activities. If, as the prosecutor believes, his repertory included extortion, he has used methods that the law denies to persons fighting cartels, but for the moment we are concerned only with the deceit that caused the universities to pay stipends to "professional" athletes. For current purposes it matters not whether the NCAA actually monopsonizes the market for players; the point of this discussion is that the prosecutor's theory makes criminals of those who consciously cheat on the rules of a private organization, even if that organization is a cartel. We pursue this point because any theory that makes criminals of cheaters raises a red flag.

Cheaters are not self-conscious champions of the public weal. They are in it for profit, as rapacious and mendacious as those who hope to collect monopoly rents. Maybe more; often members of cartels believe that monopoly serves the public interest, and they take their stand on the platform of business ethics, e.g., *National Society of Professional Engineers v. United States*, 435 U.S. 679 (1978), while cheaters' glasses have been washed with cynical acid. Only Adam Smith's invisible hand turns their self-seeking activities to public benefit. It is cause for regret if prosecutors, assuming that persons with low regard for honesty must be villains, use the criminal laws to suppress the competitive process that undermines cartels. Of course federal laws have been used to enforce cartels before; the Federal Maritime Commission is a cartel-enforcement device. Inconsistent federal laws also occur; the United States both subsidizes tobacco growers and discourages people from smoking. So if the United States simultaneously forbids cartels and forbids undermining cartels by cheating, we shall shrug our shoulders and enforce both laws, condemning practical jokes along the way. But what is it about § 1341 that labels as a crime all deceit that inflicts any loss on anyone? Firms often try to fool their competitors, surprising them with new products that enrich their treasuries at their rivals' expense. Is this mail fraud because large organizations inevitably use the mail? "Any scheme or artifice to defraud, or for obtaining money or property by means of false or fraudulent pretenses, representations, or promises" reads like a description of schemes to get money or property by fraud rather than methods of doing business that incidentally cause losses.

* * *

Reversed.

Federal prosecution of agent misbehavior under federal law does not appear, then, to be a viable option. (Ironically, just a few months after the Seventh Circuit had overturned the convictions of Walters and Bloom, an unknown assailant murdered Bloom in his Malibu home.) So far, at least, the same appears true of efforts to use general state criminal law. For example, the State of Alabama was unsuccessful in its prosecution of Jim Abernathy for supposedly "tampering with a sporting contest" by paying Auburn's Kevin Porter, who continued to play (see *Abernathy v. State*, 545 So.2d 185 (Ala.Crim.App.1988)).

The *Walters, Abernathy*, and other such cases pose the broader question whether it is appropriate to use criminal law in this sphere. Answering that question requires study and analysis of the current state of big-time college sports, a subject treated in depth in Chapters 9, 10, and 11. However, as some indication of the moral complexity of the problem, it turned out that Walter's college client, Ron Harmon, had a very dubious academic record compiled at the University of Iowa, one that likely left him ineligible under Big Ten, if not also NCAA, regulations. Academic and athletic officials who ignore such academic standards are not the subject of criminal prosecution. The question, then, is whether agents who play fast and loose with amateurism standards should be treated any differently.

As was noted at the outset of this section, since the early 1980s more and more states have enacted laws that are specifically targeted at agent dealings with college athletes.[u] (Unsurprisingly, almost every one of these states has one or more colleges that are traditional powers in either football or basketball.) A number of these statutes adopt registration programs that at least purport to ensure high-quality representation for their departing student-athletes. But with or without such a certifica-

---

[u] See Jan Stiglitz, *NCAA–Based Agent Regulation: Who are We Protecting?*, 67 North Dakota L. Rev. 215 (1991), and his more recent critique of this trend, *A Modest Proposal: Agent Deregulation*, 7 Marquette Sports L. J. 361 (1997).

Sec. D   AGENTS AND NCAA RULES

tion scheme, each of these statutes adopts one or more of the following restraints on agent dealings with college athletes.

1. Some states require an explicit warning, in bold print on the face of the agency contract, that by entering into this agreement, the player is forfeiting any further NCAA eligibility. Most of these laws give the athlete a "cooling off" period within which to change his mind and cancel the agreement (for example, Maryland law allows fifteen days).

2. A few states (such as Florida) require the agent and/or the athlete to notify the institution immediately after having signed the contract. Most, however, provide that such notification must be given to the institution (to its athletic director) a minimum number of days (for example, thirty days in Georgia) *before* the agency contract is to be signed.

3. Many states (such as Illinois) make it illegal, both civil and criminal, for an agent to give anything of value to the athlete or his family as an inducement to signing the representation contract.

4. At least ten states (Iowa, Kentucky, Louisiana, Maryland, Michigan, Mississippi, Oklahoma, Pennsylvania, Texas, and Virginia) flatly prohibit the agent from signing any contract with an athlete who has not yet completed his college eligibility. Indeed, some states (such as Texas) prohibit any contact or communication between an agent and a college player that might lead to loss of the player's eligibility:

> A registered athlete agent shall not directly contact an athlete who is participating in a team sport at an institution of higher education located in the state to discuss the athlete agent's representation of the athlete in the marketing of the athlete's athletic ability or reputation or the provision of financial services by the athlete agent, or enter into any agreement, written or oral, by which the athlete agent will represent the athlete, until after the completion of the athlete's last intercollegiate contest, including postseason games, and may not enter into an agreement before the athlete's last intercollegiate contest that purports to take effect at a time after that contest is completed.

(Texas Code, Ann. art. 8871, para. 6(b)(5).)

The most visible use of this Texas law took place in 1990 when former Heisman Trophy winner Johnny Rodgers, who worked for Howard Misle's Nebraska firm Total Economic Athletic Management (TEAM), took out for dinner and shopping in New York the mother of Andre Ware, the Houston quarterback who had just won the 1989 Heisman Trophy as a junior, and told Mrs. Ware that TEAM could make $20 million for her son if he were to leave college that year. Although neither Rodgers nor Misle had ever set foot in Texas for the purpose of recruiting Ware, both Rodgers and TEAM were fined $10,000 by the Texas Secretary of State (a Houston alumnus) for violating the above-quoted law based on what took place in New York. Could one fashion a persuasive constitutional basis for the Rodgers appeal (see *Shapero v. Kentucky Bar Ass'n*, 486 U.S. 466 (1988))?

These various restrictions on agent dealings with college athletes are enforced by a variety of sanctions, in some states against the athlete as well as the agent: not only criminal prosecution and fines, but also a right conferred on the college to sue for any damages it suffers as the result of the agent's signing of one of its athletes.[v] In Tennessee, for example, such damages include all lost television revenues, lost ticket sales from regular season athletic events, lost revenues from not qualifying for postseason athletic events such as football bowl games and NCAA tournaments, and an amount equal to three times the value of the athlete's scholarship.

The foregoing conveys the intensity of state legislative interest in the subject. The proposed federal Collegiate Athletic Integrity Act would actually go even further by making it a crime for any agent to "knowingly influence a college athlete to terminate that athlete's college eligibility," whether by "a gift or a loan of money, property, or services, or offering to procure employment" for the student athlete. All of this legislative effort poses important questions of legal policy. Should there be *any* legislative enforcement of the NCAA's rules regarding player-agent relationships? If so, which of the above models is best (including a uniform state law that may well be appearing in 1998 or 1999)? Or does the problem lie in the NCAA eligibility rules themselves, rather than in the efforts by athletes and agents to avoid them? Keep your views on that last question tentative for the moment, until we examine the entire sphere of intercollegiate athletics in Chapters 9, 10, and 11.

In conclusion, reflect for a moment about all the materials presented in the first five chapters of this book about the legal and institutional framework for the player market in professional team sports. How would you compare the value of contract, antitrust, and labor law in securing the key interests of athletes? The contributions made by players associations or agents in elevating player salaries and benefits?

---

v. As was noted earlier in this section, California's new Miller–Ayala Athlete Agents Act replaced its earlier regime of *ex ante* administrative certification with *ex post* litigation by colleges against agent rule-breakers. This was inspired by a lawsuit filed by the University of Southern California in 1995 against lawyer-agent Robert Caron, whose "runner" had provided money and other tangible benefits to several USC football stars while they were still playing college games. Caron settled USC's tort action for inducing breach of contract by agreeing to pay $50,000 to the university, and that episode helped persuade the state legislature to establish this as the general enforcement model. For the common law possibilities of such a suit in a state without such special legislation, see Richard P. Woods and Michael R. Mills, *Tortious Interference With an Athletic Scholarship: A University's Remedy for the Unscrupulous Sports Agent*, 40 Alabama L. Rev. 141 (1988), and Marianne M. Jennings and Lynn Zioiko, *Student–Athletes, Athlete Agents and Five Year Eligibility: An Environment of Contractual Interference, Trade Restraint and High–Stake Payments*, 66 U. of Detroit L. Rev. 179 (1989).

Chapter Six

SPORTS BROADCASTING, MERCHANDISING, AND INTELLECTUAL PROPERTY LAW

When spectator sports such as baseball, football, basketball, and hockey emerged in the 19th Century, live attendance was the only way that the fans could enjoy the performance and that teams could profit from the events. The same was true of other branches of the broader entertainment world: e.g., live theater and music concerts. The invention of film and recording at the turn of the century (and then the synchronization of the two) transformed the organization and economics of the entertainment industry. It took the invention of radio in the 1920s and television in the 1940s to do the same for sports (with an equal impact, of course, on filmmaking and music recording).

In the early 1960s, the vast majority of sports revenues still came from fans who attended live games. (This was true even though luxury boxes, club seats, and personal seat licenses had not yet been developed as a league device for extracting even more money from fans and communities wanting to attract or retain their teams in a world of franchise free agency.) In 1962, the NFL's first League-wide television contract (with CBS) paid the League $4.65 million, or $320,000 for each of the 14 clubs. Major League Baseball's national contract provided $3 million to its 20 teams. By 1998, the NFL's five television and cable contracts totalled $2.2 billion annually, or $75 million for each of 30 teams. The NBA's contracts generated $660 million, the MLB's $350 million, while the NHL still lagged behind at $45 million. However, in those three sports, each team reserved the right to sell broadcasts of most of its games on local stations, which in baseball generated another $550 million or so a year. (In stark contrast to football, the revenues of individual baseball clubs from that local broadcast source ranged from approximately $60 million apiece for the Yankees and the Braves to $6 million for the Royals and Expos.) By the late 1990s, then, over two-thirds of football's overall revenues came from broadcasting, nearly 50%

of baseball's and basketball's, and more than 20% of hockey's (including the latter's sizable Canadian contracts).

The immediate source of such revenues is fan (and advertiser) interest. Every year, the Super Bowl is the most-watched program on all of television. Baseball's World Series, the NBA Finals, and the NCAA's March Madness dominate their time frames, and ABC's Monday Night Football is one of the highest-priced regular programs on prime-time television. Meanwhile, local television and radio rights in sports with as many games as baseball, basketball, and hockey have long been crucial to the prosperity of the teams as well as the local stations and cable systems. National cable channels like ESPN and TNT, as well as "superstations" like Atlanta's WTBS and Chicago's WGN, which were created in the late 1970s, owe much of their success to a sporting audience whom advertisers and cable systems wish to attract.

Beginning with the NFL in the 1980s, leagues began to exploit another potential revenue source—licensing the use of team names and logos on merchandise. (The value of this asset was first demonstrated by the Major League Baseball Players Association, which began in the late 1960s to sell its members' names and licenses for use on baseball cards.) By the late 1990s, of $70 billion in national sales of this kind of commercial product, approximately $15 billion has this sports connection. Even casual sports fans love to wear shirts, caps, and other apparel with the colorful insignia of a variety of teams. With this market in mind, more and more teams are consulting design specialists to make their colors and logos even more appealing (the way that Disney and other studios do with movie characters that will eventually appear on children's clothing). The total annual sales of NFL-related merchandise is around $3.5 billion (with the NBA close behind), of which the league's licensing share is in the range of seven or eight percent (depending on the terms of the deal).

This new marketing phenomenon has not only become a lucrative asset for teams (and thence a source for rising player salaries): it is now a direct bonanza for players. All players associations now market on a group basis the right to use the names and likenesses of player-members on everything from sports cards to sporting attire. The $70 million earned annually by the MLBPA from this effort generates significant supplemental income for its members. It has also served as a union war chest for the fierce struggles we read about in Chapters 3 and 4 regarding free agency and salary caps. Meanwhile, individual stars like Shaquille O'Neal and Ken Griffey, Jr. earn a large endorsement bonus over and above the huge salaries that free agency has secured for them. In fact, Michael Jordan's $33 million contract with the Chicago Bulls for the 1997–98 season was actually less than the $45 million or so he received from his various commercial ventures off the court. The amount that companies like Nike, Reebok, and other merchandising firms are willing to pay for brand-new names was demonstrated in 1996, when Tiger Woods and Allen Iverson secured $60 million and $55 million dollar deals just as they were beginning their respective PGA and NBA careers.

Fan affection for their favorite players, teams, and leagues determines the amount of money that can be secured through broadcasting and merchandising. The law is indispensable, though, in enabling the sports world to realize significant revenues from these sources. The legal rules that make up intellectual property law initially create an exclusive property right in the broadcast of a game, the logo of a team, and the celebrity of a player—assets that would otherwise be freely available for use by a host of interested entrepreneurs. And it is antitrust law that shapes the ability of both leagues and players associations to sell their property rights at a collective premium, and then divide up the proceeds in line with membership votes.

A. RIGHT TO BROADCAST GAMES[a]

The first significant source of off-site sports revenue was radio broadcasts, particularly of baseball games in the sport that still is most suited to enjoyable *listening*. (The first big sports broadcast, one that was crucial to the popularization of radio generally, was Radio Corporation of America's (RCA's) live transmission of the 1921 heavyweight championship bout between Jack Dempsey and Georges Carpentier.) In the 1920s, major league clubs gradually overcame their qualms about the harm that radio broadcasts might do to ticket sales. If anything, easy and regular access to games over-the-air enhanced their appeal in the local community, and radio made it possible for fans across the country to enjoy pennant races and the World Series. More and more teams, then, were pleased to sell to radio stations the right to install announcers with microphones inside the ballpark to describe the events of the game to the audience at home.

Absent the law, though, radio broadcasts could not easily be made the exclusive preserve of the station that was paying for the rights. Unlike seats, in which only one person can sit at the same time, the events in a game can readily be recounted and transmitted on a host of radio frequencies without any physical interference with each other. The cost of duplication comes only in the size of the audience and thence the amount of money that any one station is prepared to pay the team for what are supposed to be *exclusive* rights.

Of course, the club could limit access to the ballpark to those stations who enjoyed broadcast rights. However, even in the 1990s, games at Fenway Park or Wrigley Field, for example, can still be easily viewed and described from rooms or rooftops in neighboring buildings. In the 1920's and 1930's, another vehicle for announcers to learn and

---

[a] The best overview of this topic is Robert Alan Garrett and Philip R. Hochberg, "Sports Broadcasting," Chapter 18 of Gary Uberstine, ed., *Law of Professional and Amateur Sports* (Deerfield Ill: Clark Boardman & Callaghan, 1991). An earlier version of this work appeared at 59 Indiana L. J. 155 (1984).

embellish what was happening on the field was Western Union, which transmitted the details by telegraph, pitch by pitch.

Indeed, a little-known fact about the early life of a recent American President is that he once was just such a "long-distance announcer." Back around 1930, Ronald Reagan used to broadcast from Des Moines the games of the Chicago White Sox and Cubs. The telegraph receiving agent would hand him a piece of paper stating "#12, out, 4–3," and young Reagan would tell his listeners about the hard hit ground ball that the second baseman had fielded and then narrowly thrown the batter out at first. In his autobiography, President Reagan recounted the dilemma he faced one day when the telegraph suddenly went dead: he had to narrate a major league record for consecutive foul balls until finally the receiver disclosed that the batter had fouled out—on the first pitch.

Reagan's announcing experience served as training for his eventual roles as movie star, labor leader (as head of the Screen Actors Guild), and President of the United States. His (and other) radio techniques also posed a significant challenge to the law, as teams sought to block this free use of their games for which clubs wanted to charge a fee for the privilege of locating an announcer inside the press box.

As we shall soon see, once games have been broadcast over the air, federal copyright law forbids anyone else rebroadcasting the particular versions of a Red Barber, Mel Allen, Vin Scully, or Ronald Reagan. Copyright law does not, however, create exclusive property in the bare events of the game—no more than it does for the events of a war, a crime, or a political convention. If ballclubs were going to enjoy and be able to license property rights in the games themselves, this right was going to have to be the product of general common law doctrine. In what might have been a path-breaking decision, *National Exhibition v. Teleflash*, 24 F.Supp. 488 (S.D.N.Y.1936), a federal district judge refused to enjoin a station from broadcasting a game via telephone from inside the Polo Grounds. (The judge noted that there was then no restriction on the face of the ticket through which the announcer had paid to gain access to the park.) The brief *Teleflash* opinion was not even reported, though, until the next crucial ruling had come down.

PITTSBURGH ATHLETIC CO. v. KQV BROADCASTING CO.

United States District Court, Western District of Pennsylvania, 1938.
24 F.Supp. 490.

SCHOONMAKER, DISTRICT JUDGE.

[For several decades prior to the construction of Three Rivers Stadium, the Pittsburgh Pirates baseball team played their home games at Forbes Field. The site of Bill Mazeroski's dramatic 1960 World Series winning home run, Forbes Field was unlike its more modern counterparts in that it was simply enclosed by fences that precluded unauthorized entry, but still permitted the game to be seen from outside vantage points. By the 1930s, though, fans were admitted to the ballpark only on condition that they not give out any news of the game while it was in progress.

The Pittsburgh Athletic Company, which owned the Pirates, contracted to give General Mills the exclusive right to broadcast play-by-play descriptions or accounts of Pirates games. General Mills in turn contracted with the National Broadcast Company (NBC) to broadcast the games over two Pittsburgh radio stations, KDKA & WWSW. At the same time, however, a rival radio station, KQV, was also broadcasting Pirates games. By stationing observers at leased vantage points outside Forbes Field, KQV received information about the progress of the games and provided simultaneous broadcasts.

The Pirates' owners sought an injunction to stop these "pirated" descriptions of their games, in which they asserted an underlying property right.]

* * *

It is perfectly clear that the exclusive right to broadcast play-by-play descriptions of the games played by the "Pirates" at their home field rests in the plaintiffs, General Mills, and the Socony-Vacuum Oil Company under the contract with the Pittsburgh Athletic Company. That is a property right of the plaintiffs with which defendant is interfering when it broadcasts the play-by-play description of the ball games obtained by the observers on the outside of the enclosure.

The plaintiffs and the defendant are using baseball news as material for profit. The Athletic Company has, at great expense, acquired and maintains a baseball park, pays the players who participate in the game, and has, as we view it, a legitimate right to capitalize on the news value of their games by selling exclusive broadcasting rights to companies which value them as affording advertising mediums for their merchandise. This right the defendant interferes with when it uses its broadcasting facilities for giving out the identical news obtained by its paid observers stationed at points outside Forbes Field for the purpose of securing information which it cannot otherwise acquire. This, in our judgment, amounts to unfair competition, and is a violation of the property rights of the plaintiffs. For it is our opinion that the Pittsburgh Athletic Company, by reason of its creation of the game, its control of the park, and its restriction of the dissemination of news therefrom, has a property right in such news, and the right to control the use thereof for a reasonable time following the games.

* * *

On the unfair competition feature of the case, we rest our opinion on the case of *International News Service v. Associated Press*, 248 U.S. 215. In that case the court enjoined the International News Service from copying news from bulletin boards and early editions of Associated Press newspapers, and selling such news so long as it had commercial value to the Associated Press. The Supreme Court said:

Regarding the news, therefore, as but the material out of which both parties are seeking to make profits at the same time and in the same field, we hardly can fail to recognize that for this purpose, and as between them, it must be regarded as quasi property, irrespective of the rights of either as against the public....

248 U.S. at 236. And again:

The right of the purchaser of a single newspaper to spread knowledge of its contents gratuitously, for any legitimate purpose not unreasonably interfering with the complainant's right to make merchandise of it, may be admitted; but to transmit that news for commercial use, in competition with complainant—which is what defendant has done and seeks to justify—is a very different matter....

248 U.S. at 239–40.

* * *

Defendant contends it is not unfairly competing with any of the plaintiffs because it obtains no compensation from a sponsor or otherwise from its baseball broadcasts. It concedes, however, that KQV seeks by its broadcast of news of baseball games to cultivate the good will of the public for its radio station. The fact that no revenue is obtained directly from the broadcast is not controlling, as these broadcasts are undoubtedly designed to aid in obtaining advertising business.

* * *

Injunction granted.

The court in *Pittsburgh Athletic* rejected the principle advanced by the KQV station (relying on *Teleflash*) that "the information [the station] received from its observers stationed on its own property without trespassing on plaintiff's property, may be lawfully broadcast by it." As we saw, the key precedent relied on by the judge was a decision by the Supreme Court in *International News Service v. Associated Press*, 248 U.S. 215 (1918). The Court found INS guilty of unfair competition when it took early East Coast versions of AP's World War I news stories from Europe and provided the news (not the stories) that same day to its own subscribers in the western United States. The Court's concern was that allowing one news service to take and sell the benefit of investigations and reporting undertaken by another would eventually eliminate the incentive of the second service to invest in that work and effort.

In the subsequent legal contest, *Pittsburgh Athletic's* reading of *INS* bested *TeleFlash's*, though with little additional analysis on the part of the trial courts that handled the later suits. (See, e.g., *Mutual Broadcasting System v. Muzak Corp.*, 177 Misc. 489, 30 N.Y.S.2d 419 (1941); *Liberty Broadcasting System v. National League Clubs*, 1952 Trade Cases

(CCH) § 67,278 (N.D.Ill.1952); *National Exhibition v. Fass*, 143 N.Y.S.2d 767 (1955); but see contra, *Loeb v. Turner*, 257 S.W.2d 800 (Tex.Civ.App. 1953).) In *Zacchini v. Scripps–Howard Broadcasting Co.*, 433 U.S. 562 (1977), a narrow Supreme Court majority cited *Pittsburgh Athletic* approvingly. The brief reference, though, came in the context of the Court's holding that it was not a violation of a television station's federal constitutional right of freedom of speech for the state courts of Ohio to find a violation of the flying Zacchini's "publicity rights" to telecast his entire 15-second "human cannonball act" on the local news. The Court was not ruling that states *must* protect such performances as a matter of their property law. As we shall see shortly, it is on a rather fragile legal reed that rests the rights to sports broadcasts that are now being sold for billions of dollars a year. In the meantime, what is your view about the similarities and the differences between baseball game broadcasts and the situation in *INS*? Between game radio broadcasts and the telecast of Zacchini's entire act from the County Fair?

Questions For Discussion

1. What is it that gives the team a property right in the broadcast of its games? Is it the fact that the game is being played in a privately owned or operated facility? If so, what about local telecasts of World Figure Skating Championships being held at the Hartford Civic Center Coliseum with television rights sold to ABC (see *Post Newsweek v. Travelers*, 510 F.Supp. 81 (D.Conn.1981))? Is it the fact that the event is being organized and staged at all? If so, can the Boston Athletic Association sell exclusive rights to one local station to telecast the Boston Marathon that is being run on public streets (see *WCVB–TV v. Boston Athletic Association*, 926 F.2d 42 (1st Cir.1991))?

2. Unlike a performance such as Zacchini's human cannonball act, the crucial feature of sporting events is that there are always at least two competitors. Thus, even after a court has decided that the game is privately owned by a team rather than freely accessible over the air, it must next decide *which* team has the right to broadcast the games.

Of course, if the teams are part of a league like Major League Baseball, these rights will be distributed according to the terms of their agreement. (For an early case in which this problem had not been anticipated by the NFL, see *Johnson-Kennedy Radio Corp. v. Chicago Bears Football Club*, 97 F.2d 223 (7th Cir.1938), where the then-Chicago Cardinals sought to block a radio broadcast of its home game with the Chicago Bears on the Bears licensed station.) Even there, one wonders whether the underlying allocation of broadcast property rights influences the terms of renewal of the league contract being negotiated between large and small market teams.

In college sports, where teams regularly play nonconference games, this issue has produced litigation. One case, *Wichita State University Intercollegiate Athletic Ass'n v. Swanson Broadcasting*, (unreported, Kansas, 1981), involved the effort by a Wichita radio station to air the broadcasts of Wichita's away games by the home team's broadcasters. The other case, *Kelly Communications v. Westinghouse Broadcasting* (unreported, Mass., 1983), involved the airing in Boston of Penn State's network radio broadcast of a football game that Penn State was playing at Boston College. Faced with claims by both the local school and the station to whom it had sold *its* broadcast rights in these games, should a court block another station airing the other team's broadcasts? In both cases, or in only one of the above?

From the 1950s into the 1990s, *Pittsburgh Athletic* was largely a non-issue in the sports world. The location and design of new stadiums and arenas made it essentially impossible to produce a broadcast of a game without access to the facility, something that teams granted only on condition that there would be no such transmission of the game without the team's consent. The issue of which of the two competing teams actually "owned" the games could readily be resolved through league rules or contracts between non-league participants. The important intellectual property issues in game broadcasts and other marketable features of sports arose under doctrine of copyright, trademark, and publicity law which we will be encountering shortly.

However, the development of new technology has recently created a new legal problem—not just under property law, but also under the First Amendment. In early 1996, the National Basketball Association filed a lawsuit against Motorola, Inc., and its joint venturer, Sports Team Analysis and Tracking System, Inc. (STATS). These two partners were producing and selling a new portable electronic pager device—SportsTrax—that provided "real-time" information about what was taking place in NBA games. A fan could keep track of every NBA game being played around the country, by punching into his SportsTrax pager the channel with the game he was interested in and seeing displayed on an inch-and-a-half screen the score, time, ball possession, and foul bonus situation. This information was updated every two minutes or so during the game, and even more often at the end of close games.

The SportsTrax equipment was manufactured and sold by Motorola (for $200 per pager). The information was compiled by STATS which was in the business of generating statistics from a variety of sports for bodies such as AP, ESPN, Fox, Turner, and numerous teams. STATS did not have data gatherers located at the games themselves: these people would have been subject to the terms of the NBA Media Pass which limits outside updates to three times per quarter. Instead, STATS hired reporters who, for $10 a game, watched or listened to broadcasts and continuously typed into their computers the shots taken and made, fouls, clock updates, and the like. That data was sent out via STATS' on-line service to a common carrier satellite which beamed the programmed information onto pagers around the country. Basketball fans who bought the pager equipment and subscribed to the SportsTrax service could stay in constant touch with their favored game(s) whether they were at work, at a party, or at home.

SportsTrax was originally developed by Motorola and STATS for baseball, for which Major League Baseball gave it a license and Business Week a salute as the 1994 product of the year. In the fall of 1994, the partners began discussions with the NBA to expand their service into basketball. The NBA was then developing its own product, called Gamestats, which collected the statistics from all games going on and provided this information to broadcasters and luxury suites at the game in question. While not yet possible, the NBA wanted to develop a capacity for Gamestats to transmit this real-time data to all other arenas, as well as to outside commercial services such as SportsTrax. However, the two sides were not able to agree on the terms of a deal. Thus Motorola and SportsTrax decided to generate and transmit NBA statistics by themselves (as described above), and without a license from the league. Some of that data would have been compiled by Gamestats and then sent out by broadcasters over the air to the SportsTrax reporters listening to the game. When SportsTrax began its basketball operation for the 1995–96 season, the NBA responded with a lawsuit.

The suit involved a host of legal issues, including under federal copyright and trademark law. The judge dismissed the latter claims as unsupported by the relevant doctrines that we shall see in the following sections. The tougher legal call was whether the SportsTrax service constituted commercial misappropriation of the NBA's property rights in its games under state common law. District Judge Preska, relying on *Pittsburgh Athletic* and other judicial readings of *International News Service*, found such misappropriation to have taken place. Admittedly, SportsTrax was not the equivalent of a broadcast of everything taking place in a game. However, it did "provide consumers of real-time NBA game data with portable, nation-wide contemporaneous, and core information about every NBA game. [Quoting the SportsTrax advertising flyer, it] 'covers it all, any game, any team, any time, anywhere.'"

The defendants immediately appealed this district court ruling to the Second Circuit and the injunction was stayed during the 1996–97 season. Not just the American Civil Liberties Union, but also the New York Times and Associated Press filed amicus briefs in support of Motorola and STATS. However, the NBA had amicus briefs from NBC, which broadcasts NBA games as well as Tom Brokaw's evening news; the network claimed that SportsTrax's continuous presentation of what was going on was the virtual recreation of NBA games on NBC and other broadcast outlets. Another amicus brief was filed by America Online, which was itself the target of an NBA lawsuit. America Online had become a purchaser of SportsTrax data which it was making available to its subscribers. The Internet is potentially a much bigger source of both consumer use and revenues than devices such as the SportsTrax pagers, and its fate would also turn on what happened in the appeal.

NATIONAL BASKETBALL ASSOCIATION v. SPORTS TEAM ANALYSIS AND TRACKING SYSTEMS (STATS) AND MOTOROLA (SPORTSTRAX)

United States Court of Appeals, Second Circuit, 1997.
105 F.3d 841.

WINTER, CIRCUIT JUDGE.

[A large part of the circuit court opinion was devoted to a significant technical question: to what extent does federal copyright law preempt any such claims under state law? As we shall see in the next section of this chapter, the live performance of sports events is not itself protected under the Copyright Act. However, in its major 1976 rewriting of that Act, Congress made it clear that the simultaneously-recorded broadcast of a game was copyrightable. Even then, copyright in the broadcast extended only to the "expression" of the game in picture and sound, not the bare "facts" of the game that were being aired. Application of this fact-expression dichotomy, as formulated in *Feist Publications v. Rural Telephone Service Co.*, 499 U.S. 340 (1991), led the district court to reject the NBA's copyright claim here.

The question, though, was whether the fact that copyright law did not specifically apply meant that state commercial misappropriation law could govern. The Second Circuit in earlier cases had read the Copyright Act's § 301 "subject matter" preemption of state law as applying to any claim that comes within the "ambit" of copyright, even though it may not meet the standards of that law (e.g., because of "fair use" as well as "fact-expression" doctrine). There had to be a significant "extra element" to the situation to preserve a state law claim.

The Second Circuit acknowledged that *INS* still permitted state law protection of "hot news" against commercial misappropriation, even though the news consisted of uncopyrightable facts. The key question posed by this case was whether the district court's reliance on *Pittsburgh Athletic* and its successors' application of *INS* placed SportsTrax inside or outside the "hot news" domain.]

* * *

In our view, the elements central to an *INS* claim are: (i) the plaintiff generates or collects information at some cost or expense; (ii) the value of the information is highly time-sensitive; (iii) the defendant's use of the information constitutes free-riding on the plaintiff's costly efforts to generate or collect it; (iv) the defendant's use of the information is in direct competition with a product or service offered by the plaintiff; (v) the ability of other parties to free-ride on the efforts of the plaintiff would so reduce the incentive to produce the product or service that its existence or quality would be substantially threatened.[8]

---

8. Some authorities have labeled this element as requiring direct competition between the defendant and the plaintiff in a primary market. "In most of the small number of cases in which the misappropriation doctrine has been determinative, the

INS is not about ethics; it is about the protection of property rights in time-sensitive information so that the information will be made available to the public by profit-seeking entrepreneurs. If services like AP were not assured of property rights in the news they pay to collect, they would cease to collect it. The ability of their competitors to appropriate their product at only nominal cost and thereby to disseminate a competing product at a lower price would destroy the incentive to collect news in the first place. The newspaper-reading public would suffer because no one would have an incentive to collect "hot news."

We therefore find the extra elements—those in addition to the elements of copyright infringement—that allow a "hot-news" claim to survive preemption are: (i) the time-sensitive value of factual information, (ii) the free-riding by a defendant, and (iii) the threat to the very existence of the product or service provided by the plaintiff.

2. THE LEGALITY OF SPORTSTRAX

We conclude that Motorola and STATS have not engaged in unlawful misappropriation under the "hot-news" test set out above. To be sure, some of the elements of a "hot-news" *INS*-claim are met. The information transmitted to SportsTrax is not precisely contemporaneous, but it is nevertheless time-sensitive. Also, the NBA does provide, or will shortly do so, information like that available through SportsTrax. It now offers a service called "Gamestats" that provides official play-by-play game sheets and half-time and final box scores within each arena. It also provides such information to the media in each arena. In the future, the NBA plans to enhance Gamestats so that it will be networked between the various arenas and will support a pager product analogous to SportsTrax. SportsTrax will of course directly compete with an enhanced Gamestats.

However, there are critical elements missing in the NBA's attempt to assert a "hot-news" *INS*-type claim. As framed by the NBA, their claim compresses and confuses three different informational products. The first product is generating the information by playing the games; the second product is transmitting live, full descriptions of those games; and the third product is collecting and retransmitting strictly factual

---

defendant's appropriation, like that in *INS*, resulted in direct competition in the plaintiffs' primary market.... Appeals to the misappropriation doctrine are almost always rejected when the appropriation does not intrude upon the plaintiff's primary market," *Restatement (Third) of Unfair Competition*, § 38, Cmt. c, at 412–13; see also *National Football League v. Delaware*, 435 F.Supp. 1372 (D.Del.1977). In that case, the NFL sued Delaware over the state's lottery which was based on NFL games. In dismissing the wrongful misappropriation claims, the court stated:

While courts have recognized that one has a right to one's own harvest, this proposition has not been construed to preclude others from profiting from demands for collateral services generated by the success of one's business venture.

Id. at 1378. The court also noted, "It is true that Delaware is thus making profits it would not make but for the existence of the NFL, but I find this difficult to distinguish from the multitude of charter bus companies who generate profit from servicing those of plaintiffs' fans who want to go to the stadium or, indeed, the sidewalk popcorn salesman who services the crowd as it surges towards the gate." Id.

400   SPORTS BROADCASTING, MERCHANDISING, ETC.   **Ch. 6**

[margin note: 2nd CIR Reverses]

information about the games. The first and second products are the NBA's primary business: producing basketball games for live attendance and licensing copyrighted broadcasts of those games. The collection and retransmission of strictly factual material about the games is a different product: e.g., box-scores in newspapers, summaries of statistics on television sports news, and real-time facts to be transmitted to pagers. In our view, the NBA has failed to show any competitive effect whatsoever from SportsTrax on the first and second products and a lack of any free-riding by SportsTrax on the third.

With regard to the NBA's primary products—producing basketball games with live attendance and licensing copyrighted broadcasts of those games—there is no evidence that anyone regards SportsTrax or the AOL site as a substitute for attending NBA games or watching them on television. In fact, Motorola markets SportsTrax as being designed "for those times when you cannot be at the arena, watch the game on TV, or listen to the radio...."

The NBA argues that the pager market is also relevant to a "hot-news" *INS*-type claim and that SportsTrax's future competition with Gamestats satisfies any missing element. We agree that there is a separate market for the real-time transmission of factual information to pagers or similar devices, such as STATS's AOL site. However, we disagree that SportsTrax is in any sense free-riding off Gamestats.

An indispensable element of an INS "hot-news" claim is free-riding by a defendant on a plaintiff's product, enabling the defendant to produce a directly competitive product for less money because it has lower costs. SportsTrax is not such a product. The use of pagers to transmit real-time information about NBA games requires: (i) the collecting of facts about the games; (ii) the transmission of these facts on a network; (iii) the assembling of them by the particular service; and (iv) the transmission of them to pagers or an on-line computer site. Appellants are in no way free-riding on Gamestats. Motorola and STATS expend their own resources to collect purely factual information generated in NBA games to transmit to SportsTrax pagers. They have their own network and assemble and transmit data themselves.

To be sure, if appellants in the future were to collect facts from an enhanced Gamestats pager to retransmit them to SportsTrax pagers, that would constitute free-riding and might well cause Gamestats to be unprofitable because it had to bear costs to collect facts that SportsTrax did not. If the appropriation of facts from one pager to another pager service were allowed, transmission of current information on NBA games to pagers or similar devices would be substantially deterred because any potential transmitter would know that the first entrant would quickly encounter a lower cost competitor free-riding on the originator's transmissions.[9]

---

[9]. It may well be that the NBA's product, when enhanced, will actually have a competitive edge because its Gamestats system will apparently be used for a number of in-stadium services as well as the pager market, resulting in a certain amount of

However, that is not the case in the instant matter. SportsTrax and Gamestats are each bearing their own costs of collecting factual information on NBA games, and, if one produces a product that is cheaper or otherwise superior to the other, that producer will prevail in the marketplace. This is obviously not the situation against which INS was intended to prevent: the potential lack of any such product or service because of the anticipation of free-riding.

For the foregoing reasons, the NBA has not shown any damage to any of its products based on free-riding by Motorola and STATS, and the NBA's misappropriation claim based on New York law is preempted.

* * *

Reversed.

Questions For Discussion

1. As a matter of federal preemption law, is the Second Circuit right in holding that state law endorsement of the NBA's claim cannot square with the federal government's occupation of the copyright field? As a matter of policy, should federal law be expanded to give the NBA exclusive control over live-time description and sale of what is going on in their games? Would any such intellectual property conferred on the league improperly intrude upon the First Amendment rights of Motorola and STATS (an issue the Second Circuit did not have to address in this case)?

2. Does *NBA-Motorola* implicitly overturn *Pittsburgh Athletic* as applied to the latter's facts? For a potential up-to-date example of this problem, recall that major boxing matches are now shown on pay-for-view, for $40 to $50 a home. There are no longer live radio broadcasts, as there were in the late 1930s when cases like *Twentieth Century Sporting Club v. Transradio Press Service, Inc.*, 165 Misc. 71, 300 N.Y.S. 159 (1937) (involving a Joe Louis fight), were being decided. There likely still are a considerable number of fans who, while they do not feel able to pay that price actually to see the fight on the screen, would like to know what is happening to Mike Tyson, for example, while his fight with Evander Holyfield is going on, rather than wait to read about it in the newspaper sports section the next morning. After *NBA-Motorola*, could (and should) a radio station be able to locate an announcer in a place where the game is being shown on pay-for-view television and describe to the radio audience the key developments in the fight as they are taking place?

B. COPYRIGHT IN THE GAME BROADCASTS

Radio is the broadcast medium that is most conducive to such "free" use of a fight or game for broadcasting purposes, absent a property right

cost-sharing. Gamestats might also have a temporal advantage in collecting and transmitting official statistics. Whether this is so does not affect our disposition of this matter, although it does demonstrate the gulf between this case and *INS*, where the free-riding created the danger of no wire service being viable.

in the team. All that the radio station needs is an announcer (like the young Reagan) with the talent to reconstruct the events of the game for the benefit of his listeners. Television, by contrast, needs cameras appropriately located next to the field so that visual images of the game can be transmitted to viewers to see for themselves at home at the same time the game is being played in the stadium. Since the team controls the facility where the game is being played, it could effectively block almost any other telecast even if it did not have legal recourse. (The exception which proves that rule is the *Boston Marathon* case we will see in a later section, where the local Boston station that had bought the telecast rights had to film the event from the same public locations that other stations had access to on the ground or in the air.) And television rights are by far the major asset that teams have to sell away from the park.

Once the game has been broadcast, this triggers the copyright brand of intellectual property. Sports fans are familiar with the statement that begins or ends every broadcast: "any rebroadcast, retransmission, or other use of the events of this game, without the express written consent of the owner, are hereby prohibited." We saw in the prior section the preemptive impact that federal copyright of game broadcasts can have on state common law rights of the league. Here we shall examine the affirmative scope of the rights conferred by copyright, and the distinctive issues posed by sports broadcasting for the copyright regime.

Most recently rewritten in the Copyright Act of 1976, 17 U.S.C.A. § 101, et. seq., copyright law finds its roots in the constitution itself. Article I, § 8, cl. 8, authorizes Congress "To promote the Progress of Science and useful Arts, by securing for limited Times to Authors and Inventors the exclusive Right to their respective Writings and Discoveries." The operating premise then and now is that only if one gives authors and inventors the exclusive right to control and license use of their works will there be sufficient incentive to invest the time, effort, and resources in production of those works for the benefit of the ultimate consumers.

Congress moved quickly to enact the first copyright statute in 1789, which gave authors of books and maps the right to block any copying of their work for 14 years after publication. The current law extends copyright protection to songs, plays, recordings, films, and radio and television broadcasts; the exclusive right (under § 106) encompasses not just duplication of the original, but also preparation of derivative works (e.g., movies out of books); sale or rental of copies of the original or the derivative work; and public performance of either. Copyright duration now lasts for the rest of the author's life plus fifty years (and where the owner is a business entity rather than a real person, the copyright term is a straight 75 years).

At the same time, there remain two key limitations on the availability and scope of such copyright protection. Section 102(a) states that the only kinds of works that can be copyrighted are "original works of authorship fixed in any tangible medium of expression," and § 102(b) says that, even for an original work of authorship, copyright protection does not "extend to any idea, procedure, process, system, method of operation, concept, principle, or discovery...."

In this statutory section we find the reasons why state common law, not federal copyright legislation, had to be appealed to for the right *to* broadcast a game. Judge Winter explained in the *NBA-Motorola* case why a live sports performance cannot amount to a "work of authorship."

> Sports events are not "authored" in any common sense of the word. There is, of course, at least at the professional level, considerable preparation for a game. However, the preparation is as much an expression of hope or faith as a determination of what will actually happen. Unlike movies, plays, television programs, or operas, athletic events are competitive and have no underlying script. Preparation may even cause mistakes to succeed, like the broken play in football that gains yardage because the opposition could not expect it. Athletic events may also result in wholly unanticipated occurrences, the most notable recent event being in a championship baseball game in which interference with a fly ball caused an umpire to signal erroneously a home run.
>
> What "authorship" there is in a sports event, moreover, must be open to copying by competitors if fans are to be attracted. If the inventor of the T-formation in football had been able to copyright it, the sport might have to come to an end instead of prospering. Even where athletic preparation most resembles authorship—figure skating, gymnastics, and, some would uncharitably say, professional wrestling—a performer who conceives and executes a particularly graceful and difficult—or, in the case of wrestling, seemingly painful—acrobatic feat cannot copyright it without impairing the underlying competition in the future. A claim of being the only athlete to perform a feat doesn't mean much if no one else is allowed to try.

105 F.3d at 846. Even when the authorized broadcast of a game has been captured on a video and/or audio tape (i.e., "fixed in a tangible medium"), copyright protection does not extend to the basic "ideas" (or facts) in the game, as opposed to their broadcast "expression." (See *Feist Publications v. Rural Telephone Service*, 499 U.S. 340 (1991), and *Miller v. Universal City Studios*, 650 F.2d 1365 (5th Cir.1981).) Thus, as long as Ronald Reagan was making up his own expression of what was happening in a Cubs or White Sox game, he was not violating the copyrighted expression of another announcer's broadcast a half inning or so earlier.

Finally, even with respect to an *expression* that has been *fixed in a tangible medium*, the defendant's action does not always constitute a copyright violation. Indeed, even if there is a strong *similarity* between the two works, the later author must be proven to have had *access* to the original work in order to support the conclusion that he copied it, rather than produced it independently. On that basis, the First Circuit rejected a copyright claim by a New England Patriots fan who had sent the team a suggested design for a new logo. The reason was that the team had not provided that example to the professional artist hired by NFL Properties to design a new logo that the fan thought was very similar to his. See *Grubb v. KMS Patriots, L.P.*, 88 F.3d 1 (1st Cir.1996). Indeed, even if there is unauthorized copying, a key doctrine now embodied in § 107 of the Copyright Act gives everyone the right to make "fair use" of a copyrighted work. The following case provides an intriguing example of an effort to appeal to fair use in the sports broadcasting context.

NEW BOSTON TELEVISION v. ENTERTAINMENT SPORTS PROGRAMMING NETWORK [ESPN]

United States District Court, District of Massachusetts, 1981.
Copy. L. Rep. (CCH) § 25,293, 215 U.S.P.Q. (BNA) 755.

ZOBEL, DISTRICT JUDGE:

[Under its contract with the Boston Red Sox and the Boston Bruins, New Boston Television held the exclusive right to broadcast Red Sox and Bruins games on its Channel 38, WSBK–TV. The Red Sox retained the copyright in the baseball telecasts, and WSBK was entitled to one-half of all royalties earned by the copyright. The copyright in the hockey telecasts was controlled jointly by WSBK and the Bruins.

Throughout the fall of 1979 and the spring of 1980, the new ESPN cable channel negotiated with WSBK to rebroadcast excerpts of the Bruins and Red Sox telecasts on its SportsCenter program. ESPN offered to exchange segments of its national programs for segments of WSBK broadcasts. WSBK offered to authorize the use of its broadcasts in exchange for payment of a fee and compliance with other conditions. However, without reaching any agreement, ESPN proceeded to use the WSBK broadcasts. After several letters of protest, WSBK filed suit for copyright infringement. ESPN asserted a number of defenses, principally fair use.]

* * *

The fair use defense is a judicially developed doctrine which is now codified in the Copyright Revision Act of 1976, 17 U.S.C. § 107. It has been defined as "a privilege in others than the owner of the copyright to use the copyrighted material in a reasonable manner without his consent; notwithstanding the monopoly granted to the owner." *Rosemont Enterprises, Inc. v. Random House, Inc.*, 366 F.2d 303, 306 (2d Cir.1966). The doctrine "offers a means of balancing the exclusive rights of the copyright holder with the public's interest in the dissemination of information affecting areas of universal concern, such as art, science, and industry." *Wainwright Securities, Inc. v. Wall Street Transcript Corp.*, 558 F.2d 91, 94 (2d Cir.1977).

Fair use is a question which depends on the facts of each particular case, evaluated in light of certain criteria: 1) the purpose and character of the use, including whether such use is of a commercial nature or is for nonprofit educational purposes; 2) the nature of the copyrighted work; 3) the amount and substantiality of the portion used in relation to the copyrighted work as a whole; and 4) the effect of the use upon the potential market for or value of the copyrighted work.

Defendants assert that as to the first of these factors, their use is primarily for "news" purposes and hence should be protected by the fair use doctrine in order to assure the public's right of access to newsworthy information. While protection of the public right of access to such information is a primary justification for the fair use defense, this right is sufficiently protected merely by enabling defendants to report the underlying facts which the plaintiff's videotapes record. It does not however permit defendants to appropriate the plaintiff's expression of that information by copying the plaintiff's films themselves. "The fair use doctrine is not a license for corporate theft, empowering a court to ignore a copyright whenever it determines the underlying work contains material of possible public importance." *Iowa State University v. American Broadcasting Cos.*, 621 F.2d 57, 61 (2d Cir.1980).

Defendants rely on *Time Incorporated v. Bernard Geis Assoc.*, 293 F.Supp. 130 (S.D.N.Y.1968), in which the Court determined that the reproduction of frames of the Zapruder film in a book inquiring into the assassination of President Kennedy was fair use. However, the unique and extraordinary nature of that historical event renders that case distinguishable from the case at bar. In addition, while the defendants in *Geis* had no opportunity to record the event themselves, defendants here are under no such impediment. Moreover, defendants are engaged in copying for commercial exploitation. That fact is not dispositive and would not preclude a finding of fair use, but it is a factor which adds to the plaintiffs' case in evaluating likelihood of their success on the merits.

Defendants assert that their use is *de minimis* because it amounts to no more than two minutes out of each videotape owned by plaintiffs. However, it is the quality of the use rather than its quantity which is determinative. The excerpts used by defendants in this case, although of relatively short duration, are the "highlights" of each broadcast and as such their use may be considered substantial.

Defendants contend that plaintiffs have failed to demonstrate that their transmission has had any effect on the present or potential market for plaintiffs' copyright in that plaintiffs have made no attempt to sell excerpts from their programming to any cable networks in the past, and have experienced no diminution in the substantial revenue that they receive from the three major television networks who do pay plaintiffs for the right to broadcast highlights on their respective news shows. Assuming it to be true that plaintiffs have made no attempt to market their broadcasts within the cable field, a fact which has not been established, this does not permit defendants to appropriate plaintiffs' copyrighted material and effectively preclude such efforts in the future. It is for plaintiffs, not defendants, to determine when and in what manner they choose to exploit their copyright. Evidence of plaintiffs' revenues from the three major networks lends further credence to their claim that defendant's use deprives them of substantial additional revenue to which they are entitled as the owners of the copyright to these materials.

* * *

Injunction granted.

Questions For Discussion

1. Do you agree with this judicial treatment of fair use? Would it be better public policy to allow television newscasts to use short clips of games, rather than just the bare facts that the sportscaster learned from watching (or listening to) the broadcasts? Is there a difference between this use and one channel using clips from another channel's newscasts? What harm, if any, is inflicted on WSBK (or the Red Sox and Bruins) from limiting intellectual property rights so as to accommodate such uses by ESPN? What do you think was the impact of this decision on the marketplace?

2. Shortly after *New Boston*, a closely divided Supreme Court, in its first major fair use decision, ruled that it was not illegal copying for television viewers to videotape shows for later viewing. See *Sony Corp. of America v. Universal City Studios*, 464 U.S. 417 (1984). What would have been your reaction to that question in light of the statutory factors you have just seen applied? How would you compare the relative impact on sports broadcasts of home taping or newscast clippings?

3. Cablevision of Michigan had the state "pay-per-view" broadcast rights for the 1990 heavyweight championship boxing match between Evander Holyfield and James "Buster" Douglas. Cablevision's rates in Kalamazoo were $35 for residences and $1,000 for sports bars. The Sports Forum, which did not want to pay the latter fee, agreed to allow one of its patrons to show on the bar's big-screen television videotapes of the fight which were brought in every few rounds by the patron's girlfriend, who was taping the fight at home. The case raised a number of technical legal questions about the ban on "interception" under the Cable Communications Policy Act of 1984. (See *Cablevision of Michigan v. Sports Palace*, 27 F.3d 566 (6th Cir.1994)). Should these actions be deemed fair or unfair uses under copyright doctrine, whether by the bar or by the patron and his friends?

The last problem brings into play another feature of copyright law—public performance. The original version of federal copyright law gave the author only the exclusive right to reproduce—i.e., to copy—the original work. (That is why an American court told Harriet Beecher Stowe, author of the mid–19th century best-seller *Uncle Tom's Cabin*, that this law did not even preclude someone else from translating and selling her book in a different language.) For the author of a play or a song, not much legal value is afforded by preventing others from publishing written versions, but not blocking them from performing the work for audiences. However, beginning in the late 19th Century, copyright law has steadily expanded to give authors exclusive control over who can transform their work into derivative versions (via various forms of new technology), and who can publicly perform the play, song, or other artistic expression. People can sing a song for free in the shower, but they must pay to do so on stage.

A particular problem that is posed in broadcasting (including of sporting events) is whether it is a public performance of a program for a business simply to play the unedited program for a public audience (not just in a club or retail store, but even on a cable transmission service). The Supreme Court's response to these issues was to adopt a narrow definition of *performance*. See *Fortnightly Corporation v. United Artists*, 392 U.S. 390 (1968), *Teleprompter Corp. v. CBS*, 415 U.S. 394 (1974), and *Twentieth Century Music v. Aiken*, 422 U.S. 151 (1975). In its new Copyright Act of 1976, Congress responded by enacting a broad § 101 definition of "public performance," which included performance or transmission of the work to "a place open to the public or at any place where a substantial number of persons outside of a normal circle of a family and its social acquaintances is gathered." At the same time, though, Congress created an exception (in § 110(5)) to this expansive definition of "public performance" for "communication of a transmission embodying a performance ... of a work by the public reception of the transmission on a single receiving apparatus of a kind commonly used in private homes." The scope and limits of this "small business" exemption have produced nearly a dozen judicial opinions about the interplay of radio music and retail stores. See, e.g., *Broadcast Music, Inc. v. Claire's Boutiques*, 949 F.2d 1482 (7th Cir.1991). Similar problems have also arisen about how to draw the line between sports broadcasts and sports blackouts.

Teams and leagues not only want to have their games broadcast, but they also want to control which games are going into which markets. For example, the National Football League, which has always had the most comprehensive rules of this kind, requires that the away games of a team be telecast live in its home city, but that home games not be telecast at "home" (i.e., within 75 miles of the home city) unless the game seats have sold out 72 hours in advance.[b] Control over the right to broadcast

---

b. This NFL television policy has a long history. Up until the 1965 season, the league required all its games to be blacked out of any local market in which a team was playing a home game. That year, though, hoping that the larger the television viewership, the greater the long-term interest in their sport, the NFL owners permitted CBS (which then broadcast all NFL games) to transmit one outside game into a market where a team was playing at home. However, the home game itself was still not telecast locally.

In 1966, the NFL agreed to a merger with the AFL whose games were then being broadcast across the country by NBC. When that league merger went into full effect in 1970, the fact that there were two teams (one in the NFL, the other in the AFL) in the New York and San Francisco Bay areas meant that the team playing on the road on any given Sunday would have its game telecast back into its home market even though the other local team was then playing at home. In addition, the fact that all NFL games were telecast by CBS and all AFL games by NBC meant that at least two games would be seen every Sunday in every market, irrespective of whether a home game was being played there. Still, though, the home game was always blacked out in its local area.

The next big change was precipitated by a controversy in Washington when the NFL

the game gives the NFL the authority to regulate what the television networks and stations do in transmission. The new technology of satellite signals and satellite dishes has, however, made it far more difficult to control what television viewers do with their receivers. That is why the NFL and other leagues (as well as pay-for-view cable systems) need to go to court in cases such as the following.

NFL v. McBEE & BRUNO'S, INC.
United States Court of Appeals, Eighth Circuit, 1986.
792 F.2d 726.

ARNOLD, CIRCUIT JUDGE.

[In 1984, the NFL sued a number of restaurants and bars in St. Louis for showing home games of the St. Louis Cardinals—games that were supposed to be blacked out in St. Louis because the team had not sold out at Busch Stadium. Most of the establishments (such as McBee & Bruno's) picked up the game signal on their satellite dish and then displayed it on the television viewing screens for customers. One defendant, Sandrinas, was able to use its high television antenna to bring in the actual broadcast from another Missouri city located approximately 100 miles away. Another defendant, Guttmann, was closed for customers on Sunday, but the owner and several of his friends watched the game at his bar with the help of his satellite dish. After the district court granted the NFL injunctive relief, defendants appealed.]

* * *

The Cardinals, a professional football team, is one of 28 teams composing the NFL, an unincorporated non-profit association through which the member clubs schedule games and manage their affairs as a group, including contracts with the three major television networks. One provision of those television contracts is that games which are not sold out within 72 hours of game time are to be "blacked out," that is, not broadcast within a 75-mile radius of the home team's playing field. Officials of the league and club testified at trial that such a rule boosts team revenue directly by increasing ticket sales and indirectly because a full stadium contributes to a more exciting television program and therefore makes the right to broadcast games more valuable.

refused to lift the blackout of home playoff game by the Redskins against the Green Bay Packers and the Dallas Cowboys at the end of the 1972 season. That winter, an angry Congress enacted a law that required that any game that had been sold out at least 72 hours before kickoff had to be available for telecast locally. See Pub.L. #93–107, § 1, 87 Stat. 350 (1973). The law was to be in effect for three years, during which time the FCC was to study the effect of local telecasts on ticket sales. After the FCC's (and other independent) studies found no such television impact on ticket sales, new legislation was introduced in 1976 that would make this federal anti-blackout law permanent. Before this bill came to a vote, though, Commissioner Pete Rozelle promised Congress that the NFL would voluntarily continue this new system for at least two years—and it has continued to be in place ever since. For a detailed depiction of NFL television practices and legal challenges to them, see Gary Roberts, *Pirating Signals of Blacked–Out Sports Events: A Historical and Policy Perspective*, 11 Columbia–VLA J. of Law & Arts 363 (1987).

Witnesses also described the process by which a live football game is telecast by the networks, in this case CBS. As television cameras capture the visual portion of the game, announcers describe and discuss the action from a sound booth of some kind. Those simultaneous audio and video signals are combined at an earth station outside the stadium. This signal—called an uplink—is transmitted up to a satellite, which then sends the signal back—called a downlink—to a network control point on Long Island. Because that signal contains no images other than those from the stadium, this stage is referred to as a "clean feed." The signal is then sent by cable to CBS studios in New York; commercials and other interruptions, such as station breaks, are inserted, and it is now described as a "dirty feed." There is another uplink to the satellite, and then a downlink to local affiliates, who insert local material and finally put the live broadcast on the air. The process apparently takes far longer to describe than to occur; at argument, counsel for the NFL called the procedure "simultaneous, instantaneous," and said that the delay between the action on the field and the broadcast by local affiliates was considerably less than two seconds.

The defendants are owners, corporate or individual, of St. Louis bar-restaurants within 75 miles of Busch Stadium, the Cardinals' home field. All defendants have satellite dish antennae that enable them to receive transmissions in the so-called C-band frequency, approximately 3200–4200 megahertz, in which the satellite sends and receives transmissions. There is no question that prior to November 19, 1984, all defendants but two picked up the clean feed (from the satellite to CBS) and thereby showed blacked-out home games of the Cardinals.

* * *

B

Defendants' ... most considerable argument is that their display of plaintiffs' blacked-out games falls into the category of non-infringing acts under Section 110(5) of the Copyright Act. Under that provision, no copyright liability can be imposed for "communication of a transmission embodying a performance ... by the public reception of the transmission on a single receiving apparatus of a kind commonly used in private homes...." The District Court rejected this argument, finding that satellite dish antennae, which in the United States are outnumbered by television sets by more than 100-to-one, were outside the statutory exemption.

According to the defendants, this ruling ignores their theory that how "the signal was captured by the antenna outside the premises" is "irrelevant." Instead, they argue, the key to Section 110(5) is whether an alleged infringer uses commercial equipment to enhance the sound or visual quality of the performance as it is perceived inside the premises. "All published cases on Section 110(5) take this approach." This interpretation ignores both the plain language of the statute and its obvious intent.

The home-use exemption was included in the 1976 Copyright Act specifically in response to the Supreme Court's decision in *Twentieth Century Music Corp. v. Aiken*, 422 U.S. 151 (1975). *Aiken* held that the owner of a small fried-chicken restaurant was not "performing" copyright works when he played a conventional radio through four in-the-ceiling speakers for the benefit of customers and employees. According to the legislative history of the 1976 Act, an act such as Aiken's would be considered a performance; to decide whether an infringement had occurred, the critical question instead would be the type of equipment used by the putative infringer. Calling "the use of a home receiver with four ordinary loudspeakers ... the outer limit of the exemption," the drafters then said:

> [T]he clause would exempt small commercial establishments whose proprietors merely bring onto their premises standard radio or television equipment and turn it on for their customers' enjoyment, but it would impose liability where the proprietor has a commercial 'sound system' installed or converts a standard home receiving apparatus ... into the equivalent of a commercial sound system.

H.R. Rep. No. 94–1476 at 87, 94th Cong., 2d Sess. Common sense alone says that it does not matter how well speakers amplify a performance if a receiver cannot pick up the signal in the first place. Moreover, both the legislative history and the plain language of the statute—which speaks of a "receiving set"—contemplate that how the signal is captured will be as much at issue under the exemption as how good the captured signal sounds or looks. There is no indication that the portion of a system which receives should be considered separately from that which displays.

The factors listed in the legislative history do speak of the size of the area where the transmission will be played and "the extent to which the receiving apparatus is altered ... for the purpose of improving the aural or visual quality of the performance." And it is true, as defendants argue, that most of the cases involving the Section 110(5) exemption deal with the enhancement factor, see, e.g., *Rodgers v. Eighty Four Lumber Co.*, 617 F.Supp. 1021, 1022–1023 (W.D.Pa.1985); *Sailor Music v. The Gap Stores, Inc.*, 516 F.Supp. 923, 924–925 (S.D.N.Y.), aff'd, 668 F.2d 84 (2d Cir.1981). The reason, however, is that these cases have to do not with interception of blacked-out television programming, where the difficulty is in intercepting a signal, but with the playing of music for which no royalties have been paid. In this sort of case, the question as a practical matter is whether the defendant establishment is of the size and kind that Congress would expect to obtain a license through a subscription music service. See *Sailor Music*, 668 F.2d at 86; *Springsteen v. Plaza Roller Dome, Inc.*, 602 F.Supp. 1113, 1119 (M.D.N.C.1985); H. Conf. Rep. No. 94–1733, 94th Cong., 2d Sess. 75, reprinted in 1976 U.S. Code Cong. & Ad. News 5810, 5816. In the present case, however, the NFL and Cardinals are not saying the bar owners can display their programs if a license fee is paid; these plaintiffs intend that their work not be performed at all outside their aegis, making the fact of reception rather than just its quality the primary consideration. The question in this instance, therefore, is how likely the average patron who watches a blacked-out Cardinals game at one of the defendant restaurants is to have the ability to watch the same game at home? If it is likely—that is, if such systems are the "kind commonly used in private homes"—then the Section 110(5) exemption applies.

However, as the District Court in this case stated:

> There are less than 1,000,000 dish systems in use, and many of these are confined to commercial establishments. The dishes do have residential use when the home is so situated that access to television station broadcasting by standard television antennae is poor. Television sets can be purchased for $100.00 or more [while] dish systems cost no less than $1,500.00 and for desired reception, $3,000.00 to $6,000.00 or more.

621 F.Supp. at 887.

Given these facts, the Court's finding that satellite dishes are not "commonly found in private homes" is not clearly erroneous. There was testimony that the number of such receivers has been growing rapidly, and while some day these antennae may be commonplace, they are not now.

C

The Copyright Act protects "original works of authorship fixed in any tangible medium," 17 U.S.C. § 102(a), including "motion pictures and other audiovisual works," 17 U.S.C. § 102(a)(6). As for live broadcasts, such as the football games at issue here, the Act states that "[a] work consisting of sounds, images, or both, that are being transmitted, is 'fixed' ... if a fixation of the work is being made simultaneously with its transmission," 17 U.S.C. § 101; "to 'transmit'" is defined as "to communicate ... by any device or process whereby images or sounds are received beyond the place from which they are sent." The defendants claim that no infringement took place because they intercepted the clean feed, and it was the dirty feed which was fixed under the Act and for which the plaintiffs sought copyright protection. In making the argument that the clean and dirty feeds represent separate works, defendants depend on the quoted definitions, as well as a third provision of Section 101 which states that each draft version of a work "prepared over a period of time," constitutes a separate work.

The District Court rejected this theory on two grounds. Not only could the argument rule out any protection for live broadcasting by satellite transmission but, the Court said, it also ignored the fact that the game, and not the inserted commercials and station breaks, constituted the work of authorship.

We agree. Plaintiffs testified copyright protection was obtained for "the game, the game action ... the noncommercial elements of the game." More important, the legislative history demonstrates a clear intent on the part of Congress to "resolve, through the definition of 'fixation' ..., the status of live broadcasts," using—coincidentally but not insignificantly—the example of a live football game. We have already discussed the near-instantaneous nature of the picture's journey from stadium to viewer; Congress surely was aware that the images and sounds from a live broadcast do not go directly from camera or microphone to a home television or radio. To hold that this transmission process nevertheless represents the performance of separate works would gut the plain purpose of the "fixation" definition, as well as distort the concept of a "work prepared over a period of time."

* * *

Affirmed.

Questions For Discussion

1. The Eighth Circuit affirmed the district court's conclusion that there were so few satellite dishes used in people's homes (less than one in 100) that the dishes did not constitute a technology "commonly used in private homes." At what percentage of homes with dishes should this ruling change? If 25% of all private homes had satellite dishes, should bars then be allowed to rebroadcast blacked-out games? What policy does this exception further that is not also in play when the number of homes having dishes is less than one percent? In any event, has the presence of satellite dishes in private homes changed significantly enough since 1986 to alter the legal situation in *McBee & Bruno's*?

2. What should have been the Court's decision with respect to Guttman, who used the satellite dish to bring the signal in to his bar for himself and his friends to watch the game? Or with respect to Sandrinas, whose customers could watch the "blacked-out" game because he had an antenna large enough to bring in the broadcast from a station 100 miles away? From the point of view of copyright doctrine or policy, are there material differences in these cases? (On the antenna issue, see also *NFL v. Rondor*, 840 F.Supp. 1160 (N.D.Ohio 1993).)

3. Another possible legal resource for leagues or broadcasters is the Federal Communications Act. Section 605(a) of that Act provides that:

> No person not being authorized by the sender shall intercept any radio communication and divulge or publish the existence, contents, substance, purport, effect, or meaning of such intercepted communication to any person ... This section shall not apply to the receiving, divulging, publishing, or utilizing the contents of any radio communication which is transmitted by any station for the use of the general public.

Does this section cover any (or all) of the situations in *McBee & Bruno's*? Would it cover the case noted earlier, *Cablevision of Michigan v. Sports Palace*, 27 F.3d 566 (6th Cir.1994), where a sports bar played on its big screen the telecast of the Holyfield–Douglas fight through tapes that were being made via home reception at residential pay-for-view rates? For an exploration of the implications of § 605 of the Communications Act, see *Quincy Cablesystems v. Sully's Bar*, 684 F.Supp. 1138 (D.Mass.1988), where Quincy sports bars were able to receive and play the signal of the New

England Sports Network (NESN) that was being transmitted by NESN to Quincy Cablevision.

An analogous legal problem, but one of far greater popular and economic significance, relates to cable television. Cable television originated in the late 1950s as a vehicle for retransmitting into rural communities a number of stations and programs that otherwise would never have been available in that area. As cable (then known as community antenna television, or CATV) expanded into larger cities whose residents wanted to improve their signal, the copyright owners of the shows being retransmitted sought compensation for what they contended were public performances by the cable systems of works that had only been licensed for the television station or network. In its first major decision in this field, *Fortnightly Corp. v. United Artists Television*, 392 U.S. 390 (1968), the Supreme Court rejected that copyright claim:

* * *

Television viewing results from combined activity by broadcasters and viewers. Both play active and indispensable roles in the process; neither is wholly passive. The broadcaster selects and procures the program to be viewed. He may produce it himself, whether "live" or with film or tape, or he may obtain it from a network or some other source. He then converts the visible images and audible sounds of the program into electronic signals, and broadcasts the signals at radio frequency for public reception. Members of the public, by means of television sets and antennas that they themselves provide, receive the broadcaster's signals and reconvert them into the visible images and audible sound of the program. The effective range of the broadcast is determined by the combined contribution of the equipment employed by the broadcaster and that supplied by the viewer.

The television broadcaster in one sense does less than the exhibitor of a motion picture or stage play; he supplies his audience not with visible images but only with electronic signals. The viewer conversely does more than a member of a theater audience; he provides the equipment to convert electronic signals into audible sound and visible images. Despite these deviations from the conventional situation contemplated by the framers of the Copyright Act, broadcasters have been judicially treated as exhibitors, and viewers as members of a theater audience. Broadcasters perform. Viewers do not perform. Thus, while both broadcaster and viewer play crucial roles in the total television process, a line is drawn between them. One is treated as active performer; the other, as passive beneficiary.

When CATV is considered in this framework, we conclude that it falls on the viewer's side of the line. Essentially, a CATV system no more than enhances the viewer's capacity to receive the broadcaster's signals; it provides a well-located antenna with an efficient connection to the viewer's television set. It is true that a CATV system plays an "active" role in making reception possible in a given area, but so do ordinary television sets and antennas. CATV equipment is powerful and sophisticated, but the basic function the equipment serves is little different from that served by the equipment generally furnished by a television viewer. If an individual erected an antenna on a hill, strung a cable to his house, and installed the necessary amplifying equipment, he would not be "performing" the programs he received on his television set. The result would be no different if several people combined to erect a cooperative antenna for the same purpose. The only difference in the case of CATV is that the antenna system is erected and owned not by its users but by an entrepreneur.

The function of CATV systems has little in common with the function of broadcasters. CATV systems do not in fact broadcast or rebroadcast. Broadcasters select the programs to be viewed; CATV systems simply carry, without editing, whatever programs they receive. Broadcasters procure programs and propagate them to the public; CATV systems receive programs that have been released to the public and carry them by private channels to additional viewers. We hold that CATV operators, like viewers and unlike broadcasters, do not perform the programs that they receive and carry.

392 U.S. at 397–401. Six years later, in *Teleprompter Corp. v. Columbia Broadcasting System*, 415 U.S. 394 (1974), the Court reiterated this verdict, even though cable systems had become much more sophisticated in transmitting signals from across the country, as well as adding and selling commercials.

During this same period, Congress had embarked on its wholesale 1976 revisions of the Copyright Act, which included several major changes in the legal treatment of cable. One was the expanded definition of "public performance" which, if it covered a local bar, would definitely include a regional cable system. At the same time, though, Congress created (in § 111(a)(3)) a special exemption for retransmission of broadcast signals by

any carrier who has no direct or indirect control over the content or selection of the primary transmission or over the particular recipients of the secondary transmission, and whose activities with respect to the secondary transmission consist solely of providing wires, cable, or other communications channels for the use of others.

The price of that exemption (or compulsory license) was a statutorily prescribed royalty to be distributed by the Copyright Royalty Tribunal to the copyright owners of sports broadcasts and other television shows.

The details and controversies surrounding this royalty system will be described later. For the moment, it is important to note that cable systems must pay such royalties only for "distant non-network" programming. Retransmission via cable of local television signals enhances rather than harms the existing returns of the local stations. So also for network programming where the financial returns of either the producers or networks have already been calculated on the assumption that a national market is being reached. The focus, then, of this licensing-royalty system was on distant and independent (non-network) stations whose programming (and advertising) were aimed at their local market, but could now be retransmitted by cable to homes across the country.

The interplay of sports broadcasting and cable transmission made it possible for a selected number of such "distant non-network" signals to become superstations, with major consequences for both the sports and the broadcasting world.[c] This became a problem particularly in baseball, and then in basketball, because (unlike the NFL) most baseball and basketball games are telecast on local stations pursuant to contract licenses from the local clubs. Efforts by sports leagues to cope with individual team broadcasts on superstations will be considered later, but the fit between such sports broadcasts and the Copyright Act has produced two major circuit court interpretations of the 1976 amendments.

The first case, *Eastern Microwave v. Doubleday Sports*, 691 F.2d 125 (2d Cir.1982), involved a suit filed by Doubleday Sports, owner of the New York Mets, against Eastern Microwave (EMI), which was a vehicle for retransmitting (via satellite) to cable systems across the country all the programs on New York's WOR television station. Included in these program offerings were the approximately 100 Mets regular season games that Doubleday had licensed WOR to carry in its local market. The Second Circuit rejected the Mets' argument that programming retransmitted by this new satellite technology did not fit with the language and intent of the Copyright Act's new compulsory license-royalty system, and thus EMI needed a license from the Mets.

* * *

The Compulsory License Scheme

Interpretation of the Act must occur in the real world of telecommunications, not in a vacuum. The centerpiece of the compromise reflected in the Act is the compulsory licensing scheme. That scheme is predicated on and presupposes a continuing ability of CATV systems to receive signals for distribution to their subscribers. Doubleday is but one of numerous copyright owners whose works may be broadcast by WOR–TV. EMI serves as a signals conduit between the performance by WOR–TV and the performance by its CATV system customers. Adoption of Doubleday's position would stand all copyright owners athwart that conduit between the original broadcast and the opportunity for subsequent performances by CATV systems. In so doing, it would defeat Congress' intent by

---

[c.] See Thomas Joseph Cryon and James S. Crane, *Sports on the Superstations: The Legal and Economic Effects*, 3 U. Miami Enter. & Sports L. J. 35 (1986).

imposing on EMI the unworkable separate negotiations with numerous copyright holders from which the Act sought to free CATV systems. Congress drew a careful balance between the rights of copyright owners and those of CATV systems, providing for payments to the former and a compulsory licensing program to insure that the latter could continue bringing a diversity of broadcasted signals to their subscribers. The public interest thus lies in a continuing supply of varied programming to viewers. Because CATV systems served by intermediate carriers cannot provide their full current programming to their subscribers without the services of those carriers, imposition of individual copyright owner negotiations on intermediate carriers would strangle CATV systems by choking off their life line to their supply of programs, would effectively restore the "freeze" on cable growth described above, and, most importantly, would frustrate the congressional intent reflected in the Act by denying CATV systems the opportunity to participate in the compulsory licensing program. After years of consideration and debate, Congress could not have intended that its work be so easily undone by the interposition of copyright owners to block exercise of the licensing program by cable systems.

The Royalty Scheme

EMI is, like all common carriers, compensated for its transmission services as such. In accord with its FCC-approved tariff, and as above indicated, EMI is paid by each CATV system in relation to the number of its subscribers up to a maximum of $3,000. The fee does not increase thereafter, regardless of the number of a CATV system's subscribers. In contrast, the royalty fee paid by each CATV system under the Act is limited to no maximum, but is entirely based on percentages of gross receipts from subscribers to the CATV service in accord with 17 U.S.C. § 111. It is undisputed that if each CATV system had its own string of microwave repeaters or satellite transponder it would be liable through the Tribunal to a copyright owner for only the one established royalty fee when and if it publicly performed the copyrighted work by making it available to its subscribers; and that such an integrated CATV system would not be liable for a second royalty fee for having itself retransmitted the original broadcast signal to its headend. We are unpersuaded by counsel's urging that a different result should obtain when a separate entity, e.g. EMI, supplies the retransmission service. That EMI is a separate entity supplies no justification for subjecting EMI to copyright liability when those same activities would not result in copyright liability if carried out by the CATV systems served by EMI. In the Act, Congress established a specific scheme for recognition of the rights of copyright owners. Under that scheme those rights are not unlimited. Neither are they rendered superior to the rights of viewers. If this court were to impose here a requirement that intermediate carriers negotiate with and pay all copyright owners for the right to retransmit their works, assuming such requirement were not impossible to meet, such action would produce a result never intended by Congress, namely a substantially increased royalty payment to copyright owners with no increase in number of viewers.

691 F.2d at 132–33.

While the Mets may have lost that initial legal battle, they ultimately won the economic war. As the contracts with stations like WOR (or WGN, WPIX and KTVT) expired, the teams involved were able to negotiate new rights fees that reflected the higher economic value derived from their station's new national market. Crucial to that effort was Ted Turner, then owner of the most "super" of all superstations, WTBS in Atlanta, as well as Atlanta's baseball Braves and basketball Hawks.

In tandem with its retransmission carrier, Southern Satellite System, WTBS developed a new method for transmitting its signal to the satellite system and thence to local cable systems. A key feature of that technology was that it made it possible for WTBS to insert different advertising in the programming transmitted to distant cable systems from that incorporated in the original programming in Atlanta. WTBS was an extremely attractive superstation for cable systems around the country precisely because it offered Braves' games in the summer and Hawks' games in the winter. The new technology permitted Turner—especially given his common ownership of both the teams and the station—to sell separate commercial time to advertisers in the local Atlanta market and in the national market. This proved a bonanza for Turner's combined broadcasting and sports empire (which in 1996 was merged into the even vaster Time Warner entertainment conglomerate).

The flip side is that WTBS was considered a severe market threat by local stations in distant markets—not simply because the stations had to compete with WTBS sports broadcasts, but also because they had to face WTBS' broadcast of the syndicated shows for which WTBS had secured the license in Atlanta, but for which the local stations had bought the supposedly exclusive license in their areas. In *Hubbard Broadcasting v. Southern Satellite Systems*, 777 F.2d 393 (8th Cir.1985), the owner of television stations in Minneapolis, Albuquerque, and St. Petersburg challenged the compatibility of this new technology and broadcasting venture with the 1976 Copyright Act regime. After analyzing and rejecting the various technical arguments, the Eighth Circuit addressed the economic core of the case:

* * *

Turner's Commercial Substitution and the Compulsory Licensing Program

> As a third theory of liability, Hubbard asserts that the commercial substitution process undertaken by Turner and facilitated by Southern impermissibly alters the careful balance achieved by Congress through the compulsory licensing system. Specifically, Hub-

bard focuses on section 111(c)(3) which provides that the compulsory license will not be applicable if the content of the particular program ... or any commercial advertising ... transmitted by the primary transmitter ... is in any way willfully altered by the cable system.... 17 U.S.C. § 111(c)(3). Here, Hubbard argues that Turner, by substituting commercials at the primary transmission stage, accomplishes indirectly what Congress has concluded cable systems cannot do directly. As a result, Hubbard contends that cable systems carrying WTBS cannot qualify for the compulsory license of section 111(c)(1) with respect to the WTBS transmission. We disagree.

In adopting section 111(c)(3), Congress concluded that to allow cable television systems to alter the primary transmission by substituting commercials would significantly alter the basic nature of the cable retransmission service, and make its function similar to that of a broadcaster. Further, the placement of substitute advertising in a program by a cable system on a "local" signal harms the advertiser and, in turn, the copyright owner, whose compensation for the work is directly related to the size of the audience that the advertiser's message is calculated to reach. On a "distant" signal, the placement of substitute advertising harms the local broadcaster in the distant market because the cable system is then competing for local broadcasting dollars without having comparable programming costs. Consequently, Congress "attempted broadly to proscribe the availability of the compulsory license if a cable system substitutes commercial messages."

Congress, in forbidding commercial substitution by cable systems, sought to ensure the competitive compatibility of the cable system and the local broadcaster. Cable systems, when retransmitting local signals, would retransmit exactly what was received and in so doing would neither undercut the local broadcaster's ability to generate local advertising revenues nor jeopardize the ability of creators of programming to receive a fair return for their product based upon the size of the audience that the advertiser's message was calculated to reach. In other words, the status quo relationship between local broadcasters and copyright holders would be protected and facilitated. With respect to distant signal retransmission, Congress sought to ensure that cable systems were not allowed, while claiming protection of the compulsory license, to compete for local advertising dollars without having to bear comparable programming costs.

As an initial matter, we emphasize that there has been no assertion on the part of Hubbard that either Southern or any cable system carrying the WTBS signal has ever substituted or in fact has ever attempted to substitute commercials originally placed on the WTBS signal by Turner. Rather, both Southern and the cable systems retransmit intact any commercials they receive from Turner on the WTBS signal. Thus, under the literal language of section

111(c)(3), no infringement based upon commercial substitution has occurred.

Additionally, we conclude that none of the concerns raised by Congress in adopting section 111(c)(3) are implicated by Turner's practices. WTBS, in placing only national advertising on the microwave signal, seeks to and in fact can economically address only the national advertising market. Turner cannot effectively address the local advertising markets served by Hubbard. Thus, Turner does not compete with Hubbard for local advertising dollars.

Further, to the extent Turner and Hubbard compete for national advertising dollars, that competition will exist regardless of Turner's current practices since even absent the microwave signal, Turner's UHF signal will continue to reach a national market and carry national advertising. And, unlike a cable system that substitutes commercials without bearing programming costs, Turner has the same types of programming costs as Hubbard.

Finally, we also conclude that Turner's development of two separate WTBS signals has no adverse impact on the interests of the copyright holders. These individuals or companies, when contracting with Turner, know that WTBS signals will be available nationwide as well as locally and are entirely free to take those steps necessary to assure that they are compensated accordingly. At bottom, no copyright holder is deceived by the extent of Turner's market or the commercial content of the signals; no advertiser reaches a smaller market than anticipated; and no local broadcaster is forced to compete with Turner on any greater level than would exist absent Turner's transmission of two television signals.

777 F.2d at 403–04.

Questions For Discussion

1. *Hubbard* concluded, then, that Satellite, WTBS, and Ted Turner's teams were entitled under federal copyright law to transmit their games on cable systems across the country. Does that ruling imply that teams in the games cannot assert their common law property rights (dating back to *Pittsburgh Athletic*) to decide whether there will be a broadcast on such a system? For example, could a small market team like the Pittsburgh Pirates sue to block WTBS from telecasting a Pirates–Braves game back into Pittsburgh? Should the answer differ depending on whether the game is being played in Pittsburgh or in Atlanta? Does the *NBA-Motorola* ruling mean that any such common law rights are now preempted by Turner's copyright in the broadcast "expression" of the game?

2. What about league rules that purport to block such transmission? In the early 1980s, for example, baseball teams in divisional playoffs in each league were permitted to broadcast their games on their local channels, but the league sold to a network (for a large fee) the exclusive right to national broadcasts. When the Braves made the 1982 National League playoffs, was

either the league or ABC entitled to block WTBS from telecasting Braves' playoff games if the WTBS telecasts were retransmitted across the country?

The superstation phenomenon, of whose legal underpinnings we have now seen glimpses, has posed major institutional and financial challenges to sports. From the point of view of the "best interests" of the league, what do you think should be its policy about whether any games should be telecast on superstations, and if so, how the revenues should be allocated? As we will see in the next chapter, from the point of view of consumer interests, there are major questions about restraints that a league might want to impose on such team-station relationships, under the watchful eye of antitrust law. In baseball, though, the situation has changed somewhat with WTBS. Ted Turner's successor, Time Warner, decided in 1997 to turn the superstation into a cable channel, one that would enable WTBS to collect a share of subscriber fees from local cable operators—in an amount that some were estimating to be about $100 million a year. However, because baseball's internal rules as well as its existing contracts with Fox and ESPN barred individual teams from broadcasting their games on national cable channels, Time Warner had to renegotiate the status of Braves games on WTBS. These are now reduced from 124 to 96 a season, with a significant increase in the $15 million payment to the league's superstation pool, and concessions by Time Warner to Fox and Disney–ABC for carriage of its channels on Time Warner's large array of cable systems.

The other side of the copyright license conferred by statute on cable transmission is that these systems must pay a statutory royalty for the shows they use. This model of a compulsory license-royalty was originally developed in the 1909 Copyright Act for music. Once a song is published, any music group has a right to perform and record it, with payment of a "mechanical" royalty set by statute and collected and distributed by the Copyright Royalty Tribunal (CRT). Congress's assumption about music, and then about cable, was that this legal regime is a more efficient technique for ensuring that consumers would have easy access to the songs they wanted to hear and the shows they wanted to watch, rather than having to rely on individual negotiations about who would get the performance license and how much should be paid for it.

The compulsory license has certainly resolved the issue of program accessibility to the nation's vast cable system. The statutory formula for royalty payments generated a total of $12 million in 1978 and had produced more than $200 million in the early 1990s. There remains, however, a running annual battle in front of the Copyright Royalty Tribunal and the D.C. Circuit about precisely how this money should be divided up among the numerous copyright owners of the rebroadcast programs. (For a representative case, see *National Broadcasting Co. v. Copyright Royalty Tribunal*, 848 F.2d 1289 (D.C.Cir.1988) (regarding the distribution of 1984 revenues).)

One obvious question is how to determine the share that should go to different program sources—sports versus syndicated series re-runs, for example. The Motion Picture Association of America has always argued for a formula based on the amount of time its producers' shows are on the air. The Joint Sports Council (representing baseball, basketball, hockey, and the NCAA) was successful, however, in persuading the CRT that a better test of the comparative market value of different programming is the shows' Nielsen ratings (on which sports have consistently scored higher). So far, though, the sports world has not won its argument that the ideal test would be the demographic makeup of the respective audiences, as measured by commercial advertiser preferences. One should not, however, overestimate the significance of this debate: in the early 1990s, when baseball's total broadcast revenues had topped $600 million, its statutory royalties from cable were approximately $20 million.

Especially when their spokesman was Fay Vincent (who came to the commissioner's office from the entertainment world), baseball has strongly objected to the principle of a statutory license and royalty for cable transmission of its games.[d] Baseball (and the other sports) would prefer to let the free market set the terms on which any of its games would be telecast. In reflecting on that fundamental issue of intellectual property law, keep the following issues in mind.

1. Are there any practical obstacles in the way of sports teams (or copyright owners of other programs) negotiating agreements for the showing of their events on cable? Any differences from the *New Boston-ESPN* case we saw earlier about game highlights on the news?

2. Are there differences between the showing of a pay-for-view boxing match, for example, in a sports bar and the showing on cable of a regular season game already licensed to be telecast on a local station? Precisely what kinds of economic losses does a team suffer by not being able to withhold its consent to the latter? Are these the kinds of losses that the law should compensate?

3. Even more basic, when Congress was revising the Copyright Act in 1976, it had three options. The first was to preserve the Supreme Court's status quo, which had deemed cable transmission not to be an infringement of copyright in sports (or other) telecasts. The second option was to make every cable transmission a copyright violation that

---

[d]. See David Prebut, *Best Interests or Self Interests: Major League Baseball's Attempt to Replace the Compulsory Licensing Scheme With Retransmission Consent*, 3 Seton Hall J. of Sports L. 111 (1993).

required agreement (for a fee) from the program owner. The third option (which Congress adopted) was to come down somewhere in-between. More than twenty years later, which of those options seems to make sense? For whom is it supposed to make sense—sports teams, cable system operators, their respective fans, or the general public interest?

C. PLAYER PUBLICITY RIGHTS[e]

Resting on the legal foundation whose key components we have just seen, broadcasts of sports events have become a great source of pleasure for fans and revenue for teams. The immediate source of those revenues, though, are advertisers trying to reach the games' audiences in order to interest them in buying the firms' products. Key figures in these commercials, as well as in the games, are celebrity athletes. That merchandising phenomenon, found not just in sports broadcasts but in every part of the marketing world, in turn rests on a different branch of intellectual property—the state law right of publicity.

Early in this century, state courts and legislatures developed a right of *privacy* that allowed people to block the use of their name and likeness in advertisements without their consent. (See *Pavesich v. New England Life Insurance*, 122 Ga. 190, 50 S.E. 68 (Ga.1905).) A contrary verdict had been rendered by the New York Court of Appeals in *Roberson v. Rochester Folding Box*, 171 N.Y. 538, 64 N.E. 442 (N.Y.1902), but the New York legislature quickly reversed that result by enacting what are now §§ 50 and 51 of the Civil Rights Law that make it actionable to use the "name, portrait or picture of any living person ... for advertising purposes, or for the purposes of trade ... without having first obtained the written consent of such person."

There were serious doubts about whether this personal protection against the psychological injury (hurt feelings) from having such an intrusion upon their private lives extended to athletes (or entertainers) who had actively sought to make themselves into celebrated public figures. Illustrative was the decision in *O'Brien v. Pabst Sales*, 124 F.2d 167 (5th Cir.1941). Davey O'Brien had been the All–American quarterback for Texas Christian University in 1938, before going on to play for the Philadelphia Eagles. In 1939, Pabst Brewing put out its annual football calendar containing college and professional schedules. At the top of the calendar was a picture of O'Brien in his TCU uniform and throwing stance, side by side with a glass of Pabst Blue Ribbon beer. Pabst had obtained O'Brien's picture from TCU's publicity department for this explicit purpose. In dismissing O'Brien's suit, the Fifth Circuit (applying Texas law) said that O'Brien, who had authorized countless

---

[e]. The concept of publicity rights has spawned a voluminous scholarly literature. Among the major recent treatments are Roberta Rosenthal Kwall, *The Right of Publicity vs. The First Amendment: A Property and Liability Rule Analysis*, 70 Indiana L. J. 47 (1994); Mark F. Grady, *A Positive Economic Theory of the Right of Publicity*, 1 UCLA Enter. L. Rev. 97 (1994); and Michael Madow, *Private Ownership of Public Image: Popular Culture and Publicity Rights*, 81 California L. Rev. 127 (1993).

mailings of his picture to the media and football fans, could not now complain of an intrusion on his privacy; that the calendar did not contain an explicit endorsement of Pabst beer by O'Brien; and that he had no independent right to sell the commercial value of his name and likeness. (See also *Hanna Mfg. v. Hillerich & Bradsby*, 78 F.2d 763 (5th Cir.1935).) The result was that such celebrated athletes as Red Grange, Joe DiMaggio, Joe Louis, Bill Tilden, and most illustrious of all, Babe Ruth, never enjoyed a right of publicity during their careers.

A decade later that legal situation was dramatically altered in another sports-related case, *Haelan Laboratories v. Topps Chewing Gum*, 202 F.2d 866 (2d Cir.1953). The dispute here was actually between two firms that had signed agreements with baseball players authorizing use of their names and pictures on cards sold with chewing gum. Haelan, the firm with the first and supposedly "exclusive" license to that effect, sued Topps for inducing breach of its contract. Topps' defense was that both sets of contracts amounted to no more than the players giving Haelan a release from liability for invasion of the privacy right not to have their feelings hurt by unconsented-to publication: under the governing New York law there was no separate right in the commercial value of one's name and likeness. A divided Second Circuit rejected that position. Besides the statutory right of privacy, there existed an independent and assignable common law right to the publicity value of one's name and picture:

> This right might be called a "right of publicity." For it is common knowledge that many prominent persons (especially actors and ballplayers), far from having their feelings bruised through public exposure of their likenesses, would feel sorely deprived if they no longer received money for authorizing advertisements, popularizing their countenances, displayed in newspapers, magazines, busses, trains and subways. This right of publicity would usually yield them no money unless it could be made the subject of an exclusive grant which barred any other advertiser from using their pictures.

202 F.2d at 868.

The judicial ruling in *Haelan* gave an entirely different *property* twist to the traditional *tort* slant to privacy doctrine. Ironically, 35 years later the Second Circuit had to acknowledge, in *Pirone v. MacMillan*, 894 F.2d 579 (2d Cir.1990), that the legal footing for *Haelan* no longer existed in New York. Pirone, a daughter of Babe Ruth, had sued MacMillan Publishing for using three pictures of Ruth (as well as pictures of Lou Gehrig, Mickey Mantle, and other baseball greats) in its 1988 Baseball Engagement Calendar. By then, though, the New York Court of Appeals had made it clear that there was no common law right of privacy or publicity separate and apart from the Civil Rights Law, whose statutory protection was limited to "any living person."

Notwithstanding its legal defeat in *Pirone*, by 1995 (the 100th anniversary of Babe Ruth's birth) the sale of Ruth's name and likeness was generating over a million dollars a year for the Ruth estate and its licensing agency. The reason is that most states now recognize an independent right of publicity, and more and more states are making it descendible. (A major ruling to this effect, involving the estate of an illustrious figure from another sphere, was *Martin Luther King, Jr. Center for Social Change v. American Heritage Products*, 250 Ga. 135, 296 S.E.2d 697 (Ga.1982).) The scope as well as the duration of such a publicity right has been extended to encompass the figure's voice (see *Bette Midler v. Ford Motor Company*, 849 F.2d 460 (9th Cir.1988)), and identifiable routines (see *Vanna White v. Samsung Electronics America*, 971 F.2d 1395, aff'd en banc, 989 F.2d 1512 (9th Cir.1993)).

Judge Jerome Frank, the author of the *Haelan* opinion, would likely be stunned to see how much money baseball players and other athletes would eventually derive from the new brand of intellectual property that his court was fashioning. For example, in the late 1960s, as part of the transformation of the Major League Baseball Players Association into a real union, the Association took over the sale of baseball card licenses and other group marketing efforts by the players. By the 1990s, the Association was realizing $70 million a year for its members from collective sales of their publicity rights. Numerous individual athletes (ironically, few of them baseball players) now reap millions of dollars from personal endorsements and merchandise—e.g., Michael Jordan, Tiger Woods, Dennis Rodman, Andre Agassi, and even Arnold Palmer whose golfing career ebbed many years ago. Indeed, a recent by-product of this combination of law and economics is that the Internal Revenue Service has established the principle that the descendible publicity right may be a taxable asset in a dead author's (or athlete's or entertainer's) estate: see *Estate of V.C. Andrews v. United States*, 850 F.Supp. 1279 (E.D.Va.1994).

While publicity rights have proven a financial bonanza for this select group of celebrity superstars, they also pose important issues of public policy. One such issue stems from the fact that enforcement of one person's publicity right constitutes a legal restriction on another's freedom of speech. And unlike copyright law, this branch of intellectual property is not aimed at developing incentives for the creation of even more speech.

The one occasion on which the Supreme Court addressed this conflict was *Zacchini v. Scripps–Howard Broadcasting*, 433 U.S. 562 (1977). As noted earlier, Hugo Zacchini was an entertainer whose "human cannonball" act had him being shot from a cannon into a net located 200 feet away. One day at an Ohio county fair where Zacchini was performing, a television reporter videotaped Zacchini's fifteen second act, which was shown on the local station's newscast that night—telling the audience that this act was a thriller that they needed to see in person to appreciate. By a narrow 5–4 majority, the Court held that enforcement of Zacchini's publicity rights under Ohio state law did not abridge the television station's First Amendment rights:

> The broadcast of a film of petitioner's entire act poses a substantial threat to the economic value of that performance.... [T]his act is the product of [Zacchini's] own talents and energy, the end result of much time, effort, and expense. Much of its economic value lies in the "right of exclusive control over the publicity given to his performance": if the public can see the act free on television, it will be less willing to pay to see it at the fair.... [T]he broadcast of petitioner's entire performance, unlike the unauthorized use of another's name for purposes of trade ... goes to the heart of petitioner's ability to earn a living as an entertainer.

433 U.S. at 575–76.

The *Zacchini* case differs in two respects from *Haelan* and its successors. The one side, emphasized by the dissent, is that this case involved a newscast, worthy of far greater constitutional protection than commercial marketing. The other side, focused on by the majority, was that this broadcast was not simply an "appropriation of an entertainer's reputation to enhance the attractiveness of a commercial product, but the appropriation of the very activity by which the entertainer acquired his reputation in the first place." Like the judge in *Pittsburgh Athletic* (which the majority alluded to here), the Court was concerned that the latter form of appropriation would dilute the performer's economic incentives to make the necessary investment in developing the skills and appeal required for an entertainment performance that the public would watch and enjoy.

The more typical and more difficult illustrations of this publicity-speech conflict are cases like *Johnny Carson v. Here's Johnny Portable Toilets*, 698 F.2d 831 (6th Cir.1983), involving the defendant's manufacture of a portable toilet called "Here's Johnny," and billed as "The World's Foremost Commodian." Clearly Carson's late-night television successors, David Letterman and Jay Leno, could use that phrase to describe Carson on their show. So far, though, the majority verdict by the courts (albeit with vigorous dissents in *Carson* and in the *Vanna White* case cited earlier) is that the use in a show's commercials of the same images of an entertainer, athlete, or other celebrity is actionable.

The sports world not only created the right of publicity but has also contributed a number of interesting cases regarding the scope and limits of such a right. Following are examples of cases where the court upheld at least the viability of a publicity claim.

1. A moisturizing shaving gel for women is marketed under the name "Crazylegs." Elroy Hirsch, one of football's all-time greats, had always been known as "Crazylegs" because of his distinctive "eggbeater" running style. The shaving gel's name was found to violate Hirsch's

publicity rights. See *Hirsch v. S.C. Johnson*, 90 Wis.2d 379, 280 N.W.2d 129 (Wis.1979).

2. Lothar Motschenbacher was a well-known racing car driver whose cars had a distinctive color style of solid red with a narrow white pinstripe. R.J. Reynolds Tobacco did a "Winston's tastes good, like a cigarette should" commercial that involved a picture of several racing cars at the track. Motschenbacher's car was in the foreground, altered in several respects (e.g., from his number 11 to 71), but not in its color style. The driver was also entitled to legal relief. See *Motschenbacher v. R.J. Reynolds Tobacco*, 498 F.2d 821 (9th Cir.1974).

3. Playgirl Magazine had a cartoon-like drawing of a nude black male seated with his gloved hands on the ropes in the corner of a boxing ring—labelled "Mystery Man," but referred to in an accompanying verse as "The Greatest." Having found a clear resemblance between Muhammad Ali and this "illustration falling somewhere between representational art and a cartoon" (and without any "informational or newsworthy dimension"), the judge found this to be a violation of Ali's celebrity publicity rights. See *Ali v. Playgirl*, 447 F.Supp. 723 (S.D.N.Y.1978).

4. A firm, T. Henricksen, manufactured and sold games called "Negamco's Major League Baseball." These games used the names and statistics of over 500 major league baseball players, identified by team, uniform number, and playing position. Based on their playing statistics, the defendant also provided computations of the relative value of players. Using this data, people could play the games (either by themselves or in neighborhood leagues) by selecting and managing the players in simulated games. The Major League Baseball Players Association (MLBPA) had recently embarked on its own venture of marketing group player licensing packages for baseball cards and commercial endorsements, at a standard price of five percent of gross sales and a minimum annual royalty amount. Those funds were divided up on a per capita basis among all MLBPA members (though occasionally stockpiled for upcoming labor disputes). The MLBPA was able to secure an injunction blocking use of the players' names and statistics in the defendant's games. See *Uhlaender v. Henricksen*, 316 F.Supp. 1277 (D.Minn.1970).

Consider now the following more recent sports cases that have had to explore both the scope and the limits of celebrity publicity rights.

Questions For Discussion

1. A set of baseball cards, described as "Cardtoons," includes caricatures of a significant number of players who are renamed Fowl Boggs, Tony Twynn, Cal Ripkenwinkle, Treasury Bonds, Ozzie Myth, Ken Spiffey, Jr., and so on, and who are said to be playing for teams such as the St. Louis Credit Cards, the Los Angeles Codgers, and the Seattle Mari–Nerds. Should the manufacturer be able to assert a "parody" defense to a publicity suit, relying on the Supreme Court's endorsement (in *Campbell v. Acuff–Rose*

Music, 510 U.S. 569 (1994)) of such "fair use" in a copyright suit about 2 Live Crew's rap music version of the Roy Orbison classic, *Pretty Woman*? Or should it be limited to a First Amendment "free speech" argument, and if so, with what results? Compare *Cardtoons v. MLB Players Association*, 868 F.Supp. 1266 (N.D.Okla.1994), with same at 95 F.3d 959 (10th Cir.1996).

2. After quarterback Joe Montana led the San Francisco 49ers to their fourth Super Bowl victory in the 1980s, the San Jose Mercury published a special Souvenir Section of the paper devoted exclusively to the 49ers. The front page of the Section had an artistic rendition of Montana. Two or three weeks later, the Mercury had this Section's pages reprinted in poster form, with each page-poster selling for $5 (though many were given away at charity functions). Montana then sued the Mercury, not with respect to the original newspaper picture and story, but just for the poster-page featuring his likeness. Was the latter a violation of Montana's publicity rights under state law? Would upholding such a state law claim violate the First Amendment rights of the newspaper? See *Montana v. San Jose Mercury News*, 34 Cal.App.4th 790, 40 Cal.Rptr.2d 639 (6th Dist.Ct.App.1995). Compare the earlier case in which a photo of wrestler Hulk Hogan was inserted at the center of a magazine, folded to accommodate the fact that it was four times the size of the regular page, and the paper was the kind that can be used for a poster on the wall. Is Hogan's claim weaker or stronger than Montana's? See *Titan Sports v. Comics World*, 870 F.2d 85 (2d Cir.1989).

3. The Oldsmobile division of General Motors did a television commercial during the 1993 NCAA basketball championship which celebrated the fact that Oldsmobile had just won Consumers Digest's "Best Buy" award for the third year in a row. The lead-in was a trivia quiz about "Who holds the record for being voted the MVP in this tournament three times in a row," and the answer was UCLA's Lew Alcindor, from 1967 through 1969. Shortly afterwards, Alcindor changed his name to Kareem Abdul-Jabbar, under which he became the NBA's all-time scoring leader and a member of basketball's Hall of Fame. Should Abdul-Jabbar be able to sue for a violation of his publicity rights consisting of this use of his former name, or is "abandonment" a defense in a case such as this? Even if the Oldsmobile ad used his current name in the quiz answer, should that type of commercial be actionable? See *Abdul-Jabbar v. General Motors Corp.*, 75 F.3d 1391 (9th Cir.1996).

Adding to the intriguing issues posed by this case, in the fall of 1997, *Kareem* Abdul-Jabbar filed another publicity rights lawsuit, this one against *Karim* Abdul-Jabbar. In the fall of 1995, Sharman Shah, then a football running back at UCLA, had also opted for that new name, and after leaving for the professional ranks, he is now earning endorsement contracts as well as a substantial salary while playing for the Miami Dolphins. The younger Karim said at the time that his name had been changed to Abdul-Jabbar for the same Muslim religious reasons that had moved the older Kareem to make the change 25 years earlier. It seems that use of the name Abdul-Jabbar as well as Alcindor is going to make an important contribution to the scope of publicity rights law.

Having gained some sense of the evolution and present topography of publicity rights, we now must consider the fundamental policy questions posed by this doctrine. Judicial creation of this new form of private intellectual property has made multi-millionaires out of Ken Griffey, Jr., Shaquille O'Neal, Greg Norman and their celebrity colleagues. It has also made it correspondingly more expensive for fans to enjoy collecting baseball cards, wearing basketball sneakers, and swinging golf clubs. Is the justification for that legal redistribution of wealth that this is a necessary incentive for development of the players' talents and performance? Or that it ensures an accurate and economic allocation of player likenesses across the spectrum of commercial products? Or is the true source a natural moral right of players (and anyone else) to control and exploit their own identities, rather than allow these to enrich others? How much force is there to these and other rationales you may think of for awarding Michael Jordan exclusive property in the image "His Airness?"

Whatever the intrinsic merits of publicity rights for players and other celebrities, creation of this new form of intellectual property posed a problem of accommodation with other branches of property law. The most pressing question involved the teams' right to broadcast games.

As we have seen, in *Zacchini* the Supreme Court characterized an entertainer's performance routine as the core feature of his publicity rights. Needless to say, sports fans are far more interested in watching Michael Jordan than Hugo Zacchini soaring through the air. A key difference, though, is that Jordan and his fellow athletes in other professional team sports are employees of their clubs and leagues who have long asserted the right to sell broadcast rights in their games for increasingly lucrative fees. The legal question is whether, just as stations and networks need a license from the club to broadcast the game (after *Pittsburgh Athletic*), the clubs also need a license from their players to allow the players' likeness and performance to be displayed on the screen. Like so many other owner-player disputes in sports, this issue simmered in baseball for years before finally surfacing in the following federal court ruling.[f]

BALTIMORE ORIOLES v. MAJOR LEAGUE BASEBALL PLAYERS ASS'N.

United States Court of Appeals, Seventh Circuit, 1986.
805 F.2d 663.

Eschbach, Senior Circuit Judge.

[Back in 1947, the baseball leagues inserted in the standard form player contract a clause by which the player agreed that his picture could be taken for still photographs, motion pictures, or television, and that all

---

[f] This issue produced a law journal piece before the judicial ruling, James W. Quinn and Irving H. Warren, *Professional Team Sports New Legal Arena: Television and the Player's Right of Publicity*, 16 Indiana L. Rev. 487 (1983) (whose lead author was also counsel for the MLBPA), and a critical review afterwards, Shelley R. Saxer, Baltimore Orioles v. MLBPA: *The Right of Publicity in Game References and Federal Copyright Protection*, 36 UCLA L. Rev. 861 (1989).

rights in these pictures would belong to the club and be usable for publicity purposes. When baseball players first began bargaining collectively in the late 1960s, language was inserted in the labor agreements stating that nothing in these agreements affected whatever rights or obligations either side might have with respect to broadcasts. Finally, in 1982 the players sent letters to both the clubs and the broadcasters saying that telecasts without their consent constituted misappropriation of the players' property right in their performance on the field.

The baseball clubs responded with a suit in an Illinois federal district court, seeking a declaration that they had the exclusive right to televised performance of major league games involving their players. When the case reached the Seventh Circuit on competing motions for summary judgment, instead of focusing on state law issues about the terms of the employment ("master and servant") relationship or the clubs' right to control broadcast of games, the Court rested its decision on the federal Copyright Act. The Act posed two distinct legal questions. The first was whether the clubs rather than the players owned copyright in the game broadcasts as "works made for hire." The second was whether any such copyright ownership by the clubs preempted state publicity law claims by the players about whether their performances could be broadcast in the first place.]

* * *

II

B. COPYRIGHT CLAIM

* * *

1. Works Made for Hire Under 17 U.S.C. § 201(b)

Our analysis begins by ascertaining whether the Clubs own a copyright in the telecasts of major league baseball games. In general, copyright in a work "vests initially in the author or authors of the work;" however, "[i]n the case of a work made for hire, the employer or other person for whom the work was prepared is considered the author ... and, unless the parties have expressly agreed otherwise in a written instrument signed by them, owns all of the rights comprised in the copyright." A work made for hire is defined in pertinent part as "a work prepared by an employee within the scope of his or her employment." Thus, an employer owns a copyright in a work if (1) the work satisfies the generally applicable requirements for copyrightability ..., (2) the work was prepared by an employee, (3) the work was prepared within the scope of the employee's employment, and (4) the parties have not expressly agreed otherwise in a signed, written instrument.

a. Copyrightability of the telecasts

[The court synopsized the key conditions for copyrightability of telecasts, citing the *McBee & Bruno's* case we read above. The opinion continued.]

* * *

Moreover, the telecasts are original works of authorship. The requirement of originality actually subsumes two separate conditions, i.e., the work must possess an independent origin and a minimal amount of creativity.[6] It is obvious that the telecasts are independent creations, rather than reproductions of earlier works.

As for the telecasts' creativity, courts long have recognized that photographing a person or filming an event involves creative labor. See, e.g., *Burrow-Giles Lithographic Co. v. Sarony*, 111 U.S. 53, 60 (1884). For example, one court held that Zapruder film of the Kennedy assassination was copyrightable because it embodied

> many elements of creativity. Among other things, Zapruder selected the kind of camera (movies, not snapshots), the kind of film (color), the kind of lens (telephoto), the area in which the pictures were to be taken, the time they were to be taken, and (after testing several sites) the spot on which the camera would be operated.

Time Inc. v. Bernard Geis Associates, 293 F.Supp. 130, 143 (S.D.N.Y. 1968). The many decisions that must be made during the broadcast of a baseball game concerning camera angles, types of shots, the use of instant replays and split screens, and shot selection similarly supply the creativity required for the copyrightability of the telecasts....

[After finding that players were employees and that playing games before an audience, "live and remote," came within the scope of their employment, the Court turned to the question of whether the clubs' presumptive ownership of these "works for hire" had been reversed by a written document. The Court quoted the relevant language from the 1947 player-contract and the 1969 and 1970 labor agreements with the MLBPA, and found nothing there that "represents an express agreement that the Players own the copyright in the telecasts. If anything they reflect the parties' express disagreement as to the copyright's ownership."]

* * *

---

6. It is important to distinguish among three separate concepts—originality, creativity, and novelty. A work is original if it is the independent creation of its author. A work is creative if it embodies some modest amount of intellectual labor. A work is novel if it differs from existing works in some relevant respect. For a work to be copyrightable, it must be original and creative, but need not be novel. (Thus, in contrast to patent law, a work that is independently produced by two separate authors may be copyrighted by both.) Although the requirements of independent creation and intellectual labor both flow from the constitutional prerequisite of authorship and the statutory reference to original works of authorship, courts often engender confusion by referring to both concepts by the term "originality." For the sake of clarity, we shall use "originality" to mean independent authorship and "creativity" to denote intellectual labor.

The Players further assert that the parties' traditional practice of devoting approximately one-third of the revenues derived from nationally televised broadcasts to the Players' pension fund establishes a genuine issue of material fact as to the ownership of the copyright in these telecasts. We disagree. The allocation of revenues from nationally televised broadcasts is determined by the parties' relative bargaining power, they can negotiate a greater or a lesser share of the national telecast revenues. Nevertheless, there is no relationship between the division of revenues from nationally televised broadcasts and the ownership of rights in those telecasts. For example, a motion picture star might negotiate to receive a certain number of "points" from a film's profits; however, that she shares in the film's profits does not mean that she owns some share of the copyright in the film. (Indeed, the producer most likely holds the copyright in the work.) Just as the ownership of points in a film's profits profit does not represent a proportionate ownership of the copyright in the film, the Players' receipt in the form of pension contributions of a certain fraction of the revenues from nationally televised broadcasts in no way suggests that they own any part of the copyright in the telecasts.

We thus conclude that there are no genuine issues of material fact as to the ownership of the copyright in the telecasts, and that the parties did not expressly agree to rebut the statutory presumption that the employer owns the copyright in a work made for hire. We, therefore, hold that the Clubs own the copyright in telecasts of major league baseball games.

2. *Preemption under 17 U.S.C. § 301(a)*

[Having found that the clubs, not the players, owned the copyright in game telecasts, the Court next turned to the question whether such owner copyright under federal law preempted player publicity rights under state law. That question turned on the wording of § 301 which was added to the Copyright Act in 1976, and whose impact we encountered in the *NBA-Motorola* decision.]

* * *

This provision sets forth two conditions that both must be satisfied for preemption of a right under state law: first, the work in which the right is asserted must be fixed in tangible form and come within the subject matter of copyright as specified in § 102. Second, the right must be equivalent to any of the rights specified in § 106.

The works in which the Players claim rights are the telecasts of major league baseball games. As established above, the telecasts are fixed in tangible form because they are recorded simultaneously with their transmission and are audiovisual works which come within the subject matter of copyright. The first condition for preemption is, therefore, satisfied.

The Players argue, however, that the works in which they claim rights are their performances, rather than the telecasts of the games in which they play, and that performances per se are not fixed in tangible form. They contend that, since the works in which they assert rights are not fixed in tangible form, their rights of publicity in their performances are not subject to preemption. We disagree. Under § 101, "[a] work is 'fixed' in a tangible medium of expression when its embodiment in a copy ..., by or under the authority of the author, is sufficiently permanent and stable to permit it to be perceived, reproduced, or otherwise communicated for a period of more than transitory duration." The Players' performances are embodied in a copy, viz, the videotape of the telecast, from which the performances can be perceived, reproduced, and otherwise communicated indefinitely. Hence, their performances are fixed in tangible form, and any property rights in the performances that are equivalent to any of the rights encompassed in a copyright are preempted.

It is, of course, true that unrecorded performances per se are not fixed in tangible form. Among the many such works not fixed in tangible form are "choreography that has never been filmed or notated, an extemporaneous speech, 'original works of authorship' communicated solely through conversations or live broadcasts, and a dramatic sketch or musical composition improvised or developed from memory and without being recorded or written down." House Report at 131, reprinted in 1976 U.S. Code Cong. & Ad. News at 5747. Because such works are not fixed in tangible form, rights in such works are not subject to preemption under § 301(a). Indeed, § 301(b), which represents the obverse of § 301(a), expressly allows the states to confer common law copyright protection upon such works, and protection has been afforded to unfixed works by some states. Nonetheless, once a performance is reduced to tangible form, there is no distinction between the performance and the recording of the performance for the purpose of preemption under § 301(a). Thus, if a baseball game were not broadcast or were telecast without being recorded, the Players' performances similarly would not be fixed in tangible form and their rights of publicity would not be subject to preemption. By virtue of being videotaped, however, the Players' performances are fixed in tangible form, and any rights of publicity in their performances that are equivalent to the rights contained in the copyright of the telecast are preempted.

The Players also contend that to be a "work[] of authorship that ... [is] fixed in a tangible medium of expression" within the scope of § 301(a), a work must be copyrightable. They assert that the works in which they claim rights, namely their performances, are not copyrightable because they lack sufficient creativity. They consequently conclude that because the works in which they claim rights are not works within the meaning of § 301(a), their rights of publicity are not subject to preemption. There is a short answer to this argument. Congress contemplated that "[a]s long as a work fits within one of the general subject matter categories of section 102 and 103, ... [section 301(a)] prevents the States from protecting it even if it fails to achieve Federal copyright because it is too minimal or lacking in originality to qualify." Hence

§ 301(a) preempts all equivalent state-law rights claimed in any work within the subject matter of copyright whether or not the work embodies any creativity. Regardless of the creativity of the Players' performances, the works in which they assert rights are copyrightable works which come within the scope of § 301(a) because of the creative contributions of the individuals responsible for recording the Players' performances. Therefore, the Players' rights of publicity in their performances are preempted if they are equivalent to any of the bundle of rights encompassed in a copyright.

b. Section 106 test

A right under state law is "equivalent" to one of the rights within the general scope of copyright if it is violated by the exercise of any of the rights set forth in § 106. That section grants the owner of a copyright the exclusive rights to reproduce (whether in original or derivative form), distribute, perform, and display the copyrighted work. Thus, a right is equivalent to one of the rights comprised by a copyright if it "is infringed by the mere act of reproduction, performance, distribution or display."

In particular, the right to "perform" an audiovisual work means the right "to show its images in any sequence or to make the sounds accompanying it audible." Thus, the right to perform an audiovisual work encompasses the right to broadcast it. Hence, a right in a work that is conferred by state law is equivalent to the right to perform a telecast of that work if the state-law right is infringed merely by broadcasting the work.

In this case, the Players claim a right of publicity in their performances. As a number of courts have held, a right of publicity in a performance is violated by a televised broadcast of the performance. See *Zacchini v. Scripps–Howard Broadcasting Co.*, 54 Ohio St. 2d 286, 376 N.E.2d 582, (1978), on remand from 433 U.S. 562 (1977)(broadcast of human cannonball act). Indeed, from the start of this litigation, the Players consistently have maintained that their rights of publicity permit them to control telecasts of their performances, and that televised broadcasts of their performances made without their consent violate their rights of publicity in their performances. Because the exercise of the Clubs' right to broadcast telecasts of the games infringes the Players' rights of publicity in their performances, the Players' rights of publicity are equivalent to at least one of the rights encompassed by copyright, viz., the right to perform an audiovisual work. Since the works in which the Players claim rights are fixed in tangible form and come within the subject matter of copyright, the Players' rights of publicity in their performances are preempted.

The Players argue that their rights of publicity in their performances are not equivalent to the rights contained in a copyright because rights of publicity and copyrights serve different interests. In their view, the purpose of federal copyright law is to secure a benefit to the public, but the purpose of state statutory or common law concerning rights of publicity is to protect individual pecuniary interests. We disagree.

The purpose of federal copyright protection is to benefit the public by encouraging works in which it is interested. To induce individuals to undertake the personal sacrifices necessary to create such works, federal copyright law extends to the authors of such works a limited monopoly to reap the rewards of their endeavors. Contrary to the Players' contention, the interest underlying the recognition of the right of publicity also is the promotion of performances that appeal to the public. The reason that state law protects individual pecuniary interests is to provide an incentive to performers to invest the time and resources required to develop such performances. *In Zacchini v. Scripps–Howard Broadcasting Co.*, 433 U.S. 562 (1977), the principal case on which the Players rely for their assertion that different interests underlie copyright and the right to publicity, the Supreme Court recognized that the interest behind federal copyright protection is the advancement of the public welfare through the encouragement of individual effort by personal gain, action for violation of the right to publicity "is closely analogous to the goals of patent and copyright law." Id. at 573. Because the right of publicity does not differ in kind from copyright, the Players' rights of publicity in their performances cannot escape preemption.

In this litigation, the Players have attempted to obtain ex post what they did not negotiate ex ante. That is to say, they seek a judicial declaration that they possess a right—the right to control the telecasts of major league baseball games—that they could not procure in bargaining with the Clubs. The Players' aim is to share in the increasingly lucrative revenues derived from the sale of television rights for over-the-air broadcasts by local stations and national networks and for distribution by subscription and pay cable services. Contrary to the Players' contention, the effect of this decision is not to grant the Clubs perpetual rights to the Players' performances. The Players remain free to attain their objective by bargaining with the Clubs for a contractual declaration that the Players own a joint or an exclusive interest in the copyright of the telecasts.

* * *

Affirmed.

Questions For Discussion

1. Recall the Supreme Court's *Zacchini* decision, in which Zacchini sued a television station for broadcasting his entire 15-second human cannonball act on the evening news. Is the implication of *Baltimore Orioles* that, if a station asserts as its defense copyright preemption rather than First Amendment speech, it could now defeat Zacchini's state publicity law claim? Was there a viable "authorship" distinction that the *Baltimore Orioles* Court could make from *Zacchini*? Should there be any difference between the situation of baseball (or other) professional athletes who are

employees, and other athletes who are not—e.g., a golfer on the PGA Tour or a college basketball player in the Final Four?

2. Now that teams (or leagues) have been found to have some level of preemptive ownership of their game telecasts, does this mean that they are entitled to take bits of the telecast tape containing an especially dramatic performance by a Dennis Rodman or a Deion Sanders and license this to filmmakers wanting to produce a docudrama like *Hoop Dreams*? To an athletic shoe manufacturer wanting to show Sanders or Rodman in a commercial advertisement? Can these uses be distinguished from what took place in *Baltimore Orioles*?

3. There is a recent decision that addressed some, though not all, of these legal issues. Titan Sports Enterprises created and operates the World Wrestling Federation (WWF), featuring among others, Hulk Hogan. Besides the live event and television broadcast, a lucrative feature of WWF has been production and sale of videotapes of its matches. Jesse "The Body" Ventura began as a wrestler with WWF in 1984, but after medical problems he switched to the role of color commentator over the air. Initially, Ventura worked under an oral contract that paid him $1,000 a week and made no mention of Titan's videotaping and sale of his broadcasts. In 1987, Ventura used a talent agent who negotiated a written agreement. While the talent agent had sought to secure Ventura some royalties from the videos, he eventually agreed to drop the issue when Titan said it did not pay this to its regular performers. This representation turned out to be untrue (not just in the case of Hulk Hogan, but a number of other wrestlers). In 1990, Ventura left to work for Titan's competitor (WCW), and he filed suit for video royalties, eventually securing a jury verdict of over $800,000.

On appeal to the Eighth Circuit, both the majority and dissenting opinions agreed that Ventura had a valid claim of fraud for the 1987–90 period. The difference of view related to the 1984–87 time frame when the royalty issue had never been mentioned in contract negotiations. One side supported Ventura's *quantum meruit* claim for that period. Even though the state courts in Minnesota (whose law governed this case) had always rejected the basic tort of privacy, the right of publicity was judged to be qualitatively different (financial rather than emotional in nature). Absent a contract waiver by Ventura of his publicity rights, he was entitled to compensation for the use and sale of his name, likeness, or performance on video. The other side was of the view that, if someone like Ventura agreed to perform on television for a specified weekly fee and no other contract conditions, he should not be able to claim later that his employer, Titan, which was staging the entire event, was unjustly enriching itself by selling videotapes of the program to fans who had not been able to see it on television. Neither side, though, had to address the *Baltimore Orioles* decision about possible federal copyright preemption of state publicity law claims, because this issue had not been raised by Titan on time.

What is your view about whether Jesse Ventura should have an underlying publicity right to control the collateral use of his performances absent express contractual permission? Does *Baltimore Orioles* (and more recently, *NBA-Motorola*) render that whole debate redundant because the Copyright

Act preempts any such state law claim? See *Ventura v. Titan Sports*, 65 F.3d 725 (8th Cir.1995).

4. Suppose the *Baltimore Orioles* decision had gone the other way. Clearly that would have made a difference in the short run, since the baseball owners and players were in their first full year of a collective agreement that was the by-product of a lengthy and acrimonious work stoppage in 1981. In the longer run, though, does the legal allocation of initial rights about game broadcasts make a material difference in later contractual outcomes? (Consider the implications of the earlier superstation example.)

D. OWNER TRADEMARK RIGHTS

This brings us to a fourth branch of intellectual property law, through which franchise owners seek to realize the celebrity value of their team's (not their players') name and identity. As was mentioned at the outset of this chapter, over the last 15 years the sale of merchandising revenues has become an increasingly significant source of sporting revenues. Sports now accounts for approximately $15 billion of the $70 billion or so that Americans spend annually on clothes, shoes, drinking glasses, and other products that come with an identifiable name and logo attached to it. The merchandise licensed by NFL Properties accounts for $3.5 billion in annual sales of more than 2,500 different items carrying a pro football association. Such licenses typically generate payment to the league itself of seven to eight percent of the gross revenues from the products in question.

Sports merchandising and sports broadcasting complement each other in generating greater fan interest in the sport. No better example could be found than a 1994 news photo of a young South African wearing a Toronto Raptors T-shirt long before this expansion NBA franchise had even acquired a player, let alone been in a game. However, just as is true of game broadcasts and player endorsements, there must be a legal underpinning to the ability of the Raptors and the NBA to extract their share of the revenue from the sale of that T-shirt. In this setting, the vehicle is yet another branch of intellectual property—trademark law, as governed by the 1946 Federal Lanham Act (15 U.S.C.A. § 1051, et seq.).

Trademarks are defined as "any word, name, symbol, or device ... used by a person ... to identify and distinguish his or her goods ... from those manufactured and sold by others and to indicate the source of the good...." Trademarks (and their equivalent, service marks) can be registered with the United States Patent and Trademark Office, in which case use by anyone else is presumed to be an infringement in a suit filed under § 32 of the Lanham Act. Even if the mark is not registered, though, an action can still be filed under § 43, which essentially codifies common law doctrine against unfair competition.

Whatever the statutory footing, the essence of a trademark claim is quite different from what we have seen of copyright and publicity right protection of the exclusive property in a team's broadcast or a player's identity. Teams do not have an absolute right to stop someone else from using their names and symbols. Rather, they can block that action only if it is likely to cause confusion or deception of consumers in the sale of competing goods.

As explained in one of the leading scholarly treatments of this subject,[g] the basic aim of trademark law is to protect consumers in their choice and use of goods. The technique for doing so is to encourage producers to develop names and other identifiers for their products—such as Coca Cola or Kleenex—that permit easy recognition of the product whose features consumers prefer. That kind of brand-name recognition gives the producers an incentive to preserve and enhance the attractive qualities of its products. It also gives imitators an incentive to use the name without necessarily matching the product quality. The role of trademark law is to bar any use of a name or symbol that is identified with a product where such use may confuse consumers in some fashion about the source and quality of the products they are seeking.

Performing in his judicial rather than in his scholarly role, the co-author of that economic treatment of trademark recently rendered a decision about a sports trademark dispute that provides an apt introduction to this branch of the law, as well as an initial look at one of the NFL franchise moves we will encounter in the next chapter.

INDIANAPOLIS COLTS v. METROPOLITAN BALTIMORE FOOTBALL CLUB

United States Court of Appeals, Seventh Circuit, 1994.
34 F.3d 410.

POSNER, CHIEF JUDGE.

[Baltimore first gained an NFL franchise in 1952, when the NFL granted permission to the unsuccessful and bankrupt Dallas Texans to move to that city. The team was renamed the Baltimore Colts. Three decades later, in 1984, the franchise-owner, Robert Irsay, moved the team to Indianapolis, literally under cover of darkness. The league, worried about the prospects of an antitrust lawsuit, decided not to block the relocation of the team. Irsay kept the team's nickname, and they are now known as the Indianapolis Colts.

For the next nine years, the citizens of Baltimore and Maryland unsuccessfully sought another NFL team, whether through relocation or expansion. In 1993, the Canadian Football League (CFL) gave Baltimore a franchise in its league, which the new owner (and his fans) wanted to name the Colts. Faced with possible legal action, the team was dubbed the Baltimore CFL Colts: using that name, the team undertook its

---

g. William M. Landes and Richard Posner, Trademark Law: An Economic Perspective, 30 J. of Law and Economics 265 (1987).

marketing efforts leading up to its initial 1994 season. Not satisfied with that variation on the old name, the Indianapolis Colts and the NFL sued (in an Indianapolis federal court) to block any use of the word "Colts" in the team name. After the district judge had granted an interim injunction, the Baltimore team appealed.]

* * *

The Baltimore team wanted to call itself the "Baltimore Colts." To improve its litigating posture (we assume), it has consented to insert "CFL" between "Baltimore" and "Colts." A glance at the merchandise in the record explains why this concession to an outraged NFL has been made so readily. On several of the items "CFL" appears in small or blurred letters. And since the Canadian Football League is not well known in the United States—and "CFL" has none of the instant recognition value of "NFL"—the inclusion of the acronym in the team's name might have little impact on potential buyers even if prominently displayed. Those who know football well know that the new "Baltimore Colts" are a new CFL team wholly unrelated to the old Baltimore Colts; know also that the rules of Canadian football are different from those of American football and that teams don't move from the NFL to the CFL as they might from one conference within the NFL to the other. But those who do not know these things—and we shall come shortly to the question whether there are many of these football illiterate—will not be warned off by the letters "CFL." The acronym is a red herring, and the real issue is whether the new Baltimore team can appropriate the name "Baltimore Colts." The entire thrust of the defendants' argument is that it can.

They make a tremendous to-do over the fact that the district judge found that the Indianapolis Colts abandoned the trademark "Baltimore Colts" when they moved to Indianapolis. Well, of course; they were no longer playing football under the name "Baltimore Colts," so could not have used the name as the team's trademark; they could have used it on merchandise but chose not to, until 1991 (another story—and not one we need tell). When a mark is abandoned, it returns to the public domain, and is appropriable anew—in principle. In practice, because "subsequent use of [an] abandoned mark may well evoke a continuing association with the prior use, those who make subsequent use may be required to take reasonable precautions to prevent confusion." J. Thomas McCarthy, *McCarthy on Trademarks and Intellectual Property* § 17.01 [2] (3d ed. 1994) at p. 17–3. This precept is especially important where, as in this case, the former owner of the abandoned mark continues to market the same product or service under a similar name, though we cannot find any previous cases of this kind. No one questions the validity of "Indianapolis Colts" as the trademark of the NFL team that plays out of Indianapolis and was formerly known as the Baltimore Colts. If "Baltimore CFL Colts" is confusingly similar to "Indianapolis Colts" by virtue of the history of the Indianapolis team and the overlapping product and geographical markets served by it and by the new Baltimore team, the latter's use of the abandoned mark would infringe the Indianapolis Colts' new mark. The Colts' abandonment of a mark confusingly similar to their new mark neither broke the continuity of the team in its different locations—it was the same team, merely having a different home base and therefore a different geographical component in its name—nor entitled a third party to pick it up and use it to confuse Colts fans, and other actual or potential consumers of products and services marketed by the Colts or by other National Football League teams, with regard to the identity, sponsorship, or league affiliation of the third party, that is, the new Baltimore team....

Against this the defendants cite to us with great insistence *Major League Baseball Properties, Inc. v. Sed Non Olet Denarius, Ltd.*, 817 F.Supp. 1103, 1128 (S.D.N.Y.1993), which, over the objection of the Los Angeles Dodgers, allowed a restaurant in Brooklyn to use the name "Brooklyn Dodger" on the ground that "the 'Brooklyn Dodgers' was a non-transportable cultural institution separate from the 'Los Angeles Dodgers.'" The defendants in our case argue that the sudden and greatly resented departure of the Baltimore Colts for Indianapolis made the name "Baltimore Colts" available to anyone who would continue the "nontransportable cultural institution" constituted by a football team located in the City of Baltimore. We think this argument very weak, and need not even try to distinguish *Sed Non Olet Denarius* since district court decisions are not authoritative in this or any court of appeals. If it were a Supreme Court decision it still would not help the defendants. The "Brooklyn Dodger" was not a baseball team, and there was no risk of confusion. The case might be relevant if the Indianapolis Colts were arguing not confusion but misappropriation: that they own the goodwill associated with the name "Baltimore Colts" and the new Baltimore team is trying to take it from them. They did make a claim of misappropriation in the district court, but that court rejected the claim and it has not been renewed on appeal. The only claim in our court is that a significant number of consumers will think the new Baltimore team the successor to, or alter ego of, or even the same team as the Baltimore Colts and therefore the Indianapolis Colts, which is the real successor. No one would think the Brooklyn Dodgers baseball team reincarnated in a restaurant.

A professional sports team is like Heraclitus's river: always changing, yet always the same. When Mr. Irsay transported his team, the Baltimore Colts, from Baltimore to Indianapolis in one night in 1984, the team remained, for a time anyway, completely intact: same players, same coaches, same front-office personnel. With the passage of time, of course, the team changed. Players retired or were traded, and were replaced. Coaches and other nonplaying personnel came and went. But as far as the record discloses there is as much institutional continuity between the Baltimore Colts of 1984 and the Indianapolis Colts of 1994 as there was between the Baltimore Colts of 1974 and the Baltimore Colts of 1984. Johnny Unitas, the Baltimore Colts' most famous player, swears in his affidavit that his old team has no connection with the Indianapolis Colts, and he has even asked the Colts to expunge his name from its record books. He is angry with Irsay for moving the team. He is entitled to his anger, but it has nothing to do with this lawsuit. The Colts were Irsay's team, it was moved intact, there is no evidence it has changed more since the move than it had in the years before. There is, in contrast, no continuity, no links contractual or otherwise, nothing but a geographical site in common, between the Baltimore Colts and the Canadian Football League team that would like to use its name. Any suggestion that there is such continuity is false and potentially misleading.

Potentially; for if everyone knows there is no contractual or institutional continuity, no pedigree or line of descent, linking the Baltimore–Indianapolis Colts and the new CFL team that wants to call itself the "Baltimore Colts" (or, grudgingly, the "Baltimore CFL Colts"), then there is no harm, at least no harm for which the Lanham Act provides a remedy, in the new Baltimore team's appropriating the name "Baltimore Colts" to play under and sell merchandise under. If not everyone knows, there is harm. Some people who might otherwise watch the Indianapolis Colts (or some other NFL team, for remember that the NFL, representing all the teams, is a coplaintiff) on television may watch the Baltimore CFL Colts instead, thinking they are the "real" Baltimore Colts, and the NFL will lose revenue. A few (doubtless very few) people who might otherwise buy tickets to an NFL game may buy tickets to a Baltimore CFL Colts game instead. Some people who might otherwise buy merchandise stamped with the name "Indianapolis Colts" or the name of some other NFL team may buy merchandise stamped "Baltimore CFL Colts," thinking it a kin of the NFL's Baltimore Colts in the glory days of Johnny Unitas rather than a newly formed team that plays Canadian football in a Canadian football league. It would be naive to suppose that no consideration of such possibilities occurred to the owners of the new Baltimore team when they were choosing a name, though there is no evidence that it was the dominant or even a major consideration.

Confusion thus is possible, and may even have been desired; but is it likely? There is great variance in consumer competence, and it would be undesirable to impoverish the lexicon of trade names merely to protect the most gullible fringe of the consuming public. The Lanham Act does not cast the net of protection so wide. The legal standard under the Act has been formulated variously, but the various formulations come down to whether it is likely that the challenged mark if permitted to be used by the defendant would cause the plaintiff to lose a substantial number of consumers. Pertinent to this determination is the similarity of the marks and of the parties' products, the knowledge of the average consumer of the product, the overlap in the parties' geographical markets, and the other factors that the cases consider. The aim is to strike a balance between, on the one hand, the interest of the seller of the new product, and of the consuming public, in an arresting, attractive, and informative name that will enable the new product to compete effectively against existing ones, and, on the other hand, the interest of existing sellers, and again of the consuming public, in consumers' being able to know exactly what they are buying without having to incur substantial costs of investigation or inquiry.

* * *

[The court then compared the market research surveys conducted by the two sides. After criticizing the methodology used by the defendant's expert, Michael Rappeport, the court analyzed the study conducted by the plaintiff's expert.]

* * *

The plaintiffs' study, conducted by Jacob Jacoby, was far more substantial and the district judge found it on the whole credible. The 28-page report with its numerous appendices has all the trappings of social scientific rigor. Interviewers showed several hundred consumers in 24 malls scattered around the country shirts and hats licensed by the defendants for sale to consumers. The shirts and hats have "Baltimore CFL Colts" stamped on them. The consumers were asked whether they were football fans, whether they watched football games on television, and whether they ever bought merchandise with a team name on it. Then they were asked, with reference to the "Baltimore CFL Colts" merchandise that they were shown, such questions as whether they knew what sport the team played, what teams it played against, what league the team was in, and whether the team or league needed someone's permission to use this name, and if so whose.... There were other questions, none however obviously loaded, and a whole other survey, the purpose of which was to control for "noise," in which another group of mallgoers was asked the identical questions about a hypothetical team unappetizingly named the "Baltimore Horses." The idea was by comparing the answers of the two groups to see whether the source of confusion was the name "Baltimore Colts" or just the name "Baltimore," in which event the injunction would do no good since no one suggests that the new Baltimore team should be forbidden to use "Baltimore" in its name, provided the following word is not "Colts."

* * *

Rappeport threw darts at Jacoby's study. Some landed wide.... But Rappeport was right to complain that the choice of "Horses" for the comparison team loaded the dice and that some of Jacoby's questions were a bit slanted. That is only to say, however, that Jacoby's survey was not perfect, and this is not news. Trials would be very short if only perfect evidence were admissible.

Jacoby's survey of consumers reactions to the "Baltimore CFL Colts" merchandise found rather astonishing levels of confusion not plausibly attributable to the presence of the name "Baltimore" alone, since "Baltimore Horses" engendered much less. (We don't like the name "Baltimore Horses," as we have said; but we doubt that a more attractive "Baltimore" name, the "Baltimore Leopards," for example, would have generated the level of confusion that "Baltimore CFL Colts" did.) Among self-identified football fans, 64% thought that the "Baltimore CFL Colts" was either the old (NFL) Baltimore Colts or the Indianapolis Colts. But perhaps this result is not so astonishing. Although most American football fans have heard of Canadian football, many probably are unfamiliar with the acronym "CFL," and as we remarked earlier it is not a very conspicuous part of the team logo stamped on the merchandise. Among fans who watch football on television, 59% displayed the same confusion; and even among those who watch football on cable television, which attracts a more educated audience on average and actually carries CFL games, 58% were confused when shown the merchandise. Among the minority not confused about who the "Baltimore CFL Colts" are, a substantial minority, ranging from 21 to 34% depending on the precise sub-sample, thought the team somehow sponsored or authorized by the Indianapolis Colts or the National Football League. It is unfortunate and perhaps a bit tricky that the sub sample of consumers likely to buy merchandise with a team name on it was not limited to consumers likely to buy merchandise with a football team's name on it; the choice of the name "Baltimore Horses" for the comparison team was unfortunate; and no doubt there are other tricks of the survey researcher's black arts that we have missed. There is the more fundamental problem, one common to almost all consumer survey research, that people are more careful when they are laying out their money than when they are answering questions.

But with all this granted, we cannot say that the district judge committed a clear error in crediting the major findings of the Jacoby study and inferring from it and the other evidence in the record that the defendants' use of the name "Baltimore CFL Colts" whether for the team or on merchandise was likely to confuse a substantial number of consumers. This means—given the defendants' failure to raise any issue concerning the respective irreparable harms from granting or denying the preliminary injunction—that the judge's finding concerning likelihood of confusion required that the injunction issue.

* * *

Affirmed.

———

As it turned out, after spending nearly $600,000 to try to keep the Colts name, the Baltimore team gave up on the eve of a full-blown trial of the consumer confusion issue. The word "Colts" was removed from all merchandise. After surveying Baltimore fans, owner Jim Speros turned down the name "Stallions" and decided to call the team just The Baltimore Football Club. Soon afterwards, though, the Baltimore Club and all other CFL franchises in the United States were disbanded. (In 1997, the NFL agreed to give the Canadian clubs in the CFL some financial support as a post-college base for developing football talent.) In the meantime, the NFL moved back to Baltimore in 1996, with the historic Cleveland Browns franchise (a story we will read about in Chapter 7). The NFL was able to persuade Browns' owner Art Modell to leave that name in Cleveland, but the League did not induce Colts owner Bob Irsay to return "Colts" to its Baltimore fans. Baltimore's football team is now called the Ravens. Ironically, though, the 50-year-old Baltimore Colts Band has continued to play under that name, which it trademarked while the Colts team was still in that city.

Questions For Discussion

1. What was the precise source of this trademark claim? Could an NFL team in a different city have objected if Baltimore had chosen its name—e.g., the Packers—for its CFL franchise? Or was the real issue that the two Colts teams were playing the same sport? For example, could the St. Louis baseball Cardinals now sue the Arizona Cardinals (or could they have sued this NFL team when it was relocated from Chicago to St. Louis under that name)? What about the overlap between the NHL New York Rangers and the MLB Texas Rangers, or the NFL Houston Oilers and the NHL Edmonton Oilers? And we should note that, in early 1997, a federal district judge refused to grant an injunction to the barnstorming Harlem Wizards basketball team to block the NBA's Washington franchise from changing its name from Bullets to Wizards: see *Harlem Wizards Entertainment Basketball, Inc. v. NBA Properties*, 952 F.Supp. 1084 (D.N.J.1997), a ruling that the plaintiff is now appealing to the Third Circuit.

2. Is the issue merely the use of the same team name? Could Baltimore have used a different nickname with the same blue and white horseshoe logo, or the same name with very different colors and logo?

3. What is the relevant market for determining "likelihood of confusion" for trademark purposes? Should it be people who identify themselves as football fans? People in Indianapolis and/or in Baltimore? People who might actually buy NFL and/or CFL merchandise?

Trademark in sports extends far beyond team names. An earlier decision addressed the question of what protection would be enjoyed by one of the sports world's most prestigious events—the Masters Golf Tournament at the National course in Augusta, Georgia. After taking over a Hilton Head, South Carolina, development named the Moss Creek Plantation, Northwestern Mutual Life Insurance decided to sponsor a Ladies Professional Golf Association (LPGA) Tournament to promote both the development and its insurance business. Since the tournament was held one week after the Augusta Masters, Northwestern named its tournament the "Ladies Masters at Moss Creek Plantation." Augusta National immediately secured an injunction blocking any use of the word "Masters." See *Augusta National v. Northwestern Mutual Life Insurance*, 193 U.S.P.Q. (BNA) 210 (S.D.Ga.1976). As the judge put it:

> [T]he use of the term "Masters" by NML in the name of its planned annual tournament, "Ladies Masters at Moss Creek Planta-

tion," is likely to confuse the public into believing that Augusta National also sponsors the women's tournament. From this factual premise, logic compels the conclusion that if Augusta National's reputation is high, defendant will be "trading" on that reputation and "reaping where it has not sown." If Augusta National's good will is of great value, defendant will be sharing in it without having contributed to its growth. Logic compels, too, the conclusion that if NML "sins," they will be "visited upon" Augusta National. If NML mismanages the tournament, Augusta National will suffer the consequences in loss of good will and reputation; and this without having a hand in it. In sum, there would be a confusion of businesses in which plaintiff would no longer be master of its own destiny.

The case presents a classic example of the reasons for the creation of equity jurisprudence calling for the exercise of the conscience of a long-footed chancellor.

193 U.S.P.Q. (BNA) at 220.

Questions For Discussion

1. In light of the *Augusta National* decision, how would you decide a case brought by the promoters of the National Invitation Tournament in New York for men's college basketball teams, against the Women's National Invitation Tournament, which is held in Amarillo, Texas, and invites eight women's college basketball teams that do not qualify for the NCAA tournament? What distinctions, if any, do you see between the two cases?

2. In his *Colts* opinion, Judge Posner referred to, but refused to be governed by, the earlier district court decision in *Major League Baseball Properties v. Sed Non Olet Denarius*, 817 F.Supp. 1103 (S.D.N.Y.1993). That case was the by-product of an even more notorious sports franchise move—the Dodgers' flight from Brooklyn to Los Angeles in 1958. Thirty years later, a few of the Dodgers fans in Brooklyn decided to open a restaurant named the Brooklyn Dodgers Sports Bar and Restaurant, dedicated to the themes of "fun, sports, and Brooklyn." Though the original nickname commemorated children "dodging" Brooklyn streetcars, the restaurant logo included a depiction of the Artful Dodger, a character from Charles Dickens' *Oliver Twist*. The restaurant did, however, draw heavily upon the illustrious history of the city's baseball team—naming dishes after famous Dodgers players and decorating the restaurant with Dodgers memorabilia. Brooklyn Dodgers merchandise, with and without the phrase "Brooklyn Bum," was available for sale.

The baseball club had registered the word "Dodgers," and had licensed merchandisers to use both "Los Angeles Dodgers" and "Brooklyn Dodgers." While the club had warned off a 1966 effort to name a Continental Football League team the Brooklyn Dodgers, it never took action against a Brooklyn restaurant named Dodgers Cafe during its operation from 1942 to 1968. In 1991, though, the Dodgers filed a trademark infringement action against the new Brooklyn Sports Bar and Restaurant.

The federal judge dismissed the claim after applying the standard trademark litigation factors:

a) Strength of the plaintiff's trademark

b) Similarity between the parties' marks

c) Proximity of their products

d) Likelihood that the plaintiff will "bridge the gap" between the two markets

e) Evidence of actual confusion

f) Presence or absence of good faith on the part of the defendant

g) Quality of defendant's services

h) Sophistication of likely purchasers

[Margin note: Kind of a balancing test. All 8 are not necessary.]

What balance would you strike among these (and any other relevant) factors in a case such as this one? Suppose that some of the (relatively few) ex-Chicago Cardinals fans had started a restaurant in Chicago bearing that name? What would be the verdict of Judge Posner and his Seventh Circuit colleagues?

3. Whatever the positive impact of the point spread on television ratings for one-sided games, the NFL and other sports leagues have always expressed displeasure about gambling on their games, given the potential for point-shaving and game-throwing. Thus, in 1976, when the Delaware State Lottery developed one of the early sports lotteries based on weekly results of NFL games, the League filed suit. Is it a violation of the NFL's trademark for a lottery to use its game scores for that purpose, whether the teams be identified by their nicknames or just their home cities? Should this constitute misappropriation of the League's reputation and good will (by analogy to the court's reasoning in the *Pittsburgh Athletic* decision reproduced earlier)? See *NFL v. Governor of the State of Delaware*, 435 F.Supp. 1372 (D.Del.1977).

In the *Colts* case, the NFL's principal motivation for suing was not the likelihood that football fans would be confused about whether they were buying tickets to watch the NFL Colts or the CFL Colts on the field. Rather, NFL Properties wanted to make sure that fans would not buy T-shirts and other paraphernalia licensed by the Baltimore CFL Colts, rather than by the Indianapolis NFL Colts. The major economic value in team names, colors, and logos is not to adorn the players uniforms in the games, but rather to market the $15 billion worth of sports-related merchandise now being sold in stores.

Use of trademark law to secure such protection poses an analytical problem. Recall that the nature and objective of trademark law is to encourage producers like Coca Cola and Augusta National to develop distinctive names and symbols to identify their products, by barring other producers from attaching the same names and symbols to other products and thence misleading consumers looking to enjoy (and pay for) their favorite soft drink or golf tournament. Producers do not, however, receive a copyright-like monopoly in their name and symbol that blocks others from using it for non-confusing purposes. Pepsi, for example, can use the words "Coca Cola" in an advertisement that tries to draw an unfavorable comparison with its own product. (So also could the CFL refer to the NFL's Super Bowl in advertising how closely-contested are CFL championship Grey Cup games.) See, by analogy, *Consumers Union of the United States v. General Signal Corp.*, 724 F.2d 1044 (2d Cir. 1983).

In the case of sports merchandising, though, what is being sold are the team names and symbols themselves, thus allowing fans wearing a T-shirt to identify with their favorite teams and sports. If the T-shirt carried the name and likeness of a celebrated athlete, the publicity right we encountered earlier does give the individual the exclusive legal authority to license or bar use of his name and likeness for that purpose. Teams or leagues, by contrast, are business organizations, and thus cannot use this legal outgrowth of the right of personal privacy. The sports world did, however, give birth to a judicial ruling that expanded trademark doctrine into a surrogate form of protection for promotional goods (for the benefit not only of sports franchises but also the equally lucrative merchandising rights of movies like E.T. and The Lion King).[h]

BOSTON PROFESSIONAL HOCKEY ASSOCIATION v. DALLAS CAP AND EMBLEM MFG., INC.

United States Court of Appeals, Fifth Circuit, 1975.
510 F.2d 1004.

RONEY, CIRCUIT JUDGE.

[Prior to this case, NHL hockey teams had organized National Hockey League Services (NHLS) to serve as their exclusive licensing agent. NHLS licensed numerous manufacturers to use the team names and symbols in various promotions, including an exclusive license with Lion Brothers Company to manufacture embroidered emblems depicting the team logos. Between 1968 and 1971, Dallas Cap & Emblem sought to obtain a similar license. Unable to do so, the company then proceeded to manufacture the emblems for sale to sporting goods stores in various states.

When the NHL teams ultimately sued for trademark infringement, their complaint alleged that Dallas Cap's manufacture and sale of the team symbols constituted (1) an infringement of the plaintiffs' registered marks in violation of 15 U.S.C.A. § 1114; (2) false designation of origin in violation of 15 U.S.C.A. § 1125; and (3) common law unfair competition. The district court held that a disclaimer informing consumers that

---

[h]. Valuable analyses of the cases and issues regarding this topic are Robert C. Denicola, *Institutional Publicity Rights: An Analysis of the Merchandising of Famous Trade Symbols*, 62 North Carolina L. Rev. 603 (1984), and Peter A. Mims, *Promotional Goods and the Functionality Doctrine: An Economic Model of Trademarks*, 63 Texas L. Rev. 639 (1984).

the products were not officially authorized by the NHL was a sufficient remedy. The NHL teams appealed.]

* * *

Nearly everyone is familiar with the artistic symbols which designate the individual teams in various professional sports. The question in this case of first impression is whether the unauthorized, intentional duplication of a professional hockey team's symbol on an embroidered emblem, to be sold to the public as a patch for attachment to clothing, violates any legal right of the team to the exclusive use of that symbol. Contrary to the decision of the district court, we hold that the team has an interest in its own individualized symbol entitled to legal protection against such unauthorized duplication.

* * *

The Case

The difficulty with this case stems from the fact that a reproduction of the trademark itself is being sold, unattached to any other goods or services. The statutory and case law of trademarks is oriented toward the use of such marks to sell something other than the mark itself. The district court thought that to give plaintiffs protection in this case would be tantamount to the creation of a copyright monopoly for designs that were not copyrighted. The copyright laws are based on an entirely different concept than the trademark laws, and contemplate that the copyrighted material, like patented ideas, will eventually pass into the public domain. The trademark laws are based on the needed protection of the public and business interests and there is no reason why trademarks should ever pass into the public domain by the mere passage of time.

Although our decision here may slightly tilt the trademark laws from the purpose of protecting the public to the protection of the business interests of plaintiffs, we think that the two become so intermeshed when viewed against the backdrop of the common law of unfair competition that both the public and plaintiffs are better served by granting the relief sought by plaintiffs.

Underlying our decision are three persuasive points. First, the major commercial value of the emblems is derived from the efforts of plaintiffs. Second, defendant sought and ostensibly would have asserted, if obtained, an exclusive right to make and sell the emblems. Third, the sale of a reproduction of the trademark itself on an emblem is an accepted use of such team symbols in connection with the type of activity in which the business of professional sports is engaged. We need not deal here with the concept of whether every artistic reproduction of the symbol would infringe upon plaintiffs' rights. We restrict ourselves to the emblems sold principally through sporting goods stores for informal use by the public in connection with sports activities and to show public allegiance to or identification with the teams themselves.

* * *

[The court turned directly to the question whether the plaintiffs had proven elements (4) and (5) of a § 1114 violation, i.e., whether the symbols were used in connection with the sale of goods and whether such use was likely to cause confusion, mistake, or deception.]

* * *

The fourth requisite of a § 1114 cause of action is that the infringing use of the registered mark must be in connection with the sale, offering for sale, distribution or advertising of any goods. Although the district court did not expressly find that plaintiffs had failed to establish element four, such a finding was implicit in the court's statement that "in the instant case, the registered trade mark is, in effect, the product itself."

Defendant is in the business of manufacturing and marketing emblems for wearing apparel. These emblems are the products, or goods, which defendant sells. When defendant causes plaintiffs' marks to be embroidered upon emblems which it later markets, defendant uses those marks in connection with the sale of goods as surely as if defendant had embroidered the marks upon knit caps. See *Boston Professional Hockey Association, Inc. v. Reliable Knitting Works,* 178 U.S.P.Q. (BNA) 274 (E.D.Wis.1973). The fact that the symbol covers the entire face of defendant's product does not alter the fact that the trademark symbol is used in connection with the sale of the product. The sports fan in his local sporting goods store purchases defendant's fabric and thread emblems because they are embroidered with the symbols of ice hockey teams. Were defendant to embroider the same fabric with the same thread in other designs, the resulting products would still be emblems for wearing apparel but they would not give trademark identification to the customer. The conclusion is inescapable that, without plaintiffs' marks, defendant would not have a market for his particular product among ice hockey fans desiring to purchase emblems embroidered with the symbols of their favorite teams. It becomes clear that defendant's use of plaintiffs' marks is in connection with the sale, offering for sale, distribution, or advertising of goods and that plaintiffs have established the fourth element of a § 1114 cause of action.

The fifth element of a cause of action for mark infringement under 15 U.S.C.A. § 1114 is that the infringing use is likely to cause confusion, or to cause mistake or to deceive. The district court decided that there was no likelihood of confusion because the usual purchaser, a sports fan in his local sporting goods store, would not be likely to think that defendant's emblems were manufactured by or had some connection with plaintiffs.... In this case, however, the district court overlooked the fact that the Act was amended to eliminate the source of origin as being the only focal point of confusion. The confusion question here is conceptually difficult. It can be said that the public buyer knew that the emblems portrayed the teams' symbols. Thus, it can be argued, the buyer is not confused or deceived. This argument misplaces the purpose of the confusion requirement. The confusion or deceit requirement is met by the fact that the defendant duplicated the protected trademarks and sold them to the public knowing that the public would identify them as being the teams' trademarks. The certain knowledge of the buyer that the source and origin of the trademark symbols were in plaintiffs satisfies the requirement of the Act. The argument that confusion must be as to the source of the manufacture of the emblem itself is unpersuasive, where the trademark, originated by the team, is the triggering mechanism for the sale of the emblem.

* * *

ADDITIONAL DEFENSES TO RELIEF

Defendant makes two arguments against an extension of Lanham Act protection to plaintiffs which need consideration. Adopting the district court's rationale, defendant asserts first, that plaintiffs' marks when embroidered on emblems for wearing apparel are functional and thus serve no trademark purpose and, second, that there is some overriding concept of free competition which, under the instant facts, would remove plaintiffs from the protective ambits of the Lanham Act.

The short answer to defendant's arguments is that the emblems sold because they bore the identifiable trademarks of plaintiffs. This fact clearly distinguishes the case from *Pagliero v. Wallace China Co.*, 198 F.2d 339 (9th Cir.1952), relied upon by the district court. *Pagliero* involved designs on chinaware which were neither trademarked, patented nor copyrighted. The court found no unfair competition on the ground that the designs were functional, that is, they connoted other than a trademark purpose. "The attractiveness and eye-appeal of the design sells the china," 198 F.2d at 343–344, not the trademark character of the designs. In the case at bar, the embroidered symbols are sold not because of any such aesthetic characteristic but because they are the trademarks of the hockey teams. Those cases which involved utilitarian articles such as pole lamps, *Sears, Roebuck & Co. v. Stiffel Co.*, 376 U.S. 225 (1964), fluorescent lighting fixtures, *Compco Corp. v. Day–Brite Lighting, Inc.*, 376 U.S. 234 (1964), and toggle clamps, *West Point Mfg. Co. v. Detroit Stamping Co.*, 222 F.2d 581, 105 U.S.P.Q. (BNA) 200 (6th Cir.1955), all involved products which had a consumer demand regardless of their source or origin. The principles involved in those cases are not applicable to a trademark symbol case where the design or symbol has no demonstrated value other than its significance as the trademark of a hockey team.

The argument that the symbols could be protected only if copyrighted likewise misses the thrust of trademark protection. A trademark is a property right which is acquired by use. *Trade-Mark Cases*, 100 U.S. 82 (1879). It differs substantially from a copyright, in both its legal genesis and its scope of federal protection. The legal cornerstone for the protection of copyrights is Article I, section 8, clause 8 of the Constitution. In the case of a copyright, an individual creates a unique design and, because the Constitutional fathers saw fit to encourage creativity, he can secure a copyright for his creation for a period of 28 years, renewable once. After the expiration of the copyright, his creation becomes part of the public domain. In the case of a trademark, however, the process is reversed. An individual selects a word or design that might otherwise be in the public domain to represent his business or product. If that word or design comes to symbolize his product or business in the public mind, the individual acquires a property right in the mark. The acquisition of such a right through use represents the passage of a word or design out of the public domain into the protective ambits of trademark law. Under the provisions of the Lanham Act, the owner of a mark acquires a protectable property interest in his mark through registration and use.

The time limit on copyright protection not being sufficient for plaintiffs' purposes, they acquainted the public with their marks and thereby created a demand for those marks. Through extensive use, plaintiffs have acquired a property right in their marks which extends to the reproduction and sale of those marks as embroidered patches for wearing apparel. What plaintiffs have acquired by use, the substantive law of trademarks as it is embodied in the Lanham Act will protect against infringement. There is no overriding policy of free competition which would remove plaintiffs, under the facts of this case, from the protective ambits of the Lanham Act.

* * *

Reversed and remanded.

Boston Hockey produced a major and still controversial expansion in the scope of trademark law, especially in contrast with the decision in *Pagliero v. Wallace China*, 198 F.2d 339 (9th Cir.1952), which had adopted the "aesthetic functionality" trademark defense for use of another product's colors and design. Indeed, in *International Order of Job's Daughters v. Lindeburg*, 633 F.2d 912 (9th Cir.1980), the Ninth Circuit reiterated its *Pagliero* precedent in preference to *Boston Hockey*, while denying relief to an organization whose decorative insignia were being reproduced and sold on the defendant's jewelry. A variety of decisions have appeared since then in the sports context (compare *NFL Properties v. Wichita Falls Sportswear*, 532 F.Supp. 651 (W.D.Wash. 1982), with *University of Pittsburgh v. Champion Products*, 566 F.Supp. 711 (W.D.Pa.1983)), as well as in the entertainment industry (see the interesting judicial back-and-forth in *Warner Bros. v. Gay Toys*, 513 F.Supp. 1066 (S.D.N.Y.1981); 658 F.2d 76 (2d Cir.1981); 553 F.Supp. 1018 (S.D.N.Y.1983); and 724 F.2d 327 (2d Cir.1983)), about whether a toymaker could adorn its cars with the same orange color and confederate flag roof as had marked the General Lee automobile in the television hit *The Dukes of Hazzard*).

There is no better illustration of the legal ambiguity in this branch of intellectual property law than a pair of encounters the First Circuit has had with the Boston Marathon. Since 1897, the Boston Marathon has been run annually on Patriots Day from Hopkinton to Boston, under the auspices of the non-profit Boston Athletic Association (BAA). The first case, *BAA v. Sullivan*, 867 F.2d 22 (1st Cir.1989), involved a Hopkinton clothing distributor and retailer who, beginning in 1978, sold T-shirts depicting the event (e.g., "1978 Boston Marathon") along with pictures of runners and the words Hopkinton–Boston. Not only did the BAA not object to this practice, but in 1985 it bought at a discount a large quantity of shirts to give away to runners and volunteers in that year's event.

However, after becoming conscious of the financial prospects from merchandise licensing, for the 1987 race the BAA sold to another producer an exclusive license to use the Boston Marathon name on shirts and other apparel. When the Hopkinton firms continued to sell their brand of shirts, the BAA and its licensee sued to block this action. Though the district court dismissed the complaint on the grounds that there was no evidence of "colorable confusion" between the competing T-shirts, the First Circuit panel reversed. While acknowledging "that a trademark, unlike a copyright or patent, is not a 'right in gross' that enables a holder to enjoin all reproduction," the court asserted that "when a manufacturer intentionally uses another's mark as a means of establishing a link in consumers' minds with the other's enterprise, and directly profits from that link, there is an unmistakable aura of deception." In this case,

> [g]iven the undisputed facts that (1) defendants intentionally referred to the Boston Marathon on its shirts, and (2) purchasers were likely to buy the shirts precisely because of that reference, we think it fair to presume that purchasers are likely to be confused about the shirt's source or sponsorship. We presume that, at the least, a sufficient number of purchasers would be likely to assume—mistakenly—that defendant's shirts had some connection with the official sponsors of the Boston Marathon. In the absence of any evidence that effectively rebuts this presumption of a "likelihood of confusion," we hold that plaintiffs are entitled to enjoin the manufacture and sale of defendant's shirts.

867 F.2d at 34.

Emboldened by this legal success, the BAA formally registered the words "Boston Marathon" in connection with the race and expanded its marketing efforts to generate more funds for enhancing the quality of the event. One such agreement was an exclusive license given to WBZ–TV, the local Channel 4 station, to telecast the race. Nevertheless, WCVB–TV, Channel 5 in Boston, continued to televise the race with cameras in helicopters and along the marathon route, and regularly used the phrase Boston Marathon before, during, and after its unauthorized telecast. The BAA went back to court, relying not on the *Pittsburgh Athletic* case, but on trademark law as interpreted in *Sullivan*. Following is the First Circuit's second treatment of this issue.

WCVB–TV v. BOSTON ATHLETIC ASS'N

United States Court of Appeals, First Circuit, 1991.
926 F.2d 42.

BREYER, CHIEF JUDGE.

* * *

[The Court initially noted the "likelihood of confusion" standard for trademark infringement cases.]

* * *

Obviously, we do not have before us the common, garden variety type of "confusion" that might arise with typical trademark infringement. This is not a heartland trademark case, where, for example, plaintiff uses the words "Big Tom" to mark his apple juice, defendant (perhaps a big man called Tom) uses the same words (or perhaps similar words, e.g., "Large Tommy") on his own apple juice label, and plaintiff says customers will confuse defendant's apple juice with his own. See, e.g., *Beer Nuts, Inc. v. Clover Club Foods Co.*, 805 F.2d 920 (10th Cir.1986) ("Beer Nuts" and "Brew Nuts" confusingly similar); 2 J. McCarthy § 23.3 at 56 ("Cases where a defendant uses an identical mark on competitive goods hardly ever find their way into the appellate reports . . . [and] are 'open and shut'. . . . "). No one here says that Channel 5 is running its own marathon on Patriot's Day, which a viewer might confuse with the BAA's famous Boston Marathon.

Rather, BAA argues that the confusion here involved is somewhat special. It points to cases where a defendant uses a plaintiff's trademark in connection with a different type of good or service and a plaintiff claims that the public will wrongly, and confusedly, think that the defendant's product somehow has the plaintiff's official "O.K." or imprimatur. The Eleventh Circuit, for example, found trademark law violated when the defendant, without authorization, used the plaintiff's football team mark, a bulldog, not in connection with a different football team, but, rather, on his beer mugs. See *University of Georgia Athletic Ass'n v. Laite*, 756 F.2d 1535 (11th Cir.1985). This circuit has found trademark law violated, when the defendant, without authorization, used this very appellant's foot race mark, "Boston Marathon," on his t-shirts, sold during the event, permitting the customer to wrongly or confusedly think that his t-shirts were somehow "official." See *Boston Athletic Ass'n v. Sullivan*, 867 F.2d 22 (1st Cir.1989). BAA goes on to say that Channel 5's use of those words will lead viewers, wrongly, and confusedly, to believe that Channel 5 (like the t-shirt seller) has a BAA license or permission or authorization to use the words, i.e., that it broadcasts with the BAA's official imprimatur. It also notes that this court, in *Sullivan*, listed circumstances that create a "rebuttable presumption" of confusion. And, it quotes language from *Sullivan*, in which this court, citing *International News Service v. Associated Press*, 248 U.S. 215 (1918), said that the defendant's t-shirts were "clearly designed to take advantage of the Boston Marathon and to benefit from the good will associated with its promotion by plaintiffs," and that defendants obtained a "free ride" at the plaintiffs' expense; they "reap where [they have] not sown." *Sullivan*, 867 F.2d at 33. Appellants say that Channel 5 is doing the same here.

In our view, the cases BAA cites, and *Sullivan* in particular, do not govern the outcome of this case. Nor can we find a likelihood of any relevant confusion here. First, the *Sullivan* opinion, taken as a whole, makes clear that the court, in using the language appellants cite, referring to a "free ride," and taking "advantage" of another's good will, did not intend to depart from ordinary principles of federal trademark law that make a finding of a "likelihood of confusion" essential to a conclusion of "violation." As a general matter, the law sometimes protects investors from the "free riding" of others; and sometimes it does not. The law, for example, gives inventors a "property right" in certain inventions for a limited period of time; see 35 U.S.C. §§ 101 et seq.; it provides copyright protection for authors; see 17 U.S.C. §§ 101 et seq.; it offers certain protections to trade secrets. See generally 2 J. McCarthy § 29.16. But, the man who clears a swamp, the developer of a neighborhood, the academic scientist, the school teacher, and millions of others, each day create "value" (over and above what they are paid) that the law permits others to receive without charge. Just how, when and where the law should protect investments in "intangible" benefits or goods is a matter that legislators typically debate, embodying the results in specific statutes, or that common law courts, carefully weighing relevant competing interests, gradually work out over time. The trademark statute does not give the appellants any "property right" in their mark except "the right to prevent confusion." And, nothing in *Sullivan* suggests the contrary.

Second, the "rebuttable presumption" of confusion that this court set forth in *Sullivan* does not apply here. We concede that the *Sullivan* court said that "there is a rebuttable presumption" of confusion "about the shirts' source or sponsorship" arising from the fact that the defendants used the words "Boston Marathon" on the shirts, which use made customers more likely to buy the shirts. The court wrote that when a manufacturer intentionally uses another's mark as a means of establishing a link in consumers' minds with the other's enterprise, and directly profits from that link, there is an unmistakable aura of deception. *Sullivan*, 867 F.2d at 35. As we read these words, they mean that the *Sullivan* record indicated that the defendant wanted to give the impression that his t-shirt was an "official" t-shirt, a fact that, in the sports world, might give a shirt, in the eyes of sports fans, a special "cachet." It makes sense to presume confusion about a relevant matter (namely,

454 SPORTS BROADCASTING, MERCHANDISING, ETC. Ch. 6

official sponsorship) from such an intent, at least in the absence of contrary evidence.

Here, however, there is no persuasive evidence of any intent to use the words "Boston Marathon" to suggest official sponsorship of Channel 5's broadcasts. To the contrary, Channel 5 offered to "broadcast whatever disclaimers" the BAA might want—"every thirty seconds, every two minutes, every ten minutes"—to make certain no one thought the channel had any special broadcasting status. Nor is there any evidence that Channel 5 might somehow profit from viewers' wrongly thinking that the BAA had authorized its broadcasts. Indeed, one would ordinarily believe that television viewers (unlike sports fans who might want to buy an official t-shirt with the name of a favorite event, team or player) wish to see the event and do not particularly care about the relation of station to event-promoter.

Third, and perhaps most importantly, the record provides us with an excellent reason for thinking that Channel 5's use of the words "Boston Marathon" would not confuse the typical Channel 5 viewer. That reason consists of the fact that those words do more than call attention to Channel 5's program; they also describe the event that Channel 5 will broadcast. Common sense suggests (consistent with the record here) that a viewer who sees those words flash upon the screen will believe simply that Channel 5 will show, or is showing, or has shown, the marathon, not that Channel 5 has some special approval from the BAA to do so. In technical trademark jargon, the use of words for descriptive purposes is called a "fair use," and the law usually permits it even if the words themselves also constitute a trademark. If, for example, a t-shirt maker placed the words "Pure Cotton" (instead of the words "Boston Marathon") on his t-shirts merely to describe the material from which the shirts were made, not even a shirt maker who had a registered trademark called "Pure Cotton" could likely enjoin their sale. As Justice Holmes pointed out many years ago, "when the mark is used in a way that does not deceive the public we see no such sanctity in the word as to prevent its being used to tell the truth." *Prestonettes Inc. v. Coty*, 264 U.S. 359, 368.

This is not a case where it is difficult to decide whether a defendant is using particular words primarily as a mark, i.e., as an "attention getting symbol," or primarily as a description. Here there is little in the record before us to suggest the former (only the large size of the words on the screen); while there is much to show the latter (timing, meaning, context, intent, and surrounding circumstances). Consequently, the appellants have shown no real likelihood of relevant confusion.

We also note that the only federal court which has decided a case nearly identical to the one before us, a case in which a station planning to televise a public parade was sued by the parade's promoter who had granted "exclusive" rights to another station, reached a conclusion similar to the one we draw here. See *Production Contractors, Inc. v. WGN Continental Broadcasting Co.*, 622 F.Supp. 1500, 1504 (N.D.Ill.

1985). Reviewing the promoter's Lanham Act claim that the "unauthorized" broadcast would create a "false impression" of sponsorship, the court concluded that it fell "far short of establishing likelihood of confusion" among viewers that the defendant station was the "official" or "authorized" broadcaster of the parade. Similarly, we do not see how Channel 5's broadcast could likely confuse viewers that it bore the imprimatur of the BAA.

* * *

Affirmed.

Questions For Discussion

1. Are there differences in the doctrinal approaches used by the First Circuit panels in the two *Boston Marathon* cases? Between the First Circuit and the Fifth Circuit's decision in *Boston Hockey*? As a tangible test, what would have been the First Circuit's response if Sullivan had followed the suggestion of the district court in *Boston Hockey* and added to its T-shirt label the notation "*Not* sponsored or authorized by the BAA?"

2. Even given the *Boston Hockey* enforcement of a quasi-property right in a team's name and label, there remain issues about precisely when that right has been infringed. Consider the following sports examples:

(a) Despite their move across the Hudson River to the Meadowlands in New Jersey, the NFL Giants retained their identity as the New York Giants. A decade later, a company began selling a line of sportswear with the inscription New Jersey GIANTS and the Giants' team colors. With that product proving especially popular among New Jersey fans of the Giants, NFL Properties filed suit. What should be the result? See *NFL Properties v. New Jersey Giants*, 637 F.Supp. 507 (D.N.J.1986).

(b) One of the distinctive and popular features of games in the American Basketball Association (ABA) was the red, white, and blue basketball introduced by its commissioner (and former NBA great), George Mikan. A sporting goods company, AMF–Voit, began producing and selling red, white, and blue basketballs, without either the ABA's name or license. Is that a trademark violation? See *ABA v. AMF Voit*, 358 F.Supp. 981 (S.D.N.Y.1973), aff'd w/o opinion, 487 F.2d 1393 (2d Cir.1973).

(c) For nearly a century, the United States Golf Association (USGA) has developed and maintained a golf handicap system, based on a player's pattern of scores adjusted for the degree of difficulty of the courses: this permitted players of different skill levels to compete on an equal basis. In 1980, Data–Max, d/b/a St. Andrews Systems, developed a computer system and telephone subscription service which, using the USGA formula, allowed golfers to receive "instant handicaps" as they entered new scores, even if they were not members of USGA-affiliated golf clubs. Does Data-Max's administration and advertisement of that service with the USGA handicap formula violate USGA's trademark rights? See *USGA v. St. Andrews Systems, Data–Max*, 749 F.2d 1028 (3d Cir.1984).

3. Are there certain uses of a party's mark which, even if they do not induce consumer confusion, might serve to disparage and misappropriate its value? One possible example is the Delaware State Lottery contest noted earlier, involving the weekly results in NFL games. (See *NFL v. Governor of Delaware*, 435 F.Supp. 1372 (D.Del.1977).) An even more egregious example involved the X-rated film *Debbie Does Dallas*, featuring a high school cheerleader engaging in sex acts while wearing a uniform strikingly similar to the well-known uniforms of the Dallas Cowgirl cheerleaders. Though the actress who played Debbie had never been a Dallas cheerleader, movie advertisements included such captions as "Starring ex-Dallas Cowgirl Cheerleader, Bambi Woods," and "You'll do more than cheer for this X–Dallas Cheerleader." Should this be held to violate not just the Cowboys' feelings, but also their trademark (with or without the advertising captions)? Should the answer turn on whether Pussycat Cinema (or the Delaware State Lottery) makes it clear that the NFL is *not* authorizing their venture? See *Dallas Cowboys Cheerleaders v. Pussycat Cinema*, 604 F.2d 200 (2d Cir. 1979).

Whatever the legal outcome of this doctrinal difference across the circuits, there is a real question about whether it makes a significant practical difference in the level of protection enjoyed by entertainment firms. Even circuit courts that apply the *Job's Daughters* (rather than the *Boston Hockey*) formulation, one that requires tangible proof of consumer confusion, are likely to receive considerable survey evidence that the latter has occurred. The reality is that, because of the current blend of legal action and industry reaction, a large part of the consuming public probably does believe that the products they are buying with merchandising names and symbols carry the authorization of the parties that created those names and symbols. On the other hand, if the law were to make it clear that any manufacturer could sell clothing with the Dallas Cowboys or Chicago Bulls name and logo on it, as long as the item carried a specific disclaimer, customers would not assume that any such product carried the *imprimatur* of the Cowboys, the Bulls, and their respective leagues. The question is which way should the law seek to shape consumer perceptions.

In a little-noticed move "inside the Beltway" in late 1995, Congress made a potentially significant change to this aspect of trademark law. The Federal Trademark Dilution Act of 1995 amended § 43 of the existing Lanham Act to grant the "owner of a *famous work*" injunctive relief (and on occasion damages) if others used its mark in ways that "cause *dilution* of the distinctive quality of the mark." The factors listed by new § 43(c) as determining whether or not a mark has become "famous" include the mark's degree of distinctiveness, the duration and extent of its use in connection with particular products and in geographic areas and trading channels, the mark's degree of recognition, and whether or not the mark had been officially registered. Section 45's new definition of "dilution" states that this is the "lessening of the capacity of a famous mark to identify and distinguish goods and services," regardless of any "likelihood of confusion, mistake, or deception."[i]

The very limited explanations offered by members of Congress for this potentially major expansion in the scope of federal trademark law is that this would be helpful to the government in securing better enforcement of famous American marks (like Coca Cola) in foreign countries, many of which have anti-dilution laws on their books and apparently object to the absence of such protection of their own marks under American law. As it turns out, approximately 25 states had previously adopted different versions of the anti-dilution principle in their legislation (which is not preempted by the Lanham Act). A recent case, *Hormel Foods Corp. v. Jim Henson Productions,* 73 F.3d 497 (2d Cir.1996) (an unsuccessful effort by Hormel to block the naming of a character Spa'am in the movie *Muppet Treasure Island*), explores the concept of "dilution" as a form of "blurring" or "tarnishing" of a trade name.

Questions For Discussion

1. In appraising the desirability for sports of such an expanded scope to federal trademark law, consider first the situation of teams and leagues. Should they be entitled to the same exclusive property rights in their names and symbols as are now given to athletes by the law of publicity rights? Even if the user of the performer's name and likeness makes it clear that its product or advertisement does not carry the performer's endorsement, this caveat will not constitute a defense to a publicity rights suit. Are there tangible distinctions between the interests of athletes as persons and teams as business entities that warrant any difference in legal treatment?

2. Consider now the interests of sports fans. Suppose that there are a large number of consumers in the sports market who would like to wear a shirt or cap with their favorite team's logo on it, but do not much care whether this is an "official" product—at least do not care enough to want to add the team's five to ten percent licensing fee to the purchase price of the merchandise. Should the law deny fans this informed choice in a competitive marketplace in order to ensure that hundreds of millions of dollars a year in licensing fees continue to be channelled to sports leagues? What affirmative social values are served by such a legal regime?

3. The Congress has actually made one (and only one) focused judgment on this score. In the Amateur Sports Act of 1978, Congress gave the U.S. Olympic Committee an explicit statutory right to prohibit commercial and promotional uses of the USOC emblem, the five interlocking rings symbolic of the Olympic Games, and the words Olympic or Olympiad, irrespective of consumer confusion about their use. In *San Francisco Arts & Athletics v. USOC,* 483 U.S. 522 (1987), a closely-divided Supreme Court

---

[i]. For an in-depth analysis of the underlying questions posed by this concept, see Simone A. Rose, *Will Atlas Shrug? Dilution Protection for "Famous" Trademarks: Anti-Competitive "Monopoly" or Earned "Property" Right,* 47 Florida L. Rev. 653 (1995).

upheld the constitutionality of the USOC using this legislation to block the staging of a Gay Olympic Games in 1982. Do you feel the Court might have decided the case differently if the USOC had sought to block the staging of a Special Olympics for the disabled? Why do you think Congress passed this law? What are your views about the merits of the legislation and its use? (For the 1996 Games in Atlanta, the USOC sold corporate sponsorships for $40 million apiece, and raised $650 million in total sponsorship and licensing fees.)[j] About its implications for the broader question of the proper interpretation of the Lanham Act (as well as state laws) with respect to sports marketing generally?

One final and intriguing note about this issue. In February 1995, Major League Baseball was in the midst of the longest labor relations dispute in sports history. This was one of the key reasons why MLB merchandising sales, which had soared from $1.5 billion in 1990 to $2.8 billion in 1993, were projected to drop to $2.1 billion in 1995. Then came another move by baseball owners that did *not* add to their popularity among fans: indeed, a USA Today editorial on the subject was titled "Baseball's Kid–Gougers."

What happened was that MLB Properties took action to block Little League players from using on their uniforms the names of major league teams such as Yankees or Dodgers. The estimated cost of licenses for uniform manufacturers was approximately $6.00 for each uniform worn by the nearly 2.5 million Little League players across the country. Counsel for MLB Properties said this action had to be taken to protect the teams' trademarks in order to avoid losing them under federal law; that it was the uniform manufacturers, not the Little Leagues, that paid the licensing fees; and that the commissioner's office was donating $1 million a year to youth baseball. Dave Montgomery, CEO of the Philadelphia Phillies and member of the MLB Properties board, said it was also crucial to protect the standards and quality of major league products: if someone wanted to use the name Phillies for a fictional baseball team in a movie, Montgomery wanted to be able to see the script to avoid licensing an offensive product.

Consider this case from the point of view of trademark law. Should a Little League team (or a movie producer) need the consent of Major League Baseball to use the team name Phillies (not Philadelphia Phillies)? How do you think Justice Breyer or Chief Judge Posner would analyze this type of case (before and after passage of the Trademark Dilution Act)?

E. GROUP MARKETING OF INTELLECTUAL PROPERTY RIGHTS

As we noted at the outset of this chapter, revenues from sports broadcasting and merchandising have soared over the last two decades.

---

[j] See Stephen M. McKelvey, *Atlanta 96: Olympic Countdown to Ambush Armageddon*, 4 Seton Hall L. J. 397 (1994).

The immediate source of those financial gains has been the increasing fan appetite for watching games at home while wearing a shirt and cap adorned with the logos of their favorite teams. The background source is a legal system that gives clubs an exclusive property right in their team's broadcasts and names. Another crucial legal feature is the ability of teams to come together to sell a single package of broadcasting and marketing rights to the highest bidder.

A key policy issue is whether these legal arrangements are in the best interests of fans of the sport and consumers of products advertised during game broadcasts or emblazoned with team logos. League-wide controls over the sale of television rights have been the principal setting for the legal debate about the compatibility of such licensing packages with antitrust law's commitment to a competitive consumer market. That crucial aspect of sports broadcasting law will be explored in the next chapter, which addresses a range of antitrust problems presented by league constraints upon *owners*. Here we shall briefly consider the antitrust issues presented by collective sales of merchandising rights, because this involves not only league sales of owner trademark rights, but also player association sales of athlete publicity rights.

This became a big issue in the fall of 1995. NFL Properties was then earning over $200 million in licensing fees from the sale of merchandise with club names and logos on it. That money was used to pay the league's operating costs and then divided equally among team owners. Jerry Jones, owner of the Dallas Cowboys, complained publicly about the fact that while the Cowboys—"America's Team"—accounted for 30% of total NFL merchandise sales, he received only one-thirtieth of the licensing revenues. Jones felt that, as an individual team-owner, if he had the right to market the Cowboys name and logo, he would be able to expand total Cowboys' sales and (needless to say) keep a lot more of the financial returns for himself. There was, however, little likelihood that Jones could persuade three quarters of his fellow owners to change the NFL rules as he wanted. Not only would such intra-league competition exacerbate revenue disparities between more popular and less popular teams, but it might well reduce the NFL's overall revenue from much larger merchandise sales.

Jones, however, figured out a way to do an end run on these NFL rules. He signed contracts with Pepsi, Nike, and American Express that licensed their use of the name, "Texas Stadium, the home of the Cowboys." Not only did these deals upset Jones' fellow owners, but also Coca Cola, Reebok, and Visa, which had paid NFL Properties handsomely for what they thought was the exclusive right to exploit the Cowboys' identity. Commissioner Paul Tagliabue filed a $300 million lawsuit against Jones for allegedly having violated the Cowboys' contractual commitment to assign to NFL Properties the sole right to market the team's name, logo, and goodwill. Jones defended the contracts claim on the grounds that the identity of Texas Stadium was qualitatively different from that of the Cowboys. He also filed a $750 million antitrust countersuit, contending that, when the league owners (including the earlier Cowboys owner Clint Murchison) had pooled all their teams' trademark rights in an entity called the NFL Trust, this constituted an illegal cartel under § 1 of the Sherman Act.

By early 1997, both Jones and Tagliabue had decided that it was in their respective best interests to settle their dispute on terms that allowed Jones to continue his deals between Texas Stadium and its licensees. This left open the substantive antitrust issue and the more fundamental policy question whether sports fans—the consumers whose welfare is supposed to be protected by both trademark and antitrust law—are being helped or harmed by league merchandising regimes that require all clubs to pool their trademark rights into an exclusive group licensing arm. Ironically, the only antitrust decisions that have been rendered in this area have involved players associations, bodies that engage in *nonexclusive* group marketing of their members' publicity rights. (There is no question that Michael Jordan, Dennis Rodman, Greg Norman, Tiger Woods, and other celebrity stars do compete against each other as individuals in this market.) And while the principal such suits have been lodged against the Major League Baseball Players Association, no court has ever mentioned baseball's antitrust exemption in this context.

As we saw earlier in this chapter, baseball—in particular, baseball player cards—were actually the occasion for judicial creation of a property-like publicity right for any kind of celebrity: see *Haelan Laboratories v. Topps Chewing Gum*, 202 F.2d 866 (2d Cir.1953). For decades, Topps Chewing Gum had dominated this market. For five dollars apiece, it signed up young players as they entered the minor leagues to a contract that gave Topps the exclusive right to use the player's name and likeness on cards that were sold alone or in combination with chewing gum or candy. This right was triggered when the player reached the major leagues and lasted for five years, at $125 a year. Topps then renewed the contracts for another small payment as they neared expiry.

Two things began to happen in the mid–1960s. One was that baseball cards' popularity and sales were rising. The other was that Marvin Miller was turning the MLBPA into a real union, one that needed an independent source of funding that the leagues would no longer supply. When Miller asked Topps for an increase in the players' returns from the cards bearing their names, pictures, and statistics, Topps declined, pointing to the contractual rights they had already secured. Miller went back to the players and persuaded all of those whose contracts were expiring not to sign for renewal. When Topps realized that soon it would no longer have all the players on its card roster, it agreed to Miller's request for payment to the Association (for per capita distribution to the players) of royalties amounting to ten percent of card sales. Topps was not prepared, though, to change from an exclusive to a non-exclusive license for its market. (By the way, the reason why baseball cards were originally sold with gum or candy was to give Topps access to candy counters in stores: after a period of consumer experience with chewing its gum, Topps decided that its best marketing strategy was to sell the cards alone, which it had the exclusive player's license to do.) That license was upheld against antitrust attacks by Topps' competitors: see *Fleer Corp. v. Topps Chewing Gum*, 658 F.2d 139 (3d Cir.1981).

Over the next 15 years, the MLBPA's marketing arm did negotiate non-exclusive group licensing arrangements with companies like Fleer, Leaf–Duncuss, and others to sell player names and pictures along with "premium" products such as stamps, games, puzzles, trivia cards and the like. (By the mid–1990s, total MLBPA marketing revenues had reached $70 million a year.) Finally, in the early 1980s, the Association set out again to turn Topps' license in its important market niche into a non-exclusive one. Once more, a key tactic was a concerted refusal by players to renew their individual contract licenses as they expired. This took the form of a modification of the MLBPA's Commercial Authorization Agreement with its members, whereby the players authorized only the Association to market their publicity rights on a group basis and agreed not to renew any existing contracts that were inconsistent with this. The stated purpose of this new MLBPA rule was to "enhance the Association's ability to negotiate a new agreement with Topps and others."

This time Topps responded with an antitrust suit, claiming violations of both §§ 1 and 2 of the Sherman Act. Following are the judge's reactions to both sides' motions for summary judgment in the case.

TOPPS CHEWING GUM v. MAJOR LEAGUE BASEBALL PLAYERS ASS'N.

United States District Court, Southern District of New York, 1986.
641 F.Supp. 1179.

CONNER, DISTRICT JUDGE.

* * *

The Supreme Court has long held that certain concerted refusals to deal or group boycotts are so likely to restrict competition without any offsetting efficiency gains that they fall within the category of per se violations of section 1.... Topps contends that the MLBPA has instigated such a group boycott and has therefore committed a per se violation of the Sherman Act.

However, while group boycotts are often listed among the categories of economic arrangements that merit per se invalidation under section 1, "[e]xactly what types of activity fall within the forbidden category is ... far from certain." *Northwest Wholesale Stationers, Inc. v. Pacific Stationery & Printing*, 472 U.S. 284, 294 (1985). Accordingly, the task of determining whether certain concerted activity is per se illegal is not always an easy one.

In *Smith v. Pro Football, Inc.*, 593 F.2d 1173 (D.C.Cir.1978), the Court of Appeals for the District of Columbia Circuit provided helpful instruction on this difficult question. The court stated:

> The classic "group boycott" is a concerted attempt by a group of competitors at one level to protect themselves from competition from non-group members who seek to compete at that level. Typically, the boycotting group combines to deprive would-be competitors of a trade relationship which they need in order to enter (or survive in) the level wherein the group operates. The group may accomplish its exclusionary purpose by inducing suppliers not to sell to potential competitors, by inducing customers not to buy from them, or, in some cases, by refusing to deal with would-be competitors themselves. In each instance, however, the hallmark of the "group boycott" is the effort of competitors to "barricade themselves from competition at their own level." It is this purpose to exclude competition that has characterized the Supreme Court's decisions invoking the group boycott per se rule.

Id. at 1178.

An examination of the leading Supreme Court cases bears out the court's analysis. For example, in *United States v. General Motors Corp.*, 384 U.S. 127 (1966), the Supreme Court found the *per se* rule applicable where some retail dealers of General Motors automobiles agreed with each other and with General Motors not to sell cars to competing discount dealers. The Court found that "[w]hat resulted was a fabric interwoven by many strands of joint action to eliminate the discounters from participation in the market." Similarly, in *Klor's, Inc. v. Broadway–Hale Stores, Inc.*, 359 U.S. 207 (1959), the Court used the per se rule where a large retail seller of appliances induced manufacturers and distributors of such products not to sell to a competing retailer. The Court stated that the alleged combination took from the plaintiff "its freedom to buy appliances in an open competitive market and drives it out of business as a dealer in the defendants' products." Finally, in *Fashion Originators' Guild of America, Inc. v. FTC*, 312 U.S. 457 (1941), the Court applied the per se rule where certain manufacturers of clothing agreed with each other not to sell their products to retailers who also purchased garments made by competing "design pirate" manufacturers. The Court stated that this combination was an attempt to exclude from the industry those manufacturers and distributors who did not conform to the rules established by the defendants.

The instant case differs from these classic cases in a number of important respects. First, in most of these cases the parties to the agreement were competitors of each other. This is a critical element. The per se rule is not applicable to boycotts that do not involve agreements among competitors. In this case, Topps does not and could not contend that the parties to the alleged boycott, the MLBPA and the major league baseball players, are in any sense competitors with each other.

Second, as noted above, in a classic group boycott, a group of businesses combine to exclude other competitors or potential competitors from their level of the market. Topps certainly does not compete with major league baseball players for the players' publicity rights. Topps merely purchases the rights from the players.

Topps contends, however, that it competes with the MLBPA for the players' publicity rights, and that the MLBPA has instigated the boycott in order to exclude Topps from the market except on those terms the MLBPA dictates. In light of facts set forth above, there can be little doubt that Topps and MLBPA are indeed engaged in a struggle for control of the players' rights. However, it is far from clear that Topps and the MLBPA compete economically at the same level of the market. Topps purchases the rights from the players and uses them in producing and marketing its products. Thus, it is a consumer of the rights. The MLBPA, on the other hand, does not purchase the rights from the players, and does not manufacture or market any products itself. It acts as an agent for the players in licensing manufacturers or distributors of products to use the rights. Thus, the MLBPA is more analogous to a wholesale distributor of the rights. Accordingly, it does not appear to function at the same level in the market as Topps.

Finally, a classic group boycott involves a type of arrangement that is so clearly and consistently anticompetitive that it is inherently illegal. As the Supreme Court stated recently, "[t]he decision to apply the per se rule turns on 'whether the practice facially appears to be one that would always or almost always tend to restrict competition and decrease output.'" *Northwest Wholesale Stationers*, 472 U.S. at 295, (quoting *Broadcast Music, Inc. v. Columbia Broadcasting Sys.*, 441 U.S. 1, 19–20 (1979)). I am not persuaded that the arrangement between the MLBPA and the players is one that clearly restricts competition. In fact, the MLBPA has made a strong argument that the arrangement will enhance competition for players' publicity rights for use on a group basis.

Because Topps has for many years managed to secure exclusive long-term licenses from nearly all minor and major league baseball players to use their photographs on trading cards sold alone or in combination with gum or candy, other companies have not been able to acquire similar licenses. Topps has by all appearances acquired its licenses by hard work and perseverance, and should not now be punished for having been successful in its competitive efforts. See, e.g., *United States v. Aluminum Co. of Am.*, 148 F.2d 416, 430 (2d Cir.1945). Nonetheless, Topps' competitors are desirous of an opportunity to acquire the rights Topps holds. Topps contends that its competitors can acquire the rights in the same way Topps does—by soliciting ballplayers when they enter the minor leagues. But Topps' competitors have indicated that they are unwilling to do so since that course "would be too expensive, would take too long, and would have too little chance of success." Thus, there is currently little competition for the rights Topps acquires through its player contracts.

However, under the arrangement created by the players and the MLBPA, the tremendous expense, inefficiency, and risk in acquiring the full bundle of rights necessary to market a complete set of baseball trading cards is eliminated. A company interested in acquiring players' publicity rights would not have to solicit a contract from every individual who becomes a professional baseball player. Instead, Topps and its competitors could purchase the necessary grants from a single agent for all of the major league players. Topps' competitors apparently find this an appealing prospect, and would bid against Topps and each other for the rights Topps now acquires with little serious competition. Topps complains that this may drive up the price of the rights. But that is the natural consequence of increased competition for a limited supply of goods, and is not a ground for concluding that the arrangement between the players and the Players Association is necessarily illegal per se.

In view of the important differences between classic group boycotts and the arrangement at issue here, I conclude that *per se* treatment is inappropriate.

* * *

The first issue in any rule of reason analysis is to define the relevant market in which the competitive impact of the defendant's actions are to be examined. The parties here have devoted little attention to this question, and to the extent they have addressed it, they disagree. The MLBPA appears to claim that the relevant market is that of publicity rights for all athletes and performers, whereas Topps contends that it is the market for the publicity rights of major league baseball players for use on a group basis. Thus, there is a disputed issue of material fact that precludes summary judgment.

Another issue in the rule of reason calculus is the intent underlying the defendant's acts. Here the MLBPA claims that its intent is to increase competition in the bidding for players' publicity rights, whereas Topps contends that the Players Association intends to obtain monopoly power over those rights. Again, this is a disputed issue of fact. Finally, rule of reason analysis looks to the effects of the defendant's acts on the relevant market. The MLBPA claims that its acts are procompetitive, while Topps asserts that it is being improperly foreclosed from competing for players' publicity rights. This is yet another question of fact. Summary judgment is obviously unavailable in these circumstances.

[For essentially the same reasons the judge dismissed the motions for summary judgment on the § 2 "monopolization" charge, and directed trials on both issues.]

* * *

Summary judgment denied.

The litigation was settled by the parties before trial, thus leaving unresolved the key legal issues posed by the case. The settlement did, however, produce a major change in the Topps-MLBPA-players relationship. Topps continued to sign individual baseball players to card licensing agreements. However, these agreements were pursuant to a new uniform contract that Topps worked out with the MLBPA, and the Association served as its members' agent for collecting and distributing their licensing fees. And under the current Topps–MLBPA contract, Topps no longer has the exclusive license to sell baseball cards.

Questions For Discussion

1. Suppose the *Topps* case had gone to trial: how would you have ruled on the antitrust rule of reason issues? Should the MLB Players Association have enjoyed antitrust immunity under either the *Flood* baseball exemption or the statutory labor exemption that we read about in Chapters 2 and 3 respectively?

2. Change the fact-situation so that the MLBPA had made itself the sole agent for all its player-members' licensing rights, and that the Association had refused to renew the contract with Topps because another card manufacturer (e.g., Fleers) was offering a large premium for an exclusive baseball cards contract. Would these hypothetical variations on the actual scenario have exposed the Association to a *per se* antitrust violation? To a much stronger rule of reason challenge?

Recall the 1995 dispute between Jerry Jones of the Cowboys and his fellow NFL owners regarding individual club versus League-wide merchandising ventures. A similar controversy was seeded in baseball in early 1997 when George Steinbrenner and his Yankees signed a $95 million sponsorship contract with Adidas. This deal promised the Yankees a far larger amount than its share of a $325 million proposal that Nike and Reebok had together offered Major League Baseball Enterprises for sponsorship of the entire League (and which Steinbrenner and a number of other owners had blocked because they felt it was too small). The general wording of the Yankees–Adidas contract was carefully framed so as not to appear to infringe upon MLB Enterprise's or Properties' exclusive authority over national and international merchandising and promotion deals. However, the Executive Council judged that the sale inside Yankee Stadium of T-shirts bearing both the Yankees and Adidas logos did not come within the Yankees autonomy in its "Home Licensing Territory." In addition, the Council insisted that the Yankees–Adidas contract must include a "subservience clause" that would subject it to any future changes in the owners Agency Agreement regarding MLB Enterprise's or Properties' authority (changes that could be adopted by a three-quarters owner majority, and thence be binding on the Yankees). For these and a number of other reasons, the Yankees and Adidas partnership filed a preemptive lawsuit in Steinbrenner's home city of Tampa, Florida, claiming that the entire MLB merchandising system violates both federal and Florida state law. Ironically, Steinbrenner's lawyer David Boies then had to leave his long-time law firm Cravath, Swaine, and Moore in New York, because Cravath's biggest client, Time Warner, had recently become the owner of the Atlanta Braves (and Hawks) when it bought Ted Turner's entertainment and sports enterprises.

Suppose that league owners in baseball or football (or other sports) were to adopt and enforce rules that blocked any loopholes in their merchandising programs that would permit "cherry-picking" by a few big-market and/or big-name teams, which might sharply reduce the ability of NFL or MLB Properties to negotiate valuable league-wide packages with sports footwear or other product companies that value a sports connection. Should Jerry Jones have been able to win his suit against his fellow NFL owners under antitrust law? Should Steinbrenner be able to sue MLB in the face of the special *Flood* baseball exemption from antitrust? Should the Little Leagues (or their uniform manufacturers) be able to sue MLB owners (including Steinbrenner) for their having insisted on a trademark license to use team names such as the Yankees? The special challenge posed to antitrust law from these and a host of other league arrangements and conflicts are the subject of the following chapter.

Chapter Seven

FRANCHISE, LEAGUE, AND COMMUNITY

In the next two chapters we shall undertake a detailed examination of how the law treats the relationship between clubs and their league.[a] The significance of this inquiry can be seen in the economic trends in sports over the last few decades. As most sports fans know, average player salaries have soared—in baseball, for example from $19,000 in 1967 to $1.3 million in 1997, and in football from $25,000 in 1967 to $800,000 in 1997. Despite such spiraling player costs, baseball and football franchises that sold for approximately $7 million in 1967 were selling for well over $200 million thirty years later.

Recognition of these financial trends is important for two reasons. First, although a more favorable legal environment has enabled players to secure a larger share of the game's revenues—player salaries have gone up somewhat more than franchise prices—the lion's share of salary increases is attributable to increases in the game's revenues that also enlarge ownership profits. Sports over the past few decades serves as an apt illustration of what the eminent British economist Alfred Marshall called the first "law" of labor economics: the employer's demand for labor is derived from the consumer's demand for the goods and services produced by that labor.

---

a. There has been a good deal of scholarly commentary in law reviews about the legal issues raised in these chapters, and we shall provide citations at the appropriate points in the text. Here we refer the reader to several valuable book-length treatments of the personalities and the economics in the background to the legal disputes: David Harris, *The League: The Rise and Decline of the NFL* (New York: Bantam Books, 1986); James Edward Miller, *The Baseball Business: Pursuing Pennants and Profits in Baltimore* (Chapel Hill, N.C.: University of North Carolina Press, 1990); Andrew Zimbalist, *Baseball and Billions* (New York: Basic Books, 1992); James Quirk and Rodney D. Fort, *Pay Dirt: The Business of Professional Team Sports* (Princeton, N.J.: Princeton U. Press, 1992); Eric M. Leifer, *Making the Majors: The Transformation of Team Sports in America* (Cambridge, Mass: Harvard U. Press, 1995); Michael N. Danielson, *Home Team: Professional Sports and the American Metropolis* (Princeton, N.J.: Princeton U. Press, 1997); and Roger C. Noll and Andrew Zimbalist, eds., *Sports, Jobs, & Taxes: The Economic Impact of Sports, Teams, and Stadiums* (New York: Brookings Inst. Press, 1997).

The second reason why we must be conscious of this explosion in team values—of the fact, for example, that the NHL charged $2 million for an expansion franchise in 1967 and $80 million in 1997—is because the law has left its imprint on that economic trend as well. The next two chapters explore the legal structure of sports ownership, both within a league and between leagues, and how this structure influences franchise values and the amount of revenue teams and leagues extract from fans who attend the games, broadcasters and advertisers that televise the games, merchandisers that draw upon the team's names and logos that are seen in the games, and communities that subsidize the facilities in which the games are played.

A. NATURE OF THE LEAGUE: A PRELIMINARY LOOK

Chapter 1 provided a glimpse of the distinctive structure of the sports league.[b] In each of the four historically "major" sports, the dominant league rests upon an elaborate contractual agreement among all the member teams—its "constitution." Each owner is given both a franchise which the team runs in its (usually) exclusive territory and a vote in the governance of the league. Through its governing bodies, the league in turn develops by-laws and rules that define the rights and obligations of all participants in the enterprise—in particular, the division of revenues from gate receipts, television contracts, and marketing of the league and team names. At the apex of this structure is a commissioner who wields broad authority to determine and enforce "the best interests of the sport," including adjudication of disputes between league participants. Illustrative of the latter role is baseball Commissioner Fay Vincent's ruling in the summer of 1991, in connection with the National League's expansion into Miami and Denver, about what proportion of the players would be contributed and expansion fees received by American League and National League clubs, respectively.

As we saw in Chapter 1, when objections are launched against the commissioner's formulation of the league's "best interests," courts have generally displayed a deferential attitude towards decisions reached through internal league councils. Courts have exhibited a much different legal posture, however, when attacks are launched against the underlying validity of the league contract—particularly challenges under antitrust law. As we saw in Chapter 3's depiction of antitrust litigation in

b. Besides several of the books cited in note a, analyses of the special economic features of sports leagues can be found in Walter C. Neale, *The Peculiar Economics of Professional Sports: A Contribution to the Theory of the Firm in Sporting Competition and in Market Competition*, 78 Quarterly J. of Econ. 1 (1964); James Quirk & Mohammed El Hodiri, "The Economic Theory of a Professional Sports League," Chapter 1 of Roger Noll, ed., *Government and the Sports Business* (Washington, D.C.: Brookings, 1974); Henry G. Demmert, *The Economics of Professional Team Sports* (Lexington, Mass.: D.C. Heath, 1973); George G. Daly, "The Baseball Player's Labor Market Revisited," Chapter 1 of Paul M. Sommers, ed., *Diamonds Are Forever: The Business of Baseball* (Washington, D.C.: Brookings, 1992); and John Vrooman, *A General Theory of Professional Sports Leagues*, 61 So. Econ. J. 971 (1995).

the players' market, there are two potential bases for legal attacks under the Sherman Antitrust Act: § 1, which bars any "contract, combination, or conspiracy ... in restraint of trade," and § 2, which bars any effort to "monopolize or attempt to monopolize" a market. In turn, three different types of challengers may surface against league practices. One group consists of third parties attempting to deal with the existing league, such as players, fans, stadiums, aspiring club owners, and television networks. The second group includes team owners who may oppose a rule or policy of their league. The third type of challenger is a new league trying to develop and maintain itself as a viable competitor to the established league. This chapter considers how the law has treated the first two groups (except for players, who were the subject of Chapter 3); the next chapter examines the third.

Chapter 3 gave a detailed picture of the manner in which § 1 of the Sherman Act enabled courts to strike down league restraints on the players market. This chapter takes another look at the antitrust "rule of reason"—here as applied to league decisions about team ownership, franchise locations, and television policies. In this setting we will also focus on a crucial legal issue that underlies all § 1 sports litigation within both the product and the labor markets. Does a sports league consist of a collection of distinct and economically competitive clubs who have come together to cooperate in some aspects of otherwise autonomous businesses—akin to NUMMI Motors, formed by General Motors and Toyota? Or is a sports league more aptly treated as a single integrated entity, analogous to a national law firm with partners based in several cities, which is thus incapable of *conspiracy* in restraint of trade when it establishes its internal operating rules and structure?[c] Logically, the "single entity" defense was potentially available against the antitrust suits by players and their associations in the 1970s.

---

c. Except for the labor exemption issue studied in Chapter 3, the "single entity" issue has produced more scholarly debate than any other question in sports law. The issue was first explored in a series of articles in the early 1980s. Compare Myron C. Grauer, *Recognition of the National Football League as a Single Entity Under Section 1 of the Sherman Act: Implications of the Consumer Welfare Model*, 82 Michigan L. Rev. 1 (1983); Gary R. Roberts, *Sports Leagues and the Sherman Act: The Use and Abuse of Section 1 to Regulate Restraints on Intraleague Rivalry*, 32 UCLA L. Rev. 219 (1984); John C. Weistart, *League Control of Market Opportunities: A Perspective on Competition and Cooperation in the Sports Industry*, 1984 Duke L. J. 1013 (all arguing for single entity treatment in most if not all sports settings); Daniel E. Lazaroff, *The Antitrust Implications of Franchise Relocation Restrictions in Professional Sports*, 53 Fordham L. Rev. 1157 (1984) (arguing against the single entity theory); and Gary R. Roberts, *The Single Entity Status of Sports Leagues Under Section 1 of the Sherman Act: An Alternative View*, 60 Tulane L. Rev. 562 (1986) (rebutting Lazaroff). A second round took place at the end of the 1980s. See Daniel E. Lazaroff, *Antitrust and Sports Leagues: Re-Examining the Threshold Questions*, 20 Arizona State L. J. 953 (1988) (against); Lee Goldman, *Sports, Antitrust, and the Single Entity Theory*, 63 Tulane L. Rev. 751 (1989) (against); Myron C. Grauer, *The Use and Misuse of the Term "Consumer Welfare": Once More to the Mat on the Issue of Single Entity Status for Sports Leagues Under Section 1 of the Sherman Act*, 64 Tulane L. Rev. 71 (1989) (in favor); Gary R. Roberts, *The Antitrust Status of Sports Leagues Revisited*, 64 Tulane L. Rev. 17 (1989) (in favor); and Michael S. Jacobs, *Professional Sports Leagues, Antitrust, and the Single-Entity Theory: A Defense of the Status Quo*, 67 Indiana L. J. 25 (1991) (against).

However, the argument was not seriously advanced by league defendants until the early 1980s, in response to § 1 antitrust suits brought by individual owners who objected to particular decisions made by their own leagues, under constitutions to which the plaintiffs themselves were parties. The basic premises to this argument were (i) that the athletic product offered by each league in the broader sports and entertainment market was jointly created by the league members who were inherently incapable of producing anything of value independently of their league; and (ii) that while each team *competed athletically* on the field in order to produce an attractive league product, they *cooperated economically* as partners within a joint venture through which they collectively created and owned the business assets of the league.

The first skirmish in this legal war over league authority versus club autonomy arose out of a 1970s dispute between the NFL and two of its club owners, Lamar Hunt of the Kansas City Chiefs and Joe Robbie of the Miami Dolphins, over the ownership by Hunt and by Robbie's wife of teams in a new North American Soccer League (NASL), the Dallas Tornadoes and Ft. Lauderdale Strikers, respectively. The NFL had long had a policy against NFL owners, team CEOs, or their immediate family members owning interests in teams in competing leagues. Under pressure from Max Winter, owner of the Minnesota Vikings, and Leonard Tose of the Philadelphia Eagles, whose clubs were facing substantial competition from NASL teams in their home cities, the NFL threatened to turn this policy into a formal rule that would force the Hunt and Robbie families to divest themselves of their NASL franchises. In terms of antitrust policy, this league restriction would have had its major impact (if any) on competition between the NFL and other professional sports leagues. However, NASL (including Hunt and Robbie) framed its legal challenge to the NFL's cross-ownership ban under § 1 of the Sherman Act. The NFL argued, and the trial court agreed, that no § 1 recourse was available against league rules that were adopted by the partners in a single league entity. In the first appellate court ruling on the "single entity" defense, the Second Circuit, in *NASL v. NFL*, 670 F.2d 1249 (2d Cir.1982), rejected it.

> ... Although NFL members ... participate jointly in many of the operations conducted by [the league] on their behalf, each member is a separately owned, discrete legal entity which does not share its expenses, capital expenditures or profits with other members. Each also derives separate revenues from certain lesser sources, which are not shared with other members, including revenues from local TV and radio, parking and concessions. A member's gate receipts varies from those of other members, depending on the size of the home city, the popularity of professional football in the area and competition for spectators offered by other entertainment, including professional soccer. As a result, profits vary from team to team.... Thus, in spite of sharing of some revenues, the financial performance of each team, while related to that of the others, does not, because of the variables in revenues and costs as between

member teams, necessarily rise or fall with that of the others. The NFL teams are separate economic entities engaged in a joint venture.

670 F.2d at 1252.

* * *

The characterization of the NFL as a single economic entity does not exempt from the Sherman Act an agreement between its members to restrain competition. To tolerate such a loophole would permit league members to escape antitrust responsibility for any restraint entered into by them that would benefit their league or enhance their ability to compete even though the benefit would be outweighed by its anticompetitive effects. Moreover, the restraint might be one adopted more for the protection of individual league members from competition than to help the league.... The sound and more just procedure is to judge the legality of such restraints according to well-recognized standards of our antitrust laws rather than permit their exemption on the ground that since they in some measure strengthen the league competitively as a "single economic entity," the combination's anticompetitive effects must be disregarded.

670 F.2d at 1257.

Because *NASL v. NFL* was only the first salvo in a long string of battles involving this fundamental issue of what a sports league is for § 1 purposes, and because it predates the landmark Supreme Court ruling in *Copperweld Corp. v. Independence Tube Corp.*, 467 U.S. 752 (1984), about what distinguishes a single entity from multiple firms, the value of this case is merely to frame the issue. At this early point in the analysis, which side seems to have the better of the argument? Is the Second Circuit correct that a joint venture rule prohibiting its partners from investing in competing businesses should be judged under antitrust law as to whether the benefits to the joint venture outweigh the injury to other businesses in which the venture's partners might invest? Keep this question in mind when you read the Second Circuit's opinion (and Justice Rehnquist's dissent from the Supreme Court's denial of certiorari) on the "rule of reason" issue in *NASL v. NFL* in the next part of this chapter.

Because the arguments on both sides of the single entity issue also directly relate to whether the specific rule being challenged meets the rule of reason test, the single entity and restraint of trade issues tend to become intertwined and blurred, making it difficult to analyze and consider either in isolation. Thus, as each of the three major areas of league governance that have come under § 1 attack are explored in this chapter—rules about team ownership, franchise location, and television and merchandising contracts—keep in mind the implications of the arguments and judicial opinions for both the single entity and rule of reason issues.

B. FRANCHISE OWNERSHIP RULES

The MLB, NBA, and NHL have no restrictions on the owners of their teams also owning franchises in other leagues. Such cross-ownership is in fact quite common: e.g., Atlanta's baseball Braves, and basketball Hawks (as well as an NHL expansion team) are all owned by Time Warner, Inc. (which acquired them in its merger with Ted Turner's broader entertainment enterprise); Chicago's baseball White Sox and basketball Bulls are owned by Jerry Reinsdorf; New York's basketball Knicks and hockey Rangers belong to Cablevision; Washington's basketball Wizards and hockey Capitols belong to Abe Pollin; Philadelphia's basketball 76ers and hockey Flyers are owned by Comcast; and baseball's Arizona Diamondbacks and hockey's Phoenix Coyotes are owned by Jerry Colangelo. However, as noted above, the NFL had a longstanding unwritten policy against any of its owners or their immediate family owning an interest in a team in another league. The validity of that league restraint under antitrust rule of reason was analyzed by the Second Circuit in the *NASL* lawsuit described earlier.

NASL v. NFL

United States Court of Appeals, Second Circuit, 1982.
670 F.2d 1249.

MANSFIELD, CIRCUIT JUDGE.

* * *

Because of the economic interdependence of major league team owners and the requirement that any sale be approved by a majority of the league members, an owner may in practice sell his franchise only to a relatively narrow group of eligible purchasers, not to any financier. The potential investor must measure up to a profile having certain characteristics. Moreover, on the supply side of the sports capital market the number of investors willing to purchase an interest in a franchise is sharply limited by the high risk, the need for active involvement in management, the significant exposure to publicity that may turn out to be negative, and the dependence on the drawing power and financial success of the other members of the league. The record thus reveals a market which, while not limited to existing or potential major sports team owners, is relatively limited in scope and is only a small fraction of the total capital funds market. The evidence further reveals that in this sports capital and skill market, owners of major professional sports teams constitute a significant portion. Indeed the existence of such a submarket and the importance of the function of existing team owners as sources of capital in that market are implicitly recognized by the defendants' proven intent in adopting the cross-ownership ban. If they believed, as NFL now argues, that all sources of capital were fungible substitutes for investment in NASL sports teams and that the ban would not significantly foreclose the supply of sports capital, they would hardly have gone to the trouble of adopting it.

Unless the ban has procompetitive effects outweighing its clear restraint on competition, therefore, it is prohibited by § 1 of the Sherman Act. That law does not require proof of the precise boundaries of the sports capital market or the exact percentage foreclosed; it is sufficient to establish, as was done here, the general outlines of a separate submarket of the capital market and that the foreclosed portion of it was likely to be significant.

NFL argues that the anticompetitive effects of the ban would be outweighed by various procompetitive effects. First it contends that the ban assures it of the undivided loyalty of its team owners in competing effectively against the NASL in the sale of tickets and broadcasting rights, and that cross-ownership might lead NFL cross-owners to soften their demands in favor of their NASL team interests. We do not question the importance of obtaining the loyalty of partners in promoting a common business venture, even if this may have some anticompetitive effect. But in the undisputed circumstances here the enormous financial success of the NFL league despite long-existing cross-ownership by some members of NASL teams demonstrates that there is no market necessity or threat of disloyalty by cross-owners which would justify the ban. Moreover, the NFL was required to come forward with proof that any legitimate purposes could not be achieved through less restrictive means. This it has failed to do. The NFL, for instance, has shown no reason why it could not remedy any conflict of interest arising out of NFL–NASL competition for broadcast rights by removing cross-owners from its broadcast rights negotiating committee.

For the same reasons we reject NFL's argument that the ban is necessary to prevent disclosure by NFL cross-owners of confidential information to NASL competitors. No evidence of the type of information characterized as "confidential" is supplied. Nor is there any showing that the NFL could not be protected against unauthorized disclosure by less restrictive means. Indeed, despite the existence of NFL cross-owners for some years there is no evidence that they have abused confidentiality or that the NFL has found it necessary to adopt confidentiality rules or sanctions. Similarly, there is no evidence that cross-ownership has subjected the personnel and resources of NFL cross-owners to conflicting or excessive demands. On the contrary, successful NFL team owners have been involved in ownership and operation of other outside businesses despite their equal potential for demands on the owners' time and resources. Moreover, a ban on cross-ownership would not insure that NFL team owners would devote any greater level of their resources to team operations than they otherwise would.

Reversed.

Interestingly, in his dissent from the Supreme Court's refusal to review this ruling, Justice Rehnquist took issue with precisely that last feature of the Second Circuit's decision.

The NFL owners are joint venturers who produce a product, professional football, which competes with other sports and other forms of entertainment in the entertainment market. Although individual NFL teams compete with one another on the playing field, they rarely compete in the marketplace. The NFL negotiates its television contracts, for example, in a single block. The revenues from broadcast rights are pooled. Indeed, the only interteam competition occurs when two teams are located in one major city, such as New York or Los Angeles. These teams compete with one another for home game attendance and local broadcast revenues. In all other respects, the league competes as a unit against other forms of entertainment.

This arrangement, like the arrangement in *Broadcast Music, Inc. v. Columbia Broadcasting System*, Inc., 441 U.S. 1 (1979), is largely a matter of necessity. If the teams were entirely independent, there could be no consistency of staffing, rules, equipment, or training. All of these are at least arguably necessary to permit the league to create an appealing product in the entertainment market. Thus, NFL football is a different product from what the NFL teams could offer independently, and the NFL, like ASCAP, is "not really a joint sales agency offering the individual goods of many sellers, but is a separate seller offering its [product], of which the individual [teams] are raw material. [The NFL], in short, made a market in which individual [teams] are inherently unable to compete fully effectively."

The cross-ownership rule, then, is a covenant by joint venturers who produce a single product not to compete with one another. The rule governing such agreements was set out over 80 years ago by Judge (later Chief Justice) Taft: A covenant not to compete is valid if "it is merely ancillary to the main purpose of a lawful contract, and necessary to protect the covenantee in the enjoyment of the legitimate fruits of the contract, or to protect him from the dangers of an unjust use of those fruits by the other party." *United States v. Addyston Pipe and Steel Co.*, 85 F. 271, 281 (6th Cir.1898), *aff'd as modified*, 175 U.S. 211 (1899).

The cross-ownership rule seems to me to meet this test. Its purposes are to minimize disputes among the owners and to prevent some owners from using the benefits of their association with the joint venture to compete against it. Participation in the league gives the owner the benefit of detailed knowledge about market conditions for professional sports, the strength and weaknesses of the other teams in the league, and the methods his co-venturers use to compete in the marketplace. It is only reasonable that the owners would seek to prevent their fellows from giving these significant assets, which are in some respects analogous to trade secrets, to their competitors.

The courts have not, to my knowledge, prohibited businesses from requiring employees to agree not to compete with their employer while they remain employed. I cannot believe the Court of Appeals would expect a law firm to countenance its partners working part time at a competing firm while remaining partners. Indeed, this Court has noted that the Rule of Reason does not prohibit a seller of a business from contracting not to compete with the buyer in a reasonable geographic area for a reasonable time *after* he has terminated his relationship with the business. It is difficult for me to understand why the cross-ownership rule is not valid under this standard.

The anticompetitive element of the restraint, as found by the Court of Appeals, is that competitors are denied access to "sports capital and skill." In defining this market, the Court of Appeals noted that although capital is fungible, the skills of successful sports entrepreneurs are not. This entrepreneurial skill, however, is precisely what each NFL owner, as co-venturer, contributes to every other owner.

* * *

In any event, it seems to me that the cross-ownership rule was narrowly drawn to vindicate the legitimate interests described above. The owners are limited only in areas where the special knowledge and skills provided by their co-owners can be expected to be of significant value. They are not prohibited from competing with the NFL in areas of the entertainment market other than professional sports. An owner may invest in television movies, rock concerts, plays, or anything else that suits his fancy.

NFL v. NASL, 459 U.S. 1074, 1077–80 (1982). Does Justice Rehnquist's reasoning change your mind about the appeals court's judgment on this score? Is consumer welfare (i.e., the price, quantity, and quality of the goods and services provided to the consuming public)—which now is the primary, if not the exclusive, goal of antitrust law—likely to be enhanced or diminished by the Second Circuit's decision?

Notwithstanding its above legal victory, the NASL suffered a fatal financial defeat in the sports marketplace in the early 1980s. However, following a very successful World Cup that took place in the United States in 1994, the new Major League Soccer (MLS) began play in 1996. Two of the key investors in this new venture are the NFL Chiefs' Lamar Hunt, with his Kansas City Wizards and Columbus Crew, and the NFL Patriots' Robert Kraft, with his New England Revolution. Understandably, the NFL did not seek to reargue the validity of its cross-ownership ban in this setting. However, in 1997, the NFL owners did pass a resolution reaffirming their previous ban on cross-ownership, which had read:

No person owning a majority interest in, or in direct or indirect operational control of, a member club may acquire any interest in another major team sport.

This time the resolution (by a 24–5 vote, with the Raiders' Al Davis abstaining) expressly carved out exceptions for NFL owners whose franchises in another league are either in the same city as their NFL team, or in a city that did not have any NFL team in its market. Thus, NFL owners are now only precluded from owning teams in a competing league if those other teams are in cities where somebody else's NFL team is located.

These exceptions were created to resolve two specific controversies confronting the league. The first arose in 1993 when the NFL's Miami Dolphins were sold by the family of Joe Robbie (which was forced to sell the team in order to pay the estate taxes due on it) to Wayne Huizenga, who already owned the baseball Florida Marlins and hockey Florida Panthers. The NFL owners tentatively approved that sale in 1994, but only on condition that Huizenga put the Dolphins' stock in trust for two years, after which he would comply with whatever cross-ownership policy the league had in place in June 1996. Motivated at least in part by fear of an antitrust suit by Huizenga if the league tried to make him sell either the Dolphins or his other two Miami-based teams, the first of the above exceptions now allows Huizenga to keep all of his teams as long as they remain in Miami. The second troublesome situation took place in 1996 when Paul Allen, owner of the NBA's Portland Trail Blazers (and also a large shareholder of Microsoft) was considering the purchase of the NFL's Seattle Seahawks. Allen's acquisition of the Seahawks would help resolve the economic and political difficulties the Seahawks were facing in Seattle and its Kingdome, as well as the tension between current owner Kenneth Behring and the league which arose from his aborted attempt in early 1996 to move the Seahawks to Los Angeles over Commissioner Paul Tagliabue's opposition. The second cross-ownership exception, which now allows NFL owners to have another league's team in a market where no NFL team is located, allowed Allen to move forward and buy the Seahawks from Behring.

Questions for Discussion

1. What lessons do the new exceptions to the NFL's cross-ownership ban teach us about the underlying reasons for this league restraint? Suppose that Huizenga were to relocate his hockey Panthers to another city, e.g., Atlanta, where the NFL Falcons are located. Or an NFL team other than Paul Allen's Seahawks were to relocate to Portland where Allen has his NBA Trail Blazers. If the NFL then stepped in to enforce its cross-ownership ban against Huizenga or Allen, would this more narrowly-targeted rule strengthen or weaken the "rule of reason" antitrust challenge to the league policy? What variables does *NASL* allow a court to consider in determining whether application of a cross-ownership restriction is lawful under the rule of reason? Are these distinctions sensible as a matter of antitrust policy?

2. Does the NFL's current iteration of the cross-ownership ban apply to NFL owners who have ownership interests in *minor* league teams in other sports? Arguably, the language of the previously unpublished resolution applied only to ownership of other major league teams. However, in 1993, when New Orleans Saints owner Tom Benson tried to purchase the Charlotte Knights of the Class AA Southern League and move it to New Orleans, Benson and Commissioner Tagliabue worked out an arrangement whereby Benson would be allowed to own the baseball team only upon condition that it play in New Orleans (a deal consistent with the exception later formalized in 1997). Does any underlying policy for the cross-ownership ban justify extending the ban to minor league teams? If so, would that policy also justify extending the ban to any other types of business interests, either sports or non-sports related? Interestingly, after the Denver Zephyrs of the Class AAA American Association moved to New Orleans in order to leave Denver vacant for the Major League expansion team, the Colorado Rockies, the Zephyrs blocked the lower-classification Knights from moving to New Orleans, and thus Benson was forced to abandon his efforts to buy the Knights. He then filed an antitrust suit in New Orleans against the National Association of Professional Baseball Leagues (the Minor Leagues) for its rule that gave the Zephyrs territorial exclusivity and the right to bump lower-classification teams out of the market. This suit, which was quickly dismissed by District Judge Martin Feldman who relied on the *Federal Baseball* exemption, presumably was filed without the knowledge or consent of Benson's fellow NFL owners.

3. Abstracting from the external legal questions, what are the pros and cons of a ban on cross-ownership from the point of view of the league itself? Unlike the NFL, the other three major sports leagues have welcomed owners from other leagues and sports. If you were the commissioner of a sports league, what policy would you advocate on this score, and why? Is the public interest enhanced or diminished by a ban on sports cross-ownership?

The NFL, again unlike other sports leagues, has also long had an unwritten policy against any NFL franchise being owned by publicly-traded corporations. (The Green Bay Packers, which has always been a not-for-profit corporation owned by citizens of Green Bay, Wisconsin, is a grandfathered exception to this league policy.) The mechanism for enforcement of this NFL rule has been the requirement that three-quarters of the clubs must approve any change in ownership of a team.

In 1987, New England Patriots owner Billy Sullivan sought to alleviate his financial distress by putting up 49% of the team in a public stock offering. The Sullivan family's financial troubles were attributable in large part to Michael Jackson's "Victory Tour" which inflicted huge losses on Billy's son, Charles "Chuck" Sullivan, the Tour's underwriter and owner of the stadium in which the Patriots played. The idea for a Patriots' stock offering came from the remarkable success enjoyed by the Boston Celtics when that team fashioned a similar limited partnership venture in 1986. However, allegedly because the NFL rule precluded public ownership, Sullivan decided in October 1988 to sell the Patriots (for $84 million) to a limited partnership largely owned by Victor Kiam. Then, when Kiam sold the Patriots to James Orthwein in 1992 for approximately $110 million, Sullivan sued the NFL for damages under the Sherman Act, claiming that absent the NFL's policy against public ownership he would have been able to retain the controlling interest in a rapidly-appreciating football asset, instead of having to sell it at a depressed price to private buyers. After a trial in December 1993, the jury awarded Sullivan $38 million in damages, which the trial judge remitted to $17 million, before trebling. The NFL appealed the verdict to the First Circuit, which rendered its first-ever sports antitrust decision.

SULLIVAN v. NATIONAL FOOTBALL LEAGUE

United States Court of Appeals, First Circuit, 1994.
34 F.3d 1091.

TORRUELLA, CIRCUIT JUDGE.

* * *

III. ISSUES ALLEGEDLY REQUIRING JUDGMENT FOR THE NFL

A. Lack of Antitrust Injury

To establish an antitrust violation under § 1 of the Sherman Act, Sullivan must prove that the NFL's public ownership policy is "in restraint of trade." Under antitrust law's "rule of reason," the NFL's policy is in restraint of trade if the anticompetitive effects of the policy outweigh the policy's legitimate business justifications. Anticompetitive effects, more commonly referred to as "injury to competition" or "harm to the competitive process," are usually measured by a reduction in output and an increase in prices in the relevant market. Injury to competition has also been described more generally in terms of decreased efficiency in the marketplace which negatively impacts consumers. Thus, an action harms the competitive process "when it obstructs the achievement of competition's basic goals—lower prices, better products, and more efficient production methods." *Town of Concord v. Boston Edison Co.*, 915 F.2d 17, 22 (1st Cir.1990).

The jury determined in this case, via a special verdict form, that the relevant market is the "nationwide market for the sale and purchase of ownership interests in the National Football League member clubs, in general, and in the New England Patriots, in particular." The jury went on to find that the NFL's policy had an "actual harmful effect" on competition in this market.

The NFL argues on appeal that Sullivan has not established the existence of any injury to competition, and thus has not established a restraint of trade that can be attributed to the NFL's ownership policy. The league's attack is two-fold, asserting (1) that NFL clubs do not compete with each other for the sale of ownership interests in their teams so there exists no competition to be injured in the first place; and (2) Sullivan did not present sufficient evidence of injury to competition from which a reasonable jury could conclude that the NFL's policy restrains trade. Although we agree with the NFL that conceptualizing the harm to competition in this case is rather difficult, precedent and deference to the jury verdict ultimately require us to reject the NFL's challenge to the finding of injury to competition.

Critically, the NFL does not challenge on appeal the jury's initial finding of the relevant market and no corresponding challenge was raised at trial.... The NFL nevertheless maintains that NFL teams do not compete against each other for the sale of their ownership interests, even if we accept that a market exists for such ownership interests.

1. *No Competition Subject to Injury as Matter of Law*

The NFL correctly points out that member clubs must cooperate in a variety of ways, and may do so lawfully, in order to make the football league a success. On the other hand, it is well established that NFL clubs also compete with each other, both on and off the field, for things like fan support, players, coaches, ticket sales, local broadcast revenues, and the sale of team paraphernalia. The question of whether competition exists between NFL teams for sale of their ownership interests, such that the NFL's ownership policy injures this competition, is ultimately a question of fact. The NFL would have us find, however, that, as a matter of law, NFL teams do not compete against each other for the sale of their ownership interests. We decline to make such a finding.

The NFL relies on a series of cases which allegedly stand for the "well established" rule that a professional sports league's restrictions on who may join the league or acquire an interest in a member club do not give rise to a claim under the antitrust laws. *Seattle Totems Hockey Club, Inc. v. National Hockey League*, 783 F.2d 1347 (9th Cir.1986); *Fishman v. Estate of Wirtz*, 807 F.2d 520 (7th Cir.1986); *Mid-South Grizzlies v. National Football League*, 720 F.2d 772, at 772 (3d Cir.1983); *Levin v. National Basketball Ass'n*, 385 F.Supp. 149 (S.D.N.Y.1974). These cases, all involving a professional sport's league's refusal to approve individual transfers of team ownership or the creation of new teams, do not stand for the broad proposition that no NFL ownership policy can injure competition. See, e.g., *North American Soccer League v. National Football League*, 670 F.2d 1249, 1259–61 (2d Cir.1982) (finding that the NFL's policy against cross-ownership of NFL teams and franchises in competing sports leagues, which also effectively barred certain owners who owned other sports franchises from purchasing NFL teams, injured competition between the NFL and competing sports leagues and thus violated § 1 of the Sherman Act).

None of the cases cited by the NFL considered the particular relevant market that was found by the jury in this case or a league policy against public ownership. *Seattle Totems* and *Mid-South Grizzlies* considered potential inter-league competition when a sports league rejected plaintiffs' applications for new league franchises. Those decisions found no injury to competition because the plaintiffs were not competing with the defendant sports leagues, but rather were seeking to join those leagues. *Mid-South Grizzlies* left open the possibility that potential intraleague competition between NFL football clubs could be harmed by the NFL's action, but found that the plaintiff in that case had not presented sufficient evidence of harm to such competition.

The *Fishman* and *Levin* cases concerned the National Basketball Association's ("NBA") rejection of plaintiffs' attempts to buy an existing team. Those cases also based their finding that there was no injury to competition on the fact that the plaintiffs were seeking to join with, rather than compete against, the NBA. Neither case considered whether competition between teams for investment capital was injured.

The important distinction to make between the cases cited by the NFL and the present case is that here Sullivan alleges that the NFL's policy against public ownership generally restricts competition between clubs for the sale of their ownership interests, whereas in the aforementioned cases, a league's refusal to approve a given sale transaction or a new team merely prevented particular outsiders from joining the league, but did not limit competition between the teams themselves. To put it another way, the NFL's public ownership policy allegedly does not merely prevent the replacement of one club owner with another—an action having little evident effect on competition—it compromises the entire process by which competition for club ownership occurs.

* * *

2. *Insufficient Evidence of Harm to Competition*

The NFL contends that Sullivan did not present sufficient evidence concerning: (1) the existence of competition between NFL clubs for the sale of ownership interests, or (2) a decrease in output, an increase in prices, a detrimental effect on efficiency or other incidents of harm to competition in the relevant market, from which a reasonable jury could conclude that the NFL's policy injured competition. Although we agree that the evidence of all these factors is rather thin, we disagree that the evidence is too thin to support a jury verdict in Sullivan's favor.

With respect to evidence of the existence of competition for the sale of ownership interests, one of Sullivan's experts, Professor Roger Noll, testified that "one of the ways in which the NFL exercises monopoly power in the market for the franchises and ownership is by excluding certain people from owning all or part—any type part of an NFL franchise." Dr. Noll explained that this "enables a group of owners, in this case, you only need eight owners, to exclude from the League and from competing with them, people who might be more effective competitors than they are." The record also contains statements from several NFL owners which could reasonably be interpreted as expressions of concern about their ability to compete with other teams in the market for investment capital in general, and for the sale of ownership interests in particular. For example, Arthur Rooney II of the Pittsburgh Steelers stated in a letter that he did not "believe that the individually or family owned teams will be able to compete with the consolidated groups."

Ralph Wilson of the Buffalo Bills stated that big corporations should not own teams because it gives them an "unfair competitive advantage" over other teams since corporations will funnel money into the team and make it "more competitive" than the other franchises. Former NFL Commissioner Pete Rozelle admitted that similar sentiments had been expressed by NFL members.

Although it is not precisely clear that the "competition" about which Noll, Rooney, and Wilson were discussing is the same competition at issue here—that is competition for the sale of ownership interests—a jury could reasonably interpret these statements as expressing a belief that the competition exists between teams for the sale of ownership interests. The statements of the two NFL owners imply that greater access to capital for all teams will put increased pressure on some teams to compete with others for that capital, and all the statements reveal that the ownership rules, particularly the rule against public ownership, are the main obstacle preventing such access. The fact that ownership by "consolidated groups" is not necessarily the same as public ownership does not affect the conclusion that teams face competitive pressure in selling their ownership interests generally to whoever might buy them. We also note that evidence of actual, present competition is not necessary as long as the evidence shows that the potential for competition exists. It would be difficult indeed to provide direct evidence of competition when the NFL effectively prohibits it.

* * *

The record also contains sufficient evidence of the normal incidents of injury to competition from the NFL's policy—reduced output, increased prices, and reduced efficiency—to support the jury's verdict. As Dr. Noll pointed out in his testimony, the NFL's policy "excludes individuals ... who might want to own a share of stock in a professional football team." Several NFL officials themselves admitted that the policy restricts the market for investment capital among NFL teams. There is thus little dispute that the NFL's ownership policy reduces the available output of ownership interests.

The NFL is correct that, in one sense, the overall pool of potential output is fixed because there are only 28 NFL teams and, although their value may fluctuate, the quantity of their ownership interests cannot. However, the NFL's public ownership policy completely wipes out a certain type of ownership interest—public ownership of stock. By restricting output in one form of ownership, the NFL is thereby reducing the output of ownership interests overall. In other words, the NFL is literally restricting the output of a product—a share in an NFL team.

There was considerable testimony concerning the price effects of the NFL policy. Both of Sullivan's experts testified that the policy depressed the price of ownership interests in NFL teams because NFL franchises would normally command a premium on the public market relative to their value in the private market, which is all that the league currently permits. Professor Noll testified that fan loyalty would push up the price of ownership interests if sales to the public were allowed. Even former Commissioner Pete Rozelle acknowledged that "it was pointed out, with justification, it has been over the years, that [the ownership policy] does restrict your market and, very likely, the price you could get for one of our franchises if you wanted to sell it, because you are eliminating a very broad market.... And they have said that there is a depression on the price they could get for their franchise."

The NFL points out that the alleged effect of its ownership policy is to reduce prices of NFL team ownership interests, rather than to raise prices which is normally the measure of an injury to competition. E.g., *Town of Concord*, 915 F.2d at 22. We acknowledge that it is not clear whether, absent some sort of dumping or predatory pricing, see, e.g., *Monahan's Marine, Inc. v. Boston Whaler, Inc.*, 866 F.2d 525, 527 (1st Cir.1989), a decrease in prices can indicate injury to competition in a relevant market. The Supreme Court has emphasized, however, that overall consumer preferences in setting output and prices is more important than higher prices and lower output, per se, in determining whether there has been an injury to competition. *NCAA v. Board of Regents*, 468 U.S. 85, 107 (1984). In this case, regardless of the exact price effects of the NFL's policy, the overall market effects of the policy are plainly unresponsive to consumer demand for ownership interests in NFL teams. Dr. Noll testified that fans are interested in buying shares in NFL teams and that the NFL's policy deprives fans of this product. Moreover, evidence was presented concerning the public offering of the Boston Celtics professional basketball team which demonstrated, according to some of the testimony, fan interest in buying ownership of professional sports teams. Thus, a jury could conclude that the NFL's policy injured competition by making the relevant market "unresponsive to consumer preference."[3]

As for overall efficiency of production in the relevant market[4] Sullivan's experts testified that the NFL's policy hindered efficiency gains, and that allowing public ownership would make for better football teams. Professor Noll stated that the NFL's public ownership policy

---

3. The NFL maintains that price and output are not affected because its ownership policy does not limit the number of games or teams, does not raise ticket prices or the prices of game telecasts and does not affect the normal consumer of the NFL's product in any other way. Such facts might be relevant to an inquiry of whether the NFL's policy harms overall efficiency, see infra note [4], but it is not relevant to whether the policy affects output and prices in the relevant market for ownership interests. Just because consumers of "NFL football" are not affected by output controls and price increases does not mean that consumers of a product in the relevant market are not so affected. In this case, two types of consumers are denied products by the NFL policy: consumers who want to buy stock of the Patriots or other teams, and consumers like Sullivan who want to "purchase" investment capital in the market for public financing.

4. Although the product at issue in the relevant market is "ownership interests," efficiency in production of that product can be measured by the value of the ownership interest. That is, an improved product produced more efficiently will be reflected in the value of the output in question (regardless of the price). In this case, the value of the product depends on the success of the Patriots' football team, the overall efficiency of its operations, and the success of the NFL in general.

prevented individuals who might be "more efficient and much better at running a professional football team" from owning teams. Dr. Noll also stated that publicly owned NFL teams would be better managed, and produce higher quality entertainment for the fans. Noll testified that the ownership rule excluded certain types of management structures which would likely be more efficient in running the teams, resulting in higher franchise values. One NFL owner, Lamar Hunt, acknowledged that increased access to capital can improve a team's operations and performance. A memorandum prepared by an NFL staff member stated that changes to the NFL's public ownership policy could contribute to each NFL team's own financial strength and viability, which in turn would benefit the entire NFL because the league has a strong interest in having strong, viable teams.

The NFL presented a large amount of evidence to the contrary and now claims on appeal that Sullivan's position was based on nothing more than sheer speculation. We have reviewed the record, however, and we cannot say that the evidence was so overwhelming that no reasonable jury could find against the NFL and in favor of Sullivan. We therefore refuse to enter judgment in favor of the NFL as a matter of law.

B. Ancillary Benefits

The NFL next argues that even if its public ownership policy injures competition in a relevant market, it should be upheld as ancillary to the legitimate joint activity that is "NFL football" and thus not violative of the Sherman Act. We take no issue with the proposition that certain joint ventures enable separate business entities to combine their skills and resources in pursuit of a common goal that cannot be effectively pursued by the venturers acting alone. See, e.g., *Broadcast Music, Inc. v. Columbia Broadcasting System, Inc.*, 441 U.S. 1 (1979). We also do not dispute that a "restraint" that is ancillary to the functioning of such a joint activity—i.e. one that is required to make the joint activity more efficient—does not necessarily violate the antitrust laws. *Broadcast Music*, 441 U.S. at 23–25; *Rothery Storage & Van Co. v. Atlas Van Lines, Inc.*, 253 U.S.App.D.C. 142, 792 F.2d 210, at 223–24 (D.C.Cir.1986); see also *Northwest Wholesale Stationers, Inc. v. Pacific Stationery & Printing Co.*, 472 U.S. 284, 295–96 (1985). We further accept, for purposes of this appeal, that rules controlling who may join a joint venture can be ancillary to a legitimate joint activity and that the NFL's own policy against public ownership constitutes one example of such an ancillary rule. Finally, we accept the NFL's claim that its public ownership policy contributes to the ability of the NFL to function as an effective sports league, and that the NFL's functioning would be impaired if publicly owned teams were permitted, because the short-term dividend interests of a club's shareholder would often conflict with the long-term interests of the league as a whole. That is, the policy avoids a detrimental conflict of interests between team shareholders and the league.

We disagree, however, that these factors are sufficient to establish as a matter of law that the NFL's ownership policy does not unreasonably restrain trade in violation of § 1 of the Sherman Act. The holdings in *Broadcast Music*, *Rothery Storage*, and *Northwest Stationers*, do not throw the "rule of reason" out the window merely because one establishes that a given practice among joint venture participants is ancillary to legitimate and efficient activity—the injury to competition must still be weighed against the purported benefits under the rule of reason....

One basic tenet of the rule of reason is that a given restriction is not reasonable, that is, its benefits cannot outweigh its harm to competition, if a reasonable, less restrictive alternative to the policy exists that would provide the same benefits as the current restraint. The record contains evidence of a clearly less restrictive alternative to the NFL's ownership policy that would yield the same benefits as the current policy. Sullivan points to one proposal to amend the current ownership policy by allowing for the sale of minority, nonvoting shares of team stock to the public with restrictions on the size of the holdings by any one individual. Dividend payments, if any, would be within the firm control of the NFL majority owner. Under such a policy, it would be reasonable for a jury to conclude that private control of member clubs is maintained, conflicts of interest are avoided, and all the other "benefits" of the NFL's joint venture arrangement are preserved while at the same time teams would have access to the market for public investment capital through the sale of ownership interests.

C. Causation of Injury in Fact

* * *

[The court here addressed and rejected the NFL's claim that Sullivan's case should have been dismissed because there was no evidence to support a finding that the NFL's policy against public ownership in fact had caused economic injury to Sullivan. The court noted that "[a]lthough the evidence of causation is not overwhelming, it is nevertheless sufficient to support the verdict." With regard to the NFL's argument that Sullivan never asked for a vote, and thus the League never actually voted on whether he could sell 49% of the team through a public offering, the court concluded that the jury had sufficient evidence to find that the parties believed that a formal vote would have been futile, and thus the NFL owners' prior practice had effectively denied Sullivan permission to issue public stock in the Patriots. With respect to the NFL's second argument, that its evidence showed that a public offering of minority shares would not have raised the $70 million necessary to keep Sullivan from having to sell the team, the court stated: "[a]lthough we share the NFL's skepticism that Sullivan would have succeeded in his public offering if the NFL had allowed him to try it, we cannot say that, as a matter of law, the evidence was so overwhelming that no reasonable jury could find that the NFL's policy harmed Sullivan by preventing him from doing something he would otherwise have been able to do."]

The NFL's arguments concerning the application of § 1 of the Sherman Act to the facts of this case raise a substantial challenge to the jury verdict and are certainly weighty enough to give us pause. Upon careful consideration of the issues, however, we find Sullivan's theory of the case to be a plausible one and ultimately find the evidence sufficient to support it. For the foregoing reasons, therefore, we see no justification, as a matter of law, for ringing the death knell on this litigation.

IV. TRIAL ERRORS

Having reviewed those issues which would have warranted a judgment in favor of the NFL, had we decided any of those issues in the NFL's favor, we now turn to the NFL's claim that it is entitled to a new trial because of allegedly erroneous jury instructions and other trial errors.

* * *

D. *Balancing Procompetitive and Anticompetitive Effects in the Relevant Market*

As we noted above, the rule of reason analysis requires a weighing of the injury and the benefits to competition attributable to a practice that allegedly violates the antitrust laws. The district court instructed the jury on its verdict form to balance the injury to competition in the relevant market with the benefits to competition in that same relevant market. The NFL protested, claiming that all procompetitive effects of its policy, even those in a market different from that in which the alleged restraint operated, should be considered. The NFL's case was premised on the claim that its policy against public ownership was an important part of the effective functioning of the league as a joint venture. Although it was not readily apparent that this beneficial effect applied to the market for ownership interests in NFL teams, the relevant market found by the jury, the NFL argued that its justification should necessarily be weighed by the jury under the rule of reason analysis. Sullivan responded, and the district court agreed, that a jury cannot be asked to compare what are essentially apples and oranges, and that it is impossible to conduct a balancing of alleged anticompetitive and procompetitive effects of a challenged practice in every definable market.

The issue of defining the proper scope of a rule of reason analysis is a deceptive body of water, containing unforeseen currents and turbulence lying just below the surface of an otherwise calm and peaceful ocean. The waters are muddied by the Supreme Court's decision in *NCAA*—one of the more extensive examples of the Court performing a rule of reason analysis—where the Court considered the value of certain procompetitive effects that existed outside of the relevant market in which the restraint operated. *NCAA*, 468 U.S. at 115–20 (considering the NCAA's interest in protecting live attendance at untelevised games and the NCAA's "legitimate and important" interest in maintaining competitive balance between amateur athletic teams as a justification for a restraint that operated in a completely different market, the market for the telecasting of collegiate football games). Other courts have demonstrated similar confusion. See, e.g., *L.A. Coliseum*, 726 F.2d at 1381,

1392, 1397, 1399 (stating that the "relevant market provides the basis on which to balance competitive harms and benefits of the restraint at issue" but then considering a wide variety of alleged benefits, and then directing the finder of fact to "balance the gain to interbrand competition against the loss of intrabrand competition", where the two types of competition operated in different markets).

To our knowledge, no authority has squarely addressed this issue. On the one hand, several courts have expressed concern over the use of wide ranging interests to justify an otherwise anticompetitive practice, and others have found particular justifications to be incomparable and not in correlation with the alleged restraint of trade. *Smith v. Pro Football, Inc.*, 193 U.S.App.D.C. 19, 593 F.2d 1173, 1186 (D.C.Cir.1978); *Brown v. Pro Football, Inc.*, 812 F.Supp. 237, 238 (D.D.C.1992); *Chicago Pro. Sports Ltd. Partnership v. National Basketball Ass'n*, 754 F.Supp. 1336, 1358 (N.D.Ill.1991). We agree that the ultimate question under the rule of reason is whether a challenged practice promotes or suppresses competition. Thus, it seems improper to validate a practice that is decidedly in restraint of trade simply because the practice produces some unrelated benefits to competition in another market.

On the other hand, several courts, including this Circuit, have found it appropriate in some cases to balance the anticompetitive effects on competition in one market with certain procompetitive benefits in other markets. See, e.g., *NCAA*, 468 U.S. at 115–20; *Grappone, Inc. v. Subaru of New England, Inc.*, 858 F.2d 792, 799 (1st Cir.1988); *M & H Tire Co. v. Hoosier Racing Tire Corp.*, 733 F.2d 973, 986 (1st Cir.1984); *L.A. Coliseum*, 726 F.2d at 1381, 1392, 1397, 1399. Moreover, the district court's argument that it would be impossible to compare the procompetitive effects of the NFL's policy in the interbrand market of competition between the NFL and other forms of entertainment, with the anticompetitive effects of the intrabrand market of competition between NFL teams for the sale of their ownership interests, is arguably refuted by the Supreme Court's holding in *Continental T.V., Inc. v. GTE Sylvania Inc.*, 433 U.S. 36 (1977). *Continental T.V.* explicitly recognized that positive effects on interbrand competition can justify anticompetitive effects on intrabrand competition. Although *Continental T.V.* can reasonably be interpreted as referring only to interbrand and intrabrand components of the same relevant market, there is also some indication that interbrand and intrabrand competition necessarily refer to distinct, yet related, markets. *Continental T.V.*, 433 U.S. at 52 n.19 ("The degree of intrabrand competition is wholly independent of the level of interbrand competition."). Arguably, the market put forward by the NFL—that is the market for NFL football in competition with other forms of entertainment—is closely related to the relevant market found by the jury such that the procompetitive benefits in one can be compared to the anticompetitive harms in the other. Clearly this question can only be answered upon a much more in-depth inquiry that we need not, nor find it appropriate to, embark upon at this time.

Finally, we note that although balancing harms and benefits in different markets may be unwieldy and confusing, such is the case with a number of balancing tests that a court or jury is expected to apply all the time.

* * *

Although the issue of the proper scope of the rule of reason analysis is more appropriately resolved in a case where it is dispositive and more fully briefed, we can draw at least one general conclusion from the case law at this point: courts should generally give a measure of latitude to antitrust defendants in their efforts to explain the procompetitive justifications for their policies and practices; however, courts should also maintain some vigilance by excluding justifications that are so unrelated to the challenged practice that they amount to a collateral attempt to salvage a practice that is decidedly in restraint of trade.

In any event, we need not enter these dangerous waters to resolve the instant dispute. The NFL wanted the jury to consider its proffered justifications for the public ownership policy—namely that the policy enhanced the NFL's ability to effectively produce and present a popular entertainment product unimpaired by the conflicting interests that public ownership would cause. These procompetitive justifications should have been considered by the jury, even under Sullivan's theory of the proper scope of the rule of reason analysis. [However], to the extent the NFL's policy strengthens and improves the league, resulting in increased competition in the market for ownership interests in NFL clubs through, for example, more valuable teams, the jury may consider the NFL's justifications as relevant factors in its rule of reason analysis. The danger of the proffered instructions on the verdict form is that they may have mislead the jury into thinking that it was precluded from considering the NFL's justifications for its ownership policy. Therefore, the relevant market language on the verdict form should be removed, or else the jury should be informed that evidence of benefits to competition in the relevant market can include evidence of benefits flowing indirectly from the public ownership policy that ultimately have a beneficial impact on competition in the relevant market itself.

[The court also found several other trial court errors that required reversal of the jury verdict; for example, the fact that the trial judge had erroneously refused to give the jury an instruction about the NFL's "equal involvement" defense, by which the league claimed that Sullivan was barred from challenging its public ownership ban because of his "complete, voluntary, and substantially equal participation" in the formulation and enforcement of the ban over his years as an NFL owner. For all of these reasons, the decision below was]

Reversed and remanded.

Questions for Discussion

1. The only market in which the court found evidence of anticompetitive effects was the "nationwide market for the sale and purchase of

ownership interests in NFL member clubs." By restricting the number of potential buyers for interests in franchises, the court acknowledged that the effect of the ban was to lower the price NFL owners could get for their teams. Is there an antitrust concern (i.e., an injury to consumer welfare) if joint venture partners impose a limitation on who can be partners, when the impact of the rule may be to depress the value of their own franchise interest? Do you agree with the court that a jury could reasonably find that NFL team owners compete against each other for the sale of their franchises?

2. The court indicated that the anticompetitive effect of the ban was that it deprived consumers of the ability to buy shares of NFL teams, and that the rule caused the league to be "unresponsive to consumer demand for ownership interests in NFL teams." Are equity interests in a business a consumer good for which antitrust law requires the business to maintain a competitive market? How would restrictions on the sale of equity interests in any partnership, joint venture, close corporation, or limited liability company (which are pervasive in our economy) fare under the rule of reason inquiry recognized in *Sullivan*? Is there something distinctive about the Patriots as compared to other business ventures in Boston?

3. Standard partnership law expressly prohibits joint venture partners from assigning their partnership interests to anyone without the unanimous consent of the other venturers, unless the partnership agreement provides otherwise. Should this basic principle of partnership law (reinforced by § 502 of the new Uniform Partnership Act) be a sufficient justification under federal antitrust law for the NFL's restrictions on who can own a league franchise?

4. Is there anything distinctive about the market for NFL franchises, or is this simply a subset of the larger capital market in which investors buy and sell ownership rights in sports franchises generally—indeed, in any part of the business world (e.g., the sale of McDonald's franchises)? Is that question relevant to a court's judgment about the competitive impact of the NFL's policy against public ownership?

5. The *Sullivan* court's view that a restraint ancillary to a legitimate underlying agreement is still fully subject to the rule of reason, and that such a restraint would be unlawful if there were a less restrictive alternative, left little independent value to the NFL's "ancillary restraint" defense. With respect to its substantive reasonability, the court agreed that the league's policy against public ownership "contributes to the ability of the NFL to function as an effective sports league," and that "the policy avoids a detrimental conflict of interest between team shareholders and the league." What precisely is the positive contribution of this rule? Consider the experience in other leagues which all have publicly-owned teams—e.g., baseball's Chicago Cubs, basketball's New York Knicks, hockey's Boston Bruins, indeed, even football's (not-for-profit corporation) Green Bay Packers. Are the league's fans, players, or other owners better or worse off because such public ownership has been permitted?

6. One of the key grounds on which the trial verdict was reversed was that the jury should have been asked to pass on Billy Sullivan's personal role in the NFL's adoption and implementation of the rule against public

ownership. How extensive must such owner involvement be in a league's rules to preclude the owner's later challenge to the rule when it is detrimental to this owner's interests? As you read the *Los Angeles Memorial Coliseum v. NFL* case later in this chapter, ask yourself how this antitrust doctrine should have been applied to Al Davis's legal challenge to the NFL's refusal to permit the Raiders' relocation from Oakland to Los Angeles.

7. The issue of whether the procompetitive effects that defendants use to offset anticompetitive harms in a relevant market must be felt in the same market as the anticompetitive harms is crucial. Does this seem like a difficult question? If the only procompetitive effects a jury could consider are those in the same market as the anticompetitive effects, how would that affect the rule of reason analysis in the player restraint cases we considered in Chapter 3? In the *NASL* case we looked at earlier in this chapter? Keep in mind the question of what procompetitive effects a jury is allowed to consider as you assess the rule of reason issues in franchise relocation and television restriction cases later in this chapter, and the cases involving NCAA rules in Chapter 10.

The second trial in Sullivan's case was held during the fall of 1995 and ended in a hung jury. Before a third trial could begin, the parties settled with the help of court-ordered mediation: the NFL paid Sullivan $11 million to drop his suit. The league's ban on public ownership remains unchanged. Meanwhile, Billy's son, Chuck Sullivan, had also filed suit against the League. Chuck Sullivan contended that when the NFL denied his father the right to do a public stock offering for the Patriots, this severely damaged the economic value of the Patriots' home field, Sullivan Stadium, owned by Chuck's Stadium Management Corporation (SMC). The fact the Sullivan family had less funds available meant it could not improve the stadium facility, lease, and revenue stream. In turn, that put SMC into bankruptcy and forced a sale of the stadium to Robert Kraft at a "bargain basement" price of $25 million. (Happily for New England football fans, Kraft's ownership of the renamed Foxboro Stadium, which had a Patriot's lease until the year 2002, gave him the leverage to block a move of the Patriots to St. Louis by its 1993 owner, James Orthwein, and then to buy the team for himself for $160 million.)

However, the First Circuit, in *Sullivan v. Tagliabue*, 25 F.3d 43 (1st Cir.1994), held that Chuck Sullivan had not suffered the kind of direct injury from the NFL's "no corporate ownership" rule that antitrust is designed to prevent, and thus he had no standing to sue. The Circuit distinguished not only the situation of Chuck's father Billy, the Patriot's owner, but also *Los Angeles Memorial Coliseum v. NFL*, 791 F.2d 1356 (9th Cir.1986), in which the L.A. Coliseum (as well as the Raiders' owner) was able successfully to sue the NFL for blocking the Raiders' move from Oakland to Los Angeles. What are the distinguishing features of the financial injuries suffered by Sullivan Stadium and the L.A.

Coliseum as a result of these NFL rules? Do these distinctions warrant the difference in legal result?

The Sullivan family's legal war against the NFL was not the only antitrust litigation to grow out of the saga of the wayward Patriots. When Billy Sullivan was forced to sell the team, Francis Murray stepped in and claimed that he held an option to purchase the Patriots from Sullivan for $63 million. When Sullivan found other buyers for a substantially higher price (illegally assisted by the NFL, according to Murray), Murray was able to obtain an injunction against that sale. Eventually, the dispute was settled with Murray agreeing to take a 49% ownership interest in an entity called KMS Patriots, which purchased the team for $84 million in 1988. The other 51% of this limited partnership was owned by Victor Kiam. The agreement between Kiam and Murray provided that Murray had the option to tender his 49% to Kiam in October 1991 for $38 million, and that if Kiam did not then make the purchase, Murray would have the right to become sole owner of the team.

Murray, meanwhile, owned 40% of another group in St. Louis that had been established to bring an NFL team to that city. When Kiam fell into financial difficulties in the early 1990s, he tried to sell his majority interest in the Patriots to James Orthwein, who also happened to be both a major creditor of Murray (holding a security interest in his 49% Patriots share) and a partner with Murray in the St. Louis venture. Thus, in 1991 Murray tendered his 49% to Kiam for $38 million, and when Kiam did not consummate the deal, Murray claimed he owned the team in its entirety. Murray then appealed to NFL commissioner Paul Tagliabue to rule (under his authority as the arbitrator of all internal league disputes) that Murray was entitled either to the $38 million from Kiam or to the team. While that arbitration process was still pending, Orthwein foreclosed on his security interest in Murray's 49%, since Murray could not pay his debt without the $38 million from Kiam. With no funds to pursue these disputes, Murray eventually settled in 1992 by selling his 49% share to Orthwein and by allowing Orthwein to purchase Kiam's 51%, making Orthwein the sole owner of the Patriots for a price of roughly $110 million. And as was noted above, Orthwein felt compelled to sell the Patriots to Robert Kraft for $160 million in 1994—with the huge increase in franchise price likely driven more by the league's new television contracts with Fox and other networks than by Orthwein's installation of Bill Parcells as the Patriots' coach.

After the jury verdict in *Sullivan* was announced, Murray filed an antitrust suit in Philadelphia against the NFL, claiming that the league's rules regarding franchise relocation and expansion, its ban on public ownership, and its requirement that internal disputes be arbitrated by the commissioner, in combination with the league's conduct in enforcing those policies, had prevented Murray from raising sufficient money to become the owner of the Patriots and then relocate the team to St. Louis. He claimed that this illegal § 1 restraint on the nationwide market for purchase and sale of ownership interests and control of NFL teams caused him to lose millions of dollars. The district judge dismissed the claim against the NFL based on the league's relocation and expansion rules, because there was no alleged impact on competition here. However, with respect to the rule against public ownership, the court denied the league's motion to dismiss.

> Plaintiffs have alleged sufficient facts to mount a § 1 challenge against the NFL's financing policy.... Plaintiffs allege that the NFL, through its financing policy denied them access to certain investment resources which in turn limited their ability to raise capital to maintain an ownership interest in the Patriots. Prospective purchasers similarly situated were also excluded from that market. Where even a single competitor is excluded from a market, an effect on interstate commerce may result....
>
> Admittedly, the anti-competitive effect of the League's financing policy is difficult to discern. The NFL continues to add expansion teams and Plaintiffs admit readily that NFL franchises "command high prices," and stadium owners and cities "compete to secure NFL franchises." Nonetheless, restrictive agreements between members of a joint venture, such as members of a football league, can under some circumstances have legitimate purposes as well as anti-competitive effects and therefore are subject to rule of reason analysis....
>
> We cannot conclude, as a matter of law, that a jury could not find that a market existed for the sale and purchase of NFL franchises or that existing franchises, or the League itself, does not compete in that market. Nor can we conclude, as a matter of law, that a rule limiting participation in that market to individuals with private financing is not anticompetitive.

Murray v. National Football League, 1996–2 Trade Cases (CCH) ¶ 71,479 (at ¶ 77,523)(E.D.Pa.1996). While this case raises many of the same questions involved in *Sullivan*, what are the procompetitive and anticompetitive effects of the NFL's ownership ban on public ownership, and how would they balance out in a rule of reason analysis? If a jury were to find the rule unlawful, how was someone in Murray's position injured by it, and how would a court instruct a jury to calculate his damages?

Both the *NASL* and *Sullivan* courts rejected the league's single entity defense. The Supreme Court has declined to take a sports league case to resolve this fundamental issue. However, two years after *NASL* was decided, but before *Sullivan*, the Supreme Court issued an important decision in *Copperweld Corp. v. Independence Tube Corp.*, 467 U.S. 752 (1984), holding that a parent corporation and its wholly-owned subsidiaries constituted a single firm for § 1 purposes; thus, "agreements" among members of this type of corporate family are not subject to any "rule of reason" scrutiny. While *Copperweld* is factually distinguishable from the sports league context, the Court's rationale in that case may be instructive in thinking about whether a league is a single entity for § 1 purposes.

The *Copperweld* Court first noted why the behavior of single entities is subject only to the § 2 bar on *monopolistic* behavior.

> [A]n efficient firm may capture unsatisfied customers from an inefficient rival, whose own ability to compete may suffer as a result. This is the rule of the marketplace and is precisely the sort of competition that promotes the consumer interests that the Sherman Act aims to foster. In part because it is sometimes difficult to distinguish robust competition from conduct with long-run anti-competitive effects, Congress authorized Sherman Act scrutiny of single firms only when they pose a danger of monopolization. Judging unilateral conduct in this manner reduces the risk that the antitrust laws will dampen the competitive zeal of a single aggressive entrepreneur.

467 U.S. at 767–68. By contrast, concerted activity on the part of several firms is subject to broader judicial scrutiny of whether this "combination" unduly "restrains trade."

> Concerted activity inherently is fraught with anticompetitive risk. It deprives the marketplace of the independent centers of decision making that competition assumes and demands. In any conspiracy, two or more entities that previously pursued their own interests separately are combining to act as one for common benefit. This not only reduces the diverse directions in which economic power is aimed but suddenly increases the economic power moving in one particular direction. Of course, such mergings of resources may well lead to efficiencies that benefit consumers, but their anticompetitive potential is sufficient to warrant scrutiny even in the absence of incipient monopoly.

467 U.S. at 768–69. In the Court's view, coordinated activity by officers or employees of the same company clearly did not fit within either the wording or the policy of § 1.

> The officers of a single firm are not separate economic actors pursuing separate economic interests, so agreements among them do not suddenly bring together economic power that was previously pursuing divergent goals. Coordination within a firm is as likely to result from an effort to compete as from an effort to stifle competition. In the marketplace, such coordination may be necessary if a business enterprise is to compete effectively....
>
> Indeed, a rule that punished coordinated conduct simply because a corporation delegated certain responsibilities to autonomous units might well discourage corporations from creating divisions with their presumed benefits. This would serve no useful purpose

but could well deprive consumers of the efficiencies that decentralized management may bring.

467 U.S. at 769–71. For precisely that same reason, coordinated relations between a parent company and its wholly-owned subsidiary had to be treated as a single entity for purposes of § 1.

> A parent and its wholly owned subsidiary have a complete unity of interests. Their objectives are common, not disparate; their general corporate actions are guided or determined not by two separate corporate consciousnesses, but one.... If a parent and a wholly owned subsidiary do "agree" to a course of action, there is not a sudden joining of economic resources that had previously served different interests, and there is no justification for § 1 scrutiny....
>
> ... [I]n reality a parent and a wholly owned subsidiary *always* have a "unity of purpose or a common design." They share a common purpose whether or not the parent kept a tight rein over the subsidiary; the parent may assert full control at any moment if the subsidiary fails to act in the parent's best interests.

467 U.S. at 771–72. Thus, the *Copperweld* Court repealed its earlier "intra-enterprise conspiracy" doctrine for having based antitrust liability on corporate form, rather than antitrust policy.

> The economic, legal, or other considerations that lead corporate management to choose one structure [unincorporated division] over the other [wholly-owned subsidiary] are not relevant to whether the enterprise's conduct seriously threatens competition. Rather, a corporation may adopt the subsidiary form for valid management and related purposes. Separate incorporation may improve management, avoid special tax problems arising from multistate operations, or serve other legitimate interests. Especially in view of the increasing complexity of corporate operations, a business enterprise should be free to structure itself in ways that serve efficiency of control, economy of operations, and other factors dictated by business judgement without increasing its exposure to antitrust liability.

467 U.S. at 772–73.

In the course of its lengthy *Sullivan* opinion, the First Circuit authored just this brief passage rejecting the NFL's *Copperweld*-based single entity argument.

> We do not agree that *Copperweld*, which found a corporation and its wholly owned subsidiary to be a single enterprise for purposes of § 1, applies to the facts of this case or affects the prior precedent concerning the NFL ... *Copperweld's* holding turned on the fact that the subsidiary of a corporation, although legally distinct from the corporation itself, "pursued the common interests of the whole rather than interests separate from those of the corporation itself." *Copperweld*, 467 U.S. at 770. As emphasized in *City of Mt. Pleasant, Iowa v. Associated Elec. Co-op., Inc.*, 838 F.2d 268 (8th Cir.1988), upon which the NFL relies for the application of *Copper-*

weld to this case, the critical inquiry is whether the alleged antitrust conspirators have a "unity of interests" or whether, instead, "any of the defendants has pursued interests diverse from those of the cooperative itself." Id. at 274–77 (defining "diverse" as "interests which tend to show that any two of the defendants are, or have been, actual or potential competitors"). As we have already noted, NFL member clubs compete in several ways off the field, which itself tends to show that the teams pursue diverse interests and thus are not a single enterprise under § 1.

Ultimately, the NFL's *Copperweld* challenge is subsumed under the question of whether or not the evidence can support a finding that NFL teams compete against each other for the sale of their ownership interests. Proof of such competition defeats both the NFL's challenge to the existence of an injury to competition and the NFL's *Copperweld* argument as well. Insufficient proof of such competition would require a judgment in favor of the NFL anyway, regardless of the implications under *Copperweld*. As we discuss below, the jury's finding that there exists competition between teams for the sale of ownership interests was based on sufficient evidence.

34 F.3d at 1099. Having read the above excerpts from *Copperweld*, the rationales offered by the First and Second Circuits for rejecting the single entity defense in *Sullivan* and *NASL*, consider the following questions.

Questions for Discussion

1. Is the issue of whether a sports league is a single firm or multiple firms for § 1 purposes one that should be decided as a matter of law by a court, or one that should be decided on a case-by-case basis by a jury as mixed law and fact? Keep in mind the Supreme Court's *Copperweld* statement that features of an enterprise that are the product of voluntary choice in the pursuit of efficiency are not relevant to the single entity question. What facts are relevant to this issue? Are these facts likely to be disputed? Are they variable from case to case or league to league, or are they largely standard in all sports league cases?

2. Recall the Supreme Court's policy arguments for rejecting the "intra-enterprise conspiracy" doctrine in the wholly-owned subsidiary corporation context. What do these imply for the case of league structures in the four major sports?[d] To what extent are the actual interests of clubs within a league unified or disparate? Inherently ordained or voluntarily negotiated? Does the degree of unity depend on the league's tradition, culture, and leadership? Compare, for example, baseball under Judge Landis in the 1920s and 1930s with baseball under Bud Selig in the 1990s. Does it depend on the degree of revenue sharing among the clubs in the league? Should the NFL,

---

[d] The implications of *Copperweld* for the antitrust status of sports leagues are a major preoccupation of the second round of scholarly debate on the single entity issue. See the later articles by Lazaroff, Goldman, Grauer, Roberts, and Jacobs cited in note c above.

which divides about 90% of its revenues according to league-determined formulas, be deemed a different "entity" than the NHL, where less than 10% of revenues are shared?[e]

3. To the extent that the interests of individual clubs are disparate instead of uniform, does this disparity result from inherent independence ("separate sources of economic power," in the words of the *Copperweld* opinion), or from the voluntary choice of an entity with a single source of economic power to use a decentralized mode of operation? What is the source of the league's and/or its clubs' economic power? What products does a sports league produce? Who owns the trademarks under which either a league (the NFL) or its teams (e.g., the Cowboys) market their product(s)? Do member clubs of a sports league compete with each other like independent oil companies or auto manufacturers, or like divisions of a single corporation in which each division's economic rewards are based on its varying performance?

4. The *Copperweld* court also noted that "[s]ubjecting a single firm's every action to judicial scrutiny for reasonableness would threaten to discourage the competitive enthusiasm that the antitrust laws seek to promote." Because leagues can operate only through agreement of all its members, not treating it as a single entity means that every league rule or action is potentially subject to rule of reason scrutiny. As a general matter, would this tend to discourage leagues from acting in ways that are good or bad for consumers? Keep this question in mind as you consider the specific rules being challenged in each case.

The established leagues whose structures and policies have figured in the decisions we have read in this and prior chapters were all fashioned long before single entity and other antitrust doctrines became so much a part of the sports world. Because they are aware of this jurisprudence, though, the organizers of new leagues have both the opportunity and the incentive to design their structures in a fashion that will insulate the league from these potential legal troubles.

The most important such new sports venture of the 1990s is Major League Soccer (MLS). Its creator, Alan Rothenberg, is a notable Los Angeles lawyer at Latham & Watkins who had been a co-owner of the Los Angeles Aztecs in the North American Soccer League, president of the Los Angeles Clippers in the NBA (whose litigation with the league we will encounter later in this chapter), and then leader of the 1994 World Soccer Cup which demonstrated the appeal of soccer in this country. Based on that legal and industry experience, Rothenberg originally designed MLS as a single limited-liability Delaware company that would itself own and operate all the teams around the country. Investors would own shares in MLS and sit on or select members of its Board of

---

[e]. See Scott E. Atkinson, Linda R. Stanley & John Tschirhart, *Revenue Sharing as an Incentive in an Agency Problem: An Example From the National Football League*, 19 RAND J. of Econ. 27 (1988).

Directors which would oversee league policy. However, personnel in the league's offices would run all the teams, sign and allocate players, coaches, general managers, and other staff, and set and collect the prices for tickets, concessions, local broadcasts, and merchandising ventures. These revenues, along with fees from national broadcasting and merchandising, would be used to pay the costs incurred by each team, not only for its players and staff, but for stadium rentals, and the like. The net profits eventually earned by MLS would be paid out as dividends to the investor-shareholders. As we saw in Chapter 3, a key feature of this plan was a cap on both team payrolls and individual salaries.

Whatever its legal promise, this design encountered a major practical problem. There were few, if any, wealthy sports fans who were prepared to put up the initial $5 million investment, plus take on the additional risk of significant start-up costs, just to be faceless investors in a league venture whose visible figures would all be in the MLS head office. Indeed, the reason why sports franchise values have escalated in value so much higher than even the Dow Jones Stock Index is because owners reap not just the financial returns from increasingly lucrative television and stadium deals, but many also get the personal pleasure of running the (hoped-for) successful team in their home town.

Thus, in order to attract the money to begin Major League Soccer in 1996, the league structure had to be significantly altered. MLS still was the formal owner of all its franchises. However, in seven of the ten cities (in particular, the larger markets such as New York, Los Angeles, and Boston), a separate special class of stock was sold to each of seven "investor-operators" who received almost full operating control over the teams in their areas. (For the moment, at least, the other three MLS teams in Tampa Bay, Dallas, and San Jose are operated, as well as owned, by the league.) In essentially the same way as he does with his NFL New England Patriots, Robert Kraft, the "investor-operator" of the MLS New England Revolution, decides who will run the front office (largely done by his family); who will be the coach; who will be the team's players; where the games will be played (in his Foxboro Stadium, along with the Patriots); and what prices will be charged for tickets, local broadcasts, merchandise, and the like. The revenues that come from these local sources are split 50–50 between the individual "investor-operator" and the league, while all revenues generated from national television and merchandising deals go to MLS (which uses this money to pay each team's player salaries as well as league expenses, and then distributes any profits or dividends to the investors in this new sports venture). The special stock owned by Kraft and other investor-operated franchises, with those rights in particular teams, can be sold to outside bidders, which allows these stock owners to reap all the capital gain (or loss) that flows out of their team's performance on the field as well as off it.

The one key feature of Rothenberg's original design that remains in place is the relationship of the league to players. Once a team decides which players it would like to have, the league negotiates and pays the contract with each player as his employer—subject to the league's reserve and team salary cap constraints. Rothenberg wanted to avoid a replay of his experience in the NASL which had been dominated by the New York Cosmos whose owner Steve Ross of Warner Communications (now Time Warner) had been prepared to offer a very lucrative contract to bring in perhaps the greatest soccer player ever, Pelé from Brazil. These restraints on the players' market are now the subject of the *Fraser* class action antitrust suit that we read about in Chapter 3. Almost certainly, that suit under § 1 would have been dismissed under the *Copperweld* single entity standard had the original organizational design of the MLS been preserved.

In fact, the pure single entity approach has been embodied in the league structure in the latest major professional sport to emerge in this country—women's basketball. This sport has not just one, but two leagues; the American Basketball League (ABL) which began play in the winter of 1996–97, and the Women's National Basketball Association (WNBA) which began in the summer of 1997. The ABL was founded by Steve Hams, Anne Cribs, and Gary Cavelli, with Cavelli serving as Chief Executive Officer. They established teams in eight cities, and operating from their head office in Palo Alto, California, hired and assigned general managers and coaches as well as players to each team. The WNBA situation is somewhat more complex because this is an offshoot of the NBA which itself is comprised of 29 separately-owned franchises. However, NBA Development (a corporate spin-off of the league whose shares are equally divided among the 29 team owners) itself created WNBA LLC (a limited liability company) that also hired and assigned all the personnel for the eight original teams. The WNBA operates pursuant to policies established by a Governing Board of eight NBA owners and NBA Commissioner David Stern (one such policy being a salary floor of $24,000 and a salary cap of $50,000 for individual player contracts). Each WNBA team is actually operated by the NBA team in whose city (and arena) the women's team is playing its games. The operating agreement gives each of the eight managing NBA franchises a designated share of the revenues (and costs) of the WNBA team for which it is directly responsible, and four of the eight WNBA board members come from this group. However, the ultimate control of the WNBA and ownership of its assets and financial returns remains in the hands of NBA Development, the entity equally-owned by the 29 NBA teams.

In their respective opening seasons, the quality of ABL talent and play was considered to be somewhat superior to the WNBA's, but its average 3,500 game attendance was only a third of the WNBA's 9,700 for its 28–game season (as well as the latter's television ratings on Fox, ESPN, and Lifetime). Notwithstanding that gap, for its second 1997–98 season, the ABL added a new team in Long Beach, California, moved its Richmond team to the much larger Philadelphia market, expanded the schedule from 40 to 44 games, and attracted a new investor, the Fortune 500 Phoenix Corporation, which paid $3 million for a 20% share of the league. The ABL also decided to reserve ten percent of its stock to be offered to players as options that could vest after three years in the league. ABL salaries averaged $80,000 (ranging from $40,000 to $150,000), with additional amounts payable as incentive bonuses and promotional appearance fees.

A key difference, of course, between women's and men's basketball is that there are now two professional leagues competing with each other not just for women players, but also for fans (and the latter's intermediaries, the television networks, merchandising firms, and sports facilities owners). As long as this remains the case within the sport, the antitrust law status of the two leagues' structures is of less importance. The situation in soccer (and the other team sports) is very different, of course, since MLS is the single major professional league in this sport in the United States. We shall have to wait and see what the judicial verdict will be in the *Fraser* litigation, as well as the fan's verdict at the box office (about which there is no guarantee, since MLS game attendance dropped from 17,400 in 1996 to 14,600 in 1997). The broader policy question, though, relates to these variations in the league structures of the ABL, the MLS (its current version, not the original plan), and the NBA (rather than the WNBA), NFL, NHL, and MLB (which itself is composed of an American and a National League). Are these simply matters of voluntary choice by financial investors, or are they fundamentally different forms of business organization and economic power in which teams should be required to compete against each other at least to some extent in their respective player and other markets?

The true nature of a sports league—as either a joint venture of independent clubs or a single entity comprised of separately managed divisions—has arisen in other contexts. For example, recall from Chapter 4 that the National Labor Relations Board held (and the Fifth Circuit agreed) that the North American Soccer League could be treated as a "joint employer" that was subject to a single bargaining unit of players represented by its Players' Association. A few years later, the USFL Players' Association brought suit against the League to collect the unpaid salaries of players for the defunct Portland Breakers' franchise. In ruling against the Players Association, the judge emphasized the difference between *joint* and *single* employer status, and held that a sports league did not exhibit the integrated operation under common ownership and management that warranted "single employer" treatment. See *USFLPA v. USFL*, 650 F.Supp. 12 (D.Or.1986). Having seen in earlier chapters the league policies that establish uniform player contracts, entry-level drafts, waiver and trade rules, and restrictions on veteran free agency and salary caps, do you agree that players left unpaid by one franchise should have no recourse against the league as a whole? Is this relevant to whether a league is a single entity for antitrust purposes?

In another case, *Professional Hockey Corp. v. World Hockey Ass'n (WHA)*, 143 Cal.App.3d 410, 191 Cal.Rptr. 773 (1983), a California court held that the representatives of each franchise on the Board of Trustees of the WHA (a corporate entity) had a fiduciary duty to act for the benefit of the league as a whole when making decisions about common league goals—in this case whether or not to approve a new league owner whose financial strength or weakness could affect the league-wide venture. The court explicitly rejected the argument that, for example, merely because the San Diego Chargers were involved in fierce athletic competition with the Los Angeles Raiders, this meant that Gene Klein, then owner of the Chargers, owed no duty of "obedience, diligence, and loyalty" to his bitter rival, Raiders' owner Al Davis.

In the *World Hockey Association* case, the court did not have to decide how far the fiduciary duty of corporate directors extends, because the judge found no factual basis for any breach of such a duty. However, under general partnership law, which treats joint ventures as a type of partnership, each partner has a fiduciary duty to place the interests of the venture above his own interests unless the partnership agreement or the other partners allow otherwise. The next case from the summer of 1992—a case we considered in Chapter 1 with reference to the authority of the commissioner—raises the question of how far that fiduciary duty of the team might go.

The National League baseball owners as a whole favored having the Chicago Cubs and the Atlanta Braves switch places in the League's eastern and western divisions, both to enhance geographic rivalries and to reduce travelling time and costs. However, the Cubs' owner, the Chicago Tribune, exercised its power under the National League constitution to veto the proposed realignment, reportedly because it feared that adding late-starting west coast games to the Cubs' schedule would detract from the television ratings of the Cubs' games broadcast on the team's corporate sibling, the Chicago superstation WGN. Commissioner Fay Vincent overrode the Cubs' veto because he believed the new alignment was in the best interests of baseball. As we saw in Chapter 1, the Cubs persuaded a federal judge in Chicago to block the Commissioner's action, and in the aftermath of Vincent's forced resignation, the matter was dropped pending a study of broader realignment in baseball. But whether or not a commissioner has authority to override individual team prerogatives, should each owner have a judicially enforceable duty to vote in favor of the interests of the league at the expense of its own team's financial rewards? If so, should the Chicago Tribune (with its Cubs and WGN), Time Warner (which owns both the Atlanta Braves and the first cable superstation, WTBS), and George Steinbrenner (who owns the New York Yankees' and enjoys a lucrative television contract with Madison Square Garden network), be under a fiduciary duty to vote in favor of sharing their teams' television revenues with poorer teams such as the Montreal Expos, the Kansas City Royals, and the Pittsburgh Pirates? How does revenue-sharing relate to the single entity issue?

This is not the end of the single entity discussion. This issue also plays a role in the cases in the next two sections, involving individual owner challenge to league restraints on franchise relocation and television contracts. Keep the above questions in mind as you read and reflect upon the judicial scrutinies of various league policies in these respective areas.

C. ADMISSION AND RELOCATION OF SPORTS FRANCHISES[f]

In the 1990s, the most impassioned debates in the sports world have been about franchise (not player) free agency. In just two years, the NFL witnessed the relocation of the Rams from Los Angeles to St. Louis, the Raiders from Los Angeles to Oakland, the decision by the Oilers to go from Houston to Nashville, and most controversial of all, the Browns move from Cleveland to Baltimore (as the Ravens). During that same period, several franchise relocations also took place within the NHL—teams moving from Minnesota to Dallas, from Quebec City to Denver (where the Avalanche won the 1996 Stanley Cup in its first season there), from Winnipeg to Phoenix, and from Hartford to Raleigh (as the Carolina Hurricanes). While no baseball or basketball relocations actually occurred, there were numerous threats of such moves (which is now a serious prospect with baseball's Minnesota Twins), most of which were successful in securing the teams new stadium or arena deals from their home communities.

This surge in actual or potential franchise relocation has forced cities and states to spend huge amounts of money on sports facilities—subsidies that will top $10 billion in the 1990s, the bulk of which was used to replace or transform stadiums and arenas built in the previous quarter century. The city of Miami, for example, built a $65 million arena in the mid–1980s to house both the NBA Heat and NHL Panthers. However, by the late 1990s, each of those teams had secured a new $150 million facility just for itself. Franchise free agency has proven to be very lucrative not just for the wealthy owners of the teams, but also for the players who can utilize their own free agency rights to extract more sizeable salary contracts from the teams that now can afford to pay even more to try to win a championship. It has not been so beneficial to the

---

f. Besides the books by Zimbalist, Quirk and Fort, and Danielson, cited in note a above, see Kenneth L. Shropshire, *The Sports Franchise Game: Cities in Pursuit of Sports Franchises, Events, Stadiums, and Arenas* (Philadelphia: Univ. of Pennsylvania Press, 1995); Charles C. Euchner, *Playing the Field: Why Sports Teams Move and Cities Fight to Keep Them* (Baltimore: John Hopkins Univ. Press, 1993); Bob Andelman, *Stadium For Rent: Tampa Bay's Quest for Major League Baseball* (Jefferson, N.C.: McFarland & Co. 1993); Kevin E. Martens, *Fair or Foul? The Survival of Small–Market Teams in Major League Baseball*, 4 Marquette Sports L. J. 323 (1994); Steven M. Crafton, *Taking the Oakland Raiders: A Theoretical Reconsideration of the Concepts of Public Use and Just Compensation*, 32 Emory L. J. 857 (1993); Richard G. Sheehan, *Keeping Score: The Economics of Big-Time Sports* (South Bend, Ind.: Diamond Communications, 1996); and Mark S. Rosenstraub, *Major League Losers: The Real Cost of Sports and Who's Paying For It* (New York: Basic Books, 1997).

taxpayers who must foot the bill for the new stadium deals—and almost always through some version of a sales tax collected from ordinary working families, rather than from higher income or capital gains taxes collected from the well-to-do who watch the games from the most luxurious seats.

The benefits secured by individual team owners sometimes also come at the expense of the league as a whole. This was not true in hockey, where Commissioner Gary Bettman and the other owners felt that the above relocations were beneficial to the NHL in its effort to secure broader exposure in southern and western markets that were without teams. The same was true of the vast majority of franchise shifts in baseball (from the 1950s into the early 1970s) and in basketball (until the mid–1980s). The major exception to that rule has been football, where Commissioner Tagliabue and NFL owners in the 1990s (as well as Rozelle and the owners in the 1980s) have judged that few, if any, of these individual owner relocation decisions were in the best interests of the league as a whole (which found itself with no team in Los Angeles, the second largest market in the country).

The internal rules and practices of each league require super-majority consent to the creation of a new franchise, and even to acceptance of the new owner of an existing franchise. Once part of the league, the franchise enjoys an exclusive right (near-exclusive in the largest markets) to operate a team in that geographic area. However, any attempt by an owner to move his club to a new location (whether or not occupied by another team) is also supposed to gain league-wide consent. That league power was used by the National League owners in baseball to block the proposed 1992 sale and move of the San Francisco Giants to the Tampa Bay area.

As we read in Chapter 2, that baseball decision sparked the *Piazza* and *Butterworth* litigation by frustrated Tampa Bay owner-investors, who sought to roll back baseball's antitrust exemption in order to attack this particular league decision under the Sherman Act. The key antitrust precedents they wanted to use were the product of a 1980s war between the NFL and Raiders' owner Al Davis, when the latter sought to move his team from Oakland to Los Angeles in the first place. There are a host of social, economic, and legal factors that have contributed to franchise free agency and taxpayer subsidy. A crucial feature, though, is antitrust doctrine whose evolution and current shape we shall now examine in detail.[g]

An early legal challenge to traditional league prerogatives came in *San Francisco Seals v. NHL*, 379 F.Supp. 966 (C.D.Cal.1974). One of the six NHL expansion franchises created in 1967, the Seals enjoyed little success in the San Francisco Bay area. In 1969, then, the team sought to

---

[g.] Besides the articles cited in note c above, see Gary R. Roberts, *The Evolving Confusion of Professional Sports Antitrust, The Rule of Reason, and the Doctrine of Ancillary Restraints*, 61 Southern Calif. L. Rev. 943 (1988), and Matthew J. Mitten and Bruce W. Burton, *Professional Sports Franchise Relocations from Private Law and Public Law Perspectives*, 56 Maryland L. Rev. 57 (1997).

move to what then was still-vacant territory in Vancouver, British Columbia. The League's Board of Governors (comprised of one representative from each team) refused to approve the move, and the Seals sued under § 1 of the Sherman Act. The trial court summarily rejected this claim in a brief decision with the following key passage:

> What then is the relevant market? I find that the relevant product market with which we are here concerned is the production of professional hockey games before live audiences, and that the relevant geographical market is the United States and Canada.
>
> Now let us examine plaintiff's relationship with the defendants within the relevant market. Plaintiff, of course, wishes to participate in this market, but not in competition with the defendants. It expects to maintain its league membership and to accept and enjoy all of the exclusive territorial benefits which the National Hockey League affords. As a member team, it will continue cooperating with the defendants in pursuit of its main purpose, i.e., producing sporting events of uniformly high quality appropriately scheduled as to both time and location so as to assure all members of the league the best financial return. In this respect, the plaintiff and defendants are acting together as one single business enterprise, competing against other similarly organized professional leagues.
>
> The main thrust of the Sherman Act is to prohibit some competitors from combining with other competitors to gain a competitive advantage over other competitors by creating impermissible restraints upon trade or commerce. It is fundamental in a section 1 violation that there must be at least two independent business entities accused of combining or conspiring to restrain trade.
>
> Within the relevant market in which we are here concerned, plaintiff and defendants are not competitors in the economic sense. It is of course true that the member teams compete among themselves athletically for championship honors, and they may even compete economically, to a greater or lesser degree, in some other market not relevant to our present inquiry. But, they are not competitors in the economic sense in this relevant market. They are, in fact, all members of a single unit competing as such with other similar professional leagues. Consequently, the organizational scheme of the National Hockey League, by which all its members are bound, imposes no restraint upon trade or commerce in this relevant market, but rather makes possible a segment of commercial activity which could hardly exist without it.

See 379 F.Supp. at 969–70.

A decade later came what has aptly been called the "Super Bowl of Sports Litigation." This was the struggle between Commissioner Pete Rozelle and the National Football League and Al Davis, owner of the Raiders, over whether or not the Raiders were free to leave Oakland, where the team had enjoyed marked athletic and financial success, and move its home base south to Los Angeles, where Davis felt his prospects were even more rosy.[h] Of the ten or so judicial rulings reported from this single sports law saga, the following decision is perhaps the most important. In reading this opinion, keep two questions in mind. One is whether the Supreme Court's then-pending *Copperweld* judgment would have made a difference in the Ninth Circuit's treatment of the "single entity" question. The other is whether this appellate panel's appraisal of the franchise movement issue under "rule of reason" antitrust analysis indicates that relocation is best left to internal league governance or should be subject to outside judicial scrutiny.

LOS ANGELES MEMORIAL COLISEUM COMM'N. v. NFL (RAIDERS I)

United States Court of Appeals, Ninth Circuit, 1984.
726 F.2d 1381.

ANDERSON, CIRCUIT JUDGE.

[This case was precipitated by the 1978 decision of Carroll Rosenbloom, owner of the Los Angeles Rams, to move his team from the Los Angeles Coliseum to Anaheim, attracted by a lucrative lease arrangement offered by that city. At the same time, Al Davis had reached a stalemate in efforts to negotiate the terms for renewal of the Raiders' lease with the Oakland Coliseum. Conversations thus began between Davis and L.A. Coliseum officials about a possible Raiders' move to the Coliseum.

Alerted to possible legal difficulties with its relocation procedures (particularly when the L.A. Coliseum filed suit to try to force the league to grant it an expansion team), the NFL moved in late 1978 to amend its rules. Rule 4.1 had defined "home territory" as extending for a 75-mile radius from the boundaries of the team's home city as designated in the NFL Constitution. (Thus, Los Angeles was still the home city of the Rams playing in Anaheim.) Rule 4.3 then provided that any team proposing to move into another's home territory needed unanimous approval from all other teams. Other relocations required only a three-quarters vote. The amended Rule 4.3 applied the three-quarters formula to all relocations regardless of the new site, thence removing the possibility of a veto by the incumbent club.

On March 1, 1980, Davis signed a "memorandum of agreement" to move the Raiders to the L.A. Coliseum. On March 10, 1980, the NFL took a vote on the proposed move (over Davis' objections). The verdict was 22–0 against, with five teams (including the Rams) abstaining.

Shortly thereafter, the Raiders joined the suit filed in 1978 by the Coliseum against the NFL. Over the objections of the NFL (and the Oakland Coliseum, which intervened as a party), Los Angeles was retained as the venue for the jury trial. After a three-month jury trial in

---

h. The Raiders case is treated in depth throughout Harris, *The League*, note a above.

1981 on liability alone, a trial that focused largely on the single entity defense, Judge Harry Pregerson, who had just become a Ninth Circuit judge, granted a directed verdict for plaintiffs on this issue and thus removed it from jury consideration. Nonetheless, the jury could not reach a rule of reason verdict and a mistrial was declared. A lengthy liability retrial in 1982 resulted in a verdict which found that the NFL's action was an unreasonable restraint of trade. An injunction was entered barring the league from blocking the Raiders' relocation, and the NFL immediately appealed. The first issue addressed by the Ninth Circuit panel was the single-entity defense.]

* * *

It is true, as the NFL contends, that the nature of an entity and its ability to combine or conspire in violation of § 1 is a fact question. It would be reversible error, then, to take the issue from the jury if reasonable minds could differ as to its resolution. Here, however, the material facts are undisputed. How the NFL is organized and the nature and extent of cooperation among the member clubs is a matter of record; the NFL Constitution and Bylaws contain the agreement. Based on the undisputed facts and the law on this subject, the district court correctly decided this issue.

The district court cited three reasons for rejecting the NFL's theory. Initially, the court recognized the logical extension of this argument was to make the League incapable of violating Sherman Act § 1 in every other subject restriction—yet courts have held the League violated § 1 in other areas. Secondly, other organizations have been found to violate § 1 though their product was "just as unitary ... and requires the same kind of cooperation from the organization's members." Finally, the district court considered the argument to be based upon the false premise that the individual NFL "clubs are not separate business entities whose products have an independent value." We agree with this reasoning.

NFL rules have been found to violate § 1 in other contexts. Most recently, the Second Circuit analyzed the NFL's rule preventing its member-owners from having ownership interests in other professional sports clubs. *North American Soccer League v. National Football League*, 670 F.2d 1249, 1257–1259 (2d Cir.1982).

* * *

Cases applying the single entity or joint venture theory in other business areas also contradict the NFL's argument. As stated by the Supreme Court.

> Nor do we find any support in reason or authority for the proposition that agreements between legally separate persons and companies to suppress competition among themselves and others can be justified by labelling the project a "joint venture." Perhaps every agreement and combination in restraint of trade could be so labeled.

Timken Roller Bearing Co. v. United States, 341 U.S. 593, 598 (1951).

* * *

The NFL is only in very limited respects an identity separate from the individual teams. It is an unincorporated, not-for-profit "association." It has a New York office run by the Commissioner, Pete Rozelle, who makes day-to-day decisions regarding League operations. Its primary functions are in the areas of scheduling, resolving disputes among players and franchises, supervising officials, discipline and public relations. The decision involved here on territorial divisions is made by the NFL Executive Committee, which is comprised of a representative of each club. Even though the individual clubs often act for the common good of the NFL, we must not lose sight of the purpose of the NFL as stated in Article I of its constitution, which is to "promote and foster the primary business of League members." Although the business interests of League members will often coincide with those of the NFL as an entity in itself, that commonality of interest exists in every cartel. As in *United States v. Sealy, Inc.*, 388 U.S. 350 (1967), we must look behind the label proffered by the defendants to determine the substance of the entity in question.

Our inquiry discloses an association of teams sufficiently independent and competitive with one another to warrant rule of reason scrutiny under § 1 of the Sherman Act. The NFL clubs are, in the words of the district court, "separate business entities whose products have an independent value." The member clubs are all independently owned. Most are corporations, some are partnerships, and apparently a few are sole proprietorships. Although a large portion of League revenue, approximately 90%, is divided equally among the teams, profits and losses are not shared, a feature common to partnerships or other "single entities." In fact, profits vary widely despite the sharing of revenue. The disparity in profits can be attributed to independent management policies regarding coaches, players, management personnel, ticket prices, concessions, luxury box seats, as well as franchise location, all of which contribute to fan support and other income sources.

In addition to being independent business entities, the NFL clubs do compete with one another off the field as well as on to acquire players, coaches, and management personnel. In certain areas of the country where two teams operate in close proximity, there is also competition for fan support, local television and local radio revenues, and media space.

These attributes operate to make each team an entity in large part distinct from the NFL. It is true that cooperation is necessary to produce a football game. However, as the district court concluded, this does not mean "that each club can produce football games only as an NFL member." This is especially evident in light of the emergence of the United States Football League.

[Just like the Second Circuit in the *NASL* case, the Ninth Circuit majority recognized that the operation of the NFL as a joint venture required a rule of reason analysis of Rule 4.3 and its application.]

* * *

In a quite general sense, the case presents the competing considerations of whether a group of businessmen can enforce an agreement with one of their co-contractors to the detriment of that co-contractor's right to do business where he pleases. More specifically, this lawsuit requires us to engage in the difficult task of analyzing the negative and positive effects of a business practice in an industry which does not readily fit into the antitrust context. Section 1 of the Sherman Act was designed to prevent agreements among competitors which eliminate or reduce competition and thereby harm consumers. Yet, as we discussed in the context of the single entity issue, the NFL teams are not true competitors, nor can they be.

The NFL's structure has both horizontal and vertical attributes. On the one hand, it can be viewed simply as an organization of 28 competitors, an example of a simple horizontal arrangement. On the other, and to the extent the NFL can be considered an entity separate from the team owners, a vertical relationship is disclosed. In this sense the owners are distributors of the NFL product, each with its own territorial division. In this context it is clear that the owners have a legitimate interest in protecting the integrity of the League itself. Collective action in areas such as League divisions, scheduling and rules must be allowed, as should other activity that aids in producing the most marketable product attainable. Nevertheless, legitimate collective action should not be construed to allow the owners to extract excess profits. In such a situation the owners would be acting as a classic cartel. Agreements among competitors, i.e., cartels, to fix prices or divide market territories are presumed illegal under § 1 because they give competitors the ability to charge unreasonable and arbitrary prices instead of setting prices by virtue of free market forces.

On its face, Rule 4.3 divides markets among the 28 teams, a practice presumed illegal, but, as we have noted, the unique structure of the NFL precludes application of the per se rule. Instead, we must examine Rule 4.3 to determine whether it reasonably serves the legitimate collective concerns of the owners or instead permits them to reap excess profits at the expense of the consuming public.

1. RELEVANT MARKET

[The court then turned to the NFL's argument that the trial judgment should be reversed on the grounds that there had been no adverse impact on the relevant market, defined in both "product" and "geographic" terms. In the court's view, the scope of the market turned on what range of products had the ability to take significant amounts of business away from the others. This required judgments about the "reasonable interchangeability" of the products for similar uses and the "cross-elasticity of demand" for one product based on price changes in the other, which in turn depended on the "economically significant" geographic area of effective competition in which these products were traded. For their case, the Raiders claimed that the relevant market consisted just of NFL football (the product) in greater Los Angeles (the geographic area). The L.A. Coliseum claimed that its market consisted of stadiums offering facilities to NFL teams across the United States. The NFL's position was that the relevant product markets consisted of all entertainment and stadium uses across the entire country.]

* * *

That NFL football has limited substitutes from a consumer standpoint is seen from evidence that the Oakland Coliseum sold out for 10 consecutive years despite having some of the highest ticket prices in the League. A similar conclusion can be drawn from the extraordinary number of television viewers-over 100 million people-that watched the 1982 Super Bowl, the ultimate NFL product. NFL football's importance to the television networks is evidenced by the approximately $2 billion they agreed to pay the League for the right to televise the games from 1982–1986. This contract reflects the networks' anticipation that the high number of television viewers who had watched NFL football in the past would continue to do so in the future.

To some extent, the NFL itself narrowly defined the relevant market by emphasizing that NFL football is a unique product which can be produced only through the joint efforts of the 28 teams. Don Shula, coach of the Miami Dolphins, underscored this point when he stated that NFL football has a different set of fans than college football.

The evidence from which the jury could have found a narrow pro football product market was balanced, however, with other evidence which tended to show the NFL competes in the first instance with other professional sports, especially those with seasons that overlap with the NFL's. On a broader level, witnesses such as Pete Rozelle and Georgia Frontierre (owner of the L.A. Rams) testified that NFL football competes with other television offerings for network business, as well as other local entertainment for attendance at the games.

In terms of the relevant geographic market, witnesses testified, in particular Al Davis, that NFL teams compete with one another off the field for fan support in those areas where teams operate in close proximity such as New York City–New Jersey, Washington, D.C.-Baltimore, and formerly San Francisco–Oakland. Davis, of course, had first-hand knowledge of this when his team was located in Oakland. Also, the San Francisco Forty–Niners and the New York Giants were paid $18 million because of the potential for harm from competing with the Oakland Raiders and the New York Jets, respectively, once those teams joined the NFL as a result of the merger with the American Football League. Al Davis also testified at length regarding the potential for competition for fan support between the Raiders and the Los Angeles Rams once his team relocated in Los Angeles.

Testimony also adequately described the parameters of the stadia market. On one level, stadia do compete with one another for the tenancy of NFL teams. Such competition is shown by the Rams' move to Anaheim. Carroll Rosenbloom was offered what he considered to be a more lucrative situation at the Big A Stadium, so he left the L.A. Coliseum. In turn, the L.A. Coliseum sought to lure existing NFL teams to Los Angeles. Competition between the L.A. Coliseum and the Oakland Coliseum for the tenancy of the Raiders resulted.

* * *

The NFL claims that it is places, not particular stadia, that compete for NFL teams. This is true to a point because the NFL grants franchises to locales (generally a city and a 75 mile radius extending from its boundary). It is the individual stadia, however, which are most directly impacted by the restrictions on team movement. A stadium is a distinct economic entity and a territory is not.

It is also undoubtedly true, as the NFL contends, that stadia attempt to contract with a variety of forms of entertainment for exhibition in their facilities. In the case of the L.A. Coliseum, this includes college football, concerts, motorcycle races and the like. An NFL football team, however, is an especially desirable tenant. The L.A. Coliseum, for example, had received the highest rent from the Rams when they played there. We find that this evidence taken as whole provided the jury with an adequate basis on which to judge the reasonableness of Rule 4.3 both as it affected competition among NFL teams and among stadia.

We conclude with one additional observation. In the context of this case in particular, we believe that market evidence, while important, should not become an end in itself. Here the exceptional nature of the industry makes precise market definition especially difficult. To a large extent the market is determined by how one defines the entity: Is the NFL a single entity or partnership which creates a product that competes with other entertainment products for the consumer (e.g., television and fans) dollar? Or is it 28 individual entities which compete with one another both on and off the field for the support of the consumers of the more narrow football product? Of course, the NFL has attributes of both examples and a variety of evidence was presented on both views. In fact, because of the exceptional structure of the League, it was not necessary for the jury to accept absolutely either the NFL's or the plaintiff's market definitions. Instead, the critical question is whether the jury could have determined that Rule 4.3 reasonably served the NFL's interest in producing and promoting its product, i.e., competing in the entertainment market, or whether Rule 4.3 harmed competition among the 28 teams to such an extent that any benefits to the League as a whole were outweighed. As we find below, there was ample evidence for the jury to reach the latter conclusion.

2. THE HISTORY AND PURPOSE OF RULE 4.3

The NFL has awarded franchises exclusive territories since the 1930s. In the early days of professional football, numerous franchises failed and many changed location in the hope of achieving economic success. League members saw exclusive territories as a means to aid stability, ensuring the owner who was attempting to establish an NFL team in a particular city that another would not move into the same area, potentially ruining them both.

Rule 4.3 is the result of that concern. Prior to its amendment in 1978, it required unanimous League approval for a move into another team's home territory. That, of course, gave each owner an exclusive territory and he could vote against a move into his territory solely because he was afraid the competition might reduce his revenue. Notably, however, the League constitution required only three-quarters approval for all other moves. The 1978 amendment removed the double-standard, and currently three-quarters approval is required for all moves.

That the purpose of Rule 4.3 was to restrain competition among the 28 teams may seem obvious and it is not surprising the NFL admitted as much at trial. It instead argues that Rule 4.3 serves a variety of legitimate League needs, including ensuring franchise stability. We must keep in mind, however, that the Supreme Court has long rejected the notion that "ruinous competition" can be a defense to a restraint of trade. Conversely, anticompetitive purpose alone is not enough to condemn Rule 4.3. The rule must actually harm competition, and that harm must be evaluated in light of the procompetitive benefits the rule might foster.

3. Ancillary Restraints and the Reasonableness of Rule 4.3

The NFL's primary argument is that it is entitled to judgment notwithstanding the verdict because under the facts and the law, Rule 4.3 is reasonable under the doctrine of ancillary restraints. The NFL's argument is inventive and perhaps it will breathe new life into this little used area of antitrust law, but we reject it for the following reasons.

The common-law ancillary restraint doctrine was, in effect, incorporated into Sherman Act § 1 analysis by Justice Taft in *United States v. Addyston Pipe & Steel Co.*, 85 F. 271 (6th Cir.1898), aff'd as modified, 175 U.S. 211 (1899). Most often discussed in the area of covenants not to compete, the doctrine teaches that some agreements which restrain competition may be valid if they are "subordinate and collateral to another legitimate transaction and necessary to make that transaction effective."

Generally, the effect of a finding of ancillary is to "remove the per se label from restraints otherwise falling within that category." R. Bork, *Ancillary Restraints and the Sherman Act*, 15 Antitrust L. J. 211, 212 (1959). We assume, with no reason to doubt, that the agreement creating the NFL is valid and the territorial divisions therein are ancillary to its main purpose of producing NFL football. The ancillary restraint must then be tested under the rule of reason, the relevance of ancillary being it "increases the probability that the restraint will be found reasonable."

As we have already noted, the rule of reason inquiry requires us to consider the harms and benefits to competition caused by the restraint and whether the putative benefits can be achieved by less restrictive means.

The competitive harms of Rule 4.3 are plain. Exclusive territories insulate each team from competition within the NFL market, in essence allowing them to set monopoly prices to the detriment of the consuming public. The rule also effectively foreclosed free competition among stadia such as the Los Angeles Coliseum that wish to secure NFL tenants. The harm from Rule 4.3 is especially acute in this case because it prevents a move by a team into another existing team's market. If the transfer is upheld, direct competition between the Rams and Raiders would presumably ensue to the benefit of all who consume the NFL product in the Los Angeles area.

The NFL argues, however, that territorial allocations are inherent in an agreement among joint venturers to produce a product. This inherent nature, the NFL asserts, flows from the need to protect each joint venturer in the "legitimate fruits of the contract, or to protect him from the dangers of an unjust use of those fruits by the other party." We agree that the nature of NFL football requires some territorial restrictions in order both to encourage participation in the venture and to secure each venturer the legitimate fruits of that participation.

Rule 4.3 aids the League, the NFL claims, in determining its overall geographical scope, regional balance and coverage of major and minor markets. Exclusive territories aid new franchises in achieving financial stability, which protects the large initial investment an owner must make to start up a football team. Stability arguably helps ensure no one team has an undue advantage on the field. Territories foster fan loyalty which in turn promotes traditional rivalries between teams, each contributing to attendance at games and television viewing.

Joint marketing decisions are surely legitimate because of the importance of television. Title 15, U.S.C. § 1291 grants the NFL an exemption from antitrust liability, if any, that might arise out of its collective negotiation of television rights with the networks. To effectuate this right, the League must be allowed to have some control over the placement of teams to ensure NFL football is popular in a diverse group of markets.

Last, there is some legitimacy to the NFL's argument that it has an interest in preventing transfers from areas before local governments, which have made a substantial investment in stadia and other facilities, can recover their expenditures. In such a situation, local confidence in the NFL is eroded, possibly resulting in a decline in interest. All these factors considered, we nevertheless are not persuaded the jury should have concluded that Rule 4.3 is a reasonable restraint of trade. The same goals can be achieved in a variety of ways which are less harmful to competition.

As noted by Justice Rehnquist, a factor in determining the reasonableness of an ancillary restraint is the "possibility of less restrictive alternatives" which could serve the same purpose. See Justice Rehnquist's dissent from the denial of certiorari in *North American Soccer League*, 459 U.S. 1074 (1982). This is a pertinent factor in all rule of reason cases. Here, the district court correctly instructed the jury to take into account the existence of less restrictive alternatives when determining the reasonableness of Rule 4.3's territorial restraint. Because there was substantial evidence going to the existence of such alternatives, we find that the jury could have reasonably concluded that the NFL should have designed its "ancillary restraint" in a manner that served its needs but did not so foreclose competition.

The NFL argues that the requirement of Rule 4.3 that three-quarters of the owners approve a franchise move is reasonable because it deters unwise team transfers. While the rule does indeed protect an owner's investment in a football franchise, no standards or durational limits are incorporated into the voting requirement to make sure that concern is satisfied. Nor are factors such as fan loyalty and team rivalries necessarily considered.

The NFL claims that its marketing and other objectives are indirectly accounted for in the voting process because the team owners vote to maximize their profits. Since the owners are guided by the desire to increase profits, they will necessarily make reasonable decisions, the NFL asserts, on such issues of whether the new location can support two teams, whether marketing needs will be adversely affected, etc. Under the present Rule 4.3, however, an owner need muster only seven friendly votes to prevent three-quarters approval for the sole reason of preventing another team from entering its market, regardless of whether the market could sustain two franchises. A basic premise of the Sherman Act is that regulation of private profit is best left to the marketplace rather than private agreement. The present case is in fact a good example of how the market itself will deter unwise moves, since a team will not lightly give up an established base of support to confront another team in its home market.

The NFL's professed interest in ensuring that cities and other local governments secure a return on their investment in stadia is undercut in two ways. First, the local governments ought to be able to protect their investment through the leases they negotiate with the teams for the use of their stadia. Second, the NFL's interest on this point may not be as important as it would have us believe because the League has in the past allowed teams to threaten a transfer to another location in order to give the team leverage in lease negotiations.

Finally, the NFL made no showing that the transfer of the Raiders to Los Angeles would have any harmful effect on the League. Los Angeles is a market large enough for the successful operation of two teams, there would be no scheduling difficulties, facilities at the L.A. Coliseum are more than adequate, and no loss of future television revenue was foreseen. Also, the NFL offered no evidence that its interest in maintaining regional balance would be adversely affected by a move of a northern California team to southern California.

It is true, as the NFL claims, that the antitrust laws are primarily concerned with the promotion of interbrand competition. To the extent the NFL is a product which competes with other forms of entertainment, including other sports, its rules governing territorial division can be said to promote interbrand competition. Under this analysis, the territorial allocations most directly suppress intrabrand, that is, NFL team versus NFL team, competition. A more direct impact on intrabrand competition does not mean, however, the restraint is reasonable. The finder of fact must still balance the gain to interbrand competition against the loss of intrabrand competition. Here, the jury could have found that the rules restricting team movement do not sufficiently promote interbrand competition to justify the negative impact on intrabrand competition.

To withstand antitrust scrutiny, restrictions on team movement should be more closely tailored to serve the needs inherent in producing the NFL "product" and competing with other forms of entertainment. An express recognition and consideration of those objective factors espoused by the NFL as important, such as population, economic projections, facilities, regional balance, etc., would be well advised. Fan loyalty and location continuity could also be considered. Al Davis in fact testified that in 1978 he proposed that the League adopt a set of objective guidelines to govern team relocation rather than continuing to utilize a subjective voting procedure.

Some sort of procedural mechanism to ensure consideration of all the above factors may also be necessary, including an opportunity for the team proposing the move to present its case. See *Silver v. New York Stock Exchange*, 373 U.S. 341 (1963) (without procedural safeguards, the collective act of the Exchange in disconnecting the wire service to a broker constituted a boycott, per se illegal under § 1); cf. *Deesen v. Professional Golfers' Ass'n*, 358 F.2d 165 (9th Cir.1966) (where PGA had reasonable rules governing eligibility of players for tournaments, there was not a § 1 violation). In the present case, for example, testimony indicated that some owners, as well as Commissioner Rozelle, dislike Al Davis and consider him a maverick. Their vote against the Raiders' move could have been motivated by animosity rather than business judgment.

Substantial evidence existed for the jury to find the restraint imposed by Rule 4.3 was not reasonably necessary to the production and sale of the NFL product. Therefore, the NFL is not entitled to judgment notwithstanding the verdict.

Affirmed.

[The appeals court majority concluded, then, that the jury's verdict about the unreasonableness of this restraint—the opinion labelled this a "paradigm fact question"—was based on adequate evidence in the record. The majority judgment elicited the following vigorous dissent, which focused on the single-entity question.]

JUDGE WILLIAMS, dissenting.

* * *

The only realistic manner in which to define what constitutes a single entity for antitrust review is to focus upon the purpose the definition is to serve. "Single entity" taken in a functional sense begins and ends with an analysis of formal organizational and operational aspects of an enterprise, reconciled with the realities of the economic competition in the marketplace. If the aim of the Sherman Act § 1 is consumer-dictated supply, unfettered by conspiracy between competing producers—and, I submit that it is—extreme caution is warranted in defining precisely what competitive units exist in the marketplace. It is equally as important to permit collaboration and concerted action among branches of a single economic entity in the marketplace with impunity from the Sherman Act § 1, as it is to police conspiracies between economic competitive entities. Nonetheless, all economic units remain susceptible to challenge under the antitrust laws from those external entities injured by acts violative of § 1, or competitive entities injured as result of monopoly, or attempted monopoly, in an industry under Sherman Act § 2 tenets.

Resolving whether the NFL is a single entity requires consideration of many factors, including formalistic aspects of operations such as ownership, overlapping directorates, joint marketing or manufacturing, legal identity, corporate law autonomy, and substantive aspects such as de facto autonomy of member clubs, chains of command over policy decisions, public perception and economic interdependency rendering otherwise independent member clubs subordinate to the integrated whole. When the entities in question are to be evaluated under the antitrust laws, the crucial criterion is whether the formally distinct member clubs compete in any economically meaningful sense in the marketplace.

* * *

The district court placed an unwarranted emphasis upon the formalistic aspects of the relationship of the NFL and the member clubs, ignoring the subtle, but yet more significant interdependency of the member clubs and the indivisibility of the clubs with the NFL. For example, the district court makes much of two such formal organizational characteristics: separate incorporation and management. But, when viewed from the mundane perspective of daily operations, emphasis upon these legal formalisms obscures the reality of life in the NFL. Only the athletic stratagems are autonomous—albeit tightly constrained by league guidelines on eligibility, medical and physical condition and exploitation of player talent. The NFL cannot truly be separated from its member clubs, which are simultaneously franchisees and franchisors. The Raiders did not, and do not now, seek to compete with the other clubs in any sense other than in their win/loss standings; they do not challenge the plethora of other ancillary regulations attendant to the league structure, including the draft, regulation and scheduling of meetings between teams, and the system of pooled and shared revenues among the clubs because they wish to remain within its beneficial ambit.

* * *

[F]unctionally distinct units that cannot produce separate, individual goods or services absent coordination are inextricably bound in an economic sense, and must adopt certain intra-league instrumentalities to regulate the whole's "downstream output." In the case of the member clubs, this "downstream output" is professional football, and the organ of regulation is the unincorporated, not-for-profit, association commonly known as the NFL. There is virtually no practical distinction between the League, administered by the appointed Commissioner, per se and the member clubs; the NFL represents to all clubs, including the Raiders, the least costly and most efficient manner of reaching day-to-day decisions regarding the production of their main, and collectively produced, product.

Although the NFL determines matters of scheduling, resolving player disciplinary matters and inter-club disputes as well as other routine matters, critical league decisions, such as the matter of franchise location, are submitted to an Executive Committee comprised of a representative of each club. There can be no instance of the Executive Committee acting in other than the collective interests of the member clubs, since by definition, that body's decisions are the consensus of NFL members. There is no distinct interest of the NFL, since it exists solely to coordinate the members' participation in the joint production of professional football.

By riveting its attention upon the "single entity" issue, as a sort of talismanic affirmative defense to the appellees' charges here, the district court overlooked the dispositive inquiry of whether Rule 4.3, as an instrument of the NFL member clubs, violated the Sherman Act § 1, by restricting any economically independent entities from supplying goods or services related to professional football to the individual clubs. I use "upstream flow" as shorthand for products and services like players and coaches, television services, potential investors and the myriad of other integrated industries; member clubs do have independent and economically significant identities apart from the collective NFL for the limited purposes of their extra-league dealings with those upstream suppliers. Thus, § 1 can and should protect the competitive aspects of player drafts, disallow cross-ownership bans and exclusive television and equipment contracts, by insuring that any one club's interaction outside the confines of intra-league regulation of production of the sport is unfettered by the working of any intraleague rule.

This is the critical distinction between cases which invalidate various intraleague rules, and those which uphold them. That member clubs compete for investors and the services of talented players is underscored by the fact that, although aggregate revenues are shared among all member clubs, there is no intra-league regulation upon the form of investment by a member club's financial backers, the dividend policy, or operating expenses and expenditures of any member for player services. League regulations comport with economic reality in this sense; courts have merely applied a similar philosophy to other aspects of the professional leagues' operations, including, inter alia, club-player relationships.

The paradox to which I return, as the root of why the NFL, as well as other sports leagues, must be regarded as a "single entity" is that the keener the on-field competition becomes, the more successful their off-the-field, and ultimately legally relevant, collaboration. The formal entities, including the member clubs—including the Raiders—which the district court ruled to be competitors cannot compete, because the only product or service which is in their separate interests to produce can only result as a fruit of their joint efforts. This systemic cooperation trickles down to all members of the league, regardless of their on-the-field record, at least to the extent of the shared revenues....

A ruling that the NFL cannot enforce Rule 4.3 is effectively ruling that it may not enforce any collective decision of its member clubs over the dissent of a club member, although this is precisely what each owner has contractually bargained for in joining the enterprise. Without power to reach collective decisions, the NFL structure becomes superfluous, and professional sports, without a cost-effective policing mechanism such as the league, will dissolve in the face of uncontrollable free-riding and loss of economies of scale.

Not only did the district court underrate the business scenario in which the member teams cooperate far more than they compete in the legally irrelevant on-field sense, but its directed verdict on the single entity issue ignored two significant aspects of the NFL's organization. First, the NFL member clubs pool their revenues to a degree unique even among sporting leagues. By focusing upon the separate calculation of profits and loss by members, the district court elevated form over substance. Profit, as currently understood in the accounting profession, is a term of art, and as such is inherently subjective, often manipulated by equity interests to serve legally irrelevant business motives. The relevant consideration, as the NFL has recognized by implementation of its shared revenue concept, is total infusion of consumer dollars into the sport, and some predictable and centrally administered allocation of those jointly earned revenues among member clubs. After that purpose, the members adopt the only workable model for earning and distributing the revenues from sale of a non-severable and indistinct product—professional football.

The product distributed by the member clubs is not analogous to ball bearings (*Timken Roller Bearing Co. v. U.S.*), mattresses (*U.S. v. Sealy, Inc.*), or groceries (*U.S. v. Topco Associates*), because stripped of the NFL rules, participation in a regulated draft, orderly schedules and league standings, professional football is indistinguishable from sand lot follies. This inescapable fact of interdependence distinguishes the NFL franchisees and professional football from other industries comprised of "separate business entities whose products have independent value."

* * *

Holding that the NFL is not a single entity, but rather an aggregation of economic competitors, is tantamount to ruling that the NFL structure is itself per se invalid under the Sherman Act § 1; this will spell the end of sporting leagues as are currently used in football, hockey, golf, soccer, basketball and countless other associations in industries with similar endemic characteristics.

To elevate formal corporate characteristics of ongoing economic entities above the substance of what purpose and function the structure serves, and what product(s) emerge from the process, would not only destroy the NFL, professional sports leagues, and the goodwill that results from continuity in national allocation of the sport throughout the country, but would create a rule of law casting all franchise/wholesale distribution relationships into inescapable doubt.

Rather than avoid creating an "exemption" from the Sherman Act for professional sporting leagues, failing to account for the substantial and unique characteristics extant in professional sports by refusing the NFL review as a single entity creates turmoil and dissolves the analytic framework within which courts scrutinize agreements under Sherman Act § 1. It is unrealistic and inaccurate to lump intra-NFL rules in with agreements binding separate economic entities which produce independent products and accrue independent revenues. Rule 4.3 is no more a restraint on trade in professional football for Sherman Act § 1 purposes, than is an intra-corporate directive regulating the location or operation of its headquarters, franchise, or branch of a multi-outlet business.

No "antitrust exemption" for the NFL would be created by holding that it is a single economic entity for purposes of regulating franchise location. Section 2 of the Sherman Act, prohibiting monopolies and attempts to monopolize, remains fully applicable to all NFL intra-league rules and activities.

Many present NFL practices, including Rule 4.3, are highly suspect under the Sherman Act § 2 prohibitions, because notwithstanding the form or substance of the NFL's style of organization and operation, some practices appear calculated to create barriers to entry for would-be rival leagues in profitable geographical markets. In short, Sherman Act § 2 is the proper curb upon the NFL's successful exploitation of its intra-firm economies of scale and competitive advantages.

* * *

As always, § 1 remains a viable theory under which those "upstream" aspects of member clubs' operations—those activities [for] which the NFL and previous courts acknowledge the individual members as economically distinct entities—could be challenged. An oft-tried, and frequently successful example of this theory has been the player draft litigation; the distinction between instances in which the NFL acts as a collective monitor of intra-league affairs, and those in which it intercedes at the behest of a member club for anti-competitive advantage over "upstream" bargaining entities outside the NFL.

The purposes for which the NFL should be viewed as a single entity, impervious to § 1 attack, must be functionally defined as those instances in which member clubs must coordinate intraleague policy and practices if the joint product is to result. Prohibiting the NFL from attempting to exploit a monopolistic position in the industry, or from cloaking concerted anti-competitive pressure upon extrinsic "upstream" suppliers in the guise of "league" restrictions, does not require that we strike ancillary terms of the franchise agreements between member clubs as anti-competitive. A principled approach requires that we distinguish one situation from the other, and protect both competitive markets for football players and television coverage, as well as the integrity of terms Al Davis agreed to as salient aspects of his arms' length negotiations with the other member clubs. Davis has received no more or less than he has bargained for, as a franchisee of the NFL.

To hold the NFL a single entity for purposes of intraleague regulation of relocation of existing franchises, thereby cutting off Sherman Act § 1 liability in this instance, is fully consistent with the prior cases that address the validity of league regulation of member clubs. In such cases, the leagues' power has consistently been upheld.

This case raised again the important question whether the single entity issue is one of fact, of law, or of mixed fact and law. Recall that in *NASL*, the appellate court reversed the trial judge's finding that the NFL was a single entity, while in *Raiders I*, despite labelling the issue one of fact, the appellate court upheld the trial judge's directed verdict against the league on this issue. Keep this procedural factor in mind as you read further single entity analyses in this chapter.

Questions for Discussion

1. Regardless of whether courts rule that the NFL (or any other league) is a single entity and thereby insulated from any § 1 antitrust scrutiny, the teams are in a reasonably close and cooperative relationship in producing and selling their games. As Justice Rehnquist stated in *NASL* (dealing with the NFL's ban on interleague cross-ownership), the success of a joint venture may require significant restrictions on each member's individual freedom of action. The Supreme Court explained in *Continental T.V., Inc. v. GTE Sylvania Inc.*, 433 U.S. 36 (1977), why such restraints can be compatible with antitrust's objective of market competition. In that case the Court rejected *per se* illegality of "vertical restraints" imposed by a manufacturer on the territories in which its distributors could market the manufacturer's products. The Court reasoned that such limitations on "intrabrand competition"—one distributor competing against another to sell a particular

manufacturer's brand of television set—may be necessary to sustain the manufacturer's competitive presence in the broader interbrand market for all brands of television sets. (For a more detailed discussion of and excerpts from *GTE Sylvania*, see Chapter 3.)

How would you apply this line of analysis to the analogous problem of a restriction imposed by a sports league on the freedom of individual clubs to change the territory in which they play their home games (in other words, distribute the league's product)? What might a team owner hope to gain, artistically or financially, from moving his club to a new location? What tangible reasons might lead other clubs to resist such a relocation? Might this depend on the degree to which league rules require the sharing of revenues from various sources? In comparing the interests of an individual owner and the group of owners, whose are more compatible with the consumer welfare that antitrust law is supposed to promote? Does your answer vary depending on the circumstances of the proposed move, and if so, what are the relevant circumstances?

2. Turning now to the specifics of the *Raiders* case, how was the jury supposed to balance effects on both interbrand and intrabrand competition? As for intrabrand competition, would the Raiders' presence in Los Angeles affect the competitive behavior of either the Rams or the Raiders? If so, would the Raiders absence from the San Francisco area affect the 49ers' competitive behavior in the opposite manner? As for interbrand competition, what does this mean? Does a "monopolist" that increases its efficiency enhance interbrand competition by making a higher quality or less expensive product, or does it diminish interbrand competition by raising barriers to entry? In the *Raiders* case, how would you have balanced the intrabrand competitive effects in Los Angeles and San Francisco and the interbrand effects in the larger entertainment market?

3. The *Raiders I* majority noted that one factor in determining reasonableness was whether or not there were less restrictive alternatives that could serve the same purpose. What does this mean? How would a jury use such an instruction in its deliberations? After the case was concluded, the NFL amended Rule 4.3 to include a list of "objective factors" that club owners should consider in deciding whether to approve a franchise relocation—for example, market size, stadium adequacy, and attendance. Had this language been in the rule prior to the teams' 22–0 vote against the Raiders move, would the rule or its application in the *Raiders* case have been less restrictive? Would it have changed any votes? What if the owners had amended Rule 4.3 to require only a majority vote to approve a relocation (or perhaps only 25% approval), but the vote was still 22–0 against? Would that rule have been less restrictive? Might it have changed any votes in the *Raiders* case?

4. The *Raiders I* majority rejected the NFL's claim that Rule 4.3 was inherently reasonable as a restraint ancillary to a larger lawful contract. The court stated that classification of a restraint as ancillary means only that the restraint is not *per se* illegal. How should a restraint's ancillary nature be considered in subsequent rule of reason analysis? What instructions should a trial court give to a jury? What inherent rights should partners in a joint venture (all of whom have a fiduciary duty to the venture) have to control

the business activity of their partners in the conduct of the venture's business?

5. Note that the dissenting judge in *Raiders I* argued that the NFL was a single entity immune from § 1 attack against franchise location decisions, but he agreed with the implicit finding in cases such as *Smith* and *Mackey* (included in Chapter 3 above) that the league is a § 1 combination with respect to its decisions about player personnel or television and merchandising matters. Does that distinction appeal to you as a matter of legal logic? As a matter of practical common sense?

The *Raiders I* decision concerned only the NFL's antitrust liability for rejecting the Raiders' proposed move to Los Angeles. Following a second trial on the damages question, the jury awarded the Raiders $11.55 million for profits lost due to the two-year delay in their move south. The NFL appealed this sizable damage award (trebled under the Sherman Act to over $34 million) on the ground that the benefits the Raiders realized by taking from the NFL the opportunity to create an expansion franchise in Los Angeles should be deducted from the team's lost profits. This produced the *Raiders II* decision, *Los Angeles Memorial Coliseum Comm'n v. NFL*, 791 F.2d 1356 (9th Cir.1986).

The Circuit court first endorsed the basic premise to the NFL's argument:

> Prior to 1980, the NFL as a whole owned the right to expand into the Los Angeles area. As evidence at both phases of the trial in this case demonstrated, the Los Angeles opportunity represented an extremely valuable expansion possibility for the league. The value of the Los Angeles opportunity arose not only from the economic potential of one of the nation's largest media markets, but also from the NFL's well-established and widely followed nation-wide entertainment product....
>
> As indicated above, the value of the league's expansion opportunities belonged to the league as a whole, or in other words, was owned in part by each franchise owner. Unquestionably, when the Raiders moved to Los Angeles, they appropriated for themselves the expansion value that had accumulated in Los Angeles. Although by moving out of Oakland the Raiders "gave back" an expansion opportunity to the NFL, the uncontradicted testimony at trial showed the Los Angeles market to be a significantly more lucrative franchise opportunity. Indeed, the Raiders' managing general partner, Al Davis, testified that the Raiders increased their value by some $25 million by moving to Los Angeles.

791 F.2d at 137. Since prior to 1980 the NFL had done nothing illegal in enhancing the value of the football market in Los Angeles, to give the Raiders all of "the accumulated value of that business opportunity" would confer on owner Davis a "windfall benefit." Instead, the differ-

ence in the value of the Los Angeles expansion opportunity (prior to 1980) and the Oakland opportunity that was now being returned to the league, had to be offset against the damages awarded to the Raiders for the two-year delay in their move to Los Angeles.

Application of this offset rule is consistent with, and indeed, virtually compelled by, this court's *Raiders 1* opinion. In analyzing the "unique" nature of professional athletic leagues vis-a-vis the antitrust laws, this panel expressly acknowledged that "the nature of NFL football requires some territorial restrictions in order both to encourage participation in the venture *and to secure each venturer the legitimate fruits of that participation.*" Here, the league owners collectively possessed the value that had accumulated in the Los Angeles expansion opportunity. This value, as indicated above, was created at least in part through the NFL's development, over the years, of a popular spectator sport with a national following. Although this panel upheld the liability jury's conclusion that Rule 4.3 as it was applied to the Raiders' move was an unreasonable restraint of trade, the opinion noted several less onerous forms of territorial restrictions that could pass muster under the rule of reason. Among these were standards restricting team movement that expressly recognized certain objective factors such as population, economic projections and the like, that the league could legitimately consider in deciding whether to permit a team to move. If such restrictions, applied in a non-arbitrary manner, would be reasonable under the Sherman Act, then *a fortiori*, a rule requiring merely an objectively-determined payment to league members as compensation for the right to take a valuable, jointly-owned franchise opportunity out of the league's hands, would also be a reasonable restriction.

791 F.2d at 1373.

Questions for Discussion

1. *Raiders I* and *Raiders II* were both decided by the same three-judge panel. The second opinion reasoned that the NFL owned the expansion market in Los Angeles, and that the Raiders' move to Los Angeles gave them a windfall benefit. Is this reasoning consistent with the first opinion's conclusions on the single-entity and rule of reason issues? Both the NFL and the Raiders filed certiorari petitions after *Raiders II*, arguing that the two decisions were irreconcilable, but the Supreme Court again declined to hear the case. See 484 U.S. 826 (1987).

2. *Raiders II* indicated that it would have been reasonable and thus legal if, instead of blocking the Raiders' move to Los Angeles, the league had merely levied a charge against the Raiders for the difference in the value of the Los Angeles and Oakland markets. How would such values be calculated? Could the Raiders refuse to pay the amount determined by the league, and then sue for treble damages under § 1, claiming that the amount charged was in fact greater than it should have been? If so, would a jury reviewing the amount of the charge substitute its own judgment of the

correct amount, or should it be instructed to give some deference to the league's determination?

3. In another part of the *Raiders II* opinion, the court reversed the jury's verdict finding that the NFL had breached a state law duty of good faith and fair dealing with the Raiders:

> The evidence presented in this case, taken as a whole, permits only one of two conclusions: either (1) neither the Raiders nor the NFL breached the duty of good faith with respect to the contemplated franchise move from Oakland to Los Angeles, or (2) both parties so breached.... The Raiders and their managing general partner Al Davis expressed, on various occasions ... their refusal to forego these relocation plans regardless of the wishes of the NFL. They in essence denied any contractual obligation to submit their relocation plans to the League for approval, and deliberately sought to avoid or circumvent the prescribed procedure for obtaining a vote of the other teams. In fact, the Raiders even notified the League, prior to the owners' vote, that they had officially and unilaterally "moved" to Los Angeles.... It cannot reasonably be maintained that the NFL's subsequent withholding of authorization, but not these actions of the Raiders, constituted a breach of the implied promise of good faith and fair dealing.

See 791 F.2d at 1361–62. Again, are *Raiders I* and *Raiders II* compatible? How does the finding that all NFL teams have reciprocal duties of good faith toward one another affect the single entity or rule of reason issues? If the NFL's disapproval of the Raiders' move violated federal antitrust law, how could the Raiders' refusal to submit their proposed move to such a vote be a breach of that duty?

4. The wave of relocations and inter-city bidding for NFL teams in the mid-1990s has generated several § 1 lawsuits against the league's revised Rule 4.3, one that was amended after *Raiders I* to include several "objective" factors the owners must consider when voting on a proposed relocation. In 1997, Al Davis and his Raiders were again suing the league, claiming that Rule 4.3 was used to block the Raiders move back to Oakland for the 1994 season, after the Los Angeles Memorial Coliseum had been greatly damaged by the Northridge Earthquake that January. In addition, the Raiders (and the City of Oakland) are seeking to prevent the NFL from applying its 60–40 gate receipt revenue-sharing rule to the portion of the personal seat license and $50 annual seat maintenance fees charged to season ticket holders that the team and the city had agreed would be used to help pay for the $175 million improvements to the Coliseum that had induced the Raiders to return to their original home. In the spring of 1997, a federal district judge refused to grant the NFL summary dismissal of either the contract or antitrust claims, which means that a new *Raiders* saga will be unfolding in the Central District of California. In addition, Victor Kiam, who had bought the New England Patriots from the Sullivan family for $85 million in 1988, is suing the league because its Rule 4.3 allegedly forced him to sell his New England Patriots in 1992 to James Orthwein for $110 million, instead of allowing him to keep the team and move it to another city (probably St. Louis). Finally, the St. Louis Tourist & Convention Center is suing the league, alleging that Rule 4.3 allowed the NFL to extract a

substantial $30 million relocation fee from the Rams (one that was not charged to the Raiders), and that this increased the cash subsidy the Center had to pay the Rams to lure them out of Los Angeles: in the fall of 1997, the trial judge dismissed the case after a lengthy trial on the basis of a lack of evidence of conspiracy, and the Center is now appealing.

Do the decisions in *Raiders I* and *II* provide support for any or all of these antitrust claims? Can the league offer a reasonable single entity defense to these cases? How would you balance the intrabrand and interbrand competitive effects in the cases involving proposed moves to St. Louis where there was no other NFL team? Does it matter that the Patriots would have moved there from a Greater Boston market with no other NFL team, but the Rams moved there from a Los Angeles market that at the time had a second team (the Raiders) playing there? In making these determinations, should juries undertake *de novo* evaluation of the competitive effects, or should they give some deference to the judgment of the league owners? Finally, should the NFL follow (and be entitled to follow) the lead of the NBA, NHL, and MLB and adopt a proposed rule that would require any team that loses a lawsuit against the league to pay for all of the latter's legal costs?

Raiders II was significant not just in sharply reducing the size of the NFL's damage liability to the Raiders, but also in offering somewhat greater support for league constraints upon unilateral team movements. The latter effect became apparent soon afterwards in litigation involving the National Basketball Association and the San Diego Clippers. The Clippers decided to move their operations from San Diego to the Los Angeles Sports Arena (which, ironically, was also owned by the Los Angeles Memorial Coliseum Commission) where the Clippers would compete for fans with the Los Angeles Lakers who were playing in their Forum. After *Raiders I*, but before *Raiders II*, the NBA decided not to risk trebled damages by refusing to schedule Clippers' games in Los Angeles. Instead, the league sued the Clippers in San Diego, seeking a judicial declaration that the league could lawfully prohibit this relocation. After the district court had summarily dismissed the league's suit, the Ninth Circuit provided yet another interpretation of its holdings in *Raiders I* and *Raiders II*.

NBA v. SAN DIEGO CLIPPERS BASKETBALL CLUB

United States Court of Appeals, Ninth Circuit, 1987.
815 F.2d 562.

FERGUSON, CIRCUIT JUDGE.

* * *

The antitrust issues are directly controlled by the two *Raiders* opinions, although the district judge had the benefit only of *Raiders I* when he rendered judgment. Collectively, the *Raiders* opinions held that rule of reason analysis governed a professional sports league's efforts to restrict franchise movement. More narrowly, however, *Raiders I* merely held that a reasonable jury could have found that the NFL's application of its franchise movement rule was an unreasonable restraint of trade. *Raiders II* confirmed that the jury's liability verdict affirmed in *Raiders I* "held Rule 4.3 [the franchise movement rule] invalid only as it was applied to the Raiders' proposed move to Los Angeles." The Clippers' and the Coliseum's efforts to characterize *Raiders I* as presenting guidelines for franchise movement rules are thus unavailing. Neither the jury's verdict in *Raiders*, nor the court's affirmance of that verdict, held that a franchise movement rule, in and of itself, was invalid under the antitrust laws ... [T]he panel set down no absolute rule for sports leagues. Instead, it examined the facts before it and concluded that the jury's conclusion that the NFL violated the antitrust laws was supported by the record.

Yet the Clippers argue, as they must to support summary judgment, that the "NBA three-quarters rule ... is illegal under *Raiders I* "—i.e., either that the NBA rule is void as a matter of law under *Raiders I*, or that the NBA has not adduced genuine issues of fact to allow the rule to stand. The Clippers assert that the rule "is illegal as applied ... [but that under *Raiders I*], a professional sports league's club relocation rule must at least be 'closely tailored' and incorporate objective standards and criteria such as population, economic projections, playing facilities, regional balance, and television revenues." ... The Clippers' confusion, and that of a number of commentators, may derive from the *Raiders I* panel's painstaking efforts to guide sports leagues toward procedures that might, in all cases, withstand antitrust analysis. The objective factors and procedures recounted by the Clippers are "well advised," and might be sufficient to demonstrate procompetitive purposes that would save the restriction from the rule of reason. They are not, however, necessary conditions to the legality of franchise relocation rules.

... As we have demonstrated, antitrust analysis under *Raiders I* indicates that the question of what restraints are reasonable is one of fact. We believe that numerous issues of fact remain.

The NBA asserts a number of genuine issues of fact: (1) the purpose of the restraint as demonstrated by the NBA's use of a variety of criteria in evaluating franchise movement, (2) the market created by professional basketball, which the NBA alleges is substantially different from that of professional football, and (3) the actual effect the NBA's limitations on movements might have on trade. The NBA's assertions, if further documented at trial, create an entirely different factual setting than that of the Raiders and the NFL. Further, as the NBA correctly notes, the antitrust issue here is vastly different than that in the *Raiders* cases: the issue here is "whether the mere requirement that a team seek [NBA] Board of Governor approval before it seizes a new franchise location violates the Sherman Act." The NBA here did not attempt to forbid the move. It scheduled the Clippers in the Sports Arena, and when faced with continued assertions of potential antitrust liability, brought this suit for declaratory relief. Given the *Raiders I* rejection of per se analysis for franchise movement rules of sports leagues, and the existence of genuine issues of fact regarding the reasonableness of the restraint, the judgment against the NBA must be reversed.

Summary judgment reversed.

After this decision had been rendered, the NBA and the Clippers settled their litigation, with the Clippers agreeing to make a substantial payment to the league for the right to remain in Los Angeles.[i] What are the broader guidelines that emerge from *Raiders* and from *Clippers* for the benefit of leagues and teams that naturally want to know *before* antitrust litigation whether a team's proposed move from one city to another can either be made or be blocked? What kind of legal liability does the league—or the club—face if it guesses incorrectly about the state and application of the law?

The issues of franchise relocation must also be viewed in tandem with the antitrust treatment of league expansion. Suppose that a city builds an expensive new sports facility in the hope of attracting a sports franchise (as St. Petersburg, Florida, built its Suncoast Dome), but no existing team is prepared to move there. However, a local entrepreneur with the appropriate background and resources has indicated firm interest in filling this vacant facility and territory, which has the requisite population and fan interest. Should the entrepreneur and/or the city have a right under antitrust law to insist that the league offer an expansion franchise?

A preliminary rehearsal of this question took place in an analogous context, in the case of *Levin v. NBA*, 385 F.Supp. 149 (S.D.N.Y.1974). The plaintiff had entered into an agreement to purchase the Boston Celtics. The NBA, like other sports leagues, required approval of such transactions by three-fourths of the other teams acting as the league's Board of Governors. The Board rejected Levin's bid to purchase the Celtics, and Levin sued. The federal district judge did not venture into the merits of the contrary views asserted by the parties about the nature and legitimacy of the grounds for rejection, which apparently were related in some way to Levin's long-standing business relationship with Sam Schulman, the maverick owner of the Seattle SuperSonics (whose signing of Spencer Haywood before he was four years out of high school had triggered the *Denver Rockets* litigation described in Chapter 3).

---

i. For analysis of both the *Raiders* damages decision and the *Clippers* liability decision, see Kenneth L. Shropshire, *Opportunistic Sports Franchise Relocations: Can Punitive Damages in Actions Based Upon Contract Strike a Balance?*, 22 Loyola of L.A. L. Rev. 569 (1989).

Instead, the judge summarily dismissed the claim on the ground that this case presented no antitrust concerns:

> While it is true that the antitrust laws apply to a professional athletic league, and that joint action by members of a league can have antitrust implications, this is not such a case. Here the plaintiffs wanted to join with those unwilling to accept them, not to compete with them, but to be partners in the operation of a sports league for plaintiffs' profit. Further, no matter which reason one credits for the rejection, it was not an anti-competitive reason. Finally, regardless of the financial impact of this rejection upon the plaintiffs, if any, the exclusion of the plaintiffs from membership in the league did not have an anticompetitive effect nor an effect upon the public interest. The Celtics continue as an operating club, and indeed are this year's champion.
>
> The law is well established that it is competition, and not individual competitors, that is protected by the antitrust laws....
>
> It is also clear that where the action the plaintiffs attack, the rejection from co-partnership, has neither anticompetitive intent nor effect, that conduct is not violative of the antitrust laws....

385 F.Supp. at 152.

Remember, though, that a decade after the equally abrupt dismissal of the *San Francisco Seals* relocation case, Al Davis was able to persuade an appellate court that he did have an antitrust right to move his Oakland Raiders team to Los Angeles. In tandem with Davis, three owners from the defunct World Football League sought to persuade a different federal appellate court that they were entitled to admission to the National Football League—not as purchasers of an existing team, but as creators of a new team. And as the main survivor of the World Football League venture in the 1970s (which generated the *Bergey* case in Chapter 2), these owners brought with their application not just a city, a stadium, and a fan base, but also a team of players looking for a league in which to play.

MID–SOUTH GRIZZLIES v. NFL

United States Court of Appeals, Third Circuit, 1983.
720 F.2d 772.

GIBBONS, CIRCUIT JUDGE.

[The Memphis Southmen were one of the few successful franchises in the World Football League, which opened in 1974 and closed midway through the 1975 season. The team then reorganized with players from two other WFL teams (the Philadelphia Bell and the Southern California Sun), named itself the Grizzlies, and applied for a franchise in the National Football League. The Grizzlies claimed that they were an established football enterprise operating in a city, Memphis, that had demonstrated strong popular demand for professional football, and was not included in the 75–mile "home territory" of any existing NFL franchise. The NFL rejected the Grizzlies' application; the reasons given were recent expansion to Seattle and Tampa, the scheduling need for an even number of teams, and an uncertain labor relationship with the NFLPA (the *Mackey* suit was still being litigated). The Grizzlies then filed an antitrust suit in Philadelphia. The suit relied not only on the Sherman Act, but also upon 15 U.S.C.A. § 1291 (Public Law 87–331), which gave professional sports leagues a limited antitrust exemption to pool and sell their television rights, and upon Public Law 89–800, which in 1966 amended § 1291 to permit the merger of the National and American Football Leagues "if such agreement increases rather than decreases the number of professional football clubs." The trial judge granted the NFL's motion for summary dismissal, and the Grizzlies appealed. The circuit court rejected the Grizzlies' claim that the additional monopoly power conferred on an expanded NFL by that special legislation imposed on the league an affirmative obligation, in effect, to share that power with franchise-seekers such as the Grizzlies. The court then turned to the question whether the NFL's rejection of the Grizzlies' application constituted a violation of the basic Sherman Act.]

* * *

... In this case there is no dispute about the requisite concert of action among the defendants. The defendants do deny injury to competition in any relevant market from their rejection of the Grizzlies' application. They urge that any limitations on actual or potential competition in any relevant market were insulated from antitrust scrutiny by the 1961 and 1966 statutes referred to, or are reasonable as a matter of law. They also urge that as a matter of law there was no competition among league members or between league members and non-members in other markets to which the Grizzlies point.

The Grizzlies identify as the relevant product market major-league professional football, and as the relevant geographic market the United States. The trial court found these markets to be relevant. The court observed as well that "[t]here is no doubt that the NFL currently has a monopoly in the United States in major league football." The Grizzlies pose as the question on this appeal "whether it can be said as a matter of law that defendants neither acquired nor maintained monopoly power over any relevant market in an unlawful manner."

As to the acquisition of dominant position and monopoly power, the facts are undisputed. Long before the Grizzlies and the World Football League came into existence, Congress authorized the merger of the two major football leagues extant in 1966, and granted to the merged league the power to pool television revenues. That congressional decision conferred on the NFL the market power which it holds in the market for professional football. Congress could not have been unaware that necessary effect of the television revenue sharing scheme which it approved for the NFL would be that all members of that league would be strengthened in their ability to bid for the best available playing and coaching personnel, to the potential disadvantage of new entrants.

* * *

... As noted above, Sherman Act liability requires an injury to competition. In this case the competition inquiry is a narrow one, because the Grizzlies are not seeking recovery as potential competitors outside the NFL. They identify as the antitrust violation the league's negative vote on their application for membership.

* * *

Assuming, without deciding, that the summary judgment record presents disputed fact issues with respect to the actual motivation of the NFL members, those disputed facts are not material, under § 1 of the Sherman Act, if the action complained of produced no injury to competition.

As to competition with NFL members in the professional football market, including the market for sale of television rights, the exclusion was patently pro-competitive, since it left the Memphis area, with a large stadium and a significant metropolitan area population, available as a site for another league's franchise, and it left the Grizzlies' organization as a potential competitor in such a league. If there was any injury to competition, actual or potential, therefore, it must have been to intra-league competition.

The NFL defendants' position is that the summary judgment record establishes conclusively the absence of competition, actual or potential, among league members. Rather, they urge, the league is a single entity, a joint venture in the presentation of the professional football spectacle.

For the most part the congressionally authorized arrangements under which the NFL functions eliminate competition among the league members. Indeed it is undisputed that on average more than 70% of each member club's revenue is shared revenue derived from sources other than operations at its home location. The Grizzlies do not challenge the legality of the NFL's revenue sharing arrangements, and seek to participate in them. The Grizzlies emphasize that there nevertheless remains a not insignificant amount of intra-league non-athletic competition. We need not, in order to affirm the summary judgment, accept entirely the NFL's position that there is no intra-league competition. Conceivably within certain geographic submarkets two league members compete with one another for ticket buyers, for local broadcast revenue, and for sale of the concession items like food and beverages and team paraphernalia. Thus rejection of a franchise application in the New York metropolitan area, for example, might require a different antitrust analysis than is suggested by this record. But the Grizzlies were obliged, when faced with the NFL denial of the existence of competition among NFL members and a potential franchisee at Memphis, to show some more than minimal level of potential competition, in the product markets in which league members might compete. They made no such showing. The record establishes that the NFL franchise nearest to Memphis is at St. Louis, Mo., over 280 miles away. There is no record evidence that professional football teams located in Memphis and in St. Louis would compete for the same ticket purchasers, for the same local broadcast outlets, in the sale of team paraphernalia, or in any other manner.

The Grizzlies contend on appeal, although they did not so contend in the trial court, that league members compete in what they call the "raw material market" for players and coaching personnel. Entirely apart from the propriety of considering a legal theory not presented in the trial court, there are major defects in this Grizzlies' argument. First, the Grizzlies exclusion from the league in no way restrained them from competing for players by forming a competitive league. Second, they fail to explain how, if their exclusion from the league reduced competition for team personnel, that reduction caused an injury to the Grizzlies' business or property.

One final Grizzlies' argument in support of their § 1 Sherman Act claim bears mentioning. Relying on the essential facilities doctrine developed in cases such as *Silver v. New York Stock Exchange*, 373 U.S. 341 (1963) and *Associated Press v. United States*, 326 U.S. 1 (1945), they urge that because the NFL is a practical monopoly it had an obligation to admit members on fair, reasonable, and equal terms, absent some procompetitive justification for their exclusion. This Grizzlies argument suffers from the same defect as the others. The essential facilities doctrine is predicated on the assumption that admission of the excluded applicant would result in additional competition, in an economic rather than athletic sense. The Grizzlies have simply failed to show how competition in any arguably relevant market would be improved if they were given a share of the NFL's monopoly power.

Since on the record before us the Grizzlies have shown no actual or potential injury to competition resulting from the rejection of their application for an NFL franchise, they cannot succeed on their § 1 Sherman Act claim.

Affirmed.

A similar antitrust suit to force expansion in hockey was summarily dismissed in *Seattle Totems v. National Hockey League*, 783 F.2d 1347 (9th Cir.1986).[j]

Questions for Discussion

1. The court concluded in *Grizzlies* that the NFL's refusal to add this new team to the league did not affect market competition because no other NFL teams were located near Memphis, a situation that differed in this

---

[j] Thomas A. Piraino, Jr., *The Antitrust Rationale For the Expansion of Professional Sports Leagues*, 57 Ohio State L. J. 1677 (1996), provides an in-depth review of the expansion issues and a critique of the *Mid-South Grizzlies* and *Seattle Totems* rulings.

respect from the league's earlier effort to block the Raiders relocation to Los Angeles. What does the reasoning of *Raiders* and *Grizzlies* imply about the legal right of the Baltimore Colts to move (in the mid-1980s) to Indianapolis, or of the St. Louis Cardinals to move to Phoenix? Alternatively, suppose that after the demise of the United States Football League (which we will examine in the next chapter), Donald Trump had sought admission to the NFL for his New Jersey Generals, bringing with him Herschel Walker and Doug Flutie to play in Yankee Stadium. If the NFL had refused to admit the Generals, did the antitrust analysis in *Raiders* and *Grizzlies* give Trump any hope of winning admission in court?

2. In any event, the Grizzlies also argued that NFL teams competed economically with one another in broader national markets—e.g., for players, coaches, and other personnel. How did the court deal with this argument? Is the court's response persuasive?

3. Many commentators react to this rather abstract antitrust demand for market competition with the feeling that it is a far bigger step for a court to order addition of a new franchise to the league than simply to require that an existing franchise be permitted to move to a more profitable site. Does that imply that a golfer (for example, a foreign golfer such as Ernie Els or Greg Norman) should have no legal right to be admitted to play in tournaments on the Professional Golfers Association Tour? (We will consider the organization of individual sports such as golf and tennis in Chapter 12.)

4. There are, of course, practical differences in the way in which new golfers and tennis players gain access to their respective tours, and the manner in which new expansion franchises are added. Generally, new golfers and tennis players are accepted for tournaments when they prove more competitive at the game than the people they replace. In contrast, new league franchises are added when owners of the existing teams agree that expansion to a particular area is in the league's best economic or political interests, and then only upon payment of huge expansion fees (as of the mid-1990s, $140 million in football and $130 million in baseball). Even if a court were inclined to support the hypothetical expansion claim by Donald Trump's New Jersey Generals, how would the judge decide that New York City was the best place for NFL expansion, and how would the judge calculate the appropriate franchise fee? Could the court be guided by how clubs now decide these issues?

Step back from these technical legal issues and consider the broader economic significance of *Raiders* and *Grizzlies* taken as a pair. Cities have been told by the courts that no new sports franchises will be created unless the league agrees to that step, something that leagues do only sparingly. Yet, the NFL's Raiders, Colts, Cardinals, Browns (Ravens), Rams, and Oilers have proved that an existing franchise has considerable leeway to move to an attractive vacant site. Is this not a significant factor in the fierce financial bidding between cities competing for a scarce number of sports franchises? The result of these bidding wars is that many teams, whether or not they move, are regularly favored with large public subsidies through luxurious new stadiums built at public expense and leased at low rentals, generous concession and parking rights, tax holidays, and even substantial direct payments. Indeed the Raiders scenario illustrated precisely that phenomenon: the City of Anaheim lured the Rams out of the L.A. Memorial Coliseum by offering Rams' owner Carroll Rosenbloom 95 acres of valuable real estate for commercial development right next to a refurbished Anaheim Stadium. Nor could Los Angeles legitimately complain about that action since the city had pioneered in this tactic in 1957 by securing 300 acres in Chavez Ravine for the Brooklyn Dodgers to come west and build their own park to replace an outmoded Ebbetts Field.[k] This leverage by clubs over communities anxious to keep or acquire a professional franchise is a textbook example of the exercise of monopoly power (lawfully-acquired or not) to drive the "price" of franchises up by artificially restricting supply in the face of growing demand.

Local governments do have some legal power with which to try to block departures of their "home" teams. One method is to enforce an existing stadium lease between the team and the city. The question is what remedy the city may receive if the team would be breaking its lease contract with the proposed move. Should the city (or its stadium authority) be entitled to injunctive relief or limited to damages for lost rental and concession revenue, an amount that presumably is more than matched by the money being offered by another community? (Recall the same issue with respect to enforcement of player contracts discussed in Chapter 2.) Interestingly, some courts have found that the city-lessor's damages from a team's breach of contract are not irreparable and that monetary damages are sufficient. Others have granted equitable relief based on the unique and irreplaceable value of the franchise. Compare *City of New York v. New York Jets*, 90 Misc.2d 311, 394 N.Y.S.2d 799 (1977), with *HMC Management v. New Orleans Basketball Club*, 375 So.2d 712 (La.App.1979).

Some interesting issues arose in recent cases involving efforts by local governments to block the Cleveland Browns from moving to Baltimore (as the Ravens), and the Seattle Seahawks from moving to Los Angeles. In both cases, the legal issues went unresolved when the disputes and the lawsuits were settled. In the Browns' case, the City of Cleveland, which owns Municipal Stadium, sued the Browns for breaching their lease which had three more years to run as of 1996, when the team was planning to move. The Browns' lease, however, was not with the City, but rather with a management corporation owned by Browns'

---

k. See Harris, *The League*, note 1 above, *passim* (describing in detail how NFL owners—including Ram's owner Carroll Rosenbloom—extracted more and more favorable stadium deals from communities anxious to attract or retain a professional football team); Miller, *The Baseball Business*, note a above, at 293–303 (describing similar negotiations undertaken by Edward Bennett Williams, owner of baseball's Baltimore Orioles, to secure a highly attractive stadium—the new Camden Yards—and lease arrangement for his team); and Neil J. Sullivan, *The Dodgers Move West* (New York: Oxford University Press, 1987) (recounting the relocation of the baseball Dodgers from Brooklyn to Los Angeles).

owner Art Modell, which two decades earlier had entered into its own deal with the City to operate the stadium. The Browns' defense, then, was that the City was not in privity with the Browns, and was not intended to be a third-party beneficiary of the lease between the Browns and the management company. Does this defense seem persuasive? If the City was precluded from suing the Browns directly under the lease, might it have had an action of some kind against Modell's management company with whom it was in contract privity? Recognizing this problem, how should a city or other governmental authority that wants to assign operational control of a stadium it owns to someone else still protect its legal rights in the stadium assets (including the franchise lease)?

In Seattle, King County sued the Seahawks in 1996 when Kenneth Behring, the team's owner, announced his plan to leave for Los Angeles with several years remaining on the team's Kingdome lease with the County. The lease contained a clause that expressly gave the County the right to obtain specific performance should the team breach it. This clause is given much of the credit for eventually persuading Behring to agree to sell the team for $200 million to Microsoft magnate Paul Allen, who promised to keep the Seahawks in Seattle (in return for a $325 million taxpayer subsidy for a new retractable-dome, football-only stadium). The defense initially offered by the Seahawks to the County's suit was that the lease was voidable because the County had allowed the Kingdome to deteriorate to where it no longer met adequate earthquake standards. (This "concern" led Behring to say he wanted to move to Los Angeles!) What would a team have to show in order to establish that a stadium had so deteriorated that the lease was voidable? Are there less drastic remedies a court could consider, short of letting a team walk away from its lease obligation? How enforceable are specific performance clauses, or very large liquidated damages clauses (such as the New Orleans Superdome lease that requires $1 million in liquidated damages for every year the Saints do not fulfill their lease obligation which runs until 2017)?

Even if granted, an injunction (or monetary damages) has only short term value. Indeed, the prospect of such injunctive enforcement or huge liquidated damages may make club-owners like Al Davis even less willing to sign long-term leases. Thus, cities have tried to devise more potent legal weapons in order to hold onto their present teams. One such weapon—eminent domain—was employed by the city of Oakland in another twist to the long-running saga of the "Lost" (and now "Refound") Raiders. The city tried to use California's extremely broad eminent domain statute to keep the Raiders in Oakland by condemning the Raiders' NFL franchise and immediately reselling it to a local owner approved by the NFL. The state trial court dismissed the city's petition, and the appeal eventually reached the California Supreme Court.

CITY OF OAKLAND v. OAKLAND RAIDERS (I)
Supreme Court of California, 1982.
32 Cal.3d 60, 183 Cal.Rptr. 673, 646 P.2d 835.

RICHARDSON, JUSTICE.

... [T]wo issues are herein presented, the first dealing with the intangible nature of the property proposed to be taken, and the second focusing on the scope of the condemning power as limited by the doctrine of public use.

* * *

Because the power to condemn is an inherent attribute of general government, we have observed that "constitutional provisions merely place limitations upon its exercise." The two constitutional restraints are that the taking be for a "public use" and that "just compensation" be paid therefor. No constitutional restriction, federal or state, purports to limit the nature of the property that may be taken by eminent domain. In contrast to the broad powers of general government, "a municipal corporation has no inherent power of eminent domain and can exercise it only when expressly authorized by law." [However, as the court read the California legislation, it granted cities the full range of eminent domain power that was permitted by the Constitution.]

* * *

Over 125 years ago, the United States Supreme Court rejected a similar claim that intangible property could not be condemned. In *The West River Bridge Company v. Dix et al.*, 47 U.S. 507, 533 (1848), the high court carefully explained:

> A distinction has been attempted ... between the power of a government to appropriate for public uses property which is corporeal ... and the like power in the government to resume or extinguish a franchise. The distinction thus attempted we regard as a refinement which has no foundation in reason, and one that, in truth, avoids the true legal or constitutional question in these causes; namely, that of the right in private persons, in the use or enjoyment of their private property, to control and actually to prohibit the power and duty of the government to advance and protect the general good. We are aware of nothing peculiar to a franchise which can class it higher, or render it more sacred, than other property. A franchise is property, and nothing more; it is incorporeal property....

A century later, the high court reaffirmed the principle. Reasoning that "the intangible acquires a value ... no different from the value of the business' physical property," it concluded that such intangibles as trade routes of a laundry were condemnable, upon payment of just compensation therefor, when properly taken for a public use. (*Kimball Laundry Co. v. United States*, 338 U.S. 1, 10–11, 16 (1949)).

* * *

For eminent domain purposes, neither the federal nor the state constitution distinguishes between property which is real or personal, tangible or intangible. Nor did the 1975 statutory revision. Bearing in mind that the Law Revision Commission, after an extensive national study, made its legislative recommendations, including a definition of condemnable property which it characterized as "the broadest possible," we conclude that our eminent domain law authorizes the taking of intangible property. To the extent that the trial court based its summary judgment on a contrary conclusion it erred.

In fairness it must be said that the trial court fully acknowledged "the intent of the Legislature to allow the taking of any type of property, real or personal, if it was in fact necessary for a public use." But the court concluded as a matter of law that (1) no statutory or charter provision specifically authorized the taking of a professional football franchise, and (2) the operation of such a franchise is not a recognized public use which would permit its taking under general condemnation law. Assuming, for purposes of discussion, the propriety of the first premise, this fact alone is insufficient to support summary judgment, and we cannot agree with the second premise which we now explore.

* * *

Is City's attempt to take and operate the Raiders' football franchise a valid public use? We have defined "public use" as "a use which concerns the whole community or promotes the general interest in its relation to any legitimate object of government." On the other hand, "It is not essential that the entire community, or even any considerable portion thereof, shall directly enjoy or participate in an improvement in order to constitute a public use." Further, while the Legislature may statutorily declare a given "use, purpose, object or function" to be a "public use" (§ 1240.010), such statutory declarations do not purport to be exclusive.

* * *

The United States Supreme Court established years ago that "what is a public use frequently and largely depends upon the facts and circumstances surrounding the particular subject-matter in regard to which the character of the use is questioned." Further, "public uses are not limited, in the modern view, to matters of mere business necessity and ordinary convenience, but may extend to matters of public health, recreation and enjoyment."

No case anywhere of which we are aware has held that a municipality can acquire and operate a professional football team. May it do so? In our view, several decisions concerning recreation appear germane. In *City of Los Angeles v. Superior Court*, 333 P.2d 745 (1959), we noted that a city's acquisition of a baseball field, with recreational facilities to be constructed thereon to be used by the city, was "obviously for proper public purposes." Similarly, in *County of Alameda v. Meadowlark Dairy Corp.*, 38 Cal.Rptr. 474 (1964), the court upheld a county's acquisition by eminent domain of lands to be used for a county fair, reasoning that "Activities which promote recreation of the public constitute a public purpose." Considerably earlier, in *Egan v. San Francisco*, 133 P. 294 (1913), in sustaining a city's power to build an opera house, we declared:

> Generally speaking, anything calculated to promote the education, the recreation or the pleasure of the public is to be included within the legitimate domain of public purposes.

The examples of Candlestick Park in San Francisco and Anaheim Stadium in Anaheim, both owned and operated by municipalities, further suggest the acceptance of the general principle that providing access to recreation to its residents in the form of spectator sports is an appropriate function of city government. In connection with the latter stadium, the appellate court upheld the power of the City of Anaheim to condemn land for parking facilities at the stadium on the ground that "the acquisition, construction, and operation of a stadium by a county or city represents a legitimate public purpose."

Several of our sister jurisdictions are in accord. [The Court here referred in particular to *New Jersey Sports & Exposition Authority v. McCrane*, 292 A.2d 580 (N.J.1971), which had laid the legal foundations for New Jersey's Meadowlands sports complex.]

* * *

The obvious difference between managing and owning the facility in which the game is played, and managing and owning the team which plays in the facility, seems legally insubstantial. If acquiring, erecting, owning and/or operating a sports stadium is a permissible municipal function, we discern no valid legal reason why owning and operating a sports franchise which fields a team to play in the stadium is not equally permissible.

* * *

From the foregoing we conclude that the acquisition and, indeed, the operation of a sports franchise may well be an appropriate municipal function. That being so, the statutes discussed herein afford City the power to acquire by eminent domain any property necessary to carry out that function.

We caution that we are not concerned with the economic or governmental wisdom of City's acquisition or management of the Raiders' franchise, but only with the legal propriety of the condemnation action. In this period of fiscal constraints, if the city fathers of Oakland in their collective wisdom elect to seek the ownership of a professional football franchise, are we to say to them nay? And, if so, on what legal ground? Constitutional? Both federal and state Constitutions permit condemnation requiring only compensation and a public use. Statutory? The applicable statutes authorize a city to take any property, real or personal. Decisional? Courts have consistently expanded the eminent domain remedy permitting property to be taken for recreational purposes with the public either as playing participants or observing spectators.

* * *

Respondents urge, further, that because the NFL constitution bars a city from holding a franchise and being a member, the expenditure of any public monies for acquisition of the Raiders' franchise cannot be deemed in the public interest. On the other hand, an affidavit filed by the NFL commissioner avers that "a brief interim ownership" by City "would not be inconsistent with the NFL Constitution...." We, of course, are not bound by such an interpretation. Assuming its validity, however, respondents answer that if City contemplates the prompt transfer to private parties of the property interests which it seeks to condemn, after such brief ownership, that transfer would vitiate any legitimate "public use" which is a prerequisite to condemnation in the first place. In turn, City points to the statute which, as previously noted, expressly authorizes that to which respondents object: "[A] person may acquire property under subdivision (a) with the intent to sell, lease, exchange or otherwise dispose of the property or an interest therein," provided such retransfer is made "subject to such reservations or restrictions as are necessary to protect or preserve the attractiveness, safety, and usefulness of the project." So long as adequate controls are imposed upon any retransfer of the condemned property, there is no reason why the "public purpose" which justifies a taking may not be so served and protected. We envision that the adequacy of any such controls can only be determined within the factual context of a specific retransfer agreement.

* * *

Reversed and remanded.

* * *

BIRD, C.J., concurring and dissenting.

The power of eminent domain claimed by the City in this case is not only novel but virtually without limit. This is troubling because the potential for abuse of such a great power is boundless. Although I am forced by the current state of the law to agree with the result reached by the majority, I have not signed their opinion because it endorses this unprecedented application of eminent domain law without even pausing to consider the ultimate consequences of their expansive decision. It should be noted that research both by the parties and by this court has failed to disclose a single case in which the legal propositions relied on here have been combined to reach a result such as that adopted by the majority.

There are two particularly disturbing questions in this case. First, does a city have the power to condemn a viable, ongoing business and sell it to another private party merely because the original owner has announced his intention to move his business to another city? For example, if a rock concert impresario, after some years of producing concerts in a municipal stadium, decides to move his productions to another city, may the city condemn his business, including his contracts with the rock stars, in order to keep the concerts at the stadium? If a small business that rents a storefront on land originally taken by the city for a redevelopment project decides to move to another city in order to expand, may the city take the business and force it to stay at its original location? May a city condemn any business that decides to seek greener pastures elsewhere under the unlimited interpretation of eminent domain law that the majority appear to approve?

Second, even if a city were legally able to do so, is it proper for a municipality to drastically invade personal property rights to further the policy interests asserted here?

The rights both of the owners of the Raiders and of its employees are threatened by the City's action. Thus, one unexplored aspect of the majority's decision is the ruling that contract rights can be taken by eminent domain. The cases relied on by the majority in support of this holding chiefly concerned inverse condemnation suits. Those cases essentially held that when a state condemns a business, the government is obligated to compensate the business owner for the value of the contract rights destroyed by the taking. In this case, the City seeks to condemn employment contracts between the Raiders and dozens of its employees. Can the City acquire personal employment contracts as simply as it can acquire a tract of land? Are an employee's rights violated by this nonconsensual taking of an employment contract or personal services agreement?

At what point in the varied and complex business relationships involved herein would this power to condemn end? In my view, this court should proceed most cautiously before placing a constitutional imprimatur upon this aspect of creeping statism. These difficult questions are deserving of more thorough attention than they have yet received in this litigation.

It strikes me as dangerous and heavy-handed for the government to take over a business, including all of its intangible assets, for the sole purpose of preventing its relocation. [However, despite her "serious misgivings about the wisdom of the City's action," Chief Justice Bird could find no tangible legal basis for not joining, "albeit reluctantly," the Court's judgment.]

Questions for Discussion

1. Is the majority correct that if it is legitimate to use eminent domain to take someone's land to build a stadium to attract a sports franchise, it is equally legitimate to use eminent domain to take a franchise (at fair compensation) in order to keep the team in the community? On the very broad scope of a government's "public use" prerogative under the federal constitution, see the Supreme Court's subsequent decision in *Hawaii Housing Auth. v. Midkiff*, 467 U.S. 229 (1984).

2. The issue raised by Chief Justice Bird, about cities "condemning" contract rights (whether employment or franchise), is an interesting one. If employees (in this case, football players) are under a personal services contract with the Oakland Raiders owned by Al Davis, are they bound by those contracts if the City of Oakland takes the team by eminent domain? Are they bound to a new owner if the City then immediately resells the team? There may be no significant difference in the impact on player rights by a transfer of franchise ownership in this fashion, as compared to a direct sale by Al Davis (or any other NFL owner). But would the City be bound by the collective bargaining agreement with the NFL Players Association, even though municipal employees are barred by California law from unionizing? And while the NFL was apparently cooperating with the City in the *Raiders* case (as part of its effort to keep the team in Oakland), would the league have a legal obligation to recognize the City or its assignee as a new partner in the league's joint venture? Or could the NFL schedule games involving the Raiders in Los Angeles and simply ignore the city's purported taking?

3. How would one measure the value of a team for purposes of providing fair compensation in the eminent domain proceedings? Is it the value of the Raiders in Oakland or in Los Angeles? With or without favorable lease offers from the two cities competing for the franchise?

The force of the *City of Oakland I* ruling was felt soon thereafter on the other side of the country. Robert Irsay, owner of the Baltimore Colts, had been negotiating with Baltimore, Phoenix, and Indianapolis to secure the best new stadium offer upon the expiry of his Baltimore Memorial Stadium lease. Immediately after the State of Maryland enacted an amendment to its eminent domain legislation that would explicitly authorize such proceedings against the Colts by the City of Baltimore, Irsay decamped late one night in moving vans that took all the Colt's personnel and tangible property to a hearty welcome in Indianapolis the next day. A federal district court in Maryland eventually ruled that Irsay had thereby eluded the reach of the Baltimore City Council's eminent domain ordinance. See *Mayor & City Council of Baltimore v. Baltimore (Colts) Football Club*, 624 F.Supp. 278 (D.Md.1985). If the intangible property to be condemned is the NFL franchise assigned in the NFL constitution to Baltimore, was this ruling correct?

Of course, only a few teams could make the sudden getaway accomplished by the Colts. States could enact explicit legislation to authorize eminent domain proceedings if a team threatened to move in the midst of negotiations for a lease renewal and improved facilities. Why then was the Oakland action not emulated by other cities that since 1982 have lost or been threatened with the loss of their teams? Part of the answer, at least, can be found in the next decision on remand from *City of Oakland I*. Here, the Raiders asserted a different constitutional argument—that the affirmative federal power "to regulate commerce ... among the several states ..." implicitly precluded state or local regulation of "those phases of the national economy which, because of the need of national uniformity, demand their regulation, if any, be prescribed by a single authority." *Southern Pacific Co. v. Arizona*, 325 U.S. 761, 767 (1945). Does football (or other sports) pass that test?[1]

CITY OF OAKLAND v. OAKLAND RAIDERS (II)

California Court of Appeals, First District, 1985.
174 Cal.App.3d 414, 220 Cal.Rptr. 153.

SABRAW, ASSOCIATE JUSTICE.

* * *

It is well established that a state may exercise eminent domain power even though by so doing it indirectly or incidentally burdens interstate commerce. Defendants, however, contend that professional football is such a nationwide business and so completely involved in interstate commerce that acquisition of a franchise by an individual state through eminent domain would impermissibly burden interstate commerce. A recent Supreme Court decision, *Partee v. San Diego Chargers Football Co.*, 194 Cal.Rptr. 367 (1983), supports this view.

Partee held that the NFL required nationally uniform regulation and that interstate commerce would be unreasonably burdened if state antitrust laws applied to a League franchise located in this state. Uniform nationwide regulation was called for because:

> Professional football's teams are dependent upon the league playing schedule for competitive play.... The necessity of a nationwide league structure for the benefit of both teams and players for effective competition is evident as is the need for a nationally uniform set of rules governing the league structure. Fragmentation of the league structure on the basis of state lines would adversely affect the success of the competitive business enterprise, and differing state antitrust decisions if applied to the enterprise would likely compel all member teams to comply with the laws of the strictest state.

The same situation is presented here. Indeed, the trial court's findings track and amplify on *Partee*. Regarding the interdependent character of the NFL, the court noted that each member team is substantially dependent for its income on every other team: League television contract proceeds are divided equally and gate receipts nearly equally; a team's drawing power is therefore a financial benefit to the other teams as well as to itself; hence the capacity and quality of the facility in which games are played is a component of the League's financial success. The court also found evidence of the necessity of a nationwide League structure: based on the above factors, each League franchise owner has an important interest in the identity, personality,

---

1. See Gray, note k above; Lisa J. Tobin–Rubio, *Eminent Domain and the Commerce Clause Defense*, 41 U. of Miami L. Rev. 1185 (1987); Edward P. Lazarus, *The Commerce Clause Limitation on the Power to Condemn a Relocating Business*, 96 Yale L. J. 1543 (1987).

financial stability, commitment, and good faith of each other owner. Thus, under League bylaws, new members must first be approved by the current members. In short, although the clubs compete to an important degree, the League is also a joint venture of its members organized for the purpose of providing entertainment nationwide. Finally, the court found that a bar to relocation on the basis of state eminent domain law would adversely affect the League enterprise. An involuntarily acquired franchise could, at the local government's pleasure, be permanently indentured to the local entity. The League's interests would be subordinated to, or at least compromised by, the new owner's allegiance to the local public interest in matters such as lease agreements, ticket prices, concessions, stadium amenities, scheduling conflicts, etc. As the trial court found, it must also be anticipated that a single precedent of eminent domain acquisition would pervade the entire League, and even the threat of its exercise elsewhere would seriously disrupt the balance of economic bargaining on stadium leases throughout the nation.

Plaintiff's proposed action would more than indirectly or incidentally regulate interstate commerce: plaintiff claims authority—pursuant to authorization found in state eminent domain statutes—to bar indefinitely defendant's business from relocating out of Oakland. This is the precise brand of parochial meddling with the national economy that the commerce clause was designed to prohibit.

As shown above, relocation of the Raiders would implicate the welfare not only of the individual team franchise, but of the entire League. The specter of such local action throughout the state or across the country demonstrates the need for uniform, national regulation. In these circumstances, ... if relocation threatens disproportionate harm to a local entity, regulation—if necessary—should come from Congress; only then can the consequences to interstate commerce be assessed and a proper balance struck to consider and serve the various interests involved in a uniform manner.

Case dismissed.

In the one case that the Raiders have lost so far, the Internal Revenue Service has persuaded the Tax Court that some $19 million the Raiders received from public authorities in the 1980s—$2 million to settle the team's "inverse condemnation" suit against Oakland for losing the above case, $7 million in "without recourse" loans from the L.A. Memorial Coliseum to erect luxury suites that were never built, and $10 million as another "without recourse" loan from the town of Irwindale which was blocked by a 1988 state law from building a $115 million facility for the Raiders—were all "taxable income" for the team. See *Milenbach v. Commissioner of Internal Revenue*, 106 T.C. 184 (1996).

With respect to the legality of Oakland's eminent domain efforts to keep the Raiders, a major constitutional ruling was handed down two years after the above decision. In *CTS Corp. v. Dynamics Corp. of Am.*, 481 U.S. 69 (1987), a divided Supreme Court held that neither the federal securities laws nor the "interstate commerce" clause preempted Indiana legislation to control hostile takeover bids launched from outside the state against corporations legally domiciled within the state. Yet the appellate court in *City of Oakland II* ruled that a local government, exercising state legislative authority, was precluded by the "dormant" commerce clause from trying to block the Raiders' move from one city to another city within the same state. Can one square this holding with *CTS Corp.* by finding an intrinsic difference in the relationship between an individual club and the overall league, as compared to the operation of our national securities market? But is any such argument on behalf of the Raiders against Oakland's eminent domain claim compatible with the Raiders' earlier position in support of its intraleague conspiracy claim against the NFL?

Now is a good time to step back from these doctrinal debates and judicial rulings in the 1980s and consider their role in the franchise controversies in the 1990s—e.g., the move of the Browns from Cleveland to Baltimore. One must not assume that the law is the sole—perhaps not even the principal--cause of franchise free agency. Baseball, for example, has long had a special exemption which until recently was assumed to protect all its decisions from antitrust challenge. That sport, however, witnessed ten team moves from the early 1950s to the early 1970s.

The most notorious incident was the shift of the beloved Dodgers from Brooklyn to Los Angeles. Ironically, the reason why Dodgers' owner Walter O'Malley took that step was that he was able to persuade only the Los Angeles, and not the New York, authorities to use their eminent domain power to assemble the land upon which he himself would build and pay for a new Dodgers Stadium in Chavez Ravine. In the mid–1980s, Jerry Reinsdorf used the credible threat of a move of his White Sox to Tampa Bay in order to force Chicago and Illinois to build (and pay for) a new $150 million Comiskey park. In the late 1990s, the Seattle Mariners used the same lever—i.e., the loss of Ken Griffey, Jr. and Randy Johnson—to get a new $400 million facility (replacing a 20–year-old, multi-sport Kingdome), that would match the Baltimore Orioles' Camden Yards, Cleveland Indians' Jacobs Field, and Texas Rangers' Ballpark at Arlington.

Football owners have, if anything, extracted even more lucrative stadium deals from their new (or current) cities. However, what is distinctive about the NFL situation is that many of these team moves have been vigorously opposed by the league as a whole (e.g., for removing professional football from Los Angeles, the second largest market in the country, and from Cleveland, the city with the highest football television ratings). It is only when there is such an internal league conflict about proposed relocation that antitrust law comes into play.

In order to strengthen the league's ability to keep teams in place, there have been numerous versions of antitrust reform introduced in Congress in the mid–1990s. The prospects for actual enactment are not that promising: for every community that loses a team another gains one. Still, the basic concepts embedded in the various bills may well be utilized by the courts (especially the Supreme Court) if it revisits and rethinks the rulings that we have just read.[m] Following are several of the major options.

(i) The first would simply remove all antitrust regulation of league decisions in this area—perhaps by treating the league as a single entity in this context at least.

(ii) A second model would grant a league such immunity from § 1 if and only if its internal relocation rules required judgment about what step was "reasonable and appropriate" after considering such factors as the levels of fan and public support for the team in its current site; levels of operating loss and the extent to which team management (rather than stadium facilities, for example) was responsible for its financial and popular failings; and the presence or absence of other teams in the current and proposed locations.

(iii) A third option would give the team or affected community the right to either judicial or arbitral scrutiny of the internal league decision on that score, but insulate the league from any antitrust liability until and unless it had refused to adhere to such an external verdict.

(iv) Another proposed step would amend antitrust and/or eminent domain law to allow the home city to "take" its current team (using its traditional name and logo), and at least gain the right to an expansion team within a specified period if prior experience in the current location satisfied the above conditions.

These and other substantive legal proposals raise an underlying institutional question. How and by whom should the judgment be made about where particular sports teams should be located: by the individual owner who is most involved in and affected by the fate of his team; by the league's governing board deciding how the move affects the interests of all teams and their owners; or by some combination of courts and lawmakers seeking to protect the interests of the affected communities? As to the latter, it is important to note that there is a community that is seeking as well as one that may be losing the team. (Indeed, recall that Oakland, St. Louis, and Baltimore which took teams from other cities in the 1990s had previously lost their own teams in the 1980s.) One point of view is that the people in Brooklyn, for example, should have had a "moral" right to keep their Dodgers, and the people in Cleveland their

---

m. See Glenn M. Wong, *Of Franchise Relocation, Expansion, and Competition in Professional Sports: The Ultimate Political Football*, 9 Seton Hall L. J. 1 (1985); Daniel S. York, *The Professional Sports Community Protection Act: Congress' Best Response to* Raiders, 38 Hastings L. J. 345 (1987); John A. Gray, *Section 1 of the Sherman Act and Control Over NFL Franchise Locations: The Problem of Opportunistic Behavior*, 25 Amer. Bus. L. J. 123 (1987); John Beisner, *Sports Franchise Relocation: Competitive Markets and Taxpayer Protection*, 6 Yale L. & Pol. Rev. 429 (1988).

Browns. An alternative view is that if the objective is to protect the broader public welfare, the ideal market test asks which city's fans are willing to pay the most either to gain or to keep the current franchise free agent.

The sports franchise market, like any other market, is shaped by a host of factors—social, economic, and legal (including much more than antitrust law). It is easy to understand why Art Modell, owner of the Cleveland Browns, and Georgia Frontiere, owner of the Los Angeles Rams, were ready to leave their large and apparently attractive markets and move to Baltimore and St. Louis. The latter two cities offered to pay all the $250 million cost of new stadiums designed for football alone, with a large number of attractive and expensive luxury boxes and club seats. In return for paying little or no rental on their long-term leases, the Rams and the (now) Ravens get to keep almost all the revenues from regular seat prices, club seat and luxury box-rentals, concessions, parking, and advertising (including the stadium name). Indeed, the teams get this revenue not just from football games, but from non-football stadium events such as music concerts. And as the final attraction, the cities offered a $50–75 million "signing bonus" to Modell and Frontiere, generated by the sale of "personal seat licenses" that were bought by fans who were willing to pay a considerable amount to gain season ticket rights in the regular seats.

However, in no other league but the NFL would such a move likely have been made. A key source of the problem is the internal rule structure (i.e., the private law) of the NFL. One such feature may well be the bar on corporate ownership that we saw contested in the *Sullivan* case. If an entertainment conglomerate such as Disney/ABC had been permitted to own the Los Angeles football franchise (as it now owns the NHL Mighty Ducks), its executives would never have taken the steps of the Rams' Frontiere or the Raiders' Davis, because these immediate gains in the company's football division would have been dwarfed by the losses inflicted by irate consumers on other parts of their entertainment operations. Indeed, it is likely that some of these corporate owners may invest in the sport not for cash profits from the team itself, but rather for the synergistic impact on the value of their much larger and more lucrative broadcasting, apparel, beverage, or other consumer businesses.

However, even an individual owner of a team in another sport (e.g., the Yankees' George Steinbrenner) would almost certainly refuse to move his team to a small market city (e.g., Nashville) in return for such a stadium payoff. (Steinbrenner, would, of course, be willing to move across the Hudson River to New Jersey, where the NFL's "New York" Giants and Jets now play their home games.) The reason is that under MLB rules, the Yankees (like the L.A. Dodgers) keep the lion's share of the valuable television revenues that the Greater New York (or Los Angeles) markets generate. The NBA Knicks and Lakers and the NHL Rangers and Mighty Ducks retain an even larger share of these big market revenues than do their baseball counterparts. Under the NFL's rules, though, the Giants and Jets have to share on an equal basis with the small market Green Bay Packers and Jacksonville Jaguars all of the television and merchandising revenues generated from their far larger markets, and (on a 60–40 basis) all of the regular gate receipts. By contrast, all stadium-related revenues—luxury suites and club seat rentals, and concessions and advertising—are retained by the home team if it is able to extract those items from the owner of the stadium. (There is a question whether personal seat licenses are the equivalent under the NFL rules of club seat rentals or regular gate receipts, and this has now produced litigation involving the league and the Raiders and Rams.) Given the choice between securing one football revenue stream, of which it keeps approximately three percent, or another, of which it keeps 100%, it is not surprising why so many NFL owners have opted for the latter.

Ironically, then, the NFL's internal revenue sharing system, one that was designed to protect smaller market teams from the competitive pressures of the bigger market teams in the players market, has actually generated movement from larger to smaller communities in the franchise market. We will consider later in this chapter whether the solution to either or both of those problems is best found in reshaping internal league revenue-sharing or external antitrust controls.

Public Subsidy of Sports Facilities and Franchises

Just as important a question, though, is why the government of St. Louis (or Baltimore and other cities recruiting teams, or Cincinnati and other cities seeking to keep their teams) is prepared to use scarce taxpayer dollars to confer such large financial benefits on team owners (and thence also on their players). In a sense, this is the policy dimension of the constitutional condition of "public use" that we read about in *City of Oakland (I)*. The Supreme Court of California concluded that if there was a public use in the city taking land to build a stadium to secure a sports team, it seemed equally a public use to take the franchise to keep the team in the stadium. That still leaves open the question whether it is a sensible—rather than just constitutional—use of public resources to make such large expenditures on the stadium in the first place.

There is an alternative method through which even limited-use football stadiums can be financed: the sale of personal seat licenses (PSL's) to people who are willing to pay for the right to attend and enjoy the games. This is the method that was employed in Charlotte to finance construction of the new stadium for the NFL expansion Carolina Panthers. As it turned out, though, once the marketability of PSL's was demonstrated in the Carolinas, other free agent owners (e.g., the Browns' Art Modell) used this device to extract their bonuses for moving the team, leaving the state and city to build the stadium out of public funds. To justify the latter step, both teams and politicians have claimed it to be a wise financial investment in the economic growth of the region. Indeed, many assert that the spillover effect of bringing a team into the community more than pays for the upfront stadium costs, and thence avoids the need to raise taxes to make these expenditures. The essence of this argument is that the presence of the team brings more people and more money into the community, that the money is spent not just at the game but at a host of surrounding businesses, that all of these expenditures and private revenues generate greater tax payments, and that these increased public revenues can be drawn upon to pay the interest and principal on the stadium bonds.

This is an issue that has sparked considerable debate among economists, with most being rather skeptical of the sports spillover thesis.[n] Perhaps the best way for our readers to reflect on this problem is to consider these two public expenditure alternatives: one city invests in a sports stadium to bring in a professional sports team, another in a campus (with buildings) to bring in a university (including a law school). What are the various revenue sources for a football team or a college? Which of these sources involve new people coming into the community to expend money that would not otherwise have been spent there? What are the kinds of jobs that are generated by teams or colleges, the nature of the incomes earned from those jobs, and where do the occupants tend to live and spend their earnings? What kinds of businesses, if any, are teams and colleges likely to attract to their community, and what would be the additional spillover effects they generate? From the point of view of economic investment analysis alone, what final scores would you give the team or the college in that competition? In addition, how would you assess the comparative social value of government expenditures on deteriorating roads and services, expanded prisons, or pay increases for school teachers and police forces?

Even if the above analysis were to cast some doubt on the relative economic impact of a team on its community (as compared to investments in education, for example), one might still judge the expenditure on sports to be a worthwhile consumption expenditure. The local residents get a chance to experience the presence of a team, just as they experience and enjoy public parks that are primarily used by residents rather than tourists. Of course, one big difference between New York City's Central Park, for example, and New Jersey's Giants Stadium is that the former is not reserved for just the people who can and do pay for season tickets (although it is also true that area football fans can watch and enjoy the Giants and Jets games on television, in the sports pages or on talk shows, and even in conversations with friends about their favorite teams). As it turns out, though, there is a significant feature in the tax treatment of these two public expenditures that also helps explain why stadium deals have taken their recent shape.[o]

[n]. See the analyses in the relevant chapters of the books by Zimbalist, Quirk and Fort, and Danielson cited in note a above, and by Shropshire, Euchner, and Rosentraub cited in note h. Two recent empirical studies are Robert Baade, *Professional Sports as Catalysts for Metropolitan Economic Development*, 18 J. of Urban Affairs 1 (1996), and Dennis Coates and Brad Humphrey, *The Growth Effects of Sports Franchises, Stadia, and Arenas*, Working Paper 97–02 (1997).

[o]. The most recent analysis of this issue is Daniel J. Lathrope, *Federal Tax Policy, Tax Subsidies, and the Financing of Professional Sports Facilities*, 38 South Texas L. Rev. 1147 (1997). See also Dennis Zimmerman, *Tax-Exempt Bonds and the Economics of Professional Sports Stadiums* (Cong. Res. Serv., Report #96–460E (1996)).

Like other long-term capital expenditures, the public money spent on sports facilities is funded through state or municipal bonds that are repaid over several decades, with regular interest payments on the outstanding principal. The interest paid on such public bonds has long been exempt from federal as well as state taxes. The result is that the interest rate required to attract investors for such tax-free public offerings is significantly less than the interest on ordinary securities, because the net after-tax return is higher on the public offering (particularly for wealthy investors with high marginal tax rates). The other side of that coin is that the federal government is, in effect, helping to fund the local project by foregoing tax revenues that it would otherwise have earned from that person's investment in another private security (assuming that this was not also tax-free). To illustrate the amount of that subsidy, it is assumed that in current financial markets the federal government is providing approximately $75 million of the $225 million expended by a state or local government through a 30-year bond.

In the 1968 Revenue Expenditure Control Act, the federal government imposed its first restraints upon such uses of state and local bonds. These bonds would be tax-free only if a non-governmental entity used no more than 25% of the bond proceeds (the Use Test) *and* if no more than 25% of the debt service (via interest on principal payment) was derived from property used directly or indirectly in a private business (the Debt Service Test). However, Congress exempted from such conditions any bonds that were used to finance sports facilities and a number of other facilities for designated "private activities." Then, the major Tax Reform Act of 1986 sought to cut back even further on such use of tax free bonds for private purposes. Both the Use and Debt Service Test figures were reduced from 25% to 10%, and "sports facilities" were removed from the "exempt facilities" category.

The authors of the latter bill did not appreciate that this new law would actually increase the value of the stadium deals that communities felt compelled to offer team owners. In order to avail themselves of that substantial federal contribution to a $225 million sports facility, the city had to put up at least 90% of the cost, and it could repay no more than ten percent of that amount from revenues generated from any use of the facility (for non-sports as well as sports events). Not only does this tax law help explain the terms of the stadium deal that Art Modell extracted from Baltimore to move his Browns there, but it also means that Cleveland residents helped fund that move through their federal tax returns.

This tax issue has now returned to Congress; in particular through legislation introduced by New York Senator Pat Moynihan, which he has titled the *Stop Tax–Exempt Arena Debt Issuance Act* (*STADIA*). This Act would simply exclude from the scope of tax-free "qualified bonds" under § 141 of the Internal Revenue Code any bonds issued for either erection or improvement of "professional sports facilities" in an amount that totalled more than $5 million. The advocates of this proposal—for example, the Senators from the Dakotas—have said that this would save their citizens from having to contribute millions of dollars every year to help finance more than $10 billion in sports facilities being erected this decade, even though there is not one major sports franchise playing in those states. The critics state that this measure would deny the people of Maryland (or Missouri or Tennessee) the freedom to decide whether it was a worthwhile expenditure of their tax resources (including use of tax-free bonds) to bring NFL teams to their communities.

What is your view of these competing positions? Would you perhaps prefer a different proposal, one that would remove any specific limits imposed just on "professional sports facilities," but instead include the latter in the broader category of qualified/tax-exempt bonds for "private activities?" For these, the overall bond amount per state in any one year is capped at the larger of $150 million or $50 per state resident. This would mean that the citizens of Maryland would have to choose between building a new stadium with these federal tax-free bonds, or using the latter device for Industrial Development Bonds (IDB's), first-time home buyer mortgages, student loans, or other activities that fit into this category. Might the Congress go even farther and permit use of tax-free bonds for sports facilities only if the teams committed *themselves* to pay off all that debt?

Whether or not any changes should be (or will be) made in the current tax, antitrust, league revenue-sharing, and other regimes we have been reading about, it is clear that their combined role in shaping franchise free agency has generated huge increases in franchise values. It is estimated that Modell's Ravens and Frontiere's Rams are now worth $100 million more than they were in their previous settings. The value of these and other teams is enhanced even more by the favorable treatment that federal tax law has long provided to the purchase and sale of sports franchises.[p]

These rather esoteric tax rules are a key part of the explanation for an otherwise puzzling phenomenon—the continued escalation in franchise prices over the last three decades while owners regularly lament the "losses" they experience in running their teams (losses that owners invariably attribute to rising player salaries). For example, in 1988 Victor Kiam purchased the New England Patriots from Billy Sullivan for $85 million (a sale that later produced the *Sullivan* litigation against the NFL). The Patriots then dropped to the bottom of the National Football

---

[p] In-depth analyses of this topic can be found in Benjamin Okner, "Taxation and Sports Enterprises," Chapter 5 of Roger G. Noll, ed., *Government and the Sports Business* (Washington, D.C.: Brookings, 1974), and Stafford Matthews, "Taxation of Sports," Chapter 22 of Gary Uberstine, ed., *Law of Professional and Amateur Sports* (Deerfield, Ill: Clark, Boardman & Callaghan, 1991) (particularly § 22.04 on "Sale or Transfer of a Sports Franchise"). For an up-to-date synopsis of the financial significance of this issue see Zimbalist, *Baseball and Billions*, note a above, at 34–36. And for a brief description of how this tax device was originally used, by the person who claims to have "invented" it, see William Veeck, *Hustler's Handbook* 328–332 (New York: Putnam, 1965).

League both on the playing field and in fan attendance. Eventually Kiam was forced to sell the team in 1992 because of its reported deficits. Surprisingly, though, the new purchaser, Jim Orthwein, paid approximately $105 million for the Patriots, and after his team continued to lose money as well as games, Orthwein resold the Patriots in 1995 to Robert Kraft for $160 million.

One key explanation for this apparent financial discrepancy stems from the way in which purchasers of a team are entitled to allocate and depreciate the assets that make up a sports franchise. Assuming that the club does not own the stadium in which it plays, the team's only tangible assets are its playing and office equipment (which is of modest value). One could plausibly argue that the bulk of the purchase price—particularly for a brand-new expansion team—should be attributed to the "franchise" itself. It is "membership" in the league that gives the team the exclusive right to play league games in its territory (usually in a publicly-owned and subsidized facility), and to share in the league's national television and marketing contracts. However, because the useful life and economic value of a franchise lasts indefinitely, it is a nondepreciable asset for tax purposes, just like the land on which stands Wrigley Field, owned by the Chicago Cubs.

Thus, beginning in the 1960s, club owners took the position that much of the purchase price should be allocated to the player contracts that came with the franchise. By the late 1970s, both the courts and Congress had accepted that theory, overriding the contrary views of the Internal Revenue Service (IRS). In *Selig v. United States*, 740 F.2d 572 (7th Cir.1984), the Seventh Circuit ruled that of the $10.8 million that Allan "Bud" Selig paid in 1969 to buy the insolvent Seattle Pilots and move them to Milwaukee (as the Brewers), $10.2 million (approximately 95%) was properly attributable to the 150 major and minor league players that came with the team. In *Laird v. United States*, 556 F.2d 1224 (5th Cir.1977), the Fifth Circuit held that of the $8.45 million paid by the Smith family in 1966 for an NFL expansion franchise in Atlanta, $3.05 million (approximately 40%) was attributable to the player contracts. (The disparity in the two rulings was due to the district court's appraisal in *Laird* of the value of the Smiths' share of the NFL's national television contract.) These appellate court rulings were not rendered until fifteen years after the original purchase of the Pilots-Brewers. In the meantime, as part of its Tax Reform Act of 1976, Congress had enacted § 1056 of the Internal Revenue Code, which created a presumption that no more than 50% of the sale price of a franchise should be attributed to its players. Currently, at least when the club's purchase price does not include a playing facility, this 50% figure operates more as a floor than as a ceiling.

The reason why this tax treatment is financially significant is that player contracts are a depreciable asset that can be amortized over the five-year period that is the typical professional career. Thus, when Robert Kraft bought the Patriots for $160 million in 1995, he could readily impute $80 million of this price to his player contracts, and thus write off $16 million each year against any operating profits earned by the team over the next five-year span. If the club's operating profits totalled less than $16 million in any one year, the extra book losses could be set off against Kraft's earnings from the other business he owns.

The Fifth Circuit in *Laird* (echoed by the Seventh Circuit in *Selig*) had rejected the IRS position that only a modest portion of the club's purchase price should be allocated to the players who came with the team:

> [I]t is clear that the players are the primary assets of a professional football club. Without them, there could not be a game. As Texas E. Schramm, the widely-respected President and General Manager of the Dallas Cowboys, testified:
>
>> The players are the principal product and it is players who are responsible for your winning. They are responsible for the fans coming to your stadium. They are responsible for the income that you receive on television.
>
> Without the players, in professional football, you don't have anything.

556 F.2d, at 1237. While players are obviously the key factor in a team's success on the field, how relevant is that fact to the tax question whether player contracts should be deemed a depreciable asset of the team? Is not the crucial athletic asset that comes with the purchase of a franchise the right to participate in the rookie draft, the salary cap system, and other features of the players market that allow teams to restock their rosters as current players leave? Keep in mind that clubs include in their operating expenses the money they spend on player salaries owed under the contracts, as well as expenditures made for scouting, drafting, and training new playing prospects (including the minor league operations in baseball and hockey). Should the buyer of a Hollywood studio be entitled to write off 50% of the purchase price as payment for the movie stars the studio has under contract for ongoing film productions (as well as deduct from taxable income all salary payments made under these contracts)?

When the concept of player depreciation first emerged on the tax accounting scene in the 1960s, the owners' practice was to write off the value of players *presently* on their rosters. When the team was later sold after these players had retired, none of the sale price would be attributed to these assets that had been fully depreciated and literally disappeared from the game. Section 1245 of the Internal Revenue Code (as amended by the 1976 Tax Reform Act) blocked that loophole. Now, if a team is sold for more than its base value after the write-off of player contracts, the gains are recaptured and taxed as of the date of sale. In effect clubs can postpone, rather than eliminate, tax liability for any operating profits the team had written off. This tax break still constitutes a valuable, long-term, interest-free "loan" from the government in the amount of the taxes that would otherwise have been payable on operating profits, analogous to the tax savings gained from contributions made to pensions and other retirement plans. And if the owner holds on to the franchise until he dies, this loan is forgiven by the government, beca\ tax law deems the heirs to assume title to this asset (and others) with . current market value as their tax base.

The tax reforms of the 1980s further reduced the legal value of this tax benefit by reducing the top marginal income tax rates for individuals and corporations from their 1970s levels of 70% and 50%, respectively, to the 40% rates that prevail in the late–1990s. On the other hand, the financial value of such a depreciable asset has increased much faster because of sharply higher franchise sale prices. An apt illustration is the sale of the Los Angeles Dodgers in 1998 for more than $300 million—30 times the amount paid by Bud Selig in 1969 for the Seattle Pilots/Milwaukee Brewers.

D. LEAGUE–WIDE TELEVISION CONTRACTS[q]

As we have noted earlier, sports revenues, especially from broadcasting and merchandising, have been soaring over the last quarter century. The immediate source of those financial gains has been an increasing fan appetite for watching games at home while wearing a shirt and cap adorned with the logos of their favorite teams. The background source is a legal regime that gives clubs an exclusive intellectual property right in their teams' broadcasts and names (which we read about in Chapter 6). Another crucial legal factor is the ability of teams to come together to sell a single package of broadcasting and marketing rights to the highest bidder. A key policy issue is whether such legal arrangements actually are in the best interests of fans of the sport and consumers of products advertised during game broadcasts or emblazoned with team logos. League-wide controls upon the sale of television rights has been the principal setting for this legal debate about the compatibility of league licensing packages and restraints with antitrust law's commitment to a competitive consumer market.

At the beginning of the 1950s, there was a legal consensus that the right to broadcast a game over the air belonged to and thus could be sold by the teams playing in the game. However, the new television medium posed a special threat to the fundamental principle of territorial exclusivity embodied in league constitutions, a principle that insulated franchise owners from intrusion by other clubs into their home markets. Broad-

---

[q.] On the broader financial and social implications of sports on television, see David A. Klatell & Norman Marcus, *Sports for Sale: Television, Money, and the Fans* (New York: Oxford University Press, 1988). For an excellent, but now factually-dated, economic analysis of televised sports, see Ira Horowitz, "Sports Broadcasting," Chapter 8 of Roger G. Noll, ed., *Government and the Sports Business* (Washington, D.C.: Brookings, 1974). See also Joan M. Chandler, "Sport as T.V. Product: A Case Study of 'Monday Night Football,'" Chapter 2 of Paul D. Staudohar & James A. Mangan, eds., *The Business of Professional Sport* (Urbana, Ill.: University of Illinois Press, 1991). The legal framework for these issues is detailed in Robert Alan Garrett & Philip R. Hochberg, "Sports Broadcasting," Chapter 11 of Gary Uberstine, ed., *Law of Professional and Amateur Sports*, note p above. The best treatment of the contemporary antitrust issues to be found is Stephen F. Ross, *An Antitrust Analysis of Sports League Contracts with Cable Networks*, 39 Emory L. J. 463 (1990).

casts of games involving the more successful teams (such as the New York Yankees in baseball and the Cleveland Browns in football) could be beamed into any part of the country. Thus, the earliest league television policy sought to limit the breadth of broadcasts of games played by any one team. This policy generated the first antitrust challenge encountered by leagues in their internal dealings—in fact, the one and only antitrust suit filed by the Justice Department against professional sports. The result of that challenge we shall read in the first case in this section.

Not long afterwards, it became evident that league-wide pooling and sale of broadcast rights would help the league enlarge the total revenues it derived from television and would permit a more equitable distribution of these funds among all clubs in the league. To facilitate such arrangements for the National Football League in particular, Congress enacted the Sports Broadcasting Act (SBA) of 1961, the first ever antitrust exemption fashioned for sports by the legislative—as opposed to the judicial—branch of our national government. The second and third decisions in this section, involving the Chicago Bulls and the NBA, depict the immense role played by sports television since the 1980s, and the complex legal and policy problems that television poses for both the leagues and their fans. By the 1990s, sports merchandising had also become a lucrative revenue source within the sports world, and thence came conflicts between teams and their leagues about who would control this asset. The first major antitrust suit filed in this area, by the Dallas Cowboys' owner Jerry Jones against the NFL, was eventually settled in 1996, leaving us here with just the sports industry problem, but no judicial resolution.

UNITED STATES v. NFL

United States District Court, Eastern District of Pennsylvania, 1953.
116 F.Supp. 319.

GRIM, DISTRICT JUDGE.

[The NFL's initial stance was to permit each individual team to contract for the telecasting (and radio broadcasting) of games in which that team was participating. However, the League's by-laws contained a blanket prohibition against teams broadcasting their games into the home territories of other teams. The Justice Department charged that this league policy constituted an agreement in restraint of trade in violation of § 1 of the Sherman Antitrust Act.]

I.

Is the provision which prevents the telecasting of outside games into the home territories of other teams on days when the other teams are playing at home illegal?

There can be little doubt that this provision constitutes a contract in restraint of trade. The market for the public exhibition of football no longer is limited to the spectators who attend the games. Since the advent of television and radio, the visual and aural projections of football games can be marketed anywhere in the world where there are television or radio facilities to transmit and receive them. When a football team agrees to restrict the projection of its games in the home areas of other teams, it thereby cuts itself off from this part of its potential market. Since the clubs of the National Football League have agreed at certain times not to project their games into the home territories of other clubs, they have given that part of their market at those certain times exclusively to other teams. In return, each of them has been given the right to market its own games without competition in its own home area under the same circumstances. The purpose and effect of this is to restrict outside competition on the part of other teams in the home area of each club. This, therefore, is a clear case of allocating marketing territories among competitors, which is a practice generally held illegal under the anti-trust laws.

An allocation of marketing territories for the purpose of restricting competition, however, is not always illegal.... The principal question in the present case is whether the particular restraints imposed by Article X are reasonable or unreasonable.

Professional football is a unique type of business. Like other professional sports which are organized on a league basis, it has problems which no other business has. The ordinary business makes every effort to sell as much of its product or services as it can. In the course of doing this it may and often does put many of its competitors out of business. The ordinary businessman is not troubled by the knowledge that he is doing so well that his competitors are being driven out of business.

Professional teams in a league, however, must not compete too well with each other, in a business way. On the playing field, of course, they must compete as hard as they can all the time. But it is not necessary and indeed it is unwise for all the teams to compete as hard as they can against each other in a business way. If all the teams should compete as hard as they can in a business way, the stronger teams would be likely to drive the weaker ones into financial failure. If this should happen not only would the weaker teams fail, but eventually the whole league, both the weaker and the stronger teams, would fail, because without a league no team can operate profitably.

It is particularly true in the National Football League that the teams should not compete too strongly with each other in a business way. The evidence shows that in the National Football League less than half the clubs over a period of years are likely to be financially successful. There are always teams in the League which are close to financial failure. Under these circumstances it is both wise and essential that rules be passed to help the weaker clubs in their competition with the stronger ones and to keep the League in fairly even balance.

The winning teams usually are the wealthier ones and unless restricted by artificial rules the rich get richer and the poor get poorer (as Commissioner Bell put it). Winning teams draw larger numbers of spectators to their games than do losing teams and from the larger gate receipts they make greater profits than do losing teams. With this greater wealth they can spend more money to obtain new players, they can pay higher salaries, and they can have better spirit among their players than can the weaker teams. With these better and happier players they will continue to win most of their games while the weaker teams will continue to lose most of their games. The weaker teams share in the prosperity of the stronger teams to a certain extent, since as visiting teams they share in the gate receipts of the stronger teams. But in time even the most enthusiastic fans of strong home teams will cease to be attracted to home games with increasingly weaker visiting teams. Thus, the net effects of allowing unrestricted business competition among the clubs are likely to be, first, the creation of greater and greater inequalities in the strength of the teams; second, the weaker teams being driven out of business; and, third, the destruction of the entire League.

In order to try to keep its teams at approximately equal strength and to protect weaker teams from stronger teams, a league theoretically might use a number of devices. It might (1) limit the bonus price which could be paid to new players, (2) give the weaker teams a prior right over stronger teams to draft new players, (3) prohibit the sale of players after a certain day in the playing season, (4) limit the number of players on each team, (5) limit the total amount of salaries which a team can pay, (6) give the lowest team in the league the right to draft a player from the highest team, when and if the highest team has won a certain number (three for instance) of consecutive championships, and (7) reasonably restrict the projection of games by radio or television into the home territories of other teams.

It is easy to see that the first six devices would make it easier for weaker teams to compete with stronger ones. The usefulness of the seventh device, however, in the protection of the weaker teams may not be so obvious, particularly since it prevents the weaker teams from televising into the home territories of the stronger teams as much as it prevents the stronger teams from telecasting into the home territories of the weaker ones. The evidence indicates that television audiences and sponsors have so little interest in games between weak teams that it is very difficult to obtain sponsors for outside telecasts of such games. Consequently, the weaker teams lose practically nothing by this television restriction. But they benefit greatly from it in that the restriction adds to their home game attendance by preventing potential spectators from staying at home to watch on television exciting outside head-on games between strong teams. The competitive position of the weaker teams is improved by this increase in home attendance, while the competitive position of the stronger teams is weakened somewhat by their inability to sell to sponsors the right to televise their desirable head-on games into the home territories of the weaker teams when the weaker teams are playing at home.

A large part of defendants' evidence was directed to the question of whether the televising of a team's own home games in that team's home territory has an adverse effect on attendance at these home games. The evidence on this point, particularly the evidence relating to the great decrease in home attendance of the Los Angeles Rams during the 1950 season when all its home games were televised at home, shows quite clearly that the telecasting of a home game into a home territory while the home game is being played has an adverse effect on the attendance at the game. This clearly indicates by implication that the telecast of an outside game, particularly a head-on game, also adversely affects attendance at a home game.

* * *

The greatest part of the defendant clubs' income is derived from the sale of tickets to games. Reasonable protection of home game attendance is essential to the very existence of the individual clubs, without which there can be no League and no professional football as we know it today.

This is not a case of one industry fighting the competition of another, as for instance coal fighting the competition of oil, or railroads fighting the competition of trucks, or moving pictures fighting the competition of television. Football provides a magnificent spectacle for television programs and television provides an excellent outlet and market for football. They both can use and indeed need each other. By working together intelligently each will be an important adjunct to the other. The objective of the clubs in agreeing to a television blackout of the home territory (except for the remote possibility of a home game telecast) during the day a home game is played is not to restrain competition among the individual clubs in the sale of television rights or competition among television stations and networks and advertisers and advertising agencies in the purchase of such rights. This particular restriction promotes competition more than it restrains it in that its immediate effect is to protect the weak teams and its ultimate effect is to preserve the League itself. By thus preserving professional football this restriction makes possible competition in the sale and purchase of television rights in situations in which the restriction does not apply.

The purposes of the Sherman Act certainly will not be served by prohibiting the defendant clubs, particularly the weaker clubs, from protecting their home gate receipts from the disastrous financial effects of invading telecasts of outside games. The member clubs of the National Football League, like those of any professional athletic league, can exist only as long as the league exists. The League is truly a unique business enterprise, which is entitled to protect its very existence by agreeing to reasonable restrictions on its member clubs. The first type of restriction imposed by Article X is a reasonable one and a legal restraint of trade.

II.

Is the restriction on telecasting outside games in home territories when the home teams are playing away games and telecasting them in their home territories illegal?

The reasonableness of this particular restriction must also be tested by its effect on the attendance and gate receipts of a team's home games.

It is obvious that on a day when the home team is playing an away game there is no gate attendance to be harmed back in its home area and the prohibition of outside telecasts within its home area cannot serve to protect gate attendance at the away game, which is played in the opponent's home territory.

Several of defendants' witnesses attempted to justify the restriction with the opinion that it is necessary in this situation to protect the home team's "good will" by which they meant that the restriction is necessary to protect the home team from loss in gate receipts at subsequent home games. However, there is not one shred of evidence, not one specific example based on actual experience, to support this opinion which, more accurately stated, is nothing more than conjecture.

It is probably true, though not proved by the evidence, that the simultaneous telecasting of an outside game and an away game in the home area of the team playing away would result in a division of the television audience between the two games. Obviously the existence or the prospect of such competition would make the television rights to the home club's away games less attractive to sponsors and consequently less profitable to the club. But this does not concern attendance at football games. Indeed, the testimony of defendants' witnesses consistently indicates that the primary reason for the restrictions in this situation actually is to enable the clubs in the home territories to sell monopoly rights to purchasers of television rights to away games.

The record in this case contains no factual justification for Article X's suppression of competing telecasts of League games when, for example, the Philadelphia Eagles' away game is being televised in its home territory. Defendants' speculation or conjecture that without such restriction gate attendance would decline a week or two later at the Eagles' home game has little probative value. Article X's restriction on this type of competition is an unreasonable and illegal restraint of trade.

Charge upheld in part.

As is clear from the opinion, the principal concern of the league as well as the district court was the perceived impact of television on the home team's game attendance, rather than on the financial value of potential television viewership and contracts. In any event, the judge issued a decree that prohibited the National Football League and its clubs from adopting any rules or entering into any television contracts that restricted the area in which any team's games would be broadcast, except into a team's home territory on the day it was playing a home game. In 1960, the American Football League (AFL) started up operations and immediately negotiated a league-wide television contract with ABC. At this time, each NFL club was still selling its television rights separately. The new NFL Commissioner, Pete Rozelle, believed that if the AFL was going to operate with the advantage of a league-wide television package, the NFL had to do the same. Such a contract, under which revenues would be shared equally by all clubs, was becoming more important to the NFL because teams in the large markets (New York, Chicago, and Los Angeles) were starting to get much greater revenues for their television rights than were teams in smaller cities (Green Bay, Pittsburgh, and Baltimore). The resulting disparity in income, coupled with competition for players from the AFL, threatened the ability of small-market clubs to field good teams. (There is today a far greater disparity in income from local television revenues in major league baseball than there was in football in the late 1950s.) Thus, Rozelle promptly negotiated a league-wide television contract with CBS. The NFL then petitioned Judge Grim to approve the new CBS contract.

However, because a provision of the NFL–CBS contract barred individual teams from selling television rights for their games to competing broadcasters, Judge Grim held (at 196 F.Supp. 445 (E.D.Pa.1961)) that the contract violated the terms of his 1953 antitrust decree. The NFL went to the Congress and persuaded it to pass the Sports Broadcasting Act (SBA). Section 1291 of the SBA states that:

> § 1291. The antitrust laws ... shall not apply to any joint agreement by or among persons engaging in or conducting the organized professional team sports of football, baseball, basketball, or hockey, by which any league of clubs ... sells or otherwise transfers all or any part of the rights of such league's member clubs in the sponsored telecasting of the games of football, baseball, basketball, or hockey as the case may be, engaged in or conducted by such clubs....

§ 1292 made it clear, though, that the antitrust immunity conferred by § 1291 was only available to league-wide television contracts that limited "black-outs" of NFL games to those areas in which a member club was playing a home game on the day of the blackout.

Questions for Discussion

1. As we saw in the *NFL* decision, the Justice Department alleged, and the court agreed, that the league's 1953 television policies constituted a "conspiracy in restraint of trade" by the clubs, in violation of § 1 of the Sherman Act. Does the SBA, which grants professional sports leagues special antitrust immunity for television contracts, constitute tacit congressional recognition of the "economically divisible" as opposed to "single entity" character of a sports league in all its other policy decisions—in particular, when the league limits the free agency enjoyed by either its players or its owners? It should be noted, though, that § 1294 stated that, with the exception of § 1291's joint broadcast agreements, nothing in the SBA:

> ... shall be deemed to change, determine, or otherwise affect the applicability or nonapplicability of the antitrust laws to any act, contract, agreement, rule, course of conduct, or other activity by, between, or among persons engaging in, conducting, or participating in the organized professional team sports of football, baseball, basketball, or hockey....

2. With respect to the § 1292 limit on "blacked-out" game broadcasts, the NFL's definition of "home territory" includes the area within a 75-mile radius of the franchise city. Does the SBA exemption cover a league requirement that a network black out broadcasts of Miami Dolphins games from a television station located 100 miles from Miami, whose primary signal reaches as close as 40 miles to Miami? See *WTWV v. NFL*, 678 F.2d 142 (11th Cir.1982). What if the signal reached Miami only after bouncing off a satellite and could be received only with a satellite dish?

3. All NFL regular season games are televised pursuant to national contracts. If the Dolphins unilaterally decided to have one of their non-sellout games blacked out in New York (assuming the network contract permitted such a black-out), so that § 1292 was triggered and the § 1291 exemption was vitiated, what would be the legal implications? Is § 1 of the Sherman Act thereby violated, and if so, in what way and by whom? Is Judge Grim's decree (which has never been lifted) violated? What if the Dolphins sold the rights to one of its pre-season home games to CBS but required that it be blacked out in both Miami and New York—would that eliminate the exemption? Would the black-out be illegal? What would happen if the visiting team sold the rights to the same game to NBC and allowed the telecast to be shown in Miami and New York?

4. Are league contracts with cable networks covered by the SBA? By its terms, § 1291 extends antitrust immunity to a league's sale of pooled-rights for "sponsored telecasting of games." The major sports cable networks such as ESPN, TNT, and SportsChannel America are funded partially by subscriber's fees and partially by advertising revenues. In addition, the transmission by cable from event to television screen fits within the term "telecasting." The legislative history of the SBA, however, casts doubt on whether Congress intended to grant antitrust immunity to any league contracts other than those with the "free" over-the-air television networks. When the SBA was enacted in 1961, its chief proponent, NFL Commissioner Pete Rozelle, told Congress that "[T]his bill covers only the free telecasting of professional sports contests, and does not cover pay TV." In 1982, then-NFL counsel (and now Commissioner) Paul Tagliabue reiterated to a Senate Committee that "the words 'sponsored telecasting' were intended to exclude pay and cable. This is clear from the legislative history and from the committee reports. So, that statute does not authorize us to pool and sell to pay and cable." In light of these comments before and after enactment of the SBA, how should a court interpret the Act with respect to the NFL's current television contracts with ESPN and TNT? With reference to the NHL's 1988–92 contract with SportsChannel America? With respect to any attempts to put the Super Bowl, or the NBA playoffs, or regular season games, on pay-per-view television?

5. If the SBA does not provide antitrust immunity for the NFL's regular season game contracts with ESPN and TNT, or the NHL's contract with SportsChannel America, do these contracts, under a rule of reason analysis, violate § 1 of the Sherman Act?

6. Does an NFL restriction on the telecasting of a playoff game or the Super Bowl violate § 1 under the reasoning of *United States v. NFL*? If such

restrictions are a violation, does the SBA exempt them? See *Blaich v. National Football League*, 212 F.Supp. 319 (S.D.N.Y.1962).

7. Does the SBA have any implications for league revenue sharing? Article 10.3 of the NFL constitution provides that all member clubs share equally in the league's television revenues. (It was a major political accomplishment of new Commissioner Pete Rozelle in 1961 to persuade the Mara family (owner of the New York Giants), George Halas (Chicago Bears), and Dan Reeves (Los Angeles Rams) to agree to this policy, which transferred significant dollar revenues from their clubs to those in smaller media markets. Similar suggestions over the years in other major sports leagues have been quickly killed by large market owners.) Even though the legislative history makes it clear that one important rationale for the SBA was to allow NFL teams to share television revenues, does the SBA's language exempt the sharing of network television revenues? If not exempt, would such network revenue sharing, or the sharing of any other type of revenue (such as local radio and television revenues, gate receipts, luxury box rental fees, parking and concessions revenues, and trademark licensing fees), be a § 1 antitrust violation?

8. Even if the SBA does not offer special antitrust shelter to a particular league television package, that gap is not necessarily filled by affirmative antitrust liability. For example, does major league baseball's judicially-fashioned antitrust immunity apply to its contract with ESPN? See, by analogy, *Henderson Broadcast Corp. v. Houston Sports Association*, 541 F.Supp. 263 (S.D.Tex.1982).

9. Section 1291 only protects league pooled-rights contracts in the "team sports of football, baseball, basketball, or hockey." If Major League Soccer were to negotiate a league-wide contract with CBS similar to the NFL's original contract in 1961, would it be protected by the SBA? Could MLS claim that it is "football," since that is what soccer is called in the rest of the world? Would the new women's American Basketball League be protected? How about the Arena Football League or the Inline Skate Hockey League? Is there any reason why any of these leagues should not have the same protection for their TV contracts as the NFL or NBA?

The more fundamental question is how judges should treat current league television policies, which have progressed far beyond the primitive state displayed to Judge Grim in 1953, under modern principles of antitrust analysis that have also become more sophisticated. Sports television revenues from contracts negotiated under the protective umbrella of the SBA have experienced phenomenal growth. The first exclusive NFL contract with CBS, beginning in 1962, paid the 14 teams an annual total of $4.65 million ($320,000 per team). Thirty-six years later, the NFL's four network and cable contracts earned its 30 teams a total of $2.2 billion ($73 million per team in 1998). Similarly, major league baseball's network contracts in the late 1960s netted a little more than $3 million per year, while the late 1990s combination of Fox and ESPN contracts paid $350 million per year (in addition to the $550 million that baseball teams cumulatively received from sales of their local broadcasting rights). In the 1980s, National Basketball Association (NBA) teams began to share in those television riches (as did their players through the salary cap arrangement). It was the NBA's television policy that finally provided a more up-to-date look at the legal issues, in a dispute that took six years, several district court opinions, and two Seventh Circuit decisions on a range of legal issues, before it was finally settled by the parties.

The dispute arose in 1991 when the NBA voted to reduce from 25 to 20 the number of games that it would allow individual teams to sell to "superstations"—local over-the-air stations whose signals are transmitted and shown on cable outlets throughout the country. There were (and are) only three major superstations in the United States—WTBS in Atlanta (showing the Hawks), WOR in New York (showing the New Jersey Nets), and WGN in Chicago (showing the Chicago Bulls). Thus, the potential impact of this rule was limited to three NBA teams. The team most directly affected was the Chicago Bulls, which for the 1991–92 season had already sold to WGN the broadcast rights in 25 games. WGN and the Bulls thus brought suit against the NBA's enforcement of the new rule, alleging that it was a horizontal agreement among the teams to limit competition among themselves in a way that restricted output in violation of § 1 of the Sherman Act.

The NBA had two basic reasons for wanting to reduce, and eventually to eliminate, superstation broadcasts of games sold by individual teams. First, because these broadcasts are shown on cable in the markets of most other NBA teams, weaker teams in smaller markets suffered revenue losses from having to compete against these superstation telecasts. These losses came in the form of both reduced ticket sales for their home games and reduced fees for the rights to televise all of their games in their local market. This competitive impact of superstation telecasts was particularly acute during the early and mid–1990s because of the tremendous popularity of the perennial NBA champion Bulls, led by Michael Jordan, Scottie Pippen, and (after 1995) Dennis Rodman. In fact, because WGN was available to about 30% of American homes, Bulls' games were viewed in an average of 650,000 homes. This was almost double the Chicago-only audience for the non-superstation Bulls' broadcasts on Chicago SportsChannel, only slightly less than TNT's usual national cable audience of 750,000 homes under its league contract, although far less than NBC's 4.7 million viewers on regular-season Sunday afternoons.

The second concern was the impact on the NBA's league-wide network contracts with NBC and TNT, totalling roughly $180 million in the 1991–92 season. (In fact, overall league revenues had soared from $128 million in the 1982–83 season, just before the owner-player agreement on a salary cap, to $700 million in 1991–92.) The value of these contracts was inevitably reduced when games televised by NBC and TNT had to compete across the country in the same time slots against superstation broadcasts of the Bulls, Nets, and/or Hawks—particularly against the popular games of the Bulls shown on WGN. The revenues generated by the league's television contracts, which are shared equally by all of the NBA teams, were a crucial component (as much as 50%) of the lower-revenue teams' income. Thus, the league felt it needed to protect the value of these network contracts by limiting superstation broadcasts.

The first NBA restrictions on its teams' sale of their broadcasting rights came in 1980, when the league permitted no more than 41 of a team's 82 regular season games to be shown on local "free" television (which could include superstations). The Bulls voted in favor of this restriction. In 1985, the league limited individual team superstation telecasts to 25 games a year, and in 1989, it barred superstation telecasts altogether on nights when an NBA game was being shown nationally on a cable network pursuant to a league contract (then with TNT). Finally, in 1990, the NBA Board of Governors adopted the rule—opposed only by the Bulls and the New Jersey Nets—that reduced the maximum number of superstation games to 20. It was this action that WGN and the Bulls sued to block.

District Judge Hubert Will found that the league's new policy, which lowered the league cap on superstation telecasts by individual teams from 25 to 20, was a violation of § 1 and was not protected by the Sports Broadcasting Act. The NBA appealed his injunction to the Seventh Circuit.

CHICAGO PROFESSIONAL SPORTS LTD. & WGN v. NBA

United States Court of Appeals, Seventh Circuit, 1992.
961 F.2d 667.

EASTERBROOK, CIRCUIT JUDGE.

* * *

[T]he Sports Broadcasting Act applies only when the league has "transferred" a right to "sponsored telecasting." Neither the NBA's contract with NBC nor its contract with Turner Network Television transfers to the network a right to limit the broadcasting of other contests. Both contracts and, so far as we can tell, the league's articles and bylaws, reserve to the individual clubs the full copyright interest in all games that the league has not sold to the networks. As the "league of clubs" has not transferred to the networks either the right to show, or the right to black out, any additional games, the Sports Broadcasting Act does not protect its 20–game rule.

The NBA protests that such an approach is arbitrary. What if the league had assumed control of all broadcast rights and licensed only 20 of the Bulls' games to WGN? That would have been a "transfer" by a "league of clubs." What could be the point of forbidding a different mechanism (the rule limiting to 20 the number of games teams may sell to superstations) that leads to the same result? Other mechanisms to achieve similar outcomes abound. The league might have put a cap of 20 superstation games in its contracts with NBC and Turner, or it might have followed the path of professional baseball and allowed unlimited broadcasting over superstations while claiming a portion of the revenues for distribution among the clubs. (Sharing of revenues occurs in all team sports, although less so in the NBA than other leagues.)

Whether there are ways to achieve the NBA's objective is not the question. Laws often treat similar things differently. One has only to think of tax law, where small differences in the form of a business reorganization have large consequences for taxation. Substance then follows form. Antitrust law is no exception: agreements among business rivals to fix prices are unlawful per se, although a merger of the same firms, even more effective in eliminating competition among them, might be approved with little ado. Such distinctions are not invariably formal. The combined business entity might achieve efficiencies unavailable to the cartelists. But then the line in the Sports Broadcasting Act is not entirely formal either. Perhaps the reason the NBA has not commandeered all of the telecasting rights and sold limited numbers of games to superstations is that it cannot obtain the approval of the clubs to do this—for a change in the allocation of rights is apt to affect the allocation of revenues, making the bargaining problem difficult with 27 clubs. A league's difficulty in rearranging its affairs to obtain the protection of the Sports Broadcasting Act is one source of protection for competition.

What the NBA might have done, it did not do. The Sports Broadcasting Act is special interest legislation, a single-industry exception to a law designed for the protection of the public. When special interests claim that they have obtained favors from Congress, a court should ask to see the bill of sale. Special interest laws do not have "spirits," and it is inappropriate to extend them to achieve more of the objective the lobbyists wanted. What the industry obtained, the courts enforce; what it did not obtain from the legislature—even if similar to something within the exception—a court should not bestow . . .

III

The merits of the case turn on the characterization of the NBA. Is a sports league a single entity? In that event its decisions about telecasting are effectively unreviewable. *Copperweld Corp. v. Independence Tube Corp.*, 467 U.S. 752 (1984). True, its operating divisions (the teams) have separate owners, but on this view the league's method of hiring capital is no more relevant than would be the decision of a single firm to obtain loans from different banks in different cities, or the decision by a large retailer to compensate managers of its stores with a percentage of the local profits. Is the NBA instead a joint venture adopting strategies that foster its competition with other entertainments? In that event pro basketball on TV is not fundamentally different from "Star Trek: The Next Generation," a series created by cooperation among many persons who are competitors at other times. Producers of a television series commit the episodes exclusively to one network (or one station in a local market) in order to compete against the offerings of other ventures. No program, indeed no producer's entire menu of programs, commands a substantial share of the market in televised entertainment. Marketing strategies such as exclusivity and limits on the number of episodes produced per year then must be understood as ways to compete rather than ways to exploit consumers. Perhaps, however, the NBA is a joint venture only in the production of games; in the hiring of inputs (from basketballs to players) and in the sale of their product, the owners are competitors. In that event the television rules look more like a reduction in output, the work of a cartel, and only an exemption from the antitrust laws permits the owners to act cooperatively.

Characterization is a creative rather than exact endeavor. Appellate review is accordingly deferential. The district court held a trial, heard the evidence, and concluded that the best characterization of the NBA is the third we have mentioned: a joint venture in the production of games but more like a cartel in the sale of its output. Whether this is the best characterization of professional sports is a subject that has divided courts and scholars for some years, making it hard to characterize the district judge's choice as clear error.

Parts of the NBA's brief verge on the argument that a sports league is a single entity as a matter of law. Justice Rehnquist's opinion dissenting from the denial of certiorari in [*NASL*] 459 U.S. 1074 (1982), supports such a position, to which *Copperweld* added weight two years later. There is a lively debate in the academic press on the subject. All agree that cooperation off the field is essential to produce intense rivalry on it—rivalry that is essential to the sport's attractiveness in a struggle with other sports, and other entertainments in general, for audience. The persons denominated owners of teams may not own them in an economic sense. Many of their actions are subject to review by the league's board, so that the "owners" may be no more than financier-managers of the league's branch offices. How much cooperation at the league level is beneficial is an interesting question in economics as well as law. See Jesse W. Markham & Paul v. Teplitz, *Baseball Economics and Public Policy* (1981). But the NBA did not contend in the district court that the NBA is a single entity, let alone that it is a single entity as a matter of law. It does no more than allude to the possibility here. Whether a sports league is a single entity for antitrust purposes has significance far beyond this case, and it would be imprudent to decide the question after such cursory dialog. Perhaps the parties will join issue more fully in the proceedings still to come in the district court. For now we treat the NBA as a joint venture, just as the parties do in the bulk of their arguments.

[The appellate panel, assuming for the sake of this case that the NBA was a joint venture governed by the rule of reason, next assessed the league's market power.]

* * *

As the NBA points out, sports is a small fraction of all entertainment on TV, and basketball a small fraction of sports televising. Viewers of basketball games do not have qualities uniquely attractive to advertisers—and if they do, the advertisers can reach them via other sports programs and many other programs too. NBC advertises basketball games during sitcoms and other programs, implying that the market in viewers extends well beyond weekend sports programming. Higher prices, the hallmark of a reduction in output, are missing: advertisers pay no more per thousand viewers of NBA basketball than they do for other sports audiences, and substantially less than they pay per thousand viewers of other entertainment. During 1990 the cost per thousand viewers (CPM) of a regular-season NBA network game was $8.17. NCAA football fetched $11.50, and viewers of prime-time programs were substantially more expensive. The CPM for "L.A. Law" was $19.34, the CPM for "Coach" $13.40. The NBA hardly has cornered the market on the viewers advertisers want to reach.

According to the NBA, this means that its rules do not injure viewers or advertisers, and it makes more sense to understand them as ways to compete against other suppliers of entertainment programming, all of which—right down to the smallest producers of syndicated programs—find it in their interest to sell exclusive rights to a small number of episodes. The NBA contends that until it tried to adopt a rational structure for television it had a much smaller audience than it does now. During 1980 and 1981 CBS carried the final game of the championship series by delayed broadcast! In 1982 only five NBA games appeared on network TV. A "restraint" that in the end expands output, serves the interests of consumers and should be applauded rather than condemned. Rules keeping some popular games off superstations may help weaker teams attract the support of their local audiences, something that (like the sharing of revenues) in the longer run promotes exciting, competitive games. Teams in smaller markets depend more on live gate to finance operations that will compete with the Bulls, Lakers, and Knicks on the court. Rivalry makes for a more attractive product, which then attracts a larger audience—the very expansion of output that the antitrust laws foster.

A market defined by TV viewers is not the only way to look at things. The district court in *NCAA* defined a market of games shown. If "basketball games" are the product, then the NBA's plan cuts output by definition even if more persons watch the fewer (and more attractive) games shown on TV. The NCAA tried to persuade the Supreme Court that the plaintiffs should be required to establish power in a viewership market. The Court replied:

> We must reject this argument for two reasons, one legal, one factual. As a matter of law, the absence of proof of market power does not justify a naked restriction on price or output.... This naked restraint on price and output requires some competitive justification even in the absence of a detailed market analysis.

468 U.S. at 109–10. Although this passage is not entirely clear, we understand it as holding that any agreement to reduce output measured by the number of televised games requires some justification—some explanation connecting the practice to consumers' benefits—before the court attempts an analysis of market power. Unless there are sound justifications, the court condemns the practice without ado, using the "quick look" version of the Rule of Reason advocated by Professor Areeda and by the Solicitor General's brief in *NCAA*.

The district court proceeded in this fashion, examining the league's justifications; finding each wanting, the judge enjoined the 20–game rule without defining a market. In this court, the league's lead-off justification is that the telecasting rule prevents the clubs from "misappropriating" a "property" right that belongs to the NBA: the right to exploit its symbols and success. The district court properly rejected this argument on two grounds. First, it mischaracterizes the NBA's articles and bylaws, which leave with the teams the intellectual property in their games. The NBA could acquire a property interest in all broadcasting rights but has not done so. The 20–game rule does not transfer any broadcasting rights to the league; instead it shortens the list of stations to which clubs may sell rights the teams concededly possess. Second, it has nothing to do with antitrust law. We want to know the effects of the TV policy on consumers' welfare, not whether the league possesses sufficient contractual rights that it has become the "owner" of the copyright. See *Continental T.V., Inc. v. GTE Sylvania Inc.*, 433 U.S. 36, 52–53 & n. 21 (1977) (rejecting an argument that legality of restraints under the antitrust laws depends on the characterization of a transaction in the law of property). A cartel could not insulate its agreement from the Sherman Act by giving certain producers contractual rights to sell to specified customers. Agreements limiting to whom, and how much, a firm may sell are the defining characteristics of cartels and may not be invoked as justifications of a cutback in output. That the NBA's cutback is only five games per year is irrelevant; long ago the Court rejected the invitation to inquire into the "reasonableness" of price and output decisions. Competition in markets, not judges, sets price and output. A court applying the Rule of Reason asks whether a practice produces net benefits for consumers; it is no answer to say that a loss is "reasonably small." (What is more, if five superstation games is tiny in relation to the volume of telecasting, the benefits from the limitation are correspondingly small.)

[The court then addressed the NBA's argument that the reduction to 20 games that might be broadcast on superstations was justified as a restraint on "free riders."]

* * *

It costs money to make a product attractive against other contenders for consumers' favor. Firms that take advantage of costly efforts without paying for them, that reap where they have not sown, reduce the payoff that the firms making the investment receive. This makes investments in design and distribution of products less attractive, to the ultimate detriment of consumers. Control of free-riding is accordingly an accepted justification for cooperation.

Three forms of free-riding characterize the Bulls' telecasting, according to the NBA. First, the contracts with NBC and TNT require these networks to advertise NBA basketball on other shows; the Bulls and WGN receive the benefit of this promotion without paying the cost. Second, the NBA has revenue-sharing devices and a draft to prop up the weaker teams. The Bulls took advantage of these while they were weak (and through the draft obtained their current stars) but, according to the league, are siphoning viewers (and thus revenues) to their own telecasts, thus diminishing the pot available for distribution to today's weaker teams. Third, the Bulls and WGN are taking a free ride on the benefits of the cooperative efforts during the 1980s to build up professional basketball as a rival to baseball and football—efforts that bore fruit just as the Bulls produced a championship team, and which the Bulls would undermine.

Free-riding is the diversion of value from a business rival's efforts without payment. [For example, suppose there are two retailers of the same brand of electronic equipment who sell in the same neighborhood. If one provides an attractive showroom and hires salespeople to explain and demonstrate the equipment, the price of the product must build in these ancillary costs. If the other retailer simply sells the equipment off the shelf, without any ancillary services, it can sell at a lower price because it avoids these costs. Consumers can thus obtain all of the ancillary services for free from the first retailer, and then buy the product from the second at the lower price; this means that the second retailer has had a "free ride" on the services of the first. However, this will either force the first retailer to stop providing the services, which is detrimental to consumer welfare, or require the manufacturer of the brand to restrict the second retailer in some fashion, to prevent its free riding.]

What gives this the name free-riding is the lack of charge.... Put the retailers in a contractual relation, however, and they could adjust their accounts so that the person providing a valuable service gets paid. When payment is possible, free-riding is not a problem because the "ride" is not free. Here lies the flaw in the NBA's story. It may (and does) charge members for value delivered. As the NBA itself emphasizes, there are substantial revenue transfers, propping up the weaker clubs in order to promote vigorous competition on the court. Without skipping a beat the NBA may change these payments to charge for the Bulls' ride. If the $40 million of advertising time that NBC will provide during the four years of its current contract also promotes WGN's games, then the league may levy a charge for each game shown on a superstation, or require the club to surrender a portion of its revenues. Major league baseball does exactly this and otherwise allows its teams access to superstations. Avoidance of free-riding therefore does not justify the NBA's 20–game limit.

Doubtless there is irony in saying that the limit violates the antitrust laws because the defendants could adopt a system of charges for making sales. Revenue-pooling and pass-over payments are the usual tools of cartels.... Charges for the privilege of putting games on superstations will lead to fewer such broadcasts; by selecting the tax carefully, the NBA could induce the Bulls to broadcast 20 games, neither more nor less, on WGN. Plaintiffs have hinted that they will ask the district court to ban all revenue-sharing procedures for telecasting. Yet we do not suppose that the Bulls are going to ask the court to hold that the draft of college players, the cap on their payroll, the distribution of revenues from the NBC and TNT contracts, and other sharing devices all violate the Sherman Act. Sharing is endemic in league sports. The prevalence of what is otherwise a hallmark of a cartel may suggest the shakiness of treating the clubs, which must cooperate to have any product to sell, as rival "producers" in the first place.

Because of the way in which issues have become separated in this litigation, we do not decide whether revenue-sharing from superstation broadcasts is consistent with the antitrust laws. Needless to say, we also do not decide whether any of the cooperative arrangements by which the league hires the services of the players comports with the Sherman Act. (The National Basketball Players Association, concerned that we might do some such thing by accident, has filed a brief urging us to guard our tongues.) It is enough to say that if the league may levy a tax on superstation broadcasts, then there is no free-riding. And if the league may not levy a tax, then a direct limit with the same effect as a tax is unjustifiable. Either way the NBA comes up short, and under *NCAA* the failure of its justifications eliminates the need for the district judge to define a market.

The NCAA argued that restrictions on the number of games telecast spread revenues and exposure among universities, helping to produce balanced competition on the field and hence making the games actually telecast more exciting, to the benefit of fans. Distributing telecasts among schools served, in the NCAA's view, as a substitute for the draft and other controls professional leagues deployed to the same end. The Supreme Court found the argument unpersuasive. It is hard to see how similar balance arguments by professional leagues, which make the most of drafts, trades, and revenue-pooling to foster exciting games, could be more compelling. Unless the Supreme Court is prepared to modify *NCAA*, the district court did not commit clear error in applying the "quick look" version of the Rule of Reason and rejecting the NBA's arguments.

Affirmed.

Ironically, as a notable law and economics scholar at Chicago, then Professor Easterbrook was counsel for the National Collegiate Athletic Association (NCAA) in its unsuccessful appeal to the Supreme Court in

NCAA v. Board of Regents of the University of Oklahoma, 468 U.S. 85 (1984) (which is reproduced and discussed in Chapter 10), a decision that is referred to at numerous points in the *WGN* opinion.[r] In that case—the only Supreme Court decision on the substantive antitrust treatment of any aspect of sports—the Court ruled that the NCAA's sale of an exclusive package of college football telecasts violated § 1 of the Sherman Act. Though the judicial opinions in *WGN* never adverted to this fact, the *NCAA* case provided the most graphic evidence we have of the economic impact of sports teams collectively restricting the sale of their television rights. In 1983, just before the Supreme Court ruling, the NCAA received and distributed to its members approximately $75 million for the eighty football games that were shown pursuant to several network contracts (on both free and cable television). In 1984, immediately after the *NCAA* decision, all the schools together received less than $60 million for broadcasts of over 200 games on different forms of television. The price paid by ABC and CBS to show a national game dropped from $1.3 million in 1983 to $600,000 or less in 1984.

Questions for Discussion

1. The trial judge had determined that the NBA functioned as a single firm in producing the league product (the games), but constituted a cartel in the marketing and selling of that product. Judge Easterbrook deferred to this finding, given that the NBA had made neither an issue of nor a clear record on the single entity defense. (As we shall soon see, Easterbrook's extensive comments on this sports law issue played a significant role in the later stages of the *WGN* litigation.) Is the district court's distinction between the league as a single firm producing, and a group of potential competitors selling, the product a plausible one? Under this theory, what league rules or policies would be immune from rule of reason review as unilateral conduct? Player restraints such as the NFL's Plan B at issue in *McNeil*? Franchise relocation restrictions like the NFL's Rule 4.3 at issue in the *Raiders* case?

2. The principal procompetitive benefit claimed by the NBA from its superstation cap was that this would prevent the Bulls from "free riding" on league efforts when they broadcast their games over the WGN superstation. Is this true? If so, does Easterbrook's opinion give the league a right to "tax" the Bulls? If the league attempted to impose such a tax, could the tax itself be a § 1 violation? Keep this in mind as well as you read further in the *WGN* saga.

Having lost this effort to implement its 20–game limit on superstation broadcasts, the NBA tried a different approach. It added a provision to its network contract with Turner Network Television (TNT) that prohibited all NBA teams from having their games televised on a

---

r. For an illuminating exchange about the virtues and vices of antitrust law generally, see Frank A. Easterbrook, *The Limits of Antitrust*, 63 Texas L. Rev. 1 (1984), and Richard S. Markovits, *The Limits to Simplifying Antitrust: A Reply to Professor Easterbrook*, 63 Texas L. Rev. 41 (1984).

superstation on the same night that another NBA game was being televised on TNT. This restraint on the ability of the Bulls and WGN to compete against other NBA games had two features that distinguished it from the 20 games-per-year limitation. First, the restriction was embodied in the league's network contract—which Judge Easterbrook had noted might possibly allow the league to utilize the SBA exemption. Second, though, the TNT network is available only to viewers who subscribe to a cable service, by contrast with NBC which is carried over the air for "free" viewing. That feature might eliminate the SBA's protection, on the theory that cable is not "sponsored telecasting" for purposes of § 1291. When the Bulls and WGN challenged this "superstation same night rule," Judge Will had to confront these two important issues affecting the scope of the SBA protection.

As to the NBA's argument that Judge Easterbrook had already endorsed the view that any restriction embodied in a league's network contract qualified for SBA protection, Judge Will disagreed (in an opinion reported at 808 F.Supp. 646 (N.D.Ill.1992)).

> [T]he NBA has taken none of the steps posited by [the Seventh Circuit] to try to obtain protection by "commandeer[ing] all of the telecasting rights" of the "27 clubs" and "rearranging its affairs" to change the clubs' "allocation of revenues." First, ... "nothing in any NBA agreement ... suggests further agreement by the teams to share their separately owned copyrights and transfer those rights, in whole or in part, to the league." ... Second, the rights to the games licensed by the Bulls to WGN have not been transferred to the league or by the league to any other party. As the Seventh Circuit affirmed, "the [SBA] applies only when the league has 'transferred' a right to 'sponsored telecasting.'" ... Third, because each team retains the right to televise on its particular over-the-air or cable outlet the *same games* that are televised by TNT, the league's transfer of rights to TNT cannot be characterized as exclusive.

808 F.Supp. at 648–49.

As to the second issue, Judge Will also ruled that the SBA would not apply, because TNT did not appear to be "sponsored telecasting."

> In its status as a cable television programming service, however, it is not clear that TNT constitutes "sponsored telecasting" as that term is used in the SBA. Although it is indeed a hybrid programming service, TNT is perhaps better characterized as subscription television for the following reasons. First, ... a viewer must pay to receive TNT through the costs of hook-up fees, monthly cable fees and even additional monthly "premium cable" fees charged by some local cable operators for TNT.... Second, TNT derives its revenues predominantly from "subscriptions" [$232 million in 1991] as opposed to advertising revenues from paying "sponsors" [$138 million in 1991]. Third, prior and subsequent legislative history demonstrates that "sponsored telecasting" as used in the SBA is limited to free commercial television as opposed to cable....

> ... "Sponsored telecasting" is not expressly defined by either the SBA or by any subsequent case law. In its report on the proposed legislation, the House Judiciary Committee noted only that "[t]he bill does not apply to closed circuit or subscription television." While the plain meaning of the term "subscription television" in 1961 might arguably have referred only to a pay-per-view service, it seems equally likely that the term "sponsored telecasting" would not have included such hybrid services as TNT and ESPN. "Sponsored telecasting" in 1961 referred to "free" television—the national network and local over-the-air broadcasting provided at no direct cost to viewers. The NBA's attempt to construe TNT as such "sponsored telecasting" simply because it contains commercial advertisements and is not offered on a pay-per-view basis is unconvincing....

808 F.Supp. at 649–50.

Because its contracts with TNT and NBC were about to expire after the 1992–93 season, the NBA did not appeal Judge Will's second ruling. Instead, the league lawyers re-read Judge Easterbrook's opinion in *WGN I* and sought to "rearrange" their affairs to achieve the same economic goals, but in a legally-insulated fashion. The NBA first amended its by-laws (with the Bulls and Nets dissenting) to have its teams confer copyright in all game telecasts on the league. Then, in its new television contract with NBC, the league assigned to NBC the exclusive right to televise all 1,100 regular season games. In return, NBC agreed that after selecting its 25 or so favored games, it would authorize the NBA to license Turner Broadcasting to telecast up to 85 games on its TNT cable and WTBS superstation channels. Then, after Turner had picked its games, the NBA could authorize individual teams to telecast the remaining games on local channels—but never on superstations. The new NBA rules also provided that, if its ban on superstation telecasts were to be struck down, a club like the Bulls that chose to use a superstation like WGN would have to pay a fee to the NBA that reflected the difference in the fair market value between local and national markets.

Needless to say, both the Bulls and WGN immediately went back to Judge Will with another antitrust claim against these new arrangements. Also with an eye to Judge Easterbrook's first opinion, the NBA now expressly raised the single entity defense, relying on *Copperweld* and its subsequent interpretation in *City of Mt. Pleasant v. Associated Elec. Coop., Inc.*, 838 F.2d 268 (8th Cir.1988). Judge Will rejected this defense, in an opinion reported at 874 F.Supp. 844 (N.D.Ill.1995).

> ... [T]he teams comprising the NBA pursue the very type of diverse interests that *Mt. Pleasant* indicated must be absent. The NBA teams are actual competitors, not only on the baseline for points, but also off the court in the market for players, coaches, managers, advertising dollars, fan support, ticket sales, and overall revenues. They keep their own profits and generally earn far more for themselves than they do through their combined efforts as a league.

Winning season games, playoffs and championships translates into greater financial prosperity for the victors. One team's gain on the court is thus generally another's loss at the bank, and while some cooperation is necessary, the profit seeking interests of one team are often contrary to those of other teams.

* * *

There is no doubt that the NBA, like any sports league, has cooperative characteristics. Mutual agreement is necessary to create the "product" of competitive basketball games and to insure its quality. Moreover, the member teams undoubtedly derive genuine financial benefit from their combined efforts. The NBA confuses, however, the necessary and beneficial cooperation of a joint venture with the unified interests of a single entity. When independent actors join in order to achieve mutual benefit, or even to accomplish what they could not on their own, the result is not automatically exempt from antitrust scrutiny.... Thus, while the unique needs and structure of the NBA demand that we carefully review its joint agreements for procompetitive effects, they do not support the conclusion that the NBA is a single entity.

874 F.Supp. at 848–50.

In the same lengthy opinion, Judge Will also found that the series of arrangements that resulted in the superstation ban were illegal, because the new regime simply accomplished through different mechanisms the exact same result that he had already held to be illegal. The assignment of copyrights to the league was a "sham," since teams ended up with the same right to broadcast all non-network games as they had held before.

The ultimate fact is that there has been no change in either the teams' rights to enter into contracts involving local and regional TV or radio transmission of NBA games and the sale of other copyrighted products, or in the league continuing in all of its contracts to act as agent for the teams and not as the owner and licensor of the copyrights.... [Thus], the nominal transfer of the various teams' copyrights to the NBA does not immunize it [under the SBA] from the application of the antitrust laws.

874 F.Supp. at 851. The judge also found that the league's assignment of exclusive broadcast rights to NBC did not bring the arrangement SBA protection; while this network contract did involve sponsored telecasting, it ran afoul of § 1292's exception to the exemption by prohibiting the telecasting of games in certain areas, by limiting NBC to 25 games, and by prohibiting the games eventually reassigned to the teams from being broadcast on superstations outside the teams' local areas.

Judge Will then found the superstation ban to be illegal under antitrust law, using a "quick-look" rule of reason analysis. He reasoned that the league's arrangement obviously restricted broadcast output, while the league had not proven any significant procompetitive benefit. The judge did endorse the NBA position that charging some fee to the

Bulls for superstation telecasts was appropriate in order to offset the free-rider effect. However, the fee could not be set at an unreasonably high level so as effectively to restrict output.

> [W]e note that any superstation fee necessarily will decrease the amount of profitability that the Bulls and WGN realize on the games shown. Yet, ... we are not concerned with the plaintiff's ability to make a profit, but instead we are concerned about the effects of the restraints on consumers. To the extent that a reasonable fee reduces the Bulls and WGN's profits, but does not reduce distribution of the product while equitably compensating the other teams for their contribution to the production of the product, we see no objection to it.

874 F.Supp. at 868–69. Judge Will ordered the NBA not to limit the Bulls to any less than 30 superstation telecasts. He left it for the parties to try to negotiate the appropriate fee for those telecasts. Failing that, future litigation would be needed to determine if any fee the NBA in fact imposed was too high because it cut back on broadcast output; if so, the NBA would still be, *de facto*, in violation of § 1.

The NBA appealed the ruling that its current superstation ban was illegal. In the fall of 1996, Judge Easterbrook issued the Seventh Circuit's second decision (reported at 95 F.3d 593 (7th Cir.1996)) in this seemingly never-ending war between the NBA and the Bulls. As Judge Easterbrook observed at the outset of his opinion, "in the six years since they filed an antitrust suit, the Chicago Bulls have won four National Basketball Association titles and an equal number of legal victories." In *WGN V* the Bulls suffered their first legal loss (though that season they still won their fifth NBA title). However, the circuit court's decision, which vacated Judge Will's prior ruling in favor of the Bulls and remanded the case back for a full-scale retrial of the antitrust issues, did not provide clearcut answers to the vast majority of questions posed in this book about this area of sports law.

The appeals court did reject the NBA's effort to fit its league rules within the Sports Broadcasting Act (SBA), through the new technique of transferring all broadcast rights to NBC and TBS/TNT, and having the latter return the vast majority of unused games to the individual teams, subject now to restrictions against selling those games to superstations like WGN. Echoing its earlier observation that the SBA must receive "beady-eyed reading" as a special interest exception to the antitrust laws, Judge Easterbrook asserted that "a league has to jump through every [SBA] hoop: partial compliance doesn't do the trick." The only way that the NBA could avail itself of the SBA was by itself taking over and selling broadcast rights in the games of the Bulls (and other) teams. However,

> by signing a contract with NBC that left the Bulls, rather than the league, with the authority to select the TV station that would broadcast the games, the NBA made its position under the SBA untenable. For as soon as the Bulls picked WGN, any effort to

control cable system retransmission of the WGN signal tripped over § 2 [of the SBA] which barred such restraints except within the home territory of clubs when they are playing.

96 F.3d at 596. There were federal taxation as well as internal managerial and political problems that blocked the league taking over this role as *licensor* of all its members teams' home broadcasts. Thus, if the league wanted to function just as *regulator* of such local team licensing, it had to do so under the scrutiny of antitrust law.

With respect to the key antitrust question whether sports leagues are "single entities" or § 1 "combinations ... in restraint of trade," Judge Easterbrook did not affirmatively rule one way or the other. However, supported by Judge Bauer, he did opine that at least for some purposes, leagues such as the NBA were sufficiently close to that organizational form that they could well be deemed a single entity. The court thus remanded the case back to a new district judge (Judge Will having died in the interim) to create a full record for legal analysis of the single entity issue in the context of league television policies. Even if the league were found not to be a single entity for that purpose, a full-blown rule of reason proceeding was required, not Judge Will's "quick-look" approach. Judge Cudahy, while concurring in the need to remand for an in-depth rule of reason treatment, expressed a somewhat different view on the single entity-sports league issue. Easterbrook's and Cudahy's opinions on the single entity issue are perhaps the most interesting and sophisticated of all the judicial musings on this issue thus far. The key portions of their diverging analyses are reproduced below.

CHICAGO PROFESSIONAL SPORTS LIMITED PARTNERSHIP & WGN v. NATIONAL BASKETBALL ASSOCIATION

United States Court of Appeals, Seventh Circuit, 1996.
95 F.3d 593.

EASTERBROOK, CIRCUIT JUDGE.

[Judge Easterbrook first addressed Judge Will's fourth ruling, that while the NBA did have the right to charge the Bulls a fee for sending its games out on a superstation, it should use as its calculation base the "outer market advertising revenues" that WGN generated from cable, and then split this in half with the Bulls. The upshot was that Judge Will cut the fee imposed by the league on the Bulls from roughly $138,000 to $35,000 a game.]

* * *

The district court's opinion concerning the fee reads like the ruling of an agency exercising a power to regulate rates. Yet the antitrust laws do not deputize district judges as one-man regulatory agencies. The core question in antitrust is output. Unless a contract reduces output in some market, to the detriment of consumers, there is no antitrust problem. A high price is not itself a violation of the Sherman Act. See *Broadcast*

Music, Inc. v. CBS, Inc., 441 U.S. 1, 9–10, 19–20, 22 n. 40 (1979); *Buffalo Broadcasting Co. v. ASCAP*, 744 F.2d 917 (2d Cir.1984). WGN and the Bulls argue that the league's fee is excessive, unfair, and the like. But they do not say that it will reduce output. They plan to go on broadcasting 30 games, more if the court will let them, even if they must pay $138,000 per telecast. Although the fee exceeds WGN's outer-market revenues, the station evidently obtains other benefits—for example, (i) the presence of Bulls games may increase the number of cable systems that carry the station, augmenting its revenues 'round the clock;' (ii) WGN slots into Bulls games ads for its other programming; and (iii) many viewers will keep WGN on after the game and watch whatever comes next. Lack of an effect on output means that the fee does not have antitrust significance. Once antitrust issues are put aside, how much the NBA charges for national telecasts is for the league to resolve under its internal governance procedures. It is no different in principle from the question how much (if any) of the live gate goes to the visiting team, who profits from the sale of cotton candy at the stadium, and how the clubs divide revenues from merchandise bearing their logos and trademarks. Courts must respect a league's disposition of these issues, just as they respect contracts and decisions by a corporation's board of directors. *Charles O. Finley & Co. v. Kuhn*, 569 F.2d 527 (7th Cir.1978); cf. *Baltimore Orioles, Inc. v. Major League Baseball Players Association*, 805 F.2d 663 (7th Cir.1986).

According to the league, the analogy to a corporate board is apt in more ways than this. The NBA concedes that it comprises 30 juridical entities—29 teams plus the national organization, each a separate corporation or partnership. The teams are not the league's subsidiaries; they have separate ownership. Nonetheless, the NBA submits, it functions as a single entity, creating a single product ("NBA Basketball") that competes with other basketball leagues (both college and professional), other sports ("Major League Baseball", "college football"), and other entertainments such as plays, movies, opera, TV shows, Disneyland, and Las Vegas. Separate ownership of the clubs promotes local boosterism, which increases interest; each ownership group also has a powerful incentive to field a better team, which makes the contests more exciting and thus more attractive. These functions of independent team ownership do not imply that the league is a cartel, however, any more than separate ownership of hamburger joints (again useful as an incentive device, see Benjamin Klein & Lester F. Saft, *The Law and Economics of Franchise Tying Contracts*, 28 J.L. & Econ. 345 (1985)) implies that McDonald's is a cartel. Whether the best analogy is to a system of franchises (no one expects a McDonald's outlet to compete with other members of the system by offering pizza) or to a corporate holding company structure (on which see *Copperweld Corp. v. Independence Tube Corp.*, 467 U.S. 752 (1984)) does not matter from this perspective. The point is that antitrust law permits, indeed encourages, cooperation inside a business organization the better to facilitate competition between that organization and other producers. To say that participants in an organization may cooperate is to say that they may control what they make and how they sell it: the producers of Star Trek may decide to release two episodes a week and grant exclusive licenses to show them, even though this reduces the number of times episodes appear on TV in a given market, just as the NBA's superstation rule does.

The district court conceded this possibility but concluded that all cooperation among separately incorporated firms is forbidden by § 1 of the Sherman Act, except to the extent *Copperweld* permits. *Copperweld*, according to the district court, "is quite narrow, and rests solely upon the fact that a parent corporation and its wholly-owned subsidiary have a 'complete unity of interest'" (quoting from 467 U.S. at 771). Although that phrase appears in *Copperweld*, the Court offered it as a statement of fact about the parent-subsidiary relation, not as a proposition of law about the limits of permissible cooperation. As a proposition of law, it would be silly. Even a single firm contains many competing interests. One division may make inputs for another's finished goods. The first division might want to sell its products directly to the market, to maximize income (and thus the salary and bonus of the division's managers); the second division might want to get its inputs from the first at a low transfer price, which would maximize the second division's paper profits. Conflicts are endemic in any multi-stage firm, such as General Motors or IBM, see Robert G. Eccles, "Transfer Pricing as a Problem of Agency," in *Principals and Agents: The Structure of Business* 151 (Pratt & Zeckhauser eds. 1985), but they do not imply that these large firms must justify all of their acts under the Rule of Reason. Or consider a partnership for the practice of law (or accounting): some lawyers would be better off with a lockstep compensation agreement under which all partners with the same seniority have the same income, but others would prosper under an "eat what you kill" system that rewards bringing new business to the firm. Partnerships have dissolved as a result of these conflicts. Yet these wrangles—every bit as violent as the dispute among the NBA's teams about how to generate and divide broadcast revenues—do not demonstrate that law firms are cartels, or subject to scrutiny under the Rule of Reason their decisions about where to open offices or which clients to serve.

Copperweld does not hold that only conflict-free enterprises may be treated as single entities. Instead it asks why the antitrust laws distinguish between unilateral and concerted action, and then assigns a parent-subsidiary group to the "unilateral" side in light of those functions. Like a single firm, the parent-subsidiary combination cooperates internally to increase efficiency. Conduct that "deprives the marketplace of the independent centers of decisionmaking that competition assumes", 467 U.S. at 769, without the efficiencies that come with integration inside a firm, go on the "concerted" side of the line. And there are entities in the middle: "mergers, joint ventures, and various vertical agreements" (id. at 768) that reduce the number of independent decisionmakers yet may improve efficiency. These are assessed under the Rule of Reason. We see no reason why a sports league cannot be treated as a single firm in this typology. It produces a single product; cooperation is essential (a league with one team would be like one hand clapping); and a league need not deprive the market of independent centers of decisionmaking. The district court's legal standard was therefore incorrect, and a judgment resting on the application of that standard is flawed.

Whether the NBA itself is more like a single firm, which would be analyzed only under § 2 of the Sherman Act, or like a joint venture, which would be subject to the Rule of Reason under § 1, is a tough question under *Copperweld*. It has characteristics of both. Unlike the colleges and universities that belong to the National Collegiate Athletic Association, which the Supreme Court treated as a joint venture in *NCAA*, the NBA has no existence independent of sports. It makes professional basketball; only it can make "NBA Basketball" games; and unlike the NCAA the NBA also "makes" teams. After this case was last here the NBA created new teams in Toronto and Vancouver, stocked with players from the 27 existing teams plus an extra helping of draft choices. All of this makes the league look like a single firm. Yet the 29 clubs, unlike GM's plants, have the right to secede (wouldn't a plant manager relish that!), and rearrange into two or three leagues. Professional sports leagues have been assembled from clubs that formerly belonged to other leagues; the National Football League and the NBA fit that description, and the teams have not surrendered their power to rearrange things yet again. Moreover, the league looks more or less like a firm depending on which facet of the business one examines. See Phillip E. Areeda, 7 *Antitrust Law* ¶ 1478d (1986). From the perspective of fans and advertisers (who use sports telecasts to reach fans), "NBA Basketball" is one product from a single source even though the Chicago Bulls and Seattle Supersonics are highly distinguishable, just as General Motors is a single firm even though a Corvette differs from a Chevrolet. But from the perspective of college basketball players who seek to sell their skills, the teams are distinct, and because the human capital of players is not readily transferable to other sports (as even Michael Jordan learned), the league looks more like a group of firms acting as a monopsony. That is why the Supreme Court found it hard to characterize the National Football League in *Brown v. Pro Football, Inc.*, 116 S.Ct. 2116, 2126 (1996): "the clubs that make up a professional sports league are not completely independent economic competitors, as they depend upon a degree of cooperation for economic survival.... In the present context, however, that circumstance makes the league more like a single bargaining employer, which analogy seems irrelevant to the legal issue before us." To say that the league is "more like a single bargaining employer" than a multi-employer unit is not to say that it necessarily is one, for every purpose.

The league wants us to come to a conclusion on this subject (six years of litigation is plenty!) and award it the victory. Yet as we remarked in 1992, "characterization is a creative rather than exact endeavor." The district court plays the leading role, followed by deferential appellate review. We are not authorized to announce and apply our own favored characterization unless the law admits of only one choice. The Supreme Court's ambivalence in *Brown*, like the disagreement among judges on similar issues, implies that more than one characterization is possible, and therefore that the district court must revisit the subject using the correct legal approach.

Most courts that have asked whether professional sports leagues should be treated like single firms or like joint ventures have preferred the joint venture characterization. E.g., *Sullivan v. NFL*, 34 F.3d 1091 (1st Cir.1994); *North American Soccer League v. NFL*, 670 F.2d 1249 (2d Cir.1982); *Smith v. Pro Football, Inc.*, 593 F.2d 1173, 1179 (D.C.Cir. 1978). But Justice Rehnquist filed a strong dissent from the denial of certiorari in the soccer case, arguing that "the league competes as a unit against other forms of entertainment", *NFL v. North American Soccer League*, 459 U.S. 1074, 1077 (1982), and the Fourth Circuit concluded that the Professional Golf Association should be treated as one firm for antitrust purposes, even though that sport is less economically integrated than the NBA. *Seabury Management, Inc. v. PGA of America, Inc.*, 878 F.Supp.771 (D.Md.1994), affirmed in relevant part, 52 F.3d 322 (4th Cir.1995). Another court of appeals has treated an electric cooperative as a single firm, *Mt. Pleasant v. Associated Electric Cooperative*, 838 F.2d 268 (8th Cir.1988), though the co-op is less integrated than a sports league. These cases do not yield a clear principle about the proper characterization of sports leagues—and we do not think that *Copperweld* imposes one "right" characterization. Sports are sufficiently diverse that it is essential to investigate their organization and ask *Copperweld's* functional question one league at a time—and perhaps one facet of a league at a time, for we do not rule out the possibility that an organization such as the NBA is best understood as one firm when selling broadcast rights to a network in competition with a thousand other producers of entertainment, but is best understood as a joint venture when curtailing competition for players who have few other market opportunities. Just as the ability of McDonald's franchises to coordinate the release of a new hamburger does not imply their ability to agree on wages for counter workers, so the ability of sports teams to agree on a TV contract need not imply an ability to set wages for players. See Jesse W. Markham & Paul V. Teplitz, *Baseball Economics and Public Policy* (1981); Arthur A. Fleisher III, Brian L. Goff & Robert D. Tollison, *The National Collegiate Athletic Association: A Study in Cartel Behavior* (1992).

However this inquiry may come out on remand, we are satisfied that the NBA is sufficiently integrated that its superstation rules may not be condemned without analysis under the full Rule of Reason. We affirmed the district court's original injunction after applying the "quick look" version because the district court had characterized the NBA as something close to a cartel, and the league had not then made a *Copperweld* argument. After considering this argument, we conclude that when acting in the broadcast market, the NBA is closer to a single firm than to a group of independent firms. This means that plaintiffs cannot prevail without establishing that the NBA possesses power in a relevant market, and that its exercise of this power has injured consumers. Even in the *NCAA* case, the first to use a bobtailed Rule of Reason, the Court satisfied itself that the NCAA possesses market power. The district court had held that there is a market in college football telecasts on Saturday afternoon in the fall, a time when other entertainments do not flourish but college football dominates. Only after holding that this was not clearly erroneous did the Court cast any burden of justification on the NCAA. 468 U.S. at 111–13; see also *International Boxing Club v. United States*, 358 U.S. 242 (1959).

Substantial market power is an indispensable ingredient of every claim under the full Rule of Reason.... During the lengthy trial of this case, the NBA argued that it lacks market power, whether the buyers are understood as the viewers of games (the way the district court characterized things in NCAA) or as advertisers, who use games to attract viewers (the way the Supreme Court characterized a related market in *Times-Picayune Publishing Co. v. United States*, 345 U.S. 594 (1953)). College football may predominate on Saturday afternoons in the fall, but there is no time slot when NBA basketball predominates. The NBA's season lasts from November through June; games are played seven days a week. This season overlaps all of the other professional and college sports, so even sports fanatics have many other options. From advertisers' perspective—likely the right one, because advertisers are the ones who actually pay for telecasts—the market is even more competitive. Advertisers seek viewers of certain demographic characteristics, and homogeneity is highly valued. A homogeneous audience facilitates targeted ads: breakfast cereals and toys for cartoon shows, household appliances and detergents for daytime soap operas, automobiles and beer for sports. If the NBA assembled for advertisers an audience that was uniquely homogeneous, or had especially high willingness-to-buy, then it might have market power even if it represented a small portion of airtime. The parties directed considerable attention to this question at trial, but the district judge declined to make any findings of fact on the subject, deeming market power irrelevant. As we see things, market power is irrelevant only if the NBA is treated as a single firm under *Copperweld*; and given the difficulty of that issue, it may be superior to approach this as a straight Rule of Reason case, which means starting with an inquiry into market power and, if there is power, proceeding to an evaluation of competitive effects.

* * *

Vacated and remanded.

CUDAHY, CIRCUIT JUDGE, concurring.

[Judge Cudahy agreed with the majority's conclusion that the "quick-look" antitrust approach that the Supreme Court had formulated and utilized in *NCAA v. Bd. of Regents of the Univ. of Oklahoma*, 468 U.S. 85 (1984), in connection with the loose NCAA alliance of colleges, should not apply to the NBA "whose separate constituents are individually owned but are closely but not completely tied economically to their organization—single entity aside, there is certainly enough concern here for the efficiency of the league as a competitor in the entertainment market to require full Rule of Reason analysis." Judge Cudahy did, however, have reservations about the way in which the majority had articulated its single entity thesis, and thus decided to express his own separate views on that topic.]

* * *

Assuming as I must that the sole goal of antitrust is efficiency or, put another way, the maximization of total societal wealth, the question whether a sports league is a "single entity" turns on whether the actions of the league have any potential to lessen economic competition among the separately owned teams.[1] The fact that teams compete on the floor is more or less irrelevant to whether they compete economically—it is only their economic competition which is germane to antitrust analysis. In principle, of course, a sports league could actually be a single firm and the individual teams could be under unified ownership and management. Such a firm would, of course, be subject to scrutiny only under § 2 of the Sherman Act and not under § 1. From the point of view of wealth maximization, a league of independently-owned teams, if it is no more likely than a single firm to make inefficient management decisions, should be treated as a single entity. The single entity question thus would boil down to "whether member clubs of a sports league have legitimate economic interests of their own, independent of the league and each other." *Sports Leagues Revisited* at 127. It follows that a sports league, no matter what its ownership structure, can make inefficient decisions only if the individual teams have some chance of economic gain at the expense of the league.

Another form of the same question is whether a sports league is more like a single firm or like a joint venture. With efficiency the sole criterion, a joint venture warrants scrutiny for at least two reasons—(1) the venture could possess market power with respect to the jointly produced product (essentially act like a single firm with monopoly power) or (2) the fact that the venturers remain competitors in other arenas might either distort the way the joint product is managed or allow the venturers to use the joint product as a smokescreen behind which to cut deals to reduce competition in the other arenas. The most convincing "single entity" argument involving the NBA is that the teams produce only the joint product of "league basketball" and that

---

1. See, e.g., Michael S. Jacobs, *Professional Sports Leagues, Antitrust and the Single-Entity Theory: a Defense of the Status Quo*, 67 Ind. L. J. 25 (1991); Gary R. Roberts, *The Antitrust Status of Sports Leagues Revisited*, 64 Tul. L. Rev. 117 (1989); Myron C. Grauer, *The Use and Misuse of the Term "Consumer Welfare": Once More to the Mat on the Issue of Single Entity Status for Sports Leagues Under Section 1 of the Sherman Act*, 64 Tul. L. Rev. 71 (1989); Lee Goldman, *Sports, Antitrust, and the Single Entity Theory*, 63 Tul. L. Rev. 751 (1989); Gary R. Roberts, *Sports Leagues and the Sherman Act: The Use and Abuse of Section 1 to Regulate Restraints on Intraleague Rivalry*, 32 UCLA L. Rev. 219 (1984), for discussions of this issue.

there is thus no significant economic competition between them. If this is the case, the argument goes, type (2) concerns drop out and only type (1) concerns remain. Type (1) concerns, of course, are exactly those appropriate for § 2 analysis of a single firm.

There are, however, flaws in this single entity argument. The assumption underlying it is that league sports are a different and more desirable product than a disorganized collection of independently arranged games between teams. For this reason, it is contended that joining sports teams into a league is efficiency-enhancing and desirable. I will accept this premise.[2] It is perhaps true, as argued by the NBA and many commentators, that sports are different from many joint ventures because the individual teams cannot, even in principle, produce the product—league sports. However, the fact that cooperation is necessary to produce league basketball does not imply that the league will necessarily produce its product in the most efficient fashion. There is potential for inefficient decisionmaking regarding the joint product of "league basketball" even when the individual teams engage in no economic activity outside of the league. This potential arises because the structure of the league is such that all "owners" of the league must be "owners" of individual teams and decisions are made by a vote of the teams. This means that the league will not necessarily make efficient decisions about the number of teams fielded or, more generally, the competitive balance among teams. Thus, the fact that several teams are required to make a league does not necessarily imply that the current makeup of the league is the most desirable or "efficient" one.

The NBA's justification for its restriction of Bulls broadcasts centers on the need to maintain a competitive balance among teams. Such a balance is needed to ensure that the league provides high quality entertainment throughout the season so as to optimize competition with other forms of entertainment. Competitive balance is not the only contributor to the entertainment value of NBA basketball, however. Fan enjoyment of league sports depends on both the opportunity to identify with a local or favorite team and the thrill of watching the best quality of play. A single firm owning all of the teams would presumably arrange for the number of teams and their locations efficiently to maximize fan enjoyment of the league season. There is, however, no reason to expect that the current team owners will necessarily make such decisions efficiently, given their individual economic interests in the financial health of their own teams.

It's not surprising that farflung fans want to watch the Bulls' superstars on a superstation. The NBA argues that the broadcasting of more Bulls games to these fans will disturb the competitive balance among teams. However, one can also speculate that, since sports viewing has become more of a television activity than an "in the flesh" activity, these fans might prefer to have a league composed of fewer, better teams

---

2. But the Green Bay Packers and the Chicago Bears played, presumably before enthusiastic crowds, before there was a National Football League.

(like the Bulls). If this were the case, league policies designed to shore up all of the current teams would be inefficient. The point, of course, is not that this speculation is necessarily correct, but that the efficient number of teams (or, more generally, the efficient competitive balance) may not be obtained as a matter of course given the current league ownership framework.

The team owners thus retain independent economic interests. This would be the case even if they did not compete for the revenues of the league. Teams do compete for broadcast revenues, however. "A conflicting economic interest between the league and an individual club can exist only when league revenues are distributed unequally among the member clubs based on club participation in the games generating the revenue." *Sports Leagues and the Sherman Act* at 297–99. When teams receive a disproportionate share of the broadcast revenues generated by their own games, such a situation exists.

The analysis of this issue is tricky, however, since decisions about how to allocate broadcasting revenues are made by the league. It may be that "member clubs of a league do not have any legitimate independent economic interests in the league product" and "each team has an ownership interest in every game" (including an equal a priori ownership interest in the broadcast rights to every game). *Sports Leagues Revisited* at 135–36. If this assumption is correct, then whatever arrangements for revenue distribution the league decides to make will be, like bonuses to successful salespeople in an ordinary firm, presumptively efficient. If, however, broadcast rights inure initially to the two teams participating in a particular game and if, as is certainly the case, some games are more attractive to fans than others, the league cannot be presumed to have made decisions allocating those broadcast revenues efficiently.

The analogy, within the context of an ordinary firm, is to allow the salespeople to vote on the bonuses each is to get. Each salesperson has some incentive, of course, to promote the overall efficiency of the firm on which his or her salary, or perhaps the value of his or her firm stock, depends and therefore to award the larger bonuses to the most productive salespersons. However, in this scenario each salesperson has two ways of maximizing personal wealth—increasing the overall efficiency of the firm and redistributing income within the firm. The result of the vote might not be to distribute bonuses in the most efficient fashion. The potential for this type of inefficiency is particularly great when, as with the NBA, the league is "the only game in town" so that a team does not have the option of going elsewhere if it is not receiving revenues commensurate with its contribution to the overall league product.[4] In any event, a group of team owners who do not share all revenues from

---

4. The hypothetical example of a team taking its broadcast rights elsewhere does seem to suggest, however, that broadcast rights are at bottom the property of the teams participating in a given game. Indeed, if the team does not own the broadcast rights to the games in which it participates, it is hard to understand what it means to own a team at all.

all games might well make decisions that do not maximize the profit of the league as a whole.[5]

As this discussion demonstrates, determining whether the potential for inefficient decisionmaking survives within a joint venture because of the independent economic interests of the partners is extraordinarily complex and confusing. For this reason, a simple, if not courageous, way out of the problem might be to establish a legal presumption that a single entity cannot exist without single ownership. To avoid the complexities and confusions of attempted analysis, one might simply ordain that combinations that lack diverse economic interests should opt for joint ownership of a single enterprise to avoid antitrust problems. On the other hand, judges may want to play economist to the extent of resisting simplifying assumptions.

In any event, sports leagues argue that they must maintain independent ownership of the teams because separate ownership enhances the appearance of competitiveness demanded by fans. But the leagues cannot really expect the courts to aid them in convincing consumers that competition exists if it really does not. If consumers want economic competition between sports teams, then independent ownership and preservation of independent economic interests is likely an efficient choice for a sports league. But that choice, as with other joint ventures, brings with it the attendant antitrust risks. The NBA cannot have it both ways.

Relating all of this to the majority's treatment of the single entity issue, I see two problems with the majority analysis. First, as already noted, divorcing the question of single entity from the question of ownership is likely to lead to messy and inconsistent application of antitrust law. The bottom line may be that the inquiry into whether separate economic interests are maintained by the participants in a joint enterprise is likely to be no easier than a full Rule of Reason analysis.

Second, some of the majority's discussion of independent interests is puzzling. The majority contends that the district court "concluded that all cooperation among separately incorporated firms is forbidden by § 1 of the Sherman Act, except to the extent *Copperweld* permits." *Copperweld* concluded that a parent corporation and its wholly-owned subsidiary have a "complete unity of interest" and hence should be treated as a single entity. Here the district court simply concluded that the NBA, because it involved cooperation between separately-owned teams, was subject to antitrust analysis. This conclusion is a far cry from deciding that all cooperation among separately incorporated firms is forbidden.

I also cannot agree with the majority's analysis of the type of "unity of interest" required for single entity status. The majority states that "even a single firm contains many competing interests." The opinion

---

5. See Herbert Hovenkamp, *Exclusive Joint Ventures and Antitrust Policy*, 1995 Colum. Bus. L. Rev. 1 (1995), for a general discussion of the ways in which joint ventures can act inefficiently either by excluding members (or, here perhaps, overincluding members) or by excluding products (superstation broadcasts, perhaps?).

goes on to cite the competition for salary and bonuses between division managers as an example. However, when *Copperweld* talks about unity of interests in the single entity context, I think it must be taken to mean unity of economic interests of the decisionmakers. See *Copperweld*, 467 U.S. at 769. A single firm does not evidence diverse economic interests to the outside world because final decisions are made by the owners or stockholders, who care only about the overall performance of the firm. Only because this is the case can single firms be assumed to behave in the canonical profit-maximizing fashion. The diverse interests mentioned in the majority opinion seem as irrelevant to the antitrust analysis as is the on-court rivalry between teams in the NBA.

Thus, when *Copperweld* refers to conduct that "deprives the marketplace of the independent centers of decisionmaking that competition assumes," it does not refer to "decisionmakers" whose economic independence is only potential. The antitrust issue is really whether, as a result of some cooperative venture, economic interests which remain independent coordinate their decisions. As *Copperweld* notes, "the officers of a single firm are not separate economic actors pursuing separate economic interests...." Id. Therefore, their joint decisionmaking is of no antitrust concern. Employees or divisions within a firm, on the other hand, may remain separate economic actors pursuing separate economic interests but they do not make the final decisions governing the firm's operations. They may compete for shares of the firm's revenues, but they do not decree how that revenue will be shared. Thus their conflict or cooperation does not pose antitrust issues either. Joint ventures, on the other hand, are subject to antitrust scrutiny precisely because separate economic interests are joined in decisionmaking, with the potential for distorted results.

As long as teams are individually owned and revenue is not shared in fixed proportion, the teams both retain independent economic interests and make decisions in concert. Where this is the case, there is a strong argument that sports leagues should be treated as joint ventures rather than single entities because there remains a potential that league policy will be made to satisfy the independent economic interests of some group of teams, rather than to maximize the overall performance of the league. Thus, it is possible, if more Bulls games were broadcast, league profits might increase. But, if the revenue from the broadcast of Bulls games goes disproportionately to the Bulls, the other league members may not vote for this more efficient result.

There may, of course, be cases in which independent ownership of the partners in a joint venture does not pose any real possibility of inefficient decisionmaking. This would be the case if the parties did not compete in any other arena and if all revenues were shared in fixed proportions among the partners. In general, however, a plausible case can be made for the proposition that independent ownership should presumptively preclude treatment as a single entity. This certainly does not mean, of course, that "all cooperation among separately incorporated firms is forbidden by § 1 of the Sherman Act," Maj. Op. at 7. It would mean only that such cooperation must ordinarily be justified under the Rule of Reason. Justification might not be more difficult than the elusive search for treatment as a single entity.

After six years of litigation on this subject, the NBA, the Bulls, and the Chicago Tribune (WGN) finally decided (in December 1996) to compromise and settle their dispute, rather than expend even more legal resources in a full-scale trial of the Rule of Reason in professional sports. (A new district judge would have had to be brought up to speed on the case because Judge Will had died in the interim.) The reported terms of the settlement permitted the Bulls to broadcast 35 of their games in the Chicago area over WGN, of which only 15 would go out over national cable as a superstation telecast. (The station would have to generate new programming, not just new commercials, for satellite distribution across the country while the 20 Bulls "home" games were being played, something that may raise some questions from the FCC for WGN, under the Telecommunications Act.) Revenues from these national broadcasts would be shared by the league getting some of the advertising spots, in return for the league dropping its proposed superstation tax. What do these terms indicate were the two sides' assessment of their relative prospects and benefits in settling rather than continuing to litigate this dispute? What we know for sure is that in the post-WGN (and post-Michael Jordan) era, the NBA was able to secure new contracts from NBC and TNT that raised the total of $275 million paid by the two networks in 1997–98 to $660 million for 1998–99 and for each of the following three seasons.

Questions for Discussion

1. With the *WGN* litigation finally at an end, what is the status of the various issues raised along the way concerning the interpretation of the SBA?

(a) What constitutes "sponsored telecasting?" Does the NFL's contract with ESPN qualify for the SBA? What about a league contract with a superstation like WTBS? With a premium channel like HBO?

(b) Does a league qualify for SBA protection if it incorporates a restriction on an individual team's sale of telecasting rights into a league contract with a network that is SBA-protected?

(c) Can a league avoid the limitations of the SBA by assigning exclusive rights in all games to the network, and then require the network to license back rights to games it does not televise to the individual clubs, but with restraints on when and how the clubs can allow their games to be telecast?

2. Almost four decades after its enactment, is the SBA good public policy toward sports broadcasting? (In considering this question, keep in mind that if a league is a single entity, the SBA is irrelevant, since league restrictions would not be agreements subject to § 1 in the first place.) What

are the benefits secured by affording sports leagues this prerogative in the sale of their television rights? What has been the SBA's effect on franchise values? What are the costs of this policy? What effects has the SBA had on the number and price of games that fans can watch (in the NFL and in the NBA)? Are there other ways to secure the legitimate interests of the clubs while reducing any harmful impact on the fans? Keep these questions and this material from professional sports in mind when we address in Chapter 10 the analogous issue within college sports, and when we read the *NCAA* decision to which Easterbrook makes reference.

3. After the second Easterbrook decision, can a league charge a fee to an individual team for utilizing any source of revenue (e.g., selling television rights or various stadium revenues) that arguably exploits the reputation and product of the league, without thereby violating antitrust law? By what standard should a court judge whether a fee is legal or illegal? What does your answer imply for the concept of a league requiring any source of revenue to be shared (outside the express authorization by the SBA)?

4. Judge Easterbrook's opinions in the *WGN* litigation illustrate the trend toward antitrust analysis founded on classic microeconomic theory, with its focus on consumer welfare, rather than the more populist approach of the pre–1970s era. In his second *WGN* opinion, Easterbrook held that market power was an essential element for a plaintiff to prove anticompetitive effects in a full-blown rule of reason case. Does the NBA have market power when selling the rights to telecast its games? What does market power mean in this context? How would a plaintiff go about proving it?

5. Judge Will indicated on several occasions that there was no evidence that superstation telecasts actually injure other NBA teams by siphoning fans away from buying their tickets or watching them on TV. Indeed, he found that superstation telecasts have actually increased general interest in the NBA nationwide, and thus enhanced the popularity of all NBA teams. If that judgment is correct, why is the NBA so adamant about abolishing superstation telecasts not controlled by the league? Are the other owners simply not as smart or perceptive as Judge Will, or do they have some ulterior unstated motive? Even more interestingly, is that factual finding relevant to the case? If the NBA was correct that superstation telecasts were cutting into the television prices charged and revenues earned by many other teams, would that suffice to legalize its limits on those telecasts under the Sherman Act?

6. The essence of the NBA's position was that "[e]fforts to limit or abolish superstation telecasts are legal because it is not unlawful for partners in a joint venture to adopt rules that limit the ways in which they are allowed to compete against one another in selling the very product that they jointly produce. Indeed, in general partnership/joint venture law there is a fiduciary duty on the partners not to compete against the venture or its other partners in the venture's line of business or to expropriate an asset belonging to the venture for the partner's own benefit [without the permission of the venture]." Is this a persuasive antitrust position?

7. We have now seen the entire range of arguments on the single entity issue, from *NASL* to *Raiders I* to *Sullivan* to *WGN V*. What is your view about whether the NFL or NBA should be treated as a single entity for

§ 1 purposes (assuming that the NCAA is *not*)? Based upon what legal standard? Might a league be a single entity for only some purposes? If so, which ones—selling the Bulls games to TNT or WGN, or purchasing Michael Jordan's services to play those games?

A broader issue raised by all cable (not just superstation) broadcasts is the alleged migration (or "siphoning") of sports events from over-the-air ("free") television to cable. Some of those sports cable telecasts are on superstations like WGN and WTBS, others are on basic cable channels like ESPN and TNT, and others are on pay cable services like Sports Channel and Prime Sports. While cable systems are now physically available to more than 95% of American homes, they are actually present in 60% of homes. It often makes economic sense for clubs or leagues to place their games on one or the other of these cable channels: an important reason why that is a feasible step is because of the variety of league rules that constrain team broadcasts on over-the-air television on certain nights or in outside markets.

Popular and political concerns have been expressed for the last 20 years about the migration of games from free to cable television. Rather than enact proposed regulations, Congress directed the Federal Communications Commission (FCC) in the Cable Television Consumer Protection and Competition Act of 1992 to do a study of the extent to which there had been any such migration. The FCC's 1994 Report on this subject concluded that there was not a siphoning problem. While there now is far more sports on cable than there was back in 1980, there is actually slightly more sports on over-the-air television as well.

Do the FCC findings square with your personal impressions as a sports viewer? More important, does the experience over the last two decades mean that we will witness the same trends in the future? Even if we do not, does the presence of more sports on cable and less on free television constitute a problem—any more than the fact that early telecasts of movies are now almost always on cable? Suppose, though, that the Super Bowl, the World Series, and the NCAA Final Four were to migrate to pay-for-view. Would the respective sports league make a lot more money at the expense of a lot fewer fans seeing these events? Even if so, is that any more a public policy problem than the fact that Mike Tyson and Evander Holyfield's heavyweight championship fights are definitely on pay-for-view, and no one in Congress objects? Or are there differences in the legal, economic, and popular situations of the NFL, by contrast with Tyson's promoter Don King, that make these cases distinguishable?

Whatever the doctrinal details of the application of the Sherman Act and Sports Broadcasting Act, the economic impact of league control over its teams' telecasts is unmistakable. No more vivid illustration can be found than what happened to the NFL's television rights as its prior four-year contracts were expiring at the end of 1993. Suddenly, Fox Broadcasting became another bidder for the rights to Sunday afternoon NFC games that CBS had held ever since the Sports Broadcasting Act had been passed. CBS was prepared to increase its rights fees from $265 to $300 million a season. However, Fox wanted to establish itself as a major network rival to CBS, NBC, and ABC and to stage a preemptive strike against the about-to-be-formed Warner and United Paramount Networks. Thus Fox stunned the NFL as much as it did CBS by winning the next NFC package for a total of $1.6 billion for four years.

Happily for the NFL Players Association, that Fox contract raised the total amount of salary money available to players under the NFL's hard cap, which was just about to come into play. Happily for John Madden, free agent bidding for his services trebled his salary to $7.5 million a year to move to Fox as its star color commentator. (Recall that networks do not have a salary cap for television performers.) The biggest gains were apparently reaped by NFL owners, as evidenced by what happened to franchise values. The NFL had set its expansion fee at $140 million for new teams in Charlotte and Jacksonville, and roughly that same amount was paid for the purchase of the Miami Dolphins by Blockbuster Entertainment's Wayne Huizenga. However, shortly after the new television deal was in place, the then lowly New England Patriots were sold for $160 million, later in 1994 the Philadelphia Eagles went for over $185 million, and in early 1995 the Tampa Bay Buccaneers were auctioned off for $195 million. And that same economic trend will be replayed following the NFL's recent and even more dramatic television deal, in which CBS' return to the football field (replacing NBC) helped drive the NFL's total television revenues from $1.1 billion in 1997 to an average of $2.2 billion for 1998 and each of the next seven seasons.

To many, the evidence seems clear that a legal regime which puts six networks, and as many cable channels, bidding against each other for the broadcast rights to a sport like professional football, whose teams have agreed not to compete against each other to get on a particular network or channel, will drive up broadcast revenues and franchise values: not just for the NFL's perennial powerhouses, the 49ers and Cowboys, and the big-market Giants, but also for the longtime doormats, the Bucs and Saints, as well as the small-market Super Bowl champions, the Green Bay Packers. The key antitrust policy question, though, is whether the current law and its economic impact enhances consumer welfare for the fans who watch the games on television and buy the products shown during commercial breaks.

Suppose that all the television networks formed a broadcast association to make single bids for league television rights (with games to be distributed across the broadcast spectrum, free and cable). The practical effect of such collaboration has been vividly displayed in bidding for Olympic television rights. All the networks in the European Community agreed on a single bid for the 1992 Summer Games from Barcelona: the result was that the International Olympic Committee received $75 million for television rights for the entire European market. By contrast, the IOC received $401 million from NBC as the outcome of competitive bidding by U.S. networks for the American market. Should sports leagues be entitled to attack such a network arrangement under antitrust law? Should the presence of the SBA, permitting cooperation by teams in the league-wide sale of broadcast rights, legitimate network cooperation in buying rights offered by the league under the SBA umbrella?

More fundamentally, recall the line of analysis sketched earlier in Chapter 3—about the consumer welfare orientation of modern antitrust law and the latitude this may imply for the exercise of monopsony power that reduces production costs ultimately passed on to consumers. Is it fair to equate the position of teams in a league collectively deciding on the allocation of or price paid for the services of players, with the position of networks purchasing from the teams in this same league the right to show these players and games to fans across the country? Or are there critical differences between the two settings that make this parallel inappropriate?

Note on Merchandising Rights

While league sale of television rights is the most visible and financially significant illustration of the foregoing issues, essentially the same questions are raised by the sale of sports merchandising rights. Here, all of the leagues have followed the lead of the NFL, and to a considerable extent centralized trademark licensing for merchandising purposes in a single league office to which every club assigns an exclusive right to market its team names and logos. By the late 1990s, the total consumer sales of merchandise bearing these league and team identities ranged from $3.5 billion for the NFL to $1.2 billion for the NHL, with the leagues receiving average royalties of approximately eight percent for licensing use of the trademark rights that we analyzed in Chapter 6. In 1996, the share of merchandise sales by individual team names and logos ranged from the Cowboys (25% of the league total), Packers (16%), and 49ers (9%) to the Buccaneers (.2%), Cardinals (.2%), and Oilers (.1%).

It was this kind of disparity that generated the dispute we read about in Chapter 6, between the NFL and the Dallas Cowboys. In the summer of 1995, Cowboys' owner Jerry Jones sold to Pepsi, Nike, and American Express the right to use the name of the Cowboys home, Texas Stadium, even though Coca Cola, Reebok, and Visa had paid NFL Properties large amounts for what was supposed to be the exclusive right to exploit the identity of the Cowboys (and other NFL teams). The league filed a $300 million lawsuit against Jones for allegedly having violated the Cowboys' contractual commitment to assign to NFL Properties the sole right to market the team's name and identity. Besides defending the contract claim on the ground that the identity of Texas Stadium was qualitatively different from that of the Cowboys, Jones filed a $750 million antitrust suit against his fellow owners, asserting that the agreement of the owners (including his Cowboys predecessor) to give that exclusive merchandising authority to NFL Properties constituted an illegal "combination ... in restraint of trade" under § 1 of the Sherman Act. In early 1997 both sides to this legal battle decided that it was in their mutual interests to drop their respective suits and to allow each to continue essentially what they had been doing. Soon thereafter, though, the Yankees and Adidas filed a similar suit against MLB for obstructing their 10–year, $95 million sponsorship deal. (The principal reason why the suit was filed in Tampa rather than in New York City may be found in the aftermath of the *Piazza* decision we read at the end of Chapter 2.) MLB responded by suspending Steinbrenner from its Executive Council and the team from membership on any league committees. Meanwhile, Steinbrenner's lawyer, David Boies, a long-time partner in Cravath, Swaine, and Moore, had to leave the firm because one of the teams being sued, the Atlanta Braves, was now owned by the entertainment giant Time Warner, Cravath's largest client.

The underlying legal and policy questions remain. The concerns expressed by NFL owners about Jones' action (and also by MLB owners about George Steinbrenner's deal with Adidas) are, among others, that such individual exploitation of the merchandising market would not only increase revenue disparities in favor of the successful and popular teams, but that it would likely reduce the overall league revenues generated even by much broader use of team names or merchandise. The latter result, at least, is precisely the goal that an antitrust-preserved competitive market is supposed to deliver to consumers—greater output at lower prices. There is no Sports Marketing Act that gives special antitrust immunity to leagues whose owners pool their team names and logos in a central league office that actually sells the right to outsiders to use them. And as we saw in the case of *Topps Chewing Gum v. MLB Players Association*, 641 F.Supp. 1179 (S.D.N.Y.1986), that we read at the end of Chapter 6, when baseball (or football) players have assigned to their players association just the *nonexclusive* right to market their publicity rights on a collective basis (e.g., for baseball or football cards), such action is subject to rule of reason antitrust scrutiny.

Consider now the Cowboys–NFL dispute (or the Yankees–MLB dispute) about individual versus league-wide control of merchandising rights, in light of the extended judicial analysis we have read about broadcasting rights. Is there a qualitative difference between the relations among owners and relations among players that should give the owners a form of antitrust immunity (e.g, as a single entity league) that is not available to the players (e.g., as a labor organization)? Should the baseball owners' long-standing antitrust exemption be applied to restraints the owners may want to apply to this recently-developed sports merchandising market? Should all leagues be given the same kind of

Sports Marketing Act protection for the concerted sale of their teams' trademark rights that leagues now have when they sell their teams' broadcast rights for "sponsored telecasting" (or should the two be equated instead by repealing the Sports Broadcasting Act)? Even if subjected to full-blown rule of reason scrutiny, are there factual differences between the merchandising and broadcasting settings that might justify different legal verdicts regarding exclusive league control over these two key revenue sources?

Note on Revenue Sharing[s]

The *WGN* case illustrates not only the impact of league policy on the sports television market, but also the relationship between league economic cooperation and the quality of the league's athletic competition. As Judge Easterbrook pointed out in *WGN I* (and the NBA then followed), a league could accomplish the same objective of protecting the revenues of the other teams without limiting the number or times of superstation game telecasts by individual teams. Instead, it could "tax" the extra revenues derived by a team from selling the rights to its games to a superstation (the amount exceeding what a purely local television station was prepared to offer for these broadcast rights).

As happened when the NBA imposed such a "tax" on the Bulls from its WGN telecasts, this type of league action would likely attract antitrust attack from the taxed team as an attempt to do indirectly what Judge Will had said the league could not do directly. However, as explained in the *WGN* litigation, if the tax was no greater than the extra revenue derived from selling to the superstation, the team would still have no disincentive to putting its games on the superstation, thus causing no reduction in output in violation of antitrust law. Suppose, though, that the NBA went further, and required that *all* revenues derived from local broadcast rights (or from stadium-related revenues like luxury box rentals, personal seat licenses, concessions and parking) must be shared among all teams—an extension of the principle of revenue sharing developed earlier by the NBA and its players association under their collectively bargained "salary cap?"

In all sports except football (which sells all television rights through league-wide contracts), the current distribution of local broadcasting revenue is a major source of inequality in club earnings. (Another source, present also in football, is the quality of the stadium lease with the local community.) The problem is especially acute in baseball, where the disparity in local broadcast revenues has risen even faster than their absolute amounts. In 1971, for example, when the 24 baseball teams earned less than $30 million from local broadcasting, the largest gap was roughly 4 to 1 (from the Dodgers' $1.8 million to the Pirates' $450,000). In 1997, when total local broadcast revenues had soared well over $500 million, the gap was 10 to 1 (from the Yankees' and Braves' $60 million to the Royals' and Expos' $6 million). Because the clubs could no longer rely on the old reserve system to

---

[s]. See Jeffrey A. Rosenthal, *The Football Answer to the Baseball Problem: Can Revenue Sharing Work?*, 5 Seton Hall L. J. 419 (1995), which explores the implications of revenue sharing in the sports franchise, television, and merchandising markets, and also in the sports labor market.

insulate equality of team playing talent from inequality in team earnings, the felt need for greater revenue sharing in major league baseball had become acute among small market teams. Understandably, the large market teams continued to resist the idea. Peter Bavasi, former president of the Toronto Blue Jays and the Cleveland Indians, recalled that when the subject of revenue sharing was brought up in league meetings, one of the owners of a large-market team would stand up, begin his comments with "Comrades!," and after embarrassed laughter the topic would quickly be dropped.

By the mid–1990s, though, there was general acceptance among the owners of the value of significantly expanding the degree of revenue sharing, which was distributing just $25 million or so of the estimated $1.2 billion in total club (rather than league) revenues. This became a significant feature of the bitter three-year labor dispute that shut down baseball in 1994, its most successful year ever, and then substantially reduced both attendance and revenues in 1995 and 1996. Ironically, the technique that was used by the small market teams to secure the acquiescence of large market owners was a variation on the players' strike weapon. Small market clubs such as the Kansas City Royals and the Montreal Expos announced that they would no longer allow broadcasts from their home stadiums of games played by visiting teams like the Yankees and Dodgers. (Whoever may have "owned" property rights in those games under the doctrines depicted in Chapter 6, the home teams had operational control over access to their facilities.) Indeed, this technique was also used to extract a larger amount being specially charged to Ted Turner for broadcasts of his Braves on Turner's WTBS superstation.

The larger market owners agreed to a new revenue-sharing formula in the spring of 1994, but only on condition that the players would accept the hard salary cap that the owners would insist upon in collective bargaining that summer, before and after the strike that eliminated that year's World Series. The players were not only strongly opposed to a hard salary cap (or tax), but were also concerned about the potential salary-constraining impact of a progressive revenue-sharing system. Finally, in December 1996, the owners ratified their agreement with the players for a 35% luxury tax on the amount that the five highest payrolls exceeded the sixth highest. The parties also agreed on a somewhat less ambitious increase in the revenue-sharing system among the owners: 60% of this new formula was applied to 1996 revenues, and it will be fully phased in by the year 2000 (by which time the net transfer amount is projected to be $70 million). Each team must designate a portion of its local revenues for payment into a league-wide pool, including gate receipts, concessions, stadium advertising, local broadcasts, and the like, minus stadium operating costs when the team, not the stadium authority, pays these. The 13 highest-earning clubs *pay* progressively more (based on their relative revenue position), and the 13 lowest-earning clubs *receive* progressively more (again based on their relative revenue positions). For the 1996 season, the Yankees paid $5.8 million and the Expos received $5.5 million: by the year 2000, it was projected that the top payment made would be $14.4 million and the top one received would be $13.5 million.

We shall have to wait and see what impact this new combination of revenue-sharing and payroll taxing is going to have on the future of major league baseball. This sport now has somewhat more revenue-sharing than basketball, significantly more than hockey, though far less than football. In appraising both the current systems and possible revisions for the future, keep the following policy issues in mind.

1. Is extensive revenue sharing fair to the teams in larger markets? Do the Yankees have a "right" to all revenues from broadcasts of their games in New York? Is there a special problem of fair treatment of the owners who recently purchased teams in larger revenue markets (for example, the Orioles that were purchased for $173 million in 1993, just as this scenario was about to play itself out)? Is there a way of dealing with that latter concern?[t]

2. Is extensive revenue sharing an efficient way to run a league, particularly from the point of view of consumer welfare? Should the league's main concern be how to divide up the current revenue pie or how to enlarge the pie? Does revenue sharing contribute to or detract from the latter objective? How could a revenue-sharing scheme be designed to maximize its contribution to revenue expansion?

3. Why would revenue sharing among owners have created concerns among players not only on the large market, but also on the small market teams? Should revenue sharing be designed (and if so, how) to minimize any constraining effect on salaries from that source, particularly if the players have agreed to a direct salary cap or tax?

4. Suppose that after considerable thought and effort a new revenue-sharing scheme was devised, it proved attractive to a majority of the owners, but it could not get the necessary three-quarters approval because of opposition from the large-market clubs. Could the commissioner step in under his "best interests of baseball" authority we studied in Chapter 1 to impose the scheme on all owners? Is there a difference between Commissioner Vincent barring George Steinbrenner from pocketing the money he received by selling Yankees' games to the Madison Square Garden cable network, and Commissioner Bowie Kuhn prohibiting Oakland A's owner Charles Finley from pocketing the money from the sale of his star players to Steinbrenner's Yankees (and to Tom Yawkey's Red Sox)? Regardless of the similarities or differences between the two cases as a matter of principle, is it likely that a commissioner would impose his revenue-sharing views in such a fashion? What does reflection on this problem suggest about the "single-entity" issue we have been tracing through this chapter?[u]

---

[t]. See Louis Kaplow, *An Economic Analysis of Legal Transitions*, 99 Harvard L. Rev. 509 (1986), for a valuable analysis of this general type of problem.

[u]. For a post-*Copperweld* argument that the degree of league revenue sharing should be crucial to the characterization of a sports league as a single entity or a joint venture, see Note, *A Substantive Test for Sherman Act Plurality: Applications for Professional Sports Leagues*, 52 U. of Chicago L. Rev. 99 (1985). Does this argument square with the Court's statement in *Copperweld* that single-entity status should not turn on the voluntary structural and operational choices of a business pursuing optimal efficiency?

The experience under the Sports Broadcasting Act may provide revealing lessons about other congressional efforts to benefit professional sports leagues. Consider these comments by Vice President Al Gore, made while he was a Senator from Tennessee, when he dissented from the Senate Commerce Committee's proposed Professional Sports Community Protection Act of 1985:

> The fundamental cause of franchise instability in professional football is scarcity of franchises. The NFL has refused to expand to meet legitimate demand and this has occasioned intense bidding by cities to lure and maintain existing franchises. Professional team owners are positioned to extract enormous benefits and subsidies from municipalities and they are taking advantage of these opportunities. So long as the NFL refuses to expand, the current situation with its frenzied bidding and disappointed sports fans will persist even if the committee bill becomes law.
>
> It is not surprising that concerned parties have looked to the Congress for help because it is an earlier Congressional waiver of the antitrust laws for the NFL that has contributed to the current problems. What is surprising is that the Committee has ignored the real cause of the problem and instead asked to further protect the NFL from the antitrust laws. To my mind, the Committee has missed the point.
>
> * * *
>
> By entering into contracts with all three networks, the NFL has been able to effectively eliminate the opportunity for a competing league to establish itself in the fall season. With no competition, they have been free to limit the available franchises and to ignore justifiable claims from municipalities for teams. Since the merger 15 years ago, the NFL has enjoyed an increase in annual television revenues per team from close to $1,500,000 in 1970 to $15 million in 1985. With the supply of franchises limited, the value of NFL franchises has increased dramatically. It is no wonder that the owners have been reluctant to establish new franchises. This would only decrease their share of available television revenues and diminish competition for, and accordingly the resale value of, their franchises.
>
> * * *
>
> While I share the Chairman's and the Committee's interest in allowing the NFL and other professional sports leagues to better control the movement of franchises, I am of the view that legislative action in that area alone does nothing to solve the real cause of the problem. If you take the simple step of limiting the NFL antitrust exemption to operate consistent with the Congress' original intention, you would establish a competitive environment which in due course would bring more professional football, including NFL franchises, to more cities. This would put a quick halt to the frenzied bidding between competing cities for the existing number of limited

franchises, which is only making owners richer, taxpayers poorer, and sports fans feel betrayed.

It is likely that the Senator was moved to make these comments by his constituents' sense of grievance about the NFL's denial of a franchise to Memphis (recall the *Grizzlies* case earlier). The merits of our Vice-President's views are explored in the following chapter.

Chapter Eight

MONOPOLY IN PROFESSIONAL SPORTS

In appraising the legal policies fashioned for professional sports by both legislatures and courts, it is of paramount importance to keep in mind that there is almost always only one major professional league in each established sport. This "monopoly" state, in turn, is the principal source of many of the conflicts that arise between the league and its constituents, and of the difficult problems that these disputes pose for traditional legal doctrines.[a]

Previous chapters have described how player salaries and franchise values have soared during the last quarter century. Underlying both trends has been a remarkable rise in the total revenues flowing into professional sports. In 1950, for example, major league baseball's revenues from all sources barely totalled $30 million. By the late 1990s, baseball's revenues surpassed $2 billion annually—a 66-fold increase. To some extent, this revenue growth was produced by increased fan attendance at games: from 21 million in the early 1950s (an average of 18,000 per game) to 65 million in 1997 (an average of more than 28,000 for a considerably larger number of games). As we saw in Chapter 6, an even greater source of financial growth in baseball has been the explosion of its broadcasting revenues: from $4 million in 1950 to more than $900 million in the late 1990s.

The same kind of financial bonanza has been experienced in football, starting in the late 1950s, and in basketball and hockey, especially since the early 1980s. The legal doctrines we have traced up to this point exert their influence upon the division of this expanding pie among the team owners themselves, between owners and players, or between owners and

---

[a] The most important legal treatment of this topic is Stephen F. Ross, *Monopoly Sports Leagues*, 73 Minnesota L. Rev. 643 (1989) (a shorter version of which appears as Chapter 8 of Paul D. Staudohar and James A. Mangan, eds., *The Business of Professional Sports* (Urbana, Ill: University of Illinois Press, 1991)). For a contrasting point of view to Ross' on many of the issues, see Thane N. Rosenbaum, *The Antitrust Implications of Professional Sports Leagues Revisited: Emerging Trends in the Modern Era*, 41 U. of Miami L. Rev. 729 (1987).

stadium authorities. This chapter considers whether the total size of the pie is due in part to the fact that there is almost always only one major league in each sport selling this product to an enthusiastic fandom—and if so, what is the law's responsibility for that state of affairs.

This broad theme is an undertone to many of the cases we have already read, in which courts applying "rule of reason" analysis under § 1 of the Sherman Act have struggled to strike an appropriate balance between the league's interest in fashioning internal rules that promote vigorous athletic competition on the field or floor, and the claims of players, fans, and communities to fair economic treatment at the hands of member clubs. Consider how some of the cases analyzed earlier would look if there had been two, three, or even four leagues presenting viable alternatives for the plaintiffs.

Players—Suppose that "Yazoo" Smith, after being drafted by the Redskins, or John Mackey, after playing out his option with the Colts, had had the option of signing with teams in other football leagues. Similarly, suppose Curt Flood had had available to him other baseball leagues in which to play when he had to decide whether to sign a contract that permitted the Cardinals to trade him to the Phillies without his consent.

Television—Suppose that there were several professional basketball leagues seeking exposure and revenue from television networks and superstations. Would the NBA still have tried to reduce the number of Bulls games on WGN? If it had done so, would the availability of other leagues and games have ameliorated the impact of the NBA's policy on television viewers who wanted to watch professional basketball?

Franchises—Suppose that the American Football League had continued as a rival to the National Football League, perhaps accompanied by one or more of the other leagues that have sought to challenge the NFL's dominance. Would there still have been only one professional football team in the Los Angeles area in the late 1970s, so that the city of Anaheim was forced to offer Rams' owner Carroll Rosenbloom 95 acres of prime real estate to induce him to move his team from the Coliseum? Or more starkly, would the NFL have left Los Angeles, the nation's second largest metropolitan area, without any team as it has done since the Rams and Raiders left for St. Louis and Oakland in the mid–1990s? In these situations, would not the AFL have moved aggressively to occupy such a lucrative market, and would not that have encouraged the NFL to try to fill that void first? Similarly, following the demise of the WFL in the mid–1970s, would not the Memphis Grizzlies have been eagerly sought after by at least one football league wanting to establish a presence in the "football-mad" South?

Products—Although league resistance to innovations that may improve the quality of the sport only rarely generates antitrust litigation on the part of product suppliers,[b] such innovation is an important value

---

b. One example is the prohibition by the Professional Golfers Association Tour

from the point of view of consumer welfare. The competitive pressures generated by a challenger league create an incentive for innovations that enhance enjoyment of the sport. Perhaps the best example is the American Basketball Association, whose heritage for professional basketball includes not only the *Oscar Robertson* case and thence veteran free agency, but also the three-point shot and the slam dunk.

Earlier chapters have described an emerging sentiment among antitrust scholars and judges such as Robert Bork, Ralph Winter, and Frank Easterbrook that courts should be loath to scrutinize closely the reasonableness of restrictive practices developed within a business enterprise. The assumption of the law and economics movement is that the best guarantee that social welfare will be enhanced rather than harmed by such arrangements is the force of market competition faced by such businesses. Courts have, however, been unwilling to embrace that position fully in sports cases because the undeniable lesson from history is that interleague competition in a single sport is very much the exception, not the rule.[c]

For example, while organized baseball regularly faced rival leagues during its first fifty years of existence, no new league has surfaced since the demise of the Federal League in 1915 (that league's principal legacy being the Supreme Court decision that produced baseball's antitrust immunity). Similarly, once the National Hockey League (formed in 1917) established its dominance in that sport in the 1920s, only one competitor has come on the scene. The World Hockey Association disappeared after only six seasons, with a 1979 agreement under which the NHL absorbed four WHA teams—the Edmonton Oilers, Winnipeg Jets, Hartford Whalers, and Quebec Nordiques—while the other WHA teams folded. In basketball, the National Basketball Association (formed in 1949) faced the short-lived American Basketball League for only the 1961–1962 season (recall from Chapter 2 the ABL's legal legacy, the *Barnett* decision), and then struggled against the American Basketball Association for nine seasons (1967–1976) before a peace treaty brought four ABA teams—the New Jersey Nets, Denver Nuggets, Indiana Pacers, and San Antonio Spurs—into the NBA, with the other ABA teams folding.

The National Football League (formed in 1920) has faced by far the most vigorous interleague competition. The most serious challenges came from the All American Football Conference, which lasted from

against players using the new, square-grooved PING irons in tournaments, a decision that produced litigation in *Bob Gilder v. PGA Tour, Inc.*, 727 F.Supp. 1333 (D.Ariz.1989), affirmed, 936 F.2d 417 (9th Cir.1991). Chapter 12 contains a detailed treatment of this issue, which has surfaced mainly on organized tours for individual sports.

[c]. Books describing that history in the several sports include Harold Seymour, *Baseball: The Early Years* (New York: Oxford University Press, 1960), and *Baseball: The Golden Years* (New York: Oxford University Press, 1971); David Cruise and Alison Griffiths, *Net Worth: Exploding the Myths of Pro Hockey* (New York: Viking Press, 1991); Terry Pluto, *Loose Balls: The Short Wild Life of the American Basketball Association* (New York: Simon and Schuster, 1990); David Harris, *The League: The Rise and Decline of the NFL* (New York: Bantam Books, 1986); and Jim Byrne, *The $1 League: The Rise and Fall of the USFL* (New York: Simon and Schuster, 1986).

1946 to 1949, when the NFL absorbed three AAFC teams—the Cleveland Browns, San Francisco 49ers, and Baltimore Colts—and then from the American Football League, whose growing impact from 1960 through 1966 led the NFL to merge with the AFL and take in all nine AFL teams (with the blessing of an express antitrust exemption granted by Congress). This larger, more powerful NFL, with its annual Super Bowl championship, had little trouble in fending off subsequent challenges from the World Football League in the mid–1970s and the United States Football League in the mid–1980s. At the present time in football, as in all the other men's professional team sports, the established league faces no visible prospect of serious competition.

While the above factual record is clear, the explanation for it is not. Does the historic tendency toward monopoly indicate that this is the "natural" state for professional sports, or does it reveal a failure to implement the legal policy against monopolization? This is the underlying question posed in the cases and materials in this chapter.

A. MONOPOLY POWER AND THE RELEVANT MARKET

The principal source of law in this area is § 2 of the Sherman Act which prohibits firms from "monopolizing [or attempting to monopolize] trade and commerce," supplemented by § 7 of the Clayton Act which forbids mergers that may tend substantially to "lessen competition or tend to create a monopoly." A monopolization charge consists of two elements: the possession of monopoly market power, and the use of unacceptable means to acquire, entrench or maintain that market power. An "attempt to monopolize" claim requires a showing that the defendant has a dangerous probability of acquiring monopoly market power and taking action with the specific intent to achieve monopoly status. In both types of § 2 claims, there are essentially two elements: the first requires market power of some degree; and the second, improper conduct that creates, entrenches, or enlarges that market power.[d] To facilitate discussion, we will focus upon the monopolization offense. Here we address the first issue—the meaning of monopoly power in the sports marketplace.

From an economic point of view, monopoly is not to be equated with "bigness" as such. Companies as huge as General Motors have learned to their chagrin that mere size is no guarantee against the forces of market competition. A firm has a measure of monopoly power only if it has the ability to raise prices significantly above marginal production costs without experiencing a decrease in profits (perhaps not even in sales). The immediate source of such market power is "inelasticity of demand": few consumers will substantially reduce their purchases of the

---

d. For a more detailed treatment of monopolization see Herbert Hovenkamp, *Economics and Federal Antitrust Law* (St. Paul, Minn.: West Publishing, 1985), pp. 135 ff.

firm's products when prices are raised or product quality (and thence costs of production) is lowered. A long-run source is "inelasticity of supply:" despite the presence of monopoly profits in this market, barriers to entry obstruct the emergence of new competitors that would give consumers an alternative source of supply.

In practice, however, it is difficult to detect and measure monopoly power in the precise economic sense of the term, and even more difficult to demonstrate such market reality in the artificial setting of a courtroom.[e] Consequently, courts have adopted a surrogate test for monopoly power: does the firm have a large majority of the total production (or sales) in the relevant market, which is defined by both a product type and a geographical area within which the products in question are viable alternatives for most buyers (or sellers)—e.g., television rights to football games in the northeastern United States, tickets to sporting events in southern California, or professional football players in the United States? (It is worth noting that this is an exercise that seems as much religious as scientific. In order to define properly the boundaries of the relevant product and geographic markets, one has to make some assessment of the demand and supply elasticities of the defendant's product, and thence the defendant's market power, but these are the very things whose difficulty of proof requires use of the surrogate "market share" test in the first place.) Once the plaintiff demonstrates a sufficiently large market share (usually somewhere over 70%), the burden shifts to the defendant to show that it does not actually have the power to raise prices above or reduce output below their competitive levels without a sharp decline in sales. Few defendants can meet the burden of proving this negative—the absence of market power.

The key task in the legal determination of monopoly power, therefore, is establishing the precise scope of the market within which the defendant is alleged to have too large a share. Defining the relevant product market is not as easy a task as it might appear. What initially looks like an insulated enclave for a particular firm if the market is viewed narrowly, often can be a strongly competitive environment when one takes account of the entire array of choices available to participants in the broader marketplace. The following case illustrates an appeals court wrestling with the geographic contours of the sports market, as the court considered a complaint by the fledgling American Football League that the National Football League had adopted tactics designed to stifle its potential rival from the outset.

AFL v. NFL

United States Court of Appeals, Fourth Circuit, 1963.
323 F.2d 124.

HAYNSWORTH, CIRCUIT JUDGE.

---

[e] See Hovenkamp, *Economics and Federal Antitrust Law*, note d above, at pp. 55 ff.

[Shortly after the American Football League (AFL) began operations in 1960, the AFL launched this antitrust suit against its established rival, the National Football League. The AFL charged that the NFL had offered expansion franchises to the cities of Dallas and Minneapolis in order to frustrate the AFL's plan to move into these two prime football sites. A trial judge dismissed the antitrust suit, and the AFL appealed.]

* * *

The National Football League was organized in 1920. For a number of years its existence was precarious. Until the last ten years, its membership was far from static, and until 1946 every major league professional football team operating in the United States was associated with it. In 1945, the All American Football Conference was organized, and it operated through the four seasons of 1946–1949 with eight teams, except that two of the teams were merged in 1949, and in the last season, there were but seven teams. Thereafter the All American Football Conference disbanded, but three of its teams were received into the National Football League, and teams franchised in those three cities, Baltimore, Cleveland and San Francisco, were operated under National League franchises when this action was commenced.

In 1959, the National Football League operated with twelve teams located in eleven cities. There were two teams in Chicago and one each in Cleveland, New York, Philadelphia, Pittsburgh, Washington, Baltimore, Detroit, Los Angeles, San Francisco, and Green Bay, Wisconsin. In 1960, two additional franchises were placed, one in Dallas and one in Minneapolis–St. Paul, the Dallas team beginning play in 1960 and the Minneapolis–St. Paul team in 1961. In 1961, one of the Chicago teams, the Cardinals, was transferred to St. Louis.

The American Football League was organized in 1959, and began with a full schedule of games in 1960. Affiliated with it were eight teams located in eight cities, Boston, Buffalo, Houston, New York, Dallas, Denver, Los Angeles and Oakland. After the 1960 season, the Los Angeles team was moved to San Diego.

* * *

[Discussion of expansion in the NFL began as early as 1956; the early favorites were Dallas and Houston because of their good weather and potential rivalry. In 1959, however, one of the applicants for a Dallas franchise, Lamar Hunt, decided to form a new league instead. By the end of 1959, the AFL had been organized with eight teams, including teams in Dallas (the Texans), Houston (the Oilers), and Minneapolis. Meanwhile, in late 1959 the NFL announced that it would grant expansion teams to Dallas (the Cowboys) and Houston in 1960, but the creation of a Houston franchise turned on the availability of an adequate stadium. The only adequate facility in Houston at the time was Rice University's stadium, and it soon became clear that a professional team would not be allowed to play in it. Thus, the NFL eliminated Houston from consideration. Instead, the prospective owners of the AFL Minneapolis franchise (who had already paid a $25,000 franchise fee to AFL founder, Lamar Hunt) withdrew from the AFL and were granted an NFL team (the Vikings).]

It thus came to pass that in the 1960 season, teams of the two leagues were in direct competition in New York, Dallas, Los Angeles, and in the San Francisco–Oakland area. Each league had teams in other cities in which there was no direct competition between the leagues. The two leagues were competing on a national basis for television coverage, outstanding players and coaches, and the games of each league competed for spectators with the televised broadcast of a game of the other.

The first and most important question on appeal, therefore, is a review of the District Court's determination of the relevant market. The District Court recognized that the two leagues and their member teams competed with each other in several ways, and that the relevant market with respect to one aspect of their competition would not necessarily be the relevant market with respect to another. Since each league recruited players and coaches throughout the nation, he concluded that the relevant market with respect to their competition in recruiting was nationwide. He necessarily found that their competition for nationwide television coverage, with a blackout only of the area in which the televised game was played, was nationwide. As for the competition for spectators, he found the relevant market to be those thirty-one metropolitan areas in the United States having a population of more than 700,000 people according to the 1960 census. This determination was based upon testimony that a metropolitan area of that size might be expected to support a major league professional football team. Indeed, [Lamar] Hunt, of the American League, had testified that a metropolitan area of 500,000 might support such a team. The District Court's determination was influenced by American's contention that the bare existence of the National League and its member teams foreclosed certain markets to it and limited its capacity to operate successfully. It is reinforced by the evidence of many applications from other cities which were actively pressed upon American, some of which, at least, were thought worthy of real consideration.

In addition to those cities in which American actually placed franchises, Hunt testified that there was substantial interest in a franchise in Vancouver, Seattle, Kansas City, Louisville, Cincinnati, Philadelphia, Jacksonville, Miami, Atlanta, St. Louis and Milwaukee. The eighth franchise was placed in Oakland only after consideration of the "strong case" made by Atlanta. In short, it abundantly appears that cities throughout the United States and one Canadian city were actively competing for league franchises, there being many more applicants than available franchises.

In this Court, the plaintiffs contend that the relevant market is composed of those seventeen cities in which National now either has operating franchises, or which it seriously considered in connection with its expansion plans in 1959. They would thus include in the relevant market New York, Chicago, Philadelphia, Cleveland, Pittsburgh, Washington, Los Angeles, San Francisco, Baltimore, Detroit and Green Bay, in which National teams were operating in 1959, plus Dallas and Minneapolis–St. Paul, in which franchises were authorized in 1960, plus Houston, Buffalo and Miami, which were considered by National for expansion, and St. Louis, to which the Chicago Cardinals were transferred in 1961 after American's first operating season. They include in the relevant market all of the closed cities in which there is a National League team, but no American League team, but exclude from the relevant market all of those closed cities in which there is an American League team but no National League team, and all of those other cities in which there is now no major league professional football team, but which would be hospitable to a franchise and which have a potential for adequate support of a professional football team. They advance the unquestioned principle that the relevant market should be geographically limited to the area in which the defendants operate, or the area in which there is effective competition between the parties.

In very different contexts, the relevant market has been found to be a single city, a group of cities, a state, or several states. In considering an attempt to monopolize, it, of course, is appropriate to limit the relevant geographic market to the area which the defendant sought to appropriate to itself, and, if monopoly power has been acquired in a separably identifiable and normally competitive market, it is irrelevant that the defendant did not possess the same monopoly power in an unrelated market elsewhere.

Plaintiff's contention here, however, is a simple fractionalization of a truly national market. Each league has teams franchised to cities on the Atlantic, on the Pacific and in the midlands. Each team in each league travels back and forth across the country to play before many different audiences in many different cities. Most of the official season games are played in a city in which there is a franchised team, but that is not invariable, and most of the preseason exhibition games are played in cities in which there is no franchised team. In locating franchises, neither league has restricted itself to any geographic section of the country or limited itself to any particular group of cities. In American's brief history, it has moved one team from Los Angeles to San Diego, and the many changes which have occurred in National's franchises belie any notion of geographic limitation.

Though we may concentrate our attention upon competition between the leagues for franchise locations and lay aside for the moment clearly national aspects of their competition for players, coaches and television coverage, location of the franchise is only a selection of a desirable site in a much broader, geographically unlimited market. It is not unlike the choice a chain store company makes when it selects a particular corner lot as the location of a new store. It preempts that lot when it acquires it for that purpose, but, as long as there are other desirable locations for similar stores in a much broader area, it cannot be said to have monopolized the area, or, in a legal sense, the lot or its immediate vicinity.

* * *

Though there may be in the nation no more than some thirty desirable sites for the location of professional football teams, those sites, scattered throughout the United States, do not constitute the relevant market. The relevant market is nationwide, though the fact that there are a limited number of desirable sites for team locations bears upon the question of National's power to monopolize the national market.

The District Court's finding that National did not have the power to monopolize the relevant market appears plainly correct. In 1959, it occupied eleven of the thirty-one apparently desirable sites for team locations, but its occupancy of some of them as New York and San Francisco–Oakland was not exclusive, for those metropolitan areas were capable of supporting more than one team. Twenty of the thirty-one potentially desirable sites were entirely open to American. Indeed, the fact that the American League was successfully launched, could stage a full schedule of games in 1960, has competed very successfully for outstanding players, and has obtained advantageous contracts for national television coverage strongly supports the District Court's finding that National did not have the power to prevent, or impede, the formation of the new league. Indeed, at the close of the 1960 season, representatives of the American League declared that the League's success was unprecedented.

American advances a theory, however, that, since the National League won Minneapolis–St. Paul in competition with American, National could have taken several other cities away from American had it undertaken to do so. This is only a theory, however, unsupported by evidence. It ignores the fact that American won Houston over National's competition, and that each league has won one and lost one in their direct competition for franchise locations. It ignores the fact that National was committed to expansion from twelve to sixteen teams in two separate steps, two teams at a time, so that it had but two franchises to place at the time American was being organized. American questions the finding that sixteen teams is a maximum that one league can efficiently accommodate, but the finding is based upon evidence and was not clearly erroneous. In short, there is no basis for a contention that the evidence required a finding that National, had it wished, could have placed a team in every location sought by American, or in a sufficient number of them to have destroyed the league.

American complains that National, the first upon the scene, had occupied the more desirable of the thirty-one potential sites for team locations. Its occupancy of New York and San Francisco–Oakland was not exclusive, however, and the fact that its teams in other locations, such as Baltimore and Washington, enjoyed a natural monopoly does not occasion a violation of the antitrust laws unless the natural monopoly power of those teams was misused to gain a competitive advantage for teams located in other cities, or for the league as a whole. It frequently happens that a first competitor in the field will acquire sites which a latecomer may think more desirable than the remaining available sites, but the firstcomer is not required to surrender any, or all, of its desirable sites to the latecomer simply to enable the latecomer to compete more effectively with it. There is no basis in antitrust laws for a contention that American, whose Boston, Buffalo, Houston, Denver and San Diego teams enjoy natural monopolies, has a right to complain that National does not surrender to it other natural monopoly locations so that they too may be enjoyed by American rather than by National. When one has acquired a natural monopoly by means which are neither exclusionary, unfair, nor predatory, he is not disempowered to defend his position fairly.

* * *

We conclude, therefore, that the District Court properly held that the plaintiffs have shown no monopolization by the National League, or its owners, of the relevant market, and no attempt or conspiracy by them, or any of them, to monopolize it or any part of it. No violation of the Sherman Act having been established, the judgment of the District Court is affirmed.

Affirmed.

Despite its lack of success in this litigation, the upstart AFL proved a worthy competitive force against the established NFL. Buoyed by the first big network television contract with ABC for regular season sports—the contract that forced the NFL to petition Congress for enactment of the Sports Broadcasting Act—the AFL undertook a dramatic bidding war for NFL players, especially star quarterbacks such as John Brodie. By 1966 the NFL was ready to make peace, and the two leagues agreed to a merger. However, in light of the Fourth Circuit's reasoning in the above decision, the leagues had grave doubts about the legality of their plans. But by dangling the promise of expansion into New Orleans to powerful committee chairs from Louisiana, Senator Russell Long and Representative Hale Boggs, the leagues were able to secure congressional blessing for this new league venture through an amendment to the Sports Broadcasting Act, 15 U.S.C.A. § 1291. We have seen this amendment discussed in Chapter 7 in the *Memphis Grizzlies* case (post-World Football League), and we will encounter it later in this chapter in litigation arising out of the demise of the United States Football League.

It is important in thinking about § 2's ban on monopolization to remember that the two elements of a violation—monopoly market power and improper conduct—are wholly separate. The conduct constituting the monopolizing act does not have to involve directly the market being monopolized. Given this doctrinal reality, why was the principal focus of *AFL v. NFL* on the geographic market in which franchises were being awarded? The fact that the alleged unlawful conduct was strategic placement of new NFL franchises and the threat to add two more in other potential AFL cities does not mean that the market being monopolized has to be the one in which franchises are granted. If you were an upstart league alleging that an established league was trying to prevent you from becoming a viable competitor, in what market would you allege that the established league clearly held monopoly (or monopsony) market power that it most wanted to maintain? In what market are the competitive effects of a second league most immediately apparent and dramatic? What do established leagues fear most from new leagues?

In assessing the presence of monopoly power, there is a *functional* as well as a *geographic* cast to the relevant market. The National Football League, for example, has regularly argued (though without much success) that professional football faces market competition from college football, as well as from professional baseball, basketball, and other sports, and that all sports face competition from movies, concerts, theater, and other forms of entertainment.[f] The major judicial precedent in this regard is *United States v. E.I. du Pont de Nemours & Co.*, 351 U.S. 377 (1956). This case involved a § 2 complaint against du Pont which produced 75% of the country's cellophane; cellophane, however, constituted just 20% of all "flexible packaging materials." The following passages indicate how the Supreme Court analyzes such market definition issues:

> Market delimitation is necessary under du Pont's theory to determine whether an alleged monopolist violates § 2. The ultimate consideration in such a determination is whether the defendants control the price and competition in the market for such part of trade or commerce as they are charged with monopolizing. Every manufacturer is the sole producer of the particular commodity it makes but its control in the above sense of the relevant market depends upon the availability of alternative commodities for buyers: i.e., whether there is a cross-elasticity of demand between cellophane and the other wrappings. This interchangeability is largely gauged by the purchase of competing products for similar uses, considering the price, characteristics and adaptability of the competing commodities.

* * *

> If a large number of buyers and sellers deal freely in a standardized product, such as salt or wheat, we have complete or pure competition. Patents, on the other hand, furnish the most familiar

---

[f]. Indeed, an antitrust complainant against the NFL also failed in his effort to characterize football tickets as merely one product available in the "general entertainment market," where such a judgment was essential to his charge that the Buffalo Bills illegally "tied" availability of season ticket packages for regular season games to the purchase of tickets for exhibition games. See *Coniglio v. Highwood Services, Inc.*, 495 F.2d 1286, 1292 (2d Cir.1974). Also, to the same effect, *Driskill v. Dallas Cowboys Football Club*, 498 F.2d 321 (5th Cir.1974); *Laing v. Minnesota Vikings Football Club*, 372 F.Supp. 59 (D.Minn.1973), affirmed, 492 F.2d 1381 (8th Cir.1974); *Pfeiffer v. New England Patriots*, 1973–1 Trade Cases ¶ 74,267, 1972 WL 647 (D.Mass.1972).

type of classic monopoly. As the producers of a standardized product bring about significant differentiations of quality, design, or packaging in the product that permit differences of use, competition becomes to a greater or less degree incomplete and the producer's power over price and competition greater over his article and its use, according to the differentiation he is able to create and maintain. A retail seller may have in one sense a monopoly on certain trade because of location, as an isolated country store or filling station, or because no one else makes a product of just the quality or attractiveness of his product, as for example in cigarettes. Thus one can theorize that we have monopolistic competition in every nonstandardized commodity with each manufacturer having power over the price and production of his own product. However, this power that, let us say, automobile or soft-drink manufacturers have over their trademarked products is not the power that makes an illegal monopoly. Illegal power must be appraised in terms of the competitive market for the product.

Determination of the competitive market for commodities depends on how different from one another are the offered commodities in character or use, how far buyers will go to substitute one commodity for another. For example, one can think of building materials as in commodity competition, but one could hardly say that brick competed with steel or wood or cement or stone in the meaning of the Sherman Act litigation; the products are too different. This is the interindustry competition emphasized by some economists. On the other hand, there are certain differences in the formulae for soft drinks, but one can hardly say that each one is an illegal monopoly.

* * *

What is called for is an appraisal of the "cross-elasticity" of demand in the trade. The varying circumstances of each case determine the result. In considering what is the relevant market for determining the control of price and competition, no more definite rule can be declared than that commodities reasonably interchangeable by consumers for the same purposes make up that "part of the trade or commerce," monopolization of which may be illegal.

351 U.S. at 380–81.

Shortly after *du Pont*, the Supreme Court rendered its second decision in the litigation involving *International Boxing Club v. United States* (at 358 U.S. 242 (1959)). In its initial decision in these proceedings, at 348 U.S. 236 (1955), the Supreme Court ruled for the first time that any sport was subject to antitrust law (thereby beginning the scenario whereby the immunity won earlier by baseball would be confined to that sport by *Flood v. Kuhn*). This second decision dealt with the merits of the antitrust complaint concerning boxing. Apparently James

Sec. A   POWER AND THE RELEVANT MARKET   605

Norris, owner of Detroit's Olympia Arena and hockey Red Wings, and Willard Wirtz, owner of Chicago's Stadium and Black Hawks, had formed the International Boxing Club (IBC) to try to dominate professional boxing. IBC used Joe Louis and Sugar Ray Robinson as the levers to win exclusive control of the champions and contenders in boxing's heavyweight, middleweight and welterweight divisions, and bought Madison Square Garden to secure control of all the major sites for big time fights. The Justice Department charged IBC with monopolizing and restraining trade in *championship* boxing, and the District Court found violations of both §§ 1 and 2 of the Sherman Act. The following is the key passage from the Supreme Court's analysis of the merits of IBC's appeal:

> Appellants launch a vigorous attack on the finding that the relevant market was the promotion of *championship* boxing contests in contrast to *all* professional boxing events. They rely primarily on *United States v. du Pont & Co.*, 351 U.S. 377 (1956).... The appellants argue that the "physical identity of the products here would seem necessarily to put them in one and the same market." They say that any boxing contest, whether championship or not, always includes one ring, two boxers and one referee, fighting under the same rules before a greater or lesser number of spectators either present at ringside or through the facilities of television, radio, or moving pictures.

We do not feel that this conclusion follows. As was also said in *du Pont*, supra, at 404:

> The 'market' ... will vary with the part of commerce under consideration. The tests are constant. That market is composed of products that have reasonable interchangeability for the purposes for which they are produced—price, use and qualities considered.

With this in mind, the lower court in the instant case found that there exists a "separate, identifiable market" for championship boxing contests. This general finding is supported by detailed findings to the effect that the average revenue from all sources for appellants' championship bouts was $154,000 compared to $40,000 for their nonchampionship programs; that television rights to one championship fight brought $100,000, in contrast to $45,000 for a nontitle fight seven months later between the same two fighters; that the average "Nielsen" ratings over a two-and-one-half-year period were 74.9% for appellants' championship contests, and 57.7% for their nonchampionship programs (reflecting a difference of several million viewers between the two types of fights); that although the revenues from movie rights for six of appellants' championship bouts totaled over $600,000, no full-length motion picture rights were sold for a non-championship contest; and that spectators pay "substantially more" for tickets to championship fights than for nontitle fights. In addition, numerous representatives of the broadcasting, motion picture and advertising industries testified to the general effect that a "particular and special demand exists among radio broadcasting and telecasting [and motion picture] companies for the rights to broadcast and telecast [and make and distribute films of] championship contests in contradistinction to similar rights to non-championship contests."

In view of these findings, we cannot say that the lower court was "clearly erroneous" in concluding that nonchampionship fights are not "reasonably interchangeable for the same purpose" as championship contests.... [C]hampionship boxing is the "cream" of the boxing business, and, as has been shown above, is a sufficiently separate part of the trade or commerce to constitute the relevant market for Sherman Act purposes.

358 U.S. at 249–52.

Questions for Discussion

1. In light of the *du Pont* and *IBC* line of analysis, how much weight should be given to the NFL's product market argument sketched earlier in antitrust litigation against the league? Recall Judge Easterbrook's observations in the *WGN* decision in Chapter 7; should the sports *television* market be treated differently from the sports *ticket* market?

2. A sports league operates in markets other than those in which it sells its product to customers—the markets for live event tickets and television and radio broadcast rights. It also sells franchises in the league and trademark licenses, and it purchases equipment and the services of coaches and players. In which of the major markets does an established league probably hold substantial market power? In which does it likely hold little market power? Does your answer hinge on unstated variables—i.e., which sport is involved, whether an upstart league is operating at the time, or whether the market is national or local (in which case market power can vary from city to city)?

3. In considering the labor or equipment markets, review the discussion of "monopsony" in Chapter 3—a buyer has so much market power over sellers of some factor of production that the latter have virtually no alternative buyers. In such a case, the monopsonist can force prices down to artificially low levels, which ultimately hurts the consumer by causing some suppliers to cut back the amount of the input they are willing to supply and thereby shifts resources toward goods and services that they are less efficient at producing and are less desired by consumers. That may, however, also benefit consumers who do buy the product by reducing the monopsonist's production costs that in some part (depending on the elasticity of demand for the product) will be passed through to consumers. If a league monopsonizes an input market, should that be as automatic a § 2 violation as if it had monopolized a product market? Or should a court have to go one step

further and determine whether the monopsony on balance benefits or injures consumers?

A final word about monopoly power and relevant markets. Recall that the definition of market power is the ability to restrict output and raise prices from levels that would be established in a competitive market. In a world in which all relevant economic data were available, it would be easy to determine if a defendant possessed monopoly market power: one would simply see if the price the defendant is charging is significantly higher than its marginal costs at the given level of output. It would not matter if, at the monopoly price level, there were other products that consumers might substitute. However, since marginal cost is in most cases almost impossible to ascertain, and demand and supply elasticity almost as difficult to prove, courts have relied on narrative tests like those we saw in *du Pont* and *International Boxing Club*. But as you are reading the cases in this chapter and trying to identify the relevant market, keep in mind that even with the apparent presence (or absence) of functional substitutes to which consumers might turn, the defendant may still have (or may not have) monopoly market power. The legal test is whether the price the defendant actually charges is substantially above its marginal cost, irrespective of whether there are functional substitutes for consumers.

Another interesting issue presented in the sports context is whether or not each major sports league, even if it does have monopoly power, is a "natural monopolist," and if so, whether or not that status protects its holder from violating § 2. A natural monopolist is one whose product is such that the market will only allow a single producer to be profitable. The most common explanation for this phenomenon is that the producer's average cost per unit of production is greater than its marginal cost at all significant levels of output. This creates a situation where two or more producers feel compelled to cut prices to near-marginal cost but below average total costs, which causes them all to lose money and eventually fold one after another. Eventually, only one producer is left, which can then charge a "monopoly" price above its average costs and thus make a profit. Does this condition characterize the market in which the NFL operates? What is the NFL's marginal cost? How does one measure a unit of output necessary to determine marginal and average costs? Would you think the NFL's average total cost is greater or less than its marginal cost? Regardless of the answers to these economic questions, are there other characteristics of professional football (or other sports) that make it inevitable that only one *major* league will survive for any long period of time? During the next few years we will have a real-world test of this question, as we watch what happens to the American Basketball League (ABL) and Women's National Basketball Association (WNBA) which brought this women's professional sport back to the United States in the late 1990s.

B. MONOPOLY RESOURCES AND MONOPOLIZING CONDUCT

The mere existence of monopoly power in the relevant market, however defined, is not sufficient to establish a violation of § 2 of the Sherman Act. As the Supreme Court put it in *United States v. Grinnell Corp.*, 384 U.S. 563, 570–71 (1966), a § 2 violation also requires "the willful acquisition or maintenance of that power as distinguished from growth or development as a consequence of a superior product, business acumen, or historic accident." Over the last century, courts have developed a sizable jurisprudence regarding how to distinguish legitimate from illegitimate sources of monopoly power.

From the point of view of antitrust policy, the question is not whether a monopolistic firm has exploited its power by raising prices or lowering output to maximize its profits. While this practice harms consumers in the short run (and may be subject to government regulation on that account), the presence of monopoly profits in a particular market often serves as an inducement to other firms to enter the market if they can, which in the long run creates a competitive environment for the benefit of consumers. Indeed, the prospect of new entry may discourage the established firm from fully exploiting its monopoly power in the first place. The true evil aimed at by antitrust law, then, is action by the monopolist that excludes others from entering or remaining in the market and providing competitive balance.

However, not all exclusionary practices warrant legal prohibition. If the size or competence of an established firm allows it to develop high quality products sold at low prices that cannot be matched by its rivals, it hardly enhances consumer welfare for a judge to penalize the firm for being so successful in its effort to satisfy its customers. The challenge in this area of antitrust law is to distinguish between those exclusionary practices by the dominant firm that benefit consumers, and hence are legally tolerable, from exclusionary practices that are anticompetitive, and thus warrant legal prohibition.

A good deal of this antitrust jurisprudence is displayed in the following cases. In sports, such litigation has been targeted at the established league's use of its control over assets vital to the emergence of a competitive sports venture. We saw this in the *AFL* case above, which involved desirable franchise cities, and in the *NASL* case in Chapter 7 (in which the charge was brought under § 1 of the Sherman Act), which involved the allegedly scarce supply of sports capital and entrepreneurial talent. The next series of decisions deals with other resources indispensable in present-day professional sports—players, facilities, and television contracts.

1. PLAYERS

Chapter 3 presented an in-depth look at the role of antitrust law in the player market. The focus of that chapter's analysis was very different from our concern here. In cases such as *Flood*, *Mackey*, and *McCourt*, the players and their associations used § 1 of the Sherman Act to attack a variety of legal practices—capsulized as the "reserve system"—that limited player mobility and bargaining leverage within the established league. This chapter examines the established leagues' use of their control over players (including control obtained through collective bargaining) to foil potential competitors by denying new leagues access to the most vital of all sports assets—player talent (especially well-known, high-quality talent).

Such control tends to be less effective in football and basketball, because every year the intercollegiate "farm clubs" in these sports "graduate" a new class of athletes of demonstrated quality and considerable renown. Perhaps this is one of the reasons why the NFL and NBA never included provisions in their player contracts that perpetually bound players to the team and prevented them from signing with teams *in a different league* (if one existed) when the contract expired. By contrast, in baseball and hockey, the intercollegiate game is much less prominent; thus the major leagues have created their own farm systems to develop player talent for parent clubs. Since a network of contract restrictions bound every young player from the time he entered the minor leagues to the time he retired from the big leagues,[g] it was crucial to the success of new leagues aspiring to big-time status to break that stranglehold. The appropriate legal vehicle was § 2 of the Sherman Act; the following decision is the principal example of its use in this context.

PHILADELPHIA WORLD HOCKEY CLUB v. PHILADELPHIA HOCKEY CLUB

United States District Court, Eastern District of Pennsylvania, 1972.
351 F.Supp. 462.

HIGGINBOTHAM, DISTRICT JUDGE.

[This decision concerned an antitrust suit filed by the fledgling World Hockey Association (WHA) against its established rival, the National Hockey League (NHL). The WHA's primary objective was to secure a federal court injunction barring the NHL and its clubs from seeking state court injunctions to prevent more than 60 NHL players who had signed WHA contracts from moving to the WHA in apparent violation of their NHL standard player contracts.[h] The trial judge provided an elaborate description of the structure of professional hockey, relations between the NHL and amateur and minor professional hockey leagues, the reserve system and the standard player contract, expansion

---

g. Bobby Orr, for example, became the "property" of the Boston Bruins when he was just 14 years old, because the Bruins, recognizing his talent, took over sponsorship of the "midget" league in which Orr was then playing in his hometown of Parry Sound, Ontario.

h. See *Boston Professional Hockey Ass'n v. Cheevers*, 348 F.Supp. 261 (D.Mass.1972), reversed on other grounds, 472 F.2d 127 (1st Cir.1972), and *Nassau Sports v. Hampson*, 355 F.Supp. 733 (D.Minn.1972) (both denying the negative injunction); contra, *Nassau Sports v. Peters*, 352 F.Supp. 870 (E.D.N.Y.1972) (granting the injunction).

In 1917, the National Hockey League was born with Montreal and Toronto as its only members. In 1924, Boston was added, followed in 1926 with Chicago, Detroit and New York. In 1967, Los Angeles, Philadelphia, Pittsburgh, California, Minnesota, and St. Louis entered the League and in 1970 Buffalo and Vancouver. In 1972, Nassau (New York) and Atlanta joined this now famous League. Since 1966, the National Hockey League has received in excess of $36,000,000 for the sale of the rights to play major league professional hockey in their league. When in 1970 the National Hockey League admitted Vancouver and Buffalo, each of these two new clubs paid in excess of $8,000,000 for the acquisition of the minor professional league clubs in their locality and for distribution to National Hockey League clubs.

[The court concluded that while hockey was probably no more a part of interstate commerce than was baseball back in 1922 when *Federal Base Ball* was decided, hockey was clearly now a business in commerce, and thus subject to antitrust law. The judge then described how almost all major league hockey players came from amateur teams governed by the Canadian Amateur Hockey Association (CAHA), although some came from U.S. clubs operating under the auspices of the Amateur Hockey Association of the United States. While traditionally NHL clubs had directly sponsored individual amateur teams in Canada, especially at the Junior A level, since 1967 there had been an umbrella NHL–CAHA agreement under which NHL clubs contributed over $1 million per year for amateur player development. At the same time, the NHL began to conduct an annual draft of 150 or so of the approximately 7,000 amateur players turning 20 years of age. Specified payments were made to CAHA club members for each player drafted, and again for each of the 45 or so players who signed an NHL contract.

Almost all newly drafted players began professional hockey in one of three minor hockey leagues—the American, Western, and Central Hockey Leagues—all of whose teams were either directly sponsored by, or had an affiliation or player loan arrangement with an NHL club. There were sharp differences in both profitability and caliber of play between the NHL and the three minor leagues. Whereas NHL teams then averaged near sellout crowds of 14,000 per game at more than $5 per ticket, minor league teams averaged 4,000 fans per game at $2.50 per ticket. These differences in gate revenues, together with the emergence of local and network television contracts, permitted NHL teams to pay their players an average annual salary of $24,000 in 1971–1972, compared to $11,000–12,000 for minor league players. Thus, while the WHA planned to recruit a significant number of players from the minor professional leagues, the judge concluded that in order to succeed the WHA also needed access to players who had developed the ability to excel in the NHL.

The major obstacle to the WHA's recruiting of NHL players was the NHL standard player contract. Under Clause 17 of that contract, the club was entitled to renew the contract on the same terms as before, with the exception of the salary amount, which was set anew each year. Since one of the terms in the existing contract was Clause 17 itself, the player contract was perpetually renewable. Similar terms were included in the standard contracts in the AHL, the WHL, and the CHL constitutions, which led the trial judge to this key finding:]

* * *

The similarities of phraseology and basic incorporation of Clause 17 in the Standard Player's Contract of the AHL, CHL, WHL, and NHL is the result of a common agreement, mutual understanding, and conspiracy by the NHL and its affiliated minor leagues to maintain a monopolistic position so strong that the NHL precludes effective competition by the entry of another major professional hockey league. Through the totality of many interlocking arrangements, including the Joint Affiliation Agreement, the Pro–Amateur Agreement, and Clause 17 in the Standard Player's Contract, the NHL perpetuates a conspiracy and combination with the intent to monopolize and which monopolizes major league professional hockey. These concerted efforts were done not solely to maintain a high level of professional competition among the NHL teams, but rather the major reason was the desire to preclude others from ever having immediate access to the reservoir of players who could become part of another major professional hockey league which could be a material and viable competitor to the NHL. In the words of Mr. Clarence Campbell, President of the NHL, part of the NHL's purpose was to make certain that the NHL would always be " ... the only major professional hockey league operating from coast-to-coast in the United States or Canada."

[In the late 1960s, there were some negotiations about the terms of this standard player contract between the NHL and its long-time president Clarence Campbell, and the new NHL Player Association under its founding leader Alan Eagleson. These labor negotiations, though, focused only on the mechanism for settling differences about salary amounts in the renewed option contract. Previously, salary disputes between teams and veteran players were adjudicated by NHL President Campbell; as of 1972, though, the NHL agreed to neutral salary arbitration. With that exception, hockey's basic reserve system remained untouched, enforced by a vigorous anti-tampering section in the NHL bylaws. Any team that publicly indicated interest in acquiring a player on another team's reserve list, let alone negotiated with that player, was subject to fines and loss of draft choices.]

* * *

The Necessity for Some Form of Reserve Clause.

Every major professional team sport utilizes some form of "reserve" clause in its standard player's contract. Some of the purported justifications for a "reserve" clause (e.g., the need for competitive balance within the league) apply to all sports. A less anti-competitive "reserve" clause than the present one may be needed in hockey.

In order to be successful, a professional hockey league normally must have some of the qualities of parity among its member teams which make other sports successful. That is, the public must believe that there is relative parity among the member teams and that each team has the opportunity of becoming a contender over a reasonable cycle of years and a reasonable chance of beating any other team on any given night.

The history of the NHL's Stanley Cup Series, the "World Series" of hockey, indicates that relative parity does not exist within the NHL. In the last twenty years, Montreal has won the Stanley Cup on twelve occasions, Toronto has won four times, Detroit has won three times, and Chicago has won once.

The founders of the WHA believe that even if the quality of the hockey played by its member teams is not as high as in the NHL, the WHA will still be successful if it can maintain sufficient parity of quality among its own teams.

* * *

[The judge then described the expansion of major-league professional hockey. The NHL, which was formed in 1917, achieved a permanent base in six cities by 1942. Not until 1967 did expansion occur, this time into six new cities. For the $2 million franchise fee, each new club obtained the right to select 20 players from the established teams' reserve lists, except for 20 protected players on each of the latter teams. Three years later, in 1970, the NHL expanded again into Buffalo and Vancouver, this time at a price of $8 million per franchise, and the clubs selected players from those left off 15–player protected lists.

In August 1971, the NHL learned of the imminent formation of the WHA. In reaction, the NHL took two major steps. One was to authorize further expansion into Atlanta and Long Island, at $6 million per franchise. Long Island was crucial because the WHA had been actively negotiating for a franchise lease in the newly-constructed Nassau Coliseum, the only site available for a hockey team in the New York metropolitan area (other than Madison Square Garden, which had an exclusive hockey lease with the NHL Rangers). When the NHL awarded a franchise to Roy Boe (who also paid $4 million in territorial indemnity to the Rangers), the Nassau Coliseum signed a lease with the NHL's New York Islanders.

The NHL's other step was to form a Legal Committee that, through the Washington law firm of Covington and Burling, coordinated vigorous enforcement of the reserve clause through injunction proceedings against NHL players seeking to move to the WHA for much higher salaries.

The WHA's response was to launch this antitrust suit against the NHL. One claim rested on § 1 of the Sherman Act. Judge Higginbotham was loath to grant an injunction to the WHA on that ground.]

* * *

On the basis of the present record as to the § 1 issues, I have some doubts on the WHA's probability of ultimate success. The sports field is in some ways a hybrid, in that it is both similarly and dissimilarly affected by the normal economic variables governing business success. For a corporation producing aluminum, any entrant in the field is a competitor. From a traditional oligopolist's or monopolist's view, one might consider any new entrant as an adversary and thus undesirable. But by the nature of a sports contest, there must always be an adversary. By analogy, who would enjoy Vida Blue blazing strikes across home plate when the batter's box was empty, or Mark Spitz' triumphs, if he were the only one in the pool. Sports teams need competition, and if there are more than two teams, some type of league is probably desirable.

For maximum customer receptivity and profit it is in the best interest of any club that its opponents not generally be viewed by the public as totally incompetent and utterly unable to compete effectively. For if the latter occurs, thousands of customers will not spend their dollars for tickets to view hundreds of games when the contest seems to present no more of a challenge than an ant confronting an elephant. Thus, if it is not possible to keep the competitive challenge of all teams within some reasonable parameters, some type of intraleague reserve clause or system may be desirable and in fact necessary.

[At the heart of the WHA's case, though, was § 2 of Sherman, which prohibited monopolization, and which Judge Higginbotham believed gave the WHA much firmer legal ground. The judge began by reviewing the history of hockey's traditional reserve system. NHL teams had always had a perpetually renewable option clause in their Standard Player's Contract, though unlike baseball, hockey players could take salary disputes with their team to Commissioner Clarence Campbell for arbitration. Judge Higginbotham viewed this arrangement, which had been fashioned by NHL owners with monopoly power, to be a clearcut violation of § 2 of Sherman. When the Players Association appeared on the scene in the late 1960s, it negotiated an understanding with the owners to substitute a neutral salary arbitrator for Commissioner Campbell. However, given the informal "handshake" style of relations between hockey owners and players (in their Player–Owner Council), it was not until March 1972 that a formal Arbitration Agreement was executed by the two sides. The judge was of the view that even this document could not modify an existing player contract without the player's express authorization or ratification. However,]

* * *

... even if, arguendo, the 1972 Arbitration Agreement is automatically incorporated into an existing individual player's contract and is not solely a device for determining salary, and even if the 1972 Arbitration Agreement expires in 1975 without having been extended by the NHL and the NHLPA (thus arguably making the reserve clause unenforceable after 1975 because no mechanism will then exist for determining the amount of compensation), I hold that in the circumstances of this case, the three year restraint following the expiration of a current contract (considering this factor along with the other numerous interlocking agreements the NHL has fashioned and shaped over the years to monopolize a hockey player's professional career) is unreasonable, and in violation of § 2 of the Sherman Act.

Finally, apart from the collective bargaining negotiations relative to the arbitration of salary, there have been no modifications of Clause 17 of the Standard Player's Contract which have altered or eliminated the basic perpetual option which the NHL has over any hockey player once he has first signed a Standard Player's Contract.

B. Monopoly Power.

In view of the impact of the reserve clause, an additional issue for determination is whether the NHL possesses monopoly power in the relevant market. In *United States v. E. I. du Pont de Nemours & Co.*, supra, 351 U.S. at 391, the Court defined monopoly power as " ... the power to control prices or exclude competition."

* * *

Here, through the use, inter alia, of (1) Standard Players' Contracts, including the "reserve clause" in paragraph 17 of that contract, (2) the agreements between the NHL and three of the major semi-professional leagues, and (3) the agreements between the professional and semi-professional leagues and the amateur leagues, it is clear that the NHL overwhelmingly controls the supply of players who are capable and available for play in a new league where the level of internal competitions fairly approaches the levels currently existing in the NHL. In an attempt to minimize the NHL's extraordinary degree of control over the players, the NHL asserts that there are many other available players who will shortly be able to play major league professional hockey. However, the relevant market place is the market place of today, not the market place of 1980 or even the market place of 1975. A monopolist may not today excuse his present predatory practices because someday in the future his total domination of the market place may be lessened.

The NHL's monopoly power is their power to control overwhelmingly the supply of hockey players who are today available for play in any major professional league. It is that total control by the NHL which I hold is proscribed by § 2 of the Sherman Act. One who builds the most modern steel mill cannot operate without an adequate supply of iron ore. The 50,000 amateur hockey players allegedly available to the WHA are the "iron ore" from which viable competition can be built. If the WHA is to compete effectively for attendance and television rights with commensurate payments, the WHA must have a "show" which is equal or nearly equal to that of the NHL today. Since the WHA is a newcomer, the quality of play need not instantly equal that of the NHL, but there must be a prospect that the product will be nearly equal in a relatively short period of time.

Of course, I recognize that the NHL has neither prevented the birth of the infant WHA nor has the NHL caused the WHA to sustain a premature demise, but monopoly power may be restrained before its full wrath is felt.

C. Willfulness & Intent.

The mere possession of monopoly power in the relevant market does not alone constitute a violation of § 2 of the Sherman Act, 15 U.S.C. § 2. There must also be "(2) the willful acquisition or maintenance of that power as distinguished from growth or development as a consequence of a superior product, business acumen, or historic accident." *United States v. Grinnell*, 384 U.S. 563, 570–71 (1966).

The activities of the NHL go beyond mere possession of monopoly power in the relevant market to breach these aforementioned prohibitions articulated in *United States v. Grinnell*.

The NHL has willfully acquired and maintained its monopoly power through the use of the many agreements detailed in Findings of Fact 35–89. Its continuing and overriding goal is to maintain a monopoly over the supply of major league professional hockey players.

The NHL employs devices such as reserve clauses, Standard Player Contracts, an NHL semi-professional league Joint-Affiliation Agreement, and control over the amateurs through the Pro-Am Agreement in which the amateurs agreed to recognize the NHL as the "sole and exclusive governing body of professional hockey." If the NHL reserve clause were valid for those players whose contracts terminated in September, 1972, then the NHL would have the power, directly or indirectly, to prevent any player under "contract" to the NHL or one of its affiliated minor professional leagues from playing with any other team or league outside the NHL System.

Upon reading the self-serving tributes for its expenditure of millions of dollars to develop amateur and minor league hockey, one might infer that the millions were spent solely for the honor and glory of amateur and minor league hockey. The NHL's motives were not quite so noble; these expenditures to develop the amateur and minor professional leagues were essential to maintain the NHL's monopolistic position.

In *American Football League v. National Football League,* the Court noted:

> In 1959 the NFL had most of the ablest players under contract. However, colleges graduate annually large numbers of talented players, and, because after the season starts professional football rosters are usually limited to around 35 players, many good players are released each year after the training season and are available to be signed by clubs in any league. Moreover, NFL players become free agents after a period of years.
>
> In contrast to the above picture of relative openness and availability of players in professional football, the NHL has a system which controls

access to all professional and semi-professional players for at least three years. As my discussion, *supra*, concerning the reserve clause conclusively demonstrates, if the operation of the NHL's current reserve clause is not restrained, the NHL's control over the players is absolute for at least three years after the expiration of any current contract. Further, the value of the minor league professional hockey players as a source of supply to the major leagues is not the equivalent of college-level players in football. Moreover, the minor league professional hockey players are likewise bound by standard player contracts which contain reserve clauses materially identical to the NHL standard player contract. Finally, the general practice is that if a minor professional league player does not make the NHL team, nevertheless he is still bound by his former minor professional league contract and is thus not free to sign with another club or any other league. These differences between the football and hockey reserve systems are crucial.

Secondary evidence of the NHL's intent to maintain its control over professional hockey is its continuing policy of expansion tied to the increasing demand for hockey in the United States and also in Canada. Of course, if even this burgeoning interest in hockey in North America could nonetheless support only one supplier, then this court would be bound to conclude that the NHL enjoys a "natural monopoly." In *Ovitron Corp. v. General Motors Corp.*, 295 F.Supp. 373, 378 (S.D.N.Y. 1969), the Court noted "the natural monopolist is entitled to compete vigorously and fairly in a struggle for a market which cannot support more than one supplier."

* * *

Keeping in mind both the many agreements employed by the National Hockey League and its continuing expansion, it is apparent that the National Hockey League's intent is and was the willful acquisition and maintenance of a position as the only major professional hockey league in the United States and Canada.

* * *

The expansion of the NHL during the WHA's formative period and the creation of the WHA itself are both responses to an increased market for the sport and thus increased economic attractiveness for those entering as well as those already in the field.

Here, I do not rely solely on the expansion of the NHL to show that it had the intent to monopolize; for the President of the NHL, Clarence Campbell, has explained his league's intent as a determined drive to assure that the NHL is 'the only major professional hockey league operating from coast to coast in the United States or Canada.'

Expansion of the NHL was one factor indicative of the wrongful intent of the older league to totally monopolize hockey and remain the only major professional hockey league operating with the United States, but expansion was only one of the several threads spun in the monopolistic fabric of the NHL to blanket players from entry to another league.

Injunction granted.

In other portions of his lengthy decision, Judge Higginbotham described negotiations about hockey's reserve clause that had taken place between the NHL and its newly formed Players Association (the NHLPA) in the previous three to four years. The NHLPA had succeeded in adding to the standard player's contract a procedure for neutral arbitration of the salary amount when a team exercised its option to renew one of its player's contracts. It was clear, though (as NHLPA Executive Director Alan Eagleson testified in *Flood v. Kuhn*), that hockey clubs continued to enjoy the same perpetually renewable rights to their players' services as was then understood to exist in baseball (prior to the *Messersmith* arbitration ruling). Because the perpetually renewable option clause was accepted by the NHLPA and included in the collective bargaining agreement, it is necessary briefly to revisit the nonstatutory labor exemption that shields collectively bargained provisions from antitrust attack (see Chapter 3), an exemption that Judge Higginbotham held did not protect the NHL in this case. The following is an excerpt from his opinion on this issue:

> From my examination of the foregoing cases (*Hutcheson*, *Allen Bradley*, *Pennington*, and *Jewel Tea*), several conclusions can be drawn. First, those cases all involved situations where the union had been sued for its active, conspiratorial role in restraining competition in a product market, and the union, not the employer, sought to invoke the labor exemptions. Here there is no evidence that the Players' Association was a joint-conspirator with the National Hockey League in creating and retaining the reserve clause. The evidence establishes the Players' Associations' persistent opposition to the present form of reserve system. The reserve clause, in fact, was more than a sturdy teenager when the Players' Association was born. The reserve clause was fathered by the NHL, and the Players' Association has repeatedly sought to exclude it in its present form.
>
> Second, the cases cited above pertained to issues which furthered the interests of the union members and on which there had been extensive collective bargaining. Again, that is not true in this litigation. The National Hockey League has not come forward with any substantial evidence which could warrant this Court finding that the reserve clause—as it presently operates in conjunction with the other interlocking agreements—was ever a subject of serious, intensive, arm's-length collective bargaining. When the Players' Association was recognized in 1967, some variation of the reserve system had existed for probably sixteen years prior thereto. Subsequent efforts by the Association to markedly revamp the reserve system have been continually rebuffed by the NHL. The discussions revolving around the Arbitration Agreements related only to resolv-

ing salary disputes, and did not in any way alter or affect the basic perpetual option of the reserve system.

Finally, even if, arguendo, there had been substantial arm's-length collective bargaining by the National Hockey League and the Players' Association to revise the perpetual option provision of the reserve clause, those negotiations would not shield the National Hockey League from liability in a suit by outside competitors who sought access to players under the control of the National Hockey League.

* * *

Even if the benefits of the labor exemptions can be extended to encompass the employer's activities, that outcome is not changed merely because the employer is a member of a multi-employer association. A multi-employer group will not be accorded any greater protections than a single employer. Though a multi-employer organization will be insulated from unfair labor practice prosecutions only if it acts in good faith and takes only the limited steps necessary to protect itself, however, restraining, anti-competitive acts will not be immunized from the Sherman Act. Cf. *Kennedy v. Long Island R.R.* (2nd Cir.1963); *Prepmore Apparel, Inc. v. Amalgamated Clothing Workers of America* (5th Cir.1970). While the employer activities in the two latter cases were not subject to the Sherman Act, the Courts clearly intimated that employer efforts to monopolize a particular product market would not be similarly treated.

... The labor exemption which could be defensively utilized by the union and employer as a shield against Sherman Act proceedings when there was bona fide collective bargaining, could not be seized upon by either party and destructively wielded as a sword by engaging in monopolistic or other anti-competitive conduct. The shield cannot be transmuted into a sword and still permit the beneficiary to invoke the narrowly carved out labor exemption from the antitrust laws. To allow and condone such conduct would frustrate Congress' carefully orchestrated efforts to harmoniously blend together two opposing public policies.

In sum, the National Hockey League, as it stands before me in the instant action, is not the most ideal candidate to be a beneficiary of the labor exemptions. The National Hockey League itself was primarily responsible for devising and perpetuating a monopoly over the system. Not only did it enforce and implement its restraints against players and member clubs of the National Hockey League, but, moreover, it sought to enforce it against outside competitors who wanted to enter the competition at the professional level.

I reject the argument that an employer (National Hockey League) can conspire with or take advantage of a union to restrain competition and seriously impair the business dealings and transactions of competitors.

351 F.Supp. at 498–500.

Questions for Discussion

1. Which of the reasons that the judge gave for not applying the labor exemption in this case seems most valid in light of the Supreme Court's ruling in *Brown* that we read in Chapter 3? Would this same result follow if a players association negotiated a full free agency system within the boundaries of its own league, but with the proviso that teams in this league enjoyed a "right of first refusal" if one of its players signed a contract with a team in a rival league? Might the answer depend on who the plaintiff is?

2. Facilitated by the above decision, the WHA's entry on the hockey scene resulted in a fierce bidding war for players that sent average salaries soaring and team balance sheets into the red. The same scenario took place in football and basketball, whose established leagues faced the challenge of new competitors without a perpetually renewable option in their standard player contracts (recall the *Barnett*, *Bergey*, and *Neely* decisions in Chapter 2). Why were teams willing to spend huge sums of money on players, irrespective of the effect on their balance sheets? Does this practice make good business sense for teams in the new league? For teams in the established league? Is there—or should there be—a legal barrier to such spending, especially by the established league? Consider the analogy of illegal "predatory pricing" by a dominant firm faced by a new rival—i.e., deliberately pricing a product below cost to force weaker firms out of the market. Should there be a similar bar to "predatory salary-paying?" If so, how would a court determine when a salary had escalated above the player's legitimate competitive market value (i.e., his marginal revenue product) and become an illegitimate predatory wage level? (Recall the "natural monopoly" market hypothesis described earlier.) And by the way, why does an established league such as the NFL, the NBA, and the NHL always choose to compete by paying higher salaries to its players, rather than by charging lower prices to its fans? The explanation is crucial to understanding the peculiar features of monopoly in sports.

3. Judge Higgenbotham also made reference to the NHL's expansion initiative, taken at the same time that the WHA was trying to establish itself, as further evidence of its intent to monopolize. Thinking back to the *AFL* case, can expansion that fills the public's growing demand for more franchises be an illegal erection of barriers to a new league's entry, by depriving any new entrant of the most attractive areas in which to locate profitable teams? From a policy standpoint, should Congress put more pressure on existing leagues to expand into areas where there is great demand, or should it act to limit the size of existing leagues in order to preserve attractive virgin markets for potential new leagues? Since all of the major leagues today have approximately 30 teams, are there enough attractive markets available for a new league to have any hope of surviving in these sports? Does this make the existing major leagues illegal monopolists for having expanded into so many cities, or natural monopolists in a market where no new league could possibly survive? Remember that the 1966 NFL–AFL merger into a single league of 26 teams was given an express congressional exemption. Was that good antitrust and/or sports policy?

4. The culmination of the legal and financial struggle between the NHL and the WHA was a 1979 agreement under which four WHA clubs moved into the NHL and the other WHA owners received monetary compensation to fold their teams. The NHL Players Association agreed not to challenge the legality of this arrangement under the Sherman Act in return for a collective agreement containing the "free agency" rules we described in the *Dale McCourt* case in Chapter 3. An almost identical scenario occurred in basketball: absorption of a number of ABA teams into the NBA with the consent of the NBA Players Association, producing the collective agreement at issue in the *Leon Wood* case (also in Chapter 3). Is consent by the players through their union a sufficient response to public policy concerns about interleague mergers? If not, who should challenge such arrangements? In what circumstances, if any, should sports mergers be allowed to occur?

2. STADIUMS

Expansion into desirable cities targeted by a new league is a favorite tactic of established leagues, not only in hockey (see *Philadelphia World Hockey Club*) and in football (see *AFL v. NFL*), but also in baseball. Indeed, major league baseball, threatened in the late 1950s by Branch Rickey's proposed Continental Baseball League, hastily undertook its first expansion in this century—into New York and Houston in the National League and Washington and Kansas City in the American League.[i]

However effective these preemptive steps may be in opposing the new sporting venture, judges understandably feel qualms about erecting absolute bars against such league action. Such a rule would forever deny fans in "virgin" cities the opportunity to secure a team in the established major league. Even assuming an upstart league came along, at best these fans would acquire a team in the less attractive league that would still be the city's only team in that sport. Ideally, there should be two or more major league teams in each sport playing in the same city, at least if the population is not so small that it effectively constitutes a natural monopoly market. Fans would then have a choice of which team to patronize and clubs would face pressure to be more efficient managers and to charge lower ticket prices. There is, however, a major obstacle to accomplishing that goal—the limited number of stadiums and arenas available for play. We have already seen that such sports facilities are typically provided by the municipality at a heavily subsidized price; sometimes the city even gives the team valuable land upon which to build a privately owned facility, such as the land the Dodgers secured in Chavez Ravine when the team was induced to move from Brooklyn to Los Angeles. The next case considers whether, once the established team has secured a stadium through either full ownership or an exclusive long-term lease, a newcomer team can demand access to this "essential facility."[j]

---

[i]. See Lance E. Davis, "Self-Regulation in Baseball: 1909–71," Chapter 10 of Roger Noll, ed., *Government and the Sports Business* (Washington D.C.: Brookings, 1974).

[j]. See generally James R. Ratner, *Should There Be an Essential Facility Doctrine?*, 21 U.C. Davis L. Rev. 327 (1988).

HECHT v. PRO–FOOTBALL, INC.

United States Court of Appeals, District of Columbia, 1977.
570 F.2d 982.

WILKEY, CIRCUIT JUDGE.

[With the successful launching of their eight-team football venture in 1960, the American Football League owners began planning in 1965 for expansion into two new cities, one of which was a current National Football League city. Hecht and his partners believed that Washington, D.C., was a prime candidate for an AFL team they wanted to start, but they needed a stadium in which to play. The one existing facility in the area, RFK Stadium, was owned by the U.S. Government, but was subject to a 30–year lease under which Pro–Football Inc.'s Redskins were the exclusive football tenant. Although the federal government's Interior Department wanted to offer a lease to an AFL franchise, the Redskins were unwilling to grant explicit permission for that step. Having lost out on expansion (the AFL went into Miami instead), Hecht sued the Redskins and the NFL, alleging a violation of § 2 of the Sherman Act. This decision considered Hecht's appeal from the trial jury's verdict in favor of the defendant.

The target of the appeal was a number of jury instructions made by the trial judge. The first concerned whether, even assuming that professional football was the appropriate product market, the entire country or only the D.C. area was the relevant geographic market.]

* * *

The relevant geographic market is "the area of effective competition," the area "in which the seller operates, and to which the purchaser can practicably turn for supplies." It is well settled that the relevant market "need not be nationwide," and that "where the relevant competitive market covers only a small area the Sherman Act may be invoked to prevent unreasonable restraints within that area." Indeed, courts have regularly identified relevant geographic markets as single cities or towns, and even portions thereof.

In this case Hecht sought to enter the market for professional football in Washington, D.C. He argues that the Redskins frustrated his entry by denying him use of RFK stadium, access to which was a condition precedent to his submitting a successful franchise application. Given this posture of the case, it seems evident that the relevant geographical market is the D.C. metropolitan area: it is here that "the seller operates;" it is here alone that the Redskins' customers (primarily, their ticket purchasers) can "practically turn" for the supply of professional football. Hecht sought to compete for these customers by obtaining a franchise of his own, and it can scarcely be doubted that "the area of effective competition" between him and the Redskins would be the nation's capital.

The trial court, however, defined the relevant geographical market as "the area of effective competition for the acquisition, location and operation of a professional football franchise in the years 1965 and 1966." It is true, of course, that Hecht had to "compete" with other cities before he could assure himself of a franchise for Washington; yet this is hardly the competition that is at issue here. Hecht is not complaining that the Redskins' restrictive covenant prevented him from entering "the national market for football franchises;" obviously, Hecht could have entered that market, notwithstanding the Redskins' lease, from any other city. Hecht is complaining, rather, that the restrictive covenant on RFK Stadium in Washington, D.C., prevented him from entering the market for professional football in Washington; this is "the area which the alleged restraints affect." The "national competition" was but a preliminary, if necessary, step to a distinctly local end. We hold, therefore, that the trial judge erred in failing to instruct the jury that the relevant geographic market is the area of metropolitan Washington, D.C., in which Hecht and the Redskins would have effectively competed for customers.[12]

Monopolistic Intent and "Natural Monopoly."

The offense of "monopolization" under Sherman Act § 2 implicates both the possession of monopoly power, "monopoly in the concrete," and an element of willfulness or intent. To demonstrate intent to monopolize, however, a plaintiff need not always prove that the defendant acquired or maintained his monopoly power by means of exclusionary, unfair, or predatory acts. At least since *Alcoa*, it has been clear that the requisite intent can be inferred if a defendant maintains his power by conscious and willful business policies, however legal, that inevitably result in the exclusion or limitation of actual or potential competition. In accordance with *Alcoa*, Hecht requested an instruction that the jury could find monopolistic intent if it found that the Redskins had consciously engaged in acts or contracts, whether lawful or unlawful, that "maintained and protected" their monopoly over professional football in Washington. The trial judge refused to give this instruction. Instead, he ruled that the *Alcoa* theory of intent (viz., an inference of monopolistic intent without a showing of specific unfair practices) was not available to Hecht unless he proved that the Washington metropolitan area could support two professional football teams. We hold that this instruction was error.

In order to explain the trial judge's chain of reasoning, it is necessary to elaborate somewhat the teaching of *Alcoa*. In that opinion, Judge

---

12. These customers would include potential season ticket holders and occasional ticket buyers, and, to a lesser extent, purchasers of local radio and pre-season television broadcasting rights. Most of a professional football team's broadcasting revenue, of course, derives from the national television contract, which is negotiated by the league. As testimony at trial indicated, however, individual teams have very little control over the revenue they derive from this contract, and thus the most important factor in considering location of a franchise is the potential "gate" in the home city. For this reason, national television audiences and national television contract revenues should be ignored in ascertaining the relevant market here....

Hand recognized, as noted above, that monopolistic intent may be inferred from conscious business practices that inevitably produce or maintain monopoly power. Judge Hand also recognized, of course, that there are situations in which an inference of monopolistic intent absent a showing of specific unfair practices would be improper. One such situation is where defendant has a "natural monopoly" where, in Judge Hand's words, "[a] market [is] so limited that it is impossible to produce at all and meet the cost of production except by a plant large enough to supply the whole demand."[26] In the wake of *Alcoa*, accordingly, a substantial body of case law has developed, holding that the "characteristics of a natural monopoly make it inappropriate to apply the usual rule that success in driving competitors from the market is evidence of illegal monopolization." These cases hold, in short, that a natural monopolist does not violate § 2 unless he "acquired or maintained [his] power through the use of means which are 'exclusionary, unfair or predatory.'" In this case, therefore, the trial judge properly told the jury that if it found the Redskins to have a natural monopoly, "such a monopoly does not violate the antitrust laws unless it was acquired or maintained by exclusionary, unfair, or predatory means."

The trial judge further instructed the jury, however, that Hecht bore the burden of proving that the Redskins did not have a natural monopoly.

* * *

This part of the instruction, we think, was incorrect. It is the clear thrust of *Alcoa* that, once a plaintiff has proven the defendant's maintenance of its monopoly power through conscious business practices, a rebuttable presumption is established that defendant has the requisite intent to monopolize. The defendant can defeat this presumption by showing that it had monopoly, as some have greatness, "thrust upon it,"—that its power derives from "superior skill, foresight and industry" or (as is particularly relevant here) from the advantages of natural monopoly conditions. Both the Supreme Court and the lower courts have echoed this position. We are not called upon in this case to elaborate the various circumstances under which the burden of proof in § 2 cases might shift to defendant; we hold merely that when, as here, a defendant seeks to avoid a charge of monopolization by asserting that it has a natural monopoly owing to the market's inability to support two competitors, the defendant, and not the plaintiff, bears the burden of proof on that score.

This holding finds firm grounding in antitrust policy. To hold otherwise could effectively mean that a defendant is entitled to remain

---

26. *United States v. Aluminum Co. of America*, 148 F.2d at 430. See C. Kaysen & D. Turner, *Antitrust Policy* 191 (1959):

Natural monopoly. In the economic sense, natural monopoly is monopoly resulting from economies of scale, a relationship between the size of the market and the size of the most efficient firm such that one firm of efficient size can produce all or more than the market can take at a remunerative price, and can continually expand its capacity at less cost than that of a new firm entering the business.

free of competition unless the plaintiff can prove, not only that he would be a viable competitor, but also that he and defendant both would survive. This result would be ironic indeed: we cannot say that it is in the public interest to have the incumbent as its sole theatre, or its sole newspaper, or its sole football team, merely because the incumbent got there first. Assuming that there is no identity of performance, the public has an obvious interest in competition, "even though that competition be an elimination bout." "It has been the law for centuries," Justice Holmes once wrote, "that a man may set up a business in a small country town, too small to support more than one, although thereby he expects and intends to ruin some one already there, and succeeds in his intent." The newcomer and the incumbent may both succeed, or either or both may fail; this is what competition is all about.

Essential Facility.

Hecht contends that the District Court erred in failing to give his requested instruction concerning the "essential facility" doctrine. We agree. The essential facility doctrine, also called the "bottleneck principle," states that "where facilities cannot practicably be duplicated by would-be competitors, those in possession of them must allow them to be shared on fair terms. It is illegal restraint of trade to foreclose the scarce facility."[36] This principle of antitrust law derives from the Supreme Court's 1912 decision in *United States v. Terminal R. R. Ass'n*,[37] and was recently reaffirmed in *Otter Tail Power Co. v. United States*;[38] the principle has regularly been invoked by the lower courts. To be "essential" a facility need not be indispensable; it is sufficient if duplication of the facility would be economically infeasible and if denial of its use inflicts a severe handicap on potential market entrants. Necessarily, this principle must be carefully delimited: the antitrust laws do not require that an essential facility be shared if such sharing would be impractical

---

36. A. D. Neale, *The Antitrust Laws of the United States* 67 (2d ed. 1970); id. at 66–69, 127–31. See L. A. Sullivan, *Antitrust* 131 (1977):

[I]f a group of competitors, acting in concert, operate a common facility and if due to natural advantage, custom, or restrictions of scale, it is not feasible for excluded competitors to duplicate the facility, the competitors who operate the facility must give access to the excluded competitors on reasonable, non-discriminatory terms.

37. 224 U.S. 383 (1912). In *Terminal R.R.*, a group of railroads had won control of all railroad switching facilities in St. Louis; topographical factors prevented potential competitors from gaining access to the city via other routes. The Court held:

[W]hen, as here, the inherent conditions are such as to prohibit any other reasonable means of entering the city, the combination of every such facility under the exclusive ownership and control of less than all of the companies under compulsion to use them violates both the first and second sections of the [Sherman Act].

The Court ordered the railroads to amend their agreement to provide "for the admission of any existing or future railroad to joint ownership and control of the combined terminal properties" on equal terms.

38. 410 U.S. 366, 377–78 (1973). In *Otter Tail*, municipalities sought to compete with defendant power company by building their own electric facilities. The municipalities could not afford to construct their own subtransmission lines, however, and defendant refused to "wheel" power for them over its own lines. The court found that Otter Tail's subtransmission lines were a scarce facility and that its refusal to share them violated § 2.

or would inhibit the defendant's ability to serve its customers adequately.

In this case Hecht presented evidence that RFK stadium is the only stadium in the D.C. metropolitan area that is suitable for the exhibition of professional football games. He also presented evidence that proper agreements regarding locker facilities, practice sessions, choice of playing dates, and so forth would have made sharing of the stadium practical and convenient. Accordingly, Hecht requested an instruction that if the jury found (1) that use of RFK stadium was essential to the operation of a professional football team in Washington; (2) that such stadium facilities could not practicably be duplicated by potential competitors; (3) that another team could use RFK stadium in the Redskins' absence without interfering with the Redskins' use; and (4) that the restrictive covenant in the lease prevented equitable sharing of the stadium by potential competitors, then the jury must find the restrictive covenant to constitute a contract in unreasonable restraint of trade, in violation of Sherman Act §§ 1 and 2. This instruction was substantially correct and failure to give it was prejudicial error.

Remanded for new trial.

Unfortunately for Hecht, despite the above ruling (which was the second appellate court reversal of a judgment for the Redskins—the first overturned a summary judgment on state action grounds, cited at 444 F.2d 931 (D.C.Cir.1971)), he still had evidentiary problems. The two main defenses upon which the Redskins would have relied during retrial were that the University of Maryland's Byrd Stadium just outside Washington in College Park was a suitable alternative that Hecht could have used, and that Hecht was not in fact injured because the AFL would have never given him a franchise in the first place. (The second defense was supported by the testimony of all of the AFL owners in the early 1960s, most of whom since that time had become partners of the Redskins in the NFL, with Barron Hilton, former owner of the Los Angeles/San Diego Chargers, being the exception.) Because of this, Hecht finally agreed to settle the case in 1979, about nine years after it had been filed, for $200,000.

Questions for Discussion

1. If you were counsel for an NFL team negotiating a lease with a local stadium authority, would you seek an exclusivity clause of the type the Redskins had, in light of *Hecht*? Even if it turned out that § 2 prevented the team from enforcing that provision, might it still have some value to the NFL team in the event a team in a new league sought to obtain a lease?

2. In *Fishman v. Estate of Wirtz*, 807 F.2d 520 (7th Cir.1986) (with Judge Easterbrook dissenting at length), the court considered a claim that Chicago Stadium was an "essential facility" for the NBA Chicago Bulls, which could not lawfully be withheld from Fishman, a prospective buyer of

the Bulls, by the Wirtz family (owners of the Stadium and the NHL Chicago Black Hawks) in their competition to purchase the Bulls (in 1972, for $3.3 million). What is the appropriate antitrust verdict?

In *USFL v. NFL*, 634 F.Supp. 1155, 1176–80 (S.D.N.Y.1986), the district judge granted summary judgment to the defendant NFL against a feature of the USFL's wide-ranging antitrust claim—the allegation that NFL teams had hampered efforts by potential USFL franchises to play in stadiums where NFL teams had leases. Most of the alleged offenders were NFL teams that leased municipally-owned stadiums (for example, the Minneapolis Humphrey Metrodome, the Detroit-area Pontiac Silverdome, Pittsburgh's Three Rivers Stadium, and Denver's Mile High Stadium). The judge held that any NFL team's effort to persuade the public stadium authority not to grant a lease to a USFL rival, or at least a lease on unfavorable terms, was insulated from antitrust scrutiny by the *Noerr–Pennington* doctrine. That doctrine, based on a pair of Supreme Court decisions bearing these names, holds that a private actor's effort to persuade a public body to exercise its prerogative favorably to the petitioner's position cannot violate the Sherman Act even if done for an anticompetitive purpose. The USFL did not appeal this feature of the trial judge's ruling, which held that such First Amendment immunity to antitrust regulation applied to municipal decisions made in a commercial or a proprietary (as well as in a regulatory) capacity. (The Second Circuit's opinion on the USFL's appeal of other aspects of this litigation is reproduced later in this chapter.)

A more recent judicial ruling addressed the same problem of a team using its control over a facility to secure control in a sports market, though this time in the merchandising side of the business. The suit was actually filed under the Illinois Antitrust Act, but the Illinois state courts have interpreted this statute as being substantively identical to the Sherman Act.

WEINBERG v. CHICAGO BLACKHAWK HOCKEY TEAM

Appellate Court of Illinois, First District, Third Division, 1995.
274 Ill.App.3d 637, 210 Ill.Dec. 860, 653 N.E.2d 1322.

RIZZI, JUSTICE.

[Mark Weinberg had created an unofficial program for the Chicago Blackhawks home games, *The Blue Line*, which he sold outside Chicago Stadium. *The Blue Line* soon began to outsell the Blackhawks' own program, *Face Off*, which was available inside the stadium. Weinberg periodically asked the Blackhawks for media credentials and press access to team practices, press conferences, and post-game interviews, as well as to the packets of statistical material, player photographs, and the like that were periodically passed out to the media. The Blackhawks always refused these requests, with one official allegedly having said that "I don't think we want to set aside credentials for a publication that is conceivably competing against *Goal* [the predecessor to *Face Off*]."

Weinberg filed suit alleging that the Blackhawks had violated § 3(3), the "anti-monopoly" provision of the Illinois statute that was modelled on § 2 of the Sherman Act. After the trial judge granted summary dismissal of the claims, which were based on both "monopoly leveraging" and "essential facilities" doctrines, Weinberg appealed.]

* * *

Monopoly leveraging occurs where a party has monopoly power in one market, and uses this power to extract a competitive advantage in a second market. In the present case, plaintiffs allege that the Blackhawks are using their monopoly power in professional hockey in Chicago to gain a competitive edge in the sale of game day programs by illegally refusing to deal with plaintiffs.

In order to state a claim for monopoly leveraging under § 3(3) of the Act, a plaintiff must allege (1) that defendant has monopoly power in one market, (2) that defendant used this power to exact a competitive advantage for itself in a second market (3) that the competitive advantage was not won on competitive merits, but rather stemmed from a coercive use of the monopoly power in the first market, (4) that the defendant acted with the intent to gain the unwarranted advantage in the second market and (5) the anti-competitive conduct resulted in a lessening of competition.

In the present case, we believe plaintiffs' complaint adequately contains allegations of fact supporting a finding of all the necessary elements. As to the first element, the Blackhawks unquestionably have monopoly power in National Hockey League hockey in Chicago. We note that a professional sports team, like the Blackhawks, is an absolutely unique entity providing the public with an absolutely unique product. The second element, concerning the use of monopoly power to gain an advantage in a second market, is established by the allegations relating to the Blackhawks' refusal to grant plaintiffs media credentials and press access to prevent *The Blue Line* from competing with *Face Off*. The same allegations satisfy the third element. The advantage *Face Off* has acquired was achieved not through pro-competitive efficiencies, but rather through denying plaintiffs access to the Blackhawks' games. The fourth element, intent, is supplied by the quote from the assistant director of public relations wherein he stated: "I don't think we want to set aside credentials for a publication that is conceivably competing against *Goal*."

The only remaining element under the monopoly leveraging theory is whether plaintiffs have sufficiently alleged that the Blackhawks' course of conduct has had an anti-competitive effect.... The complaint clearly states that the Blackhawks have effectively excluded *The Blue*

Line from the immediate and intimate access to the games and players to which the Blackhawks' own publication enjoys and to which one would reasonably expect any game day program to have. From the very existence of media credentials, press boxes, press rooms and press conferences, we can reasonably infer that a publication without access to these credentials, locations and events is less competitive than it would otherwise be. Through the course of conduct alleged in the complaint, plaintiffs are unable to obtain the quality of photographs, reports and interviews, including answers to plaintiffs' own questions which they would otherwise have. Denying such access necessarily makes *The Blue Line* less competitive.

It is no answer to argue as the Blackhawks have that *The Blue Line* easily outsells their own publication. First and foremost, such information is not contained in plaintiffs' complaint and it is to the four corners of plaintiffs' complaint which we look in reviewing a motion to dismiss for failing to state a cause of action. Moreover, an inquiry into whether competition has been harmed is not a mere exercise in bean counting. One of the primary goals of antitrust legislation is to enhance consumer welfare. Accordingly, if *The Blue Line* cannot put forth its best program due to the monopolistic practices being engaged in by the Blackhawks, then its readers, however many, are suffering an anti-competitive effect. Consumer welfare is measured as much, if not more so, by the quality of a product as it is by the quantity being sold.

* * *

The plaintiffs here prevail for another reason. Plaintiffs' complaint also states a cause of action based on the essential facilities doctrine. The impetus behind this doctrine is the fear that a monopolist will be able to extend monopoly power from one market to another. *MCI Communications v. American Tel. & Tel. Co.* 708 F.2d 1081, 1132 (7th Cir.1983). Antitrust laws, therefore, require that a party controlling an essential facility provide access to that facility on non-discriminatory terms.

To state a cause of action under § 3(3) of the Act based on the essential facilities doctrine, a plaintiff must allege (1) control of the essential facility by a monopolist, (2) a competitor's inability to practically or reasonably duplicate the essential facility, (3) the denial of the use of the facility to a competitor, (4) the feasibility of providing the facility and (5) that denial has had an anti-competitive effect.

In the present case, plaintiffs have sufficiently alleged facts to support all five elements. First, plaintiffs have alleged that the Blackhawks have exclusive control over the granting of media credentials, access to the players and coaching staff and attendance at games, practices, press conferences and post game interviews. Second, the above allegation gives rise to the reasonable inference that plaintiffs cannot reasonably duplicate the access to the games, players and so forth. Third, plaintiffs have clearly alleged that they have been denied the use of the facility they are seeking. Fourth, the feasibility of providing the facility is demonstrated by the allegations that such access is regularly granted to others. Finally, as stated above, we believe that the complaint gives rise to the reasonable inference that the denial of access complained of has had the anti-competitive effect of lessening the quality of plaintiffs' publication.

The Blackhawks make much out of the fact that the plaintiffs are not seeking the use of a physical facility, but access which they argue is intangible. We fail to see any real significance in this distinction. Moreover, what plaintiffs really sought was use of the Chicago Stadium, which while sadly is no longer standing, certainly was at the time a physical facility.

* * *

Reversed and remanded.

Questions For Discussion

1. The antitrust offense of monopolization requires that defendants possess (or are very likely to acquire) monopoly market power. Apparently, in this case, the plaintiff's *The Blue Line* was greatly outselling the Black Hawks' official program. On what basis, then, might the Black Hawks be found in violation of this monopoly standard? Is the relevant market something that goes beyond the sale of game day programs in or around the arena? On remand, how should the jury decide this case?

---

3. TELEVISION CONTRACTS

The last essential ingredient for a viable sports league is a reasonably lucrative television contract. This source of guaranteed revenue is needed not so much to pay the new league's stadium rentals and administrative expenses, as to pay the players for whose services the new league is bidding against its entrenched rival. The 1961 Sports Broadcasting Act permitted the NFL (and other leagues) to sell in a single exclusive package the right to televise their games. The amounts received by leagues from networks for these television rights have risen at a remarkable pace: from approximately $325,000 per club in the NFL's first exclusive network contract in 1962 to $70 million a year in 1998, under contracts with three "free" and two cable networks. A practical question is whether *not* having such a television deal presents an insurmountable barrier to any new league. A second question is whether there is anything the law can or will do about this barrier. The next case offers some extended judicial reflections on the latter question.

USFL v. NFL[k]

United States Court of Appeals, Second Circuit, 1988.
842 F.2d 1335.

WINTER, CIRCUIT JUDGE.

[As we saw earlier, challenges launched against the National Football League's dominance of professional football by the American Foot-

---

k. On the rise and demise of both the USFL and its lawsuit, see Byrne, *The $1*

ball League in the 1960s and the World Football League in the 1970s produced important antitrust (and player contract) decisions. This pattern continued with the United States Football League's abortive challenge in the 1980s. The USFL began as a spring football league in March 1983, bolstered by television contracts with ABC and ESPN. However, after losing $200 million in three years, the league played its last game in July 1985. At the urging of Donald Trump, owner of the New Jersey Generals, the USFL made an effort to move to a fall schedule in 1986, supposedly the more natural time for fans to watch football. However, the League was unable to secure a network television contract and it folded. Blaming the NFL for its failure, the USFL sued.

Though the case did go to trial and the jury found that the NFL had violated § 2 of the Sherman Act by monopolizing the market for professional football in the United States, the USFL won only a Pyrrhic victory because the jury's damage verdict was for just $1.00 (which was trebled by statute to $3.00). An important factor was that the jury rejected the USFL's principal allegation—that the NFL had denied the USFL access to the essential resource of network television. The following decision deals with the USFL's appeal on that issue.]

THE HISTORY OF MAJOR-LEAGUE PROFESSIONAL FOOTBALL.

* * *

The USFL was founded in May 1982 by David Dixon as a league that would play spring football. The league began play in March 1983 with teams in Birmingham, Boston, Chicago, Denver, Los Angeles, Michigan, New Jersey, Oakland, Philadelphia, Phoenix, Tampa and Washington. In part because of the location of its teams in major television markets, the USFL was able to obtain multimillion dollar network and cable television contracts with ABC and ESPN. Nevertheless, for reasons explored in detail infra, the USFL demonstrated little stability. Over its three seasons of spring football (one of which was a "lame-duck" season commenced after an announced decision to shift to fall play), the USFL clubs played in twenty-two cities, and had thirty-nine principal owners. None of the majority owners of an original USFL team was a majority owner by 1986 when a planned fall schedule was aborted by the $1.00 verdict.

* * *

THE NFL'S TELEVISION CONTRACTS.

[Here the court traced the history of the NFL's relationship with television, noting that the growth of the league was closely related to the growth of television. Prior to 1961, NFL teams sold their TV rights

---

League, note c above. The legal issues are presented in Lori J. Brown, *The Battle: From the Playing Field to the Courtroom—* United States Football League v. National Football League, 18 Toledo U. L. Rev. 871 (1987).

individually. However, following the AFL's league-wide network contract with ABC in 1960, Commissioner Rozelle negotiated a league contract with CBS under which the NFL pooled all the clubs' TV rights and sold them as a package, and then divided the revenues equally among the teams. One reason for that step was to maintain competitive balance on the field by not allowing revenue disparities among the teams to get too great. However, before the CBS contract could be implemented, the 1953 antitrust decision in *United States v. NFL* that we read in Chapter 7 forced the NFL to secure a special antitrust exemption from Congress (the Sports Broadcasting Act of 1961), which permitted pooled-rights league contracts with networks for "sponsored telecasting."

The NFL's contract with CBS earned it $4,650,000 per year in 1962 and 1963, amounts that jumped to $14 million per year in 1964 and 1965. In 1964, the AFL switched from ABC to NBC with a five-year, $36 million deal. In 1966, Congress amended the Sports Broadcasting Act to permit the NFL and AFL to merge, after being specifically informed that the new combined league would maintain television contracts with at least two networks. In 1970, the NFL entered into its long-running contract with ABC to televise a game on Monday nights. The NFL's relationship with the three networks was maintained through the USFL's emergence, producing total television revenues of $186 million in 1970–73, $268 million in 1974–77, $646 million in 1978–81, and over $2.1 billion in 1982–86.]

* * *

The ABC, CBS and NBC contracts from 1970 onward have given each network rights of first negotiation and first refusal to decide whether to continue its NFL contract for subsequent years. The NFL's 1982–86 contracts were nonexclusive and did not forbid a network from televising another football league's games at any time when it was not broadcasting NFL games.... Because the NFL was forbidden by its network contracts to televise games on cable, cable television contracts were open to a competing league, although such contracts are less lucrative than network contracts. When the NFL's network contracts expired in 1981 and 1986, the networks were free to contract with a competing league's games for all time slots.

* * *

Management of the USFL.

The USFL was conceived and organized in 1981 to play in the spring rather than the fall. Its founders believed that public demand for football was not satisfied by the NFL's and the colleges' fall seasons; that cable television, which could not televise NFL games under the existing NFL-network contracts, would offer unique opportunities for television revenues and exposure; that a spring football league would face limited competition; that there was a sufficient supply of football players for two leagues; and that a spring league could draft college players and put them on the field even before the NFL draft.

The USFL's founders placed a high priority on the fans' perception of the quality of play. They intended to use major stadiums and to hire well-known coaches. At the same time, they wanted the league to control costs. For its first season, therefore, the USFL established budget guidelines for player salaries of between $1.3 and $1.5 million per team.

The USFL's founders did not seek to obtain a television contract for fall play. Before fielding a team, however, the USFL received bids for a spring television contract from ABC and NBC and from two cable networks, ESPN and the Turner Broadcasting System. The league entered a four-year contract with ABC, and a two-year contract with ESPN. The ABC agreement provided for ABC to pay the USFL $18 million for the 1983 and 1984 seasons, with options exercisable by ABC at $14 million for 1985 and at $18 million for 1986. ESPN contracted to televise USFL games for two years at rights fees of $4 million for 1983 and $7 million for 1984. The USFL began with eight of its twelve teams in the nation's top ten television markets. The ABC contract required the USFL to field teams in the three largest television markets (New York, Los Angeles and Chicago) and in at least four of the five other top-ten television markets in which teams were originally located (Philadelphia, Boston, Detroit, San Francisco/Oakland and Washington).

The USFL's first year of play, 1983, was a mixed success. The league received extensive media exposure when it signed Heisman Trophy winner Herschel Walker to a three-year, $3,250,000 contract. The Nielsen television rating for the first week of games was 14.2, a figure comparable to NFL ratings. As the season went on, however, the USFL's television ratings declined; average television ratings for the year were 6.23 on ABC and 3.28 on ESPN. Average attendance for the year was approximately 25,000. Nevertheless, these figures were consistent with the league's and networks' preseason projections.

On the financial side, the picture was not as bright. The USFL lost a total of almost $40 million, or an average of $3.3 million per team. The league had projected losses of only about $2 million per year for each team over the first three years. The unanticipated financial losses were chiefly the result of the failure to stay within the original salary guidelines. Indeed, in a November 1983 letter to other owners, Tad Taube of the Oakland team warned that: "If we are not successful in establishing player [salary] caps I can guarantee you that there will not be a USFL within three years, irrespective of improved revenue [from] television.... We have sighted the enemy and they are us!"

The USFL's second year was marked by change. Four teams shifted locations. For example, the owner of the Chicago franchise exchanged that franchise for the Phoenix franchise, taking his winning Chicago coach and players while the original Phoenix team moved to Chicago under a new owner. The league, over the objection of some owners, expanded from twelve teams to eighteen. Five of the original owners left the league. Some of the new owners, notably Donald Trump of the New Jersey Generals, believed that the USFL ought to play in the fall.

Thereafter, the issue of when to play became divisive, and several owners came to believe that Trump was trying to bring about a merger with the NFL that would include only some USFL teams.

The NFL introduced extensive evidence designed to prove that the USFL followed Trump's merger strategy, and that this strategy ultimately caused the USFL's downfall. The merger strategy, the NFL argued, involved escalating financial competition for players as a means of putting pressure on NFL expenses, playing in the fall to impair NFL television revenues, shifting USFL franchises out of cities where NFL teams played into cities thought to be logical expansion (through merger) cities for the NFL, and, finally, bringing the antitrust litigation now before us.

Throughout the second half of 1983 and early 1984, several USFL owners escalated spending on player salaries. USFL teams, for example, signed established NFL players such as running back Joe Cribbs and defensive back Gary Barbaro. Trump, in particular, signed a number of players who were still under contract with the NFL to future contracts, including superstar Lawrence Taylor of the New York Giants. USFL owners also signed many top players coming out of college, for example, wide receiver Anthony Carter and quarterback Jim Kelly. The USFL's spending on players greatly outpaced its revenues. The owner of the Los Angeles team, for example, committed the team to $13.1 million in salaries and bonuses for just one season. He even entered into a multiyear, $40 million contract with just one player, Steve Young of Brigham Young University.

By the end of the 1984 season, USFL franchises in two of the top three television markets, Chicago and Los Angeles, had failed, and only four of the original owners remained in the league. The league was not a failure as entertainment, however. Despite a decline in the USFL's television ratings to 5.7 on ABC and 2.8 on ESPN, ABC exercised its option to carry the USFL in the spring of 1985 at $14 million and offered a new contract worth $175 million for four years in the spring beginning in 1986. ESPN offered a contract worth $70 million over three years.

Nevertheless, during an August 1984 owners' meeting, the USFL decided to move to the fall in 1986. This decision was made despite: (i) ABC's warning that such a move would breach its contract for the spring of 1985 and 1986; (ii) the contrary recommendations of a management consulting firm, McKinsey & Company, which the USFL had retained for $600,000 to consider the advisability of a fall season; and (iii) the contrary recommendations of the USFL's directors of operations and marketing.

Moreover, Eddie Einhorn, a USFL owner who was to represent the USFL in negotiations to secure a network contract for the fall, warned that moving from large television markets to "merger" cities too quickly might preclude the securing of a network contract. Nevertheless, in the ensuing months, the USFL withdrew from Chicago, Detroit, Philadelphia, Pittsburgh and Washington, D.C.—each a large television market with an NFL team—and moved into Baltimore (which had lost its NFL team in 1984) and Orlando (which had no NFL team). Through mergers, the USFL bolstered franchises in Oakland (which had lost the NFL Raiders to Los Angeles) and Phoenix (which had been discussed as a possible NFL expansion city). The decision to move to the fall damaged the USFL's relations with ABC and ESPN. The former withheld a significant portion of the USFL's rights fees for the 1985 season, while the latter demanded a renegotiation of its proposed 1985–87 USFL contract.

In October 1984, the instant litigation was begun. The USFL's 1985 "lame-duck" spring season appears to have been affected adversely by the now publicly announced move to the fall. The league's television ratings declined to 4.1 on ABC and 2.0 on ESPN. By the end of the season, several owners had withdrawn financial support for their teams, and a number of clubs were no longer meeting their payrolls and other bills. The USFL scheduled eight teams for its fall 1986 season, which was ultimately cancelled after the verdict in this case. Only one team (New Jersey), was in a top-ten television market. One other team (Tampa Bay) was in a top-twenty market. Three teams were located in Florida (Jacksonville, Orlando and Tampa Bay) but only one was west of the Mississippi River (Phoenix). In three years, USFL teams had left fourteen of the twenty-two cities in which they had played.

* * *

[At trial, the jury found that the NFL had violated § 2 of the Sherman Act in a number of ways. One violation was an effort to co-opt potential USFL owners such as Donald Trump or franchise locations such as Oakland (a strategy sketched in a presentation to NFL executives by Harvard Business School Professor Michael Porter, called "Conquering the USFL"). Another was expanding NFL rosters from 45 to 49 players and conducting a draft of USFL players, in line with a memorandum prepared by NFL labor negotiator Jack Donlan, called "Spending the USFL Dollar" by bidding up player salaries. But the jury rejected the USFL argument that the NFL had monopolized access to television in the fall, a key predicate to the USFL's damages claim. The following is the appellate court's analysis of that crucial issue.]

1. *Liability*

A. *The Sports Broadcasting Act.*

[The court considered the USFL's contention that the NFL's contracts with all three networks violated Judge Grim's 1953 injunction, and was not saved by the Sports Broadcasting Act which, the USFL said, limited a league to only one network. After looking at both the unambiguous statutory language and the legislative history, the court concluded that the SBA did not limit a league to only one network.]

* * *

In any event, the passage of the 1966 NFL–AFL merger statute provides conclusive evidence that Congress did not intend the 1961 Act to prohibit NFL contracts with more than one network. When considering this legislation, Congress was explicitly informed that the merged league would continue to broadcast its games on "at least 2 networks,"[18] and no concern whatsoever was expressed in Congress that such conduct was either undesirable or would go beyond the scope of the 1961 Act's exemption. Moreover, while permitting the merger, Congress added a further limitation to the exemption to protect high school games from televised competition with the NFL. The lack of a "one network" limitation in the 1966 merger bill thus dooms the USFL's claims. Accordingly, we hold that the mere existence of the NFL contracts with the three networks does not violate the antitrust laws. Having made this determination, we need not consider whether the decree in *United States v. National Football League* has any collateral-estoppel effect.

B. *The "Dilution Effect."*

* * *

Because the [USFL's next two] claims are based on the so-called "dilution effect" of the NFL's contracts with the three networks, a separate discussion of the concept of a "dilution effect" and its role in the professional football industry is necessary.

The term "dilution effect" comes from a CBS business study ordered by Neil Pilson, CBS Sports' President, and completed in June 1984. CBS conducted the study because it was apprehensive over ABC's signing a USFL fall contract and desired the leverage a second league would afford it in its negotiations with the NFL. The study estimated the economic impact on CBS of the televising of USFL games in the fall under various scenarios....

As explained by Pilson, the value of a USFL fall contract to CBS was determined (in simplified fashion) as follows. From the estimated gross advertising revenues would be subtracted estimates of: (i) expenses related to production; (ii) losses in revenues that would otherwise have

---

18. During the hearings on the merger bill, Commissioner Rozelle testified "that because of the logistics of handling perhaps 13 or 14 games on a Sunday afternoon, [the NFL] would require at least 2 networks." In response to the question of whether New York City residents would be able to see professional football on television when the other New York club was playing a home game, Rozelle said that the league would try to do so, "which is why I feel we will probably have to go to two networks, to assure that each of the 26 or 28 teams has all of its road games brought back to its home city." Moreover, the NFL and AFL submitted a memorandum to the subcommittee concerning whether the merger would result in reduced broadcasts of football games:

Because a single network cannot practicably establish as many as twenty-eight regional networks and because the expanded league desires to maintain its present level of club television income, the plan contemplates the continued use of two networks by the expanded league, e.g., on a conference or other divisional basis. Thus, both during the period prior to the expiration of the existing television contracts and afterwards, it is contemplated that there will be continued home viewer access to duplicate broadcasts, including telecasts of other league games into home cities on days when the home team is playing at home.

been earned by programs preempted by USFL games, or "preemptive impact"; (iii) decreases in advertising revenues from NFL games resulting from the addition of USFL games, or "dilution effect"; and (iv) rights fees to the USFL. Pilson testified that when these estimates were made in June 1984, the resultant calculation, CBS's profit, was negative. The USFL argues that, but for the "dilution effect" of $50 million, the sum would have been sufficiently positive to make a USFL contract attractive. The USFL assumes that the "dilution effect" was experienced equally by all three networks and thus concludes that the effect of NFL's network contracts was to exclude all competition.

The district court instructed the jury to analyze the NFL's television contracts in light of the CBS study. Specifically, the jury was told to consider "[t]he high NFL rights fees charged to the networks, which plaintiffs allege triggered a dilution effect that makes it economically infeasible for any network to offer a satisfactory television contract to any professional football league other than the NFL." The jury rejected the USFL's claims as to the "dilution effect" in finding that the NFL had not monopolized a television submarket, that the NFL television contracts were not an unreasonable restraint, and that the NFL did not have the power to exclude a competing league from obtaining a network contract. There was ample evidence to support these conclusions.

First, the USFL concedes, as it must, that the "dilution effect" is nonexistent when the NFL network contracts expire and negotiations over new contracts are under way.... The district court's instructions directed the jury to consider the length of these contracts, then five years, in determining whether they were reasonable. Its verdict, therefore, is dispositive because the duration of the contracts was hardly unreasonable as a matter of law.

Second, there was no evidence that the result of the calculations described above would be the same for ABC as for CBS. ABC's contract was largely confined to televising a single NFL game in prime time on a weekday night. Its Sundays were free of football, and it would not encounter the scheduling problems faced by CBS in televising both NFL and USFL games on Sunday afternoons. ABC was thus free to schedule games so as to maximize revenue.... The USFL, which bore the burden of proof on this issue, called two witnesses from ABC in a position to testify about the "dilution effect" on ABC. Neither witness was questioned about the "dilution effect." Both did testify, however, that the USFL's exodus from major television markets and its other difficulties greatly diminished the value of USFL telecasts by 1985 and 1986.

Third, the conduct of the NFL and the networks indicates that neither believed their contracts to be exclusionary. Notwithstanding the early opinion of the NFL's Moyer about a network without a contract being an "open invitation to a new league," the NFL's actual conduct displayed no marked desire to lock up all three networks. Prime-time weekday telecasts were offered to NBC and CBS, both of whom already had NFL contracts, before ABC was approached. It was the testimony of both the ABC executives and CBS's Pilson, elicited by counsel for the USFL, that Rozelle routinely used the threat of leaving them without an NFL contract in order to extract from them the largest possible rights fees. If the "dilution effect" theory of exclusion were correct, the NFL could not credibly threaten to leave one network without a contract. If the theory were correct, moreover, the last network to sign with the NFL would have a bargaining advantage because its agreement would be essential to the NFL's monopoly, much as the owner of the last lot in a tract of land needed for a construction project can demand the highest price. In the NFL-network negotiations, the opposite was the case, and the last network to sign was at a bargaining disadvantage. Thus, in 1982, the NFL first signed agreements with ABC and NBC and then approached CBS. According to Pilson, CBS regarded itself as being in a very disadvantageous bargaining position. As a result, CBS paid $736 million for the new contract, an increase of more than 100% over its previous contract. On the basis of this evidence, therefore, the jury would have been hard-pressed to conclude that the NFL needed a contract with CBS to freeze out a competing league, a circumstance that would have precluded a credible threat to leave CBS without a contract and the resultant hefty increase in rights fees.

Fourth, even if the "dilution effect" theory were alive and well in 1986, the jury could have found that that "effect" was not a cause of the USFL's failure to get a network contract in that year. The CBS study was made in 1984 and was based on estimates of revenues that were plainly excessive given the circumstances of 1986. Immediately after the study was completed, the Supreme Court decided *National Collegiate Athletic Association v. Board of Regents*, 468 U.S. 85 (1984), invalidating the NCAA's exclusive control over the televising of college football games. This decision had the effect of multiplying greatly the number of college games telecast and of reducing advertising revenue generally for football games. An ABC witness also testified there was a proliferation of sporting events on network and cable television after the fall of 1984 that also reduced the advertising fees that could be charged for professional football. In addition, there were the problems of the USFL itself. The league had failed to establish fan loyalty in most places because of repeated franchise moves. Most importantly, the USFL had abandoned most major television markets, thereby rendering telecasts of its games much less valuable than had been estimated by the earlier CBS study. Finally, the disagreements among the USFL owners, the financial condition of some of the franchises, and the "lame-duck" spring season of 1985 further lessened the value of USFL telecasts in 1986. In fact, Pilson himself testified that by 1986 the events described above had rendered the "dilution effect" irrelevant to CBS's decision not to televise the USFL. In light of this evidence, the jury was free to conclude that the revenues to be expected from USFL telecasts were so low that no network would purchase them even if there were no "dilution effect."

C. "Intent and Effect" Charge.

We now consider the district court's instruction regarding liability on the USFL's television-related claims. The USFL contends that it should not have been required to show that the intent and effect of the NFL's television contracts with the major networks were exclusionary (rather than simply intent or effect) in order to prove a § 2 claim....

The district court gave the following charge with respect to the USFL's § 2 television-related claims:

> A company may not be found to have wilfully acquired or maintained monopoly power if it has acquired that power solely through the exercise of superior foresight and skill or because of natural advantages ... or because of economic or technological efficiency; ... or by laws passed by Congress.... In this regard, you should be aware that in 1966 Congress passed a law permitting the merger of the two major football leagues then existing.... Accordingly, I instruct you that the 1966 merger of the AFL and the NFL cannot be the basis for inferring that the NFL acquired monopoly power unlawfully. In addition, in 1961 Congress passed a statute that provides that a contract between a professional sports league and a television network for the sale of pooled telecast rights is not a restraint of trade in violation of the antitrust laws. Accordingly, I instruct you that the making of these contracts by the NFL with the television networks constitutes the lawful acquisition of power, [e]ven if you were to find that these contracts gave the NFL monopoly power, unless you found that the intent and effect of these agreements is to exclude a competing league or its members from selling any of their television rights.

This instruction was consistent with the Sports Broadcasting Act, discussed infra, as exempting from antitrust scrutiny a league's pooled-rights contracts with networks unless they constitute illegal monopolization or an unreasonable restraint of trade so far as competing leagues are concerned. More importantly, the intent-and-effect charge was consistent with the legal standards for illegal monopolization under § 2.

The Supreme Court has repeatedly defined monopolization as the "willful acquisition or maintenance" of monopoly power. The willfulness element certainly requires proof of intent. Proof of effect is required by definition alone to satisfy the "acquisition or maintenance" requirement.

A requirement that both intent and effect be proven is necessary to enable a trier of fact to make the critical distinction between conduct that defeats a competitor because of efficiency and consumer satisfaction, and conduct that "not only (1) tends to impair the opportunities of rivals, but also (2) either does not further competition on the merits or does so in an unnecessarily restrictive way." Hopes and dreams alone cannot support a § 2 claim of monopolization. If they did, the nationwide advertisement "Ford wants to be your car company" would constitute an open-and-shut § 2 case. Success alone is not enough or the antitrust laws would have their greatest impact on the most efficient entrepreneurs and would injure rather than protect consumers.

Proof of intent and effect is also of evidentiary value. Distinguishing between efficient and predatory conduct is extremely difficult because it is frequently the case that "[c]ompetitive and exclusionary conduct look alike." Evidence of intent and effect helps the trier of fact to evaluate the actual effect of challenged business practices in light of the intent of those who resort to such practices....

The present case is in fact a useful example of the intent-and-effect approach to determining whether certain practices are predatory. [T]he jury's conclusion that the NFL's three network contracts were not exclusionary was supported by evidence that a quality league could either have overcome the "dilution effect" or have acquired a contract when the NFL's contracts expired. The conduct of the NFL itself and the networks showed their disbelief in any exclusionary effect by the NFL's threatening to leave a network without NFL games and the networks' taking the threat seriously. The evidence also supported the conclusion that when the NFL locked up the third network, CBS, in the 1982 negotiations, it did so to obtain $736 million in rights fees, not to exclude competitors.

* * *

D. *Legitimate Business Opportunities and Profit–Maximization Charge.*

The USFL further argues that the district court erroneously charged the jury that the NFL's three network contracts were lawful if motivated by any "legitimate" purpose, including profit maximization. The pertinent charge reads as follows:

> Plaintiffs allege that the NFL coerced the networks not to give the plaintiffs a contract.... So long as they have a legitimate business purpose in doing so, defendants have no duty to limit themselves in entering into the television contracts so that other football leagues would have an easier time entering the market, or to foresee that other leagues might do so, or for any reasons to decline a profitable business opportunity.

This charge was consistent with settled precedent. "[A] firm with lawful monopoly power has no general duty to help its competitors, whether by holding a price umbrella over their heads or by otherwise pulling its competitive punches." A monopolist may not, of course, use its market power, whether obtained lawfully or not, to prevent or impede competition in the relevant market. The jury was thus properly instructed that:

> A monopoly achieved or maintained as a result of ... legitimate good business practices is not unlawful. A monopolist has the same right to compete as any other company. Under the antitrust laws, a monopolist is encouraged to compete vigorously with its competitors and to remain responsive to the needs and demands of its customers.

At the same time, a monopolist cannot use its lawfully acquired power to maintain its monopoly. In addition, there is nothing in the antitrust laws that requires a monopolist to act against its own self interest so long as the monopolist does not at the same time exercise its power to maintain that power. Thus, a monopolist is under no duty affirmatively to help or aid its competitors and is free to set as its legitimate goal the maximization of its own profits so long as it does not exercise its power to maintain that power.

The USFL challenges this charge on the ground that setting prices at a profit-maximizing level is an anticompetitive act. We disagree. Prices not based on superior efficiency do not injure competitors, but rather invite competitive entry. As we stated in *Berkey Photo* [*Inc. v. Eastman Kodak Co.*, 603 F.2d 263, 274 (2d Cir. 1979)]:

> Setting a high price may be a use of monopoly power, but it is not in itself anticompetitive. Indeed, although a monopolist may be expected to charge a somewhat higher price than would prevail in a competitive market, there is probably no better way for it to guarantee that its dominance will be challenged than by greedily extracting the highest price it can.

* * *

H. Essential–Facilities Charge.

Finally, the USFL contends that it was held to an improperly high standard of proof on its "essential-facilities" claim. We set out the pertinent charge:

> Plaintiffs allege that defendants violated Sections [1] and [2] of the Sherman Act by conspiring to and in fact denying plaintiffs access to a satisfactory national broadcast television contract for future seasons, with any one of the three networks. The legal basis for this particular claim by plaintiffs is that a network contract is an essential facility which the USFL or any other professional football league needs in order to compete in major league professional football. You should only consider this claim if you have already found, pursuant to my earlier instructions, that defendants possess monopoly power in a relevant market or submarket. If you have not found that defendants possess monopoly power, you must return a verdict in defendants' favor on this claim. In order to prove their essential "facilities" claim, plaintiffs must prove all of the following elements by a preponderance of the evidence: First: That a national broadcast television contract with at least one of the three networks, CBS, NBC or ABC, is essential to the ability of a professional football league to compete successfully in the United States; Second[:] that potential competitors of the NFL cannot as a practical matter duplicate the benefits of a network contract; Third: That the defendants control access to each of the three networks, that is, the defendants themselves have the ability by their actions to deny actual or potential competitors, such as the USFL, access to national

broadcast television—access to a national broadcast television contract; Fourth: That the defendants through their actions have exercised their ability to deny actual or potential competitors access to a national broadcast television contract by denying the USFL such access; Fifth: That a national broadcast television contract between one or more of the networks and a professional football league other than the NFL would not interfere with any of the defendants' lawful dealings with those networks.

The USFL argues first that this charge erred in failing to distinguish between a network television contract in the spring and one in the fall. The charge did, however, address the USFL's denial of "access to a satisfactory national broadcast contract for future seasons." The jury was well aware of the USFL's claim that a spring contract was unsatisfactory as an "inferior facility" or "minor league." It thus either rejected that characterization of spring football or rejected the USFL's claim that the NFL could deny the USFL access to a network in the fall. The spring-fall issue was thus before the jury.

The USFL next claims that it was error for the district court to require a showing of monopoly power in a relevant submarket or market before considering the essential-facilities claim. We fail to see why the USFL challenges this instruction because the jury did find monopoly power in a relevant market and therefore did consider the essential-facilities claim. Had the challenged instruction been omitted, the verdict would have been exactly the same.

[On the basis of this analysis of the television liability issue, the appeals court found no reason to overturn the jury's purely nominal damage award for other antitrust violations found against the NFL. The court also rejected the USFL's request to use these antitrust findings as a basis for sweeping injunctive relief—restructuring the NFL into two leagues, each limited to a single network contract.]

* * *

What the USFL seeks is essentially a judicial restructuring of major-league professional football to allow it to enter. Because of the explicit congressional authorization in 1966 for the NFL-AFL merger and single-league operation, the USFL does not attack the league structure directly. Instead, the USFL asks us to prevent networks from broadcasting, and fans from watching, NFL games in the hope that they will turn to the USFL. Absent a showing of an unlawful barrier to entry, however, new sports leagues must be prepared to make the investment of time, effort and money that develops interest and fan loyalty and results in an attractive product for the media. The jury in the present case obviously found that patient development of a loyal following among fans and an adherence to an original plan that offered long-run gains were lacking in the USFL. Instead, the USFL quickly changed to a strategy of competition with the NFL in the fall, hoping thereby to force a merger of a few USFL teams into the NFL. That led to a movement of USFL teams out of large television markets and a resultant reduction in value of USFL games to television. As USFL owner and negotiator Einhorn predicted, abandoning major television markets precluded the possibility of obtaining a network contract. The USFL hoped, however, that if a merger did not occur, a jury verdict in the instant litigation followed by a decree effectively forcing a network to televise its product would save the day. Instead, the jury found that the failure of the USFL was not the result of the NFL's television contracts but of its own decision to seek entry into the NFL on the cheap.

Verdict affirmed.

Following this appellate decision, the NFL argued that the USFL was not a "prevailing plaintiff" in this litigation and hence was not entitled to have the NFL pay its attorney fees as mandated by the Clayton Act. The trial judge held (at 704 F.Supp. 474 (S.D.N.Y.1989)) that notwithstanding the USFL's inability to persuade the jury of financial damages from the NFL's actions—as opposed to the USFL's managerial mistakes—the jury had found significant enough violations of the Sherman Act by the NFL to warrant a fee award to the USFL's attorneys of $5.5 million.

Questions for Discussion

1. The jury awarded the USFL only $1 in damages because it believed that irrespective of the NFL's illegal monopolizing behavior, the USFL's business strategy and conduct was such that it would have failed anyway. However, if the purpose of private antitrust actions is to encourage private enforcement, and the NFL was found to be an illegal monopoly, why was the court unwilling to grant the USFL's requested injunction that would have forced the NFL to divide into two independent leagues? Is the court's reasoning persuasive? Would consumer welfare and competition have been benefitted by granting the requested relief?

2. After the AFL's successful merger with the NFL in the late 1960s, and the partial mergers of the WHA into the NHL and the ABA into the NBA, many felt that acquiring a team in an upstart league was a good investment, not because it was likely to earn a profit and become a viable long-term business, but because eventually the established league would either buy-off or merge with the teams in the new league. Was this the strategy of David Dixon and the founders of the USFL? How about Donald Trump and the second wave of USFL owners? After the result in the *USFL* case, do you believe that this is still a viable strategy?

3. Should the law allow an established league to merge with all or some of the clubs in an upstart league? Under what circumstances would you permit such a merger? What is the likely alternative if such a merger is not permitted? Why did the NFL not try to merge with or buy-off the USFL?

Since the demise of the USFL, no new leagues have risen up to challenge the established major league organizations in football, baseball, basketball, and hockey. Several new leagues *have* come along, either as minor leagues in one of these four sports (e.g., the two developmental leagues in men's basketball) or as a prospective major league in a newly emerging sport (e.g., MLS in soccer, and the ABL and WNBA in women's basketball). However, it appears that the market position of the four major sports leagues is so well entrenched that only the most brave or foolhardy would try to compete directly against any of them at the highest level.

C. BREAK UP THE BIG LEAGUES?

Having added this final piece to the existing legal mosaic of professional league sports, step back and speculate about a possible future course for the game. In particular, consider a position that has been seriously advanced by some scholars,[1] that the major leagues within each sport should be broken up into three or four separate leagues that would compete against each other (on the model of the judicial break-up of AT&T's historic monopoly over telephone services[m]). The following questions will help focus your analysis of this proposal and its implications for our understanding of the status quo in sports.

1. To what extent are the legal, economic, and personal conflicts seen in prior chapters attributable to the fact that there is only one established league in each sport (including Major League Baseball)?

2. Is there any prospect of competitive leagues emerging on their own to challenge seriously the dominant power within any sport? Why has no upstart league in any sport ever been able to survive for more than a few years as a viable counterweight to the market power of the established league?

3. Is the current sports monopoly attributable in significant measure to barriers created by the "exclusionary" conduct of the established leagues or barriers deriving from the variety of special legal prerogatives and immunities that we have seen extended to the various leagues? By the way, why have government officials in the federal and state legislative, executive, and judicial branches of government been forthcoming with so many privileges and subsidies for the dominant sports leagues?

4. Alternatively, is the more likely explanation for the uniform pattern displayed in all sports over the last century that sports is a natural monopoly? We mean "natural" not only in the strict econo-

---

[1.] In particular, by Stephen Ross in the articles cited in note 1 above.

[m.] *United States v. American Telephone and Telegraph Company*, 552 F.Supp. 131 (D.D.C.1982). See Glen O. Robinson, *The Titanic Remembered: AT&T and the Changing World of Telecommunications*, 5 Yale J. on Reg. 517 (1988), for a review of the AT&T litigation and break-up.

mist's definition of that term,[n] but also in the practical sense that the essence of sports is competition, the high point of athletic competition is the crowning of a champion, and the league whose champion is generally recognized by fans as supreme inevitably receives the lion's share of gate attendance and television revenues—funds the league can use to attract the best players to its teams and thereby reinforce its dominant image with fans. In other words, is a single "major" league what sports consumers really want? As noted earlier, the emergence in the late 1990s of both an ABL and a WNBA in women's professional basketball will provide a vivid test of this hypothesis on both the court and at the box office.

5. Whatever your diagnosis of the causes of the current sports monopoly, would it be desirable—would it be feasible—for Congress or an antitrust court to break up the established leagues, all of whose current divisions enjoy "big league" status in the popular mind? Each such division would be made an independent entity headed by its own commissioner: no agreements would be permitted with the other new leagues for allocation of players or franchises, or sale of television rights and marketing licenses. If that policy course were to be followed, should the several new leagues be entitled to (or required to) cooperate in staging a single championship playoff? In effect, should the Super Bowl or the World Series be deemed an "essential facility" that must be made accessible to each league in order to preserve a competitive sports marketplace (by analogy to the appeals court ruling in *Aspen Highlands Skiing Corp. v. Aspen Skiing Co.*, 738 F.2d 1509 (10th Cir.1984), affirmed on somewhat different grounds, 472 U.S. 585 (1985))?

6. Among the different constituencies observed in earlier chapters—owners, players, players associations, agents, municipalities, television networks, and fans—who would win and who would lose from such a dramatically different structure to the sports world? Why?

7. If each major league is judged to be a natural monopoly which it is neither desirable nor feasible to break up, should Congress deal with the economic problems created in the sports world in the manner that natural monopolies have historically been treated? A federal regulatory commission would be established to determine (or at least approve) how many franchises there would be, where they would be located, who would be allowed to own them, what television rights could be sold and for how much, how much trademarks and logos could be licensed for, the length of the season, and many other important decisions that a monopolist would otherwise make against the best interests of the public. What are the pros and cons of having sports governed by such an agency?

---

n. See John Cirace, *An Economic Analysis of Antitrust Law's Natural Monopoly Cases*, 88 West Virginia L. Rev. 677 (1986).

The foregoing is a purely speculative exercise, at least for the foreseeable future. Nevertheless, reflecting upon this possible "brave new world" of competitive sports leagues is important to cast into sharper relief the economic and human conflicts, and the resulting legal puzzles, depicted in the previous chapters. Recall the case of *Rose v. Giamatti*, with which this book began. What is the ultimate source of the commissioner's authority to define the "best interests of the sport?" Is such authority purely private or public, or is it some blend of the two? How does George Will's observation—that the courts should stay out of sports—look to you now?

Chapter Nine

INTERCOLLEGIATE SPORTS: DUE PROCESS AND ACADEMIC INTEGRITY

We now begin exploring the law's impact on intercollegiate sports. As in professional sports, the last quarter century has witnessed an explosion of litigation by the people and institutions involved in intercollegiate athletics. There are interesting similarities and contrasts between college sports and their professional counterparts. Whatever points of comparison are emphasized, the materials presented in the next three chapters from the world of college athletics cast light on the broader role of law in shaping the governance of all sports.[a]

For our legal purposes, the telling comparison is not how the game is played on field or floor, even though the rules of football, for example, are essentially the same in the NFL and the Big Ten. Rather, the key common feature to professional and college sports that has helped fuel

---

[a] The subject of college sports has produced a growing number of popular book-length treatments. These books, typically written by journalists, exhibit a rather jaundiced attitude towards various features of intercollegiate athletics, an attitude that is visible in titles such as *A Hundred Yard Lie*, *Win At Any Cost*, and *Undue Process*. While these and other books provide interesting glimpses of the real life practices that lead to litigation and judicial opinions, a more balanced picture of the fundamental issues can be found in scholarly works such as John R. Thelin, *Games Colleges Play: Scandal and Reform in Intercollegiate Athletics* (Baltimore, MD: Johns Hopkins University Press, 1994); Wilford S. Bayley and Taylor D. Littleton, *Athletics and Academe: An Anatomy of Abuses and a Prescription for Reform* (New York: American Council on Education, MacMillan Publishing, 1991); Symposium, The Reform of Big–Time Intercollegiate Athletics, 20 Capital L. Rev. 541 (1991); Rodney K. Smith, *An Academic Game Plan for Reforming Big–Time Intercollegiate Athletics*, Denver U. L. Rev. 213 (1990); and John C. Weistart, *Legal Accountability and the NCAA*, 10 J. of Col. and Univ. L. 167 (1983). Perhaps the most informative of the more popular books are Murray Sperber, *College Sports Inc., The Athletic Department Versus the University* (New York: Henry Holt, 1990); Gary Funk, *Major Violation: The Unbalanced Priorities in Athletics and Academics* (Champaign, Ill: Leisure Press, 1991); Don Yaeger and Douglas S. Looney, *Under the Tarnished Dome: How Notre Dame Betrayed Its Ideals for Football Glory* (New York: Simon & Schuster, 1993); and most recently, Walter Byers, with Charles Hammer, *Unsportsmanlike Conduct: Exploiting College Athletes* (Ann Arbor, Mich.: University of Michigan Press, 1995) (whose lead author was the first full-time Executive Director of the NCAA).

litigation in both arenas is the vast sum of money generated from fans intensely interested in watching the games, whether live or on television.

An especially vivid number is the $1.7 billion-dollar contract signed by the Columbia Broadcasting System (CBS) with the National Collegiate Athletic Association (NCAA) to televise the Division I basketball tournament—sports fans' annual March Madness—for eight years. Postseason college football bowl games generate $100 million a year in revenues for participating schools and their conferences. The top football programs (not just Notre Dame and Michigan, but Florida and Washington) earn $14–15 million a year in profits for their schools, and the top men's basketball programs (like Louisville, Indiana and North Carolina) earn $5–7 million a season. In aggregate, major college sports (Division I, and Division I–A in football) generate nearly $2.5 billion dollars in annual revenues, nearly half from football programs. It is estimated that the capitalized economic value of big-time college sports at Michigan, Notre Dame, Florida, and the like is in the $200–$250 million range, putting these programs in the upper echelons of all sports franchises.[b]

These soaring financial figures have jeopardized the principles that supposedly make intercollegiate sports unique. Article I of the NCAA's constitution proclaims:

> The competitive athletics programs of member institutions are designed to be a vital part of the education system. A basic purpose of this Association is to maintain intercollegiate athletics as an integral part of the education program and the athlete as an integral part of the student body and, by so doing, retain a clear line of demarcation between intercollegiate athletics and professional sports.

However, the financial temptation of this commercial athletic venture often creates serious tension with the NCAA's stated purpose of conducting intercollegiate sports "in a manner designed to protect and enhance the physical and educational welfare of student-athletes" (Article 2.2). In particular, the prospect of lucrative championship teams makes it difficult to treat student-athletes as "amateurs" whose participation is "motivated primarily by education and by the physical, mental, and social benefits" of athletics, and who are to "be protected from exploitation by professional and commercial enterprises" (Article 2.6).

Beneath the surface of these stated objectives, intercollegiate sports has much the same structural features as we earlier saw exhibited by professional sports. The NCAA has approximately 900 member-colleges and universities. The Association was formed early in the twentieth century in response to the dangerous state of college football.[c] In 1906,

---

b. The principal source of financial data for intercollegiate sports is Daniel L. Fulks, *Revenues and Expenses of Division I and II Intercollegiate Athletic Programs: Financial Trends and Relationships—1995* (Overland Park, Kan.: NCAA, 1996). Richard G. Sheehan, *Keeping Score: The Economics of Big-Time Sports* (South Bend, Ind.: Diamond Communications, 1996), especially Chapter 11, "Colleges—Financial Rankings or Going for the Green," also provides valuable analyses of these data and their economic implications.

c. A first-rate historical treatment of the early years of intercollegiate sports is Ronald Smith, *Sports and Freedom: The*

with nearly 20 fatal and 150 seriously disabling injuries befalling participants in college football games every year, President Theodore Roosevelt called together the heads of major universities to get them to agree on a set of playing rules that would outlaw dangerous tactics such as the "flying wedge." After considerable bickering, the schools agreed to create the NCAA as a forum for reshaping the rules for football (e.g., bringing in the forward pass), and later for standardizing the rules for basketball and other sports.

With respect to the rules of the game *off* the field, Association members agreed upon broad principles of student amateurism in college sports. However, for decades the operating constitutional regime was "home rule" by each institution in determining what these principles meant for admission, academic progress, and financial assistance of its student-athletes. Only after World War II, and an initially unsuccessful effort to implement a "Sanity Code" intended to eliminate perennial abuses in college programs, did the NCAA members agree to empower the Association (and its newly-hired Executive Director, Walter Byers) with authority over the *enterprise* (and not merely the *game*) of college sports. Four decades later, the NCAA Manual consists of 500 pages of intricate regulations authored, interpreted, and enforced by a complex interplay of the legislative, executive, and judicial branches of the Association.

Just as was historically true in professional sports, establishing a detailed body of private law for the governance of intercollegiate sports has been the preserve of the colleges and universities who, along with the conferences to which they belong, constitute the membership of the Association. Unsurprisingly, the member schools have displayed a strong interest in maintaining NCAA objectives such as the principles of "equity in competition" (Article 2.7) and "economy of athletics program operation" (Article 2.13). This institutional interest has become much more intense recently because athletic program expenditures have been rising even faster than revenues. In 1989, for example, the University of Michigan had a football team that won the Rose Bowl and a basketball team that won the NCAA championship, but the school had a $2 million deficit in its overall athletic budget. Together, the two revenue-producing sports, football and men's basketball, can produce profits ranging as high as $15–$20 million, but a considerable number of schools show a loss even in these two supposedly lucrative sports programs.

These dollar amounts on their balance sheets generate intense concerns among school officials who collectively decide what constitutes the "best interests" of intercollegiate sports. That institutional perspective inevitably clashes with the interests not only of dissident NCAA members, but also of athletes and coaches whose sporting careers are governed by the NCAA regime, but who have no vote in the formulation or enforcement of NCAA policy. The last three decades have witnessed growing recourse to the courts by people dissatisfied with the decisions

Rise of Big–Time College Athletics (New York: Oxford University Press, 1988).

made within the NCAA hierarchy. The cases and materials in this chapter depict both the judicial response to specific conflicts, and the uneasy equilibrium in the autonomy the law has left to the NCAA in governing the college sports enterprise.

A. THE TARKANIAN SAGA[d]

The most celebrated legal challenge to NCAA autonomy was launched by Jerry Tarkanian, then of the University of Nevada at Las Vegas (UNLV). After a successful but contentious career at Long Beach State, in the fall of 1973 Tarkanian was recruited to be head coach for the struggling UNLV basketball program. On his arrival, Tarkanian found that the NCAA had embarked on a full-scale examination of rule violations by UNLV. The investigation lasted four years, during which time Tarkanian took his Running Rebels to a 29–3 regular season record and the Final Four championship playoffs in 1977. At the end of that season, however, UNLV announced that, pursuant to an NCAA directive, the school was suspending Tarkanian for two years because he had been found personally guilty of major violations of NCAA rules.

The two main charges against Tarkanian were that he had arranged for payment of a flight home for one of his players, and that he had arranged for an instructor to give another player a passing grade in a course the player did not attend. The NCAA investigators asserted that these infractions had been disclosed by the player and the instructor. Upon learning of the charges, Tarkanian, the University, and the Nevada Attorney General's office undertook their own investigations and obtained contrary affidavits from both the alleged participants and several corroborating witnesses. But production of this new material simply elicited a new and more serious charge against Tarkanian, that he had pressured witnesses to give false evidence in NCAA proceedings.

At Tarkanian's hearing before the NCAA's Committee on Infractions, the evidence against him consisted merely of assertions made by NCAA staff investigators of what they recalled people saying to them in the previous three years, matched against the affidavits and supporting documents offered by Tarkanian and UNLV. No oral testimony or cross-examination of witnesses was permitted. At the end of the proceeding, after a private consultation with the enforcement staff, the five-member Committee (of which the chair and two other members were law professors) found that the violations had occurred. The Committee put UNLV's basketball program on probation for two years and required the university to suspend Tarkanian as coach for those two years or face further penalties. UNLV's appeal to the NCAA Council was dismissed a

---

d. A revealing look at the entire Tarkanian case, written from a pro-Tarkanian vantage point, is Don Yaeger, *Shark Attack: Jerry Tarkanian and His Battle With the NCAA and UNLV* (New York: Harper Collins, 1992). A scholarly treatment of the legal issues is John P. Sahl, *College Athletes and Due Process Protection: What's Left After* NCAA v. Tarkanian, 21 Arizona St. L. J. 621 (1989).

few months later. (Tarkanian himself had no right of appeal, since he was not a member of the NCAA.)

As a state university, UNLV was required by both federal constitutional and state statutory law to give Tarkanian, its tenured coach, a hearing before suspending him. Although the hearing officer did not believe that any violations had occurred, he concluded that UNLV had no choice but to suspend Tarkanian if the school wanted to remain part of the NCAA. On the eve of his suspension, Tarkanian went to court, eventually suing both UNLV and the NCAA. The Nevada courts found that the NCAA proceedings had denied Tarkanian "due process." Operating on the assumption that the NCAA was a "state actor" governed by the federal constitution, the trial court issued injunctions barring UNLV's suspension of Tarkanian and NCAA retaliation against UNLV. The Nevada Supreme Court affirmed. The case finally reached the United States Supreme Court in 1988; by then Tarkanian had one of the highest winning percentages of all active coaches in college basketball (and had become Nevada's highest paid public employee), and the Supreme Court had considerably narrowed its view of what constitutes "state action."

NATIONAL COLLEGIATE ATHLETIC ASS'N. v. TARKANIAN

Supreme Court of the United States, 1988.
488 U.S. 179, 109 S.Ct. 454, 102 L.Ed.2d 469.

JUSTICE STEVENS for the Court.

* * *

II

Embedded in our Fourteenth Amendment jurisprudence is a dichotomy between state action, which is subject to scrutiny under the Amendment's Due Process Clause, and private conduct, against which the Amendment affords no shield, no matter how unfair that conduct may be. As a general matter the protections of the Fourteenth Amendment do not extend to "private conduct abridging individual rights." *Burton v. Wilmington Parking Authority*, 365 U.S. 715, 722 (1961).

"Careful adherence to the 'state action' requirement preserves an area of individual freedom by limiting the reach of federal law" and avoids the imposition of responsibility on a State for conduct it could not control. When Congress enacted § 1983 as the statutory remedy for violations of the Constitution, it specified that the conduct at issue must have occurred "under color of" state law; thus, liability attaches only to those wrongdoers "who carry a badge of authority of a State and represent it in some capacity, whether they act in accordance with their authority or misuse it." *Monroe v. Pape*, 365 U.S. 167, 172 (1961). As we stated in *United States v. Classic*, 313 U.S. 299, 326 (1941):

> Misuse of power, possessed by virtue of state law and made possible only because the wrongdoer is clothed with the authority of state law, is action taken "under color of" state law.

In this case Tarkanian argues that the NCAA was a state actor because it misused power that it possessed by virtue of state law. He claims specifically that UNLV delegated its own functions to the NCAA, clothing the Association with authority both to adopt rules governing UNLV's athletic programs and to enforce those rules on behalf of UNLV. Similarly, the Nevada Supreme Court held that UNLV had delegated its authority over personnel decisions to the NCAA. Therefore, the court reasoned, the two entities acted jointly to deprive Tarkanian of liberty and property interests, making the NCAA as well as UNLV a state actor.

These contentions fundamentally misconstrue the facts of this case. In the typical case raising a state action issue, a private party has taken the decisive step that caused the harm to the plaintiff, and the question is whether the State was sufficiently involved to treat that decisive conduct as state action. This may occur if the State creates the legal framework governing the conduct; if it delegates its authority to the private actor; or sometimes if it knowingly accepts the benefits derived from unconstitutional behavior. Thus, in the usual case we ask whether the State provided a mantle of authority that enhanced the power of the harm-causing individual actor.

This case uniquely mirrors the traditional state action case. Here the final act challenged by Tarkanian—his suspension—was committed by UNLV. A state university without question is a state actor. When it decides to impose a serious disciplinary sanction upon one of its tenured employees, it must comply with the terms of the Due Process Clause of the Fourteenth Amendment to the Federal Constitution. Thus when UNLV notified Tarkanian that he was being separated from all relations with the University's basketball program, it acted under color of state law within the meaning of 42 U.S.C. § 1983.

The mirror image presented in this case requires us to step through an analytical looking glass to resolve it. Clearly UNLV's conduct was influenced by the rules and recommendations of the NCAA, the private party. But it was UNLV, the state entity, that actually suspended Tarkanian. Thus the question is not whether UNLV participated to a critical extent in the NCAA's activities, but whether UNLV's actions in compliance with the NCAA rules and recommendations turned the NCAA's conduct into state action.

We examine first the relationship between UNLV and the NCAA regarding the NCAA's rulemaking. UNLV is among the NCAA's members and participated in promulgating the Association's rules; it must be assumed, therefore, that Nevada had some impact on the NCAA's policy determinations. Yet the NCAA's several hundred other public and private member institutions each similarly affected those policies. Those institutions, the vast majority of which were located in States other than Nevada, did not act under color of Nevada law. It necessarily follows that the source of the legislation adopted by the NCAA is not Nevada but the collective membership, speaking through an organization that is independent of any particular State.

State action nonetheless might lie if UNLV, by embracing the NCAA's rules, transformed them into state rules and the NCAA into a state actor. UNLV engaged in state action when it adopted the NCAA's rules to govern its own behavior, but that would be true even if UNLV had taken no part in the promulgation of those rules. In *Bates v. State Bar of Arizona*, 433 U.S. 350 (1977), we established that the State Supreme Court's enforcement of disciplinary rules transgressed by members of its own bar was state action. Those rules had been adopted in toto from the American Bar Association Code of Professional Responsibility. It does not follow, however, that the ABA's formulation of those disciplinary rules was state action. The State Supreme Court retained plenary power to reexamine those standards and, if necessary, to reject them and promulgate its own. So here, UNLV retained the authority to withdraw from the NCAA and establish its own standards. The University alternatively could have stayed in the Association and worked through the Association's legislative process to amend rules or standards it deemed harsh, unfair, or unwieldy.[15] Neither UNLV's decision to adopt the NCAA's standards nor its minor role in their formulation is a sufficient reason for concluding that the NCAA was acting under color of Nevada law when it promulgated standards governing athlete recruitment, eligibility, and academic performance.

Tarkanian further asserts that the NCAA's investigation, enforcement proceedings, and consequent recommendations constituted state action because they resulted from a delegation of power by UNLV. UNLV, as an NCAA member, subscribed to the statement in the Association's bylaws that NCAA "enforcement procedures are an essential part of the intercollegiate athletic program of each member institution." It is, of course, true that a state may delegate authority to a private party and thereby make that party a state actor. Thus, we recently held that a private physician who had contracted with a state prison to attend to the inmates' medical needs was a state actor. But UNLV delegated no power to the NCAA to take specific action against any University employee. The commitment by UNLV to adhere to NCAA enforcement procedures was enforceable only by sanctions that the NCAA might impose on UNLV itself.

Indeed, the notion that UNLV's promise to cooperate in the NCAA enforcement proceedings was tantamount to a partnership agreement or the transfer of certain University powers to the NCAA is belied by the history of this case. It is quite obvious that UNLV used its best efforts to retain its winning coach—a goal diametrically opposed to the NCAA's interest in ascertaining the truth of its investigators' reports. During the

---

15. Furthermore, the NCAA's bylaws permit review of penalties, even after they are imposed, "upon a showing of newly discovered evidence which is directly related to the findings in the case, or that there was a prejudicial error in the procedure which was followed in the processing of the case by the Committee." UNLV could have sought such a review, perhaps on the theory that the NCAA's investigator was biased against Tarkanian, as the Nevada trial court found in 1984. The NCAA Committee on Infractions was authorized to "reduce or eliminate any penalty" if the University had prevailed.

several years that the NCAA investigated the alleged violations, the NCAA and UNLV acted much more like adversaries than like partners engaged in a dispassionate search for the truth. The NCAA cannot be regarded as an agent of UNLV for purposes of that proceeding. It is more correctly characterized as an agent of its remaining members which, as competitors of UNLV, had an interest in the effective and evenhanded enforcement of NCAA's recruitment standards. Just as a state-compensated public defender acts in a private capacity when she represents a private client in a conflict against the State, the NCAA is properly viewed as a private actor at odds with the State when it represents the interests of its entire membership in an investigation of one public university.

The NCAA enjoyed no governmental powers to facilitate its investigation. It had no power to subpoena witnesses, to impose contempt sanctions, or to assert sovereign authority over any individual. Its greatest authority was to threaten sanctions against UNLV, with the ultimate sanction being expulsion of the University from membership. Contrary to the premise of the Nevada Supreme Court's opinion, the NCAA did not—indeed, could not—directly discipline Tarkanian or any other state university employee.[18] The express terms of the Confidential Report did not demand the suspension unconditionally; rather, it requested "the University ... to show cause" why the NCAA should not impose additional penalties if UNLV declines to suspend Tarkanian. Even the University's vice president acknowledged that the Report gave the University options other than suspension: UNLV could have retained Tarkanian and risked additional sanctions, perhaps even expulsion from the NCAA, or it could have withdrawn voluntarily from the Association.

Finally, Tarkanian argues that the power of the NCAA is so great that the UNLV had no practical alternative to compliance with its demands. We are not at all sure this is true,[19] but even if we assume that

---

18. Tarkanian urges us to hold, as did the Nevada Supreme Court, that the NCAA by its rules and enforcement procedures has usurped a traditional, essential state function. Quite properly, he does not point to the NCAA's overriding function of fostering amateur athletics at the college level. For while we have described that function as "critical," *NCAA v. Board of Regents of the University of Oklahoma*, 468 U.S. 85, 120 (1984), by no means is it a traditional, let alone an exclusive, state function. Cf. *San Francisco Arts & Athletics, Inc. v. United States Olympic Committee*, 483 U.S. 522, 545, (1987) ("Neither the conduct nor the coordination of amateur sports has been a traditional government function."). Tarkanian argues instead that the NCAA has assumed the state's traditional and exclusive power to discipline its employees. "[A]s to state employees connected with intercollegiate athletics, the NCAA requires that its standards, procedures and determinations become the State's standards, procedures and determinations for disciplining state employees," he contends. "The State is obligated to impose NCAA standards, procedures and determinations making the NCAA a joint participant in the State's suspension of Tarkanian." This argument overlooks the fact that the NCAA's own legislation prohibits it from taking any direct action against Tarkanian. Moreover, suspension of Tarkanian is one of many recommendations in the Confidential Report. Those recommendations as a whole were intended to bring UNLV's basketball program into compliance with NCAA rules. Suspension of Tarkanian was but one means toward achieving that goal.

19. The University's desire to remain a powerhouse among the nation's college basketball teams is understandable, and non-membership in the NCAA obviously would thwart that goal. But that UNLV's options

a private monopolist can impose its will on a state agency by a threatened refusal to deal with it, it does not follow that such a private party is therefore acting under color of state law.

In final analysis the question is whether "the conduct allegedly causing the deprivation of a federal right [can] be fairly attributable to the State." It would be ironic indeed to conclude that the NCAA's imposition of sanctions against UNLV—sanctions that UNLV and its counsel, including the Attorney General of Nevada, steadfastly opposed during protracted adversary proceedings—is fairly attributable to the State of Nevada. It would be more appropriate to conclude that UNLV has conducted its athletic program under color of the policies adopted by the NCAA, rather than that those policies were developed and enforced under color of Nevada law.

Reversed.

JUSTICE WHITE dissented and filed an opinion in which JUSTICES BRENNAN, MARSHALL and O'CONNOR joined.

All agree that UNLV, a public university, is a state actor, and that the suspension of Jerry Tarkanian, a public employee, was state action. The question here is whether the NCAA acted jointly with UNLV in suspending Tarkanian and thereby also became a state actor. I would hold that it did.

I agree with the majority that this case is different on its facts from many of our prior state action cases. As the majority notes, in our "typical case raising a state action issue, a private party has taken the decisive step that caused the harm to the plaintiff." In this case, however, which in the majority's view "uniquely mirrors the traditional state action case," the final act that caused the harm to Tarkanian was committed, not by a private party, but by a party conceded to be a state actor. Because of this difference, the majority finds it necessary to "step through an analytical looking glass" to evaluate whether the NCAA was a state actor.

But the situation presented by this case is not unknown to us and certainly is not unique. In both *Adickes v. S.H. Kress & Co.*, 398 U.S. 144 (1970), and *Dennis v. Sparks*, 449 U.S. 24 (1980), we faced the question of whether private parties could be held to be state actors in cases in which the final or decisive act was carried out by a state official. In both cases we held that the private parties could be found to be state actors, if they were "jointly engaged with state officials in the challenged action."

The facts of *Dennis* are illustrative. In *Dennis*, a state trial judge enjoined the production of minerals from oil leases owned by the plaintiff. The injunction was later dissolved on appeal as having been issued illegally. The plaintiff then filed suit under 42 U.S.C. § 1983, alleging that the judge had conspired with the party seeking the original injunction—a private corporation—the sole owner of the corporation,

were unpalatable does not mean that they were nonexistent.

and the two sureties on the injunction bond to deprive the plaintiff of due process by corruptly issuing the injunction. We held unanimously that under the facts as alleged the private parties were state actors because they were "willful participant[s] in joint action with the State or its agents." . . .

On the facts of the present case, the NCAA acted jointly with UNLV in suspending Tarkanian. First, Tarkanian was suspended for violations of NCAA rules, which UNLV embraced in its agreement with the NCAA. As the Nevada Supreme Court found in its first opinion in this case, "[a]s a member of the NCAA, UNLV contractually agrees to administer its athletic program in accordance with NCAA legislation." Indeed, NCAA rules provide that NCAA "enforcement procedures are an essential part of the intercollegiate athletic program of each member institution."

Second, the NCAA and UNLV also agreed that the NCAA would conduct the hearings concerning violations of its rules. Although UNLV conducted its own investigation into the recruiting violations alleged by the NCAA, the NCAA procedures provide that it is the NCAA Committee on Infractions that "determine[s] facts related to alleged violations," subject to an appeal to the NCAA Council. As a result of this agreement, the NCAA conducted the very hearings the Nevada Supreme Court held to have violated Tarkanian's right to procedural due process.

Third, the NCAA and UNLV agreed that the findings of fact made by the NCAA at the hearings it conducted would be binding on UNLV. By becoming a member of the NCAA, UNLV did more than merely "promise to cooperate in the NCAA enforcement proceedings." It agreed, as the University Hearing Officer appointed to rule on Tarkanian's suspension expressly found, to accept the NCAA's "findings of fact as in some way superior to [its] own." By the terms of UNLV's membership in the NCAA, the NCAA's findings were final and not subject to further review by any other body, and it was for that reason that UNLV suspended Tarkanian, despite concluding that many of those findings were wrong.

In short, it was the NCAA's findings that Tarkanian had violated NCAA rules, made at NCAA-conducted hearings, all of which were agreed to by UNLV in its membership agreement with the NCAA, that resulted in Tarkanian's suspension by UNLV. On these facts, the NCAA was "jointly engaged with [UNLV] officials in the challenged action," and therefore was a state actor.

* * *

The majority states in conclusion that "[i]t would be ironic indeed to conclude that the NCAA's imposition of sanctions against UNLV—sanctions that UNLV and its counsel, including the Attorney General of Nevada, steadfastly opposed during protracted adversary proceedings—is fairly attributable to the State of Nevada." I agree. Had UNLV refused to suspend Tarkanian, and the NCAA responded by imposing sanctions against UNLV, it would be hard indeed to find any state action that harmed Tarkanian. But that is not this case. Here, UNLV did suspend Tarkanian, and it did so because it embraced the NCAA rules governing conduct of its athletic program and adopted the results of the hearings conducted by the NCAA concerning Tarkanian, as it had agreed that it would. Under these facts, I would find that the NCAA acted jointly with UNLV and therefore is a state actor.

While the NCAA won this major legal victory over Tarkanian, it was not thereby able to remove him from the college basketball court. Further litigation in the lower courts kept Tarkanian in place through the 1989–1990 season, which UNLV capped with its first national championship. (Tarkanian's coaching contract entitled him to ten percent of the $1.4 million UNLV won from the NCAA's tournament.) In the summer of 1990, UNLV and the NCAA reached a settlement whereby UNLV accepted additional probation for its basketball team in lieu of suspending Tarkanian, the coach. However, this ban on television and post-season appearances was postponed until the 1991–1992 season. It was the Duke Blue Devils, not NCAA investigators, who ended Tarkanian's bid in March 1991 for an unbeaten season and a second consecutive national championship. In the summer of 1991, faced with further troubles, including public criticism from UNLV's president and another major NCAA investigation (this one involving the recruiting of Lloyd Daniels in the mid–1980s), Tarkanian finally announced his intention to resign from UNLV in 1992, eighteen years after he began. Although his basketball team had lost its major stars to the NBA, Tarkanian's final season was highly successful—UNLV finished the regular season ranked seventh in the national polls. But because of offenses allegedly committed in the mid–1970s, this unheralded group of players was denied the chance to play for the NCAA's 1992 basketball championship.

The U.S. Supreme Court has settled the NCAA's status as a matter of legal doctrine, but important questions of constitutional principle remain. In the 1970s the lower courts treated the NCAA as a "state actor" in connection with both private and public universities. See, e.g., *Howard University v. NCAA*, 510 F.2d 213 (D.C.Cir.1975). After the Supreme Court's "state action" trilogy in 1982,[e] the Fourth Circuit reversed the judicial course in *Arlosoroff v. NCAA*, 746 F.2d 1019 (4th Cir.1984): the appeals court held the NCAA to be a private actor and thereby dismissed a constitutional challenge against an NCAA rule restricting the eligibility of foreigners brought by a student at Duke

---

e. The three decisions were *Rendell–Baker v. Kohn*, 457 U.S. 830 (1982); *Lugar v. Edmondson Oil Company, Inc.*, 457 U.S. 922 (1982); and *Blum v. Yaretsky*, 457 U.S. 991 (1982).

University, a private institution. The *Tarkanian* case was the first major case in the 1980s involving a state university.

Suppose that the Supreme Court had found the NCAA to be a "state actor" that owed constitutional due process to Tarkanian (as UNLV, a public university, clearly did owe its employee). What legal obligations were riding on this label? Courts have interpreted the Fourteenth Amendment due process requirement to require that governmental action meet minimum standards of fairness such as adequate notice or an opportunity to be heard before the state makes a decision. To succeed on a due process claim under the Fourteenth Amendment, a litigant must prove that state action has deprived him or her of a liberty or property interest and that the procedures employed by the state were less than what was "due." There is a developed (and confusing) jurisprudence defining liberty or property interests and the procedures mandated by the Constitution in specific circumstances. Generally, state law determines whether a litigant has a protected property interest, and federal constitutional law determines the amount of required process.[f]

In *Tarkanian* the Nevada Supreme Court held that Tarkanian's contractual relationship with UNLV, a state institution, created a protected property interest in his tenured coaching job. See *Tarkanian v. NCAA*, 103 Nev. 331, 741 P.2d 1345 (1987). That ruling was based on Supreme Court jurisprudence that if state law provides "a legitimate claim of entitlement" to a job, a protected property interest exists. See *Board of Regents of State Colleges v. Roth*, 408 U.S. 564 (1972) (ruling that a non-tenured instructor at a state university had no property interest in his position because state law created no legitimate basis for him to claim that he was entitled to renewal of his contract). The Nevada Supreme Court also found that Tarkanian's liberty interests were implicated because termination of his employment would stigmatize him and alter or extinguish a "right or status previously recognized by state law" (quoting *Paul v. Davis*, 424 U.S. 693 (1976)).

As we will see later in this chapter, courts before *Tarkanian* struggled with the question whether student-athletes have a property interest in their intercollegiate athletic eligibility, as a means of obtaining either a career in professional sports or at least a college education. Some courts answered in the affirmative. See, e.g., *Hall v. University of Minnesota*, 530 F.Supp. 104 (D.Minn.1982) (finding that college eligibility was a protected property interest because it was an essential step on the way to a professional sports career). Most courts, however, refused to find a property interest in athletic eligibility, believing that a college athlete's prospects for securing professional employment were too "speculative and not of constitutional dimensions." *Colorado Seminary v. NCAA*, 417 F.Supp. 885 (D.Colo.1976), affirmed, 570 F.2d 320 (10th Cir.1978).[g]

f. See generally, Laurence H. Tribe, *American Constitutional Law*, 2d ed., §§ 10–9 to 10–14, at 685–718 (Mineola, NY: Foundation Press, 1988).

g. See Brian L. Porto, *Balancing Due Process and Academic Integrity In Intercol-*

The Nevada Supreme Court also ruled that, as a matter of federal law, the NCAA did not provide the requisite amount of process in its investigation of Tarkanian. The court found that, at a minimum, the evidence against Tarkanian collected during interviews conducted by the NCAA enforcement staff should have been in the form of written affidavits, relying on an oft-cited passage from the Supreme Court about what factors courts should balance in determining the procedures required in a given situation:

> First, the private interest that will be affected by the official action; second, the risk of erroneous deprivation of such interest through the procedures used, and the probable value, if any, of additional or substitute safeguards; and finally, the Government's interest, including the function involved and the fiscal and administrative burdens that the additional or substitute procedural requirement would entail.

Mathews v. Eldridge, 424 U.S. 319, 335 (1976). When considering legal challenges to NCAA revocation of the eligibility of student-athletes, those courts that have treated the NCAA as a state actor have generally found NCAA procedures to be adequate under the Due Process Clause. See, e.g., *Regents of the University of Minnesota v. NCAA*, 560 F.2d 352 (8th Cir.1977); *Howard University v. NCAA*, 510 F.2d 213 (D.C.Cir. 1975); *Justice v. NCAA*, 577 F.Supp. 356 (D.Ariz.1983). Although *Tarkanian* bars federal due process claims against the NCAA, these cases may be relevant in determining the procedures required by state statutes (which we will examine later in this chapter) imposing due process requirements on the NCAA. In addition, the constitutional analysis in the cases cited presumably still applies to suits brought by students or coaches against public universities, which are state actors. A recent case upholding the legal viability of such a claim is *Campanelli v. Bockrath*, 100 F.3d 1476 (9th Cir.1996) in which the circuit panel ruled that Lou Campanelli, the former coach of the University of California at Berkeley's men's basketball team, had the right to *Roth* procedural due process when the university not only fired him from his job (as the contract permitted), but when the athletic director publicly accused Campanelli of abusive tirades at his players (to a degree that had allegedly made point guard Jason Kidd physically ill).

Questions for Discussion

1. In appraising the merits of the *Tarkanian* ruling, consider the following issues:

(i) Should NCAA action toward a student-athlete at a private school such as Duke or Notre Dame be treated any differently under the Constitution than a baseball commissioner's action toward a Pete Rose or a George Steinbrenner? Is there anything special about the function of regulating sports in educational institutions? Are there any material

legiate Athletics: The Scholarship Athlete's Property Interest in Eligibility, 62 Indiana L. J. 1151 (1987).

differences in the structures of the NCAA and of a professional sports league and in the manner in which the respective members conduct their athletic businesses? And by the way, after *Tarkanian*, would a successor to Melissa Ludtke (whom we read about in Chapter 1) likely win a suit to gain access of women reporters to the New York Yankees clubhouse? Note that the public-private relationship in *Ludtke* was the reverse of the relationship in *Tarkanian*.

(ii) When the NCAA takes action against a state university such as UNLV or UCLA, is there a stronger case for judicial scrutiny than when the Association imposes sanctions on its private members? How much choice did UNLV have to defy the NCAA and respect Tarkanian's due process rights? On the other hand, could the NCAA afford to have different procedural rules for disciplining state and private schools and their personnel? Are there legal instruments more appropriate than the Constitution for challenging NCAA restraints on institutional or personal choices?

(iii) What if the policies of the NCAA were targeted not at its members or their students and staff, but rather at outside parties? We saw one potential example of such a conflict in Chapter 1, involving the NCAA's concern about gambling on college games. In early 1997, the Association was seriously considering adoption of a rule that would deny press credentials for championship events to newspapers (such as USA Today) that printed advertisements of "tout and tip sheet" services. Indeed, some Association members advocated such a ban for the much larger part of the media world that publishes game odds or point spreads, and that even have "experts" telling their readers or viewers which team to pick against the spread. Suppose that the NCAA, faced with another college gambling scandal, were to adopt such a policy. Would USA Today and others have a viable First Amendment claim against the NCAA? Would it make a difference if the Final Four were being staged in a public sports facility, and/or that one or more of the contenders was from a public university? Might (or should) the Supreme Court's *Tarkanian* "state action" verdict have been different if riding on the case were USA Today's First Amendment rights, rather than Jerry Tarkanian's due process claim?

2. Suppose that UNLV had not been able to reach a settlement with the NCAA and had eventually suspended Tarkanian (after the Supreme Court's ruling). Would Tarkanian have had any legal remedies against UNLV? Since UNLV clearly is a state actor, could Tarkanian have sued the university for violating his due process rights by acceding to the demands of a private association to deprive him of a protected property right without a hearing, especially when the university doubted the factual basis for the NCAA's demand? If such a suit succeeded, what remedies would be available? Would the threat of such remedies place public colleges that belong to the NCAA in a Catch–22 situation when the NCAA orders one of their employees disciplined—either do it and violate the constitution or refuse and face NCAA sanctions? Could private schools follow the NCAA's directives without legal consequence? What are the possible implications for the NCAA of such a dual legal standard?

3. Whether or not Tarkanian could have sustained such a suit against UNLV, could he successfully have sued the NCAA, not for itself denying him due process, but for inducing UNLV to breach his constitutional rights under his employment contract? (Recall the tort action brought by the Toronto Blue Jays against the Boston Celtics in the Danny Ainge case in Chapter 2, and by USC against college player agent Robert Caron in Chapter 5.) There is limited support for such a legal claim against the NCAA in the preliminary injunction ruling in *Regents of the University of Minnesota v. NCAA*, 422 F.Supp. 1158 (D.Minn.1976), which involved a basketball player who had sold his complimentary tickets at more than their face value. The court of appeals set aside the injunction on the specific facts of the case, and expressed no view about the general legal principle. See 560 F.2d 352 (8th Cir.1977). Is such a claim consistent with the state action policies underlying *Tarkanian*?

The case, *NCAA v. Hornung*, 754 S.W.2d 855 (Ky.1988), drawn from a quite different side of the intercollegiate sports enterprise, illustrates both the strengths and weaknesses of such a tort claim against the NCAA as an "outside" third party allegedly interfering with the plaintiff's rights *vis-a-vis* a public university. Paul Hornung was the Heisman Trophy quarterback for Notre Dame, and then a star running back who helped the Green Bay Packers win several Super Bowls in the 1960s. However, Hornung's professional career was marred by the disclosure that he had been betting on Packers' games (to win), for which he was suspended for a season by NFL Commissioner Pete Rozelle. When he retired from the game, Hornung became a sports broadcaster, as well as a notable "playboy" figure in popular Miller Beer commercials. In 1982, Ted Turner's new Atlanta superstation WTBS secured from the NCAA the right to broadcast a package of college football games that season. Although Turner was inclined to make Hornung the color analyst for these games, the NCAA exercised its rights under its contract with WTBS to veto Hornung for that role.

Hornung sued and won a $1.1 million jury verdict against the NCAA for having "improperly" interfered with his potential contractual relationship with WTBS. On appeal, the Supreme Court of Kentucky ruled that the issue in this area of torts/contracts law was not whether the NCAA had "reasonable justification" for its actions, but whether the organization had acted "in good faith" in pursuit of its legally-protected interests, rather than out of malice and ill will towards Hornung. Because the evidence showed that NCAA officials were concerned about associating college football with Hornung's image as a gambler, playboy, and professional football player, this barred a suit by Hornung, even though the NCAA was itself selling Miller commercials and electing Hornung to the College Football Hall of Fame.

In light of *Hornung*, how far could the commissioner of baseball go in barring Pete Rose from working for firms doing business with Major League Baseball? Recall the cases noted in Chapter 1 in which Commissioner Bowie Kuhn banned Willie Mays and Mickey Mantle from associating with baseball teams because they worked for Atlantic City casinos. Similarly, could the NCAA bar Jerry Tarkanian from ever working in any capacity for an NCAA member school (inside or outside the athletic department)? Is there a difference between "interfering" with a prospective employment opportunity and ordering suspension or dismissal of someone already employed (as the NCAA did to Tarkanian)?

At a more fundamental level, both the Pete Rose and the Paul Hornung cases reveal the difficulties with characterizing these litigants as third parties. On the one hand, players and coaches neither make the rules nor appoint the commissioners who govern professional and intercollegiate sports. On the other hand, they sign contracts with their teams that incorporate by reference the league's or association's governing rules and authorities. The question, then, is how much the courts should defer to judgments made by the league or association about the "best interests" of its sport, when these judgments will defeat the contractual expectations of individuals who have no role in this private governing structure. Suppose, for example, that a professional league or college conference exercised its contractual right to reject a television analyst on the ground that he was openly gay. Under the *Hornung* standard, is such a veto legal?

As just a preliminary glimpse of the substantive issues that lead to litigation about NCAA procedures, recall that the rule allegedly broken in the *University of Minnesota* case (mentioned above) dealt with the players' complimentary game tickets. The evolution of NCAA policy regarding such tickets displays the constant tug of war between rule-making at the NCAA and temptations felt on campus. The NCAA's initial rule simply permitted each player to receive four tickets for every game in which his team participated. While players were prohibited from selling their tickets, many players broke that rule in return for substantial payments, especially for more attractive games. The NCAA then instituted a "pass" system under which the players could list four people who had to identify themselves at the gate to obtain their seats for the game. This system made it more difficult, but by no means impossible, for players to sell (to school boosters, for example) a favored position on the pass list. Eventually, the NCAA turned to the current rule, which specifies that three of the four passes must be designated for the player's family members or fellow students. Is this a sensible solution? What exactly is the problem?

B. PROCEDURAL DUE PROCESS[h]

As the preceding section indicates, the Supreme Court's insulation of the NCAA from direct constitutional constraints did not end the

---

h. For an extended journalistic critique of NCAA procedures, see Don Yaeger, *Un-*

debate about the obligations that this organization owes to its constituents. After the NCAA initiated its action against *Tarkanian* in 1977, Congress conducted a lengthy inquiry into NCAA enforcement procedures. The resulting Report[i] threatened legislation unless the NCAA voluntarily improved its procedures (and in certain respects the Association did so). Following the Supreme Court's *Tarkanian* decision in 1988, a number of states (including Nebraska, Florida, Illinois, and, not surprisingly, Nevada) passed legislation requiring the NCAA to comply with federal and state due process principles as a matter of statutory law.

The Nebraska and Nevada laws provide an interesting comparison in legislative approaches to this issue. Instead of specifying the procedures necessary to afford due process, the Nebraska legislation, passed in 1990, required only that "all proceedings of a collegiate athletic association, college, or university that may result in the imposition of a penalty for violation of such association's rule or legislation shall comply with due process of law as guaranteed by the Constitution of Nebraska and laws of Nebraska." The procedures the NCAA had to follow were to be derived from general Nebraska case law defining due process, which presumably is influenced by federal constitutional precedents such as *Mathews v. Eldridge*. That left open the key question, though, of whether the procedures appropriate for NCAA investigations are those used for administrative determination of welfare entitlements or those used by courts in resolving criminal charges. The Nebraska statute allowed the parties to sue the NCAA for injunctive relief or damages, and made NCAA decisions and penalties reviewable in state court like the decisions of state agencies.

In contrast, the Nevada legislation, passed in 1991, noted that "substantial monetary loss, serious disruption of athletic programs and significant damage to reputations and careers result from the imposition of sanctions on member institutions, its employees, [and] student-athletes . . . for violations of [NCAA] rules." In an NCAA proceeding which results in the imposition of a sanction for violation of an NCAA rule, "all parties against whom a sanction may be imposed must be afforded an opportunity for a hearing after reasonable notice." The law also provides that 1) the NCAA must give detailed notice of the charge against the

due Process: The NCAA's Injustice For All (Champaign, Ill.: Sagamore Publishing, 1991). Contrasting scholarly views are presented by Frank Remington, "NCAA Rule Enforcement Procedures," Chapter 12 of Gary Uberstine, ed., *Law of Professional and Amateur Sports* (Deerfield, Ill.: Clark, Boardman, and Callaghan, 1991) (the author was a long-time member of the NCAA Committee on Infractions as well as an eminent criminal law professor at Wisconsin Law School), and Burton F. Brody, *NCAA Rules and Their Enforcement: Not Spare the Rod and Spoil the Child; Rather Switch the Values and Spare the Sport*, 1982 Arizona St. L. J. 109. For a recent, in-depth analysis of the NCAA's rule-making rather than rule-enforcing procedures, see John R. Allison, *Rule-Making Accuracy in the NCAA and its Member Institutions: Do Their Decisional Structures and Processes Promote Educational Primacy for the Student Athlete?*, 44 Kansas L. Rev. 1 (1995).

i. *NCAA Enforcement Program*: Hearings Before the Subcomm. on Oversight and Investigation of the Comm. on Interstate and Foreign Commerce, House of Representatives, 95th Cong., 2d Sess. (1978).

party; 2) the party charged with violating an NCAA rule may be represented by counsel and "is entitled to respond to all witnesses and evidence related to the allegations against him and may call witnesses on his own behalf"; 3) "all written statements introduced as evidence at a proceeding must be notarized and signed under oath by the person making the statement"; 4) a record must be kept of all the proceedings; 5) parties may make objections to evidence; 6) the adjudicator must be impartial and avoid ex parte communications with the parties; 7) "the decision and findings of fact must be based on substantial evidence in the record, and must be supported by a preponderance of such evidence"; and 8) NCAA sanctions must be "reasonable in light of the nature and gravity of the violation" and "consistent with penalties and sanctions previously imposed" by the NCAA. Like the Nebraska statute, the Nevada legislation offers injunctive and damage remedies to those harmed by violations of these procedures, as well as affording judicial review of the merits of the NCAA decision.

In 1990, the NCAA received information which suggested that UNLV had again violated NCAA rules—this time by the recruiting of basketball player Lloyd Daniels by Coach Jerry Tarkanian and his assistants. Both NCAA and UNLV staff conducted investigations of these allegations as the prelude to a hearing before the NCAA Committee on Infractions scheduled for late September, 1991. That summer, Tarkanian and his colleagues filed written requests with the NCAA asking for compliance with Nevada law; in particular, seeking advance copies of any documents that the NCAA intended to use and any exculpatory statements obtained during the investigation, with a right to confront all witnesses in a public hearing in front of an independent and impartial entity. Faced with that request, the NCAA went to federal court, asking for a ruling that the Nevada law was unconstitutional because of its obstruction of national uniformity in the enforcement of NCAA rules. The district court granted the NCAA an injunction against any use of the state law, and the Governor of Nevada appealed to the Ninth Circuit.[j]

THE NATIONAL COLLEGIATE ATHLETIC ASS'N v. ROBERT F. MILLER, GOVERNOR, STATE OF NEVADA, ET AL.

United States Court of Appeals, Ninth Circuit, 1993.
10 F.3d 633.

FERNANDEZ, CIRCUIT JUDGE.

* * *

Whenever an alleged rules violation is reported to the NCAA, the matter is handled pursuant to the enforcement program. The enforce-

---

[j]. See Sherry Young, *The NCAA Enforcement Program and Due Process: The Case for Internal Reform*, 43 Syracuse L. Rev. 747 (1992), and Sherry Young, *Is "Due Process" Unconstitutional? The NCAA Wins Round One in Its Fight Against Regulation of its Enforcement Proceedings*, 25 Arizona State L. J. 841 (1993).

ment program is administered by the Committee on Infractions, which establishes investigation procedures that must later be approved by the NCAA Council and the full membership of the NCAA. The Manual details the procedures that must be followed in processing an infractions case.

The first step in the process is for the enforcement staff to notify the institution in question that the NCAA is making a preliminary inquiry into the institution's athletics policies and practices. If the enforcement staff determines that a possible rule violation has occurred, it sends an official inquiry letter to the chief executive officer of the institution. The official inquiry must include a statement of the NCAA rule alleged to have been violated and the details of each separate allegation. The enforcement staff must also provide the institution and other involved individuals with the names of the principals involved and the names, addresses and telephone numbers of any people contacted during the NCAA investigation. The institution is required to notify past or present staff members or prospective, past, or present student-athletes who may be affected by the charges that they have the opportunity to submit any information they desire to the Committee and that they and their personal legal counsel may appear before the Committee. The institution is also required to investigate the charges and to indicate whether it feels that the allegations are substantially correct. It may also submit written evidence to support its response to the official inquiry.

After the institution has submitted its written response to the official inquiry in a case involving a major violation, the enforcement staff must "prepare a summary statement of the case that indicates the status of each allegation and identifies the individuals upon whom and the information upon which the staff will rely in presenting the case." The summary is presented to the Committee, the institution, and all other affected individuals before the Committee hearing. The institution and affected individuals and their legal counsel are permitted to review any memoranda or documents upon which the enforcement staff will rely in the presentation of its case, but only at the NCAA national office.

Prior to the Committee on Infractions hearing, prehearing conferences are held with the NCAA staff, the institution and all affected individuals and their legal counsel. At those meetings, the NCAA staff is required to provide all of the information upon which it intends to rely at the hearing. All involved parties review the relevant documents. Areas of factual dispute are identified. Unsupported allegations may be withdrawn and the institution and affected individuals can determine whether they need to conduct any further interviews in order to supplement their responses to the official inquiry.

The Committee on Infractions hearing consists of a detailed presentation of the case by the enforcement staff followed by a response from the institution and any affected individuals (or their legal representatives) who desire to respond. After the hearing, the Committee members privately make their determinations of fact, determine appropriate corrective action, if any, and prepare their written report. The institution is entitled to appeal the Committee's findings of fact and any corrective action taken against it to the NCAA Council.

In 1991, the Nevada legislature enacted the Statute. Essentially, the Statute requires any national collegiate athletic association to provide a Nevada institution, employee, student-athlete, or booster who is accused of a rules infraction with certain procedural due process protections during an enforcement proceeding in which sanctions may be imposed. Many of the procedures required by the Statute are not included in the NCAA enforcement program. For example, the NCAA does not provide the accused with the right to confront all witnesses, the right to have all written statements signed under oath and notarized, the right to have an official record kept of all proceedings, or the right to judicial review of a Committee decision.

[The Court then described the history of this dispute, and then turned to the constitutional issues.]

* * *

A. Legal Standards

The Supreme Court has outlined a two-tiered approach to analyzing state economic regulations under the Commerce Clause.

> When a state statute directly regulates or discriminates against interstate commerce, or when its effect is to favor in-state economic interests over out-of-state interests, we have generally struck down the statute without further inquiry. When, however, a statute has only indirect effects on interstate commerce and regulates evenhandedly, we have examined whether the State's interest is legitimate and whether the burden on interstate commerce clearly exceeds the local benefits.

Healy v. Beer Institute, 491 U.S. 324, 337 n. 14 (1989) (quoting *Brown-Forman Distillers Corp. v. New York State Liquor Auth.*, 476 U.S. 573, 579 (1986)). Applying this test, we must first ask whether the Statute: 1) directly regulates interstate commerce; 2) discriminates against interstate commerce; or 3) favors in-state economic interests over out-of-state interests. If the Statute does any of these things, it violates the Commerce Clause per se, and we must strike it down without further inquiry. If we determine that the Statute has only indirect effects on interstate commerce and that it regulates evenhandedly, then we must apply the balancing test.

B. The Statute Violates the Commerce Clause Per Se

The district court held that the Statute does not violate the Commerce Clause per se because it does not directly discriminate against interstate commerce or favor in-state economic interests over out-of-state interests. That holding was error because discrimination and economic protectionism are not the sole tests. The court should also have considered whether the Statute directly regulates interstate commerce.

It is clear that the Statute is directed at interstate commerce and only interstate commerce. By its terms, it regulates only interstate organizations, i.e., national collegiate athletic associations which have member institutions in 40 or more states. Moreover, courts have consistently held that the NCAA, which seems to be the only organization regulated by the Statute, is engaged in interstate commerce in numerous ways. It markets interstate intercollegiate athletic competition. See *NCAA v. Board of Regents of Univ. of Okla.*, 468 U.S. 85 (1984) (finding by implication that NCAA was engaged in interstate commerce and was subject to antitrust regulation). The NCAA schedules events that call for transportation of teams across state lines and it governs nationwide amateur athlete recruiting and controls bids for lucrative national and regional television broadcasting of college athletics. Thus, the Statute regulates only interstate organizations which are engaged in interstate commerce, and it does so directly. In fact, it applies no such panoply of procedural rights to voluntary organizations which operate wholly within the State of Nevada.

The Statute would have a profound effect on the way the NCAA enforces its rules and regulates the integrity of its product. The district court found that in order for the NCAA to accomplish its goals, the "enforcement procedures must be applied even-handedly and uniformly on a national basis." That finding is not only correct, but is also consistent with the Supreme Court's statement that the integrity of the NCAA's product cannot be preserved "except by mutual agreement; if an institution adopted [its own athlete eligibility regulations] unilaterally, its effectiveness as a competitor on the playing field might soon be destroyed." *Board of Regents of Univ. of Okla.*, 468 U.S. at 102.

In order to avoid liability under the Statute, the NCAA would be forced to adopt Nevada's procedural rules for Nevada schools. Therefore, if the NCAA wished to have the uniform enforcement procedures that it needs to accomplish its fundamental goals and to simultaneously avoid liability under the Statute, it would have to apply Nevada's procedures to enforcement proceedings throughout the country.

The practical requirement that the NCAA would have to use the Statute in enforcement proceedings in every state in the union runs afoul of the Commerce Clause in two ways. First, "a statute that directly controls commerce occurring wholly outside the boundaries of a State exceeds the inherent limits of the enacting State's authority and is invalid regardless of whether the statute's extraterritorial reach was intended by the legislature. The critical inquiry is whether the practical effect of the regulation is to control conduct beyond the boundaries of the State." *Healy*, 491 U.S. at 336.

The Statute would force the NCAA to regulate the integrity of its product in every state according to Nevada's procedural rules. Thus, if a university in state X ("U of X") engaged in illicit practices while recruiting a high school quarterback from state Y, the NCAA would have to conduct its enforcement proceeding according to Nevada law in order to maintain uniformity in its rules. Nevada procedures do not allow the Committee on Infractions to consider some types of evidence, like hearsay and unsworn affidavits, that it can consider under the NCAA Bylaws. As a result, if its case against the U of X were based on unsworn affidavits from unavailable witnesses, the NCAA might not have enough admissible evidence to prove that there was a violation of the recruiting rules. The NCAA could be forced to allow the U of X to use an illegally recruited quarterback from state Y because it could not prove a rules violation under the strictures of Nevada law. In this way, the Statute could control the regulation of the integrity of a product in interstate commerce that occurs wholly outside Nevada's borders. That sort of extraterritorial effect is forbidden by the Commerce Clause.

The Statute's extraterritorial reach also violates the Commerce Clause because of its potential interaction or conflict with similar statutes in other jurisdictions. "Generally speaking, the Commerce Clause protects against inconsistent legislation arising from the projection of one state regulatory regime into the jurisdiction of another State." *Healy*, 491 U.S. at 336–37.

Nevada is not the only state that has enacted or could enact legislation that establishes procedural rules for NCAA enforcement proceedings. Florida, Illinois, and Nebraska have also adopted due process statutes and similar legislation has been introduced in five other states. Those statutes could easily subject the NCAA to conflicting requirements. For example, suppose that state X required proof of an infraction beyond a reasonable doubt, while state Y only required clear and convincing evidence, and state Z required infractions to be proven by a preponderance of the evidence. Given that the NCAA must have uniform enforcement procedures in order to accomplish its fundamental goals, its operation would be disrupted because it could not possibly comply with all three statutes. Nor would it do to say that it need only comply with the most stringent burden of persuasion (beyond a reasonable doubt), for a state with a less stringent standard might well consider its standard a maximum as well as a minimum. The serious risk of inconsistent obligations wrought by the extraterritorial effect of the Statute demonstrates why it constitutes a per se violation of the Commerce Clause.

Under *Brown-Forman*, 476 U.S. at 579, when a state law directly regulates interstate commerce, it can generally be struck down without further inquiry. The Statute directly regulates interstate commerce and runs afoul of the Commerce Clause both because it regulates a product in interstate commerce beyond Nevada's state boundaries, and because it puts the NCAA, and whatever other national collegiate athletic associations may exist, in jeopardy of being subjected to inconsistent legislation arising from the injection of Nevada's regulatory scheme into the jurisdiction of other states. Because the Statute violates the Commerce Clause per se, we need not balance the burden on interstate commerce against the local benefit derived from the Statute.[8]

8. If balancing were necessary or appropriate, the balance struck by the learned

CONCLUSION

We appreciate Nevada's interest in assuring that its citizens and institutions will be treated fairly. However, the authority it seeks here goes to the heart of the NCAA and threatens to tear that heart out. Consistency among members must exist if an organization of this type is to thrive, or even exist. Procedural changes at the border of every state would as surely disrupt the NCAA as changes in train length at each state's border would disrupt a railroad. See *Southern Pac. Co. v. Arizona,* 325 U.S. 761 (1945). It takes no extended lucubration to discover that. If the procedures of the NCAA are "to be regulated at all, national uniformity in the regulation adopted, such as only Congress can prescribe, is practically indispensable.... " Id. at 771. In short, when weighed against the Constitution, the Statute must be found wanting. It violates the Commerce Clause.

Affirmed.

By the time the Ninth Circuit had issued its *Miller* decision, Tarkanian and his associates had left the UNLV basketball program. After a brief stint with the San Antonio Spurs and then a period in retirement, Tarkanian went back to college coaching at Fresno State in California. In the meantime, though, Tarkanian (and his wife) had filed yet another lawsuit against the NCAA, alleging that the Association had "wrongfully attempted to force him out of college coaching." In 1997, the Supreme Court of Nevada ruled that this case could go to trial in Las Vegas: see *NCAA v. Tarkanian,* 113 Nev. 610, 939 P.2d 1049 (1997). Facing that prospect, the NCAA agreed in early 1998 to settle their quarter-century battle with Tarkanian by paying him $2.5 million in damages.

Questions For Discussion

1. Suppose that Nevada were to amend its legislation to make its requirements applicable to all athletic associations (including intrastate high school sports federations), and to remove the ban on NCAA expulsion of Nevada colleges if the NCAA preferred not to comply with these procedural restrictions. Would those revisions materially reduce the impact of this brand of state regulation? Alternatively, suppose the Nebraska statute required the NCAA to satisfy the "due process" requirements of the federal, not the state, constitution in its disciplinary actions against Nebraska college players and personnel. Would (should) any of these changes alter the judicial verdict under the dormant Commerce Clause?

2. A major Commerce Clause decision is *CTS Corp. v. Dynamics Corp. of Am.,* 481 U.S. 69 (1987), which involved an Indiana law that regulated tender offers made for Indiana-chartered corporations, whether or not the offer came from in-state or out-of-state bidders. The Supreme Court upheld

---

trial judge was exactly right. If the NCAA is suffering from a procedural disease, Nevada's attempted cure is as likely to destroy the patient as it is to banish the disease. It is not an example of permissible praxis.

the Indiana law against the constitutional argument that the state had unduly interfered with the national securities market. Are there differences between the sports industry and the securities industry that might explain why the court in *Miller* did not even cite *CTS Corp.*?

3. Suppose that Nevada (following the lead of Montana) enacted a statute that forbade wrongful dismissal or suspension of employees working in the state, and specified in the law what kind of due process must be extended to employees before such disciplinary action could be taken. Can such a law be applied to national corporations that have employees working in the state? Would the answer differ if the employer—perhaps a securities firm—belonged to a national association that required alternative dispute resolution procedures for employees suspected of specific offenses, such as fraud? Again, is there a difference between employment in sports and employment in other industries that is relevant to the issues of constitutional federalism?

4. Recall from Chapter 1 the decision in *Hill v. NCAA & Stanford Univ.*, 26 Cal.Rptr.2d 834, 7 Cal.4th 1, 865 P.2d 633 (1994), in which the Supreme Court of California ruled that the NCAA's program of random drug testing of college athletes did not violate their privacy rights under the California state constitution. The *Hill* decision did, however, expressly affirm that this privacy clause (and perhaps other constitutional constraints) barred private as well as public entities from unduly infringing on the rights of California citizens. Thus, to the extent that privacy, due process, equal protection, and other claims under the California (or other state) constitution extend to private action, are the NCAA's rules and procedures subject to challenge, or would the dormant commerce clause doctrine relied on in *Miller* insulate the NCAA from any such state constitutional limits? In particular, suppose California were either to amend its constitution (e.g., by popular referendum) or pass legislation that precluded random drug-testing of either high school or college students, with no exceptions for athletes. Is such a state initiative barred by *Miller*? Does your verdict differ if the target of NCAA tests are performance-enhancing drugs such as anabolic steroids, or mind-altering drugs such as marijuana?

If *Miller* governs, state efforts to regulate NCAA enforcement *procedures* are likely not to be constitutionally permissible. However, in the early 1990s, former Rep. Tom McMillan introduced legislation in Congress that would have required the NCAA to provide "due process" in all enforcement proceedings. While such national legislation would not be subject to dormant Commerce Clause attack, it raised both practical and policy questions about what role the law and courts should play in securing fair and effective "law" enforcement by a private body. In any event, in response to the popular and political pressures reflected in the McMillan proposal, the NCAA appointed a blue-ribbon committee to review its procedures. The Special Committee, which was headed by Rex Lee (former U.S. Solicitor–General and the NCAA's counsel in the *Tarkanian* appeal before the Supreme Court) and included former Chief

Justice Warren Burger, announced its recommendations in late 1991. As we will see, some of the proposals are being implemented.

These developments cast a somewhat different light on the question posed earlier about whether or not it is necessary to constitutionalize the NCAA to secure proper safeguards for its members. After all, why would the member-schools of the NCAA tolerate procedures that truly deny them "due process"? The answer, at least in part, lies in the regular scandals that afflict the world of college sports.

Two of the most widely publicized scandals from the 1980s produced litigation. One involved the football program at Southern Methodist University (SMU),[k] which was revived under the leadership of Ron Meyer (who, ironically, had previously been a coaching colleague of Jerry Tarkanian at UNLV). In order to recruit star high school prospects (such as Eric Dickerson who gave SMU the best five-year record in college football in the early 1980s), the SMU athletic staff and a cadre of Dallas boosters instituted a program of bonus payments to high school seniors to induce them to sign letters of intent to enroll at SMU. They also made regular monthly payments to SMU players and arranged for a Dallas dealership to provide expensive cars to star players. It was later learned that these expenditures had been authorized by William Clements during his tenure as Chairman of the SMU Board of Governors, between Clements' two terms as governor of Texas. As we shall see in the next chapter, the NCAA's imposition of the "death penalty"[l] on SMU football produced an important antitrust challenge to the NCAA's authority.

Shortly after SMU's practices and penalties became public, the even more successful and prestigious Kentucky basketball program was literally enveloped in scandal.[m] Inside an Emery delivery envelope addressed by Kentucky assistant coach Dwayne Casey to the father of Chris Mills, one of the nation's most heavily-recruited basketball players in the spring of 1988, was a basketball video tape—and $1,000 in cash. National publicity about this discovery by Emery's Los Angeles warehouse staff precipitated an NCAA investigation that also uncovered apparent cheating on the ACT college entrance examination by Eric Manuel, another star Kentucky recruit that year. Manuel, who scored only three (out of a possible 36) when he first took the ACT in his native Georgia, received an 18 the next time he took the test, in Kentucky. Investigation of the second answer sheet revealed that almost every one of Manuel's answers (right or wrong) were identical to those of another Kentucky student

---

k. See David Whitford, *A Payroll to Meet: A Story of Greed, Corruption and Football at SMU* (New York: MacMillan, 1989).

l. The "death penalty" rule (in NCAA By-law Art. 19.6.2.3.2(a)) allows the NCAA to terminate for two years a school's program in a sport in which a major rules violation is committed within five years of another major rules violation in any sport.

m. See Alexander Wolff & Armen Keteyian, *Raw Recruits: The High Stakes Game Colleges Play to Get Their Basketball Stars—And What It Costs to Win* (New York: Simon and Schuster, 1990).

sitting behind him. Still another Kentucky recruit, Shawn Kemp, was caught with jewelry that had been reported stolen from a teammate, Sean Sutton, son of Kentucky coach Eddie Sutton. Despite these and other unpleasantries, Kentucky basketball escaped the "death penalty" after the school fired its athletic director and coaching staff. (The assistant coach, Casey, sued Emery for its handling of the envelope and the money, and apparently received a lucrative settlement.) The new coach was Rick Pitino, who was wooed away from the NBA's New York Knicks with a multi-million dollar contract. By the spring of 1996, Pitino had brought yet another NCAA title back to Kentucky, before leaving again for the NBA Celtics.

The SMU and Kentucky cases are just the tip of the iceberg of what is taking place in big-time college sports. During the 1980s alone, more than half of the 105 Division I-A schools received sanctions, and many were put on probation and banned from post-season play.[n] The problem is not merely that schools violate the numerous technical requirements of a voluminous NCAA rulebook. In a 1989 survey of NFL players, one-third admitted that they had received cash payments while in college, and half said that they knew teammates who had received money under the table.[o] Coaches such as Bobby Knight of Indiana (and also Jerry Tarkanian) publicly lamented that top high school basketball prospects were being offered financial packages of $100,000 or more to choose one school over its competitors. Even legitimate recruiting expenditures (such as departmental salaries and travel expenses) can cost as much as $50,000 for each athlete who enrolls in the school. Rick Pitino's million dollar compensation package when he was coaching at Kentucky, as well as Steve Spurrier's new contract after leading Florida to the 1996 football championship, put them just slightly ahead of other college luminaries such as John Thompson at Georgetown and Bobby Bowden at Florida State. (These packages include not only salary, but also revenues from shoe contracts, radio and television shows, summer clinics, and speaking engagements across the country.)

Why are institutions prepared to expend this much money on sports—$15 million in 1995 for the average Division I athletic program, and just under $40 million for the largest? The explanation is complex. While many Division I programs apparently suffer a financial loss from athletic operations, the institutions retain the programs because of the tremendous marketing, public relations, and political benefits that athletics generate. However, there are limits on the amount that schools can afford to lose in subsidizing their "auxiliary" athletic programs, and the only way to limit those losses (or for some schools, to maximize their profits) is to have winning football and men's basketball teams that frequently appear on television and regularly fill their stadiums and arenas with paying fans. (Recall that the top football programs can earn $15 million in profits per season, and the top basketball programs $7 million a year; the downside is that 30% of the programs lose an average

n. See Bayley & Littleton, *Athletics and Academe*, note 1 above, at 25.

o. See Sperber, *College Sports Inc.*, note 1 above, at 257.

of $1 million in football and $225,000 in basketball.) In addition, the intangible public relations value of these programs are greatly increased when the school's teams are winning.

Given the multi-million dollar differences between the winning and losing "revenue-sport" programs, as well as the intangible benefits from victory, institutions put great pressure on their coaches and athletic department personnel to win games. And because their careers, reputations, and chances for celebrity status are at stake, many coaches and others involved in athletics succumb to the temptation to bend or break the rules to attract the best athletes to their schools and keep them eligible once they are there.[p] This is why the NCAA decided after World War II that it would no longer rely on voluntary "home rule" adherence to the Association's principles. An enforcement staff of one employee in the early 1950s became three by the late 1960s and now consists of 15 full-time employees; the NCAA has even used ex-FBI agents as part-time investigators. The enforcement problem faced by the NCAA (and thence by courts and legislatures scrutinizing the NCAA) is that the targets of the NCAA rulebook are "crimes without victims"—consensual behavior that takes place in private and is very hard to detect and deter even for governments that can use compulsory investigative techniques unavailable to a private body such as the NCAA.

A case that illustrates the problem is *Berst v. Chipman*, 232 Kan. 180, 653 P.2d 107 (1982), involving an NCAA investigation of the University of Alabama's recruiting of high school basketball star Bobby Lee Hurt. The Birmingham Post wrote a series of stories about the case (both before and after the NCAA investigation), stories that eventually produced libel suits against the Post by Hurt and his high school principal. The Post then sought to compel discovery of the NCAA's investigative files, which contained several off-the-record statements made to NCAA staff.

In the eyes of the court,

> ... [T]his case presents a conflict between highly valued interests. On the one hand there is an interest in confidentiality, both to prevent embarrassment to persons who have relied on pledges of secrecy in disclosing information to the NCAA or about whom information in the file may relate, and to promote the public interest in the supervision of intercollegiate athletics to prevent corruption in that area and retain a clear line of demarcation between college athletics and professional sports. On the other hand is the interest in disclosure of all facts relevant to the petitioners' defense in the libel action which will contribute to a full and fair determination of the issues in that case.

---

p. One should not think this is a recent phenomenon. The first intercollegiate sporting event was a Harvard–Yale rowing regatta in 1852. In the second such competition between these schools in 1855, Harvard included an ex-student in its crew. See Smith, *Sports and Freedom*, note c above, at 176.

653 P.2d at 116. How would you resolve this conflict? Is there a compromise that would serve the key interests of both sides?

Although NCAA records that are directly material can usually be discovered in litigation, and are often subject to protective orders requiring litigants to keep the contents confidential, a more troubling prospect for the NCAA is that its investigative records (or those compiled by its conferences and member schools) might be published pursuant to state "freedom of information" laws that allow private parties (usually newspapers) access to most "public records." Such laws present two questions. First, are the NCAA's files "public records"? (A state institution's files almost surely are public.) See *Kneeland v. NCAA*, 850 F.2d 224 (5th Cir.1988) (holding NCAA and Southwest Conference documents compiled during investigations of the SMU "death penalty" case not to be "public records" under the Texas Open Records Act). Second, if they are public records, does the state law provide any exceptions that allow these files to be kept confidential? See *Combined Communications Corp. of Oklahoma v. Boger*, 689 F.Supp. 1065 (W.D.Okla.1988) (holding that there is no public right of access to a state university's letter of intent under the First Amendment or the Oklahoma Open Records Act). However these questions are resolved, the underlying policy issues are often the same for both freedom of information laws and discovery demands in the litigation. What impact would public disclosure of such records have on the ability of the NCAA or its members to investigate infractions?

Does the value placed by NCAA investigators on off-the-record tips help explain the procedures we saw used in *Tarkanian*? Is it justifiable for the NCAA to use such unattributed material in a hearing about alleged rules violation? The following provision from the NCAA Manual states the Association's present policy.

> 32.6.5.5.1 *Information from Confidential Sources*. In presenting information and evidence for consideration by the committee during an institutional hearing, the enforcement staff shall present only information that can be attributed to individuals who are willing to be identified. Information obtained from individuals not wishing to be identified shall not be relied upon by the committee in making findings of violations. Such confidential sources shall not be identified to either the Committee on Infractions or the institution.

Another issue relating to NCAA power has been the extent to which courts should protect the rights of student-athletes (and of coaches such as Tarkanian) against an organization whose only constituent members are colleges and universities.[q] To many, it seems especially unfair, for

[q.] For a critique of the historical exclusion of student-athletes from NCAA decision-making, see Rodney K. Smith, *The National Collegiate Athletic Association's Death Penalty: How Educators Punish*

example, when the NCAA sanctions an athletic program for violations that occurred several years earlier. As a result, student-athletes who had nothing to do with the infractions now lose their chance to compete in post-season games or on national television. This happened to the 1991–92 UNLV basketball team which was not allowed to play in the NCAA tournament because of rules violations committed fifteen years earlier, and to the SMU football team which received the "death penalty" for earlier rules violations.

In 1987 Hersey Hawkins and his Bradley University teammates sued the NCAA after it barred the team from the NCAA basketball tournament because of earlier school violations. The players asserted that imposing such a penalty on them was so fundamentally unfair that it violated the Equal Protection and Due Process Clauses of the Constitution. The district court dismissed the suit on the grounds that no fundamental rights were implicated and that the NCAA had a rational basis for imposing penalties on innocent players in order to maintain the integrity of intercollegiate athletics. See *Hawkins v. NCAA*, 652 F.Supp. 602 (C.D.Ill.1987). Today, presumably the suit would also be dismissed pursuant to the *Tarkanian* decision because NCAA sanctions are not state action. However, the case raises the basic policy questions whether it is fair for student-athletes to be penalized for "crimes" committed by others, and if not, whether the NCAA could alter its enforcement procedures to avoid such unfairness while effectively enforcing its substantive rules.

Another question is what procedural protection the NCAA should provide to players or coaches accused of violations. The NCAA recently adopted several protections for individual students (and coaches) who may lose their eligibility to play (or coach) intercollegiate sports. For example, players and coaches have the right to be represented by legal counsel during an interview with NCAA investigators (Article 32.3.5) and to participate with counsel at Committee on Infractions hearings in which their eligibility (or employment) is at stake (Article 32.6.4). However, only staff members faced with disciplinary sanctions have the right of appeal to the NCAA Council; the university must exercise the right to appeal a denial of its student-athlete's eligibility (Article 32.8.3). Are these changes sufficient? If not, what alternatives exist that would also provide effective enforcement of NCAA rules?

In 1991, a Special Committee appointed by the NCAA to review its investigative and adjudicative process recommended major changes in the Association's procedures.[r] The Committee suggested that the NCAA use retired judges to serve as hearing officers in order to determine whether violations have occurred, based on taped transcripts of investigative interviews and legal arguments. The Committee on Infractions would no longer determine whether wrongdoing has in fact occurred, but

Themselves and Others, 62 Indiana L. J. 985, 1050–57 (1985).

r. See *Report and Recommendations of the Special Committee to Review the NCAA Enforcement and Infractions Process* (Overland Park, Kan.: NCAA, 1991).

would decide only whether to accept or alter the penalties recommended by the hearing officer. Jerry Tarkanian's reaction to the Committee Report was that his case "has been a catalyst for bringing this reform about. This is a magnificent day for those who want and expect fairness within the most powerful athletic body in the world."

As it turned out, the NCAA adopted some, but by no means all, of the Committee's recommendations. But even if all of the proposals were now in the NCAA rule book (e.g., the use of retired judges to determine violations), was Tarkanian right in his applause? Should the accused also have a right to confront and cross-examine witnesses who provide evidence to be used in this hearing process? If so, does the NCAA need a subpoena power to force recalcitrant witnesses to testify? Should the NCAA have that power, and if so, would that turn the Association back into a "state actor"? The crucial theme that runs through all these cases and questions is the extent to which expanded procedural rights for the targets of NCAA investigations are compatible with effective enforcement of NCAA rules regulating the multi-billion dollar world of intercollegiate sports.

C. ELIGIBILITY REQUIREMENTS

Reflection on that last question, the enforcement costs of due process, brings into focus the content and value of the rules that the NCAA is trying to enforce in the first place. The bulk of the NCAA's investigations and penalties involve promises made to players in recruiting and money or benefits received while they are in college. The NCAA deems these practices improper and "illegal" because they violate the basic principles stated earlier—that intercollegiate sports, unlike professional sports, are an integral part of the academic mission of the college, played by students for the love of the game (i.e., as "amateurs") rather than for pay. To define the meaning of a "student amateur athlete" takes several hundred pages in the NCAA Manual. The scandals at Southern Methodist University and the University of Kentucky epitomize the continual threat to the *amateur* quality of intercollegiate sports. A contemporaneous scandal at the University of Georgia revealed the sometimes dubious *academic* quality of this enterprise.[s]

The case of *Kemp v. Ervin*, 651 F.Supp. 495 (N.D.Ga.1986), was a lawsuit by an instructor at the University of Georgia who was fired for speaking out about practices used by the university to maintain its football players' academic eligibility. Jan Kemp was the coordinating instructor of English in Georgia's Division of Developmental Studies, which provided remedial education to academically underqualified students to whom the school had granted special admission. Athletic director and football coach Vince Dooley regularly used this program for many of his recruits (sometimes twenty or more players in a single year).

---

[s] See Francis X. Dealy, Jr., *Win At Any Cost: The Sellout of College Athletics* 78–95 (New York: Birch Lane Press, 1990).

Dooley's intervention resulted in Herschel Walker's admission via this program in 1980, a week *after* Walker had starred for Georgia in his first game as a supposed freshman playing against Tennessee. In December 1981, the school promoted nine football players out of the developmental program into regular academic studies in order to keep them eligible for the New Year's Day Sugar Bowl, even though all the players had received D's in remedial English and school policy required a grade of C to exit the remedial program.

Kemp, leading a protest by the Division's faculty, complained about the implications of this practice for the academic treatment of the school's African–American football players (more than 60% of the players in the program were black). Kemp attacked decisions made by her supervisor, Dr. Leroy Ervin, head of Developmental Studies, who was African–American, and Ervin's supervisor, Dr. Virginia Trotter, the University's Vice President of Academic Affairs (and former Undersecretary of Education for President Gerald Ford). After receiving Kemp's letter of protest, Ervin (with Trotter's support) removed Kemp from her position as English coordinator and then refused to renew her oral contract as an instructor in the Division. Ervin apparently called Kemp "a liar and bigot," and asked her whether she thought she was more important to the school than a football player. Kemp, after attempting suicide, eventually sued and won a $2.6 million verdict against Ervin, Trotter, and the University of Georgia. Following the defendants' appeal, a settlement reduced the award to a $1 million cash payment and Kemp's reinstatement.

Kemp v. Ervin dramatically portrays the problem of maintaining the academic quality of intercollegiate sports. Widespread publicity about the scandal and litigation coincided with the NCAA's effort to enhance academic standards for both admission to and scholarly progress at the school. The NCAA's proposal, in turn, produced heated controversy about the disparate impact of these new standards on African–American athletes. The following decisions and text provide a snapshot of the key NCAA judgments about who should be academically eligible to play in intercollegiate sports, and the practical problems and conflicts generated by these official judgments. While several of the early cases were filed against the NCAA under the "state action" constitutional rubric that the Supreme Court later removed in *Tarkanian*, the substantive issues remain—now challenged under different branches of federal and state law.

1. ADMISSION STANDARDS: PROPOSITION 48

NCAA rules specify the academic credentials required from athletes who graduate from high school and want to play in intercollegiate athletics. In the athletic setting, as in university admissions generally, a continuing struggle has been waged over the use of standardized admissions tests.[t] In its early days, the NCAA followed a policy of college

---

t. For an account of the earlier debates, see Ron Waicukauski, *The Regulation of*

"home rule" in making the judgment about whether or not to admit athletes into the school's classes. At its 1964 Convention, though, the membership adopted a "1.6 Predictor Rule," one that conditioned eligibility for participating in intercollegiate sports upon the student-athlete's academic prospects for meeting a minimum 1.6 predicted grade point average (GPA) in college. This prediction would be based on the student's high school GPA and class ranking, combined with the Scholastic Aptitude Test (SAT) or American College Test (ACT), as assessed through expectancy tables that incorporated statistics for over 40,000 students at more than 80 colleges. The debate about the impact of this rule surfaced in the federal courts in a case involving Centenary College's effort to play a center who had not met this 1.6 Predictor standard—Robert Parish, who would later lead the Boston Celtics to three NBA championships in the 1980s.

PARISH v. NCAA

United States District Court, Western District of Louisiana, 1973.
361 F.Supp. 1220.

DAWKINS, CHIEF JUDGE.

* * *

Parish, 7' 1" in height, denominated a "super-athlete," was recognized during his last high school year by national magazines, newspapers, and sports columnists as probably the number one or number two leading basketball prospect in the United States, in the manner of Wilt Chamberlain and Lew Alcindor. He was named to several All–American high school teams and chosen by the Basketball News as the number one high school graduate basketball player in the country. Of course, he was recruited, even courted, by almost every major college in the nation.

In order to fulfill the requirements of NCAA's 1.600 Rule, Parish took the ACT twice, his score being an 8. Regrettably, before achieving such prominence, he had been somewhat deprived, both educationally and economically; and probably began to aspire ambitiously toward a full higher education only after "the baskets began to swish." With this score, most colleges "backed off" because they felt Parish could not meet the 1.600 requirement.

* * *

With these facts before us, we now turn to the recruitment of Robert Parish by Centenary. NCAA, knowing that he was going to be a highly recruited prospect, had familiarized itself with Parish's high school record before the summer of 1972, well prior to his being signed to an athletic scholarship contract by Centenary. During June of 1972, NCAA received information that Centenary was going to sign Parish, and one of its representatives, Berst, called then Coach Wallace and asked him how Parish was going to predict a 1.600 score. Wallace replied that the school

Academic Standards in Intercollegiate Athletics, 1982 Arizona L. J. 79.

was going to convert the ACT test score to an SAT score, whereupon Berst informed him this was prohibited by the rules. Subsequently, NCAA advised Centenary through its coaching staff and its Director of Athletics (who has "resigned" since the controversy arose), orally and by written correspondence, that the College could not convert ACT scores to SAT scores. As "water runs from a duck's back," so did these warnings fall on deaf ears and failed to prevent Centenary's Athletic Department successfully from proceeding with its efforts to sign Parish upon a scholarship contract.

The College signed Parish August 17, 1972, to a four-year athletic scholarship. It is interesting to note that Centenary's athletic agents-in-charge informed Parish that this scholarship award was made " ... in accordance with the provisions of the Constitution of the National Collegiate Athletic Association, pertaining to the principles of amateurism, sound economic standards, and financial aid to student athletes."

Subsequently, Centenary informed NCAA that in taking such action it had converted test scores of other athletes at the school, i.e., the remaining plaintiffs in this action. It is worthy of note that, as stated, even by using the most favorable conversion table, as did Centenary, Parish still failed to predict 1.600. Ironically, he and all other plaintiffs have maintained a higher scholastic grade-point average throughout their respective college careers than required by the Rule.

* * *

Now, unfortunately, we have before us the single, not so simple, question of whether we should issue a preliminary injunction against defendants—a "Hobson's choice," which we do not relish at all, considering the empathy we hold for all of these competing interests: 1) the careers of these young athletes; 2) their present and future prospects; 3) the outstanding degree of culture contributed by the institution known as Centenary College, locally, regionally, and nationally, since well before the War Between the States; and finally, 4) the nationwide elevation of scholastic and athletic standards developed by NCAA for so many years.

* * *

Addressing the merits, even if [education] is a right or privilege protected by the Constitution, we hold that the 1.600 Rule withstands the denial of equal protection attack because it has a rational relationship to legitimate State (or national) purposes. Obviously, the challenged action by NCAA is not subject to strict judicial scrutiny. Therefore, we turn to the traditional standard of review which requires only that the NCAA's system be shown to bear some rational relationship to legitimate purposes. NCAA adopted the 1.600 Rule as a means of insuring that the athlete be an integral part of the student body and to maintain intercollegiate athletics as an integral part of the education program. Mr. Byars, of NCAA, summarized the need for these rules, as establishing a minimum standard which would prevent exploitation of athletes by the college or university, that is, setting up and agreeing to the prediction process by NCAA's members in order to prevent recruitment for athletic purposes alone of young men who had relatively poor chances of obtaining academic degrees; to encourage institutions with lower standards to elevate those standards to be more compatible with other institutions; and to discourage the unsound academic and economic practices of the past which had allowed indiscriminate granting of scholarships, resulting in too many athletes dropping out after their freshman or sophomore years. This rule was adopted to prevent abuses and at the time it was thought that this rule would solve the problem.

Notwithstanding, NCAA now has determined (since its action involving Centenary, Parish, and his teammates) that the rule was inadequate. This is based upon the fact that the 1.600 Rule was repealed and the 2.00 Rule was enacted in its stead. In *Associated Students v. NCAA* (May 25, 1973, Civil No. S–2754, E.D. Cal.), Judge McBride stated:

> Without deciding the question, it appears that this classification is reasonably related to the purposes of the 1.600 Rule.

However, he concluded that the 1.600 Rule, as interpreted by Official Interpretation 418 (O.I. 418) did not meet muster as to equal protection constitutional requirements. We agree that the 1.600 Rule's classification is reasonable, not arbitrary, and rests upon a ground having a fair and substantial relation to NCAA's object in enacting the legislation, so that all persons similarly circumstanced shall be treated alike, i.e., the Rule bears a rational relationship to the legitimate purposes for which it was enacted. Although application of the Rule may produce seemingly unreasonable results in certain situations, this is not unusual, for use of generalized rules frequently produces irrational results in isolated circumstances. Such results do not condemn those rules under traditional equal protection scrutiny. Here, NCAA has advanced one step at a time, addressing itself to the phase of the problem which then seems most acute to it.

Plaintiffs also presented evidence to show that the SAT and ACT tests discriminated against all of them in some form. One (Parish) came from a minority group, one from a rural school, etc. This type of evidence was rejected as having no weight in *Murray v. West Baton Rouge Parish School Board*, 472 F.2d 438 (5th Cir.1973):

> Plaintiffs have made a broad-based attack on the use of psychological testing at Port Allen Elementary School. The focus of the attack appears to be that the tests are being used to discriminate against the black students. There is absolutely no evidence that the testing is being used to foster segregation in the class rooms, ... and despite conclusionary allegations to the contrary, there is no evidence whatsoever that the tests are being administered in a discriminatory manner. If, as plaintiffs claim, there are a few black students whose educational progress has been wrongly retarded because of this testing, it is most unfortunate. But as a federal court we cannot intervene absent some well defined constitutional deprivation. There is no factual showing that the tests are culturally

biased, discriminatorily conceived, or even that they had a discriminatory effect. That the tests might not be an educationally valid one for a few individual children does not, in and of itself, give rise to constitutional deprivation. On the record before us, we can find no constitutional fault with the testing in the Port Allen Elementary School.

We take judicial notice of the fact that, at the time in question, the particular tests involved here under NCAA's Rule 1.600 were administered throughout the nation; almost every college in the United States required a score from one test or the other for admission purposes. We, therefore, must reject plaintiffs' claim as to this issue. We also note that members of the black race have been perhaps the greatest beneficiaries of numerically disproportionate participation in intercollegiate athletics; and they have done so under the aegis of the 1.600 Rule.

In *Associated Students*, supra, the Court stated:

* * *

Bearing in mind that the central purpose of the 1.600 Rule is to insure that the individual who participates in intercollegiate athletics is capable of succeeding academically at the college level, this new classification is overinclusive and not rationally related to the objective of the rule insofar as it declares ineligible not only those student athletes who fail to predict a minimum 1.600 grade point average and who have not yet completed their first year in college, and not only those student athletes who fail to achieve a minimum 1.600 grade point average for the first year in college, but additionally those student athletes who demonstrated by the conclusion of the first year that they have the ability to achieve academic success by actually earning at least a 1.600 grade point average. Once a student has an earned grade point average achieved over a reasonable period of time, then it is unreasonable, in light of the purposes of the rule, to impose sanctions against the student based on the fact that he failed to predict a certain grade point average. Instead, any sanctions imposed should be predicated on the actual grade point average attained by the student.

* * *

With this conclusion, we respectfully but regretfully disagree. It is our considered view that the Court in the just quoted decision overlooked the fact that one of the purposes of the official interpretation of the 1.600 Rule is to prevent schools from granting scholarships to those students who, after taking part in testing procedures, do not show a possibility of attaining a degree before entering college.

Under that decision, all member schools could recruit all those athletes whose entrance examinations did not predict successful graduation and then, if they did obtain a higher grade-point average than 1.600 after the first year in school, they would be entitled to participate in NCAA sponsored athletic events thenceforth. The Court's decision there effectively would prevent enforcement of the 1.600 Rule, which the Court already had determined to be rational in order to achieve NCAA's stated objective.

We cannot fathom how the official interpretation creates a classification which is in nonconformance with equal protection standards. In order to meet that objective, determination of eligibility must be made at the time of application and certification; to make it at a later date simply destroys the classification which the Court already had conceded to be reasonable. This decision in effect would allow colleges to recruit ineligible athletes and hope they will meet graduation prediction standards after their first year grades are in, thus becoming eligible for their entire collegiate athletic life. As stated, it is our considered opinion that NCAA's official interpretation of its 1.600 Rule does not create a classification which violates the equal protection requirements of the Constitution.

Case dismissed.

While the court's decision in favor of the NCAA was upheld on appeal (see *Parish v. NCAA*, 506 F.2d 1028 (5th Cir.1975)), the NCAA repealed the 1.600 Rule in the early 1970s (at the request of Ivy League members). Instead, scholarship athletes were required to have only a minimum 2.0 GPA from high school. Twenty-five years later, Robert Parish played his final season in the NBA, helping the Chicago Bulls win yet another championship in the 1996–97 season. That same year, the NCAA again faced a challenge against a much more controversial eligibility rule, via a *Shaw-Cureton* class action suit filed by the Trial Lawyers for Public Service under Title VI of the Civil Rights Act.

The two named plaintiffs, Leatrice Shaw and Tai Kwan Cureton, had graduated with honors from their Philadelphia high school in June 1996, ranking 5th and 27th respectively in their senior year class of 305 students. Both Shaw and Cureton were also topflight track and field runners who had been actively recruited by Division I colleges around the country. However, the NCAA now had a new eligibility regime, colloquially referred to as Proposition 48, which also required minimum SAT or ACT scores that Shaw and Cureton had not met. Shaw still secured an athletic scholarship as a "partial qualifier" with Miami University's Division I track and field team, although she was not able to compete in her 1996–97 freshman year. Cureton's athletic ineligibility as a freshman rendered him unattractive to Division I schools, and thus he ended up at Division III Wheaton College which does not offer any athletic scholarships.

Understanding the evolution and controversy over Proposition 48 since the early 1980s is crucial to one's evaluation of its legal defensibility and policy merits in present-day college sports. Proposition 48 (embodied in Article 14–3 of the Manual) was adopted by the NCAA in 1983, establishing a much tougher set of academic standards for athletic eligibility. Student-athletes still had to have at least a 2.00 GPA at high school, but this now had to come from core academic courses in English, mathematics, science and other subjects specified and investigated by the NCAA. Even such a high school record was not sufficient. No matter how high their GPA and class ranking, student-athletes also had to score a minimum of 700 on the SAT or 15 on the ACT. Two of the cases that epitomized popular concerns about academic integrity in big-time college sports involved Chris Washburn at North Carolina State and John Williams at Tulane. Even though Washburn and Williams had each scored just 470 on SAT (with the maximum at 1600, and 400 as the minimum figure received just by writing one's name on the exam sheet), they were hotly recruited by more than 100 colleges because of their basketball prowess, and eventually enrolled at NC State and Tulane whose average SAT scores in that freshman class were 1020 and 1120, respectively.

Proposition 48 was initially developed by a group of college athletic notables, including Penn State's football coach Joe Paterno, Indiana's basketball coach Bobby Knight, North Carolina's basketball coach Dean Smith, and Michigan Athletic Director Dan Canham. (One key figure was Georgia's football coach Vince Dooley, who was then seeking to address the consequences of the Jan Kemp case described above, and the fact that this had made Georgia and its Southeastern Conference (SEC) colleagues adopt stiffer athletic admission standards at their institutions.) The proposal was then endorsed by a special President's Committee headed by Harvard's Derek Bok, Notre Dame's Father Theodore Hesburgh, Miami's Edward Foote, and Southern Methodist's Donald Shield. Adoption of such a binding rule—in particular, the SAT minimum—was, however, vigorously opposed by the leaders of historically black colleges (such as Grambling and Jackson State), who recognized that average African American SAT scores were more than 200 points lower than white scores, and that in 1982 they had just passed the 700 mark for the first time. Proposition 48 was also counselled against by the head of the Educational Testing Service that administered this system, who had always contended that SAT scores should be an important factor, but not an absolute requirement, for college admissions. However, with the support of some important black athletes such as Arthur Ashe, Proposition 48 was adopted by the NCAA at its 1983 convention, to become effective in 1986.

Unlike the 1.6 Predictor Rule in the *Parish* case, the original version of Proposition 48 did not make the SAT (or GPA) minimum an absolute barrier to college sports. A student-athlete who met either of, though not both, the SAT and GPA criteria was deemed a "partial qualifier" who could still enroll in college on an athletic scholarship. However, he (or she) was not eligible to play (though he could practice) during the freshman year, during which he had to demonstrate satisfactory progress in the college's academic program. Two early examples of partial qualifiers were Rumeal Robinson and Terry Mills, who together starred on

Michigan's 1989 Final Four championship team and went on to play in the NBA.

In the late 1980s, though, the NCAA membership passed Proposition 42 which would bar colleges from giving any financial aid to partial qualifiers during their freshman year. Proposition 42's disparate impact on blacks (who made up about 90% of the 600 partial qualifiers each year) made this version of the eligibility rule even more controversial than the original. A protest movement led by Georgetown University's John Thompson produced yet another amendment, Proposition 26, which left partial qualifiers eligible for non-athletic, need-based, financial aid.

In 1992, the NCAA further tightened up on athlete eligibility standards by adopting a Proposition 16 that had been recommended by the President's Commission, now a key part of the Association's policymaking structure. For Division I colleges, the minimum high school GPA standard was raised from 2.00 to 2.5 in 13, not just 11, core academic courses. Athletes who had higher than minimum test scores could have a somewhat lower GPA (and vice versa): e.g., the minimum GPA was 2.00 for an athlete who scored 900 on the SAT. However, both the commission and the membership rejected a recommendation by the NCAA's Academic Requirements Committee (based on empirical research) that the best predictor of college performance was a weighted average of the two factors, with no absolute minimum in either. The 700 SAT score and 2.0 GPA remained the floor.

Debates within the NCAA continued throughout the 1990s. At the 1995 convention, the rules were changed back to permit partial qualifiers to receive athletic scholarships (not just need-based aid) and to practice, though not play, during their freshmen years. However, the definition of "partial qualifiers" was itself tightened. No longer was a student who met the minimum standard for either factor partially qualified. A new coordinated scale was created that required minimum performance in both areas. For example, a student who scored below a 600 SAT (or a 2.0 GPA) could not be a partial qualifier for a scholarship, even if he had scored a 4.0 GPA (or 1600 SAT). The NCAA also had to adjust all its SAT standards to reflect the recentered and higher figures adopted by ETS that year. The original 700 SAT (now the Scholastic *Assessment* Test) cut-off point is now at 820.

At that same 1991 convention, the membership (by a very close 168–155 vote) rejected a proposal by the Black Coaches Association to allow partial qualifiers to have a fourth year of athletic eligibility in their fifth year of enrollment at the school, if the student by then was making "satisfactory progress" towards his undergraduate degree. (As we shall see in the next section, it is quite common for student-athletes who meet the Proposition 48 standard for admission to college to take an extra year or two on the way to a degree if they have missed a season of competition because of injuries, talent deficiencies, and the like.) However, at the 1997 convention, the membership (by a somewhat wider 173–

145 margin) adopted Proposition 68 which gives partial qualifiers a fourth year of athletic competition, but only if they have actually received their college degree in four years, and are then playing their sport while pursuing a second degree.

With the above as historical background, consider now several options for NCAA admissions policy.[u]

1. Should the NCAA have a flat admissions eligibility rule like it now has for Division I members (and a variation for Division II), or should all schools have the flexibility of Division III members to set their own admissions standards for student-athletes? What are the relevant factors that might explain these variations in athletic policy within the NCAA?

2. If there is to be any such across-the-board standard, should it be based only on a GPA in a core high school curriculum (with the NCAA specifying what is "core" for academic purposes)? Or should a minimum SAT score also be required? If there is going to be a combination (i.e., a weighted average) of the two, should a minimum number be specified for each (something that was not done in the earlier 1.6 Predictor Rule)? What reasons might NCAA members have for insisting on an SAT minimum even for a student-athlete whose high school grades and class ranking are quite high?

3. If there is to be a weighted average rule, should this also be adjusted to the average qualifications of the particular college's freshman class? In other words, should Duke and Stanford have to reach a higher admissions floor for their student athletes than the UNLV and Centenary College programs that we saw figuring in earlier cases, let alone the Gramblings and Jackson States which have long objected to Proposition 48's requirement of a minimum SAT score for their student athletes that is higher than the average scores of their overall student bodies?

4. If a student does not meet the NCAA's academic standards, should that preclude just athletic participation, athletic financial aid, need-based financial aid to a student-athlete, or all of the above? In reflecting on the "partial qualifier" category, what are the relevant benefits and burdens to the student who is told he can practice but not compete during his freshman year? But if that athlete does apparently make "academic progress" in his freshman and later years, should he be entitled to a fourth year of eligibility even if (like

---

u. For early and contrasting views of two prominent black scholars in the original debate, see Linda S. Greene, *The New NCAA Rules of the Game: Academic Integrity or Racism?*, 28 St. Louis Univ. L. J. 101 (1984), and Harry Edwards, "The Collegiate Athletic Arms Race: Origins and Implications of the 'Rule 48' Controversy," in Richard Lapchick, ed., *Fractured Focus: Sport as a Reflection of Society* 21–43 (Lexington, Mass: D.C. Heath, 1986). For a more recent statement about Proposition 48, see Kenneth L. Shropshire, *Color-Blind Propositions: Race, the SAT, & the NCAA*, 8 Stanford Law & Pol. Rev. 141 (Winter 1997). On the broader range of racial issues, see Timothy Davis, *The Myth of the Superspade: The Persistence of Racism in College Athletics*, 22 Fordham Urban L. J. 615 (1995).

many students and athletes) he has not graduated with an initial degree after four years in college?

5. Would it be preferable for the NCAA to return to its very old regime, under which all freshmen students were unable to compete in intercollegiate sports, regardless of their high school GPA or SAT scores, and regardless of whether they were attending college on athletic scholarship?

In grappling with these questions, consider also the relevance and implications of the following data.[v]

1. In 1996, the average freshman SAT score was 1013, with males at 1034 and females at 995. Asian Americans, at 1052, had the highest average score of any ethnic group, with whites slightly behind at 1049. Mexican–Americans averaged 914, Puerto Ricans 897, and African–Americans 856. The African–American SAT deficit is slightly larger on the mathematical than on the verbal test. The SAT gap between African–American and white student-athletes is somewhat smaller than it is within the general student body.

2. Among student-athletes who were admitted to college in 1984 and 1985 (the years before Proposition 48 came into effect), 52% of white athletes and 27% of African–American athletes had graduated five years later. The 700 SAT minimum would have excluded 41% of these African–American graduates and five percent of the whites.

3. Of freshman athletes who did not qualify under Proposition 48 in its first five years of operation, approximately 85% were African–American. Of these, approximately 85% were ineligible because they failed to meet the minimum SAT requirement (rather than the GPA).

4. The percentage of African–Americans among scholarship athletes dropped sharply in 1986, Proposition 48's first year of operation, from 24% in 1984 and 1985 to 19% in 1986. However, the figures improved in 1987 to 21%, and had reached 28% in 1993, significantly higher than they had been before (and far greater than the ten percent African–American share of all college students). In Division I schools, African–Americans now comprise 6.6% of all students, 25% of athletes on scholarship, 46% of football players, and 60% of men's basketball players.

5. Graduation rates have risen as well. Of student-athletes who entered college in 1983, 51% graduated within the next six years; whereas of those who entered in 1989, 58% had graduated by

---

[v]. These data are drawn from the 1991 Report of the College Board (which administers the SAT), the series of reports by the American Institute for Research from its 1987–1988 *National Study of Intercollegiate Athletics* (conducted for the NCAA's President's Commission and released in 1989), another series of reports by the NCAA's own *Academic Performance Study* (released in 1991), and most recently, NCAA Research Report 96–01, *A Longitudinal Analysis of NCAA Division I Graduation Rates Data* (1996).

1996. That seven percentage point gain among all student-athletes was topped by an 11% gain (from 35% to 46%) by African-American student-athletes. To put these athlete figures into perspective, though, overall student graduation rates rose from 51% to 56% in that same period, and that overall percentage point gain was also exceeded by the eight percent rise (from 30% to 38%) in overall African–American graduation rates.

The foregoing racial disparities in SAT scores, and thence the impact of Proposition 48, pose not just policy concerns for often intense debates within the NCAA. They now also pose a legal problem under civil rights law, which itself has undergone major changes since the days of the *Parish* case. A legal challenge has finally been launched against Proposition 48, in the *Shaw-Cureton* class action suit filed in early 1997.

Such a civil rights claim might be lodged on either constitutional or statutory grounds. After *Tarkanian*, the NCAA is not a state actor and thus is not directly subject to the Fourteenth Amendment. Suppose, however, that a constitutional challenge were aimed at state universities that adhere to Proposition 48. This scenario potentially raises the same legal questions as we posed after the *Tarkanian* opinion. Can the NCAA sanction a state institution for failing to follow NCAA admissions standards that might violate student-athletes' constitutional rights? If not, could the NCAA afford to enforce these minimum admission standards against only its private college members?

These questions are relevant, however, only if Proposition 48 constitutes discrimination in the constitutional sense. The major obstacle to such a finding is *Washington v. Davis*, 426 U.S. 229 (1976), which requires *intentional* discrimination for a violation of constitutional equal protection. Could one argue that because NCAA members *knew* of the racial disparities in SAT scores, and nonetheless adopted (and have since tightened up on) Proposition 48 over vehement objections from black colleges, that their action amounted to *intentional* discrimination?

A second possible basis for a legal challenge to Proposition 48 is Title VI of the federal Civil Rights Act, which provides that "no person shall, on the grounds of race, color, or national origin, be excluded from participation in, be denied the benefit of, or be subjected to discrimination under any program receiving any federal financial assistance."[w]

---

[w] In the mid–1980s, there was a major legal and political controversy about whether Title VI covered only the specific program or activity that received federal funding, or the entire institution that obtained such aid. In *Grove City College v. Bell*, 465 U.S. 555 (1984), the U.S. Supreme Court opted for the former interpretation, but in 1988 Congress overrode President Reagan's veto and enacted the Civil Rights Restoration Act which explicitly expanded the law's scope to include the institution as a whole. Thus, all colleges receiving federal financial assistance for any program (virtually every school receives some federal aid) are subject to Title VI. In *Shaw-Cureton*, though, the NCAA has claimed that Title VI does not apply to its policies, at least when challenged by private litigants.

Under this federal *statutory* law, it is sufficient for a finding of illegal discrimination that use of SAT scores has had a disparate *impact* on blacks, regardless of whether these eligibility criteria were adopted for purposes of disparate *treatment* of blacks. See *Griggs v. Duke Power Co.*, 401 U.S. 424 (1971) (so interpreting Title VII, the employment part of the Civil Rights Act), and *Groves v. Alabama State Board of Education*, 776 F.Supp. 1518 (M.D.Ala.1991) (applying Title VII jurisprudence to a Title VI attack on minimum SAT scores for admission to a state teachers' college). See also *Sharif by Salahuddin v. New York State Educ. Dept.*, 709 F.Supp. 345 (S.D.N.Y.1989) (finding that Title IX of the federal Education Amendments of 1972 was violated by the State of New York when it used SAT scores alone, rather than a combination of high school GPA and SAT, to award college scholarships based on academic achievement in high school, because the SAT (though not the GPA) scores of female students had been consistently lower than those of male students). This was the ground relied on by Trial Lawyers for Public Justice in their *Shaw-Cureton* class action suit.

Once a plaintiff shows a disparate impact, the burden shifts to the defendant to justify continued use of the practice in question. For the last several years, there has been a heated legal and political debate about the nature and extent of the required justification, a debate that has been focused on *employment* practices of businesses that are challenged under Title VII of the Civil Rights Act. In its path-breaking *Griggs* decision in the 1970s, the Supreme Court said that the touchstone is "business necessity," and that the employer must "show that any given requirement [has] a manifest relationship to the employment in question" (401 U.S. at 432). Nearly two decades later, in *Wards Cove Packing Co. v. Atonio*, 490 U.S. 642, 659 (1989), the Rehnquist Supreme Court articulated a more relaxed "business justification" test, under which it was sufficient that "a challenged practice serves, in a significant way, the legitimate employment goals of the employer," rather than having to be demonstrably "essential to effective job performance" (as the Court had stated earlier in *Dothard v. Rawlinson*, 433 U.S. 321, 331 (1977)). The *Wards Cove* decision sparked a two-year struggle between former President Bush and the Democratic Congress, which ended in 1991 when the President finally signed a new Civil Rights Act. In disparate impact cases, the law now requires the defendant "to demonstrate that the challenged practice is job-related to the position in question and consistent with business necessity." Pub. L. No. 102–66 (codified at 42 U.S.C.A. § 1981) (1991).

In light of the historical evolution of disparate impact standards in Title VII employment cases, how should a court appraise the legality of the NCAA's Proposition 48 against the *Cureton-Shaw* Title VI challenge described earlier? In particular, what is the appropriate reference point for determining whether there is a disparate impact in the first place? Should it be the proportion of African–American and white high school athletes who fail the minimum eligibility requirements, or the impact on the proportion of African–American and white athletes who secure college scholarships in any event? This question is crucial because the percentage of blacks among student-athletes in NCAA schools had become higher by 1993 than it was in 1985 before Proposition 48 came into effect. (As noted earlier, the percentage of blacks has risen considerably higher in football and men's basketball, and less so in other sports. What does this tell us about the "market" for college athletes?) It appears, then, that the black athletes who fail to satisfy the minimum eligibility requirements of Proposition 48 are being replaced by other blacks who do pass these tests.

However, in a narrow 5–4 decision in *Connecticut v. Teal*, 457 U.S. 440 (1982), the Supreme Court rejected such a "bottom line" defense to a Title VII lawsuit. The plaintiffs were African-American state employees who had failed in disproportionate numbers a preliminary test for promotion; the Court rejected the State of Connecticut's defense that its affirmative action program ensured that a proportionate number of African-American employees (though not the plaintiffs) were in fact promoted.[x] Does this ruling make sense, either as a general matter or when you consider its possible application under Title VI to decisions made by educational institutions in the admission of student-athletes (or of all students for that matter)?

Assume for the sake of argument that Proposition 48 has had a "disparate impact" under the relevant legal criteria. The question, then, is whether the NCAA could establish that SAT scores are "related to the practice in question and consistent with [educational] necessity" (according to the new Civil Rights Act wording). Answering this question first requires value judgments about the nature and purpose of the athletic position for which SAT scores are used as a screening criterion. (Is it relevant, for example, that noted African-American educators such as Harry Edwards of Berkeley and Henry Gates of Harvard have defended Proposition 48 as a motivator for high school athletes who might otherwise *not* secure college athletic scholarships?) It would also require careful empirical assessment of any available statistical data to determine the correlation (if any) between the NCAA's minimum SAT scores and academic performance in college. Finally, one must consider whether, if the NCAA and its members have violated the Civil Rights Act by establishing minimum SAT scores for athletic scholarship eligibility, it would also be illegal for any college to use minimum test scores in its normal admissions process.

The other key feature of Proposition 48 is its insistence upon a minimum GPA in at least 13 "core courses" in high school to permit a student to compete in college sports in his or her freshman year. Ironically, this initially much less controversial provision has already

x. See Martha Chamallas, *Evolving Conceptions of Equality Under Title VII: Disparate Impact and the Demise of the Bottom Line Principle*, 31 UCLA L. Rev. 305 (1983).

was governed by the ADA, as a private body that "*operates* . . . a place of public accommodation." The NCAA's certification rules function as a "ticket" for effective student-athlete use of Michigan State's physical facilities, because the rules determine whether the university can give them financial support, coaching, practice time, and competitive performance in athletic events taking place in those facilities.

The judge then turned to the crucial substantive issue whether the NCAA bylaws and procedures had the effect of "screening" Ganden out of college sports because of his learning disability, and if so, whether the NCAA had refused to take reasonable steps to accommodate its standards to Ganden's disability.]

* * *

1. DISCRIMINATION ON THE BASIS OF DISABILITY.

The court rejects the NCAA's contention that Ganden cannot establish a causal link between its denial of Ganden's waiver application and his learning disability. The NCAA asserts that it denied Ganden's waiver application because he failed to meet the minimum eligibility requirements through his combined GPA and ACT scores. In support, the NCAA cites to *Sandison v. Michigan High School Athletic Ass'n*, 64 F.3d 1026 (6th Cir.1995), in which two learning disabled students argued that a high school athletic association's age limitation excluded them from competition on the basis of their disabilities. Dismissing their claims under the ADA and the Rehabilitation Act of 1973, *Sandison* explained that "the plaintiffs' respective learning disability does not prevent the two students from meeting the age requirements, the passage of time does . . ." Id. at 1033 & 1036; *Johannesen v. NCAA*, No. 96 C 197 PHX ROS, p. 7 (D.C.Ariz.1996).

The court respectfully disagrees with this analysis. In implementing civil rights legislation for the disabled, Congress recognized that discrimination on the basis of a disability is "most often the product, not of invidious animus, but rather of thoughtlessness and indifference—of benign neglect." *Alexander v. Choate*, 469 U.S. 287, 297 & n. 12 (1985). Accordingly, the ADA and Rehabilitation Act focus on whether the defendant has provided a reasonable accommodation to an individual on the basis of a known disability.[10] In the instant case, the evidence strongly suggests that Ganden failed to take the requisite "core courses" or satisfy the remaining eligibility criteria because of his disability.[11]

---

10. In respect to Ganden's claim under section 12182(b)(2)(A)(i), the provision expressly prohibits eligibility criteria that "screen out or tend to screen out" persons on the basis of their disability. Because the NCAA's definition of "core course" explicitly excludes special education, compensatory and remedial courses, this definition provides at least a prima facie case of a disparate impact on learning disabled students. Although the NCAA considered some of his remedial courses as "core," it did not consider all of his remedial courses as "core." If the NCAA had considered these two remaining remedial courses as "core," he would have satisfied the GPA standard.

11. Each of Ganden's counselors testified that Ganden's disability required him to take remedial courses in order to succeed at college preparatory courses. These witnesses also explained that summer school courses were not an option for Ganden. In addition, Ganden has presented evidence of

When they reviewed his waiver application, the NCAA Subcommittee was aware of this condition and how it affected his ability to meet their eligibility requirements. Consequently, Ganden has presented a strong prima facie case that there is a causal link between the NCAA refusal to certify Ganden a "qualifier" and his learning disability.

2. REASONABLE MODIFICATIONS.

The court next addresses whether Ganden's requested modifications are reasonable or would "fundamentally alter" the nature of the privilege or accommodation to which he has been denied access. In determining whether reasonable accommodations have been provided under Title III, precedent interpreting the Rehabilitation Act and Title II of the ADA are instructive. *Vande Zande v. Wisc. Dept. of Admin.*, 44 F.3d 538, 542 (7th Cir.1995); see *Allison v. Dept. of Corrections*, 94 F.3d 494, 497 (8th Cir.1996). In particular, the Title III analysis is identical to the analysis determining whether a disabled plaintiff is "otherwise qualified" to participate in a program under the other statutes. See *Johnson v. Florida High School Activities Ass'n, Inc.*, 899 F.Supp. 579, 583 n. 5 (M.D.Fl.1995). Under each provision, a modification is unreasonable if it imposes an "undue financial and administrative burden" or requires a "fundamental alteration" in the nature of the privilege or program. Id.; see *Pottgen v. Missouri State High School Activities Ass'n*, 40 F.3d 926, 930 (8th Cir.1994).

This analysis requires that the court examine the particular eligibility criteria and the nature of the privilege that it monitors. The criteria at issue are the minimum GPA requirements and the "core course" definition that is instrumental in computing a student's GPA. The privilege at issue is the NCAA's intercollegiate athletic program. Ganden narrowly characterizes this privilege as swimming competitions. However, this cramped view ignores the broader nature and role of NCAA intercollegiate athletics. The NCAA is not merely a swimming group, but an integral part of the college community. The NCAA was created to promote the concept of the student-athlete through both athletic excellence and academic development. It offers its competitors more than an opportunity to swim, but also to represent the NCAA's member institutions. Towards this general purpose of the privilege, the eligibility requirements (1) insure that student-athletes are representative of the college community and not recruited solely for athletics; (2) insure that a student-athlete is academically prepared to succeed at college; and (3) preserve amateurism in intercollegiate sports.

As an initial matter, the court does not believe that any alteration to the NCAA's eligibility requirements would "fundamentally alter" the nature of the privilege offered. In support of this position, the NCAA cites to two recent decisions holding that any waiver to an age cap for high school sports leagues would "fundamentally alter" the high school

the severity of his decoding disability and its effect on his academic performance. The record also indicates that assistance tailored toward his disability has permitted him to significantly improve his academic performance.

programs. See *Sandison*, 64 F.3d 1026 (Title II); *Pottgen*, 40 F.3d 926 (Title II). First, those cases found that requiring an individual assessment of each overage student would constitute an undue burden for the defendant. *Sandison*, 64 F.3d at 1034; see also *Pottgen*, 40 F.3d at 931 (refusing to assess eligibility criteria in light of plaintiffs' circumstances because it would [require] exhaustive evidentiary investigation by defendant for each disabled student). In contrast, the NCAA already has instituted an individual assessment process particularly intended to review student-athletes academic records and abilities. More importantly, the court believes that these decisions failed to adequately analyze the purposes of the act in light of the specific claims for modifications; i.e., the circumstances of the plaintiff and learning disabled students. *Johnson*, 899 F.Supp. at 584. Rather, these courts simply asked whether the eligibility requirement served any important interests of the program. Like most rationally created procedural requirements, the court found that the age requirement did, and concluded that any alteration to those rules would fundamentally alter the program. *Pottgen*, 40 F.3d at 930 ("Waiving an essential eligibility standard would constitute a fundamental alteration in the nature of the [athletic] program."); see *Sandison*, 64 F.3d at 1035.

This analysis ignores the central issue under the ADA: Are reasonable accommodations possible in light of the disability. See *Johnson*, 899 F.Supp. at 584. Reasonable accommodation is a fact-bound inquiry, see *Sandison*, 64 F.3d at 1034, looking to whether the modification required for the plaintiff would "do violence to the admittedly salutary purposes underlying the [] rule." *Pottgen*, 40 F.3d at 932 (dissent). Therefore, a court must look to the underlying purposes of an eligibility requirement to determine if the modification would undermine those purposes in the circumstances of the plaintiff. Otherwise, any modification of a rule rationally tailored to the denied privilege would be unreasonable.

Although the court does not believe that any modification to the NCAA's eligibility requirements would "fundamentally alter" the nature of its accommodation, the court finds that Ganden does not have a reasonable likelihood of demonstrating that his requested modification would not "fundamentally alter" that accommodation. There is little doubt that the GPA and "core course" requirements generally serve important interests of the NCAA athletics. Because of its dual mission, the NCAA has an important interest in insuring that its student-athletes are prepared to succeed at college. Whatever criticism one may level at GPA and the national standardized tests, these provide significant objective predictors of a student's ability to succeed at college. The "core course" criteria further serves the dual interest of insuring the integrity of that GPA and independently insuring that the student has covered the minimum subject matter required for college.

However, in the case of learning disabled students, the NCAA may be able to serve these purposes and insure that a student has the necessary academic capabilities through consideration of additional factors. In fact, through its waiver application process, the NCAA provides such individualized consideration. In the case of learning disabled students, a generally improving academic record may indicate that prior remedial courses adequately substituted for earlier "core courses," even if not qualitatively and quantitatively identical to other "core courses." In such circumstances, some remedial courses may have served the same role as approved "core courses" to other students. Therefore, the record indicates that Title III requires the NCAA to consider a students' progress in his or her IEP courses and overall high school career.

Ganden could only satisfy the required GPA if the Subcommittee actually counted his two LRC courses as "core:" if the Subcommittee replaced other "core course" grades with the grades from the LRC courses. However, in contrast to Ganden's other remedial courses, neither of the LRC courses appear remotely similar to the subject areas of "core courses." While Title III may require the NCAA to count courses as "core" even if they are not substantively identical to approved "core courses," it does not require the NCAA to count courses with little substantive similarity. Whatever skills such a course may provide to the student, they cannot be said to substitute for earlier "core courses." Similarly, the grades from such courses do not provide valid indications of the student's academic potential. Based upon the current record, the court finds that this modification would "fundamentally alter" the privilege of participation in intercollegiate swimming.

The court also finds that lowering the minimum GPA for Ganden would "fundamentally alter" the nature of the privilege. Unlike a modification to the "core course" definition, lowering the GPA minimum directly removes the NCAA's primary objective tool to determine a student's academic capabilities. While circumstances may exist where such a modification are necessary, the court finds that it is generally unreasonable to require the NCAA to lower this basic standard. Instead, Title III would focus on less drastic modifications affecting the computation of the GPA, such as modifications to the "core course" requirement.

As Ganden argues, Title III requires the NCAA to individually assess his request for modifications. However, the NCAA provided such an assessment. The Subcommittee reviewed Ganden's case for over one hour. It received an application prepared by a member institution with a strong interest in procuring a waiver on his behalf. This package included his academic record, a psychological report focusing on his disability as well as his efforts and successes in overcoming it, and arguments on his behalf from MSU. In addition, the record indicates that the Subcommittee was aware of the Department of Justice's efforts and arguments on his behalf. After this review, the Subcommittee accommodated Ganden through granting him "partial qualifier" status.

While there is some doubt whether the NCAA actually counted Ganden's three "Basic" courses as "core" in consideration of his disability or MSU's reliance argument, the record reveals that the Subcommittee did consider Ganden's disability, his efforts to overcome it, and his impressive academic gains during his final two years of high school.

Even though he did not meet the minimum GPA, it still granted Ganden "partial qualifier" status. Title III does not require the NCAA to simply abandon its eligibility requirements, but only to make reasonable modifications to them. The record reveals that the NCAA did precisely that.

* * *

4. Conclusion.

Although Ganden has demonstrated some likelihood of success on the merits with respect to questions of subject matter jurisdiction, the court finds that he has not shown a reasonable likelihood of success on the critical allegation that the NCAA's denial of his waiver application constituted "discrimination" under § 12182(b)(2) of Title III....

Injunction denied.

In the fall of 1997, shortly before Ganden was to begin varsity swimming for Michigan State in his sophomore year, the Department of Justice announced that its Civil Rights Division had concluded that the NCAA's eligibility rules and procedures did not adequately accommodate the situation and needs of Ganden and other learning-disabled athletes. The remedies proposed by the Department for this alleged ADA violation were an additional fourth year of eligibility for Ganden and 33 other learning-disabled athletes who had lost their freshman athletic year, plus financial compensation for Ganden and four others who had filed complaints under this federal law. The NCAA did not immediately accede to this proposal, and was especially concerned about changing its rules to grant a fourth year of athletic eligibility to a Ganden, but not to a Shaw or Cureton who had failed to meet the Proposition 48 standard for other reasons.

Absent a voluntary settlement of this issue by the NCAA and the Justice Department, there almost certainly will be another legal attack on Proposition 48, this one initiated by the federal government. In assessing the legal prospects, we should also note that shortly after the *Ganden* decision came down, another federal district judge reached a contrary result. Toure Butler was diagnosed with a learning disability in the seventh grade and had received special education services throughout his high school time in Everett, Washington. However, the NCAA refused to count a number of his "support" courses (in American History, for example) as "core," which meant that Butler did not reach the 13–core course number and his GPA fell below the Proposition 48 minimum. The result was that Butler did not even secure the "partial qualifier" status of Ganden, which meant that he could not even practice or receive financial aid during his freshman year at the University of Washington which had recruited Butler as a star football player. Supported by the Department of Justice, Butler went to court, claiming that his Cascade High School "support" courses were academically sufficient, and that his grades in them raised his GPA comfortably above the minimum level. The unpublished opinion of the federal district judge in Washington (*Butler v. NCAA*, Case No. 96–1656D (W.D.Wash.1996)), was principally devoted to explaining why the NCAA did "operate" a facility of "public accommodation," and thus was subject to the ADA. For purposes of this request for a preliminary injunction in November, 1996, the judge simply said that Butler's ADA claim had sufficient merit to warrant such relief. As it turned out, the Huskies decided to redshirt Butler for his freshman year, and thence preserve four full years of college play for him if he wins the case on the merits. What the ultimate appellate (or NCAA) verdict about this set of issues will be, only time will tell.

Questions For Discussion

1. Did the NCAA process do everything that could "reasonably" accommodate Ganden's disability under its Proposition 48 requirements? What lessons does this case provide about the benefits and burdens of this academic constraint on competing in college sports?

2. Prodded by the Justice Department, the NCAA has made some further modifications to the Proposition 48 rules that we saw in operation in *Ganden*. Besides relaxing somewhat the constraints on college recruiting visits made by the learning disabled during their senior year, a student like Ganden can now meet the academic course requirement by taking some additional courses in the summer after graduating from high school, and thence be able to play college football or other sports that fall. Is that an appropriate measure from the perspective of either college sports or high school education?

3. As noted earlier, the NCAA's judgment about the academic quality of an apparently "special education" course is reached by comparing the course's ultimate intellectual content (though not its pace and format) to the content of the basic course offered in that same high school. One concern raised about that procedure is that it may still exclude "remedial" courses offered in an elite college preparatory school, although the latter's content seems significantly stronger than the basic courses in that subject at the normal high school. Is there any way in which that problem can be accommodated? Is there any difference between that problem and the use of a common GPA figure for grades at every school around the country, with no adjustment for the quality of individual institutions?

4. Compare the NCAA's treatment of Ganden and other learning-disabled students under the "core course" GPA feature of Proposition 48, and its treatment of Shaw, Cureton, and other African-Americans under the SAT feature. Should there be a special review process that might waive the SAT minimum score for students whose GPA was near the top of her class in high school? What are the similarities and differences between SAT and GPA scores? Between African-Americans and the disabled?

Two other controversies about the operation of Proposition 48 illustrate the difficulties with any system of external regulation, irrespective of the substantive content. The first involved a student-athlete named Chris Rohe who was neither African–American nor learning-disabled. Rohe had been both a star player on the state football champion in Minnesota and also a star student in his high school, graduating with a 3.96 GPA. However, after being admitted to the Air Force Academy where Rohe wanted both to play football and become a pilot, the student learned that he had been academically disqualified by the NCAA because his Grade 10 English course had been labeled "Developing Study Skills" by his high school. The NCAA Initial–Eligibility Committee was not persuaded by the high school principal's assertion that this course actually taught grammar, reading, and language skills in an academically rigorous manner. Only after the school altered the course title to "Basic English II" was the Committee prepared to treat it as "core" for purposes of Proposition 48 (though too late to save Rohe's freshman year on the Academy football team).

The Rohe case illustrates the huge administrative difficulty faced by a single NCAA body trying to appraise the true academic value of courses taught by tens of thousands of high schools to millions of students around the country. (Part of the NCAA's attraction to the SAT and ACT systems may well be the fact that these are standard tests administered by a single body responsible for their content and application.) A second case and controversy, involving the Southeastern College of the Assemblies of God, illustrates the fact that no matter how elaborate the rules and regulations, people still have the incentives to do what is needed to evade, not just to avoid, them.

High school student-athletes who do not qualify under Proposition 48 can legitimately avoid part of the consequence by getting a junior college degree that then permits them to study and play at an NCAA school for at least two seasons. In the early 1990s, Southeastern became a popular resource for student-athletes and their prospective coaches. Southeastern was based in Lakeland, Florida, but offered some of its courses by correspondence to students who could write their exams in front of a proctor with a teaching certificate. There were no limits placed on the number and timing of courses and exams, because Southeastern understandably believed that its principal student body—those planning to be preachers or teachers—would voluntarily honor principles of academic integrity. By the mid–1990s, though, it turned out that 60 or so Division I schools had football or basketball players who had supposedly taken Southeastern courses such as "Old Testament Survey," and then had written exams in front of their college coaches (most of whom held teaching certificates). After three Baylor assistant football coaches had been convicted of federal wire and mail fraud for faking such Southeastern results, Southeastern was forced to put significant restraints on its program, and the NCAA amended its By-laws to require any nonqualifying high school graduate to give up his first season in Division I football and basketball even if he had obtained a legitimate junior college degree.

2. ACADEMIC PROGRESS

Rohe, Southeastern, and other cases have led numerous commentators (including both the Governor of Minnesota and USA Today's editorial page) to state that the NCAA should stop "micro-managing" public and private high schools who were doing their job of educating the nation's children, and instead should concentrate on making sure that the teaching and grading of courses by the Association's own college membership meet serious academic standards. The NCAA does have a set of rules designed to ensure that student-athletes successfully advance through the college's academic program and ultimately graduate. Article 14.4 of the NCAA Manual spells out the minimum course and GPA requirements that student-athletes must meet to show "satisfactory academic progress" at each stage in their college career in order to maintain their eligibility to play. Ironically, the following case (like Rohe, also from Minnesota) offers an unusual twist on this source of concern within major college sports.

HALL v. UNIVERSITY OF MINNESOTA
United States District Court, District of Minnesota, 1982.
530 F.Supp. 104.

LORD, CHIEF JUDGE.

[Mark Hall was an African–American student-athlete who had starred on the University of Minnesota basketball team. For his first three years on the team, Hall was enrolled in a non-B.A. degree program of the University's General College, where he had accumulated 90 credits. While Hall met the Big Ten standards for grade point average and credit numbers, he needed to be enrolled in a degree course to play his senior year in 1981–82. Hall sought admission to the school's University Without Walls (UWW) Degree Program and was accepted by the admission committee for the Program's introductory stage. However, the Program Director intervened and vetoed Hill's admission, based to a large extent on concerns expressed by the General College Dean about the academic integrity as well as quality of Hall's stay and performance there. Hall went to federal district court with credible evidence that he was likely to be an early round NBA draft choice that spring, but only if he was able to play and develop in his senior year at Minnesota. The question, though, was whether he was thereby entitled to enroll in a program in which it was assumed he would not be staying for another year or two to complete and graduate.]

* * *

A student's interest in attending a university is a property right protected by due process. The defendant asserts that while in cases of expulsion, public education may be a property right, in cases of nonadmission, public education is but a mere privilege. However, the right versus privilege distinction has long been abandoned in the area of due process. And in any event, even though the plaintiff was denied admission, the circumstances of this case make it more like an expulsion case than a non-admission case. The plaintiff lost existing scholarship rights; he cannot enroll in another college without sitting out one year of competition under athletic rules; and although he has attended the defendant University for several years, he may no longer register for day classes at the defendant University.

But to say that due process applies in the area of a student's interest in attending a university does not finish the analysis. One must answer the question of what process is due. "Due process is flexible and calls for such procedural protection as the particular situation demands." *Morrissey v. Brewer*, 408 U.S. 471, 481 (1972). Factors balanced to determine what process is due are: 1) the private interest affected by the action; 2) the risk of an erroneous deprivation of such interest through the procedures used and the value of additional procedural safeguards; and (3) the government's interest involved, including fiscal and administrative burdens.

The private interest at stake here, although ostensibly academic, is the plaintiff's ability to obtain a "no cut" contract with the National Basketball Association. The bachelor of arts, while a mark of achievement and distinction, does not in and of itself assure the applicant a means of earning a living. This applicant seems to recognize this and has opted to use his college career as a means of entry into professional sports as do many college athletes. His basketball career will be little affected by the absence or presence of a bachelor of arts degree. This plaintiff has put all of his "eggs" into the "basket" of professional basketball. The plaintiff would suffer a substantial loss if his career objectives were impaired.

The government's interest, i.e., the defendant University's interest, is the administrative burden of requiring a hearing or other due process safeguards for every rejection of every student who applies to the University. This burden would be tremendous and this Court would not require the defendant University to shoulder it.

The key factor in this case which weighs heavily in the plaintiff's favor is the risk of an erroneous deprivation given the nature of the proceedings used in processing the plaintiff's application. This Court is aware that in the area of academic decisions, judicial interference must be minimal. However, an academic decision is based upon established academic criteria. In this case, the plaintiff's applications to the UWW were treated very differently than all other applications. The directors intervened in the process and provided the admissions committee with allegations concerning the plaintiff's conduct, a facet of the proceedings that taints this "academic" process and turns it into something much like a disciplinary proceeding. Given this aspect of the proceedings, it would appear that the plaintiff should have at least been notified that allegations had been made regarding his conduct so that he could have presented evidence in his own behalf. Without this safeguard, there exists a chance that the plaintiff may have been wrongfully accused of actions which then form the basis for his rejection.

This is not to say that all applicants who are rejected by the defendant University must be given an opportunity to rebut evidence used in evaluating a college application; however, if the defendant University intends to interject evidence concerning allegations of improper conduct of the applicant into the admissions process, it must provide the applicant an opportunity to give his or her side of the story.

Finally, one must consider all that has occurred in light of the standards utilized by the Courts in this Circuit in evaluating the propriety of issuing a preliminary injunction. Four factors determine whether a preliminary injunction should issue. They are: (1) the threat of irreparable harm to the moving party, (2) the state of balance between that harm and the injury that granting the injunction will inflict on other parties, (3) the public interest, and (4) the probability that the movant will succeed on the merits of the claim.

With respect to the first factor, if the plaintiff is not eligible to play basketball by January 4, 1982, he will not play his senior year. This poses a substantial threat to his chances for a "no cut" contract in the National Basketball Association, according to his coach, and his overall aspirations regarding a career as a professional basketball player. It would be difficult indeed to measure the loss to the plaintiff in terms of dollars and cents. The injury is substantial and not really capable of an accurate monetary prediction. Thus, it would be irreparable.

The harm to the other parties, i.e., the defendant University, is difficult to assess. On the one hand, this Court doubts that the University men's intercollegiate varsity basketball team and coaching staff would characterize the reinstatement of the plaintiff to the team in terms of "harm." But the defendant University's academic wing argues that if this Court orders the plaintiff into a degree program, its academic standards and integrity would be undermined. The plaintiff and his fellow athletes were never recruited on the basis of scholarship and it was never envisioned they would be on the Dean's List. Consequently we must view with some skepticism the defendant University's claim, regarding academic integrity. This Court is not saying that athletes are incapable of scholarship; however they are given little incentive to be scholars and few persons care how the student athlete performs academically, including many of the athletes themselves. The exceptionally talented student athlete is led to perceive the basketball, football, and other athletic programs as farm teams and proving grounds for professional sports leagues. It well may be true that a good academic program for the athlete is made virtually impossible by the demands of their sport at the college level. If this situation causes harm to the University, it is because they have fostered it and the institution rather than the individual should suffer the consequence.

It appears from the record that there is a "tug of war" going on over this plaintiff. The academicians are pulling toward higher standards of achievement for all students while the athletic department must tug in the direction of fielding teams who contribute to paying a substantial share of the university's budget. In this tug of war the academic department will suffer substantially no ill effects if it loses. On the other hand, the athletic department, directors, coaches and personnel under this system are charged with the responsibility of at least maintaining and fielding teams which are capable of competing with the best in their conference or in the nation. This Court is not called upon to determine any long term solution to the dilemma posed. It is called upon to determine if the rights of an individual caught up in the struggle have been violated.

* * *

Injunction granted.

Is the above message the kind that judges should send to college administrators about student-athletes? Recalling the Jan Kemp case, how often do you think college officials are too rigorous in enforcing internal academic standards and thereby threatening a star athlete's eligibility?

Or is the case of Ronnie Harmon at the University of Iowa more representative of what actually goes on?[z] Apparently Harmon maintained a 1.62 GPA at Iowa with help from courses such as billiards, soccer, bowling, and football coaching. To try to meet the minimum 1.85 GPA required by the Big Ten, Harmon took a summer school course in watercolor painting, but he received only a D. Yet Iowa ignored both Big Ten requirements and the NCAA rule that students must obtain course credits that demonstrate real progress toward a degree. What eventually cost Harmon his eligibility was his acceptance of cash advances from agents Norby Walters and Lloyd Bloom in return for signing a contract with them.

Consider also the case of Brent Fullwood, a star running back at Auburn University and another Walters and Bloom client whose litigation was described in Chapter 5. The NFL had Fullwood and other potential draft picks take the standard Wunderlic Personality Test of general verbal, mathematical, and spatial reasoning skills. On a scale that deems a person scoring 25 or higher as having "management potential," someone scoring 14 as qualified for a janitorial job, and someone scoring 10 as "functionally illiterate," Fullwood, who was enrolled for four years at Auburn, scored only a 9.

Faced with mounting criticism about such cases, the NCAA continues to refine and enforce its requirement that athletes make meaningful

---

z. We saw Harmon earlier in Chapter 5, in a legal battle with his ill-starred agents, Norby Walters and Lloyd Bloom. An account of the entire Walters–Bloom affair, including the sorry academic performance of Harmon and many other clients of these agents, is Chris Mortenson, *Playing for Keeps: How One Man Kept the Mob from Sinking Its Hooks into Pro Football* (New York: Simon and Schuster, 1991).

progress toward a legitimate degree in the institution.[aa] An offshoot of this NCAA effort has been a proliferation of "sports management" courses taught by members of the athletic department. That development, in turn, raises the question whether playing the sport should itself be considered a key component of a college degree program, presumably accompanied by a few academic courses. Before dismissing this option, compare the requirements for college degree programs in music, dance, the visual arts, and architecture. Why not allow students to major in football, or basketball, or in athletics generally?[bb] What place should sports—in particular, *intercollegiate* sports—have in American college life?[cc]

3. AGE AND EXPERIENCE

Having been admitted to and performed acceptably in the college's academic program, the student-athlete is permitted to participate in intercollegiate competition for no more than four seasons in any one sport (see Article 14.2). This eligibility period expires after five calendar years from first registration, with a variety of exceptions for the Peace Corps, church missions, pregnancy, and international sports competition (the Olympics and the Pan–American games). A special rule states that "any participation . . . in organized sports competition . . . after the student's 20th birthday and prior to full-time enrollment in a collegiate

aa. The limits of this "academic progress" standard were, however, vividly illustrated by two incidents, both involving Australian "student" athletes. Andrew Gaze came to Seton Hall in the fall of 1988, enrolled in courses such as First Aid, Creative Motion, and Youth Activities, and led Seton Hall to its first-ever NCAA basketball final in the spring of 1989 (which the team lost to Michigan in the final seconds of overtime). Immediately after the game, Gaze went back to Melbourne to play for his father's professional basketball team. More recently, in the midst of the 1995 college softball season, UCLA recruited Tanya Harding from Queenland, Australia, and she was able to lead the Lady Bruins to victory in the 1995 College World Series in women's softball. (This was not the *Tonya* Harding who became a notorious figure after the attack on her figure-skating rival Nancy Kerrigan just before the 1994 Winter Olympics, an episode we shall read about in Chapter 12.) Harding also returned to Australia without ever having taken a UCLA exam, let alone having earned an academic credit during her brief stint there.

bb. In thinking about that issue, consider the implications of these two pieces of data. First, the odds of a high school athlete making a Division I college team are approximately 1 in 16 in football and 1 in 40 in basketball, and the odds of these college players going on to play for a professional team are just 1 in 75 in football and 1 in 70 in basketball. (These odds were calculated from 1989 figures presented in Bayley & Littleton, *Athletics and Academe*, note 1 above, at 84.) On the other hand, a study done by Clifford Adelman of the Office of Research of the U.S. Department of Education, *Light and Shadows on College Athletes: College Transcripts and Labor Market History* (1990), traced the experience of college athletes who did not go on to professional sports as part of a larger national cohort of the high school class of 1972. By 1986, when the class had reached the average age of 32, students who had played intercollegiate sports (including blacks) had fared significantly better in subsequent employment than had their non-athlete counterparts. In contrast, the students who had fared worst economically were performing arts majors.

cc. See Robert Simon, *Fair Play: Sports, Values, and Society* (Boulder, Colo.: Westview Press, 1991), in particular, Chapter 4, "Do Intercollegiate Sports Belong on Campus?"; Gregory M. Travalio, *Values and Schizophrenia in University Athletics*, 20 Capital Univ. L. Rev. 587 (1991); and Rodney K. Smith, *When Ignorance Is Not Bliss: In Search of Racial and Gender Equity In Intercollegiate Athletics*, 61 Missouri L. Rev. 329, 332–47 (1996), for thoughtful discussions of the last issue.

institution shall count as one year of varsity competition in that sport" (Article 14.2.5). *Butts v. NCAA & LaSalle University*, 751 F.2d 609 (3d Cir.1984), illustrates both the general rationale for the rule and the problems it can cause when placed side by side with the NCAA's academic admission requirements.

Albert Butts, an outstanding high school basketball player in Philadelphia, who had deficiencies in his academic record, spent both his senior year and an extra year enrolled in a private Virginia preparatory school (on scholarship). Butts' twentieth birthday took place during that second year. Having enrolled in and played for three years at LaSalle University, Butts sued to avoid the "competition after 20 rule"; he argued that the rule discriminated against him on account of both age and race. The district court concluded that Butts had shown a strong likelihood that the by-law has a racially disparate impact, and thus that he could make out a prima facie case under civil rights law, but that the NCAA had advanced a legitimate, nondiscriminatory reason for the by-law:

> [T]he bylaw is designed and intended to promote equality of competition among its members at each level so as to prevent college athletics and access to athletic scholarships from being dominated by more mature, older, more experienced players, and to discourage high school students from delaying their entrance into college in order to develop and mature their athletic skills.

On appeal, Judge Higginbotham began his opinion with this capsule history of basketball:

> Though there have been many changes since, in December of 1891, James Naismith first nailed two peach baskets to the balcony ten feet above the floor at the International Young Men's Christian Association Training School, now Springfield College, Springfield, Massachusetts, basketball is still the only major sport of strictly United States origin. The game was an almost instant success at the scholastic level. However, not surprisingly, it was the "acceptance by Yale in 1894 that induced other institutions to follow suit." In these early years the rules of the game varied greatly from institution to institution, with Cornell, for example, playing with 50 men per side. The first collegiate basketball game with five men on a side was played on March 20, 1897 between Yale University and the University of Pennsylvania. Approximately eight years after the first intercollegiate basketball game the NCAA was born and since then it has played an important role in the regulation of amateur collegiate sports. It had adopted and promulgated playing rules, standards of amateurism, standards for academic eligibility, regulations concerning recruitment of athletes, and rules governing the size of athletic squads and coaching staffs. During the eighty years since the NCAA's birth, collegiate basketball and the NCAA have grown as dominant institutions in America at a level which Naismith could never have contemplated when he invented this sport to appease the

students at Springfield who were bored with "the Swedish, German and French forms of calisthenics of that period," and because he wanted to "fill the void that existed between football and baseball."

751 F.2d at 612. The judge then synopsized the core features of the policy debate about this issue:

> When stripped of legal verbiage, the competing interests in this case are those of: (1) a talented young man who fervently desires to show his athletic prowess—not primarily for success in academia but for what could be the success on the highly remunerative courts of the National Basketball Association; (2) a distinguished college that would like to demonstrate its highest excellence on the basketball floor and thereby rise as close as it can to a local, regional or maybe even a national championship; and (3) a powerful collegiate association which, according to its brief, wants to thwart "professionalism" in college sports, "maintain intercollegiate athletics as an integral part of the educational process," and "ensure that athletes are representative of, and thus an integral part of, the student body as a whole."
>
> Despite the exalted nomenclature which today's basketball aficionado might use in describing the college game, with its adroit "full-court press" defensive maneuver, or the exhilarating offensive "slam dunks," "high percentage shooters" from the outside, "good moves" to the basket, and players who can go "either way," we recognize that there is far more involved in this case than merely the joy of the sport. At stake are the size of Mr. Butts' future bank account, the additional luster that could be added to LaSalle's legend of success in basketball, and the limits of the NCAA's power to curb "a persistent and perhaps inevitable desire to 'win at all costs,'" and prevent "a wide range of competitive excesses that prove harmful to students and institutions alike."

751 F.2d at 602–13. However, the circuit court was not prepared to reverse the district court's ruling at this preliminary stage of the proceedings.

As we have observed throughout this chapter, the *Butts* (and other) decisions raise two different kinds of questions. One is whether such a hands-off judicial posture is appropriate towards such private regulation. The second is whether the NCAA policy itself is sound. What are your views on both of these scores?

Litigation initiated in the 1990s has utilized another legal vehicle to try to challenge age restraints on participation in sports. Rather than equal protection under the constitution or federal civil rights legislation which were tried unsuccessfully in *Butts*, these more recent claims have been filed under the Rehabilitation Act of 1993 and the Americans with Disabilities Act of 1990 (which we have already encountered in *Ganden* in connection with the NCAA's Proposition 16 academic requirements for athletic eligibility). Here the claim is that the impact of early learning disability on academic progress can turn the general age limit into a discriminatory barrier to such disabled persons, absent efforts to provide "reasonable accommodation" to the personal history and current situation in individual cases. The following decision—involving high school, not college sports—captures the significant debate this problem has generated about the scope of federal disability protection.

POTTGEN v. THE MISSOURI STATE HIGH SCHOOL ACTIVITIES ASSOCIATION

United States Court of Appeals, Eighth Circuit, 1994.
40 F.3d 926.

BEAM, CIRCUIT JUDGE.

[The Missouri State High School Activities Association (MSHSAA) bars high school students who have reached the age of 19 before their school year begins from participating in interscholastic sports during that year. Edward Pottgen had been forced to repeat two years in early elementary school due to what was later diagnosed as a learning disability. With the help of specialized educational services, Pottgen's learning problems were resolved and he was able to progress through regular high school classes at the normal rate. The two years he lost earlier, though, meant that Pottgen had reached 19 shortly before his senior year in high school. That meant he was ineligible to play baseball on the high school team of which he had been a member for the previous three years.

Pottgen petitioned the MSHSAA for an exemption from the age rule, but the Association refused to grant him a disability-based waiver. Pottgen went off to federal district court and secured an injunction against applying the MSHSAA rule to him, based on the Rehabilitation Act and the Americans with Disabilities Act. On appeal, the judges agreed that the key question under both Acts was whether the age limit and its application to Pottgen was an "essential eligibility requirement" for high school sports.]

* * *

We find that MSHSAA has demonstrated that the age limit is an essential eligibility requirement in a high school interscholastic program. An age limit helps reduce the competitive advantage flowing to teams using older athletes; protects younger athletes from harm; discourages student athletes from delaying their education to gain athletic maturity; and prevents over-zealous coaches from engaging in repeated red-shirting to gain a competitive advantage. These purposes are of immense importance in any interscholastic sports program.

Even though Pottgen cannot meet this essential eligibility requirement, he is "otherwise qualified" if reasonable accommodations would enable him to meet the age limit. See *School Bd. of Nassau County v.*

Arline, 480 U.S. 273, 287 n. 17 (1987); *Kohl v. Woodhaven Learning Ctr.*, 865 F.2d 930, 936 (8th Cir.1989). Reasonable accommodations do not require an institution "to lower or to effect substantial modifications of standards to accommodate a handicapped person." *Southeastern Community College v. Davis*, 442 U.S. 397, 413 (1979). Accommodations are not reasonable if they impose "undue financial and administrative burdens" or if they require a "fundamental alteration in the nature of [the] program." *Arline*, 480 U.S. at 287 n.17 (citations omitted).

Since Pottgen is already older than the MSHSAA age limit, the only possible accommodation is to waive the essential requirement itself.[4] Although Pottgen contends an age limit waiver is a reasonable accommodation based on his disability, we disagree. Waiving an essential eligibility standard would constitute a fundamental alteration in the nature of the baseball program. Other than waiving the age limit, no manner, method, or means is available which would permit Pottgen to satisfy the age limit. Consequently, no reasonable accommodations exist.

Since Pottgen can never meet the essential eligibility requirement, he is not an "otherwise qualified" individual. Section 504 was designed only to extend protection to those potentially able to meet the essential eligibility requirements of a program or activity. See *Beauford v. Father Flanagan's Boys' Home*, 831 F.2d 768 (8th Cir.1987). As a result, the district court erred by granting the injunction based on Pottgen's Rehabilitation Act claim.

2. Title II of the ADA

* * *

To determine whether Pottgen was a "qualified individual" for ADA purposes, the district court conducted an individualized inquiry into the necessity of the age limit in Pottgen's case. Such an individualized inquiry is inappropriate at this stage. Instead, to determine whether Pottgen is a "qualified individual" under the ADA, we must first determine whether the age limit is an essential eligibility requirement by reviewing the importance of the requirement to the interscholastic baseball program. If this requirement is essential, we then determine whether Pottgen meets this requirement with or without modification. It is at this later stage that the ADA requires an individualized inquiry.

The dissent disagrees with this holding and would impose an individualized "essential eligibility requirement" inquiry at the first stage. We think this is not required, and for good reason. A public entity could never know the outer boundaries of its "services, programs or activities." A requirement could be deemed essential for one person with a disability but immaterial for another similarly, but not identically,

---

4. Other accommodations may exist when a younger student realizes that he will not be able to meet the age requirement when he is a senior. For example, MSHSAA allows eighth grade students to participate on a high school team if they will be ineligible as a high school senior. This accommodation permits students to play for four years at the high school level.

situated individual. MSHSAA's interscholastic baseball program demonstrates this proposition. The dissent admits that the age requirement is "admittedly salutary" but believes it must fall away for Pottgen because an individualized fact-finding inquiry found him "not appreciably larger than the average eighteen-year-old" and not "a threat to the safety of others." If this is the query, MSHSAA would need to establish a fact-finding mechanism for each individual seeking to attack a program requirement. At that time, MSHSAA would have to show the essential nature of each allegedly offending program requirement as it applies to the complaining individual. The dissent's approach requires thorough evidentiary hearings at each stage of the process. Clearly the ADA imposes no such duty. Indeed, such an approach flies in the face of the *Arline* Court's statement that "accommodation is not reasonable if it either imposes 'undue financial and administrative burdens' [on the public entity] or requires 'a fundamental alteration in the nature of [the] program.'" 480 U.S. at 287 n.17.

Consistent with our Rehabilitation Act analysis, we find MSHSAA has demonstrated that the age limit is an essential eligibility requirement of the interscholastic baseball program. Again, Pottgen alleges he can meet the eligibility requirement if MSHSAA waives it for him. In conformity with our previous finding, we conclude that this is not a reasonable modification.

Thus, we find that Pottgen is not a "qualified individual" under the ADA. The district court erred in granting a preliminary injunction based on recovery under this Act.

* * *

Reversed and remanded.

ARNOLD, CHIEF JUDGE, dissenting.

In my view, the courts are obligated by statute to look at plaintiffs as individuals before they decide whether someone can meet the essential requirements of an eligibility rule like the one before us in the present case. Such an individualized inquiry, I believe, shows that the age requirement, as applied to Ed Pottgen, is not essential to the goals of the Missouri State High School Activities Association. I therefore respectfully dissent.

I have little to add to Judge Shaw's excellent opinion for the District Court. For me, this case is largely controlled by the words of the Americans With Disabilities Act of 1990, 42 U.S.C. § 12132, and by regulations issued under the Act. The statute provides, in relevant part, that

> no qualified individual with a disability shall, by reason of such disability, be excluded from participation in or be denied the benefits of the services, programs, or activities of a public entity, or be subjected to discrimination by any such entity.

There is no doubt that Ed Pottgen has a learning disability (for which he is now adequately compensating), and that, by reason of this disability, he has become unable to meet the Activities Association's age requirements. The Court today holds, however, that Ed is not a "qualified individual."

The statute itself defines this term. "Qualified individual with a disability" means

> an individual with a disability, who, with or without reasonable modifications to rules, policies, or practices ... meets the essential eligibility requirements for ... participation in programs or activities provided by a public entity.

42 U.S.C.A. § 12131(2). So, by the express words of Congress, it is not necessary for a person to meet all eligibility requirements. Instead, if a proposed modification of those requirements is "reasonable," a person can be a "qualified individual." The question therefore is whether it is "reasonable" to require the Activities Association to modify or waive the age requirement in the case of Ed Pottgen. The age criterion would not have to be abandoned completely: Ed would have been eligible if the requirement had been modified by only thirty-five days. He was that close to complete and literal compliance with all of the Activities Association's rules.

I agree with the Court that if a requirement is "essential" to a program or activity, a waiver or modification of that requirement would not be "reasonable" within the meaning of the statute. But how do we determine what is "essential"? The regulations interpreting the statute are of some help in answering that question. Under 28 C.F.R. § 35.130(b)(7) (1994),

> A public entity shall make reasonable modifications in policies, practices, or procedures when the modifications are necessary to avoid discrimination on the basis of disability, unless the public entity can demonstrate that making the modifications would fundamentally alter the nature of the service, program, or activity.

Was high-school baseball competition in Missouri fundamentally altered when Ed Pottgen was allowed to play one more year? I think not, and here the District Court's findings of fact become important. According to the Activities Association itself, there are three reasons for the age requirement. First, there is a desire to protect the safety of younger athletes against whom an older athlete might compete. Second, the Association wishes to reduce the competitive advantage that results when older students play, because of their presumed greater maturity. And third, the Association wishes to discourage students from delaying their education to gain athletic maturity. There is no contention whatever in the present case that Ed Pottgen deliberately repeated the first and third grades in order to make himself eligible to play baseball another year at age nineteen. The District Court found, moreover, "that any competitive advantage resulting from plaintiff's age is de minimis." The Court further found that the Activities Association made no individualized review of plaintiff's circumstances and gave no consideration to the issue of safety when it denied plaintiff's request for a waiver of the age rule. Finally, the Court found that "plaintiff does not appear to constitute a threat to the safety of others." Plaintiff is not appreciably larger than the average eighteen-year-old.

In other words, the age requirement could be modified for this individual player without doing violence to the admittedly salutary purposes underlying the age rule. But instead of looking at the rule's operation in the individual case of Ed Pottgen, both the Activities Association and this Court simply recite the rule's general justifications (which are not in dispute) and mechanically apply it across the board. But if a rule can be modified without doing violence to its essential purposes, as the District Court has found in the present case, I do not believe that it can be "essential" to the nature of the program or activity to refuse to modify the rule.

The Court avoids this issue by holding that "an individualized inquiry into the necessity of the age limit in Pottgen's case ... is inappropriate...." With respect, I find no such principle in the words of the statute. If an eligibility requirement can be reasonably modified to make someone eligible, that person is a qualified individual. In determining this issue, it seems to me entirely appropriate to focus on the effect that modification of the requirement for the individual in question would have on the nature of the program. When the case is looked at from this point of view, it becomes clear that the Association could easily bend to accommodate Ed Pottgen without breaking anything essential. For these reasons, I would affirm the preliminary injunction entered by the District Court.

A subsequent case, *Sandison v. Michigan High School Athletic Association*, 64 F.3d 1026 (6th Cir.1995), followed much the same path as the majority in *Pottgen*. Because of a learning disability, Ronald Sandison fell behind his Michigan counterparts right at the kindergarten stage. However, through special programs that have been developed for problems such as Sandison's "auditory input disability, which hampered [his] ability to distinguish between similar sounds," Sandison's problems were solved and he was able to attend and graduate from the regular high school. However, the student did not get to his final high school year until he was 19, and thus was ineligible to continue on the school's track and field team under a Michigan High School Athletic Association's rule that was essentially the same as Missouri's.

Sandison won injunctive relief from a federal judge who concluded that individualized reasonable accommodation was needed for learning disabled students, and that a waiver in Sandison's case would have been reasonable: (i) because he was not a star athlete as some older students might be, and (ii) track and field was not a contact sport that posed risks of injury from overage and oversized students. On appeal, the Sixth

Circuit reversed that verdict for essentially the same reasons as the Eighth Circuit majority in *Pottgen*. The following passage captures their rationale for rejecting the view of the district court judge and Judge Arnold in his *Pottgen* dissent that only *individualized* accommodation was reasonable for these age-based eligibility rules.

But the district court erred in finding that waiver of Regulation I § 2 constituted a reasonable accommodation. First, we agree with the court in *Pottgen* that waiver of the age restriction fundamentally alters the sports program. Due to the usual ages of first-year high school students, high school sports programs generally involve competitors between fourteen and eighteen years of age. Removing the age restriction injects into competition students older than the vast majority of other students, and the record shows that the older students are generally more physically mature than younger students. Expanding the sports program to include older students works a fundamental alteration.

Second, although the plaintiffs assert that introducing their average athletic skills into track and cross-country competition would not fundamentally alter the program, the record does not reveal how the MHSAA, or anyone, can make that competitive unfairness determination without an undue burden. The MHSAA's expert explained that five factors weigh in deciding whether an athlete possessed an unfair competitive advantage due to age: chronological age, physical maturity, athletic experience, athletic skill level, and mental ability to process sports strategy. It is plainly an undue burden to require high school coaches and hired physicians to determine whether these factors render a student's age an unfair competitive advantage. The determination would have to be made relative to the skill level of each participating member of opposing teams and the team as a unit. And of course each team member and the team as a unit would present a different skill level. Indeed, the determination would also have to be made relative to the skill level of the would-be athlete whom the older student displaced from the team. It is unreasonable to call upon coaches and physicians to make these near-impossible determinations.

Finally, we note that there is a significant peculiarity in trying to characterize the waiver of the age restriction as a "reasonable accommodation" of the plaintiffs' respective learning disability. Ordinarily, an accommodation of an individual's disability operates so that the disability is overcome and the disability no longer prevents the individual from participating. In this case, although playing high school sports undoubtedly helped the plaintiffs progress through high school, the waiver of the age restriction is not directed at helping them overcome learning disabilities; the waiver merely removes the age ceiling as an obstacle.

64 F.3d at 1035.

While the ultimate verdicts were the same, the circuit court opinions in *Pottgen* and *Sandison* adopted a much more limited reading of the "reasonable accommodation" standard in federal disability law than did the district court opinion in *Ganden* which we read earlier. We shall have to wait to see the Supreme Court's eventual judgment on a legal issue that has much broader implications for disability claims lodged outside the sports context. In the meantime, the facts of these cases (and *Butts*) give us a somewhat more informed base upon which to judge the appropriateness of age restraints on otherwise eligible students participating in sports. What are your views on that score?

D. JUDICIAL SCRUTINY OF INSTITUTIONAL DECISIONS

We now turn to the question whether and to what extent courts should engage in serious independent scrutiny of the judgments made about these issues within the college athletic establishment. This is an issue similar to the one we encountered in Chapter 1, regarding legal challenges to commissioner judgments about the best interests of their professional sports.

Gulf South Conference v. Boyd, 369 So.2d 553 (Ala.1979), involved a college football player, Julian Boyd, who had entered Division II Livingston University in the fall of 1975 under a one-year scholarship. At the end of the year, Boyd was suffering from an asthmatic condition. Thus, he refused Livingston's offer to renew his scholarship, dropped out of school, and attended a junior college in his home town. Two years later, Boyd wanted to go to college to play football for Troy State, a Livingston rival in the Gulf South Conference. The GSC Commissioner declared Boyd ineligible to play for Troy State, under a GSC rule that prohibited transfers except, among other things, when "a GSC member does not renew the grant-in-aid of an eligible athlete." Boyd went to court to reverse this ruling, but was faced with a Supreme Court of Alabama precedent, *Scott v. Kilpatrick*, 286 Ala. 129, 237 So.2d 652 (Ala.1970), which had held that the courts should not intervene in the internal affairs of a high school athletic association. This time the state Supreme Court made it clear that

> ... [t]here is a vast difference between high school football and college football. A high school athlete receives no present economic benefit from playing high school football, his only economic benefit being the possibility of his receiving an offer of a college scholarship. The *Scott* case held that such a possibility was too speculative to recognize as a property right. In contrast, the college athlete receives a scholarship of substantial pecuniary value to engage in college sports. Such scholarships often cover the complete cost of attending a college or university; therefore, the right to be eligible to participate in college athletics cannot be viewed as a mere speculative interest, but is a property right of present economic value.

The contention by the GSC that the lower court did not have jurisdiction basically stems from a body of common law involving private associations. See Chaffee, *The Internal Affairs of Associations Not For Profit*, 43 Harv. L. Rev. 993 (1930). The general rule is that courts should not interfere with the internal management of such associations. The theory behind this non-interference doctrine is that the individual members of such associations have the freedom to choose their associates and the conditions of their association; further, it is argued, judicial review of the affairs of such associations would violate this basic principle of the freedom to associate. Still another justification asserted for the existence of the non-interference doctrine is that the rules and regulations upon which these associations operate are often unclear, and the courts would have no available standard upon which to determine the reasonableness of their rules. Even though we recognize the existence of this non-interference principle, nevertheless this Court has sanctioned judicial review when the actions of an association are the result of fraud, lack of jurisdiction, collusion, arbitrariness, or are in violation of or contravene any principle of public policy.

We hold that the general non-interference doctrine concerning voluntary associations does not apply to cases involving disputes between college athletes themselves and college athletic associations. There is a cogent reason for this position. In such cases the athlete himself is not even a member of the athletic association; therefore, the basic "freedom of association" principle behind the non-interference rule is not present. The athlete himself has no voice or bargaining power concerning the rules and regulations adopted by the athletic associations because he is not a member, yet he stands to be substantially affected, and even damaged, by an association ruling declaring him to be ineligible to participate in intercollegiate athletics. Thus he may be deprived of the property right eligibility to participate in intercollegiate athletics.

369 So.2d at 556–57. The court went on to state that while Livingston had offered to renew the scholarship, Boyd had not accepted the offer; thus, the scholarship was not renewed, and under the GSC rule, "Boyd became a free agent and was free to sign with whatever school he chose."

A similar judicial sentiment was expressed in *California State University, Hayward (CSUH) v. NCAA*, 47 Cal.App.3d 533, 121 Cal.Rptr. 85 (1975). The NCAA had suspended CSUH from play in any post-season college championships, because the school had adopted a different interpretation than the Association's of the "1.6 Predictor Rule" for academic eligibility (the rule that we saw at issue in the *Robert Parish* case). An appellate court in California stated that, even though CSUH was itself a member of the NCAA (by contrast with Boyd's "outsider" position in the GSC), it had the same right to assert in court that the Association had "failed to abide by its own rules or the laws of the land" as did the member of a trade union or medical association.

As to the claim that CSUH's interest is not sufficiently substantial to justify judicial intervention due to a mere expectancy of participation in championship events, it has already been discussed that a violation by an association of its own bylaws and constitution or of the laws of the land justifies judicial intervention. Further, that CSUH had, and has, more than a mere expectancy that some of its athletes would earn the opportunity to participate in NCAA championship events but for the suspension is evidenced by the fact that at the time of both the hearing on the temporary restraining order and the hearing on the preliminary injunction, there were upcoming NCAA championship events in which CSUH students, without the imposed suspension, were eligible to compete. Additionally, the decision of the NCAA necessarily affects more than just the possibility of being precluded from championship events. The sanction of indefinite probation affects the reputation of CSUH and its entire athletic program, and thereby also affects CSUH's ability to recruit athletes. Judicial notice may be taken that state schools such as CSUH are deeply involved in fielding and promoting athletic teams with concurrent expenditures of time, energy and resources. The school provides and pays for the coaches, supplies and equipment. It finances, equips, trains and fields the teams. And, its funds pay the NCAA membership dues. The contention that CSUH has no substantial interest to justify judicial intervention lacks merit.

121 Cal.Rptr. at 89–90.

Despite the sentiments expressed in *Boyd* and *Hayward*, there are limits to the protections athletes (or coaches) can secure through judicial interpretation of NCAA rules. The reason is that even if the NCAA loses a particular case, it can simply rewrite the rules to make them crystal-clear in support of the same policy. For example, Article 11.2 of the NCAA Manual requires that all contractual agreements or appointments for coaching staffs stipulate that coaches found in violation of NCAA regulations are subject to discipline pursuant to NCAA enforcement procedures, including suspension without pay and even dismissal for "deliberate and serious violations."

Therefore, enduring protections for individuals can be secured only through legal tools that establish binding rights and obligations that cannot be altered by internal NCAA procedures. Even after *Tarkanian*, in which the Supreme Court removed federal constitutional scrutiny of the NCAA, there remain several such tools. The next case exemplifies the use of attempted *tort* litigation in a situation that vividly evokes the academic concerns about the world of big-time college sports.

ROSS v. CREIGHTON UNIV.

United States District Court, Northern District of Illinois, 1990.
740 F.Supp. 1319.

NORDBERG, DISTRICT JUDGE.

One day in July 1987, Kevin Ross, a former college basketball player, barricaded himself in a high-rise hotel room in downtown Chicago and threw assorted pieces of furniture out the window. As Ross currently recalls it, the defenestrated furniture "symbolized" the employees of Creighton University, whose alleged misdeeds he blames for the onset of this "major depressive episode." Ross now sues the university in contract and tort. The gist of Ross's Amended Complaint is that Creighton caused this episode and otherwise injured him by recruiting him to attend the school on a basketball scholarship while knowing that Ross, who scored nine points out of a possible 36 on the American College Test, was pitifully unprepared to attend Creighton, which is a private school whose average student in the year Ross matriculated, 1978, scored 23.2 points on the ACT.

Complaint

Ross, who is six feet and nine inches tall, was a high school basketball star in Kansas City, Kansas, when Creighton recruited him. Creighton knew that Ross could not handle college-level studies, but kept him eligible for the basketball team by recommending that he enroll in "bonehead" (Ross's description) courses, such as ceramics, marksmanship, and the respective theories of basketball, track and field, and football. Under its rules, the university would not have accepted the pursuit of this esoteric curriculum by a non-athlete. After four years, when his basketball eligibility expired, Ross had earned only 96 of the 128 credits required to graduate, maintaining a "D" average. His reading skills were those of a seventh-grader; his overall language skills, those of a fourth-grader.

In order to get Ross remedial education, representatives of Creighton made arrangements for Ross to attend Chicago's Westside Preparatory School, an elementary and high school whose founder, Marva Collins, has drawn national attention for her abilities as an educator. As its name suggests, Westside Prep is a school for children, not for adults. Ross says that Creighton representatives made four trips to Chicago to discuss Ross's enrollment. The agreement to enroll Ross is spelled out in a letter dated July 29, 1982, from Collins to Creighton's athletic director. The letter, countersigned by a Creighton official and returned to Collins, obligated Creighton to pay for Ross's tuition, special tutoring, books and living expenses. Ross attended Westside in 1982 and 1983. He later attended Roosevelt University, also located in Chicago, but dropped out after 1985 for want of money. Ross's furniture-throwing outburst took place on July 23, 1987. He was arrested and ordered to make restitution in the amount of $7,500.

* * *

Ross's Tort Claim

... Ross says [his tort] claim is a hybrid of "negligent infliction of emotional distress" and "educational malpractice." These strands of tort law "intertwine" to form the novel tort of "negligence in recruiting and repeatedly re-enrolling an athlete utterly incapable—without substantial tutoring and other support—of performing the academic work required to make educational progress," exacerbated by the enrollment of plaintiff in a school with children half his age and size. Before considering the merits of this tort, the Court must unravel its separate threads.

Educational malpractice is a tort theory beloved of commentators, but not of courts. While often proposed as a remedy for those who think themselves wronged by educators (see, e.g., J. Elson, *A Common Law Remedy for the Educational Harms Caused by Incompetent or Careless Teaching*, 73 Nw. U. L. Rev. 641 (1978)), educational malpractice has been repeatedly rejected by the American courts.

* * *

Whether to create a cause of action for educational malpractice is, of course, a question for the Court, which determines as a matter of law whether a duty runs from defendant to plaintiff. It is a matter of considering sound social policy, guided by looking to " '[t]he likelihood of injury, the magnitude of the burden of guarding against it and the consequences of placing that burden upon defendant.' "

* * *

This Court believes the same general concerns would lead the Illinois courts to reject the tort of educational malpractice. Admittedly, the term "educational malpractice" has a seductive ring to it; after all, if doctors, lawyers, accountants and other professionals can be held liable for failing to exercise due care, why can't teachers? The answer is that the nature of education radically differs from other professions. Education is an intensely collaborative process, requiring the interaction of student with teacher. A good student can learn from a poor teacher; a poor student can close his mind to a good teacher. Without effort by a student, he cannot be educated. Good teaching methods may vary with the needs of the individual student. In other professions, by contrast, client cooperation is far less important; given a modicum of cooperation, a competent professional in other fields can control the results obtained. But in education, the ultimate responsibility for success remains always with the student. Both the process and the result are subjective, and proof or disproof extremely difficult.

* * *

It also must be remembered that education is a service rendered on an immensely greater scale than other professional services. If every failed student could seek tort damages against any teacher, administrator and school he feels may have shortchanged him at some point in his education, the courts could be deluged and schools shut down. The Court believes that Illinois courts would avert the flood and the educational loss. This is not to say that the mere worry that litigation will increase justifies a court's refusal to remedy a wrong; it is to say that the real danger of an unrestrained multiplication of lawsuits shows the disutility of the proposed remedy. If poor education (or student laziness) is to be corrected, a common law action for negligence is not a practical means of going about it.

* * *

[Having rejected both the general tort of educational malpractice and Ross' claim for negligent infliction of emotional distress, the court then asked whether Ross nonetheless has a cause] of action that is sui generis? Ross argues that he does, contending that "the present case is so unique and egregious that, despite the lack of precedent, a cause of action should be found to exist." Ross basically argues that a special tort be created for the benefit of student athletes, or more precisely, for the benefit of student athletes whose academic performance would not have qualified them to be students had they not been athletes. In Ross's view, "The present case does not question classroom methodology or the competence of instruction. Rather the issue is whether Plaintiff should ever have been admitted to Creighton and whether, once admitted, Creighton had a duty to truly educate Plaintiff and not simply to maintain his eligibility for basketball.... "

Ross's inability to plead a cause of action under existing law strongly counsels against creating a new cause of action in his favor. Rules serve little purpose if they are not reasonably predictable and if they do not apply across the board, for one cannot conform behavior to the unknowable. See A. Scalia, *The Rule of Law as a Law of Rules*, 56 U. Chicago L. Rev. 1175, 1178–79 (1989). Even a new rule declared through the evolutionary process of the common law ought fairly be deduced from existing doctrine—something that cannot be said for Ross's claim. The policy reasons considered by the Illinois courts further counsel against recognition of this new duty. Schools would be forced to undertake the delphic science of diagnosing the mental condition of potential recruits. And why should the cause of action be limited to student athletes? Shouldn't all students who actually pay tuition also have an equal right to recover if they are negligently admitted, and once negligently admitted, have a right to recover if the school negligently counsels and educates them? To allow Ross to recover might redress a wrong (assuming, for sake of argument, that he was in fact exploited), but it would also endanger the admissions prospects of thousands of marginal students, as schools scrambled to factor into their admissions calculations whether a potentially "negligent admission" now could cost unforeseeable tort damages later. The Court should not and will not craft a new tort for Ross.

[On appeal, the Seventh Circuit Court of Appeals upheld the summary dismissal of Ross' tort theory of educational malpractice, but took a somewhat different view of Ross' contract claim.]

ROSS v. CREIGHTON UNIV.
United States Court of Appeals, Seventh Circuit, 1992.
957 F.2d 410.

RIPPLE, CIRCUIT JUDGE.

* * *

It is held generally in the United States that the "basic legal relation between a student and a private university or college is contractual in nature. The catalogues, bulletins, circulars, and regulations of the institution made available to the matriculant become a part of the contract." Indeed, there seems to be "no dissent" from this proposition. As the district court correctly noted, Illinois recognizes that the relationship between a student and an educational institution is, in some of its aspects, contractual. It is quite clear, however, that Illinois would not recognize all aspects of a university-student relationship as subject to remedy through a contract action. "A contract between a private institution and a student confers duties upon both parties which cannot be arbitrarily disregarded and may be judicially enforced." However, "a decision of the school authorities relating to the academic qualification of the students will not be reviewed.... Courts are not qualified to pass an opinion as to the attainments of a student ... and ... courts will not review a decision of the school authorities relating to academic qualifications of the students."

There is no question, we believe, that Illinois would adhere to the great weight of authority and bar any attempt to repackage an educational malpractice claim as a contract claim. As several courts have noted, the policy concerns that preclude a cause of action for educational malpractice apply with equal force to bar a breach of contract claim attacking the general quality of an education. "Where the essence of the complaint is that the school breached its agreement by failing to provide an effective education, the court is again asked to evaluate the course of instruction ... [and] is similarly called upon to review the soundness of the method of teaching that has been adopted by an educational institution."

To state a claim for breach of contract, the plaintiff must do more than simply allege that the education was not good enough. Instead, he must point to an identifiable contractual promise that the defendant failed to honor. Thus, ... if the defendant took tuition money and then provided no education, or alternately, promised a set number of hours of instruction and then failed to deliver, a breach of contract action may be available. See *Zumbrun v. University of Southern California*, 101 Cal. Rptr. 499 (1972) (breach of contract action allowed against university when professor declined to give lectures and final exam, and all students received a grade of "B"). Similarly, a breach of contract action might exist if a student enrolled in a course explicitly promising instruction that would qualify him as a journeyman, but in which the fundamentals necessary to attain that skill were not even presented. In these cases, the essence of the plaintiff's complaint would not be that the institution failed to perform adequately a promised educational service, but rather that it failed to perform that service at all. Ruling on this issue would not require an inquiry into the nuances of educational processes and theories, but rather an objective assessment of whether the institution made a good faith effort to perform on its promise.

We read Mr. Ross' complaint to allege more than a failure of the University to provide him with an education of a certain quality. Rather, he alleges that the University knew that he was not qualified academically to participate in its curriculum. Nevertheless, it made a specific promise that he would be able to participate in a meaningful way in that program because it would provide certain specific services to him. Finally, he alleges that the University breached its promise by reneging on its commitment to provide those services and, consequently, effectively cutting him off from any participation in and benefit from the University's academic program. To adjudicate such a claim, the court would not be required to determine whether Creighton had breached its contract with Mr. Ross by providing deficient academic services. Rather, its inquiry would be limited to whether the University had provided any real access to its academic curriculum at all.

Accordingly, we must disagree respectfully with our colleague in the district court as to whether the contract counts of the complaint can be dismissed at the pleadings stage. In our view, the allegations of the complaint are sufficient to warrant further proceedings. We emphasize, however, the narrow ground of our disagreement. We agree—indeed we emphasize—that courts should not "take on the job of supervising the relationship between colleges and student-athletes or creating in effect a new relationship between them." We also recognize a formal university-student contract is rarely employed and, consequently, "the general nature and terms of the agreement are usually implied, with specific terms to be found in the university bulletin and other publications; custom and usages can also become specific terms by implication." Nevertheless, we believe that the district court can adjudicate Mr. Ross' specific and narrow claim that he was barred from any participation in and benefit from the University's academic program without second-guessing the professional judgment of the University faculty on academic matters.

Affirmed in part, remanded in part.

A similar case involved contract and tort claims by Terrell Jackson in a dispute with Drake University. *Jackson v. Drake University*, 778 F.Supp. 1490 (S.D.Iowa 1991). Jackson claimed that when he was recruited by Drake basketball coach Tom Abatemarco, he was promised both the right to play basketball and an environment conducive to high academic achievement. When Jackson got to Drake, the coaches allegedly pressured him to take easy courses and hand in plagiarized papers, and denied him adequate study time. When Jackson complained about the situation, Abatemarco was said to have harassed him at practice, called him foul names, and made him run extra drills and do extra exercises. In the middle of his sophomore year, Jackson quit the team. He filed suit against the school alleging breach of contract, negligent educational malpractice, negligent misrepresentation in recruiting, and fraud. The court dismissed the contract claim because the entitlements upon which it was based, especially the right to play basketball, were not expressly contained in Jackson's scholarship documents. Citing *Ross,* the court dismissed the educational malpractice claim as not a viable tort in Iowa. The court did order trial of the negligent misrepresentation and fraud claims, according to the following legal specifications:

> To properly state a claim of negligent misrepresentation, Jackson must allege that the defendant, in the course of its business or profession or employment, supplied false information for the guidance of others in their business transactions, that the information was justifiably relied on by the plaintiff, and the defendant failed to exercise reasonable care or competence in communicating the information. To state a claim for fraud, Jackson must allege a material misrepresentation, made knowingly, with the intent to induce Jackson to act, upon which he justifiably relied, with damages.

778 F.Supp. at 1494.

Questions for Discussion

1. If courts are unwilling to allow tort claims by student-athletes, and are prepared to accept contract claims only for explicit and specific promises, how will future scholarship agreements be worded? Should courts allow suits for breach of alleged verbal promises (for example, by recruiters) that are not contained in the written agreement?

2. Can one distinguish between a university's legal and educational obligations to the general student body[ee] and its obligations to student-athletes, especially those on athletic scholarships in revenue-producing football and basketball? In what legal direction should the factual differences incline courts?[ff]

3. After reading this and earlier cases, and from exposure to the general media, are you comfortable with the judicial conclusion in *Ross* that supervision of educational quality is best left to the NCAA "which presumably possesses the staff and expertise to carry out the job"?

---

ee. See John G. Culhane, *Reinvigorating Educational Malpractice Claims: A Representational Focus,* 67 Washington L. Rev. 349 (1992).

ff. As for athletes, see Timothy Davis, *Examining Educational Malpractice Jurisprudence: Should a Cause of Action Be Created for Student Athletes?,* 69 Denver U. L. Rev. 57 (1992), and Harold B. Hilborn, *Student Athletes and Judicial Inconsistency: Establishing a Duty to Educate as a Means of Fostering Meaningful Reform of Intercollegiate Athletics,* 89 Northwestern U. L. Rev. 741 (1995).

Congress has not been prepared to place full reliance on the NCAA. Over the NCAA's opposition, a Student–Athlete Right–to–Know Act was enacted in 1990 (Pub. Law 101–542, Title I, §§ 102, 104 (Nov. 8, 1990) (codified at 20 U.S.C.A. § 1092(e) (1991)). This Act, which was propelled through the Congress by Senator Bill Bradley and Representative Tom McMillan, two former basketball All–Americans and Rhodes Scholars, requires the Department of Education to assemble and publish comparative athlete graduation rates at different colleges. With this bill pending, the NCAA adopted a similar regulation of its own (Articles 13.3 and 30.1), under which these data are to be collected and distilled into a form that must be given to athletes and their families.

The reports issued every year, entitled *NCAA Division I Graduation Rates*, offer a statistical perspective on the educational problem to which these measures are addressed. The report for the 1996–97 academic year, for example, listed graduation rates of those who enrolled as freshmen in 1990–91 (thus allowing six years for securing the four year degree). For all students in Division–I schools, the graduation rate was 56%, while the student-athlete rate was slightly higher at 58%. (It should be noted that that student-athlete graduation rates are still significantly lower than the 75% to 80% rate for those students who attend school full-time for up to five consecutive years, the situation of almost all college athletes.) Both athlete and overall rates are up significantly from the 51% level just before Proposition 48 went into effect.

Broken down into ethnic categories, the athlete graduation rate ranges from 46% for African-Americans, to 52% for Hispanic–Americans, to 62% for whites, to 64% for Asian–Americans. There is also a significant disparity between male and female graduation rates: e.g., 59% of black female athletes and 70% of white female athletes had graduated, as compared to 43% of black male athletes and 57% of white male athletes. The one demographic group, though, in which athletes perform worse than regular students are white males, 53% of whose athletes graduate versus 55% overall. The single biggest sports deficit is within men's basketball, whose average graduation rate is just 45%, up from 38% five years earlier, but much lower than women's basketball (65%) or even football (52%). And recall what we saw earlier, that only one of 70 players on Division I basketball teams ever played a game in the NBA.

The foregoing figures capsulize the record at Division I schools taken as a whole. The several hundred pages of the reports are principally devoted to recording the situation at each school. Unsurprisingly, graduation records of individual colleges vary dramatically above and below the 58% Division I average. In appraising these reports from individual schools, it is important both to compare the academic performance of athletes to that of the school's general student body, and even then not to place too much weight on a single year in which the relatively small number of athletes may do exceptionally well or poorly. Thus, the NCAA's academic champions designated by the 1995–96 and 1996–97 reports were Oregon State and Prairie View, respectively, with 96% and 100% athlete graduation rates that were far above general student rates in those respective years. In the other year, though, Oregon State had a 61% athlete rate (in 1996–97), while Prairie View's was as low as 27% (in 1995–96). Viewing the two years together, it turns out that Division I schools such as Duke, Notre Dame, Boston College, and a few others are consistently in the 85–90% athlete graduation rate, which at Boston College, at least, is slightly higher than the overall graduation rate. By contrast, schools such as Houston U. have very low athlete graduation rates (24% and 33% in those years), but this is not that far below the general student rate (35% in each year). A true student-athlete problem at a school is not when its athlete graduation rates are below Duke's, for example, but below that school's own general student rates. Here, the concerns should be felt at a Clemson or UCLA which had gaps in their athlete and student graduation rates that ranged from 15% to 30% (in those two years at least).

There remains a serious question about whether publication and distribution of comparative athlete-student graduation data within and among different schools is likely to create incentives to improve the educational situation for athletes. (Following publication of the 1996 Report, Oregon State issued T-shirts proclaiming "National Champions, Beavers, 1996"; however, it also replaced that year's football coach whose players may have been graduating, but who had not been able to end the school's 26-year streak of losing seasons, the longest in Division I–A football.) Some have suggested that schools should also be required to provide data regarding the odds of a college athlete going on to a professional sports career (see note bb above), with a view to motivating student-athletes to work at least as hard in the classroom as on the field. Is development by both Congress and the NCAA of such a database for "informed consent" by college applicants (and their parents) a sufficient answer to those who advocate educational malpractice suits by athletes such as Kevin Ross? (For example, would informed consent preclude patients from suing hospitals for medical malpractice? See *Tunkl v. Regents of the Univ. of California*, 60 Cal.2d 92, 32 Cal.Rptr. 33, 383 P.2d 441 (1963).)

Consider yet another possible solution, designed to provide even stronger institutional incentives than publication of graduation rates. Suppose that the NCAA abolished all of its mandatory rules regarding which athletes can be admitted to college and how they must progress academically while at school. Instead, athletes would take a standardized test (such as the Graduate Record Exam (GRE) also administered by ETS) when they finish their third (or fourth) year of college. If the athlete received at least a certain minimum score on this test of knowledge and skill acquired while at college, the school would be entitled to offer a scholarship to his replacement. If, however, the athlete failed (or refused to take) the test, the college would lose one of its scholarships in that sport for the next four years. How might this regime influence relations between the athletic and the academic departments in the university?

In March 1991, the Report of the Knight Foundation's blue-ribbon Commission on Intercollegiate Athletics was issued—*Keeping Faith with the Student–Athlete: A New Model for Intercollegiate Athletics.* The following passage captures the Commission's model for reforming college sports:

> The reform we seek takes shape around what the Commission calls the "one-plus-three" model. It consists of the "one"—presidential control—directed toward the "three"—academic integrity, financial integrity and accountability through certification. This model is fully consistent with the university as a context for vigorous and exciting intercollegiate competition. It also serves to bond athletics to the purposes of the university in a way that provides a new framework for their conduct.

You have now been exposed to a variety of materials concerning the problems of academic integrity and due process in college sports. Has this chapter left you confident that we can entrust responsibility for these issues to college presidents? Are there parallels with the questions posed earlier about the role of commissioners in determining the "best interests" of professional sports? These questions may be even more urgent when we confront in the next chapter the problem of financial integrity in an increasingly commercialized world of intercollegiate athletics.

Chapter Ten

INTERCOLLEGIATE SPORTS: COMMERCIALISM AND AMATEURISM

The previous chapter traced the tension between the NCAA's efforts to foster academic values in intercollegiate sports and the interests of the students and coaches who are affected by the definition and enforcement of NCAA rules. This chapter considers the even starker conflict between the amateur ideal and the commercial reality of big-time college sports, and explores the availability of contract, antitrust, and other legal regimes to parties who dislike the balances struck within the NCAA.[a]

In Chapter 9 we mentioned the large sums of money being generated by and spent on college sports in the 1990s; perhaps the most remarkable figure is the $1.7 *billion*, eight-year television contract for the NCAA's men's basketball tournament. Just 30 years ago the television rights for this tournament earned a mere $190,000, and as late as 1981 the television rights were sold for $9 million per year. In 1997, CBS paid the NCAA $215 million to bring March Madness into American homes. In 1995, total sports revenues reached just under $40 million for one particular school, and an average of over $15 million apiece for the 108 Division I–A schools.[b] Division I (I–A in football) consists of schools with large programs in football and men's basketball, which earn almost all the *direct* athletic revenues for their schools—an average of approximately $9 million from the two sports together for the Division 1–A

---

a. Besides the works cited in the opening footnote of the previous chapter, see Nand Hart–Nibbing & Clement Cottingham, *The Political Economy of College Sports*, (Lexington, Mass.: D.C. Heath, 1986); Paul R. Lawrence, *Unsportsmanlike Conduct: The National Collegiate Athletic Association and the Business of College Football* (New York: Praeger, 1987); Arthur A. Fleisher III, Brian L. Goff & Robert D. Tollison, *The National Collegiate Athletic Association: A Study in Cartel Behavior* (Chicago: University of Chicago Press, 1992); Richard B. McKenzie & E. Thomas Sullivan, *Does the NCAA Exploit College Athletes?: An Economics and Legal Interpretation*, 32 Antitrust Bulletin 373 (Summer 1987).

b. Many of the figures in this and the next paragraph are drawn from Daniel L. Fulks, *Revenues and Expenses of Intercollegiate Athletics Programs: Financial Trends and Relationships—1995* (Overland Park, Kan. NCAA, 1996).

schools in 1995. This can be compared to the total of $825,000 per school from all the other men's and women's sports combined (of which $135,000 comes from women's basketball). Schools such as Notre Dame, Michigan, and Florida earn $14 to 15 million in profits from football alone, and Indiana and North Carolina $5 to $7 million in profits from men's basketball.

Unfortunately for NCAA members, though, accompanying these expanding revenues has been a corresponding escalation in expenditures on intercollegiate sports. Though the big-time programs earn the lion's share of sports revenues, the average Division I–A school ended with only a modest surplus of $1.2 million from athletics. The average balance sheet for schools in all other NCAA Divisions showed a deficit; for example, the typical school in Division I–AA lost $500,000 on sports. Indeed, while football and men's basketball usually produce profits for their schools, even in these two sports many of the larger universities have experienced substantial deficits in recent years. When one includes expenditures on sports that produce little or no revenue on their own (e.g., swimming), approximately 15% of Division I–A schools reported an athletic deficit in 1995, averaging $1.8 million apiece.[c]

The foregoing financial figures produce an obvious interest on the part of schools in the success of the NCAA in realizing its principle of *Economy of Athletics Program Operation*:

> Intercollegiate athletics programs shall be administered in keeping with prudent management and fiscal practices to assure the financial stability necessary for providing student-athletes with adequate opportunities for athletic competition as an integral part of a quality educational experience.

(Article 2.13) A host of NCAA rules are designed to implement this policy, as well as the principle of "Competitive Equity" which "assures that individual student-athletes in institutions would not be prevented unfairly from achieving the benefits inherent in participation in intercollegiate athletics" (Article 2.7). The most important such NCAA rules set out to define who is an "amateur" eligible to compete in college sports,

---

c. These are the financial figures reflected in university accounts and reported to the NCAA. Tracking and calculating surpluses or deficits from college sports is a difficult exercise because there is no firm consensus about what revenues or expenditures are properly attributable to a school's athletic program. How much of the university's general overhead—ranging from the president's office to the library to campus security—should be allocated to athletics? What is the true cost to a college of admitting a scholarship athlete into its classes and its housing and eating facilities, and will this cost tend to be more or less than the tuition and room and board fees charged to ordinary students (the latter being the figure depicted as the sports expenditure in university accounts)? How much of the revenues from game concessions, souvenirs, and alumni donations should be credited to the athletic department? There is considerable disparity in the accounting methods and judgments used by different schools with respect to these and a host of other questions posed in this area. The limited amount of in-depth scholarly investigation of the institutions' books finds that schools tend to understate significantly the revenues and correspondingly overstate the expenses from sports: see Fleisher, et al., *The NCAA: A Study in Cartel Behavior*, note a above, at 73–94. This empirical finding accords with the expectations of economists that people in charge of any non-profit enterprise will minimize book profits from their programs. What is the likely source of that non-profit managerial incentive? If valid, what are its implications for the world of college sports?

and to ban receipt by student-athletes of any extra benefits beyond those permitted by the rules. The first part of this chapter completes our presentation of the main components of the NCAA Manual, with selected cases illustrating the rules in operation. We then turn to the various legal approaches that have been used to challenge these NCAA policies, not only by players and coaches, but also by the fans whose patronage (either at the gate or on television) finances the large college sports establishment.

A. NCAA ELIGIBILITY RULES[d]

1. PAY BEFORE COLLEGE

A key "general principle" (stated at the outset of Article 12) that underlies much NCAA regulation is that "only an *amateur* student-athlete is eligible for intercollegiate participation in a particular sport," so as to "maintain a clear line of demarcation between college athletics and professional sports." Article 12 goes on to provide that an athlete "loses amateur status and thus shall not be eligible for intercollegiate competition" in a number of specified ways. For example, athletes lose their eligibility not just by payment "in any form for the sport," but also by "a promise of pay even if such pay is to be received following completion of intercollegiate athletic competition."

A perennial problem faced by the NCAA concerns hockey players from Canada, many of whom play major Junior A hockey under Canadian Amateur Hockey Association (CAHA) auspices which permit teams to pay room and board and educational expenses for their players (who often live away from home). Until the early 1970s, NCAA by-laws simply made any Canadian Junior A hockey player ineligible for U.S. college hockey. That "official interpretation" by the NCAA of its rules was struck down by a district judge in *Buckton v. NCAA*, 366 F.Supp. 1152 (D.Mass.1973), as unconstitutional discrimination against aliens. In 1974, the NCAA substituted a new interpretation of the term "pay" to include "educational expenses not permitted by governing legislation of this Association ... [and any] expenses received from an outside amateur sports team ... in excess of actual and necessary travel and meal expenses and apparel or equipment ... for practice and game competition ..." (Article 12.1.2(e)). This new formula produced a struggle between the NCAA and Denver University, which culminated in the following case.

COLORADO SEMINARY (UNIV. OF DENVER) v. NCAA

United States District Court, District of Colorado, 1976.
417 F.Supp. 885, aff'd, 570 F.2d 320 (10th Cir.1978).

ARRAJ, CHIEF JUDGE.

[In 1973, Denver U. had won the NCAA hockey championship with a team led by several Canadian players. Both the University Chancellor

---

d. See Timothy Davis, *Intercollegiate Athletics: Competing Models and Conflicting Realities*, 25 Rutgers L. J. 269 (1994).

and Coach Murray Armstrong refused to characterize these star players as "professionals" who were ineligible to play for the university simply because they had received the same room and board for playing for a Canadian amateur team before college as they were receiving from Denver U. while playing at college. As a result, the NCAA imposed sanctions on Denver U. which not only barred the school from future television and post-season appearances, but demanded return of the 1973 championship trophy and revenues. Denver and the players went off to court, asserting that their constitutional rights had been violated. As in *Buckton*, the district court in this pre-*Tarkanian* era believed that the NCAA was a "state actor" governed by the constitution. However, citing *Parish v. NCAA*, 506 F.2d 1028 (5th Cir.1975), the judge dismissed the due process claim, because he found no independent constitutional right to play sports as part of one's college education, even as training for a possible professional concern. The court then addressed a novel equal protection claim advanced by the players.]

* * *

It is first asserted that the prohibition on receipt of compensation for expenses other than travel and one meal from an outside source discriminates between various classes of student-athletes, Canadian and American, poor and rich, rural and city. The gist of the claims of discrimination against these shifting and sometime vague classes is that poor rural students, most commonly Canadian, must move to cities where amateur hockey is being played to be able to participate and, to be able to live, must accept compensation from the teams for such expenses as room and board.

It is now well established that the right to an education, though important, is not so fundamental as to require strict scrutiny of classifications allegedly affecting that right, *San Antonio Independent School District v. Rodriguez*, 411 U.S. 1 (1973)....

The same court which struck down the previous official interpretations in *Buckton* while utilizing strict scrutiny has subsequently found, and we believe correctly, that the present classifications in the interpretations apply to all hockey players of all nationalities and are not based on alienage or any other basis requiring strict scrutiny. Indeed, [one of the student-plaintiffs here, Falcone] is an American whose eligibility was lost for having accepted compensation for room and board expenses from an American amateur team. Accordingly, the plaintiff[s][are] entitled to have the NCAA's eligibility regulations invalidated only if they bear no rational relationship to that organization's legitimate objectives.

The objectives of the NCAA have been previously stated. They include maintaining intercollegiate athletics as an integral part of the educational program and the athlete as an integral part of the student body. In furtherance of these objectives Article 3, § 1 of the NCAA constitution requires in substance that any aid received with minor exceptions be administered by the student-athlete's educational institution....

There is some merit to the argument that those student-athletes who received aid from an outside team while in school were in a substantially similar position to those receiving aid from their school for the same expenses. But this is not to say that the restrictions have no "fair and substantial relation to the object of the legislation." Although explanations for the restrictions have not been presented, an obvious reason would be to avoid the practical difficulties of monitoring and controlling aid received from a nonmember, over which the Association could exercise no authority. It might also be pointed out that it was these student-athletes the NCAA determined to immediately reinstate.

The situation of those student-athletes receiving aid from outside sources while not in school is entirely different. The court in *Jones v. National Collegiate Athletic Association* [392 F.Supp. 295 (D.Mass.1975)] observed that play during the periods while not in school cannot be considered as coincidental to or in conjunction with obtaining an education.

* * *

We concur in the holding of the court in *Jones* [*v. NCAA*, 392 F.Supp. 295 (D.Mass.1975)], that the present regulations do not unconstitutionally discriminate against those in any of the classes suggested by plaintiffs, particularly not against those plaintiffs receiving compensation for room and board while not in school.

The court is not oblivious to the less advantageous position in which a student-athlete without means may be placed by the effect of the NCAA regulations. But neither the Equal Protection Clause of the Fourteenth Amendment, nor the counterpart equal protection requirement embodied in the Fifth Amendment, guarantees "absolute equality or precisely equal advantages." This Court cannot use the Constitution as a vehicle to alleviate the consequences of differences in economic circumstances that exist wholly apart from any NCAA action.

[The court then turned to the University's claim that the level of sanctions imposed by the NCAA on Denver "irrationally discriminated" against it when compared with milder penalties imposed on schools like Michigan and Minnesota for more serious incidents. After reviewing the specifics of Denver's charge, the opinion continued.]

* * *

This court is one of expressly limited jurisdiction whose statutory duties do not include sitting as a final arbiter of disputes between an association and its membership. A disturbing aspect of this litigation is the attempt to rely upon the federal judiciary to resolve essentially private disputes because of the refusal of the Association and member institution to deal with each other on a reasoning and where necessary compromising basis.

* * *

Most importantly, because of the refusal of Association and member institution to cooperate, student-athletes in all sports must suffer the consequences. We cannot constitutionalize amateur sports to protect their interests. The result may well be to develop new levels of cynicism in young students who are so often the pawns in the games of power between associations, and associations and member institutions. But if nothing else, this case may well demonstrate that defiance in the name of principle can prove to be inflexibility disguised as a virtue.

Case dismissed.

Given the stringency of the NCAA's definition of an "amateur" student-athlete as applied to Canadian hockey players wanting to play U.S. college hockey, should NCAA rules have permitted Danny Ainge to play basketball for Brigham Young University while he was also playing third base for the Toronto Blue Jays (as we saw in Chapter 2)? What are the policy reasons that would justify the NCAA labelling as a "professional" only those student-athletes who have been paid to play in the same sport rather than a different sport they are now playing at college?

The *Buckton* case mentioned earlier did find it unconstitutional for the NCAA to limit *Canadian* (rather than "professional") students playing on intercollegiate hockey teams. Should U.S. colleges be able to restrict the presence of foreign players on their college teams, or at least the availability of athletic scholarships for them? This is a much more substantial question in the 1990s because foreign athletes have become a far bigger presence in American college sports.

While there are few such foreign figures in American-style football, there are a growing number in basketball—following a trail blazed by Hakeem Olajuwon when he came from Nigeria in the early 1980s to play college ball for Houston University, before going on to play for the NBA Houston Rockets. Foreigners make up far larger proportions of the squads in hockey, soccer, track and field, swimming, golf, and tennis than in basketball, let alone football. (In the men's singles draw of the 1995 NCAA tennis championship, 33 out of the 64 players were foreign.) This practice first became popular in the 1970s when the University of Texas at El Paso (UTEP) won several NCAA track and field titles by importing star long-distance runners from Africa, several of whom were more than 30 years old. The NCAA responded with a 1980 rule that takes away one year of college eligibility for every year of organized competition after the age of 20. So far, though, no cap has been placed on the number of foreign athletes as such.

A key reason why coming to American colleges is so attractive to athletes from other countries is that very few of their home universities have significant athletic programs. Development of athletic talent abroad is reserved for independent amateur or athletic organizations devoted solely to sports. Unsurprisingly then, viewers of the 1996 Olympics in Atlanta saw a considerable number of medal winners from other countries who had (or still were) competing on U.S. college teams in their respective sports. Some observers (such as American Olympic hero Carl Lewis) have objected to this practice, seeing it as a form of U.S. subsidy (whether public or private) to foreigners who take college scholarships away from American students, and are then taught how to beat their American competitors at the Olympics, Wimbledon, and other settings. Why is it that so many U.S. schools find it so important to bring in foreign student-athletes for a free education? Would it be desirable for the NCAA to bar or limit this practice by its members? Would any such policy be consistent with either American constitutional principles or international trade policy?

2. PAY AT COLLEGE

Although the NCAA has drawn a line against the typical kind of compensation, like that provided to Canadian Junior A hockey players, the Association's rules make it clear that "[p]ay is the receipt of funds, awards or benefits not permitted by the governing legislation of the Association for participation in athletics" (Article 12.02.3), and that a "grant-in-aid administered by an educational institution is not considered to be pay ..., provided it does not exceed the [Association's] financial aid limitations" (Article 12.01.4). Article 15 of the NCAA Manual then uses twenty pages to spell out the precise kind of tuition, fees, room and board, and books that a college may provide as financial aid to its athletes. Article 16 is equally detailed regarding permissible "awards, benefits and expenses." A crucial rule, Article 16.02.03, bans "extra benefits" for student-athletes—i.e., benefits not "generally available to the institution's students." (This is the rule that Jerry Tarkanian allegedly violated by reimbursing the air fare home for one of his UNLV players.) A recurring issue is how to treat athletes who, while receiving an athletic scholarship, are also able to draw on external sources of financial support while at college.

WILEY v. NCAA

United States Court of Appeals, Tenth Circuit, 1979.
612 F.2d 473.

McKay, Circuit Judge.

Wiley was a student-athlete at the University of Kansas. Coming from a desperately poor background, he sought to meet his education costs through a federal Basic Education Opportunity Grant (BEOG) pursuant to 20 U.S.C. § 1070a. He was awarded $1,400 for the 1975–1976 school year. In addition, he received an athletic scholarship from the University of Kansas in the amount of $2,621. In the spring of 1976, plaintiff was declared ineligible to compete in intercollegiate athletic events because his athletic award plus his BEOG exceeded National Collegiate Athletic Association (NCAA) limitations. The University of Kansas unsuccessfully appealed to the NCAA to restore plaintiff's eligibility but did not pursue its right to appeal further.

Wiley then brought suit in the United States District Court for the District of Kansas to enjoin, inter alia, the inclusion of his BEOG in the calculation of the maximum financial assistance permissible under the NCAA Constitution. He alleged violation of the Equal Protection Clause and the Supremacy Clause.

[The district judge found that the inclusion of Wiley's BEOG in the calculation of maximum student aid from Kansas violated his equal protection rights, because this rule bore no rational relationship to the NCAA's policy objective of preserving college amateurism. While Wiley was able, then, to complete his Kansas track and field career on a full athletic scholarship along with the BEOG, the Tenth Circuit decided to hear and uphold the NCAA's appeal even after Wiley had graduated.]

* * *

We observe that the case does not implicate the right to a college education, or even to participate in intercollegiate athletics. Wiley's interest is instead the right to attend college and play sports under a certain favorable financing arrangement, i. e., a full athletic scholarship plus a full BEOG grant.[6]

* * *

This court has consistently found that, unless clearly defined constitutional principles are at issue, the suits of student-athletes displeased with high school athletic association or NCAA rules do not present substantial federal questions. In light of *Hagans* [*v. Lavine*, 415 U.S. 528 (1974)], language contained in these cases may be too sweeping if applied where access to an education or other similarly substantial interest is at stake. Nonetheless, we find neither Wiley's personal interest nor the character of the alleged misclassification, even under *Hagans*, to require alteration of our cases.

Appeal upheld.

---

6. Wiley admits to several available options that would have permitted attending college. Wiley insists that "[a]s a student with complete need at the university, [he would be] entitled to $3,800 aid" from various programs. Indeed, Wiley could have remained on the university's track team and under NCAA rules met his residual needs through federal educational loans or other student loans. Wiley was also free under NCAA rules to obtain employment during periods either before or between his years in college. Finally, while it may have required an "austere" life style, Wiley could have survived in college on his athletic scholarship alone. The athletic scholarship available to Wiley in 1975–1976 included tuition, books, housing, food and, had Wiley chosen to do various jobs for the athletic department, $15.00 per month extra.

HOLLOWAY, CIRCUIT JUDGE dissenting.

* * *

Everyone concerned admits that neither a suspect classification nor deprivation of a fundamental constitutional right is involved in this case. But even so, Wiley is a person entitled to "equal protection" against state action under a rule not rationally related to a legitimate purpose of the acting agency.

* * *

Under the NCAA rule a student-athlete may receive a full grant even though his or her parents are millionaires and are providing any level of support. Student-athletes also can receive without penalty government payments under the GI Bill of Rights, military reserve training programs, the War Orphans Educational Program, Social Security Insurance Program and Non–Service–Connected Veteran's Death Pension Program. Thus, the rule distinguishes between student-athletes receiving money from BEOG's and those receiving money from their parents or these government sources.

The NCAA regulations concerning limitations on aid to athletes, as applicable here, clearly have as their principal purpose the promotion of amateurism in athletics by prohibiting pay for play. The NCAA concludes, and I think permissibly, that any aid which can be manipulated by the university or its supporters to supplement the basic athletic grant-in-aid to student-athletes falls into the play-for-pay category. The regulations also seem to prevent one member institution from using its access to economic resources (through endowment funds, alumni or otherwise) to obtain an advantage over other member institutions in the fielding of athletic teams. These are legitimate purposes, I believe. The question then is whether the regulation applied here is rationally related to these purposes.

Appellants argue that the exclusion of the assistance received from parents, from the GI Bill of Rights, or from social security, veterans or other death benefits is justified as "earned" by the athlete or the athlete's family prior to matriculation. That does not explain, of course, the exclusion of payments for student-athletes' participation in military reserve training programs. What is foreclosed or taken into account in determining the amount of assistance permitted is payment for employment of the student during the semester or term time, and all grants and scholarships (government or otherwise) that possibly can be controlled by the university or its athletic supporters. Thus, the line drawn is to permit support that is totally beyond the control of the university and its supporters, that has no possible relationship to the student's athletic ability or participation, that does not provide an advantage to one university over another, and that can have no bearing upon the principal aim of the regulations prohibiting pay for play.

The key question then becomes whether the university or its supporters can manipulate the BEOG's, and, perhaps, whether these grants are more available to students in some member universities than in others. The BEOG legislation provides a minimum base of financial support for economically deprived college students. BEOG's are based solely on need, considering only the resources the student's family can be expected to provide. Athletic ability or participation is totally irrelevant to the grants; neither is scholastic nor other ability a factor. The program operates under an entitlement concept that all eligible students receive awards without regard to any other student financial aid. The student apparently may attend any college or university. It has been described as a "G.I. Bill for all Americans." All this appears to be admitted by the NCAA and the other appellants, who have appended to their reply brief a letter setting out much of that policy, written by the Chief of the Program Policy and Analysis Branch of the Department of Health, Education & Welfare.

A university can enter into an agreement with the United States Commissioner of Education to administer the BEOG's, and to calculate and disburse funds to qualifying students enrolled in that institution. But disbursement must be in accordance with very strict requirements of federal regulations; these requirements eliminate the exercise of any significant discretion. Under statutory and regulatory BEOG guidelines the university cannot administer the grants in a manner calculated to benefit student-athletes without violating federal law.

There was absolutely no indication that the University of Kansas could manipulate the BEOG program to provide any semblance of pay for play. Applications need not be made through any university; Wiley applied for his grant through a public library in Maryland. Neither is there any indication that the University of Kansas, nor any other university member of the NCAA, could derive a special benefit from the BEOG's that would help the institution secure an advantage over any similar institution in the recruitment of or assistance to student-athletes. The NCAA appears to have recognized these conclusions because it has now changed its regulations to permit student-athletes to receive BEOG grants along with athletic scholarships.

Wiley is not entitled to a university education as a fundamental right, and certainly not to participation in college athletics, but as a member of an identifiable class he is protected under the Equal Protection Clause from arbitrary state action. Although the test to be applied in this instance is the "rational relationship" test, requiring great deference to the formulators, this appears to be one of those perhaps rare cases in which there is no rational basis for the NCAA's rule. I would affirm the district court decision.

After the Supreme Court's ruling in *Tarkanian* (see Chapter 9) that the NCAA is not a state actor, the Association's rules now appear to be immune from direct constitutional challenges. Does this mean that the NCAA is now free to adopt "irrational" rules without fear of judicial review? Might a court be tempted to read *Tarkanian* as applying only to challenges of NCAA disciplinary procedures, but not to cases involving substantive NCAA rules affecting important constitutional rights? If not, is there any other legal theory that an "ineligible" player (especially one at a private school) might use to challenge an "irrational" NCAA rule?

Ironically, as indicated by the dissent, the NCAA was in the process of reversing its position about this issue at the same time as the case was being litigated. Prior to 1992, poor student-athletes could and did apply for Pell Grants from the government, but because NCAA rules did not let them keep the grants for themselves, the money was paid to their school's athletic departments. This was so, even though an NCAA-commissioned survey had disclosed that more than 60% of black football and basketball players, and 40% of white athletes in these revenue-producing sports, reported that they had less than $25 per month for personal expenses while at college.[e] Many member schools had still opposed efforts to amend the rule to allow students to keep up to $1,700 of their Pell Grants, not because the schools felt that poor athletes did not need the money, but because the institutions could not afford to lose this source of revenue. However, by a 1992 amendment, Division I student-athletes were permitted to "receive a Pell Grant in combination with other institutional financial aid, provided the overall grant does not exceed the value of a full grant-in-aid plus $1700...." (Article 15.2.4.1). Is this a sensible resolution of the problem?

Recall from the *Wiley* dissent that the stated purpose of the NCAA's ban on various types of financial assistance to student-athletes is to prevent institutions and their boosters from manipulating the amount of money awarded to star players. Besides cash payments to athletes, the NCAA strictly forbids any benefits "in kind" over and above the carefully delineated grant-in-aid for tuition, fees, books, and room and board. Article 16 spends fifteen pages of the NCAA Manual elaborating on the general principle that "extra benefits" may not be provided to athletes and their families or friends if the same benefit is not "generally available to the institution's students or their relatives or friends." This rule prohibits, for example, a school from providing athletes with notebook paper or pocket calculators, or a coach from giving an injured player a ride (even to class or practice); also, student-athletes cannot receive complimentary tickets to an awards dinner for their parents or spouses, transportation home during holidays or for family emergencies, free long-distance telephone calls, pay TV movies charged to an athlete's hotel bill for a road game, or legal assistance for any personal problem with the law. After much adverse publicity, the NCAA recently amended this rule to allow athletes to receive transportation to and from a teammate's funeral (Art. 16.10.1.5), and (from a panel of up to three designated faculty or staff members) advice about their prospective professional careers (Art. 16.3.2(e)). A very sizable proportion of the

---

[e]. See American Institutes for Research, *Studies of Intercollegiate Athletics, Report No. 3: The Experiences of Black Intercollegiate Athletes at NCAA Division I Institutions* (Palo Alto, Cal.: AIR, 1989).

infractions found by the NCAA enforcement branch rests on violations of this rule. Do these cases trivialize NCAA policy, or is there a need for such close scrutiny of benefits for student-athletes?

An alternative method for providing such "extra benefits" above the student-athlete's room and board would be for the students to earn the money themselves through part-time jobs. However, Article 15.2.6 of the NCAA rules had always blocked this route by deeming any earnings from student-athlete employment during the school term to be counted as part of the scholarship itself, and thence included in the calculation of when the college's "full grant-in-aid has been reached." Only athletes who received no scholarships at all were permitted to "earn legitimate income in excess of a full grant-in-aid," and even then only if no one from the athletic department had helped arrange the job.

Finally, after an extended debate on the issue, the January 1997 Convention amended this rule to permit student-athletes to work for pay during the school year, although the amount of money that the student could earn was limited to the difference between scholarship benefits and the normal cost of attending the college (including travel expenses to and from home), estimated as normally around $2,000. This Proposition 62 passed by a close margin, with a majority of Division I–A members voting against. Then, in the summer of 1997, the newly-established Division I Board of Directors voted to postpone the institution of this new rule for at least one year.

Several concerns have long been expressed about part-time employment of student-athletes. One concern is that it would be very difficult to prevent athletic departments and their supporters from arranging "jobs" with lucrative pay for little or no work for star athletes (and schools located in less promising labor markets would face strong pressures to do so to meet that external competitive disadvantage). Another is that adding part-time employment to the lengthy time spent on playing, practicing, and training for the sport would detract from academic work by not-so-stellar students. Are you persuaded by these concerns? Should they be met by simply increasing the value of the athletic scholarship itself? At whose expense?

As yet another example of the scope of NCAA restraints on activities that might give student-athletes simply reputational rather than financial rewards, Rule 12.5.2 prohibits them from having their name or picture on any product that is being sold, even if the student gets no renumeration for it. Thus, in 1985, Steve Alford, star guard of Indiana's NCAA champion basketball team (and now head coach at Southwest Missouri State University), was suspended for one game that season because he had allowed his photograph to be included on a calendar that was sold for charity by a school sorority. In the fall of 1994, the NCAA told Florida's offensive lineman Anthony Ingrassi that he had violated this "reputational" rule because his restaurant column in the student newspaper, "Anthony's Digest," had given favorable reviews to several area restaurants.

In the spring of 1996, Northwestern's star running back and Rose Bowl hero Darnell Autry filed a tort suit against the NCAA because he had been offered a part in a supernatural movie thriller titled *The 18th Angel*. The Association said that this violated Rule 12.5.2.3.4 which states that "the individual performance of a student-athlete may not be used in a commercial movie . . ." While the Cook County circuit court granted Autry a preliminary injunction, his eligibility would have been at severe risk if he had appeared in the movie and the NCAA then won the case on the merits. Before the trial, though, the Association's Eligibility Committee granted Autry a special waiver on the basis that as a theater major in college, his appearance in the film was something that many theater majors might do, and thus not related to his athletic ability. The vast majority of student-athletes who do not have this particular college major cannot take advantage of that special exception. What justifications can be offered for an NCAA policy that may apply in cases such as Alford's, Ingrassi's, and Autry's?

That same Rule 12.5.2 entitles member schools to use their student-athletes' names, pictures, and images in various ways that help support and finance the schools' educational activities. Thus, in 1994, the University of Kansas' star basketball center Greg Ostertag, who was relying on public assistance to support his wife and child, was the major attraction on the "Big O" t-shirts, dolls, and other merchandise that the university sold to Kansas fans. Grant Hill, then a star on the Duke basketball Blue Devils, was featured on Duke sweatsuits bearing his name and likeness. However, Hill was told by his coach Mike Krzyzewski that he could get one for his father Calvin Hill only if Grant paid the full $120 price at the Duke book store.

This merchandising effort by schools was sparked by the public visibility of Michigan's "Fab Five" basketball team in the early 1990s. Faced with objections from Michigan teammates Chris Webber and Juwan Howard, the NCAA did amend Rule 12.5.2 to bar the *sale*, though not the *distribution*, of trading cards bearing the student-athlete's name or picture. What has become quite common, though, is for a college to sell team jerseys that bear the number of the star player on this or prior year's teams: e.g., the University of Florida earned sizeable sums in the 1996-97 academic year from the sale of jerseys bearing #7, the number of quarterback and Heisman Trophy winner Danny Wuerffel who led his Gators team to the school's first-ever national football title that year. Recall, though, the law regarding celebrity publicity rights that we explored in Chapter 6, which has generated huge financial benefits for professional athletes such as Michael Jordan and Tiger Woods. Would either Hill, or Ostertag, or even Wuerffel have been able to claim violation of these rights by their institutions while they were in college—

presumably via suits filed after they had left school?[f] Would it be a defense to such a suit that the standard letter-of-intent and scholarship agreement incorporated by reference the NCAA Rules, presumably including the rule that authorizes school use of names and likenesses? (Indeed, suppose that the scholarship contract made it clear that the player's athletic *alma mater* retained the right to use his image in future merchandising deals even after the student-athlete had become a professional celebrity such as Michael Jordan or Tiger Woods.) And as you read the later decisions in this chapter, consider whether an NCAA rule that secures such automatic licensing of player publicity rights to their schools constitutes a "combination ... in restraint of trade" in violation of antitrust law.

3. PROFESSIONAL CONTRACTS

Under NCAA rules, an athlete loses amateur status not only for receiving pay or a promise of pay for current athletic competition, but also for "sign[ing] a contract or commitment of any kind to play professional athletics" in the future (Article 12.1.1(c)). Recall the *Neely* case in Chapter 2, in which the Houston Oilers tried to keep confidential their signing of Ralph Neely so that he could play for the Oklahoma Sooners in a New Year's bowl game. The next case also illustrates this rule in operation.

SHELTON v. NCAA
United States Court of Appeals, Ninth Circuit, 1976.
539 F.2d 1197.

WRIGHT, CIRCUIT JUDGE.

The principal issue in this appeal is whether the NCAA rule declaring ineligible for intercollegiate athletics in a particular sport any student who has ever signed a contract to play that professional sport violates the Equal Protection Clause of the constitution.

The basic facts are not in dispute. The NCAA constitution declares as one of its goals the promotion and preservation of amateurism in college athletics. In order to advance this goal, the NCAA constitution contains a rule which distinguishes between amateur and professional athletes on the basis of whether an individual has signed a contract to play professional sports. The rule provides that a student who has signed such a contract, regardless of its enforceability, is ineligible to participate in intercollegiate athletics in that sport.

Appellee Shelton does not deny that he signed a professional contract with an American Basketball Association team which resulted in his being declared ineligible by Oregon State University. Indeed, he contends that the contract is unenforceable because he was induced to sign it by fraud and undue influence. The legal enforceability of the contract is the subject of a separate action brought by Shelton against

---

f. See James S. Thompson, *University Trading Cards: Do College Athletes Enjoy a Common Law Right to Publicity?*, 4 Seton Hall J. of Sports L. 143 (1994), and Vladimir P. Belo, *The Shirts Off Their Backs: Colleges Getting Away With Violating the Right of Publicity?*, 19 Hastings Comm.Ent. L. J. 133 (1996).

the professional team which is now pending before the district court. Shelton urges that the NCAA rule making him ineligible despite the alleged defects in the contract creates an impermissible classification in violation of the Equal Protection Clause. He wants the rule suspended while his litigation and the college basketball season continue.

Our review on such questions is limited. None of the parties contends that the NCAA rule infringes upon a fundamental right which would necessitate strict judicial scrutiny. Instead, we must examine the rule to determine whether it rationally furthers some legitimate purpose. If it does, then our review is complete.

The rule purports to promote and protect amateurism in intercollegiate athletics. None of the parties seriously contends that this goal is illegitimate. Instead they dispute the means chosen by the NCAA to achieve it.

Shelton believes that it is unreasonable to treat as a professional one who alleges that the contract which he signed is unenforceable. In effect, he contends that the NCAA rule is overinclusive because if he is successful in his other action and the contract is declared unenforceable he is not nor would he ever have been a professional.

In a similar case two years ago, *Associated Students, Inc. v. NCAA*, 493 F.2d 1251 (9th Cir.1974), this court reviewed another NCAA eligibility rule which was challenged on equal protection grounds. We recognized that the application of such rules may produce unreasonable results in certain situations. Nonetheless, we found that the rule did not violate the equal protection clause. Moreover, we did so although we recognized that the rule and its enforcement provisions might not be the best means for achieving the desired goal. It is not judicial business to tell a voluntary athletic association how best to formulate or enforce its rules.

We believe that the present appeal is controlled by *Associated Students*. The general rule under which Shelton was declared ineligible may from time to time produce unfortunate results. If an individual were subsequently successful in gaining a legal declaration that a professional contract was in fact void from its inception, a ruling that he was ineligible in the interim between his signing and the court's judgment might cause hardship. But the potential hardship does not make the rule irrational or unrelated to its goal. Moreover, hardship could be avoided by not signing a pro-contract. Reliance on a signed contract as an indication that a student's amateur status has been compromised is rationally related to the goal of preserving amateurism in intercollegiate athletics.

While our function is to determine only if the NCAA has selected a method of protecting amateurism which is reasonably related to that goal, an examination of the alternatives suggested by Shelton supports the conclusion that the rule in question withstands an equal protection challenge. Shelton argues that the rule should allow for cases such as his own where alleged defects in formation of the contract render it a nullity. The NCAA and its member institutions cannot simply take an athlete's word that his signed contract is void. An eligibility rule limited to contracts that would withstand a court test would be no rule at all. One could sign a contract, then allege that it was unenforceable and participate at will in college athletics while maintaining an option to enter the professional ranks at any time. Clearly, this would obliterate any remaining distinctions between amateur and professional athletes.

The alternative would be extremely burdensome. In the context of this appeal, for instance, the NCAA and its member institutions would be placed in the position of having to predict the outcome of Shelton's action against the professional basketball team. In order to do so they would likely have to undertake extensive investigations of the facts and time consuming hearings involving the parties. Even then, they would have no assurance that their decision would be compatible with the ultimate determination of the courts.

We hold that an effort to avoid this tangled set of affairs through the use of an easily applied and generally reliable criterion is rationally related to a legitimate purpose and does not, therefore, violate the equal protection clause.

Case dismissed.

After *Shelton*, the NCAA amended the rule to make clear that merely *signing* a professional contract will cost the student-athlete his amateur status, "regardless of [the contract's] legal enforceability or any consideration received" (Article 12.1.3). If *Tarkanian* had not foreclosed a constitutional challenge, would this rule be rationally related to a legitimate objective? What is the objective? Are there circumstances under which the application of this rule would not further the objective? Should the NCAA be required to create exceptions for every conceivable irrational application of a rule that is generally reasonable?

Whatever the merits of this NCAA policy, it is now clear that any player who reaches an agreement with a professional team thereby gives up his amateur status and eligibility to play for a college in that sport. As we saw in Chapter 5, more recent controversies have focused on the NCAA's extension of such "professional" status to encompass any player who signs a contract with an agent and/or opts to be drafted by a professional team.

Player drafts pose a problem of the interplay of professional and college sports, one that can be and has been handled in different fashions. The earliest a player can now be drafted in hockey is when he reaches the age of 18; in baseball and basketball when he graduates from high school; and in football three years after he graduates from high school. Under MLB and NHL rules, any team can draft a player who satisfies that league's eligibility conditions, irrespective of whether the player opts into the draft. If the player chooses to go on to college instead of playing professionally (usually in the minor leagues for a period), he is entitled to do so, and the team drafting him loses its rights to that draft pick after a certain point. (This fact gives some players considerably greater leverage in extracting a more generous signing bonus offer from the drafting team.) In football and basketball, though, it has always been assumed that college teams will provide the training and development of future professional athletes: that is why players become automatically eligible for the NFL and NBA drafts only after they have used up their four years in college play. Spurred by antitrust challenges in the 1970s, the NBA allowed players to opt into the draft earlier, and the NFL eventually followed suit (though the latter league still limits that option to players who have used up three years of college eligibility).

However, prior to 1994, making themselves subject to a professional league draft immediately cost basketball and football (though not baseball and hockey) players their college eligibility, under NCAA Article 12.2.4.2, which labelled a player "professional" if he "asks to be placed on the draft list ... of a professional league in that sport." This rule risked considerable hardship to college players who were not picked as high as they expected, or perhaps not drafted at all. As we shall see later in this chapter, the denial to such players of any option to return to college to play ball, and thence either to improve their draft prospect and/or to secure a college degree, led to two antitrust suits against the NCAA: *Banks v. NCAA*, 977 F.2d 1081 (7th Cir.1992), and *Gaines v. NCAA*, 746 F.Supp. 738 (M.D.Tenn.1990). Hence, in 1994 the NCAA voted to amend this rule to allow basketball players to declare themselves available for the NBA draft once (but only once) during their college careers. (Because of opposition from football programs, the NCAA membership rejected its Committee's recommendation that the same opportunity be extended to football players opting into the NFL draft.) The player then had 30 days after the NBA draft to decide whether to accept a professional contract and renounce his college eligibility, or instead to retain his eligibility and return to play for his college team. Because the drafted player had the option of returning to college, this gave the player somewhat greater leverage in negotiating with the team that had drafted him. Thus, the NBA's own rules were amended to extend the drafting team's exclusive rights to underclassmen until their college eligibility had expired. The college coaches, in turn, used this NBA move as the ammunition with which to prod the NCAA to cut back its eligibility rule in 1997. Now, only players who have not been picked by any team in the two-round NBA draft would be able to continue playing college ball.

Another key component of this NCAA "professionalism" doctrine is that it deems a player ineligible if he or she has "ever agreed (orally or in writing) to be represented by an agent for the purpose of marketing his or her athletic ability or reputation in that sport" (Article 12.3.1). In Chapter 5, we explored the sports law problems posed by agents such as Norby Walters, who paid players money while they were still in college and covered up that tangible professional status of their clients while they still were in school. Under NCAA rules, though, it is equally disqualifying for a player to hire (and agree to pay) the best-qualified and most ethical of agents in order to discover what their true professional athletic value is (and some states have even made it criminal for the agent to reach such an agreement with players who have not given up their college eligibility). To help fill that gap, not just the schools, but also the NBA and NFL have now set up advisory committees to give interested players a prediction (though not a guarantee) of where they would likely be drafted that year. However, to receive independent advice while still not forfeiting his future college eligibility—not only before the draft, but afterwards when contract offers are being made—the player must hire someone who is billed as the "family advisor," and who is not authorized to "negotiate" on behalf of the athlete with the drafting team.

In the mid- to late–1990s, approximately thirty to forty players elected to be part of each year's NBA and NFL drafts. In basketball especially, the top picks are usually underclassmen. (The 1997 drafts were the exception to that rule, with Wake Forest's Tim Duncan, a senior, being the first pick in the NBA draft, while Ohio State's Orlando Pace, a junior, was first in the NFL.) Indeed, not only college freshmen such as Stephon Marbury, but high school seniors such as Kevin Garnett are being picked high in the NBA draft. On the other hand, every year roughly half the players who have opted-into these drafts are not selected; of those players not drafted, very few seek to return to their school, even in basketball where this is permitted.

The current regime raises a number of questions, whether viewed from the perspective of college teams, professional teams, or the players themselves. What are the various professional, financial, and personal factors that should influence a player's decision about whether to opt into the professional draft before finishing his college eligibility? Do you think Proposition 48 played any role in the decision by high school stars such as Kevin Garnett and Kobe Bryant to opt into the NBA's 1996 and 1997 drafts? From the point of view of college coaches like Georgetown's John Thompson, clearly they would like to keep a sophomore player like Allen Iverson in college, rather than lose him to the Philadelphia 76ers as the top 1996 draft pick. However, does it help or harm the NBA to have not only Iverson, but his underclassmen predecessors such as Joe Smith, Glenn Robinson, Chris Webber, and Shaquille O'Neal come out of school early to be the first picks in their respective drafts? Does the current system of rookie salary caps and veteran free agency encourage or discourage such moves?

The NCAA's strict definition of "amateur" status is supposed to "maintain a clear line of demarcation between college athletics and professional sports." In that regard, is there a defensible reason for the very different treatment afforded to baseball players who are drafted by an MLB team after three years in college (which by itself does not cost them their college eligibility), basketball players who elect into the NBA draft (who can now retrieve their eligibility only if no team picks them), and football players (who give up any college football future when they opt in to the NFL draft)? With respect to any or all of the leagues, should a player be free to hire a real "agent" to determine his true market value in professional sports before deciding whether to enter or return to college sports?[g] Indeed, suppose a player is picked low in the draft, is offered and signs a contract to play with that team eventually (but with no money paid now), and wants to return to college to finish both his athletic and academic careers there. Is it vital for the NCAA to bar any such contract for *future* professional services in order to maintain its "clear line of demarcation" from professional leagues? (Recall the Chapter 2 case of Danny Ainge who played professional baseball for the Toronto Blue Jays at the same time that he was playing college basketball for Brigham Young University.) What exactly is the demarcation line between an NCAA football venture such as Ohio State's (which Orlando Pace left in 1997), and the NFL's St. Louis Rams (which Pace joined as the league's number one draft pick that year)? Certainly, there is a great deal of movement of highly-paid coaches (such as Rick Pitino and Jimmy Johnson) between these two settings, with the college programs often outbidding the professional teams for highly-valued coaches' services. The broader issue that runs through all of these questions and cases in this chapter is whether, given the financial stakes now riding on big-time college sports, courts should defer to NCAA efforts to maintain the *amateur* status of its players (as opposed to the *academic* status we addressed in the prior chapter).

B. JUDICIAL READING OF THE SCHOLARSHIP CONTRACT[h]

Having seen a variety of NCAA rules in operation, we now consider the legal resources still available to aggrieved parties who wish to challenge NCAA policies after the Supreme Court's *Tarkanian* decision sharply inhibited constitutional attacks. Just as in professional sports, one possible route is to ask for an independent judicial interpretation of the contractual relationship between the parties, consisting of both the contract between student (or coach) and institution and, in the background, the implicit contract among the institutions making up the

---

g. See Marianne M. Jennings & Lynn Zioko, *Student–Athletes, Athlete Agents and Five Year Eligibility: An Environment of Contractual Interference, Trade Restraint and High–Stake Payments*, 66 Univ. of Detroit L. Rev. 179 (1989).

h. For careful analyses of the legal issues presented by these cases, see Michael J. Cozzillio, *The Athletic Scholarship and the College National Letter of Intent: A Contract By Any Other Name*, 35 Wayne L. Rev. 1275 (1989); Alfred Dennis Mathewson, *Intercollegiate Athletics and the Assignment of Legal Rights*, 35 St. Louis Univ. L. J. 39 (1990); and Timothy Davis, *Student-Athlete Prospective Economic Interests: Contractual Dimensions*, 19 Thurgood Marshall L. Rev. 585 (1994).

TAYLOR v. WAKE FOREST
Court of Appeals of North Carolina, 1972.
16 N.C.App. 117, 191 S.E.2d 379.

CAMPBELL, JUDGE.

[Gregg Taylor was recruited by and signed a letter of intent to play football for Wake Forest University. The grant-in-aid, or athletic scholarship, provided as follows:

This Grant, if awarded, will be for 4 years provided I conduct myself in accordance with the rules of the Conference, the NCAA, and the Institution. I agree to maintain eligibility for intercollegiate athletics under both Conference and Institutional rules. Training rules for intercollegiate athletics are considered rules of the Institution, and I agree to abide by them. If injured while participating in athletics supervised by a member of the coaching staff, the Grant or Scholarship will be honored; and the medical expenses will be paid by the Athletic Department. This grant, when approved, is awarded for academic and athletic achievement and is not to be interpreted as employment in any manner whatsoever.

Taylor played for Wake Forest's football team in his freshman year. During the fall semester he compiled a grade point average of 1.0 (out of 4.0), far below the 1.35 the school required all students to have at the end of the freshman year. Taylor did not attend the spring football practices, and his GPA for the spring semester rose to 1.9. He then decided not to play football in the fall of his sophomore year; his GPA rose again, to 2.4.

Because of his refusal to play football, Wake Forest's Scholarship Committee, on the recommendation of the Faculty Athletic Committee, revoked his scholarship as of the end of his sophomore year. Taylor nevertheless remained at Wake Forest and graduated on time. He sued to recover $5,500 in expenses incurred during his last two years because he had lost his scholarship. Faced with Wake Forest's motion for summary dismissal, Taylor contended that under the relevant contract doctrines there was a genuine issue for a jury to determine—whether or not he had "acted reasonably and in good faith in refusing to participate in the football program at Wake Forest when such participation interfered with reasonable academic progress."]

* * *

The plaintiffs' position depends upon a construction of the contractual agreement between plaintiffs and Wake Forest. As stated in the affidavit of George J. Taylor, the position of the plaintiffs is that it was orally agreed between plaintiffs and the representative of Wake Forest that:

> [I]n the event of any conflict between educational achievement and athletic involvement, participation in athletic activities could be limited or eliminated to the extent necessary to assure reasonable academic progress.

And plaintiffs were to be the judge as to what "reasonable academic progress" constituted.

We do not agree with the position taken by plaintiffs. The scholarship application filed by Gregg Taylor provided:

> I agree to maintain eligibility for intercollegiate athletics under both Conference and Institutional rules. Training rules for intercollegiate athletics are considered rules of the Institution, and I agree to abide by them.

Both Gregg Taylor and his father knew that the application was for "Football Grant–In–Aid Or A Scholarship," and that the scholarship was "awarded for academic and athletic achievement." It would be a strained construction of the contract that would enable the plaintiffs to determine the "reasonable academic progress" of Gregg Taylor. Gregg Taylor, in consideration of the scholarship award, agreed to maintain his athletic eligibility and this meant both physically and scholastically. As long as his grade average equaled or exceeded the requirements of Wake Forest, he was maintaining his scholastic eligibility for athletics. Participation in and attendance at practice were required to maintain his physical eligibility. When he refused to do so in the absence of any injury or excuse other than to devote more time to studies, he was not complying with his contractual obligations.

Summary judgment granted.

Questions for Discussion

1. Some time after *Taylor* (and after a similar verdict in *Begley v. Mercer University*, 367 F.Supp. 908 (E.D.Tenn.1973)), the NCAA amended its rules to provide that "where a student's athletic ability is taken into consideration in any degree in awarding financial aid, such aid shall not be awarded in excess of one academic year" (Article 15.3.3.1). While high school athletes may be informed that the practice of the athletic department is to recommend renewal of financial aid, this rule explicitly forbids any assurance that renewal is automatic (even for an athlete who suffers a career-ending injury). Why does the NCAA impose these constraints on its own members' freedom of action? Can these constraints be justified?

2. Under what circumstances is it ethically and legally appropriate for a school not to renew a scholarship for a student who has neither exhausted eligibility nor graduated? Because he or she was a poor player? Injured? Academically ineligible? Missed practice once a week in order to attend chemistry lab? If the school refuses to renew the scholarship for an inappropriate reason, does the student-athlete have any legal remedy against the school? Would your answer differ if the NCAA had not prohibited its member schools from assuring their student-athletes automatic renewal of their scholarships?

3. Recall the prior discussion about the growing number of players who are leaving college early to play professional ball, and the NCAA rules that have (not very successfully) sought to reduce those numbers by taking away the college eligibility of anyone who opts into the draft (football) or anyone who is actually selected in the draft (basketball). Suppose a college was to add a condition to its standard scholarship terms that required future Orlando Paces or Allen Iversons who accept that scholarship in their first year to complete their full four years of play at the school, or perhaps have to pay over a certain proportion of their professional earnings during the years they still "owed" the school. The college athletic director might say that he is asking for no more than the standard renewable options that musicians, for example, must give their record companies as part of the contract for their first recording. Should such a contract term be enforceable against student athletes (or student musicians or actors with college scholarships)? Should one's judgment depend on whether the decision is made by individual universities like Ohio State and Georgetown, or the NCAA membership as a whole?

Another college contracts issue produced the following lawsuit. In the spring of 1989, Bryan Fortay, quarterback of his East Brunswick, N.J., high school team, was one of the most-heavily recruited football players in the country. The University of Miami Hurricanes' football coach, Jimmy Johnson, persuaded Fortay to sign a letter of intent with Miami by allegedly promising Fortay that Johnson would never leave the school, and that after playing behind current Hurricanes' quarterback, Craig Erickson, Fortay would be the next to fill that starting position, following in the line from Jim Kelly to Bernie Kosar to Vince Testaverde to Steve Walsh, all of whom became NFL quarterbacks.

Three weeks later, Johnson stunned everyone with the news that he was leaving Miami to become head coach of the NFL Dallas Cowboys, which had just been bought by Johnson's old Arkansas Razorbacks' teammate Jerry Jones. Miami quickly installed Washington State's Dennis Erickson as Johnson's successor, and Erickson persuaded Fortay not to switch schools (which would cost him two years' eligibility if done without Miami's consent) by allegedly promising Fortay that he would be Miami's starter and Erickson's first Heisman winner. Unfortunately for Fortay, Erickson eventually installed Gino Torretta as Miami quarterback, and Torretta took the Hurricanes to another national championship and himself to the Heisman Trophy.

Fortay left Miami to play for Rutgers in his home state, but by the time he became eligible to play there he was not able to distinguish himself on the college football field. Fortay did, however, file a $10 million breach of contract suit against Miami. The suit relied on detailed transcripts of his and his parents' conversations with Johnson and Erickson. The University contends these transcripts are based on tape recordings, and unconsented-to tapings of conversations are illegal under Florida, though not New Jersey, law. A federal district judge in Miami rejected those parts of Fortay's suit which rely on either the written scholarship contract or a claimed employment relationship. He has, however, said that Fortay's claim of a violation of oral promises in the recruiting relationship can go to trial. The case was, however, dropped by Fortay before trial.

Should oral promises by a college recruiter to the effect that the coach will not be leaving or that the player will be a starting quarterback be legally enforceable? Are these any different from promises about academic issues, e.g., available courses, majors, or tutors?

A fully-informed appraisal of the scholarship contract term we saw in *Taylor* requires an understanding of the constraints imposed on players such as Fortay. Once the student-athlete enrolls in the school, NCAA rules erect a significant hurdle to the athlete choosing to transfer to another school.[i] No athletic representative of another college may contact the student-athlete without permission from his current college (Article 13.1.1.3). Without such permission, no financial aid can be provided to a transferee until at least one year has passed. And even with permission from the first institution, the basic rule (in Article 14.6.1) is that a transferring student in Division I is ineligible to compete in football, basketball, or ice hockey until after a full academic year in residence at the new school. (Recall that there is a maximum player eligibility period of five calendar years.) The NCAA's transfer regulations take up ten pages in its Manual. The following case concerns a student-athlete who thought that he had found a loophole in these regulations.

ENGLISH v. NCAA
Court of Appeals of Louisiana, Fourth Circuit, 1983.
439 So.2d 1218.

SCHOTT, JUDGE.

* * *

[Jon English, a highly rated high school quarterback, was recruited by and enrolled at Michigan State for the 1979–1980 school year. Realizing that his playing prospects at Michigan State were poor, English dropped out for a year to enroll at a junior college in Pittsburgh, the city in which his father was an assistant college football coach. English then went to Iowa State, where he played in the fall seasons of 1981 and 1982. After having little success at Iowa, English spent the winter and spring of 1983 at a junior college in New Orleans, and then sought to enroll and play for Tulane in the fall of 1983, a school where his father was now head coach. English considered himself eligible because the NCAA rule at the time, as well as the summary of the rule

---

i. See Michael J. Cozzillio, *The Athletic Scholarship and the College National Letter of Intent: A Contract by Any Other Name*, 35 Wayne L. Rev. 1275 (1989).

in the NCAA Guide for the College–Bound Student–Athlete, referred to a year elapsing "since the transfer from the *first* four-year college." Having failed to persuade the NCAA of his position, English brought suit.]

* * *

Plaintiff's due process argument is based on the theory that the NCAA did not adequately inform him of the rules regarding his eligibility. He argues that the rule as quoted in the NCAA Guide literally entitled him to play ball with Tulane in 1983 because a year had elapsed since his transfer from the first four-year college, Michigan State, in 1980. Thus, he attacks the interpretation placed on the rule by William Hunt, head of the NCAA's Legislation and Enforcement Section, as being unreasonable in defining "first" to be the last four-year college. He argues further that the Guide's references to residence and semester hours completed at junior colleges further confuse the transfer rule and create further ambiguity. Finally, he rejects the notion that he would have sought further interpretation of the rule even if he had read the introduction because it was so clear to him that he was eligible.

The record does not support this argument. First, it is clear from the testimony of plaintiff's father, Coach English, that there was from the very beginning a question in plaintiff's mind about his eligibility notwithstanding the way he wanted to read the rule. He was plainly aware of the underlying and laudable policy of the NCAA to prevent a student from playing for two different colleges in successive years. Second, while he pretends to a sincere belief that the rule plainly declared him eligible, his first move after seeing the rule was to raise a question about it with his father who in turn raised questions about it with Petersen and Wall. He was squarely in the teeth of the Guide's introduction, i.e., he had questions about NCAA legislation, and was obliged to contact the NCAA national office for answers. But he failed to avail himself of this opportunity. Instead, he embarked on a course which he knew was perilous and preferred to take a chance that somehow his interpretation might be accepted by the NCAA.

It is well to note here that plaintiff was determined to play for his father at Tulane if at all possible. His prospects at Iowa State, as at Michigan State previously, were poor and not at all conducive to his being considered for a professional football contract upon his graduation from college. He explained that his skills as a quarterback could be best developed under the tutelage of his father who was a pass oriented coach. Since this would be his last year of college ball it was important for him to make the most of it. Only his interpretation of the transfer rule would make all of this possible.

We find Hunt's interpretation of the rule to be absolutely correct. The rule is dealing with a present college attempting to certify a player as eligible when he has played for a previous college. It contemplates two colleges, the first and the second. If one plays for a college one year he can't play for another college the next year. He must sit out for a year after playing for the first college. The rule does not and need not concern itself with the bizarre kind of a situation where one had played for yet a third college in the distant past. Reduced to its simplest terms a player may not jump from one college to another in successive years. We repeat that plaintiff on his own and again after speaking to his father was generally aware of the rule's meaning and while hoping to have found a loophole had questions about his theory.

* * *

There is no support in the record for plaintiff's contention that the NCAA was arbitrary, capricious, unfair, or discriminatory in dealing with his case. Had he inquired of the NCAA as to his plans before he left Iowa State he would have been told that he could not play at another college in 1983. Some 900 colleges belong to the NCAA and thousands of players abide by its rules. They do so voluntarily apparently convinced that constraints on their freedom to move about from college to college are a fair price to pay for protection against the evils which would emerge from untrammeled recruiting practices and uncontrolled pirating of players among the colleges. The word "arbitrary" connotes acting without reason or judgment, or determined by whim or caprice. "Capricious" is virtually synonymous. The record reflects that the NCAA, in adopting and implementing the transfer rule at issue here, acted quite reasonably in its efforts to prevent players from jumping from one school to another in successive years. Plaintiff was not dealt with unfairly. He was the victim only of his own plans and his own hope for special treatment. As to discrimination, Hunt testified that in all his years with the NCAA he never saw a case like plaintiff's and plaintiff failed to produce proof of any case like his which would provide a basis for his charge. He did show that some years ago the NCAA adopted the present rule to add the "first four-year college" language to close a loophole which previously existed and which enabled players to move from one four year college to another in successive years, but this is not plaintiff's situation and his charge of discrimination gets no support from these facts.

* * *

Appeal dismissed.

BARRY, JUSTICE, dissenting.

This case involves a very unique and isolated situation involving a very narrow question of interpretation of one word in an NCAA bylaw which may determine the eligibility for a student-athlete's last year of intercollegiate football competition.

* * *

[After reviewing the relevant materials and agreeing with English's reading of the rule, the dissent continued.]

The NCAA virtually controls football in over 900 colleges. Its purpose is to regulate sports programs and maintain the integrity of amateur athletics. Member schools must adhere to rigid rules or suffer severe sanctions. Considering the NCAA's enormous control (and its laudable purposes), it must also bear some burden to account for its heavy hand options.

Along with the NCAA's privileges goes the duty to provide clear and accurate information when disseminating its many rules and regulations. Jon English's interpretation of [the NCAA rule] was reasonable because the language is clear. His conclusion was supported by Mr. Wall. "First" still means "first," not "last," contrary to what Mr. Hunt would have us believe. What the NCAA intended, and what it published, were two different things. "Intent" is immaterial when the expression is unambiguous.

The majority's opinion is a Monday morning quarterback's opinion of what should be, but wasn't; what was intended, but not expressed. The NCAA goofed on the English language (no pun intended). Jon English relied on the NCAA bylaw and changed his position to his detriment. He was supported and encouraged in his belief by his more sophisticated superiors. Surely he has a right to protect his interests based on these extraordinary facts. That right should permit his eligibility [the NCAA rule].

A subsequent decision, *McHale v. Cornell Univ.*, 620 F.Supp. 67 (N.D.N.Y.1985), refused to read an exception into this non-transfer NCAA rule, even for the case of a student-athlete who had dropped out of the University of Maryland where he had been playing football on scholarship, then moved to Cornell for purely academic reasons (and without a scholarship), but was barred from playing Ivy League football in his senior year.

Certainly this NCAA rule would seem very odd if it restricted student participation in other extracurricular college activities. No one would have been concerned if Jon English wanted just to be the reporter covering sports for the Tulane school newspaper, or to participate in a college drama group. The historic reason why the NCAA felt compelled to adopt such strict controls on mobility for student-athletes was its concern about the practice of "tramp athletes." One of the most highly publicized of these "tramp" incidents occurred in the 1890 when Fielding Yost, then a third-year law student at West Virginia, enrolled as a freshman at Lafayette on a Wednesday in order to help Lafayette's football team beat its arch-rival Pennsylvania that Saturday. Yost then withdrew from Lafayette in time to return to West Virginia for classes on Monday. (He later became one of the most successful head coaches in college football history, at Michigan.) Today, the stated reason for retaining the rule is the fear that top athletes enrolled at one college will constantly be recruited by other schools. Once a student-athlete chooses a school and signs a letter of intent, the NCAA wants the student to be left alone to pursue his or her studies and sports without being wooed by other schools, who might also be tempted to offer improper inducements. Are these legitimate concerns that justify a transfer rule?

Note also the breadth of the transfer rule. Is a two-year ban on eligibility without the consent of the "home team" university excessive? Or even a full one-year ban if the student-athlete transfers with his prior school's consent? How does such a restriction likely affect the treatment received by athletes from their current schools? Why is this two (or one) year hiatus on eligibility applied only to athletes in college football, basketball, and ice hockey? What should be the operation of the rule in cases where the program is put on NCAA probation? When a player's personal circumstances or relationship with the coach changes? When the head coach leaves a particular school, especially in the case of a student who has signed a letter of intent but not yet even enrolled at the school?

Now consider the implications of *Taylor* and *English* read together. The NCAA members have all agreed that any scholarship offered to a student-athlete must reserve for the college the freedom to terminate that scholarship at the end of each academic year, and then replace the athlete by someone else on that team's roster. That same contract, though, bars the athlete from transferring to play for another NCAA member for at least one year, and for two years if the college chooses not to waive its rights. Even if this college sports version of the "reserve system" cannot likely be justified on *academic* grounds, might it pass muster on *athletic* grounds: i.e., does barring talented players moving from one school to another enhance or reduce competitive balance in the college game? (It should be noted that the NCAA has not imposed similar contract terms on college coaches.) Perhaps the legal vehicle for scrutinizing such a restraint of college athletes is not contract or (after *Tarkanian*) constitutional, but antitrust law.

C. ANTITRUST SCRUTINY OF NCAA RULES[j]

The cases examined so far have all involved efforts by individual players or institutions to retain athletes' eligibility to participate in intercollegiate sports within the framework of NCAA rules. These cases reflect a recurring tension between the expectations and the obligations generated in the relationship between the athlete (or coach) and the school and the school's commitment to the NCAA. The reason why that tension is so strong, and why the school ultimately feels compelled to live by the edicts of the NCAA, is because the school could not otherwise participate in major college sports—in the NCAA basketball tournament,

---

[j]. The major scholarly articles in this area are Lee Goldman, *Sports and Antitrust: Should College Athletes Be Paid to Play?*, 65 Notre Dame L. Rev. 206 (1990); and Gary R.Roberts, *The NCAA, Antitrust, and Consumer Welfare*, 70 Tulane L. Rev. 2631 (1996). Other valuable analyses include Note (by George Kokkines), *Sherman Act Invalidation of the NCAA Amateurism Rules*, 105 Harvard L. Rev. 1299 (1992). John C. Weistart, *Antitrust Issues in the Regulation of College Sports*, 5 J. of College & Univ. L. 77 (1978–79), and Note, *Tackling Intercollegiate Athletics: An Antitrust Analysis*, 87 Yale L. J. 655 (1978).

football bowl games, and other post-season championships. All colleges with major athletic programs are members of the NCAA, and they have all agreed to abide by the NCAA's rules and not to play against any school the Association declares ineligible. A question that underlies the various cases and issues we shall now be reading about is whether membership in the NCAA should be deemed an "essential facility" for schools wanting to participate in "big-time" college athletics, and what antitrust standards should be used to assess the Association's denial or removal of a school's membership (e.g., through the "death penalty").

1. PRODUCT MARKET

In earlier chapters, we saw numerous challenges under antitrust law to comparable structures agreed to by the owners of teams in each sport's only professional league. A similar antitrust attack against one key aspect of the intercollegiate structure was launched in the early 1980s. Intriguingly, this suit was filed by two universities that were part of the group of football powers that comprised the College Football Association (CFA), and who were chafing under the restrictive television policies adopted by the NCAA's broader membership. (The CFA consisted of virtually all Division I–A football institutions except for the members of the Big Ten and Pac–Ten conferences, which had separate television contracts.) The Supreme Court's opinion in this case is the only Supreme Court decision to consider how to apply substantive antitrust law to the sports industry.

NCAA v. BOARD OF REGENTS OF THE UNIV. OF OKLAHOMA & UNIV. OF GEORGIA ATHLETIC ASS'N.

Supreme Court of the United States, 1984.
468 U.S. 85, 104 S.Ct. 2948, 82 L.Ed.2d 70.

JUSTICE STEVENS for the Court.

* * *

History of the NCAA Television Plan

In 1938, the University of Pennsylvania televised one of its home games.[3] From 1940 through the 1950 season all of Pennsylvania's home games were televised. That was the beginning of the relationship between television and college football.

On January 11, 1951, a three-person "Television Committee," appointed during the preceding year, delivered a report to the NCAA's annual convention in Dallas. Based on preliminary surveys, the committee had concluded that "television does have an adverse effect on college football attendance and unless brought under some control threatens to seriously harm the nation's overall athletic and physical system." The

---

[3]. According to the NCAA football television committee's 1981 briefing book: "As far as is known, there were [then] six television sets in Philadelphia: and all were tuned to the game."

report emphasized that "the television problem is truly a national one and requires collective action by the colleges."

[In 1951 the NCAA adopted a television plan that permitted only one game per week to be broadcast in each area, and limited each school to two television appearances per season. The University of Pennsylvania at first insisted on televising all its home games, but after the NCAA declared it a member in bad standing and the four schools scheduled to play at Pennsylvania that year threatened to cancel the games, the school agreed to follow the NCAA plan.

Studies in each of the next five years indicated that television had an adverse effect on attendance. The NCAA continued to formulate a television policy for all its members. From the mid-1960s to the late 1970s, ABC held the exclusive network right to broadcast college football games. In 1981, the NCAA negotiated four-year agreements with both ABC and CBS, under which each network could broadcast 14 games per season in return for an annual $33 million apiece. In addition, the NCAA granted Turner Broadcasting System (TBS) exclusive cable rights for a limited number of games, for $9 million a year.

The "appearance requirements and limitations" followed the same pattern as before. Under the new contracts, over a two-year cycle each network had to carry games showing at least 82 NCAA members, with six being the maximum number for any one college team (and only four on national coverage). The NCAA's rules, as reflected in the network contracts, also barred any individual member from selling its own team's broadcast rights.

However, the CFA members were unhappy with these restraints, and they negotiated a different contract with NBC that gave these "big-time" college football powers both more appearances and more money. The NCAA threatened any team that allowed its game to be broadcast on NBC with sanctions, not only against their football program, but against all their sports. Thus, the Universities of Oklahoma and Georgia filed suit in an Oklahoma federal district court, and secured an injunction against any effort by the NCAA to interfere with CFA's dealings with NBC. The Supreme Court agreed to hear the NCAA's appeal.]

* * *

II

There can be no doubt that the challenged practices of the NCAA constitute a "restraint of trade" in the sense that they limit members' freedom to negotiate and enter into their own television contracts. In that sense, however, every contract is a restraint of trade, and as we have repeatedly recognized, the Sherman Act was intended to prohibit only unreasonable restraints of trade.

It is also undeniable that these practices share characteristics of restraints we have previously held unreasonable. The NCAA is an association of schools which compete against each other to attract television revenues, not to mention fans and athletes. As the District

Court found, the policies of the NCAA with respect to television rights are ultimately controlled by the vote of member institutions. By participating in an association which prevents member institutions from competing against each other on the basis of price or kind of television rights that can be offered to broadcasters, the NCAA member institutions have created a horizontal restraint—an agreement among competitors on the way in which they will compete with one another. A restraint of this type has often been held to be unreasonable as a matter of law. Because it places a ceiling on the number of games member institutions may televise, the horizontal agreement places an artificial limit on the quantity of televised football that is available to broadcasters and consumers. By restraining the quantity of television rights available for sale, the challenged practices create a limitation on output; our cases have held that such limitations are unreasonable restraints of trade. Moreover, the District Court found that the minimum aggregate price in fact operates to preclude any price negotiation between broadcasters and institutions, thereby constituting horizontal price fixing, perhaps the paradigm of an unreasonable restraint of trade.

Horizontal price fixing and output limitation are ordinarily condemned as a matter of law under an "illegal per se" approach because the probability that these practices are anticompetitive is so high; a per se rule is applied when "the practice facially appears to be one that would always or almost always tend to restrict competition and decrease output." In such circumstances a restraint is presumed unreasonable without inquiry into the particular market context in which it is found. Nevertheless, we have decided that it would be inappropriate to apply a per se rule to this case. This decision is not based on a lack of judicial experience with this type of arrangement, on the fact that the NCAA is organized as a nonprofit entity, or on our respect for the NCAA's historic role in the preservation and encouragement of intercollegiate amateur athletics. Rather, what is critical is that this case involves an industry in which horizontal restraints on competition are essential if the product is to be available at all.

As Judge Bork has noted: "[S]ome activities can only be carried out jointly. Perhaps the leading example is league sports. When a league of professional lacrosse teams is formed, it would be pointless to declare their cooperation illegal on the ground that there are no other professional lacrosse teams." R. Bork, *The Antitrust Paradox* 278 (1978). What the NCAA and its member institutions market in this case is competition itself—contests between competing institutions. Of course, this would be completely ineffective if there were no rules on which the competitors agreed to create and define the competition to be marketed. A myriad of rules affecting such matters as the size of the field, the number of players on a team, and the extent to which physical violence is to be encouraged or proscribed, all must be agreed upon, and all restrain the manner in which institutions compete. Moreover, the NCAA seeks to market a particular brand of football—college football. The identification of this "product" with an academic tradition differentiates college football from and makes it more popular than professional sports to which it might otherwise be comparable, such as, for example, minor league baseball. In order to preserve the character and quality of the "product," athletes must not be paid, must be required to attend class, and the like. And the integrity of the "product" cannot be preserved except by mutual agreement; if an institution adopted such restrictions unilaterally, its effectiveness as a competitor on the playing field might soon be destroyed. Thus, the NCAA plays a vital role in enabling college football to preserve its character, and as a result enables a product to be marketed which might otherwise be unavailable. In performing this role, its actions widen consumer choice—not only the choices available to sports fans but also those available to athletes—and hence can be viewed as procompetitive....

Respondents concede that the great majority of the NCAA's regulations enhance competition among member institutions. Thus, despite the fact that this case involves restraints on the ability of member institutions to compete in terms of price and output, a fair evaluation of their competitive character requires consideration of the NCAA's justifications for the restraints.

Our analysis of this case under the Rule of Reason, of course, does not change the ultimate focus of our inquiry.... Under the Sherman Act the criterion to be used in judging the validity of a restraint on trade is its impact on competition.

III

Because it restrains price and output, the NCAA's television plan has a significant potential for anticompetitive effects.[28] The findings of the District Court indicate that this potential has been realized. The District Court found that if member institutions were free to sell television rights, many more games would be shown on television, and that the NCAA's output restriction has the effect of raising the price the networks pay for television rights. Moreover, the court found that by fixing a price for television rights to all games, the NCAA creates a price structure that is unresponsive to viewer demand and unrelated to the prices that would prevail in a competitive market. And, of course, since as a practical matter all member institutions need NCAA approval, members have no real choice but to adhere to the NCAA's television controls.

28. In this connection, it is not without significance that Congress felt the need to grant professional sports an exemption from the antitrust laws for joint marketing of television rights. See 15 U.S.C. §§ 1291–1295. The legislative history of this exemption demonstrates Congress' recognition that agreements among league members to sell television rights in a cooperative fashion could run afoul of the Sherman Act, and in particular reflects its awareness of the decision in *United States v. National Football League*, 116 F.Supp. 319 (E.D.Pa.1953), which held that an agreement between the teams of the National Football League that each team would not permit stations within 75 miles of the home city of another team to telecast its games on a day when that team was playing at home violated § 1 of the Sherman Act.

The anticompetitive consequences of this arrangement are apparent. Individual competitors lose their freedom to compete. Price is higher and output lower than they would otherwise be, and both are unresponsive to consumer preference.[33] This latter point is perhaps the most significant, since "Congress designed the Sherman Act as a 'consumer welfare prescription.'" A restraint that has the effect of reducing the importance of consumer preference in setting price and output is not consistent with this fundamental goal of antitrust law.[34] Restrictions on price and output are the paradigmatic examples of restraints of trade that the Sherman Act was intended to prohibit. At the same time, the television plan eliminates competitors from the market, since only those broadcasters able to bid on television rights covering the entire NCAA can compete. Thus, as the District Court found, many telecasts that would occur in a competitive market are foreclosed by the NCAA's plan.

Petitioner argues, however, that its television plan can have no significant anticompetitive effect since the record indicates that it has no market power—no ability to alter the interaction of supply and demand in the market. We must reject this argument for two reasons, one legal, one factual.

As a matter of law, the absence of proof of market power does not justify a naked restriction on price or output. To the contrary, when there is an agreement not to compete in terms of price or output, "no elaborate industry analysis is required to demonstrate the anticompetitive character of such an agreement." Petitioner does not quarrel with the District Court's finding that price and output are not responsive to demand. Thus the plan is inconsistent with the Sherman Act's command that price and supply be responsive to consumer preference. We have never required proof of market power in such a case. This naked restraint on price and output requires some competitive justification even in the absence of a detailed market analysis. As a factual matter, it is evident that petitioner does possess market power. The District Court employed the correct test for determining whether college football broadcasts constitute a separate market—whether there are other products

---

33. The District Court provided a vivid example of this system in practice:

A clear example of the failure of the rights fees paid to respond to market forces occurred in the fall of 1981. On one weekend of that year, Oklahoma was scheduled to play a football game with the University of Southern California. Both Oklahoma and USC have long had outstanding football programs, and indeed, both teams were ranked among the top five teams in the country by the wire service polls. ABC chose to televise the game along with several others on a regional basis. A game between two schools which are not well-known for their football programs, Citadel and Appalachian State, was carried on four of ABC's local affiliated stations. The USC–Oklahoma contest was carried on over 200 stations. Yet, incredibly, all four of these teams received exactly the same amount of money for the right to televise their games.

34. As the District Court observed:

Perhaps the most pernicious aspect is that under the controls, the market is not responsive to viewer preference. Every witness who testified on the matter confirmed that the consumers, the viewers of college football television, receive absolutely no benefit from the controls. Many games for which there is a large viewer demand are kept from the viewers, and many games for which there is little if any demand are nonetheless televised.

that are reasonably substitutable for televised NCAA football games. Petitioner's argument that it cannot obtain supracompetitive prices from broadcasters since advertisers, and hence broadcasters, can switch from college football to other types of programming simply ignores the findings of the District Court. It found that intercollegiate football telecasts generate an audience uniquely attractive to advertisers and that competitors are unable to offer programming that can attract a similar audience. These findings amply support its conclusion that the NCAA possesses market power. Indeed, the District Court's subsidiary finding that advertisers will pay a premium price per viewer to reach audiences watching college football because of their demographic characteristics is vivid evidence of the uniqueness of this product. Moreover, the District Court's market analysis is firmly supported by our decision in *International Boxing Club v. United States*, 358 U.S. 242 (1959), that championship boxing events are uniquely attractive to fans and hence constitute a market separate from that for non-championship events. Thus, respondents have demonstrated that there is a separate market for telecasts of college football which "rest[s] on generic qualities differentiating" viewers. It inexorably follows that if college football broadcasts be defined as a separate market—and we are convinced they are—then the NCAA's complete control over those broadcasts provides a solid basis for the District Court's conclusion that the NCAA possesses market power with respect to those broadcasts. "When a product is controlled by one interest, without substitutes available in the market, there is monopoly power." *United States v. E.I. du Pont de Nemours & Co.*, 351 U.S. 377, 394 (1956).

Thus, the NCAA television plan on its face constitutes a restraint upon the operation of a free market, and the findings of the District Court establish that it has operated to raise price and reduce output. Under the Rule of Reason, these hallmarks of anticompetitive behavior place upon petitioner a heavy burden of establishing an affirmative defense which competitively justifies this apparent deviation from the operations of a free market.

IV

[P]etitioner argues that its television plan constitutes a cooperative "joint venture" which assists in the marketing of broadcast rights and hence is procompetitive....

The District Court did not find that the NCAA's television plan produced any procompetitive efficiencies which enhanced the competitiveness of college football television rights; to the contrary it concluded that NCAA football could be marketed just as effectively without the television plan. There is therefore no predicate in the findings for petitioner's efficiency justification. Indeed, petitioner's argument is refuted by the District Court's finding concerning price and output. If the NCAA's television plan produced procompetitive efficiencies, the plan would increase output and reduce the price of televised games. The District Court's contrary findings accordingly undermine petitioner's position. In light of these findings, it cannot be said that "the agreement on price is necessary to market the product at all." ... Here production has been limited, not enhanced. No individual school is free to televise its own games without restraint. The NCAA's efficiency justification is not supported by the record.

Neither is the NCAA's television plan necessary to enable the NCAA to penetrate the market through an attractive package sale. Since broadcasting rights to college football constitute a unique product for which there is no ready substitute, there is no need for collective action in order to enable the product to compete against its nonexistent competitors. This is borne out by the District Court's finding that the NCAA's television reduces the volume of television rights sold.

V

Throughout the history of its regulation of intercollegiate football telecasts, the NCAA has indicated its concern with protecting live attendance. This concern, it should be noted, is not with protecting live attendance at games which are shown on television; that type of interest is not at issue in this case. Rather, the concern is that fan interest in a televised game may adversely affect ticket sales for games that will not appear on television.[56]

Although studies in the 1950s provided some support for the thesis that live attendance would suffer if unlimited television were permitted, the District Court found that there was no evidence to support that theory in today's market....

There is, however, a more fundamental reason for rejecting this defense. The NCAA's argument that its television plan is necessary to protect live attendance is not based on a desire to maintain the integrity of college football as a distinct and attractive product, but rather on a fear that the product will not prove sufficiently attractive to draw live attendance when faced with competition from televised games. At bottom the NCAA's position is that ticket sales for most college games are unable to compete in a free market. The television plan protects ticket sales by limiting output—just as any monopolist increases revenues by reducing output. By seeking to insulate live ticket sales from the full spectrum of competition because of its assumption that the product itself is insufficiently attractive to consumers, petitioner forwards a justification that is inconsistent with the basic policy of the Sherman Act. "[T]he Rule of Reason does not support a defense based on the assumption that competition itself is unreasonable." *National Society of Professional Engineers v. United States*, 435 U.S. 679, 696 (1978).

56. The NCAA's plan is not even arguably related to a desire to protect live attendance by ensuring that a game is not televised in the area where it is to be played. No cooperative action is necessary for that kind of "blackout." The home team can always refuse to sell the right to telecast its game to stations in the immediate area. The NCAA does not now and never has justified its television plan by an interest in assisting schools in "blacking out" their home games in the areas in which they are played.

VI

Petitioner argues that the interest in maintaining a competitive balance among amateur athletic teams is legitimate and important and that it justifies the regulations challenged in this case. We agree with the first part of the argument but not the second.

Our decision not to apply a per se rule to this case rests in large part on our recognition that a certain degree of cooperation is necessary if the type of competition that petitioner and its member institutions seek to market is to be preserved. It is reasonable to assume that most of the regulatory controls of the NCAA are justifiable means of fostering competition among amateur athletic teams and therefore procompetitive because they enhance public interest in intercollegiate athletics. The specific restraints on football telecasts that are challenged in this case do not, however, fit into the same mold as do rules defining the conditions of the contest, the eligibility of participants, or the manner in which members of a joint enterprise shall share the responsibilities and the benefits of the total venture.

The NCAA does not claim that its television plan has equalized or is intended to equalize competition within any one league.[62] The plan is nationwide in scope and there is no single league or tournament in which all college football teams complete. There is no evidence of any intent to equalize the strength of teams in Division I–A with those in Division II or Division III, and not even a colorable basis for giving colleges that have no football program at all a voice in the management of the revenues generated by the football programs at other schools.[63] The interest in maintaining a competitive balance that is asserted by the NCAA as a justification for regulating all television of intercollegiate football is not related to any neutral standard or to any readily identifiable group of competitors.

---

62. It seems unlikely, for example, that there would have been a greater disparity between the football prowess of Ohio State University and that of Northwestern University in recent years without the NCAA's television plan. The District Court found that in fact the NCAA has been strikingly unsuccessful if it has indeed attempted to prevent the emergence of a "power elite" in intercollegiate football. Moreover, the District Court's finding that there would be more local and regional telecasts without the NCAA controls means that Northwestern could well have generated more television income in a free market than was obtained under the NCAA regime.

63. Indeed, the District Court found that the basic reason the television plan has endured is that the NCAA is in effect controlled by schools that are not restrained by the plan:

The plaintiffs and other CFA members attempted to persuade the majority of NCAA members that NCAA had gone far beyond its legitimate role in football television. Not surprisingly, none of the CFA proposals were adopted. Instead the membership uniformly adopted the proposals of the NCAA administration which "legitimized" NCAA's exercises of power. The result was not surprising in light of the makeup of the voting membership. Of approximately 800 voting members of the NCAA, 500 or so are in Divisions II and III and are not subjected to NCAA television controls. Of the 275 Division I members, only 187 play football, and only 135 were members of Division I–A at the time of the January Convention. Division I–A was made up of the most prominent football-playing schools, and those schools account for most of the football games shown on network television. Therefore, of some 850 voting members, less than 150 suffer any direct restriction on their right to sell football games to television.

The television plan is not even arguably tailored to serve such an interest. It does not regulate the amount of money that any college may spend on its football program, nor the way in which the colleges may use the revenues that are generated by their football programs, whether derived from the sale of television rights, the sale of tickets, or the sale of concessions or program advertising. The plan simply imposes a restriction on one source of revenue that is more important to some colleges than to others. There is no evidence that this restriction produces any greater measure of equality throughout the NCAA than would a restriction on alumni donations, tuition rates, or any other revenue producing activity. At the same time, as the District Court found, the NCAA imposes a variety of other restrictions designed to preserve amateurism which are much better tailored to the goal of competitive balance than is the television plan, and which are "clearly sufficient" to preserve competitive balance to the extent it is within the NCAA's power to do so. And much more than speculation supported the District Court's findings on this score. No other NCAA sport employs a similar plan, and in particular the court found that in the most closely analogous sport, college basketball, competitive balance has been maintained without resort to a restrictive television plan.

Perhaps the most important reason for rejecting the argument that the interest in competitive balance is served by the television plan is the District Court's unambiguous and well supported finding that many more games would be televised in a free market than under the NCAA plan. The hypothesis that legitimates the maintenance of competitive balance as a procompetitive justification under the Rule of Reason is that equal competition will maximize consumer demand for the product. The finding that consumption will materially increase if the controls are removed is a compelling demonstration that they do not in fact serve any such legitimate purpose.[68]

VII

The NCAA plays a critical role in the maintenance of a revered tradition of amateurism in college sports. There can be no question but that it needs ample latitude to play that role, or that the preservation of the student-athlete in higher education adds richness and diversity to intercollegiate athletics and is entirely consistent with the goals of the Sherman Act. But consistent with the Sherman Act, the role of the NCAA must be to preserve a tradition that might otherwise die; rules that restrict output are hardly consistent with this role. Today we hold only that the record supports the District Court's conclusion that by curtailing output and blunting the ability of member institutions to respond to consumer preference, the NCAA has restricted rather than

---

68. This is true not only for television viewers, but also for athletes. The District Court's finding that the television exposure of all schools would increase in the absence of the NCAA's television plan means that smaller institutions appealing to essentially local or regional markets would get more exposure if the plan is enjoined, enhancing their ability to compete for student athletes.

enhanced the place of intercollegiate athletics in the Nation's life. Accordingly, the judgment of the Court of Appeals is

Affirmed.

JUSTICE WHITE with whom JUSTICE REHNQUIST joins, dissenting.

* * *

I

"While it would be fanciful to suggest that colleges are not concerned about the profitability of their ventures, it is clear that other, non-commercial goals play a central role in their sports programs." J. Weistart & C. Lowell, *The Law of Sports* § 5.12 (1979). The NCAA's member institutions have designed their competitive athletic programs "to be a vital part of the educational system." Deviations from this goal, produced by a persistent and perhaps inevitable desire to "win at all costs," have in the past led, and continue to lead, to a wide range of competitive excesses that prove harmful to students and institutions alike....

The NCAA, in short, "exist[s] primarily to enhance the contribution made by amateur athletic competition to the process of higher education as distinguished from realizing maximum return on it as an entertainment commodity." In pursuing this goal, the organization and its members seek to provide a public good—a viable system of amateur athletics—that most likely could not be provided in a perfectly competitive market. "Without regulation, the desire of member institutions to remain athletically competitive would lead them to engage in activities that deny amateurism to the public. No single institution could confidently enforce its own standards since it could not trust its competitors to do the same." Note, *Antitrust and Nonprofit Entities*, 94 Harv. L. Rev. 802, 817–18 (1981). The history of intercollegiate athletics prior to the advent of the NCAA provides ample support for this conclusion. By mitigating what appears to be a clear failure of the free market to serve the ends and goals of higher education, the NCAA ensures the continued availability of a unique and valuable product, the very existence of which might well be threatened by unbridled competition in the economic sphere.

In pursuit of its fundamental goal and others related to it, the NCAA imposes numerous controls on intercollegiate athletic competition among its members, many of which "are similar to those which are summarily condemned when undertaken in a more traditional business setting." J. Weistart & C. Lowell, *supra*, at § 5.12.b. Thus, the NCAA has promulgated and enforced rules limiting both the compensation of student-athletes, and the number of coaches a school may hire for its football and basketball programs; it also has prohibited athletes who formerly have been compensated for playing from participating in intercollegiate competition, restricted the number of athletic scholarships its members may award, and established minimum academic standards for recipients of those scholarships; and it has pervasively regulated the recruitment process, student eligibility, practice schedules, squad size, the number of games played, and many other aspects of intercollegiate athletics. One clear effect of most, if not all, of these regulations is to prevent institutions with competitively and economically successful programs from taking advantage of their success by expanding their programs, improving the quality of the product they offer, and increasing their sports revenues. Yet each of these regulations represents a desirable and legitimate attempt "to keep university athletics from becoming professionalized to the extent that profit making objectives would overshadow educational objectives." Significantly, neither the Court of Appeals nor this Court questions the validity of these regulations under the Rule of Reason.

Notwithstanding the contrary conclusion of the District Court, and the majority, I do not believe that the restraint under consideration in this case—the NCAA's television plan—differs fundamentally for antitrust purposes from the other seemingly anticompetitive aspects of the organization's broader program of self-regulation. The television plan, like many of the NCAA's actions, furthers several complementary ends. Specifically, the plan is designed "to reduce, insofar as possible, the adverse effects of live television ... upon football game attendance and, in turn, upon the athletic and related educational programs dependent upon the proceeds therefrom; to spread football television participation among as many colleges as practicable; to reflect properly the image of universities as educational institutions; to promote college football through the use of television, to advance the overall interests of intercollegiate athletics, and to provide college football television to the public to the extent compatible with these other objectives." More generally, in my view, the television plan reflects the NCAA's fundamental policy of preserving amateurism and integrating athletics and education. Nor does the District Court's finding that the plan is intended to maximize television revenues, warrant any implication that the NCAA and its member institutions pursue this goal without regard to the organization's stated policies.

* * *

[I]t is essential at this point to emphasize that neither the Court of Appeals nor this Court purports to hold that the NCAA may not (1) require its members who televise their games to pool and share the compensation received among themselves, with other schools, and with the NCAA; (2) limit the number of times any member may arrange to have its games shown on television; or (3) enforce reasonable blackout rules to avoid head-to-head competition for television audiences. As I shall demonstrate, the Court wisely and correctly does not condemn such regulations. What the Court does affirm is the Court of Appeals' judgment that the NCAA may not limit the number of games that are broadcast on television and that it may not contract for an overall price that has the effect of setting the price for individual game broadcast rights. I disagree with the Court in these respects.

* * *

III

Even if I were convinced that the District Court did not err in failing to look to total viewership, as opposed to the number of televised games, when measuring output and anticompetitive effect and in failing fully to consider whether the NCAA possesses power to fix the package price, as opposed to the distribution of that package price among participating teams, I would nevertheless hold that the television plan passes muster under the Rule of Reason. The NCAA argues strenuously that the plan and the network contracts "are part of a joint venture among many of the nation's universities to create a product—high-quality college football—and offer that product in a way attractive to both fans in the stadiums and viewers on [television]. The cooperation in producing the product makes it more competitive against other [television] (and live) attractions." The Court recognizes that, "[i]f the NCAA faced 'interbrand' competition from available substitutes, then certain forms of collective action might be appropriate in order to enhance its ability to compete." It rejects the NCAA's proffered procompetitive justification, however, on the ground that college football is a unique product for which there are no available substitutes and "there is no need for collective action in order to enable the product to compete against its nonexistent competitors." This proposition is singularly unpersuasive.

It is one thing to say that "NCAA football is a unique product," that "intercollegiate football telecasts generate an audience uniquely attractive to advertisers and that competitors are unable to offer programming that can attract a similar audience." It is quite another, in my view, to say that maintenance or enhancement of the quality of NCAA football telecasts is unnecessary to enable those telecasts to compete effectively against other forms of entertainment. The NCAA has no monopoly power when competing against other types of entertainment. Should the quality of the NCAA's product "deteriorate to any perceptible degree or should the cost of 'using' its product rise, some fans undoubtedly would turn to another form of entertainment.... Because of the broad possibilities for alternative forms of entertainment," the NCAA "properly belongs in the broader 'entertainment' market rather than in ... [a] narrower marke[t]" like sports or football.

The NCAA has suggested a number of plausible ways in which its television plan might enhance the ability of college football telecasts to compete against other forms of entertainment. Although the District Court did conclude that the plan is "not necessary for effective marketing of the product," its finding was directed only at the question whether college football telecasts would continue in the absence of the plan. It made no explicit findings concerning the effect of the plan on viewership and thus did not reject the factual premise of the NCAA's argument that the plan might enhance competition by increasing the market penetration of NCAA football. The District Court's finding that network coverage of NCAA football would likely decrease if the plan were struck down, in fact, strongly suggests the validity of the NCAA's position. On the record now before the Court, therefore, I am not prepared to conclude that the restraints imposed by the NCAA's television plan are "such as may suppress or even destroy competition" rather than "such as merely regulat[e] and perhaps thereby promot[e] competition."

IV

Finally, I return to the point with which I began—the essentially noneconomic nature of the NCAA's program of self-regulation. Like Judge Barrett, who dissented in the Court of Appeals, I believe that the lower courts "erred by subjugating the NCAA's educational goals (and, coincidentally, those which Oklahoma and Georgia insist must be maintained in any event) to the purely competitive commercialism of [an] 'every school for itself' approach to television contract bargaining." Although the NCAA does not enjoy blanket immunity from the antitrust laws, it is important to remember that the Sherman Act "is aimed primarily at combinations having commercial objectives and is applied only to a very limited extent to organizations ... which normally have other objectives." *Klor's Inc. v. Broadway–Hale Stores, Inc.*, 359 U.S. 207, 213, n. 7 (1959).

The fact that a restraint operates on nonprofit educational institutions as distinguished from business entities is as "relevant in determining whether that particular restraint violates the Sherman Act" as is the fact that a restraint affects a profession rather than a business. The legitimate noneconomic goals of colleges and universities should not be ignored in analyzing restraints imposed by associations of such institutions on their members, and these noneconomic goals "may require that a particular practice, which could properly be viewed as a violation of the Sherman Act in another context, be treated differently." The Court of Appeals, like the District Court, flatly refused to consider what it termed "noneconomic" justifications advanced by the NCAA in support of the television plan. It was of the view that our decision in *National Society of Professional Engineers v. United States*, 435 U.S. 679 (1978), precludes reliance on noneconomic factors in assessing the reasonableness of the television plan. This view was mistaken, and I note that the Court does not in so many words repeat this error.

Professional Engineers did make clear that antitrust analysis usually turns on "competitive conditions" and "economic conceptions." Ordinarily, "the inquiry mandated by the Rule of Reason is whether the challenged agreement is one that promotes competition or one that suppresses competition." The purpose of antitrust analysis, the Court emphasized, "is to form a judgment about the competitive significance of the restraint; it is not to decide whether a policy favoring competition is in the public interest, or in the interest of the members of an industry." Broadly read, these statements suggest that noneconomic values like the promotion of amateurism and fundamental educational objectives could not save the television plan from condemnation under the Sherman Act. But these statements were made in response to "public interest" justifications proffered in defense of a ban on competitive bidding imposed by practitioners engaged in standard, profit-motivated commercial activities. The primarily noneconomic values pursued by educational institutions differ fundamentally from the "overriding commercial purpose of [the] day-to-day activities" of engineers, lawyers, doctors, and businessmen, and neither *Professional Engineers* nor any other decision of this Court suggests that associations of nonprofit educational institutions must defend their self-regulatory restraints solely in terms of their competitive impact, without regard for the legitimate noneconomic values they promote.

When these values are factored into the balance, the NCAA's television plan seems eminently reasonable. Most fundamentally, the plan fosters the goal of amateurism by spreading revenues among various schools and reducing the financial incentives toward professionalism. As the Court observes, the NCAA imposes a variety of restrictions perhaps better suited than the television plan for the preservation of amateurism. Although the NCAA does attempt vigorously to enforce these restrictions, the vast potential for abuse suggests that measures, like the television plan, designed to limit the rewards of professionalism are fully consistent with, and essential to the attainment of, the NCAA's objectives.... The collateral consequences of the spreading of regional and national appearances among a number of schools are many: the television plan, like the ban on compensating student-athletes, may well encourage students to choose their schools, at least in part, on the basis of educational quality by reducing the perceived economic element of the choice; it helps ensure the economic viability of athletic programs at a wide variety of schools with weaker football teams; and it "promot[es] competitive football among many and varied amateur teams nationwide." These important contributions, I believe, are sufficient to offset any minimal anticompetitive effects of the television plan.

The majority and dissenting opinions in the preceding case are among the most important in this book, both because they constitute a primer on the application of antitrust law and its rule of reason to the peculiar business of marketing athletically competitive sports entertainment, and because they highlight the fundamental conflict of values that permeates all of the legal policy issues surrounding college athletics. The questions raised and/or left unresolved by the decision in the *Board of Regents* case are among the most complex and confounding in all of the law of sports.

Perhaps the most important question about intercollegiate sports is how to reconcile the conflict between academic and amateur values and commercial market values. Both the majority and dissent recognize that the NCAA's promotion of amateur and educational goals is legitimate.

From that premise, the dissent argued that this "higher" goal justifies virtually any agreement among NCAA members about producing and marketing their various sports. The majority opinion, however, appears to draw a sharp line of demarcation between rules defining the nature of the product (the hundreds of pages of rules described earlier about academic eligibility and recruiting and compensating players)—which likely are lawful because they allow the NCAA schools to offer a unique type of product—and rules regarding how the schools market and sell their games, which must conform to antitrust restrictions against collaboration to reduce output and raise prices. Is it sensible for the majority to distinguish between the labor market for student-athletes and the product market for fans? Or is the dissent correct that the NCAA should be free to govern both the labor and product markets in college sports? If neither view is appealing, how should courts determine when a set of rules that promote competing values should escape the antitrust requirement of market competition?

This question is complicated by the fact that while most college officials involved in athletics truly believe that amateurism and academics are important values, maximizing revenue is undeniably a crucial factor in athletic decision-making at every Division I school. If colleges must compete for revenues, the financial (and public relations) benefits of winning (and the consequences of losing) are magnified. Thus, by requiring schools to be economic competitors in the product market, the Court has created a huge incentive for schools and coaches to win, which jeopardizes the standards designed to promote amateurism and academics. Does the Supreme Court draw the proper balance between these competing values in the application of antitrust law? How should courts balance these values in determining when different athletic programs should be required to compete and when they should be allowed to cooperate?

Questions for Discussion

1. Recall the Supreme Court's judgment in *Professional Engineers* (see Chapter 3) that only Congress, not private producers, should be allowed to structure an industry on the premise that other values are more important than market competition. Is Justice White's dissent correct that nonprofit entities such as colleges should be exempt from this rule? Or is the majority correct that the NCAA cannot lawfully decide to stifle competition in order to promote what its members (with their own economic interests) perceive to be in the best interests of their educational mission? In thinking about this question, ask yourself how antitrust law should apply to an agreement by the only three hospitals in a city, all of which are nonprofit, to fix common prices for their medical services or not to perform certain types of controversial medical procedures. Should universities be allowed to agree to hire professors only at defined salaries and benefits?

2. Given the requirement that colleges compete in selling their product (at least through television), are there any steps the NCAA can take to alleviate the adverse effects that such competition has on the academic and

amateur values it seeks to foster in student athletics? The dissent suggests some possibilities, such as forced sharing of all revenues and limiting each school's number of television appearances. Would such steps be lawful under the majority opinion? Why has the NCAA not adopted these or similar measures?[k]

3. Putting aside the question of whether and when it is appropriate to allow alternative social values to trump market competition, the majority suggests that many NCAA rules are actually procompetitive because they are important to the creation of a unique product that would not otherwise be available—amateur athletics. Is college football intrinsically different from NFL football? Is college tennis intrinsically different from professional tennis? Are you persuaded by the Court's arguments that the NCAA's television rules did not significantly contribute to the preservation of amateur athletics?

4. After this decision, the CFA (as well as the Pac–Ten and Big Ten conferences) entered into network contracts that gave exclusive network rights to broadcast members' football games and thus prevented individual schools from negotiating their own television deals. (Almost every college basketball conference has negotiated similar television packages.) If, as the Court holds, any agreement among different colleges that has the effect (indeed, the express purpose) of reducing output and raising prices violates the rule of reason, would the CFA's contracts be any more legal than the NCAA's? See *Regents of the Univ. of Calif. v. American Broadcasting Cos.*, 747 F.2d 511 (9th Cir.1984); and *Association of Independent Television Stations, Inc. v. College Football Ass'n.*, 637 F.Supp. 1289 (W.D.Okl.1986).

Justice White noted in his dissent that the antitrust victory won by these CFA members might come back to haunt the CFA in its own dealings with the television networks. In the immediate aftermath of the *Board of Regents* ruling, the price of network television packages, which had risen from $1.1 million in 1952, to $5 million per year in the early 1960s, to $75 million per year in the early 1980s, dropped sharply in value. Although there were nearly three times as many college football games on television in 1984 as in 1983 (under a CFA contract with ABC, a Big Ten/Pac Ten contract with CBS, and a host of deals between individual schools and cable networks or television sports distributors), the price per game was cut from just under $1 million to $250,000 (and total game attendance rose marginally). Not until 1990 was the CFA able to negotiate a $70 million per year deal with ABC and ESPN, to go along

---

k. In fact, legislation was introduced in Congress in 1991 (the *Collegiate Athletic Reform Act*) to try to prod the NCAA down that path. This bill, authored by Representative Tom McMillan (who had been an All–American basketball player, a Rhodes scholar, and an NBA performer of note), would grant the NCAA a carefully tailored exemption from the antitrust restraints imposed by the Supreme Court in *Board of Regents*. In return, the NCAA would have to adopt a revenue distribution plan that rewarded schools for the *academic* performances of their student-athletes, rather than their teams' win-loss records. For a defense of this proposal by its author, see Tom McMillan, *Out of Bounds* (New York: Simon and Schuster, 1992). What are your views, in light of the materials in Chapter 9 as well as the *NCAA* decision itself?

with the Big Ten/Pac Ten package (which by now had been awarded to ABC). Toward the end of those negotiations, Notre Dame broke away and signed a separate 5-year, $35 million deal with NBC for the rights to telecast its home games, to the great displeasure of its fellow CFA members (though the CFA did not retaliate against Notre Dame by boycotting their NBC games).[1]

In the early 1990s, the Federal Trade Commission (FTC) considered a complaint that the CFA's exclusive contract with ABC and ESPN violated the Sherman Act. The FTC, though, can enforce antitrust laws only against an entity that is "organized to carry on business for its own profit or that of its members" (see 15 U.S.C. § 44 (1988)). There was then a difficult question of whether that wording did encompass the CFA; for this or other reasons, the FTC eventually chose not to initiate proceedings against the CFA. Regardless of the scope of the FTC's *administrative* jurisdiction, the key *substantive* question remains: whether or not the CFA-ABC television package should have been judged a "restraint of trade" under § 1 of the Sherman Act (in a complaint filed in court by the Justice Department, for example). In that regard, note that the NCAA, the CFA, and intercollegiate sports generally do not enjoy the protective exemption from antitrust enjoyed by professional sports' television packages under the Sports Broadcasting Act (SBA) at issue in the *WGN* decision in Chapter 6. Ironically, the NFL invited the NCAA to co-sponsor the SBA and be included in the list of protected organizations, but NCAA officials, believing that their policies were beyond antitrust question, declined. The NCAA's only statutory protection is § 1293 of the SBA, which rescinds the exemption for a professional league if its games are telecast into any area where a college game is being played on a Saturday.

In basketball, by contrast with football, the NCAA has long conducted a national championship tournament for which it sells exclusive network and cable coverage to CBS and ESPN respectively. As noted earlier, the annual value of the television rights for the men's basketball finals has risen from $9 million in 1981 to $215 million in 1997. For the past decade, many people have advocated a single post-season tournament for football; not simply to produce an undisputed champion for college football fame, but also to generate significantly greater revenue than the current $100 million or so now earned by all the schools in bowl games.

No one has ever claimed that the members of the NCAA have violated antitrust law by agreeing to create the championship tournaments in various sports, with the organization selling broadcast rights to

1. For initial analysis of the *Board of Regents* decision and its impact, see David Greenspan, *College Football's Biggest Fumble: The Economic Impact of the Supreme Court's Decision in* National Collegiate Athletic Association v. Board of Regents of the University of Oklahoma, 33 Antitrust Bulletin 1 (Spring 1988). For a later treatment, see D. Kent Meyers and Ira Horowitz, *Private Enforcement of the Antitrust Laws Works Occasionally:* Board of Regents of the University of Oklahoma v. NCAA, *A Case in Point,* 48 Oklahoma L. Rev. 669 (1995), authored by the chief counsel and the expert witness for the Oklahoma Regents, respectively.

the event. What has evoked legal concerns, though, is a new football Bowl Alliance that was fashioned in the mid-1990s. The Alliance was initially created by agreement among four of the major Division I-A football conferences (the SEC, ACC, Big East, and now Big-Twelve), as well as Notre Dame. Bids were submitted to the Alliance by the dozen or so existing bowls, and the Fiesta, Sugar, and Orange Bowls were selected as the highest bidders. (The Rose Bowl and its long-time conference partners, the Big Ten and Pacific Ten, were not part of the original Alliance.) Each of these bowls would get the hoped for "national championship" game once every three years, matching the two top-ranked teams within the Alliance; the other two bowls would get games matching the other member conference champions, Notre Dame (if it won at least six games), and one or more other "at large" teams selected by the bowls. Team rankings would be determined by combining the Associated Press sportswriter poll and CNN-USA Today coaches poll at the end of the regular season.

In sum, rather than let each individual bowl bid for participants in its game, with each school accepting or rejecting those competitive market bids, the Alliance pooled the post-season game rights of all its members, and required the Bowls to buy the right to stage those games from a single seller. This scheme was touted by the Alliance leaders not just as the best way to produce a college football champion, but also as a vehicle for increasing bowl revenues and pay-outs for team members. In fact, bowl game ticket prices and television rights did increase sharply when the Alliance regime came into operation. For these and other reasons, in 1996 the Rose Bowl and its two conference partners agreed to join a new Super Alliance championship beginning with the 1998 football season.

In early 1996, the Antitrust Division of the Justice Department did conduct a quiet investigation of whether this Super Alliance constituted an illegal "combination ... in restraint of trade" under the Sherman Act. While the Justice Department dropped this investigation in 1996 (for unstated reasons in that election year), the matter returned to public view at the end of the 1996 football season. The Western Athletic Conference (WAC) asked for a congressional investigation of an Alliance arrangement that had excluded its member Brigham Young from the lucrative Alliance bowl games, even though BYU had ended the regular season ranked number five in the polls with its 13-1 record. Following congressional hearings in May, 1997, the Bowl Alliance offered a virtual guarantee to the WAC (and also to Conference USA) that their champions would appear in one of these bowl games if they were in the top five of regular season ratings. That proposal, however, evoked a strong objection from Notre Dame whose odds of appearing in such a bowl would drop sharply if it were not in the top five because of preferential guarantees given to conference champions who might well be below the independent Notre Dame in these same rankings. Despite these political difficulties, the new Super Alliance appeared to be on track for the 1998 season, especially given the sharp increase in fees that ABC offered to Alliance members to broadcast these championship bowl games.

Questions for Discussion

1. The Bowl Alliance raises a number of antitrust questions. Did the exclusion of the WAC and BYU constitute an illegal boycott of a possible contender for the national championship? What about the exclusion of the Cotton Bowl or Citrus Bowl, for example, from any opportunity to stage the championship game? Does the sharp rise in ticket prices, television rights, and sponsorship fees (or any one of the above), and thence pay-outs to participating teams and conferences, stem just from the greater consumer appeal of this new joint product, an annual college football championship game? Or are these higher prices at least in part the result of the Alliance's market power that flows out of its members pooling the most attractive post-season football viewing rights? Even if the latter is true, should it be a violation of antitrust for a group of conferences and bowls to agree to stage a football championship, if there is no such violation by the NCAA when it conducts and sells its basketball Final Four and other national college sports championships? Is there any less restrictive alternative that might better accommodate the procompetitive benefits of a new championship football game and the alleged anticompetitive impact on consumers of the current Alliance regime?

2. Returning now to *Board of Regents*, the majority opinion asserted that the complaining universities, Oklahoma and Georgia, had no real choice but to adhere to the NCAA's television rules. Recall, however, that in *Tarkanian* the Court found that the NCAA was not a "state actor" in ordering UNLV to suspend Coach Tarkanian because, the Court reasoned, UNLV had a choice, "however unpalatable," whether to comply with the NCAA's directives. Are these judicial observations, just four years apart, incompatible? Or is there a difference in the circumstances (legal or factual) that explains these contrasting sentiments?

3. What implications, if any, does the *Board of Regents* decision have for the question of whether professional sports leagues should be treated as single entities for § 1 "conspiracy" purposes? Are there material differences between the structure and product of the NFL or NBA and that of the NCAA?

4. The *Board of Regents* ruling involved the use of antitrust law to eliminate restrictive agreements that affected the supply and price of a product offered to consumers, the principal constituency of antitrust policy. What often is a key step in rule of reason analysis is the determination of the market in which the defendant's product competes. Study the majority opinion closely. Does the Court indicate whether any one league's games should be considered as just one of the many sports and entertainment products that compete for consumer patronage, either at the live gate or on the television screen?

The world of college sports has experienced the same surge in revenues from product merchandising as we read about in Chapter 6 relating to professional sports. In the early 1980s, the total retail market for products identified with college athletics was under $100 million a year, most of which was sold in college book stores or other outlets on campus. By the mid–1990s, the college market was over $2.5 billion a year, the vast bulk sold in retail stores and chains. The average royalty rates of around eight percent earned some 20 schools more than a million dollars each per year, with Michigan reportedly the highest at $6 million (though most assumed that Notre Dame, which does not disclose its revenues, was even higher). When schools appear in major football bowls or Final Four basketball championships, the financial value of their deals and offers from Nike, Reebok, and other merchandisers jumps sharply. However, college sports, in stark contrast to professional sports, does not have a central NCAA Properties arm to manage these merchandising deals and distribute the revenues among all its members. Perhaps one reason is that the *Board of Regents* decision we have just read was being rendered at the same time that athletic merchandising was taking off. However, as of late 1997, the same group of conference commissioners that had put together the Bowl Alliance was trying to establish a trademark pooling and licensing enterprise for their member schools. We shall have to wait and see whether any such merchandising venture will emerge, and if so, how it will stand up to antitrust scrutiny.

Let us turn away from antitrust law for a moment. The Internal Revenue Service has treated revenues derived from intercollegiate sports telecasts—as well as from gate receipts—as non-taxable income earned by colleges and universities that are non-profit enterprises. The IRS has accepted the schools' argument that, for purposes of §§ 511–513 of the Internal Revenue Code, college sports are "related" to the institutions' tax-exempt educational purposes.[m] In the winter of 1992, however, the IRS ruled that funds received from the corporate sponsors of a bowl game (for example, from Mobil Oil for the Cotton Bowl) were unrelated and therefore taxable. (Presumably this would also encompass merchandising deals signed by Ohio State and Florida State that license Burger King to incorporate their "fight songs" in its commercials.) Competing bills have been introduced in the Congress that would either overturn this ruling or extend it to all television revenues from college sports. Which of these options makes the most sense as a matter of tax policy? Educational policy? Sports policy?

---

[m] See David Williams, *Is the Federal Government Suiting Up to Play in the Reform Game?*, 20 Capital Univ. L. Rev. 621, 625–26 (1991).

2. COACHING MARKET

The sports industry provides the major judicial evidence that the product market is not the exclusive concern of antitrust law, and that § 1 prohibits unreasonable restraints on the labor market (at least absent the *Brown* labor exemption drawn from federal labor law policy). The labor market in intercollegiate sports includes both players and coaches.

The operation of the college coaching market vividly demonstrates what free agency can do for those who make a difference between winning and losing programs. Total compensation for college football and basketball coaches includes not only base salary, but also shoe contracts, radio and television shows, summer athletic clinics (often at the school's facilities), endorsements, and speaking engagements. Earnings from all these sources for well-known college coaches such as Bobby Bowden and Joe Paterno in football, and Mike Krzyzewski and John Thompson in basketball, are now in the range of $1 million dollars per year—roughly four times the earnings of their university presidents. Indeed, in the summer of 1997, Steve Spurrier negotiated a six-year contract extension at Florida that guaranteed him approximately $2 million a year. Top college coaches in football and basketball now make sums that are comparable to those paid to most professional coaches, because there is competition between as well as within these two branches of the respective sports for the most-talented and visible coaching personalities.

In late 1989, the NCAA created a Cost Reduction Committee to address what many of its members felt was a "catastrophic cost spiral" affecting their athletic programs. Individual institutions were feeling the pressure to spend more money to recruit high quality coaches and players in order to stay athletically competitive with their rivals (in the words of the NCAA, "to keep up with Joneses"). This was so, even though financial reports were indicating that many schools were losing significant amounts of money from this effort. The NCAA's Raiborn Report for the 1981–85 period found that 42% of Division I institutions were incurring athletic deficits, at an average of $842,000 apiece. The problem was not declining revenues, but rather spiraling costs. The average Division I program's $4.6 million expenditures in 1985 were nearly three times higher than the 1973 average.

The Cost Reduction Committee made a number of recommendations at the 1992 NCAA Convention to address this cost problem. While no salary cap was imposed on coaches generally, all coaches were required to get the *written* approval of school officials for their outside income from the kinds of sources noted above. More importantly, the Convention adopted the Committee's proposed "Restricted Earnings Coach Rule." This new Rule 11.02.03 required that one of the limited number of coaches allowed each school in each sport (with the exception of football) be designated as a "restricted earnings coach." A salary limit was set for the latter position at $12,000 during the academic year and

$4,000 during the summer months—which was said to be roughly equivalent to the average amounts that schools had previously paid to those designated as "graduate assistant coaches." The NCAA Rule figure did not vary with earnings and living costs in different communities, and was not to be adjusted annually to inflation.

In basketball, the Rule limited each team to one head coach, two assistants, and one restricted earnings coach. A number of coaches who were designated for the latter role had previously been earning $60,000 to $70,000 a year. Early on, the new rule produced the following strange spectacle: when Duke's head coach Krzyzewski (whose total annual earnings were around $1 million) became sick during the 1994–95 season, he was replaced in that role by the long-time, but now part-time, restricted earnings coach Pete Gaudet who was paid $12,000 (down dramatically from the $71,000 he had earned in the previous year). Gaudet could and did have another part-time job teaching physical education. However, that job was also subject to close NCAA scrutiny: Gaudet had to be demonstrably qualified for that teaching function; his physical education rate of pay had to be the same as was paid to his counterparts in that role; and the actual portion of the physical education salary that he received had to be proportionate to the ratio of time spent on that function, by comparison to the time spent coaching the Blue Devils.

Gaudet, along with other restricted earnings coaches in basketball, became part of a class action antitrust suit. Two decades earlier, there had been an unsuccessful suit against another NCAA rule that had imposed limits on the size of coaching staffs, a ceiling that had required especially sizeable football programs to dismiss a number of their assistants. See *Hennessey v. NCAA*, 564 F.2d 1136 (5th Cir.1977). Since then, though, the Supreme Court had made it clear in *Board of Regents* that antitrust not only governed NCAA regulations, it also made some of them illegal. Thus, the following decision by a federal district judge considers the implications of antitrust doctrine in the 1990s for such an NCAA cost reduction effort.

LAW v. NATIONAL COLLEGIATE ATHLETIC ASSOCIATION

United States District Court, District of Kansas, 1995.
902 F.Supp. 1394.

VRATIL, DISTRICT JUDGE.

[The first part of the judge's opinion detailed the evolution and content of the "restricted earnings" rule. The judge quoted Committee Chair Gene Corrigan, commissioner of the ACC and later president of the NCAA, as characterizing his task as "this gigantic attempt to save intercollegiate athletics from itself"—meaning that "a collaborative effort among NCAA members was required to maintain a level playing field because unilateral cost reduction efforts by individual members were ineffectual." The following passage from the opinion elaborated further on this NCAA argument.

Another member of the Cost Reduction Committee explained this point further. Donna Lopiano testified that if one educational institution cuts costs, and its athletic competitor does not make the same reductions, the latter will be more competitive on the field than the former. To illustrate, if institution "A" unilaterally cuts its number of scholarships from 85 (the number permitted in Division I–A) to 50, institution "A" necessarily becomes less competitive than institutions that use 85 scholarships to recruit their teams. Similarly, if NCAA legislation allows 10 football coaches, and institution "A" unilaterally reduces that number to 2 football coaches, then the schools with 10 coaches will have a valuable recruiting tool, in that they will be able to offer better coach-student ratios and guarantee more individualized attention for the student-athlete's experience. Ms. Lopiano further testified that when an institution loses athletic contests due to an "unlevel playing field," it suffers diminished revenues because it loses spectators, has disconcerted alumni and experiences other disadvantageous effects. The concept of a "level playing field" has frequently been referred to in this litigation as "competitive equity."

The NCAA's constitution describes the concept of competitive equity in this way:

> The Principle of Competitive Equity. The structure and programs of the Association and the activities of its members shall promote opportunity for equity in competition to assure that individual student-athletes and institutions will not be prevented unfairly from achieving the benefits inherent in participation in intercollegiate athletics.

NCAA 1994–95 Manual, Const. 2.9.

902 F.Supp. at 1399, n.4. Judge Vratil then reviewed the evolution of antitrust jurisprudence in the Supreme Court, relying in particular on the following passage quoted from *Board of Regents*, to reject the plaintiff coaches' argument that this NCAA restricted earnings rule must be struck down as a case of horizontal college price-fixing that was *per se* illegal.

> A myriad of rules affecting such matters as the size of the field, the number of players on a team, and the extent to which physical violence is to be encouraged or proscribed, all must be agreed upon, and all restrain the manner in which institutions compete. Moreover, the NCAA seeks to market a particular brand of [sports]—college [sports]. The identification of this "product" with an academic tradition differentiates college [sports] from and makes [them] more popular than professional sports to which [they] might otherwise be comparable.... In order to preserve the character and quality of the "product," athletes must not be paid, must be required to attend class, and the like. And the integrity of the "product" cannot be preserved except by mutual agreement; if an institution adopted such restrictions unilaterally, its effectiveness as

a competitor on the playing field might soon be destroyed. Thus, the NCAA plays a vital role in enabling college [sports] to preserve [their] character, and as a result enables a product to be marketed which might otherwise be unavailable.

468 U.S. 85, at 101–02. However, while *Board of Regents* did make clear "that the NCAA's 'vital role' in making college sports available to the public entitles it to a rule of reason review," the Supreme Court did not intend "to give the NCAA carte blanche in imposing restraints of trade on its member institutions or other parties because of its role in the marketplace." With that as background, Judge Vratil addressed the substantive effects of this NCAA restraint "under the rubric of the rule of reason."]

* * *

D. Effects of the Restricted Earnings Coach Rule

The NCAA first argues that the Restricted Earnings Coach Rule has no anticompetitive effect because restricted earnings coaches may avoid the restraining effect of the rule by obtaining coaching positions with high school teams, non-NCAA college teams, NCAA Division II or III teams, overseas teams or, in fact, by obtaining other employment not related to their coaching duties.[11] At best, this argument amounts to an assertion that because Division I restricted earnings coach positions represent such a small portion of the market, the NCAA has no market power in this arena and thus its restraint can have no adverse competitive impact.

This argument by the NCAA is wholly unconvincing. The absence of proof of market power does not foreclose a finding of anticompetitive behavior under the Sherman Act. See *Board of Regents*, 468 U.S. at 109. In fact, where there is an agreement not to compete in terms of price, " 'no elaborate industry analysis is required to demonstrate the anticompetitive character of such an agreement.' " Id. (quoting *National Soc'y of Professional Engineers v. United States*, 435 U.S. 679, 692, (1978)). Where a restraint runs counter to the Sherman Act's requirement that price be responsive to consumer preference, proof of market power is unnecessary because such an agreement's anticompetitive character is evident. See *Board of Regents*, 468 U.S. at 110.

The NCAA acknowledges that before the rule was enacted, some restricted earnings coaches were paid $60,000 to $70,000—apparently because the schools that employed them believed their services were worth that amount. Controlling such responses to consumer preference was in fact the very objective which the NCAA sought to achieve in

---

11. Defendant's argument—essentially that price-fixing victims can simply go elsewhere and get a job in another part of the economy that is not fixed—is, of course, absurd and cannot carry the day for the NCAA in this litigation. See, e.g., *Roman v. Cessna Aircraft Co.*, 55 F.3d 542, 544 (10th Cir.1995) ("plaintiffs whose opportunities in the employment market have been impaired by an anticompetitive agreement directed at them as a particular segment of employees have suffered an antitrust injury under the governing standard").

enacting the rule. Sometimes the rule of reason may be applied "in the twinkling of an eye," Id. at 109 n.39; and this is surely one such case. Because the Restricted Earnings Coach Rule specifically prohibits the free operation of a market responsive to demand and is thus inconsistent with the Sherman Act's mandates, it is not necessary for the Court to undertake an extensive market analysis to determine that the rule has had an anticompetitive effect on the market for coaching services.

The NCAA next argues that its regulation may even be procompetitive because, if the NCAA does not collapse as a result of its skyrocketing costs, it will be able to continue providing the product of college basketball and there will thus continue to be jobs available in the market for basketball coaches. For all its alarming rhetoric, however, the NCAA has offered no compelling evidence that its member institutions are on the brink of financial disaster or that the *de minimus* effect which reducing the salaries of the lowest paid member of each school's coaching staff by a few thousand dollars would pull them back from the abyss. Moreover, even if the situation of intercollegiate athletics was every bit as dire as the NCAA makes it out to be in resisting the coaches' challenge to the Restricted Earnings Coach Rule, the NCAA's argument—that the regulation is procompetitive because it will help the NCAA schools stay in the black so that they can continue providing intercollegiate athletics at all—cannot succeed.

The market for coaching services is different from the market for intercollegiate sports. In the market for coaching services, coaches are the producers and schools are the consumers, whereas in the market for intercollegiate sports, the schools become the producers and the public the consumers. Procompetitive justifications for price-fixing must apply to the same market in which the restraint is found, not to some other market. See *United States v. Topco Assoc., Inc.*, 405 U.S. 596 (1972) (competition "cannot be foreclosed with respect to one sector of the economy because certain private citizens or groups believe that such foreclosure might promote greater competition in a more important sector of the economy"); *United States v. Philadelphia Nat'l Bank*, 374 U.S. 321 (1963) (anticompetitive effects in one market cannot be justified by procompetitive consequences in another); *Sullivan v. National Football League*, 34 F.3d 1091, 1112 (1st Cir.1994) (it seems "improper to validate a practice that is decidedly in restraint of trade simply because the practice produces some unrelated benefits to competition in another market"). If price-fixing buyers were allowed to justify their actions by claiming procompetitive benefits in the product market, they would almost always be able to do so by arguing that the restraint was designed to reduce their costs and thereby make them collectively more competitive sellers. To permit such a justification would be to give businesses a blanket exemption from the antitrust laws and a practically limitless license to engage in horizontal price-fixing aimed at suppliers. This license the Court will not issue—even in the unique context of intercollegiate athletics.

E. NCAA JUSTIFICATIONS FOR THE RESTRICTED EARNINGS COACH RULE

Because the Restricted Earnings Coach Rule constitutes a restraint on the operation of a free market, and because the uncontroverted facts demonstrate that its effect has been to stabilize and, in some cases, depress prices in the market for coaching services, the rule of reason next places on the NCAA a "heavy burden of establishing an affirmative defense which competitively justifies" this infringement on the Sherman Act's protected domain. See *Board of Regents*, 468 U.S. at 113.

The NCAA attempts to carry its burden by emphasizing the importance of maintaining a level playing field in the sports arena, retaining and fostering the spirit of amateurism which is one of college athletics' defining characteristics, and protecting NCAA member institutions from self-imposed, ruinous cost increases.[12] In doing so, the NCAA relies heavily on two earlier cases which held that NCAA coaching restrictions were not inconsistent with the antitrust laws and were, in fact, legitimate and necessary means of maintaining competitive equity and the other values the NCAA seeks to protect. Those cases are: *Board of Regents of the Univ. of Oklahoma v. National Collegiate Athletic Ass'n*, 561 P.2d 499 (Okla.1977) ("Oklahoma Board of Regents"), and *Hennessey v. National Collegiate Athletic Ass'n*, 564 F.2d 1136 (5th Cir.1977).

The *Hennessey* case and the *Oklahoma Board of Regents* case, decided well before the Supreme Court issued its opinion in *Board of Regents*, were both challenges to an NCAA bylaw adopted in 1976 that limited the number of Division I football and basketball coaches member institutions could employ. In upholding the bylaw, the Fifth Circuit in *Hennessey* and the Oklahoma Supreme Court in *Oklahoma Board of Regents* both gave deference to the NCAA's motives in enacting the challenged restriction. In *Hennessey*, the court noted that plaintiffs had presented no evidence that the NCAA intended to injure the affected coaches by adopting the bylaw and that, to the contrary, "the fundamental objective in mind was to preserve and foster competition in intercollegiate athletics—by curtailing, as it were, potentially monopolistic practices by the more powerful—and to reorient the programs into their traditional role as amateur sports operating as part of the educational processes." *Hennessey*, 564 F.2d at 1153. The NCAA, of course, asserts the same motivating objective in this litigation.

---

12. The NCAA also asserts that by enforcing the Restricted Earnings Coach Rule it is maintaining an "entry-level" position for coaches who are young and/or inexperienced in the field. By enacting the salary cap, the NCAA sought to level the playing field by weeding out more experienced and seasoned coaches; ostensibly, more experienced coaches would not be willing to work for only $16,000 per year. However, the NCAA has introduced no evidence whatsoever that its method has been effective in making more opportunities available for younger or more inexperienced coaches. Nor has it introduced evidence that any seasoned coaches who were drawing $60,000 to $70,000 under the old salary regime have ceded their positions to the younger and more inexperienced coaches waiting to fill their shoes. In fact, the NCAA has not introduced evidence of a single restricted earnings coaching position which has been made available to a younger, more inexperienced coach that would not have been available in the previously unrestricted market for coaching services.

Significantly, in attempting to balance the NCAA's professed good intentions with the anticompetitive nature of the coaching restriction, the *Hennessey* court noted that on the evidence presented, it was difficult to determine what the actual effects of the restriction would be, since the rule had only been in effect for one month. The court recognized that one possible consequence of that bylaw would be to "stabilize, if not depress, the compensation which any assistant coach can obtain for his services." However, the court concluded that if that should happen and actual experience under the bylaw run counter to the NCAA's expectations and good intentions, a court could certainly consider that evidence in reevaluating the restraint in a later case.

In contrast to the bylaw at issue in *Hennessey*, the explicit intent of the Restricted Earnings Coach Rule at issue here was both to stabilize and depress the compensation of restricted earnings coaches. This Court therefore does not need the experience of time which the *Hennessey* court felt it was lacking in order to make a judgment about the potential effects of the restraint. Moreover, we believe that the *Hennessey* court placed undue emphasis on the NCAA's stated good intentions—not only in light of the Supreme Court's clear articulation of the proper antitrust analysis in *Board of Regents*, but also in light of clearly established precedent existing at the time of the *Hennessey* decision itself. Although intent is relevant in helping a court interpret facts and predict consequences in this type of case, "a good intention will [not] save an otherwise objectionable regulation...." *Chicago Board of Trade*, 246 U.S. at 238.

[The Court also distinguished *Oklahoma Board of Regents*.]

* * *

The Supreme Court in *Board of Regents*, however, clarified that the burden of proof in an antitrust case is somewhat different from what the Oklahoma court articulated: under the rule of reason, the proponent— not the challenger—of a facially anticompetitive measure carries "a heavy burden of establishing an affirmative defense which competitively justifies [such an] apparent deviation from the operations of a free market." *Board of Regents*, 468 U.S. at 113. The NCAA has repeatedly and vigorously urged this Court to shift the burden and require the coaches here to "prove a negative"—that the Restricted Earnings Coach Rule is unjustifiable under rule of reason antitrust analysis. In support, the NCAA quotes the following language from *Board of Regents*:

> It is reasonable to assume that most of the regulatory controls of the NCAA are justifiable means of fostering competition among amateur athletic teams and therefore procompetitive because they enhance public interest in intercollegiate athletics. The specific restraints on football telecasts that are challenged in this case do not, however, fit into the same mold as do rules defining the conditions of the contest, the eligibility of participants, or the manner in which members of a joint enterprise shall share the responsibilities and the benefits of the total venture.

Id. at 117. This language does not create a presumption of reasonableness for any regulation the NCAA chooses to enact, nor does it alter the burden of proof. Rather, the Court's general observation merely reiterates its previous comment that certain regulations which may restrain economic competition—rules dictating the size of the field, the number of players on each team, the extent to which physical violence should be allowed, that athletes should not be paid and that they must attend class—are crucial to the well-being of amateur athletic competition. Moreover, the regulations referred to by the *Board of Regents* court are qualitatively a far cry from a regulation limiting the amount of compensation a professional coach, or even a graduate student assistant coach, can earn as a livelihood for providing services to NCAA member schools.

In this litigation, the NCAA attempts to obtain leniency for its restricted earnings salary cap by characterizing it as a noncommercial regulation. The NCAA cites the district court's opinion in *Board of Regents* to support its position that noncommercial activities of the NCAA are reasonable methods of preserving competition in college sports. Finding previous cases regarding noncommercial NCAA regulations inapposite to its evaluation of the commercial restrictions on television contracts at issue, the court in that case noted,

> Several courts have analyzed the non-commercial activities of NCAA and concluded that they were reasonable methods of preserving and regulating competition in intercollegiate football.... However, none of these cases dealt with the commercial activities of NCAA. These [commercial] activities are far different from regulations governing the size of coaching staffs or rules on academic eligibility. There is only a tenuous relationship between such non-commercial regulations and the marketplace. Moreover, the non-commercial regulations relate more directly and effectively to the preservation of competitive balance. In this case, the commercial activities of NCAA have a direct and substantial anti-competitive effect on the marketplace, and contribute only indirectly, if at all, to the legitimate non-commercial goals of NCAA.

Board of Regents of the Univ. of Oklahoma v. National Collegiate Athletic Ass'n, 546 F.Supp. 1276, 1316 (W.D.Okla.1982). The NCAA has not persuaded this Court that the relationship between the Restricted Earnings Coach Rule's salary cap and prices in the market for coaching services is at all tenuous or indirect. On the contrary, the relationship is direct, substantial and demonstrable. As the NCAA admits, the rule is directly responsible for a reduction in certain coaches' salaries. Furthermore, the NCAA has not demonstrated through any plausible evidence that the rule's restraint relates directly and effectively to the preservation of competitive balance, amateurism or any other legitimate, noncommercial goal; instead, it offers only argument on this point. It is far from clear to this Court that the act of imposing a ceiling on the salaries of one class of employees in the labor market could possibly be characterized as "noncommercial," especially given the NCAA's express purpose of cutting costs in doing so.

While the Supreme Court in *Board of Regents* accepted competitive balance as a legitimate objective for the NCAA and was willing to assume that most NCAA regulations are justifiable means of accomplishing that objective, the Court required that regulations with anticompetitive effects be somehow related or tailored to the interests they purport to protect. Because the television restrictions in that case were not closely tailored to the NCAA's proffered justifications regarding competitive balance and amateurism—the same justifications the NCAA offers here—the Court invalidated the restraints. For purposes of this motion, the Court accepts that cost-cutting measures are needed, that amateurism and competitive equity should be maintained, and that retaining a coaching position for an entry-level coach benefits both coaches and NCAA member institutions. Nevertheless, the NCAA has not demonstrated the necessary link between these stated objectives and the Restricted Earnings Coach Rule.

"Even if an anticompetitive restraint is intended to achieve a legitimate objective, the restraint only survives a rule of reason analysis if it is reasonably necessary to achieve the legitimate objectives proffered by the defendant." *Brown University*, 5 F.3d at 678–79. To determine if a restraint is reasonably necessary, a court first examines whether the restraint furthers the legitimate objectives, and then whether comparable benefits could be achieved through substantially less restrictive means.

The NCAA has not cleared the first of these two hurdles. As noted previously, the NCAA has offered no evidence that the Restricted Earnings Coach Rule furthers its stated objectives at all. The NCAA's stated objectives are to level the playing field to obtain competitive equity, to provide for an entry-level coaching position and to cut costs. The NCAA has submitted no evidence to this Court that requiring schools to pay their fourth-ranked basketball coaches all the same low salary levels the playing field in any significant way, especially when there is no limit on how disparately the three more senior coaches may be paid by competitor schools. Similarly, the NCAA has presented no evidence that the restricted earnings coach positions are now more likely to be filled by young or inexperienced coaches than they were when salaries were competitive.

Nor has the NCAA offered any evidence that the Restricted Earnings Coach Rule really achieves an overall reduction in costs; as stipulated by the parties, nothing in the Restricted Earnings Coach Rule prevents NCAA schools from spending money saved (if any) from fixing the restricted earnings coach's salary on some other aspect of their basketball programs, such as increasing the head coach's salary. Because the NCAA has failed to meet its burden of establishing that the Restricted Earnings Coach Rule actually promotes a legitimate, procompetitive objective, it is unnecessary for plaintiffs to demonstrate that the Restricted Earnings Coach Rule is the least restrictive alternative available to the NCAA to achieve its stated goals or that comparable benefits could be achieved through viable, less restrictive means.

Because the Restricted Earnings Coach Rule is a restraint of trade as prohibited by the Sherman Act, the NCAA bears a heavy burden in this case to establish that the restraint enhances competition or, in other words, promotes a legitimate, procompetitive goal. On this record, the Court finds that the NCAA has not met this weighty burden and that plaintiffs are entitled to judgment as a matter of law on the issue of liability.

Summary judgment granted.

In January 1996, Judge Vratil issued a permanent injunction against NCAA maintenance of this "restricted earnings" rule for basketball coaches. The NCAA then sought to appeal the lower court ruling, but the Tenth Circuit refused to address the substantive merits for procedural reasons. The case then went back to Judge Vratil who certified it as a class action and scheduled the damages trial for April 1998. Just as this book was going to press in early 1998, the Tenth Circuit came down with its decision in *Law v. NCAA*, 134 F.3d 1010 (10th Cir.1998). Applying a "quick look" version of rule of reason analysis, the court upheld Judge Vratil's summary antitrust judgment and permanent injunction against the NCAA's "restricted earnings" rule.[n] Trial for damages was scheduled for April 1998.

Questions For Discussion

1. In compliance with the *Law* ruling, the NCAA Council removed its earnings limit for the third assistant basketball coach. Some NCAA members are now considering whether to have the Association simply abolish this additional coaching position, rather than pay individually-negotiated salaries. Would that rule square with Judge Vratil's analysis of the relevant antitrust law, including the Fifth Circuit's 1977 ruling in *Hennessey* and the Supreme Court's subsequent decision in *Board of Regents*? Is there a plausible distinction between an NCAA cap on coaching salaries and one on the number of coaching positions? Between coaching positions and athletic scholarship positions?

2. Would it be more sensible and legally defensible for the NCAA to establish uniform rules governing all coaching (and athletic director) positions? Perhaps the Association might adopt a cap on the total amount of salary that can be paid to all the coaches of each team, and maybe even a limit on how much can be paid to the individual head coach. They might also require that additional revenue generated from shoe contracts, broadcast shows, summer athletic clinics, and the like be channelled into the school's coffers to help defray athletic and other program expenses. What are the

---

n. The Tenth Circuit's opinion relied on both the Supreme Court's broader antitrust approach in *Board of Regents,* and on the first scholarly analysis of these coaching restraints, by Gary R. Roberts, *The NCAA, Antitrust, and Consumer Welfare,* note j above. In a companion decision, *Law v. NCAA*, 134 F.3d 1025 (10th Cir.1998), the circuit panel reversed some of the earlier procedural sanctions that the district judge had imposed on the NCAA during the course of this litigation.

pros and cons of such a Cost Reduction rule from the point of view of both sports policy and antitrust doctrine?

3. Judge Vratil rejected as without factual support the NCAA's defense of its coaching salary cap as necessary to preserve the fiscal solvency of colleges. She also rejected the argument on the legal ground that an anticompetitive restraint on the labor market could not be supported by procompetitive justifications in the product market for college sports. Is this legal position compatible with the host of antitrust cases we have read from professional sports? Would it permit the NCAA to justify the host of regulations we have already seen on student-athlete eligibility? Most important, would it permit the strict limits we are about to see on athletic scholarships and other compensation?

3. ATHLETES MARKET[o]

At one point in her *Law* decision, Judge Vratil responded to the NCAA's argument that its restricted earnings coach rule "preserves the spirit of amateurism" in college sports. The judge acknowledged that earlier precedents had afforded the NCAA "plenty of room under the antitrust law in order to preserve the amateur character of intercollegiate sports contests." She pointed out, though, that these cases were "about ensuring that college players—student-athletes—are amateurs; they are not about preserving the amateurism of coaches by capping their salaries ..." Indeed, Article 2.8 of the NCAA's own Manual defined amateurism just with reference to the athletes.

> Student-athletes shall be amateur in an intercollegiate sport, and their participation should be motivated primarily by education and by the physical, mental and social benefits to be derived. Student participation in intercollegiate athletics is an avocation, and student-athletes should be protected from exploitation by professional and commercial enterprises.

We saw earlier in this chapter the array of restrictions the NCAA has imposed on both players and colleges to ensure that students participate in college athletics simply as an educational "avocation," rather than for professional or commercial "exploitation." However, we have just read decisions that struck down NCAA restraints on what colleges can pay their coaches and how many of the games the students are playing can be offered to the networks to broadcast over the air. The question remains, then, why restraints on the players are to be treated as qualitatively different under the law.

One circuit court case that considered an antitrust challenge to such NCAA policies was *McCormack v. NCAA*, 845 F.2d 1338 (5th Cir.1988). This case involved a class action brought by a lawyer-alumnus of Southern Methodist University (SMU), who complained on behalf of the school's alumni, cheerleaders, and athletes about the "death penalty" the NCAA imposed on the SMU football program in 1981 for repeated

---

o. For an exploration of these issues, see Peter C. Carstensen & Paul Olszowka, *Antitrust Law, Student–Athletes, and the NCAA: Limiting the Scope and Conduct of Private Economic Regulation*, 1995 Wisconsin L. Rev. 545.

major infractions of NCAA rules prohibiting payments and extra benefits to athletes.[p] The Fifth Circuit spent most of its *McCormack* opinion doubting whether McCormack or the class he claimed to represent had standing to complain of an antitrust violation here. However, assuming for the sake of argument that at least the players might have standing to challenge NCAA restraints on compensation of student-athletes, the Fifth Circuit panel briefly addressed the merits of such a claim. After describing the *Board of Regents* decision and quoting the key passage in the Supreme Court's opinion that we also saw quoted in *Law* above, the *McCormack* panel stated:

> The NCAA markets college football as a product distinct from professional football. The eligibility rules create the product and allow its survival in the face of commercializing pressures. The goal of the NCAA is to integrate athletics with academics. Its requirements reasonably further this goal.

845 F.2d at 1344–45. The plaintiffs had pointed out that "the NCAA permits some compensation through scholarships and allows a student to be a professional in one sport and an amateur in another." The court was not persuaded that those factors "undermined the rationality of the eligibility requirement. That the NCAA has not distilled amateurism to its purest form does not mean that its attempts to maintain a mixture containing some amateur elements are unreasonable."

A more direct and substantial antitrust challenge to this key feature of NCAA policy was mounted by Ralph Nader's Public Citizens Litigation Group on behalf of Braxston Banks, a former Notre Dame football player. This suit targeted the NCAA eligibility rules that deny "amateur status" to any player who "enters into a professional draft or an agreement with an agent ... to negotiate a professional contract" (Article 12.1.1(f)). This is the rule that courts and legislatures attempted to enforce against agents to protect colleges from premature loss of their players (see Chapter 5).[q] The question posed in the *Banks* litigation is whether the underlying NCAA policy unreasonably deprives college players of the opportunity to participate in the draft and receive the advice and representation of an agent.

p. For the facts of the SMU case, see Chapter 9, and also David Whitford, *A Payroll to Meet: A Story of Greed, Corruption and Football at SMU* (New York: MacMillan, 1989).

q. Recall in particular, the case of Norby Walters and Lloyd Bloom, which is recounted in Chris Mortenson, *Playing for Keeps: How One Man Kept the Mob From Sinking Its Hooks Into Pro Football* (New York: Simon and Schuster, 1991). In fact, Walters and Bloom sought to have their criminal indictment quashed on the ground that the NCAA rules whose violations the agents and their clients had concealed were themselves illegal under antitrust law. The district court tersely rejected this argument in a decision that focused primarily on mail fraud issues. See *United States v. Walters & Bloom*, 711 F.Supp. 1435 (N.D.Ill.1989).

BANKS v. NCAA
United States Court of Appeals, Seventh Circuit, 1992.
977 F.2d 1081.

COFFEY, CIRCUIT JUDGE.

[Braxston Banks entered Notre Dame in 1986 as a highly rated football prospect. By the end of his freshman year he was the starting fullback on the varsity team. But Banks injured his knee early in his sophomore year and started only a handful of games during that season and the next one. Banks decided to sit out his entire senior year (1989) to give his knee a chance to recover fully. By that time, Banks' classmate, Anthony Johnson, had become Notre Dame's starting fullback and the top-rated NFL prospect at that position.

In the winter of 1990, Banks debated whether to turn professional with Johnson or to return to Notre Dame for a fifth year, for which he was eligible under NCAA rules and for which Notre Dame was ready to give him another year's full scholarship. After extensive discussions with NFL scouts and a player-agent known to his family, Banks decided in March 1990 to enter the NFL draft and to sign a representation agreement with the agent. To make himself eligible for the draft, the NFL required Banks to sign a form whereby he "irrevocably renounced any and all remaining college eligibility." As far as the NCAA was concerned, its own By-laws 12.2.4 and 12.3 dictated that either of Banks' actions—entering the draft or signing an agent representation contract—would cost Banks his future college eligibility.

Unfortunately, the condition of Banks' knee hampered his performance at the NFL tryout camp in Indianapolis in early April. Thus no team selected Banks in any of the twelve rounds of the late April draft, and no team was willing to sign him to a free-agent contract. Though Banks returned to Notre Dame in the summer of 1990 to finish his degree, the NCAA would not give him a waiver from its rules to permit Banks to play for Notre Dame that fall. As a result, Banks launched this antitrust suit against the NCAA. The judge granted the NCAA's motion under Rule 12(b)(6) for summary dismissal because of Banks' failure to state a valid antitrust claim.]

* * *

IV. RULE 12(B)(6) DISMISSAL OF A RULE-OF-REASON CASE

Banks' primary contention on appeal is that because the record is not thoroughly developed, it was inappropriate for the district court to decide that the NCAA no-draft and no-agent rules were pro-competitive in ruling on a Rule 12(b)(6) motion to dismiss.... The district court decided the case not on the basis of the relative anti-competitive effect of the rules versus the pro-competitive impact, but on the ground of Banks' absolute failure to allege an anti-competitive effect.... Since the district judge's decision was based on Banks' failure to allege an anti-competitive effect on an identifiable market, the argument that the court improperly determined that the rules were reasonable on a motion to dismiss is without merit.

V. THE VALIDITY OF THE ANTITRUST CLAIM

* * *

[Plaintiff's] allegations identify two markets: (1) NCAA football players who enter the draft and/or employ an agent and (2) college institutions that are members of the NCAA. Another reading of the complaint might even have deduced a third market, the NFL player recruitment market. But regardless of how charitably the complaint is read, it has failed to define an anti-competitive effect of the alleged restraints on the markets.

The dissent reasons that Banks has alleged that the NCAA no-draft rule has an anti-competitive effect in the market for college football players. The dissent claims this anti-competitive effect is the no-draft rule "foreclosing players 'from choosing a major college football team based on the willingness of the institution to waive or change [the no-draft] rule.'" This allegation can at best be described as inaccurate and further fails to allege an anti-competitive impact. First, as Banks states in his amended complaint, the NCAA has adopted the no-draft, no-agent, and other substantive rules to which all NCAA member institutions "have agreed, and do in fact, adhere." Contrary to Banks' erroneous allegation, an NCAA member institution may not waive or change the no-draft rule at its discretion, for it is rather obvious that only the National Collegiate Athletic Association can waive or change one of its substantive rules. Any school that sought to waive or change the rules would forfeit its ability to participate in NCAA sanctioned events.

Second, as the district court held, the complaint has failed to allege an anti-competitive impact. The failure results from Banks' inability to explain how the no-draft rule restrains trade in the college football labor market. The NCAA Rules seek to promote fair competition, encourage the educational pursuits of student-athletes and prevent commercialism....

As the Supreme Court in *Board of Regents* stated: "most of the regulatory controls of the NCAA [are] a justifiable means of fostering competition among the amateur athletic teams and therefore are pro-competitive because they enhance public interest in intercollegiate athletics." The Court further explained:

> The NCAA seeks to market a particular brand of football—college football. The identification of this "product" with an academic tradition differentiates college football from and makes it more popular than professional sports to which it might otherwise be comparable, such as, for example, minor league baseball. In order to preserve the character and quality of the "product," athletes must not be paid, must be required to attend class, and the like. And the integrity of the "product" cannot be preserved except by mutual agreement; if an institution adopted such restrictions unilaterally (restrictions on eligibility rules), its effectiveness as a competitor on the playing field might soon be destroyed. Thus, the NCAA plays a

vital role in enabling college football to preserve its character, and as a result enables a product to be marketed which might otherwise be unavailable. In performing this role, its actions widen consumer choice—not only the choices available to sports fans but also those available to athletes—and hence can be viewed as procompetitive.

468 U.S. at 102.

The no-draft rule has no more impact on the market for college football players than other NCAA eligibility requirements such as grades, semester hours carried, or requiring a high school diploma. They all constitute eligibility requirements essential to participation in NCAA sponsored amateur athletic competition. Banks might just as well have alleged that only permitting a student five calendar years in which to participate in four seasons of intercollegiate athletics restrains trade. Banks' allegation that the no-draft rule restrains trade is absurd. None of the NCAA rules affecting college football eligibility restrain trade in the market for college players because the NCAA does not exist as a minor league training ground for future NFL players but rather to provide an opportunity for competition among amateur students pursuing a collegiate education.[12] Because the no-draft rule represents a desirable and legitimate attempt "to keep university athletics from becoming professionalized to the extent that profit making objectives would overshadow educational objectives," the no-draft rule and other like NCAA regulations preserve the bright line of demarcation between college and "play for pay" football. We consider college football players as student-athletes simultaneously pursuing academic degrees that will prepare them to enter the employment market in non-athletic occupations, and hold that the regulations of the NCAA are designed to preserve the honesty and integrity of intercollegiate athletics and foster fair competition among the participating amateur college students.

In order for the NCAA Rules to be considered a restraint of trade in violation of § 1 of the Sherman Act, Banks must allege that the no-draft and no-agent rules are terms of employment that diminish competition in the employment market (i.e., college football).

The dissent refers to NCAA member colleges as "purchasers of labor" in the college football player market and the players as "suppliers" in this market.[13] After likening colleges to "purchasers of labor,"

---

12. This conclusion is buttressed by the fact that a very small number of college athletes go on to participate in professional athletics. Of the over 12,000 Division I-A college football players, less than 300 go on to the NFL each year. In fact, it has been calculated that of the elite 336 players drafted each year, only 49 percent make NFL teams and after 5 years only 35 percent are still with an NFL team.

13. We disagree with Banks' allegation in paragraph 22(c) of his Amended Complaint that the NCAA no-draft and no-agent Rules give the college player only one realistic chance of being drafted in the NFL, because the college player (1) can enter the draft any time during his college career (Tommy Maddox of UCLA was just drafted by Denver although he had two more years of eligibility); (2) enter the draft, then play for another league like the CFL, WFL, or ARENA or even sit out for a year and then reenter the draft (Bo Jackson was a first round draft choice of Tampa Bay, but he chose to play baseball instead, the next year he was drafted by the Los Angeles Raiders

Affirmed.

FLAUM, CIRCUIT JUDGE, concurring in part and dissenting in part.

* * *

As the NCAA concedes, Banks defined two markets in his complaint, only one of which it is necessary to address here: the nationwide labor market for college football players. NCAA member colleges are the purchasers of labor in this market, and the players are the suppliers. The players agree to compete in football games sponsored by the colleges, games that typically garner the colleges a profit, in exchange for tuition, room, board and other benefits.

It is hardly a revelation that colleges fiercely compete for the most promising high school football players—the players who, incidentally, are most likely to feel constrained by the challenged rules two or three years down the line. If the no-draft rule were scuttled, colleges that promised their athletes the opportunity to test the waters in the NFL draft before their eligibility expired, and return if things didn't work out, would be more attractive to athletes than colleges that declined to offer the same opportunity. The no-draft rule eliminates this potential element of competition among colleges, the purchasers of labor in the college football labor market. It categorically rules out a term of employment that players, the suppliers of labor in that market, would find advantageous.

* * *

It should come as no surprise that the no-draft rule operates to the detriment of the players, and that colleges benefit from the fact that their athletes feel tied to the institution for four years. Consider, for example, athletes who are known in the vernacular as "bubble" players. These athletes are excellent competitors at the collegiate level, but for various reasons are considered less than certain NFL prospects. Bubble players who wish to market their wares in the professional market after their sophomore or junior year will forego entry into the NFL draft because, if they are not selected (or fail to join a team after being selected), the rule will prevent them from returning to college to hone their skills and try again in subsequent years. See Note, *Sherman Act Invalidation of the NCAA Amateurism Rules*, 105 Harv. L. Rev. 1299, 1311 (1992). The rule permits colleges to squeeze out of their players one or two more years of service, years the colleges might have lost had the ability to enter the draft without consequence to eligibility been the subject of bargaining between athletes and colleges. The rule thereby distorts the "price" of labor in the college football labor market to the detriment of players.

The NCAA disputes this characterization, maintaining that the no-draft rule is not "anticompetitive" as the term is employed under the Sherman Act. At the heart of its argument is the contention that "there is no price competition as such among colleges for players because the 'price,' the value of grant-in-aid, is determined by the school's tuition, room, and board, not by the supply of and demand for players." This analysis of the college football labor market is partially correct; in that market, players exchange their labor for in-kind benefits, not cash. At least ideally. But see Johnson, *Defense Against the NCAA*, U.S. News & World Rep., Jan. 13, 1992, at 25 (improper cash payments made to football players at Auburn University); Johnson, *Playing for Pay in Texas*, Newsweek, Mar. 16, 1987, at 32 (same at Southern Methodist University).

It is unrealistic, however, to suggest that the value of those in-kind benefits is limited solely to tuition, room and board. If this were true, the best football players would attend the most expensive private universities that would admit them, for these universities would offer, under the NCAA's analysis, the most "valuable" compensation for their services. Assuming some regional loyalties, private colleges such as Syracuse University, the University of Southern California, and Notre Dame would consistently outrecruit public colleges such as Penn State, UCLA and the University of Michigan. As anyone familiar with college football well knows, this is not the case. The reason is simple. Athletes look to more than tuition, room and board when determining which college has offered them the most attractive package of in-kind benefits. Some athletes look primarily to the reputation of a particular program or coach as a "feeder" into the NFL; others believe that the quality of a university's academic program and the commitment of the coaching staff to scholarly pursuits is more important. Some athletes look to whether a college will offer them a cushy, high-paying job during the summer or school year; others might be attracted by state-of-the-art training facilities. And some athletes, if given the chance, would look to whether a college would allow them to enter the NFL draft and return if they did not join a professional team.

All of these things—with the exception of the last item—are "terms of employment" that currently sweeten the pot for athletes choosing among college football programs. They provide, apart from tuition, room and board, the means by which colleges, as purchasers of labor, attract and compensate their players, the suppliers of labor. That the medium of exchange is non-monetary does not alter the fact that these benefits constitute the "price" of labor in the college football market, or that the categorical elimination of one of those benefits harms competition in that market. The NCAA's protestations notwithstanding, there can be no doubt that Banks has alleged an anticompetitive effect in a relevant market.

* * *

Banks easily clears the threshold ["of connecting the injury claimed to the purposes of the antitrust laws"]. The no-draft rule, as noted, is anticompetitive because it constitutes an agreement among colleges to eliminate an element of competition in the college football labor market. The purposes of the antitrust laws are served when employers are prevented from tampering with the employment market in this precise way. "Just as antitrust law seeks to preserve the free market opportunities of buyers and sellers of goods, so also it seeks to do the same for buyers and sellers of employment services...." Banks' injury—namely, the revocation of his eligibility and consequent loss of his athletic scholarship during his final year at Notre Dame—"flows from" the precise anticompetitive aspects of the NCAA rules that he set out in his complaint.

The NCAA also raises the issue of harm to consumers; it contends that Banks' complaint is deficient because it does not "reasonably support the inference that consumers are harmed by the operation of the no-draft and no-agent rules." Whether harm to consumers is the sine qua non of antitrust injury is an issue over which there is currently a split in this circuit. Some of our cases hold that a plaintiff, to satisfy the antitrust injury requirement, must demonstrate that the challenged practice causing him harm also harms consumers by reducing output or raising prices. *Stamatakis Indus., Inc. v. King*, 965 F.2d 469, 471 (7th Cir.1992); *Chicago Professional Sports Ltd. Partnership v. National Basketball Ass'n*, 961 F.2d 667, 670 (7th Cir.1992). Others hold that application of the antitrust laws "does not depend in each particular case upon the ultimate demonstrable consumer effect." *Fishman v. Estate of Wirtz*, 807 F.2d 520, 536 (7th Cir.1986); see also *Chicago Professional Sports*, 961 F.2d at 677 (Cudahy, J., concurring).

One can dispense with the NCAA's contention without choosing sides in this dispute. To see why, it is important first to identify the consumers and the market at issue in this case. By "consumers," the NCAA apparently means people who watch college football. These individuals certainly are consumers in the college football product market, but the market at issue here is the college football labor market, and the NCAA member colleges are consumers in that market. It would be counterintuitive to require Banks to demonstrate that the no-draft and no-agent rules harm the colleges, the very entities that established those rules. I doubt very strongly that the rule laid out in *Chicago Professional Sports*, to the extent it is valid elsewhere, was intended to apply in this context. Concerted action among consumers that lowers prices harms competition as much as concerted action among producers that raises prices. The distinction should be irrelevant to any discussion of antitrust injury. Professors Areeda and Turner, when discussing the right of laborers to challenge antitrust violations in the labor market, put things nicely:

> It would be perverse ... to hold that the very object of the law's solicitude and the persons most directly concerned—perhaps the only persons concerned—could not challenge the restraint.... The standing of such plaintiffs is undoubted and seldom challenged.

Banks has alleged that the NCAA rules harm competition to the detriment of producers in the college football labor market, and that his injuries are directly related to that harm. This is sufficient to establish "antitrust injury" in this context.

I add here a caveat to avert any potential misunderstandings. My point is only that Banks has properly alleged an anticompetitive effect in a relevant market and has demonstrated antitrust injury, and hence that his damages action should survive the NCAA's motion to dismiss. But this is, of course, only the first step. To ultimately prevail, Banks also must demonstrate, under the rule of reason, that the no-agent and no-draft rules, despite their anticompetitive effects, are not "justifiable means of fostering competition among amateur athletic teams and therefore procompetitive" on the whole. It may very well be that the no-draft and no-agent rules are essential to the survival of college football as a distinct and viable product, in which case Banks would lose. A lively debate has arisen among those who have already considered this matter. I opt not to join the fray here, for I think it unwise to weigh pro-and anticompetitive effects under the rule of reason on a motion to dismiss.

Today's decision, by holding that Banks has not alleged that the rules are anticompetitive in the first instance, deprives him of the opportunity to join this issue on remand. As I have discussed, it is difficult to reconcile this holding with a sound reading of Banks' complaint. On a broader level, I am also concerned that today's decision—unintentionally, to be sure, for it suggests that a "more artfully drafted complaint" could have alleged an anticompetitive effect in this market—will provide comfort to the NCAA's incredulous assertion that its eligibility rules are "noncommercial." The NCAA would have us believe that intercollegiate athletic contests are about spirit, competition, camaraderie, sportsmanship, hard work (which they certainly are) ... and nothing else. Players play for the fun of it, colleges get a kick out of entertaining the student body and alumni, but the relationship between players and colleges is positively noncommercial. It is consoling to buy into these myths, for they remind us of a more innocent era—an era where recruiting scandals were virtually unknown, where amateurism was more a reality than an ideal, and where post-season bowl games were named for commodities, not corporations. On the flip side, it is disquieting to think of college football as a business, of colleges as the purchasers of labor, and of athletes as the suppliers.

The NCAA continues to purvey, even in this case, an outmoded image of intercollegiate sports that no longer jibes with reality. The times have changed. College football is a terrific American institution that generates abundant nonpecuniary benefits for players and fans, but it is also a vast commercial venture that yields substantial profits for colleges. The games provide fans with entertaining contests to watch, and athletes with an opportunity to display and develop their strength, skills and character, but they are saleable products nonetheless. An athlete's participation offers all of the rewards that attend vigorous competition in organized sport, but it is also labor, labor for which the athlete is recompensed. The no-draft and no-agent rules may, ultimately, pass muster under the rule of reason. But, putting the adequacy of Banks' complaint to the side, contending that they have no commercial effect on competition in the college football labor market, or that there is no market of that type at all, is chimerical:

> The true stake is this decades-long gentleman's agreement between the NFL and the college powers-that-be that has kept all but a handful of football playing collegians from turning pro before their four-year use to their schools is exhausted. The pros get a free farm system that supplies them with well-trained, much publicized employees. The colleges get to keep their players the equivalent of barefoot and pregnant.

Klein, *College Football: Keeping 'em Barefoot*, Wall St. J., Sept. 4, 1987, at 15.

When confronted with the clash between soothing nostalgia and distressing reality, it is oftentimes difficult to resist the call of tennis champion Andre Agassi, who when hawking cameras off the court tells us that "image is everything." But we must remember that Agassi's domain, at least in this instance, is television. What may be true there is decidedly not under the lens of the antitrust laws. Having found that Banks has cleared the threshold of alleging an anticompetitive effect in a relevant market, I would reverse the district court's dismissal of his damages action and remand for further proceedings.

Questions for Discussion

1. Was the holding in *Banks*[r] based upon a deficiency in pleadings, or upon the court's view that the nature of college sports made it impossible for a student-athlete to formulate an antitrust claim against the NCAA's amateurism and academic eligibility rules? If the former, how should Banks have crafted his complaint to satisfy the court? If the latter, do you agree with that substantive position?

2. The *Banks* majority argued that if the NCAA's "no draft" and "no agent" rules were held illegal under § 1, the same fate must befall all other NCAA eligibility requirements. If a court found unreasonable the NCAA's bar against Banks' returning for his senior year, must the same antitrust verdict follow for the NCAA rules that limit Notre Dame's (and other colleges') financial expenditures for athletes to reimbursement of standard educational expenses? Or can these two features of NCAA "amateurism" be distinguished under the antitrust Rule of Reason?

3. Should the long-standing NCAA ban on payments to college athletes be maintained,[s] or should each school determine whether this is how it wants to conduct its athletic program? Consider these two analogies to the situation of college athletes. Suppose that the owners of a professional sports

---

r. An almost identical suit was resolved in the same manner as *Banks* by a district court in Tennessee. See *Gaines v. NCAA*, 746 F.Supp. 738 (M.D.Tenn.1990). For a trenchant critique of the district court decision in *Banks*, see Ethan Lock, *Unreasonable NCAA Eligibility Rules Send Braxston Banks Truckin*, 20 Capital Univ. L. Rev. 643 (1991).

s. For contrasting views on this question, compare Goldman, *Sports and Antitrust*, note j above (no), with Rodney K. Smith, *An Academic Game Plan for Reforming Big–Time Intercollegiate Athletics*, 67 Denver U. L. Rev. 213, at 274–77 (yes).

league (one without a players union) adopted a league-wide policy limiting the salaries and bonuses that teams could pay to their draft picks. Would this policy be acceptable under the antitrust Rule of Reason (assuming that the league is not a single entity)? Alternatively, suppose that the nation's universities agreed on the amount and terms of academic scholarships they would give to students. On the amount of money they would pay to teaching and research assistants? On the amount of money that teaching hospitals would offer to prospective interns and residents? Would any such intercollegiate agreement be acceptable under antitrust law? See *United States v. Brown Univ., et al*, 5 F.3d 658 (3d Cir.1993). Is there anything distinctive about the student-athlete, by comparison to these examples?[t]

As the *Banks* court acknowledges, the case illustrates a phenomenon of broader significance for the role of sports in higher education. Only a tiny number of college athletes can make a career of professional sports. The odds of a Division I college player making the cut as a rookie on a professional team are one in 75 in football and one in 70 in basketball.[u] Fortunately, Banks had the ability and motivation to return to college and secure a degree to equip him for a different career path. Too often, though, that is not the result of the student-athlete's stay in college.

With respect to the specific NCAA rule at issue in *Banks*, there have been some changes made since the litigation. As mentioned earlier, the 1994 Convention accepted a Committee recommendation to allow basketball players to opt into the NBA draft, but to regain their college eligibility within 30 days after the draft if they did not like the point at which they had been selected or the contract offer made by the drafting team. (The college football programs blocked any such changes for their players, such as Banks.) Eligibility would still be lost if the player hired an "agent" to advise him about whether to go into the draft and/or to negotiate favorable offers with the drafting club. In 1997, though, the NCAA significantly diluted that option for basketball players, after the NBA rules were changed to give the team drafting an underclassman the exclusive right to that player until one year after his college eligibility had expired. The NCAA now says that if a basketball player opts in and is actually selected by an NBA team (even with the last pick in the entire draft), his college eligibility can never be retrieved.

This particular NCAA rule is not, however, triggered in baseball or hockey, because in those sports players (even prior to college graduation) do not have to *elect* to be part of the draft selection pool. That option can significantly enhance the bargaining leverage of a draft pick, as illustrated by the experience of Brien Taylor, a young high school graduate

---

t. For an in-depth analysis of these issues and comparisons, see Matthew J. Mitten, *University Price Competition For Elite Students and Athletes: Illusions and Realities*, 36 South Texas L. Rev. 59 (1995).

u. These odds were calculated from 1989 figures presented in Wilford S. Bailey & Taylor D. Littleton, *Athletics and Academe: An Anatomy of Abuses and a Prescription for Reform* 84 (New York: MacMillan, 1991).

selected by the Yankees as the first pick in the 1991 baseball draft. After a summer of negotiating with the Yankees (via his mother, assisted by "family advisor" Scott Boras), Taylor, on the eve of his final enrollment date for junior college, extracted a contract from the Yankees with what was then an unprecedented $1.5 million signing bonus. The source of this leverage for Taylor (and other baseball draftees) is not so much the NCAA rules that permit the players still to go to college to play, but rather the Major League Baseball rules that cost a drafting team like the Yankees their pick if he does choose to go to college. Thus, in the winter of 1992, the major league owners unilaterally amended their draft rules to extend and preserve the drafting team's right to such high school picks throughout the player's college career. However, even though the draft itself is not part of the MLB collective agreement, baseball's labor arbitrator George Nicolau ruled that this action by the owners violated the agreement because it infringed upon the rights of veteran players. Increasing the value of a rookie draft pick that might have to be given up by a team signing a higher level free agent would likely reduce somewhat the salaries that other teams would bid to move a free agent.

In *Banks*, the Seventh Circuit majority relied heavily on the Supreme Court's oft-cited dictum in *Board of Regents*—that restraints on college dealings with athletes (rather than with television networks) are designed to develop and market college sports as an activity played by student amateurs—a product that is clearly demarcated from professional sports in consumer appeal. From the very beginning[v] the NCAA philosophy has been that

> [a]n amateur in athletics is one that enters and takes part in athletic contests purely in obedience to the play impulse or for the satisfaction of purely play motives and for the exercise, training, and social pleasures derived. The natural or primary attitude of mind and motives in play determines amateurism.

This philosophy initially led the NCAA to prohibit "the offering of inducements to players to enter colleges or universities because of their athletic abilities and of supporting or maintaining players while students on account of their athletic abilities." As late as 1935, the NCAA Code on Recruiting and Subsidizing of Athletes banned participation in intercollegiate athletics by anyone who had ever "received a loan, scholarship aid, remission of fees, or employment, primarily because he is an athlete, through channels not open to non-athletes equally with athletes." Only after extensive struggles in the late 1940s and early 1950s did the current NCAA regime emerge, under which member schools are permitted to offer scholarships that pay student-athletes their tuition, fees, books, and room and board, supplemented by general need-based financial assistance, and often by extensive and costly academic tutoring. In

---

v. For an account of the historical evolution of the NCAA's philosophy of amateurism, see Lawrence, *Unsportsmanlike Conduct*, note a above.

light of this evolution of its policy, can the NCAA claim that college athletes are truly "amateurs" for purposes of antitrust law, and that the product it offers to fans is distinctive in that respect from professional sports? Or are college athletes in the revenue sports (Division I men's basketball and Division I–A football) really professionals who, instead of being paid cash in amounts based on free market negotiations, are paid in kind, through fixed amounts of educational services determined by a producer-employer trade association? At the same time, suppose that a court were to find illegal under the Sherman Antitrust Act the battery of rules in the NCAA Manual specifying the "amateur" flavor of college sports. Does it follow that the "academic" features of NCAA eligibility rules—e.g., Proposition 48—would also be legally improper?

On the way to reaching its *Banks* ruling that denied college players antitrust rights against the NCAA, the majority asserted that student-athletes were not *employees* (and thus there was no labor market in which colleges might have been competing for their services). The contrary view, of course, is that the presence of NCAA rules barring schools from competing for athletes with cash payments or other non-scholarship benefits actually demonstrated that the absence of a current market here is the product of the NCAA restraints on trade, rather than the inherent nature of college-student-athlete relationships. Whatever one's verdict on that score, if the *Banks* decision were to be followed and extended (in particular, by the Supreme Court), the successors to Braxston Banks would end up with significantly fewer legal rights than the heirs to Anthony Brown and his development squad football players in *Brown v. Pro Football, Inc.*, 518 U.S. 231 (1996), which we read in Chapter 3. College football (and other) players would have no rights under labor as well as antitrust law (or constitutional law, post-*Tarkanian*) to address their concerns with NCAA policies.

The question of whether an athlete playing intercollegiate sports for a college or a scholarship should be treated as an *employee* of the institution arises in a variety of contexts. For example, as we shall see in Chapter 13, a severely injured and permanently disabled athlete may want to file a claim for workers' compensation on the ground that the injury "arose out of and in the course of employment." See *Rensing v. Indiana State Univ.*, 437 N.E.2d 78 (Ind.App.1982), aff'd, 444 N.E.2d 1170 (Ind.1983). Similarly, under current income tax law (§ 117(b)(2) of the Internal Revenue Code), the portion of an athletic scholarship that covers room and board, but not tuition, fees, and books, is deemed to be *taxable* income for services performed.[w]

Turning now to the National Labor Relations Act, if a group of student-athletes are employees, they would have the right under § 7 to "engage in concerted activities for purposes of collective bargaining or

---

w. See David Williams, note m above, at 623–24 (1991).

mutual aid or protection"—i.e., the same right to organize, negotiate, and strike as professional athletes. As employees, college athletes would also be entitled to minimum wage, occupational safety, and the host of other protections now offered workers under federal and state *employment* law. There are no NLRB decisions addressing the status of college athletes under this law. Until recently, though, any such legal option would likely have been precluded by the precedent of *Cedars–Sinai Medical Center and Cedars–Sinai Housestaff Ass'n*, 223 NLRB 251 (1976). There, the Nixon–Ford National Labor Relations Board ruled that because medical residency programs were designed to provide in-house training for future doctors, the residents could not be deemed employees for purposes of collective bargaining with the hospital about the pay and conditions under which they worked (often for 80 hours or more per week). However, a number of state Public Employee Relations Boards (PERBs) have reached the opposite conclusion with respect to residents working in publicly-owned hospitals (which are not covered by the NLRA), and the Clinton Board will be readdressing this question in a case involving the merger of a public and a private hospital in Boston. Indeed, another analogous case is also working its way up to the Labor Board, involving unfair labor practice charges filed by a graduate assistants organization against Yale University: the University asserts that graduate assistants are there for educational purposes only, but the assistants assert that they have a right to negotiate collectively the pay and conditions provided for the teaching work they do for the school.

For our purposes here, there are two questions about the interplay of law and sports law policy. With respect to each of these categories—medical residents, graduate assistants, and college football players—should the NLRB maintain or remove this hard-and-fast line between educational objectives and labor (or employment) law rights? Next, consider the real-life situation of college football players, as compared not just to professional players, but also to college cafeteria workers (who are unionized at Yale and elsewhere). How much time does each group spend "working" in their respective roles; how much control is exercised by the organization over the kind of work they do and how much direct supervision is given to their performance; how mandatory are the conditions established for the rewards offered for the work; and how much net value does the organization itself realize from the work each group performs?

The public policy issues posed by college sports are not simply whether courts should interpret federal antitrust and/or labor law so as to afford college athletes (as well as college coaches and broadcasters) greater legal leverage in securing better deals from big-time athletic programs. The more fundamental question is whether at least some college athletes are actually being treated unfairly under the current "amateur" regime.

On the surface, the answer seems clear to many. Economists, for example, have applied to college sports the same economic analysis that has been used to appraise the labor markets in professional team sports.[x] One first determines the marginal *athletic* productivity of individual players—i.e., their contribution to team victories—and then their marginal *revenue* productivity—the impact of victories on team revenues. One can then compare the figure for the player's marginal revenue productivity with the actual compensation by the team to the player. Such a mode of analysis has long been used to document the huge differences made by the move from the reserve system to free agency in baseball in empowering players to extract this economic premium for their talent, rather than leave it in the pockets of owners.

When that same kind of analysis was done for college sports, it was estimated that in the late 1980s, each additional victory in football earned the school $300,000, and in men's basketball $45,000. For football players selected in the NFL draft during that same period, their marginal revenue productivity while at college was approximately $500,000 a season, while for basketball players selected in the NBA draft, the figure was $1 million. Patrick Ewing is estimated to have generated $12 million in additional revenues for Georgetown during his four years there in the early 1980s, when overall college basketball revenues were significantly lower than they are today. Obviously, there is a huge gap between the economic value of such players to their college programs, and the cost of their athletic scholarships—ranging from $10,000 to $30,000 a season, depending on whether the tuition being waived is at a public or private college. Indeed, it is not just financial revenues, but even the number and quality of admission applications that can rise with athletic renown. Thus, Patrick Ewing also helped generate a 47% increase in Georgetown applications and a 40 point rise in its freshman SAT scores, while Doug Flutie's stay at Boston College sent its SAT scores up by 110 points. These empirical findings provide further support for those who have long proposed that athletes should be offered at least a modest stipend over and above their tuition and room and board. This would, in effect, "pay" the players the money that would allow them to enjoy the amenities of college life, in return for working 30 or so hours a week training for, practicing, and playing football and basketball games that may generate $15 to $20 million in profits for their schools.

Implementation of such a stipend policy would require adoption of a new NCAA rule that spelled out the amounts and conditions of any such payments permitted by member-institutions. Indeed, there is a significant legal obstacle to the NCAA taking any such legislative action. Once schools began to make some direct cash payments to athletes for playing their sport, it would be far more difficult for their lawyers to invoke the

---

x. See Robert W. Brown, *An Estimate of the Rent Generated by a Premium College Football Player*, 31 Economic Inquiry 671 (1993); Robert W. Brown, *Measuring Cartel Rents in the College Basketball Recruitment Market*, 26 Applied Economics 27 (1994); and Arthur Padilla and David Baumer, *Big Time College Sports: Management and Economic Issues*, J. Sport & Soc. Issues 123 (May, 1994).

rubric of "amateur" college sports as a defense against antitrust challenges. (It may not be that plausible for the NCAA to argue that college sports still are a distinctive product offered to consumer fans because they are just a "little" professional.) If the courts (with or without such a new stipend rule) were to rethink *McCormack* and *Banks* and strike down the NCAA's *amateur* (though not necessarily its *academic*) regulations, this would create free agent bidding by colleges for players as we now watch in professional sports every off-season. Star high school football and basketball players may well end up with much the same kind of signing bonuses that are now regularly paid to high school baseball players when they go directly into the professional leagues. Unless student-athletes were also judged to be "employees" under the NLRA, there could be no labor union empowered to waive any such antitrust rights by agreeing to a salary cap for college programs.

There is, however, a fundamental difference between college football, for example, and major league baseball. Whereas baseball's historic reserve system put more money into the pockets of wealthy team owners (such as the Dodgers' Walter O'Malley and the Cardinals' Gussie Busch), NCAA rules permit "exploitation" of star college athletes by not-for-profit educational institutions such as Notre Dame and Florida. Big-time college sports has become a highly commercialized enterprise, generating $40 million a year for the most successful programs, and $2.5 billion in total for NCAA members. However, the revenues thereby generated (almost all by football and men's basketball) go into the university's coffers to be spent on its programs.

The vast majority of such revenues are spent on *athletic* rather than on *academic* programs. (The exception that corroborates the rule is Notre Dame, which has dedicated all the revenues from its lucrative NBC television contract to the school's academic life.) Even universities such as Michigan, which not only fills its 106,000–seat football stadium, but also generates sizable returns from its men's basketball team, has occasionally experienced million-dollar deficits in its overall athletic budget. Part of this deficit is due to large expenditures made for athletic department salaries and amenities. Most of the money, though, goes to support the other 15 to 30 athletic programs offered by the school. When star football and basketball players are limited to $10,000–$30,000 scholarships, which represents only a fraction of their actual economic value to the school, the college is then able to award the same scholarships to marginal players on these teams, as well as to all the players on non-revenue-producing teams. (Ironically, it is the latter two categories, not the first, that typically use that scholarship to earn an academic degree.[y]) In fact, at many schools the general student body also benefits

---

[y]. Indeed, one reform proposal would "pay" college athletes by giving an additional sixth year of scholarship assistance to those who may have exhausted their athletic eligibility (which can include a fifth "redshirt" year), but have not yet received a college degree. See Rodney K. Smith, *When Ignorance Is Not Bliss: In Search of Racial and Gender Equity In Intercollegiate Athletics*, 61 Missouri L. Rev. 329 (1996). Such a measure, which is now barred by NCAA rules, poses the same distributional questions as are noted in the text.

by gaining access to elaborate facilities that they can use to play intramural sports.

These features of college sports raise quite different distributional issues than what we saw earlier with the owner-player conflicts in professional sports. The vast majority of college football and men's basketball players are from African–American and/or lower income families. Both of these demographic categories are significantly under-represented in the general university student body, and among those playing non-revenue sports. In effect, the current NCAA rules produce a transfer of the wealth generated by poor and/or black students playing revenue-producing college sports such as football, to middle and upper class white student-athletes playing sports such as tennis. However, before making one's judgment about the "equity" of this result, we need to read the materials in the next chapter about an even more fundamental redistribution that the law has produced in the world of college sports.

Chapter Eleven

INTERCOLLEGIATE SPORTS: GENDER EQUITY[a]

No feature of college sports—perhaps of any part of the sports world—has witnessed a greater impact from the law than the surge in athletic opportunities and resources for women student-athletes over the last quarter century. In the early 1970s, only a small share of student-athletes were female, and they received just two percent of the athletic budget. Women were much more likely to be found in cheerleader groups on the sidelines than competing on the playing field itself. Women's sports in college did not even come within the purview of the NCAA. Instead, there was a separate and severely underfunded Association of Intercollegiate Athletic Women (AIAW).

Then, in 1972, the Congress passed and President Nixon signed an Education Amendment Act that included a new Title IX.

> No person ... shall, on the basis of sex, be excluded from participation in, be denied the benefit of, or be subjected to discrimination under any education program or activity receiving federal financial assistance.

In 1974, the Congress rejected an amendment from Republican Senator John Tower (and one that was pressed for by the NCAA leadership) that would have excluded revenue-generating college sports from the purview of Title IX's coverage of "education program or activity." In the late 1970s, President Carter's administration issued Regulations and Policy Interpretations designed to flesh out Title IX's implications for sports in college and high school.

---

[a]. Popular accounts of the emergence of women in sports are Mariah Burton Nelson, *Are We Winning Yet? How Women Are Changing Sports and How Sports Are Changing Women* (New York: Random House, 1991), and David F. Salter, *Crashing the Old Boys Network: The Tragedies and Triumphs of Girls and Women in Sports,* (Westport, Conn.: Praeger, 1996). A thoughtful analysis of the philosophical complexities of gender equality in sports is Robert Simon, *Fair Play in Sports, Values and Society* (Boulder, Colo. Westview Press, 1991), in particular Chapter 6, "Sex Equality in Sports." Deborah Rhode, *Gender and Justice*, 300–04 (Cambridge, Mass.: Harvard University Press, 1989), situates the issues posed by women, sports, and law within broader legal and feminist debates about gender discrimination.

However, in the early 1980s, the Supreme Court secured for sports essentially the same result that Senator Tower had been aiming at. In *Grove City College v. Bell*, 465 U.S. 555 (1984), the Court read Title IX as governing only the specific college programs that received federal financial assistance—funding that was not offered to the athletic departments. Not until the Civil Rights Restoration Act of 1987 (20 U.S.C.A. § 1681, et seq. (1988)) explicitly extended Title IX's coverage to *all* the programs of an educational institution that received *any* federal aid (including grants on loans to its students) did Title IX come fully into play for college sports. Then, in the early 1990s, the Supreme Court sharply raised the legal stakes in these disputes by permitting private suits for damages and attorney fees by any woman asserting that she had been personally harmed by the school's violation of Title IX. See *Franklin v. Gwinnett County Public Schools*, 503 U.S. 60 (1992) (involving a high school student's claim of sexual harassment by a teacher). This set off a wave of Title IX suits in the mid-1990s, with the plaintiffs winning almost all of the judicial rulings.[b]

A quarter century after Title IX was first enacted, the proponents of women's sports seemed to have won the legal battle, as well as much of the war inside the athletic departments. As of 1996, more than 35% of high school and college athletes were women (though still receiving less than 25% of the overall athletic budget). By this time, though, such gains had intensified the efforts of women to secure the same 50% share of athletic positions that they make up of the general student body, as well as the resistance of male groups who have experienced cost-conscious college administrators pursuing this more equal female-male athletic ratio by cutting back on the number of men's teams and positions. The debate about Title IX provides an important new perspective on the world of college sports, and also a valuable window into the broader social debate about the values and trade-offs in anti-discrimination and affirmative action policies.

b. Title IX has recently generated even more voluminous literature than it has litigation. The major pieces include Diane Heckman, *Women & Athletics: A Twenty Year Perspective on Title IX*, 9 U. of Miami Enter. & Sports L. Rev. 21 (1992); B. Glenn George, *Miles to Go and Promises to Keep: A Case Study in Title IX*, 64 U. Colorado L. Rev. 535 (1993); Diane Heckman, *The Explosion of Title IX Legal Activity in Intercollegiate Athletics During 1992–93: Defining the "Equal Opportunity" Standard*, 3 Detroit College of Law Rev. 953 (1994); Jill K. Johnson, *Title IX and Intercollegiate Athletics: Current Judicial Interpretation of the Standards of Compliance*, 74 Boston U. L. Rev. 533 (1994); Catherine Pieroneck, *A Clash of Titans: College Football v. Title IX*, 20 J. Coll. & Univ. L. 351 (1994); Melody Harris, *Hitting 'Em Where It Hurts: Using Title IX Litigation to Bring Gender Equity to Athletics*, 72 Denver U. L. Rev. 57 (1994); Jennifer L. Henderson, *Gender Equity in Intercollegiate Athletics: A Commitment to Fairness*, 5 Seton Hall J. Sport L. 133 (1995); B. Glenn George, *Who Plays and Who Pays: Defining Equity in Intercollegiate Athletics*, 1995 Wis. L. Rev. 647; Rodney K. Smith, *When Ignorance is Not Bliss: In Search of Racial and Gender Equity in Intercollegiate Athletics*, 61 Missouri L. Rev. 329 (1996); and a Symposium in the 1996 volume of the Duke Journal of Gender Law and Policy, which has a number of substantial pieces, including John C. Weistart, *Can Gender Equity Find a Place in Commercialized College Sports?*, 3 Duke J. of Gender Law and Pol. 191 (1996). A recent non-lawyer appraisal of the issues is Louis M. Guenin, *Distributive Justice in Competitive Access to Intercollegiate Athletic Teams Segregated by Sex*, 16 Studies in Philosophy and Religion 347 (1997).

A. PRE–TITLE IX IN ACTION

Before we delve into the Title IX jurisprudence fashioned in the 1990s, it is helpful to gain some perspective on the issues by looking at a decision that addressed the gender equity problem in sports in the 1980s, while Title IX was in abeyance. This case was brought in 1982 by female athletes and coaches at Washington State University, who claimed that the school's distribution of athletic opportunities and resources violated both the "Equal Rights Amendment" to the state constitution and the statutory "Law Against Discrimination."

BLAIR v. WASHINGTON STATE UNIV.
Supreme Court of Washington (en banc), 1987.
108 Wash.2d 558, 740 P.2d 1379.

DOLLIVER, JUSTICE.

[The key findings of fact made by the trial judge were that in 1980–81, men's athletic programs received total funding of approximately $3.02 million, and women's programs $690,000 (or 19% of the total). The majority of the male funding ($1.91 million) came from revenues earned by male sports through gate receipts, broadcast revenues, and the like: football alone generated $1.43 million. The bulk of women's sports funds came from legislative appropriations ($450,000): only $11,000 was earned from gate admissions. During the previous seven years, the number of male athletic positions had risen by 115, while women's had dropped by nine. This disparity in both positions and scholarships ($480,000 for male athletes and $150,000 for women) made it clear to the judge that Washington State had engaged in "unlawful sex discrimination" in its treatment of women's athletics.

> The non-emphasis on the women's athletic program was demonstrated in many ways, some subtle, some not so subtle.... The message came through loud and clear, women's teams were low priority.... [T]he net result was an entirely different sort of participation opportunity for the athletes.

The plaintiffs, however, filed an appeal of two key features of the trial judge's injunctive remedy for those violations, the details of which the Supreme Court described as follows.]

* * *

The court entered a detailed injunction to remedy the violations. With respect to funding, the court ordered the women's program must receive 37.5% of the University's financial support given to intercollegiate athletics during the year 1982–1983. The required minimum percentage for women increased each year by 2 percent until it corresponded to the percentage of women undergraduates at the University, 44 percent at the time of the injunction. The trial court provided, however, the level of support for women's athletics was not required to exceed by more than 3 percent the actual participation rate of women in intercollegiate athletics at the University, excluding football participation from the comparison. The injunction prohibited the total budget for women's athletics ever to be less than the base budget of $841,145 for 1981–1982, unless the expenditures for men's athletics were correspondingly reduced.

The injunction also specified:

> In determining the level of University financial support of intercollegiate athletics for purposes of the above calculation, the term "University financial support" shall not include revenue generated by or attributable to any specific sport or program. Such excluded sources of revenue shall specifically include gate receipts, conference revenues, guarantees, sale of media rights, concession and novelty sales at games, coach and athlete work projects, and donations attributable to a sport or program.

The injunction apportioned the funding for athletic scholarships in a similar manner. . . .

The court also ordered the University to allow for increased participation opportunities until female participation, again excluding football participation from the comparison, reached a level commensurate with the proportion of female undergraduate students. The court noted female participation had increased in recent years and stated in its memorandum opinion, "[t]he change in the last ten years is dramatic, and it seems possible that parity will soon arrive."

The court further required the University to take affirmative steps to make opportunities to generate revenue equally available to men's and women's programs, stating:

> Because past sex discrimination has afforded women's teams and coaches less opportunity to generate revenue, the University should take affirmative action in providing additional personnel with such knowledge and experience.

The trial court required the University to appoint a [sex equity committee, comprised of students, coaches, and administrators,] to monitor the application of the funding formulas and other elements of the injunction.

* * *

A. Football Exclusion

The first issue raised by the plaintiffs is whether the trial court abused its discretion in creating an injunctive remedy which excluded football from its calculations for participation opportunities, scholarships, and distribution of nonrevenue funds. We conclude the trial court did abuse its discretion and reverse on this issue. The Equal Rights Amendment and the Law Against Discrimination prohibit such an exclusion.

* * *

The recognized purpose of the Equal Rights Amendment is to end special treatment for or discrimination against either sex. This absolute mandate of equality does not, however, bar affirmative governmental efforts to create equality in fact; governmental actions favoring one sex which are intended solely to ameliorate the effects of past discrimination do not implicate the Equal Rights Amendment.

Neither party disputes that the intercollegiate athletics program at Washington State University is subject to the Equal Rights Amendment and the Law Against Discrimination. The trial court found that the operation of the program resulted in discriminatory treatment of women and the women's athletic program in violation of these laws. Football is a large and essential part of intercollegiate athletics at the University. To exclude football, an all male program, from the scope of the Equal Rights Amendment would only serve to perpetuate the discriminatory policies and diminished opportunities for women.

The trial court attempted to explain the exclusion of football by stating football was a sport "unique in many respects, the combination of which distinguished it from all other collegiate sports...." The court identified such distinguishing characteristics as the number of participants, scholarships, and coaches, amount of equipment and facilities, income generated, media interest, spectator attendance, and publicity generated for the University as a whole. The court concluded:

> Because of the unique function performed by football, it should not be compared to any other sport at the University. Because football is operated for profit under business principles, ... football should not be included in determining whether sex equity exists ...

We do not believe, however, these or any other characteristics of football justify its exclusion from the scope of the injunction remedying violations of the Equal Rights Amendment. It is stating the obvious to observe the Equal Rights Amendment contains no exception for football. The exclusion of football would prevent sex equity from ever being achieved since men would always be guaranteed many more participation opportunities than women, despite any efforts by the teams, the sex equity committee, or the program to promote women's athletics under the injunction.

B. Revenue Retention

The plaintiffs also challenge the portion of the injunction excluding from the division of university financial support the revenue generated by any specific sport or program. The injunction allows each sport to reap the benefit of the revenues it generates. We hold the trial court did not abuse its discretion. Exclusion of sports-generated revenue from the calculations of university financial support is not prohibited under applicable state law and can be supported by several policy considerations. We affirm this portion of the trial court's injunction.

* * *

The trial court's funding plan provides incentive for all sports to develop revenue-generating capability of their own. As the trial court stated in its findings of fact and conclusions of law:

> There is an incentive to coaches and to a lesser extent their athletes to produce as much income as possible from all sources because they are the persons who first benefit from such income. The funding plan encourages the sports to fund their expenses through their own efforts, rather than depend upon direct legislative appropriations.
>
> The injunction specifically requires the sex equity committee to recommend ways to encourage and promote women's sports to increase their own revenues; the funding plan would further promote such a goal. The plan thus requires the University to create equal opportunity to raise revenue for men's and women's sports.
>
> The funding plan allows disproportionate expenses of any particular sports program to be derived from the program itself. The plan is also gender neutral. It provides a solution which does not violate the Equal Rights Amendment and encourages revenue development for all sports while accommodating the needs of the sports program incurring the greatest expenses at this time.

Our decision upholding the trial court's conclusion regarding sports-generated revenues does not in any way modify the University's obligation to achieve sex equity under the Equal Rights Amendment. The trial court's minimum requirements for participation opportunities and scholarships, already discussed, must be achieved; the court's guidelines for distribution of nonrevenue funds must be followed, and the remaining portions of the injunction, including promotion and development of women's sports, must be observed.

In addition, our conclusion allowing each sport to use the revenues it generates does not, of course, require the sport to do so. The record reflects the football program was transferring $150,000 or more per year from its revenues to the women's program before the injunction was entered. We encourage such practices to continue, along with other efforts to foster cooperation within the department.

We therefore reverse the trial court's exclusion of football from its calculations for participation opportunities and scholarships and affirm the trial court's decision to exclude sports-generated revenues from its distribution of financial support. We emphasize the portion of the injunction requiring additional promotion of women's sports and development of their revenue-generating capability and encourage continued cooperation and efforts to bring the University's intercollegiate athletic program into compliance with the Equal Rights Amendment.

* * *

Reversed in part.

Questions for Discussion

1. What difference is there between the trial court's exclusion of football as such from the gender equation, and the appellate court's exclusion of all revenues generated by football? If revenues earned by each sport could lawfully be excluded from the determination of whether women's sports were being treated unequally, and if the football program was actually earning a profit which the university was using to subsidize other sports, what was the basis for the judicial finding of a university violation? How would the overall athletic program differ after the court's requirements were met? Would there merely be many more women participants in sports that have very little money to spend? Who would bear the burden of a judicial decision that requires a school to bring in more women participants in intercollegiate sports?

There is a revealing aftermath to the *Blair* case. In the 1989-90 academic year, two years after the state Supreme Court decision, female athletes still comprised just 37% of the total at Washington State, and only 33% at the University of Washington which was also governed by that state law ruling. By 1995-96, the female athlete shares at the two institutions had risen to 47% and 46% respectively (though Washington State's female enrollment share was 47%, while Washington's was 50%). A key source of those gains was a law passed by the state legislature at the end of the 1980s which allowed (and funded) state universities to grant tuition and fee waivers to female student-athletes (pursuant to an approved gender equity plan). However, while *de facto* equality has been reached at these two institutions in female-male athletic participation and scholarships, there remains a substantial disparity in total expenditures per student. In 1995-96, Washington State spent an average of $10,100 on its female athletes and $14,300 on males (59%-41%), and the disparity was almost the same at Washington (61%-39%) ($12,400 and $19,300). The reason for this contrast between participation and funding is that a large part of the increase in women's sports at those two schools has been in low-cost rowing. Indeed, in 1995-96 Washington had as large a women's rowing crew (126 members) as it had on its men's football roster. While Washington State University still had a sizable gap in those two sports' numbers (103 in women's rowing and 152 in football), the athletic department had created gender equity by cutting the number of men's teams to five, by comparison with eight in women's sports. Keep these developments in Washington's college sports in mind as you now begin to read the cases and controversies under Title IX.

B. ADMINISTRATIVE DEVELOPMENT OF TITLE IX

As we saw above, Title IX simply states a very general statutory prohibition of sex-based exclusion from participation, denial of benefits, or discrimination under educational programs. There was very little congressional material (e.g., no Committee Report) about what was envisaged for the bill as a whole, and only two mentions of college sports in the entire congressional deliberations. The Act did go on to state that Title IX was not to

> ... be interpreted to require any educational institution to grant preferential or disparate treatment to the members of one sex on account of an imbalance which may exist with respect to the total number or percentage of persons of that sex participating in or receiving the benefits of any federally supported program or activity, in comparison with the total number or percentage of persons of that sex in any community, state, section, or other area: Provided, that this subsection shall not be construed to prevent the consideration in any hearing or proceeding under this chapter of statistical evidence tending to show that such an imbalance exists with respect to the participation in, or receipt of the benefits of, any such program or activity by the members of one sex.

Even the latter provision did no more than reject pure statistical disparities as themselves a violation of the statute; such statistical material can be and is regularly used (along with other factors) to find "discrimination."

In 1975, pursuant to a Congressional directive, the Health, Education and Welfare Department (HEW) promulgated regulations that further spelled out the implications of Title IX, including its application to athletic programs. Over the next three years, HEW received more than one hundred complaints under the Act. In response to this onslaught, HEW's Office of Civil Rights (OCR) issued a Policy Interpretation in 1979 which elaborated in much greater detail the meaning of equal educational opportunity, including in college and high school sports programs. That same year, Congress split HEW into a Department of Health and Human Services (HHS) and a Department of Education (DED). The latter department, through its OCR, took principal responsibility for the administration of Title IX.

As in the statute itself, the Title IX Regulations began by stating that the statutory requirement of "equality" was not necessarily violated by "unequal aggregate expenditures for members of each sex or unequal expenditures for male and female teams." 51 Fed. Reg. 20,524 (1986). Instead, the test for compliance is a comparison of the

> ... availability, quality and kinds of benefits, opportunities and treatment afforded members of both sexes. Institutions will be in compliance if the compared program components are equivalent, that is, equal or equal in effect. Under this standard, identical benefits, opportunities or treatment are not required, provided the overall effect of any differences is negligible.

44 Fed. Reg. 71,415 (1979). For purposes of judging whether there actually is "equal athletic opportunity," the federal regulations direct that the amounts spent on athletic scholarships be on a "substantially

proportional basis to the number of male and female participants in the institution's athletic programs," 44 Fed. Reg. 71,414 (1979). In addition, the following program factors must be taken into account:

1. Whether the selection of sports and levels of competition effectively accommodate the interests and abilities of members of both sexes;

2. Provision of equipment and supplies;

3. Scheduling of games and practice time;

4. Travel and per diem allowance;

5. Opportunity to receive coaching and academic tutoring;

6. Assignment and compensation of coaches and tutors;

7. Provision of locker rooms, practice and competitive facilities;

8. Provision of medical training services;

9. Provision of housing and dining facilities and services;

10. Publicity.

34 C.F.R. § 106.41(c) (1990)

There have been three different categories of Title IX complaints about sex discrimination in educational athletic programs. One involves the claim that there has been an unequal allocation of *resources*, and thence of opportunities for women to play on women's-only teams—with that gender separation of teams being the standard practice in college sports. The second involves unequal treatment in the *administration* of such women's programs—in particular, disparity in pay and benefits offered to the (often-male) coaches of the women's teams. The third category involves denial of *access* by female (or occasionally male) athletes to teams that the school has chosen to confine to one sex in that particular sport.

The bulk of the cases and controversies have arisen in the first category, and here the oft-cited feature of the OCR Policy Interpretation reads as follows:

(1) Whether intercollegiate level participation opportunities for male and female students are provided in numbers substantially proportionate to their respective enrollments; or

(2) Where the members of one sex have been and are underrepresented among intercollegiate athletes, whether the institution can show a history and continuing practice of program expansion which is demonstrably responsive to the developing interest and abilities of the members of that sex; or

(3) Where the members of one sex are underrepresented among intercollegiate athletes, and the institution cannot show a continuing practice of program expansion such as that cited above, whether it can be demonstrated that the interests and abilities of the

members of that sex have been fully and effectively accommodated by the present program.

As we shall see, the presence of such an administrative interpretation is very important in the courts as well, because of the major Supreme Court statement in *Chevron U.S.A. v. Natural Resources Defense Council*, 467 U.S. 837 (1984), that courts must defer to interpretations of a statute by the agency to whom Congress has delegated administrative responsibility, unless the agency's reading is "arbitrary, capricious, or significantly contrary to the Statute." With the above as background, we now turn to the key disputes and judicial rulings in these three areas of Title IX jurisprudence.

C. RESOURCES

The dispute that has produced the most judicial writing about Title IX involved Brown University. The Ivy League, of which Brown is a member, is the setting where college sports first began in the 1850s, and where American-style football evolved in the 1870s. Not until the late 1960s and early 1970s did Ivy League universities integrate their undergraduate colleges by accepting women into their academic as well as athletic programs. By that time, the Ivy League was no longer part of the NCAA's highly-commercialized Division I–A branch of college sports, and it did not give athletic scholarships as such to its students.

Ironically, though, by the 1990s, Ivy League schools were providing more varsity athletic opportunities to both their female and male students than schools in any other college conference. Under the 1995 Equity in Athletics Disclosure Act, schools must provide both the OCR and the public with relevant data about participation in and financing of their male and female athletic programs. The first such report, for the 1995–96 academic year, disclosed that while Washington State University had the same 47% ratio of female-athletes to female students, it had eight female and five male teams. Harvard University, by contrast, had a slight disparity in those two ratios, 40% to 44%, but it provided a total of 41 intercollegiate teams to its students (20 female and 21 male teams). Princeton had almost as many teams as Harvard, and offered varsity athletic positions to 24% of all women students (for which the Division I average is three percent for women students, and five percent for male students).

In 1971, Brown University merged with Pembroke College, a women's-only school. One of the early steps in that joint venture was to increase substantially the athletic opportunities for its new female students; by 1977, Brown had created 14 women's varsity teams. However, over the next decade, just a single women's team was added, such that by 1991–92 Brown had 15 women's teams and 16 men's teams. Again because of football, the total number of positions on the teams were 328 for women (37%) and 566 for men (63%).

This was the time, though, when NCAA members were engaged in a Cost Reduction program (the effort that generated the "restricted earnings coach" rule and the *Law* litigation we read about in Chapter 10). Like a number of schools, the Brown administration announced that it was going to reduce its athletic budget by cutting four varsity sports—two women's teams in volleyball and gymnastics (which would generate savings of approximately $37,000 and $24,000) and two men's teams in water polo and golf (which would save $9,000 and $7,000 respectively). While significantly more dollars were cut from the women's than the men's programs, the relative number of team positions remained essentially the same, at 37%–63%; however, women now made up approximately 48% of Brown's student body. The university told the team members that they could continue playing in those sports as "intercollegiate clubs," but without financial assistance or support services from the school, and likely with sharply reduced opportunities to play varsity teams at other schools. The members of the women's teams (led by Amy Cohen) chose, instead, to file suit under Title IX, and they won a preliminary injunction against Brown's elimination of the women's varsity teams. Brown appealed that decision, and received the first circuit court opinion about how Title IX applied to the college sports world.

COHEN v. BROWN UNIVERSITY

United States Court of Appeals, First Circuit, 1993.
991 F.2d 888.

SELYA, CIRCUIT JUDGE.

* * *

I. BROWN ATHLETICS: AN OVERVIEW

College athletics, particularly in the realm of football and basketball, has traditionally occupied a prominent role in American sports and American society. For college students, athletics offers an opportunity to execute leadership skills, learn teamwork, build self-confidence, and perfect self-discipline. In addition, for many student-athletes, physical skills are a passport to college admissions and scholarships, allowing them to attend otherwise inaccessible schools. These opportunities, and the lessons learned on the playing fields, are invaluable in attaining career and life successes in and out of professional sports.

The highway of opportunity runs in both directions. Not only student-athletes, but universities, too, benefit from the magic of intercollegiate sports. Successful teams generate television revenues and gate receipts which often fund significant percentages of a university's overall athletic program, offering students the opportunity to partake of sports that are not financially self-sustaining. Even those institutions whose teams do not fill the grandstands of cavernous stadiums or attract national television exposure benefit from increased student and alumni cohesion and the support it engenders. Thus, universities nurture the legends, great or small, inhering in their athletic past, polishing the hardware that adorns field-house trophy cases and reliving heroic exploits in the pages of alumni magazines.

In these terms, Brown will never be confused with Notre Dame or the more muscular members of the Big Ten. Although its football team did play in the 1916 Rose Bowl and its men's basketball team won the Ivy League championship as recently as 1986, Brown's athletic program has only occasionally achieved national prominence or, for that matter, enjoyed sustained success. Moreover, at Brown, as at most schools, women are a relatively inconspicuous part of the storied athletic past. Historically, colleges limited athletics to the male sphere, leaving those few women's teams that sprouted to scrounge for resources.

* * *

III. Title IX and Collegiate Athletics

* * *

A. *Scope of Title IX.*

At its inception, the broad proscriptive language of Title IX caused considerable consternation in the academic world. The academy's anxiety chiefly centered around identifying which individual programs, particularly in terms of athletics, might come within the scope of the discrimination provision, and, relatedly, how the government would determine compliance. The gridiron fueled these concerns: for many schools, the men's football budget far exceeded that of any other sport, and men's athletics as a whole received the lion's share of dedicated resources—a share that, typically, was vastly disproportionate to the percentage of men in the student body.

[The judge then described the evolution of the Title IX legislation and its administrative interpretation. After quoting the key passage from the OCR Policy Interpretation set out above, the court continued.]

* * *

... The first benchmark furnishes a safe harbor for those institutions that have distributed athletic opportunities in numbers "substantially proportionate" to the gender composition of their student bodies. Thus, a university which does not wish to engage in extensive compliance analysis may stay on the sunny side of Title IX simply by maintaining gender parity between its student body and its athletic lineup.

The second and third parts of the accommodation test recognize that there are circumstances under which, as a practical matter, something short of this proportionality is a satisfactory proxy for gender balance. For example, so long as a university is continually expanding athletic opportunities in an ongoing effort to meet the needs of the underrepresented gender, and persists in this approach as interest and ability levels in its student body and secondary feeder schools rise, benchmark two is satisfied and Title IX does not require that the university leap to complete gender parity in a single bound. Or, if a school has a student body in which one sex is demonstrably less interested in athletics, Title IX does not require that the school create teams for, or rain money upon, otherwise disinterested students; rather, the third benchmark is satisfied if the underrepresented sex's discernible interests are fully and effectively accommodated.[13]

It seems unlikely, even in this day and age, that the athletic establishments of many coeducational universities reflect the gender balance of their student bodies. Similarly, the recent boom in Title IX suits suggests that, in an era of fiscal austerity, few universities are prone to expand athletic opportunities. It is not surprising, then, that schools more often than not attempt to manage the rigors of Title IX by satisfying the interests and abilities of the underrepresented gender, that is, by meeting the third benchmark of the accommodation test. Yet, this benchmark sets a high standard: it demands not merely some accommodation, but full and effective accommodation. If there is sufficient interest and ability among members of the statistically underrepresented gender, not slaked by existing programs, an institution necessarily fails this prong of the test.

Although the full-and-effective-accommodation standard is high, it is not absolute. Even when male athletic opportunities outnumber female athletic opportunities, and the university has not met the first benchmark (substantial statistical proportionality) or the second benchmark (continuing program expansion) of the accommodation test, the mere fact that there are some female students interested in a sport does not ipso facto require the school to provide a varsity team in order to comply with the third benchmark. Rather, the institution can satisfy the third benchmark by ensuring participatory opportunities at the intercollegiate level when, and to the extent that, there is "sufficient interest and ability among the members of the excluded sex to sustain a viable team and a reasonable expectation of intercollegiate competition for that team...." Staying on top of the problem is not sport for the short-winded: the institution must remain vigilant, "upgrading the competitive opportunities available to the historically disadvantaged sex as warranted by developing abilities among the athletes of that sex," until the opportunities for, and levels of, competition are equivalent by gender.[15]

13. OCR also lists a series of illustrative justifications for the disparate treatment of men's and women's athletic teams, including (1) sports that require more resources because of the nature of the game (e.g., contact sports generally require more equipment), (2) special circumstances, such as an influx of first-year players, that may require an extraordinary infusion of resources, (3) special operational expenses (e.g., crowd control at a basketball tournament), as long as special operational expense needs are met for both genders and (4) affirmative measures to remedy past limitations on athletic opportunities for one gender.

15. If in the course of adding and upgrading teams, a university attains gender parity between its athletic program and its student body, it meets the first benchmark of the accommodation test. But, Title IX does not require that a school pour ever-increasing sums into its athletic establishment. If a university prefers to take another route, it can also bring itself into compliance with the first benchmark of the accommodation test by subtraction and downgrading, that is, by reducing opportu-

Brown argues that DED's Policy Interpretation, construed as we have just outlined, goes so far afield that it countervails the enabling legislation. Brown suggests that, to the extent students' interests in athletics are disproportionate by gender, colleges should be allowed to meet those interests incompletely as long as the school's response is in direct proportion to the comparative levels of interest. Put bluntly, Brown reads the "full" out of the duty to accommodate "fully and effectively." It argues instead that an institution satisfactorily accommodates female athletes if it allocates athletic opportunities to women in accordance with the ratio of interested and able women to interested and able men, regardless of the number of unserved women or the percentage of the student body that they comprise.

Because this is mountainous terrain, an example may serve to clarify the distinction between Brown's proposal and our understanding of the law. Suppose a university (Oooh U.) has a student body consisting of 1,000 men and 1,000 women, a one to one ratio. If 500 men and 250 women are able and interested athletes, the ratio of interested men to interested women is two to one. Brown takes the position that both the actual gender composition of the student body and whether there is unmet interest among the underrepresented gender are irrelevant; in order to satisfy the third benchmark, Oooh U. must only provide athletic opportunities in line with the two to one interested athlete ratio, say, 100 slots for men and 50 slots for women. Under this view, the interest of 200 women would be unmet—but there would be no Title IX violation.

We think that Brown's perception of the Title IX universe is myopic. The fact that the overrepresented gender is less than fully accommodated will not, in and of itself, excuse a shortfall in the provision of opportunities for the underrepresented gender. Rather, the law requires that, in the absence of continuing program expansion (benchmark two), schools either meet benchmark one by providing athletic opportunities in proportion to the gender composition of the student body (in Oooh U.'s case, a roughly equal number of slots for men and women, as the student body is equally divided), or meet benchmark three by fully accommodating interested athletes among the underrepresented sex (providing, at Oooh U., 250 slots for women).

In the final analysis, Brown's view is wrong on two scores. It is wrong as a matter of law, for DED's Policy Interpretation, which requires full accommodation of the underrepresented gender, draws its essence from the statute. Whether Brown's concept might be thought more attractive, or whether we, if writing on a pristine page, would craft the regulation in a manner different than the agency, are not very important considerations. Because the agency's rendition stands upon a plausible, if not inevitable, reading of Title IX, we are obligated to enforce the regulation according to its tenor.

nities for the overrepresented gender while keeping opportunities stable for the underrepresented gender (or reducing them to a much lesser extent).

Brown's reading of Title IX is legally flawed for yet another reason. It proceeds from the premise that the agency's third benchmark countervails Title IX. But, this particular imprecation of the third benchmark overlooks the accommodation test's general purpose: to determine whether a student has been "excluded from participation in, [or] denied the benefits of" an athletic program "on the basis of sex...." While any single element of this tripartite test, in isolation, might not achieve the goal set by the statute, the test as a whole is reasonably constructed to implement the statute. No more is exigible.

As it happens, Brown's view is also poor policy for, in the long run, a rule such as Brown advances would likely make it more difficult for colleges to ensure that they have complied with Title IX. Given that the survey of interests and abilities would begin under circumstances where men's athletic teams have a considerable head start, such a rule would almost certainly blunt the exhortation that schools should "take into account the nationally increasing levels of women's interests and abilities" and avoid "disadvantaging members of an underrepresented sex...."

Brown's proposal would also aggravate the quantification problems that are inevitably bound up with Title IX. Student plaintiffs, who carry the burden of proof on this issue, as well as universities monitoring self-compliance, would be required to assess the level of interest in both the male and female student populations and determine comparatively how completely the university was serving the interests of each sex. By contrast, as we read the accommodation test's third benchmark, it requires a relatively simple assessment of whether there is unmet need in the underrepresented gender that rises to a level sufficient to warrant a new team or the upgrading of an existing team. We think the simpler reading is far more serviceable.

Furthermore, by moving away from OCR's third benchmark, which focuses on the levels of interest and ability extant in the student body, Brown's theory invites thorny questions as to the appropriate survey population, whether from the university, typical feeder schools, or the regional community. In that way, Brown's proposal would do little more than overcomplicate an already complex equation.

We will not paint the lily. Brown's approach cannot withstand scrutiny on either legal or policy grounds. We conclude that DED's Policy Interpretation means exactly what it says. This plain meaning is a proper, permissible rendition of the statute.

* * *

D. Summing Up.

We summarize succinctly, beginning with the probability of plaintiffs' success. In an era where the practices of higher education must adjust to stunted revenues, careening costs, and changing demographics, colleges might well be obliged to curb spending on programs, like athletics, that do not lie at the epicenter of their institutional mission.

Title IX does not purport to override financial necessity. Yet, the pruning of athletic budgets cannot take place solely in comptrollers' offices, isolated from the legislative and regulatory imperatives that Title IX imposes.

This case aptly illustrates the point. Brown earnestly professes that it has done no more than slash women's and men's athletics by approximately the same degree, and, indeed, the raw numbers lend partial credence to that characterization.[23] But, Brown's claim overlooks the shortcomings that plagued its program before it took blade in hand. If a school, like Brown, eschews the first two benchmarks of the accommodation test, electing to stray from substantial proportionality and failing to march uninterruptedly in the direction of equal athletic opportunity, it must comply with the third benchmark. To do so, the school must fully and effectively accommodate the underrepresented gender's interests and abilities, even if that requires it to give the underrepresented gender (in this case, women) what amounts to a larger slice of a shrinking athletic-opportunity pie.

The record reveals that the court below paid heed to these realities. It properly recognized that even balanced use of the budget-paring knife runs afoul of Title IX where, as here, the fruits of a university's athletic program remain ill-distributed after the trimming takes place. Because the district court understood this principle, and because its findings of fact as to the case's probable outcome are based on substantial evidence, the court's determination that plaintiffs are likely to succeed on the merits is inexpugnable.

Injunction affirmed.

Two months after the *Brown* decision, the Tenth Circuit rendered a similar judgment in a suit involving Colorado State University (CSU): *Roberts v. Colorado State Bd. of Agriculture*, 998 F.2d 824 (10th Cir. 1993). In 1992, CSU announced that it was eliminating both the men's varsity baseball program (with its fifty-five players) and the women's varsity softball team (with its eighteen players). These cutbacks left in place the ten percentage point differential between the female share of student enrollment and of varsity athletes. The women's softball team secured an injunction under Title IX against Colorado's State Board of Agriculture (the government entity in charge of the state university), prohibiting this cutback in the women's side of the school's athletic program.

---

23. We note, however, that while the cuts proposed by Brown eliminate a roughly equal number of athletic opportunities for women as for men, those cuts subtract roughly four times more money from the budget for female pancratiasts than from the budget for their male counterparts. And, as a noted playwright once observed, "where there is no money, there is no change of any kind." Moss Hart, *Act One* (1959).

The lawsuits against *Brown* and *Colorado State* (as well as *Indiana U. of Penn.*) all involved challenges to university decisions to eliminate certain women's varsity sports as part of broader cutbacks in the schools' athletic programs. In the summer of 1993, settlements were reached in two pending class action suits (against California State University and the University of Texas) that had asserted a right under Title IX to have new women's sports added to the athletic programs. In both cases, the schools settled the litigation by promising that within the next several years, their respective ratios of female and male athletes would be brought to no less than five percentage points of the female-male ratios in the student bodies. To some extent this goal would be accomplished by adding more women's sports, paid for by increasing the athletic budgets (for example, through increased student fees). The remaining disparity would be eliminated by reducing the number of male varsity athletes (partly by cutting back on the number of non-scholarship "walk-on" members of male teams, such as football).

Unsurprisingly, male athletes also began to file lawsuits challenging what they perceived to be a gender-related disparity in cutbacks of athletic programs by universities who were worried about litigation by female athletes. Among the suits initiated in 1993 was one brought by the male swimmers at the University of Illinois. Faced with a $600,000 budgetary deficit in its athletic program, the University decided to cut four varsity teams—men's and women's diving, men's fencing, and men's swimming. The selection criteria included such factors as team costs, competitive success, and student and spectator interest in the sports. It was conceded, though, that a major reason why women's swimming was not cut along with the men's program was the administration's concern about Title IX liability. While the University's student body was 44% women, its female varsity athletes comprised only 23% of the total. Members of the men's swimming team then filed suit, contending that they were the victims of reverse discrimination that violated both Title IX and the Equal Protection provisions of the Constitution. After losing in the district court, the men's team appealed to the Seventh Circuit which rendered the first appellate ruling about this variation on the equal sporting rights theme.

KELLEY v. UNIVERSITY OF ILLINOIS

United States Court of Appeals, Seventh Circuit, 1994.
35 F.3d 265.

CUMMINGS, CIRCUIT JUDGE.

* * *

III.

The University's decision not to terminate the woman's swimming program was—given the requirements of Title IX and the applicable regulation and policy interpretation—extremely prudent. The percentage of women involved in intercollegiate athletics at the University of Illinois is substantially lower than the percentage of women enrolled at the school. If the University had terminated the women's swimming program, it would have been vulnerable to a finding that it was in violation of Title IX. Female participation would have continued to be substantially disproportionate to female enrollment, and women with a demonstrated interest in an intercollegiate athletic activity and demonstrated ability to compete at the intercollegiate level would be left without an opportunity to participate in their sport. The University could, however, eliminate the men's swimming program without violating Title IX since even after eliminating the program, men's participation in athletics would continue to be more than substantially proportionate to their presence in the University's student body. And as the caselaw makes clear, if the percentage of student-athletes of a particular sex is substantially proportionate to the percentage of students of that sex in the general student population, the athletic interests of that sex are presumed to have been accommodated. The University's decision to retain the women's swimming program—even though budget constraints required that the men's program be terminated—was a reasonable response to the requirements of the applicable regulation and policy interpretation.

Plaintiffs contend, however, that the applicable regulation and policy interpretation pervert Title IX. Title IX, plaintiffs contend, "ha[s] through some alchemy of bureaucratic regulation been transformed from a statute which prohibits discrimination on the basis of sex into a statute that mandates discrimination against males ..." Or, as plaintiffs put it later: "If a university is required by Title IX to eliminate men from varsity athletic competition ..., then the same Title IX [sh]ould require the university to eliminate women from the academic departments where they are over[-]represented. Such a result would be ridiculous."

We agree that such a result would be ridiculous. But Congress itself recognized that addressing discrimination in athletics presented a unique set of problems not raised in areas such as employment and academics. Congress therefore specifically directed the agency in charge of administering Title IX to issue, with respect to "intercollegiate athletic activities," regulations containing "reasonable provisions considering the nature of particular sports." Pub.L. No. 93–380, 88 Stat. 484, 612. And where Congress has specifically delegated to an agency the responsibility to articulate standards governing a particular area, we must accord the ensuing regulation considerable deference. *Chevron U.S.A. v. Natural Resources Defense Council, Inc.*, 467 U.S. 837, 844 (1984) (Where Congress has expressly delegated to an agency the power to "elucidate a specific provision of a statute by regulation," the resulting regulations should be given "controlling weight unless they are arbitrary, capricious, or manifestly contrary to the statute.")

The regulation at issue here is neither "arbitrary ... [n]or manifestly contrary to the statute." The regulation provides that notwithstanding Title IX's requirement that "[n]o person ... shall, on the basis of sex, be excluded from participation in any ... activity," a school may "sponsor separate teams for members of each sex where selection for such teams is based upon competitive skill or the activity involved is a contact sport."[5] Such a provision is not at odds with the purpose of Title IX and we do not understand plaintiffs to argue that it is. And since [the regulation] is not manifestly contrary to the objectives of Title IX, this court must accord it deference. Plaintiffs, while they concede the validity of [the regulation], argue that the substantial proportionality test contained in the agency's policy interpretation of that regulation establishes a gender-based quota system, a scheme they allege is contrary to the mandates of Title IX. But the policy interpretation does not, as plaintiffs suggest, mandate statistical balancing. Rather the policy interpretation merely creates a presumption that a school is in compliance with Title IX and the applicable regulation when it achieves such a statistical balance. Even if substantial proportionality has not been achieved, a school may establish that it is in compliance by demonstrating either that it has a continuing practice of increasing the athletic opportunities of the underrepresented sex or that its existing programs effectively accommodate the interests of that sex.

Moreover, once it is agreed Title IX does not require that all teams be co-ed—a point the plaintiffs concede—and that 34 C.F.R. § 106.41 is therefore a valid regulation, schools must be provided some means of establishing that despite offering single-sex teams, they have provided "equal athletic opportunit[ies] ... for both sexes." Undoubtedly the agency responsible for enforcement of the statute could have required schools to sponsor a women's program for every men's program offered and vice versa. Requiring parallel teams would certainly have been the simplest method of ensuring equality of opportunity—and plaintiffs would doubtless have preferred this approach since, had it been adopted, the men's swimming program would likely have been saved. It was not unreasonable, however, for the agency to reject this course of action. Requiring parallel teams is a rigid approach that denies schools the flexibility to respond to the differing athletic interests of men and women.[8] It was perfectly acceptable, therefore, for the agency to chart a different course and adopt an enforcement scheme that measures compliance by analyzing how a school has allocated its various athletic resources.

This Court must defer to an agency's interpretation of its regulations if the interpretation is reasonable, a standard the policy interpretation at issue here meets. Measuring compliance through an evaluation of a school's allocation of its athletic resources allows schools flexibility in meeting the athletic interests of their students and increases the chance that the actual interests of those students will be met. And if compliance with Title IX is to be measured through this sort of analysis, it is only practical that schools be given some clear way to establish that they have

---

5. Congress would indeed be surprised to learn that Title IX mandated co-ed football teams.

8. Requiring parallel teams would, for example, require the University either to terminate the football program or to begin a women's team, even if female students had little interest in that sport but had great interest in other sports.

satisfied the requirements of the statute. The substantial proportionality contained in Benchmark 1 merely establishes such a safe harbor.

Since the policy interpretation maps out a reasonable approach to measuring compliance with Title IX, this Court does not have the authority to condemn it. Plaintiffs' claim that the University of Illinois violated Title IX when it terminated the men's swimming program is, therefore, rejected. The University's actions were consistent with the statute and the applicable regulation and policy interpretation. And despite plaintiffs' assertions to the contrary, neither the regulation nor the policy interpretation run afoul of the dictates of Title IX.

IV.

Plaintiffs' final argument is that the defendants' decision to eliminate the men's swimming program while retaining the women's program denied them equal protection of law as guaranteed by the Fourteenth Amendment. While the effect of Title IX and the relevant regulation and policy interpretation is that institutions will sometimes consider gender when decreasing their athletic offerings, this limited consideration of sex does not violate the Constitution. Congress has broad powers under the Due Process Clause of the Fifth Amendment to remedy past discrimination. *Metro Broadcasting, Inc. v. Federal Communications Comm'n*, 497 U.S. 547, 565–566 (1990). Even absent a specific finding that discrimination has occurred, remedial measures mandated by Congress are "constitutionally permissible to the extent that they serve important governmental objectives . . . and are substantially related to achievement of those ends." Id. at 565; see also *Mississippi University for Women v. Hogan*, 458 U.S. 718, 728 (1982). There is no doubt but that removing the legacy of sexual discrimination—including discrimination in the provision of extra-curricular offerings such as athletics—from our nation's educational institutions is an important governmental objective. We do not understand plaintiffs to argue otherwise.

Plaintiffs' complaint appears, instead, to be that the remedial measures required by Title IX and the applicable regulation and policy interpretation are not substantially related to their purported goal. Plaintiffs contend that the applicable rules allow "the University to . . . improve its statistics without adding any opportunities for women . . .," an outcome they suggest is unconstitutional. But to survive constitutional scrutiny, Title IX need not require—as plaintiffs would have us believe—that the opportunities for the under-represented group be continually expanded. Title IX's stated objective is not to ensure that the athletic opportunities available to women increase. Rather its avowed purpose is to prohibit educational institutions from discriminating on the basis of sex. And the remedial scheme established by Title IX and the applicable regulation and policy interpretation are clearly substantially related to this end. Allowing a school to consider gender when determining which athletic programs to terminate ensures that in instances where overall athletic opportunities decrease, the actual opportunities available to the under-represented gender do not. And since the remedial scheme here at issue directly protects the interest of the disproportionately burdened gender, it passes constitutional muster.

* * *

Affirmed.

This first wave of decisions under Title IX involved requests for preliminary injunctions and/or summary judgments from one side or the other. Brown University's athletic program was also the subject of the first full-scale trial of a Title IX case. By this time, Amy Cohen and her gymnastic and volleyball classmates had long since graduated from Brown. However, the lawsuit was now a class action on behalf of all present and future Brown women students who might want to participate in intercollegiate sports. While the percentage of women among Brown's varsity athletes had increased slightly from 37% in 1990–91 to 38% in 1993–94, the percentage of women in Brown's classes had gone from 48% to 51% in that same period. Thus, while Brown had 16 varsity *teams* for both men and women students-athletes, there was a 13 point gap between the percentage of women team *members* and students. Even in the Ivy League, football was the single biggest factor: while Brown had 125 varsity football players, rowing was its largest women's team, with just 50 crew members.

Brown now pressed an argument that had been alluded to in earlier cases—that the latter gap actually reflected a disparity in male and female student *interests* in varsity sports, and that Brown's programs provided more than "equal accommodation" to the female interests. The trial judge rejected this argument: in his view, not only was measurement of such true student interests inherently difficult, but it was legally irrelevant under the OCR standard. Since Brown had stopped expanding women's sports, while still leaving this statistical disparity between its female athlete and student ratios, the university had to meet all existing women student interests and abilities in any particular varsity sport (which clearly existed at Brown in volleyball and gymnastics).

The reaction of Brown President Vartan Gregorian to the trial verdict was that this reading of Title IX was "tantamount to quotas," something that had certainly lost their political appeal by the mid–1990s. In filing their appeal, Brown's counsel also placed some hope in two major Equal Protection decisions rendered by the Supreme Court since the First Circuit's prior *Cohen* decision. In *Adarand Constructors, Inc. v. Pena*, 515 U.S. 200 (1995), the Court had overruled *Metro Broadcasting v. FCC*, 497 U.S. 547 (1990) (a case that had been relied on by the First Circuit in *Cohen*); the Court now requires that even benign federal affirmative action programs in favor of previously discriminated-against groups—there a racial group—have to pass the same "strict scrutiny" standard that is applied to negative state discrimination. A year later came *United States v. Virginia*, 518 U.S. 515 (1996), which dealt with the state of Virginia's effort to preserve its all-male Virginia Military Institute (VMI), and to offer women with military aspirations a female-only program instead. In this case, the Supreme Court did not utilize the traditional "intermediate scrutiny" to judge whether gender-based classifications were "substantially related to an important government objective." Instead, the Court majority subjected Virginia's actions to "skeptical scrutiny of official action denying rights or opportunities based on sex" (518 U.S. at ___), and eventually concluded that the state did not provide the "exceedingly persuasive justification" needed for its exclusion of women applicants from VMI.

While Justice Scalia in *Virginia* accused the Court majority of having "drastically revised our established standards for reviewing sex-based classifications" (*id.* at 2291), Brown University asserted that *Virginia* and *Adarand* required the First Circuit to take a second look at the application of Title IX to its case. The following opinion (by a new circuit panel) produced the first Title IX division within an appeals court.

COHEN v. BROWN UNIVERSITY
United States Court of Appeals, First Circuit, 1996.
101 F.3d 155.

BOWNES, CIRCUIT JUDGE.

* * *

IV.

Brown contends that the district court misconstrued and misapplied the three-part [Title IX] test. Specifically, Brown argues that the district court's interpretation and application of the test is irreconcilable with the statute, the regulation, and the agency's interpretation of the law, and effectively renders Title IX an "affirmative action statute" that mandates preferential treatment for women by imposing quotas in excess of women's relative interests and abilities in athletics. Brown asserts, in the alternative, that if the district court properly construed the test, then the test itself violates Title IX and the United States Constitution.

We emphasize two points at the outset. First, notwithstanding Brown's persistent invocation of the inflammatory terms "affirmative action," "preference," and "quota," this is not an affirmative action case. Second, Brown's efforts to evade the controlling authority of *Cohen II* by recasting its core legal arguments as challenges to the "district court's interpretation" of the law are unavailing; the primary arguments raised here have already been litigated and decided adversely to Brown in the prior appeal.

A.

Brown's talismanic incantation of "affirmative action" has no legal application to this case and is not helpful to Brown's cause. While "affirmative action" may have different connotations as a matter of politics, as a matter of law, its meaning is more circumscribed. True affirmative action cases have historically involved a voluntary undertaking to remedy discrimination (as in a program implemented by a governmental body, or by a private employer or institution), by means of specific group-based preferences or numerical goals, and a specific timetable for achieving those goals. See *Adarand*, 115 S.Ct. 2097 (1995) (remanding for review under strict scrutiny a challenge to a federal statute establishing a government-wide goal for awarding to minority businesses not less than 5% of the total value of all prime contracts and subcontracts for each fiscal year); *Metro Broadcasting v. FCC*, 497 U.S. 547 (1990) (upholding a federal program requiring race-based preferences); *City of Richmond v. J.A. Croson Co.*, 488 U.S. 469 (1989) (striking down a municipal set-aside program requiring that 30% of the city's construction dollars be paid to racial minority subcontractors on an annual basis); *Johnson v. Transportation Agency*, 480 U.S. 616 (1987) (upholding a temporary program authorizing a county agency to consider sex and race as factors in making promotions in order to achieve a statistically measurable improvement in the representation of women and minorities in major job classifications in which they had been historically underrepresented); *Wygant v. Jackson Bd. of Educ.*, 476 U.S. 267 (1986) (striking down a collective-bargaining faculty lay-off provision requiring preferential treatment for certain racial minorities); *Fullilove v. Klutznick*, 448 U.S. 448 (1980) (upholding a federal program requiring state and local recipients of federal public works grants to set aside 10% of funds for procuring goods and services from minority business enterprises); *United Steelworkers v. Weber*, 443 U.S. 193 (1979) (upholding a collective bargaining agreement that set aside for blacks half the places in a new training program until the percentage of blacks among skilled workers at the plant was commensurate with the percentage of blacks in the local labor force); *Regents of the Univ. of Cal. v. Bakke*, 438 U.S. 265 (1978) (striking down a state medical school's admissions policy that set aside 16 of its places for racial minorities).

Title IX is not an affirmative action statute; it is an anti-discrimination statute, modeled explicitly after another anti-discrimination statute, Title VI. No aspect of the Title IX regime at issue in this case—inclusive of the statute, the relevant regulation, and the pertinent agency documents—mandates gender-based preferences or quotas, or specific timetables for implementing numerical goals.

Like other anti-discrimination statutory schemes, the Title IX regime permits affirmative action. In addition, Title IX, like other anti-discrimination schemes, permits an inference that a significant gender-based statistical disparity may indicate the existence of discrimination. Consistent with the school desegregation cases, the question of substantial proportionality under the Policy Interpretation's three-part test is merely the starting point for analysis, rather than the conclusion; a rebuttable presumption, rather than an inflexible requirement. See, e.g., *Swann v. Charlotte–Mecklenburg Bd. of Educ.*, 402 U.S. 1, 25 (1971). In short, the substantial proportionality test is but one aspect of the inquiry into whether an institution's athletics program complies with Title IX.

Also consistent with the school desegregation cases, the substantial proportionality test of prong one is applied under the Title IX framework, not mechanically, but case-by-case, in a fact-specific manner. As with other anti-discrimination regimes, Title IX neither mandates a finding of discrimination based solely upon a gender-based statistical disparity, see *Cohen II*, 991 F.2d at 895, nor prohibits gender-conscious remedial measures....

Another important distinction between this case and affirmative action cases is that the district court's remedy requiring Brown to accommodate fully and effectively the athletics interests and abilities of its women students does not raise the concerns underlying the Supreme Court's requirement of a particularized factual predicate to justify voluntary affirmative action plans. In reviewing equal protection challenges to such plans, the Court is concerned that government bodies are reaching out to implement race-or gender-conscious remedial measures that are "ageless in their reach into the past, and timeless in their ability to affect the future," *Wygant*, 476 U.S. at 276, on the basis of facts insufficient to support a prima facie case of a constitutional or statutory violation, *Croson*, 488 U.S. at 500, to the benefit of unidentified victims of past discrimination, see id. at 469; *Wygant*, 476 U.S. at 276. Accordingly, the Court has taken the position that voluntary affirmative action plans cannot be constitutionally justified absent a particularized factual predicate demonstrating the existence of "identified discrimination," see *Croson*, 488 U.S. at 500–06, because "societal discrimination, without more, is too amorphous a basis for imposing a racially classified remedy," *Wygant*, 476 U.S. at 276.

From a constitutional standpoint, the case before us is altogether different. Here, gender-conscious relief was ordered by an Article III court, constitutionally compelled to have before it litigants with standing to raise the cause of action alleged; for the purpose of providing relief upon a duly adjudicated determination that specific defendants had discriminated against a certified class of women in violation of a federal anti-discrimination statute; based upon findings of fact that were subject to the Federal Rules of Evidence. The factual problem presented in affirmative action cases is, "Does the evidence support a finding of discrimination such that race-or gender-conscious remedial measures are appropriate?" We find these multiple indicia of reliability and specificity to be sufficient to answer that question in the affirmative.

From the mere fact that a remedy flowing from a judicial determination of discrimination is gender-conscious, it does not follow that the remedy constitutes "affirmative action." Nor does a "reverse discrimination" claim arise every time an anti-discrimination statute is enforced. While some gender-conscious relief may adversely impact one gender—a fact that has not been demonstrated in this case—that alone would not make the relief "affirmative action" or the consequence of that relief "reverse discrimination." To the contrary, race-and gender-conscious remedies are both appropriate and constitutionally permissible under a federal anti-discrimination regime, although such remedial measures are still subject to equal protection review.

* * *

[The court then retraced and reaffirmed the earlier *Cohen* panel's treatment of the Title IX regulatory issues. In particular, the majority here specifically rejected Brown's principal argument—that the existing demands of its women students for varsity athletic opportunities were being accommodated as much if not more than were the demands of its male students. This position, the Court said, did not satisfy the third prong of the Policy Interpretation which required "full and effective" accommodation of all the athletic demands of the currently under-represented female student. The court dismissed Brown's effort to use the Title VII equal employment opportunity analogy to try to paint the Policy Interpretation as creating an illegitimate quota system in the athletic sphere.]

E.

* * *

It is imperative to recognize that athletics presents a distinctly different situation from admissions and employment and requires a different analysis in order to determine the existence vel non of discrimination. While the Title IX regime permits institutions to maintain gender-segregated teams, the law does not require that student-athletes attending institutions receiving federal funds must compete on gender-segregated teams; nor does the law require that institutions provide completely gender-integrated athletics programs. To the extent that Title IX allows institutions to maintain single-sex teams and gender-segregated athletics programs, men and women do not compete against each other for places on team rosters. Accordingly, and notwithstanding Brown's protestations to the contrary, the Title VII concept of the "qualified pool" has no place in a Title IX analysis of equal athletics opportunities for male and female athletes because women are not "qualified" to compete for positions on men's teams, and vice-versa. In addition, the concept of "preference" does not have the same meaning, or raise the same equality concerns, as it does in the employment and admissions contexts.

Brown's approach fails to recognize that, because gender-segregated teams are the norm in intercollegiate athletics programs, athletics differs from admissions and employment in analytically material ways. In providing for gender-segregated teams, intercollegiate athletics programs necessarily allocate opportunities separately for male and female students, and, thus, any inquiry into a claim of gender discrimination must compare the athletics participation opportunities provided for men with those provided for women. For this reason, and because recruitment of interested athletes is at the discretion of the institution, there is a risk that the institution will recruit only enough women to fill positions in a program that already underrepresents women, and that the smaller size of the women's program will have the effect of discouraging women's participation.

In this unique context, Title IX operates to ensure that the gender-segregated allocation of athletics opportunities does not disadvantage either gender. Rather than create a quota or preference, this unavoidably gender-conscious comparison merely provides for the allocation of athletics resources and participation opportunities between the sexes in a nondiscriminatory manner....

In contrast to the employment and admissions contexts, in the athletics context, gender is not an irrelevant characteristic. Courts and institutions must have some way of determining whether an institution complies with the mandate of Title IX and its supporting regulations to provide equal athletics opportunities for both genders, despite the fact that the institution maintains single-sex teams, and some way of fashioning a remedy upon a determination that the institution does not equally and effectively accommodate the interests and abilities of both genders....

* * *

F.

Brown has contended throughout this litigation that the significant disparity in athletics opportunities for men and women at Brown is the result of a gender-based differential in the level of interest in sports and that the district court's application of the three-part test requires universities to provide athletics opportunities for women to an extent that exceeds their relative interests and abilities in sports. Thus, at the heart of this litigation is the question whether Title IX permits Brown to deny its female students equal opportunity to participate in sports, based upon its unproven assertion that the district court's finding of a significant disparity in athletics opportunities for male and female students reflects, not discrimination in Brown's intercollegiate athletics program, but a lack of interest on the part of its female students that is unrelated to a lack of opportunities.

We view Brown's argument that women are less interested than men in participating in intercollegiate athletics, as well as its conclusion that institutions should be required to accommodate the interests and abilities of its female students only to the extent that it accommodates the interests and abilities of its male students, with great suspicion. To assert that Title IX permits institutions to provide fewer athletics participation opportunities for women than for men, based upon the premise that women are less interested in sports than are men, is (among other things) to ignore the fact that Title IX was enacted in order to remedy discrimination that results from stereotyped notions of women's interests and abilities.

Interest and ability rarely develop in a vacuum; they evolve as a function of opportunity and experience. The Policy Interpretation recognizes that women's lower rate of participation in athletics reflects women's historical lack of opportunities to participate in sports. See 44 Fed. Reg. at 71,419 ("Participation in intercollegiate sports has historically been emphasized for men but not women. Partially as a consequence of this, participation rates of women are far below those of men").

Moreover, the Supreme Court has repeatedly condemned gender-based discrimination based upon "archaic and overbroad generalizations" about women. *Schlesinger v. Ballard*, 419 U.S. 498, 508 (1975). See, e.g., *Mississippi Univ. for Women v. Hogan*, 458 U.S. 718, 725 (1982); *Califano v. Webster*, 430 U.S. 313, 317 (1977); *Frontiero v. Richardson*, 411 U.S. 677, 684–86 (1973). The Court has been especially critical of the use of statistical evidence offered to prove generalized, stereotypical notions about men and women. For example, in holding that Oklahoma's 3.2% beer statute invidiously discriminated against males 18–20 years of age, the Court in *Craig v. Boren*, 429 U.S. 190, 208–209 (1976), stressed that "the principles embodied in the Equal Protection Clause are not to be rendered inapplicable by statistically measured but loose-fitting generalities." . . .

Thus, there exists the danger that, rather than providing a true measure of women's interest in sports, statistical evidence purporting to reflect women's interest instead provides only a measure of the very discrimination that is and has been the basis for women's lack of opportunity to participate in sports. Prong three requires some kind of evidence of interest in athletics, and the Title IX framework permits the use of statistical evidence in assessing the level of interest in sports.[15]

---

15. Under the Policy Interpretation, institutions may determine the athletic interests and abilities of students by nondiscriminatory methods of their choosing provided:

    a. The processes take into account the nationally increasing levels of women's interests and abilities;

    b. The methods of determining interest and ability do not disadvantage the members of an underrepresented sex;

    c. The methods of determining ability take into account team performance records; and

    d. The methods are responsive to the expressed interests of students capable of intercollegiate competition who are members of an underrepresented sex.

44 Fed. Reg. at 71,417.

The 1990 version of the Title IX Athletics Investigator's Manual, an internal agency document, instructs investigating officials to consider, inter alia, the following: (i) any institutional surveys or assessments of students' athletics interests and abilities, see Valerie M. Bonnette & Lamar Daniel, *Department of Education, Title IX Athletics Investigator's Manual* at 22 (1990); (ii) the "expressed interests" of the underrepresented gender, id. at 25; (iii) other programs indicative of interests and abilities, such as club and intramural sports, sports programs at "feeder" schools, community and regional sports programs, and physical education classes, id.

As the district court noted, however, the agency characterizes surveys as a "simple way to identify which additional sports might appropriately be created to achieve compliance.... Thus, a survey of interests would follow a determination that an institution does not satisfy prong three; it would not be utilized to make that determination in the first instance." *Cohen III*, 897 F.Supp. at 210 n.51; see 1990 *Investigator's Manual* at 27 (explaining that a survey or assessment of interests and abilities is not required by the Title IX regulation or the Policy Interpretation but may be required as part of a remedy when OCR has conclud-

Nevertheless, to allow a numbers-based lack-of-interest defense to become the instrument of further discrimination against the underrepresented gender would pervert the remedial purpose of Title IX. We conclude that, even if it can be empirically demonstrated that, at a particular time, women have less interest in sports than do men, such evidence, standing alone, cannot justify providing fewer athletics opportunities for women than for men. Furthermore, such evidence is completely irrelevant where, as here, viable and successful women's varsity teams have been demoted or eliminated. We emphasize that, on the facts of this case, Brown's lack-of-interest arguments are of no consequence. As the prior panel recognized, while the question of full and effective accommodation of athletics interests and abilities is potentially a complicated issue where plaintiffs seek to create a new team or to elevate to varsity status a team that has never competed in varsity competition, no such difficulty is presented here, where plaintiffs seek to reinstate what were successful university-funded teams right up until the moment the teams were demoted....[16]

On these facts, Brown's failure to accommodate fully and effectively the interests and abilities of the underrepresented gender is clearly established. See *Clarification Memorandum* at 8 ("If an institution has recently eliminated a viable team from the intercollegiate program, OCR will find that there is sufficient interest, ability, and available competition to sustain an intercollegiate team in that sport unless an institution can provide strong evidence that interest, ability or available competition no longer exists."); id. at 8–9 n.2 ("While [other] indications of interest may be helpful to OCR in ascertaining likely interest on campus, particularly in the absence of more direct indicia[,] an institution is expected to meet the actual interests and abilities of its students and admitted students."). Under these circumstances, the district court's finding that there are interested women able to compete at the university-funded varsity level is clearly correct. Finally, the tremendous growth in women's participation in sports since Title IX was enacted disproves Brown's argument that women are less interested in sports for reasons unrelated to lack of opportunity. See, e.g., Mike Tharp et al., *Sports crazy! Ready, set, go. Why we love our games*, U.S. News & World Report, July 15, 1996, at 33–34 (attributing to Title IX the explosive growth of women's participation in sports and the debunking of "the traditional myth that women aren't interested in sports").

ed that an institution's current program does not equally effectively accommodate the interests and abilities of students).

16. The district court found that the women's gymnastics team had won the Ivy League championship in 1989–90 and was a "thriving university-funded varsity team prior to the 1991 demotion;" that the donor-funded women's fencing team had been successful for many years and that its request to be upgraded to varsity status had been supported by the athletics director at the time; that the donor-funded women's ski team had been consistently competitive despite a meager budget; and that the club-status women's water polo team had demonstrated the interest and ability to compete at full varsity status. *Cohen III*, 879 F.Supp. at 190.

Brown's relative interests approach is not a reasonable interpretation of the three-part test. This approach contravenes the purpose of the statute and the regulation because it does not permit an institution or a district court to remedy a gender-based disparity in athletics participation opportunities. Instead, this approach freezes that disparity by law, thereby disadvantaging further the underrepresented gender. Had Congress intended to entrench, rather than change, the status quo—with its historical emphasis on men's participation opportunities to the detriment of women's opportunities—it need not have gone to all the trouble of enacting Title IX.

V.

In the first appeal, this court rejected Brown's Fifth Amendment equal protection challenge to the statutory scheme. Here, Brown argues that its challenge is to the decision of the district court. As Brown puts it, "the [equal protection] violation arises from the court's holding that Title IX requires the imposition of quotas, preferential treatment, and disparate treatment in the absence of a compelling state interest and a determination that the remedial measure is 'narrowly tailored' to serve that interest." Reply Br. at 18 (citing *Adarand*, 115 S.Ct. at 2117).

[The court then addressed and rejected Brown's argument that when *Adarand* reversed *Metro Broadcasting* and required strict scrutiny of federal affirmative action measures for minorities, the Supreme Court thereby removed a key underpinning of *Cohen I* which (relying on *Metro Broadcasting*) had applied "intermediate scrutiny" in assessing Title IX and its Policy Interpretation. The majority in *Cohen II* was satisfied that intermediate scrutiny was still the appropriate "equal protection" standard for assessing gender (as opposed to racial) classifications. That was especially the case here, where the gender-based standard was embodied in a district court remedy for violation of an anti-discrimination law, rather than the legislatively-mandated preferences that were at issue in both *Metro Broadcasting* and *Adarand*.]

* * *

Under intermediate scrutiny, the burden of demonstrating an exceedingly persuasive justification for a government-imposed, gender-conscious classification is met by showing that the classification serves important governmental objectives, and that the means employed are substantially related to the achievement of those objectives. E.g., *Hogan*, 458 U.S. at 724. Applying that test, it is clear that the district court's remedial order passes constitutional muster.

We find that the first part of the test is satisfied. The governmental objectives of "avoiding the use of federal resources to support discriminatory practices," and "providing individual citizens effective protection against those practices," *Cannon*, 441 U.S. at 704, are clearly important objectives. We also find that judicial enforcement of federal anti-discrimination statutes is at least an important governmental objective.

Applying the second prong of the intermediate scrutiny test, we find that the means employed by the district court in fashioning relief for the statutory violation are clearly substantially related to these important objectives. Intermediate scrutiny does not require that there be no other way to accomplish the objectives, but even if that were the standard, it would be satisfied in the unique context presented by the application of Title IX to athletics.

As explained previously, Title IX as it applies to athletics is distinct from other anti-discrimination regimes in that it is impossible to determine compliance or to devise a remedy without counting and comparing opportunities with gender explicitly in mind. Even under the individual rights theory of equal protection, reaffirmed in *Adarand*, 115 S.Ct. at 2112 (the equal protection guarantee "protects persons, not groups"), the only way to determine whether the rights of an individual athlete have been violated and what relief is necessary to remedy the violation is to engage in an explicitly gender-conscious comparison. Accordingly, even assuming that the three-part test creates a gender classification that favors women, allowing consideration of gender in determining the remedy for a Title IX violation serves the important objective of "ensuring that in instances where overall athletic opportunities decrease, the actual opportunities available to the underrepresented gender do not." *Kelley*, 35 F.3d at 272. In addition, a gender-conscious remedial scheme is constitutionally permissible if it directly protects the interests of the disproportionately burdened gender. See Hogan, 458 U.S. at 728 ("In limited circumstances, a gender-based classification favoring one sex can be justified if it intentionally and directly assists members of the sex that is disproportionately burdened").

Under Brown's interpretation of the three-part test, there can never be a remedy for a violation of Title IX's equal opportunity mandate. In concluding that the district court's interpretation and application of the three-part test creates a quota, Brown errs, in part, because it fails to recognize that (i) the substantial proportionality test of prong one is only the starting point, and not the conclusion, of the analysis; and (ii) prong three is not implicated unless a gender-based disparity with respect to athletics participation opportunities has been shown to exist. Where such a disparity has been established, the inquiry under prong three is whether the athletics interests and abilities of the underrepresented gender are fully and effectively accommodated, such that the institution may be found to comply with Title IX, notwithstanding the disparity.

Of course, a remedy that requires an institution to cut, add, or elevate the status of athletes or entire teams may impact the genders differently, but this will be so only if there is a gender-based disparity with respect to athletics opportunities to begin with, which is the only circumstance in which prong three comes into play. Here, however, it has not been shown that Brown's men students will be disadvantaged by the full and effective accommodation of the athletics interests and abilities of its women students.

VII.

[While the circuit court majority upheld the district court's ruling that Brown's athletic program was in violation of Title IX, the panel refused to endorse the remedial order that required Brown to upgrade its existing women's gymnastics, fencing, skiing, and water polo teams to university-funded varsity status. The Court said that Brown should have the option to cut back, instead, on its men's varsity slots in order to put itself in compliance with the law.]

* * *

There can be no doubt that Title IX has changed the face of women's sports as well as our society's interest in and attitude toward women athletes and women's sports. See, e.g., Frank DeFord, *The Women of Atlanta*, Newsweek, June 10, 1996, at 62–71; Tharp, supra, at 33; Robert Kuttner, *Vicious Circle of Exclusion*, Washington Post, September 4, 1996, at A15. In addition, there is ample evidence that increased athletics participation opportunities for women and young girls, available as a result of Title IX enforcement, have had salutary effects in other areas of societal concern.

One need look no further than the impressive performances of our country's women athletes in the 1996 Olympic Summer Games to see that Title IX has had a dramatic and positive impact on the capabilities of our women athletes, particularly in team sports. These Olympians represent the first full generation of women to grow up under the aegis of Title IX. The unprecedented success of these athletes is due, in no small measure, to Title IX's beneficent effects on women's sports, as the athletes themselves have acknowledged time and again. What stimulated this remarkable change in the quality of women's athletic competition was not a sudden, anomalous upsurge in women's interest in sports, but the enforcement of Title IX's mandate of gender equity in sports.

Affirmed in part, reversed in part, and remanded for further proceedings. No costs on appeal to either party.

TORRUELLA, CHIEF JUDGE (Dissenting).

Because I am not persuaded that the majority's view represents the state of the law today, I respectfully dissent.

* * *

II. BROWN'S EQUAL PROTECTION CHALLENGE

Appellees have argued that the three-prong test does not create a gender classification because the classification applies to both women and men. Although I agree that by its words, the test would apply to men at institutions where they are proportionately underrepresented in intercollegiate athletics, I cannot accept the argument that, via this provision, the Government does not classify its citizens by gender.... The fact of gender-conscious classification, even with equal enforcement with respect to both genders, requires the application of a higher level of scrutiny than rational basis review. We cannot pretend that an interpretation of a statute that contains explicit categorization according to gender and that has intentional gender-conscious effect does not represent gender-based government action. Equal Protection is implicated where the claim is made that a classification made by the government intentionally subjects an individual to treatment different from similarly situated individuals based on an impermissible characteristic, such as race, national origin, or gender.

A. The District Court's Construction of the Three-Prong Test

1. Prong One

A central issue in this case is the manner in which athletic "participation opportunities" are counted. During the 1990–91 academic year, Brown fielded 16 men's and 15 women's varsity teams on which 566 men and 328 women participated. By the 1993–94 year, there were 12 university-funded men's teams and 13 university funded women's teams. These teams included 479 men and 312 women. Based on an analysis of membership in varsity teams, the district court concluded that there existed a disparity between female participation in intercollegiate athletics and female student enrollment.

Even assuming that membership numbers in varsity sports is a reasonable proxy for participation opportunities—a view with which I do not concur—contact sports should be eliminated from the calculus. The regulation at 34 C.F.R. § 106.41 (1995)(b) provides that an academic institution may operate separate teams for members of each sex "where selection of such teams is based upon competitive skill or the activity involved is a contact sport." 34 C.F.R. § 106.41(b). When a team is sponsored only for one sex, however, and where "athletic opportunities for members of that sex have previously been limited, members of the excluded sex must be allowed to try-out for the team offered unless the sport involved is a contact sport," id. The regulation, therefore, allows schools to operate single-sex teams in contact sports. In counting participation opportunities, therefore, it does not make sense to include in the calculus athletes participating in contact sports that include only men's teams. For example, if a university chooses to sponsor a football team, it is permitted to sponsor only a men's team. Not all sports are the same and the university should be given the flexibility to determine which activities are most beneficial to its student body. By including in its accounting a contact sport that requires very large numbers of participants, e.g., football, the district court skews the number of athletic participants—making it impossible for the university to provide both men's and women's teams in other sports.

If the athletes competing in sports for which the university is permitted to field single-sex teams are excluded from the calculation of participation rates, the proportion of women participants would increase dramatically and prong one might be satisfied. If so, the inquiry ends and Brown should be judged to be in compliance.

2. Prong Two

The district court concluded, and the majority appears to agree, that Brown failed to satisfy prong two because "merely reducing program offerings to the overrepresented gender does not constitute program expansion for the underrepresented gender." This is a curious result because the entire three-prong test is based on relative participation rates. Prong one, for example, requires that participation opportunities be provided proportionately to enrollment, but does not mandate any absolute number of such opportunities. The district court's conclusion with respect to prong two, however, implies that a school must not only demonstrate that the proportion of women in their program is growing over time, it must also show that the absolute number of women participating is increasing.[26]

Under the district court's interpretation, a school facing budgetary constraints must, in order to comply with prong two, increase the opportunities available to the underrepresented gender, even if it cannot afford to do so. Rather than respecting the school's right to determine the role athletics will play in the future—including reducing the opportunities available to the formerly overrepresented gender to ensure proportionate opportunities—the district court and the majority demand that the absolute number of opportunities provided to the underrepresented gender be increased. I see no possible justification for this interpretation—the regulation is intended to protect against discrimination, not to promote athletics on college campuses. A school is not required to sponsor an athletic program of any particular size. It is not for the courts, or the legislature, for that matter, to mandate programs of a given size. The most that can be demanded is that athletics be provided in a non-discriminatory manner.

* * *

3. Prong Three

Prong three of the three-prong test states that, where an institution does not comply with prongs one or two, compliance will be assessed on the basis of

> whether it can be demonstrated that the interests and abilities of the members of the [proportionately underrepresented] sex have been fully and effectively accommodated by the present program.

44 Fed. Reg. 71,413, 71,418 (December 11, 1979).

According to the district court, Brown's athletics program violates prong three because members of the proportionately underrepresented sex have demonstrated interest sufficient for a university-funded varsity team that is not in fact being funded. The district court asserts that this

---

26. This requirement presents a dilemma for a school in which women are less interested in athletics, as Brown contends is the case. Under such conditions, a school may be unable to succeed under the second prong because there may not be enough interested female students to achieve a continuing increase in the number of female participants.

is not a quota. Brown, on the other hand, argues that prong three is satisfied when (1) the interests and abilities of members of the proportionately underrepresented gender (2) are accommodated to the same degree as the proportionately overrepresented gender.

The district court's narrow, literal interpretation should be rejected because prong three cannot be read in isolation. First, as Brown points out, the Regulation that includes prong three provides that, in assessing compliance under the regulation, "the governing principle in this area is that the athletic interests and abilities of male and female students be equally effectively accommodated." *Policy Interpretation*, 44 Fed. Reg. 71,413, 71,414. Thus, Brown contends, to meet "fully"—in an absolute sense—the interests and abilities of an underrepresented gender, while unmet interest among the overrepresented gender continues, would contravene the governing principle of "equally effective accommodation" of the interests and abilities of students of both genders.

It is also worthwhile to note that to "fully" accommodate the interests and abilities of the underrepresented sex is an extraordinarily high—perhaps impossibly so—requirement. How could an academic institution with a large and diverse student body ever "fully" accommodate the athletic interests of its students? Under even the largest athletic program, it would be surprising to find that there is not a single student who would prefer to participate in athletics but does not do so because the school does not offer a program in the particular sport that interests the student. To read fully in an absolute sense would make the third prong virtually impossible to satisfy and, therefore, an irrelevant addition to the test.

This difficulty was recognized in *Cohen II*, which stated that "the mere fact that there are some female students interested in a sport does not ipso facto require the school to provide a varsity team in order to comply with the third benchmark." *Cohen II* 991 F.2d at 898. The balance that *Cohen II* advocates would require the institution to ensure "participatory opportunities ... when, and to the extent that, there is sufficient interest and ability among the members of the excluded sex to sustain a viable team." Id. (internal citations omitted). This standard may be practical for certain sports that require large teams, but what of individual sports? A "viable" tennis team may require only a single player. The same could be said of any individual sport, including golf, track and field, cycling, fencing, archery, and so on. Therefore, we still have the problem that to "fully accommodate" the interests of the underrepresented sex may be impossible under the district court's interpretation.

In light of the above, Brown argues that prong three is in fact ambiguous with respect to whether "fully" means (1) an institution must meet 100% of the underrepresented gender's unmet reasonable interest and ability, or (2) an institution must meet the underrepresented gender's unmet reasonable interest and ability as fully as it meets those of the overrepresented gender. I agree with Brown that, in the context of OCR's Policy Interpretation, prong three is susceptible to at least these two plausible interpretations.

Additionally, § 1681(a), a provision enacted by Congress as part of Title IX itself, casts doubt on the district court's reading of prong three. 20 U.S.C. § 1681(a) (1988). As Brown points out, Title IX, of which the Policy Interpretation is an administrative interpretation, contains language that prohibits the ordering of preferential treatment on the basis of gender due to a failure of a program to substantially mirror the gender ratio of an institution. Specifically, with respect to Title IX's guarantee that no person shall be excluded on the basis of sex from "participation in, denied the benefits of or subjected to discrimination under any education program or activity receiving Federal financial assistance," 20 U.S.C. § 1681(a),

> nothing contained [therein] shall be interpreted to require any educational institution to grant preferential or disparate treatment to the members of one sex on account of an imbalance which may exist with respect to the total number or percentage of persons of the sex participating in or receiving the benefits of any federally supported program or activity, in comparison with the total number or percentage of persons of that sex in any community.

Id. § 1681(b). Section 1681(b) provides yet another reason why the district court's reading of prong three is troublesome and why Brown's reading is a reasonable alternative.

Since the applicable regulation, 34 C.F.R. § 106.41, and policy interpretation, 44 Fed. Reg. 71,418, are not manifestly contrary to the objectives of Title IX, and Congress has specifically delegated to an agency the responsibility to articulate standards governing a particular area, we must accord the ensuing regulation considerable deference. *Chevron, U.S.A. v. Natural Resources Defense Council, Inc.*, 467 U.S. 837, 844 (1984). That notwithstanding, where—as here—the resulting regulation is susceptible to more than one reasonable interpretation, we owe no such deference to the interpretation chosen where the choice is made not by the agency but by the district court. Therefore, like other cases of statutory interpretation, we should review the district court's reading de novo.

B. The District Court's Interpretation and the Resulting Equal Protection Problem

The district court's interpretation of prongs one and three creates an Equal Protection problem, which I analyze in two steps. First, the district court's interpretation creates a quota scheme. Second, even assuming such a quota scheme is otherwise constitutional, appellees have not pointed to an "exceedingly persuasive justification," see *Virginia*, 116 S.Ct. at 2274, for this particular quota scheme.

1. The Quota

I believe that the three prong test, as the district court interprets it, is a quota. I am in square disagreement with the majority, who believe that "no aspect of the Title IX regime at issue in this case ... mandates gender-based preferences or quotas." Put another way, I agree that "Title IX is not an affirmative action statute," but I believe that is exactly what the district court has made of it. As interpreted by the district court, the test constitutes an affirmative action, quota-based scheme.

I am less interested in the actual term "quota" than the legally cognizable characteristics that render a quota scheme impermissible. And those characteristics are present here in spades. I am not persuaded by the majority's argument that the three-part test does not constitute a quota because it does not permit an agency or court to find a violation solely on the basis of prong one of the test; instead, an institution must also fail prongs two and three. As Brown rightly argues, the district court's application of the three-prong test requires Brown to allocate its athletic resources to meet the as-yet-unmet interest of a member of the underrepresented sex, women in this case, while simultaneously neglecting any unmet interest among individuals of the overrepresented sex. To the extent that the rate of interest in athletics diverges between men and women at any institution, the district court's interpretation would require that such an institution treat an individual male student's athletic interest and an individual female student's athletic interest completely differently: one student's reasonable interest would have to be met, by law, while meeting the other student's interest would only aggravate the lack of proportionality giving rise to the legal duty. "The injury in cases of this kind is that a 'discriminatory classification prevents ... competition on an equal footing.'" *Adarand*, 115 S.Ct. at 2104 (quoting *Northeast Fla. Chapter, Assoc'd Gen'l Contractors of America v. Jacksonville*, 508 U.S. 656, 666 (1993)). As a result, individual male and female students would be precluded from competing against each other for scarce resources; they would instead compete only against members of their own gender. Cf. *Hopwood v. Texas*, 78 F.3d 932, 943–46 (5th Cir.1996) (concluding that not only would government action precluding competition between individuals of different races for law school admissions be unconstitutional, but in fact even partial consideration of race among other factors would be unconstitutional).

The majority claims that "neither the Policy Interpretation nor the district court's interpretation of it, mandates statistical balancing." The logic of this position escapes me. A school can satisfy the test in three ways. The first prong is met if the school provides participation opportunities for male and female students in numbers substantially proportionate to their enrollments. This prong surely requires statistical balancing. The second prong is satisfied if an institution that cannot meet prong one can show a "continuing practice of program expansion which is demonstrably responsive to the developing interest and abilities of the members of the underrepresented sex." 44 Fed. Reg. at 71,418. It can hardly be denied that this prong requires statistical balancing as it is essentially a test that requires the school to show that it is moving in the direction of satisfying the first prong. Establishing that a school is moving inexorably closer to satisfying a requirement that demands statistical balancing can only be done by demonstrating an improvement in the statistical balance. In other words, the second prong also requires balancing. Finally, the third prong, interpreted as the majority advocates, dispenses with statistical balancing only because it chooses to accord zero weight to one side of the balance. Even a single person with a reasonable unmet interest defeats compliance. This standard, in fact, goes farther than the straightforward quota test of prong one. According to the district court, the unmet interests of the underrepresented sex must be completely accommodated before any of the interest of the overrepresented gender can be accommodated.[28]

A pragmatic overview of the effect of the three-prong test leads me to reject the majority's claim that the three-prong test does not amount to a quota because it involves multiple prongs. In my view it is the result of the test, and not the number of steps involved, that should determine if a quota system exists. Regardless of how many steps are involved, the fact remains that the test requires proportionate participation opportunities for both sexes (prong one) unless one sex is simply not interested in participating (prong three). It seems to me that a quota with an exception for situations in which there are insufficient interested students to allow the school to meet it remains a quota. All of the negative effects of a quota remain,[29] and the school can escape the quota under prong three only by offering preferential treatment to the group that has demonstrated less interest in athletics.

2. "Extremely Persuasive Justification" Test

In view of the quota scheme adopted by the district court, and Congress' specific disavowal of any intent to require quotas as part of Title IX, appellees have not met their burden of showing an "exceedingly persuasive justification" for this gender-conscious exercise of government authority. As recently set forth in *Virginia*, "parties who seek to defend gender-based government action must demonstrate an 'exceedingly persuasive justification' for that action." *Virginia*, 116 S.Ct. at 2274. While the Supreme Court in Virginia acknowledged that "physical differences between men and women ... are enduring," id. at 2276, it went on to state that such "'inherent differences' between men and

---

28. The problem with the majority's argument can be illustrated with a hypothetical college admissions policy that would require proportionality between the gender ratio of the local student aged population and that of admitted students. This policy is comparable to prong one of the three prong test and is, without a doubt, a quota. It is no less a quota if an exception exists for schools whose gender ratio differs from that of the local population but which admit every applicant of the underrepresented gender. It remains a quota because the school is forced to admit every female applicant until it reaches the requisite proportion. Similarly, the district court's interpretation requires the school to accommodate the interests of every female student until proportionality is reached.

29. Nor does the second prong of the test change the analysis. That prong merely recognizes that a school may not be able to meet the quotas of the first or third prong immediately, and therefore deems it sufficient to show program expansion that is responsive to the interests of the underrepresented sex.

women, we have come to appreciate, remain cause for celebration, but not for ... artificial constraints on an individual's opportunity." Id.

Neither appellees nor the district court have demonstrated an "exceedingly persuasive justification" for the government action that the district court has directed in this case. In fact, appellees have failed to point to any congressional statement or indication of intent regarding a proportional representation scheme as applied by the district court. While they point to Congress' decision to delegate authority to the relevant agencies, this does not amount to a genuine ... exceedingly persuasive justification in light of § 1681(b)'s "no quota" provision. We are left with the explanations discussed in *Cohen II* to the effect that Congress conducted hearings on the subject of discrimination against women in education. There is little more than that, because Congress adopted Title IX as a floor amendment without committee hearings or reports.

I believe that the district court's interpretation of the Policy Interpretation's three-prong test poses serious constitutional difficulties. "Where an otherwise acceptable construction of a statute would raise serious constitutional problems, [we] construe the statute to avoid such problems unless such construction is plainly contrary to the intent of Congress." *Edward J. DeBartolo Corp. v. Florida Gulf Coast Bldg. & Constr. Trades Council*, 485 U.S. 568 (1988); see *NLRB v. Catholic Bishop of Chicago*, 440 U.S. 490, 507 (1979). To the extent that Congress expressed a specific intent germane to the district court's interpretation, Congress, if anything, expressed an aversion to quotas as a method to enforce Title IX. As a result, I opt for Brown's construction of prong three, which, as we have discussed, infra, is also a reasonable reading.

Accordingly, I would reverse and remand for further proceedings.

III. Evidentiary Issues

In disputes over the representation of women in athletic programs, it is inevitable that statistical evidence will be relevant. There is simply no other way to assess participation rates, interest levels, and abilities. The majority opinion, however, offers inconsistent guidance with respect to the role of statistics in Title IX claims. Early in the opinion, the majority approvingly cites to the statistical evaluations conducted in *Cohen I*, *Cohen II*, and *Cohen III*. The figures in question demonstrate that women's participation in athletics is less than proportional to their enrollment. Later in the opinion, however, when the level of interest among women at Brown is at issue, the court adopts a much more critical attitude towards statistical evidence: "There exists the danger that, rather than providing a true measure of women's interest in sports, statistical evidence purporting to reflect women's interest instead provides only a measure of the very discrimination that is and has been the basis for women's lack of opportunity." In other words, evidence of differential levels of interest is not to be credited because it may simply reflect the result of past discrimination.

The refusal to accept surveys of interest levels as evidence of interest raises the question of what indicators might be used. The majority offers no guidance to a school seeking to assess the levels of interest of its students. Although the three-prong test, even as interpreted by the district court, appears to allow the school the opportunity to show a lack of interest, the majority rejects the best—and perhaps the only—mechanism for making such a showing.

Brown claims that the district court erred in excluding evidence pertaining to the relative athletic interests of men and women at the university. Brown sought to introduce the NCAA Gender Equity Study and the results of an undergraduate poll on student interest in athletics, but was not permitted to do so. The majority is unsympathetic to Brown's claim that the disparity between athletic opportunities for men and women reflect a gender-based difference in interest levels. Indeed, despite Brown's attempt to present evidence in support of its claim, the majority characterizes Brown's argument as an "unproven assertion."[30]

Furthermore, the majority recognizes that institutions are entitled to use any nondiscriminatory method of their choosing to determine athletic interests. If statistical evidence of interest levels is not to be considered by courts, however, there is no way for schools to determine whether they are in compliance. Any studies or surveys they might conduct in order to assess their own compliance would, in the event of litigation, be deemed irrelevant. Regardless of the efforts made by the academic institution, the specter of a lawsuit would be ever-present.

In addition, the majority has put the power to control athletics and the provision of athletic resources in the hands of the underrepresented gender. Virtually every other aspect of college life is entrusted to the institution, but athletics has now been carved out as an exception and the university is no longer in full control of its program. Unless the two genders participate equally in athletics, members of the underrepresented sex would have the ability to demand a varsity level team at any time if they can show sufficient interest. Apparently no weight is given to the sustainability of the interest, the cost of the sport, the university's view on the desirability of the sport, and so on.

IV. First Amendment Issue

Finally, it is important to remember that Brown University is a private institution with a constitutionally protected First Amendment

---

30. Among the evidence submitted by Brown are: (i) admissions data showing greater athletic interest among male applicants than female applicants; (ii) college board data showing greater athletic interest and prior participation rates by prospective male applicants than female applicants; (iii) data from the Cooperative Institutional Research Program at UCLA indicating greater athletic interest among men than women; (iv) an independent telephone survey of 500 randomly selected Brown undergraduates that reveals that Brown offers women participation opportunities in excess of their representation in the pool of interested, qualified students; (v) intramural and club participation rates that demonstrate higher participation rates among men than women; (vi) walk-on and try-out numbers that reflect a greater interest among men than women; (vii) high school participation rates that show a much lower rate of participation among females than among males; (viii) the NCAA Gender Equity Committee data showing that women across the country participate in athletics at a lower rate than men.

right to choose its curriculum. Athletics are part of that curriculum. Although the protections of the First Amendment cannot be used to justify discrimination, this court should not forget that it has a duty to protect a private institution's right to mould its own educational environment.

The majority pays lip service to these concerns in the final pages of its long opinion, stating that " 'we are a society that cherishes academic freedom and recognizes that universities deserve great leeway in their operations.' " Majority Opinion at 69 (quoting *Cohen II*, 991 F.2d at 906), and "our respect for academic freedom and reluctance to interject ourselves into the conduct of university affairs counsels that we give universities as much freedom as possible." Despite these statements, however, the majority in its opinion today, and the district court before it, have failed to give Brown University freedom to craft its own athletic program and to choose the priorities of that program. Instead, they have established a legal rule that straightjackets college athletics programs by curtailing their freedom to choose the sports they offer.

In the spring of 1997, the Supreme Court declined Brown University's invitation to use the *Cohen* case as its first occasion to address the complexities of Title IX in the world of college sports.[c] Brown thus filed

---

c. We should note that a Louisiana district court judge within the Fifth Circuit rejected the major legal premise to the *Cohen* opinion, though she ultimately reached the same verdict on the specific facts of her case. See *Pederson v. Louisiana State University*, 912 F.Supp. 892 (M.D.La.1996). Louisiana State had first created a football team in 1893, a baseball team in 1908, and several other men's varsity sports after that. Not until 1977, though, did LSU create its first women's varsity teams: volleyball, gymnastics, basketball, tennis, and swimming, to which golf was added in 1979 and track and field in 1981. Women's fastpitch softball was also made a varsity sport in 1979, but then dropped in 1982 for no express reasons. By the 1990s, LSU's student body was 49% female, but its varsity athletes just 29% female. In 1993, pursuant to a Southeastern Conference mandate (which LSU had initially opposed), the school announced that it would be creating women's varsity soccer and softball. Play in soccer had begun in 1995 on a limited basis, and softball, with a coach hired, was planned to start in the spring of 1997. However, this lawsuit was filed in 1994 by female student-athletes in those sports who wanted quicker and stronger action from the school.

In the course of her lengthy opinion, Judge Rebecca Doherty disagreed with the circuit court decisions in *Cohen I* and *Roberts* that had endorsed the OCR's Title IX Policy Interpretation, with its proportionality standard between female athletes and female students. In the judge's opinion, it was a mistake to assume that "the same percentage of [the school's] male population as its female population has the ability to participate and the interest or desire to participate in sports at the same competitive level" (p. 913). However, because here LSU had produced no "credible evidence to establish what the interests and abilities of its student population are" (p. 915), the school was found liable based on the combination of overall statistical disparity, demonstrated interest and ability in these particular sports among at least some of its current students, and the lack of ongoing expansion of athletic opportunities for its female students as a whole. However, while Judge Doherty was prepared to issue injunctive relief for the future, she rejected this first-ever request by student-athletes for monetary damages under Title IX. On the assumption that Title IX authorized damages only for *intentional* violations, the Judge said that while this question is "a very close one," LSU's violations were not intentional. "Rather, they are a result of arrogant ignorance, confusion regarding the practical requirements of the law, and a

with the district court its proposal about how it would comply with the judge's ruling. Another 60 positions were to be added to the school's female rosters; in particular, by upgrading to varsity status the existing club teams in women's lightweight crew, equestrian, and water polo. While no men's teams were to be eliminated, a number of positions would be cut from several teams, and a cap would be imposed upon the number of athletes permitted on each male team (as well as a minimum floor on the number of positions on the women's teams). The result would be that Brown's previous 13–percentage point gap between the female-athlete and female-student ratios would be cut to one percentage point, well within the five percent range accepted by the OCR.

Interestingly, at around that same time, the data required by the Equity in Athletics Disclosure Act were released, and it turned out that at three Division I schools, the female athlete ratios were more than five points *above* their student ratios—in the military academies. At the Air Force Academy, women comprised 15% of the student body and 26% of the athletes; at Navy, the figures were 14% and 22%, and at Army, 12% and 19%.

Two lines of inquiry must be pursued in considering this vital issue in both sports and higher education. One is strictly legal in character: what *must* colleges now do in their varsity athletic programs? The other is about the underlying policy question: what *should* colleges do, either the same or more or less than what the circuit courts have endorsed in *Cohen* and the other cases?

With respect to the first problem, look again at the wording of both Title IX's ban on gender discrimination in education, and the Departmental regulation requiring "effective accommodation of the interests and abilities of members of both sexes in sports." Compare these to the more detailed Policy Interpretation by the Office of Civil Rights. Is the latter administrative interpretation actually compatible with the wording of the statute and its regulations? Even if it is a *rational* interpretation (as three circuits have affirmed), would a different interpretation also be compatible with the wording and intention of Title IX? That question of statutory construction is crucial because it dictates whether a President alone, or only Congress and the President together, can change the legal course in this area.

The underlying policy question is whether the existing legal benchmark should be retained or revised, and if the latter, in which direction. One key fact is that, faced with a combination of Title IX and budget crunches, universities have now cumulatively eliminated 140 men's wrestling teams, 100 men's gymnastic teams, and 65 men's swimming

remarkably outdated view of women and athletics which created the byproduct of resistance to change" (p. 918).

teams. These steps have made the public and the politicians vividly aware of the costs as well as the benefits of this law. A recent example was the decision of Boston University to terminate its football program at the end of the 1997 season, a program that had begun in 1884 and had won the Division I–AA title as late as 1993. A few years earlier, B.U. had eliminated men's baseball while retaining women's softball (as well as its revenue-generating NCAA champion men's hockey team). Ironically, the NCAA reduced to 13 the permissible number of scholarships for men's basketball (though leaving the women's team at 15) at the same time as it was securing a $1.75 *billion* contract from CBS to telecast its men's basketball championship tournament through 2001–02. Critics of Title IX in the Congress as well as in athletic departments point to these developments as evidence of the disparate impact of Title IX's current proportionality standard.

Proponents of Title IX, such as Donna Lopiano, Executive Director of the Women's Sports Foundation, are equally critical of this elimination of various men's sports, but they say that the real culprit is not Title IX, but college football. In the early 1990s, the NCAA reduced the maximum number of football scholarships at Division I–A schools to 85. This scholarship figure, though, remains nearly double the size of the rosters that NFL teams take to the Super Bowl. In addition, most schools have another 40 to 50 non-scholarship players on their squads, "walk-ons" who want to spend their extracurricular time practicing football and hoping for a chance to get on the field for a game. Lopiano and other defenders of Title IX contend, then, that the solution is simply for colleges to stop spending so much of their money on football programs, so that they can better accommodate the interests of both women and men students in other sports.

In appraising these conflicting views about the distribution of college athletic positions among female and male students, we must also be aware of other distributional data regarding college sports. One important aspect is the revenue factor described in Chapter 10. Football, at least in Division I–A, is the dominant revenue source for college sports, with men's basketball the only other major contributor. The most recent NCAA Report on *Revenues and Expenses of Intercollegiate Athletics: 1995* reported that the average Division I–A men's athletic program had a $2.5 million profit on a $9.8 million revenue stream, while the average women's program had a $1.7 million deficit, over and above its nearly $600,000 in total revenues. The average Division I–A football program took in $6.4 million (and one program actually topped $22 million), and produced $2.35 million in profits for the school. The average men's basketball team earned $2.2 million in revenues and $1.3 million in profits. The average women's basketball team generated $135,000 in total revenues and had a $415,000 deficit: only four Division I women's teams made even modest profits in 1995.

While a significant proportion (roughly one-third) of college football and basketball programs do spend more than they earn, even here their revenues cover a substantially higher proportion of the programs' costs than do non-revenue sports (men's or women's). In aggregate terms, colleges *spend* roughly $2 on men's sports for every $1 spent on women's sports: however, the same schools *earn* $13 from their men's varsity teams for every $1 earned from their women's teams. Recall the ruling of the Washington Supreme Court in *Blair*, that Washington State was entitled under the state law to exclude from its calculations of the relative contribution made by the *school* to its men's and women's athletic programs the amounts generated by each *sport* from fans who watched the games as spectators or television viewers, or who contributed to the programs as alumni and booster club members. Should that same formula be applied to Washington State (and Brown) under federal Title IX?

Another distributional factor in the college sports world relates to race. In 1994–95, African-American men made up 65% of the rosters of Division I basketball teams and 51% of Division I–A football teams. Together with track and field, these three sports accounted for 92% of the positions occupied by male black athletes. African–American women found 81% of their athletic positions in basketball and track. At the same time, while women who comprise half the student body have just over 35% of scholarship athletes, blacks who comprise nine percent of the students account for 25% of the athletes. To what extent, if any, do these numbers suggest any tension between the policies embodied in Title IX and Title VI of the Civil Rights Act regarding fair treatment of different demographic groups within college sports?

Finally, what should be the policy treatment of the principal argument advanced by Brown in the *Cohen* litigation—that the apparent disparity between the female proportion of its student body and the female proportion of its varsity athletes was attributable not to discriminatory exclusion by the school, but rather to divergent male and female student interests in varsity sports as an extracurricular activity (with male students often not having the same interests as women in other extracurricular activities such as theater or dance)? Among the measures of student interest advanced by Brown's counsel were variations in participation rates on high school teams or college intramural teams, as well as surveys of interest among the college student body. (While the relative interest of Brown's female freshmen applicants in intercollegiate sports was significantly less than women's 38% share of actual team rosters, women made up 91% and 66% respectively of freshmen interest in the school's dancing and music programs.) One such study was done for Colorado University regarding its freshmen and transfer students during the orientation week: it disclosed that 15% of the male and eight percent of the female students were interested in varsity sports, 30% to 21% in club sports, and 44% to 54% in intramural sports. And in American high schools, whereas women made up just five percent of high school athletes in 1971, this figure jumped to 18% in 1972 (the year that Title IX was enacted) and 30% in 1977; it was at 37%–38% in the mid-1990s, roughly the same ratio as in colleges.

Certainly, Title IX is phrased to guarantee women an equal opportunity to participate in college athletics (and other educational programs), not to require actual equality in participation, irrespective of variations in real interests. A key question, though, is whether the above statistical snapshots simply reflect longstanding cultural attitudes towards women aspiring to reach athletic heights, a social attitude that the law must try to overcome rather than simply accommodate. There is also a question, though, of how long such an affirmative form of government regulation should be pursued and enforced in the face of existing interests. Once Title IX and Title VI have succeeded in creating a large critical mass of female or minority participation in college sports (or broader educational and workplace settings), should the regulations be relaxed to permit more individual choice in the college marketplace? Indeed, one suggestion has been made to modify the Equity and Athletics Disclosure Act to follow the lead of the Student–Athlete Right-to-Know Act we read about at the end of Chapter 9.[d] Every student applicant (not just every scholarship athlete) would have to be told not just of the school's athlete graduation rates, but also of its female-male (and minority-white) participation rates in college sports. Is such a measure likely to suffice now as the vehicle for implementing Title IX (and if not, when)? One final question about variations in athletic interests among students: should schools like the University of Illinois be forced to bar male "walk-on" students from being added to their football rosters, in order to preserve teams for scholarship athletes in *men's* swimming and fencing?

Shortly after the Supreme Court refused to address the Title IX issues posed by the *Cohen* case, the National Women's Law Center (NWLC) raised a new issue about the application of Title IX to college sports. In a complaint filed with the U.S. Department of Education in June 1997 (25 years after Title IX became law), NWLC charged 25 universities with having failed to provide their women athletes with a proportionate share of athletic scholarship funding. The Title IX standard appealed to here would require women athletes to receive the same proportion of their college's expenditures on athletic scholarships as the female share of all the school's athletes, not the whole student body. Even with this narrower benchmark, Vanderbilt was alleged to have spent each year $6,750 less per female athlete than Title IX required, with Boston University having a $3,754 gap, Wake Forest $3,665, Duke $2,603, all the way down to South Carolina State at $1,001. B.U.'s removal of its 65 football positions and scholarships will presumably eliminate the problem at its school. However, NWLC asserts that the gap at Vanderbilt, for example, means that the average woman athlete there receives $25,000 less in scholarship assistance over a four year college career than does her male counterpart.

d. See Rodney K. Smith, *When Ignorance is Not Bliss: In Search of Racial and Gender Equity in Intercollegiate Athletics*, note b above, at 371–72.

News accounts regarding this complaint (which was still at an early stage when this book was going to press) have suggested that the problem stems to some extent from the interplay of Title IX and NCAA rules, not just from individual school policies. The NCAA distinguishes between two different kinds of sports: one labelled "head count," which requires full scholarships for any athlete receiving one, and the other "equivalency," which permits partial scholarships that divide up the available maximum numbers among a large roster of players. Football, with its 85 permitted full scholarships, is the major "head count" sport, with basketball (at 13 scholarships) being the only other men's sport in this category. The four women's head count sports—basketball (15), volleyball (12), gymnastics (12), and tennis (8)—together comprise 47 positions. If these were the only sports involved, the award of 98 full-time scholarships (68%) to male athletes and 47 (or 32%) to female, would seem to satisfy the Title IX proportionality test on this score.

However, what has been happening over the last decade is that colleges have both reduced the number of positions they have offered on the men's "equivalency" teams (as well as reducing the number of "walk-on" football players without scholarships), and significantly increased the number of equivalency positions offered on women's teams—in order to place themselves closer to compliance with the *Cohen* standard of female student *participation* in intercollegiate sports. This tactic has, however, increased the likelihood that the share of scholarship dollars going to the total number of female athletes will be significantly less than their share of the overall athlete group. One possible solution, of course, is to raise the number of equivalency scholarships permitted for female sports, but this has raised a concern among Division I schools which do not play lucrative Division I-A football that they will be at a competitive disadvantage to those competitors in their non-revenue-generating female sports. Needless to say, the remedy favored by NWLC and its supporters is to cut back sharply on the total number of football head count scholarships.

D. ADMINISTRATION

Whatever one's verdict about the current legal and policy debates in this area, there is little doubt that Title IX has been a great success in affording dramatically greater opportunities for women athletes and their fans. In 1971–72, just before Title IX was enacted, there were 300,000 female athletes in high school and 30,000 in college. Twenty-five years later, in 1996–97 there were 2.4 million females playing in high school and 110,000 playing for college varsity teams. Indeed, 1997 witnessed the birth of two new professional women's basketball leagues, the ABL and the WNBA, who now vigorously compete for both the athletes and the fans generated by Final Four broadcasts of the NCAA's women's (as well as men's) championships in March each year.

Ironically, though, while Title IX ushered in this huge expansion in female *participation* in college (and high school) sports, that same era witnessed a marked decline in women's share of the *administration* of these athletic programs. Again, the bare figures tell the story. In the early 1970s, women comprised more than 90% of both the coaches and administrators of women's teams and programs. Women now coach 50% of female teams (and just two percent of male teams), and make up only 35% of overall college athletic administrative staff.

The source of this trend is easy to trace. In the early 1970s, the "separate but unequal" women's athletic programs formed their own body, the Association of Intercollegiate Athletics for Women (AIAW), to play a role analogous to that of the NCAA in the governance of women's sports. In the late 1970s, though, the NCAA, having failed in its effort to roll back Title IX's coverage of college sports, decided to take control of the now-burgeoning women's sports programs. Thanks to its greater financial resources and television exposure, the NCAA was successful in its quest. After failing in an antitrust suit, see *AIAW v. NCAA*, 558 F.Supp. 487 (D.D.C.1983), affirmed, 735 F.2d 577 (D.C.Cir.1984), the AIAW folded in 1982.

At the same time, most schools integrated their men's and women's programs under a single administrative director. Almost invariably, the men's athletic director, a man, became the overall athletic director, and the women's athletic director, a woman, either became his assistant or saw her position eliminated altogether. In the coaching sphere, the men's teams almost always had a male coach (the fewer than two percent of men's teams with a female coach tended to be in sports such as tennis and swimming). However, the women's teams had begun to generate greater resources and exposure, and thence became attractive to male coaches who gradually filled approximately 50% of these positions.

A broader philosophical question was posed by these historical developments. Many feminists looked back fondly on the era of the AIAW as exhibiting the possibility of a distinctive women's voice in the governance of sports.[e] Among the features they pointed to were the AIAW's promotion of a wide range of sports for student participants, without special regard to those that are the most exciting for spectators (to pay) to watch; the equal division of television revenues among all schools, not just among the winning programs; and the denial of special scholarships for athletics as such. (Ironically, that last feature of the AIAW philosophy had to be dropped in the face of threatened Title IX litigation by women athletes who wanted the same kind of scholarship aid as was available to male college athletes.) The questions remain, though, of whether these tenets of the AIAW's philosophy exhibit a distinctively "female" tone, and whether they would be of enduring value for the policies of a now-integrated NCAA.

e. See Ann Uhlir, *Athletics and the University: The Post-Woman's Era*, Academe 25 (July–August, 1987); R. Vivian Carpenter & Linda Jean Acosta, *Back to the Future: Reform with a Woman's Voice*, Academe 23 (January–February, 1991); and Wendy Olson, *Beyond Title IX: Toward an Agenda for Women and Sports in the 1990s*, 3 Yale J. of L. & Fem. 105 (1991).

The more immediate financial and legal concerns relate to the disparity in pay between the coaches of male and female teams. As we saw in Chapter Ten, the coaches of men's basketball and football teams are by far the highest paid. A national survey of 1996–97 pay rates in selected sports found that the *median* earnings for Division I-A basketball coaches was $290,000 and in football $268,000. (The *average* earnings in these sports would be significantly higher, given that 13 basketball and 12 football coaches made more than $500,000 a season.) The number three earnings category was women's basketball at $98,000, and then came men's baseball at $80,000. Women's softball coaches earned a median $45,000, which put them in the same $40,000–$55,000 range of coaches of both male and female teams in the other surveyed sports, soccer, track, swimming, gymnastics, and volleyball. That last sport was the only one in which the median coach of the women's team (at $48,000) earned slightly more than the median coach of the men's team (at $47,000).

Not just Title IX, but also the federal Equal Pay Act, provides a possible source of legal challenge to this apparent discrepancy.[f] Such a suit was filed in 1993 by Marianne Stanley, coach of the women's basketball team at the University of Southern California. Stanley had been offered a substantial salary increase at the end of the 1992–93 season, but the amount was still significantly less than what USC was paying George Raveling, its men's basketball coach. When negotiations between USC and Stanley reached a deadlock in the summer of 1993, USC decided to replace Stanley as coach of its women's team. Stanley responded with a lawsuit that alleged violation by the university of a number of federal and state laws. Following is a portion of the Ninth Circuit's decision about Stanley's request for a preliminary injunction that would reinstate her in the USC coaching position.

STANLEY v. UNIVERSITY OF SOUTHERN CALIFORNIA

United States Court of Appeals, Ninth Circuit, 1994.
13 F.3d 1313.

ALARCON, CIRCUIT JUDGE.

[In April 1993, the USC women's basketball coach, Marianne Stanley, began negotiations with Athletic Director Michael Garrett on a new contract to replace her four-year deal that was to expire on June 30. Under her old contract, Stanley had earned $60,000 per year plus a $6,000 annual housing allowance, a total which was far below the six-figure compensation package enjoyed by USC's men's basketball coach, George Raveling. Initially, Garrett offered Stanley a three-year contract at $80,000 (plus the $6,000 housing allowance) for the first year, increas-

---

f. For an intriguing analysis of the broader questions posed by the athletic case, see Vicki Schultz, *Telling Stories About Women and Work: Judicial Interpretations of Sex Segregation in the Workplace in Title VII Cases Raising the Lack of Interest Argument*, 103 Harvard L. Rev. 1750 (1990).

ing by $10,000 per year in the second and third years. Stanley characterized the offer as "an insult" and continued to ask for a three-year contract that would eventually pay her the equivalent of what Raveling was earning. Her counsel later specifically asked for a three-year deal starting at $88,000 and increasing to $112,000 in the third year, plus lucrative incentive provisions and radio and television shows that spotlighted the women's team.

After the negotiations turned acrimonious, on June 21 Garrett amended his offer to a one-year deal at $90,000 (along with the housing allowance). In a phone conversation between Garrett and Stanley on July 13, Stanley reiterated her insistence that she earn what Raveling was making, and Garrett told her that she had until the end of that day to accept or reject the one-year, $90,000 offer. When Stanley failed to respond formally to that offer, Garrett sent her a memorandum on July 15 effectively terminating her employment. Stanley then sought legal counsel and filed suit against the University, based primarily on the Equal Pay Act, alleging that her firing was in retaliation for her exercise of rights under that statute. The district court denied Stanley's preliminary injunction which would have reinstated her as the head coach pending the litigation. Stanley appealed this decision.]

* * *

III. Discussion

The gravamen of Coach Stanley's multiple claims against USC is her contention that she is entitled to pay equal to that provided to Coach Raveling for his services as head coach of the men's basketball team because the position of head coach of the women's team "requires equal skill, effort, and responsibility, and [is performed] under similar working conditions." She asserts that USC discriminated against her because of her sex by rejecting her request. She also maintains that USC retaliated against her because of her request for equal pay for herself and her assistant coaches. According to Coach Stanley, USC retaliated by withdrawing the offer of a three-year contract and instead presenting her with a new offer of a one-year contract at less pay than that received by Coach Raveling.

We begin our analysis mindful of the fact that we are reviewing the denial of a preliminary injunction. There has been no trial in this matter. Because the hearing on the preliminary injunction occurred 21 days after the action was filed in state court, discovery had not been completed. Our prediction of the probability of success on the merits is based on the limited offer of proof that was possible under the circumstances. We obviously cannot now evaluate the persuasive impact of the evidence that the parties may bring forth at trial.

* * *

B. *There Has Been No Clear Showing of a Probability of Success on the Merits of Coach Stanley's Claim for Injunctive Relief.*

* * *

1. Merits of Coach Stanley's Claim of Denial of Equal Pay for Equal Work.

The district court concluded that Coach Stanley had failed to demonstrate that there is a likelihood that she would prevail on the merits of her claim of a denial of equal pay for equal work because she failed to present facts clearly showing that USC was guilty of sex discrimination in its negotiations for a new employment contract. The thrust of Coach Stanley's argument in this appeal is that she is entitled, as a matter of law, "to make the same salary as was paid to the Head Men's Basketball Coach at USC." None of the authorities she has cited supports this theory.

In her reply brief, Coach Stanley asserts that she has "never said or argued in any of her submissions that the compensation of the men's and women's basketball coaches at USC or elsewhere must be identical." Coach Stanley accuses USC of mischaracterizing her position. This argument ignores her insistence to Garrett that she was entitled to the "same salary" received by Coach Raveling. The denotation of the word "same" is "identical." Webster's Third New International Dictionary 2007.

In her reply brief, Coach Stanley asserts that she merely seeks equal pay for equal work. In *Hein v. Oregon College of Education*, 718 F.2d 910 (9th Cir.1983), we stated that to recover under the Equal Pay Act of 1963, 29 U.S.C. § 206(d)(1) (1988), "a plaintiff must prove that an employer is paying different wages to employees of the opposite sex for equal work." We concluded that the jobs need not be identical, but they must be "substantially equal."

The EPA prohibits discrimination in wages "between employees on the basis of sex ... for equal work, on jobs the performance of which requires equal skill, effort, and responsibility, and which are performed under similar working conditions." 29 U.S.C. § 206(d)(1) (1988). Each of these components must be substantially equal to state a claim.

Coach Stanley has not offered proof to contradict the evidence proffered by USC that demonstrates the differences in the responsibilities of the persons who serve as head coaches of the women's and men's basketball teams. Coach Raveling's responsibilities as head coach of the men's basketball team require substantial public relations and promotional activities to generate revenue for USC. These efforts resulted in revenue that is 90 times greater than the revenue generated by the women's basketball team. Coach Raveling was required to conduct twelve outside speaking engagements per year, to be accessible to the media for interviews, and to participate in certain activities designed to produce donations and endorsements for the USC Athletic Department in general. Coach Stanley's position as head coach did not require her to engage in the same intense level of promotional and revenue-raising activities. This quantitative dissimilarity in responsibilities justifies a different level of pay for the head coach of the women's basketball team. See *Horner v. Mary Inst.*, 613 F.2d 706, 713–14 (8th Cir.1980) (evidence that male physical education teacher had a different job from a female physical education teacher because he was responsible for curriculum precluded finding that jobs were substantially similar; court may consider whether job requires more experience, training, and ability to determine whether jobs require substantially equal skill under EPA).

The evidence presented by USC also showed that Coach Raveling had substantially different qualifications and experience related to his public relations and revenue-generation skills than Coach Stanley. Coach Raveling received educational training in marketing, and worked in that field for nine years. Coach Raveling has been employed by USC three years longer than Coach Stanley. He has been a college basketball coach for 31 years, while Coach Stanley has had 17 years experience as a basketball coach. Coach Raveling had served as a member of the NCAA Subcommittee on Recruiting. Coach Raveling also is the respected author of two bestselling novels. He has performed as an actor in a feature movie, and has appeared on national television to discuss recruiting of student athletes. Coach Stanley does not have the same degree of experience in these varied activities. Employers may reward professional experience and education without violating the EPA.

Coach Raveling's national television appearances and motion picture presence, as well as his reputation as an author, make him a desirable public relations representative for USC. An employer may consider the marketplace value of the skills of a particular individual when determining his or her salary. *Horner,* 613 F.2d at 714. Unequal wages that reflect market conditions of supply and demand are not prohibited by the EPA. *EEOC v. Madison Community Unit Sch. Dist. No. 12,* 818 F.2d 577, 580 (7th Cir.1987).

The record also demonstrates that the USC men's basketball team generated greater attendance, more media interest, larger donations, and produced substantially more revenue than the women's basketball team.[1] As a result, USC placed greater pressure on Coach Raveling to promote his team and to win. The responsibility to produce a large amount of

---

1. The total average attendance per women's team game during Coach Stanley's tenure was 751 as compared to 4,035 for the men's team during the same period. The average sales of season ticket passes to faculty and staff for women's games were 13, while the average sales for men's games were 130. Alumni and other fans, on average, purchased 71 passes for women's home games as compared to over 1,200 season passes for men's home games during the same period. A season pass to the men's home games was more than double the price of a season pass to women's home games.

The same disparity exists with respect to media interest in the men's and women's basketball teams. Television and radio stations paid USC to broadcast the men's basketball games; all of the home games and many games off campus were broadcast on network or cable stations. All of the games were broadcast on commercial radio. Approximately three of the women's basketball games were broadcast on cable stations as part of a contract package that also covered several other sports.

Donations and endowments were likewise greater for the men's basketball team, totalling $66,916 during the time period of Coach Stanley's contract, as compared to $4,288 for the women's basketball team. The same was true for revenue production. While the women's basketball team produced a total revenue of $50,262 during Coach Stanley's four years, the men's team generated $4,725,784 during the same time period.

revenue is evidence of a substantial difference in responsibility. See *Jacobs v. College of William and Mary*, 517 F.Supp. 791, 797 (E.D.Va. 1980) (duty to produce revenue demonstrates that coaching jobs are not substantially equal), aff'd without opinion, 661 F.2d 922 (4th Cir.), cert. denied, 454 U.S. 1033 (1981).

Coach Stanley did not offer evidence to rebut USC's justification for paying Coach Raveling a higher salary. Instead, she alleged that the women's team generates revenue, and that she is under a great deal of pressure to win.[2]

We agree with the district court in *Jacobs* that revenue generation is an important factor that may be considered in justifying greater pay. We are also of the view that the relative amount of revenue generated should be considered in determining whether responsibilities and working conditions are substantially equal. The fact that the men's basketball team at USC generates 90 times the revenue than that produced by the women's team adequately demonstrates that Coach Raveling was under greater pressure to win and to promote his team than Coach Stanley was subject to as head coach of the women's team.

Coach Stanley's reliance on *Burkey v. Marshall County Board of Education*, 513 F.Supp. 1084 (N.D.W.Va.1981), and *EEOC v. Madison Community Unit School District No. 12*, 818 F.2d 577 (7th Cir.1987), to support her claim of sex discrimination is misplaced. In *Burkey*, the women coaches were "uniformly paid one-half (1/2) of the salary which male coaches of comparable or identical boys' junior high school sports were paid." Here, however, Coach Stanley has not shown that her responsibilities were identical.

Coach Stanley argues that *Jacobs* is distinguishable because, in that matter, the head basketball coach of the women's team was not required to produce any revenue. Coach Stanley appears to suggest that a difference in the amount of revenue generated by the men's and women's teams should be ignored by the court in comparing the respective coaching positions. We disagree.

In *Madison*, the Seventh Circuit held that the plaintiff established a prima facie EPA claim because "male and female coaches alike testified that the skill, effort, and responsibility required were the same and the working conditions [were] also the same—not merely similar—which is all the Act requires." In the instant matter, the uncontradicted evidence shows that Coach Raveling's responsibilities, as head coach of the men's basketball team, differed substantially from the duties imposed upon Coach Stanley.

---

2. Coach Stanley also alleged that, as head coach, she had won four national women's basketball championships, but that Coach Raveling had won none. In addition, while head coach at USC, Coach Stanley was named PAC–10 Coach-of-the-Year in 1993 and the women's basketball team played in the last three NCAA Tournaments and advanced to the NCAA Sweet Sixteen in 1993 and the NCAA Elite Eight in 1992. She also described numerous speaking engagements in which she had participated.

Coach Stanley contends that the failure to allocate funds in the promotion of women's basketball team demonstrated gender discrimination. She appears to argue that USC's failure to pay her a salary equal to that of Coach Raveling was the result of USC's "failure to market and promote the women's basketball team." The only evidence Coach Stanley presented in support of this argument is that USC failed to provide the women's team with a poster containing the schedule of games, but had done so for the men's team. This single bit of evidence does not demonstrate that Coach Stanley was denied equal pay for equal work. Instead, it demonstrates, at best, a business decision to allocate USC resources to the team that generates the most revenue.

The district court also was "unconvinced" by Coach Stanley's claim that USC's disparate promotion of men's and women's basketball teams had "caused the enormous differences in spectator interest and revenue production." The court rejected Coach Stanley's assertion that the differences were due to societal discrimination and that this was evidence of a prima facie case under the EPA. The court reasoned that societal discrimination in preferring to witness men's sports in greater numbers cannot be attributed to USC. We agree.

At this preliminary stage of these proceedings, the record does not support a finding that gender was the reason that USC paid a higher salary to Coach Raveling as head coach of the men's basketball team than it offered Coach Stanley as head coach of the women's basketball team. Garrett's affidavit supports the district court's conclusion that the head coach position of the men's team was not substantially equal to the head coach position of the women's team. The record shows that there were significant differences between Coach Stanley's and Coach Raveling's public relations skills, credentials, experience, and qualifications; there also were substantial differences between their responsibilities and working conditions. The district court's finding that the head coach positions were not substantially equal is not a "clear error of judgment."

* * *

Affirmed.

After losing this appeal, Stanley filled in during the 1995–96 season at Stanford, temporarily replacing the university's women's basketball coach who had taken a year's leave of absence to coach the women's team at the 1996 Atlanta Olympics. Stanley was then hired to coach the University of California at Berkeley team, beginning in the 1996–97 season. Her lawsuit against USC was still pending in early 1998, with Stanley seeking just monetary damages. So also was a suit filed by the women's basketball coach at Howard University, Sonya Tyler, who had won a $2.4 million damage verdict from a District of Columbia jury (reduced by the trial judge to $1.1 million, including $300,000 for emotional distress). Tyler had sued under both the Equal Pay Act and

Title IX, as well as under the D.C. Human Rights Act, complaining that she was paid just $44,000 in annual salary, while the coach of Howard's men's team, former NBA player Butch Beard, received $78,000 a year. The Tyler case was under appeal before the D.C. Circuit Court. Meanwhile, in October, 1997, the federal Equal Employment Opportunity Commission (EEOC) issued interpretation guidelines relating to disparities in college coaching salaries, which the coaches of women's teams have read as enhancing the prospects for their gender discrimination claims in this area.

These coaching cases pose a number of legal questions. What kinds of differences in responsibilities and qualifications between the women's and men's teams' coaching jobs should suffice to block Stanley, Tyler, and others from claiming "equal pay for equal work" under the Equal Pay Act? Is such a disparity between the coaching positions for the men's and women's team itself evidence of a violation of Title IX by the college; in particular, because the creation of such administrative disparities violates the school's obligation to offer equal opportunity to its female and male *athletes*? Should a male coach of a women's basketball team have the same rights as Stanley and Tyler? The female coach of a man's team? What are (or should be) the prospects for suit by a woman who has been denied a position as a football coach, when the woman, though never having played football, had a successful coaching record in a variety of sports? See *Oates v. District of Columbia*, 647 F.Supp. 1079 (D.D.C.1986), aff'd, 824 F.2d 87 (D.C.Cir.1987). Or of a woman who sought a job as athletic director of a school's program whose main popular attractions were football and men's basketball? See *Wynn v. Columbus Municipal Separate School Dist.*, 692 F.Supp. 672 (N.D.Miss. 1988). And, by the way, what is the social significance of the fact that the Division I–A salary survey mentioned above found that the median salary of athletic directors was $158,000, but the median salary of University Deans of Arts and Sciences is approximately $115,000?

E. ACCESS

An even more fundamental question lurks beneath the surface of the legal and policy issues we have addressed thus far, regarding gender equity in college sports. All of the cases we have read have assumed that there is to be a women's and a men's team in basketball and other college sports (with football the one conspicuous exception). Such segregation of black and white athletes would never be suggested as an appropriate solution to the issues of racial disparity raised by Proposition 48 and other NCAA policies considered in the previous two chapters. It is intriguing, then, that there has been little discussion or debate about gender segregation in college sports.[g]

The tacit assumption of both the administrative and judicial reading of Title IX is that colleges will establish *separate* teams for their female

---

[g.] But for an extended critique by a feminist scholar, see Karen L. Tokarz, *Separate but Unequal Educational Sports Programs: The Need for a New Theory of Equality*, 1 Berkeley Women's L. J. 201 (1985).

and male students, and that the institution must then provide *equal* positions and support for their women's and men's teams. The federal Regulations adopted under Title IX in 1975 were quite frank on this point.

> (b) *Separate teams.* Notwithstanding the requirements of paragraph (a) of this section, a recipient may operate or sponsor separate teams for members of each sex where selection for such teams is based upon competitive skill or the activity involved is a contact sport. However, where a recipient operates or sponsors a team in a particular sport for members of one sex but operates or sponsors no such team for members of the other sex, and athletic opportunities for members of that sex have previously been limited, members of the excluded sex must be allowed to try-out for the team offered unless the sport involved is a contact sport. For the purposes of this part, contact sports include boxing, wrestling, rugby, ice hockey, football, basketball and other sports the purpose or major activity of which involves bodily contact.

After having been named as one of the 25 schools in the scholarship disparity complaint filed by NWLC in June 1997, Duke University found itself the target of yet another Title IX suit in September, 1997—this one filed by a woman who claimed that she had not been given a fair opportunity to make the Duke football team.

Heather Mercer had been the place-kicker for her Yorktown Heights high school team which won the New York State Class B championship in 1993, with Mercer named as the third-team All-State place-kicker. After enrolling at Duke in the fall of 1994, Mercer sought to make the Blue Devils football squad. She not only attended all Duke team practices and off-season training programs, but also summer place-kicking camps operated by the former West Virginia All–American Paul Woodside and by former Washington Redskins All–Pro Mark Moseley, both of whom were quoted as saying that Mercer had the talent to make a college team. At the end of Duke's 1995 spring training session, Mercer was the first place-kicker selected by the "rising seniors" to play in the Blue-White game, and her last-minute, 28-yard field goal won the game for the Blues. While Blue Devils coach Fred Goldsmith apparently said after that game that Mercer had made the team (for the first time in Division I college football history), she was not invited to the team's summer football camp, nor permitted that fall to wear a football uniform and sit on the sidelines even during home games (an opportunity given to all male walk-ons, including place-kickers). When that situation continued into her 1997 senior year, Mercer sued Duke under Title IX, seeking monetary damages for her exclusion which Mercer said she would use to create a scholarship fund for future female place-kickers.

It will take some considerable time for the Mercer (and the NWLC) complaints against Duke to be resolved. Even if female successors to Mercer do eventually kick field goals and extra points in college football games, no one (including the NWLC) believes they will make up any significant share of the rosters on football (or other male) teams. The assumption in college (if not junior high or high school) sports is that female students have to have their own separate teams in order to have an equal opportunity to participate in this college activity.[h] However, not just with respect to blacks and whites, but also women and men in just about every other college program, such "separate but equal" treatment would be highly suspect under both Title IX and the constitutional model of integration as the way to secure equal protection, ever since *Brown v. Board of Education*, 347 U.S. 483 (1954).

A case, *Haffer v. Temple Univ.*, 678 F.Supp. 517 (E.D.Pa.1987), did face one aspect of this question. During the early 1980s, when Title IX was temporarily removed from college sports by the Supreme Court's *Grove City College* ruling, Temple was sued under the Pennsylvania Equal Rights Amendment, as well as under the federal Constitution's Fourteenth Amendment, for having denied "equal protection" to its female students by providing them just one third of varsity athletic positions, even though women made up one half of the student body. In seeking summary dismissal of this suit, one position advanced by Temple was that its offer of separate female teams to women "constitutes discrimination in favor of, not against, women." The following brief passage from the district court's opinion captures that Temple thesis and the judge's response to it.

> If the University sponsored a unisex sports program, virtually no women would participate in intercollegiate athletics. Therefore the existence of a separate women's program is a form of preferential treatment. Temple analogizes to a hypothetical case in the racial area:
>
>> Suppose, for example, that Temple had an overall enrollment which was sixteen percent black but, finding that virtually no black students were able to meet the regular admissions standards for the physics program, instituted a special admissions track to increase the number of black students in that program from zero to ten percent. Could black applicants then successfully challenge this effort as a violation of the Equal Protection Clause[?].... The plaintiffs are challenging Temple's affirmative efforts in *extending* benefits to women on the theory that Temple has not gone far enough.
>
> This argument misses the mark. In the above example, black students were not precluded from applying to the regular admissions program. The separate track represents an additional opportunity to join the physics program. However, the physics program and the men's athletic program are not analogous: both black and white students may apply to the general physics program; only men may try out for the men's sports teams. Thus, the women's teams do not

---

h. See Rodney K. Smith, *Solving the Title IX Conundrum With Women's Football*, 38 South Texas L. Rev. 1057 (1997).

represent an additional opportunity for women to play intercollegiate sports, but rather the only opportunity for women to play intercollegiate sports....

678 F.Supp. at 527.

After losing on this and other arguments made for summary dismissal, Temple settled the case midway through trial, in June 1988. Under a consent decree, the school agreed to raise the female proportion of its student-athletes to over 40%, to award athletic scholarships to women in proportion to their athletic participation, and to keep budget expenditures for female programs within ten percentage points of female athletic participation. The situation at the school in 1995–96 was that Temple had nine male and 11 female sports; women made up 55% of the student body and 43% of athletic scholarships and positions; and average expenditures per female athlete were just under $13,000, and for male athletes just over $21,000.

There is an additional ironic feature to the Temple case. In 1991, the faculty voted to drop its football program on the ground that this sport was responsible for half of the large deficit in the school's athletic budget. In contrast to Boston University, the Temple administration resisted that pressure, arguing that the football team was beginning to win and that revenues were projected to grow sharply in the new Big East football conference. A university spokesman was quoted in the Chronicle of Higher Education as saying, "Now is not the time to eliminate football. It's time to cash in on the investment we have made." In the aftermath of yet another dismal team record in 1992, with some prodding from Bill Cosby, Temple's most famous alumnus, the university installed as its new coach Ron Dickerson, the only black head coach in any Division I–A football program at that time (though Dickerson was gone by the end of 1997).

Returning now to the underlying questions of principle, the *Haffer* decision and the Title IX Regulation quoted above both asserted that schools *may*, not that they *must*, establish separate teams for their female as well as their male students. Suppose that Temple (or Brown, or Illinois, or Washington State) had responded to the judicial rulings we have read by directing that all of their varsity teams (including football) should be fully integrated by gender as well as race, with the only qualification for play being ability. What would be the likely impact of such a college athletic policy? Should such action be legal under the federal or state constitutions, as well as Title IX? Even if they were legally free to take such action, do college presidents face market disincentives that bar any such step?

While these issues of gender integration of sports are untested in college athletics, this is a different matter in high school and elementary school sports. Indeed, female student athletes at this level have on occasion filed suit under Title IX to require their schools to integrate the teams in certain sports. The following decision illustrates the judicial response.

HOOVER v. MEIKLEJOHN
United States District Court, District of Colorado, 1977.
430 F.Supp. 164.

MATSCH, DISTRICT JUDGE.

[The plaintiff, a 16–year–old eleventh grade student, was barred from playing for her public high school's junior varsity soccer team. She challenged a rule adopted by the Colorado High School Activities Association that limited soccer (but not baseball or cross country running) to males. The Association had relied on advice from its medical committee that girls playing soccer on mixed-sex teams risked their health and safety.]

* * *

Primarily, the committee was concerned with risks attendant upon collisions in the course of play. While the rules of soccer prohibit body contact (except for a brush-type shoulder block when moving toward the ball), there are frequent instances when players collide in their endeavors to "head" the ball. In those instances, contact is generally in the upper body area.

There is agreement that after puberty the female body has a higher ratio of adipose tissue to lean body weight as compared with the male, and females have less bone density than males. It is also true that, when matured, the male skeletal construct provides a natural advantage over females in the mechanics of running. Accordingly, applying the formula of force equals mass times acceleration, a collision between a male and a female of equal weights, running at full speed, would tend to be to the disadvantage of the female. It is also true that while males as a class tend to have an advantage in strength and speed over females as a class, the range of differences among individuals in both sexes is greater than the average differences between the sexes. The association has not established any eligibility criteria for participation in interscholastic soccer, excepting for sex. Accordingly, any male of any size and weight has the opportunity to be on an interscholastic team and no female is allowed to play, regardless of her size, weight, condition or skill.

* * *

The defendants on the board of education and the professional educators in control of the activities association have concluded that the game of soccer is among those which serve an educational purpose and governmental funds have been provided for it. It is a matter of common knowledge that athletics are a recognized aspect of the educational program offered at American colleges and universities and that many of them offer scholarships to males and females for their agreement to participate in intercollegiate sports competition. Such offers result from organized recruiting programs directed toward those who have demonstrated their abilities on high school teams. Accordingly, the chance to play in athletic games may have an importance to the individual far greater than the obvious momentary pleasure of the game.

Accordingly, the claim of the plaintiff class in this case is properly characterized as a denial of an equal educational opportunity.

* * *

Brown v. Board of Education, 347 U.S. 483 (1954), held that blacks were denied a constitutionally protected equality when they were forced to attend schools established only for those of the same race. As suggested by Justice Brennan in *Frontiero v. Richardson*, 411 U.S. 677, 686 (1973), a classification according to sex is comparable to race in that it is "an immutable characteristic determined solely by the accident of birth."

* * *

The Supreme Court has exhibited an obvious reluctance to label sex as a "suspect" classification because the consequences of the application of the many "invidious" discrimination precedents to all separations by sex could lead to some absurd results. For example, would the Constitution preclude separate public toilets?

* * *

In a very recent Supreme Court opinion, *Craig v. Boren*, 429 U.S. 190 (1976), Mr. Justice Brennan, writing for the Court, attempted to define a new standard of review, saying:

> To withstand constitutional challenge, previous cases establish that classifications by gender must serve important governmental objectives and must be substantially related to achievement of those objectives.

That language may be considered a "middle-tier approach," requiring something between "legitimate" and "compelling," viz., "important," and something more than a "rational" relationship but less perhaps than "strict scrutiny," viz., "substantially" related.

* * *

... Because of its flexibility and sensitivity to the notion of equality itself, [the following three-pronged] method of analysis is particularly appropriate to the present case.

1. The Importance of the Opportunity Being Unequally Burdened or Denied

The opportunity not merely burdened but completely denied to the plaintiff and the class she represents is the chance to compete in soccer as a part of a high school educational experience. Whether such games should be made available at public expense is not an issue. The content of an educational program is completely within the majoritarian control through the representatives on the school board. But, whether it is algebra or athletics, that which is provided must be open to all. The Court in *Brown* expressed a constitutional concern for equality in educational opportunity and this controversy is squarely within that area of concern. Accordingly, without reference to any label that would place this opportunity on one of two or more "tiers," it must be given a great importance to Donna Hoover and every other individual within her class. Surely it is of greater significance than the buying of beer, considered in *Craig*, supra.

2. THE STRENGTH OF THE STATE INTEREST SERVED IN DENYING IT

The defendants in this case have sought to support the exclusionary rule by asserting the state interest in the protection of females from injury in this sport. While the evidence in this case has shown that males as a class tend to have an advantage in strength and speed over females as a class and that a collision between a male and a female would tend to be to the disadvantage of the female, the evidence also shows that the range of differences among individuals in both sexes is greater than the average differences between the sexes. The failure to establish any physical criteria to protect small or weak males from the injurious effects of competition with larger or stronger males destroys the credibility of the reasoning urged in support of the sex classification. Accordingly, to the extent that governmental concern for the health and safety of anyone who knowingly and voluntarily exposes himself or herself to possible injury can ever be an acceptable area of intrusion on individual liberty, there is no rationality in limiting this patronizing protection to females who want to play soccer.

3. THE CHARACTER OF THE GROUP WHOSE OPPORTUNITIES ARE DENIED

Women and girls constitute a majority of the people in this country. To be effective citizens, they must be permitted full participation in the educational programs designed for that purpose. To deny females equal access to athletics supported by public funds is to permit manipulation of governmental power for a masculine advantage.

Egalitarianism is the philosophical foundation of our political process and the principle which energizes the equal protection clause of the Fourteenth Amendment. The emergence of female interest in an active involvement in all aspects of our society requires abandonment of many historical stereotypes. Any notion that young women are so inherently weak, delicate or physically inadequate that the state must protect them from the folly of participation in vigorous athletics is a cultural anachronism unrelated to reality. The Constitution does not permit the use of governmental power to control or limit cultural changes or to prescribe masculine and feminine roles.

It is an inescapable conclusion that the complete denial of any opportunity to play interscholastic soccer is a violation of the plaintiff's right to equal protection of the law under the Fourteenth Amendment. This same conclusion would be required under even the minimal "rational relationship" standard of review applied to classifications which are not suspect and do not involve fundamental rights. The governmental purpose in fielding a soccer team is to enhance the secondary school educational experience. The exclusion of girls to protect them from injury cannot be considered to be in furtherance of that educational objective. If the purpose of the exclusionary rule is the protection of health, safety and welfare of the students, it is arbitrary to consider only the general physiological differences between males and females as classes without any regard for the wide range of individual variants within each class.

While Rule XXI is invalid under either method of analysis, there is a difference between them which is revealed in considering both the remedy required here and the possible ramifications of this case for future controversies.

There is no contention in this case that the Constitution compels soccer competition with teams composed of the best players, regardless of sex. Donna Hoover sought a chance to play on the boys' team only because there is no girls' team. The parties here agree that the effective equalization of athletic opportunities for members of both sexes would be better served by comparable teams for members of each sex and that under current circumstances mixed-sex teams would probably be dominated by males. Accordingly, it is conceded that "separate but equal" teams would satisfy the equality of opportunity required by the Constitution. The "separate but equal" doctrine was articulated in *Plessy v. Ferguson*, 163 U.S. 537 (1896), approving racial separation in transportation facilities. The doctrine was rejected for education in *Brown*, supra, upon the conclusion that racial separation was inherently unequal because it involved a stigmatizing inferiority for the minority race. No such effect is conceivable for a separation of athletic teams by sex.

* * *

Given the lack of athletic opportunity for females in past years, the encouragement of female involvement in sports is a legitimate objective and separation of teams may promote that purpose. It may also justify the sanction of some sports only for females, of which volleyball may be an example.

Separate soccer teams for males and females would meet the constitutional requirement of equal opportunity if the teams were given substantially equal support and if they had substantially comparable programs. There may be differences depending upon the effects of such neutral factors as the level of student interest and geographic locations. Accordingly, the standard should be one of comparability, not absolute equality.

In arriving at the conclusion that the defendants are in violation of the Fourteenth Amendment by providing interscholastic soccer only for male high school students, I am aware that there will be many concerned about the ramifications of this ruling. Football, ice hockey and wrestling are also made available only for males in Colorado, and volleyball is provided only for females. While there is now no reason to rule beyond the specific controversy presented by the evidence, it would seem appropriate to make some general observations about constitutional concerns in athletic programs supported by public funds.

The applicability of so fundamental a constitutional principle as equal educational opportunity should not depend upon anything so mutable as customs, usages, protective equipment and rules of play. The courts do not have competence to determine what games are appropriate for the schools or which, if any, teams should be separated by sex. What the courts can and must do is to insure that those who do make those decisions act with an awareness of what the Constitution does and does not require of them. Accordingly, it must be made clear that there is no constitutional requirement for the schools to provide any athletic program, as it is clear that there is no constitutional requirement to provide any public education. What is required is that whatever opportunity is made available be open to all on equal terms. It must also be made clear that the mandate of equality of opportunity does not dictate a disregard of differences in talents and abilities among individuals. There is no right to a position on an athletic team. There is a right to compete for it on equal terms.

* * *

Order granted.

Questions for Discussion

1. What actions does this ruling allow Colorado high schools to take? Consider each of the following scenarios: (1) a school allows girls to try out for the school's only soccer team, but over a period of several years few girls try out and none make the team; (2) a school requires half the players on the school's only soccer team to be girls; (3) a school has both boys' and girls' soccer teams, but disbands the girls' team when only three girls come out for the team, and then refuses to let the three girls try out for the boys' team; (4) a school has a boys-only soccer team and a girls-only field hockey team (each team has the same number of players).

2. In the 1990s, unlike the 1970s, few would argue that mixed soccer poses a serious risk of injury to young girls. But what about football or ice hockey? Should either of these sports be mixed-sex or just single sex? How should the court rule in a case involving a sixteen-year-old girl who wants to try out for the men's wrestling team when the school has no girl's wrestling program? See *Saint v. Nebraska School Activities Ass'n*, 684 F.Supp. 626 (D.Neb.1988). How about a case in which a young woman sues to be permitted to compete in the regional Golden Gloves boxing competition? See *Lafler v. Athletic Board of Control*, 536 F.Supp. 104 (W.D.Mich.1982).

3. The opposite question arises if a boy wishes to participate in a sport for which his school offers only a girls' team—for example, in field hockey or volleyball. Should courts allow boys to try out for spots on a "girls'" team if there is no boys' team in that sport? What would likely happen if that were

the rule? Should it matter whether the sport is a "contact sport?" Compare *Kleczek v. Rhode Island Interscholastic League,* 612 A.2d 734 (R.I.1992) (holding that boys do not have any right to play on the girls' field hockey team), with *Williams v. School District of Bethlehem,* 799 F.Supp. 513 (E.D.Pa.1992), rev'd, 998 F.2d 168 (3d Cir.1993) (holding that it is a factual question whether field hockey is a "contact sport" that would justify a girl's-only team under Title IX).

4. The Kentucky High School Athletic Association (KHSAA) serves as the agent of the Kentucky State Board for Elementary and Secondary Education, for regulation of interscholastic sports in Kentucky. The KHSAA grants official "sanction" to a sport for purposes of creating a state tournament only when the sport has secured interest in participation among at least 25% of member schools (though such sanction is preserved as long as at least 15% of members maintain their participation). The KHSAA had sanctioned ten sports for boys, including baseball, and eight for girls, including slow-pitch softball. The latter sport was first approved in 1982, after a school survey found that 44% of Association members wanted to play it. A 1988 survey found just nine percent membership interest in girl's fast-pitch softball, which had risen to 17% (or 50 schools around the state) by 1992. Because the minimum 25% figure had not been met, the KHSAA refused to grant "sanction" to the sport. Member schools did retain the freedom to compete among themselves in such a non-sanctioned sport, and girls had the freedom to play on a boy's baseball team if their member schools did not offer girl's fast-pitch softball.

Lori Ann Horner and eleven other female student athletes in Kentucky filed suit against both the KHSAA and its parent Board, alleging that the failure to sanction girl's fast-pitch softball violated both their Equal Protection and Title IX rights. The tangible concern was that in college sports, both the NCAA and the NAIA had sanctioned girl's fast-pitch, but not slow-pitch, softball. This meant that Kentucky girls who were playing softball were at a disadvantage relative to their classmates in other sanctioned sports (boy's or girl's) in securing athletic scholarships when they went to college. Should the KHSAA's "25 percent" rule be found in violation of the constitutional right to equal protection? Or of the Title IX jurisprudence we have seen in OCR Regulations and *Cohen* and other circuit court opinions? See *Horner v. Kentucky High School Athletic Ass'n,* 43 F.3d 265 (6th Cir.1994).

In *Clark v. Arizona Interscholastic Ass'n.,* 695 F.2d 1126 (9th Cir.1982), a group of boys sued when they were barred by Arizona rules from playing on their school's volleyball team, which was limited to girls. In dismissing the suit, the court asserted:

> As discussed above, the governmental interest claimed is redressing past discrimination against women in athletics and promoting equality of athletic opportunity between the sexes. There is no question that this is a legitimate and important governmental interest.

The only question that remains, then, is whether the exclusion of boys is substantially related to this interest. The question really asks whether any real differences exist between boys and girls which justify the exclusion; i.e., are there differences which would prevent realization of the goal if the exclusion were not allowed.

The record makes clear that due to average physiological differences, males would displace females to a substantial extent if they were allowed to compete for positions on the volleyball team. Thus, athletic opportunities for women would be diminished. As discussed above, there is no question that the Supreme Court allows for these average real differences between the sexes to be recognized or that they allow gender to be used as a proxy in this sense if it is an accurate proxy. This is not a situation where the classification rests on "'archaic and overbroad' generalizations" or "the baggage of sexual stereotypes." Nor is this a situation involving invidious discrimination against women, or stigmatization of women. The [Arizona Interscholastic Association] is simply recognizing the physiological fact that males would have an undue advantage competing against women for positions on the volleyball team. The situation here is one where there is clearly a substantial relationship between the exclusion of males from the team and the goal of redressing past discrimination and providing equal opportunities for women.

We recognize that specific athletic opportunities could be equalized more fully in a number of ways. For example, participation could be limited on the basis of specific physical characteristics other than sex, a separate boys' team could be provided, a junior varsity squad might be added, or boys' participation could be allowed but only in limited numbers. The existence of these alternatives shows only that the exclusion of boys is not necessary to achieve the desired goal. It does not mean that the required substantial relationship does not exist....

In this case, the alternative chosen may not maximize equality, and may represent trade-offs between equality and practicality. But since absolute necessity is not the standard, and absolute equality of opportunity in every sport is not the mandate, even the existence of wiser alternatives than the one chosen does not serve to invalidate the policy here since it is substantially related to the goal. That is all the standard demands. While equality in specific sports is a worthwhile ideal, it should not be purchased at the expense of ultimate equality of opportunity to participate in sports. As common sense would advise against this, neither does the Constitution demand it.

695 F.2d, at 1131. Do you agree with the court's reasoning? When, if ever, should sports teams be integrated by gender (as they clearly must be by race)? Does your answer differ depending on whether the level of play is elementary school, high school, college, or professional (recall that private sports activities are covered by the Civil Rights Act)? Is there a stigma of female athletic inferiority created by "separate but equal"

teams? If teams were integrated by gender and selected on the basis of ability alone, would this enhance or reduce equality of athletic opportunity? How much of the current differential between female and male athletic performance is due to physiology, and how much is due to resources and socialization?[i] Is integration the ideal way for aspiring female athletes to overcome the latter obstacles?

F. AFTERTHOUGHTS

Let us step back from the specifics of Title IX jurisprudence and consider the lessons from the last three chapters about the role that the law (private NCAA law, as well as public law) can play in shaping the world of sports. For example, the NCAA's Proposition 48 rules have had a far bigger impact on what student athletes learn in high school than its "academic progress" rules on what they learn in college (and we shall have to see whether the *Student-Athlete Right-to-Know Act* will fill the educational malpractice vacuum left by *Ross*). The core course requirement in Proposition 48 has to be significantly accommodated to the situation of the "learning disabled" by reason of the *Americans With Disabilities Act*, but so far at least, Title VI of the *Civil Rights Act* has not generated any such accommodation to African–American performance on college admissions tests. The Supreme Court's *NCAA* decision has generated a more competitive and product-laden market for college sports fans, but the interpretation by lower courts of the *NCAA* opinion has left untouched the Association's restraints on the market for players (though not for coaches). At the same time, Title IX has had a profound impact on female participation in sports, not just in college (and high school), but now in professional sports as well. Whatever one's views about the substantive issues posed in each of these legal settings, college sports offers a graphic illustration of the differences the law can make in the real world.

These cases also illustrate some of the tensions generated by these different legal regimes. Certainly, college football and men's basketball have become multi-billion dollar business ventures. Yet, however attractive and lucrative these sports are in the consumer market, the athletes who perform on the field or court are deemed to be amateurs who play simply for the love of the game, as part of their education rather than for monetary reward. While coaches and athletic directors have reaped a significant part of the revenues generated within these two sports, the bulk of the money is used to fund non-revenue sports—partly for male students, though now even more for females (and in both cases, primarily white students from higher income families).

This poses an even more fundamental question. Should the premiums realized from these "amateur-commercial" sports be spent by colleges on their *academic* rather than their *athletic* programs? Or is it

---

i. See Brian J. Whipp & Susan A. Ward, *Will Women Soon Outrun Men?*, 355 Nature 25 (Jan. 2, 1992).

true, as some observers contend, that participation in varsity sports is actually a significant part of the education of students (as much as courses in the fine arts or the performing arts)? With Ivy League schools such as Brown very much the exception rather than the rule, just four percent of the college student body now participates in varsity sports, though student tuition and/or activity fees are used to cover the often significant deficits in many athletic programs. Others have suggested that the schools that make up the NCAA should adopt a rule that imposes a total budgetary cap on the amount that each member can spend on each sport, with athletic scholarships having to be paid for by the revenues actually generated by the sport in question. The result would be that students playing men's golf or women's tennis would not get a free ride through college, no more than writers for the student newspaper or musicians in the school band. The gender equity objectives of Title IX would be pursued by distributing the resulting profits from football and men's basketball (eventually perhaps women's basketball as well) into women's *studies* rather than women's *sports*.

Is this "brave new world" more compatible with the philosophy of the NCAA quoted and relied on in so many of the cases in this and the previous two chapters? Or would it ruin college sports to the detriment not only of the athletic establishment, but also of the athletes and fans who derive so much enjoyment from the games? What are your thoughts at the end of this extended examination of the impact of both money and law on the world of intercollegiate athletics?

Chapter Twelve

INDIVIDUAL SPORTS

This chapter introduces a different part of the sports world: sports played by individual competitors rather than by teams, sports played in tournaments rather than in leagues. More and more, sports such as golf, tennis, auto racing, boxing, track and field, and bowling have been able to tap spectator interest and generate large revenues from live attendance, television broadcasts, and merchandising arrangements. A by-product of this expanding financial success has been increasing litigation.

Individual sports pose the same challenge to courts as do professional and college team sports. How can one accommodate private regulation designed to foster vigorous and appealing athletic competition with public laws designed to protect both participants and outsiders from the misguided or arbitrary exercise of power by those in charge of the sport? This chapter presents a number of judicial variations on this perennial theme, all drawn from the world of individual sports.

As a prelude to these case selections, it is useful to underline some of the distinctive characteristics exhibited by individual sports off (rather than on) the field.

1. Most important, the athletes compete as individuals rather than as members of a team. In the eyes of the law, this makes tennis players, for example, independent contractors rather than employees.

2. In several sports, the players have organized themselves into associations that govern their respective sports in the best interests of the performers, as contrasted with team sports where the dominant forces are the owners who contribute financial capital. The pioneer in this respect has been the Tournament Players Division of the Professional Golfers Association (PGA Tour).

3. Fan interest focuses much more on individual tournaments than on season-long championship races. The tours in several sports have developed systems for accumulation of points from each event that entitle the top players to participate in a lucrative final event,

such as the Association of Tennis Professionals (ATP's) Masters' Championship. However, much greater fan and media interest is aroused by the "Grand Slam" events. Hence, authorities in charge of a tournament such as the Masters in golf, Wimbledon in tennis, and the Indianapolis 500 in auto racing, have a great deal of clout in their sports, while sponsors of lesser-known tournaments have substantial economic concerns about how tour officials and players treat their events.

4. For decades, many of the major individual sports (though not boxing, golf, or auto racing) were fully committed to the ideal of "amateurism"—athletes playing simply for the love of the game. These sports excluded from major events any players who openly earned their living from playing the sport. However, unlike college football and men's basketball, the tennis world in the early 1970s, and track and field in the early 1980s, responded to the growth of "under the table" payments to top stars in a profitable sports enterprise by accepting professionalism among their performers.

5. The combination of the large sums of money generated by a sport and the professional status of its athletes produces a demand for sports agents. Individual sports have been the setting for some of the most prominent and successful sports agents—Mark McCormack, for example, who represented Arnold Palmer and Jack Nicklaus, and Donald Dell, who represented Arthur Ashe and Jimmy Connors. This agency work served as the stepping stone for McCormack's International Management Group (IMG) and Dell's ProServ to become major forces in the business of individual sports, managing and promoting the same tournaments their clients played in—which evoked some delicate questions about how these many-sided relationships could be meshed.

6. Equipment used in individual sports usually plays a much larger role than in team sports in determining who wins the contest—most conspicuously, the engines in racing cars, but also the rackets, clubs, and balls used in tennis and golf. Many equipment manufacturers have a major financial stake in having their products used on professional tours because of the influence star athletes exert on purchases by the general sporting public. Thus, manufacturers are another group with a distinct economic interest in decisions about the rules of the game.

7. The professional and college sports examined in previous chapters are played by teams located almost entirely in the United States. (The exceptions are two baseball teams, two basketball teams, and six hockey teams based in Canada, a country whose laws are similar to those in the United States.) In contrast, several of the major individual sports have a large share of their events set in (as in tennis), or players drawn from (as in golf), numerous countries around the world. Moreover, track and field and swimming, for example, are governed by international federations that control

access to the Olympic Games, which every four years capture the attention of athletes and fans around the world. This international dimension to individual sports poses a major challenge to American judges asked to apply and enforce domestic laws.

The foregoing provides a capsule summary of the distinctive real-world flavor of individual sports. The cases in this chapter exhibit some of the legal differences that these factual distinctions can make.

A. UMPIRING THE GAME

A revealing illustration of the extent of sports litigation is that, in the 1980s, auto racing produced *two* appellate court decisions about whether aggrieved contestants could go to court to try to snatch victory from the jaws of defeat. In both cases, suit was brought against the National Association of Stock Car Auto Racing (NASCAR). NASCAR was originally created back in 1947 by a young auto mechanic, Bill France, as a vehicle for organized stock car racing in several southeastern states. Fifty years later, the third generation of the France family was still owning and operating a for-profit organization whose major Winston Cup series (sponsored by the R.J. Reynolds tobacco company since 1971) had expanded across the country. Attendance at these races averages 180,000 an event, or nearly 6 million a season, with total revenues from all sources reportedly exceeding $2 billion (thus in the same range as football and baseball). To participate in these very popular and lucrative racing events, the racing team had to be a member of and pay an annual licensing fee to NASCAR. Membership does not, however, entitle one to elect NASCAR officials or participate in its decisions.

CROUCH v. NASCAR
United States Court of Appeals, Second Circuit, 1988.
845 F.2d 397.

MESKILL, CIRCUIT JUDGE.

[The plaintiff, Crouch, was declared the victor in a 1985 stock car race held in Vermont under the auspices of NASCAR. Another driver, LaJoie, actually crossed the finish line ahead of Crouch but was disqualified by the NASCAR official at the track. LaJoie appealed the official scorer's verdict to NASCAR headquarters on the ground that the scorer had improperly penalized him a lap during a restart of the race; this missing lap had led to LaJoie's disqualification for allegedly passing Crouch's car in the face of the yellow accident caution flag displayed later in the race. NASCAR headquarters first characterized the track rulings as an appealable "scoring," rather than an unappealable "race procedure" decision, and then, after reviewing the race tapes, declared LaJoie the victor.

Crouch took the matter to court even though, under the NASCAR constitution, competitors in all races were required to sign entry forms that stipulated that everyone agreed to abide by the decisions of officials relating to the event and "that such decisions are non-appealable and non-litigable." The trial judge nonetheless upheld Crouch's claim on the theory that NASCAR's interpretation and application of its rules—in particular its characterization of this dispute as a "scoring" rather than a "race procedure" matter—was "unreasonable and arbitrary." NASCAR and LaJoie appealed to the Second Circuit.]

* * *

The threshold issue that we must resolve is the proper standard for judicial review of NASCAR's interpretation of its own rules. Our decision in *Koszela v. National Association of Stock Car Auto Racing, Inc.*, 646 F.2d 749 (2d Cir.1981), provides some guidance. In that case, we considered claims that NASCAR misapplied its rules in determining the rightful winner of two races and that its decisions regarding the two races were arbitrary and clearly erroneous. We first reasoned that the principle of judicial noninterference set forth in the law of voluntary associations was not strictly applicable, noting that NASCAR was a for-profit company that completely dominated the field of stock car racing and that its members have no rights whatsoever with respect to the internal governance of the organization. We added, however, that a reviewing court is not free to reexamine the correctness of the official track decisions in question because NASCAR's rules "do not provide for any administrative appeal, much less judicial review, of official decisions." We also noted that the only provision granting a competitor the right to challenge occurrences at the track is the protest mechanism, and that "this provision is not intended to be a device by which disappointed competitors may challenge an official's interpretation of the rules or the application of the rules to the facts." We accordingly refused to reexamine the correctness of the official track decisions in question.

In the instant case, the district court cited *Koszela*, and concluded that because of the considerations discussed in that case it was "precluded from reviewing the official decisions of NASCAR officials with respect to the Catamount race." It added that "[t]o allow competitors to challenge the assessment of lap and time penalties or the timing and scoring of laps would result in the same type of protracted disputes that the finality rule is meant to prevent.... By according final weight to the official NASCAR track decisions, this court avoids placing itself in the position of 'super-referee.'"

The court also concluded, however, that the considerations that preclude review of the correctness of the official track decisions do not necessarily prevent the review of the procedures used to implement these decisions. The court added that "[w]hile courts may be hesitant to unnecessarily interject themselves into the private affairs of an association, where the association enforces its rules in a manner that is unreasonable or arbitrary courts may intervene." In applying this standard, the court did not defer to NASCAR's judgment that under its rules, the disputed actions of the local track officials did not constitute the imposition of a lap or time penalty, or to NASCAR's decision that disqualification is not a race procedure decision. Rather, the court apparently believed that under its adopted standard, it was appropriate to undertake a *de novo* review of the NASCAR rules in order to determine whether the national NASCAR officials had acted unreasonably or arbitrarily by reviewing the local track officials' decisions.

* * *

The court's decision in *Charles O. Finley & Co. v. Kuhn*, 569 F.2d 527 (7th Cir.1978), is relevant. In that case, the court concluded that a waiver of recourse to the courts that was signed by the major league baseball clubs was valid, noting that such a waiver coincides with the common law standard disallowing court interference. The court added that there are exceptions to this general rule of nonreviewability of the actions of private associations, however, "1) where the rules, regulations or judgments of the association are in contravention to the laws of the land or in disregard of the charter or bylaws of the association and 2) where the association had failed to follow the basic rudiments of due process of law."

* * *

In the instant case, Crouch and Wright are not claiming that they were deprived of any procedural safeguards or that their due process rights were violated, however. Rather, the crux of their complaint is that NASCAR improperly provided LaJoie with a procedural safeguard, i.e., review of the local track officials' decisions by the NASCAR headquarters. In fact, LaJoie maintains that if the district court correctly held that the local track officials' actions constituted a disqualification, then he was entitled to be informed of the disqualification and to have the disqualification decision reviewed by NASCAR headquarters pursuant to Section 13 of the rulebook. Section 13 provides that all violations of NASCAR rules are to be reported in writing to the NASCAR Vice President for Competition, and that this Vice President can review these reported violations. We therefore do not believe that the cases discussing the occasional need for a court to intervene in the internal affairs of an association because of the lack of adequate safeguards support the district court's decision.

Although here there was no allegation of inadequate procedural protections, the district court still thought that it was appropriate to conduct its own analysis of NASCAR's interpretation of its procedural rules. Moreover, despite the court's recognition that NASCAR possesses considerable stock car racing expertise upon which it may rely in interpreting its own rules, the court apparently did not give much weight to that expertise in reaching its decision that NASCAR acted unreasonably by overturning a race procedure decision made by a local track official. Rather, the court evidently felt that in order to determine whether NASCAR acted unreasonably or arbitrarily, it should itself delve into NASCAR's rulebook and decide *de novo* whether the lap 68–71 incident involved a disqualification, and whether a disqualification constitutes a lap and time penalty and is therefore a nonreviewable race procedure decision.

We believe the district court erred in making this inquiry. As the Seventh Circuit noted [in *Finley*] when rejecting the argument that the Commissioner of Baseball's actions were "procedurally unfair," certain standards, such as "the best interests of baseball, [and] the interests of the morale of the players and the honor of the game . . . are not necessarily familiar to courts and obviously require some expertise in their application." The court accordingly proclaimed that the judiciary should not be professional baseball's "umpire and governor." We believe that federal courts are equally unfamiliar with standards such as "race procedure decision" and "lap and time penalty," and thus should decline the plaintiffs' invitation to become the "super-scorer" for stock car racing disputes. Furthermore, there is no contention that NASCAR acted "in disregard of [its] charter or bylaws." Rather, plaintiffs-appellees contend essentially that NASCAR misinterpreted its own internal regulations. Accordingly, we conclude that the district court should have deferred to NASCAR's interpretation of its own rules in the absence of an allegation that NASCAR acted in bad faith or in violation of any local, state or federal laws. . . . We believe that adopting any lower standard for reviewing an organization's interpretation of its own procedural rules would create too great a danger that courts will become mired down in what has been called the "dismal swamp"—the area of a group's activity concerning which only the group can speak competently. Indeed, the district court's admitted confusion about the proper interpretation of NASCAR Rule 13–5 is one illustration of how perilously close the court came to the edge of the swamp under its adopted standard of review. As we acknowledged in *Koszela*, "[u]ltimately, the solution for unauthorized or improper officiating lies not in individual challenges seeking to undo what has been done, but rather in pressure brought upon the officials in charge by drivers, owners, fans, and even NASCAR to improve the caliber of [NASCAR's supervision of races]."

* * *

Indeed, the district court implicitly acknowledged that the national officials acted in good faith. Specifically, the court noted that the national officials believed that the local officials' decision to penalize LaJoie in connection with the lap 68–71 incident resulted in part from the scoring error the local officials made in connection with the lap 1–2 incident. The national officials therefore thought it was appropriate to correct both decisions. Moreover, as we noted in *Koszela*, it is common practice to refer race procedure questions to the national NASCAR office. We thus believe that the district court should have deferred to NASCAR's interpretation of its own rules, under which NASCAR had the authority to review and decide the disputed issues.

Reversed.

Questions for Discussion

1. What is the formal legal source of a court's authority to review decisions made by a sport's ruling body—especially about who has won an event? Should the court have dismissed Crouch's suit, regardless of the asserted grounds, because Crouch apparently had agreed (through both his membership in NASCAR and his entry form for the Vermont race) that he would not appeal adverse decisions to the courts? In an earlier decision, *Koszela v. NASCAR*, 646 F.2d 749 (2d Cir.1981), the Second Circuit stated:

> The policies supporting [judicial] noninterference are considerably weaker where the organization is "primarily a business run for profit" in which the " 'members' have no rights whatsoever with respect to the internal governance of the organization." Moreover, NASCAR's complete dominance in the field of stock car racing leaves competitors little choice but to join. Where an organization has achieved such a "stranglehold," rigid adherence to a "hands off" policy is inappropriate. See Chafee, *The Internal Affairs of Associations Not for Profit*, Harv. L. Rev. 993, 1021–23 (1930).

646 F.2d at 754. In that light, compare the judicial treatment of NASCAR in *Crouch* to the treatment of decisions rendered by baseball commissioners in the *Finley*, *Turner*, and *Chicago Cubs* cases discussed in Chapter 1.

2. If courts are prepared to intervene at least upon occasion, what are the appropriate occasions? Is it relevant, for example, that Crouch was at first named the winner at the end of the race and that he challenged a later decision made at NASCAR headquarters that reversed the scorer's decision made at the track? Is it significant that, in *Koszela*, a similar scenario took place but that the decision made at headquarters reversing Koszela's announced victory at the race site was rendered by the Competition Director without hearing from either of the contestants (a hearing would take place only upon further appeal to the NASCAR Commission)?

B. ELIGIBILITY TO PLAY

Before players can win races or tournaments, they must be eligible to compete in the first place. One of the major functions of the organization in charge of any sport is to determine who can play in each event. In team sports, the key decisions are made by the management of each team, which decides whether to keep an existing player or to bring in a replacement. In individual sports such as golf and tennis, these decisions are now made by a body composed of, or at least accountable to, the players themselves. In a similar setting, medicine, the Supreme Court has questioned the delegation of authority to committees of doctors to judge whether one of the members of their specialty should gain or retain staff privileges in a hospital where they might compete for the same patients.[a] Judicial concern is likely to be even greater in the world of sports, where there is no compelling need to protect patients from risky medical treatment.

---

[a]. See *Patrick v. Burget*, 486 U.S. 94 (1988). See also James F. Blumstein and Frank A. Sloan, *Antitrust and Hospital Peer Review*, 51 L. and Contemp. Prob. 7 (1988).

The legal response to this problem is best glimpsed through the world of professional golf, which has undergone a lengthy evolution toward its present regime of player control.[b] Golf came to the United States in the late nineteenth century with the creation of several clubs in the northeast. In 1894, two clubs, St. Andrews and Newport Country Club, both staged a "national" amateur championship within weeks of each other, each championship producing different winners. To eliminate the confusion and produce one national amateur championship, the Country Club in Brookline, Mass., the Chicago Golf Club, and the Shinnecock Hills Club in Long Island, N.Y., joined with the two tournament clubs to charter the U.S. Golfers Association (USGA). The USGA staged its first Open Championship at St. Andrews in 1895 to accompany the first U.S. Amateur Championship.

Almost all of the rising number of clubs employed professionals to keep the course in playing condition, to sell and store equipment, and to teach members how to play the game. In 1916, club professionals formed the Professional Golfers' Association (PGA), which staged its own professional championship and, during the 1920s and 1930s, coordinated golf tournaments in several cities. Most of these tournaments were held in the south in the winter, and most of the players were club professionals whose northern clubs were closed for that same winter. While there were a few golfing greats who successfully concentrated on tournament golf alone—Walter Hagen, Gene Sarazan, Sam Snead, Byron Nelson, and Ben Hogan—there rarely was a shortage of tournament slots for professionals who wanted to enter.

The situation began to change in the 1950s when the combination of spectator interest and television broadcasting brought much more money into the game—by 1958, total PGA Tour prize money surpassed $1 million. For the first time, PGA Tour officials found that the qualifying event held early in the week of each tournament was not sufficient to reduce the number of entrants to a manageable field. New eligibility rules, which still favored club professionals, resulted in many tournament players being dropped from the Tour roster. One such player, Herb Deesen, brought an antitrust suit, *Deesen v. PGA*, 358 F.2d 165 (9th Cir.1966), one of the earliest substantive antitrust decisions rendered about any sport.

By the time Deesen had ended his unsuccessful legal challenge to PGA Tour eligibility rules in 1966, the character of the golf enterprise had undergone another major change. Although Tour revenues were still

---

b. For a comprehensive picture of the development of the professional golf tours, see Al Barkow, *The History of the PGA Tour* (New York: Doubleday, 1989). The definitive history of the game of golf is Robert Browning, *A History of Golf: The Royal and Ancient Game* (London: J.M. Dent & Sons, Ltd., 1955). For detailed analysis of the current tours, IMG Chairman Mark McCormack's annual survey of the PGA Tour provides a constantly revised and updated version of such information. See Mark H. McCormack, *The World of Professional Golf* (Cleveland: International Merchandising Corporation, 1997). See also William Wartman, *Playing Through: Behind the Scenes on the PGA Tour* (New York: William Morrow and Company, Inc., 1990).

soaring—to $5 million in prize money by the late 1960s—new stars of the game, such as Arnold Palmer, Jack Nicklaus, and Gary Player had become impatient with the continuing role of club professionals. The result was formation of the Tournament Players Division (TPD) of the PGA, which took full charge of the Tour under a commissioner (now, Tim Finchem) ultimately accountable to players on the tour.

Coincident with this constitutional change was a new set of eligibility rules that sharply reduced access to tournaments for club professionals and based admission to the Tour on successful completion of qualifying school and competition. Spots for newcomers (many of whom now come from the lower-ranking Nike Tour, formerly the Ben Hogan Tour) were created by dropping from the eligibility list players who had placed near the bottom of tour winnings in the prior year. This new system produced yet another antitrust challenge and the closest judicial look yet at tour limits on player eligibility.

WESER v. PGA

United States District Court, Northern District of Illinois, 1979.
1979–2 Trade Cases (CCH) ¶ 78,180.

MARSHALL, DISTRICT JUDGE.

[Between 1949 and 1958, Emil Weser participated in tournament golf as a PGA-approved player—an individual eligible to compete on the pro tour. The PGA terminated his status as an approved player in 1958. Although he did participate in some non-TPD/PGA tournaments, Weser maintained his involvement with golf primarily through the operation of his driving range and golf shop where he gave golf instructions. In 1976, Weser decided to become active in tournament golf again and to enter the Western Open tournament. The Western Open tournament was co-sponsored by the Western Golf Association (WGA) and the TPD. The WGA and the TPD entered into a written agreement on September 29, 1975, which provided that "[p]layers eligible to apply to enter the Tournament shall be those prescribed in the TPD Tournament Regulations." The TPD Tournament Regulations established ten categories of persons eligible to participate in TPD co-sponsored events. Eligibility for entry into the Western Open was limited to members of the TPD, members of professional golfers' associations that were recognized by the TPD, the Illinois section PGA champion, the head professional at Butler National (the course where the 1976 Western Open was played), 19 members of the Illinois section of the PGA, and the PGA National club professional champion.

Weser had never been a member of the PGA or the TPD. Because he did not fit into any of the eligibility categories, he did not submit the entry form for the Western Open. Instead, he sued the PGA, the TPD, and the WGA for alleged violations of the antitrust laws. This was the district court's ruling on a motion for summary dismissal.]

ELIGIBILITY REQUIREMENTS

* * *

Defendants have asserted that the purpose for the eligibility requirements is not to exclude able competitors from the field of professional golf but rather is to foster competition by guaranteeing to sponsors, participants, and spectators that the golfers participating in tournaments are of the highest caliber. There is no evidence that this purpose is illusory and the regulations support it. The golfing proficiency of each member is constantly reviewed. When a member is consistently defeated in tournament play he must prove his competence as if he were a new player. The regulations, at least on their face, are designed to allow only those golfers of proven ability to participate in TPD events. This purpose is not exclusionary; rather the restrictions are intended to foster the highest degree of competition. Therefore, the proper standard to apply in this case is the rule of reason.

"The focus of an inquiry under the rule of reason is whether the restraint imposed is justified by legitimate business purposes, and is no more restrictive than necessary." The restraint that plaintiff has complained of is the "membership" requirement of the TPD regulations. First it should be noted that membership in the PGA and the TPD are not the only methods for gaining admission into a TPD cosponsored event. Foreign professional golfers are permitted to compete provided the golf association they belong to is recognized by the TPD. Also, the sponsor organization is allowed to invite up to eight non-members to compete in the tournament which they sponsor. However, these other methods for admission into the golf event are *de minimis* compared to the number of positions on the field which are available to members of the TPD and PGA. The proper inquiry is whether there is a legitimate business purpose for limiting the players to members of the PGA and the TPD.

Limit on Number of Players

Defendants have provided sufficient evidence which shows that the number of participants in a one-day tournament of professional golf is limited to between 144 and 156 players by the physical and extrinsic factors of the course. Each tournament golf course consists of 18 holes which are played in two waves, one wave starting from the first tee and the second from the tenth. These waves then interchange starting positions after they complete their first nine holes. It takes approximately 4.5 hours for a player to finish the entire 18 holes. Normally, the first two waves start out at 7:30 a.m. and the second two waves of the day start out at noon. It takes approximately two hours to get the last group in a wave off its first tee. The last group in the wave that starts at noon therefore actually tees off around 2:00 p.m. and would be expected to finish at about 6:30 p.m. Each of the four waves consists of 12 to 13 groups of three players. Thus if 12 groups comprise a wave, 144 players can be accommodated in one day; if 13 groups make up the wave, 156 players can participate. This evidence has not been controverted by plaintiff.

In addition the number of days the tournament may last at each golf course is controlled by the limited resources available to the sponsor. Defendants assert that the tournaments are generally played at private clubs across the country. Any time allotted by the club for a tournament results in the members of that club being deprived of the use of their golf course. At the present time, an 18–hole qualifying competition is held on the Monday preceding the major event if more than 144 applications from "qualified" golfers are received. Therefore many tournaments require a minimum of five days to complete. Many of the TPD tournaments are sponsored by civic and charitable organizations. Functions such as marshalling and scorekeeping are performed by volunteers of these sponsor organizations and the number of available volunteers is naturally limited. Plaintiff has not disputed these facts. We therefore conclude that there are legitimate business reasons for limiting the number of participants in a golf tournament.

Method to Select Players

The next inquiry is whether the method selected by defendants to limit the number of participants is reasonable or whether less restraining alternatives are available. All persons falling into one of the categories set forth in the TPD eligibility regulations are permitted to compete in the Monday pretournament qualifying rounds. Therefore the natural starting place for determining if the field is limited in a manner consistent with the anti-trust laws is with the TPD's eligibility regulations. These regulations will be considered reasonable if they are consistent with the stated purpose of the TPD—to foster competition at the highest level. But if the regulations permit entry to some golfers who have not proven their competitive ability, while denying it to others, or if the regulations are so restrictive that those persons who have proven their competitive ability are refused entry into the tournaments in order to favor less qualified members, the regulation may not be reasonable.

The 1977 TPD regulations set forth ten categories of persons who are eligible to compete in TPD co-sponsored tournaments. The first category consists of "members in good standing of TPD." The methods for becoming a member in the TPD are set forth in the TPD bylaws. The 1977 bylaws specify six divisions of persons who are eligible to apply for membership in the TPD.... These classifications ultimately break down into three categories: approved tournament players, certain PGA members, and major tournament winners. The only method for becoming an "approved tournament player" is to successfully complete a TPD qualifying school. Those PGA members who may join the TPD on the strength of their PGA membership are full-time head professionals. The third category consists of some of the major tournament winners; however, there is clearly a built-in bias for those who participate in the PGA Club Professional Championship, a tournament sponsored by the PGA.

Plaintiff alleges that completing the TPD school is not a reasonable method for determining if one has the requisite skills for competing in the individual tournaments. He has asserted that the schools are held in a limited area of the country each year, and that golfers will fluctuate in ability depending upon the location of the school. However the papers show that the 1977 fall qualifying school, unlike those in years past, was divided into three parts; sectional qualifying, regional qualifying, and then final qualifying rounds. The sectional rounds were scheduled in 24 different locations, the regionals in four areas, and then the final competition in one location. This evidence has not been expanded upon by either the plaintiff or the defendants.

In addition the papers reveal that the number of persons who may "successfully" complete the school is determined to some extent by the number of openings on the tour. This type of subjective qualifying seems inconsistent with the entire scheme of the TPD and verges on a vertical group boycott as we have before defined that phrase. The effect of this practice would be to restrict entrance of new players in favor of the old pros, and has no relationship to competence.

As we noted in our denial of plaintiff's motion for preliminary injunction, there also seems to be some question of the reasonableness of allowing Class–A PGA members into the TPD without requiring them to complete the TPD school. The defendants have asserted that the 1977 amendments to the regulations restrict automatic eligibility to Class–A PGA members who are also full-time head professionals, and that this amendment alleviates our prior concern. Whether these individuals are given a higher priority than their skills would prove, were they required to complete the TPD school, is still an issue which must be resolved in order to determine whether the regulations coincide with the purpose of the TPD.

Two of the four remaining categories of persons who may apply for membership in the TPD are geared to the PGA Club Professional Championship. While these persons have undoubtedly proven their ability in tournament golf, we are concerned with the separation of this tournament from other major golf events. Although the sixth category permits automatic eligibility for "winners" of the World Series of Golf, the U.S. Open, the Masters and British Open, there is a definite bias for players in the PGA Championship—in addition to the "winner" of the PGA Championship tournament, the 25 lowest scoring golfers are also automatically eligible. The fifth category of persons who may apply for membership without completing the TPD school are "all current PGA Section Champions." Again the relationship between the PGA and competitive ability has not been sufficiently explained.

The same problems arise in the nine remaining categories of the TPD tournament eligibility regulations. Many of the categories are tied to the PGA and/or the PGA Championship Tournament. Although the skill of these members is not questioned, the differentiation between these members and others similarly situated but unaffiliated with the PGA is questionable and is still a material fact in issue....

Partial dismissal granted.

Questions for Discussion

1. Notice that *Weser* was decided in 1979, during the same period that the Supreme Court was redefining the antitrust Rule of Reason in cases like *Professional Engineers, Broadcast Music, GTE Sylvania,* and *Northwest Wholesale Stationers* (see Chapter 3), none of which were cited in the above opinion. The *Weser* court said that the issue under the Rule of Reason was whether the PGA restraint "was justified by legitimate business purposes and was no more restrictive than necessary." Is this test compatible with the current "procompetitive vs. anticompetitive effects" formula that seeks to balance efficiency benefits from a particular restraint against consumer welfare injury from increased market power? How should *Weser* have been analyzed and resolved under the modern approach?

2. Is it appropriate for a court to decide whether each of the various categories for tournament eligibility furthers the stated TPD purpose of "foster[ing] competition at the highest levels"? To what extent should courts defer to the judgment of the private governing association on this issue? Is the *Weser* court's approach in this respect consistent with that adopted in *Crouch v. NASCAR*?

The winter of 1997–98 witnessed a major legal battle between the PGA Tour and golfer Casey Martin regarding the application of the Americans With Disabilities Act to this sport. Ironically, Martin had been the teammate of Tiger Woods on the Stanford University team that had won the NCAA golf championship in 1994. As we noted back in Chapter One, for many decades African Americans such as Charles Sifford were not allowed to play in PGA events that were limited by the original 1916 Charter to "members of the Caucasion race."[c] However, as the Congress and the nation were debating enactment of a federal Civil Rights Act in the early 1960s, the PGA amended its constitution to eliminate that racial bar, thus permitting Woods to become golf's big star of the late 1990s.

The issues presented by the Casey Martin case were far more complicated. Martin suffers from the Klippel–Trenauney–Weber syndrome, a congenital malformation of his veins that curtailed blood circulation and thus gradually atrophied the calf muscles and tibia bones in his right leg. Notwithstanding this condition and the resulting pain, Martin exhibited real skills in playing golf, a sport that typically permits the amateur golfer to ride a cart rather than to walk from shot to shot. Thus, during the NCAA championship victory, Martin was permitted to use a cart when he was experiencing severe pain.

After graduating from college (where he had been an Academic All-American), Martin decided to try professional golf even though his leg condition was significantly worsening, and he was even facing the risk of

---

[c]. See Charlie Sifford with James Gullo, *"Just Let Me Play": The Story of Charlie Sifford, the First Black PGA Golfer* (Latham, N.Y.: British American Publishing, 1992).

amputation if he happened to step into the wrong place (e.g., a hole). Martin also faced the constraints of PGA Tour rules that governed professional golf. In particular, players on the regular PGA Tour and the lower-level Nike Tour are not allowed to ride carts (though these are used to move players considerable distances from the 9th to the 10th holes, or to go back to hit shots that have been found out of bounds). By contrast, golfers on the Senior Tour (limited to those aged 50 or more) are allowed to ride carts at all times, though only a small number do exercise that option.

When Martin sought to make the PGA Tour in its Qualifying Event in December 1997, he was permitted (indeed required) to use a cart in the early rounds that had a large number of players. As one of the small number whose scores put them in the final rounds, Martin would have been blocked from riding in the cart at that stage in the event. However, Martin's lawyer went off to court and secured a preliminary injunction against enforcement of this rule against him. From that legal base, Martin narrowly missed making the regular Tour, but he did qualify for the Nike Tour. Indeed, with considerable media attention, Martin won the season's first Nike tournament (and a $40,000 purse) in early January 1998. Then Martin and his lawyers went back to court in February to try to win a permanent ruling on this issue.

The source of Martin's legal claim was the Americans With Disabilities Act of 1990, which expanded into the private sector essentially the same legal standards embodied in the Rehabilitation Act of 1973. In Chapter 9, we read cases considering the application of these laws to college and high school sports, *Ganden v. NCAA,* 1996 WL 680,000 (N.D.Ill.1996), and *Pottgen v. The Missouri High School Association,* 40 F.3d 926 (8th Cir.1994), and we will read another decision, *Knapp v. Northwestern University,* 101 F.3d 473 (7th Cir.1996), in Chapter 13. Like college athletes, Martin was not an "employee" of the PGA Tour, and thus the law applied to the latter body (or to the NCAA) only if it was operating a place of "publuic accommodation." In the *Martin* case, U.S. Magistrate Judge Thomas Coffin found that the PGA Tour was a "commercial enterprise" rather than a "bona fide private membership club," and rejected the Tour's argument that golf courses were governed by the ADA only with respect to the space made available to spectators behind the ropes rather than to eligible players out on the course. The judge noted by analogy that a physically disabled manager of a baseball team would have an ADA right to reasonable accommodation of his access to the team's dugout when visiting another team's stadium even though spectators in the stands were not allowed to enter it.

Since there was no doubt that Martin suffered from severe physical disability, the next legal question was whether permitting him to use a cart was a "reasonable accommodation" to that condition, or instead would substantially alter the game by giving Martin a competitive advantage over his fellow Tour members (e.g., Tiger Woods) who had to walk rather than ride from shot to shot. A number of major golfing figures, led by Arnold Palmer, Jack Nicklaus, and Ken Venturi, testified in favor of the PGA rule as one designed to preserve golf as "a game of stamina." Judge Coffin, however, disagreed, and rejected the PGA's argument that full adherence by everyone to its "walking rule" was necessary to fairly "inject the element of fatigue into the skill of shotmaking." The judge found, first, that in normal circumstances there is almost no fatigue factor generated from golfers walking an average of five miles over five hours (and in the case of professionals, with caddies carrying their clubs). Next, when exhaustion did occur (e.g., to Ken Venturi when he almost had to give up on the final 36-round of his memorable 1964 U.S. Open victory), this was attributable to high heat (e.g., of 100 degrees) and humidity and resulting dehydration, something that affected the non-walking spectators as much as the walking golfers. Finally, Martin's use of a cart did not give him a competitive advantage. When the judge examined the specifics of Martin's situation, he found that Martin was still at a significant disadvantage due to his pain and risk of serious injury, e.g., when he got in and out of the cart, walked to and from his shot, and occasionally had to hit his ball from traps, woods, and streams. Judge Coffin thus granted Martin a permanent order allowing him the cart accommodation on the Tour (not just Nike's, but also regular PGA Tour events for which he might receive sponsor exemptions).

As this book was going to press, the PGA Tour announced that it would be appealing the decision, but it would not be asking for a stay of Judge Coffin's order. Thus, by the time readers have begun to reflect on the validity of this ruling, we will have had a chance to see whether the ADA has given Casey Martin either a real opportunity or a real advantage in professional golf. Following are some of the questions raised by the *Martin* case (not just for the circuit court panel, but also for PGA authorities and fans) about the application of the ADA and other antidiscrimination legislation to professional sports.

Questions for Discussion

1. Should either the ADA or Title II of the Civil Rights Act, which bars racial and gender discrimination, be found to apply to golf (or tennis or auto racing) as a "place of public accommodation"? Does allowing a golfer with a condition such as Martin's to use a cart give him an unfair advantage in a tournament? Should decisions such as these be left entirely up to the private Tour, or be subject to at least some outside legal scrutiny? And whatever the judgment made under public law, should Tour authorities find it to be in the best interests of their particular sport to alter their rules (and, if so, how) to accommodate golfers such as a Casey Martin?

2. Suppose that a top-flight woman player wanted to take her chances on the much more lucrative men's PGA Tour (where the total prize money in 1997 was $75 million in 45 official events), rather than play only on the Ladies PGA Tour (where the total prize money was only $30 million). If Jack Nicklaus and Hale Irwin can now participate in both regular and senior men's golf tour events, why cannot Annika Sorenstam and Laura Davies play in events on both the women's and the men's tours? Alternatively,

could a young male golfer claim a legal right to play on either the women's or the senior men's tour? Are there any relevant legal or philosophical differences between these two claims?

3. One noteworthy case crystallizes many of the issues inherent in gender-based tours. Dr. Renee Richards, formerly a ranking men's tennis player, underwent a transsexual operation to become female. Richards then attempted to enter the women's field in the 1977 U.S. Open. The USTA adopted the Barr sex-chromatin test, which would detect male chromosomes, shortly after Dr. Richards filed for tournament entry. Richards then sought and was granted an injunction against application of the test on the ground of violation of New York human rights laws. While the court felt that use of this test was justifiable to prevent fraud against women competitors (men masquerading as women), it held that the Barr test should not be used as the sole criterion. *Richards v. USTA*, 93 Misc.2d 713, 400 N.Y.S.2d 267 (1977). Specifically, the court found that Dr. Richards was female externally, internally, endocrinologically, somatically, psychologically, and socially. Thus the USTA's use of the Barr test to exclude a participant who was a woman by so many other standards constituted illegal discrimination. Other than the phobias of tour officials or prospective audiences, does a sports tour have any legitimate grounds for excluding a transsexual? If size and muscle power are significant factors affecting truly equal competition, could the USTA not have adopted a direct standard of size and weight? Should the golf and tennis tours follow the example of boxing and classify competitors according to physical size rather than according to gender?

4. In the late 1980s, the PGA Tour adopted a controversial revision in its rules that denied general eligibility for tour events (above a specified number of sponsor invitations) to foreign players who did not commit themselves to play at least fifteen times on the American tour. Australian players such as Greg Norman were prepared to make that commitment, but star Europeans such as Nick Faldo and Seve Ballesteros were not, because of the conflicting demands of their expanding European tour. Indeed, in 1995, the PGA Tour revised its sponsor exemption rule to permit such invitations to European players only if they had played a minimum of eleven events on the European Tour. What are the objectives and likely effects of these PGA Tour policies? Should a player, whether American or foreign, have an antitrust claim if he is denied the opportunity to play in an event for these reasons, but has satisfied the tour's basic playing ability and accomplishment tests—i.e., victories and earnings?

5. Should the PGA Tour be entitled to alter its current rules and make it a condition of membership and playing rights on the Tour that each player must grant to the Tour's marketing arm the right to offer the player's name and likeness as part of a group licensing package sold by the PGA Tour to manufacturers of golf clubs, clothes, or other paraphernalia? Suppose that a player objected because he had sold (or wanted to sell) an exclusive endorsement to a manufacturer of a different product line. Suppose that the firm insisted on its endorsement rights because it was a sponsor of the tournament that the player wanted to enter. See *Greenleaf v. Brunswick-Balke-Collender Co.*, 79 F.Supp. 362 (E.D.Pa.1947), and *Washington State Bowling Proprietors Ass'n. v. Pacific Lanes Inc.*, 356 F.2d 371 (9th Cir.1966).

C. DISCIPLINARY AUTHORITY OF THE TOUR

Once courts intervene to protect the right of individual players to compete in golf (or tennis or bowling) tournaments, inevitably courts will be drawn into tour actions that terminate the eligibility of existing players, whether through suspension or permanent expulsion.[d] The pioneering case in this area came from the Ladies PGA Tour. In 1950, after the men's PGA had rebuffed their request in the 1940s for a separate women's division within that organization, women golfers created their own tour composed of eleven tournaments and eleven participants. The LPGA struggled through the 1950s and the 1960s, but in 1972 it appeared to have made a major gain in financial backing and popular status. That year, the Colgate Company, sponsor of the highly-rated Dinah Shore television show, decided to create the Dinah Shore Golf Classic, which became one of the Grand Slam events on the women's tour. In the same year, though, one of the top LPGA players, Jane Blalock, was suspended by her peers for her alleged practice of moving her ball during play.

BLALOCK v. LPGA

United States District Court, Northern District of Georgia, 1973.
359 F.Supp. 1260.

MOYE, DISTRICT JUDGE.

[Following several complaints from competitors, the LPGA tournament director appointed four observers to watch Jane Blalock play during a May 1972 tournament in Louisville. The observers agreed that Blalock was, indeed, moving her ball, including advancing her ball on the green after she had cleaned it. A meeting was convened of the Tour Executive Board which was comprised of five players—Cynthia Sullivan, Judy Rankin, Linda Craft, Penny Zavichas, and Sharon Miller. The Board initially found Blalock guilty of cheating during play, fined her $500, and placed her on probation for the rest of the season. Two weeks later, the Executive Board reconvened, with two other players from the Tour's tournament committee, and changed the penalty to a suspension for one full year. Blalock sued, alleging an illegal group boycott under federal antitrust law.]

* * *

Measured by the standard set forth in [previous cases], the Court finds that the purpose and effect of the arrangement in this case (the agreement by defendants Sullivan, Rankin, Craft, Zavichas and Miller to suspend plaintiff from defendant LPGA for one year) was to exclude plaintiff from the market, and is therefore a "naked restraint of trade."

---

d. On the legal and policy questions, see John C. Weistart, *Player Discipline in Professional Sports: The Antitrust Issues*, 18 William and Mary L. Rev. 703 (1977), and Robert H. Heidt, *"Don't Talk of Fairness": The Chicago School's Approach Toward Disciplining Professional Athletes*, 61 Indiana L. J. 53 (1985).

Plaintiff is a member in good standing of defendant LPGA. Suspension therefrom is tantamount to total exclusion from the market of professional golf. Not only would plaintiff be excluded from LPGA sponsored tournaments, but, as defendant LPGA's Constitution and By-Laws provide in Article VIII:

> A member of the Ladies Professional Golf Association may not compete for prize money in a tournament, professional-amateur, or qualifying event that is not co-sponsored by the LPGA Tournament Players Corporation, or approved in writing by the LPGA Executive Director....

The suspension was imposed upon plaintiff by defendants Sullivan, Rankin, Craft, Zavichas and Miller in the exercise of their completely unfettered, subjective discretion, as is evident from the fact that they had initially imposed upon plaintiff only probation and a fine, but then, without hearing from plaintiff, determined to impose the suspension at issue here. Furthermore, the suspension was imposed by competitors of plaintiff who stand to gain financially from plaintiff's exclusion from the market.

The Court therefore determines that the arrangement in this case is illegal per se. Consequently, it is not necessary that it inquire as to the reasonableness of the suspension.

* * *

Defendants have cited the cases of *Molinas v. National Basketball Association*, 190 F.Supp. 241 (S.D.N.Y.1961), and *Deesen v. Professional Golfers' Association of America* 358 F.2d 165 (9th Cir.1966). The Court finds these cases to be inapposite. The facts in *Molinas* demonstrate that Molinas, a professional basketball player, was suspended by the president of the National Basketball Association who was acting pursuant to a clause in Molinas's contract and a league rule prohibiting gambling. The suspension was not imposed by Molinas's competitors.

In the *Deesen* case, Deesen, a professional golfer and a member of the Professional Golfers' Association, had his approved tournament player status terminated by the PGA's national tournament committee. The national tournament committee was largely composed of non-competitors of Deesen (the only exception being Bob Rosburg). Furthermore, the Court of Appeals relied heavily on the fact that notwithstanding that Deesen's tournament status had been terminated, Deesen was not completely excluded from the market (tournaments) as he could still participate therein, if he chose to become a golf teacher employed by a golf club. The termination in *Deesen* was based upon virtually a mathematical application of pre-determined standards. It did not involve a completely unfettered, subjective and discretionary determination of an exclusionary sanction by a tribunal wholly composed of competitors, as here....

Partial summary judgment granted.

Questions for Discussion

1. Look closely at the doctrinal analysis employed in *Blalock*, a case arising early in the evolution of sports antitrust law. Would a present-day court treat this as a question of *per se* illegality, in light of the last twenty years of sports antitrust jurisprudence? Would Rule of Reason analysis make any difference in the final result?

After *Blalock*, most tours, including the LPGA's, altered their disciplinary procedures to ensure that the ultimate decision-makers are not solely fellow tour competitors of the player being charged. The typical present-day disciplinary model was at issue in the next antitrust suit, *O'Grady v. PGA*, 1986 WL 15389, 1986–2 Trade Cases (CCH) ¶ 67,361 (S.D.Cal.1986). O'Grady had been fined $500 by PGA Commissioner Deane Beman for insulting a worker at a New Orleans tournament. O'Grady was so infuriated by his discipline that he publicly described Beman as a dictator worse than Hitler, Mussolini, or Richard Nixon. O'Grady also made a disparaging comment about the Riviera Golf and Country Club, the site of the Los Angeles Open: O'Grady said that, while Riviera had once been "really great," it was now like a "cheap public course that today would make a great runway for LAX." Beman then fined O'Grady an additional $5,000 and suspended him from the tour for the next six weeks (and six golf tournaments) for "conduct unbecoming" a PGA Tour member. Having lost his appeal to the Tour's Appeals Committee (comprised of one tournament player and two non-players, the Chairman of the Tournament Policy Board and the President of the PGA), O'Grady filed an antitrust suit, relying on *Blalock*. The trial judge quoted the following testimony from Jack Nicklaus about the meaning of "conduct unbecoming a professional golfer":

> [B]asically, what it really amounts to is the PGA of America has always had a Code of Ethics and the PGA Tour has always had a Code of Ethics. We felt for the best interests of the game the players should conduct themselves in a manner that is in the best interests of the game. It is in the best interest of the tour. It is a collective image. The best interests of PGA of America, of all the club pros in the country, to be able to [omitted] our position with the sponsor, our position with television, our position dealing with the public in general. I think it is important that the image of the player and the tour be for the good of the Association.

* * *

> If the rules were not there and the players headed in any direction they wanted to head, first of all we would not have had an Association, we would not have had a tour, as we know it, nor do I think the public would have accepted us in the direction they have, which I think is good. Television contracts we have. The sponsors we have. Everything I think has grown largely because we, as an Association, have worked together for one common goal, which is for the benefit of the tour.

The judge then dismissed O'Grady's antitrust suit:

> Mr. O'Grady would better serve himself by polishing his clubs and his golfing skills which are apparently very considerable, and leave off his temptation for verbal engagements.

Do you agree? In a team sport such as the NFL, for example, suppose that the Patriots' Zeke Mowatt had publicly attacked Commissioner Paul Tagliabue as a "dictator" for fining him in the aftermath of the Lisa Olsen incident described in Chapter 1. Should Tagliabue be able to penalize Mowatt for this added offense? Or suppose that Charles Barkley had publicly criticized the parquet basketball floor in the Boston Garden as "old, in poor shape, and giving the Celtics an unfair advantage because they know where the ruts and cracks are." Is this a disciplinary offense?

2. Recall the cases and problems in Chapter 1. Should baseball and football have a procedure for appealing disciplinary rulings by their commissioners as the *O'Grady* case exemplifies in golf (and as also exists in tennis)? Of course, when there is a players association with a collective bargaining agreement, the suspended player (for example, Steve Howe) may be able to take the case to arbitration. But outside the union context, should Pete Rose have had an avenue to appeal a decision by Bart Giamatti, or George Steinbrenner one by Fay Vincent?

3. Would courts uniformly find discipline imposed by boards made up of peers or competitors to be antitrust violations, regardless of the disciplined athlete's conduct? Consider the 1997 case, when professional stock car driver Jerry Eckman and his car owner Bill Orndorff were both suspended for two years and fined $25,000 by the National Hot Rod Association. During a routine warm-up for first-round qualifying at a June race in Columbus, Ohio, Eckman's car exploded. Fortunately no other drivers or fans were injured, although many were in the vicinity of the car. A test done on the car's fuel revealed that it had been spiked with nitrous oxide, a highly volatile and banned fuel additive. Had the decision to suspend Eckman and Orndorff been made by a committee of drivers or car owners, or by a neutral committee at the insistence of drivers concerned for their safety, would a court reach the same result as it did in *Blalock*? What distinctions are there between the two cases that might justify a different result?

In thinking about tour disciplinary authority, consider the following case, one of the most important in modern American sports. On April 27, 1967, Muhammad Ali, the world's heavyweight boxing champion and most celebrated athlete, refused to be inducted into the U.S. armed forces on the ground of a conscientious religious objection. On April 28, 1967, the New York State Athletic Commission revoked Ali's license to box, and all the other state commissions soon followed suit. Ali's suit against the New York commission was then dismissed on administrative law grounds. See *Muhammad Ali v. State Athletic Commission of New York*, 308 F.Supp. 11 (S.D.N.Y.1969):

* * *

The visibly barbaric aspects of prize fighting, together with only slightly concealed vices of other kinds, led New York and other States to ban the activity altogether during long periods of modern history. For some time, however, relaxing its scarcely questionable power of total prohibition, New York, again like other States, has permitted the so-called sport, but subjected it to sweeping and rigorous controls administered by a State Athletic Commission. It is much too late in our constitutional history to dwell long upon the obviously sweeping powers of the State to regulate an activity of this kind. The scope of occupational licensing and supervision must vary, of course, with the nature of the business and its impacts. Whether the variations be deemed differences of kind or merely "of degree," it is plain that some fields, including the one before us, are subject to broad powers for the determination and application of state policy judgments.

The peculiar mix of mystique and big business characterizing the world of professional sports is nowhere more complex and bemusing than in the "boxing game." Even judges have some awareness of the brutal, corrupt and dirty chapters in the history of this subject. On the other hand, the blood, sweat and smoke of the fight arena have been the ingredients for producing folk heroes, enshrined as models for the young as well as shrewd investments for others. All such diverse things are reflected in the broad mandate of the Athletic Commission—which is required to watch out for "fixes," for sharp managerial practices and for other corrupt devices while it strives to follow the loftier and still cherished ideals of a simpler age reflected in the notion of a "clean sport." To implement its various objectives, the Commission is entitled to wide freedom both for expert technical controls and for more romantic, even "mid-Victorian" judgments of moral, quasi-aesthetic value.

308 F.Supp. at 16 (citations omitted). Not until the Supreme Court sustained Ali's constitutional freedom of religion claim and voided his subsequent conviction for draft evasion was he permitted by state authorities to return to the ring.[e]

Questions for Discussion

1. Suppose that a golfer or tennis player had claimed the same exemption from the draft as did Ali. Or suppose that the player had merely attacked the president's war policy in as vigorous a tone as Mac O'Grady employed against Deane Beman. Are either or both of these actions valid (i.e., procompetitive) grounds under antitrust law for suspension of the player from a privately-governed tour whose officials believe the player's conduct to be harmful to the best interests of their sport?

2. A different kind of disciplinary problem arose in 1983 in tennis. The Argentinian star Guillermo Vilas was discovered to have been paid $60,000 to appear at a tournament in Rotterdam. The Men's International Professional Tennis Council (MIPTC), then the governing authority for the men's

---

[e]. See Thomas Hauser, *Muhammad Ali: His Life and Times* 142–202 (New York: Simon and Schuster, 1991). On the broader issues posed by the sport of boxing and its regulation (both internally and by state boxing commissions), see Jeffrey T. Sammons, *Beyond the Ring: The Role of Boxing in American Society* (Urbana, Ill.: Univ. of Illinois Press, 1990).

tour, fined Vilas $20,000 and suspended him for a year for violating its rule against appearance money or guarantees. Vilas exercised his right under the MIPTC constitution to appeal this decision to a three-member panel composed of one person selected by Vilas, another by MIPTC officials, and the third by these two nominees (all panel members were selected from a larger MIPTC roster). The panel confirmed the Council's finding of a rules violation by Vilas and upheld the fine but revoked the suspension, because this was the first time that the Council had enforced its rule against the growing practice of paying appearance fees to star attractions. Vilas paid the modest fine and the matter was closed.

Suppose, though, that the suspension had been upheld and Vilas had proceeded with his threatened antitrust suit against the MIPTC. How does a rule that bars individual tournaments from paying individual players more than the official prize money stand up under antitrust scrutiny? Such a rule has always been the norm in men's and women's golf and women's tennis, but as we shall see, the rule has recently been relaxed somewhat in men's tennis. To what extent does such a rule serve the interests of players (those who are regularly paid appearance fees and those who are not), of tournaments, and of fans?

D. ORGANIZING A SPORTS TOUR

The phenomenon of appearance money is best understood within the broader evolution of tennis (and other non-team) tournament tours. Lawn tennis, as the game was first called, was invented in the 1870s. The All England Lawn Tennis Club staged the first Wimbledon Championship in 1877 and the United States Lawn Tennis Association (now the USTA) staged its first championship in 1881. In 1900, twelve countries agreed to play for the Davis Cup, and in 1913 the national associations from these and other countries formed the International Lawn Tennis Federation (now the ITF) as the game's world-wide governing authority.

Amateurism was the Federation's central principle. Unlike golf tournaments, "open" tennis championships were *not* open to players who earned their living from the game. Once top players established their reputations, they had to drop out of "Grand Slam" competition and barnstorm around the world playing exhibition matches. Beginning with Suzanne Lenglen in the 1920s, this was the path followed by superstars such as Bill Tilden, Don Budge, Jack Kramer, Pancho Gonzales, and Rod Laver. Meanwhile, ITF tennis had developed into a regime of "shamateurism," as it was labeled. Tournament organizers and national associations had always been permitted to pay players their travel expenses for an event, but it became common practice to pay sums substantially above actual expenses to the top players—in effect, appearance guarantees.

Some tournament tennis players were thus able to make a reasonably decent living from the sport—considerably better than college football players on scholarship, but not as good as avowedly professional golfers on the PGA Tour. By the 1960s, some tennis authorities—

particularly the British—wanted to end this hypocrisy and make their events truly "open," but they were always out-voted within the ITF by authorities in smaller countries that were worried about losing money and control. The political logjam was broken not by litigation, but by market competition. In the mid–1960s, Lamar Hunt, fresh from his success with the American Football League, organized a new venture, World Championship Tennis (WCT), which successfully recruited most of the top players to a professional tour promising both serious competition and sizable prize money. Faced with that threat, in 1968 the All England Lawn Tennis Club declared Wimbledon open to professionals, and the USTA immediately followed suit with its U.S. Open.

These actions ushered in an era of top-flight tennis, fast-growing spectator and television revenues, constant controversy about the structure of the sport, and periodic litigation among parties fighting for a larger share of the pie. The following are some of the highlights of that history.[f]

In 1968, the ITF voted to allow professionals to enter Grand Slam events and Davis Cup competition. The Federation also developed its own set of Grand Prix tournaments to compete against the WCT Tour. Scheduling conflicts and competition for players between the two tours promoted a fierce rivalry; the ITF, after failing to negotiate cooperation in scheduling with the WCT, banned all WCT pros from ITF events. The absence of the WCT pros from the 1972 Grand Slams promoted a truce between the tours; WCT and ITF officials resolved their conflict by literally dividing the calendar between them.

In 1972, the male players created an Association of Tennis Professionals (ATP), whose first presidents were Cliff Drysdale and Arthur Ashe and first executive director was Jack Kramer. Conflict between the ATP and the ITF produced another boycott of Wimbledon in 1973 by players supporting one of their members, who had been suspended by the ITF for not playing for his country in the Davis Cup competition.

Soon thereafter, with the help of Donald Dell—Arthur Ashe's agent and the founder of ProServ—the ATP and the ITF agreed to create the Men's International Professional Tennis Council (MIPTC) to run the men's game, with each given three places on the Council's governing board. The MIPTC later became a tripartite body with three board

---

[f]. The best treatment of the emergence of the present-day tennis tour is Richard Evans, *Open Tennis: 1968–1989* (New York: Viking, 1990). Other historical portrayals of the professional tennis circuits are Bud Collins, *My Life With the Pros* (New York: E.P. Dutton, 1989); Jack Kramer with Frank Deford, *The Game: My 40 Years in Tennis* (New York: G.P. Putnam & Sons, 1979); and Pam Shriver, Frank Deford & Susan Adams, *Passing Shots* (New York: McGraw–Hill, 1987). Narrower time frames are described in John Feinstein, *Hard Courts: Real Life on the Professional Tennis Tours* (New York: Villard Books, 1992), and Rich Koster, *The Tennis Bubble: Big–Money Tennis, How It Grew and Where It's Going* (New York: Quadrangle/The New York Times Book Company, 1976). The legal picture prior to the decision excerpted in this section is described in George Matanias, Thomas Cryar & David Johnson, *A Critical Look at Professional Tennis Under Antitrust Law*, 4 Enter. & Sports L. J. 57 (1987).

members added to represent the various tournaments and their directors.

Meanwhile, women players had not been faring nearly as well as men financially—women's prizes often amounted to only about 10% of those offered to men in the same Grand Prix tournament events. In response, a new Women's Tennis Association (WTA) was formed, led by Billie Jean King as President and Gladys Heldman as Executive Director. The new WTA successfully launched the Virginia Slims women's tour under the sponsorship of the Phillip Morris Tobacco Company. This challenge to the tennis establishment produced threats of expulsion of women members from Grand Slam tournaments and litigation in response (see *Heldman v. USLTA*, 354 F.Supp. 1241 (S.D.N.Y.1973)), until the ITF finally agreed with the WTA to create a Women's International Professional Tennis Council (WIPTC) to govern the women's game.

In 1974, yet another entrant appeared on the scene, World Team Tennis (WTT), which offered fans a schedule of matches between teams of players representing different cities. After the WTT recruited star players such as Jimmy Connors and Evonne Goolagong, the MIPTC threatened suspension of any players deserting its tour. That threat produced yet another lawsuit, *Jimmy Connors v. Arthur Ashe* (ATP President) and his colleagues, a suit that was dropped when the MIPTC backed down.

In fact, the new WTT model of teams playing in a league did not prove to be a serious threat to the traditional practice of individual players competing by and for themselves in tournaments. By the mid–1980s, the basic structure of present-day tennis had emerged. Tennis players drawn from around the world competed in tournaments staged around the world. Most tournaments consisted of separate events held on the men's and women's tours respectively; however, the four Grand Slam Tournaments (the Australian, French, All England (Wimbledon), and U.S. Opens) and a few other tournaments had both men's and women's competitions. Each tournament was staged by a local body with financial support from a local sponsor, but the tour as a whole had a general corporate sponsor. The men's tour, in particular, devised an elaborate system of ranking players by their overall performance throughout the year, paying bonus money for players who did best on tour events and staging a lucrative year-end Masters Tournament for the best players on the tour that year.

Along with these wider and more lucrative tournament opportunities came an extensive array of regulations by tour authorities, regulations that were embodied in contractual commitments signed by any player who wanted to appear in a tournament and by any organization that wanted to stage a tour event. Recall one example of such regulation—the ban on fees paid by an individual tournament to players in order to guarantee their appearance at that event. Instead, the tours sought to ensure widespread participation in tournaments by requiring each player to enter a minimum number of events (at least fourteen on the men's tour), and by offering a bonus pool created by contributions from each tournament.

These devices were felt necessary because star players such as John McEnroe and Chris Evert were constantly offered the chance to play in brief exhibition events that paid large sums of money with no risk to their computer rankings. Thus, the tours also imposed stringent limits on when players could perform in special events that conflicted with tournaments and on the ability of any party involved in conducting an official tournament to stage a special event off of the tour.

A particular target of such regulations were organizations such as Donald Dell's ProServ and Mark McCormack's International Management Group (IMG). ProServ and IMG initially emerged as agencies representing star tennis and golf players, but soon developed the ability to assist, manage, and even stage tour events themselves. Believing that this mix of functions involved a potential conflict of interest (Donald Dell even served as color commentator on telecasts of tournaments involving his clients), the MIPTC barred a player agency from conducting tournaments which, it was feared, would have an unfair advantage in getting the agency's clients to appear at their tour events. (In fact, it was this apparent conflict of interest that led Dell's partners, Lee Fentress and Frank Craighill, to leave ProServ and create their own organization, Advantage International.)

We have provided the foregoing detail about the evolution and structure of the tennis tour as backdrop for the one appellate court decision that addresses the compatibility with American antitrust law of tour organization of individual sports (which in the case of tennis, but not golf, is an international structure). This litigation was actually initiated by the Volvo Corporation which had been the general sponsor of the men's tour as the latter evolved in the late 1970s and early 1980s, before being outbid for sponsorship by Nabisco Brands. Some time after the suit began, the MIPTC satisfied Volvo's concerns by giving favorable schedule treatment to the latter's New England tournament. By then, however, ProServ and IMG had become parties to the litigation and continued the legal attack on MIPTC regulation. After a federal district judge in New York granted summary dismissal of the suit, the plaintiffs appealed to the Second Circuit.

VOLVO NORTH AM. CORP. v. MEN'S INT'L PROFESSIONAL TENNIS COUNCIL (MIPTC)

United States Court of Appeals, Second Circuit, 1988.
857 F.2d 55.

PIERCE, CIRCUIT JUDGE.

[The first question was whether Volvo, IMG, and ProServ had standing under antitrust law to challenge components of the MIPTC system to which they themselves were parties.]

* * *

Appellants claim on appeal that "MIPTC coordinates horizontal competitors banding together to eliminate competition among themselves and to use their collective power to limit the competitive opportunities of outsiders." In other words, appellants view MIPTC as a vehicle through which certain entities, primarily other tournament owners and producers, have established a cartel in the market for men's professional tennis; allegedly, this cartel has not only limited output and raised prices in the market for men's professional tennis events, but has also used its market power to inhibit competition from the owners and producers of Special Events. ProServ and IMG claim that the cartel has injured them, in their capacities as owners and producers of Special Events, (1) by restricting their ability to obtain a sufficient supply of players' services for Special Events; (2) by causing them to own and produce fewer Special Events than they otherwise would have owned and produced; and (3) by causing the Special Events that they have owned and produced to be less profitable than these events otherwise would have been. Volvo claims similar injuries as a potential owner and producer of Special Events. In addition, all three appellants claim that they have been injured ... because compliance with MIPTC's rules has prevented them from competing "freely and vigorously with the events owned and produced by the defendants and their co-conspirators."

In response ... MIPTC raises the following argument in one form or another: if appellants' theory is correct, and MIPTC is the vehicle through which tournament owners and producers have organized a cartel in the market for men's professional tennis, then appellants lack standing to challenge the cartel because, as owners and producers of sanctioned tournaments, appellants themselves are members of the cartel who stand to benefit from the cartel's unlawful activity. Taken to its logical conclusion, appellees' argument suggests that we adopt a per se rule prohibiting putative cartel members from asserting antitrust claims against other members of the cartel.

We decline to adopt a rule precluding cartel members from raising antitrust challenges against the cartel. As one commentator has noted, "even absent legal restraint the cartel is inherently more fragile than the single-firm monopolist. The interests of the cartel as a whole often diverge substantially from the interests of individual members." H. Hovenkamp, *Economics and Federal Antitrust Law* § 4.1, at 83 (1985) ("Hovenkamp"). Individual members of the cartel may face different costs; some may be more efficient than others, and "some may produce slightly different products, which cost either a little less or a little more than the product sold by other cartel members." Thus, even though a particular trade restraint adopted by a cartel presumably operates to the cartel's aggregate benefit, the restraint may operate to the detriment of an individual member.... To the extent a cartel member credibly asserts that it would be better off if it were free to compete—such that the member's interest coincides with the public interest in vigorous competition—we believe that the individual cartel member satisfies the antitrust injury requirement....

2. APPLYING ANTITRUST INJURY ANALYSIS

a. *MIPTC's Administration of the Grand Prix Circuit*

As noted above, appellants claim that, in administering the Grand Prix, MIPTC has denied appellants "the opportunity to produce tennis events in the manner they seek with respect to matters such as site location, player compensation and scheduling." In response, appellees argue that, to the extent appellants themselves are owners and producers of events sanctioned by MIPTC, they "are only helped by rules minimizing scheduling conflicts," and that "the MIPTC rule limiting the amount of prize money which can be awarded by an event ... cannot possibly hurt appellants in their association with MIPTC sanctioned events" because appellants stand to "benefit from a ceiling on one of the key costs of running an event."

For the following reasons, we conclude that appellants have standing to challenge the administration of the Grand Prix circuit. Because the individual cartel member's interests may diverge from the interests of the cartel as a whole, MIPTC's decisions relating to site location and scheduling might not work to appellants' advantage, even though appellants are owners and producers of sanctioned events. Appellants claim that MIPTC uses its power "to shield tournaments favored by MIPTC from the rigors of competition," and, in our view, this allegation satisfies the antitrust injury requirement. Moreover, as Volvo argues on appeal, the rule limiting the amount of prize money that may be awarded by sanctioned events may injure appellants, as owners and producers of such events, by preventing them from "compet[ing] against other Grand Prix events for the services of highly ranked players by offering more prize money." Once again, although a particular rule may work to the aggregate benefit of the owners and producers of sanctioned events, it may not benefit an individual owner or producer such as Volvo, ProServ, or IMG. Thus, because appellants' individual interests may coincide with the public interest in promoting competition, we believe that appellants have satisfied the first element of the standing analysis.

* * *

c. *Commitment Agreements*

The amended complaint alleges that the Commitment Agreements inhibit men's professional tennis players from competing in Special Events. Appellees counter the attack on the Commitment Agreements by arguing, first, that "appellants stand only to gain from each of the alleged restrictions on the market for men's tennis playing services," because "any incentives for players to sell their services to the Grand Prix ... can only benefit appellants" in their capacity as owners and producers of MIPTC-sanctioned events....

Notwithstanding the foregoing arguments, we conclude that appellants have standing to challenge the Commitment Agreements. As alleged, the Commitment Agreements discourage players from participating in non-sanctioned events and, therefore, increase the cost of producing these events. Accordingly, IMG and ProServ, in their capacities as owners and producers of non-sanctioned Special Events, may have suffered "injury of the type the antitrust laws were intended to prevent." Moreover, by restricting the supply of players available for non-sanctioned events, the Commitment Agreements also discourage owners and producers from disassociating themselves from MIPTC. To the extent that owners and producers of sanctioned events, such as Volvo, would otherwise find it in their economic interests to compete against the alleged tennis cartel, these owners and producers also have suffered the type of injuries the antitrust laws were intended to forestall. Thus, in our view, all three appellants have satisfied the element of antitrust injury.

[For similar reasons, the court upheld the plaintiffs' standing to challenge the MIPTC rules requiring tournament contributions to the bonus pool and restricting special events. The court then turned to the merits of the plaintiffs' antitrust claims. The court first held that the MIPTC, made up of representatives of players, tournaments, and national tennis associations, was the type of joint venture that was capable of an antitrust conspiracy, explicitly following judicial precedents that had characterized the NCAA and professional leagues as multiple rather than single entities for purposes of § 1 of the Sherman Antitrust Act. After noting that the plaintiffs had attacked as horizontal price-fixing the MIPTC rule that specified prize money ranges for different kinds of tournaments, the court made the following comment about the reasonableness of such a practice.]

* * *

Assuming that appellants succeed in proving the foregoing allegations, however, we express no opinion at this time as to whether appellees' conduct should be condemned as per se unlawful or, instead, should be analyzed under the Rule of Reason. Normally, "agreements among competitors to fix prices on their individual goods and services are among those concerted activities" that are considered per se illegal under § 1 of the Sherman Act. The relevant inquiry, however, involves more than "a question simply of determining whether two or more potential competitors have literally 'fixed' a 'price.'" Instead, "'price fixing' is a shorthand way of describing certain categories of business behavior to which the per se rule has been held applicable." Moreover, we recognize that professional sporting events cannot exist unless the producers of such events agree to cooperate with one another to a certain extent, and that the antitrust laws do not condemn such agreements when coordination is essential if the activity is to be carried out at all. Thus, on remand, the district court should carefully consider whatever arguments appellees may offer in support of their practices relating to player compensation before deciding whether the per se rule or the Rule of Reason should apply.

[The appeals court made essentially the same judgment about the plaintiff's attack on MIPTC's allocation of different dates to different tour sites and sponsors: this practice could constitute an illegal horizontal division of the tournament market, but no decision was made about whether the MIPTC practice was per se illegal or possibly justifiable under the rule of reason. With respect to the charge that eligibility conditions imposed by the MIPTC on players constituted a potential group boycott, the Appeals Court stated:]

* * *

According to appellant ProServ, "the Grand Prix tournaments have collectively agreed not to permit the participation by any player who fails to accept the conditions the group imposes upon the player's activities for an entire year." Thus, men's professional tennis players "confront through the Commitment Agreements a horizontal agreement among competing producers of tennis tournaments setting forth the terms under which they will collectively decline to deal with the players."

Judge Duffy considered the Commitment Agreements to be "essentially employment contracts that require employee players to play only for MIPTC for thirty-six weeks a year." The court then stated that "[e]mployers may impose reasonable employment conditions for a reasonable period of time," and that "[e]ven accepting plaintiffs' assertion that creating an independent tennis event series is not feasible during the remaining weeks of the year, I cannot find that an exclusive employment contract for thirty-six weeks a year is imposed for an unreasonable length of time."

In our view, the amended complaint adequately alleges that appellees have threatened to engage in a group boycott or concerted refusal to deal. Generally, a group boycott is "an agreement by two or more persons not to do business with other individuals, or to do business with them only on specified terms." To prevail on a group boycott or refusal to deal claim, a plaintiff must demonstrate that the defendant intends to restrain competition, or to enhance or expand his monopoly, and has acted coercively.

Whether the threatened boycott alleged in the amended complaint [should be legally appraised by a per se rule] is a matter for the district court to consider in due course.

[Finally, the court reinstated the appellant's claim that the MIPTC's organization and operation of men's tennis potentially constituted an illegal monopoly under § 2 of the Sherman Act.]

* * *

The offense of monopolization under § 2 of the Sherman Act consists of two elements: (1) the possession of monopoly power in the relevant market; and (2) the willful acquisition or maintenance of that power, as distinguished from growth or development as a consequence of a superior product, business acumen, or historic accident. *Aspen Skiing Co. v. Aspen Highlands Skiing Corp.*, 472 U.S. 585, 596 n. 19, (1985). Appellants clearly have alleged that MIPTC possesses monopoly power over the production of first-rate men's professional tennis events. Paragraph 50 of the amended complaint, for example, alleges that in 1985 the top one hundred men's professional tennis players all signed Commitment Agreements. Moreover, the amended complaint alleges that appellees have willfully maintained their monopoly power (1) by merging with WCT in 1983; (2) by requiring players to sign Commitment Agreements; and (3) by requiring owners of sanctioned events to contribute to the bonus pool. Although the facts may eventually bear out the district court's conclusion that MIPTC has not willfully maintained its monopoly power, and that MIPTC instead has benefited from "the recent historical development of men's professional tennis," we do not believe that the district court was correct to draw this conclusion on a motion to dismiss.

Appeal granted.

The appellate court thus upheld the plaintiffs' appeal, reinstated the plaintiffs' antitrust suit, and returned the case to the district court for trial on the merits. As has happened with almost every lawsuit launched in the world of tennis, the litigants in *Volvo* soon settled the case without its legal merits ever being reached in court. Volvo turned its sponsorship attention to the European golf tour (where, by the way, it insisted upon adoption of the ban on appearance fees that previously had rewarded players such as Nick Faldo, Seve Ballesteros, and Ian Woosnam). Player agencies such as ProServ and IMG agreed, after a three year phase-out period, not to be involved in ownership of tournaments, while the MIPTC relaxed its rule to allow agencies to sell television and sponsorship rights on a men's tour that itself was changing sharply in character.

In 1990, the ATP broke away from the MIPTC and decided to stage its own tour run by and for the players. Many prominent players felt that the MIPTC governing board had been unresponsive to their concerns about a tour that had become too long and dispersed to permit regular genuine competition among the top stars. The new regime left the ITF with its four Grand Slam tournaments and the Davis Cup competition, and a new $6 million Grand Slam Championship (featuring the top 16 performers from that year's Grand Slam events) to be staged just after the ATP's season-ending World Championship in November of each year. The ATP Tour is divided into 21 Championship Series events (with prize money ranging from $825,000 to $2.7 million) and 53 World Series events (with minimum prize money of $235,000). All top-ten ranked players are required to play in at least 11 of the 21 Championship events, and the ATP has guaranteed to each such tournament that at least six top-ten players will participate. In addition, none of its players are permitted to perform in another tournament or special event in competition with the Championship Series. With respect to World Series events for which there is no such commitment or protection, the ATP now allows such tournaments to pay appearance fees. The first such above-the-board fees were paid by the San Francisco tournament in

February of 1990: Andre Agassi received $175,000 to appear and $32,000 to win.

Hamilton Jordan, the first Executive Director of the ATP Tour (and formerly Chief of Staff to President Jimmy Carter), lauded this new venture as "one stop shopping" for men's tennis, through which "the pie would get bigger and everybody would benefit." Not only has the tour managed to secure a rich sponsorship deal with IBM, but the ATP has sold (through IMG) its worldwide television rights on a package basis for $110 million a year. For the ATP membership, at least, the outcome has been a happy one: fewer commitments from individual players and a tour whose prize money topped $80 million in 1997 (exclusive of the bonus pool, appearance money, and Grand Slam events). Women tennis players have observed these developments with envy, as they play a total of 57 events including the four Grand Slam tournaments (as compared with 74 for the men excluding the ITF's Grand Slam and Grand Slam Cup events), for $40 million in total prize money in 1997, which is roughly half that on the men's tour. A combination of division within the WTA ranks and contractual commitments to outside sponsors have blocked for the time being any similar venture for the women tennis players.

We have sketched the foregoing developments within tennis in order to pose anew the legal questions that were not finally addressed in *Volvo*.

1. Does the appearance money issue look any different when viewed with this broader historical perspective?

2. Why should individual players—especially the best players—be required to appear at a specified number of tour events around the world (in addition to participation by many in four two-week Grand Slam tournaments, the year-long Davis Cup competition, and the season-ending tour championships)? Should this rule pass the Rule of Reason test?

3. Why should players be barred from participating in special non-tour events held at the same time as Championship Series events, or within a specified distance of contemporaneous World Series events? At this time, players who violate these rules are simply fined by the governing body (the ATP or the WITPC), and the fines are paid by the special event sponsors as part of the appearance money guarantee. This is what happened to Monica Seles in 1991, when she played at a New Jersey exhibition shortly after her mysterious absence from Wimbledon. What if the ATP or the WITPC put more teeth in this rule by suspending a player for several months for such an infraction? Could the player or the event promoter sue?

4. Is the collective sale of television rights on behalf of the entire tour—with proceeds divided among individual tournaments—consistent with the antitrust doctrines we saw applied to professional leagues in Chapter 7 (in the *WGN* case) and to college sports in Chapter 10 (in the *Oklahoma–Georgia* case)?

5. Would it be legal for the ATP membership to boycott ITF events—on the ground, for example, that most of the money now earned by the USTA from the U.S. Open is paid not as prize money to professional players, but used to fund the USTA's broader activities promoting tennis in this country?

6. Recall the *Sims v. Argovitz* case from Chapter 5 and related questions about conflicts of interest affecting sports lawyer-agents and their player-clients. Does that material justify tour concern about the fact that, for example, Donald Dell and ProServ were at one and the same time the manager of Volvo's annual New England tennis tournament and the agent of Jimmy Connors and others whom Volvo wanted to play in the tournament?

7. In assessing each of these questions, should the tour organizations in each sport—i.e., the ATP or the PGA—be treated as a single entity offering a single product that must compete in the broader sports and entertainment market, and thus be insulated from § 1 scrutiny of its internal decisions and restrictions?

The foregoing questions are as relevant to golf as to the tennis tours. While private litigation may not soon be forthcoming from among the players, sponsors, broadcasters, and others who participate in and profit from the current tours, the Justice Department and the Federal Trade Commission (FTC) are empowered to launch such proceedings on behalf of the general public. Indeed, an ongoing FTC investigation made the sports pages at the end of 1994 in connection with the rise and quick fall of a proposed World Golf Tour. This Tour was the brainchild of Greg Norman and his fellow Australian, Rupert Murdoch, owner of Fox Broadcasting. Their idea was to have the top 30 golfers in the world play an additional championship tour comprised of eight tournaments scattered throughout the year. Four of these events would be scheduled just before the four majors: half would be in the United States and half elsewhere in the world. All would have total purses of $3 million, with minimum guarantees for all participants. Much of the money would come from Fox, which, as part of its effort to become a major sports network and cable system, would telecast the events in the United States and elsewhere around the world.

While many of the top golfers, American and non-American, expressed interest in both this competition and its rewards, the PGA Tour stated that, under its rules, it was entitled to an exclusive commitment to its tour by its own playing members. In particular, the "conflicting events" rule bars PGA Tour members from taking part in U.S. golf events that conflict with the PGA schedule from January through October (even lesser tournaments that attract few star performers), while the "television release" rule requires PGA Tour consent to any Tour members appearing on non-PGA golf events televised in this country.

In mid-1995, Norman said that he was abandoning his plans for the World Tour because he did not want to jeopardize the success of the

PGA Tour. In September, the FTC announced that it had terminated its investigation of the PGA without any legal action—a decision that then-Senate Majority Leader Bob Dole and a number of his colleagues had been pressing for. Should the antitrust inquiry have been dropped? Would the PGA Tour rules pass or fail the rule of reason test? If not, should the PGA Tour be granted a special antitrust exemption by Congress to preserve its current status? In thinking about these questions, consider the broader issues of whether the restrictive organization of one (non-team) sport unduly burdens the sports market, and whether American antitrust law enforcement should target a sport such as tennis that (by contrast with golf) operates on a world-wide basis.

Golf, tennis, bowling, and the various auto racing sports are unified under a central governing authority. (In 1996, though, Indy open-wheel car racing split into two competing tours organized under separate governing authorities—Championship Auto Racing Teams (CART) and the upstart Indy Racing League (IRL), headed by Indianapolis Motor Speedway President Tony George.) Boxing, on the other hand, has historically been subject to a patchwork of inconsistent state regulation. The lack of uniformity effectively penalized those states that took substantive action to reduce the economic exploitation and personal injury faced by boxers. In 1996, after several futile efforts over many years to establish federal regulation of the sport, Congress finally passed the Professional Boxing Safety Act (PBSA), codified at 15 U.S.C.A. §§ 6301 et seq.

The PBSA attempts to deal with several perceived problems. First, it establishes minimum safety and procedural standards that must be met before a match can be sanctioned by a state boxing commission (§§ 6304 & 6306). Second, the Act provides that no match may be held in a state that does not have a boxing commission unless it is supervised by a commission in another state and subject to guidelines promulgated by the Association of Boxing Commissions (ABC) (§ 6303). Third, the Act attacks conflicts of interest by prohibiting anyone involved with the regulation of boxing in any state from receiving any compensation from anyone who either is involved in staging boxing matches or has an interest in an active professional boxer (§ 6308); it creates a fine of up to $20,000 and up to one-year imprisonment for anyone violating this provision (§ 6309(b)). Finally, the Act requires state boxing commissions to honor suspensions imposed by a sister state commission if the suspension was for (a) a knockout or consecutive losses; (b) a physical deficiency; (c) failing a drug test; or (d) using a false name or ID card (§ 6306(a)(2)).

This last provision became an issue after the 1997 heavyweight championship fight in Las Vegas between Mike Tyson and Evander Holyfield. Tyson was suspended by the Nevada State Boxing Commission the week after he was disqualified for biting off a section of Holyfield's ear during the match. Although the grounds for the suspension were not among those that trigger the PBSA requirement that other commissions honor the suspension, most state commissions across the country (with the exception of Florida's) announced that they would honor the suspension nonetheless, in compliance with the spirit of the PBSA. Section 6306(b) of the Act provides that a state commission may allow a boxer under suspension in another state to fight in its state if either the grounds for the suspension are not on the list noted above or the boxer appeals and the commission finds that the suspension was "without sufficient grounds, for an improper purpose, or not related to the health and safety of the boxer or the purposes of this chapter." Would it violate the PBSA for another state not to allow Tyson to fight, based on the Nevada suspension? (Interestingly, it is also unlikely that Tyson could fight in another country, since one of the terms of his parole from prison after being convicted of rape years earlier was that he not leave the country without permission of the parole authorities in Indiana.)

Who do you think gained the most (and lost the most) as a result of passage of the PBSA? Does the federal government's involvement in regulating an industry historically governed by the states concern you? Should this statute survive commerce clause scrutiny as the regulation of what might appear to be purely intrastate affairs? Or do you think Congress should go further and establish a federal commission that replaces the state commissions and/or creates a federal "boxing czar?"

A final issue concerns not market restraints, but gender disparities. Among the Grand Slam tournaments comprising both men's and women's events, Wimbledon and the French Open (but not the United States or Australian Opens) pay smaller prize money for the women's than the men's championship. Is that practice discriminatory? Is it relevant that the separate men's tennis tour now offers two and a half times the prize money as the women's tour (this is also true of the PGA versus the LPGA golf tours)? What accounts for these large differentials in the financial rewards for the typical male and female athletes (Martina Hingis and Annika Sorenstam being exceptions that prove the rule)? Does this have any bearing on the questions posed in Chapter 11 about college sports under Title IX—for example, whether the men's and women's basketball programs should receive equal financial support?

E. REGULATING PLAYING EQUIPMENT

An additional source of protagonists and controversies is the manufacture of equipment used in a sport. The design of tennis rackets and golf clubs is an obvious target of tour regulation because of the impact that playing equipment can have on athletic competition. But private regulation of the tools that put individual athletes at an advantage displays the historical tensions felt by organizations whose manifest purpose is to serve the welfare of the game, but that also serve the entrepreneurial interests of participants.

One of the first cases in which a court grappled with these issues was *STP Corporation v. United States Auto Club (USAC)*, 286 F.Supp. 146 (S.D.Ind.1968). In the sport of auto racing, the USAC functioned not as the promoter of races such as the Indianapolis 500, but as a non-profit body that merely sanctioned events, licensed participants, and regulated the safety and appeal of the races—including providing specifications for racing car engines. In the 1967 Indy 500, Studebaker's new turbine-powered car proved to be much faster than traditional piston-driven engines (although the Studebaker Turbocar had to drop out near the end of that race because of gear box troubles). Shortly thereafter, the USAC introduced a rule that limited the size of turbine-powered engines in order to make them equivalent in speed to piston-powered cars. In dismissing an antitrust suit brought by STP, Studebaker's subsidiary in charge of its racing program, a district judge held that such USAC rulemaking was perfectly acceptable under the rule of reason:

> One of the purposes of the USAC is to encourage the sport of automobile racing, which is a highly competitive sport of a very technical nature. The quickest way to bring about the demise of racing would be to permit a situation that developed for one car with superior qualities or such superior capabilities as to eliminate competition. It would be somewhat like allowing one basketball team to have a large hoop at one end of the court and a small regulation size basketball hoop at the other end for the other team. In order to have a continuation of racing, the Court concludes that USAC acted reasonably in trying to bring about an equivalency between the piston-powered automobiles with turbine-powered cars according to a formula that was prepared and cemented after consultation with those who are considered most expert in the field.... The making of competitive rules is something that any governing body of an organization such as USAC has a right to do. Such action goes to the very purpose of its existence, i.e., to encourage competitive racing.

286 F.Supp. at 151.

Ten years later, a similar dispute arose in tennis with two added features. Unlike the USAC, the U.S. Tennis Association itself ran several major tournaments, including the lucrative U.S. Open. In this case, the USTA adopted a new equipment rule issued by the International Tennis Federation (ITF), which had traditionally exercised responsibility to establish a single set of rules governing tennis matches wherever played.

GUNTER HARZ SPORTS v. USTA

United States District Court, District of Nebraska, 1981.
511 F.Supp. 1103.

SCHATZ, DISTRICT JUDGE.

[The ITF had banned a German manufacturer's new model of tennis racket—called the "spaghetti racket" because it had two layers of vertical strings, one on each side of the horizontal strings. The effect of this "double-stringing" was to impart a very powerful topspin to a tennis ball, such that when the ball hit the ground in front of a player, it would bounce sharply over his head. When the racket first appeared in European tournaments, it helped produce several astonishing upsets of star players by low-ranked opponents. In the face of a threatened player boycott of the 1977 French Open, the ITF issued a temporary emergency ban of this racket pending in-depth study of its effects; when the study was completed, the ITF permanently banned the double-strung racket. The ITF stated that "the spirit of this rule is to prevent undue spin on the ball that would result in a change in the character of the game." After the USTA had endorsed and adopted both ITF regulations, the racket manufacturer sued the USTA in Nebraska.]

* * *

While the Sherman Act is primarily aimed at conduct which has commercial objectives, ample authority exists for finding the activities of the USTA subject to § 1. Non-profit voluntary associations which sanction and regulate professional sporting tournaments, races and other contests have been held subject to the antitrust laws in the exercise of their rule-making authority. Similarly, non-profit amateur athletic associations formed for the primary purpose of promoting amateur athletics have been found subject to the prohibitions of § 1 of the Sherman Act. Courts have proceeded on the theory that while each such sanctioning organization has the primary noncommercial purpose of promoting organized sports in an orderly fashion, "its subsequent actions in carrying out its laudable objectives could trigger the applicability of the Sherman Act if such conduct restrained interstate trade or commerce in an unreasonable manner."

* * *

The actions of the USTA in this case clearly cannot be characterized as the traditional type of group boycott to which the per se doctrine has been applied. The Court accepts plaintiff's contention that the USTA entered into a Sherman Act "agreement" when it joined other member nations of the ITF in the adoption of Rule 4 of the Rules of Tennis, and when it agreed to follow the temporary ban of double-strung rackets. However, the Court rejects any suggestion of "agreement," as that term is used in the Sherman Act, between the USTA or the ITF and any distributors or manufacturers of tennis equipment to prevent the plaintiff from competing in the sale or distribution of rackets or stringing systems. Totally lacking in this case is an agreement between "business competitors in the traditional sense." Nor can the actions of the USTA in adopting a rule defining tennis rackets be labeled as lacking in "any redeeming virtue."

Where the purpose of a "group boycott" has been to protect fair competition in sports and games, courts have eschewed a per se analysis in favor of an inquiry into the reasonableness of the restraint under the circumstances.

* * *

Defendants contend that the actions of the USTA are exempt from this type of analysis under the circumstances of this case because the ITF actually initiated and promulgated the temporary ban and Rule 4, while the USTA was forced to adopt the rule as a condition of its membership. The Court finds that contention without merit.... "[C]ourts have uniformly rejected any defense that an antitrust violation was 'forced' onto the defendant," and the "Supreme Court has held that 'acquiescence in an illegal scheme is as much a violation of the Sherman Act as the creation and promotion of one.'"

The Constitution of the USTA provides that it is "an independent tennis organization and as such cannot take any action at the request of any international tennis body which is inconsistent with the provisions of its Certificate of Incorporation or any By–Laws or Standing Orders issued hereunder." As an independent tennis organization the USTA's membership in the ITF is voluntary, and it cannot take any action at the request of the ITF, or as a condition of its membership in the ITF, which is a violation of the antitrust laws of the United States and escape liability.

* * *

Turning to an analysis of the actions of the USTA under the rule of reason, the Court specifically finds that the collective action of the USTA, ITF, and other member national associations of the ITF was intended to accomplish the legitimate goals of preserving the essential character and integrity of the game of tennis as it had always been played, and preserving competition by attempting to conduct the game in an orderly fashion. The record is totally devoid of any evidence from which an intent to injure the plaintiff or any other manufacturer or distributor of tennis equipment can be inferred. As noted previously, the Court finds no agreement between the USTA or ITF and any manufacturer or distributor of tennis equipment to exclude plaintiff from competing in the market for rackets or stringing systems.

The evidence shows that the ITF solicited, received, and acted upon comments and suggestions from equipment manufacturers, including Fischer and Harz. The original draft of the proposed rule was revised partly in response to comments of manufacturers suggesting that many conventional rackets on the market would be banned by the original draft of the proposed rule, although such rackets did nothing to alter the character of the game. However, the Court finds nothing impermissible in such communication or response. Both the USTA and the ITF had the right to solicit such information and act upon it in attempting to make reasonable informed decisions concerning racket specifications and in attempting to draft the rule so that it would be the least restrictive of technological improvements and developments, but still address the legitimate concern that such development not adversely alter the character of the game of tennis as it had been played historically or artificially enhance the skill and ability of players, thereby harming the integrity of competitive tennis.

Secondly, the Court concludes that the actions of the USTA and the ITF were reasonably related to the goals discussed above. In reaching that conclusion, the Court is not to substitute its own judgment for that of the ITF or the USTA. It is irrelevant whether the Court might or might not independently reach the same decision based on the same evidence. In this regard, the Court agrees with the characterization of the latitude to be given a sanctioning organization contained in *STP Corp. v. United States Auto Club*:

> ... A membership organization ... must be left to legislate its own rules and its own guidelines for participation of its members for the purposes for which it was created so long as that legislation is not done in an unreasonable manner and without malice or intention to harm a single member or segment of membership. Such membership organizations have the right to adopt such rules to protect their very existence.

Plaintiff contends that the actions of the ITF in enacting the temporary ban on double-strung rackets were arbitrary because the basis for the ban was a false and misleading assessment by the German Federation of a study made by the Braunschweig Technical University on the effect of double-strung rackets, and a playing demonstration using poor copies of the Fischer double-strung racket, not strung according to Fischer's specifications on stringing tension.

The Court finds that despite the actual conclusion of the Braunschweig study that double stringing did not revolutionize the character of the game and should not be banned, the study's findings did lend support to the concerns which prompted the temporary ban. The study found that strokes at high speed, as well as stroke types which primarily utilized cross strings, could be played under certain conditions only; that double stringing resulted in strokes with a very strong spin being played almost exclusively since those strokes were most effective; and that on red gravel and coarse fiber courts, when high topspin strokes were played in the baseline area, balls could bounce over the back fence and such balls could only be returned when hit right after they bounced.

* * *

Contrary to plaintiff's assertions, the Court finds that the ITF's temporary ban bore a rational relationship to its goal of attempting to conduct organized tennis competitions in an orderly fashion. The COM at Barcelona acted not only on the basis of the demonstration, and the German Federation's assessment of the Braunschweig study, but also on the basis of actual and threatened players' strikes against use of the double-strung racket, publicity concerning upsets of high-ranking players by virtual unknowns using double-strung rackets, and adverse reports of several national federations based on their experience with the racket in match play and in training situations. This evidence provided an objective basis from which the COM could have concluded that a temporary freeze on the use of the rackets was necessary pending further investigation and subsequent action by the ITF Council.

* * *

The Court finds that a rule on racket specifications designed to prohibit rackets which impart exaggerated topspin to the ball on impact is rationally related to the goal of preserving the character of the game of tennis. In this regard, the Court especially credits the testimony of Cliff Drysdale and Vic Braden, who are both highly qualified to testify as experts on the subject....

Both Drysdale and Braden testified that the ability to impart topspin to a ball is one of the most important skills in the game of tennis. As Braden put it, being able to hit topspin is the "name of the game." Drysdale testified that it was his opinion that a player who has never been able to hit topspin with a conventional racket could, with a double-strung racket, be able to hit great topspin lobs by making a very small adjustment in the way he hit the ball. Drysdale also testified that an average player using a double-strung racket would be able to serve much more effectively than with a conventional racket, making it more difficult for an opponent to return a serve and correspondingly more difficult to get the ball into play.

Similarly, Braden testified that because a player using a double-strung racket could increase spin on a serve, there would not be many service returns, which would change the character of the game tremendously. As a result, the game would lend itself to people who develop a very efficient serve with a double-strung racket. Clearly, the ITF and the USTA could rationally consider a racket's artificial enhancement of fundamental skills of the game a threat to the integrity and character of tennis as it has been historically played.

Drysdale and Braden testified that widespread use of the double-strung rackets could change the character of the game in a number of other ways as well. Since other shots with double-strung rackets are substantially less effective than topspin shots, Drysdale testified that the end result would be a situation where everyone would be playing almost exclusively topspin shots. This tendency to adopt a similar style would reduce the variety of the game as it has been traditionally played, resulting in decreased spectator interest. Additionally, the result of the topspin that a double-strung racket can impart to the ball is a ball that bounces considerably higher, causing an opponent to move back to or past the baseline to get into a position where he can contact the ball. This also prevents an opponent from aggressively "attacking" by coming to the net. In Drysdale's opinion, players being forced to back away from the net would result in administrators of the game either having to expand the dimensions of the court or changing the composition of the ball in some way to accommodate the differences caused by the racket.

Braden also testified to his assumption that as people using double-strung rackets became proficient in hitting topspin lobs, court dimensions and structures would have to be changed. Braden's research indicated that on a typical 120-foot court with a twelve foot fence, a topspin lob hit hard enough with a spaghetti racket could force an opponent to climb to a nine-foot height against the back fence.

While plaintiff presented witnesses who testified that use of double-strung rackets would not change the character of the game, as previously noted, the Court infers from the expert testimony of Drysdale and Braden that the ITF and USTA could have reasonably concluded that rackets or stringing that impart excessive topspin to the ball alter the character of the game. This is all that is necessary since the Court is not to substitute its independent judgment for the ITF or the USTA in weighing the relative opinions of expert witnesses.

The Court also concludes that the actions of the USTA in honoring the temporary ban and adopting Rule 4 were not more extensive than necessary to serve the legitimate goals of the USTA and ITF. Based on the players' strikes and walkouts occasioned by use of the double-strung racket, the Court concludes that the temporary freeze on the use of double-strung rackets in sanctioned play was no more extensive than necessary to further the legitimate goal of conducting the game in an orderly fashion, especially in view of the provision that member nations could apply for permission to experiment with the racket at club level. The Court finds it reasonable for the ITF and USTA to have concluded that the alternative of taking no action and letting the racket have a twenty-four month trial period would not have furthered that goal.

Rule 4 itself was narrowly drawn to proscribe only rackets and stringing systems that imparted exaggerated topspin to the ball, since the ITF concluded that it was that feature which changed the character of the game. The breadth of the rule was additionally narrowed by provision of appeal procedures whereby a racket that failed to conform to the face of the rule could be approved under the standard that it did not impart exaggerated topspin to the ball or change the character of the game.

* * *

Suit dismissed.

[In a brief unpublished *per curiam* decision, the Eighth Circuit upheld the district court decision on the merits, while making clear that the USTA, notwithstanding its non-profit status, was governed by antitrust law in making decisions such as this adoption of an ITF rule of the game.]

Despite the favorable precedents in the *STP* and *Gunter Harz* cases, in the late 1980s both the USGA and the PGA Tour became embroiled in serious antitrust litigation involving the new square-grooved (or U-shaped) golfing irons. Traditionally, grooves in golfing irons have been shaped like a "V" that angle to a point embedded in the face of the club. In the early 1980s, the USGA and the Royal and Ancient Golf Club of St. Andrew's, Scotland (the rule-making authority for golf outside the United States), had relaxed their traditional ban on square grooves (which are shaped like a "U" inside the iron's face). This provided a major market opportunity for a new club manufacturer, Karsten Manufacturing. Karsten Sollheim, head of the firm, designed a new Ping Eye2 golf iron whose U-shaped grooves helped make it the country's best selling golf club, generating revenues of $100 million per year.

According to golf's ruling authorities, the problem was that the new square-grooved club imparted much more backspin to the ball, especially with shorter irons used to hit balls out of the rough. PGA Tour players such as Jack Nicklaus, Tom Watson, and Greg Norman protested that Ping iron users such as Mark Calcavecchia gained an unfair playing advantage: long but less accurate drivers off the tee did not have to pay the usual price of less control over approach shots hit from the rough toward the pin on the green. The response of the USGA was to adopt a new formula for club design that required a slightly broader gap between the grooves on the surface of the iron. While Karsten initiated an antitrust suit against this USGA rule, he eventually settled on the terms that the firm would manufacture all its new clubs in accordance with USGA specifications, but all existing Ping clubs would be grandfathered as acceptable to the USGA.

Neither the Tournament Players Division (TPD) of the PGA Tour nor its commissioner, Deane Beman, was prepared to accept that compromise. Instead, they instituted a ban on the use of any square-grooved irons in PGA Tour events. Because this was the first time that the PGA Tour itself had imposed special restrictions on equipment used in its tournaments, the step generated some procedural complications. Broader tour decisions such as this were normally made by the TPD's Policy Board, which was composed of ten directors—four players elected by the tour membership, three officials from the PGA, and three independent directors. Since the first seven directors all had endorsement agreements with other golf equipment manufacturers, they abstained from voting on the new rule to avoid the possible conflicts of interest. The three independent directors voted unanimously for the proposed new rule. However, such a small number of votes did not square with the Board's existing quorum rule. Thus, a new meeting was scheduled, at which all members voted to change the procedural requirements for such cases, and the same independent directors again voted for the ban on U-shaped irons.

Unsurprisingly, this course of events produced another lawsuit. The lead plaintiffs were Tour golfers who had used (and been paid to endorse) Ping Eye2 irons, but an additional plaintiff (and the party financing the entire litigation) was Karsten Manufacturing. The plaintiffs won a temporary injunction that banned PGA Tour enforcement of the Tour rule pending trial on the merits in early 1993. See *Gilder v. PGA Tour, Inc.*, 727 F.Supp. 1333 (D.Ariz.1989), affirmed, 936 F.2d 417 (9th Cir.1991). On the eve of trial in April 1993, this $100 million lawsuit was settled on the basis that Ping irons could be used on the PGA Tour but that the Tour Policy Board would establish an independent committee to evaluate the acceptability of golf equipment—including square-grooved irons—for tour competition. That led to the creation of a permanent Tour Equipment Advisory Committee, made up of five outside consultants who have both an interest in golf and a scientific background that enables them to make judgments about the effect of equipment modifications on the game. There has been no effort, however, to reinstate the rule against square-grooved irons, and they are now regularly used on the tour.

Questions for Discussion[g]

1. Remember that present-day Rule of Reason analysis requires courts to balance procompetitive benefits against anticompetitive harms. How would a sports governing body's decision to ban double-stringed tennis rackets or square-grooved golf irons be analyzed under that test? Do the statements in *Gunter Harz* and *STP Corporation* that courts should defer to the good faith judgment of governing bodies make sense for purposes of such balancing of competitive effects? Is a different test appropriate in reviewing the decisions of private sports regulatory bodies? Is the procedural history of the PGA Tour's ban on square-grooved irons relevant to such an analysis? What facts should the plaintiffs in *Gilder* have had to establish at trial to warrant a finding that the ban on square-grooved irons violated the antitrust Rule of Reason? And by the way, who are the multiple parties to the "conspiracy," or are these rules the conduct of a single entity immune from §1 attack?

2. How could Karsten establish that significant damages would be inflicted on its business if Tour players are not allowed to use the firm's irons in PGA Tour tournaments? Do Bob Gilder, Mark Calcavecchia, and others actually pay for their Ping Eye2 irons?

3. Does the prior question imply that the USGA and the USTA, with their broader regulatory reach, are more exposed to antitrust litigation about their equipment rules than are the PGA Tour and the ATP? Or do the latter bodies display a characteristic antitrust exposure of their own?

4. Suppose that the ATP adopted a rule banning use of racket frame designs that imparted high levels of speed and power to the ball, especially on the serve. Why might the ATP be tempted to pass such a rule? Should adoption of such a rule be subject to antitrust challenge by either racket manufacturers or players? More so than if the ATP responded to the growing number of 130 miles-per-hour serves by shortening the service court, or by allowing only one serve per point?

g. Besides the cases mentioned in the text, other relevant precedents include *Weight–Rite Golf Corp. v. United States Golf Ass'n*, 1990 WL 145594, 1990–2 Trade Cases (CCH) ¶ 69,181 (M.D.Fla.1990) (injunction request), and 766 F.Supp. 1104 (M.D.Fla.1991) (final decision), and *Eureka Urethane, Inc. v. Professional Bowlers Ass'n. of Am.*, 746 F.Supp. 915 (E.D.Mo. 1990).

5. Should the PGA Tour consider adopting a standardized golf ball for all its tournaments—a ball designed not to fly as far as existing balls? What practical arguments would be advanced within the Tour for and against such action? Would this be a risky legal step? Should it matter whether the Tour periodically sold to the highest bidder the exclusive right to manufacture and market the ball used in its events (with the PGA Tour distributing the proceeds among Tour members either *per capita* or *pro rata*, depending on the players' performance during the year)?

6. How should a court deal with litigation by a manufacturer complaining that a professional sports league (or the NCAA) had banned its type of equipment from being used in the league's games (like aluminum bats by MCB)? In the early 1980s, a manufacturer that had developed a laser-beam device to measure for first downs in football brought a § 1 antitrust claim against the NFL for refusing to allow a home team to use the device in its games. In an unpublished opinion, the district court in San Antonio summarily dismissed the case on the ground that the NFL decision had no anticompetitive effects. *Carlock v. NFL*, Case #SA–79–CA–133 (W.D.Tex. 1982).

> The NFL's refusal to purchase the plaintiffs' invention was merely a business decision made by an entity charged with the orderly and uniform implementation of the rules of professional football. The decision was based on the League's own business judgment, in consideration of numerous factors, including public acceptance of the chain-and-stakes technique for measuring the progress of the football, the undesirability of over-elaboration of officiating techniques, risks of technical failure, additional cluttering of sidelines, additional training problems, line-of-sight problems, and the costs required for the purchase of such equipment. Disappointed by their rejection, the plaintiffs simply seek to have this court substitute its business judgment for that of the NFL, which the plaintiffs believe failed to appreciate the merits of their invention.
>
> Any purchasing decision by any organization, regardless of its form, has some effect on market conditions. The antitrust laws afford product sellers the right to compete for the sale of their products, but the antitrust laws are not designed to guarantee sales of their products. There is simply no antitrust principle that requires any buyer to purchase and make use of an unwanted product simply because the buyer's failure to do so might negatively affect an individual seller or have some effect on the market for the sale of that product.

Is this reasoning persuasive? Does it say anything about the single entity issue discussed in Chapter 7? Is the court's analysis applicable to cases involving governing bodies for individual sports?

F. OLYMPIC SPORTS

A recurring theme in this chapter is the tension between external legal regulation and internal governance of a sport, especially where the sport is international and the regulation is carried out by an American court. That tension is sharply heightened for the various sports that make up the quadrennial Olympic Games, which are followed with great interest by billions of fans around the world. To understand these issues, one must first understand the extraordinarily complex structure that governs Olympic sports.[h]

At the apex of the Olympic structure is the International Olympic Committee (IOC), which controls the Olympic Games. The IOC in turn entrusts the various national Olympic committees with determination of which athletes will compete in the Olympics. In the United States, this governing body is the United States Olympic Committee (USOC). Under the Amateur Sports Act of 1978, 36 U.S.C.A. § 371 et seq., the USOC is charged with overseeing all matters relating to U.S. participation in both the Olympic and Pan American Games, as well as with performing several other specific functions related to the promotion of "amateur athletic activity" in the United States.

Each sport is separately governed by its own international sports federation, now over 40 in number, each of which conducts its own world championships and sanctions other independently operated contests. Eligibility standards for participation in any contest sponsored or sanctioned by an international federation are established and enforced by the federation. Eligibility for participation in the Olympic Games was originally defined by the IOC in the Olympic Charter, but that responsibility has now been delegated (through Rule 45 of the Olympic Charter) to the international federation that governs each sport, as long as the federation complies with the IOC's requirements. Thus, responsibility for establishing and enforcing criteria for participation in all but unsanctioned events rests exclusively with the various international federations.

As with the IOC, operating under the umbrella of the international federation in each sport is a national federation that exercises many of the eligibility and promotional functions of the international body. The national federation in each sport holds the qualifying events that determine which athletes are to represent the country in the Olympic Games (and in many sports, the world championships sponsored by the international federation). The Amateur Sports Act of 1978 instructs the USOC to recognize an appropriate national governing body in each sport. The Act empowers these governing bodies to perform various functions related to their sports: to conduct "amateur athletic competition" in the United States; to sanction other such competitions inside and outside the United States; to determine eligibility standards for participation in such competitions; to select the athletes to represent the United States in the Olympic and Pan American Games; to represent the United States in the international federation; and generally to govern all "amateur athletic activities" in their respective sports in the United States.

h. A valuable scholarly history of the Olympic games is Alan Guttman, *The Olympics: A History of the Modern Games* (Urbana, Ill.: University of Illinois Press, 1992). A highly critical journalistic treatment of the way the Olympics are now run is Vyv Simson & Andrew Jennings, *The Lords of the Rings* (London: Simon & Schuster, 1992).

A crucial legal issue is when, under what legal theories, and under what standard of review an American court should overturn a decision by one of these governing bodies. The following highly publicized case depicts some of the key legal arguments that have been made about this issue.

DEFRANTZ v. UNITED STATES OLYMPIC COMMITTEE (USOC)

United States District Court, District of Columbia, 1980.
492 F.Supp. 1181.

JOHN H. PRATT, DISTRICT JUDGE.

Plaintiffs, 25 athletes and one member of the Executive Board of defendant United States Olympic Committee (USOC), have moved for an injunction barring defendant USOC from carrying out a resolution, adopted by the USOC House of Delegates on April 12, 1980, not to send an American team to participate in the Games of the XXII Olympiad to be held in Moscow in the summer of 1980. Plaintiffs allege that in preventing American athletes from competing in the Summer Olympics, defendant has exceeded its statutory powers and has abridged plaintiffs' constitutional rights.

* * *

According to its Rules and By-laws, the International Olympic Committee (IOC) governs the Olympic movement and owns the rights of the Olympic games. IOC Rules provide that National Olympic Committees (NOC) may be established "as the sole authorities responsible for the representation of the respective countries at the Olympic Games," so long as the NOC's rules and regulations are approved by the IOC. The USOC is one such National Olympic Committee.

The USOC is a corporation created and granted a federal charter by Congress in 1950. This charter was revised by the Amateur Sports Act of 1978. Under this statute, defendant USOC has "exclusive jurisdiction" and authority over participation and representation of the United States in the Olympic Games.

* * *

On December 27, 1979, the Soviet Union launched an invasion of its neighbor, Afghanistan. That country's ruler was deposed and killed and a new government was installed. . . .

President Carter termed the invasion a threat to the security of the Persian Gulf area as well as a threat to world peace and stability, and he moved to take direct sanctions against the Soviet Union. These sanctions included a curtailment of agricultural and high technology exports to the Soviet Union, and restrictions on commerce with the Soviets. The Administration also turned its attention to a boycott of the summer

Olympic Games [in Moscow] as a further sanction against the Soviet Union.

* * *

[The President put great pressure on the USOC not to send a team to the 1980 Games, even to the point of threatening to withhold federal funding from the USOC, to revoke its tax exemptions, and to invoke the International Emergency Economic Powers Act to forbid any athletes from traveling to the Soviet Union during the games. In addition, the House of Representatives passed a resolution, by a vote of 386 to 12, opposing U.S. participation in the Games.]

* * *

[On April 12, 1980], [a]fter what USOC President Kane describes in his affidavit as "full, open, complete and orderly debate by advocates of each motion," the House of Delegates, on a secret ballot passed, by a vote of 1,604 to 798, a resolution [declaring that the USOC would not send a team to Moscow unless international conditions changed dramatically.]

* * *

1. The Amateur Sports Act of 1978

Plaintiffs allege in their complaint that by its decision not to send an American team to compete in the summer Olympic Games in Moscow, defendant USOC has violated the Amateur Sports Act of 1978.... Reduced to their essentials, these allegations are that the Act does not give, and that Congress intended to deny, the USOC the authority to decide not to enter an American team in the Olympics, except perhaps for sports-related reasons, and that the Act guarantees to certain athletes [a right to compete in the Olympic Games.] ...

* * *

The principal substantive powers of the USOC are found in § 375(a) of the Act.[12] In determining whether the USOC's authority under the Act encompasses the right to decide not to participate in an Olympic contest, we must read these provisions in the context in which they were written. In writing this legislation, Congress did not create a new relationship between the USOC and the IOC. Rather, it recognized an already long-existing relationship between the two and statutorily legitimized that

---

12. They are to: "(1) serve as the coordinating body for amateur athletic activity in the United States directly relating to international amateur athletic competition; (2) represent the United States as its national Olympic committee in relations with the International Olympic Committee ...; (3) organize, finance, and control the representation of the United States in the competitions and events of the Olympic Games ... and obtain, either directly or by delegation to the appropriation national governing body, amateur representation for summer games." 36 U.S.C. § 375(a)(1), (2), (3). The "objects and purposes" section of the Act includes the provision, also found in the 1950 Act, that the USOC shall "exercise exclusive jurisdiction ... over all matters pertaining to the participation of the United States in the Olympic Games ... including the representation of the United States in such games." Id., § 374(3).

relationship with a federal charter and federal incorporation.[13] The legislative history demonstrates Congressional awareness that the USOC and its predecessors, as the National Olympic Committee for the United States, have had a continuing relationship with the IOC since 1896. Congress was necessarily aware that a National Olympic Committee is a creation and a creature of the International Olympic Committee, to whose rules and regulations it must conform. The NOC gets its power and its authority from the IOC, the sole proprietor and owner of the Olympic Games.

In view of Congress' obvious awareness of these facts, we would expect that if Congress intended to limit or deny to the USOC powers it already enjoyed as a National Olympic Committee, such limitation or denial would be clear and explicit. No such language appears in the statute. Indeed, far from precluding this authority, the language of the statute appears to embrace it. For example, the "objects and purposes" section of the Act speaks in broad terms, stating that the USOC shall exercise "exclusive jurisdiction" over " ... all matters pertaining to the participation of the United States in the Olympic Games.... " We read this broadly stated purpose in conjunction with the specific power conferred on the USOC by the Act to "represent the United States as its national Olympic committee in relations with the International Olympic Committee," and in conjunction with the IOC Rules and By-laws, which provide that "representation" includes the decision to participate. In doing so, we find a compatibility and not a conflict between the Act and the IOC Rules on the issue of the authority of the USOC to decide whether or not to accept an invitation to field an American team at the Olympics. The language of the statute is broad enough to confer this authority, and we find that Congress must have intended that the USOC exercise that authority in this area, which it already enjoyed because of its long-standing relationship with the IOC. We accordingly conclude that the USOC has the authority to decide not to send an American team to the Olympics.

Plaintiffs next argue that if the USOC does have the authority to decide not to accept an invitation to send an American team to the Moscow Olympics, that decision must be based on "sports-related considerations." In support of their argument, plaintiffs point to §§ 392(a)(5) and (b) of the Act, which plaintiffs acknowledge "are not in terms applicable to the USOC," but rather concern situations in which national governing bodies of various sports, which are subordinate to the USOC, are asked to sanction the holding of international competitions below the level of the Olympic or Pan American Games in the United States or the participation of the United States athletes in such competition abroad. These sections provide that a national governing body may

---

13. To the extent the USOC was granted extended power by the 1978 Act, the legislative history makes clear, and the plaintiffs do not dispute the fact, that these powers were primarily designed to give the USOC supervisory authority over United States amateur athletic groups in order to eliminate the numerous and frequent jurisdictional squabbles among schools, athletic groups and various national sports governing bodies.

withhold its sanctions only upon clear and convincing evidence that holding or participating in the competition "would be detrimental to the best interests of the sport." Plaintiffs argue by analogy that a similar "sports-related" limitation must attach to any authority the USOC might have to decide not to participate in an Olympic competition. We cannot agree.

The provision on which plaintiffs place reliance by analogy is specifically concerned with eliminating the feuding between various amateur athletic organizations and national governing bodies which for so long characterized amateur athletics. As all parties recognize, this friction, such as the well-publicized power struggles between the NCAA and the AAU, was a major reason for passage of the Act, and the provisions plaintiffs cite, among others, are aimed at eliminating this senseless strife, which the Senate and House Committee reports indicate had dramatically harmed the ability of the United States to compete effectively in international competition. In order to eliminate this internecine squabbling, the Act elevated the USOC to a supervisory role over the various amateur athletic organizations, and provided that the USOC establish procedures for the swift and equitable settlement of these disputes. As indicated above, it also directed that the national governing bodies of the various sports could only withhold their approvals of international competition for sports-related reasons. Previously, many of these bodies had withheld their sanction of certain athletic competitions in order to further their own interests at the expense of other groups and to the detriment of athletes wishing to participate.

In brief, this sports-related limitation is intimately tied to the specific purpose of curbing the arbitrary and unrestrained power of various athletic organizations subordinate to the USOC not to allow athletes to compete in international competition below the level of the Olympic Games and the Pan American Games. This purpose has nothing to do with a decision by the USOC to exercise authority granted by the IOC to decide not to participate in an Olympic competition.

* * *

We therefore conclude that the USOC not only had the authority to decide not to send an American team to the summer Olympics, but also that it could do so for reasons not directly related to sports considerations.

(b) Athletes' Statutory Right to Compete in the Olympics

* * *

Plaintiffs argue that the Report of the President's Commission on Olympic Sports, which was the starting point for the legislation proposed, and the legislative history support their argument that the statute confers an enforceable right on plaintiffs to compete in Olympic competition. Again, we are compelled to disagree with plaintiffs.

The legislative history and the statute are clear that the "right to compete," which plaintiffs refer to, is in the context of the numerous jurisdictional disputes between various athletic bodies, such as the NCAA and the AAU, which we have just discussed, and which was a major impetus for the Amateur Sports Act of 1978. Plaintiffs recognize that a major purpose of the Act was to eliminate such disputes. However, they go on to argue that the Report which highlighted the need for strengthening the USOC in order to eliminate this feuding, made a finding that there is little difference between an athlete denied the right to compete because of a boycott and an athlete denied the right to compete because of jurisdictional bickering.

The short answer is that although the Congress may have borrowed heavily from the Report of the President's Commission, it did not enact the Report. Instead, it enacted a statute and that statute relates a "right to compete" to the elimination of jurisdictional disputes between amateur athletic groups, which for petty and groundless reasons have often deprived athletes of the opportunity to enter a particular competition....

The Senate Report makes clear that the language relied on by plaintiffs is not designed to provide any substantive guarantees, let alone a Bill of Rights. Further, to the extent that any guarantees of a right to compete are included in the USOC Constitution as a result of this provision, they do not include a right that amateur athletes may compete in the Olympic Games despite a decision by the USOC House of Delegates not to accept an invitation to enter an American team in the competition. This provision simply was not designed to extend so far. Rather, it was designed to remedy the jurisdictional disputes among amateur athletic bodies, not disputes between athletes and the USOC itself over the exercise of the USOC's discretion not to participate in the Olympics.

* * *

Because we conclude that the rights plaintiffs seek to enforce do not exist in the Act, and because the legislative history of the Act nowhere allows the implication of a private right of action, we find that plaintiffs have no implied private right of action under the Amateur Sports Act of 1978 to maintain this suit.

2. Constitutional Claims

Plaintiffs have alleged that the decision of the USOC not to enter an American team in the summer Olympics has violated certain rights guaranteed to plaintiffs under the First, Fifth and Ninth Amendments to the United States Constitution....

(a) State Action

Although federally chartered, defendant is a private organization. Because the Due Process Clause of the Fifth Amendment, on which plaintiffs place great reliance, applies only to actions by the federal government, plaintiffs must show that the USOC vote is a "governmental act," i.e., state action. In defining state action, the courts have fashioned two guidelines. The first involves an inquiry into whether the state

> ... has so far insinuated itself into a position of interdependence with (the private entity) that it must be recognized as a joint participant in the challenged activity.

Here, there is no such intermingling, and there is no factual justification for finding that the federal government and the USOC enjoyed the "symbiotic relationship" which courts have required to find state action. The USOC has received no federal funding[25] and it exists and operates independently of the federal government. Its chartering statute gives it "exclusive jurisdiction" over "all matters pertaining to the participation of the United States in the Olympic Games.... " 36 U.S.C. § 374(3). To be sure, the Act does link the USOC and the federal government to the extent it requires the USOC to submit an annual report to the President and the Congress. But this hardly converts such an independent relationship to a "joint participation."

The second guideline fashioned by the courts involves an inquiry of whether:

> ... there is a sufficiently close nexus between the state and the challenged action of the regulated entity so that the action of the latter may be fairly treated as that of the state itself.

> ... In the instant case, there was no requirement that any federal government body approve actions by the USOC before they become effective.

Plaintiffs argue that by the actions of certain federal officials, the federal government initiated, encouraged, and approved of the result reached (i.e., the vote of the USOC not to send an American team to the summer Olympics). Plaintiffs advance a novel theory. Essentially, their argument is that the campaign of governmental persuasion, personally led by President Carter, crossed the line from "governmental recommendation," which plaintiffs find acceptable and presumably necessary to the operation of our form of government, into the area of "affirmative pressure that effectively places the government's prestige behind the challenged action," and thus, results in state action. We cannot agree.

* * *

Here there is no [requisite governmental] control. The USOC is an independent body, and nothing in its chartering statute gives the federal government the right to control that body or its officers. Furthermore, the facts here do not indicate that the federal government was able to exercise any type of "de facto "control over the USOC. The USOC

---

25. Federal funds were authorized under the Amateur Sports Act of 1978 but have never been appropriated. But the mere receipt of federal funds by a private entity, without more, is not enough to convert that entity's activity into state action. *Spark v. Catholic University of America*, 510 F.2d 1277 (D.C.Cir.1975).

decided by a secret ballot of its House of Delegates. The federal government may have had the power to prevent the athletes from participating in the Olympics even if the USOC had voted to allow them to participate, but it did not have the power to make them vote in a certain way. All it had was the power of persuasion. We cannot equate this with control. To do so in cases of this type would be to open the door and usher the courts into what we believe is a largely nonjusticiable realm, where they would find themselves in the untenable position of determining whether a certain level, intensity, or type of "Presidential" or "Administration" or "political" pressure amounts to sufficient control over a private entity so as to invoke federal jurisdiction.

We accordingly find that the decision of the USOC not to send an American team to the summer Olympics was not state action, and therefore, does not give rise to an actionable claim for the infringements of the constitutional rights alleged.

(b) Constitutionally Protected Rights

... Were we to find state action in this case, we would conclude that defendant USOC has violated no constitutionally protected right of plaintiffs.

We note that other courts have considered the right to compete in amateur athletics and have found no deprivation of constitutionally protected rights. As the Government has pointed out in *Parish v. National Collegiate Athletic Association*, 506 F.2d 1028 (5th Cir.1975), basketball players sought an injunction to prevent the NCAA from enforcing its ruling declaring certain athletes ineligible to compete in tournaments and televised games. The court stated that:

> the privilege of participation in interscholastic activities must be deemed to fall ... outside the protection of due process.

Plaintiffs have been unable to draw our attention to any court decision which finds that the rights allegedly violated here enjoy constitutional protection, and we can find none. Plaintiffs would expand the constitutionally-protected scope of liberty and self-expression to include the denial of an amateur athlete's right to compete in an Olympic contest when that denial was the result of a decision by a supervisory athletic organization acting well within the limits of its authority. Defendant has not denied plaintiffs the right to engage in every amateur athletic competition. Defendant has not denied plaintiffs the right to engage in their chosen occupation. Defendant has not even denied plaintiffs the right to travel, only the right to travel for one specific purpose. We can find no justification and no authority for the expansive reading of the Constitution which plaintiffs urge. To find as plaintiffs recommend would be to open the floodgates to a torrent of lawsuits. The courts have correctly recognized that many of life's disappointments, even major ones, do not enjoy constitutional protection. This is one such instance.

Case dismissed.

Questions for Discussion

1. Should the federal government be able to enact a law delegating what in many countries is a governmental function to a private group, then exert enormous political pressure on that group to make a certain decision, and still argue that there is insufficient government involvement to trigger constitutional protections for those adversely affected by that decision? The courts have uniformly refused to recognize as state action the decisions of any of the national or international athletic governing bodies. See, e.g., *Behagen v. Amateur Basketball Ass'n of the United States*, 884 F.2d 524 (10th Cir.1989); *International Olympic Comm. v. San Francisco Arts & Athletics*, 781 F.2d 733 (9th Cir.1986), affirmed, 483 U.S. 522 (1987). Thus, like the NCAA after the *Tarkanian* decision in Chapter 9, these organizations are not required to provide constitutional due process or equal protection to those affected by their decisions. Does this mean that these bodies can do whatever they want? Could the USOC decide not to send a team to the Olympics in retaliation for an IOC decision not to award the Games to an American city, or because the IOC refused to enter a licensing agreement with an American company? If constitutional arguments are unavailable, are there any other legal claims disappointed athletes could make?

2. One question stemming from the Amateur Sports Act is the extent to which the USOC, a national sports governing body, or its international counterparts, are subject to American antitrust law. The cases presented earlier in this chapter involved antitrust review of a variety of decisions made by the bodies governing professional tours in tennis, golf, and auto racing. The only case so far to challenge a sports federation decision on antitrust grounds was brought in 1989 by Carol Cady and John Powell against The Athletics Congress (TAC) of the USA (as of December, 1992, USA Track and Field). TAC had suspended the athletes for participating in an unsanctioned track meet in South Africa, which was then under an International Amateur Athletic Federation (IAAF) boycott due to its apartheid policies. In an unpublished decision, the district court held that TAC's action was within the scope of the power vested in it by Congress through the Amateur Sports Act and thus was exempt from antitrust challenge. Was this the proper result? What if TAC suspended an athlete for participating in a track meet that TAC had declined to sanction because the meet was held on the same day as a meet sponsored by TAC itself (see Rule 53(iii) of the IAAF Handbook)?

The most controversial decisions by sports federations involve athlete eligibility—either establishing eligibility standards, which is done by the international federation, or applying the standards in individual cases, which can be done by the international or national bodies. The most hotly debated eligibility issue in recent years has involved the use of performance-enhancing drugs and the procedures for testing for these drugs (particularly steroids).[i] The 1990s witnessed a major case and

---

i. See, for example, Dr. Robert L. Voy with Kirk D. Deeter, *Drugs, Sports, and Politics* (Champaign, Ill.: Leisure Press, 1991); and Don H. Catlin and Thomas H.

controversy in which American courts wrestled with the question of what role our law could play in shaping enforcement of anti-drug rules by international sports agencies.[j]

REYNOLDS v. INTERNATIONAL AMATEUR ATHLETIC FEDERATION

United States District Court, Southern District of Ohio, 1992.
841 F.Supp. 1444.

KINNEARY, DISTRICT JUDGE.

[Harold "Butch" Reynolds was the world track and field record holder at 400 meters who had won the silver medal at the 1988 Olympic Games in Seoul, Korea. However, following the "Herulis meet" event in Monte Carlo, Monaco, on August 12, 1990, Reynolds was randomly selected to provide a urine sample. In October 1990, Reynolds was informed that he had tested positively for the anabolic steroid nandrolone, and was suspended by the IAAF for two years, which would cost him a spot in the 1992 Olympic Games in Barcelona, Spain.

Reynolds went to federal court in his home state of Ohio, arguing that the test results were erroneous—based in part on the fact that a urine sample from an August 19 track meet had tested negative. The district judge dismissed this initial legal proceeding on the ground that Reynolds first had to use the athletic system's administrative process. Reynolds thus sought an arbitration hearing pursuant to the Amateur Sports Act of 1978 and the constitution of the U.S. Olympic Committee (USOC). Following a hearing in June 1991, the arbitrator issued an opinion that exonerated Reynolds from the charge of steroid use.

> The arbitrator finds that the Respondent's suspension of Mr. Reynolds was improper; that there is clear and convincing evidence that the "A" sample and the "B" sample did not emanate from the same person and the "B" sample did not confirm the "A" sample; that there is substantial evidence that neither the "A" sample or the "B" sample emanated from the Claimant; and that Claimant should be declared eligible to compete in the qualifying rounds for the World Game Championships on June 12, 1991.

However, both TAC and the IAAF refused to accept this ruling, because it had not complied with the adjudicative procedures under IAAF Rule 59, which were initially administered by the domestic track and field body (in the U.S., this was TAC). Reynolds thus asked TAC to conduct a hearing which took place that September. After 12 hours of hearing and two weeks of deliberation, the three person TAC panel also exonerated Reynolds.

Murray, *Performance-Enhancing Drugs, Fair Competition, and Olympic Sports,* 276 J. of American Medical Association 231 (July 17, 1996).

[j]. For an analysis of this case, see Jill J. Newman, *The Race Does Not Always go to the Stronger or Faster Man ... But to the One Who Goes to Court: An Examination of Reynolds v. International Amateur Athletic Fed'n, et al.,* 1 The Sports Lawyers J. 205 (1994).

> The panel, after hearing the matters before it, the testimony of witnesses and expert witnesses from both sides, documents and exhibits, hereby finds that Mr. Harry "Butch" Reynolds has cast substantial doubt on the validity of the drug test attributed to him. The panel finds that the "B" sample positive result reported by the Lafarge Laboratory has been impeached by clear and convincing evidence.

This time, the IAAF refused to accept the TAC verdict and, under its Rule 20, ordered yet another arbitration of this dispute. In a two-day hearing in London, England, on May 11–12, 1992, counsel for TAC and the IAAF presented their respective positions; after just two hours of deliberations, the three-member panel issued a perfectly typed seven-page decision that found "no doubt" about Reynolds' guilt.

The Olympic trials to select members of the U.S. track and field team for the Games in Barcelona were to be held just two weeks later. Thus, Reynolds went back to court in Ohio, suing the IAAF for breach of contract, defamation, tortious interference with a business relationship, and denial of contractual due process. The IAAF refused to participate in these proceedings, contending that an American court had no jurisdiction over its international regime. This time, the district judge found that Reynolds' claim satisfied Ohio's "long-arm" statutory jurisdiction, which covered nonresident defendents who "transact any business in the state," or who "cause tortious injury" to someone in the state even by out-of-state actions, as long as the defendant regularly engages in business in the state. This finding raised the more fundamental question of whether such a state jurisdictional rule complied with the Due Process standard in the U.S. Constitution, one that requires out-of-state defendents to have sufficient contact with the state such "that the maintenance of the suit does not offend 'traditional notions of fair play and substantial justice.'" *International Shoe Co. v. Washington*, 326 U.S. 310, 316 (1945).]

* * *

I. Personal Jurisdiction of This Court Over the IAAF

The Court believes that it may constitutionally exercise personal jurisdiction over the IAAF. Initially, the Court must sharply reject the IAAF and TAC's position that the IAAF is not subject to the jurisdiction of *any* court *anywhere* in the world. At the hearing, TAC's counsel expressed the view that the IAAF is "infallible" and its decisions must not be reviewable by this Court—or any other. Indeed, IAAF vice president Arne Ljungqvist has been quoted as stating:

> Civil courts create a lot of problems for our anti-doping work, but we have said we don't care in the least what they say. We have our rules, and they are supreme....

... It is simply an unacceptable position that the courts of this country cannot protect the individual rights of United States citizens where those rights are threatened by an association which has significant contacts with this country, which exercises significant control over both athletes and athletic events in this country, which acts through an agent organization in this country,[6] and which gains significant revenue from its contracts with United States companies.

Regarding the inquiry which this Court must make ..., it is manifest that the IAAF has purposefully availed itself of the privilege of acting in Ohio, and has caused direct consequences to the Plaintiff in Ohio. This Court has previously listed in detail the facts supporting this conclusion and they will not be recounted here. Suffice it to say, as a general matter, Ohio athletes are subject to the Rules of the IAAF, the IAAF gains substantial revenue from the activities of these athletes, and the IAAF has recognized a track and field event to be held in Ohio. With respect to Mr. Reynolds specifically, the IAAF has contributed expense money so that Mr. Reynolds could compete in two events recognized by the IAAF, has published arguably defamatory statements which were circulated in Ohio publications, and has committed acts which may be found to have tortiously interfered with Mr. Reynolds' business relationships with both United States and Ohio companies.

Furthermore, this Court believes that as the IAAF acts through its member organizations, it is reasonable to subject the IAAF to jurisdiction anywhere its member organizations may be subject to suit. The evidence before the Court establishes that the IAAF distributes money to athletes through its member organizations, notifies athletes of positive drug test results through its member organizations, and provides adjudication of disputed drug test results in the first instance through its member organizations. Essentially, the IAAF refuses to have any contact with individual athletes, instead forcing such athletes to approach the IAAF through the national organizations. Thus, this Court holds, as the Tenth Circuit held in *Behagen v. Amateur Basketball Ass'n*, [744 F.2d 731 (10th Cir.1984)], that an international organization which acts through its members may be subject to the jurisdiction of a particular court based upon a member's contacts with, and activity in, the forum. Where, as here, the member organization has intervened as a Defendant in the action, the exercise of personal jurisdiction is beyond question.

* * *

In accordance with all of the foregoing ..., this Court holds that the IAAF's failure to enter a timely objection to personal jurisdiction, which failure resulted in the inability of the Plaintiff to obtain the necessary discovery to establish the facts upon which he asserts the jurisdiction of

---

6. The Court finds untenable what is apparently the tactic of the IAAF to insulate itself from the jurisdiction of any court: despite the incredible power and influence which it directly wields over track and field athletics in the United States and throughout the world, the IAAF continually maintains that it has no direct contact with any country or athlete, and that it only acts or has any outside contact through its member organizations, such as TAC. While that may be true, it must then be conceded that TAC is an agent of the IAAF and personal jurisdiction may be found to exist through TAC's contacts with this forum.

this Court rests, results in the waiver of the IAAF's right to contest the personal jurisdiction of this Court....

II. THE PRELIMINARY INJUNCTION

* * *

The issue of greatest import to this Court, to the parties, and to *amicus*, is the threat of the IAAF to "contaminate," or in other words, suspend any athlete who competes against Mr. Reynolds knowing that he is currently deemed ineligible to participate in IAAF track and field events. The Court not only finds the threat unconvincing, it finds it to be an inappropriate consideration to weigh against the harm which will befall Mr. Reynolds if he is wrongfully prevented from participating in track and field competitions due to his IAAF Ineligibility status.

The IAAF's threat is unconvincing for several reasons. First, it is not at all clear that IAAF's contamination rule is mandatory in nature. Indeed, documents and testimony adduced at the preliminary injunction hearing cast considerable doubt upon this proposition, and lead this Court to conclude that it is not always strictly enforced. Furthermore, it is equally unclear that the IAAF would attempt to prevent United States track and field athletes uninvolved in this litigation from participating in the Olympics on the basis of Rule 53(ii) alone. The loss of some of the event's top competitors, the resulting public outcry, and the possible loss of substantial revenue to the IAAF, all lead this Court to conclude that widespread "contamination" of American athletes by the IAAF is unlikely.

Even if, however, this Court considered such contamination to be the likely result if an injunction were to issue, the Court finds such a threat *by the Defendant IAAF* to be an entirely inappropriate consideration. It is, of course, axiomatic that in considering the merits of a preliminary injunction, the Court must consider whether the injunction will harm others. However, it is the impassioned conviction of the Court that such harm to others does not, and indeed, should not, include harm to others *caused by the voluntary and intentional acts of the Defendant*. To hold otherwise would be to allow the IAAF to hold the entire American Olympic team against an unfavorable decision from this Court....

This Court also believes that Reynolds has established a likelihood of success on the merits of his claims. With respect to the validity of the drug test performed at the Lafarge Laboratory on the urine sample provided by Reynolds in Monte Carlo, this Court believes—as did the American Arbitration Association arbitrator and the TAC hearing panel—that Reynolds has created a substantial doubt as to the accuracy of the reported results. Not only did Reynolds' expert testify as to numerous deficiencies in the Lafarge Laboratories' testing procedure,[9] he also

---

9. For instance, Plaintiff's expert testified that the laboratory failed to attach proper chain of custody documentation to the urine samples provided by Reynolds,

testified as to several inconsistencies with the actual test results which make it highly unlikely that both samples actually originated with Mr. Reynolds.[10] Finally, and perhaps most egregious of all, Plaintiff's expert testified that nandrolone is known to remain in an individual's body for a considerable period of time, and the fact that Reynolds' urine allegedly tested positive for two metabolites of nandrolone on August 12, 1990, and tested negative for nandrolone one week later on August 19, 1990, casts considerable doubt on the validity of the August 12 test.

With respect to the claims in Reynolds Complaint, the Court finds it likely that they are meritorious. First, it appears likely that a contractual relationship exists between the Plaintiff and both the IAAF and TAC, and it further appears that the IAAF breached this contract when it departed from its own guidelines and regulations regarding appropriate drug testing procedures. Second, it appears likely that the IAAF—with disregard for its own policy of confidentiality—maliciously released to the world media information that Reynolds had tested positive for the steroid nandrolone *before* Reynolds was accorded a hearing before TAC as prescribed by IAAF rules. It is reasonable to infer that the IAAF knew that such information would cause third parties to void existing endorsement contracts and prevent others from entering into such contracts. As such, Reynolds is likely to succeed on his claim of defamation and tortious interference with a business relationship.

* * *

Injunction granted.

The court in *Reynolds* enjoined the IAAF and TAC "from interfering, impeding, threatening to impede or interfere in any way [with] the Plaintiff's ability to compete in all international and national amateur track and field competitions, including but not limited to the 1992 United States Olympic Trials and 1992 Summer Olympic Games, as a result of or in any manner connected with tests on any sample of urine attributed to him from the August 12, 1990 Herculis '90 International Track and Field Meet in Monte Carlo, Monaco." After two frantic days of appeals, in which a Sixth Circuit judge stayed the injunction, Justice Stevens reinstated the injunction, and the full Supreme Court declined to reconsider Justice Stevens' order, (see 505 U.S. 1301 (1992)), TAC allowed Reynolds to run in the 400–meter race at the Olympic trials in New Orleans, at which Reynolds qualified only as an alternate on the 4x400 meter relay team. However, the USOC refused to grant Reynolds

---

failed to use an "internal standard" to assist it in interpreting the results, and failed to use a positive quality control.

10. Plaintiff's expert testified that the "picture" of naturally occurring steroids should be relatively the same for both samples of urine if, as alleged, they were both supplied by Reynolds. He concluded, however, that because the naturally occurring steroids in the two samples created extremely different "pictures," the two could not have originated with the same individual.

credentials to travel with the U.S. Olympic team to Barcelona, based on the IAAF's refusal to allow him to compete there despite the injunction. After the Olympics, the IAAF announced that because of Reynolds' legal challenge, it was extending his suspension from August 1992 through the end of that year.

In December 1992, Judge Kinneary, finding that the IAAF had "purposefully avoided the truth," entered a default damages award of $27.3 million (approximately $7 million in compensatory damages and $20 million in punitive damages), and made his earlier injunction permanent. Because of this damage award, the IAAF threatened for a time to extend Reynolds' suspension again beyond December 31, 1992, but it never acted on that threat. Still, Reynolds was faced with the practical problem of how to enforce his $27 million judgment. Could he attach assets that the IAAF might have or accrue in the United States for future track meets, such as the 1996 Olympic Games in Atlanta? Could he attach assets of TAC (now UST&F), the U.S. track federation, and a member of the IAAF? Could IAAF officials be arrested for contempt when they enter the United States for failing to abide by the court's injunctions? Reynolds eventually chose a different route. He began garnishment proceedings against four American corporations (including Coca–Cola) that owed the IAAF money for sponsorship deals. The IAAF moved to quash the garnishment proceedings and set aside the default judgments of damages and injunctive relief on the ground that the district court lacked personal jurisdiction over it. The district court predictably denied this motion, and the IAAF appealed. Following is the Sixth Circuit's opinion.

REYNOLDS v. INTERNATIONAL AMATEUR ATHLETIC FEDERATION

United States Court of Appeals, Sixth Circuit, 1994.
23 F.3d 1110.

LIVELY, SENIOR CIRCUIT JUDGE.

* * *

The IAAF is an unincorporated association based in London, England, and is made up of track and field organizations representing 205 nations and territories. Its purpose is to coordinate and control track and field athletes and competitions throughout the world. The IAAF has no offices in the United States, and holds no track meets in Ohio, where Reynolds brought this action. One member of the IAAF is The Athletics Congress of the United States, Inc. (TAC) [now USA Track and Field], the United States national governing body for track and field.

* * *

When determining whether there is personal jurisdiction over a defendant, a federal court must apply the law of the state in which it sits, subject to constitutional limitations....

* * *

Under the Constitution, personal jurisdiction over a defendant arises from "certain minimum contacts with [the forum] such that maintenance of the suit does not offend 'traditional notions of fair play and substantial justice.'" Depending on the type of minimum contacts in a case, personal jurisdiction can be either general or specific. Reynolds relies on specific jurisdiction because he claims that jurisdiction arose out of the IAAF's alleged wrongful acts in Ohio.

The Sixth Circuit has established a three-part test for determining whether specific jurisdiction may be exercised: First, the defendant must purposefully avail himself of the privilege of acting in the forum state or causing a consequence in the forum state. Second, the cause of action must arise from the defendant's activities there. Finally, the acts of the defendant or consequences caused by the defendant must have a substantial enough connection with the forum to make the exercise of jurisdiction over the defendant reasonable.

* * *

IV.

This court reviews issues of personal jurisdiction de novo. Nevertheless, this appeal is from denial of the IAAF's Rule 60(b) motion to set aside a default judgment. We review the denial of that motion under the abuse of discretion standard.

A.

The district court held that TAC was the agent of the IAAF and that TAC had sufficient minimum contacts with Ohio to bring the IAAF under the "transacting business" provisions of the Ohio long-arm statute. The IAAF insists that TAC, though a member of the IAAF, is an autonomous body that acts for itself within the United States. The record is to the contrary. TAC represents the IAAF in dealings with American athletes who participate in international events. Its bylaws state that "[t]he purposes of this Congress are to act as the national governing body for athletes in the United States, and to act as the IAAF member in the United States." TAC's president, Frank Greenberg, testified that TAC is "the exclusive representative of [the IAAF] in this country," and that "part of that obligation, part of being the named representative is that [TAC] must follow [IAAF] rules."

Furthermore, the facts in this case demonstrate the IAAF's control over TAC. After receiving the results of the two urine tests and after suspending Reynolds, the IAAF did not notify Reynolds. Instead it told TAC to notify Reynolds and look into the matter, even though the meet involved was sponsored by the IAAF. Reynolds requested documents directly from the IAAF, but the IAAF told Reynolds that all document requests must be made through TAC. As a result, all IAAF documents that Reynolds received came through TAC. Moreover, after the Supreme Court held that Reynolds could compete in the U.S. Olympic Trials, the IAAF told TAC to "take all necessary steps to ensure that Mr. Reynolds does not so compete." While it is true that TAC supported Reynolds at the London Arbitration, it was not there on his behalf, but as a member of the IAAF that was responding under the IAAF's rules. Thus, we agree with the district court that TAC is an agent of the IAAF.

Nevertheless, unless TAC had minimum contacts with Ohio in relation to the "contract" between the IAAF and Reynolds, the court erred in premising jurisdiction of TAC's agency.

B.

The Supreme Court has spoken with respect to the significance of a contractual relationship between an in-state plaintiff and an out-of-state defendant. The Court has held that a contract with an out-of-state party, standing alone, is not sufficient to establish minimum contacts. *Burger King Corp. v. Rudzewicz*, 471 U.S. 462, 478 (1985). Instead, to determine whether a party purposefully availed itself of a forum a court must evaluate "prior negotiations and contemplated future consequences, along with the terms of the contract and the parties' actual course of dealing...." Id. at 479. In the instant case, there were no negotiations between Reynolds and the IAAF prior to "execution" of the contract. The IAAF arguably had a minimal course of dealing with Reynolds in Ohio, providing money to Reynolds in Ohio to travel to track events. However, there is no real evidence that a contract was negotiated in Ohio, created in Ohio, performed in Ohio, or breached in Ohio. See *LAK, Inc. v. Deer Creek Enterprises*, 885 F.2d 1293, 1300 (6th Cir.1989) (place where contractual obligation is incurred is important factor for determining personal jurisdiction).

Without further evidence concerning the purported contract, we are unable to agree that the district court had personal jurisdiction over the IAAF on the contract claims, either based on its own activities or those of TAC.

Moreover, the IAAF could not reasonably anticipate being sued in Ohio because of its alleged business dealings with Reynolds. It did not regularly transact or solicit business in Ohio or engage "in any other persistent course of conduct" there. O.R.C. § 2307.382(A)(4). The IAAF cannot foresee being required to defend in every forum where one of its athletes is present.... Instead, minimum contacts can only be formed by "an action of the defendant purposefully directed toward the forum State." *Asahi Metal Industry v. Superior Court of California*, 480 U.S. 102, 112 (1987).

The IAAF's contact with Ohio through letters and phone calls was also insufficient to support jurisdiction.... It is the "quality" of such contacts, "not their number or their status as pre-or post-agreement communications" that determines whether they constitute purposeful availment. *LAK*, 885 F.2d at 1301. That quality is missing here.

In short, the IAAF is based in England, owns no property and transacts no business in Ohio, and does not supervise U.S. athletes in Ohio or elsewhere. Its contacts with Reynolds in Ohio are superficial, and are insufficient to create the requisite minimum contacts for personal jurisdiction.

Even if the IAAF purposefully availed itself of Ohio privileges, the claims against the IAAF must arise out of the IAAF's activities in Ohio. In general, "[a]n action will be deemed not to have arisen from the defendant's contacts with the forum state only when they are unrelated to the operative facts of the controversy." *Creech v. Roberts*, 908 F.2d 75, 80 (6th Cir.1990). The controversial urine sample was taken in Monaco, analyzed in France, and confirmed by an arbitration hearing in England.... All of the activities relied upon by the district court as taking place in Ohio occurred after the activities in Europe upon which Reynolds bases his contract claims. These activities do not constitute a basis for finding personal jurisdiction under subsection (1) for "transacting business" in Ohio.

V.

The district court found that the IAAF was subject to personal jurisdiction under the provision of the Ohio long-arm statute which provides that a party is amenable to suit by "causing tortious injury in this state ... by an act outside this state." O.R.C. § 2307.382(A)(6). A tort action can be brought in the location where the injury is suffered. *Lachman v. Bank of Louisiana*, 510 F.Supp. 753 (N.D.Ohio 1981). Reynolds claimed a loss of more than $4,000,000 in Ohio because of the IAAF's false press release and the district court specifically found that the injury to Reynolds was in Ohio....

* * *

Reynolds argues ... that his claims arose out of the IAAF's connection with Ohio because the IAAF intentionally defamed him and interfered with his Ohio business relationships. Under this theory, the IAAF knew that the worldwide media would carry the report and that the brunt of the injury would occur in Ohio.

Even accepting that the IAAF could foresee that its report would be disseminated in Ohio, however, the IAAF would not be subject to personal jurisdiction in Ohio. *Madara v. Hall*, 916 F.2d 1510, 1519 (11th Cir.1990) (defendant's knowledge that independent publisher might publish defamatory statements in California does not create personal jurisdiction). The press release that the IAAF issued in London did not directly accuse Reynolds of using forbidden substances. It recited the fact that the Paris laboratory had reported a positive drug test and that Reynolds had been suspended and offered a hearing. We cannot hold that this act of the IAAF satisfied the requirements of the Ohio statute, or that permitting the IAAF to be sued in Ohio for the press release would comport with due process.

VI.

[The court here rejected Reynolds' claim that the IAAF waived objecting to the court's jurisdiction when TAC, without IAAF encouragement, intervened on its own initiative to raise the jurisdictional issue.]

CONCLUSION

In conclusion, we do not believe that holding the IAAF amenable to suit in an Ohio court under the facts of this case comports with "traditional notions of fair play and substantial justice." *Asahi Metal Industry*, 480 U.S. at 113. The IAAF stated in its brief and at oral argument that it will not challenge the jurisdiction of English courts to determine the validity of the London Arbitration award if Reynolds seeks to have it set aside in the courts of that country.

* * *

Reversed.

Questions For Discussion

1. The Sixth Circuit did not hold that an international governing federation would never be subject to the personal jurisdiction of any American court; it held only that, on the facts of this case, the IAAF was not subject to the jurisdiction of the Ohio courts. Given this decision, under what circumstances would (or should) an international governing body be subject to a state's jurisdiction in cases like *Reynolds*? Consider the following scenarios:

    1. Reynolds sues the IAAF in Georgia where the IAAF, the USOC, and other federations were engaged in extensive preparation for the 1996 Olympics.

    2. Reynolds sues the IAAF in Indiana where TAC's (now UST&F's) headquarters and offices are located.

    3. Reynolds sues the IAAF in New York where several corporations that sponsor IAAF events and TV networks that purchase television rights to IAAF events are headquartered? Would it matter if the contracts with these entities were negotiated or signed in New York?

    4. Reynolds sues the IAAF in California where the IAAF has sanctioned track meets and held its own World Track & Field Championships in the past.

    5. Reynolds sues the IAAF in Ohio, but the meet at which he was alleged to have tested positive occurred in Texas, and the laboratory at which the sample was tested was located in Louisiana. What if the meet or the laboratory were in Ohio?

In each of these situations, would a court have to proceed under principles of general or specific jurisdiction? From a policy standpoint, should that matter?

2. How significant was it to the Sixth Circuit's decision that the IAAF agreed to submit to the jurisdiction of the English courts to review the validity of the IAAF's arbitration panel award?

3. Should courts in the United States—or in any country—review and overturn the decisions of an international sports governing body? If so, under what standard of review and on what grounds? The IAAF contends that if the courts of every nation could overturn its decisions, the Federation could not govern effectively because national political interests would influ-

ence many courts to overturn any IAAF decision contrary to the interests of their country's athletes. Compare this argument to those invoked in the cases discussed in Chapter 2 after *Flood* (*Partee*, *Hebert*, *Matuszak*), and in *NCAA v. Miller* in Chapter 9, in which the courts blocked state laws from governing national sports organizations in the United States.

4. How should the courts of individual countries (or states) deal with international (or national) sports governing bodies? Would every sports governing body be fair and impartial if it were immune to judicial scrutiny? Would courts in every country (or state) be fair and impartial, as well as sufficiently uniform and consistent, in overseeing sports governing bodies? In answering, consider the disclosure in 1995 that the Chinese women's track and swimming teams had set new standards in their events with the aid of performance-enhancing substances (just as the East Germans did in the 1970s and 1980s). What would the American reaction be if a Chinese (or an East German) court had ruled that the IAAF or FINA (the international swimming federation) drug-testing procedures had violated that country's standards of fairness and accuracy and ordered their athletes reinstated for the Olympics? Should American judicial rulings receive different weight in the world of international sports?

5. After the *Reynolds* judgment in the trial court was rendered, the IOC undertook to bring about major reforms within the International Court of Arbitration for Sport (ICAS) in Lausanne, Switzerland, which has been recognized by roughly half the international governing federations (though still not by the IAAF) as the exclusive and binding dispute resolution mechanism for all such cases and controversies involving athletes (instead of federation-appointed arbitration panels such as the one convened in *Reynolds*). Most important among these reforms was the creation of an independent, 20–person council to oversee the operation of the ICAS, the division of the ICAS into trial and appellate divisions, and the broadening of geographical representation to include arbitrators from outside of Europe. Although the Sixth Circuit did not mention this development in its opinion, do you think it might have played a role in its decision to limit athlete access to national courts for de novo review of arbitration decisions?

An incident reminiscent of the *Reynolds* case involving American swimmer Jessica Foschi put an intriguing twist on the role of national tribunals in overseeing the rules and decisions of international sports federations. Many of the federations have rules that automatically result in discipline if an athlete tests positive for a banned substance even if it is established that the athlete was not aware of having ingested that substance—a "strict liability" rule. After the 1995 U.S. national swimming championships in Pasadena, California, Foschi tested positive for the anabolic steroid mesterolone. USS, the national swimming federation, held lengthy hearings and ultimately found that, while Foschi did test positive, she had "no knowledge of the manner in which the banned substance entered her body." Nonetheless, USS invalidated her times at the Nationals, imposed a two-year probation on her, and declared that if

Foschi ever tested positive again for any banned substance, she would be barred for life. Feeling that these penalties were too harsh, Foschi filed a petition for arbitration with the American Arbitration Association (AAA) pursuant to USS rules.

The issue presented to the three AAA arbitrators was whether USS could impose sanctions on a swimmer whom they found was completely innocent of *knowingly* taking a banned substance, even though the test was valid and the substance was in her body. USS claimed that, under the rules of FINA, the international federation, once an illegal drug has been found in an athlete's body through valid testing, a penalty must be imposed regardless of the athlete's guilt or innocence in taking it. Witnesses testified that the underlying FINA theory was that no guilty party should ever go free, even if that meant some innocents would be punished.

The arbitration panel concluded that this strict liability interpretation of FINA rules was wrong, particularly in light of prior instances in which positive tests had not resulted in the mandatory penalties specified by the Rules. For example, in 1996, an Australian swimmer who tested positive for a similar drug was given only a "strong warning." Thus, the panel found that a national body has the flexibility to make the penalty fit the facts of the case. The arbitrators went on to say that even if the rules were otherwise, given that nobody disputed that Foschi was without fault, "the imposition of any sanction on [Foschi] so deeply offends our deeply rooted and historical concepts of fundamental fairness so as to be arbitrary and capricious." The panel ruled, therefore, that USS was barred from taking any action to interfere with Foschi's right to compete. This decision that strict liability rules were illegal and unenforceable was consistent with the rulings of courts in Switzerland (involving sprinter Sandra Gasser), England (involving tennis players Mats Wilander and Karel Novacek), and Germany (involving sprinter Katrin Krabbe, whom the court found had knowingly taken the drug and thus upheld a suspension, but also made clear that the finding of guilt by the athlete was essential to its result).

Notwithstanding this arbitration ruling, in June 1996, FINA imposed a two-year suspension on Foschi, retroactive to August 1995, which effectively precluded her participation in the 1996 Olympics (although she had already failed to make the U.S. team). Foschi did appeal the FINA decision to the International Court of Arbitration for Sport (ICAS), which has now been accepted by roughly half of the international sports federations (including FINA) as the final arbiter in such areas. In this case, the arbitration panel ruled that, even absent strict liability, the athlete had to meet a stiff standard of disproving any responsibility (including negligence) for ingestion of the forbidden substance, a standard that Foschi was unable to meet. However, the panel did reduce the length of her suspension to six months and awarded Foschi $10,000 toward her legal costs. Immediately after this decision, FINA amended its rules, not to eliminate or qualify its strict liability standard, but to increase the automatic penalty for testing positive for a banned substance from two to four years.

Whether the standard imposed on athletes is strict liability or the onus of disproving any responsibility, *Foschi* and similar cases continue to pose the basic question presented in *Reynolds*. Can and should an international governing body be able to adopt and implement eligibility rules for their respective sports without the courts or administrative agencies in individual countries (whether in the United States or China) being empowered to overturn decisions because the rules in question offend legal standards or norms of that country?

In grappling with these dilemmas, the care and integrity of a sport's governing body are crucial. Consider a story told in *The Lords of the Rings*.[k] Apparently, IAAF president Primo Nebiolo and his assistant Luciano Barra, both Italians, arranged with Italian field judges to add almost one-half meter to the long jump of Italy's Giovanni Evangelisti in the 1987 world track and field championships in Rome so that he could win the bronze medal ahead of Larry Myricks of the United States—all in retaliation for what the Italians regarded as a bad foot-fault call made against Evangelisti at the world indoor championships the previous year in Indianapolis. Eventually the IAAF, over great resistance by Nebiolo, stripped Evangelisti of the bronze medal after the Italian Olympic Committee had exposed the cheating with the help of a video tape that had inadvertently been left running while an official tampered with the long jump measuring device.

The *Reynolds* incident was part of a larger rift that had existed between Nebiolo and economically powerful United States track officials—in particular, long-time TAC executive director and IAAF vice-president Ollan Cassell, whom Nebiolo regarded as the greatest political threat to his presidency of the IAAF. Some privately suggested that the IAAF's intransigence in the *Reynolds* case was merely part of an overall effort by Nebiolo to embarrass TAC at every opportunity in the international track community. If this story is true, does it affect your opinion on whether domestic courts should intervene in the decisions of international sports federations?

After the *Reynolds* judgment was entered by the district court, the IAAF notified UST&F that it should make every effort to have *Reynolds* reversed, because if American courts exercised jurisdiction over international sports governing bodies, it might have jeopardized holding the 1996 Olympics in Atlanta, where international officials could have been subject to court sanctions for contempt. How should American courts respond to a "threat" that, unless they refuse to interfere in the affairs of international sports federations, the United States may not be allowed

---

k. See Simson & Jennings, *The Lords of the Rings*, note 8 above, at 164–83.

to host international athletic competitions? How should UST&F or the USOC respond? How should Congress and the President respond?

Perhaps the most heavily-publicized sports episode in the 1990s involved Tonya Harding and figure skating. As sports fans and non-sports fans well remember, Nancy Kerrigan, Harding's major U.S. figure skating competitor, was assaulted on January 6, 1994, just before the U.S. Figure Skating Championships that were being held in Detroit. That event would not only crown the U.S. champion, but would also select the two American competitors in the upcoming Olympic figure skating competition in Norway. Kerrigan did not skate in Detroit; Harding won the championship and a spot on the Olympic team. Kerrigan was also selected for the team on the assumption that her leg injury would be healed in time for the Olympics.

Several days later, it was discovered that the assault on Kerrigan had been arranged and carried out by Oregon friends of Jeff Gillooly, Harding's recently-divorced husband who had gone back to live with her in Portland. Harding initially denied to the police and the public that either she or Gillooly had been involved in the conspiracy. Later in January, though, faced with conflicting evidence from the police, Harding changed her story: she said shortly after her return to Portland that she had learned of Gillooly's participation after the fact. Harding denied, however, any personal knowledge of or participation in arranging the initial assault.

Faced with Harding's accusation, Gillooly soon reached a plea bargain with Oregon authorities, one feature of which was his statement that Harding had in fact known of and approved the assault before it took place. Harding continued to deny that accusation, and claimed that her earlier false story had been motivated, among other things, by fear of physical abuse by Gillooly (who had abused her in the past).

While criminal investigation of Harding's involvement was going on, the President of the U.S. Figure Skating Association (USFSA) appointed a five-member panel to investigate this incident. On February 5, 1994, the panel found reasonable grounds for charging Harding with involvement in the conspiracy before the fact as well as for false denial after the fact. This conduct, the panel said, might constitute violation of figure skating's Code of Ethics, which requires "the highest standard of fairness, ethical behavior and general good sportsmanship." If guilty, Harding risked loss of her USFSA membership privileges for "acts, statements, or conduct detrimental to the welfare of figure skating." Under the USFSA's Rules of Procedure, Harding was entitled to a hearing before the panel no earlier than March 8th (30 days later), with a right of appeal to the USFSA Executive Council and then to an independent arbitrator from the roster of the American Arbitration Association.

By the time these USFSA disciplinary proceedings could have been completed, the February Olympic games in Norway would long have been over. Under its own Charter, the U.S. Olympic Committee gained direct jurisdiction over the athletes at the beginning of February, when their selection for the Olympic team was formally conveyed to the USOC by the National Governing Body (NGB) for each sport (i.e., the USFSA for figure skating). Thus, the USOC scheduled a disciplinary hearing of its own in the Harding case. This hearing was to be held in Norway in mid-February before the USOC Games Administration Board, which would determine whether Harding had failed to conduct herself "in such a manner that you would bring credit and honor to yourself, your teammates, your National Governing Board, the United States Olympic Committee, and the United States of America."

Harding and her counsel immediately sought an order from an Oregon state judge to prevent the USOC from holding this hearing. After the legal issues had been explored in a court hearing—in particular, the fact that the wording of the USOC's disciplinary jurisdiction seemed to point to events that took place while athletes were on the team, but not before—the USOC agreed to cancel its hearing and to allow Harding to skate in Lillehammer. Before one of the largest audiences in the history of American television, Nancy Kerrigan won figure skating's silver medal, while Harding finished eighth.

When Harding returned to the United States, the USFSA scheduled its disciplinary hearing for mid-March in Colorado. The USFSA wanted a decision rendered before the World Figure Skating Championships, which were to be held in Tokyo at the end of March. However, Harding's legal team went back to court in Oregon and got an order barring the USFSA hearing on this date. The ground was that this schedule did not give Harding sufficient time to develop and present her own case, particularly in view of the ongoing criminal investigation in Oregon.

Just before Harding was to fly to Tokyo, she accepted a plea bargain agreement with the Portland District Attorney. Under that agreement, Harding pleaded guilty to "hindering prosecution" of the case after the assault, but did not admit to any involvement in planning the assault beforehand. Harding received three years probation, paid approximately $150,000 in fines, had to perform 500 hours of community service, and her Class C felony conviction was to be removed from her record following three years of good behavior. The District Attorney insisted, and Harding agreed, that she resign from the USFSA and no longer skate competitively. There were, however, no legal bars to Harding skating in any ice show that is prepared to use (and pay for) her services.

Following completion of criminal proceedings, the Oregon judge permitted the USFSA to conduct its hearing at the end of June 1994. Harding, having decided to give up competitive skating, resigned from the USFSA and chose not to appear at the disciplinary hearing. The USFSA's position, though, was that it still had jurisdiction to consider charges that someone had violated its rules while a member. After reviewing the voluminous written record assembled in the police investigation, the Hearing Panel concluded that Harding did have prior knowledge of the planned assault on Kerrigan, that she had made calls and provided funds to assist in the attack, and that she had concealed these facts afterwards. On this basis, the Panel found that Harding had violated the USFSA Code of Ethics (which requires members "to exemplify the highest standards of fairness, ethical behavior, and genuine good sportsmanship in any of their relations with others"), stripped her of the 1994 National Women's Figure Skating Championship title, and permanently banned her from USFSA membership.

The one sports law point about which there seems no doubt is that, if Harding in fact was involved in or knew of the original assault, this constituted grounds for discipline. Taking such action off the ice to get rid of one's major competitor on the ice would seem an obvious threat to the integrity and welfare of the sport. Less obvious, are answers to the following questions:

1. With respect to the assault itself, should the sports authority have to hold off its actions until after the criminal investigation has run its course? If yes, what should be the effect of a decision not to prosecute? Of a jury acquittal? Of judicial dismissal of charges on some ground not related to the merits?

2. Should the standard of proof in the sports proceeding be proof beyond all reasonable doubt, clear and convincing evidence, preponderance of the evidence, or reasonable grounds for belief?

3. With respect to after-the-fact knowledge, should either denial of or failure to reveal a criminal offense constitute a violation of the athletic code of conduct? Should the answer differ if the offense was connected or unconnected to the sport? If the offender was or was not a family member? If part of the athlete's motivation was fear of spousal abuse?

4. Would you alter the procedural relations between athletes, the USFSA (or other NGB's), and the USOC so as better to handle cases such as Harding's? How could this be done while still protecting the due process rights of the athlete?

5. If, as rumor has it, the $27 million verdict won by Butch Reynolds against the IAAF (which had not yet been reversed) was a major factor in the decision by the USOC and USFSA not to challenge the interim decisions by Oregon judges, does this alter your views about the *Reynolds'* proceedings?

As recently as 1984, Article 26 of the IOC's Olympic Charter declared that "[t]o be eligible for participation in the Olympic Games, a competitor must ... not have received any financial rewards or material benefit in connection with his or her sports participation." Cynics have attributed the origin of this "amateurism" rule to the desire of the English upper classes (who were responsible for reviving the Olympic games in 1896) to exclude working class people, who could not afford to devote all of their time to unremunerated sporting competition.[l] In recent years, however, faced with the reality that governments in many countries heavily subsidize athletes and training programs, the Charter was changed to drop this prohibition, and under Article 45 eligibility standards for the Olympics are now left entirely to the international federation that governs each sport. (Hence, the IAAF had the power to declare Reynolds ineligible for the 1992 Games in Barcelona.)

Most federations, whose sports do not offer opportunities for large income or endorsements, still cling to a strict amateurism requirement (which does not bar government subsidies). Others, such as the IAAF, still formally require amateurism, but allow athletes to circumvent that principle by creating, through an athlete's national federation, a "trust fund" into which all money earned by the athlete is deposited and then distributed as "a subvention to an athlete to assist him in the expenses incurred in training for or participation in any competition" (IAAF Rule 16; TAC Regulation 9). Training "expenses" are liberally construed to include all transportation, food, housing, insurance, and other normal living expenses. When athletes retire, the balance in their trust funds becomes theirs to spend as they wish.[m]

Still other federations (for example, those in tennis and basketball) have completely abandoned any pretense of amateurism—Michael Jordan and Steffi Graf have now participated in the Olympics. Should the concept of amateurism required for Olympic eligibility be defined by individual federations, or should there be a uniform standard in all sports? What is the policy behind excluding some of the world's best athletes because they earn money from their athletic prowess? If there is some value to this policy, should it apply to governmental subsidies of athletes, or to college athletic scholarships (a uniquely American phenomenon)?

Finally, a recurring issue in Olympic sports has been whether all the participants in women's events are really women. We alluded to this issue earlier in this chapter, in connection with the case of *Richards v. USTA*, 93 Misc.2d 713, 400 N.Y.S.2d 267 (1977), in which a New York judge held that the USTA could not rely solely on the Barr sex-chromatin test to exclude a recently operated-on transsexual from the Women's Division of the U.S. Tennis Open. Since the 1960s, both the

---

[l]. See Guttman, *The Olympics*, note h above.

[m]. For insights into how this new system affected the life of America's most famous Olympic athlete, see Carl Lewis with Jeffrey Marx, *Inside Track: My Professional Life in Amateur Track and Field* (New York: Simon and Schuster, 1990).

USOC and most international federations have used the Barr test to try to detect competitors who are not actually female—especially in response to charges and controversies about athletes from behind the old Iron Curtain. Is there anything that American courts can or should feel authorized to do about USOC or IOC use of the Barr test to exclude otherwise apparently female athletes from competing in future Olympic Games?

Chapter Thirteen

PERSONAL INJURY FROM SPORTS

Participants in sporting events experience not only the thrill of victory and the agony of defeat, but occasionally a tragic injury that befalls one of the athletes. Highly publicized examples include the permanent crippling of Detroit Lions' tackle, Mike Utley, in an NFL game in the fall of 1991, and the collapse and death of Loyola Marymount star, Hank Gathers, in a college basketball game in the winter of 1990. Indeed, even a fan may fall victim, as when a spectator was struck by a fatal bolt of lightning while out on the golf course watching the 1991 U.S. Open.

Unsurprisingly, many serious athletic injuries generate conflicts that find their way into the legal system.[a] At the heart of this area of the law is society's concern about violent contact and personal injury. In the last quarter century there has been a sharp increase in the number of victims seeking legal redress for their injuries, sending liability insurance premiums spiraling.[b] That same phenomenon has been visible in the area of sports injuries.

Sports, however, pose a unique problem to the law of personal injury. The aim of a sporting event is to produce spirited athletic competition on the field or floor. In sports such as boxing, football, and hockey, a central feature of the contest is the infliction of violent contact on the opponent. In other sports, such as basketball and baseball, such contact is an expected risk, if not a desired outcome, of intense competition.[c] Even sports such as golf that are intrinsically non-violent for their

---

a. Useful overviews of this topic can be found in two chapters of Gary Uberstine, ed., *Law of Professional and Amateur Sports* (Deerfield, Ill.: Clark, Boardman, and Callaghan, 1991), Chapter 14 by Raymond L. Yasser, "Liability for Sports Injuries," and Chapter 15 by Chris J. Carlsen, "Violence in Professional Sports."

b. For a comprehensive analysis of the tort "crisis," see the two volume report done for the American Law Institute, Reporters' Study, *Enterprise Responsibility for Personal Injury* (Philadelphia: ALI, 1991), for which one of the editors of this book, Weiler, served as Chief Reporter.

c. Indeed, back in 1920 the Cleveland Indians' Ray Chapman who was killed

participants may inflict harmful contacts upon the spectators. This characteristic feature of sports requires the law to undertake a delicate balancing act when it tailors for use in sports litigation the standards of liability developed to govern relationships in very different aspects of life.

A. TORTS AND SPORTS

The special problems that sports pose to tort litigation are displayed most vividly in cases in which an injured athlete files suit against another athlete whose actions during the game allegedly caused the injury. The decisions in this section exemplify the current judicial response to such cases.[d]

HACKBART v. CINCINNATI BENGALS & CHARLES CLARK

United States District Court, District of Colorado, 1977.
435 F.Supp. 352.

MATSCH, DISTRICT JUDGE.

[In the first exhibition game of the 1973 NFL football season, Dale Hackbart, a veteran free safety for the Denver Broncos, attempted on a pass interception to block Charles "Booby" Clark, a rookie running back for the Cincinnati Bengals. As the play continued upfield, Clark, "acting out of anger and frustration, but without a specific intent to injure," hit Hackbart on the back of the head with his forearm. No official observed the blow and no penalty was called.

Although Hackbart experienced soreness, he continued to play in that game and the rest of the exhibition season before being released by the Broncos. Hackbart then sought medical assistance and was diagnosed as having a neck injury. When that medical information was provided to the Broncos, the team paid Hackbart his full 1973 salary, pursuant to the injury clause in the NFL standard player contract. Hackbart then filed a tort suit against both Clark and the Bengals. At issue was whether these facts could support a viable tort claim. For the following reasons, the trial judge ruled for the defendants.]

* * *

Football is a recognized game which is widely played as a sport. Commonly, teams are organized by high schools and colleges and games are played according to rules provided by associations of such schools.

The basic design of the game is the same at the high school, college and professional levels. The differences are largely reflective of the fact

---

when struck on the head by a pitch thrown by the Yankees' Carl Mays. For an insightful philosophical analysis of the ethics of bodily contact sports, see Robert Simon, *Fair Play: Sports, Values, and Society* 53–70 (Boulder, Colo.: Westview Press, 1991).

d. The best scholarly treatment of the legal issues posed by these cases is Daniel E. Lazaroff, *Torts and Sports: Participant Liability to Co–Participants for Injuries Sustained During Competition*, 7 Univ. of Miami Ent. & Sports L. Rev. 191 (1990).

that at each level the players have increased physical abilities, improved skills and differing motivations.

Football is a contest for territory. The objective of the offensive team is to move the ball through the defending team's area and across the vertical plane of the goal line. The defensive players seek to prevent that movement with their bodies. Each attempted movement involves collisions between the bodies of offensive and defensive players with considerable force and with differing areas of contact. The most obvious characteristic of the game is that all of the players engage in violent physical behavior.

The rules of play which govern the method and style by which the NFL teams compete include limitations on the manner in which players may strike or otherwise physically contact opposing players. During 1973, the rules were enforced by six officials on the playing field. The primary sanction for a violation was territorial, with the amounts of yardage lost being dependent upon the particular infraction. Players were also subject to expulsion from the game and to monetary penalties imposed by the league commissioner.

The written rules are difficult to understand and, because of the speed and violence of the game, their application is often a matter of subjective evaluation of the circumstances. Officials differ with each other in their rulings. The players are not specifically instructed in the interpretation of the rules, and they acquire their working knowledge of them only from the actual experience of enforcement by the game officials during contests.

Many violations of the rules do occur during each game. Ordinarily each team receives several yardage penalties, but many fouls go undetected or undeclared by the officials.

Disabling injuries are also common occurrences in each contest. Hospitalization and surgery are frequently required for repairs. Protective clothing is worn by all players, but it is often inadequate to prevent bodily damage. Professional football players are conditioned to "play with pain" and they are expected to perform even though they are hurt. The standard player contract imposes an obligation to play when the club physician determines that an injured player has the requisite physical ability.

The violence of professional football is carefully orchestrated. Both offensive and defensive players must be extremely aggressive in their actions and they must play with a reckless abandonment of self-protective instincts. The coaches make studied and deliberate efforts to build the emotional levels of their players to what some call a "controlled rage."

John Ralston, the 1973 Broncos coach, testified that the pre-game psychological preparation should be designed to generate an emotion equivalent to that which would be experienced by a father whose family had been endangered by another driver who had attempted to force the family car off the edge of a mountain road. The precise pitch of motivation for the players at the beginning of the game should be the feeling of that father when, after overtaking and stopping the offending vehicle, he is about to open the door to take revenge upon the person of the other driver.

The large and noisy crowds in attendance at the games contribute to the emotional levels of the players. Quick changes in the fortunes of the teams, the shock of violent collisions and the intensity of the competition make behavioral control extremely difficult, and it is not uncommon for players to "flare up" and begin fighting. The record made at this trial indicates that such incidents as that which gave rise to this action are not so unusual as to be unexpected in any NFL game.

The end product of all of the organization and effort involved in the professional football industry is an exhibition of highly developed individual skills in coordinated team competition for the benefit of large numbers of paying spectators, together with radio and television audiences. It is appropriate to infer that while some of those persons are attracted by the individual skills and precision performances of the teams, the appeal to others is the spectacle of savagery.

Plaintiff's Theories of Liability

This case is controlled by the law of Colorado. While a theory of intentional misconduct is barred by the applicable statute of limitations, the plaintiff contends that Charles Clark's foul was so far outside of the rules of play and accepted practices of professional football that it should be characterized as reckless misconduct within the principles of § 500 of the *Restatement of Torts, 2d*.

Alternatively, the plaintiff claims that his injury was at least the result of a negligent act by the defendant. The difference in these contentions is but a difference in degree. Both theories are dependent upon a definition of a duty to the plaintiff and an objective standard of conduct based upon the hypothetical reasonably prudent person. Thus, the question is what would a reasonably prudent professional football player be expected to do under the circumstances confronting Charles Clark in this incident?

* * *

It is wholly incongruous to talk about a professional football player's duty of care for the safety of opposing players when he has been trained and motivated to be heedless of injury to himself. The character of NFL competition negates any notion that the playing conduct can be circumscribed by any standard of reasonableness.

Both theories of liability are also subject to the recognized defenses of consent and assumption of the risk. Here the question is what would a professional football player in the plaintiff's circumstances reasonably expect to encounter in a professional contest?

All of the witnesses with playing or coaching experience in the NFL agreed that players are urged to avoid penalties. The emphasis, however, is on the unfavorable effects of the loss of yardage, not the safety of the players. It is undisputed that no game is without penalties and that players frequently lose control in surges of emotion.

The conflict in the testimony is the difference in the witnesses' opinions as to whether Mr. Clark's act of striking the plaintiff on the back of the head in reaction to anger and frustration can be considered as "a part of the game." Several former players denounced this incident and said that Mr. Clark's conduct could not be considered customary or acceptable.

It is noteworthy that while this incident was clearly shown on the Denver Broncos' defensive game films, which were routinely reviewed by the defensive players and coaching staff, none of them made it a matter of special attention or concern.

Upon all of the evidence, my finding is that the level of violence and the frequency of emotional outbursts in NFL football games are such that Dale Hackbart must have recognized and accepted the risk that he would be injured by such an act as that committed by the defendant Clark on September 16, 1973. Accordingly, the plaintiff must be held to have assumed the risk of such an occurrence. Therefore, even if the defendant breached a duty which he owed to the plaintiff, there can be no recovery because of assumption of the risk.

* * *

THE APPLICATION OF TORT PRINCIPLES TO PROFESSIONAL
FOOTBALL. A QUESTION OF SOCIAL POLICY

The business of the law of torts is to fix the dividing line between those cases in which a man is liable for harm which he has done, and those in which he is not. Justice O. W. Holmes, *The Common Law* (1881).

While the foregoing findings of fact and conclusions of law are determinative of the claim made by Dale Hackbart against Charles Clark and his employer, this case raises the larger question of whether playing field action in the business of professional football should become a subject for the business of the courts.

To compensate the injured at the expense of the wrongdoer, the courts have been compelled to construct principles of social policy. Through the processes of trial and error the judicial branch of government has historically evolved the common law principles which necessarily affect behavior in many contexts. The potential threat of liability for damages can have a significant deterrent effect and private civil actions are an important mechanism for societal control of human conduct. In recent years the pace of technical progress has accelerated and human conflicts have intensified. The resulting need to expand the body of governing law with greater rapidity and certainty than can be achieved through the litigation process has been met by legislation and administrative regulation. That is particularly true of industrial injuries. The coal mines became subject to the Federal Coal Mine Safety Act. The railroads have long been governed by the Federal Employers Liability Act and the Safety Appliance Act. The Occupational Health and Safety Act has broad application.

To this time professional football has been a self-regulated industry. The only protection which NFL contract players have beyond self-defense and real or threatened retaliation is that which is provided by the league rules and sanctions. It may well be true that what has been provided is inadequate and that these young athletes have been exploited and subjected to risks which should be unacceptable in our social order. In this respect, it is interesting to compare football with boxing. Because of the essential brutality of the contest, prize fighting has been held to be unlawful unless conducted under the sanction and authority of a governmental commission.

Football has been presumed to be lawful and, indeed, professional football has received the implicit approval of government because these contests take place in arenas owned by local governments and the revenues are subject to taxation. Like coal mining and railroading, professional football is hazardous to the health and welfare of those who are employed as players.

What is the interest of the larger community in limiting the violence of professional football? That question concerns not only the protection of the participants, but also the effects of such violence on those who observe it. Can the courts answer this question? I think not. An ordinary citizen is entitled to protection according to the usages of the society in which he lives, and in the context of common community standards there can be no question but that Mr. Clark's blow here would generate civil liability. It would involve a criminal sanction if the requisite intent were present. The difference here is that this blow was delivered on the field of play during the course of action in a regularly scheduled professional football game. The Illinois court was concerned with the safety of high school athletes in *Nabozny v. Barnhill*, 334 N.E.2d 258 (Ill.App.1975), and said (at 260):

> This court believes that the law should not place unreasonable burdens on the free and vigorous participation in sports by our youth. However, we also believe that organized, athletic competition does not exist in a vacuum. Rather, some of the restraints of civilization must accompany every athlete onto the playing field. One of the educational benefits of organized athletic competition to our youth is the development of discipline and self control.

The difficulty with that view as applied to professional football is that to decide which restraints should be made applicable is a task for which the courts are not well suited. There is no discernible code of conduct for NFL players. The dictionary definition of a sportsman is one who abides by the rules of a contest and accepts victory or defeat graciously. That is not the prevalent attitude in professional football.

There are no Athenian virtues in this form of athletics. The NFL has substituted the morality of the battlefield for that of the playing field, and the "restraints of civilization" have been left on the sidelines.

Mr. Justice Holmes' simple statement of the function of tort law and the evidentiary record now before me clearly reveal the density of the thicket in which the courts would become entangled if they undertook the task of allocation of fault in professional football games. The NFL rules of play are so legalistic in their statement and so difficult of application because of the speed and violence of the play that the differences between violations which could fairly be called deliberate, reckless or outrageous and those which are "fair play" would be so small and subjective as to be incapable of articulation. The question of causation would be extremely difficult in view of the frequency of forceful collisions. The volume of such litigation would be enormous and it is reasonable to expect that the court systems of the many states in which NFL games are played would develop differing and conflicting principles of law. It is highly unlikely that the NFL could continue to produce anything like the present games under such multiple systems of overview by judges and juries. If there is to be any governmental involvement in this industry, it is a matter which can be best considered by the legislative branch.

My conclusion that the civil courts cannot be expected to control the violence in professional football is limited by the facts of the case before me. I have considered only a claim for an injury resulting from a blow, without weaponry, delivered emotionally without a specific intent to injure, in the course of regular play in a league-approved game involving adult, contract players. Football as a commercial enterprise is something quite different from athletics as an extension of the academic experience and what I have said here may have no applicability in other areas of physical competition.

Judgment for defendants.

[On appeal, the Tenth Circuit Court of Appeals reversed. While the court appeared to concede that negligence actions based on "unreasonable risks of harm" were inapplicable to a game like football, its ruling adopted a different view of intentional torts.]

HACKBART v. CINCINNATI BENGALS, INC.

United States Court of Appeals, Tenth Circuit, 1979.
601 F.2d 516.

Doyle, Circuit Judge.

* * *

[T]he evidence shows that there are rules of the game which prohibit the intentional striking of blows. Thus, Article 1, Item 1, Subsection C, provides that:

All players are prohibited from striking on the head, face or neck with the heel, back or side of the hand, wrist, forearm, elbow or clasped hands.

Thus the very conduct which was present here is expressly prohibited by the rule which is quoted above.

The general customs of football do not approve the intentional punching or striking of others. That this is prohibited was supported by the testimony of all of the witnesses. They testified that the intentional striking of a player in the face or from the rear is prohibited by the playing rules as well as the general customs of the game. Punching or hitting with the arms is prohibited. Undoubtedly these restraints are intended to establish reasonable boundaries so that one football player cannot intentionally inflict a serious injury on another. Therefore, the notion is not correct that all reason has been abandoned, whereby the only possible remedy for the person who has been the victim of an unlawful blow is retaliation.

* * *

Is the Standard of Reckless Disregard of the Rights of Others Applicable to the Present Situation?

The *Restatement of Torts Second*, § 500, distinguishes between reckless and negligent misconduct. Reckless misconduct differs from negligence, according to the authors, in that negligence consists of mere inadvertence, lack of skillfulness or failure to take precautions; reckless misconduct, on the other hand, involves a choice or adoption of a course of action either with knowledge of the danger or with knowledge of facts which would disclose this danger to a reasonable man. Recklessness also differs in that it consists of intentionally doing an act with knowledge not only that it contains a risk of harm to others as does negligence, but that it actually involves a risk substantially greater in magnitude than is necessary in the case of negligence. The authors explain the difference, therefore, in the degree of risk by saying that the difference is so significant as to amount to a difference in kind.

Subsection (f) also distinguishes between reckless misconduct and intentional wrongdoing. To be reckless the act must have been intended by the actor. At the same time, the actor does not intend to cause the harm which results from it. It is enough that he realized, or from the facts should have realized, that there was a strong probability that harm would result even though he may hope or expect that this conduct will prove harmless. Nevertheless, existence of probability is different from substantial certainty which is an ingredient of intent to cause the harm which results from the act.

Therefore, recklessness exists where a person knows that the act is harmful but fails to realize that it will produce the extreme harm which it did produce. It is in this respect that recklessness and intentional conduct differ in degree.

In the case at bar the defendant Clark admittedly acted impulsively and in the heat of anger, and even though it could be said from the admitted facts that he intended the act, it could also be said that he did not intend to inflict serious injury which resulted from the blow which he struck.

In ruling that recklessness is the appropriate standard and that assault and battery is not the exclusive one, we are saying that these two liability concepts are not necessarily opposed one to the other. Rather, recklessness under § 500 of the Restatement might be regarded, for the purpose of analysis at least, as a lesser included act.

Assault and battery, having originated in a common law writ, is narrower than recklessness in its scope. In essence, two definitions enter into it. The assault is an attempt coupled with the present ability to commit a violent harm against another. Battery is the unprivileged or unlawful touching of another. Assault and battery then call for an intent, as does recklessness. But in recklessness the intent is to do the act, but without an intent to cause the particular harm. It is enough if the actor knows that there is a strong probability that harm will result. Thus, the definition fits perfectly the fact situation here.

Reversed.

After the appellate court remanded the case for trial, the case was settled with payment of $200,000 to Hackbart.

Questions for Discussion

1. Look closely at the legal standards used in both the trial and the appellate opinions. In what situations would the trial judge *permit* a tort suit by the injured athlete against another participant? In what situations would the appeals court specifically *exclude* such suits? What does "reckless misconduct" mean and how does this concept differ from either intentional or negligent misconduct? How would one illustrate the difference in examples drawn not just from football, but from boxing, baseball, or other sports?

As the next case shows, the courts have had to struggle to utilize the policy of assumption of risk in the sports arena, because this legal concept has fallen from favor in tort law generally.

ORDWAY v. CASELLA
Court of Appeals of California, Fourth District, 1988.
198 Cal.App.3d 98, 243 Cal.Rptr. 536.

CROSBY, ASSOCIATE JUSTICE.

Does reasonable implied assumption of risk remain a viable defense after the adoption of comparative fault? We hold it does.

I

Judy Casella, a veteran jockey who had ridden in 500 professional horse races without incident, was thrown from her mount and further injured when the equine fell and rolled over her during a quarterhorse race at Los Alamitos Race Course on January 3, 1983. The tragic chain of events began when Over Shadow, owned by petitioner Homer Ordway, tangled with another steed, Speedy Ball, who then stumbled in front of Casella's horse. The California Horse Racing Board determined the jockey riding Over Shadow violated a board rule by "crossing over without sufficient clearance, causing interference," and he was suspended for five racing days. Alleging "negligence, carelessness and unlawful conduct," Casella sued the riders, trainers, and owners of Over Shadow and Speedy Ball.

II

The initial question is whether the doctrine of reasonable implied assumption of risk survives in the era of comparative fault. We had occasion to touch on the subject once before, but a resolution of the matter was not essential to that decision. It is now, however; and the answer is, "Yes."

Courts and legal scholars have traditionally recognized three forms of assumption of risk. Express assumption of risk is exactly what the term describes: Where "the potential plaintiff agrees not to expect the potential defendant to act carefully, thus eliminating the potential defendant's duty of care, and acknowledging the possibility of negligent wrongdoing," the potential plaintiff has expressly assumed the risk of injury.

Reasonable implied assumption of risk is the inferred agreement to relieve a potential defendant of a duty of care based on the potential plaintiff's reasonable conduct in encountering a known danger. A second variety of implied assumption of risk is labeled unreasonable. After a brief prefatory digression, we will explain the importance of the distinction between them in determining the rights of the parties.

The relationship between the concepts of implied assumption of risk and contributory negligence has been the source of some confusion. The two doctrines are quite separate in one sense, but overlap in another. More than thirty years ago, our Supreme Court explained the basic differences between them as follows:

> The defenses of assumption of risk and contributory negligence are based on different theories. Contributory negligence arises from a [plaintiff's] lack of due care. The defense of assumption of risk, on the other hand, will negative liability regardless of the fact that plaintiff may have acted with due care. It is available when there has been a voluntary acceptance of a risk and such acceptance, whether express or implied, has been made with knowledge and appreciation of the risk.

In *Li v. Yellow Cab Co.*, 532 P.2d 1226 (Cal.1975), the court "recognized [that the doctrine of assumption of risk] in fact is made up of at least two distinct defenses. 'To simplify greatly, it has been observed ... that in one kind of situation, to wit, where a plaintiff unreasonably undertakes to encounter a specific known risk imposed by a defendant's negligence, plaintiff's conduct, although he may encounter that risk in a prudent manner, is in reality a form of contributory negligence.... Other kinds of situations within the doctrine of assumption of risk are those, for example, where plaintiff is held to agree to relieve defendant of an obligation of reasonable conduct toward him. Such a situation would not involve contributory negligence, but rather a reduction of defendant's duty of care." The court determined that unreasonable assumption of risk should be merged with the theory of contributory negligence under comparative fault principles; i.e., while an injured party who unreasonably assumed a risk may recover, the damages will nonetheless be reduced by the percentage of fault attributed to him or her.

Li did not specifically determine whether a defense based on reasonable implied assumption of risk should survive the adoption of comparative fault, and the court has not had occasion to confront the issue since. Several other divisions of the Court of Appeal have, however.

In *Segoviano v. Housing Authority*, 191 Cal.Rptr. 578 (1983), a player was injured during an amateur flag football game when an opponent, in violation of the rules, pushed him out of bounds. Ruling on an in limine motion, the trial court precluded the defendant, the institutional sponsor of the game, from relying on assumption of risk to defeat the plaintiff's claim. The plaintiff prevailed, but the jury discounted his award by 30% under comparative fault instructions.

Rejecting the notion "that a plaintiff who has reasonably assumed a risk may not recover damages because that form of assumption of risk negates defendant's duty of care to the plaintiff," *Segoviano* held that only express assumption of risk remained a viable defense after *Li*. The appellate panel conceded *Li* explicitly merged only unreasonable assumption of risk into the concept of contributory negligence; but it concluded that where "the plaintiff's conduct [is] entirely reasonable under all of the circumstances, we find no basis in reason or equity for barring his recovery. Elimination of [reasonable implied assumption of risk] as a separate defense avoids punishing reasonable conduct." Accordingly, the court not only reversed the judgment but also held the plaintiff's recovery could not be reduced under comparative fault principles because his implied assumption of the risk of injury in a flag football game was reasonable and, as a matter of law, provided no basis for apportionment of the damages.

Having studied the problem anew, we remain unpersuaded by *Segoviano's* holding. In our view, that opinion turned the law on its head. If plaintiff reasonably consented to participate in a touch football game, how could defendant's sponsorship of the contest be any less reasonable? Plaintiff and defendant had an equal opportunity to anticipate the over-exuberance of one of the participants and the potential for injury. There is no principled basis upon which any responsibility should be assigned to the defendant under those circumstances. The defendant merely provided plaintiff with the chance to play; he was the one who chose to risk an injury. There is also a strong policy basis for absolving the defendant in such circumstances: encouragement of persons and entities to provide opportunities to engage in sports and recreational activities without fear of suits by the participating beneficiaries.

The correct analysis is this: The doctrine of reasonable implied assumption of risk is only another way of stating that the defendant's duty of care has been reduced in proportion to the hazards attendant to the event. Where no duty of care is owed with respect to a particular mishap, there can be no breach; consequently, as a matter of law, a personal injury plaintiff who has voluntarily—and reasonably—assumed the risk cannot prevail. Or stated another way, the individual who knowingly and voluntarily assumes a risk, whether for recreational enjoyment, economic reward, or some similar purpose, is deemed to have agreed to reduce the defendant's duty of care.

The *Segoviano* court may have been misled because the distinction between the "reasonable" and "unreasonable" plaintiff is superficially anomalous: The former's civil action is barred while the latter's is allowed to go to judgment, reduced only in proportion to fault. But the explanation has nothing to do with rewarding or punishing a plaintiff, as *Segoviano* suggests. Rather, it is found in the expectation of the defendant. He or she is permitted to ignore reasonably assumed risks and is not required to take extraordinary precautions with respect to them. The defendant must, however, anticipate that some risks will be unreasonably undertaken, and a failure to guard against those may result in liability.

For example, borrowing from an old legal saw, "[Because a] drunken man is as much entitled to a safe street, as a sober one, and much more in need of it" (*Robinson v. Pioche*, 5 Cal.460, 461 (1855)), sidewalks should be constructed with safety in mind. If they are negligently built, inebriety will not bar a pedestrian's lawsuit for injury, although it may reduce his recovery.

Those who have taken a remunerative or recreational risk with a conscious awareness of all it entails, however, are on their own. A circus need not provide a net for an aerialist who does not want one. The owner of a dangerous piece of property, Niagara Falls for example, will have a complete defense to an action by a Hollywood stuntperson who, encased in a barrel, elects to enter the river above the falls. But the garden-variety inattentive member of the public who passes through a gate negligently left open, in the misguided belief that the water above the falls is safe for swimming, will only suffer a proportionate reduction in damages. A defendant must, under appropriate circumstances, anticipate the fool (which is merely another way of describing the careless and negligent).

The conduct of the stuntperson is "reasonable" in the eyes of the law, but not that of the negligent bather. Concededly, it does sound strange to decree that unreasonable plaintiffs may recover and reasonable ones may not; but the problem is not of law but semantics. If the "reasonable-unreasonable" labels were simply changed to "knowing and intelligent" versus "negligent or careless," the concepts would be more easily understood.

* * *

III

Having concluded that the doctrine of reasonable implied assumption of risk is alive and well, we discuss in this section its preclusive impact on Casella's lawsuit, specifically whether her action could be maintained on a theory of recklessness....

Historically, the doctrine of assumption of risk has provided a defense only to actions for negligence. It has little or no application in the case of intentional or reckless conduct. The reason is this: While a potential plaintiff who engages in dangerous activity is "held to have consented to the injury-causing events which are known, apparent or reasonably foreseeable consequences of the participation ... participants do not consent to acts [by others] which are reckless or intentional." While the line between negligent and intentional conduct is frequently obscured in sports injury litigation, we are satisfied it was not crossed here.

First, Casella's complaint alleged only that her injuries were caused by "the negligent, careless and unlawful manner in which the Defendants ... rode, ... owned and trained the horses, Over Shadow and Speedy Ball." She never used the words "reckless" or "intentional"; and neither expression would accurately characterize the defendant jockeys' conduct, as she herself described it. Her declaration in opposition to Ordway's motion for summary judgment explained, "[Over Shadow's jockey] severely guided his horse inside and in doing so crossed over and in front of other horses without looking to see whether he could safely do so. His horse crossed in front of Speedy Ball [whose jockey] did not take evasive action and the horses' legs tangled resulting in Speedy Ball tripping and falling onto the track ... directly [in front of my mount]." Casella's own assessment of the accident presents a classic case of negligence, i.e., a failure to exercise due care. But by participating in the horse race, she relieved others of any duty to conform their conduct to a standard that would exempt her from the risks inherent in a sport where large and swift animals bearing human cargo are locked in close proximity under great stress and excitement.

Casella seeks to avoid the negligence hurdle by equating suspension of one of the defendant jockeys for violation of California Horse Racing Board Rule No. 1699 (the equine equivalent of an unsafe lane change) with intentional conduct. We are not persuaded. Mens rea plays no part in the board rule. The penalty is levied when an infraction occurs; no evidence was presented to the trial court which suggested a jockey is suspended only where the conduct is determined to have been intentional.

Casella's allegations are legally indistinguishable from those found insufficient in *Turcotte v. Fell*, [502 N.E.2d 964 (1986)]. There, a jockey was injured in an accident very similar to Casella's. He sued his fellow competitor, who had been sanctioned for violating New York's foul riding rule, and the owner of the horse he rode. The trial court dismissed the complaint because there were "no allegations of [the defendant jockey's] wanton, reckless, or intentional conduct." The high court of New York unanimously affirmed the dismissal, noting that the plaintiff's failure to allege intentional conduct by the defendant rider was fatal to his cause of action:

> As the [foul riding] rule recognizes, bumping and jostling are normal incidents of the sport. They are not ... flagrant infractions unrelated to the normal method of playing the game and done without any competitive purpose. Plaintiff does not claim that [the other jockey] intentionally or recklessly bumped him, he claims only that as a result of carelessness, [the defendant] failed to control his mount.... [A] professional clearly understands the usual incidents of competition resulting from carelessness, particularly those which result from the customarily accepted method of playing the sport, and accepts them. They are within the known, apparent and foreseeable dangers of the sport and not actionable....

Casella's allegations also stand in sharp contrast to the facts in two other recent professional sports injury actions, *Hackbart v. Cincinnati Bengals, Inc.*, 601 F.2d 516 (10th Cir.1979), and *Tomjanovich v. California Sports, Inc.*, (S.D. Tex., Oct. 10, 1979, No. 78–243) (1994). In *Tomjanovich*, a professional basketball player was severely injured when an opposing player deliberately struck a vicious blow to his face. Tomjanovich sued in federal district court in Texas, and the law of California was applied. The verdict in his favor was in excess of $2 million. The matter settled pending appeal.

A verdict for Tomjanovich was clearly proper. He did assume the risk of being hit in the face by a flying elbow in the course of defending against an opponent's jump shot, suffering a painful insult to his instep by a size–16 foot descending with a rebound, or even being knocked to the court by the sheer momentum of a seven-footer driving home a slam dunk. But the scope of his consent did not extend to an intentional blow considerably beyond the expected risks inherent in basketball. Intentional fouls are part of that game. But where the intent is to injure and the force used is far greater than necessary to accomplish a legitimate objective within the scope of play, a defendant may not prevail on an assumption of risk defense.

* * *

Despite Casella's disingenuous assertion that "I did not consider at the time of this race that I was participating in a dangerous activity," professional riders must realize that accidents are always possible and not uncommon. The degree of the risk anticipated varies, of course, from sport to sport. In prize fighting bodily harm is to be expected, but pugilists do not consent to be stabbed or shot in the ring. At the other extreme, in bridge or table tennis bodily harm is not contemplated at all. The correct rule is this: If the defendant's actions, even those which might cause incidental physical damage in some sports, are within the ordinary expectations of the participants—such as blocking in football, checking in hockey, knock-out punches in boxing, and aggressive riding in horse racing—no cause of action can succeed based on a resulting injury.[8]

It is of no moment that the participants may be penalized for these actions by the officials. Routine rule violations, such as clipping in football, low blows in boxing, and fouls in horse races are common occurrences and within the parameters of the athletes' expectations.

Here defendant jockeys were attempting to win a horse race. There has never been any suggestion that they, much less the owners of their horses, were motivated by a desire to injure plaintiff. Defendants' conduct, while perhaps negligent, was within the range to be anticipated by the other riders, or should have been. As a professional rider, Casella reasonably assumed the risk of her tragic injury. As with other persons who reasonably assume similar risks, her remedy was to purchase insurance from her athletic income beforehand, not to pursue a lawsuit against her counterparts in the sport afterward. The action, accordingly, is barred as a matter of law.

Summary dismissal granted.

American courts generally have adopted the rule that tort liability in an athletic contest must rest on reckless disregard of safety. As the Supreme Judicial Court of Massachusetts put it in *Gauvin v. Clark*, 404 Mass. 450, 537 N.E.2d 94 (1989) (a case involving severe abdominal injuries inflicted by a "butt-end" with the stick in a college hockey game):

> Allowing the imposition of liability in cases of reckless disregard of safety diminishes the need for players to seek retaliation during the game or future games. Precluding the imposition of liability in cases of negligence without reckless misconduct furthers the policy that "[v]igorous and active participation in sporting events should not be chilled by the threat of litigation."

Some courts, however, do permit suits predicated on negligence, although the standard of legal negligence is greatly modified to accommodate the normal risks of the game. This doctrinal position was expressed by the Missouri Court of Appeals in *Niemczyk v. Burleson*, 538

---

8. A borderline situation is presented by knock-out punches in hockey. They are quite common, but not officially condoned as part of the game. Reasonable minds might differ as to them. Tossing one's opponent out of the ring in professional wrestling is also a gray area. These sorts of cases are jury material.

S.W.2d 737, 741–42 (Mo.App.1976) (a case involving a collision on the basepaths in a women's softball game):

> Material factors include the specific game involved, the ages and physical attributes of the participants, their respective skills at the game and their knowledge of its rules and customs, their status as amateurs or professionals, the type of risks which inhere in the game and those which are outside the realm of reasonable anticipation, the presence or absence of protective uniforms or equipment, the degree of zest with which the game is being played, and doubtless others.

538 S.W.2d at 741–42.

A closely divided Wisconsin Supreme Court became the first court at this level to adopt the general negligence standard for litigation about injuries in competitive sports. See *Lestina v. West Bend Mutual Insurance Co.*, 176 Wis.2d 901, 501 N.W.2d 28 (Wis.1993) (involving a collision between a goalie and a forward in a men's, over–30, recreational soccer league). The Wisconsin court did make clear, though, that the reason for endorsing negligence, rather than recklessness, as the governing rule in this context was that the former standard was flexible enough to accommodate the distinctive features of the particular sport in which the injury occurred:

> The very fact that an injury is sustained during the course of a game in which the participants voluntarily engaged, and in which the likelihood of bodily contact and injury could reasonably be foreseen, materially affects the manner in which each player's conduct is to be evaluated under the negligence standard. To determine whether a player's conduct constitutes actionable negligence (or contributory negligence), the fact finder should consider such material factors as the sport involved; the rules and regulations governing the sport; the generally accepted customs and practices of the sport (including the types of conduct and level of violence generally accepted); the risks inherent in the game and those that are outside the realm of anticipation; the presence of protective equipment or uniforms; and the facts and circumstances of the particular case, including the ages and physical attributes of the participants, the participants' respective skills at the game, and the participants' knowledge of the rules and customs.

Id. at 33. It is uncertain, though, how much influence this decision by even a well-regarded Wisconsin Supreme Court will have in other states. For example, a year later the New Jersey Supreme Court endorsed the "reckless disregard" standard, reversing the lower court which had adopted Wisconsin's negligence doctrine instead. See *Crawn v. Campo*, 136 N.J. 494, 643 A.2d 600 (1994).

Violent acts do take place in the sports arena that are clearly beyond the pale of the game and the law. A notable example occurred in 1965 when Juan Marichal of the San Francisco Giants, upset at having been deliberately grazed by Los Angeles Dodgers' catcher John Roseboro's throw back to the mound, turned and struck Roseboro with his bat. After Marichal was suspended and fined by the league, Roseboro sued Marichal and collected $7,500 out of court. But what is the appropriate legal treatment of the following "closer calls?"

1. A pitcher throws a ball far inside the plate and strikes the batter who has come up to the plate after the previous batter had hit a three-run home run.

2. A runner from first base slides, with spikes up, into the second baseman some distance away from the base, to break up a double play in a close late-inning game. (See *Bourque v. Duplechin*, 331 So.2d 40 (La.App.1976).)

3. A hard-hitting football free safety "blind sides" a wide receiver running a post pattern across the middle of the field, just after the ball has passed over both their heads.[e]

In *Ordway*, the court alluded to a notorious 1977 incident involving the Los Angeles Lakers' Kermit Washington and the Houston Rockets' Rudy Tomjanovich. Tomjanovich, who was trying to act as a peacemaker in a set-to between Washington and the Rockets' Kevin Kunnert, was punched in the face by Washington, fell, and struck his head on the court. Kareem Abdul–Jabbar testified that the sound was "like a watermelon being dropped on a cement floor." The resulting skull fracture, concussion, and facial injuries effectively ended Tomjanovich's playing career with the Rockets (though he later came back to coach them to the NBA championship).[f] Washington was clearly liable in tort to Tomjanovich. But should Tomjanovich have been able to sue and collect from the Lakers—the "deep pocket" able to pay substantial monetary damages (including damages to the Rockets for the loss of Tomjanovich's services)? The legal criterion for imposing such "vicarious liability" on an employer is whether the harmful action on the part of Washington was "within the scope of his employment" with the Lakers. Precisely the same issue was posed about the San Francisco Giants' liability to John Roseboro or the Cincinnati Bengals' liability to Dale Hackbart. What additional facts might be relevant to that judgment? (An earlier decision on this issue is *Averill v. Luttrell*, 44 Tenn.App. 56, 311 S.W.2d 812

---

[e]. The most notorious hit of this kind was inflicted by the Oakland Raiders' Jack Tatum on New England Patriots' wide receiver Darryl Stingley in the late 1970s. Stingley suffered a broken neck and was permanently paralyzed as a result of the hit. See John Underwood, *The Death of an American Game: The Crisis in Football* 45–46 (Boston: Little Brown, 1979); see also Jack Tatum with William Kushner, *They Call Me Assassin* (New York: Everest House, 1979).

[f]. For a detailed account see David Halberstam, *The Breaks of the Game* 199–216 (New York: Alfred Knopf, 1981). The Jabbar quote in the text comes from a Note on the *Tomjanovich* case at 23 American Trial Lawyer's Assoc. L. Rep. 107 (1980).

(1957), in which a catcher slugged a batter from behind after the batter, irate at several "brush-back" pitches, had thrown his bat at the pitcher.)

Courts have applied essentially the same doctrines to immunize clubs from liability for spectator injuries that flow from the normal risks of the game: for example, being hit by a foul ball (see *Schentzel v. Philadelphia National League Club*, 173 Pa.Super. 179, 96 A.2d 181 (1953)), or by a hockey puck (see *Pestalozzi v. Philadelphia Flyers*, 394 Pa.Super. 420, 576 A.2d 72 (1990)). On the other hand, a California appellate court ruled recently that the team could be liable for a foul ball injury if a jury found that the team had increased the inherent risks of injury to spectators by having the club's "mascot cavorting in the stands and distracting the [fan's] attention, while the game was in progress." See *Lowe v. California League of Professional Baseball*, 56 Cal.App.4th 112, 65 Cal.Rptr.2d 105 (1997).

An interesting variant on liability for spectator's injuries is *Manning v. Grimsley*, 643 F.2d 20 (1st Cir.1981). Baltimore Orioles' pitcher Ross Grimsley, while warming up during a game against the Boston Red Sox at Fenway Park, was being heckled by fans in the right field bleachers who were separated from the visitors' bullpen by a wire mesh fence. At the end of his warmup, Grimsley threw a ball hard at the fence, aimed at the hecklers. Unfortunately the ball passed through the mesh and struck and injured Manning, a fan who was not one of the hecklers. Is Grimsley liable to Manning? For the tort of battery or for negligence? Are the Orioles vicariously liable for either tort?

Return now to the more fundamental question posed by all these cases. Why, for example, does the plaintiff in *Ordway* assume the risk of negligent riding by another jockey on the racetrack, but not the risk of careless driving on the highway (perhaps by the same jockey on the way to the track)? For the last several decades the objectives of the general tort regime have undergone a major reevaluation. Until World War II, most judges and commentators tacitly assumed that the role of tort law was to mete out corrective justice between the individual parties involved in a particular case. Presently, however, the intellectual consensus seems to be that our complex and expensive system of tort litigation and liability insurance constitutes a form of enterprise responsibility for personal injury. (Sharp disagreement remains about whether the law's priority should be compensation or prevention of injury.) Which of these visions suits the special case of torts in sports? Should the answers be the same for professional sports as for playground sports?

B. CRIMINAL LAW AND SPORTS VIOLENCE

Hockey has generated the most serious concern and extensive litigation about injuries inflicted by participants. The reason is that in hockey, while "roughing" and "fighting" are considered violations of the rules of the game that call for penalties of two and five minutes respectively, these infractions do not evoke the ejections, suspensions, and fines meted out in other sports (e.g., basketball). Hockey owners believe that a certain amount of fighting helps win games and fans—recall the "Broad Street Bullies" reputation of the Stanley Cup-winning Philadelphia Flyers in the mid-1970s. The problem is that when fights break out between two players, especially when one combatant is bigger and tougher than the other, there is always a danger the fight will escalate, especially through the use of sticks. Sometimes stick swinging inflicts injuries that precipitate tort litigation. See *Babych v. McRae & Quebec Nordiques*, 41 Conn.Sup. 280, 567 A.2d 1269 (1989). Occasionally, the scene is bloody enough to yield criminal prosecutions.[g]

Perhaps the most highly-publicized such event took place in a 1969 exhibition game in Ottawa between the Boston Bruins and the St. Louis Blues. Ted Green, a star defenseman and "enforcer" for the Bruins, swung and hit the Blues' Wayne Maki on the head, drawing a delayed penalty signal from the referee. Maki then turned and speared Green in the abdomen with his stick. Green retaliated by swinging his stick at Maki's shoulder. Maki ended the fray by hitting Green on the head with his stick, which fractured Green's skull and required the insertion of a steel plate in his head. Although Green returned to play with the Bruins the next season, he was never the star player he was before the incident (though he later became head coach of the Edmonton Oilers).

Ontario authorities were so upset by this incident that they filed criminal charges against both Maki and Green. In separate decisions, the provincial court judges who tried the cases acquitted both players. In *Regina v. Green*, 16 D.L.R.3d 137 (Ont.1971), the judge commented as follows about Green's "consent" defense to the charge of simple assault:

> There is no doubt that the players who enter the hockey arena consent to a great number of assaults on their person, because the game of hockey as it is played in the National Hockey League, which is the league I am dealing with, could not possibly be played at the speed at which it is played and with the force and vigour with which it is played, and with the competition that enters into it, unless there were a great number of what would in normal circumstances be called assaults, but which are not heard of. No hockey player enters onto the ice of the National Hockey League without consenting to and without knowledge of the possibility that he is going to be hit in one of many ways once he is on that ice.
>
> I think it is notable that Mr. Maki in his evidence, when he was questioned about the fact that he was struck in the face by Mr. Green's glove, said this had happened to him hundreds of times. I think within our experience we can come to the conclusion that this

---

g. The best treatment of this topic is Richard Horrow, *Sports Violence: The Interaction Between Private Law-Making and the Criminal Law* (Westport, Conn.: Greenwood Pub., 1980). See also Carlsen, note 1 above; Note, *Sports Violence as Criminal Assault: Development of The Doctrine by Canadian Courts*, 1986 Duke L. J. 1030; Gilles Letourneau & Antoine Monganas, *Violence in Sports: Evidentiary Problems in Criminal Prosecution*, 16 Osgoode Hall L. J. 577 (1978); and Note, *Consent in Criminal Law: Violence in Sports*, 75 Mich. L. Rev. 148 (1975).

is an extremely ordinary happening in a hockey game and the players really think nothing of it. If you go in behind the net with a defenseman, particularly one who is trying to defend his zone, and you are struck in the face by that player's glove, a penalty might be called against him, but you do not really think anything of it; it is one of the types of risk one assumes.

One now gets the most difficult problem of all, in my opinion: since it is assumed and understood that there are numerous what would normally be called assaults in the course of a hockey game, but which are really not assaults because of the consent of the players in the type of game being played, where do you draw the line? It is very difficult in my opinion for a player who is playing hockey with all the force, vigour and strength at his command, who is engaged in the rough and tumble of the game, very often in a rough situation in the corner of the rink, suddenly to stop and say, "I must not do that. I must not follow up on this because maybe it is an assault; maybe I am committing an assault." I do not think that any of the actions that would normally be considered assaults in ordinary walks of life can possibly be, within the context that I am considering, considered assaults at all.

In *Regina v. Maki*, 14 D.L.R.3d 164 (Ont.1970), the trial judge expressed a somewhat different view regarding the charge of assault causing bodily harm:

If the fact situation in this case had been such that no doubt was raised in my mind regarding self-defense, I would not have hesitate[d] to convict the accused. The defense of consent would in my opinion have failed. Although no criminal charges have been laid in the past pertaining to athletic events in this country, I can see no reason why they could not be in the future where the circumstances warrant and the relevant authorities deem it advisable to do so. No sports league, no matter how well organized or self-policed it may be, should thereby render the players in that league immune from criminal prosecution....

Thus all players, when they step onto a playing field or ice surface, assume certain risks and hazards of the sport, and in most cases the defense of consent as set out in § 230 of the *Criminal Code* would be applicable. But as stated above there is a question of degree involved, and no athlete should be presumed to accept malicious, unprovoked or overly violent attack. Bastin, J., states it this way in *Agar v. Canning*, 54 W.W.R. 302 at p. 305; affirmed, 55 W.W.R. 384:

But a little reflection will establish that some limit must be placed on a player's immunity from liability. Each case must be decided on its own facts so it is difficult, if not impossible, to decide how the line is to be drawn in every circumstance. But injuries inflicted in circumstances which show a definite resolve to cause serious injury to another, even when there is provocation and in the heat of the game, should not fall within the scope of the implied consent.

The adoption of such principles in the future, would, I feel certain, be a benefit to the players, of course, to the general public peace and, in particular, to young aspiring athletes who look to the professionals for guidance and example.

The result in the second case, however, was the same: Maki was acquitted on the ground that there was at least "reasonable doubt" about whether he had used more than proportionate force in self defense.

Other courts have been unwilling to convict hockey players of criminal offenses, both in Ontario, see *Regina v. Maloney*, 28 C.C.C. 323 (Ont.1976), and in the United States, see *State v. Forbes* (unreported), which produced a hung jury. But in 1988, Dino Ciccarelli, then of the Minnesota North Stars, spent one day in a Toronto jail for having clubbed the Maple Leafs' Luke Richardson twice on the head (fortunately, by this time the NHL required players to wear helmets).

The policy question posed by these cases was brought to the floor of the U.S. Congress in 1980 when Representative Ronald Mottl of Ohio proposed a Sports Violence Act, which would have created a new federal criminal offense of "Excessive violence during professional sporting events:"

(a) Whoever, as a player in a professional sports event, knowingly uses excessive physical force and thereby causes a risk of significant bodily injury to another person involved in that event shall be fined not more than $5,000 or imprisoned not more than one year, or both.

(b) As used in this section, the term—

(1) "excessive physical force" means physical force that—

(A) has no reasonable relationship to the competitive goals of the sport;

(B) is unreasonably violent; and

(C) could not be reasonably foreseen, or was not consented to, by the injured person, as a normal hazard to such person's involvement in such sports events; and

(2) "professional sports event" means a paid admission contest, in or affecting interstate or foreign commerce, of players paid for their participation."

This bill, vigorously opposed by the commissioners of all the major sports leagues, died in committee.

Questions for Discussion

1. Did the acquittal of Maki on self-defense grounds mean that Green did inflict a battery on Maki? Or vice versa? Did the judge in *Green* imply

that we are not always expected to control ourselves—so long as we are playing sports?

2. Would the factual issues, such as consent, raised by these incidents be more easily resolvable if the Sports Violence Act had passed? Would a Sports Violence Act serve as a criminal court test run, at taxpayers' expense, for potential tort claims by injured athletes?

3. Why did the major sports commissioners oppose the Sports Violence Act? Does this imply that federal intervention to deal with sports violence is or is not in the best interests of the game?[h]

C. WORKERS' COMPENSATION FOR ATHLETES[i]

Workers' compensation is yet another legal instrument for dealing with sports injuries, designed not to punish an offender but to compensate the victim. Workers' compensation programs, which exist in every state in the United States (and in every province in Canada), pay defined benefits to employees who suffer "accidental injury arising out of and in the course of employment" (the standard statutory phrase), regardless of whether anyone was at fault in the incident. These statutory benefits, financed by the employer, typically cover medical treatment, physical and vocational rehabilitation, and earnings replacement pegged to the average wage in the state. For employment relationships and injuries covered by workers' compensation, this program is the exclusive legal remedy against the employer who is insulated by statute from tort suit by the injured employee. In the sports setting, the potential availability of workers' compensation generates an ambivalent attitude among the parties. In some cases the athlete seeks coverage and the club resists; in others, the tactical positions are reversed. The following cases provide a sample of the legal arguments regularly advanced on both sides.

1. COLLEGE ATHLETES[j]

The next case, involving an injury in intercollegiate football, recalls themes we explored earlier regarding the status of college athletes, the

---

h. See Horrow, *Sports Violence*, note 8 above, the book which was actually the source of this policy idea. For variations on this proposal, see Chris J. Carlsen & Matthew Shane Walker, *The Sports Court: A Private System to Deter Violence in Professional Sports*, 55 Southern Cal. L. Rev. 399 (1982), and Ronald A. DeNicola & Scott Mendeloff, *Controlling Violence in Professional Sports: Rule Reform and the Federal Professional Sports Violence Commission*, 21 Duquesne L. Rev. 843 (1983).

i. See Gerald Herz & Robert C. Baker, "Professional Athletes and the Law of Workers' Compensation," Chapter 16 of Uberstine, ed., *Law of Professional and Amateur Sports*, note 1 above, for a synopsis of this topic. The multi-volume treatise by Arthur Larson, *The Law of Workers' Compensation* (Desk Edition) (New York: Matthew Bender, 1992), is the authoritative and comprehensive statement of the law in this area, including the application of workers' compensation to injured athletes.

j. Mark R. Whitmore, *Denying Scholarship Athletes Workers' Compensation: Do Courts Punt Away a Statutory Right?*, 6 Iowa L. Rev. 763 (1991), is the most recent and comprehensive analysis of this issue. An earlier treatment is Mark Alan Atkinson, *Workers' Compensation and College Athletics: Should Universities Be Responsible for Athletes Who Incur Serious Injuries?*, 10 J. of Col. & Univ. Law 197 (1983–84).

nature of their relationship with their schools, and the true character of big-time college sports.

RENSING v. INDIANA STATE UNIV.
Court of Appeals of Indiana, Fourth District, 1982.
437 N.E.2d 78.

[Fred Rensing, a varsity football player at Indiana State University, was rendered a quadriplegic by a tragic injury in spring practice in 1976. At the time Rensing was on full scholarship—the standard NCAA "grant-in-aid" providing free tuition, fees, room and board, books, tutoring, and a limited number of game tickets. This scholarship was renewable by the university each year, for up to four years, as long as Rensing "actively participated in football competition." After his injury, Rensing sought and was denied workers' compensation benefits from Indiana's Industrial Board. This appeal to the courts followed.]

MILLER, PRESIDING JUDGE.

* * *

Thus, in the instant case the central question is not whether our Legislature has specifically excluded college sports participants from the coverage of the Act, since it is apparent the Legislature has not expressed such an intention, but rather whether there was a "written or implied" employment contract within the meaning of the Act which obligated Rensing to play football in return for the scholarship he received.

Viewing the facts adduced in the case at bar, the conclusion is inescapable the Trustees did contract with Rensing to play football, regardless of whether one views the various documents submitted to Rensing and signed by him as constituting an express contract, or merely as evidence of the parties' understanding in support of an implied contractual relationship. In this regard, we note the settled law that "[a]ny benefit, commonly the subject of pecuniary compensation, which one, not intending it as a gift, confers on another, who accepts it, is adequate foundation for a legally implied or created promise to render back its value." The parties' financial aid "agreement," noted above, clearly anticipated not only that Rensing would play football in return for his scholarship, but also provided that in the event Rensing suffered an injury during supervised play that would make him "unable to continue to participate" in the opinion of the University doctor, the Trustees would ask him to assist in other tasks to the extent of his ability. The benefits would continue so long as Rensing was "otherwise eligible to compete." In light of such uncontradicted evidence, we can find no merit in the Trustees' suggestion Rensing's benefits were only a gift or "grant" intended to further the young man's education, particularly in light of the fact our Legislature has expressly recognized that scholarships or similar benefits may be viewed as pay pursuant to a "contract of hire" in the analogous context of unemployment benefits.

Additionally, the Trustees also retained their right to terminate their agreement for Rensing's services under certain prescribed conditions, a factor tending to distinguish his grant from an outright gift and which has previously been noted by this Court as a significant indicia of an employer-employee or master-servant relationship.

* * *

From these facts, the conclusion is compelling that Rensing and the Trustees bargained for an exchange in the manner of employer and employee of Rensing's football talents for certain scholarship benefits. Admittedly, the issue we resolve herein is novel to Indiana. In fact, our research of the appropriate law throughout the country reveals only three cases which are particularly relevant. In *Van Horn v. Industrial Accident Commission*, 33 Cal.Rptr. 169 (1963), the California Court of Appeals held that the widow and minor children of a college football team member, who was killed in a plane crash while returning with squad members from a game, were entitled to his death benefits since he had received an athletic scholarship plus a job and, therefore, was rendering services within the meaning of the California Workmen's Compensation Act. The sole question before the Court was whether the decedent was an employee of the college within the meaning of the California's Workmen's Compensation Act so as to render the college liable thereunder for the death benefits to his dependents. In ruling affirmatively for the widow and her children the Court noted that "[t]he only inference to be drawn from the evidence is that the decedent received the 'scholarship' because of his athletic prowess and participation. The form of remuneration is immaterial. A court will look through form to determine whether consideration has been paid for services."

* * *

The Colorado Supreme Court has addressed the issue considered herein on two separate occasions reaching different results (with the same analysis) on these occasions. In *State Compensation Insurance Fund v. Industrial Comm.*, 314 P.2d 288 (Colo.1957), a college student who had received an athletic scholarship for his tuition plus a part-time job was fatally injured while playing in a college football game. The Colorado Supreme Court denied his beneficiaries' claims for death benefits under the Colorado Workmen's Compensation Act, holding that the evidence failed to establish that at the time of injury he was under a contract of hire to play football. Rather, his scholarship and part-time job were not based upon his athletic ability or participation on the football team. Lacking such a contract, the Colorado Supreme Court held there was no basis for a compensation claim. "Since the evidence does not disclose any contractual obligation to play football, then the employer-employee relationship does not exist and there is no contract which supports a claim for compensation under the [Colorado Workmen's Compensation Act]."

The Colorado Supreme Court used the same analysis to find in favor of the student-athlete in *University of Denver v. Nemeth*, 257 P.2d 423 (Colo.1953). In *Nemeth*, the Court held a college student could be compensated under Colorado's Workmen's Compensation Act for injuries sustained during the spring football practice because in that case the student's employment by the University of Denver as the manager of its tennis courts was contingent upon his participation on the football team. In reaching this result, the Court emphasized that a contract existed requiring the University of Denver to employ Nemeth as long as he was on the football team and further noted the testimony of one witness who stated that "the man who produced in football would get the meals and a job." Since Nemeth's employment by the University was dependent on his playing football and he could not retain his job without playing football, the Court held Nemeth was an employee of the University. Thus, his injury during spring practice was an incident of his employment, and therefore, was compensable under the Colorado Workmen's Compensation Act.

While the facts of *Van Horn* and *Nemeth* are distinguishable from the case at bar to the degree that Rensing did not receive a non-athletic job in return for his football prowess, we feel such a distinction is not significant in view of the language of our statute discussed supra. The evidence presented in those two cases is comparable to that introduced before the Industrial Board in the case at bar in that in all three cases the "student-athlete" received benefits from a university solely because of his athletic ability and participation on a football team. If that ability declined and he did not make the team or if he quit the team for some other reason, the benefits he received would be terminated. As noted above, the evidence in the case at bar clearly demonstrates that the benefits received by Rensing were conditioned upon his athletic ability and team participation. Consequently, the scholarship constituted a contract for hire within IC 22–3–6–1(b) and created an employer-employee relationship between the Trustees and Rensing.

* * *

[Turning then to the issue whether Rensing's employment was simply casual, the judge found that] for the team members football is a daily routine for 16 weeks each year. Additionally, during the "off-season" the "student-athlete" must daily work out to maintain his physical skills and attributes, thereby enhancing his eligibility for the team which is the basis for his scholarship. The University fields a major college football team and participates in a major college conference, the Missouri Valley Conference. In addition, the Trustees employ a large athletic department to administer the University's intercollegiate athletic program (in addition to physical education classes) and a sizable football coaching staff whose primary responsibility is to produce the best possible team so as to generate the largest possible income and whose teaching responsibilities to the general student body are, at best, of secondary importance. With regard to Rensing specifically, Coach

Harp actively recruited him—his appearance at the University was not happenstance, liable to chance or an accident. In light of these facts Rensing's employment by the University was not "casual."

* * *

Decision reversed.

[The University appealed to the Supreme Court of Indiana, which took quite a different view of the situation.]

RENSING v. INDIANA STATE UNIV.

Supreme Court of Indiana, 1983.
444 N.E.2d 1170.

HUNTER, JUSTICE.

It is clear that while a determination of the existence of an employee-employer relationship is a complex matter involving many factors, the primary consideration is that there was an intent that a contract of employment, either express or implied, did exist. In other words, there must be a mutual belief that an employer-employee relationship did exist. It is evident from the documents which formed the agreement in this case that there was no intent to enter into an employee-employer relationship at the time the parties entered into the agreement.

In this case, the National Collegiate Athletic Association's (NCAA) constitution and bylaws were incorporated by reference into the agreements. A fundamental policy of the NCAA, which is stated in its constitution, is that intercollegiate sports are viewed as part of the educational system and are clearly distinguished from the professional sports business. The NCAA has strict rules against "taking pay" for sports or sporting activities. Any student who does accept pay is ineligible for further play at an NCAA member school in the sport for which he takes pay. Furthermore, an institution cannot, in any way, condition financial aid on a student's ability as an athlete. The fundamental concerns behind the policies of the NCAA are that intercollegiate athletics must be maintained as a part of the educational program and student-athletes are integral parts of the institution's student body. An athlete receiving financial aid is still first and foremost a student. All of these NCAA requirements designed to prohibit student-athletes from receiving pay for participation in their sport were incorporated into the financial aid agreements Rensing and his parents signed.

Furthermore, there is evidence that the financial aid which Rensing received was not considered by the parties involved to be pay or income. Rensing was given free tuition, room, board, laboratory fees and a book allowance. These benefits were not considered to be "pay" by the University or by the NCAA since they did not affect Rensing's or the University's eligibility status under NCAA rules. Rensing did not consider the benefits as income as he did not report them for income tax purposes. The Internal Revenue Service has ruled that scholarship recipients are not taxed on their scholarship proceeds and there is no distinction made between athletic and academic scholarships.

As far as scholarships are concerned, we find that our Indiana General Assembly clearly has recognized a distinction between the power to award financial aid to students and the power to hire employees since the former power was specifically granted to the Boards of Trustees of state educational institutions with the specific limitation that the award be reasonably related to the educational purposes and objectives of the institution and in the best interests of the institution and the state.

Furthermore, we find that Ind.Code § 22–4–6–2 is not applicable to scholarship benefits. In that statute, which deals with contributions by employers to unemployment insurance, employers are directed to include "all individuals attending an established school ... who, in lieu of remuneration for such services, receive either meals, lodging, books, tuition or other education facilities." Here, Rensing was not working at a regular job for the University. The scholarship benefits he received were not given him in lieu of pay for remuneration for his services in playing football any more than academic scholarship benefits were given to other students for their high scores on tests or class assignments. Rather, in both cases, the students received benefits based upon their past demonstrated ability in various areas to enable them to pursue opportunities for higher education as well as to further progress in their own fields of endeavor.

Scholarships are given to students in a wide range of artistic, academic and athletic areas. None of these recipients is covered under Ind.Code § 22–4–6–2, supra, unless the student holds a regular job for the institution in addition to the scholarship. The statute would apply to students who work for the University and perform services not integrally connected with the institution's educational program and for which, if the student were not available, the University would have to hire outsiders, e.g., workers in the laundry, bookstore, etc. Scholarship recipients are considered to be students seeking advanced educational opportunities and are not considered to be professional athletes, musicians or artists employed by the University for their skills in their respective areas.

* * *

All of the above facts show that in this case, Rensing did not receive "pay" for playing football at the University within the meaning of the Workmen's Compensation Act; therefore, an essential element of the employer-employee relationship was missing in addition to the lack of intent. Furthermore, under the applicable rules of the NCAA, Rensing's benefits could not be reduced or withdrawn because of his athletic ability or his contribution to the team's success. Thus, the ordinary employer's right to discharge on the basis of performance was also missing. While there was an agreement between Rensing and the Trustees which established certain obligations for both parties, the agreement was not a contract of employment. Since at least three important factors indicative of an employee-employer relationship are absent in this case, we find it is not necessary to consider other factors which may or may not be present.

We find that the evidence here shows that Rensing enrolled at Indiana State University as a full time student seeking advanced educational opportunities. He was not considered to be a professional athlete who was being paid for his athletic ability. In fact, the benefits Rensing received were subject to strict regulations by the NCAA which were designed to protect his amateur status. Rensing held no other job with the University and therefore cannot be considered an "employee" of the University within the meaning of the Workmen's Compensation Act.

It is our conclusion of law, under the facts here, including all rules and regulations of the University and the NCAA governing student athletes, that the appellant shall be considered only as a student athlete and not as an employee within the meaning of the Workmen's Compensation Act.

Vacated.

In a subsequent case, *Coleman v. Western Michigan University*, 125 Mich.App. 35, 336 N.W.2d 224 (1983), which also involved an injured college football player on full scholarship, the Michigan Court of Appeals listed what it considered the relevant factors for determining whether an employment relationship existed as a matter of "economic reality":

> (1) the proposed employer's right to control or dictate the activities of the proposed employees; (2) the proposed employer's right to discipline or fire the proposed employee; (3) the payment of "wages" and, particularly, the extent to which the proposed employee is dependent upon the payment of wages or other benefits for his daily living expenses; and (4) whether the task performed by the proposed employee was "an integral part" of the proposed employer's business. None of the foregoing factors is by itself dispositive. Each factor must be considered in turn, and all of them then taken into account in determining the existence of an employment relationship.

How would you assess the status of a scholarship athlete in light of these factors? Does your answer depend on whether the athlete is injured in a revenue-producing sport such as football or basketball, or a non-revenue producing sport such as lacrosse or gymnastics?[k]

---

k. For contrasting views on this issue, see (besides the articles cited in note 11 above) Ray Yasser, *Are Scholarship Athletes At Big-Time Programs Really University Employees?—You Bet They Are!*, 9 Black L. J. 65 (1984), and Harry M. Cross, *The College Athlete and the Institution*, 38 Law & Contemp. Probs. 151 (Winter–Spring, 1973).

Note on NCAA Insurance

Some states, such as California and Florida, have specifically excluded college athletes from workers' compensation coverage. Nevada, in contrast, has included injured athletes at least for purposes of medical benefits, and in Nebraska a bill has been proposed to provide full workers compensation coverage to the state's college athletes. Under the common law standards of the employment relationship, the 1990s have witnessed an ongoing legal debate about whether an injured college athlete is an employee for purposes of workers compensation. Back in 1974, Texas Christian University's Kent Waldrop was permanently paralyzed from his spine down as a result of an injury inflicted in a football game against Alabama. Nearly two decades later, in 1993, the Texas Workers Compensation Commission ruled that Waldrop was an employee of TCU, who had been paid for playing through his grant-in-aid scholarship. As an injured employee, Waldrop would then be entitled to reimbursement of his medical expenses and a lifetime disability pension. However, TCU's insurer, the Texas Employers Insurance Association, in Receivership, appealed the decision to the state court where the dispute was presented *de novo* to a civil jury in the fall of 1997. By a 10–2 margin, the jury reversed the Commission and deemed Waldrop's scholarship to be an "award of excellence" in the school's educational program, rather than payment for his services as an employee. Waldrop is now appealing that verdict.

One's judgment about the most sensible and equitable policy in this area depends to some extent on the availability of alternative avenues of redress for injured athletes. In response to initiatives taking place in state courts and legislatures, in the early 1980s the NCAA developed a Catastrophic Insurance Plan for NCAA member-institutions.[1] The policy covered players, coaches, managers and cheerleaders who were injured while participating in intercollegiate sports and required at least $25,000 worth of medical care or suffered permanent loss of speech, hearing, sight, or use of hands or feet. The policy compensated actual economic loss—medical and rehabilitation expenses and lost earnings (up to $1,500 per month), less amounts received by the victim from other sources of insurance. The insurer was entitled to a lien for its payments against 50% of tort damages (less legal expenses) collected by the athlete from third-party wrongdoers.

---

1. See National Sports Underwriters, Ltd., *NCAA Athletics Insurance Programs Pamphlet* (Overland Park, Kan.: NCAA, 1991). Ironically, as we noted at the outset of Chapter 9, the reason why the NCAA was created in 1906 was national concern—in particular, by President Theodore Roosevelt—about high fatality and injury rates in college football (averaging 20 fatalities and 150 serious permanent disabilities a year). See Ronald Smith, *Sports and Freedom: The Rise of Big-Time College Athletics* 191, 208 (New York: Oxford University Press, 1988). The initial role of this new governing body for college sports was to develop playing rules that would make football less dangerous for students to play. Not until eighty years had passed did the NCAA finally address the question whether some of the revenues from the increasingly lucrative world of college sports should be spent to look after the needs of the victims of fatal or paralyzing athletic injuries—now only three or four per year in all college sports.

This insurance policy had a remarkably low premium rate: coverage for all of its athletes cost a school between $2,000 and $8,000, depending on the number and type of intercollegiate sports at the school. However, the NCAA Manual left the decision whether to purchase coverage up to each institution, and many schools elected not to pay the premium.

The disastrous consequences of this NCAA deference to member autonomy soon became visible. In the fall of 1985, Marc Buoniconti, a sophomore linebacker at the Citadel (and son of former Miami Dolphins All–Pro linebacker Nick Buoniconti), suffered a broken neck, crushed spinal cord, and permanent paralysis when he tackled a runner in a game against East Tennessee State. The Citadel had opted not to pay the $5,000 premium required for its coverage against such a devastating injury. Buoniconti sued the school, its trainer, and its team physician for negligently allowing him to play that day: Buoniconti had been injured the week before, had been held out of practice with a sore neck, and had a special elastic strap attached to the front of his helmet and his shoulder pad. A week before trial, the Citadel (and its employee-trainer) settled for $800,000. At trial, the jury rejected a medical malpractice claim against the doctor. After similar incidents at other schools—in particular, a paralyzing injury inflicted on Roy Lee (Chucky) Mullins at Mississippi State in a 1989 football game against Vanderbilt (Mullins died two years later)—the NCAA finally decided in 1991 (against some heated objections) to spend part of its $1 billion television bonanza from the men's basketball tournament to guarantee such catastrophic injury coverage at all member-institutions.

Unlike workers' compensation, the NCAA insurance plan is not the legally exclusive remedy for college athletes (although if an injured player such as Buoniconti wants to avail himself of these benefits, he must agree to forego the right to sue the university or the NCAA). The value of the right to sue was vividly illustrated by the highly-publicized tragedy involving Hank Gathers, basketball star at Loyola Marymount.[m]

Gathers, who was voted to some 1989 All–American teams in his junior year (as the nation's leading scorer and rebounder), decided to forego the NBA draft and return to college for a final year, both to help his team reach the Final Four and to help himself become a "lottery" pick in the next draft. In an early season game in December, however, Gathers collapsed on the court, and tests indicated that he had an abnormal heart rhythm. The team physician, Dr. Vernon Hattori, a cardiologist, prescribed the drug Inderal to control Gathers' heart rhythm, and Gathers missed only two games. The school purchased a defibrillator, an instrument for restoring the heart beat, and kept it at courtside.

In his early games, Gathers experienced sluggishness and fatigue—normal side effects of Inderal. Following conversations with Gathers and

---

[m.] The Gathers case inspired a fine scholarly article by Cathy J. Jones, *College Athletes: Illness or Injury and the Decision to Return to Play*, 40 Buffalo L. Rev. 113 (1992).

Loyola coach Paul Westhead, Dr. Hattori gradually reduced the Inderal dosage from 240 to 40 milligrams per day. Gathers' play sharply improved towards All–American caliber, and Loyola became one of the top-ranked teams in the country. However, in the conference championship game in March 1990, Gathers, after making a slam dunk, collapsed on court and died two hours later of heart failure. For some reason, the defibrillator had not been used immediately.

Gathers left behind him in the ghetto of north Philadelphia a mother, brothers and sisters, and a young son. They would not receive any of the benefits of the NCAA catastrophic injury policy nor would they get anything from the $1 million disability policy Gathers purchased to cover himself during his senior year: Gathers did not pay the extra $800 premium for a death rider. Instead, the family launched a $32 million wrongful death action against Loyola, Westhead, Hattori, and others. The litigation was settled in 1992 for a total of $2.6 million—$1 million from Dr. Hattori (the dollar limit on his malpractice liability insurance) and $1.6 million from Loyola on behalf of its employees.

Several months after the Gathers tragedy, the NCAA introduced a new disability insurance policy for "exceptional athletes" who have demonstrated their potential to play professional football, basketball, and baseball (but not hockey, at least not yet).[n] This policy is designed to protect athletes against the loss of expected future earnings in these sports should they suffer an injury or illness while still in college. The policy does not require death or total disability: any disability will suffice if it prevents professional play for up to three seasons after the end of the athlete's college eligibility.

The maximum coverages (and maximum premiums) per player are $2.7 million ($24,750) for basketball, $1.8 million ($25,000) for football, and $900,000 ($12,000) for baseball. To help players pay these premiums, the NCAA has arranged a loan program with a Missouri bank. The loans can be repaid either when the athlete signs a professional contract or when the athlete is injured and collects the insurance. Eligibility for this policy is limited to athletes projected by the NCAA and its underwriter as potential first round picks in the basketball or baseball drafts, and first or second round picks in football.

What motivated the NCAA to provide this kind of disability coverage? How does it fit with the NCAA's objective of maintaining a clear demarcation between college and professional sports?

2. PROFESSIONAL ATHLETES[o]

While hockey has contributed the vast majority of sports cases to the criminal courts, football has been the prime sports contributor to workers' compensation claims. An interesting case surfaced in 1991 when

---

[n]. See National Sports Underwriters, Ltd., *NCAA Exceptional Student–Athlete Disability Insurance Program* (Overland Park, Kan.: NCAA, 1991).

[o]. See Herz & Baker, *Professional Athletes and Workers' Compensation*, note i above.

Doug Williams, the quarterback for the 1987 Super Bowl champion Washington Redskins, won an estimated $1 million compensation award for a back injury suffered in 1989 while he was working out on a treadmill machine. The Redskins contested the claim on the ground that the injury, which occurred during the off-season in Williams' Louisiana home, did not "arise out of and in the course of employment." The D.C. hearing examiner disagreed, however, because the Redskins had asked Williams to undertake this conditioning program and had helped him obtain the treadmill. The size of the examiner's award was due to the fact that Williams, now a high school athletic director and coach, would receive the statutory maximum of $513 per week for this permanent disability for as long as his earnings in his new job did not exceed the $1.1 million salary level of his 1989 Redskins contract. Williams eventually settled the case in return for a substantial lump sum payment by the Redskins, and he has now gone back to his *alma mater* Grambling to try to fill the coaching shoes of Eddie Robinson, whose teams had won the most games of any college coach in this sport.

Football produces so many workers' compensation cases because the players absorb continuous bodily pounding in games and scrimmages, which inflicts permanent physical impairments on a large percentage of the participants. The following decision illustrates a club trying to use this very feature of football life to argue that a former player's condition was not due to an "accident" within the meaning of the legislation.

PALMER v. KANSAS CITY CHIEFS

Court of Appeals of Missouri, Western District, 1981.
621 S.W.2d 350.

SHANGLER, JUDGE.

The employer Kansas City Chiefs Football Club appeals from a judgment which affirms the award of compensation by the Industrial Commission to claimant Palmer. The claimant, an offensive guard on the employer professional football team, was injured in the execution of a play in the course of a scheduled game. The administrative law judge found against Palmer, but the Industrial Commission on review of the transcript reversed that decision and entered an award for Palmer for injury to the back. The award of the Industrial Commission rests on the determination that the injury was from an abnormal strain in the course of the employment duty, and so the result of accident within the sense of § 287.020.2.

The normal function of an offensive guard according to Palmer is to block on runs and pass plays. The injury resulted during the execution of a run. The play called was a left trap. The assignment of the offensive guard in such a play is to drive the oncoming defensive tackle—in this instance, one Larry Hand—out of position so as to create a hole for the ballcarrier. The offensive guard executes the play by an opening step and then a position behind the center to apply a block to the defensive tackle as he comes through. The success of the maneuver depends upon the ability of the offensive guard to remain lower than the defensive player. The team had run that play with apparent success several times during the game, but on this occasion the defensive player diagnosed the play as it developed and stunted its effect. In the course of that defensive tactic, the claimant Palmer was injured. The claimant described that sequence:

> Larry [Hand] saw the play coming, stepped down inside ... to close the play, which is a defensive procedure to keep the offensive lineman from moving him out.... "It was a situation where he got *considerably lower than I did*, and as I said, closed down the gap, and *before I had the opportunity to get low enough again to block him*, I was right on top of him, and he came up through me, and he *was underneath my pads. I just was actually off balance and had not had the opportunity to make the play work right for me*, and he drove up through me, you know, stopping me completely, and created, I felt a numbing sensation all through my upper body which would *attribute to the position I was in and him coming up through my body underneath my pads.*"

* * *

The claimant disclosed on cross-examination that professional play was the culmination of football experience which began in junior high school and extended through the university. He acknowledged he had become an accomplished professional football blocker, that when the task was done proficiently, he succeeded in the assignment against the defensive player, but sometimes the opponent bested him.

* * *

The award of the Industrial Commission for compensation rests on the determination that the injury was the result of an abnormal strain. The law treats an abnormal strain as an accident and the resultant violence to the physical structure of the body as an injury within § 287.020.[2] The abnormal strain, the unforeseen event (the accident), by this analysis of workers compensation liability, amounts to the performance of the work in an abnormal manner or in a manner not routine. Work done in an awkward or unbalanced posture, albeit in the performance of a normal duty which subjects the worker to an excessive stress and produces an unexpected strain, results in a compensable injury under this principle. The right to compensation, nevertheless, rests on accident, an element of recovery not proved either by the fact of injury or from stresses usually incident to the work performance. The burden remains on the claimant to prove both the accident and injury, the occupational cause and effect, the unexpected event and the resultant trauma.

2. Section 287.020.2: The word "accident" as used in this chapter shall ... be construed to mean an unexpected or unforeseen event happening suddenly and violently, with or without human fault, and producing at the time objective symptoms of an injury.

The appeal presents a question of law: whether the evidence shows an accident within the terms of the compensation law. In that assessment we are bound by the determinations of fact by the Industrial Commission drawn reasonably from the evidence and accord the employee favored with the award their full intendment.

The award of the Industrial Commission rests expressly on the excerpt of the Palmer testimony that the injury resulted when defensive lineman Hand diagnosed the trap and took countermeasure to nullify the play....

The majority of the Industrial Commission applied the abnormal strain analysis to find an accidental injury:

> The Commission finds that in this particular instance the claimant's injury was caused by his unusual and abnormal position due to being thrown off balance, rather than the result of the actual play or assignment he was attempting to complete. As the employee testified, this instance was different and distinct from all others he had made before because he "just was actually off balance and had not the opportunity to make the play work right for me."

To invoke the abnormal strain doctrine the claimant must show that the usual occupation was done in an unusual manner or that the work was not the usual occupational task or that some other unexpected source of strain produced the injury. Thus, the critical component of the finding of fact on which the Industrial Commission rests award is: "As the employee testified, this instance was different and distinct from all others he had made before because he 'just was actually off balance and had not the opportunity to make the play work right for me.'"

* * *

The testimony by claimant Palmer stated, iterated and then reiterated was that the trap block assignment on the event of injury was "a block similar to the blocks that [he had] done many times against defensive people," that a block was "a normal assignment that was made in practice, after practice, after practice, after practice, and game, after game, after game, after game," that the block "was something which [he] had done on many occasions in [his] professional as well as [his] college career." These variants [among the others] on that theme of testimony, all straightforward and uncontradicted, simply do not allow the inference of fact found by the Industrial Commission majority as a predicate for liability that "this instance was different and distinct from all others he had made before." An inference inconsistent with the facts from which it is drawn fails as probative evidence.

The Industrial Commission majority also found as fact that the injury of the claimant was caused by a loss of balance in the execution of the block assignment—the other corollary of accident by abnormal strain....

The claimant acknowledged that an assignment to block was, in each instance, a test of proficiency between the offensive lineman and the defensive lineman which Palmer would sometimes win and sometimes lose. In the course of the schedule, Palmer came up against "equally proficient, tough, defensive men." The technique he employed varied "according to the type and quality and caliber" of the opponent. When he performed the assignment with skill, he "[blew] that defensive man out of the way." In a trap block, "the object of the offensive guard is to get underneath the defensive lineman's pads and drive him out of the hole." The critical tactic on the trap play in question was "to stay lower than him [defensive lineman Hand], but the opponent sensed the trap, got underneath the pads of the claimant, "drove up through [him]," and Palmer felt an injury. Palmer acknowledged repeatedly that he had executed that assignment many times, only this was one of the occasions the defensive man bested him—"got to [Palmer] before [Palmer] could get to him." The only distinction between this occasion and the others, he acknowledged, was the injury Palmer "just had a bad result."

The record as a whole conclusively shows, therefore, that the function of a professional football lineman in a trap play is to maneuver the other player, to exploit his vulnerable posture. The lineman who establishes the lower stance succeeds. The unsuccessful lineman Palmer in this instance can be jostled off balance. The method and purpose of that perfected skill are to find the opponent in an unexpected posture. The most accomplished among them, as Palmer concedes, will prevail only some of the times. The off balance position the claimant describes [and the Industrial Commission majority adopt as a premise for liability], therefore, was as usual an incident of the block assignment as not. This instance of play execution was no different than the many others, except for a bad result—this time, Palmer was injured. The *off balance* posture, therefore, was not an unexpected occupational event, but rather as customary as not. Whatever strain resulted was an expected incident of the usual work task done in the usual way....

The original decision entered by the hearing judicial officer [and overruled by the Industrial Commission majority] denied the claim on the separate ground that injury was a normal incident of a professional football game. That is a fact acknowledged by claimant Palmer. That is also a fact of judicial notice. Despite the advances in the design of protective equipment under the tutelage of sports medicine, football remains a dangerous pastime fraught with expectation of injury. The compensation law protects against injury the result of accident, that is: trauma from an *unexpected or unforeseen* event in the usual course of occupation, § 287.020.2. That enactment simply does not contemplate that the deliberate collision between human bodies constitutes an accident or that injury in the usual course of such an occupation is caused by an unexpected event.

* * *

Compensation denied.

Questions for Discussion

1. Is this decision (as well as *Rowe v. Baltimore Colts*, 53 Md.App. 526, 454 A.2d 872 (1983)) an unwarranted effort by the court to introduce into workers' compensation, supposedly an accessible source of guaranteed benefits for occupational injuries, the same kinds of consensual limitations we saw earlier in tort cases such as *Hackbart*? Would Judge Shangler's reasoning exclude payment of compensation benefits to construction laborers with lower back problems or jackhammer operators with wrist and arm conditions? On the other hand, would extension to sports of the "cumulative trauma" basis for workers' compensation entitlement (see *Sielicki v. New York Yankees*, 388 So.2d 25 (Fla.Dist.Ct.App.1980)) mean that virtually every football player could collect benefits on retirement from the sport?

Most reported judicial decisions regarding professional athletes and workers' compensation have actually involved the athletes' efforts, resisted by their clubs, to be *excluded* from coverage. The reason is that while workers' compensation benefits are guaranteed, they are also modest—because the benefits are just a portion of earnings of ordinary workers. At the same time as it mandates these specified benefits, the legislation ordains that this program will be the *exclusive* remedy for occupational injuries, at least to the extent of taking away the employee's right to sue the employer (or fellow employees). Although some states (e.g., Massachusetts) specifically exclude certain categories of athletes, there is no blanket exclusion of professional athletes. As the court put it in *Bayless v. Philadelphia Phillies*, 472 F.Supp. 625 (E.D.Pa. 1979):

> Finally, plaintiff argues that the Workmen's Compensation Act was not intended to apply to "high priced athletes." But the Act makes no such distinction. It applies to all employees regardless of their earnings. If professional athletes were excluded from coverage, then hundreds and possibly thousands of low as well as high priced athletes on Major and Minor League Teams would be deprived of the humanitarian benefits and protection the Act affords. My research has failed to disclose any cases excluding professional sports or players from Workmen's Compensation coverage. "A professional baseball league is a 'business operated for gain or profit' within the meaning of a compensation act, so as to entitle one employed as a player on one of the constituent clubs to compensation for injuries sustained in the course of employment."

472 F.Supp. at 631. However, a number of doctrines have evolved to limit the scope of workers' compensation exclusivity and to permit certain kinds of tort claims to proceed. The following case is illustrative.

GAMBRELL v. KANSAS CITY CHIEFS
Court of Appeals of Missouri, Kansas City District, 1978.
562 S.W.2d 163.

WASSERSTROM, JUDGE.

[William Gambrell was a 1974 draft pick of the Kansas City Chiefs. When he reported to training camp, he was examined by team doctors and found fit to play. However, in an early exhibition game against the Rams, Gambrell suffered a permanently disabling injury to his back and neck. He filed for workers' compensation benefits and was awarded $5,250, which the Chiefs paid. Shortly thereafter, Gambrell filed a multi-million dollar lawsuit, charging fraud and deceit by the Chiefs and the team doctors. He alleged that the doctors knew or should have known of a pre-existing physical disability, but that they deliberately concealed the disability from Gambrell to induce him to play for the Chiefs. This decision dealt with the Chiefs' motion for summary dismissal on the ground that this was an accidental injury covered by workers' compensation.]

* * *

An appropriate starting point for a discussion of plaintiff's first and major proposition is the underlying philosophy of Workmen's Compensation legislation. This legislation rests on the foundation concept of the social desirability of giving employees a sure and speedy means of compensation for injuries suffered in the course of employment without the necessity of proving fault on the part of the employer. By way of exchange consideration to the employer, these Acts provide compensation in only a relatively modest amount and protect the employer by making that compensation exclusive of all other remedies....

This exclusivity, however, is qualified by a rule accepted in most jurisdictions that the Act bars common law suits for only those damages covered by the Act and for which compensation is made available under its provisions. This rule is followed in Missouri. Thus, under this rule the employee is still free despite the Act to bring suit at common law for wrongs not comprehended within the Workmen's Compensation Act, such as false imprisonment and defamation.

Most of the cases relied upon by plaintiff fall in this category. Thus, *Skelton v. W. T. Grant Company*, 331 F.2d 593 (5th Cir.1964) was an action for false arrest where the employee claimed damages for embarrassment and humiliation. *Braman v. Walthall*, 215 Ark.582, 225 S.W.2d 342 (1949), was a suit for slander in which the employee alleged damages for mental anguish, humiliation and damage to reputation. In each of those cases cited by plaintiff, and others like them, the damages for which the employee sought recovery were other than (or at least only to a very slight extent) physical injuries to the body of the type intended to be compensated by the pattern of the Workmen's Compensation Act.

The application of the rule just mentioned becomes much more difficult in a case by an employee for fraud and deceit where the plaintiff employee alleges that some fraud on the part of the employer interrelated with a bodily injury suffered by the employee in the course of his employment. Larson, a leading authority on the subject of Workmen's Compensation, discusses this problem at Section 68.32, p. 13–22, of his work where he cites and discusses decisions on this question from many jurisdictions and summarizes as follows: "The cases involving allegations of deceit, fraud, and false representation can best be sorted out by distinguishing those in which the deceit precedes and helps produce the injury, and those in which the deceit follows the injury and produces a second injury or loss." Representative of the latter class of cases, which are not precluded by the Workmen's Compensation Act, is *Ramey v. General Petroleum Corporation*, 343 P.2d 787 (Cal.App.1959), a case cited and relied upon by plaintiff in this case. In *Ramey*, the plaintiff employee was caused by misrepresentations to wait beyond the period of limitations before bringing suit against a third party defendant, and he sued both his employer and the third party for conspiracy to defraud him. The employer's defense of exclusivity of the Workmen's Compensation Act was held not effective in its favor "under the peculiar circumstances alleged." As pointed out by Larson, the court in *Ramey* "sharply distinguished between the two injuries involved; first, the personal and physical injury compensated by the act; and second, the fraud injury destroying a valuable right of action against the third party by causing it to lapse because of the running of the statute of limitations." Larson explains that cases falling within this group are not precluded by the Workmen's Compensation Act because "the alleged deceit has acted, not upon plaintiff's physical condition, but upon his legal rights under the compensation act."

The case at bar does not fall within the category just discussed but rather within Larson's first category "in which the deceit precedes and helps produce the injury." As to this category, which represents the situation with which we are dealing here, Larson states at page 13–22: "In the first category, a tort action has usually been found barred, since the deceit, so to speak, merges into the injury for which a compensation remedy is provided." Larson's conclusion is persuasive and is supported by his analysis of the cases on the subject. A repetition of that full analysis in this opinion would be redundant.

The conclusion that plaintiff's present common law action is precluded by the Workmen's Compensation Act remains valid despite the fact that plaintiff in Counts II and IV prays for punitive damages. True enough, the Act makes no provision for punitive damages, but that omission was intentional and does not prevent the compensation remedy from being exclusive. This point is well treated in *Roof v. Velsicol Chemical Corporation*, 380 F.Supp. 1373, 1374 (D.C.Ohio 1974) where the court held:

> The Ohio courts have apparently recognized no exception for actions demanding punitive damages only. Nor would such an exception be

consistent with Ohio Workmen's Compensation Act. This Act provides statutory rights to relatively speedy and moderate reimbursement to workmen for injury sustained in work related activities. These rights were substituted for all previously available remedies, on the theory that partial reimbursement is more socially desirable than the uncertainty of litigation for full compensation in such cases. To allow both compensation under the Workmen's Compensation Act and an action for punitive damages would clearly frustrate Ohio's policy of partial reimbursement.

* * *

Nor does plaintiff's allegation of conspiracy require any different result. No matter how his cause of action be framed, his claim ultimately reduces to one for bodily injuries for which compensation can be and actually has been had by plaintiff under the Workmen's Compensation Act.

Summary dismissal granted.

An Illinois appellate court issued a significant decision, *Albrecht v. The Industrial Commission*, 271 Ill.App.3d 756, 648 N.E.2d 923 (1995), about the application to professional athletes of the "wage loss" version of workers compensation benefits for permanently disabled employees. Ted Albrecht, an offensive lineman, was the first round draft pick of the Chicago Bears in 1977, and he started every game for the Bears during the next five seasons. Unfortunately, Albrecht suffered a permanent back injury in 1982 which forced him to retire from football at the end of that year. Beginning in 1983, he started a travel service business and performed as a sportscaster, earning around $80,000 a year from 1983 to 1985 (though only $36,000 in 1986), considerably less than the $130,000 salary Albrecht had made with the Bears in 1982.

Albrecht filed for "wage loss" benefits under the provision in the Illinois Workers Compensation Act that entitled someone who had been "partially incapacitated from pursuing his usual and customary line of employment ... [to] receive compensation for the duration of his disability ... equal to two-thirds of the difference between the amount he would be able to earn in the full performance of his duties in the occupation in which he was engaged at the time of the accident and the average amount he is earning ... in some suitable employment after the accident." However, the state Industrial Commission accepted the argument of the Bears that this statutory provision could not be applied in professional football, because careers there were too contingent and too speculative to permit the judgment that it was an injury that "incapacitated [a player] from pursuing his usual and customary line of employment." The Court found this administrative ruling to be invalid as a matter of law. While football players did not have a guarantee of an ongoing position on a team's roster, the same is true of most at-will employment. In the case of a starting offensive lineman like Albrecht, there was sufficient likelihood of continued play for the future that one could and should find that it was the injury which ended his career well short of the ten-year average duration for someone in his position.

The Court then found that the base for calculating the wage differential from 1983 onward should be Albrecht's $130,000 salary in 1982, rather than the higher average salaries NFL linemen were gaining after that year (to a considerable extent because by then USFL teams were competing for their services). An intriguing omission from the Court's opinion is any intimation that these wage loss benefits would cease in 1988, for example, ten years after Albrecht's NFL career had begun.

Albrecht and other such cases have sparked concern among football owners about application of the standard workers' compensation benefit structure to football players with high salaries and short careers. The NFL has pressed some state legislatures to revise their laws and place special limits on the financial benefits payable to players with permanent physical disabilities. (In 1997, for example, the league was trying to get California to exclude from workers compensation coverage any athletes who made more than $200,000 a season, a rule that would preclude the claim filed that year by Joe Montana for a disabling condition generated by his career with the San Francisco 49ers and Kansas City Chiefs.) Should states be receptive to this NFL argument? Should they tell the league that if it wants relief from the normal operation of workers compensation, it must accept exemption of the game from any feature of these laws. Would that step be in the best interests of either owners or players?

Owners and players in professional sports do have the ability to address the problem of how best to compensate injured athletes through collective bargaining. The law of torts and workers' compensation serves as the base point for such privately-negotiated disability benefits, just as Social Security and Medicare do for negotiated retirement protection. The NFL has long had such a program, titled the Bert Bell NFL Retirement Plan. Besides pension benefits for players who reach a defined retirement age, the Bell Plan also guarantees a modest flow of income for players who become permanently and totally disabled (not just from football). Disputes can and do arise in the operation and administration of the Plan, which must be resolved in accordance with the federal Employee Retirement and Income Security Act (ERISA). The following case shows the Eighth Circuit grappling with an issue of some significance to football players.

BRUMM v. BERT BELL NFL RETIREMENT PLAN

United States Court of Appeals, Eighth Circuit, 1993.
995 F.2d 1433.

ARNOLD, CIRCUIT JUDGE.

[Donald Brumm played in the NFL from 1963 to 1972. Like most professional football players, Brumm sustained a number of injuries to his back and knees during his decade-long career. Following his retirement from football, Brumm worked as a truck driver. In 1977 Brumm was involved in a highway accident from which he suffered a back injury. At the time, the treating physician noted that Brumm had a pre-existing back condition called traumatic spondylolisthesis—forward displacement of one vertebra over another—which stemmed from his football experience. Several years later Brumm became unable to work at all because of his constant back pain, and he was awarded Social Security disability benefits.

Brumm applied for additional benefits under the Bell Plan. The Plan made two kinds of benefits available to former players who were "totally and permanently disabled." Level 1 Benefits of $4,000 a month were paid if the disability was due to "a football injury incurred while an Active Player." Level 2 benefits were paid if the total disability "resulted from other than a football injury." After a period of medical investigation and administrative debate, the Bell Plan Board decided that Brumm's disability was at least partly attributable to his football career. However, the Board had just received a decision rendered by the arbitrator under the Plan (and the NFL collective agreement), Sam Kagel. In a case involving several other former NFL players, Kagel ruled that Level 1 benefits were payable only to a player who "incurred his disability from one identifiable football injury," and he became totally and permanently disabled "within a reasonable time after leaving football." All other totally and permanently disabled players received only Level 2 benefits.

Brumm filed suit challenging this ruling. After a district judge granted the Bell Plan's motion for summary dismissal, Brumm appealed. Under ERISA jurisprudence, a plan's denial of benefits was subject to *de novo* review in court unless the terms of the plan explicitly gave its administrative board discretionary authority. See *Firestone Tire & Rubber Co. v. Bruch*, 489 U.S. 101, 115 (1989). Because the Bell Board had been explicitly granted such authority under the NFL Plan, its decisions could be reversed in court only if they were "arbitrary and capricious." See *Bidwill v. Garvey*, 943 F.2d 498, 505 (4th Cir.1991). With that backdrop, the Court addressed the issues presented by the *Brumm* case.]

* * *

The § 5.1 language at issue here has not changed since 1979. The two-tier system was established in 1977 after three years of collective bargaining on the issue. It is not surprising that the players and the owners disagree as to the intended meaning of the key language differentiating Level 1 from Level 2, because, in the negotiations leading up to adoption of the relevant language, each side's proposals were repeatedly rejected by the other. The players proposed a two-tier system that was truly "football" versus "non-football", just as Brumm proposes the scheme should be interpreted: Level 1 benefits would be awarded for disability related to football, and Level 2 benefits would be awarded for disability resultant from any non-football incident or illness, i.e., if a "player had a heart attack or was hit by a car." The owners, on the other hand, proposed that the higher level of benefits should be awarded only if the injury caused the player to be totally and permanently disabled at the time of the injury. Even given the historical context in which the two-tier system evolved and was adopted, it is impossible in light of conflicting accounts to say with any certainty precisely what the parties finally agreed to as the appropriate distinction between Level 1 and Level 2 benefits. (It is as if, given their inability reach a consensus on the proper differentiation between the two levels of benefits, the parties purposefully adopted this ambiguous language, for which each side could claim victory and then hope for the best when the Board was construing it in a given case.) In January, 1979, the Board adopted a resolution that would provide for an award of the higher level of benefits "only in favor of Players who suffer football related injury as distinguished from a non-football injury or illness." This resolution seems to us to be closer to the players' position than that of the owners because it appears to endorse a "football" versus "non-football" basis for differentiation between the benefit levels.

Applying *Finley v. Special Agents Mut. Benefit Ass'n*, 957 F.2d 617, 621 (8th Cir.1992), we examine first the goals of the Plan. While the district court held that the Board's construction of § 5.1 was consistent with the Plan's goal to "provide disability benefits for former football players", the opinion offers no indication as to how the court divined this goal, one which, whether actually a goal or not, provides no real insight into the proper interpretation of § 5.1. The district court went on to discuss the three types of benefits provided by the Plan and observed that if § 5.1 were given Brumm's proposed construction, "Level 2 T & P benefits [would be] almost unnecessary" because "almost every claimant would qualify for Level 1 T & P benefits." The district court considered reasonable the Board's differentiation "between those whose disability can be traced to a single injury and those whose disability is the result of a football career's overall impact on the body, making the body more susceptible to injury later in life."

We are not convinced by this reasoning. First, we do not believe that Brumm's proposed construction would render Level 2 benefits obsolete. Such benefits would still be awarded to former football players who became disabled as a result of any of a great variety of non-football illnesses or incidents. Second, we simply disagree with the pronouncement of reasonableness of the differentiation between a single football injury and one resulting from a football career's overall impact on the body when the history of negotiation over 5.1, while admittedly inconclusive, tends to indicate a football versus non-football distinction instead. It is certainly more reasonable to differentiate between football injuries and non-football injuries, as the language of § 5.1 appears, at first glance, to do.

If the Plan's goal is to take care of the players as part of their compensation for investing themselves in the sport, players who suffer a series of football injuries resulting in disability are as entitled to consideration as those suffering a single disabling injury. Besides, the Board's construction of the benefits scheme seems inconsistent with Plan goals to the extent that we assume the Plan sought to meet the reasonable expectations of Plan participants familiar with the type and prevalence of cumulative injuries incurred by those in their profession, as well as the reasonable expectations of those reading a plan whose benefits scheme appears simply to differentiate between football and non-football disability. The considerable difference between the dollar value of benefits paid to Level 1 recipients ($4,000/month) and Level 2 recipients ($750/month) also undermines the district court's support of the Board's scheme. For a player who suffers a single football injury to receive more than five times the amount of a player who suffers a cumulative football injury strikes us as more than a little odd. If, on the other hand, a true football versus non-football distinction is represented by the two-tier scheme, those standing to receive only Level 2 benefits would receive some support from their participation in the Plan, but considerably less than if the disability was a result of their contribution to the sport. We are unconvinced that the Board's interpretation of § 5.1 is consistent with Plan goals.

Under *Finley* we next consider whether the Board's interpretation renders any Plan language redundant or internally inconsistent. We cannot say that it does.

Thirdly, we ask whether the Plan's interpretation meets the substantive and procedural requirements of ERISA. We conclude that the Plan failed to meet the ERISA requirement that the Summary Plan Description be sufficiently accurate and comprehensive. The ERISA statutory scheme mandates that a plan description "shall be sufficiently accurate and comprehensive to reasonably apprise such participants and beneficiaries of their rights and obligations under the plan." 29 U.S.C. § 1022(a)(1). Subsection 6 of that section further provides that the eligibility requirements for participation and benefits shall be included in any summary plan description of the full plan. The description must not mislead, misinform, or fail to inform participants and beneficiaries of the requirements of the full plan. See *Genter v. Acme Scale & Supply Co.*, 776 F.2d 1180, 1185 (3d Cir.1985). The district court found that the summary description of the NFL Plan complied with these standards. We disagree.

Because the summary plan description, as well as the Plan itself, is silent as to the meaning of "a football injury incurred while an Active

Player," it fails to inform participants that this means a single, identifiable injury. As noted above, at first blush the § 5.1 language, quoted in the summary plan description, appears to draw a football versus non-football distinction. A participant—particularly one without knowledge of the history of conflict over this issue—will surely assume that this is the basis of differentiation between Level 1 and Level 2 benefits. It is hard to imagine a participant who, after reading the language in both the Plan and the summary plan description, would assume that a single, identifiable football injury was necessary in order to qualify for the higher level of benefits. Language stating that a disability resulting from more than one football injury makes a participant ineligible for the highest level of benefits would have been adequate to apprise participants of this limitation and should have been included in the summary. The case for inclusion of such an explicit statement is strengthened when one considers that the single-injury limitation, now sanctioned by the Kagel arbitration, will likely be commonly invoked to deny benefits to career football players who suffer numerous and cumulative disabling injuries over the course of their careers. The summary plan description for the Bert Bell NFL Retirement Plan does not comply with ERISA.

The fourth *Finley* consideration is whether the Board has, in the past, interpreted the section at issue consistently with the construction under consideration. It appears that § 5.1 has not always been interpreted to require a single, identifiable football injury. Indeed, because the Board trustees' deadlock regarding the proper interpretation of § 5.1 led to the Kagel arbitration, we know that this criterion was not imposed consistently prior to that time. While disability claims are difficult to compare, we note that some Plan participants who have been granted Level 1 football benefits, including William Wayne Frazier, Charles Warner, and Otis Armstrong, suffered more than one football injury. That is, each suffered what is considered to be a sort of primary injury, subsequently returned to football, and eventually was re-injured and had to leave the sport. Thus, while each can identify a primary injury, each cannot truly say that he suffered a single disabling injury. These inconsistencies undermine the purported reasonableness of the Board's current construction that requires a single, identifiable football injury.

Most compelling, perhaps, in this case is our analysis under the final *Finley* consideration: Whether the Plan interpretation is contrary to the Plan's clear language. We conclude that the interpretation applied in Brumm's case, if not flatly contrary to the language of the Plan, represents at the least a startling construction. To require that disability result from a single, identifiable football injury when the relevant Plan language speaks of "a football injury incurred while an Active player" is to place undue and inappropriate emphasis on the word "a". "Injury" can mean either an "act or a result involving an impairment or destruction of ... health" Webster's Third New International Dictionary (1986). Therefore, the key phrase from § 5.1, "a football injury", could refer to either a single injury (act) or a cumulative one (result). The apparent dichotomy set up by § 5.1—between "results from a football injury" and "results from other than a football injury"—is consistent with the latter meaning. In sum, we believe that the Board's proposed construction of the relevant language impermissibly crossed the line between interpretation and amendment.

Having considered it in light of the criteria set out in *Finley*, we conclude that the Board's construction of § 5.1 is unreasonable. We therefore find that the Board arbitrarily and capriciously denied Brumm Level 1 benefits.

Reversed and remanded.

In the 1992–93 NFL negotiations that we saw settle the Chapter 3 *McNeil* suit with a combination of veteran free agency plus a salary cap, the parties agreed to spend a significant amount of the players' share of league revenues on improved retirement and disability benefits—now reaching as high as $13,000 a month (or $156,000 a year) for players like the New England Patriots' wide receiver, Darryl Stingley, who was paralyzed for life when hit by the Raiders' Jack Tatum in a 1977 game. The potential implications of the *Brumm* decision for player access to this more generous Bell Fund were graphically displayed in a federal district court ruling in *Sween v. Bert Bell NFL Player Retirement Plan*, 961 F.Supp. 1381 (S.D.Cal.1997).

Walter Sweeney was a star offensive guard with the San Diego Chargers in the 1960s and early 1970s—making the Pro Bowl in nine out of the 11 years he spent with that team. To enhance the play of Sweeney (and other Chargers), the team physicians and trainers had regularly prescribed use of amphetamines, barbiturates, and anabolic steroids. By the time his career ended, though, Sweeney had become addicted to a combination of these performance-enhancing drugs along with alcohol, marijuana, and cocaine. After he left football, this addiction left Sweeney unable to work consistently and support himself. Eventually Sweeney applied for disability benefits from the Bell Fund and was awarded a $1,800 a month pension for non-football related disability (as well as treatment for his drug addiction). Sweeney appealed and won a finding from the judge that his disability was in part attributable to his football career; in particular to the Chargers succumbing to "incredible pressure to win" by prescribing performance-enhancing drugs that "caught a player [Sweeney] who may be unusually susceptible to chemical dependency." Not only was Sweeney awarded full level 1 disability benefits for the future, but also payment of benefits (and interest) for the bulk of the years since he retired in 1976—more than $2 million.

The NFL Players Association, which is ultimately responsible for this Fund (whose League payroll costs must be covered by the salary cap), immediately announced it would appeal this *Sweeney* decision. One of the reasons for the Association's concern is that the Raiders' Jack Tatum, the person whose hit permanently paralyzed Darryl Stingley in

1977, has himself now applied for full disability benefits, citing the disabling mental anguish that his brutal tackle of Stingley has had on Tatum's life.

D. BACK TO TORTS

1. MEDICAL MALPRACTICE

A number of jurisdictions have recently permitted tort suits against employers for intentional infliction of physical injury, including deliberate concealment of medical information. In the sports context, a California appeals court upheld the player's tort claim in *Krueger v. San Francisco Forty Niners,* 189 Cal.App.3d 823, 234 Cal.Rptr. 579 (1987). The 49ers' team doctor had consistently refrained from telling Krueger, the team's All–Pro tackle, of the serious long-term risks Krueger faced from continuing to play despite a series of knee injuries and operations. The court stated that deliberate failure by a team to disclose foreseeable risks to injured players, at least if done to induce them to keep playing, amounted to the tort of fraudulent concealment and was actionable despite the exclusivity provision in the workers' compensation statute. A year later Krueger settled the litigation for more than $1 million from the 49ers.

Another potential escape valve from workers' compensation exclusivity is the "dual capacity" doctrine. This doctrine was first articulated in *Duprey v. Shane,* 39 Cal.2d 781, 249 P.2d 8 (1952), in which medical malpractice was alleged against the plaintiff's employer. In permitting the tort suit, the California Supreme Court reasoned that the workers' compensation statute barred employee suits against the employer only in its capacity as employer; the statute would not preclude suits against the employer in a different capacity—as provider of medical services. This doctrine has subsequently been extended to several other contexts (for example, the employer as product manufacturer, see *Bell v. Industrial Vangas, Inc.,* 30 Cal.3d 268, 179 Cal.Rptr. 30, 637 P.2d 266 (1981)), and has been adopted in other states. However, in its parent jurisdiction, California, the dual capacity doctrine was repealed by legislation in 1982. For that reason, in *Hendy v. Losse,* 54 Cal.3d 723, 1 Cal.Rptr.2d 543, 819 P.2d 1 (1991), the California Supreme Court held that Hendy—who was injured in 1976 while playing for the San Diego Chargers and later reinjured and permanently disabled when the Chargers' team physician, Dr. Losse, sent him back to play too early—could not maintain a tort action against the Chargers or Dr. Losse.

Because the employer bears workers' compensation liability and pays for this insurance coverage, the employer (and its employees, such as Dr. Losse) gets the benefit of statutory protection from tort suits. In many athletic situations, however, the team doctor is an "independent contractor" and thus is potentially exposed to suit, such as in the following case brought by two Chicago Bears players.

BRYANT v. FOX & CHICAGO BEARS
Court of Appeals of Illinois, First District, 1987.
162 Ill.App.3d 46, 113 Ill.Dec. 790, 515 N.E.2d 775.

JIGNATI, JUSTICE.

* * *

The documents before the trial court established the following facts concerning the relationship between the Bears and Dr. Fox. Dr. Fox was retained by the Bears in 1947 to render medical care to injured Bears' players. He was required to treat all injured players upon request, both during the regular season and the off season, and to report the treatment to the Bears' management. All anticipated treatment and surgery were discussed with the player and the Bears, either of whom could veto the proposed action. Dr. Fox did not bill the individual players for treatment. The record further shows that the agreement between the Bears and Dr. Fox required him to perform preseason physicals, which took place at Illinois Masonic Hospital. He was to attend all regular season games but could send a substitute subject to the Bears' approval. Dr. Fox was not obligated to attend preseason games or practices, but could do so at his convenience.

With respect to compensation and benefits, the record shows that Dr. Fox was paid an annual retainer of $12,000 which covered the preseason physicals and all treatment other than surgery. If surgery was required, Dr. Fox received fees for each surgery based upon the nature of the injury, the time involved and the complexity of the procedure. According to his discovery deposition, Dr. Fox had a very busy practice aside from the Bears and the compensation paid to him by the Bears represented "very much less" than 10% of his income. Unlike employees of the Bears, Dr. Fox was not offered group medical insurance, life insurance or paid vacations, and was not invited to participate in the pension and profit-sharing plan. He was not provided with W-2 forms and the Bears never made Social Security deductions from his compensation. Dr. Fox stated that he considered himself to be an employee of Lakeview Orthopedic Associates, Ltd., and received W-2 forms from that corporation.

As previously stated, the exclusive-remedy provision bars an employee from bringing a common-law negligence action against a co-employee. It has been recognized that there is no clear line of demarcation between the status of employee and independent contractor. Illinois Appellate Court in *Lister v. Industrial Commission*, 500 N.E.2d 134 (Ill.1986), stated a number of relevant factors in determining such status including the following: "[The] right to control the manner in which work is done; method of payment; right to discharge; skill required in the work to be done; who provides tools, materials, or equipment; whether the workmen's occupation is related to that of the alleged employer; and whether the alleged employer deducted for withholding tax." The single most important factor in determining the parties' relationship is the right to control the manner in which the work is done. An independent contractor has been defined as one who undertakes to produce a given result, without being controlled as to the method by which he attains that result.

* * *

In our view, the facts before the trial court on the Bears' motion to dismiss were insufficient to establish as a matter of law that Dr. Fox was an employee rather than an independent contractor. Although Dr. Fox was to treat injured players upon request, the evidence presented by the plaintiffs shows that the Bears were given little control over Dr. Fox's actions in accomplishing this result. He could send a substitute to regular season games if his attendance was not possible and was not obligated to attend practices or preseason games. Preseason physicals took place at Illinois Masonic Hospital using equipment belonging to the hospital. Although Dr. Fox was paid a relatively small retainer covering routine medical services, he would bill the Bears separately for each surgery he performed. Significantly, the plaintiffs presented evidence showing that the Bears did not withhold Social Security from Dr. Fox's compensation and did not provide him with W-2 forms. Dr. Fox stated that he received W-2 forms from Lakeview Orthopedic Associates, Ltd., and considered himself to be an employee of that corporation. A very small percentage of his practice was devoted to treating Bears' players. Finally, unlike employees of the Bears, Dr. Fox was not provided with benefits such as medical or life insurance, or a pension and profit-sharing plan.

Motion for dismissal denied.

Though the legal focus of the last several cases was on different techniques through which athletes could mount viable tort suits in the face of workers' compensation exclusivity, a common denominator in the actual litigation in *Bryant, Krueger, Buoniconti* and *Gathers* is that a principal target of the suit is the team physician. Several other notable athletes have successfully sued their team doctors for medical malpractice in the treatment (or non-treatment) of their injuries:

1. Dick Butkus, the Chicago Bears All-Pro linebacker, collected a $600,000 settlement for harm caused by cortisone injections into his injured knee.

2. Bill Walton, the Portland Trail Blazers All-Pro center, collected a substantial amount from the team doctor (not from the Blazers) for the use of pain killers that aggravated his injured foot in 1977 and severely limited his subsequent career.[p]

p. See Halberstam, *The Breaks of the Game*, note f above, at 242–262, for a detailed account of the relationship between Walton and Dr. Bob Cook, the Blazers' team physician.

3. Kenny Easley, the Seattle Seahawks' All–Pro safety, sued and collected from both the team doctor and the drug manufacturer after the drug he took for an injured ankle caused severe kidney damage and cut short his career.

4. Mike Robitaille, a defenseman for the Vancouver Canucks, won a substantial court award because the team and its doctor dismissed his complaints about an injury as purely mental, and subsequent play had permanently damaged his spinal cord. See *Robitaille v. Vancouver Hockey Club*, 3 W.W.R. 481 (B.C.C.A.1981).

5. In *Classen v. Izquierdo*, 137 Misc.2d 489, 520 N.Y.S.2d 999 (1987), the court denied summary dismissal (based on assumption of risk) in a suit brought by the widow of a boxer who died in the tenth round of a 1979 boxing match at Madison Square Garden, after the ringside physician (appointed by the State Athletic Commission, not the Garden) examined the fighter at the end of the ninth round and let the match continue.

Why are so many medical malpractice suits brought by athletes against team doctors? Is this merely symptomatic of a broader explosion in malpractice claims? Or do special features of sports aggravate this problem? If the latter, are there any available cures?[q]

2. DEFECTIVE PRODUCTS AND HAZARDOUS FACILITIES

Besides the team physician, an attractive third-party target for a tort suit by an injured player is the manufacturer of a product used in the game. Indeed, much of the "crisis" in products liability litigation and insurance costs generally has been fueled by suits brought by employees entitled to workers' compensation benefits.[r] Such litigation was facilitated by judicial adoption in the 1960s of strict liability for defective products, and by judicial expansion in the 1970s of what is considered a legally "defective" design or warning of product hazards. No sports product has been affected more by such suits than the helmets used in football, hockey, and elsewhere. The following case is illustrative.

BYRNS v. RIDDELL, INC.
Supreme Court of Arizona, 1976.
113 Ariz. 264, 550 P.2d 1065.

[After being injured by a blow to the head during a football game, the appellant, Byrns, sued the manufacturer of his football helmet. After

---

[q.] For the general issues posed by medical injuries and medical malpractice, see Paul C. Weiler, *Medical Malpractice on Trial* (Cambridge, Mass: Harvard University Press, 1991). For the distinctive issues posed by medical treatment of athletes and their injuries, see Jones, *College Athletes*, note m, above; Joseph H. King, Jr., *The Duty and Standard of Care for Team Physicians*, 18 Houston L. Rev. 657 (1981); Charles V. Russell, *Legal and Ethical Conflicts Arising from the Team Physician's Dual Obligations to the Athlete and Management*, 10 Seton Hall Legis. J. 299 (1987); and Matthew J. Mitten, *Team Physicians and Competitive Athletes: Allocating Legal Responsibility for Athletic Injuries*, 55 U. Pittsburgh L. Rev. 129 (1993).

[r.] See W. Kip Viscusi, *Reforming Products Liability* 182–86 (Cambridge, Mass: Harvard University Press, 1991); and Paul C. Weiler, *Workers' Compensation and Product Liability: The Interaction of a Tort and a Non–Tort Regime*, 50 Ohio St. L. J. 825 (1989).

extended testimony from witnesses about the nature of the impact and the design of the helmet, the defendant was granted a directed verdict, and Byrns appealed.]

HAYS, JUSTICE.

* * *

The law of strict liability in tort has followed a steady course of development since its early foundations in the case of *Greenman v. Yuba Power Products, Inc.*, 377 P.2d 897 (1963). This court, in its decision in *O.S. Stapley Co. v. Miller*, 447 P.2d 248 (1968), adopted the theory of strict liability set forth in *Restatement (Second) of Torts* § 402A (1965). In view of the steady growth in this area of the law, coupled with the singularity of the facts in this case, a further review and analysis of the law of strict liability in tort is necessary. It is to this analysis that we first turn our attention.

The California Supreme Court in a recent decision in the case of *Cronin v. J.B.E. Olson Corp.*, 501 P.2d 1153 (1972), rejected the "requirement that a plaintiff also prove that the defect made the product 'unreasonably dangerous' ..." a standard set forth in *Restatement (Second) of Torts* § 402A (1965). In *O.S. Stapley*, supra, we specifically adopted Restatement (Second) of Torts § 402A and its concept of an "unreasonably dangerous" defect, and as such rejected the California approach.

The term "unreasonably dangerous" has been considered by many courts in the jurisdictions that have adopted § 402A. A recent survey of cases which considered the concept of an "unreasonably dangerous" defect states that this concept is especially effective as a means of limiting the strict tort liability doctrine "in cases in which the issue is the nature of the duty of a manufacturer with respect to safe design, or in situations in which injury does not follow as a matter of course from the defect, and in which there are serious questions as to the effect to be given harm producing conduct or misuse on the part of the injured person."

The United States District Court, Eastern District of Pennsylvania, adopted the following test of "unreasonable danger": "whether a reasonable manufacturer would continue to market his product in the same condition as he sold it to the plaintiff With knowledge of the potential dangerous consequences the trial just revealed." The court went on to state: "And in measuring the likelihood of harm one may consider the obviousness of the defect since it is reasonable to assume that the user of an obviously defective product will exercise special care in its operation, and consequently the likelihood of harm diminishes." Comment (i) Restatement (Second) of Torts § 402A further defines the element of an unreasonably dangerous defect from the viewpoint of the consumer in the following language:

The article sold must be dangerous to an extent beyond that which would be contemplated by the ordinary consumer who purchases it, with the ordinary knowledge common to the community as to its characteristics.

* * *

The court in *Dorsey* subscribed to the following factor analysis prepared by Dean Wade to determine if a defect is unreasonably dangerous:

(1) the usefulness and desirability of the product, (2) the availability of other and safer products to meet the same need, (3) the likelihood of injury and its probable seriousness, (4) the obviousness of the danger, (5) common knowledge and normal public expectation of the danger (particularly for established products), (6) the avoidability of injury by care in use of the product (including the effect of instructions or warnings), and (7) the ability to eliminate the danger without seriously impairing the usefulness of the product or making it unduly expensive.

We must add a note of caution at this point. No all-encompassing rule can be stated with respect to the applicability of strict liability in tort to a given set of facts. Each case must be decided on its own merits. The foregoing analysis is offered as an approach to the question of whether a defect is unreasonably dangerous.

* * *

The facts in this case as presented by appellant establish the possibility of a defect in the sling design of the TK–2 suspension system. This defect is established by the testimony of [witnesses] Irving and Rappleayea regarding a series of tests conducted by them and measured by a standard known as the Z90.1 impact test. Rappleayea further established the defect based on his experience in testing the TK–2 while employed by appellee. This evidence is sufficient to raise the likelihood that reasonable men may reach different conclusions on the issue of an unreasonably dangerous defect in the sling design of the TK–2 helmet. The "bottoming out" defect might be of a type that a reasonable consumer would not contemplate.

There is a question of fact as to the place of impact, with a resulting question of causation in terms of the relationship between the impact and the injury. There is also a question as to the possibility of a substantial change in condition caused by the addition of a face mask manufactured and installed by someone other than appellee.

* * *

We hold that appellant established the presence of a defect in the helmet at the time it left the hands of the seller to the extent that reasonable minds could reach different conclusions as to that question of fact. Furthermore, we hold that appellant provided sufficient proof that a defect caused appellant's injury. The issue of causation is one of fact for the jury to decide.

The trial court concluded that the film, as a matter of law, left no reasonable doubt as to the place of impact, thus ruling that the appellant failed to show causation between the impact and the injury. We have carefully reviewed the portion of the moving picture film which contains the "onside" kick and cannot arrive at the same conclusion. The film is at best inconclusive on the question of the point of impact and in fact shows possible contact by two opposing players. We also note that Coach Hakes' testimony was similarly inconclusive in that he merely stated that appellant and an opposing player hit "head-to-head." The jury must be permitted to determine the issue of causation since there is a likelihood that reasonable minds could differ on the interpretation of the game film.

Appeal granted.

Questions for Discussion

1. In *Everett v. Bucky Warren, Inc.*, 376 Mass. 280, 380 N.E.2d 653 (1978), the court listed several factors to be considered in determining whether the design of a hockey helmet was defective: "the gravity of the danger posed by the challenged design, the likelihood that such danger would occur, the mechanical feasibility of a safer alternative design, the cost of an improved design, and the adverse consequences to the product and to the consumer that would result from an alternative design." *Bryns* and *Everett* purport to use the Restatement (Second) of Tort's new mandate for *strict* products liability. How, if at all, does this doctrinal standard differ in practice from traditional negligence analysis? Is the threat of product litigation responsible for the sharp drop in the number of U.S. helmet manufacturers during the 1970s and 1980s?

2. In the summer of 1992, the National Hockey League changed its rules to make it no longer mandatory for players to wear helmets during the game. The NHL's objective was to encourage fan recognition of star players and thereby promote popular identification with the league's product. In Chapter 4 we asked whether the fact that the NHL took this step unilaterally, without first bargaining with the NHLPA, made this change illegal under federal labor law. Here we ask whether there might be a possible tort action if a young player, tempted by the prospect of a lucrative marketing deal, decided to play without a helmet and suffered severe brain damage when struck by a blow to the head. (In a number of jurisdictions, its NHL team is not subject to state or provincial workers' compensation law. But even if the local team is covered, does this statutory bar against suing the player's "employer" preclude a suit against the NHL itself?)

Still another potential third-party target of liability for player injuries is the owner of the facility in which the game was played and whose hazardous condition may have contributed to the injury. The following case involved the Yankees' Elliot Maddox, who was injured on a wet

Shea Stadium surface. The legal issue posed was whether the doctrine of "assumption of risk," which traditionally applied to sports but not to employment, should be a defense to a suit by a professional athlete.

MADDOX v. CITY OF NEW YORK

Supreme Court of New York, Appellate Division, 1985.
108 A.D.2d 42, 487 N.Y.S.2d 354.

PER CURIAM.

* * *

At an examination before trial, plaintiff Elliot Maddox (Maddox) said that after he chased and caught up with the ball in right centerfield and while he was in the process of throwing the ball back into the infield, his "left foot hit I guess it was a wet spot and took off" and his "right foot was stuck in the water, a mud puddle and wouldn't move and therefore, my right knee buckled." Maddox admitted that a game scheduled for the night before the accident had been canceled because of the weather and poor field conditions. He further admitted that earlier in the game in question he had observed the centerfield to be "awfully wet" with "some mud" and had even noticed "some standing water" above the grass line when he "went over after a fly ball once into right center." Maddox also stated that he had previously played on a wet field. Although Maddox claimed to have informed an unidentified grounds crew member of the aforementioned condition, he did not contend that he had requested not to play or to send in a replacement.

* * *

It has long been established in this State that participants in athletic events assume the risk of injury normally associated with the sport. Although, as Special Term noted, these cases essentially deal with amateur sports, we find no reason in the case at bar to depart from the stated rule.

In his examination before trial, Maddox admitted that he knew centerfield and right centerfield to be wet, that he continued to play ball in spite of this awareness and that he sustained injury after falling on a wet spot in right centerfield. Here, where the danger of falling on the wet playing field was obvious, it makes no sense to relieve plaintiffs from the effects of the doctrine of assumption of risk merely because Maddox was a professional, and not an amateur, player. To do so would be to hold a seasoned professional who is handsomely paid for his endeavors to a lower standard of care and place him in a more advantageous position than a less-seasoned amateur who receives no remuneration whatsoever. Simply stated, as long as there are, as here, open stadiums, natural grass fields, and rain, playing on an open wet field is part of the game of baseball, both for an amateur and a professional athlete. As much as one may sympathize with Maddox, the fact is that there is no cogent reason for holding assumption of risk inapplicable at bar and since the action accrued prior to September 1, 1975, as Special Term noted, that doctrine completely bars recovery.[1]

In an effort to avoid being called out at first base, however, Maddox argues that the assumption of risk doctrine is inapplicable at bar since his employer violated a "non-delegable duty with respect to the furnishing of a safe place to work," and in any event, his superiors forced him "to either work under unsafe conditions or abandon his work." We find these arguments unpersuasive.

It is quite true that a defense of assumption of risk (or contributory negligence) is unavailable to an employer who violates his statutory duty to supply an employee with a safe place to work. Nevertheless, to avail himself of a statute's protection, a plaintiff must demonstrate that he is within the class of persons the statute was designed to protect.

The applicable statutory provision at bar, Labor Law § 200, has its genesis in the Labor Law of 1909.... Clearly the purpose of these provisions was to protect a worker engaged in industry, and there is nothing in the subsequent amendments to these provisions or the legislative history that evinces an intent on the part of the Legislature to expand the class of protected individuals to include baseball players. Indeed, the language of present-day § 200 would suggest precisely the opposite.

Initially, it bears noting that Labor Law § 200(1) does not expand coverage to workplaces beyond those enumerated in the predecessor § 20–b, cited above, but simply continues coverage to "[a]ll places to which this chapter applies." Furthermore, language added to subdivision 1 in 1962 ... suggests a continuing legislative concern for manual workers. Finally, the heading of § 200, a factor to be considered when interpreting the meaning of a statute entitled "General duty to protect the health and safety of employees; enforcement," and the statute defines an "[e]mployee" as "a mechanic, workingman or laborer working for another for hire" (Labor Law § 2[5]). Engaged as he was in the "national pastime," Maddox can hardly be characterized as a mechanic, working person or laborer. Accordingly, from all indications, Maddox does not fall within the protected class of individuals, and the remedy, if any is indicated, is for legislative, not judicial action.

Even assuming, arguendo, that Maddox was within the class of protected individuals, he still could not invoke the protection of the statute. Although plaintiffs' complaints (each verified by an attorney) refer to defendants' failure, inter alia, to provide a safe workplace and properly construct, design and maintain the stadium, their motion papers fail to substantiate any fault on the part of Maddox's employer—a requisite to the invocation of § 200—which resulted in the wet condition

---

1. When the Legislature enacted the comparative negligence statute (CPLR 1411), effective September 1, 1975, it abolished the doctrine of assumption of risk and contributory negligence as absolute bars to a plaintiff's recovery. Currently, assumption of risk and contributory negligence are termed "culpable conduct" and, if proven, operate only to proportionately reduce a plaintiff's recovery.

of the playing field. We point out that defendants' motions were motions for summary judgment and it was incumbent upon Maddox to come forward with evidence that the accident resulted from defendants' breach of a duty to provide a workplace that was "so constructed, equipped, arranged, operated and conducted as to provide reasonable and adequate protection to the lives, health and safety of all persons employed therein" and not simply from the elements or other risks normally associated with the sport. This, plaintiffs failed to do.

Plaintiffs' second argument must also fail for lack of proof. It is indeed true, as Special Term noted, that continuation on a job after being directed by a superior to proceed under circumstances recognized as dangerous does not constitute assumption of the risk as a matter of law. Had Maddox been ordered to continue playing ball after informing his superiors of a dangerous condition, the results at bar might well have been different. The fact is, however, that there is not a scintilla of evidence in the record that Maddox was directed by a superior to continue playing after making known the field conditions or that he even requested to be relieved from playing. In fact, he merely contended in papers submitted at nisi prius that he informed an unidentified grounds crew member (or members) of the condition, and that he had previously commented to the team manager "a couple of times . . . if the field was wet." Hence, on these motions for summary judgment, the proof offered by plaintiffs was insufficient to create a genuine issue of fact as to Maddox's assumption of the risk and Special Term erred in denying the motions, incorrectly inferring that Maddox "was acting within the confines of a superior's instructions."

Summary dismissal granted.

Another case, *Heldman v. Uniroyal, Inc.*, 53 Ohio App.2d 21, 371 N.E.2d 557 (1977), framed as a suit about an allegedly defective product rather than a hazardous facility, yielded a similar result. Julie Heldman, while playing Virginia Wade in the Weightman Cup tennis competition between the United States and Great Britain, fell and severely injured her knee on Uniroyal's patented Roll–a–Way court surface. Heldman and other players had noted and complained about blistering and bubbling of the court surface, a problem that had been aggravated by rainfall collected in the seams. The court of appeals reversed a jury verdict in Heldman's favor, apparently on the ground that as a professional athlete she had a greater obligation than the recreational player to learn of hazardous conditions: professionals cannot simply follow the adage that "the show must go on." Is the judicial response to the *Maddox* and *Heldman* suits appropriate? What is the object of tort law in such cases?

Another unsuccessful tort action was launched by Hall–of–Famer Bubba Smith, who sued the Tampa Bay Sports Authority and the NFL after he suffered a career-ending knee injury when he crashed into and became entangled with the sideline downs marker. A jury rejected

Smith's claim of defective equipment and negligent supervision of the markers.

E. DISABILITY AND THE RIGHT TO PLAY

Up to now we have examined the legal remedies available to players who have been hurt. Besides providing compensation after the fact, the law also seeks to provide incentives for the adoption of measures that will avoid injury before the fact. Suppose one measure adopted by a league is to screen out players with conditions that might make the player more susceptible to injury. Can these players obtain legal relief?

Illustrative of the legal dilemma is a case involving Mark Seay, who was another athlete playing for a Los Angeles college at the same time as Hank Gathers. Seay, the star wide receiver for the Long Beach State College football team, was struck by a stray bullet meant for a street gang member. Seay lost a kidney, and the bullet remained lodged near his heart. The school refused to allow Seay to return to the football team because of the risk of aggravating his injury. Seay sued, and on the eve of trial in March 1990, the school relented and allowed him to play football again—but only in return for a signed waiver of liability.[s]

Precisely what source of legal relief might be available to someone such as Seay? One possibility is antitrust law. In the mid-1970s Greg Neeld starred in Canadian Junior A hockey even though he had sight in only one eye. Anticipating Neeld's wish to play professional hockey, the National Hockey League adopted a rule that rendered ineligible "any player with only one eye, or one of whose eyes has a vision of only 3-60ths or under." Neeld sued the NHL under the Sherman Antitrust Act and alleged that this rule amounted to an illegal concerted boycott of his services by the clubs. The Ninth Circuit Court of Appeals summarily dismissed the claim:

> Here, however, the record amply supports the reasonableness of the by-law. We agree with the District Court's conclusion that the primary purpose and direct effect of the League's by-law was not anticompetitive but rather safety.
>
> Neeld argues that if the rule of reason is applied then summary judgment was inappropriate because of alleged material issues of fact. Specifically, he contends the affidavits establish a disputed issue of fact whether a certain "safety mask" (designed especially for Neeld) would adequately protect Neeld from further injury.... Even assuming for purposes of argument that the adequacy of the "safety mask" for Neeld's protection is disputed, summary judgment was still appropriate since that fact alone would not affect the outcome of this case.

---

s. The combination of the *Gathers* and the *Seay* cases inspired the article by Jones, *College Athletes,* note m above. Another insightful analysis of this legal dilemma is Steven K. Derian, *Of Hank Gathers and Mark Seay: Who Decides Which Risks an Athlete Is Allowed to Undertake?*, 5 UCLA J. of Ed. (1991).

The by-law is not motivated by anticompetitiveness and Neeld does not actually contend that it is. Further, any anticompetitive effect is at most *de minimis,* and incidental to the primary purpose of promoting safety, both for Neeld, who lost his eye in a hockey game, and for all players who play with or against him. We take judicial notice that ice hockey is a very rough physical contact sport, and that there is bound to be danger to players who happen to be on Neeld's blind side, no matter how well his mask may protect his one good eye. Also of some importance and legitimate concern to the League and its members is the possibility of being sued for personal injuries to Neeld himself or to others, if Neeld is permitted to play.

Neeld v. NHL, 594 F.2d 1297, 1300 (9th Cir.1979).

The next case illustrates a more precisely-tailored and more promising avenue of legal attack, using federal legislation that bars discrimination against the disabled. Section 504 of the federal Rehabilitation Act of 1973 prohibits anyone that offers a "program or activity receiving federal financial assistance" from "excluding from participation in, denying the benefits of, or subjecting to discrimination under" the program any "otherwise qualified individual with a disability—solely by reason of her or his disability." College sports are governed by the Rehabilitation Act because all colleges receive, directly or indirectly (e.g., via student grants or loans), some federal aid. Professional sports are governed by essentially the same substantive requirements of the Americans With Disabilities Act of 1990 (ADA), which applies to a broad spectrum of private industry.

This branch of antidiscrimination law poses some difficult questions about what is the meaning of disability and what kinds of accommodations one can reasonably expect for them. The statutory definition of "disability" (originally called "handicap") is someone who "has a physical or mental impairment which substantially limits one or more of her or his major life activities." Regulations promulgated under the Rehabilitation Act define major life activities to encompass "functions such as caring for one's self, performing manual tasks, walking, seeing, hearing, speaking, breathing, learning, and working." The regulations issued under the ADA added this interpretive note: " 'Major life activities' are those basic activities that the average person in the general population can perform with little or no difficulty." In newsworthy litigation that took place in the fall of 1996, a federal appeals court finally had to address the question of whether and how these legal standards constrained decisions by athletic authorities to prohibit athletes with certain physical conditions from playing for their teams.

KNAPP v. NORTHWESTERN UNIVERSITY

United States Court of Appeals, Seventh Circuit, 1996.
101 F.3d 473.

EVANS, CIRCUIT JUDGE.

Nicholas Knapp wants to play NCAA basketball for Northwestern University—so badly that he is willing to face an increased risk of death to do so. Knapp is a competent, intelligent adult capable of assessing whether playing intercollegiate basketball is worth the risk to his heart and possible death, and to him the risk is acceptable. Usually, competent, intelligent adults are allowed to make such decisions. This is especially true when, as here, the individual's family approves of the decision and the individual and his parents are willing to sign liability waivers regarding the worst-case scenario should it occur.

Northwestern, however, refuses to allow Knapp to play on or even practice with its men's basketball team. Knapp, currently a sophomore at Northwestern, has the basketball skills to play at the intercollegiate level, but he has never taken the court for his team. Although Northwestern does not restrict him from playing pick-up basketball games, using recreational facilities on campus, or exerting himself physically on his own, the university disqualified Knapp from playing on its intercollegiate basketball team. The issue in this case boils down to whether the school—because of § 504 of the Rehabilitation Act of 1973, as amended, 29 U.S.C. § 794—will be forced to let Knapp don a purple uniform and take the floor as a member of Northwestern's basketball team.

Prior to his senior year of high school Knapp was rated among the best basketball players in Illinois. He was recruited by numerous universities, including Northwestern. At the end of Knapp's junior year at Peoria's Woodruff High School, Northwestern orally offered him an athletic scholarship to play basketball. Knapp orally accepted the offer.

A few weeks into his senior year, Knapp suffered sudden cardiac death—meaning his heart stopped—during a pick-up basketball game. Paramedics used cardiopulmonary resuscitation, defibrillation (i.e., electric shocks), and injections of drugs to bring Knapp back to life. A few weeks later, doctors implanted an internal cardioverter-defibrillator in Knapp's abdomen. The device detects heart arrhythmia and delivers a shock to convert the abnormal heart rhythm back to normal. In other words, if Knapp's heart stops again the device is supposed to restart it.

On the day following his sudden cardiac death, Northwestern informed Knapp and his family that whatever the ultimate medical decision, Northwestern would honor its commitment for a scholarship. Seven weeks after his collapse Knapp signed a national letter of intent to attend Northwestern.

Knapp did not play basketball during his senior year in high school, but he was always a superb student, and in June 1995 he graduated as the valedictorian of his class. In September 1995 he enrolled as a Northwestern student.

On November 7, 1995, Dr. Howard Sweeney, Northwestern's head team physician, declared Knapp ineligible to participate on Northwestern's men's basketball team for the 1995–96 school year. Dr. Sweeney based his decision on Knapp's medical records in which several treating physicians recommended that Knapp not play competitive basketball, the report of team physician Dr. Mark Gardner following a physical examination of Knapp, published guidelines and recommendations following

We acknowledge that intercollegiate sports can be an important part of the college learning experience for both athletes and many cheering students—especially at a Big Ten school. Knapp has indicated that such is the case for him. But not every student thinks so. Numerous college students graduate each year having neither participated in nor attended an intercollegiate sporting event. Their sheepskins are no less valuable because of the lack of intercollegiate sports in their lives. Not playing intercollegiate sports does not mean they have not learned. Playing or enjoying intercollegiate sports therefore cannot be held out as a necessary part of learning for all students.

* * *

Because intercollegiate athletics may be one part of the major life activity of learning for certain students, the parties here have framed the analysis of what constitutes a major life activity into a choice between a subjective test or an objective test—whether we look at what constitutes learning for Nick Knapp or what constitutes learning in general for the average person. The Rehabilitation Act and the regulations promulgated under it give little guidance regarding whether the determination of what constitutes a major life activity turns on an objective or subjective standard. And while we have previously said that whether a person is disabled is "an individualized inquiry, best suited to a case-by-case determination," we have also indicated that "the definition of 'major life activity' in the regulations 'cannot be interpreted to include working at the specific job of one's choice,' " *Byrne v. Board of Educ., School of West Allis–West Milwaukee*, 979 F.2d 560, 565 (7th Cir.1992)....

We decline to define the major life activity of learning in such a way that the Act applies whenever someone wants to play intercollegiate athletics. A "major life activity," as defined in the regulations, is a basic function of life "such as caring for one's self, performing manual tasks, walking, seeing, hearing, speaking, breathing, learning, and working." 34 C.F.R. at 104.3(j)(2)(ii); 45 C.F.R. at 84.3(j)(2)(ii). These are basic functions, not more specific ones such as being an astronaut, working as a firefighter, driving a race car, or learning by playing Big Ten basketball.

However, major life activities are defined in a more individualized manner during the "substantial limitation" analysis, where, according to *Byrne*, 979 F.2d at 565, we look at whether the particular impairment constitutes a significant barrier for the particular person. What impairment will significantly impede learning for a person obtaining her third doctorate is not the same as one which would affect the average tenth grader's ability to learn. But any narrowing of what constitutes learning for a particular individual occurs within reasonable limits—coverage of the Rehabilitation Act is not open-ended or based on every dream or desire that a person may have. Not every impairment that affects an individual's major life activities is a substantially limiting impairment. The key obviously is the extent to which the impairment restricts the major life activity. *Roth v. Lutheran General Hospital*, 57 F.3d 1446,

1454 (7th Cir.1995). For that individual, "the impairment must limit [learning] generally." *Byrne*, 979 F.2d at 565. Just as "it is well established that an inability to perform a particular job for a particular employer is not sufficient to establish a handicap [in regard to working]," the inability to engage in a particular activity for a particular university is not sufficient to establish a disability in regard to education.... An impairment that interferes with an individual's ability to perform a particular function, but does not significantly decrease that individual's ability to obtain a satisfactory education otherwise, does not substantially limit the major life activity of learning. *Welsh*, 977 F.2d at 1418.

Because learning through playing intercollegiate basketball is only one part of the education available to Knapp at Northwestern, even under a subjective standard, Knapp's ability to learn is not substantially limited. Knapp's scholarship continues, allowing him access to all academic and—except for intercollegiate basketball—all nonacademic services and activities available to other Northwestern students, in addition to all other services available to scholarship athletes. Although perhaps not as great a learning experience as actually playing, it is even possible that Knapp may "learn" through the basketball team in a role other than as a player. Knapp is an intelligent student and athlete, and the inability to play intercollegiate basketball at Northwestern forecloses only a small portion of his collegiate opportunities.... Knapp has not shown that his education and training limit him to do nothing but play basketball. The fact that Knapp's goal of playing intercollegiate basketball is frustrated does not substantially limit his education. The Rehabilitation Act does not guarantee an individual the exact educational experience that he may desire, just a fair one. Consequently, we hold that Knapp as a matter of law is not disabled within the meaning of the Rehabilitation Act.

Even if we were inclined to find Knapp disabled under the Rehabilitation Act, he would still come up short because we also hold as a matter of law that he is not, under the statute, "otherwise qualified" to play intercollegiate basketball at Northwestern. A qualified disabled person, with respect to postsecondary education services, is a "person who meets the academic and technical standards requisite to admission or participation in the [school's] education program or activity." An explanatory note to the regulations states that the term "technical standards" means "all nonacademic admissions criteria that are essential to participation in the program in question."

Section 794 does not compel educational institutions to disregard the disabilities of disabled persons. *Southeastern Community College v. Davis*, 442 U.S. 397, 405 (1979). It requires only that an "otherwise qualified" disabled person not be excluded from participation in a federally funded program solely because of the disability. Id. In other words, although a disability is not a permissible ground for assuming an inability to function in a particular context, the disability is not thrown out when considering if the person is qualified for the position sought.

Id. at 405–6. "An otherwise qualified person is one who is able to meet all of a program's requirements in spite of his handicap," id. at 406, with reasonable accommodation, see *School Bd. of Nassau County, Fla. v. Arline*, 480 U.S. 273, at 287–88 n. 17 (1987) ("when a handicapped person is not able to perform the essential functions of the job, the court must also consider whether any reasonable accommodation by the employer would enable the handicapped person to perform those functions").

Legitimate physical qualifications may in fact be essential to participation in particular programs. *Southeastern*, 442 U.S. at 407.

Paragraph (k) of § 84.3 defines the term "qualified handicapped [now, disabled] person." Throughout the regulation, this term is used instead of the statutory term "otherwise qualified handicapped person." The Department believes that the omission of the word "otherwise" is necessary in order to comport with the intent of the statute because, read literally, "otherwise" qualified handicapped persons include persons who are qualified except for their handicap, rather than in spite of their handicap. Under such a literal reading, a blind person possessing all the qualifications for driving a bus except sight could be said to be "otherwise qualified" for the job of driving. Clearly, such a result was not intended by Congress. In all other respects, the terms "qualified" and "otherwise qualified" are intended to be interchangeable.

A significant risk of personal physical injury can disqualify a person from a position if the risk cannot be eliminated. *Chiari v. City of League City*, 920 F.2d 311, 317 (5th Cir.1991). But more than merely an elevated risk of injury is required before disqualification is appropriate. *Mantolete v. Bolger*, 767 F.2d 1416, 1424 (9th Cir.1985). Any physical qualification based on risk of future injury must be examined with special care if the Rehabilitation Act is not to be circumvented, since almost all disabled individuals are at a greater risk of injury. *Bentivegna v. United States Dept. of Labor*, 694 F.2d 619, 622 (9th Cir.1982).

In *Mantolete*, the Ninth Circuit addressed the standard to apply in determining if an individual is otherwise physically qualified to perform an activity when the possibility of future injury exists:

> In some cases, a job requirement that screens out qualified handicapped individuals on the basis of possible future injury is necessary. However, we hold that in order to exclude such individuals, there must be a showing of a reasonable probability of substantial harm. Such a determination cannot be based merely on an employer's subjective evaluation or, except in cases of a most apparent nature, merely on medical reports. The question is whether, in light of the individual's work history and medical history, employment of that individual would pose a reasonable probability of substantial harm....
>
> In applying this standard, an employer must gather all relevant information regarding the applicant's work history and medical history, and independently assess both the probability and severity

of potential injury. This involves, of course, a case-by-case analysis of the applicant and the particular job.

767 F.2d at 1422; see *Chiari*, 920 F.2d at 317 (disabled person not qualified for job if there is genuine substantial risk that worker could be injured or could injure others and employer cannot modify job to eliminate risk). We agree this is the appropriate standard. We now turn, however, to who should make such an assessment.

In this case, the severity of the potential injury is as high as it could be—death. In regard to the probability of injury, Dr. John H. McAnulty, one of Knapp's experts, testified at the injunction hearing that the annual risk of death to Knapp as a result of his cardiac condition under a worst-case scenario is 2.4 percent and that playing intercollegiate basketball would elevate this annual risk to 2.93 percent, or one in 34. In other words, if 34 Nick Knapps played basketball for a year, chances are one would die. Dr. Brian Olshansky, another expert for Knapp, put Knapp's risk of death for the 1996–97 basketball season at no greater than one in 100. These estimates took into account Knapp's internal defibrillator, apparently the only "accommodation" possible for Knapp's condition. Although the doctors indicated that these numbers were merely estimates, all agreed that the risk to Knapp is higher than to the average male collegiate basketball player. Knapp's experts believed it was an acceptable level of risk.

Northwestern's experts agreed with the school's team doctors that Knapp's participation in competitive Big Ten basketball presented an unacceptable level of risk. According to Dr. Barry J. Maron, one of Northwestern's experts, based on a 10-year study, the risk of nontraumatic death for the average male college basketball player is one in 28,818. Dr. Maron further testified that participation in intercollegiate basketball significantly increases Knapp's risk of death, although he believed the precise risk could not be quantified. Dr. Douglas J. Zipes agreed. According to both Drs. Zipes and Maron, the most important fact in assessing Knapp's current risk of sudden cardiac death while playing intercollegiate basketball is the fact that his previous sudden cardiac death was induced by playing basketball.

Knapp's and Northwestern's experts disagreed on the effect of the passage of time on the likelihood that Knapp would suffer another sudden cardiac death. Almost all experts agreed that the internal defibrillator had never been tested under conditions like an intercollegiate basketball game or practice and that it was unclear whether the device would actually work under the stress and physical conditions of a high-intensity sport. Dr. Olshansky, though, indicated that biweekly "interrogations" of the defibrillator would minimize the risk of its failure. Knapp has had his defibrillator checked on a regular basis and has had no problems with it.

The district court judge in this case believed that in the face of conflicting opinion evidence regarding risk, and the fact that no scientific data existed to quantify that risk, the decision on whether Knapp should play falls in the lap of the court:

> We have nothing more exotic here than highly qualified experts, in agreement on all the basic scientific principles and differing only in their medical judgment on the final question.... All possess the education, training and experience required to become experts and none disputes the expertise of the others. The range of disagreement is extremely narrow, confined only to the dimensions of the risk of recurrence and the effect of the passage of time on that risk.... My task is to consider all the opinions and determine which are most persuasive. It is what the trial of disputes such as this will sometimes require. It might have been better to have left the choice to a panel of physicians, but Congress left it with the courts and the random assignment of this case has left it here with me.
>
> ... I again find the opinions of Drs. McAnulty, Rink and Olshansky to be persuasive and I find that the risk to Nicholas Knapp of a repeat episode is not substantial.

We disagree with the district court's legal determination that such decisions are to be made by the courts and believe instead that medical determinations of this sort are best left to team doctors and universities as long as they are made with reason and rationality and with full regard to possible and reasonable accommodations. In cases such as ours, where Northwestern has examined both Knapp and his medical records, has considered his medical history and the relation between his prior sudden cardiac death and the possibility of future occurrences, has considered the severity of the potential injury, and has rationally and reasonably reviewed consensus medical opinions or recommendations in the pertinent field—regardless whether conflicting medical opinions exist—the university has the right to determine that an individual is not otherwise medically qualified to play without violating the Rehabilitation Act. The place of the court in such cases is to make sure that the decision-maker has reasonably considered and relied upon sufficient evidence specific to the individual and the potential injury, not to determine on its own which evidence it believes is more persuasive.

* * *

In *Arline*, where a school teacher with tuberculosis was fired and thereafter sued her employer under the Rehabilitation Act, the Supreme Court stated that an "otherwise qualified" inquiry must be individualized and should include

> "... facts, based on reasonable medical judgments given the state of medical knowledge, about (a) the nature of the risk ... , (b) the duration of the risk ..., [and] (c) the severity of the risk...."
>
> In making these findings, the courts normally should defer to the reasonable medical judgments of public health officials.

Arline, 480 U.S. at 287–88. The Court, however, refrained from addressing the deferential weight of the medical judgments of private physicians on which the employer relied. Id. Although the Bethesda Conferences were not convened by public health officials and such guidelines should not substitute for individualized assessment of an athlete's particular physical condition, the consensus recommendations of several physicians in a certain field do carry weight and support the Northwestern team doctors' individualized assessment of Knapp.

We do not believe that, in cases where medical experts disagree in their assessment of the extent of a real risk of serious harm or death, Congress intended that the courts—neutral arbiters but generally less skilled in medicine than the experts involved—should make the final medical decision. Instead, in the midst of conflicting expert testimony regarding the degree of serious risk of harm or death, the court's place is to ensure that the exclusion or disqualification of an individual was individualized, reasonably made, and based upon competent medical evidence. So long as these factors exist, it will be the rare case regarding participation in athletics where a court may substitute its judgment for that of the school's team physicians.

* * *

In closing, we wish to make clear that we are not saying Northwestern's decision necessarily is the right decision. We say only that it is not an illegal one under the Rehabilitation Act. On the same facts, another team physician at another university, reviewing the same medical history, physical evaluation, and medical recommendations, might reasonably decide that Knapp met the physical qualifications for playing on an intercollegiate basketball team. Simply put, all universities need not evaluate risk the same way. What we say in this case is that if substantial evidence supports the decision-maker—here Northwestern—that decision must be respected.

Section 794 prohibits authorities from deciding without significant medical support that certain activities are too risky for a disabled person. Decisions of this sort cannot rest on paternalistic concerns. Knapp, who is an adult, is not in need of paternalistic decisions regarding his health, and his parents—more entitled to be paternalistic toward him than Northwestern—approve of his decision. See *Wright* at 794 (Columbia's decision not to allow student with sight in only one eye to play football "contrary to the express wishes of his parents who, together with their son, have reached a rational decision concerning the risk involved"). In regard to cases involving risk of future injury, a school's perception of the threat of such injury cannot be based on unfounded fears or stereotypes; it must be based on objective evidence. *Chiari*, 920 F.2d at 317. But here, where Northwestern acted rationally and reasonably rather than paternalistically, no Rehabilitation Act violation has occurred. The Rehabilitation Act "is carefully structured to replace ... reflexive actions to actual or perceived handicaps with actions based on reasoned and medically sound judgments...." *Arline*, 480 U.S. at 284–85.

Reversed.

Having lost in the courts, Knapp rejected Northwestern's offer of a free education without basketball, and instead accepted a scholarship from Northeastern Illinois where he was to begin playing (as well as studying) in the 1997–98 season.

Questions for Discussion

1. District Judge Zagel had earlier ruled that college sports was a "major life activity" for someone like Knapp. The judge was not persuaded by Northwestern's argument that it was sufficient for Knapp's life that he was still able to go to college (on an athletic scholarship the school was still providing), and that Knapp could play golf or join in an orchestra instead of choosing basketball as his extracurricular activity. "Because competitive basketball is an important and integral part of Knapp's education and learning experience, I find that intercollegiate basketball is a major life activity for him."

Do you agree with the circuit court or the district court's position on this score? Suppose that Northwestern (or another college) decided that it could not offer a scholarship providing free tuition and room and board to someone whom it judged to be disabled from playing on its team; would that fact have changed the circuit court verdict? Suppose that Knapp had experienced his cardiac arrest after starring in college basketball and being drafted in the first round by an NBA team: is the chance to play professional basketball a "major life activity"? (By the way, Terry Cummings of the Seattle SuperSonics has played several years since being diagnosed with an arrhythmic heart condition that requires regular medication.) Based on what you saw regarding college sports in Chapters 9, 10, and 11, should any (or all) of these sports be treated the same or differently from professional sports for purposes of this specific issue?

2. Turning now to the question whether Knapp was "otherwise qualified" to play basketball, both the district and the circuit courts agreed that this statutory condition would not be satisfied if there was a "genuine and substantial risk of injury" from this activity. Their disagreement was about whether Northwestern's admittedly reasonable assessment on that score was sufficient, or whether the college had to persuade the court that its appraisal was more reasonable than that of Knapp and his medical experts. Which of these positions is most compatible with the legislative policy? Could one argue that if a judge believed that Knapp and his experts' assessment of his medical risk was reasonable, this should be dispositive even if the college physician's views seemed somewhat more likely?

3. Consider again the *Neeld* case of a hockey player who had lost the sight in one eye for reasons that were unrelated to the sport, and was barred from playing in the National Hockey League. Alternatively, a football player who lost use of one eye while an infant is now being barred from playing college football. In each case, is the team's concern that a hockey or football collision could cost the player his other eye and thus produce total blindness?

How does this situation compare with the one in *Knapp*? Abstracting from the issue of "major life activity," is there the kind of "genuine and substantial risk of injury" that would sustain such a team policy under either the ADA or the Rehabilitation Act? See *Wright v. Columbia University*, 520 F.Supp. 789 (E.D.Pa.1981).

In the *Wright* case noted above, both Wright and his parents made it clear that they were "willing to release Columbia from potential liability it might incur by virtue of [Wright's] participation in the football program." Is this fact relevant to a legal judgment about whether the school's policy is discriminatory under federal law? Should a league be entitled to insist on such waivers of liability as a condition for eligibility of players who have a disability? Consider the reasoning in the next case.[t]

WAGENBLAST v. ODESSA SCHOOL DISTRICT

Supreme Court of Washington, 1988.
110 Wash.2d 845, 758 P.2d 968.

ANDERSON, JUSTICE.

[Several school districts in the state of Washington, including Odessa and Seattle, adopted a policy that any student who wanted to participate in interscholastic athletics (as well as their parents or guardians) must sign a standard form that purported to release the school district from "liability resulting from ordinary negligence that may arise in connection with the school district's interscholastic activities programs." Several students filed suit asking the state courts to declare these releases invalid. This was the response of the Washington Supreme Court.]

* * *

We hold that the exculpatory releases from any future school district negligence are invalid because they violate public policy.

The courts have generally recognized that, subject to certain exceptions, parties may contract that one shall not be liable for his or her own negligence to another. As Prosser and Keeton explain:

> It is quite possible for the parties expressly to agree in advance that the defendant is under no obligation of care for the benefit of the plaintiff, and shall not be liable for the consequences of conduct which would otherwise be negligent. There is in the ordinary case no public policy which prevents the parties from contracting as they see fit, as to whether the plaintiff will undertake the responsibility of looking out for himself.

---

[t] For academic commentary, see Andrew Manno, *A High Price to Compete: The Feasibility and Effect of Waivers Used to Protect Schools from Liability for Injuries to Athletes with High Medical Risks*, 79 Kentucky L. J. 867 (1991).

In accordance with the foregoing general rule, appellate decisions in this state have upheld exculpatory agreements where the subject was a toboggan slide, a scuba diving class, mountain climbing instruction, an automobile demolition derby, and ski jumping.

As Prosser and Keeton further observe, however, there are instances where public policy reasons for preserving an obligation of care owed by one person to another outweigh our traditional regard for the freedom to contract. Courts in this century are generally agreed on several such categories of cases.

Courts, for example, are usually reluctant to allow those charged with a public duty, which includes the obligation to use reasonable care, to rid themselves of that obligation by contract. Thus, where the defendant is a common carrier, an innkeeper, a professional bailee, a public utility, or the like, an agreement discharging the defendant's performance will not ordinarily be given effect. Implicit in such decisions is the notion that the service performed is one of importance to the public, and that a certain standard of performance is therefore required.

Courts generally also hold that an employer cannot require an employee to sign a contract releasing the employer from liability for job-related injuries caused by the employer's negligence. Such decisions are grounded on the recognition that the disparity of bargaining power between employer and employee forces the employee to accept such agreements.

Consistent with these general views, this court has held that a bank which rents out safety deposit boxes cannot, by contract, exempt itself from liability for its own negligence, and that if the circumstances of a particular case suggest that a gas company has a duty to inspect the pipes and fittings belonging to the owner of the building, any contractual limitation on that duty would be against public policy.

This court has also gone beyond these usually accepted categories to hold future releases invalid in other circumstances as well. It has struck down a lease provision exculpating a public housing authority from liability for injuries caused by the authority's negligence and has also struck down a landlord's exculpatory clause relating to common areas in a multi-family dwelling complex.

In reaching these decisions, this court has focused at times on disparity of bargaining power, at times on the importance of the service provided, and at other times on other factors. In reviewing these decisions, it is apparent that the court has not always been particularly clear on what rationale it used to decide what type of release was and was not violative of "public policy." Undoubtedly, it has been much easier for courts to simply declare releases violative of public policy in a given situation than to state a principled basis for so holding.

Probably the best exposition of the test to be applied in determining whether exculpatory agreements violate public policy is that stated by the California Supreme Court. In writing for a unanimous court, the late

Justice Tobriner outlined the factors in *Tunkl v. Regents of Univ. of Cal.*, 383 P.2d 441 (1963):

> Thus the attempted but invalid exemption involves a transaction which exhibits some or all of the following characteristics. It concerns a business of a type generally thought suitable for public regulation. The party seeking exculpation is engaged in performing a service of great importance to the public, which is often a matter of practical necessity for some members of the public. The party holds himself out as willing to perform this service for any member of the public who seeks it, or at least for any member coming within certain established standards. As a result of the essential nature of the service, in the economic setting of the transaction, the party invoking exculpation possesses a decisive advantage of bargaining strength against any member of the public who seeks his services. In exercising a superior bargaining power the party confronts the public with a standardized adhesion contract of exculpation, and makes no provision whereby a purchaser may pay additional reasonable fees and obtain protection against negligence. Finally, as a result of the transaction, the person or property of the purchaser is placed under the control of the seller, subject to the risk of carelessness by the seller or his agents.

Obviously, the more of the foregoing six characteristics that appear in a given exculpatory agreement case, the more likely the agreement is to be declared invalid on public policy grounds. In the consolidated cases before us, all of the characteristics are present in each case. We separately, then, examine each of these six characteristics as applied to the cases before us.

1. The agreement concerns an endeavor of a type generally thought suitable for public regulation.

Regulation of governmental entities usually means self-regulation. Thus, the Legislature has by statute granted to each school board the authority to control, supervise, and regulate the conduct of interscholastic athletics. In some situations, a school board is permitted, in turn, to delegate this authority to the Washington Interscholastic Activities Association (WIAA) or to another voluntary nonprofit entity. In the cases before us, both school boards look to the WIAA for regulation of interscholastic sports. The WIAA handbook contains an extensive constitution with rules for such athletic endeavors. These rules cover numerous topics, including student eligibility standards, athletic awards, insurance, coaches, officials, tournaments and state championships. Special regulations for each sport cover such topics as turnout schedules, regular season game or meet limitations, and various areas of regulation peculiar to the sport, including the rule book governing the sport.

Clearly then, interscholastic sports in Washington are extensively regulated, and are a fit subject for such regulation.

2. The party seeking exculpation is engaged in performing a service of great importance to the public, which is often a matter of practical necessity for some members of the public.

This court has held that public school students have no fundamental right to participate in interscholastic athletics. Nonetheless, the court also has observed that the justification advanced for interscholastic athletics is their educational and cultural value. As the testimony of then Seattle School Superintendent Robert Nelson and others amply demonstrate, interscholastic athletics is part and parcel of the overall educational scheme in Washington. The total expenditure of time, effort and money on these endeavors makes this clear. The importance of these programs to the public is substantive; they represent a significant tie of the public at large to our system of public education. Nor can the importance of these programs to certain students be denied; as Superintendent Nelson agreed, some students undoubtedly remain in school and maintain their academic standing only because they can participate in these programs. Given this emphasis on sports by the public and the school system, it would be unrealistic to expect students to view athletics as an activity entirely separate and apart from the remainder of their schooling.[1]

This court observed in *McCutcheon v. United Homes Corp.*, 486 P.2d 1093 (1971), that it makes little sense to insist that a worker have a safe place to work but at the same time to deny that worker a safe place to live. There is likewise little logic in insisting that one who entrusts personal property to a bank for safekeeping in a deposit box must be protected from the bank's negligence while denying such protection to a student who entrusts his or her person to the coaches, trainers, bus drivers and other agents of a school sports program.

In sum, under any rational view of the subject, interscholastic sports in public schools are a matter of public importance in this jurisdiction.

3. Such party holds itself out as willing to perform this service for any member of the public who seeks it, or at least for any member coming within certain established standards.

Implicit in the nature of interscholastic sports is the notion that such programs are open to all students who meet certain skill and eligibility standards. This conclusion finds direct support in the testimony of former Superintendent Nelson and the WIAA eligibility and nondiscrimination policies set forth in the WIAA handbook.

4. Because of the essential nature of the service, in the economic setting of the transaction, the party invoking exculpation possesses a decisive advantage of bargaining strength against any member of the public who seeks the services.

---

[1]. This intimate relationship between interscholastic sports and other aspects of public education serves to distinguish this case from those involving private adult education for hazardous activities, e.g., skydiving and mountain climbing.

Not only have interscholastic sports become of considerable importance to students and the general public alike, but in most instances there exists no alternative program of organized competition. For instance, former Superintendent Nelson knew of no alternative to the Seattle School District's wrestling program. While outside alternatives exist for some activities, they possess little of the inherent allure of interscholastic competition. Many students cannot afford private programs or the private schools where such releases might not be employed. In this regard, school districts have near-monopoly power. And, because such programs have become important to student participants, school districts possess a clear and disparate bargaining strength when they insist that students and their parents sign these releases.

5. In exercising a superior bargaining power, the party confronts the public with a standardized adhesion contract of exculpation, and makes no provision whereby a purchaser may pay additional reasonable fees and obtain protection against negligence.

Both school districts admit to an unwavering policy regarding these releases; no student athlete will be allowed to participate in any program without first signing the release form as written by the school district. In both of these cases, students and their parents unsuccessfully attempted to modify the forms by deleting the release language. In both cases, the school district rejected the attempted modifications. Student-athletes and their parents or guardians have no alternative but to sign the standard release forms provided to them or have the student barred from the program.

6. The person or property of members of the public seeking such services must be placed under the control of the furnisher of the services, subject to the risk of carelessness on the part of the furnisher, its employees or agents.

A school district owes a duty to its students to employ ordinary care and to anticipate reasonably foreseeable dangers so as to take precautions for protecting the children in its custody from such dangers. This duty extends to students engaged in interscholastic sports. As a natural incident to the relationship of a student athlete and his or her coach, the student athlete is usually placed under the coach's considerable degree of control. The student is thus subject to the risk that the school district or its agent will breach this duty of care.

In sum, the attempted releases in the cases before us exhibit all six of the characteristics denominated in *Tunkl v. Regents of Univ. of Cal.* Because of this, and for the aforesaid reasons, we hold that the releases in these consolidated cases are invalid as against public policy.

Declaration granted.

Questions for Discussion

1. In light of what you have read earlier in the chapter, precisely how much legal significance is there to an explicit release by players of a team's

or league's liability for "ordinary negligence" for injury during a sporting event?

2. Do you agree with the Washington court's view of what is sensible public policy towards such contractual releases by high school athletes? Is the same view appropriate for releases by college athletes? Professional athletes? Consider the following waiver NFL teams sometimes demand from their players:

NFL
Waiver and Release

1. I have been informed by the Club physician that I have the following physical condition(s).

2. The physical condition(s) set forth above existed prior to the date of the physical examination for the current season.

3. I have received a full explanation from the Club physician that to continue to play professional football may result in deterioration of such pre-existing physical condition(s) rendering me physically unable to perform the services required of me by my NFL Player Contract executed this date.

4. I fully understand the possible consequences of playing professional football with the physical condition(s) set forth in paragraph 1 above. Nevertheless, I desire to continue to play professional football and hereby assume the risk of the matters set forth in paragraph 3 above.

5. Because I desire to play professional football for the Club, I hereby waive and release the Club, the Club physician, its trainers and the National Football League from any and all liability and responsibility in the event I become physically unable to perform the services required of me by my NFL Player Contract executed this date because of a deterioration or aggravation of the physical condition(s) set forth in paragraph 1 above.

How would the *Odessa* court treat this release form?

3. Would your verdict differ if the school district (or college or professional team) provided and paid for catastrophic injury insurance (such as the NCAA policy described earlier) in return for *mandatory* waiver of tort liability? As an inducement for a *voluntary* waiver of liability?[u]

---

[u]. For a broader discussion of these questions, see Jeffrey O'Connell, *A "Neo No–Fault" Contract in Lieu of Tort: Preaccident Guarantees of Postaccident Settlement Offers,* 73 California L.Rev. 898 (1985).

Index

References are to Pages

AGENTS, 322–388, 739–741, 780–793
Agencies,
  Advantage International, 888
  Associate Management Enterprises (FAME), 354
  International Management Group (IMG), 323, 354, 865, 888, 893, 894
  Misle's Total Economic Athletic Management (TEAM), 370
  ProServ, 323, 354, 865, 886, 888, 893, 895
  Talent Services, Inc. (TSI), 353, 354
  Total Economic Athletic Management (TEAM), 387
  World Sports & Entertainment, Inc. (WSE), 374
Breakdown in agent-player relationships, 343–360
Competence of, 343–346
Conflicts of interest, 350–355
Fee formulas, 317–320
Individuals,
  Abernathy, Jim, 380, 386
  Argovitz, Jerry, 353, 354
  Blank, Brad, 349
  Bloom, Lloyd, 355, 359, 373–75, 380–381, 386, 701, 781
  Boras, Scott, 174, 793
  Caron, Robert, 388, 660
  Childers, John, 353–354
  Cindrich, Ralph, 349
  Clements, Kathy, 359
  Collins, Thomas, 364, 370
  Condon, Tom, 370
  Craighill, Frank, 888
  Dell, Donald, 323, 865, 886, 888, 895
  Fagan, Dan, 331
  Falk, David, 323, 334, 354
  Fentress, Lee, 346, 888
  Franzese, Michael, 359
  Franzese, Sonny, 359
  Hendricks firm, 349
  Hendricks, Randy, 323
  Kapstein, Jerry, 354
  Kickliter, George, 356
  McCormack, Mark, 323, 865, 888

AGENTS, 322–388, 739–741, 780–793 —Cont'd
Individuals—Cont'd
  Misle, Howard, 370, 387
  Morris, William, 322
  Rona, Barry, 375
  Senkovich, Jr., Joe, 371
  Sorkin, Richard, 343
  Steinberg, Leigh, 323, 355
  Trope, Mike, 381
  Walters, Norby, 335, 359, 373–375, 380–381, 386, 701, 740, 793
  Wells, Lloyd, 353
  Woolf, Bob, 322, 347–348
  Woy, Bucky, 348–349
  Zinn, Leo, 343–344
  Zucker, Steve, 359
Interplay of agent and union representation, 324–342
Media depiction of *Jerry Maguire*, 322–323
Recruiting of college athletes, 351–360, 380–388, 739–741, 780–793
Regulation of, 360–388, 739–741, 780–793
  By legislation, 360–362, 380–388
  By NCAA, 373–375, 380–388, 739–741, 780–793
  By players unions, 362–379

AIDS
See HIV

ALCOHOL
See Drugs

AMATEUR SPORTS ACT, 457, 907–915

AMERICAN BASKETBALL ASSOCIATION (ABA)
See Basketball, Professional Leagues and Teams

AMERICAN BASKETBALL LEAGUE (ABL)
See Basketball, Professional Leagues and Teams

AMERICAN LEAGUE
See Baseball, Leagues and Teams, Major League Baseball

ANABOLIC STEROIDS
See Drugs

References are to Pages

ANNOUNCERS, SPORTS
See Media

ANTITRUST DOCTRINE
Ancillary restraints, 509–511, 518–519
Essential facility, 624–625, 628–629, 640–642
General principles of Sherman Act, 150–153, 156–160
Labor exemption,
    Antitrust in labor market, 154–156
    Interleague restraints, 617–619
    Interplay with labor law, 188–194
    League restraints on unionized players, 194–227
Monopoly power, 596–597, 613–616, 622–625, 627–629, 892–893
Per Se rule, 156–159, 162–163, 180–181
Rule of reason, 156–159, 163–172, 181–183, 469, 471, 506–512, 517–518, 550–554, 561–565, 576, 751–763, 899–903
Scope of market, 596–597, 613–616, 622–625, 627–629, 892–893
Single entity status of leagues, 469–471, 491–500, 504–505, 513–517, 560–561, 572–584, 568–570
Sports Broadcasting Act exemption, 554–560, 567–568, 570–571, 591

ANTITRUST IN SPORTS
Baseball's exemption, 125–149
Car racing, equipment, 897–898
College Sports,
    Athletes market, 780–792
    Coaches market, 770–780
    Television and merchandising market, 750–769
Golf,
    Disciplinary power, 880–885
    Eligibility to play, 871–876
    Equipment, 903–906
    Participation in other tours, 895–896
Interleague competition for,
    Cities, 597–602
    Players, 608–620
    Stadiums, 620–629
    Television contracts, 629–643
Professional league restraints,
    Corporate ownership, 477–491
    Cross-ownership, 472–477
    Expansion, 524–529
    Franchise relocation, 500–549
    Gambling rules, 32–36
    Merchandising deals, 459–460, 465–466, 586–588
    Rookie drafts, 160–176
    Salary caps, 176–178, 186–188
    Television contracts, 549–586, 629–643
    Union control of player agents, 362–379
    Union sale of player publicity rights, 460–465
    Veteran free agency, 178–186

ARBITRATION, 101–105, 228–233, 240–255, 297–304, 326–329, 335–342, 375–379, 925–928
Eligibility for Olympics, 925–928
    American Arbitration Association (AAA), 927
    International Court of Arbitration for Sports (ICAS), 926–927
Grievances under collective agreements
    Scope and limits of reserve system, 240–255
    Owner collusion, 228–233
    Player commitments, 101–105, 326–329
Judicial review, 297–304
Regulation of Agents, 375–379
Salary disputes, 335–342

ARENAS
See Stadiums and Arenas

ASSOCIATION OF TENNIS PROFESSIONALS (ATP)
See Tennis

ASSUMPTION OF RISK
See Tort Law

AUTOMOBILE RACING
See Racing, Automobile

BARGAINING
See Collective Bargaining; Labor Law

BASEBALL
Agents
Boras, Scott, 174, 793
Childers, John, 353, 354
Hendricks, Randy, 323
Kapstein, Jerry, 354
Rona, Barry, 375
Woolf, Bob, 322, 347–348
History
"Black Sox" scandal, 9, 31–32, 36, 125
Historians,
    Seymour, Harold, 124
Leagues and Teams
Continental League, 100, 620
    Challenge to MLB, 100
    Founder,
        Rickey, Branch, 100, 620
Federal League, 120
    Buffalo team, 120
Japanese Baseball League, 100, 230, 349
    Yakuit Swallows, 230, 349
Little League, 458, 466
Major League Baseball,
    Antitrust Exemption, 126–149
    Arbitrators,
        Collins, Daniel, 375–376, 379
        Nicolau, George, 230–234, 793
        Roberts, Tom, 230–234, 303
        Seitz, Peter, 241–242, 248, 298, 303
        St. Antoine, Ted, 349
    Collective bargaining, 228–237, 239–241, 248, 278–281, 314–321
    Owner collusion, 228–237

BASEBALL—Cont'd
Major League Baseball—Cont'd
  Commissioners,
    Chandler, Albert "Happy", 32, 73
    Giamatti, Bart, 3–7, 38, 80, 883
    Kuhn, Bowie, 13–22, 26, 32, 40, 41, 48, 54, 80, 81, 248, 275, 303–304, 590, 661
    Landis, Kenesaw Mountain, 9–12, 31, 32, 36, 73, 494
    Selig, Allen "Bud", 2, 25, 28, 494, 547, 549
    Ueberroth, Peter, 26, 32, 42, 54, 74, 228–229, 237, 248, 279
    Vincent, Francis "Fay", 5, 23–25, 27, 28, 40, 42–48, 232, 468, 499, 590, 883
  Drug policy, 38–56
  Farm system, 12–13
  MLB Players Association,
    Fehr, Don, 40
    Miller, Marvin, 8, 54, 230, 237, 239, 271, 275, 299–300, 313, 460
  MLB Player Relations Committee,
    Grebey, Ray, 275
    MacPhail, Lee, 54
    Rona, Barry, 375
  National Brotherhood of Baseball Players, 239
  League expansion, 23, 25
  League Presidents,
    Budig, Gene, 29
    Coleman, Leonard, 29
    Feeney, Charles S., 326
    Johnson, Byron "Ban", 7
    White, Bill, 23
  Major League Agreement, 27–28
  Management,
    Bavasi, Peter, 589
    Campanis, Al, 74, 75
    Montgomery, Dave, 458
    O'Malley, Peter, 74
  Managers,
    Durocher, Leo, 32
    Gaston, Cito, 74
    LaRussa, Tony, 255
    Martin, Billy, 49
    Mathewson, Christy, 125
    Michael, Gene, 40
    Rose, Pete, 49
    Showalter, Bucky, 40
  Media and,
    Journalists and media sources,
      Ludtke, Melissa, 80–86, 659
      Koppel, Ted, 74
      Nightline (ABC), 74
      Sports Illustrated, 75, 81
      Will, George, 6, 86, 645
    Locker room policy, 79–86
  Mediators,
    Usery, William, 280
  Minor leagues,
    See this topic, Leagues and Teams, Minor Leagues

BASEBALL—Cont'd
Major League Baseball—Cont'd
  Minority statistics, 74
  MLB Properties, 458, 465–466
  Option clause, 99
  Owners,
    Angelos, Peter, 29, 296
    Ball, Phil, 10
    Busch, Gussie, 797
    Chicago Tribune, 499
    Colangelo, Jerry, 472
    Cox, William, 32, 38
    Finley, Charles, 13–21, 248, 304, 590
    Frazee, Harry, 7
    Kroc, Joan, 354
    Kroc, Ray, 275
    Lurie, Bob, 21, 141
    Magowan, Peter, 141
    O'Malley, Walter, 540, 797
    Pittsburgh Athletic Company, 393
    Reinsdorf, Jerry, 25, 28, 472, 540
    Rickey, Branch, 12, 73
    Schott, Marge, 1, 75, 77
    Selig, Allen "Bud", 2, 25, 28, 494, 547, 549
    Steinbrenner, George, 13, 28, 32, 38, 40, 98, 237, 465–466, 542, 587, 590, 658, 883
    Time Warner, 318, 466, 472, 497, 499, 587
    Turner, Ted, 13, 21, 22, 248, 275, 318, 417, 420, 466, 472, 589
    Veeck, Bill, 73
    Walt Disney, 47
    Williams, Edward Bennett, 530
    Yawkey, Tom, 590
  Player transfers, legality, 9
  Realignment of divisions, 23, 25
  Reserve system, 12–22, 91–95
  Revenue Sharing, 588–590
  Revenues, 236–237, 389–390, 588–589, 593
  Salaries, 239, 270–271, 314, 321
  Salary arbitration, 341–342
  Standard player contract provisions
    Professional Baseball Agreement (PBA), 147–149
    PBA Player Development Contract (PDC), 147
    Uniform Player Contract, 241
  Umpires,
    Hirschbeck, John, 29, 30, 297
    Postema, Pam, 140
Minor leagues,
  Associations,
    National Association of Professional Baseball Leagues, 147–148, 174, 477
  Leagues
    American Association, 477
    Southern League, 477
  Owners,
    Diekou, John, 148

INDEX

References are to Pages

BASEBALL—Cont'd
Minor leagues—Cont'd
  Associations—Cont'd
    Teams,
      Charlotte Knights (Class AA), 148, 477
      Denver Zephyrs (AAA), 148, 477
Negro League, 73, 306
Northern Baseball League, 174
  Teams,
    St. Paul Saints, 174

Players
Aikens, Willie, 40
Ainge, Danny, 89–91, 99, 660, 728, 741
Alomar, Roberto, 1, 29, 30, 31, 297
Bayless, Patrick, 969
Belle, Albert, 38, 236, 270, 323
Bennett, Fred, 10–12
Benson, Kris, 173
Blue, Vida, 13, 14, 40, 41
Bonds, Barry, 141
Bowa, Larry, 230
Boyd, Dennis "Oil Can", 329
Bush, Mike, 314
Campanella, Roy, 127 n.r
Canseco, Jose, 49, 379
Chapman, Ray, 934, n.c
Chase, Hal, 120, 125
Clark, Jack, 233
Cordero, Wil, 1, 85, 86
Dawson, Andre, 229, 230
DiMaggio, Joe, 423
Doby, Larry, 73
Drew, J.D., 174
Drysdale, Don, 230
Dykstra, Lenny, 38, 49
Fingers, Rollie, 13–14
Fisk, Carlton, 233
Flood, Curt, 127, 594
Gardella, Danny, 74
Gedman, Rich, 233
Gehrig, Lou, 125, 294, 296, 423
Gibson, Josh, 73
Gibson, Kirk, 229, 231, 232
Gooden, Dwight, 39
Griffey, Jr., Ken, 294, 390, 428, 540
Grimsley, Ross, 951
Hernandez, Keith, 353
Howe, Steve, 40, 42–47, 48, 49, 51, 883
Horner, Bob, 230, 348–349
Hunter, Jim "Catfish", 13 , 303
Jackson, Reggie, 13
Jackson, Shoeless Joe, 36
Jenkins, Ferguson, 47–48
Jethroe, Sam, 73–74, 305–306
Johnson, Randy, 540
Knapp, Nicholas, 990
Koufax, Sandy, 230
Lajoie, Napoleon, 91–92, 94
Lamp, Dennis, 279
Lee, Travis, 173
Maddox, Elliot, 985–986
Maddux, Greg, 294
Mantle, Mickey, 32, 49, 423, 661

BASEBALL—Cont'd
Marichal, Juan, 950
Martin, Jerry, 40
Matthews, Gary, 21–22
Mays, Carl, 7–9
Mays, Willie, 32, 661
Mazeroski, Bill, 392
McNally, Dave, 241
Mesa, Jose, 86
Messersmith, Andy, 241, 314
Moore, Alvin, 326
Morris, Jack, 229, 233
Nixon, Otis, 48–49
Ott, Mel, 127 n.r
Paige, Satchel, 73, 127 n.r
Parker, Dave, 48, 54
Parrish, Lance, 229, 233
Perez, Pascual, 48
Phillips, Tony, 47
Piazza, Mike, 141
Raines, Tim, 229, 230, 233
Reed, Rick, 314
Ripken, Cal, 294, 296
Robinson, Jackie, 73, 74, 127, n.r, 306–306
Rose, Pete, 3–7, 21, 35, 36, 38, 80, 237, 658, 661, 883
Roseboro, John, 950
Rudi, Joe, 13–14
Ruth, Babe, 7, 119, 423
Schmidt, Mike, 230
Seaver, Tom, 233, 279
Sielicki, John, 969
Sisler, George, 125
Smith, Lonnie, 49
Strawberry, Darryl, 39, 85
Taylor, Brien, 792–793
Thomas, Frank, 294
Walker, Larry, 29
White, Matt, 173
Wiggins, Alan, 40
Wilson, Earl, 322
Wilson, Willie, 41, 51
Winfield, Dave, 28, 32

BASKETBALL
Agents
Collins, Thomas, 364, 370
Fagan, Dan, 331
Falk, David, 323, 334, 354
Fentress, Lee, 346
College
Coaches,
  Men's teams,
    Abatemarco, Tom, 718–719
    Alford, Steve, 734–735
    Beard, Butch, 851
    Campanelli, Lou, 658
    Casey, Dwayne, 670–671
    Dambrot, Keith, 75–76
    Gaudet, Pete, 771
    Knight, Bobby, 671, 682
    Krzyzewski, Mike, 735, 770–771
    Pitino, Rick, 671, 741
    Raveling, George, 845–846

INDEX

References are to Pages

BASKETBALL—Cont'd
Coaches—Cont'd
  Men's teams—Cont'd
    Smith, Dean, 682
    Sutton, Eddie, 671
    Tarkanian, Jerry, 649–650, 656–659, 661, 663, 668, 670–671, 673, 675, 729, 768
    Thompson, John, 354, 671, 683, 740, 770
    Westhead, Paul, 963–964
  Women's teams,
    Stanley, Marianne, 845–846, 850–851
    Tyler, Sonya, 850–851
Team Physicians
  Hattori, Dr. Vernon, 963–964
Television rights, 660, 700
Players
Abdul–Jabbar, Kareem (see also Lew Alcindor), 364, 427, 950
Abdul–Rauf, Mahmoud (see also Chris Jackson), 1, 76, 77
Ainge, Danny, 89–91, 99, 660, 728, 741
Alcindor, Lew (see also Kareem Abdul–Jabbar), 427, 667
Alford, Steve, 734–735
Allen, Lucius, 364
Barkley, Charles, 883
Barnett, Dick, 95, 98–99
Barry, Rick, 112
Beard, Butch, 851
Bias, Len, 49, 346
Bird, Larry, 316, 320
Bradley, Bill, 720
Bradley, Charles, 81
Brisker, John, 27
Bryant, Kobe, 740
Butts, Albert, 703–704
Camby, Marcus, 355
Chamberlain, Wilt, 667
Chapman, Rex, 354
Cummings, Terry, 364, 1000
Cunningham, Billy, 106, 112
Daniels, Lloyd, 663
Douglas, Sherman, 105
Dudley, Chris, 208, 210, 315, 331–335
Duncan, Tim, 740
Ehlo, Craig, 331
English, Alex, 364
Ewing, Patrick, 238, 316, 354, 796
Garnett, Kevin, 740
Gathers, Hank, 934, 963–964
Gaze, Andrew, 701, n.aa
Grant, Horace, 332
Green, A.C., 331
Hall, Mark, 698
Hawkins, Connie, 35
Hawkins, Hersey, 674
Haywood, Spencer, 175, 524
Hill, Grant, 735
Howard, Juwan, 332–323, 334–335, 354, 735
Hurt, Bobby Lee, 672
Iverson, Allen, 53, 354, 390, 740, 744

BASKETBALL—Cont'd
Jackson, Chris (see also Mahmoud Abdul–Rauf), 76, 77
Jackson, Terrell, 718–719
Jackson, Tracy, 81
Johnson, Dennis, 316
Johnson, Earvin "Magic", 71, 72
Jordan, Michael, 38, 227, 238, 270, 316, 319, 321, 323, 324, 333, 354, 390, 424, 428, 558, 582, 584, 734–735, 932
Kemp, Shawn, 671
Kidd, Jason, 658
Kukoc, Tony, 331
Kunnert, Kevin, 950
Malone, Karl, 71
Manuel, Eric, 670
Marbury, Stephon, 740
Mayberry, Lee, 323
Maxwell, Vernon, 31
McHale, Kevin, 316
McKey, Derrick, 356, 380
McMillan, Tom, 669, 720
Mikan, George, 455
Mills, Chris, 670
Mills, Terry, 682
Moe, Doug, 35–36
Molinas, Jack, 32–34
Mourning, Alonzo, 323, 334–335, 354
Olajuwon, Hakeem, 77, 728
O'Neal, Shaquille, 173, 227, 323, 390, 428, 740
Ostertag, Greg, 735
Parish, Robert, 85, 316, 677, 681
Pippen, Scottie, 85, 321, 558
Perkins, Sam, 77
Rajda, Dino, 100
Robertson, Oscar, 595
Robinson, Glenn, 740
Robinson, Rumeal, 682
Rodman, Dennis, 29, 31, 424, 435, 460, 558
Ross, Kevin, 721
Sampson, Ralph, 364
Sellers, Brad, 356
Shaw, Brian, 101, 105, 106, 328
Smith, Joe, 740
Sprewell, Latrell, 1, 30–31
Sutton, Sean, 671
Tomjanovich, Rudy, 31, 118, 950
Walton, Bill, 981
Washburn, Chris, 682
Washington, Kermit, 31, 118, 950
Webber, Chris, 735, 740
Williams, John "Hot Rod", 36, 323, 682
Wood, Leon, 201–204, 320
Professional Leagues and Teams
American Basketball Association (ABA), 27, 100, 106, 112, 175, 455, 595, 843
  Commissioners,
    George Mikan, 455
  Rivalry with NBA, 100, 112
American Basketball League (ABL)(men), 35, 95–98
  Owner,
    Steinbrenner, George, 98

INDEX

References are to Pages

BASKETBALL—Cont'd
American Basketball League (ABL) (women), 497–498, 557, 607, 643–644
    Founders,
        Cavelli, Gary, 497
        Cribs, Anne, 497
        Hams, Steve, 497
    Investor,
        Phoenix Corp., 497
European Basketball, 100
Harlem Globetrotters, 35
Harlem Wizards, 443
Messaggero Roma, Il, 101
National Basketball Association (NBA)
    Arbitration, 30–31, 86, 101
    Arbitrator,
        Feerick, John, 31, 86
    Coaches,
        Auerbach, Arnold "Red", 89
        Carlesimo, P.J., 30
        McLendon, John, 97
        Moe, Doug, 35–36
        Pitino, Rick, 671, 741
        Riley, Pat, 255, 334–335
    Collective bargaining, 201, 208–209, 239–241, 316–321, 331–335
    Commissioners,
        Kennedy, Walter, 27, 175
        O'Brien, Larry, 315
        Stern, David, 29, 30, 36, 74, 76–77, 315, 332–336, 497
    Draft, 175–176
    Drug policy, 52–53
    Free agency, 208–210
        "No-trade", 106
        Option clauses, 99
    NBA Players Association
        Fleisher, Larry, 208, 239, 315, 354
        Gourdine, Simon, 227, 233
        Grantham, Charles, 208, 223, 364
        Hunter, Billy, 30
        Lanier, Bob, 53
    Management,
        Biasone, Dan, 96
        NBA Board of Governors, 27
        Podoloff, Maurice, 32–34
        Rothenberg, Alan, 453
    Marketing,
        NBA Properties, Inc., 407
    Media and,
        Rodman, Dennis, 29, 31
    Officials,
        Kantner, Dee, 77
        Palmer, Violet, 77
    Owners,
        Allen, Paul, 476
        Cablevision, 472
        Comcast, 472
        Pollin, Abe, 472
        Reinsdorf, Jerry, 25, 29, 472, 540
        Schulman, Sam, 524
        Time Warner, 318, 472, 497, 499, 587
        Turner, Ted [see Baseball Owners]
    Revenues, 389–390, 557–558

BASKETBALL—Cont'd
National Basketball Association (NBA)—Cont'd
    Rivalry with ABA, 112
    Salaries, 239, 271, 314–321, 323
    Salary cap, 201–204; 208–210, 314–321, 329–335
    Standard Player Contract Provisions, Uniform Player Contract, 30
Women's National Basketball Association (WNBA), 497–498, 607, 643–644, 843
    NBA Development, 498

BOXERS
Ali, Muhammad, 426, 883–884
Carpentier, Georges, 390
Dempsey, Jack, 390
Douglas, James "Buster", 406, 412
Holyfield, Evander, 86, 401, 406, 412, 584, 896
Louis, Joe, 401, 423, 605
Morrison, Tommy, 72
Robinson, Sugar Ray, 605
Tyson, Mike, 2, 5, 86, 401, 584, 896

BOXING
Association of Boxing Commissions (ABC), 896
Competitions,
    Golden Gloves, 859
Professional Boxing Safety Act (PBSA), 896–897
Promoters,
    King, Don, 2, 36, 584
Promotional organizations,
    International Boxing Club (IBC), 604–605
        Norris, James, 604–605
        Wirtz, Willard, 605

BROADCASTING
See Media

CANADIAN AMATEUR HOCKEY ASSOCIATION
See Hockey

CANADIAN FOOTBALL LEAGUE
See Football, Professional Leagues and Teams

CLUBS
See Franchises, General

COLLECTIVE BARGAINING
See Labor Law

COLLEGE ATHLETICS
See Intercollegiate Athletics

COLLEGE FOOTBALL ASSOCIATION
See Football, College

COLLEGE SPORTS
See Intercollegiate Athletics

INDEX

References are to Pages

COLLEGE SPORTS—Cont'd
For teams and athletes, see various sports, College

COLLEGES AND UNIVERSITIES
Institutions,
    Air Force Academy, 697, 839
    Alabama, 380, 672, 962
    Arkansas, 353, 744
    Army, 839
    Auburn University, 356, 380, 701
    Baylor, 697
    Boston College, 1, 36–38, 396, 721, 796
    Boston University, 840, 842, 854
    Bradley University, 674
    Brigham Young University, 89, 728, 741, 767–768
    Brown University, 808–809, 819–820, 853, 854, 863
    California State University, 815
    California State University, Hayward (CSUH), 712
    Centenary College, 677, 684
    Central Michigan University, 69
    Citadel University, 963
    Clemson, 721
    Colorado State University, 814, 841
    Columbia University, 1001
    Cornell University, 703, 748
    Creighton University, 713
    Denver University, 725
    Drake University, 718
    Duke University, 656, 658, 684, 721, 735, 771, 842, 852
    East Tennessee State, 963
    Florida State, 36, 38, 174, 355, 671, 769, 790
    Fresno State, 668
    Georgetown University, 671, 683, 740, 796
    Georgia, 175, 682, 768
    Grambling, 682, 684, 965
    Harvard University, 682, 688, 808
    Howard University, 850–851
    Illinois, 815, 854
    Indiana, 647, 671, 682, 724, 734
    Indiana State University, 956, 958–59
    Iowa State, 745
    Jackson State, 682, 684
    Lafayette University, 748
    LaSalle University, 703, 704
    Livingston University, 711–712
    Long Beach State College, 649, 989
    Louisiana State University (LSU), 838–839, n.c
    Louisville, 647
    Loyola Marymount University, 934, 963–964
    Maryland, 36, 346
    Michigan State University, 56, 689–690, 695, 745
    Mississippi State, 963
    Missouri State University, 934
    Navy, 839

COLLEGES AND UNIVERSITIES—Cont'd
Institutions—Cont'd
    Nebraska, 85, 359
    North Carolina University, 35, 647, 682, 724
    Northwestern University, 36, 735, 990, 1000
    Notre Dame, 359, 647, 658, 660, 682, 721, 724, 766–767, 769, 781, 791, 797
    Ohio State University, 740, 741, 769
    Oklahoma, 107, 736, 768
    Oregon State University, 720–721
    Pembroke College, 808
    Penn State University, 395–396, 682
    Prairie View, 720–721
    Princeton, 808
    Rutgers, 744
    Seton Hall University, 702, n.aa
    South Carolina State, 842
    Southeastern College of the Assemblies of God, 697
    Southern California, 355, 388, 660, 845–846
    Southern Methodist University, 670, 671, 673–674, 675, 682, 780
    Springfield College, 703
    Stanford University, 57, 65, 684, 850
    Syracuse University, 36
    Temple University, 853–854
    Tennessee, 356, 676
    Texas Christian University, 422, 962
    Troy State University, 711
    Tulane University, 36, 682, 745
    University of California, Berkeley, 658, 688, 850
    University of California, Los Angeles (UCLA), 659, 702, n.aa, 721
    University of Colorado, 65
    University of Detroit, 175
    University of Florida, 647, 724, 734–735, 770, 797
    University of Georgia, 175, 675–676
    University of Houston, 387, 721, 728
    University of Illinois, 815, 842
    University of Iowa, 35, 356, 373, 386, 701
    University of Kansas, 729, 735
    University of Kentucky, 670, 671, 675
    University of Maryland, 748
    University of Massachusetts, 355
    University of Miami, 38, 172, 681, 682, 744
    University of Michigan, 647, 648, 682, 683, 724, 735, 748, 769, 797
    University of Minnesota, 697, 698
    University of Mississippi, 106–107
    University of Nevada at Las Vegas (UNLV), 649–650, 656–659, 663, 668, 670, 674, 684, 729, 768
    University of Oklahoma, 107–108
    University of Oregon, 161
    University of Pennsylvania, 703, 748
    University of Texas, 815

INDEX

COLLEGES AND UNIVERSITIES—Cont'd
Institutions—Cont'd
  University of Texas at El Paso, 728
  University of Washington, 359, 647, 695, 805
  Vanderbilt University, 842, 963
  Virginia Military Institute, 820
  Virginia University, 349
  Wake Forest University, 740, 842
  Washington State University, 744, 801, 805, 808, 854
  West Virginia, 748, 852
  Western Michigan University, 961
  Wheaton College, 681
  Yale University, 703, 795
Presidents,
  Bok, Derek (Harvard), 682
  Hesburgh, Father Theodore (Notre Dame), 682
  Foote, Edward (Miami), 682
  Gregorian, Vartan (Brown), 819
  Shield, Donald (SMU), 682
Professors and University Officials,
  Canham, Dan (Michigan), 682
  Clements, William (SMU), 670
  Edwards, Harry (Berkeley), 688
  Ervin, Dr. Leroy (Georgia), 676
  Gates, Henry (Harvard), 688
  Kemp, Jan (Georgia), 675–676, 682, 701
  Trotter, Dr. Virginia (Georgia), 676

COMMERCE CLAUSE
See Constitutional Law

COMMISSIONERS
Authority of, 6–31
Discipline of Players,
  Domestic abuse, 1, 85–86
  Drugs, 38–71
  Gambling, 2–6, 31–38
  Gun possession, 47, 53
  Violence on court or field, 1, 29–31
History of, 2
Interests of Sport, 1–86
Individuals,
  Beman, Deane (golf), 882, 884, 904
  Bettman, Gary (NHL), 200, 317, 341, 501
  Campbell, Clarence (NHL), 611, 613, 616
  Chandler, Albert "Happy" (MLB), 32, 73
  Finchem, Tim (golf), 872
  Giamatti, Bart (MLB), 3–7, 38, 80, 883
  Kennedy, Walter (NBA), 27, 175
  Kuhn, Bowie (MLB), 13–22, 26, 32, 40, 41, 48, 54, 80, 241, 248, 275, 303–304, 590, 661
  Landis, Kenesaw Mountain (MLB), 9–12, 31, 32, 36, 73, 494
  Mikan, George (ABA), 455
  O'Brien, Larry (NBA), 315

COMMISSIONERS—Cont'd
Individuals—Cont'd
  Rozelle, Pete (NFL), 32, 50, 54, 74, 107, 315, 408, 481–482, 501–502, 507, 554–556, 631, 635, 637, 660
  Selig, Allen "Bud" (MLB), 2, 25, 28, 494, 547, 549
  Stern, David (NBA), 29, 30, 36, 74, 76–77, 315, 332–336, 497
  Tagliabue, Paul (NFL), 51, 52, 78, 80, 117, 315, 330, 459–460, 476–477, 501, 556, 883
  Ueberroth, Peter (MLB), 26, 32, 42, 54, 74, 217, 227, 228–229, 237, 248, 279
  Vincent, Francis "Fay" (MLB), 5, 23–24, 27, 28, 40, 42–48, 232, 421, 468, 499, 590, 883
Voiding trades, 13–21

CONGRESS, UNITED STATES
1994 Senate Baseball hearings, 28
Members of,
  Boggs, Hale, 602
  Bradley, Bill, 720
  Culver, John, 374
  Dole, Bob, 896
  Gore, Al, 591
  Hatch, Orrin, 146
  Long, Russell, 602
  McMillan, Tom, 669, 720, 765, n.k
  Metzenbaum, Howard, 28
  Mottl, Ronald, 954
  Moynihan, Daniel, 146, 498, 545
  Tower, John, 799–800
  Wagner, Robert, 7

CONSTITUTIONAL LAW
Commerce Clause, 139–142
Due Process, 589–616
  See also Intercollegiate Sports
Eminent Domain, 531–540
Equal Protection, 677–681, 729–732, 736–738, 801–805, 820–839, 853–854, 855–862
  See also Intercollegiate Sports
Federal preemption of state regulation
  NCAA, 662–669
  Professional leagues, 537–539
Freedom of Speech, 75–76
Privacy Rights
  College and High School Drug Testing, 57–71
State Actors
  NCAA, 649–660
  USOC, 907–915
  Yankee Stadium, 80–84
Substantive Due Process, 698–701, 725–728
  See also Intercollegiate Sports

CONTRACT LAW
College scholarship contracts, 741–749
Conceptions of, 91–119
Future contracts, 112–117
Injunctions, 89–101

INDEX

References are to Pages

CONTRACT LAW—Cont'd
Mutuality, 91–95
Options, 98–101
Player-agent contracts, 343–355
    Fiduciary obligations, 350–355
Standard player, 91–96
    Baseball, 91–95
    Basketball, 95–96
Unclean hands, 106–112
Waivers of personal injury liability, 955–979

CONTRACTS
See Agents

COPYRIGHT LAW
See Intellectual Property Law

CRIMINAL LAW
Assault Causing Bodily Harm, 951–955
Proposed Sports Violence Act, 954–955

DISABILITY
See Discrimination

DISCIPLINE
See Commissioners

DISCRIMINATION
    See also Constitutional Law/Equal Protection and Gender Equity
Disabled, 71–72, 690–696, 704–711, 876–878, 989–1006
Race, 72–79, 676–688, 720–721, 798
Religion, 76–77, 883–884
Sex
    Females, 79–85, 140, 799–863, 878–879, 897
    Homosexuals, 72
    Transsexuals, 879, 932–933
Statutes
    Americans with Disabilities Act, 72–79, 691–696, 704–711, 862, 877–878, 990
    Equity in Athletics Disclosure Act, 839
    New York State Human Rights Act, 140
    Pennsylvania Equal Rights Amendment, 853–854
    Rehabilitation Act of 1973, 704, 990–1005
    Title VI of Civil Rights Act, 681, 686–688, 862
    Title VII of Civil Rights Act, 77–78, 140
    Title IX of Education Amendment Act of 1972, 799–862

DIVERS
Louganis, Greg, 71

DOCTORS
See Torts, Medical Malpractice; and various sports, team physicians

DOMESTIC VIOLENCE
See Commissioners, Disciplinary powers, Domestic abuse; See also Women and Sports, Physical abuse by male athletes

DRAFTS
See various sports, Draft

DRUGS
Alcohol, 39, 49
Amphetamines, 978
Anabolic Steroids, 49, 669, 915–920, 926–928, 978
Arbitration over, 54–56
Artificial Introduction of Testosterone, 69–70
Barbiturates, 978
"Blood-doping" drugs, 69
Cocaine, 42–48, 978
Marijuana, 51, 53, 669, 978
Regulation of, 38–71
    MLB, 41–47
    NBA, 52, 53
    NCAA, 56–65
    NFL, 50–53
    NHL, 53
Studies,
    Substance Use and Abuse Habits of College Student–Athletes, 68
Testing for,
    In college athletes, 56–65, 669
    In college students, 669
    In high school athletes, 65–68
    In high school students, 669
    Olympics, 56, 915–920, 926–928
    Professional sports, 53–56
Treatment for, 42–46
Use,
    By collegiate athletes, 56–65
    By high school athletes, 65–68
    By non-team athletes, 69–71
    By professional athletes, 38–56
    By Olympic athletes, 56, 915–920, 926–928

DUE PROCESS
See Constitutional Law

ECONOMISTS
Marshall, Alfred, 467
Noll, Roger, 480–483

ELIGIBILITY RULES
See NCAA

EMINENT DOMAIN, 531–540

EQUAL PROTECTION CLAUSE
See Constitutional law

EQUAL RIGHTS AMENDMENT
See Discrimination, Legislation

EQUIPMENT, 897–906, 982–985
See also various sports, equipment

FEDERAL TRADE COMMISSION
See Antitrust

FIGURE SKATING
Skaters
    Harding, Tonya, 929–931

1016 INDEX

References are to Pages

FIGURE SKATING—Cont'd
Skaters—Cont'd
    Kerrigan, Nancy, 929–931
U.S. Figure Skating Association (USFSA), 929–931
World Figure Skating Championship, 930

FINES AND SUSPENSIONS
See Commissioners, Disciplinary power; Commissioners, Discipline of players

FOOTBALL
Agents
    Abernathy, Jim, 380, 386
    Argovitz, Jerry, 353, 354
    Blank, Brad, 349
    Cindrich, Ralph, 349
    Steinberg, Leigh, 323, 355
    Zinn, Leo, 343, 344
College
Associations
    College Football Association (CFA), 750, 765, 766
Coaches,
    Bowden, Bobby, 671, 770
    Dickerson, Ron, 854
    Dooley, Vince, 675–676, 682
    Erickson, Dennis, 774
    Goldsmith, Fred, 852
    Johnson, Jimmy, 741
    Meyer, Ron, 670
    Osborne, Tom, 85
    Paterno, Joe, 682, 770
    Robinson, Eddie, 965
    Spurrier, Steve, 671, 770
    Walsh, Bill, 172
    Yost, Fielding, 748
Equipment Manufacturers
Riddell, Inc, 982
Players
Abdul–Jabbar, Karim (see also Sharman Shah), 427
Aikman, Troy, 224, 330
Albrecht, Ted, 972–973
Alzado, Lyle, 49
Anderson, Gary, 353
Autry, Darnell, 735
Ball, Jerry, 356
Banks, Braxston, 781, 791, 794
Barbaro, Gary, 633
Bergey, Bill, 113
Bledsoe, Drew, 187, 320
Boyd, Julian, 711–712
Brodie, John, 602
Brown, Anthony, 211, 320, 794
Brumm, Donald, 974
Buoniconti, Marc, 963
Buoniconti, Nick, 963
Butkus, Dick, 981
Butler, Toure, 695–696
Byrns, Kevin, 983
Carr, Roger, 257
Carter, Anthony, 633
Clark, Charles "Booby", 935

FOOTBALL—Cont'd
Clements, Tom, 359
Condon, Tom, 370
Cox, Brian, 78–79
Cribbs, Joe, 633
Crowder, Randy, 50, 51
Dawson, Dermontti, 371
Dickerson, Eric, 670
Dorsett, Tony, 294
Dubose, Doug, 359
Dutton, John, 249–250
Easley, Kenny, 982
Elway, John, 311
English, Jon, 744, 748
Erickson, Craig, 744
Farrior, James "Patsie", 349
Favre, Brett, 319
Flowers, Charles, 106–107
Flutie, Doug, 529, 796
Fortay, Bryan, 744
Frost, Scott, 85
Fullwood, Brent, 356, 375, 701
Gambrell, William, 970
Grange, Red, 423
Hackbart, Dale, 935, 950
Hand, Larry, 966
Harmon, Ron, 356, 373–374, 386, 701
Hebert, Bobby, 140
Hendy, John, 979
Hill, Calvin, 735
Hirsch, Elroy "Crazylegs", 425
Holmes, Clayton, 51
Hornung, Paul, 32, 38, 660–661
Hurst, Maurice, 80
Ingrassi, Anthony, 734–735
Irvin, Michael, 1, 86, 330
Jackson, Keith, 185
Johns, Paul, 259
Johnson, Bob, 113
Jones, Gordon, 353
Karras, Alex, 32, 38
Kelly, Jim, 311, 633, 794
King, Brandon, 36
Kosar, Bernie, 744
Krueger, Charles, 979
Largent, Steve, 259
LeBaron, Eddie, 290
Lett, Leon, 1
Lundy, Dennis, 36
Mackey, John, 179, 192, 197, 594
Marino, Dan, 311
Marshall, Wilbur, 312
Matthews, Shane, 36
Mayes, Rufus, 113
McCullum, Sam, 257
McGee, Tim, 356, 359
McNeil, Freeman, 206
Milanovich, Scott, 36
Montana, Joe, 254, 311, 427, 973
Moon, Warren, 1, 85
Morris, Ron, 356
Moseley, Mark, 852
Mowatt, Zeke, 80, 883
Mullins, Roy Lee (Chucky), 963

INDEX

References are to Pages

FOOTBALL—Cont'd
Neely, Ralph, 107, 112, 736
O'Brien, Davey, 422, 423
Orr, Terry, 312, 314
Pace, Orlando, 740, 741, 744
Palmer, Gery D., 965
Parrish, Lemar, 343–345
Partee, Dennis, 139
Pastorini, Dante, 329
Peterson, James, 306–307
Phillips, Lawrence, 85, 86
Pickens, Bruce, 371
Porter, Kevin, 380, 386
Reese, Don, 50, 51
Rensing, Fred, 956, 958–959
Rodgers, Johnny, 387
Rogers, Don, 49
Rogers, Reggie, 49, 356, 359
Rohe, Chris, 636
Sanders, Deion, 102, 315, 330, 435
Seay, Mark, 989
Shah, Sharman (see also Abdul-Jabbar, Karim), 427
Sims, Billy, 350
Simms, Phil, 316
Slaughter, Webster, 185
Smith, Bubba, 988–989
Smith, Emmitt, 330
Smith, James "Yazoo", 161, 594
Smith, Jerry, 71
Spurrier, Steve, 671, 770
Stingley, Darryl, 208, 950, 978–979
Sweeney, Walter, 978
Tatum, Jack, 950, 978–979
Taylor, Gregg, 742
Taylor, Laurence, 294, 633
Testaverde, Vince, 744
Torretta, Gino, 744
Trumpy, Bob, 113
Utley, Mike, 934
Veris, Garin, 185
Waldrop, Kent, 962
Walker, Byron, 259
Walker, Herschel, 175, 529, 676
Walsh, Steve, 744
Ware, Andre, 387
White, Danny, 311
White, Reggie, 185, 207
Williams, Doug, 313, 881
Wisnewski, Steve, 79
Woodside, Paul, 852
Woodson, Rod, 356
Wuerffel, Danny, 735
Yost, Fielding, 748
Young, Steve, 633
Zimmerman, Gary, 200
Organizations
St. Louis Tourist & Convention Center, 521
Professional Leagues and Teams
All American Football Conference, 595–596
  Baltimore Colts, 596
  Cleveland Browns, 596
  San Francisco 49ers, 596

FOOTBALL—Cont'd
American Football League, 594, 596–602, 621, 625, 630, 638
  Challenge to NFL, 100, 111, 596, 602
  College player drafts, 107
  Merger with NFL, 596–602, 619, 631, 642
  Owners,
    Adams, K.S. "Bud", 108
    Davis, Al (see NFL owners)
    Barron, Hilton, 625
    Hunt, Lamar (see NFL owners)
    Klein, Gene (see NFL owners)
    Sullivan, Billy (see NFL owners)
    Wilson, Ralph (see NFL owners)
  Potential owner,
    Hecht, Norman, 621–625
  Teams,
    Dallas Texans, 100, 401, 545
    Houston Oilers, 107–108, 545
    Los Angeles Chargers, 107
  Television contracts, 389–390, 557–558, 585, 629–631
Arena Football League, 509
Bands,
  Baltimore Colts Band, 443
Canadian Football League (CFL),
  Owners,
    Speros, Jim, 442
  Teams,
    Baltimore CFL Colts, 437–442
    Winnipeg Blue Bombers, 100
National Football League (NFL),
  Arbitration, 249–250
    Arbitrator Luskin, 249
    Arbitrator Kagel, 974
  Coaches,
    Belichuk, Bill, 117
    Brown, Paul, 113, 172
    Carroll, Pete, 187
    Johnson, Jimmy, 112, 172, 331, 741
    Landry, Tom, 172
    Lombardi, Vince, 172
    Noll, Chuck, 172
    Parcells, Bill, 79, 88, 112, 116–117, 172, 187, 255, 331, 349, 490
    Patera, Jack, 256–257
    Rhome, Jerry, 257
    Shula, Don, 172, 507
    Switzer, Barry, 49
    Walsh, Bill, 113, 172, 176
    Wyche, Sam, 80
  Collective bargaining, 207–208, 239–241, 248–249, 271–272, 315–316, 329–330
  Commissioners,
    Rozelle, Pete, 32, 50, 54, 74, 107, 315, 408, 481–482, 501–502, 507, 554–556, 631, 635, 637, 660
    Tagliabue, Paul, 51, 52, 78, 80, 117, 315, 330, 459–460, 476–477, 501, 556, 883
  "Development squad" system, 154–155, 176–178

INDEX

References are to Pages

FOOTBALL—Cont'd
National Football League (NFL)—Cont'd
Doctors,
    See this topic, Physicians
Draft, 160–176
Drug Policy, 50–53
Eminent domain, 531–540
Employer retaliation, 256–262
Free agency, 178–186, 234–236
Labor unions and negotiators,
    NFL Management Council,
        Donlan, Jack, 54, 290, 634
        LeBaron, Eddie, 290
    NFL Players Association
        Condon, Tom, 370
        Berthelson, Richard, 307
        Garvey, Ed, 239, 271, 315, 319
        Kennedy, Harold, 307
        Mackey, John, 179, 182
        McNeil, Freeman, 206
        Upshaw, Gene, 54, 315, 319
Management,
    McCormick, Mike, 257
    Rooney, Arthur, 480–481
    Schramm, Texas E., 548
    Sullivan, Charles ("Chuck"), 477–489
    Thompson, John, 257
Marketing,
    NFL Properties, 314, 455, 459, 466, 586–587
Media and,
    Journalists and media sources,
        Boston Herald, 80
        Olson, Lisa, 80, 86
        Toms, Denise, 80
        USA Today, 80
    Locker room policy, 80–86
Merger with AFL, 542–550, 586
Option clause, 99–100
Owners,
    Allen, Paul, 476, 531
    Adams, K.S. "Bud", 108
    Behring, Kenneth, 476, 531
    Benson, Tom, 148, 477
    Braman, Norman, 208
    Cooke, Jack Kent, 313
    Davis, Al, 197, 489, 499, 501–503, 507, 521, 531, 537, 542
    Frontiere, Georgia, 507, 542, 546
    Halas, George, 557
    Huizenga, Wayne, 476
    Hunt, Lamar, 470, 475, 483, 598–599
    Irsay, Bob, 437, 443
    Jones, Jerry, 330, 459–460, 465–466, 550, 586–587, 744
    Kiam, Victor, 478, 490, 521, 546
    Klein, Gene, 499
    Kraft, Robert, 117, 186–187, 318, 475, 490, 496, 547–548
    Mara, Wellington, 107, 557
    Modell, Art, 318, 443, 531, 542–543, 546
    Murchison, Clint, 460

FOOTBALL—Cont'd
National Football League (NFL)—Cont'd
Owners—Cont'd
    Orthwein, James, 478, 490, 521, 546
    Reeves, Dan, 557
    Robbie, Joe, 470
    Rosenbloom, Carroll, 503, 508, 530, 546
    Sullivan, Billy, 477–491, 521, 546
    Tose, Leonard, 470
    Winter, Max, 470
Physicians,
Fox, Theodore, 980
Losse, Gary, 979
Tennant, Forrest, 54
Plan B, 184–185, 206–207
Player contracts, 87–119
Retirement Plans,
    Bert Bell NFL Retirement Plan, 973–979
Revenues, 389–390, 436, 557–558, 585, 629–631
Rozelle Rule, 179–183, 194–197
Salaries,
    Salary averages, 239, 323
    Salary caps, 176–178, 314–321, 329–330
NFL Quarterback Club, 314
United States Football League (USFL), 100, 175, 200, 350, 353, 498, 505, 529, 596, 602, 626, 629–643
Founder,
    Dixon, David, 630
Owners,
    Argovitz, Jerry, 350, 353
    Einhorn, Eddie, 633, 642
    Klein, Gene, 353
    Taubo, Ted, 576
    Trump, Donald, 122, 483, 529, 632–634
Players,
    Barbaro, Gary, 633
    Carter, Anthony, 633
    Cribbs, Joe, 633
    Flutie, Doug, 529
    Kelly, Jim, 633
    Walker, Herschel, 529
    Young, Steve, 633
Teams,
    Houston Gamblers, 350
    New Jersey Generals, 122, 483, 529, 630
    Portland Breakers, 498
    Tampa Bay Bandits, 353
World Football League (WFL), 100, 112–113, 344, 498, 505, 529, 596, 602, 626, 629–643
Challenge to NFL, 100, 112–113
Teams,
    Jacksonville Sharks, 344
    Memphis Southmen (and Grizzlies), 525, 594
    Philadelphia Bell, 525
    Southern California Sun, 525

INDEX

References are to Pages

FOOTBALL—Cont'd
National Football League (NFL)—Cont'd
    World Football League (WFL)—Cont'd
        Teams—Cont'd
            Virginia Ambassadors, 113

FRANCHISES, GENERAL, 467–549
Admissions to leagues, 524–529
Characterization of, 467–471
Cross-ownership of, 470–477
Public corporate ownership of, 477–491
Public subsidy of, 543–549
Relocation of, 500–546
Tax treatment of, 546–549

FREE AGENCY, 88, 178–188, 204–209, 228–237, 240–250, 297–304
See also various sports, Free agency

FREE SPEECH
See Constitutional Law, First Amendment

GAMBLING
    See also Commissioner, Discipline, Betting and Gambling
Baseball players, 3–7, 31–38, 124–125
Basketball players, 36
"Black Sox" scandal, 9, 31–32, 36, 125
Football players, 1, 36–38
On college games, 659

GENDER EQUITY, 79–86, 799–863, 878–879
Access, 851–862
Administration, 843–851
Resources, 808–843
Societal effects, 862–863

GOLF
Antitrust, 872–876, 880–882, 895–896
Associations,
    Ladies Professional Golfers' Association (LPGA), 443, 878, 880, 882
    Professional Golfers' Association (PGA), 871–872
    U.S. Golfers Association (USGA), 455, 871, 903–905
    Western Golf Association (WGA), 872
Clubs,
    Augusta National, 443–445
    Brookline Country Club, 871
    Butler National, 872
    Chicago Golf Club, 871
    Newport Country Club, 871
    Riviera Golf and Country Club, 882
    Royal and Ancient Golf Club of St. Andrew's, 871, 903
    Shinnecock Hills Club in Long Island, 871
College,
    Stanford, 876
Commissioners,
    Beman, Deane, 882, 884, 904
    Finchem, Tim, 872
Disciplinary authority of Tour, 880–883
Discrimination, racial, 876
Eligibility rules and scrutiny, 870–876

GOLF—Cont'd
Eligibility for foreign players, 879
Eligibility for handicapped players, 72, 79, 876–878
    Americans With Disabilities Act, 72, 79, 877
Equipment, 865, 903–906
    Manufacturers,
        Data-Max, d/b/a St. Andrews Systems, 455
        Karsten Manufacturing, 904–905
    Regulations, 903–906
Foreign players, 879
Origins and Evolution of Tours, 871, 880
Sponsors,
    Colgate Company, 880
    Northwestern Mutual Life, 443
Tournaments,
    Dinah Shore Golf Classic, 880
    Los Angeles Open, 882
    Masters, 443, 865
    United States Amateur Championship, 871
    Western Open tournament, 872
Tour Managment,
    Appeals Committee, 882
    Equipment Advisory Committee, 905
    Policy Board, 882, 904–905
Tours,
    Ben Hogan Tour, 872
    Ladies Professional Golfers Association (LPGA) Tour, 878, 880, 882
    Nike Tour, 872, 877
    Professional Golfers Association (PGA) Tour, 79, 512, 529, 575, 594–595, 864, 871, 872, 876–878, 879, 882, 885, 895, 896, 903–905, 906
    Senior Tour, 877
    World Golf Tour, 895–896
        Murdoch, Rupert, 895
        Norman, Greg, 895

GOLFERS
Ballesteros, Seve, 879, 893
Blalock, Jane, 880
Calcavecchia, Mark, 904–905
Craft, Linda, 880
Davies, Laura, 878
Deesen, Herb, 871
Els, Ernie, 529
Faldo, Nick, 879, 893
Gilder, Bob, 905
Hagen, Walter, 871
Hogan, Ben, 79, 871
Irwin, Hale, 878
Martin, Casey, 79, 876–878
Miller, Sharon, 880
Nelson, Byron, 871
Nicklaus, Jack, 865, 872, 877–878, 882, 904
Norman, Greg, 428, 460, 529, 879, 895
O'Grady, Mac, 882, 884
Palmer, Arnold, 79, 323, 424, 865, 872, 877
Player, Gary, 872
Rankin, Judy, 880

INDEX

References are to Pages

GOLFERS—Cont'd
Rhodes, Ted, 79
Sarazan, Gene, 871
Sifford, Charles, 79, 876
Snead, Sam, 871
Sorenstam, Annika, 878, 897
Sullivan, Cynthia, 880
Venturi, Ken, 877–878
Watson, Tom, 904
Weser, Emil, 872
Woods, Tiger, 79, 323, 390, 424, 460, 735–736, 876
Woosnam, Ian, 893
Zavichas, Penny, 880

GRIEVANCES
See Arbitration; Labor Law

GUN POSSESSION
See Commissioner, Discipline of players

HIGH SCHOOL
Athletes,
    Acton, James, 65–68
    Bryant, Kobe, 740
    Fortay, Bryan, 744
    Garnett, Kevin, 740
    Horner, Lori Ann, 860
    Mercer, Heather, 852
    Pottgen, Edward, 709
    Sandison, Ronald, 709
    Wagenblast, Alex, 1001
Drug policy, 65–68
Gender equity, 854–862
Schools,
    Bethlehem School District, 860
    Cascade High School, 695
    Naperville North High School, 689
    Odessa School District, 1001
    Vernonia School District, 65–67
    Yorktown Heights, 852
Sports authorities,
    Colorado High School Activities Association, 855
    Kentucky High School Athletic Association (KHSAA), 860
    Kentucky State Board for Elementary and Secondary Education, 860
    Michigan High School Athletic Association, 709
    Missouri State High School Activities Association (MSHSAA), 705
    Nebraska School Activities Association, 859
    Rhode Island Interscholastic League, 860

HIV VIRUS
Effect on sports participation, 71–72
Testing for, 71–72

HOCKEY, ICE
Agents
Sorkin, Richard, 343
Woolf, Bob, 322, 347–348

HOCKEY, ICE—Cont'd
Associations
Amateur Hockey Association of the United States, 610
Canadian Amateur Hockey Association (CAHA), 610, 725
Canadian Junior A Hockey, 989
Inline Skate Hockey League, 557
College
Coaches,
    Armstrong, Murray, 726
Teams,
    Denver University, 726
Players
Brown, Andrew, 347
Bourque, Raymond, 336–337, 341
Bure, Pavel, 100
Ciccarelli, Dino, 954
Daigle, Alexander, 320
Fuhr, Grant, 53
Goldsworthy, Bill, 71
Green, Ted, 952, 954
Gretzky, Wayne, 20, 119
Howe, Gordie, 305
Hull, Bobby, 305
Kariya, Paul, 320
Lemieux, Mario, 319
Lidster, Doug, 111
Lindros, Eric, 20, 173, 320
Maki, Wayne, 952, 954
McCourt, Dale, 199
McTavish, Craig, 49
Messier, Mark, 111
Nedved, Petr, 111
Neeld, Greg, 989–990
Orr, Bobby, 609
Richardson, Luke, 954
Robitaille, Mike, 954
Tikkanen, Esa, 111
Vachon, Rogatien, 199
Professional leagues and teams
National Hockey League
    Antitrust, 199–200, 609–620
    Coaches,
        Bowman, Scotty, 255
        Keenan, Mike, 88, 111–112
    Collective bargaining, 199–200, 335–341
    Commissioners (or President),
        Bettman, Gary, 111–112, 200, 317, 341, 501
        Campbell, Clarence, 611, 613, 616
        Ziegler, John, 20
    Drug Policy, 53
    Equipment,
        Helmet rule, 985
    Free agency, 199–200
    "lifetime reserve system", 99
    Labor unions,
        NHL Coaches Association, 255
        NHL Players Association
            Eagleson, Alan, 239, 354, 611, 617
            Goodenow, Bob, 200, 341
        National Hockey League Services ("NHLS"), 446

INDEX

References are to Pages

HOCKEY, ICE—Cont'd
National Hockey League—Cont'd
  Owners,
    Boe, Roy, 612
    Cablevision, 472
    Colangelo, Jerry, 472
    Comcast, 472
    Disney/ABC, 542
    Huizenga, Wayne, 476
    Norris, James, 604–605
    Pollin, Abe, 472
    Willard Wirtz, 605, 626
  Revenues, 389–390
  Rivalry with WHA, 100, 609–616, 619, 620
  Salaries, 200, 239, 319–320, 323
  Team relocations, 500
World Hockey Association (WHA), 100, 175, 347, 595, 609–620
  Draft Eligibility, 175
  Rivalry with NHL, 100, 609–620
  Teams,
    Edmonton Oilers, 595
    Hartford Whalers, 595
    Indianapolis Pacers, 347
    Quebec Nordiques, 595
    Winnipeg Jets, 595

ICE SKATING
See Figure Skating

INCOME TAX FRAUD
See Criminal Law

INJURIES
See Tort Law

INTELLECTUAL PROPERTY IN SPORTS BROADCASTING AND MERCHANDISING, 389–466, 549–590, 750–769
  Broadcast revenues,
    Professional leagues, 389–390, 557–558, 584–585
    College sports, 751, 765–766
  Cable television, 413–422
  Common law right to broadcast games, 391–401
    Sports on Internet, 396–401
  Copyright in game broadcasts, 401–422
    Doctrinal base, 402–403, 406–407, 413–415
    Fair use, 403–406
    Public performance, 406–413
  Group sale of intellectual property, 458–466, 549–586, 629–642, 750–769
    See also Antitrust
    Broadcasting, 549–586, 629–642, 750–768
    Merchandising, 465–466, 586–588, 769
  Owner trademark rights, 436–458
    Consumer confusion, 437–443, 446–456
    Doctrinal base, 436–437, 443–446

INTELLECTUAL PROPERTY IN SPORTS BROADCASTING AND MERCHANDISING, 389–466, 549–590, 750–769—Cont'd
  Owner trademark rights—Cont'd
    Trademark dilution, 456–458
  Player publicity rights, 422–436
    Doctrinal base, 422–428
    Interplay with copyright, 428–436
  Sharing of revenues from broadcasting and merchandising, 588–590

INTERCOLLEGIATE ATHLETICS, 646–672, 723–798, 779–863
  See also NCAA
  Academics, 675–702, 720–721
    Eligibility, 675–698
    Progress toward graduation, 698–702
    Student-athlete graduation rates, 720–721
  Age and athletic experience, 702–711
  Amateurism, 670–72, 702–711
    Pay before college, 725–729
    Pay at college: Grants–In–Aid, 729–736
    Professional contracts, 736–738
    Professional drafts, 738–739, 781–793
    Relations with agents, 739–741, 781–793
  College transfer, 745–749
  Gender Equity, 799–863
    Access to and integration of teams, 851–862
    Administrative positions, 843–851
    Athletic positions, 808–841
    Evolution of Title IX, 799–800, 805–808
    Scholarship funding, 842–843
    Under state law, 801–805
  Revenues and costs, 647–648, 671–672, 723–724, 765–766
  Statistics re athletic revenues and positions by gender, 800, 805, 808–809, 839–841, 843–845, 851, 854
  Sources of Judicial Scrutiny
    Antitrust, 749, 792
    Civil rights laws, 681–696, 704–711, 805–862
    Contract, 741–749
    Constitution (federal and state), 649–660, 662–669, 677–681, 698–701, 711–713, 725–728, 729–733, 736–738, 801–805, 820–839, 853–854, 855–862
    Labor law, 792–795
    Torts (educational malpractice), 713–719

INTERNATIONAL AMATEUR ATHLETICS FEDERATION (IAAF), 915–917, 920–921, 925–926, 928, 931–932
  International Court of Arbitration for Sport, 926–927

INTERNATIONAL AMATEUR ATHLETICS FEDERATION (IAAF), 915–917, 920–921, 925–926, 928, 931–932—Cont'd
Officials,
    Barra, Luciano, 928
    Cassell, Ollan, 928
    Nebiolo, Primo, 928
Sponsors
    Coca Cola, 921

INTERNATIONAL ATHLETICS
See Olympics; various sports

INTERNATIONAL OLYMPIC COMMITTEE (IOC)
See Olympics

LABOR EXEMPTION
See Antitrust

LABOR LAW, 225–314, 326–329
Application to professional sports, 250–254
Arbitration under labor agreement, 101–105, 228–233, 240–250, 297–304, 326–329
    See also Arbitration
Canadian labor law, 267, 295–296
Creation of player free agency, 240–250
Duty of fair representation, 304–310
Duty to bargain in good faith, 279–289
    Obligation to provide relevant information, 274–278
    Unilateral action on mandatory or permissive subjects of bargaining, 281–289
Economic conflict and right to strike, 289–297
Employer retaliation against union supporters, 255–262, 290–294
General principles, 240, 250–251, 256–258, 262–263, 267–268, 271–274, 289–291, 297–298, 304–305, 310–313
Judicial review of arbitration awards, 298–304
League-wide appropriate units, 262–267
National Labor Relations Board (NLRB), 239, 240, 250, 254, 256, 262, 263, 267, 268, 275, 280–281, 287, 290, 293, 306
    Gould, William, 281
    Silverman, Daniel, 279
National Right-to-Work Legal Defense Foundation, 312
Supervisors: umpires or coaches, 254–255
Union certification, 262–267
Union exclusive bargaining authority, 267–272, 362–279
    Control of agents, 362–379
Union security and union dues, 310–315

LADIES PROFESSIONAL GOLFERS ASSOCIATION (LPGA)
See Golf

LEAGUES
See various sports

LIABILITY FOR INJURIES
See Tort Law

MAJOR LEAGUE BASEBALL
See Baseball, Professional Leagues and Teams

MARKET POWER
See Antitrust; Monopoly; Merchandising

MEDIA
    See also Intellectual Property
Announcers, sports,
    Albert, Marv, 86
    Allen, Mel, 392
    Barber, Red, 392
    Dell, Donald, 888
    Madden, John, 224, 585
    Reagan, Ronald, 392
    Scully, Vin, 392
Broadcasting, 391–422, 549–586, 750–768
Celebrities, Non–Sports,
    2 Live Crew, 427
    Carson, Johnny, 425
    Cosby, Bill, 854
    Cruise, Tom, 224, 270
    Gaye, Marvin, 355
    Jackson, Michael, 477
    Labelle, Patti, 355
    Leno, Jay, 425
    Letterman, David, 224, 425
    Orbison, Roy, 427
    Rawls, Lou, 355
    Russell, Lillian, 95
    Scorsese, Martin, 36
    Seinfeld, Jerry, 270
    Travolta, John (SAG), 224
    Vandross, Luther, 355
    Wagner, Johanna, 95
    Warwick, Dionne, 355
    Willis, Bruce, 270
    Zacchini, Hugo, 395, 424–425, 428
Copyright,
    See Intellectual Property, Copyright
Equipment and media,
    Gamestats, 396–397
    SportsTrax, 396–397
    Sports Team Analysis and Tracking System, Inc. (STATS), 396–397
Journalists,
    Koppel, Ted, 74
    Ludtke, Melissa, 80–86, 659
    Olson, Lisa, 80, 86
    Toms, Denise, 80
    Will, George, 6, 86, 645
Labor unions,
    Alliance of Motion Pictures and Television Producers (AMPTP), 224
    American Federation of Television and Radio Artists, 224
    Screen Actors Guild, 224

References are to Pages

MEDIA—Cont'd
Legislation,
    Cable Communications Policy Act of 1984, 406
    Cable Television Consumer Protection and Competition Act of 1992, 584
    Sports Broadcasting Act of 1961, 550, 555–557, 567–571, 573, 582–584, 586, 588, 591, 602, 629, 634–635, 766
Newspapers,
    Associated Press, 394, 767
    Birmingham Post, 672
    Boston Globe, 54
    Boston Herald, 80
    San Jose Mercury, 427
    USA Today, 37, 80, 658, 698
Radio networks and stations,
    Radio Corporation of America (RCA's), 391
Studio and network organizations,
    Motion Picture Association of America, 421
Television,
    Cable Networks and Superstations,
        Cable News Network (CNN), 767
        Cablevision of Michigan, 372
        ESPN, 75, 390, 396, 404, 420, 454, 508, 509, 532, 574, 765–766
        KTVT, 417
        Lifetime, 454
        Madison Square Garden cable network, 499, 558–559, 566, 568
        New England Sports Network (NESN), 413
        Prime Sports, 532, 584
        Quincy Cablevision, 413
        SportsChannel America, 556, 584
        Turner Network Television (TNT), 390, 556, 558–559, 566–568, 582, 584
        WGN Continental Broadcasting Company (Chicago), 23, 390, 417, 499, 558–559, 566, 568, 570–572, 582–584, 588, 594
        WOR, 415, 417, 558
        WPIX, 417
        WSBK, 404, 406
        WTBS, 318, 390, 417, 419, 420, 558, 582, 584, 589, 660
    Executives and station owners,
        Chicago Tribune (WGN), 530
        Murdoch, Rupert, 895
        Pilson, Neil, 635–637
        Time Warner, 419, 420
        Turner, Ted (TNT and WTBS), 396, 417, 419–420, 660
    Networks and Local stations,
        ABC, 47, 407, 554, 566, 585, 602, 630–637, 639–640, 765, 766, 768
        Chicago SportsChannel, 558

MEDIA—Cont'd
Television—Cont'd
    Networks and Local stations—Cont'd
        Columbia Broadcasting System (CBS), 224, 389, 407, 555–557, 562, 566, 585, 631, 635–637, 639–640, 765
        Disney–ABC, 420
        Fox Broadcasting, 111, 207, 224, 396, 420, 497, 557, 585, 895
        National Broadcast Company ("NBC"), 224, 397, 407, 556, 558–560, 562, 564–565, 568–570, 582, 585–586, 631–632, 636–637, 640, 766, 797
        New Boston Television, 404
    Rights/Contracts
        AFL, 631
        College Sports (NCAA), 566, 765–768
        League-wide contracts, 549
        MLB, 588
        NBA, 582
        NFL, 224, 585, 629, 631
    Olympics, 586
    Satellite transmission, 407–420

MEDICINE AND MEDICAL MALPRACTICE
See Tort Law

MERCHANDISING AND LICENSING, 422–428, 436–466, 586–588, 769
    See also Intellectual Property
Arrangements with companies,
    Adidas, 465, 587
    All–Pro Graphics, 344
    American Express, 459, 586
    Burger King, 769
    Cardtoons, 426
    Coca Cola, 437, 445–446, 459, 586
    Dallas Cap & Emblem, 446
    Fleer, 461, 465
    General Motors, 427
    Haelan Laboratories, 423
    Kleenex, 437
    Leaf–Duncuss, 461
    Lion Brothers Company, 446
    MacMillan Publishing, 423
    Miller Beer, 660
    Nike, 390, 459, 465, 586
    Pabst Brewing, 427
    Pepsi, 459, 586
    Reebok, 346, 390, 461, 465, 586
    R.J. Reynolds Tobacco, 426
    Topps, 423, 460–461, 465
    Visa, 459, 586
For leagues,
    MLB Properties, 458, 465–466
    National Hockey League Services, 446
    NFL Properties, 436, 445, 459–460, 466, 586–587

INDEX

References are to Pages

MINORITY DISCRIMINATION
See Discrimination, Race, Gender

MONOPOLY
See also Antitrust
Breaking up professional leagues, 643–645
Essential facilities doctrine, 620, 624–625, 640–641
Interleague competition, 594–607
Players, control over, 608–620
Relevant product market and, 596–607
Stadiums/arenas, control over, 620–629
Television controls, 629–643

NATIONAL BASKETBALL ASSOCIATION
See Basketball, Professional Leagues and Teams

NATIONAL BASKETBALL PLAYERS ASSOCIATION
See Basketball, Professional Leagues and Teams, National Basketball Association, Labor unions and negotiators

NATIONAL COLLEGIATE ATHLETIC ASSOCIATION (NCAA)
See also Intercollegiate Athletics
Academic Rules, 677–702
    1.6 Predictor Rule, 677–681
    Proposition 48 Rule, 681–697
        SAT minimum, 681–688
        Core course requirement, 688–696
    Satisfactory Academic Progress Rule, 698–702
Administration
    Byers, Walter, 648
    Corrigan, Gene, 771
Age and athletic experience rules, 702–711
Agent recruiting of athletes, 355–360, 380–388, 739–741, 781–793
Amateurism rules, 725–739, 780–792
    Pay before college, 725–729
    Pay at college: Grants–In–Aid, 729–736
    Professional contracts, 736–738
    Professional drafts, 738–739, 781–793
Antitrust scrutiny of rules, 750–792
    Athletes market, 780–792
    Coaches market, 770–780
    Product market (including television), 750–769
College transfer and eligibility rules, 745–749
Constitutional status, 649–669
    Non-state actor under federal constitution, 649–660
    Insulation from state regulation, 663–669
Drug use and drug testing rules, 56–65
Federal regulations
    Americans with Disabilities Act, 688–696, 704–711, 862
    Civil Rights Act
        Title VI
        Title VII, 77–78

NATIONAL COLLEGIATE ATHLETIC ASSOCIATION (NCAA)—Cont'd
Federal regulations—Cont'd
    Civil Rights Act—Cont'd
        Title IX, 80, 799–863
    Civil Rights Restoration Act, 800
    Equity in Athletics Disclosure Act
    Student–Athlete Right-to-Know Act, 720–721, 862
Foreign student-athletes, 728–729
Gender discrimination, 799–863
    See also, Discrimination, Gender Equity
    Athletic positions, 808–941
    Coaching positions, 843–851
    Integration of teams, 851–862
    Scholarship funding for female and male teams, 842–843
Injuries, 955–964
    NCAA Catastrophic Insurance Plan, 962–963
Judicial Reading of Scholarship Contracts, 741–749
Procedural due process, 661–674
Television plans and rules, 565–566, 576, 750–768

NATIONAL FOOTBALL LEAGUE
See Football, Professional leagues and Teams

NATIONAL LABOR RELATIONS ACT
See Labor Law

NATIONAL LABOR RELATIONS BOARD
See Labor Law

NO–CUT CONTRACTS
See Contract Law

NORTH AMERICAN SOCCER LEAGUE (NASL)
See Soccer, Professional Leagues and Teams

OLYMPICS
Amateurism, 932–933
Drug Regulation and Testing, 56, 915–920, 926–928
Eligibility and Discipline, 929–931
Gay Olympic Games, 458
International Court of Arbitration for Sport (ICAS), 926–927
International Olympic Committee (IOC), 586, 907, 915, 926, 931, 933
Interplay of domestic and international law, 921–926, 926–928
Legislation relating to,
    Amateur Sports Act, 907, 915
Television rights, 586
United States Olympic Committee, 457, 907, 915–916, 920, 925, 929–931, 933
    Judicial Scrutiny, 908–915

References are to Pages

OWNERS
See Franchises, General; and the various sports, Professional Leagues and Teams

PHYSICAL ABUSE
See Commissioners, Disciplinary powers, Domestic abuse

PLAYER AGENTS
See Agents
　See also, various sports, Agents

PLAYER CONTRACTS
See Contract Law

PLAYER DRAFT
See, various sports, Draft

PLAYER MARKETS
See various sports

PLAYER SALARIES
See Salaries, see also various sports, Salaries

PLAYERS ASSOCIATION
See under respective sports, MBLPA, NBPA, NHLPA, NFLPA, NASLPA

PRESIDENTS, UNITED STATES
Bush, George, 687
Carter, James 799, 894
Clinton, William, 281, 795
Ford, Gerald, 676
Nixon, Richard, 795, 799
Reagan, Ronald, 392
Roosevelt, Theodore, 648, 962, n.1
Wilson, Woodrow, 189

PROFESSIONAL GOLFERS ASSOCIATION
See Golf

PUBLICITY RIGHTS
See Intellectual Property

RACE DISCRIMINATION
See Discrimination, Race

RACING, AUTOMOBILE
Administration,
　George, Tony, 896
Drivers,
　Motschenbacher, Lothar, 426
Equipment manufacturers,
　Studebaker, 898
Leagues and teams,
　Championship Auto Racing Teams (CART), 896
　Indy Racing League (IRL), 896
　NASCAR, 866
　　Creator,
　　　France, Bill, 866
　　Drivers,
　　　Crouch, Robert, 866–867, 870
　　　Eckman, Jerry, 883
　　　Koszela, John, 870
　　　LaJoie, Randy, 866–867

RACING, AUTOMOBILE—Cont'd
Leagues and teams—Cont'd
　NASCAR—Cont'd
　　Drivers—Cont'd
　　　Richmond, Tim, 71
　　National Hot Rod Association, 883
　　Races,
　　　Winston Cup, 866
　　Sponsors,
　　　R.J. Reynolds tobacco company, 866
　United States Auto Club (USAC), 898
Owners,
　Orndorff, Bill, 883
Races,
　Indianapolis 500, 865, 898
Status under the law, 866–870

RACING, BICYCLE
Dutch cycling team, 69

RACING, HORSE, 942
Riders,
　Casella, Judy, 942

RACISM
See Discrimination, Race

REPORTERS
See Media, Journalists; See also various sports, Media

RESERVE SYSTEM
See various sports

RESTRAINT OF TRADE
See Antitrust

REVENUE SHARING, FRANCHISES AND LEAGUES
See various sports

ROWING, 805

SALARIES
Caps, 186–188, 201, 207–209, 329–335
Restraints on individal levels, 176–178, 187, 210–211, 319–321
Taxes, 317

SEX DISCRIMINATION
See Discrimination, gender

SHERMAN ACT
See Antitrust

SKATING, ICE
See Figure Skating

SOCCER
Antitrust, 186–188
Professional Leagues and Teams
Federation Internationale de Football Association (FIFA), 187–188
Major League Soccer, 186–188, 240, 266, 319, 475, 495–498, 557, 643
　Administration,
　　Alan Rothenberg, 186, 495–497

INDEX

References are to Pages

SOCCER—Cont'd
Major League Soccer—Cont'd
  Investors/Owners
    Kraft, Robert, 186, 475, 496
    Hunt, Lamar, 475
  Players Association, 240
  Salary cap, 187
  Teams
    Columbus Crew, 475
    Kansas City Wizards, 475
    New England Revolution, 475, 496
North American Soccer League (NASL), 186, 263–267, 268–270, 470–475
  Labor union,
    North American Soccer League Players Association (NASLPA), 263, 268
  Owners,
    Hunt, Lamar (see NFL owners)
    Robbie, Joe (see NFL owners)
    Ross, Steve, 497
    Rothenberg, Alan, 495
    Trump, Donald, 529, 632–634
  Players,
    Pele, 497
  Teams
    Dallas Tornadoes, 470
    Ft. Lauderdale Strikers, 470
    Los Angeles Aztecs, 495
    New York Cosmos, 497
    Toronto Metros, 263
    Vancouver Whitecaps, 263
United States Soccer Federation, 187–188, n.f
World Soccer Cup, 495

SOFTBALL, 702

SPORTS BROADCASTING ACT
See Media, Broadcasting

STADIUMS AND ARENAS
Individual,
  Anaheim Stadium, 508, 530, 534
  The Ballpark at Arlington, 540
  Baltimore's Oriole Park at Camden Yards, 296–297, 530, 540
  Baltimore Memorial Stadium, 537
  Boston Garden, 883
  Busch Stadium, 408
  Charlotte's Erickson Stadium, 543
  Chicago Stadium, 605, 625–626, 629
  Cleveland's Jacobs Field, 540
  Comiskey Park, 540
  Denver's Mile High Stadium, 626
  Detroit's Olympia Arena, 605
  Dodgers Stadium, 530, 540, 620
  Ebbetts Field, 530
  Fenway Park, 391, 951
  Forbes Field, 392
  Foxboro Stadium, 489, 496
  Hartford Civic Center Coliseum, 395
  Long Island Nassau Coliseum, 612
  Los Angeles Memorial Coliseum, 489, 503, 508, 510–511, 521, 530, 539

STADIUMS AND ARENAS—Cont'd
Individual—Cont'd
  Los Angeles Sports Arena, 522–523
  Madison Square Garden, 605, 612
  Minneapolis' Humphrey Metrodome, 626
  New Jersey's Giants Stadium, 544
  New Orleans Superdome, 54, 531
  Oakland Coliseum, 503, 508
  Pittsburgh's Three Rivers Stadium, 392, 626
  Pontiac Silverdome, 626
  Rice University Stadium, 598
  San Francisco's Candlestick (now 3–Com) Park, 141, 146, 297, 534
  Seattle Kingdome, 476, 531, 540
  Shea Stadium, 279, 986
  St. Petersburg's Suncoast Dome, 141, 146, 524
  Sullivan Stadium, 489
  Texas Stadium, 586
  Toronto SkyDome, 295–296
  University of Maryland's Byrd Stadium, 625
  Washington RFK Stadium, 312, 621–622, 625
  Wrigley Field, 391, 547
  Yankee Stadium, 81, 279, 529
Owners,
  Kraft, Robert, (see NFL owners)
  Los Angeles Memorial Coliseum, 532
  Norris, James, 605
  Stadium Management Corporation (SMC), 489
  Wirtz, Willard, 605
Public subsidy of, 546–549
Revenues,
  Club seats, 389
  Luxury boxes, 389
  Personal seat licenses (PSL's), 389, 542

STEROIDS
See Drugs

STRIKES
See Labor Law

SWIMMERS
Foschi, Jessica, 926, 928
Ganden, Chad, 689–690, 695–696

SWIMMING
USS (national swimming federation), 926–927
FINA (international swimming federation), 926–927

TAXATION
Bonds, tax-free, 543–546
Depreciation of player contracts, 546–549
Revenue Expenditure Control Act of 1968, 545
Tax Reform Act of 1976, 547–548
Tax Reform Act of 1986, 541

INDEX

References are to Pages

TELEVISION
See Media

TENNIS
Amateurism, 885–887
Antitrust, 811–817
Clubs
    All England Lawn Tennis Club, 885
Disciplinary actions, 884–885
Equipment and Rules, 898–903
Players associations,
    Association of Tennis Professionals (ATP), 865, 893–895, 905
        Management,
            Ashe, Arthur, 886
            Drysdale, Cliff, 886
            Jordan, Hamilton, 894
            Kramer, Jack, 886
Sponsors,
    IBM, 894
    Nabisco Brands, 888
    Phillip Morris Tobacco Company, 887
    Volvo Corporation, 888, 893
Tour history, 885–888, 893–894
Tournaments,
    Davis Cup, 886, 893–894
    French Open, 897, 899
    Grand Slam, 886–887, 893
    Masters' Championship, 865
    U.S. Open, 886, 898, 932
    Virginia Slims women's tour, 887
    Wimbledon, 729, 865, 885–886, 894, 897
Tours and rulemaking authorities,
    International Lawn Tennis Federation, 885
    International Tennis Federation, 893–895, 898–899, 903
    Men's International Professional Tennis Council (MIPTC), 884–888, 893
    United States Tennis Association (USTA), 879, 885–886, 898, 903, 905, 932
    Women's International Professional Tennis Council (WIPTC), 887, 894
    Women's Tennis Association (WTA), 887, 894
        Heldman, Gladys, 887
        King, Billie Jean, 887
    World Championship Tennis (WCT), 886–887
        Lamar Hunt, 886
    World Team Tennis (WTT), 887
Transsexuals in, 879

TENNIS PLAYERS
Agassi, Andre, 424, 894
Ashe, Arthur, 71, 323, 682, 865, 886–887
Budge, Don, 885
Connors, Jimmy, 865, 887, 895
Evert, Chris, 888
Gonzales, Pancho, 885
Goolagong, Evonne, 887
Graf, Steffi, 932

TENNIS PLAYERS—Cont'd
Heldman, Julie, 988
Hingis, Martina, 897
King, Billie Jean, 887
Kramer, Jack, 885
Laver, Rod, 885
Lenglen, Suzanne, 885
McEnroe, John, 888
Novacek, Karel, 927
Richards, Renee (Richard), 879
Sampras, Pete, 323
Seles, Monica, 894
Tilden, Bill, 423, 885
Vilas, Guillermo, 884
Wade, Virginia, 988
Wilander, Mats, 927

TITLE VII
See Discrimination, Legislation

TITLE IX
See Discrimination, Legislation

TORT LAW, 935–951, 979–989
Assault and battery, 935–942, 948–951
Assumption of risk, 942–948
Claims by student-athletes, 962–963
Defective products, 942–948
Discrimination against the disabled, 990–1001
Hazardous facilities, 985–989
Intentional torts, 950–951
Medical malpractice, 979–982
Negligence or recklessness, 935–942
Waivers of liability, 1000–1006
Worker's compensation and tort exclusion, 955–979

TRACK AND FIELD
Associations,
    Boston Athletic Association (BAA), 395, 451
Athletes,
    Cady, Carol, 915
    Cureton, Tai Kwan, 681, 691, 696
    Evangelisti, Giovanni, 928
    Farmer–Patrick, Sandra, 70
    Gasser, Sandra, 927
    Krabbe, Katrin, 927
    Johnson, Ben, 39, 49
    Lewis, Carl, 39, 744
    Myricks, Larry, 928
    Powell, John, 915
    Reynolds, Butch, 916–926
    Sandison, Ronald, 709
    Shaw, Leatrice, 681, 691, 696
    Slaney, Mary Decker, 70
College Teams,
    Kansas, 729
    Miami University, 681
    University of Texas at El Paso (UTEP), 725
Events,
    Boston Marathon, 395, 451

TRACK AND FIELD—Cont'd
Organizations,
    The Athletics Congress (TAC) of the USA, 915, 916–917, 920–921, 928
    USA Track and Field (UST & F), 915, 921, 925, 928–929

TRADEMARK LAW
See Intellectual Property

UNFAIR LABOR PRACTICES
See Labor Law

UNIONS
See Labor Law

UNITED STATES FOOTBALL LEAGUE (USFL)
See Football, Professional Leagues and Teams

UNITED STATES OLYMPIC COMMITTEE (USOC)
See Olympics

UNITED STATES TENNIS ASSOCIATION (USTA)
See Tennis, Organizations

VICE PRESIDENTS, UNITED STATES
Gore, Al, 591–592

VIOLENCE IN SPORTS
See Commissioners, Discipline of Players

WOMEN SPORTS ORGANIZATIONS
    See also Discrimination/Sex and Gender Equity
Association of Intercollegiate Athletic Women (AIAW), 798, 844

WOMEN SPORTS ORGANIZATIONS—Cont'd
Basketball,
    See Basketball, Professional Leagues and Teams, American Basketball League (ABL) and Women's National Basketball Association (WNBA)
National Women's Law Center, 842–843
NBA Officials, 77
Women's Sports Foundation, 840
    Executive Director
        Lopiano, Donna, 840

WOMEN'S TENNIS ASSOCIATION
See Tennis, Organizations

WORKERS COMPENSATION, 955–979
Claims by college athletes, 955–964
    Employees or Not, 955–961
        Absence of Coverage and Tort Suits, 962–964
        NCAA Catastrophic Insurance Plan, 962–963
Claims by professional athletes, 964–979
    Limits on Exclusivity, 969–972
    Private NFL Disability Plan, 974–979
    Scope of Accident, 965–969
    Scope of Employment, 964–965
    Wage Loss Calculation, 972–973

WORLD FOOTBALL LEAGUE
See Football, Professional Leagues and Teams

WORLD HOCKEY ASSOCIATION
See Hockey, Leagues and Teams

WRESTLING
World Wrestling Federation (WWF), 435
Wrestlers,
    Hogan, Hulk, 427
    Ventura, Jesse "The Body", 435
Wrestling Operators,
    Titan Sports Enterprises, 435